sylvius 4 *Free Download Instructions*

Sylvius 4 is provided as a downloadable program that you save on your local computer. You only need to download the program once—it will then run from your computer and does not require an Internet connection after the initial installation.

To download sylvius 4, follow these instructions:

1. Scratch below to reveal your unique download code.
2. Go to http://www.sinauer.com/sylvius4
3. Follow the instructions to download and register the program. (Requires a valid email address.)

Scratch below to reveal your download code:

Important Note: If this code has been revealed, it may have already been used, and may no longer be valid. Each code can be used by only one person. If this code is no longer valid, you can purchase a new code online at: http://www.sinauer.com/sylvius4.

Principles of Cognitive Neuroscience

Companion Website

www.sinauer.com/cogneuro

The *Principles of Cognitive Neuroscience* companion website features review and study tools to help you master the material presented in the textbook. Access to the site is free of charge and requires no access code.

The site includes:

- **Chapter Summaries:** Concise overviews of the important topics covered in each chapter.

- **Flashcards:** Flashcard activities help you master the extensive vocabulary of cognitive neuroscience. Each chapter's set of flashcards includes all the key terms introduced in that chapter.

- **Animations:** A collection of detailed animations that depict some of the key processes and structures discussed in the textbook.

- **Online Quizzes:** For each chapter of the textbook, the companion website includes a multiple-choice quiz that covers all the main topics presented in the chapter. Your instructor may assign these quizzes, or they may be made available to you as self-study tools. (Instructor registration is required for student access to the quizzes.)

PRINCIPLES OF
Cognitive Neuroscience

PRINCIPLES OF
Cognitive Neuroscience

Dale Purves

Elizabeth M. Brannon

Roberto Cabeza

Scott A. Huettel

Kevin S. LaBar

Michael L. Platt

Marty G. Woldorff

Center for Cognitive Neuroscience
Duke University

Sinauer Associates, Inc. • Publishers
Sunderland, Massachusetts U.S.A.

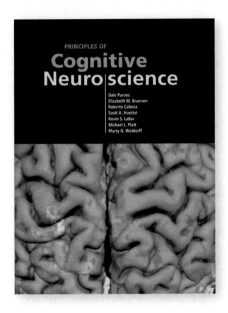

The Cover

Pictured on the cover is a portion of an fMRI image showing areas of reduced activation during performance of a visual search task. Image courtesy of Scott A. Huettel.

Address inquiries and orders to
 Sinauer Associates, Inc.
 23 Plumtree Road
 Sunderland, MA 01375 U.S.A.

www.sinauer.com
FAX: 413-549-1118
orders@sinauer.com
publish@sinauer.com

Library of Congress Cataloging-in-Publication Data

Principles of cognitive neuroscience / Dale Purves ... [et al.].
    p. ; cm.
  Includes bibliographical references and index.
  ISBN 978-0-87893-694-6 (clothbound)
 1. Cognitive neuroscience. I. Purves, Dale.
  [DNLM: 1. Brain—physiology. 2. Mental Processes—physiology.
 3. Neuropsychology. WL 300 P9565 2008]

QP360.5.P73 2008
612.8′233—dc22   2007039757

Printed in U.S.A.

5 4 3 2 1

Contents in Brief

Contents

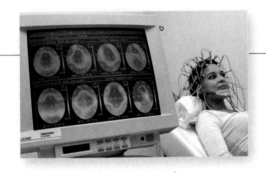

UNIT II

Principles of Sensory Processing and Perception 85

UNIT III

Principles of Motor Processing and Motor Behavior 199

UNIT IV

Principles of Attention 247

UNIT V

Principles of Memory 325

UNIT VI

Principles of Emotion and Social Cognition 431

UNIT VII

Principles of Symbolic Representation 509

UNIT VIII

Principles of Executive Processing 577

UNIT IX

Evolution and Development of Cognitive Functions, Including Consciousness 641

28 Consciousness 705

Appendix: Neural Signaling 729

Preface

The creation of this book has been a highly collaborative effort, one that unfolded over several years as we taught cognitive neuroscience courses to undergraduate and graduate students at Duke University. Initially, each chapter was drafted by the one among us with relatively more expertise in the relevant area. The chapters were then revised during a series of interactive iterations based on extensive comments, suggestions, and improvements from among the authorship. This process of vetting and revision was abetted by additional advice from many other expert colleagues named in the Acknowledgments. Especially important was the incorporation of changes based on frank feedback on the draft chapters from our students. Some topics led to debates among our group that mirrored controversies in the larger field. If the arguments and discussions we experienced come through in the text, so much the better.

Our goal has been not simply to summarize the received wisdom in this rapidly evolving field, but rather to set the stage for future advances in cognitive neuroscience, many of which will be made by those currently studying in institutions all around the world. As important as it may be to elucidate the present status of cognitive neuroscience, it is at least as important to provide a strong sense of the direction the field might take in the future to achieve the still distant goal of understanding the brain and its higher-order operations.

Principles of Cognitive Neuroscience Unit Editors

UNIT I: Roberto Cabeza, Dale Purves, Marty G. Woldorff

UNIT II: Dale Purves

UNIT III: Michael L. Platt

UNIT IV: Marty G. Woldorff

UNIT V: Roberto Cabeza

UNIT VI: Kevin S. LaBar

UNIT VII: Dale Purves, Elizabeth M. Brannon

UNIT VIII: Scott A. Huettel

UNIT IX: Elizabeth M. Brannon, Michael L. Platt, Dale Purves

Acknowledgments

We are greatly indebted to the numerous colleagues whose work we have represented—with accuracy we hope, despite the simplifications that a book like this demands. Many of these researchers as well as others among our colleagues provided valuable suggestions and criticisms about the presentation of specific issues and controversies.

We particularly wish to thank John Allman, Patricia Bauer, Catalin Buhusi, Robert O. Deaner, Mark D'Esposito, Sarah Donohue, Tineke Grent-'t-Jong, Guven Guzeldere, Ben Hayden, Hiroshi Imamizu, Andrew Krystal, Beau Lotto, Warren Meck, Ravi Menon, Karen Meyerhoff, Jamie Morris, Kevin Pelphrey, Ken Roberts, Stephen Shepherd, David V. Smith, Jared Stokes, Jim Voyvodic, Karli K. Watson, Bill Wojtach, and Vince Wu.

We also benefited enormously from the several classes of Duke University graduate and undergraduate students who provided feedback on the draft versions of the chapters that we used in our teaching over the last few years. Despite this plethora of help, it is of course understood that any errors are attributable to the authors and are not the responsibility of our critics and advisors.

Special thanks are due Len White and George Augustine for their creation of the Appendix on neural signaling, and to Mark Williams and Len White for allowing us to include their *Sylvius 4* tutorial as an adjunct to the book. Thanks are also due the authors and editors of *Neuroscience*—in particular to George Augustine, David Fitzpatrick, Anthony LaMantia, Bill Hall, Len White, and Mark Williams—for much valuable information and art developed over the several editions of that complementary book.

Finally, we are enormously grateful to Carol Wigg and Stephanie Hiebert for their expert copyediting; to Kathaleen Emerson, Laura Green, Julie HawkOwl, and Chelsea Holabird for their skill and patience in preparing the book for production; to Christopher Small and Jefferson Johnson for their fine production work; to David McIntyre for his imaginative efforts in obtaining photographs and other images; to Craig Durant and Dragonfly Studios for their expeditious preparation of the illustrations, with special thanks to Joanne Delphia and Joan Gemme at Sinauer Associates for their efforts on the art program; and to Graig Donini for managing the entire project with tact, determination, and high standards.

Supplements to accompany
Principles of Cognitive Neuroscience

For the Student

Companion Website (www.sinauer.com/cogneuro)

The *Principles of Cognitive Neuroscience* companion website features review and study resources to help students master the material presented in the textbook. Access to the site is free of charge and requires no access code. (Instructor registration is required for students to access the online quizzes.) Features of the site include Chapter Outlines, Chapter Summaries, Online Quizzes, Animations, Flashcard Activities, and a complete Glossary. (See the inside front cover for additional information.)

Sylvius 4: *An Interactive Atlas and Visual Glossary of Human Neuroanatomy*

(Free download; access code provided with every new copy of the text)

S. Mark Williams, Leonard E. White, and Andrew C. Mace

Sylvius 4 provides a unique digital learning environment for exploring and understanding the structure of the human central nervous system. *Sylvius* features fully annotated surface views of the human brain, as well as interactive tools for dissecting the central nervous system and viewing fully annotated cross-sections of preserved specimens and living subjects imaged by magnetic resonance. (See the inside front cover for additional information and download instructions.)

For the Instructor

Instructor's Resource Library

The *Principles of Cognitive Neuroscience* Instructor's Resource Library includes a variety of resources to help instructors in developing their course and delivering lectures. The Library includes:

- Textbook Figures andTables: All the figures and tables from the textbook are provided in JPEG format (both high- and low-resolution).
- PowerPoint® Presentations: All the figures and tables from each chapter are provided on PowerPoint slides, making it easy for instructors to add figures to their presentations.
- *Sylvius* Image Library: A range of images from the companion program *Sylvius 4* are provided in PowerPoint® format.
- Quiz Questions: All of the questions from the companion website's online quizzes are provided in Microsoft Word format.
- Animations: All of the animations from the companion website are provided as Flash files. The animations are also provided on PowerPoint® slides for easy integration into instructor presentations.

Introduction: What Is Cognitive Neuroscience?

Cognitive neuroscience is a relatively new scientific field that has arisen from the marriage of *neuroscience*, a biomedical field of study that focuses on animal nervous systems and that by any measure has flourished both conceptually and technically during the past century; and *cognitive psychology*, a discipline rooted in the long-standing interest of natural philosophers and psychologists in understanding human mental processes. The rationale for this union is the perception in both camps that many human brain functions that only a few years ago were considered to be beyond the reach of neuroscientific methods and theory are in fact amenable to an approach that combines the best of both traditions.

Neuroscience

Nervous systems are found in all but the simplest animals. The field of **neuroscience** is concerned with how the nervous systems of humans and other animals are organized and how they function. Over the years, neuroscientists have used many different methods and a wide variety of non-human animal studies to advance the field. Indeed, successes in neuroscience have typically involved relatively simple model systems, explored with methods and a mindset that are aptly described as "reductionist" (i.e., using techniques and a perspectives that seek to explain neural processes in terms of their component parts and elemental functions). The most important questions in neuroscience that have been addressed during the last century thus include:

■ How do the cells of the nervous system function as signaling devices in anatomical, electrophysiological, and molecular terms?

■ How do nerve cells come together in the circuits (i.e., ensembles of nerve cells) that underlie virtually all neural functions and behaviors?

■ How are these neural circuits organized into systems in humans and other animals?

A basic understanding of the answers to these questions is fundamental to cognitive neuroscience. Introducing this information in the context of the anatomy of the human nervous system is the goal of Chapter 1.

Cognitive Psychology

In addition to mediating sensory and motor functions, the brains of human beings, non-human primates, and (in varying degrees) other animals with highly evolved brains exhibit abilities that are loosely referred to as **cognitive functions**. Cognitive functions include perception, the organization of complex motor behaviors, attention, learning and memory, emotions and their social import, language and other symbolic representations, reasoning, decision making, problem solving, consciousness, and other abilities that are of special interest because they lie at the core of understanding the nature of *Homo sapiens*. On these topics, classical neuroscience has been relatively silent, primarily because of the large gulf between the molecular, cellular, and circuit-level analyses of most mainstream neuroscience and the more complex interactions that underlie human cognitive functions. With few exceptions, the study of these "higher" functions was left to philosophy in centuries past, and, in the nineteenth and much of the twentieth centuries, to the subfield of psychology called **cognitive psychology**.

Like neuroscience, psychology is a diverse field that has always included information gleaned from non-human animal models as well as human subjects. In contrast to the reductionist goals of most neuroscience, however, the goal of psychology has been to understand mental functions and behavior as such rather than the cellular and molecular underpinnings of these phenomena. The great natural philosophers of the eighteenth century were largely content to speculate about human cognitive abilities without concern for experimental evidence, of which there was in any case very little. By the nineteenth century, however, those drawn to the same philosophical interests had become convinced that such matters could and should be studied by means of experimental observation. Examples of such individuals include Wilhelm Wundt, Hermann Helmholtz, Hermann Ebbinghaus, Gustav Fechner, and Ernst Weber, all of whom figure in later chapters. As a result of such work, psychology gradually distinguished itself as a scientific discipline in its own right.

Cognitive psychology, as described in Chapter 2, emerged as the subfield of psychology specifically devoted to higher human brain functions. The reason for singling out humans in this quest is that **cognition**, which literally means "the faculty of knowing," has always been considered a largely (some would say exclusively) human faculty. Thus, for better or worse, cognitive psychology has *de facto* been the branch of psychology devoted primarily to understanding the cognitive properties, abilities, and behaviors of humans as opposed to other animals. In particular, cognitive psychology studies those aspects of human mentation that entail conscious awareness, perception, and thought as opposed to those brain processes and behaviors usually described as simple, unconscious and automatic reflexes.

Cognitive Neuroscience

Because the nominally higher-order brain functions and associated behaviors—the concerns of cognitive psychology—ultimately depend on the molecular, cellular, and circuit-level machinery that has been the focus of neuroscience, it now makes sense to transcend the historical distinctions of these two fields by joining them in a common enterprise. This convergence defines **cognitive neuroscience**.

Despite their separate histories and traditions, the impetus in recent decades to bring together neuroscience and cognitive psychology has been strong. As more and more basic problems in neuroscience were solved to a reasonable level of satisfaction and as powerful new research tools were developed, scientists in this field increasingly aspired to understand a wider range of human brain functions. At the same time, cognitive psychology increasingly aspired to closer ties with the concepts and methods of neuroscience as a means of advancing its long-standing agenda of understanding human mental processes.

As described in Chapter 3, further impetus came from the introduction some 25 years ago of methods that allow investigators to image and otherwise measure normal human brain activity as subjects perform various tasks. The rapid emergence of cognitive neuroscience over the last two decades is an expression of what many see as the next logical step for both neuroscience and cognitive psychology, driven by powerful new methods for noninvasive studies of the brain. Further incentive is provided by the many unanswered questions about how the cognitive functions of the brain work, and thus the promise of new insights and principles. The union of neuroscience and cognitive psychology has been, and continues to be, motivated by the exciting possibility of better understanding complex human brain functions that have puzzled thinkers for centuries.

As in any marriage, cognitive neuroscience is characterized by considerable optimism and the hope that this melding of interests and skills will bear fruit. It is, of course, too soon to say how fully these expectations will be met, but the new field has so far proven an exciting one for its practitioners, leading to new insights into problems raised by the remarkable abilities of the human brain—problems that thinkers of all sorts have long wished to understand and resolve.

About This Book

Understanding higher human brain functions depends on a good working knowledge of the facts of neuroscience, the perspectives of cognitive psychology, and the methods now used by cognitive neuroscientists. An overview of these subjects is presented in the three chapters comprising Unit I. Each of the remaining eight units covers a single major topic, and together these topics define the substance and breadth of cognitive neuroscience as it is practiced today. Our purpose is to provide an account of the issues cognitive neuroscientists are concerned with presently, the matters they have more or less agreed upon, and—most important—the questions that remain unsettled.

The format of the chapters is straightforward and should be self-explanatory. Each begins with a brief introduction to the material covered and ends with a brief summary. Most chapters include boxed material that is no less important than the running text but covers issues that are more or less self-contained or that do not fit readily into the narrative flow. Finally, references to useful reviews, important original papers, and books are given at the end of each chapter. This selected guide to the literature is not intended to be comprehensive, but does indicate reasonable starting points.

The chapters that follow are not meant simply to inform readers about the rapidly growing canon of cognitive neuroscience, but to make clear the nature of the many challenges that remain. We hope that students—in the broadest sense of this term—will be stimulated to enter the fray, contributing to a rapidly evolving field that will eventually shape how we think about our fellow human beings and ourselves.

UNIT I

Principles of Neuroscience and Their Importance in Studying Cognitive Functions

This unit is intended to provide the basic information needed to tackle the diverse aspects of cognitive neuroscience outlined in the Introduction. Given the importance of understanding the functional and structural properties of the human nervous system, Chapter 1 briefly reviews the cellular composition of the nervous system: how neurons signal, how they interconnect to form neural circuits, and how neural circuits are organized into neural systems. Because the anatomy of the human nervous system, and particularly that of the brain, is integral to the study of cognitive neuroscience, Chapter 1 also introduces the basic neuroanatomical vocabulary that is essential to the rest of the book.

Chapter 2 summarizes the rich heritage of cognitive psychology, a corpus that is as important as neuroscientific principles for understanding the material in the units that follow. Finally, Chapter 3 reviews the major ways cognitive neuroscientists study brain functions, ranging from electrophysiological assessment of individual neurons to studies of patients with deficits arising from damage to specific brain regions. The imaging technologies that have revolutionized our ability to study the living, behaving brain are also described in some detail, as it is these technologies that in many ways are responsible for the emergence of cognitive neuroscience as a new field. ∎

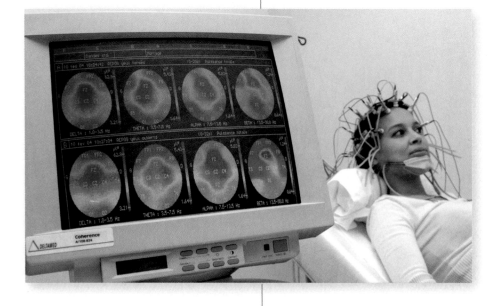

1

The Human Nervous System

Introduction

Understanding of the range of issues that cognitive neuroscience presents must ultimately be based on a working knowledge of the structure and function of the human nervous system, the brain in particular. The focus in this first chapter is thus on how the elements of the nervous system are organized into the circuits of the major sensory, motor, and associational systems that underlie higher brain functions. The chapter begins with a brief account of the nature of nerve cells and nerve cell signaling properties. For those who wish to learn more about this aspect of neuroscience, a detailed account of how neurons generate action potentials and how this information is transmitted by means of synaptic connections between neurons is included in the book's Appendix on neural signaling. The goal in what follows is to introduce the main features of nervous system structure and function at a level appropriate to understanding the material in the rest of the book. This understanding does not demand a detailed knowledge of cellular neurobiology, but does require familiarity with the nature of nerve cells, with general ways neural signaling occurs, and most especially with the organization of the human nervous system. Given its complexity, mastering human neuroanatomy presents a daunting challenge that is mastered only over time; this chapter is intended to provide a foundation for this ongoing task.

Cellular Components of the Nervous System

The fact that **cells** are the elements that make up all animal tissues was recognized early in the nineteenth century. Not until well into the twentieth century, however, did neuroscientists finally agree that the nervous system, like all other organ systems, is comprised of these fundamental units, and that the cells of the nervous system are exceptional only in some details. Pioneering histological studies led to the further consensus that the cells of the nervous system can be divided into two broad categories:

■ **Nerve cells**, or **neurons**, are specialized to generate and propagate electrical signals over distances that can be up to a meter or more in humans. Information transmitted in the form of these electrical signals is the basis of sensation, behavior, and physiological processes in all animals; it is also the source of the cognitive abilities that reach their most complex expression in human beings. Our current understanding of this signaling process represents one of the more dramatic success stories in modern biology.

■ **Neuroglial cells** comprise a variety of cell types that support and hold together nervous tissue; they are frequently referred to simply as **glia**—the Greek word for "glue"—and they play a variety of important roles in neural function. In contrast to neurons, neuroglial cells are not capable of electrical signaling, but some types (notably the *Schwann cells*, discussed later in the chapter) have a crucial effect on the speed at which a neuron's electrical signals travel.

Like other cells, each nerve cell has a **cell body** containing a nucleus and **organelles** (endoplasmic reticulum, ribosomes, Golgi apparatus, and mitochondria), and other organelles that are essential to the function of all cells (**Figure 1.1**). The distinguishing features of nerve cells arise from their specialization for *intercellular communication*. Neurons are characterized by a single, often quite long extension from the cell body called an **axon**, and by shorter branches called **dendrites** (also called *dendritic branches* or *dendritic processes*). The axon's purpose is to convey information, usually in the form of electrical impulses, over distances that range from millimeters to meters in the case axons that extend from the spinal cord to the arms and legs. Dendrites receive information from the axonal endings arising from other nerve cells.

Neurons in humans and other mammals are unusual in their extraordinary numbers; the human brain alone is estimated to contain some 100 billion neurons and several times as many neuroglial supporting cells. The neurons that make up the human nervous system also display a much greater range of dis-

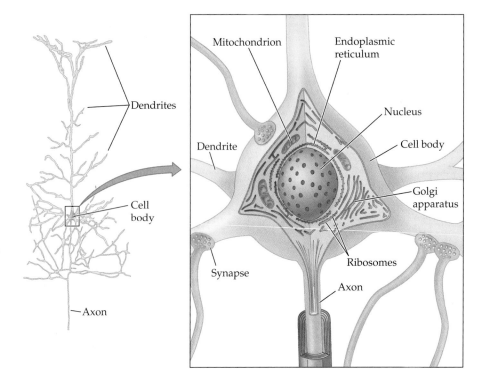

Figure 1.1 Major features of nerve cells (neurons). The drawing on the left shows a typical neuron, identifying the cell body (soma), its dendritic arborization, and the initial part of its axon. The blowup is of the vicinity of the nerve cell body and shows the variety of organelles neurons share with other cell types as well as the axonal, dendritic, and synaptic specializations that make them unique.

tinct cell types than the cells of other organ systems, whether this judgment is made on the basis of neuronal morphology or their variety of physiological properties. (The liver, in contrast, is an example of a more typical organ that has a far more uniform cellular makeup.) This structural and functional diversity, and the rich interconnection of nerve cells to form intricate signaling ensembles called **neuronal circuits**, is the foundation on which all human behaviors and cognitive functions are built.

Nerve Cells and Their Signaling Functions

The transfer of information from one neuron to another is typically mediated by a variety of **neurotransmitters**. These molecules are released from **synapses** and change the electrical potential across the membrane of the neuron they contact. As a rule, many nerve cells converge on a single target neuron, and the terminal axon branches of each neuron typically diverge to contract a number of other target neurons. The convergent input onto a neuron at any moment is integrated, or "read out," at the point of origin of the axon from the cell body—a region called the **axon hillock**—and determines whether or not the target neuron will carry the signal forward to its own target cells.

The mechanism that carries signals to additional target cells is called the **action potential**, a self-regenerating wave of electrical activity that propagates from its point of initiation at the axon hillock to the synaptic endings at the axon's terminus. Specialization for signal conduction is reflected in many aspects of axons, including a variety of proteins present in axonal membranes—**ion channels** and **ion pumps**—that are dedicated to supporting action potential propagation. The energy that ion pumps expend maintaining ionic gradients in the face of signaling is the primary reason that neurons are so metabolically costly. In addition to other nerve cells in the brain and the rest of the central nervous system, the target cells contacted by axonal endings include the autonomic ganglion cells, muscle cells, and glandular cells throughout the body. A detailed account of neural signaling and the membrane properties that enable action potentials is provided in the Appendix.

In addition to the axon, the other salient morphological feature of most nerve cells is the number and arrangement of their dendrites. Dendritic geometries range from a very small minority of neurons that lack dendrites altogether to neurons with elaborate *dendritic arborizations* that resemble the branching patterns of a mature tree (**Figure 1.2**). Dendrites, together with the cell body, provide the major site for the synaptic contacts from other nerve cells.

An important functional feature enabled by the morphological diversity of neuronal dendritic geometries is that the number of inputs that a particular neuron receives is generally proportional to the complexity of its dendritic arborization: nerve cells that lack dendrites are innervated by just one or a few other nerve cells, whereas those with increasingly elaborate dendrites are contacted by a commensurately larger number of other neurons. The number of inputs received by a single human neuron varies from 1 to about 100,000. This range reflects a fundamental purpose of the different nerve cell types—namely, to integrate information from other neurons. The number of inputs to a given neuron is therefore an important determinant of its function.

As already mentioned, the endings of neuronal axons are specialized to transfer information onto the dendrites and cell bodies of the neurons they contact by the release of neurotransmitter substances. When an action potential arrives at these axon terminals, the associated change in the membrane potential of the terminal causes the secretion of neurotransmitter molecules. Typically, the *presynaptic terminal* of the axon (also called a *synaptic bouton*) is immediately adjacent to an elaborate complementary *postsynaptic specialization*

(A)

(B)

(C)

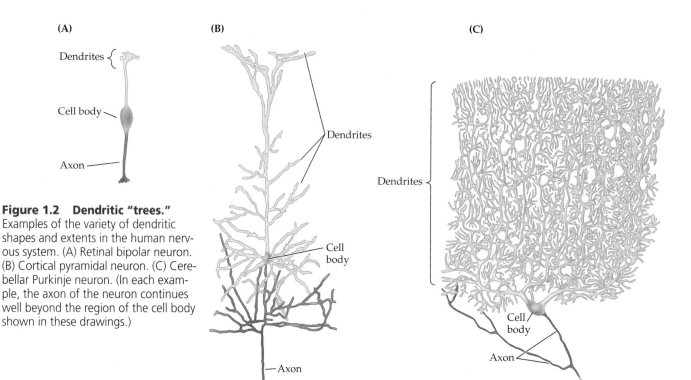

Figure 1.2 Dendritic "trees."
Examples of the variety of dendritic shapes and extents in the human nervous system. (A) Retinal bipolar neuron. (B) Cortical pyramidal neuron. (C) Cerebellar Purkinje neuron. (In each example, the axon of the neuron continues well beyond the region of the cell body shown in these drawings.)

of the dendrite or cell body of the contacted cell. There is, however, no physical continuity between the pre- and postsynaptic elements at such chemical **synapses*** (**Figure 1.3**; see also Figure 1.1).

Synaptic communication between two neurons occurs by the diffusion of neurotransmitter molecules from the presynaptic terminal across an intervening space called the **synaptic cleft** where the molecules bind to **neurotransmitter receptors**, which are proteins embedded in the membrane of the postsynaptic specialization. The synaptic contacts on dendrites and cell bodies are actually a special elaboration of the secretory apparatus found in many types of non-neural cells, such as the cells of the pancreas that secrete insulin or the cells of the gut that secrete digestive enzymes. The secretory organelles in the presynaptic terminal of chemical synapses are called **synaptic vesicles** and they are each filled with several thousand neurotransmitter molecules (see Figure 1.3).

The binding of neurotransmitters to receptors opens or closes ion channels in the postsynaptic membrane, which as noted changes the postsynaptic membrane potential; these potential changes are, in the aggregate, the information that is read out at the axon hillock, determining whether or not the contacted cell fires an action potential or remains silent. This overall process is the common currency of signaling throughout the nervous system.

Obviously this brief account only begins to describe the enormous effort over more than a century that neuroscientists have devoted to understanding the mechanisms of neural signaling. These well established signaling processes form the foundation for pursuing the questions that confront cognitive neuroscientists. Students who wish to learn more about these fundamental

---

*In the brain, and elsewhere in the nervous system, a small minority of the neural contacts are *electrical synapses* that operate quite differently from chemical synapses; they are not discussed here because of their rarity and their specialized function, but they are covered briefly in the Appendix (see Figure A13A).

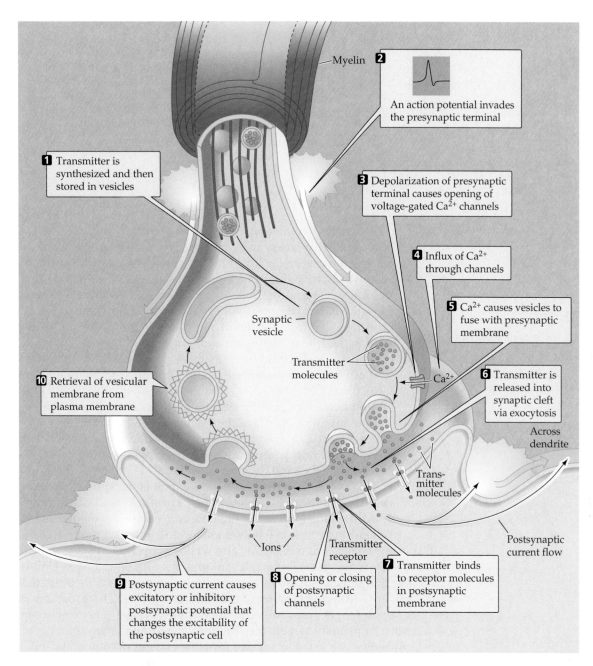

1 Transmitter is synthesized and then stored in vesicles

Myelin

2 An action potential invades the presynaptic terminal

3 Depolarization of presynaptic terminal causes opening of voltage-gated Ca^{2+} channels

4 Influx of Ca^{2+} through channels

5 Ca^{2+} causes vesicles to fuse with presynaptic membrane

Synaptic vesicle

Transmitter molecules

Ca^{2+}

6 Transmitter is released into synaptic cleft via exocytosis

10 Retrieval of vesicular membrane from plasma membrane

Across dendrite

Transmitter molecules

Postsynaptic current flow

Ions

Transmitter receptor

9 Postsynaptic current causes excitatory or inhibitory postsynaptic potential that changes the excitability of the postsynaptic cell

8 Opening or closing of postsynaptic channels

7 Transmitter binds to receptor molecules in postsynaptic membrane

processes, or who simply want to review the mechanisms of neural signaling in more detail, should consult the material on cellular neurophysiology and neurotransmission in the Appendix.

Functional Organization of the Human Nervous System

Neural circuits

All cognitive functions depend on the operation of groups of interconnected neurons called **neural circuits**. Although the arrangement of neural circuits varies greatly according to the function of the different components of the nervous system, certain features and the relevant terminology are common to all neural circuitry.

Figure 1.3   A chemical synapse.
This schematic diagram details the sequence of events initiated when an action potential arrives at the presynaptic axon terminal. The subsequent transfer of information to the postsynaptic specialization is accomplished by a variety of neurotransmitter molecules that cross the synaptic cleft and bind to receptor molecules embedded in the membrane of the postsynaptic cell.

(A)

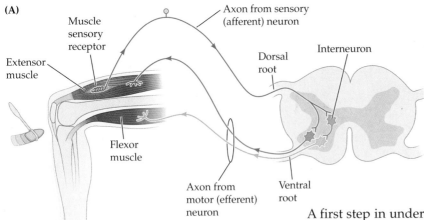

Figure 1.4 An example of a simple neural circuit. (A) The elements of the myotatic stretch reflex (the "knee-jerk" reflex). (B) Diagram showing the ability to record electrophysiological responses from each element during the execution of the reflex in an experimental animal, thus revealing the detailed function of its constituent neurons.

(B)

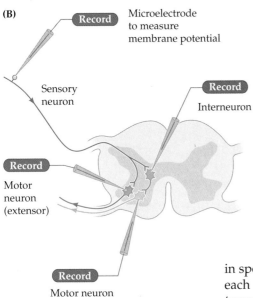

A first step in understanding neural circuitry is nomenclature. Nerve cells that carry information *centrally*—that is, toward the central nervous system (the brain or spinal cord) or, more generally, toward any neural processing structure—are called **afferent neurons**. Nerve cells that carry information *peripherally*, away from the central nervous system (or away from the structure in question), are called **efferent neurons**. These terms are mainly used in describing the inputs and outputs of the brain; within the brain itself, and within the cerebral cortex in particular, the question of whether signals are traveling centrally or peripherally is largely moot.

Nerve cells that participate only in the local aspects of a circuit, as in many components of the brain, are called **interneurons** (or, alternatively, *local circuit neurons*). These three classes—afferent neurons, efferent neurons, and interneurons—are the basic constituents of all neural circuits.

One simple example of a neural circuit is the **spinal reflex arc**; the most familiar of these is the "knee-jerk" response (**Figure 1.4A**). The afferent limb of the reflex arc comprises bipolar **sensory neurons** whose cell bodies are located in dorsal root ganglia of the spinal cord (see below) and whose peripheral axons terminate in special sensory receptors in the relevant muscles. (As described in Unit II, each of the five senses employs different, highly specialized receptors that *transduce* energy in the environment into neural signals.) The processes of these bipolar afferent neurons run centrally to contact target nerve cells in the spinal cord. The primary targets cord are **motor neurons** in the spinal cord, which in turn give rise to the axons that form the efferent portion of the reflex arc. One group of these efferent motor neurons projects to flexor muscles in the limb, and the other to extensor muscles.

The third element of the spinal reflex circuit is the interneurons of the spinal cord, which serve a *modulatory function*—a feature common to the local neurons in many neural circuits. The interneurons of this "knee-jerk" circuit receive synaptic contacts from the afferent sensory neurons and make synapses on the efferent motor neurons that project to the flexor muscles (i.e., muscles that cause the limb to fold up, as in bending the arm at the elbow or the leg at the knee). The synaptic connections between the sensory afferents and the extensor efferents are **excitatory**, causing the extensor muscles to contract, which thus extends the arm or leg; conversely, the interneurons activated by the afferents are **inhibitory**, and their activation by the afferent axons diminishes electrical activity in motor neurons, causing the flexor muscles to become less active (**Box 1A**). The result is a complementary activation of the synergist muscles and inactivation of the antagonist muscles that control the

■ BOX 1A Intracellular Recording from Nerve Cells

All neural signaling depends on changes in the permeability of nerve cell membranes to different ions. Such changes in ion permeability alter the distribution of electrical charges across the neuronal membrane, thus changing the *membrane potential* of the affected neurons. The most informative—but not always the most feasible—way to observe the events underlying neural signaling is to insert a microelectrode into the cell that directly measures the electrical potential across the neuronal membrane. A typical microelectrode used in such **intracellular recording** is a piece of glass tubing pulled to a fine point with an opening of less than 1 micron in diameter; the electrode is then filled with a good electrical conductor. This conductive core can then be connected to a voltmeter (an oscilloscope) that records the transmembrane voltage of the nerve cell over time.

When a microelectrode is inserted through the membrane of a neuron, it records a negative potential, indicating that the cell has a means of generating a constant voltage across its membrane when it is at rest. This voltage, called the *resting membrane potential*, depends on the type of neuron being examined, but it is always a small fraction of a volt (typically –50 to –100 mV). *Action potentials represent transient changes in the resting membrane potential of neurons.*

An electrical current can be injected by inserting a second microelectrode into the same neuron and connecting that electrode to a battery. (In the natural course of events, such a stimulating current would emanate from the action of neurotransmitter molecules on postsynaptic neurons, or from sensory receptor activation; see figure.) If the polarity of the current delivered in this way makes the membrane potential more negative (called **hyperpolarization**), nothing dramatic happens. The membrane potential simply changes in proportion to the magnitude of the injected current. Such hyperpolarizing responses do not engage the action potential mechanism and are therefore called *passive electrical responses*.

A much different phenomenon is seen if current of the opposite polarity is delivered, so that the membrane potential of the nerve cell becomes more positive than the resting potential (called **depolarization**). In this case, at a certain level of membrane potential called the **threshold potential**, an action potential occurs. The action potential is an active response generated by the membrane properties of neurons. It appears on an oscilloscope as a brief (1–5 ms) change from negative to positive in the transmembrane potential. Importantly, the amplitude ("height") of the action potential is independent of the magnitude of the current used to evoke it; that is, larger currents do not elicit larger action potentials. The action potentials of a given neuron are therefore said to be *all-or-none*, because they occur either fully or not at all. However, if the amplitude or duration of the stimulus current is increased sufficiently, multiple action potentials occur. Thus the intensity of a stimulus is encoded in the *frequency* of action potentials rather than in their amplitude.

Intracellular electrodes, as noted in the text, can record synaptic potentials and receptor potentials when the electrode is near synapses or sensory receptors, respectively. A chemical synapse that releases a transmitter molecule whose interaction with postsynaptic receptors brings the membrane potential of the contacted neuron closer to the threshold of action potential initiation by depolarization is called an *excitatory synapse* (producing an *excitatory postsynaptic potential*, or *EPP*), whereas a transmitter that acts to hyperpolarize the postsynaptic membrane (or simply stabilizes it at the resting level) is called an *inhibitory synapse*.

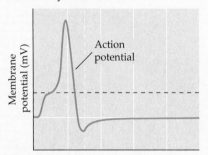

(A) Sensory neuron

Action potential

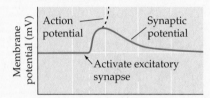

(B) Motor neuron (extensor)

Action potential — Synaptic potential

Activate excitatory synapse

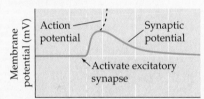

(C) Interneuron

Action potential — Synaptic potential

Activate excitatory synapse

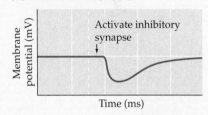

(D) Motor neuron (flexor)

Activate inhibitory synapse

Time (ms)

The membrane potential changes apparent with intracellular recording from neurons, as might be obtained from the arrangement shown in Figure 1.4B. Such changes, which are shown as they would be recorded on an oscilloscope, are the basis of all neuronal signaling. (A) An acton potential. (B,C) Dashed lines indicate the onset of the action potential that would normally be elicited by these excitatory synaptic potentials. (D) An inhibitory synaptic potential.

position of the leg. The net result is that when the muscles connected to the patellar tendon are briefly stretched by the tap of the reflex hammer, the leg extends.

A more detailed picture of the events underlying a stretch reflex or any other neural circuit can be obtained by electrophysiological recording (**Figure 1.4B**).

Electrophysiological recording has been and continues to be a mainstay of modern neuroscience, including cognitive neuroscience (see Chapter 3). There are two basic approaches to measuring electrical activity at the cellular level: extracellular recording, where an electrode is placed *near* the nerve cell of interest to detect action potential activity; and intracellular recording, where the electrode is placed *inside* the cell and records changes in membrane potential, as seen in Box 1A. Extracellular recordings detect only action potentials, the all-or-nothing changes in the potential across nerve cell membranes that convey information from one point to another in the nervous system alluded to earlier; such recordings are widely used in studies of cognitive functions in non-human primates and, to a limited extent, in humans during neurosurgery. Intracellular recordings are more revealing because they detect the graded **synaptic potentials** that trigger action potentials, but are difficult to do in living animals (although this sort of recording can be done). These triggering potentials also arise at sensory receptors in the periphery, where they are called **receptor potentials**. The changes in membrane potential that together are the basis of neural signaling can thus be measured from each element of the circuit before, during, and after a stimulus occurs. By comparing the onset, duration, and frequency of receptor, synaptic and action potential activity in each cell, a detailed functional picture of any circuit can be established (see Figure 1.4B and Box 1A).

Neural systems

Neural circuits are typically grouped together to form **neural systems** that serve broad functional purposes (**Figure 1.5**). The most obvious of these systems are:

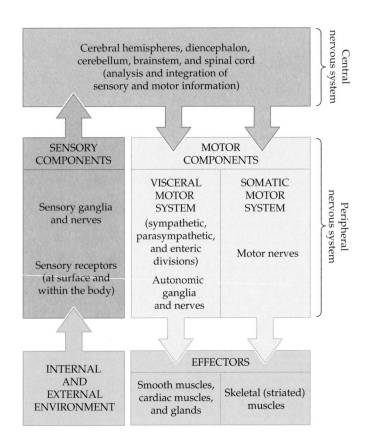

Figure 1.5 Organization of the human nervous system. This schematic diagram illustrates the flow of information through the central and peripheral components of the human nervous system. Stimuli from the environment send signals to the brain and spinal cord (the *central nervous system*) via the *sensory* components of the *peripheral nervous system*. Processing circuits in the central nervous system interpret the significance of this sensory input and in turn send signals via the *motor* elements of the peripheral nervous system. These signals result in (i.e., "effect") a large array of actions, both voluntary and involuntary, which are carried out by the body's muscles and glands.

1. The **sensory systems** (visual, auditory, mechanosensory, and chemosensory; see Unit II) that acquire and process information from the environment.

2. The **motor systems** (see Unit III) that allow an animal to respond to sensory and stored information by activating **effectors**—muscles or glands. The motor neurons that activate the skeletal muscles to generate body movement make up the **somatic motor system,** whereas those that govern cardiac muscle, the smooth muscles of the gut and other organs, and the glands comprise the **visceral** or **autonomic motor system**.

The majority of neurons and neural circuits, however, lie between these relatively well-defined input and output systems. These are collectively referred to as **associational systems**. It is the associational systems at the level of the cerebral cortex, together with their subcortical components, that mediate the functions of greatest interest to cognitive neuroscience, and will be the subjects of Units IV through IX.

Structural Organization of the Human Nervous System

The central and peripheral nervous systems

In addition to these broad functional distinctions, the nervous system of humans and other vertebrates is conventionally divided anatomically into *central* and *peripheral* components (**Figure 1.6**). The **central nervous system**

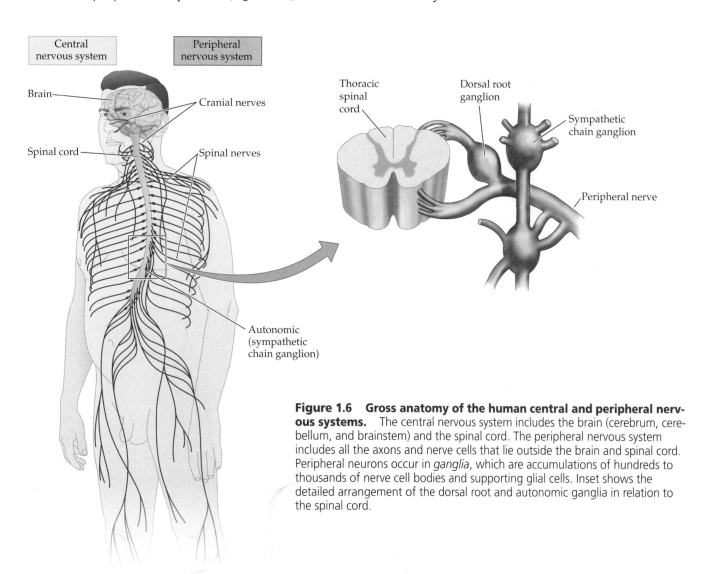

Figure 1.6 Gross anatomy of the human central and peripheral nervous systems.   The central nervous system includes the brain (cerebrum, cerebellum, and brainstem) and the spinal cord. The peripheral nervous system includes all the axons and nerve cells that lie outside the brain and spinal cord. Peripheral neurons occur in *ganglia*, which are accumulations of hundreds to thousands of nerve cell bodies and supporting glial cells. Inset shows the detailed arrangement of the dorsal root and autonomic ganglia in relation to the spinal cord.

includes the **brain** (cerebrum, cerebellum, and brainstem) and the **spinal cord**. The **peripheral nervous system** comprises all the axons and nerve cells that lie outside the brain and spinal cord. Even in humans, rather surprisingly, more neurons are estimated to be in the peripheral nervous system (mostly in the gut) than in the brain. These peripheral neurons are located in **ganglia**, which are local accumulations (hundreds to thousands) of nerve cell bodies and supporting glial cells. The axons of the peripheral nervous system are gathered into **nerves** (bundles of axons and supporting cells); nerves can arise from the brainstem, spinal cord, or sensory and autonomic ganglia.

Within the central nervous system, nerve cells are arranged in two general configurations (**Figure 1.7A**). **Nuclei** are relatively compact accumulations of

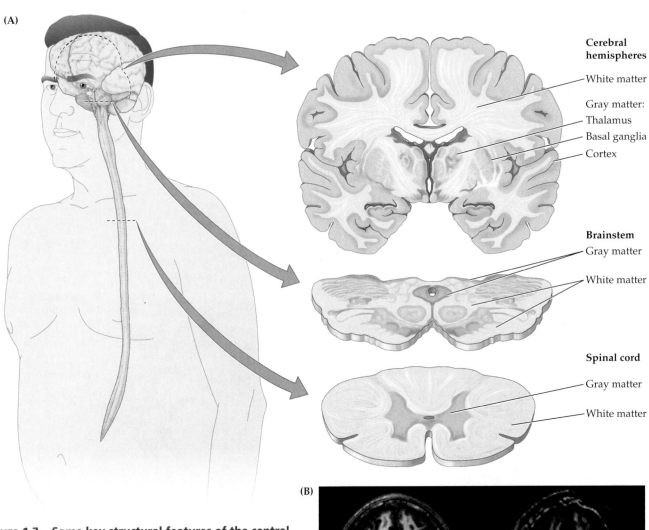

(A)

Cerebral hemispheres

White matter

Gray matter:

Thalamus

Basal ganglia

Cortex

Brainstem

Gray matter

White matter

Spinal cord

Gray matter

White matter

(B)

Figure 1.7 Some key structural features of the central nervous system. (A) Distinctions between gray matter and white matter in the brain and spinal cord. The coronal section through the cerebral hemispheres indicates the cerebral cortex and some of the major subcortical nuclei that will be of particular interest in later chapters. (B) The major white matter tracts of the cerebrum are seen in a horizontal magnetic resonance imaging section (left); various tracts can be functionally distinguished (different colors) using a method called diffusion tensor imaging (right). (Magnetic resonance imaging (MRI) techniques are explained in Chapter 3.) (B courtesy of the Johns Hopkins Medical Institute, Laboratory of Brain Anatomical MRI.)

THE HUMAN NERVOUS SYSTEM ■ 17

neurons that have functionally related inputs and outputs; these collections of hundreds to hundreds of thousands or even millions of nerve cell bodies and their connections are found throughout the brain and spinal cord. In general, nuclei define the functional organization of the central nervous system at the **subcortical** level (i.e., the components of the brain that lie beneath the cerebral cortex). In contrast, the **cerebral cortex** is the sheetlike, folded array of millions to billions of nerve cells that covers the surfaces of the cerebral hemispheres and cerebellum. (The term *cortex*—plural, *cortices*—is from the Latin for "bark" or "shell" and refers the outer layer of a structure.)

Axons in the central nervous system are gathered into **tracts**, which are in this sense equivalent to peripheral nerves (**Figure 1.7B**). Within a tract, glial cells of the central nervous system, called *oligodendrocytes*, envelop the central axons. In much the same way, another type of glial cells known as *Schwann cells* wrap the peripheral nerves. Envelopment of axons by oligodendrocytes and Schwann cells gives rise to a multilayered, membranous coating called **myelin** (see Figure 1.1) that surrounds many central and peripheral axons. Myelin exerts important effects on the transmission of neural signals by increasing the speed at which action potentials are conducted along axons (see the Appendix).

Two other key histological terms are used to distinguish nuclei and cortices from axon tracts: **gray matter** refers to the nuclei and/or cortices, which are rich in neuronal cell bodies and synapses; **white matter** refers to axon tracts. These names arose from the color of the respective regions in the postmortem brain. The relative whiteness of the axon tracts arises from the predominance of myelinated axons in the major central nervous system pathways.

A final feature of the overall organization of the human nervous system concerns the various types of the ganglia in the peripheral nervous system. **Sensory ganglia** (singular, *ganglion*) lie adjacent to either the spinal cord (where they are referred to as **dorsal root ganglia**; see Figure 1.6) or the brainstem (where they are called **cranial nerve ganglia;** see Figure 1.9). As mentioned, the nerve cells in sensory ganglia send axons to the periphery that end in (or on) specialized receptors that transduce information about a wide variety of stimuli.

The organization of **autonomic ganglia** in the visceral or autonomic motor division of the peripheral nervous system is a bit more complicated. Visceral motor neurons in the brainstem and spinal cord form synapses with peripheral motor neurons that lie in these ganglia. In the **sympathetic division** of the autonomic motor system, the ganglia are along or in front of the vertebral column (see Figure 1.6) and send axons to a variety of peripheral targets (blood vessels, piloerector muscles, heart, lungs, and many more). In the **parasympathetic division**, the ganglia are found within the organs they innervate, which generally receive input from the sympathetic division as well. Broadly speaking, *sympathetic activity* prepares the organism for the expenditure of metabolic energy, whereas *parasympathetic activity* initiates processes that conserve or store energy.

One major component of the visceral motor system is the **enteric division** (some neuroscientists prefer to think of it as a more or less separate system) made up of numerous small ganglia scattered throughout the wall of the gut. The ganglia of the enteric division modulate processes specifically concerned with digestion.

Major Subdivisions of the Central Nervous System

The central nervous system is considered to have seven basic parts: the **spinal cord, medulla, pons, midbrain, cerebellum, diencephalon,** and the two **cerebral hemispheres** (**Figure 1.8**). The medulla, pons, and midbrain are collectively called the **brainstem**; the diencephalon and cerebral hemispheres are collectively called the **forebrain**.

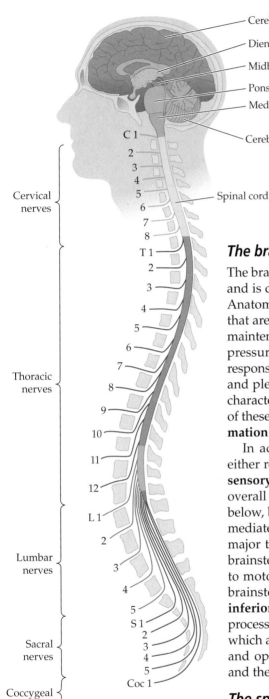

Cerebrum ⎤
Diencephalon ⎦ Forebrain

Midbrain ⎤
Pons ⎬ Brainstem
Medulla ⎦

Cerebellum

C 1
2
3
4
5
6
7
8

Spinal cord

Cervical nerves

T 1
2
3
4
5
6
7
8
9
10
11
12

Thoracic nerves

L 1
2
3
4
5

Lumbar nerves

S 1
2
3
4
5

Sacral nerves

Coc 1

Coccygeal nerve

Figure 1.8 Subdivisions of the human central nervous system.   This lateral view indicates the seven major components of the central nervous system (right) and the five different segmental levels of the vertebral column that encase the spinal cord (left). Spinal (or segmental) nerves from the spinal cord pass through foramina (openings) in the spinal column to innervate much of the body.

The brainstem

The brainstem lies between the forebrain and the upper end of the spinal cord and is conventionally divided into *midbrain, pons,* and *medulla* (**Figure 1.9A**). Anatomically, it is a highly complex structure that houses many of the nuclei that are in immediate control of those reflex functions most important for the maintenance of life. These include the reflexes that determine heart rate, blood pressure, breathing rate, the coughing and vomiting responses, digestive responses, level of consciousness (see Chapter 28), and basic aspects of reward and pleasure (see Chapters 23 and 24). The brainstem's internal structure is characterized by the presence of the nuclei that mediate these functions. Many of these nuclei are located in the core of the brainstem, called the **reticular formation** (**Figure 1.9B**).

In addition, the brainstem houses the nuclei of the **cranial nerves** that either receive input from **cranial sensory ganglia** via their respective **cranial sensory nerves** or give rise to axons that form the **cranial motor nerves**. (The overall structure is thus basically the same as that of the spinal cord described below, but the gray matter is no longer so clearly collected into dorsal, intermediate, and ventral regions.) In addition, the brainstem is the conduit for the major tracts that either relay sensory information from the spinal cord and brainstem to the forebrain, or relay motor commands from the forebrain back to motor neurons in the brainstem and spinal cord. Other structures in the brainstem that will figure importantly in later chapters are the **superior** and **inferior colliculi**, which figure in the control of eye movements and auditory processing, respectively; and the **substantia nigra** and **ventral tegmental area**, which are important in the brain's processing of *reward* (i.e., determining goals and optimal outcomes, the behaviors most appropriate to achieving them, and the feedback when desired goals and outcomes have been achieved).

The spinal cord

The spinal cord extends caudally (tailward) from the brainstem, running from the medullary-spinal junction at about the level of the first cervical vertebra to about the level of the twelfth thoracic vertebra (see Figure 1.8). The vertebral column—and the spinal cord contained within it—is divided into **cervical, thoracic, lumbar, sacral,** and **coccygeal** regions. Each of these segments gives rise to peripheral nerves called the **spinal** (or **segmental**) **nerves** that innervate much of the body. Sensory information carried by the afferent axons in the spinal nerves enters the cord via the **dorsal roots**, and motor commands carried by the efferent axons leave the cord via the **ventral roots** (see Figure 1.4). Once the dorsal and ventral roots join, sensory and motor axons (with some exceptions) travel together in the spinal nerves.

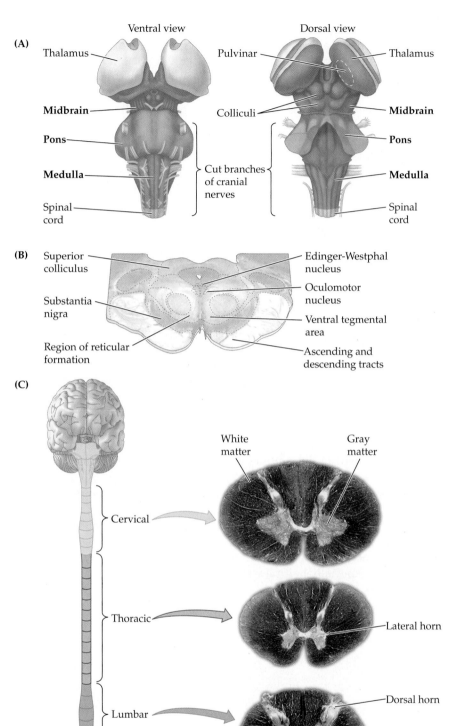

(A)

Ventral view

Thalamus

Midbrain

Pons

Medulla

Spinal cord

Cut branches of cranial nerves

Dorsal view

Pulvinar

Colliculi

Thalamus

Midbrain

Pons

Medulla

Spinal cord

(B)

Superior colliculus

Substantia nigra

Region of reticular formation

Edinger-Westphal nucleus

Oculomotor nucleus

Ventral tegmental area

Ascending and descending tracts

(C)

White matter

Gray matter

Cervical

Thoracic — Lateral horn

Lumbar — Dorsal horn

Ventral horn

Sacral

Figure 1.9 Human brainstem and spinal cord. (A) Ventral and dorsal views showing the three major divisions (boldface type) of the brainstem. The structure rostral to the midbrain is the diencephalon. (B) Cross section of the brainstem at the level of the midbrain, indicating the reticular formation, the cranial nerve nuclei visible at this level, the major ascending and descending tracts, and other structures of special importance for cognitive issues. (C) Organization of the spinal cord, indicating the major subdivisions of the spinal cord gray matter and the major ascending and descending tracts.

The interior of the cord is formed by gray matter, which is surrounded by white matter (see Figure 1.7). In transverse sections, the gray matter is conventionally divided into dorsal (posterior), lateral, and ventral (anterior) "horns" (**Figure 1.9C**). The neurons of the **dorsal horns** receive sensory information that enters the spinal cord via the dorsal roots of the spinal nerves. The **lateral horns** are present primarily in the thoracic region, and contain the visceral motor neurons that project to the sympathetic ganglia. The **ventral horns** contain the cell bodies of motor neurons that send axons via the ventral roots of the spinal nerves to terminate in striated (skeletal) muscles.

The white matter of the spinal cord represents a complex collection of axon tracts related to specific functions. Thus some of these tracts carry ascending (i.e., going toward the brain) sensory information from the body's mechanoreceptors, while others include axons that travel from the cerebral cortex and brainstem to contact spinal motor neurons and interneurons. Still others carry information locally between spinal cord levels to better coordinate motor actions.

Surface features of the brain

Although these various features of the peripheral nervous system, spinal cord, and brainstem are all relevant to aspects of cognitive neuroscience, the anatomy of the brain itself is especially pertinent, and the organization of the cerebral cortex that covers its surface is particularly important. Many of the key features of the human brain are apparent simply from examining the cortex. The major structures visible in this way are the **cerebral hemispheres**, the **cerebellum**, and the medullary (caudal) portion of the brainstem. In addition to the large size of the cerebral hemispheres—they comprise about 85 percent of the brain by weight—their surface is highly folded (**Figure 1.10A**). Neuroanatomists and evolutionary biologists have argued for at least a century about the significance of cerebral convolutions, without reaching any clear resolution. All agree, however, that the infolding of the cerebral hemispheres allows a great deal more cortical surface area (about 1.6 square meters on average) to exist within the confines of the cranium than would otherwise be possible.

The convex convolutions of the brain are known as **gyri** (singular, *gyrus*), and the concavities between the gyri are called **sulci** (singular, *sulcus*) or, if they are especially deep, **fissures**. The brain's sulci and gyri figure heavily in the description of cognitive functions. The most important of the gyri are shown in **Figure 1.10B**; although this figure may seem overly detailed at this point, it will be especially helpful when particular brain regions are discussed in later chapters.

Figure 1.10 Surface view of the human brain.   (A) The left cerebral hemisphere in lateral view (the front of the brain is to the left). (B) Identification of some of the major gyri and other features of the brain surface that will be important landmarks in later chapters.

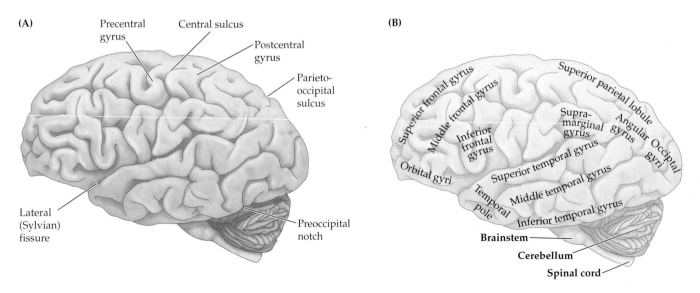

Despite its convolutions, the surface of the cerebral hemispheres is a continuous sheet of neurons and supporting cells about 2 millimeters thick called the **cerebral cortex** (recall that the term "cortex" is Latin for "bark" or "shell"). The sheet is layered in a manner that varies from one region to another, and although they remain poorly understood, these differences are functionally important. Some of these differences and the generic organization of cortical circuitry (which is central to all cognitive functions) are described in **Box 1B**.

The lateral surface view of the human brain in Figure 1.10 is also the best perspective from which to appreciate the **lobes** of the cerebral hemispheres, which are again essential descriptors in discussing cognitive functions. Each hemisphere is conventionally divided into four such lobes, named for the bones of the skull that overlie them: the **frontal**, **parietal**, **temporal**, and **occipital lobes** (**Figure 1.11A,B**). The frontal lobe is the most anterior, and is separated from the parietal lobe by the **central sulcus**. The central sulcus is an especially important landmark because it distinguishes the motor cortices anterior to it from the sensory cortices posterior to it. A particularly important feature of the frontal lobe is the **precentral gyrus**. (The prefix *pre-*, when used anatomically, refers to a structure that is anterior to, or in front of, another.) The cortex of the precentral gyrus is referred to as the **motor cortex** and contains neurons whose axons project to the motor neurons in the brainstem and spinal cord that innervate the skeletal muscles. The temporal lobe extends almost as far anterior as the frontal lobe but is inferior to (underneath) it, the two lobes being separated by the **lateral** (or **Sylvian**) **fissure**. The uppermost region of the temporal lobe contains cortex concerned with audition; the infe-

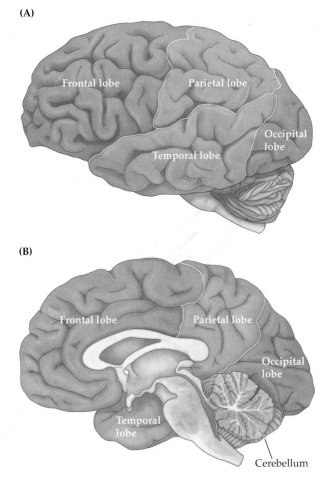

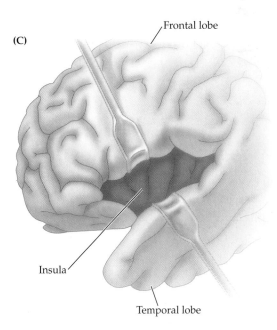

Figure 1.11 Four lobes of the human brain. (A) The lobes as seen from the lateral surface of the left hemisphere. (B) The lobes as seen from the medial surface. (C) Location of the insula.

■ BOX 1B Canonical Organization of the Cerebral Cortex

Because cognitive functions are so closely tied to the cerebral cortex, a general understanding of cortical structure and the organization of its canonical circuitry is especially important. Most of the cortex that covers the cerebral hemispheres is **neocortex**, defined as cortex that has six cellular layers, or *laminae* (singular, *lamina*).

Each layer comprises more or less distinctive populations of cells based on their different densities, sizes, shapes, inputs, and outputs. The layers are designated by numerals 1–6 (or, alternatively, Roman numerals I–VI), with letters for laminar subdivisions (thus, layers 4a, 4b, and 4c in the primary visual cortex).

Nerve cell bodies are rich in basophilic elements such as the cell nucleus and ribosomes, which therefore tend to stain darkly with chemically basic nerve cell stains such as cresyl violet acetate. These so-called *Nissl stains* (named after Franz Nissl, who first described this technique when he was a medical student in nineteenth-century Germany) provide a dramatic picture of brain structure at the histo-

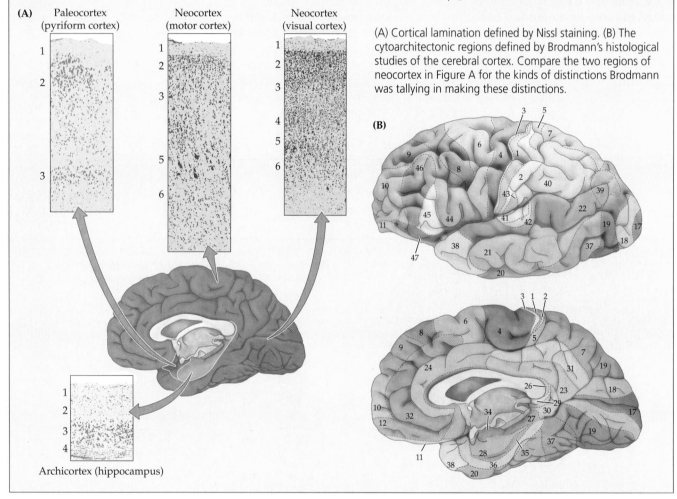

(A) Cortical lamination defined by Nissl staining. (B) The cytoarchitectonic regions defined by Brodmann's histological studies of the cerebral cortex. Compare the two regions of neocortex in Figure A for the kinds of distinctions Brodmann was tallying in making these distinctions.

rior portions deal with high-order visual information, object recognition, and categorization among other functions. Hidden beneath the frontal and temporal lobes is the **insula,** which can be seen only if these two lobes are pulled apart or removed (**Figure 1.11C**). The insular cortex is largely concerned with visceral and autonomic function, including taste and its relationship to emotional responses.

The parietal lobe lies posterior to (behind) the central sulcus and superior to (above) the lateral fissure. The **postcentral gyrus**, the most anterior gyrus in the

logical (microscopic) level. The most striking feature revealed in this way is the distinctive cortical lamination evident in humans and other mammals (Figure A).

Neocortex has six layers, but other brain regions have fewer. The infolded cortex of the hippocampus, for example, has only four laminae. The hippocampal cortex is regarded as evolutionarily more primitive and is therefore called *archicortex* to distinguish it from the six-layered neocortex. (All mammals have a well-developed hippocampus, but many have relatively rudimentary neocortex.) Another type of cortex, *paleocortex*, generally has three layers and is found on the ventral surface of the cerebral hemispheres and along the parahippocampal gyrus in the medial temporal lobe. The functional significance of different numbers of laminae in neo-

cortex, archicortex, and paleocortex is not known, although it seems likely that the greater number of layers in neocortex reflects that more complex processing takes place there than in archicortex or paleocortex.

To a considerable degree, cortical lamination corresponds to the predominance of different neuronal types, and generally different input/output characteristics. For example, neocortical layer 4 is typically rich in *stellate neurons* which have locally ramifying axons; and in the primary sensory cortices, these neurons receive input from the thalamus, the major sensory relay from the peripheral nervous system. Layer 5, and to a lesser degree layer 6, contain large *pyramidal neurons* whose axons typically leave the cortex. The generally smaller pyramidal neurons in layers 2 and 3 (which are not as distinct as their differing numeral assignments suggest) have primarily connections to and from other cortical regions (called *corticocortical connections*), and layer 1 contains mainly axons and dendrites, with few nerve cell bodies present.

Despite the overall uniformity of neocortical lamination, regional differences based on laminar features have long been apparent, allowing investigators to identify anatomically distinct subdivisions of the cerebral cortex (Figure B). Early in the twentieth century, the German neurologist Korbinian Brodmann described about 50

such distinct regions, which he called *cytoarchitectonic area*; today they are more commonly referred to as *Brodmann areas* (the phrase "cytoarchitectonic area" simply being jargon for a cortical region defined by a specific distribution of neurons as revealed with Nissl stains). Brodmann defined these regions with little or no knowledge of their functional significance. Eventually, however, studies of patients in whom one or more cortical areas had been damaged, along with much other evidence, showed that many of the regions neuroanatomists had identified on histological grounds are also functionally distinct.

These variations notwithstanding, the circuitry of all cortical regions has common features. First, each cortical layer has a primary source of inputs and a primary output target. Second, each area has connections in the vertical axis (called *columnar* or *radial* connections), as well as connections in the horizontal axis (*lateral* connections). Third, cells with similar functions tend to be arrayed in vertically aligned groups that span all of the cortical layers and receive inputs that are often segregated into radial or columnar bands. Finally, interneurons within specific cortical layers give rise to extensive local axons that extend horizontally in the cortex, often linking functionally similar groups of cells. The circuitry of any particular cortical region tends to be a variation on this canonical pattern of inputs, outputs, and vertical and horizontal patterns of connectivity (Figure C). The similarity of neocortical structure and circuit organization across the entire cerebrum suggests that there must be a common denominator of cortical operation, although no one has yet deciphered what this is.

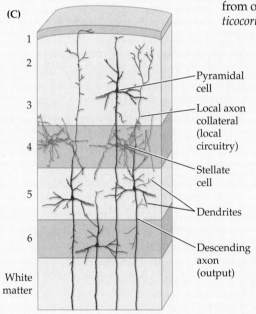

(C)

1
2
3
4
5
6

White matter

Pyramidal cell

Local axon collateral (local circuitry)

Stellate cell

Dendrites

Descending axon (output)

(C) The canonical pattern of neocortical circuitry.

parietal lobe, harbors cortex that is concerned with somatic (bodily) sensation; this area is therefore referred to as the **somatic sensory cortex**. Other regions of the parietal lobe mediate aspects of attention, aspects of language, and a variety of other functions. The boundary between the parietal lobe and the occipital lobe (the most posterior of the hemispheric lobes) is a somewhat arbitrary line from the parieto-occipital sulcus to the preoccipital "notch." The occipital lobe, only a small part of which is apparent from the lateral surface of the brain, is primarily concerned with the initial processing of visual information.

Figure 1.12 Ventral view of the human brain. Some brain structures, including the olfactory tract and the optic chiasm, are best seen from this ventral ("bottom-up") perspective.

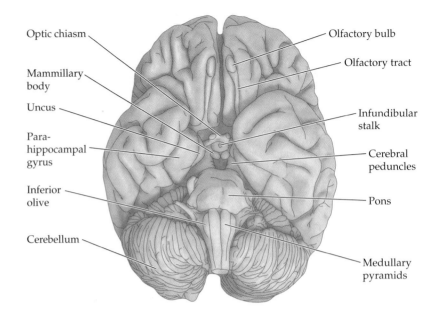

In addition to their roles in primary motor and sensory processing, each cortical lobe has characteristic cognitive functions. Very broadly speaking, the frontal lobes are critical in organizing and planning responses to stimuli, the parietal lobes in attending to stimuli, the temporal lobes in recognizing stimuli, and the occipital lobes in vision.

Other surface features of the brain are best seen from a ventral perspective (**Figure 1.12**). Extending along the inferior (lower) surface of the frontal lobe near the midline are the **olfactory tracts**, which arise from enlargements at their anterior ends called the **olfactory bulbs**. The olfactory bulbs receive input from neurons in the epithelial lining of the nasal cavity; the axons from these neurons make up the **olfactory nerve** (the first of 12 cranial nerves). On the ventromedial surface of the temporal lobe, the **parahippocampal gyrus** conceals the **hippocampus**, a highly convoluted cortical structure that figures importantly in certain kinds of memory. Medial (i.e., closer to the brain's center) to the parahippocampal gyrus is the **uncus**, a protrusion that includes the **pyriform cortex**. The pyriform cortex is the target of the olfactory tract and processes olfactory information.

In the central region of the ventral surface of the forebrain is the **optic chiasm**; immediately posterior to it lies the ventral surface of the **hypothalamus**, including the base of the **pituitary gland** and the **mammillary bodies**. Posterior to the hypothalamus are two large tracts, oriented roughly rostral–caudally ("nose to tail"), the **cerebral peduncles**. These tracts contain axons from the cerebral hemispheres that project to the motor neurons in the brainstem and into the lateral and ventral columns of the spinal cord, as well as axons traveling to forebrain structures. Finally, the ventral surfaces of the pons, medulla, and cerebellar hemispheres are all readily apparent on the ventral surface of the brain.

When the two cerebral hemispheres of the brain are pulled apart and the underlying brainstem divided by cutting in the midline, all the brain's major subdivisions plus a number of additional structures are visible on the medial surface of the hemispheres (**Figure 1.13A,B**; see also Figure 1.11B). In this view, the frontal lobe extends forward from the central sulcus, the medial end of which can just be seen. The **parieto-occipital sulcus**, running from the superior to the inferior aspect of the hemisphere, separates the parietal and occipital lobes. The **calcarine sulcus** marks the location of the primary visual cortex on the medial surface of the occipital lobe, running at very nearly a right angle

Figure 1.13 View of the brain surface after separating the hemispheres in the midline. (A) An overview of the major features visible after bisecting the brain in the midsagittal plane (see Box 1C). (B) The major gyri, sulci, and other features visible in this view after removal of the brainstem. (C) Blowup of region of the diencephalon, indicating the thalamus and some of the major landmarks that will be important in later chapters.

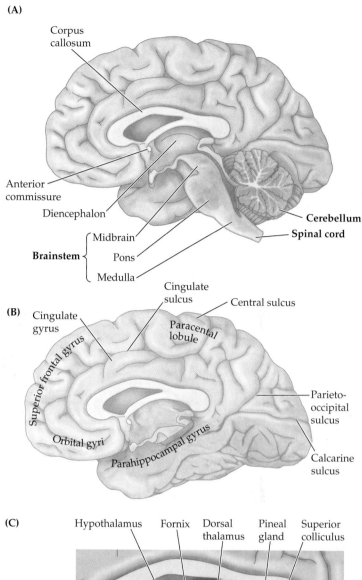

(A)

(B)

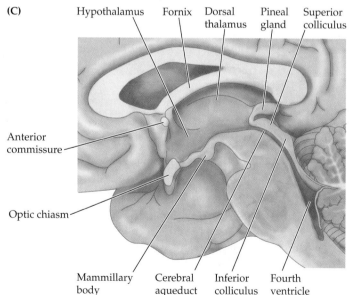

(C)

from the parieto-occipital sulcus. A long, roughly horizontal sulcus, the **cingulate sulcus**, extends across the medial surface of the frontal and parietal lobes. The prominent gyrus below it, the **cingulate gyrus**, along with the cortex adjacent to it, is part of the *limbic system* (*limbic* means border or edge), a neural circuit that will figure in subsequent discussions of emotion and social cognition. These structures are also important in the regulation of visceral motor activity, which is closely tied to emotional expression. Finally, ventral to the cingulate gyrus is the midsagittal surface of the **corpus callosum**, a massive white matter tract that is the major route for the transfer of information between the two hemispheres.

Although parts of the diencephalon, brainstem, and cerebellum are visible on the ventral surface of the brain, their overall structure is especially clear looking at the medial surface. From this perspective, the diencephalon can be seen to consist of two parts (**Figure 1.13C**). The **thalamus**, the largest component of the diencephalon, comprises a number of nuclear subdivisions, all of which relay information to the cerebral cortex from other parts of the brain; the most posterior part of the thalamus is called the **pulvinar** (see Figure 1.9A), which is important in visual attention. The **hypothalamus**, a small but crucial part of the diencephalon, is devoted to the control of homeostatic (stability-maintaining) and reproductive functions, often over natural cycles such as days or months. The hypothalamus is intimately related, both structurally and functionally, to the **pituitary gland**, an endocrine organ whose posterior part is attached to the hypothalamus by the pituitary stalk.

The midbrain, which can be seen only in this medial view, lies caudal to the thalamus; as noted, the superior and inferior colliculi define the midbrain's dorsal (back-facing) surface, or *tectum* ("roof"). Several midbrain nuclei, including the substantia nigra, lie in the ventral portion or **tegmentum** of the midbrain (*tegmentum* means "covering"). The **pons** ("bridge") lies caudal to the midbrain along the midsagittal surface, and the **cerebellum** lies over the pons, just beneath the occipital lobe of the cerebral hemispheres; in fact the pons is largely a collection of nerve cell axons and nuclei related to the cerebellum.

(A)

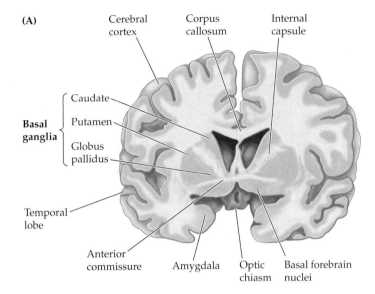

Cerebral cortex
Corpus callosum
Internal capsule

Basal ganglia
  Caudate
  Putamen
  Globus pallidus

Temporal lobe

Anterior commissure
Amygdala
Optic chiasm
Basal forebrain nuclei

(B)

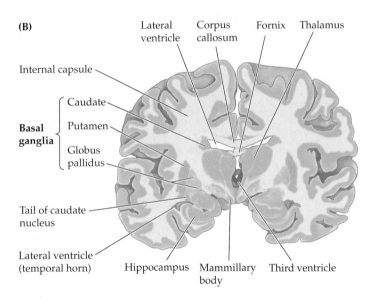

Lateral ventricle
Corpus callosum
Fornix
Thalamus

Internal capsule

Basal ganglia
  Caudate
  Putamen
  Globus pallidus

Tail of caudate nucleus

Lateral ventricle (temporal horn)
Hippocampus
Mammillary body
Third ventricle

(C)

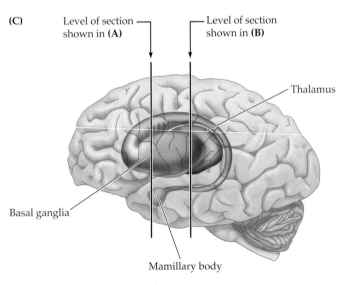

Level of section shown in **(A)**
Level of section shown in **(B)**

Thalamus

Basal ganglia

Mamillary body

The cerebellum's major function is coordination of motor activity, posture, and equilibrium, although it is implicated in some cognitive functions as well. From the midsagittal surface, the most visible feature of the cerebellum is the **cerebellar cortex**, a continuous, layered sheet of cells folded into ridges and valleys called **folia**.

Finally, the most caudal structure seen from the midsagittal surface of the brain is the **medulla**, which merges into the spinal cord.

Internal features of the brain

Many structures are not visible from any brain surface but are apparent when the organ is cut in sections and examined grossly (i.e., with the unaided eye), or, as is commonly done, stained with one of a variety of chemical agents that highlight different structures, such as the stains for myelin that accentuate the brain's white matter tracts. Understanding this **sectional anatomy** is especially pertinent to cognitive neuroscience because internal structures can be seen quite easily in the sections routinely generated by the noninvasive brain imaging techniques that will be described in detail in Chapter 3. Modern brain imaging methods are far more widely used today than the examination of postmortem brain sections in the pathology laboratory (see Figure 1.7B). Thus a major challenge—and a basic requirement in cognitive neuroscience—is learning to move easily from surface neuroanatomy to recognizing the brain's internal structures. **Box 1C** provides a brief overview of some anatomical terminology needed for this of correlational thinking about the brain as a whole and in sections.

In any plane of section through the forebrain, the cerebral cortex is evident as a thin layer of neural tissue that covers the entire cerebrum (**Figure 1.14A**). The largest structures embedded within the cerebral hemispheres are two nuclei called the **caudate** and **putamen** (together these nuclei are referred to as the **striatum**), which are closely associated with another nucleus called the **globus pallidus** (**Figure 1.14B**). Because of the related location and function of these three nuclei, they are referred to collectively as the **basal ganglia** (the use of the term *ganglia* in this case

Figure 1.14 Internal brain structures seen in coronal sections. These coronal views reveal important structures in the deep gray matter of the brain. (A) This section passes through the basal ganglia (caudate, putamen, and globus pallidus) and the amygdala. (B) This more posterior coronal section includes the thalamus. All of these structures are of major significance in cognitive studies. (C) This "transparent" lateral view shows the approximate locations of the sections in (A) and (B).

■ BOX 1C **Anatomical Terminology**

An obstacle in understanding the internal structure of the brain is the sometimes confusing use of the nomenclature used to specify anatomical locations. Although many of the same terms are used to describe spatial orientation in the brain as are used for the anatomical description of the rest of the body, the meanings of some of the terms differ. For the body, the anatomical terms in common use refer to the long axis, which is more or less straight. The long axis of the central nervous system, however, has a bend in it. Thus, when describing the brain, the simplest terms are *anterior* and *posterior*, which indicate the direction of the front (face) and back of the head, respectively. However, the somewhat more difficult terms *rostral* and *caudal* are also used for some descriptions; *rostral* indicates the direction toward the nose (Latin, *rostrum*, "beak") and caudal toward the "tail" (*caudum*), which refers to the base of the skull. When applied to the long axis of the body, the distinctions anterior–posterior and rostral–caudal are synonymous, both indicating "top to tail"; however because of the bend in the axis of the nervous system, they have somewhat

different meanings in brain anatomy, as indicated in Figure A. This discrepancy is not a major problem, but one needs to be aware of it.

A similar situation applies to the terms *dorsal* and *ventral*. When speaking of the body or spinal cord axes, *dorsal* refers to the back (Latin, *dorsum*) and *ventral* to the front, or belly (*ventrum*). When referring to the brain, however, *dorsal* refers to the upper and *ventral* to the lower surface of the brain (Figure A). Other spatial descriptions apply in the same way to the brain and the body. These include *medial* and *lateral*, toward the midline (center) or to the side (left or right); and *inferior* and *superior*, above and below.

More significant for cognitive neuroscience is the terminology applied to *sections* (i.e., slices) of the brain, either those made by a knife in the neuropathology lab, or the sections that are now routinely visualized by non-invasive brain imaging techniques (see Chapter 3). By convention, sections of the brain that are parallel to the ros-

tral–caudal axis are referred to as *horizontal sections* (Figure B). Sections taken in the plane that divides the brain's two hemispheres are called *sagittal*, and these can be further categorized as *midsagittal, median*, or *paramedian* according to whether a section is at the midline (midsagittal), near the midline (median), or at some distance from the midline (paramedian). Sections in the plane of the face are called *frontal* or *coronal*.

Although it will not figure significantly in the chapters that follow here, the sectional terminology for the spinal cord is based on the terms used in considering sections of the body as a whole. Thus the plane of section perpendicular to the long axis of the body or spinal cord is called a *transverse* (or "cross"), section, whereas sections parallel to the long axis of the body or spinal cord are called *longitudinal*. In a transverse section through the spinal cord, the terms dorsal and ventral axes and the anterior and posterior axes indicate the same directions.

(A) A bend in the long axis of the nervous system arose as humans evolved upright posture, leading to an angle of about 120° between the long axis of the brainstem and that of the rest of the brain. As explained here, this evolutionary fact introduces some special considerations in describing anatomical location in the brain. (B) The major planes of section used in cutting or imaging the brain.

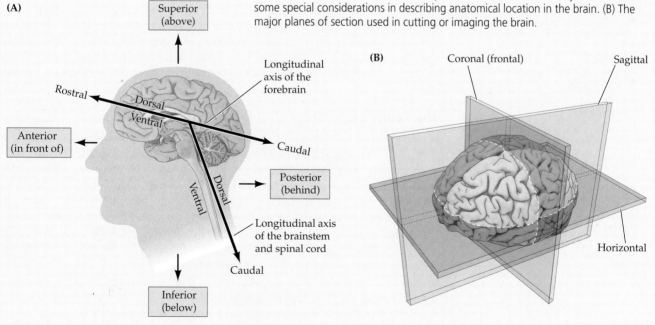

is an exception to the usual usage of this word described earlier in its application to collections of peripheral nerve cells; this idiosyncratic use is historical and refers to a collection of related nuclear structures). As can be imagined from studying **Figure 1.14C**, the basal ganglia are visible in horizontal sections through the mid-dorsal to mid-ventral portion of the forebrain, in frontal sections from just rostral to the uncus to the level of the diencephalon, and in all paramedian sagittal sections.

The neurons in the large nuclear complexes of the basal ganglia receive input from the cerebral cortex and participate in the organization and guidance of complex motor functions and well as many other cortical feedback loops, many of which are relevant to a range of cognitive functions. In the base of the forebrain, ventral to the basal ganglia, are several smaller clusters of nerve cells known as the **septal** or **basal forebrain nuclei**. The function of these latter nuclei is not well understood, but they are of particular interest because of their involvement in the early signs and symptoms of Alzheimer's disease.

The other clearly discernible structure visible in coronal sections through the cerebral hemispheres at the level shown in Figure 1.14B is the **amygdala**, a collection of nuclei that lies in front of the hippocampus in the anterior pole of the temporal lobe. Some of nuclei of the amygdala are especially important in emotional processing.

In addition to these cortical and nuclear structures, the internal anatomy of the brain shows the major axon tracts alluded to earlier. As already mentioned, the two cerebral hemispheres are interconnected by the **corpus callosum**, which is apparent in the majority of coronal sections; in some anterior sections, the much smaller **anterior commissure**, another interhemispheric tract, can also be seen (see Figure 1.14A). Another tract that will be pertinent in later chapters is the **fornix,** which interconnects the hippocampus and the hypothalamus (see Figure 1.14B). Finally, axons descending from and ascending to the cerebral cortex assemble into another very large and extensive tract called the **internal capsule**. The internal capsule lies just lateral to the thalamus (thus the name internal capsule, since it forms a sort of "capsule" around the thalamus), and many internal capsule axons arise from or terminate in the dorsal thalamus. As might be expected from its location, the internal capsule is most obvious in frontal sections through the middle third of the rostral–caudal extent of forebrain, or in horizontal sections through the level of the thalamus. The axons of internal capsule enter the cerebral peduncles that connect the cerebral hemispheres to the brainstem. Thus, the internal capsule is the major pathway linking the cerebral cortex to the rest of the brain and spinal cord.

The ventricular system

It is important to be familiar with another feature of the internal anatomy of the brain: the **ventricular system,** the location of which is particularly helpful in interpreting noninvasive brain images (**Figure 1.15**). The **ventricles** of the brain are a series of interconnected, fluid-filled spaces that lie deep in the forebrain and brainstem. Ventricles are the adult reflection of the open space (the *lumen*) of the embryonic neural tube, around which the central nervous system initially develops (see Chapter 27). The largest of these spaces are the **lateral ventricles** (one within each of the cerebral hemispheres). The lateral ventricles are best seen in frontal sections, where their ventral surface is defined by the basal ganglia, their dorsal surface by the corpus callosum, and their medial surface by the **septum pellucidum** (a membranous tissue sheet that forms part of the midline sagittal surface of the cerebral hemispheres).

(A)

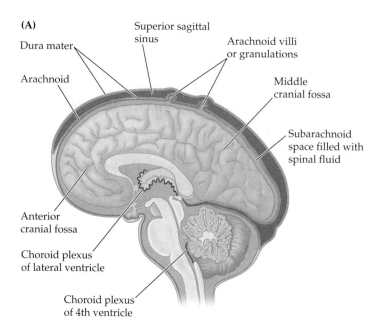

Superior sagittal sinus

Dura mater

Arachnoid villi or granulations

Arachnoid

Middle cranial fossa

Subarachnoid space filled with spinal fluid

Anterior cranial fossa

Choroid plexus of lateral ventricle

Choroid plexus of 4th ventricle

Figure 1.15 The ventricular system. The ventricles are a series of interconnected spaces deep in the forebrain and brainstem. These spaces are filled with cerebrospinal fluid. (A) Lateral view showing the main features of the system. (B) This "transparent" lateral view shows the ventricular system as a whole. (C) Another "transparent" view of the ventricles, this one from the brain's dorsal surface, looking downward.

(B)

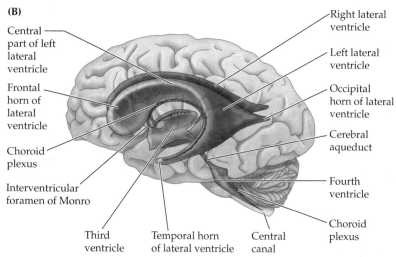

Central part of left lateral ventricle

Frontal horn of lateral ventricle

Choroid plexus

Interventricular foramen of Monro

Third ventricle

Temporal horn of lateral ventricle

Central canal

Right lateral ventricle

Left lateral ventricle

Occipital horn of lateral ventricle

Cerebral aqueduct

Fourth ventricle

Choroid plexus

(C)

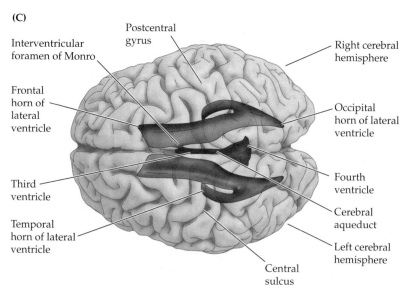

Interventricular foramen of Monro

Postcentral gyrus

Frontal horn of lateral ventricle

Third ventricle

Temporal horn of lateral ventricle

Central sulcus

Right cerebral hemisphere

Occipital horn of lateral ventricle

Fourth ventricle

Cerebral aqueduct

Left cerebral hemisphere

The **third ventricle** forms a narrow midline space between the right and left thalamus, and communicates with the lateral ventricles through a small opening (the *interventricular foramen*) at the anterior end of the third ventricle. The third ventricle is continuous caudally with the **cerebral aqueduct**, which runs though the midbrain. At its caudal end, the aqueduct opens into the **fourth ventricle**, a larger space in the dorsal pons and medulla. The fourth ventricle narrows caudally to form the central canal of the spinal cord.

The ventricles are filled with **cerebrospinal fluid**, and the lateral, third, and fourth ventricles are the sites of the **choroid plexus**, which produces this fluid. Cerebrospinal fluid percolates through the ventricular system and flows into the subarachnoid space through perforations in the thin covering of the fourth ventricle; it is eventually absorbed by specialized structures called arachnoid villi, and is thus returned to the venous circulation. Although the ventricles have no obvious function other than serving as conduits for the circulation of cerebrospinal fluid, their locations provide excellent landmarks in deciphering brain sections.

The Brain's Blood Supply

As will be apparent in later units, much insight into cognitive functions has come from the clinical consequences of **stroke**, a generic term that refers to the clinical and neuropathological results of interrupting the blood supply to one or another region of the brain. Such interruptions can be the result of occlusion (obstruction) of an artery, or hemorrhage (bleeding) from a blood vessel that ruptures. The resulting damage is referred to as a **brain lesion**, a term that also refers to damage from other causes, including trauma and tumors.

The blood supply of the brain is particularly significant because neurons are more sensitive to oxygen deprivation than other kinds of cells, which generally have lower rates of metabolism. Brain tissue deprived of oxygen and glucose as a result of compromised blood supply is especially likely to sustain transient or permanent damage. Even a brief loss of blood supply (a few minutes), referred to as **ischemia**, can cause cellular changes that, if not quickly reversed, lead to cell death.

The human brain receives blood from two sources: the **internal carotid arteries**, which arise at the point in the neck where the common carotid arteries bifurcate (diverge); and the **vertebral arteries** (**Figure 1.16**). The internal carotid arteries branch to form two major cerebral arteries, the **anterior** and **middle cerebral arteries**. The right and left vertebral arteries come together at the level of the pons on the ventral surface of the brainstem to form the midline **basilar artery**. The basilar artery in turn joins the blood supply originating from the internal carotids in an arterial ring at the base of the brain called the **circle of Willis** (see the enlargement in Figure 1.16; the actual arrangement varies among individuals, but this depiction is typical). The **posterior cerebral arteries** arise at this confluence, as do two small bridging arteries, the **anterior** and **posterior communicating arteries**. Conjoining the two major sources of cerebral vascular supply via the circle of Willis presumably improves the chances that at least some regions of the brain will continue to receive blood if one of the major arteries becomes occluded.

The anterior and middle cerebral arteries form what is referred to clinically as the **anterior circulation** of the forebrain. Each of these arteries gives rise to branches that supply the cortex and to branches that penetrate the basal surface of the brain and supply deep structures such as the basal ganglia, thalamus, and internal capsule. The **posterior circulation** of the brain comprises the **posterior cerebral**, **basilar**, and **vertebral arteries**, which supply the posterior cerebral cortex, midbrain, and brainstem. Although these and many

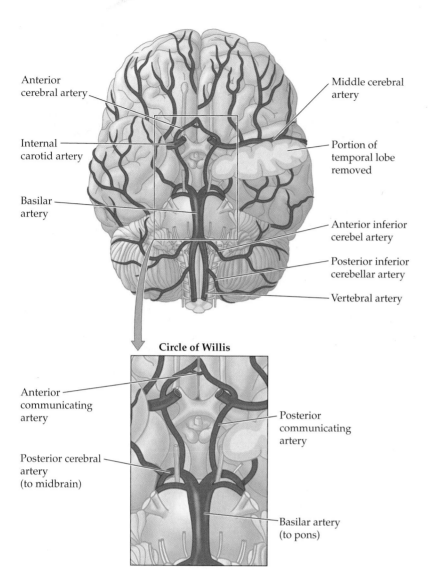

Anterior
cerebral artery

Internal
carotid artery

Basilar
artery

Middle cerebral
artery

Portion of
temporal lobe
removed

Anterior inferior
cerebel artery

Posterior inferior
cerebellar artery

Vertebral artery

Circle of Willis

Anterior
communicating
artery

Posterior cerebral
artery
(to midbrain)

Posterior
communicating
artery

Basilar artery
(to pons)

Figure 1.16   Major arteries of the brain.
The primary features of the vessels that supply
blood to the brain are seen here from the ventral
perspective. The enlargement shows the circle of
Willis, a ring of arteries at the base of the brain.

other details of brain vasculature are primarily important in clinical practice, some knowledge of the brain's blood supply is helpful in understanding a variety of issues in cognitive neuroscience. Historically, the functional consequences of compromised blood supply have provided a great deal of information about the location of various cognitive functions in the human brain, and today neurological patients continue to be a valuable source of information about brain functions pertinent to cognitive neuroscience.

Summary

1. The brain and the rest of the human nervous system include a large number of neuron types that carry out an enormous range of functions using electrical signals—action potentials, synaptic potentials, and receptor potentials. These signals are the common currency of neural functions in all animals that have nervous systems.

2. Interconnected neurons form functional associations called neural circuits that in turn make up the neural systems and subsystems that ultimately mediate cognitive functions such as perception; attention; memory; emotion and social cognition; language and symbolic representation; executive control and reasoning; and a host of other functions that define the higher-order operation of the human brain.

3. A good working knowledge of the elements of brain structure and of the basic physiology of its component nerve cells is essential in understanding how the human brain functions.

Additional Reading

Depending on their background knowledge of neuroscience, readers may find it helpful to review the primer on electrical signaling presented in the Appendix, which provides a resource for more thoroughly understanding the cellular and molecular physiology of the neural signaling that underlies cognitive functions.

With respect to a better and more detailed understanding of human anatomy, the downloadable Sylvius 4 tutorial that comes with this book is a user-friendly resource that readers will find very helpful.

For a more detailed review of these and other issues in neuroscience see:

PURVES, D., G. A. AUGUSTINE, D. FITZPATRICK, W. C. HALL, A.-S. LaMANTIA, J. O. McNAMARA AND L. E. WHITE (2008) *Neuroscience*, 4th Ed. Sunderland, MA: Sinauer.

2

Relevant Principles of Cognitive Psychology

Introduction

Cognitive psychology refers to the time-honored effort to understand the acquisition, retention, and use of the information that allows us and other animals to produce successful behavior in complex and challenging environments. "Information" is sometimes used as a synonym for "knowledge," but the narrow meaning of "knowledge" in the sense of things learned does not begin to do justice to the far broader perspective that today drives the field of cognitive psychology. Informally, *information* is defined as changes in a system (biological or otherwise) that result in altered behavior. Formally, information is defined mathematically, in terms of the reliability of communication within or between systems. Both definitions are important in cognitive psychology. The behaviorist school, which was influential in the early to mid-twentieth century, explicitly limited theorizing in this field to observable stimuli and responses. More recently, however, cognitive scientists have attempted to rationalize information processing in terms of the mental processes and representations assumed to occur in the inchoate and still poorly understood neural circuits that link stimuli and behavioral responses. But the main questions still concern how human beings acquire, manipulate, and use information in the context of perception, movement, attention, memory, emotion, language, decision making, and problem solving. In pursuit of these goals, cognitive neuroscience has co-opted the methods of modern neuroscience that are described in Chapter 3. The goal of this chapter is to briefly review the rich heritage of ideas in cognitive psychology on which the relatively recent emergence of cognitive neuroscience is conceptually based.

Major Themes in Cognitive Psychology

Behaviorism and information theory

Although extraordinarily popular today, the study of mental content and processes was not always accepted as a valid research topic in psychology.

From about 1910 through the 1950s, American psychology was dominated by **behaviorism**, which espoused the view that the study of behavior should be limited to explanations couched in terms of observable stimuli and responses, without reference to the processing in what was loosely referred to as "the mind." During the 1960s, behaviorism's popularity waned, mainly because its paradigms could not account for a number of important aspects of behavior, including the obvious limitations of human performance; the contributions of innate mechanisms to animal learning; the role of mental strategies in memory; and the rapid forms of learning described by Gestalt psychologists (see below). In what has been dubbed the "cognitive manifesto," Noam Chomsky at the Massachusetts Institute of Technology argued convincingly in 1959 that behaviorism could never explain the structural and generative properties of mental phenomena such as human language. Adding to this disaffection was the emergence of neurobiology as a discipline in its own right, a field whose ongoing success in understanding neural functions could no longer be ignored.

Even during the 1940s heyday of behaviorism, new approaches to psychological research were developing based on evidence that information processing can be quantified, and that there are principled limits to the amount of information that can be transmitted through communication channels such as telephone lines (**Box 2A**). Pioneering work in **information theory** eventually led scientists to the conclusion that humans, like telephone lines, must be limited in the number of simultaneous messages they can process. That conclusion led in turn to the notion that the human mind must require "filters" to

■ BOX 2A Information Theory

Higher-order human brain function involves first and foremost the transfer and processing of information. It is not surprising, therefore, that the vast knowledge about information processing generated by nonbiological fields such as telecommunications, computer science, and statistics has been of increasing interest to cognitive neuroscientists.

Claude Shannon, an engineer and mathematician working at Bell Labs in New Jersey, first proposed the principles of modern information theory in 1948. Shannon wanted to reduce the problem of the capacity for communication over phone lines—or any other "channels"—to a formal mathematical statement of channel capacity; that is, to reduce *information* to a measurable physical quantity like volume or mass. Shannon's theory thus considered information in the terms of *bits*, the fundamental currency of the digital technology that was just beginning to emerge as a basis for computation in the pioneering work of giants like

John von Neumann and Alan Turing. In redefining the concept of information, Shannon borrowed the term *entropy* from thermodynamics to quantify informational quality in terms of statistical disorder. When the statistical disorder (i.e., entropy) of the channel capacity is maximal (i.e., there is little probability of any randomly chosen message being exactly the same as any other), the potential for encoding information in the system is also maximal. Conversely, when the entropy of an information processing system is low, the capability of the system is also low, since all its capacity is being used to convey a single message.

Given that the transfer and processing of information in the brain occurs primarily by means of all-or-none electrical signals (action potentials) transmitted over channels (nerve fibers) that resemble other physical communication networks, cognitive psychologists and neuroscientists have paid increasing attention to information theory. They have used in-

formation theory to consider problems as diverse as the efficient layout of the brain's cortical regions; the efficient coding of information in sequences of action potentials; the analysis of natural scenes, and the statistical organization of perceptual spaces. The concepts of information theory are so basic, they apply to all these diverse aspects of neuroscience, and are likely to be increasingly useful as the relatively new field of cognitive neuroscience grows in sophistication.

References

MacKay, D. J. C. (2003) *Information Theory, Inference and Learning Algorithms.* Cambridge: Cambridge University Press.

Shannon, C. E. (1948) A mathematical theory of communication. *Bell System Tech. J.* 27: 379–423 (July) 623–656 (October).

Shannon, C. E. and W. Weaver (1963) *The Mathematical Theory of Communication.* Champaign-Urbana: University of Illinois Press.

block out or attenuate irrelevant messages. Communications engineering also contributed to the development of **signal detection theory**, which provides an important framework for the psychophysical measurement of human performance (see Box 5A).

Yet another stimulus for the new approaches of postbehaviorist cognitive psychology was research in **artificial intelligence** (**AI**), which showed that computers can solve complex problems using strategies much the same as those employed by people. A key example was the demonstration in the 1950s that computers could prove simple mathematical theorems, an ability that had previously been considered to be quintessentially human. This sort of work showed that there need be nothing unscientific or mystical about studying unobserved mental processes, because strategies that seemed similar could be unambiguously described as a quantifiable series of symbolic operations.

The "computer metaphor" was that brain circuitry is the hardware, and mental processing strategies are the software. Although now regarded as simplistic, at the time this metaphor provided a powerful antidote to behaviorist objections to the concept of "mental content" as too vague to be studied scientifically. The long-held notion of the "mind" became defined for many researchers as **processes** (operations) acting on **representations** (symbols). Whereas card-carrying behaviorists had assiduously avoided references to mind or mental content, cognitive psychologists after the 1950s increasingly proposed theories of mental processes and representations that sought to shed light on the connections between stimuli and responses that behaviorists had so vociferously eschewed (**Figure 2.1**).

An analogy sometimes used to describe these new perspectives compares the challenge facing cognitive psychology to inferring what happens inside a factory that cannot be entered. In this circumstance, one could make an informed guess about what was happening inside simply by watching what went into the factory and what eventually came out. If raw timber went in and wooden chairs came out, a reasonable guess would be that sawing, sanding, drilling, nailing, and painting were among the processes and mechanisms transpiring inside. Likewise, on the basis of observable stimuli and responses, cognitive psychologists could attempt to infer the processes and mechanisms underlying various cognitive functions.

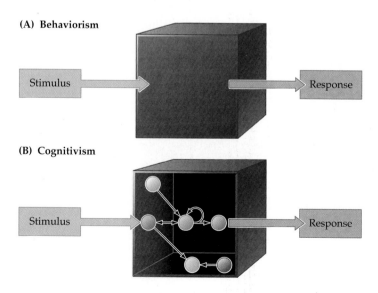

(A) Behaviorism

Stimulus → Response

(B) Cognitivism

Stimulus → Response

Figure 2.1 Two approaches to the study of the human mind. (A) Behaviorists tried to explain behavior using only stimuli and responses, avoiding any reference to the underlying mental processes (the "black box"). (B) In contrast, cognitive psychologists have sought to develop theories about mental processes (black arrows) and their representations (colored circles), at least in general terms.

Now imagine that an outside observer could manipulate what goes into the factory in various ways. Would increasing the input of wood increase the output of chairs? Up to what point might this increase hold? If an overload eventually decreased the number or quality of chairs coming out, a limitation of some sort inside the factory would be implied. By observing the effects of such manipulations, it would be possible to make more refined guesses about the factory's operations. This sort of thinking led to research approaches that manipulate stimuli and then measure what happens to the speed and quality of the output. But as this analogy suggests, it would be far better to look inside the "factory" (i.e., the brain) to understand the relevant processes directly. The enormous effort to develop ways to do this, and the ongoing shift over the last 25 years from the more traditional approaches of cognitive psychology to the approaches now practiced in cognitive neuroscience, are described in the next chapter.

The Gestalt school

Even before the rise of postbehaviorist cognitive psychology and the newer thinking it entailed, behaviorism was resisted by a group of psychologists with a very different approach to understanding behavior. The most famous representatives of this **Gestalt school** were Max Wertheimer, Wolfgang Köhler, and Kurt Kofka, a trio of German psychologists who emigrated to the United States in the 1920s and 1930s. The noun *Gestalt* means "the whole" in German, and the underlying assumption of the Gestalt school is that psychological phenomena are better understood when viewed as organized wholes than when broken down into their component parts.

The Gestalt school's greatest influences have been in the domains of perception and problem solving. In perception, Gestalt psychologists emphasized that what a person "sees" when looking at relatively complex figures and scenes is often different from their perception of the individual elements that constitute such a scene (**Figure 2.2**). For example, Wertheimer noted that when two lights flash in sequence, observers often perceive motion, even though no "real" motion has occurred (he called this effect the *phi phenomenon*). More generally, percepts tend to have an organization that transcends the physical organization of the stimuli. Gestalt psychologists described these organizing principles in terms of "Gestalt laws." For example, the "law of proximity" states that observers tend to perceive as units stimuli that are close to each other.

In the realm of problem solving, one contribution of the Gestalt school was the identification of problems that resist a step-by-step analytic solution but can be solved by *insight*—that is, a solution that seems to come suddenly and

Figure 2.2 Gestalt thinking in cognitive psychology. Stimuli illustrating Gestalt laws of proximity, similarity, closure, continuation, and form.

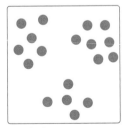

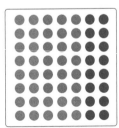

Proximity:
Elements that are closer in space are grouped together

Similarity:
Elements that are similar to each other are grouped together

Closure:
The curved lines are seen as forming an oval behind the triangle and the square rather than as two separate curved lines

Good continuation:
Seen as a curved line crossing a straight line rather than two broken lines touching on a corner

Good form:
Seen as an arrow rather than as a triangle on top of a rectangle

as a "whole" rather than gradually through a series of steps. A well known insight problem is *Duncker's candle task*, illustrated in **Figure 2.3** (see Figure 25.6 for the solution to this problem). Gestalt psychologists noticed that an obstacle in solving this kind of problem is *functional fixedness*, a tendency always to use objects and concepts in their usual way. In the candle problem, the subject must overcome functional fixedness and realize that what is currently a container can also function as a platform. More generally, solving insight problems requires *restructuring* them in order to see the elements of the problem and their relationships in a novel way. Because restructuring occurs suddenly, the person working out the answer may not feel that any progress has been made until the instant in which the answer emerges (the *Eureka!* moment). One study of problem solving in algebra showed that participants knew they were close to a solution about 15 seconds before reaching it; they did not have this anticipatory sense in the case of insight problems.

Few contemporary psychologists would identify themselves as either behaviorists or as members of the Gestalt school. Nonetheless, the inheritance from both these ways of thinking about how stimuli generate behavioral responses remains both visible and valuable.

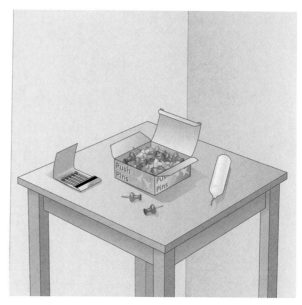

Figure 2.3 Duncker's candle problem. On a table in front of you are a candle, a matchbook, and a box of tacks. How can you mount a lit candle on the wall using only these objects?

Indirect measurement and models

Before the advent of the neurobiological tools (see Chapter 3) that now allow us to "look inside the factory," cognitive psychologists developed a number of indirect measuring methods and models, many of which are still widely influential. Among the most important of these methods is to measure **response times**, or how fast the processing for a given task occurs. (This would be analogous to measuring how long the factory takes to make a chair.) Assuming that performing a particular cognitive task involves a series of sequential and more or less independent processing stages, response times can be used to make inferences about each of these stages. The assumption is that the events underlying any form of cognitive processing take time, and that the time required by a multicomponent process will be more or less the sum of the time taken by each component. This idea was first proposed by the Dutch physiologist and ophthalmologist Franciscus Donders in 1868 and was revived by cognitive psychologists in the 1970s.

A good example of the use of response times in this framework is a study carried out in the late 1960s by Saul Sternberg, then working at Bell Labs; the problem is known today as *Sternberg's task*. Participants are presented with a "memory set" of 1–6 digits and, subsequently, a single digit "probe." The task is to respond as quickly as possible when asked whether or not the probe is part of the memory set. As shown in **Figure 2.4A**, response times increase linearly with the number of digits in the memory set, each digit adding about 40 milliseconds to the response time. According to Sternberg, response times in this task reflect four steps: perceiving the probe; comparing the probe to each item in the memory set; deciding whether or not there is a match; and generating the response (**Figure 2.4B**). Given this **sequential processing model**, it follows that each probe-to-item comparison takes around 40 milliseconds, and that the intercept with the ordinate at 400 milliseconds in Figure 2.4A (the projected minimum processing time) reflects the combined time taken by all four stages. Consistent with this idea, presenting degraded probes instead of intact probes (changing the input to the factory in our analogy), which should alter

(A)

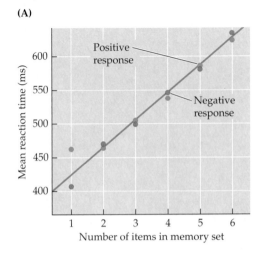

(B)

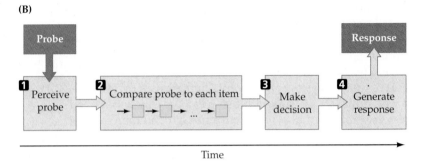

Figure 2.4 Sternberg's task. (A) Response times in this task are a function of the number of items in the memory set (see text). (B) The mental processing stages proposed by Sternberg. (A after Sternberg 1966.)

only the encoding process, affects the intercept but not the slope (rate of increase) of the function. This experiment illustrates one of the ways cognitive psychologists have tested hypotheses about processes and representations.

Although processing models of this sort can be useful, they have some obvious limitations. First, there is no reason to assume that the steps in cognitive processing tasks are sequential; indeed, given what we now know about neural processing, this scenario is unlikely. As described in **Box 2B** and the following unit on perception, **connectionist models** provide more accommodating framework by assuming **parallel distributed processing** across a number of "channels" or pathways. Second, in many instances altering one processing stage affects other stages, undermining the assumption of the independence of processing steps (and implying connectivity among parallel pathways and processing stages, which has also been amply confirmed by neurobiological studies). For example, remembering past events involves three stages: searching for memories, retrieving them, and assessing their accuracy. Yet altering any one of these stages usually affects the others. In such cases, it is difficult to attribute response time differences to changes in any one stage. Third, although there is abundant evidence that processing a particular item is affected by previous processing of the same item and by current processing of related items, processing models do not take into account the obvious effects of context described in the following section. Finally, processing models are awkward when applied to complex cognitive processes that unfold over minutes, hours, or longer, such as many decision-making and problem-solving tasks. In these instances, **accuracy of performance** measures, or even verbal descriptions of internal processes, can be more useful than response times.

Cognitive psychology as practiced today uses sequential processing models, connectionist models, and a variety of other conceptual frameworks. In the sections that follow, the legacy of cognitive psychology in cognitive neuroscience is discussed more specifically in terms of the major cognitive functions that are the focus of the remaining units. The point of the following overviews is to introduce some general ideas and terms derived from cognitive psychology that will be pertinent for the remainder of the book.

Perception

Perception is primarily defined as the conscious awareness of the external and internal environment generated by neural processing carried out by the human sensory systems. This awareness entails a series of basic qualities gen-

■ BOX 2B Connectionist Models

Unlike sequential processing models, **connectionist models** assume that information processing occurs in parallel across a large number of distributed units. For this reason, these models are also known as **parallel distributed processing (PDP) models.** The units, or *nodes*, in connectionist schemes are linked in a network, much as neurons are interconnected in the brain. Thus connectionist models are also known as **neural network models.**

An example is the model of written-word recognition developed by James McClelland and his colleague David Rummelhart at Carnegie Mellon University. Like other connectionist models, it is a network consisting of layers of units. The units of the *input layer* receive information from the environment; in this example, each input unit receives visual information and responds to one particular feature of a written letter (e.g., a horizontal line). The *output layer* consists of units that indicate the outcomes of the processing within the network. Given that this is a model of word recognition, the output units correspond to all the words the model can recognize. Finally, input and output units are connected through one or more *hidden layers,* so called because their units are "invisible" from the "outside." For simplicity, the model in the example here shows only a few letter features, fewer letters, and even fewer words.

The network shown responds to only the *first letter* of the words; similar networks would be required to recognize each of the other letters. The connections between units can be excitatory or inhibitory. Some excitatory and inhibitory connections in the figure are obvious. For example, the letter A excites the word ABLE but inhibits the word TRAP because ABLE starts with an

A but TRAP does not. The inhibitory connections among the units within the same layer ensure that one option will tend to "win out" over the others. Activation flows not only from input to output layers but also from output to input layers (e.g., the excitatory connection from ABLE to the letter A).

To see how the model works, consider the sentence "John packed his suitcase and left for a trip." Before such a network reaches the end of the sentence, the node for the word "trip" is activated by semantic associations from the words "suitcase" and "left" (not shown in the figure). This activation facilitates the identification of the letters T, R, I, and P and thus the corre-

sponding feature detectors. At the same time, activation flows in the opposite direction from feature to letter to word detectors in the input layer. A strength of models like this is that they specify how conceptually driven processing and data-driven processing might interact. Another strength is that they entail a built-in learning mechanism: the modification of connection weights represents stored information that alters the output. In computer simulations, networks are often "trained" using *supervised learning algorithms* such as *backpropagation,* in which the actual output (e.g., TRAP) is compared to the desired output

(Continued on next page)

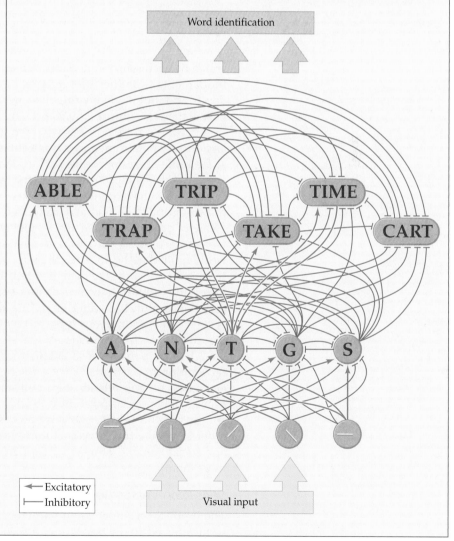

A connectionist model for written word recognition. Note that the feature and letter units stand only for the first position in the four-letter words. (After McClelland and Rummelhart 1981.)

■ BOX 2B (continued)

(e.g., TRIP) and the weights of the connections from the layers below are modified to reduce subsequent errors.

Learning can also be *unsupervised* when, for example, the strength of the connection between units is automatically increased whenever the units are simultaneously active (a process called *Hebbian learning*; see Chapter 13).

PDP models are attractive in cognitive neuroscience because changing the strength of synaptic connections through individual experience or natural selection is clearly the major way nervous systems store information (as discussed in Chapters 1, 13, and 27). The assumption that knowledge is not stored in a single location but is distributed across numerous sites is also consistent with much neurobiological evidence. Local damage to either the brain or a connectionist model typically degrades performance but doesn't abolish it altogether, a phenomenon called *graceful degradation*.

At the same time, connectionist models have several limitations, including difficulty accounting for rule-based processes in human reasoning; difficulty discerning the strategies being used to solve problems by examining weight patterns of the trained network architecture; and, consequently, difficulty distinguishing among alternative models of the same cognitive process. These caveats notwithstanding, connectionist models have provided cognitive scientists with important insights and a powerful tool.

References

HAYKIN, S. (1998) *Neural Networks: A Comprehensive Foundation*, 2nd Ed. New York: Prentice-Hall.

MCCLELLAND, J. L., D. E. RUMELHART AND G. E. HINTON (2002) The appeal of parallel distributed processing. In *Foundations of Cognitive Psychology: Core Reading*, D. J. Levitin (ed.). Cambridge, MA: MIT Press, pp. 57–91.

MCCLELLAND, J. L., D. E. RUMELHART AND THE PDP RESEARCH GROUP (1986) *Parallel Distributed Processing: Explorations in the Microstructure of Cognition*. Volume 2: *Psychological and Biological Models*. Cambridge, MA: MIT Press.

RUMELHART, D. E., J. L. MCCLELLAND AND THE PDP RESEARCH GROUP (1986) *Parallel Distributed Processing: Explorations in the Microstructure of Cognition*. Volume 1: *Foundations*. Cambridge, MA: MIT Press.

erated by each sensory modality, sometimes referred to as *qualia*. In vision, the fundamental qualities of perceptual awareness are brightness, color, form, depth, and motion; in hearing they are loudness, pitch, and timbre; the qualia of somatic sensation are touch, pressure and pain.

A natural intuition is that what we see, hear, feel, taste, or smell is more or less directly determined by a translation of the stimuli impinging on receptors at the input stages of the sensory system in question. A corollary is that what we perceive is a representation of the real world. But virtually all approaches to perception have indicated that this perspective is misleading, and that colors, forms, pitches, loudness, tactile sensations, and other qualities that we are aware of do not accord in any simple way with the physical properties of the world. Recognition of this odd relationship between percepts and the real world has led to the idea that the information generated by the initial stages of sensory processing is refined, molded, and added onto by other factors. These factors include the recent activity of the sensory system in question; prior experience with the stimulus in question; the context in which a stimulus occurs; contemporaneous input from other sensory systems; and the physiological state of the perceiver.

What we perceive also entails more complex processes that lead to the recognition of particular objects (faces, tools, other animals, and so on) and awareness of their relationships and significance. These increasingly complex aspects of conscious awareness quickly transcend the notion of perception as simply the end result of sensory processing and clearly depend on a host of other cognitive functions including learning, memory, emotional reactions, and social context. Thus what we perceive is, in the end, determined by far more than sensory input.

Sensation versus perception

The input-level information gathered by sensory receptors has historically been referred to as "sensation" by cognitive psychologists, and its neural underpinnings as "bottom-up processing," to distinguish this neural activity from the end product of the "higher-order processing" taking place in the brain—which can then influence the processing going on elsewhere in the brain or in the rest of the nervous system in a "top-down" manner. However, bottom-up and top-down processing are difficult to separate in any practical sense, and distinguishing sensations from perceptions does violence to the ordinary meaning of these words, which are generally used synonymously. Thus the nomenclature for perception inherited from cognitive psychology, while useful and widely applied, has some pitfalls that need to be recognized from the outset and used with caution.

Exploring perception in psychological terms

It is safe to assume that the major goal of perception is to enable conscious consideration of objects and conditions in the environment as a means of facilitating successful behavior, and thus the well-being of the individual and ultimately the species doing the perceiving. Nonetheless, the generation of percepts is far from understood. The most completely studied aspects of the sensory processes that culminate in perception are, not surprisingly, the structure and function of the peripheral mechanisms by which the relevant forms of energy in the environment (light energy, sound energy, chemical energy, etc.) are converted into neural signals. This has been the province of modern neurobiology. Understanding the central mechanisms of sensory processing has also been a major focus of neurobiologists, and much relevant anatomy and physiology has been documented. Cognitive psychologists, however, have long been interested in understanding the broader strategies involved in the percepts generated by sensory processing and have made many contributions that continue to influence the direction of cognitive neuroscience.

Historically, one line of thinking has explored the idea that the underlying strategy of sensory processing might be a sort of **template matching** between patterns of sensory stimulation and stored information about objects and conditions experienced in the past. That is, perceiving objects as such might depend on matching new stimuli to those previously seen and stored, perhaps using a template of some sort. Despite its intuitive appeal, this proposition quickly runs into problems. The variability of the sensory patterns we recognize is so great that it is difficult to imagine that we store templates for all of them. Beyond this objection, the qualities of perception that underlie the recognition of specific objects and conditions (color, pitch, touch, pain, etc.) are not easily rationalized in terms of a matching template scheme. For example, to say that we see something as red because it matches a stored template of previously seen red surfaces is a circular argument.

A related concept of a general strategy that could underlie perception is **feature detection**. The idea in this case is that, instead of trying to match the full sensory pattern to a stored representation, component features of the stimulus are detected separately and combined only later by higher-order processing into representations that might then be used in the process of recognizing objects and conditions to guide behavior. A feature detection scheme would reduce the number of required representations, since one class of feature detector could analyze many sorts of objects (e.g., a "vertical line" detector would respond to the vertical components of any stimulus pattern). By focusing on basic perceptual qualities, this sort of scheme avoids some of the problems of template matching. A further attraction of feature detection is that it accords with abundant neurological evidence that sensory neurons do indeed respond to simple properties such as the orientation of a line in a visual stimulus. To account for the recognition of complex real-world objects in these terms, the psychologist Irving Biederman at the University of Southern

California imagined further detectors for simple three-dimensional shapes, such as straight and curved cylinders, rectangular objects, and cones. He called these object components **geons** (short for "geometric icons"), the idea being that, just as two-dimensional shapes are defined by lines, three-dimensional objects might be defined of geon-like features.

But feature detection is also beset with problems. The major obstacle in this approach to understanding perception is that the so-called "features" of stimuli are inherently ambiguous with respect to their sources in the real world; for example, a given line projected onto the retina can, as described in Chapter 5, arise from an infinite set of real-world lines at different distances, of different sizes, and in different orientations. To make matters worse, many perceptual qualities do not have any corresponding "features" in either the stimulus or the world. Examples are color and pain, as explained in Chapters 5 and 7. Despite its intuitive attraction as a basis for perception, feature detection, like template matching, is an insufficient framework for rationalizing sensory experience, and fares even worse in dealing with percepts that do not arise directly from sensory input (such as perceptual awareness of thoughts, memories, and emotions).

Another general mechanism that could help explain the generation of percepts dates back more than a century and builds specifically on the influence of **prior experience**. Recognizing that sensory stimuli alone are generally unable to specify their real-world sources, Hermann Helmholtz proposed in the late nineteenth century that an observer's expectations about the most likely objects represented by ambiguous stimuli could modulate sensory processing in higher centers in the brain. Such expectations could arise from accumulated knowledge, memories of recent experiences, the surrounding context, or many other factors. Thus, as illustrated in **Figure 2.5A**, prior experience with animals (Dalmatians in particular) helps generate a meaningful perception of this complex visual image; in **Figure 2.5B**, the distorted words are more easily perceived when they have been recently encountered (if in this case the observer had recently read a passage that defined the phrase "top down"); and in **Figure 2.5C** the context determines whether the identical stimulus is perceived as an "H" or an "A."

These and other examples make plain that perceptions are very much subject to what the nervous system has experienced in the past and what it is doing concurrently as it processes peripheral sensory information. How such influences are implemented in the nervous system is very much a matter of debate and the current research described in Unit II.

Attention

Attention refers to the focusing of mental "processing resources" on a particular physical stimulus, task, thought, memory, feeling, or other mental content. In thinking about attention and its underpinnings, cognitive psychologists have tended to concentrate on several key aspects of this broad phenomenon, including the kind of stimuli that govern attentiveness, the selective character of attention, and the enhancement of information processing as a function of attention. As in the case of perception, this heritage from cognitive psychology strongly influences the way attention is now being studied by cognitive neuroscientists.

(A)

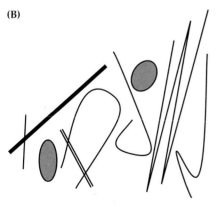

(B)

(C)

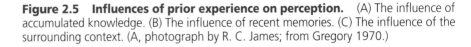

Figure 2.5 Influences of prior experience on perception. (A) The influence of accumulated knowledge. (B) The influence of recent memories. (C) The influence of the surrounding context. (A, photograph by R. C. James; from Gregory 1970.)

Exploring attention in psychological terms

In seeking to understand the underlying strategies of attention, many cognitive psychologists have focused on the sort of stimuli that elicit attentiveness. An obvious distinction is the attention generated by sensory stimuli arising from the environment (exogenous stimuli) and stimuli that arise from some aspect of ongoing brain activity not directly related to sensory processing (endogenous stimuli). An example of **exogenous attention** is the response to a ringing phone: when a phone rings, people immediately turn to it in a more or less automatic *orienting response* that is equally obvious in non-human animals. In contrast, **endogenous attention** is determined by the goals, desires, and/or expectations of the person doing the attending. Thus a person expecting an important phone call may be specifically attentive to any sound stimulus coming from the direction of the phone, or might hear a distant ringing that others would not.

Attentional selectivity

Another aspect of attention that cognitive psychologists have focused on is its *selectivity*, or the way attention can be directed to a specific stimulus. The standard (and now rather tired) example of selective attention is the **cocktail party effect**. Imagine a noisy party where several conversations are going on at the same time. Despite these unfavorable circumstances, people can listen to what the person they are conversing with is saying and not the other conversations. This phenomenon illustrates ability to attend one potential source of information while ignoring others. Psychologists have studied the basis of selective attention in a number of ways, but often by examining whether processing of a stream of information is enhanced by attention. For instance, many classic studies in cognitive psychology have investigated attention to auditory messages under circumstances aimed at simulating the cocktail party effect. Using headphones, two different messages can be presented to the left and right ears (the technique is called *dichotic listening*) and the participants are asked to attend to only one of them. The subjects in such experiments are then typically asked to perform a task based on the attended message, such as to repeating the message out loud as soon as they hear it (called *shadowing*).

In similar studies of selective attention in vision, subjects are asked to covertly attend (i.e., watch without moving their eyes) a particular spatial location on a screen; sensory processing (using reaction times for instance) in the attended and unattended locations can then be measured and compared. The result of such studies is that neural processing is faster for attended stimuli than unattended ones. This sort of observation suggests that attention can be moved to different locations, much as a spotlight can be moved across a darkened scene (an analogy often used in discussing attention). The faster responses to stimuli in the attended location are thus believed to reflect more rapid neural processing "under the spotlight."

Levels of attention

Cognitive psychologists (and more recently, using other means, cognitive neuroscientists) have also explored the **level** at which attention influences stimulus processing. For example, to what degree are the unattended messages in a dichotic listening experiment processed before the information they contain is simply lost? In the case of auditory messages that entail language, this question has often been considered in terms of the processing stages in language comprehension (**Figure 2.6**). The attentional "decision" to select information for further processing might occur only after the most basic sensory analysis (*early selection*); after some semantic analyses (*middle selection*); or after the message had been fully processed and reached awareness (*late selection*).

Figure 2.6 Early-, middle-, and late-stage selection by attention. When assessing material to be further processed during a task that involves language comprehension, early-stage selection requires only sensory analysis, whereas late-stage selection requires semantic processing and, ultimately, awareness. (After Johnston and Heinz 1978.)

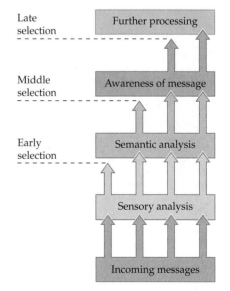

Whereas some evidence supports determination of the degree of information processing by early selection, other data implicate middle and late selection. Consistent with early selection, the participants typically remember very little about the unattended message in dichotic listening experiments (in some studies, subjects didn't remember an unattended word even when it was repeated many times). Nonetheless, participants can usually detect other changes in the message, such as the shift from male to female voice. This sort of observation suggests that the unattended message receives only very cursory sensory analysis, and that more complex information in the unattended channels is simply lost. However, subjects can readily detect words in the unattended channel if they are particularly relevant, such the subject's name. Moreover, a study by psychologist Anne Treisman at Princeton showed that participants can spontaneously switch to shadow the unattended message if it helps make sense of the unattended message. This and other evidence provides support for the existence of middle and late influences on attention as well as early selection mechanisms to determine what information is to be further processed by the brain.

These basic concepts inherited from cognitive psychology—the idea of distinct categories of attentional processing related to exogenous and endogenous stimuli; the notion of an attentional "spotlight" that can be selectively directed to information of interest and ecological importance; and the concept of different levels at which attention can influence the degree of information processing—continue to inform and shape the cognitive neuroscience of attention today.

Memory

In its broadest sense, **memory** refers to the mechanisms whereby past experiences influence present behavior. Memory researchers typically distinguish between *memory stores* that hold information for different periods, and *memory processes* that operate on this stored information. A century of neurobiological research has led to a reasonably good understanding of the mechanisms by which experience alters neural circuitry; the term *learning* refers specifically to the processes by which experience acts on neural circuitry to generate memories. Exactly how and where information is stored and how it is retrieved are less clear, however, and are the subject of much current research in both psychology and neuroscience. What follows summarizes the major concepts and approaches to memory derived from the long-standing effort to understand this central cognitive function in psychological terms.

Exploring memory in psychological terms

Figure 2.7 summarizes the conventional distinction made by psychologists among memory stores based on how much information they can hold and how long they can hold it. The term **sensory memory** refers to a store that is thought of as receiving information from sensory systems and very briefly holding a large amount of "pre-categorical" (i.e., not yet interpreted) information. As indicated by the multiple arrows in the figure, the presumption is that the different sensory modalities generate independent stores. This more or less immediate sensory memory store for vision has been called *iconic memory*, and for audition, *echoic memory*. Although most information in sensory memory is quickly lost (i.e., forgotten), a small amount is "selected" for short-term memory storage and further processing.

Short-term memory typically holds relatively few pieces of information for several tens of seconds. By continually refreshing this information (as in remembering a phone number by repeating it to ourselves until a pencil can be

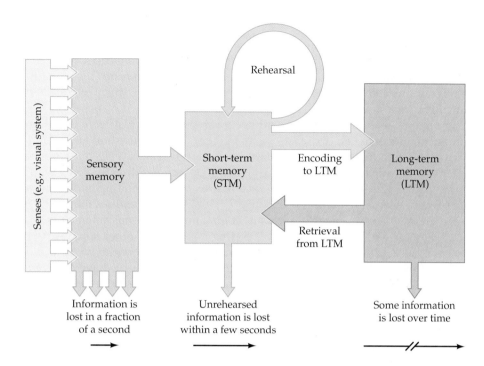

Figure 2.7 A standard psychological model of memory storage.
Sensory memory holds a large amount of sensory information in pre-categorical format for a brief period (fractions of a second). Short-term memory "selects" a subset of this information and holds items of categorized information for a longer period (seconds). Long-term memory in turn holds a further subset of information for much longer (years to decades).

found to write it down), **rehearsal** can keep information in short-term memory for as long as it is needed. The amount of information short-term memory can hold, as well as the speed with which this information can be transferred to it from sensory memory, depends on the size of each informational unit. Although the capacity is somewhere on the order of 5–9 units of information in ordinary circumstances (think again of a phone number), the size of each unit or *chunk* can vary dramatically. Large units can be created by combining several smaller units, a process known as **chunking**. Chunking is thought to explain why people have far better short-term memory skills for information in domains they know intimately. For example, chess masters have tremendous short-term memory capacity for valid positions on a chess board (meaningful chunks), but only a normal capacity for remembering randomly arranged board positions. Information in short-term memory has been taken to be held in a *categorical format*, which requires the integration of incoming sensory information with prior knowledge stored in long-term memory.

Rehearsal and chunking are only two examples of the processes that operate on information stored in short-term memory; thus, short-term memory should not be conceived as a passive buffer, but as a dynamic system with interacting subcomponents. Because of the dynamic and complex nature of short-term memory, most memory researchers today prefer the term "working memory." The cognitive and neural mechanisms of working memory are described in Chapter 16.

Finally, **long-term memory** holds a vast amount of information for much longer periods as it accumulates information encoded by and transferred from short-term memory stores. As described in Unit V, long-term memory comprises different kinds of memories, including memories of personally experienced events (**episodic memory**), knowledge about language and facts (**semantic memory**), changes in perceptual representations (**perceptual priming**), and representations supporting cognitive and motor skills (**procedural memory**). As described in Chapters 14 and 15, psychologists also categorize long-term memories as those that can be verbally reported (**declarative memory**) and those that can not (**nondeclarative memory**).

Memory processing

Cognitive psychologists have generally posited four phases of memory processing: **encoding** (the creation of memory traces as a consequence experience); **retrieval** (the recovery of memory traces); **consolidation** (the strengthening of memory traces following encoding); and **storage** (the persistence of memory traces over time).

Memory encoding and retrieval occur at specific points in time and are quite amenable to behavioral research. In contrast, consolidation and storage are protracted processes without clear behavioral manifestations, and are difficult to investigate without measuring neural processes directly. Thus cognitive psychologists have tended to focus mainly on the encoding and retrieval processes. Assessing memory consolidation and storage requires the methods of cognitive neuroscience; these aspects of memory are discussed in Unit V.

A key question about memory encoding concerns whether some sorts of experience lead to better subsequent memory of the material to which a subject was exposed than others. According to what psychologists have called the **levels of processing framework**, semantic processing leads to better retention than non-semantic (perceptual) processing. Consistent with this view, attending to the meaning of words (e.g., deciding if they refer to living versus non-living things) yields better subsequent memory for the words than attending to their phonological or orthographic characteristics (e.g., whether they have one or two syllables or are written all in capital letters). At least part of the rationale for this phenomenon is the same as in the chess example: people are much better at remembering things that they are interested in and familiar with than things they are not. Semantic encoding appears to lead to good subsequent memory regardless of whether participants know (**intentional learning**) or do not know (**incidental learning**) that their memory will be tested later. Evidently, what matters is not what participants *try to do* but what they *actually do*. But even though semantic processing generally leads to better memory than non-semantic processing, this is not always the case. For example, when a memory test emphasizes perceptual aspects of the information, perceptual encoding may yield better memory than semantic encoding. Thus, the kind of encoding that works best depends on the nature of the retrieval test. This finding supports the notion of **transfer-appropriate processing**, which postulates that better memory is partly a function of the overlap between encoding and retrieval.

Testing memory retrieval

In studying how people retrieve memories, psychologists make a basic distinction between explicit and implicit memory challenges. **Explicit memory tests** ask participants to remember information about a particular event. They may be asked to remember *what* happened (**item memory test**), or *where*, *when*, or *how* it happened (**source memory tests**). Retrieval is taken to involve a series of related processes that start with the processing of the **retrieval cue** (a hint provided by the test or the environment) and the formulation of a query. Guided by the query, a **memory search** is believed to generate one or more candidate answers, which are then evaluated for appropriateness and accuracy (the **monitoring** process). In this scheme, incorrect answers are used to refine the query until a solution is found or the search is abandoned.

Implicit memory tests ask participants to perform a task that is seemingly unrelated to the encoding event, but that nonetheless reveals memory of it. For example, the experimenter might ask participants to complete a word stem (e.g., WIN___) with the words that first comes to mind, and would then measure memory as a tendency to complete these stems with previously studied words (e.g., "window"). Such tests measure memory in terms of a facilitated processing of studied items compared to non-studied items (e.g., "winter"). This facilitation is known as **priming**.

Thus a significant framework for thinking about memory has been inherited from cognitive psychology. The notion that short- and long-term memory capacity are quite distinct entities and the existence of different types of memory processing and memory retrieval have been the subject of much important work in this field.

Emotion and Social Cognition

Emotion refers to a variety of mental states and associated physiological reactions described by terms such as happiness, anger, or sadness. A classic approach to emotion research has been to assume the existence of a discrete set of basic emotional states. This idea was first articulated by Charles Darwin in his 1872 book *The Expression of the Emotions in Man and Animals*. Darwin noted that different emotions are associated with specific facial expressions and that these expressions are consistent across different cultures. The contemporary psychologist Paul Ekman at the University of California at San Francisco further codified this perspective by proposing the existence of six basic **facial expressions of emotion** (surprise, fear, disgust, anger, happiness, and sadness). When photos of these expressions are shown in various countries around the world, people from very different cultures all agree on their meaning (**Figure 2.8A**).

Another general categorization scheme describes emotions in terms of two distinct *dimensions*. One dimension, called **valence,** describes a continuum from the most negative emotional states to the most positive. For example, anger is a negative emotion, whereas happiness is a positive emotion. The second dimension, called **arousal**, describes a continuum from extreme calm to extreme excitement (**Figure 2.8B**). Anger, for example, involves greater arousal than sadness, even though both emotions are negative in valence. The arousal dimension also emphasizes the link to the autonomic manifestations of emotions, which as explained in Chapter 17, presents a way of monitoring emotional responses. A variety of psychological studies have shown that both valence and arousal are important factors in understanding and evaluating emotional effects.

Exploring emotions in psychological terms

The expression "seeing the world though rose-colored glasses" epitomizes the obvious fact that our emotions can alter perceptual and other cognitive processes. Emotion research in cognitive psychology has generally aimed at understanding not only the nature of emotional processes, but how emotion affects other cognitive functions such as perception, memory, reasoning, and decision making.

The effects of emotion can be beneficial or detrimental, depending on the goal of the task. For example, emotion can enhance visual processing in the spatial location where an arousing stimulus is located. This effect makes adaptive sense, as fear, for instance, could help detect a potential predator (e.g. a snake on a tree branch) by facilitating perceptual processing (e.g. different shades of green). However, excessively arousing stimuli can also disrupt normal sensory processing. Psychologists have shown that witnesses to an armed robbery understandably tend to focus on the weapon; they mostly fail to process (and thus cannot remember) the face of the perpetrator. In general, emotional events, whether positive or negative, tend to be better remembered than neutral events. The mechanism of this effect presumably reflects adaptation (i.e., a change in normal responsiveness) of the relevant

(A)

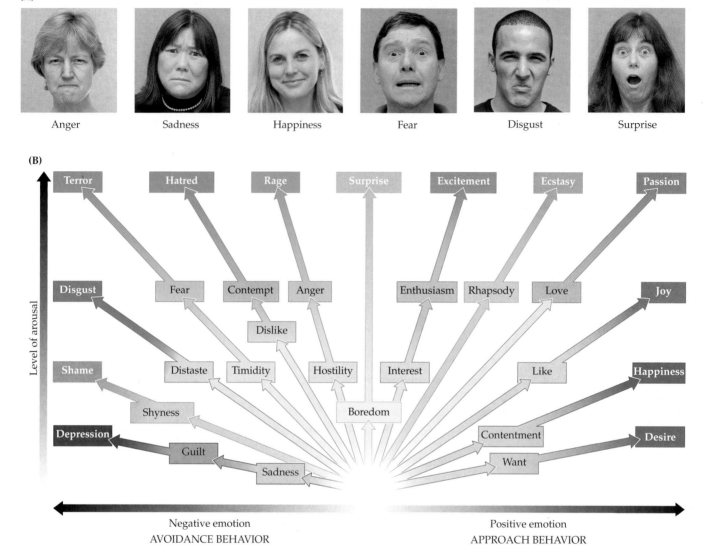

Figure 2.8 The psychology of emotion. (A) Facial expressions conveying these basic human emotions are recognized by people across all cultures. (B) Emotions can be described as functions of arousal and valence. (A, photographs by D. McIntyre; B after Kissin 1986.)

memory systems. Such adaptation again makes good biological sense, since in nature events associated with positive emotions (pleasure at finding food) or negative emotions (fear after spotting a predator) are relevant to survival. The effects of emotions on our ability to reason clearly is also an everyday experience.

Given the importance of human interactions in cognitive psychology, many studies have explored **social cognition**, which refers to the cognitive processes (perception, attention, memory, etc.) as they apply to and influence social information and social responses. Facial expressions have again provided a focus in examining the psychology of social interaction and communication. When people see a face, they quickly perceive and infer a large amount of socially relevant information, including the age, gender, race, and attractiveness of the person. By processing the person's gaze, they can infer what the person is attending to, and can often make a well-informed guess about what the person is thinking about. For example, it is obviously important to know whether the person you're interacting with is friendly or hostile, and facial expressions often reveal this. Socially relevant information is also extracted from movements and other aspects of "body language."

A related concept derived from cognitive psychology concerns **theory of mind**, a term that refers to an individual's understanding that different people have different mental states, beliefs, and intentions, and to the ability just mentioned to infer what these might be. Much work has also been directed to the question of whether other animals have these abilities. Whether non-human primates have a theory of mind remains a subject of considerable debate. Also of interest is the question of the age at which a theory of mind develops in children. Theory of mind development in children has been investigated using the so called *Sally/Anne test*, in which the experimenter produces a skit using two dolls. Sally puts a marble into her basket and leaves the scene. While Sally is away, Anne takes the marble out of the basket and puts it into her box. Sally then returns and the child being tested is asked where Sally will look for the marble. By the age of 4, normal children answer correctly that Sally will look in the basket because she does not know that Anne moved the marble to the box. As will be discussed in Chapter 19, however, autistic children have difficulty with this task, reflecting a deficit in theory of mind.

Although emotions and the social aspects of cognition have generally received less attention from psychologists over the years than many other cognitive functions, cognitive psychology research on these topics in recent decades has provided many of the core concepts in cognitive neuroscience today.

Symbolic Representation

Symbolic representation refers to a broad set of cognitive skills by which ideas are communicated using agreed-on stimuli (symbols) that stand for distinctive objects, conditions, or concepts. Obvious examples are words that stand for objects; words that stand for conditions and concepts; and numbers that stand for object quantities and the parsing of time. As used in psychology, **representation** refers more specifically to the way the brain encodes and processes such information. Cognitive psychologists have explored many sorts of mental representations, but two categories of symbolic representation have been of special interest: representations in language, and pre-linguistic representations of object quantity and time. Both of these cognitive abilities have been central to the emergence of human culture. Moreover, their presumptive antecedents can be observed in the parallel behaviors of many non-human animals, which have also been of great interest to cognitive psychologists.

Symbolic representation in language

Human **language** is defined as a system of vocal communication among groups that have interacted sufficiently to have developed a common set of speech sounds. Although also of interest in psychology, communication by written symbols is less important and relatively recent in human history. Whereas human language as we now understand it is thought to have originated on the order of 100,000 years ago, writing dates back only about 6000 years. Even among the approximately 6000 languages spoken in the world today, only about 200 have corresponding writing systems.

As described in Chapter 20, elementary speech sounds called *phones* are combined to produce more complex units such as syllables, words, sentences, and complete narratives. These basic phonic stimuli are perceived as the speech sounds we actually hear, called *phonemes*. Much of the classical work on the psychology of language has focused on how these elements of speech are processed and understood. A major obstacle in such work is that phonemes do not bear a simple relation to physical sounds, so that ranges of physically different sounds are perceived as being the same phoneme (**Figure 2.9**). More-

Figure 2.9 Physically different speech sound stimuli are perceived as the same phoneme. When sound stimuli such as /ba/, /da/, and /ga/ are gradually varied using synthesized speech, perception changes rapidly at the boundaries between phonemes, but remains stable over a wide range of acceptable stimuli for each phoneme. (After Liberman et al. 1957.)

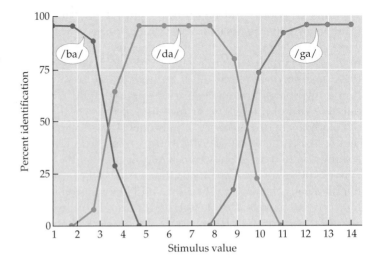

over, the, same physical stimulus associated with a phoneme can sound quite different to a listener depending on the phonemes that come just before or after it. To make matters even more complicated, in normal speech the phonemes are articulated in close succession (called *co-articulation*), altering the physical output of the same vowel sound. Despite these daunting facts, psychological studies of language show that we can accurately recognize as many as 50 phones per second when listening to speech.

With the exception of onomatopoetic words like *click, meow,* and *hum,* the combination of phonemes that make up words is arbitrary: there is no intrinsic link between the sounds constituting a word and the meaning to which it refers. A few dozen phonemes that vary from language to language are combined to create thousands of words that can be thought of as consisting of one or more **morphemes**, defined as the smallest linguistic units that convey meaning. For example, the word "immeasurable" consists of three morphemes: *im* (a prefix), *measure* (the stem), and *able* (a suffix).

Several words may have the same basic meaning, and refer to the same lexical unit or **lexeme**. For instance, the verbs *being, been, am, is, are, was,* and *were* all refer to the same lexeme, *to be.* Lexemes have been taken by some investigators to be the key elements in making verbal associations, and to correspond to the nodes of semantic memory networks (see Box 2B).

The rules by which words are correctly used and combined into sentences are called **grammar** and **syntax**, respectively. Psychologists and linguists have long sought rules that are pertinent to all of the world's languages. Whether such a **universal grammar** exists remains an open and quite controversial issue. Whereas the quest for a universal grammar focuses on the core structure of language uncontaminated by its many particulars, cognitive psychologists are also interested in *performance*—the actual behavior speakers generate. For example, although native speakers typically use valid phrase structures (the correct use of grammar and syntax is referred to as language *competence*), people tend to use only a few of the innumerable valid phrases that are possible. This repetitive usage is presumably the norm because it allows for faster and more automatic performance and understanding. Employing certain syntactic structures increases the chances of using them again, and thus individuals develop linguistic habits. Unlike competence, performance is affected by the limitations of cognitive processes such as perception, attention, and memory.

As discussed in Chapter 20, perhaps the major issue in the cognitive psychology of language today is whether the human ability to associate new words with objects and concepts ad infinitum distinguishes human language from the systems of social communication used by many other animals.

The representation of time and number

Although there are words for them, time and number are fundamentally non-verbal aspects of cognition. Language-based symbols are used when needed, but these are not essential to mental representations of time and number. In most day-to-day activities (such as waiting for an elevator or for a teapot to boil), humans have an approximate sense of how much time has passed without having to look at a clock or think explicitly in terms of seconds or minutes. The situation for number is similar: although symbols are often used to represent quantity, the human mind can process such concepts using representations that are independent of language.

The human sense of time operates over many different scales and involves a variety of neural systems. **Circadian timing** refers to mechanisms that organize homeostatic processes over the 24-hour light–dark cycle. **Interval timing** allows humans (and other animals) to track durations of seconds to minutes with surprising accuracy. Interval timing is particularly important for many kinds of decision making, and it pervades cognitive operations. There is, however, much ongoing debate over how the brain times intervals. It is not clear whether there is a central internal clock for interval timing, or how this process is related to the myriad functions in the nervous system that require temporal specificity. As described in Chapter 22, although great progress has been made in sorting out the physiology and anatomy of circadian processes, time and its uses in cognitive processing remain poorly understood. In sum, however, cognitive psychology has not only informed the field of symbolic representation but remains a major (if not the major) way of exploring these difficult issues.

Executive Processing

It goes without saying that human cognition is not simply a collection of discrete abilities dedicated to the challenges of perceiving objects, remembering past events, or manipulating symbols. A hallmark of human mentation is that people use these abilities either together or selectively based on individual goals, the constraints of the environment at any given moment, and many other factors. The cognitive functions that allow this flexible and goal-directed control are collectively called **executive processes.** The psychologically defined processes that control the flow of information in the nervous system include **initiation, inhibition, task-shifting,** and **monitoring** (that is, monitoring the environment and the consequences of behavior as humans and other animals interact with their surroundings). A general way of conceiving executive processes lies in the etymology of the word "executive," which comes from the Latin for "to carry out"—a term that aptly reflects the transition from brain processing to behavioral action. In this conception, executive processes consist of a set of organizational tools that we and other animals use to *decide* between potential courses of behavior, to *reason* about accumulated information, and to *solve* novel and complex problems.

Decision making

We are continually faced with the need to make decisions. Some of these decisions reflect the demands of the world around us and are based on sensory information; the awareness of making them may or may not enter our consciousness. Other decisions reflect current goals (personal, social or otherwise), as when we consciously decide to purchase one item and not another.

Still others entail long reflection and have lasting, even momentous consequences, such as the decision about a career path or marriage.

In principle, making a decision involves gathering information and weighing evidence pertinent to the options (again, these processes are not necessarily conscious). Theoretical economists interested in psychology tend to create **normative models** that describe the process that would underlie ideal (fully rational) decision making. The canonical normative model is based on **expected utility**, which states that decisions should ideally be made by multiplying the subjective worth of different outcomes by their probability of occurrence. Not surprisingly, normative models don't do a very good job of accounting for observed decision-making behavior. For instance, people gamble on slot machines or buy lottery tickets, even though both behaviors will cost them money in the long run. Well-off people often buy insurance for losses that they could readily afford to sustain, while less wealthy individuals fail to buy insurance that would protect them from potentially catastrophic losses. Decisions are also influenced by **framing effects** (effectively, the context in which the decision is being made); for example, research has shown that a person is more likely to drive across town to save $10 on a $20 purchase than on a $500 purchase, even though the costs and benefits are exactly the same in each case.

In the past several decades, cognitive psychologists, behavioral economists, and others have explored ways in which decisions systematically deviate from the ideal, creating **descriptive models** of decision making that better fit the rather peculiar ways in which people actually behave. Among other strategies, descriptive models introduce **heuristics**, or rules, for decision making that simplify complex situations (e.g., determining the value of a house by multiplying its square footage by a constant). Investigators using **game theory** have also examined decision making in interactive situations in new ways. Imagine, for instance that you and nine other people are brought into a room, told that you cannot communicate with each other, and asked to write down a number between 1 and 10. If your number is not chosen by someone else, you will win $100. But if you choose the same number as another person, you receive nothing. What number do you choose and why? Interactive games like this provide a rich environment for this sort of research because they bring several executive processes into play (e.g., evaluating rewards, planning strategy, thinking about others' goals and selecting a best response). Most real-world decisions are similarly complex, and cognitive psychologists and economists are collaborating on ever-more realistic models of decision making.

Reasoning and problem solving

Many of the most complex challenges humans face involve reasoning and problem solving. Cognitive psychologists have worked extensively in these domains, not least because of their practical applications. Imagine a marketer whose company is about to launch a new cell phone. How does the marketer ensure that an appropriate audience learns about the new product? How should the instrument be styled? What features should be bundled with the phone? These questions require reasoning and problem-solving skills, and no single feature distinguishes these cognitive functions. In both cases, there is an initial state, a goal state, and a set of potential operators; often there are obstacles that preclude a direct path between the initial and goal states (**Figure 2.10**). In situations where the rules are known and possible actions are highly constrained (think again of chess), the term "reasoning" is usually applied; when the rules are murky and the number of possible actions is large (as in marketing a new cell phone), the term "problem solving" is used, and the set of possible actions is referred to as the problem space.

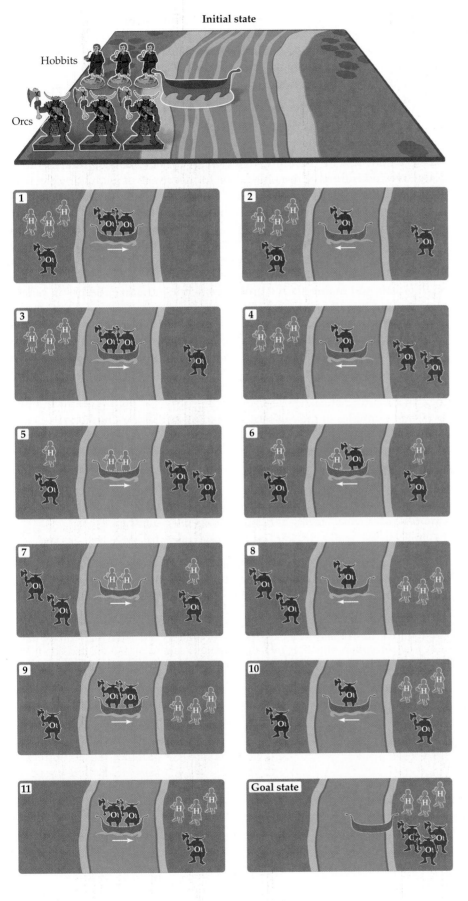

Figure 2.10 The Hobbits-and-Orcs problem. In this famous logic problem, the initial state consists of three harmless creatures (here, Hobbits) and three vicious ones (Orcs) on the same side of a river; the goal state is to get all six of them on the opposite river bank. The operators are the boat crossings; the obstacles are (1) a boat that holds only two passengers at a time, and (2) a constraint that there never be more Orcs than Hobbits in the boat or on either side of the river. Note that solving the problem requires backtracking (move number 6).

Some problems can be solved by **trial and error** or **brute force** approaches. A brute force approach that moves closer and closer to the goal is called a **hill climbing**. Other problems can only be solved by recognizing an obstacle and **backtracking** (see, for instance, move number 6 in Figure 2.10). When backtracking occurs and the solution suddenly becomes apparent, there is often an experience of **insight** (see the earlier discussion of insight in the context of Gestalt psychology).

In contrast to brute force approaches to solving a problem, reasoning describes problem solving that is both deliberate and explicitly rational. A classic distinction in reasoning is between the approaches referred to as **deductive** and **inductive** reasoning. The former involves evaluating the truth of a conclusion from a set of premises, whereas the latter involves generalizing from a set of cases to an overarching rule. People are generally much more adept at solving problems that involve inductive rather than deductive reasoning, perhaps explaining why the deductive abilities of Sherlock Holmes continue to fascinate us. Cognitive psychology studies of deductive and inductive reasoning suggest that deductive reasoning depends more heavily on linguistic and manipulative processes, while inductive reasoning reflects planning and hypothesis testing.

Despite the many advances made in the realm of cognitive psychology, the field has remained relatively poor in tools that would allow scientists to explore human mental processes directly. The explosion of the biomedical field of neuroscience and the advent of some remarkable new technologies in the last decades of the twentieth century set the stage for the emergence of cognitive neuroscience. These scientific approaches, the nature of the new tools, and examples of their use are the subject of the next chapter.

Summary

1. The heritage of cognitive psychology is both rich and important, providing experimental observations, theoretical frameworks, and insights into the human mental processes that remain highly influential in cognitive neuroscience today.

2. During the last century, work in cognitive psychology has moved—in fits and starts, to be sure—from a stance in which little or no attempt was made to consider the processes intervening between stimulus and response (the perspective typified most dramatically by early twentieth century behaviorism) to the view that many aspects of these processes can be inferred from the measurement of simple variables such as response time and the accuracy of performance.

3. Powerful new ideas such as information theory and connectionist theory have introduced substantially new frameworks for thinking about old questions in the areas of perception, attention, memory, emotions, language, and the decision-making and problem-solving abilities referred to as "executive processes."

Additional Reading

Reviews

CLIFTON, C. JR. AND S. A. DUFFY (2001) Sentence and text comprehension: Roles of linguistic structure. *Annu. Rev. Psychol.* 52: 167–196.

LOGAN, G. D. (2004) Cumulative progress in formal theories of attention. *Annu. Rev. Psychol.* 55: 207–234.

MARKMAN, A. B. AND D. GENTNER (2001) Thinking. *Annu. Rev. Psychol.* 52: 223–247.

NAIRNE, J. S. (2002) Remembering over the short term: The case against the standard model. *Annu. Rev. Psychol.* 53: 53–81.

PASHLER, H., J. C. JOHNSTON AND E. RUTHRUFF (2001) Attention and performance. *Annu. Rev. Psychol.* 52: 629–651.

RUSSEL, J. A., J. A. BACHOROWSKI AND J. M. FERNÁNDEZ-DOLS (2003) Facial and vocal expressions of emotion. *Annu. Rev. Psychol.* 54: 329–349.

TULVING, E. (2002) Episodic memory: From mind to brain. *Annu. Rev. Psychol.* 53: 1–25.

Important Original Papers

ATKINSON, R. C. AND R. M. SHIFFRIN (1968) Human memory: A proposed system and its control processes. In *The Psychology of Learning and Motivation: Advances in Research and Theory*, Vol. 2. K. W. Spence (ed.) New York: Academic Press, pp. 88–195.

CHERRY, E. C. (1953) Some experiments on the recognition of speech, with one and with two ears. *J. Acoust. Soc. Amer.* 25: 975–979.

CRAIK, F. I. AND E. TULVING (1975) Depth of processing and the retention of words in episodic memory. *J. Exp. Psychol. (General)* 104: 268–294.

POSNER, M. I., C. R. R. SNYDER AND B. J. DAVIDSON (1980) Attention and the detection of signals. *J. Exp. Psychol. (General)* 109: 160–174.

RUSSEL, C. AND J. DRIVER (2005) New indirect measures of "inattentive" visual grouping in a change-detection task. *Percep. Psychophys.* 67: 606–623.

STERNBERG, S. (1966) High-speed memory scanning in human memory. *Science* 153: 652–654.

TVERSKY, A. AND D. KAHNEMAN (1974) Judgment under uncertainty: Heuristics and biases. *Science* 185: 3–20.

WESTHEIMER, G. (1999) Gestalt theory reconfigured: Max Wertheimer's anticipation of recent developments in visual neuroscience. *Perception* 28: 5–15.

Books

GARDNER, H. (1985) *The Mind's New Science: A History of the Cognitive Revolution*. New York: Basic Books.

GREGORY, R. (1970) *The Intelligent Eye*. New York: McGraw-Hill.

KÖHLER, W. (1947) *Gestalt Psychology: An Introduction to New Concepts in Modern Psychology*. Reissued 1992, London: Liveright.

POSNER, M. I. (1978) *Chronometric Explorations of Mind*. Hillsdale, NJ: Lawrence Erlbaum.

WILLINGHAM, D. W. (2007) *Cognition: The Thinking Animal*, 3rd Ed. Upper Saddle River, NJ: Prentice-Hall.

3

Exploring Cognitive Processes in Neural Terms

■ **Brain Perturbations Shed Light on Cognitive Functions 57**

■ **Measuring Neural Activity during Cognitive Processing 64**

■ **Assembling Evidence and Delineating Mechanisms 78**

Introduction

The overarching goal of the field of cognitive neuroscience is to explain mental processes and behavior in terms of the structure and function of relevant regions of the brain and the rest of the nervous system. The contributions of cognitive psychology reviewed in Chapter 2 emphasized the importance of measuring behavioral responses as a means of inferring what transpires as the nervous system translates stimuli into appropriate actions. Such measures have for the most part focused on the speed and/or accuracy of performance, and have provided insights into the cognitive processing accomplished by the nervous system. By applying these psychological paradigms in conjunction with techniques and methods derived from neurobiology, neuropharmacology, neurology, neurosurgery, and psychiatry, investigators have increasingly been able to directly relate the biology of brain functions to the abstract mental functions studied by cognitive psychologists.

Neurobiologically based approaches can be divided into two broad categories: studying changes in cognitive behavior when the brain has been perturbed in some way, and measuring brain activity while cognitive tasks are being performed. Perhaps the most informative perturbations of brain function for cognitive neuroscience have been those due to brain lesions. Although obvious limitations are imposed by the idiosyncrasies of brain trauma, stroke, and disease, if damage to a brain area or system disrupts a cognitive function, it is likely that the damaged region is involved in some critical way in the performance of that function. Based on this same conceptual framework, temporary pharmacological and electrical perturbations have also been used to advantage in both human subjects and experimental animals. The second approach—measuring normal brain activity while the subject is engaged in a cognitive task—takes advantage of a variety of recently available electrophysiological and imaging techniques in both humans and animals. Both of these approaches have altered and accelerated our understanding of the higher human brain functions that are the focus of cognitive neuroscience.

Brain Perturbations Shed Light on Cognitive Functions

Perturbations imposed by trauma or disease

The technique of **clinical-pathological correlations** is the oldest method for understanding the neural basis of cognitive function and has been a mainstay of neurology and neurosurgery for more than a century. This approach was first accomplished by correlating a patient's signs, symptoms, and behavior during life with the location of **brain lesions** discovered after the patient died and the brain was examined at autopsy. Brain lesions can arise from a stroke that destroys a particular region of cortex (see Chapter 1), from traumatic injury, from tumors, or from various brain diseases. Many examples of clinical-pathological correlations are considered in later chapters, including the seminal work that associated language functions with specific regions in the left hemisphere (Chapter 21); patients with frontal lobe damage whose cognitive deficits revealed the importance of this part of the brain in planning and judgment (Chapter 24); and patients whose lesions provided fundamental insights into the neural basis of perception (Chapters 5–7), attentional control (Chapter 12), memory (Chapter 13), and emotion (Chapter 17).

A major limitation of the lesion approach, however, is that brain damage in humans is the result of many factors that are not under the control of the experimenter. In the case of strokes, for example, these factors include how long ago the stroke occurred, which specific artery was blocked, which brain area(s) that artery supplied, and whether other arteries were still able to supply some blood to the affected area. Although stroke-induced lesions can be relatively focal, they necessarily respect vascular rather than functional boundaries, and thus can influence multiple cognitive functions. Moreover, the distribution of brain regions supporting cognitive functions varies among individuals, which can make it difficult to generalize results. This variability can be addressed to some degree by combining information about the locus of damage across a group of patients, allowing researchers to delineate the affected region that is common to the loss of a particular function (**Figure 3.1**). The region of overlap among a group of patients more accurately defines the part of the brain relevant to the cognitive function at issue.

Another way researchers have more specifically defined the relationship between brain damage and resulting deficits in cognitive functions is by making restricted electrolytic or surgical lesions in experimental animals, including in non-human primates. This approach allows the researcher to much more specifically control the location and extent of brain damage, limiting it to specific functional areas. There are, however, some disadvantages to this approach. The training and assessment of animals carrying out cognitive tasks is considerably more difficult than similar studies in humans, and making deliberate lesions in the brains of healthy animals raises ethical concerns. Nevertheless, the use of carefully controlled brain lesions in experimental animals has provided important data to complement that derived from neuropsychological studies in humans.

Clinical-pathological correlation studies remain highly informative in cognitive neuroscience. Their continued relevance has been greatly augmented by modern neuroimaging methods that allow brain lesions to be localized with considerable precision in living, functional patients who are still available for detailed behavioral testing. Early knowledge of the exact site of a lesion can inform such testing in a far more focused way than when the definitive localization of the lesion could only be attained postmortem. These new methods of imaging brain structure are fundamental to the field of cognitive neuroscience, and are described in **Box 3A**.

Pharmacological perturbations

Perturbation studies of cognitive function have also been carried out by means of **pharmacological manipulation**. As described in Chapter 1 and the Appendix, signaling between neurons involves the release of and response to neurotransmitter molecules at synapses. Many drugs interfere with these processes and can thereby perturb cognitive functions. Cognitive neuroscientists have

Left dorsal prefrontal

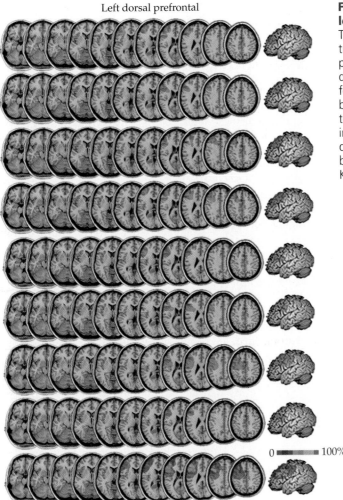

0 ▬▬ 100%

Figure 3.1 Combining information across subjects better localizes the brain region underlying a cognitive deficit. These images show the areas of damage determined from structural magnetic resonance brain images (see Box 3A) for eight patients with a common cognitive loss (the prefrontal syndrome described in Chapter 23). Each row shows the extent of damage for a given patient; each column is from a comparable level in the brain, from inferior on the left to superior on the right. The bottom row shows the area of brain damage the eight subjects have in common. The scale shows the percentage of subjects with damage in each location. This sort of analysis helps specify the brain region that is critical to a given function. (Courtesy of Robert Knight.)

taken advantage of **psychoactive drugs**—caffeine, cocaine, antidepressants, and a host of others—to gain insight into the pharmacology and synaptic physiology of these functions both in humans and experimental animals.

Pharmacological studies in humans have taken two main forms. The first approach has been to examine the influence of chronic drug use or abuse on cognitive processes, taking advantage of the unfortunate prevalence of these disorders. An example is the cognitive impairments apparent in cocaine addicts, which include changes in the mental processes related to reward evaluation (i.e., a person's ability to properly assess the positive or negative value of events and behaviors). Impaired reward evaluation in turn affects the ability to make self-protecting decisions and to formulate and pursue successful life strategies. Cocaine and other drugs of abuse lead to specific changes in neurotransmission in the brain systems that underlie these functions. Cocaine specifically activates dopamine receptors, altering the physiology of the *midbrain dopamine system*, which is known to play a major role in reward evaluation (see Chapter 24). Although the dysfunction that leads to addiction is still not completely understood, the altered sense of reward associated with both the cocaine "high" and with cocaine addiction is clear. Chronic use leads to drug tolerance and the need for increasing amounts of the drug in order to achieve the same pharmacological effect—with further negative consequences. (On a less problematic level, this sort of pharmacological adaptation is familiar to habitual coffee drinkers, who need more caffeine to achieve the

■ BOX 3A Structural Brain Imaging Techniques

Until relatively recently, images of the human brain, whether of patients or of normal subjects, provided only limited information to clinicians and researchers. For a long time, the best noninvasive imaging methodology available used conventional X-ray techniques, which do not image soft tissue structures such as the brain very well and do not provide three-dimensional image information. Although the addition of vascular contrast agents (dyes containing radio-opaque materials such as barium salts) improved the visualization of lesioned tissue, the intrinsic two-dimensional nature of conventional X-rays (i.e., giving a net density through imaged tissue only at one particular angle) still limited the anatomical resolution of brain tissue. Beginning in the 1970s, however, the development of a variety of imaging methods that revealed brain structure (and, somewhat later, brain physiology) with ever-increasing detail revolutionized neuroscience, from clinical diagnostics to research on cognitive processes.

The first technological breakthrough was the development of **computerized tomography** (**CT**). CT uses a movable X-ray tube that is rotated around the patient's head (Figure A). Rather than acquiring a single image, as in conventional X-ray images, a CT scan gathers *intensity information* gleaned from multiple angles around the patient's head. These data are entered into a matrix and the radiodensity at each point in the three-dimensional space of the head is calculated. Using sensitive detectors and digital signal processing techniques, small differences in radiodensity can be converted into 3-D image information for the full volume of the head. In addition, the computed matrix can generate "slices," or *tomograms* (*tomo* means "cut" or "slice"), visualizing internal structures in various planes throughout the brain (Figure A, inset), transformed to provide views from any angle. Since many brain structures are best seen in a particular plane, this ability is a tremendous advantage.

Today, CT imaging for research purposes has been largely superceded by **magnetic resonance imaging** (**MRI**; Figure B), although CT remains important in many clinical applications because it is faster and cheaper than MRI.

The essentials of the mechanism by which *magnetic resonance* produces *images* can be understood in terms of the three concepts reflected in the phrase itself:

■ *Magnetic:* Consider a compass needle. At rest, the needle is aligned with the Earth's magnetic field (i.e., along a north–south axis). Similarly, when a person is inside an MRI scanner, protons in hydrogen atoms of the brain become aligned with the very strong magnetic field of the scanner. Perturbations away from this alignment provide a source signal that can be measured, analyzed, and used to construct an image.

■ *Resonance:* This difficult concept is the foundation of MRI. *Resonance* refers to the ability of a system to absorb energy delivered at a particular frequency. A macroscopic example is a child on a playground swing. Given a single push, even a strong one, the resulting movement is brief and diminishes quickly. In contrast, repeated small pushes at the right frequency (i.e., a push each time the person reaches the apogee of their arc) allows the system to absorb the imparted energy effectively, such that the child will soon be swinging back and forth with great excursion. In the same way, protons in a strong magnetic field will efficiently absorb energy when the energy is delivered at a particular *resonant frequency*. During a process called *excitation,* the MRI scanner emits energy in the form of radio waves at precisely the resonant frequency of protons. After a few milliseconds, the radio-wave energy is turned off, whereupon the protons begin to release the energy they absorbed. This released energy—the *MR signal*—is measured by electromagnetic detectors around the head or other part of the body.

■ *Imaging:* In order to create an image from the MR signal, electromagnetic coils in the scanner can cause the

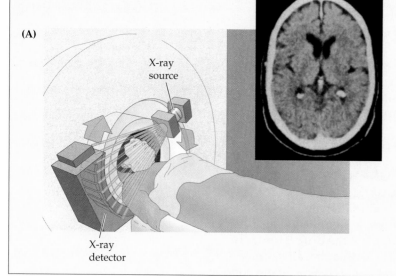

(A)

X-ray source

X-ray detector

Computerized tomography. During a CT scan, an X-ray source is rotated around the patient's head while detectors measure the intensity of the rays transmitted through the head at each imaged angle. Computer algorithms combine the opacity data from these multiple imaging angles to reconstruct the opacity at each point within the volume of the head. In addition, the detectors used in CT are more sensitive than conventional film, thereby allowing shorter imaging times and less radiation exposure. Inset shows a CT scan of a horizontal section of a normal adult brain.

magnetic field to differ in strength along specific directions. By varying these magnetic field *gradients* in a systematic way along the *x*, *y*, and *z* axes of the volume to be imaged, the MR signal is caused to vary correspondingly and systematically along these axes. This complex variation in the signal emitted by the brain or other tissue is decoded by sophisticated computer analysis to create an image that reflects the proton density as well as the density of other tissue characteristics throughout the imaged volume. Because these characteristics are different for gray matter, white matter, the fluid in the ventricles, and other neural tissues (see Chapter 1), a great deal of neuroanatomical detail becomes apparent.

The spatial resolution of MR images depends on the strength of the magnetic field, the strength of the gradient coils, and the type of images being collected. Currently, most clinical scanners have field strengths of 1.5 Tesla, which provides a resolution of structure of 1 mm or less. Many new scanners, especially those used for research purposes,

have field strengths of 3 Tesla or higher, often along with high-performance magnetic gradient coils that improve the structural imaging resolution to the level of fractions of a millimeter. These enhanced performance characteristics also facilitate the acquisition of high-speed images of functional brain activity, as described later in the chapter.

It should be apparent from this description that MRI has a number of important features that have made it an extraordinarily valuable tool in cognitive neuroscience. First, it is noninvasive; subjects are simply exposed to a strong magnetic field and radio waves that are harmless to brain tissues (although patients have been injured by unsecured ferromagnetic objects being pulled into the MR scanner). Second, MR images of brain tissue are of extremely high resolution compared to those obtainable using other techniques (compare the insets in Figures A and B for MRI and CT images, respectively). Third, by varying the gradient and

radio-frequency pulse parameters, MRI scanners can be used to generate images that are sensitive to many different aspects of brain structure. For example, although certain imaging parameters enable the acquisition of pictures that delineate gray matter and white matter in detail, the use of other parameters enable the generation of images in which gray and white matter are invisible but in which the brain's vasculature stands out.

Lastly, varying other parameters of MR scanning sequences enables a determination of the direction of water diffusion for each voxel (i.e., imaging volume unit) of imaged brain tissue. Because of the fatty nature of myelin, water tends to diffuse more along fiber tracts than across them, but in no special direction in other components of brain tissue. This technique—known as *diffusion tensor imaging* (DTI)—enables imaging of fiber tracts at higher resolution than in conventional MRI. Such information can indicate the connectivity of brain areas relevant to specific cognitive functions.

References

HOUNSFIELD, G. N. (1980) Computed medical imaging. *Science* 210: 22–28.

HUETTEL, S., A. W. SONG AND G. MCCARTHY (2004) *Functional Magnetic Resonance Imaging.* Sunderland, MA: Sinauer.

OLDENDORF, W. AND W. OLDENDORF JR. (1988) *Basics of Magnetic Resonance Imaging.* Boston: Kluwer Academic.

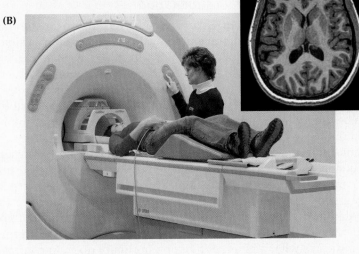

(B)

Magnetic resonance imaging. A typical 1.5-Tesla MR scanner is shown. The inset shows a horizontal MR image of a normal adult brain. Note the extraordinary clarity with which the different soft tissue types and regions of the brain can be seen, and how much more detail is seen compared to the CT image in Figure A.

same stimulatory effect than do people who drink coffee only occasionally.) Studies of the effects of cocaine have been critical in understanding of the regions of the brain and the cellular mechanisms involved in the normal sense of reward, as described in Chapters 18 and 24.

More controlled pharmacological perturbation studies take place in experimental settings in which a drug is administered acutely and its effects monitored. In this manner it is possible to study, for example, the effects of nicotine on cognitive functions, another arena that has been of great interest because of its social and health implications. Nicotine affects neurotransmission mediated by acetylcholine, interacting with cognitive processes that include mood, attention, memory, and appetite, as well as neurological processes that can lead to addiction. The nicotine molecule is an acetylcholine **agonist**—that is, its molecular structure is similar to that of acetylcholine, and so nicotine acts directly on acetylcholine receptors. (Drugs that act on receptors in a manner similar to a neurotransmitter are agonists, whereas drugs that disrupt neurotransmission by blocking receptors are called **antagonists**.) When coupled with information derived from neuropharmacological studies in experimental animals and in vitro systems, pharmacological manipulation can lead to inferences about the contribution of the relevant neurotransmitter system to the cognitive processes they affect.

A disadvantage of administering drugs systemically (i.e., by injecting into the bloodsteam) for understanding cognitive processes is the relative lack of specificity of drug effects. Much of the brain (along with the other organs of the body) is exposed to the agent, and sorting out the effects of different brain systems can be difficult. A more specific intervention is to inject substances directly into specific brain areas of an experimental animal. This approach usually involves surgically implanting a cannula or other drug delivery system that can administer defined amounts of the experimental agent locally and in a highly controlled manner. For example, agonists and antagonists of *biogenic amines*—drugs that alter the effects of neurotransmitters such as dopamine and serotonin—have been injected into midbrain regions involved in reward processing to study the cognitive functions subserved by this key region (see above). Such studies have provided insight into the actions of a range of drugs now used to treat disorders such as depression and schizophrenia and, by implication, into the cognitive functions that go awry in these disorders.

Perturbation by intracranial brain stimulation

A very different way of perturbing brain function is **direct electrical stimulation** of a specific brain region, a technique used by pioneering neurophysiologists beginning in the late nineteenth century. This approach involves placing electrodes onto or into the brain of an experimental animal or a human patient during a neurosurgical procedure. Electrodes may be placed transiently (i.e., just for the duration of the surgery) or chronically (for an extended period). Electrodes can be used to record the brain's electrical activity and to administer electrical stimuli.

In experimental animals, chronically implanted electrodes allow researchers to assess the function of individual neurons or groups of neurons as the animal (typically a monkey) carries out a cognitive task it has been trained to perform. By altering the strength of the stimulus applied, the effects on the local neuronal population can be varied to provide additional information. For example, moderate levels of stimulation can activate neurons and trigger behavior that indicates what a given population normally does. In contrast, strong stimulation tends to disrupt normal function, and thus can indicate how the loss of that neuronal population would affect specific cognitive processes. Used in this way, electrical stimulation can effectively create a transient "lesion."

Although intracranial stimulation techniques are obviously invasive, they are sometimes used in humans to enable neurosurgeons to map the functions of brain regions they are considering operating on or near. For instance, mapping by mild electrical stimulation paired with recording is often undertaken in patients with intractable epilepsy, a disorder characterized by occasional chaotic electrical activity in the cerebral cortex (i.e., seizures). Whereas the vast majority of epileptic seizures can be controlled with medication, in severe cases the condition becomes a serious threat to the patient's well-being; these cases can often be treated by surgically removing the focus of abnormal activity. To accurately determine the origin of seizure activity prior to surgery, and to help determine the function of a specific brain site to be excised, electrical grids (multiple-sensor arrays for both electrical stimulation and recording) are placed on the relevant portion of cortical surface. In this way, the specific source of the abnormality can be determined and subsequently removed, with minimal damage to adjacent regions of normal cortex. Similarly, if a brain tumor must be excised, cortical mapping helps ensure that important cognitive functions will be minimally compromised by the surgery.

Perturbation by extracranial brain stimulation

Although disrupting neural processing by local electrical stimulation can be informative, its use in humans is obviously limited to patients with serious medical problems. A far less invasive approach that can be used to disrupt cognitive processing in normal subjects is **transcranial magnetic stimulation** (**TMS**). In this technique, a strong but transient magnetic field is generated over a region of the scalp by passing a strong electrical current through a set of coils (**Figure 3.2**). The rapidly changing magnetic field in the coil induces a transient electrical field in the underlying brain tissue. The resulting flow of current temporarily disrupts local neural processing, creating a reversible brain "lesion" limited to that underlying area and causing a temporary disruption of cognitive processing in that brain region, much as would direct electrical stimulation.

Several approaches are used to apply TMS to the study of the effects of neural stimulation on cognitive processes. One technique is to apply a series of TMS pulses (e.g., one per second) over several minutes. The influence of such repetitive TMS (rTMS) stimulation on a cognitive function of interest can then be examined by behavioral tests that can be administered up to several hours after the TMS application. Studies using this approach have shown that stimulation can either reduce or improve performance on tasks involving the stimulated area, depending on the role of that area in the task.

Another approach is to deliver a single TMS pulse to a brain area at various specific times during the course of a task trial (the pulse can be delivered just before a stimulus, for example, or at some particular number of milliseconds after a stimulus) and study the interference or enhancement on the task performance. An advantage of this latter approach is that it provides greater tem-

Figure 3.2 Transcranial magnetic stimulation (TMS).   A coil for passing a strong electrical current is placed over a subject's left prefrontal lobe in this example. The position of the figure-8 coil with respect to the underlying brain is shown diagrammatically in the middle panel and overlain on a CT scan in the right panel; contour lines indicate the depth of stimulation. A common yardstick used to set the appropriate strength of stimulation for an individual is the power that needs to be delivered to the hand area of motor cortex in the frontal lobe that elicits a muscle twitch in the hand. (From George et al. 1999.)

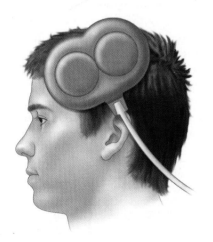
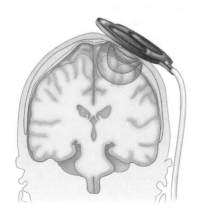
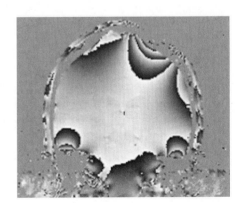

poral resolution in assessing the role of the brain area in question in the cognitive task.

There are several important drawbacks to TMS. First, as indicated in Figure 3.2, TMS tends to affect a relatively large area. Second, transcranial stimulation can only be delivered effectively to relatively superficial brain regions—primarily the more superficial regions of the cerebral cortex. Third, concurrent stimulation of the scalp and head muscles can occur, especially when attempting to stimulate certain brain regions. Such side effects can be uncomfortable and even painful; for example, stimulating the temporal lobe typically results in uncomfortable stimulation of the overlying temporalis muscle. Finally, although TMS is in principle noninvasive, the stimulation entails some risk (e.g., it can trigger a seizure). These problems notwithstanding, the ability to transiently disrupt brain function in normal subjects provides an important additional tool in the quest to understand the neural bases of cognitive functions.

Measuring Neural Activity during Cognitive Processing

Beyond making inferences about cognitive brain functions from various types of brain perturbations, another approach to understanding the relationship between cognitive functions and the neural processes that give rise to them is to *measure brain activity* while a subject performs specific cognitive tasks. There are a number of ways that neural activity can be recorded and measured in both humans and experimental animals, and today these methods are a mainstay of cognitive research.

Direct electrophysiological recording from neurons

In experimental animals, the most commonly used approach for measuring neural activity is **electrophysiological recording** of neuronal activity, a method that has its roots in the pioneering physiological work of the late nineteenth century. The most popular modern use of this general technique has been **single-unit electrical recording**, which entails measuring the action potentials produced by individual neurons (**Figure 3.3**). Such recording is done with fine tungsten or steel electrodes that are inserted into the cerebral cortex or deeper brain structures. Because the electrodes are coated with nonconducting material except at the tip, the electrical activity associated with action potentials generated by neurons near the tip are recorded *extracellularly* as a deflection on an oscilloscope or other device that measures voltage as a function of time.* Depending on the size of the electrode and its placement, the firing from several neighboring neurons can be picked up concurrently, which is advantageous in gleaning information about the behavior of small populations of nerve cells.

Until relatively recently, single-unit recording was usually carried out on anesthetized animals, which precluded experiments on cognitive functions that depend on being conscious and able to execute behaviors that indicate, for example, what the animal is perceiving or attending to. In recent years, however, electrophysiological experiments have increasingly focused on studies in awake, behaving animals that have been trained to do specific tasks. Some months prior to such experiments, researchers implant recording elec-

---

*As described in Box 1A, if hollow, electrolyte-filled glass electrodes (with a much finer tip than metal electrodes) are used, *intracellular* neuronal recordings from cortical and other brain structures are also possible. Such recordings provide information about synaptic potentials and other transmembrane potential changes, as well as recording action potentials.

(A)

(B)

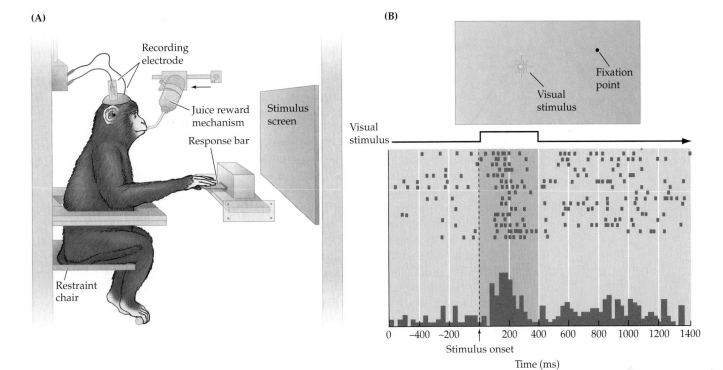

trodes in the area of interest in the animal's brain (see Figure 3.3). Typically, a movable electrode holder with an advancing mechanism is fixed to the skull over a surgically exposed brain area; after recovery from the surgery, this device allows the electrode to record from different parts and depths of the brain region below. By recording and analyzing the activity of many different neurons in a series of experimental sessions in which the animal carries out cognitive tasks it has been trained to do for a reward, insight into the underlying neural processes can be obtained.

Although single-unit data can be acquired and analyzed in many ways, there are two especially useful approaches. In studies of neuronal responses to stimuli (e.g., a light flash or a sound burst), the neuronal firing pattern across time in response to the stimulus is acquired in the form of a **peristimulus histogram**. As shown in Figure 3.3B, a stimulus is presented a number of times, each time serving as a **trial**. The neuron's responsiveness to the stimulus is determined by temporally aligning the action potentials elicited by each of the trials and then summing the spikes across trials into a histogram time-locked to the stimulus. Such an approach averages out random background firing when applied over enough trials, giving a much clearer picture of the response specifically related to the stimulus processing with respect to the task being performed. More generally, the approach of summing or averaging of the brain responses that are time-locked to repeated occurrences of various events is also used in other brain activity recording methods (to be described later).

Another way to analyze single-unit electrophysiological data is by neuronal **tuning curves**. In this approach, a stimulus is varied along some dimension (e.g., the orientation of a line while recording from neurons in visual cortex, or the frequency of a tone while recording from auditory cortex), and the strength of the response is plotted (usually in terms of spikes per second) as a function of the stimulus parameter being varied. The resulting curve defines the **selective sensitivity** of the cell to some values of that stimulus parameter relative to others.

Figure 3.3 Recording single-unit activity in an awake, behaving monkey. (A) An example of the experimental setup and recording apparatus. In this case, the monkey has been trained to press a lever for a juice reward. (B) The data recordings in this example are made from a neuron in the visual cortex. As the monkey is presented with visual stimuli and performs a visual task (in this case, moving the eyes to a particular location), the neuron responds with action potentials that are recorded as ticks on what is known as a *raster plot*. In such a plot, each row corresponds to a single trial and displays a tick for each recorded action potential following a single presentation of the stimulus. These responses are summed vertically across the trials aligned in time with the stimulus onset (i.e., time-locked), yielding a *peristimulus histogram* of the responses to stimulation (bottom). In this way the activity of neurons can be related to stimulus processing and the demands of the task being performed. (B after Colby et al. 1996.)

In most neural electrophysiological recording, single electrodes are used and only one brain region is investigated in each animal. Recently, however, researchers have started to employ *multielectrode recording arrays* to evaluate the concurrent responsiveness of sets of neurons in a given area of the brain or in related brain regions. For example, a single electrode might have multiple recording points along its length or protruding from its end, enabling the investigator to record simultaneously from multiple neurons distributed across the brain region of interest, such as across different cortical layers. Some researchers have been able to set up two or more such recording rigs, enabling them to measure neuronal activity simultaneously from widely separated but related regions of the brain. Simultaneously recorded data gathered using these approaches can then be analyzed with correlational computer algorithms to assess how neuronal activity in different parts of a putative neural circuit interact in subserving a particular cognitive function.

Many cognitive functions can be studied with these electrophysiological methods. Some of the more basic functions such as those underlying the sensory processing described in Unit II are generally amenable to study in non-primate experimental animal such as rats (or cats, although relatively few researchers today use cats as experimental subjects). However, studies of more complex functions (such as attention, memory, and symbolic representation) are most often and most effectively undertaken in monkeys. Monkeys are expensive to obtain and maintain, however, and, as already mentioned, their use in such experiments raises serious ethical considerations. Moreover, it can take weeks or even months to train a monkey to do tasks that would take a human minutes to master.

Of course, some cognitive functions—such as those involving language or abstract reasoning—can only be studied in humans. Accordingly, over the years there has been great interest in taking advantage of circumstances in which intracranial electrophysiological recording can be performed in humans (e.g., during the cortical mapping procedures that are medically necessary in treating some patients with epilepsy or other neurological lesions). Although the restrictions are obviously great, recordings of brain activity taken under such circumstances have provided important information about a variety of cognitive functions (see example on language and speech in Chapter 21). But even more attractive has been the development of *noninvasive* recording methods.

Noninvasive electrical recording in humans

Ever since the German psychiatrist Hans Berger discovered "brain waves" in the 1920s, a preeminent way of studying human brain activity associated with cognitive processes has been **electroencephalographic (EEG) recording**. Compared to the methods described in the previous section, EEG recordings are fully noninvasive, although they have other limitations. The method makes use of a set surface electrodes, ranging in number from only a few to as many as 256, which typically are embedded in an elastic cap and applied to the scalp (**Figure 3.4A**). The electrodes are brought into good electrical contact with the skin by means of a conducting gel or salt paste and the pressure from the elasticity of the cap, usually in conjunction with a bit of gentle rubbing of the scalp with a stick placed through a small hole in the back of the electrode.

The voltages at each electrode, along with that of a reference electrode placed over a site at some distance from the brain area of interest (often the mastoid bone behind the ear), are fed into differential amplifiers. The amplifiers enhance the voltage differences between each electrode and the reference electrode; the output of the amplifier is then digitized and recorded for subsequent analysis. Fluctuating voltages recorded over the brain by such electroencephalographic recordings generally vary between -100 and $+100$ μV,

(A)

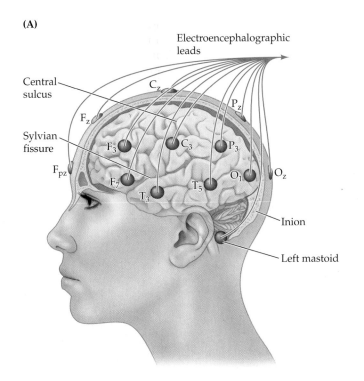

(B)

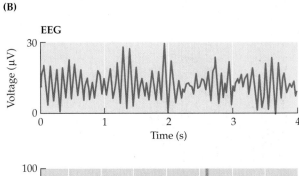

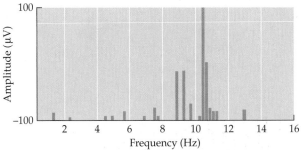

Figure 3.4 Electroencephalographic recording (EEG). (A) A subject undergoes an electoencephalogram. (B) Electrical potentials are recorded at different positions over the scalp relative to the voltage at a reference electrode. Historically, scalp locations are typically described with respect to a standardized nomenclature known as the International 10-20 or 10-10 system, in which letters indicate position on the scalp with respect to underlying cortical regions (F, frontal; P, parietal; T, temporal; O, occipital; C, central) and numbers indicate a general position with respect to the midline (odd numbers are on the left, even numbers on the right; the suffix "z" indicates placement along the midline). The electrical potential recording from each electrode is somewhat different because each primarily samples the electrical activity of large populations of neurons in the subjacent brain regions relative to a reference electrode site (here, on the left mastoid, behind the left ear). (B) Ongoing EEG activity in a normal subject with the eyes closed, a circumstance that elicits predominant activity near 10 Hz (in the alpha frequency band), as indicated in the graph at the bottom of the panel.

with a mean amplitude between 10 and 30 μV. The frequency of the fluctuations ranges from a few cycles per second to 70 Hz or more (**Figure 3.4B**).

The ongoing EEG signals are widely used in clinical settings to assess various aspects of brain function. Their most common uses are in diagnosing epilepsy and in evaluating sleep physiology and sleep disorders (see Chapters 10 and 28). In general, the signals are analyzed in terms of the power in various **frequency bands** at each electrode location, the major bands of interest being delta (<4 Hz), theta (4–8 Hz), alpha (8–12 Hz), beta (12–20 Hz), gamma (30–70 Hz), and, more recently, "high gamma" (70 to around 150 Hz). The relative power in these bands, along with other aspects of the EEG, can be used to assess arousal level, sleep stages, and the chaotic activity associated with epilepsy.

For purposes of understanding cognitive functions, however, a limitation of the ongoing EEG record is that it reflects the summed activity of *all* ongoing processes in the brain region monitored by the electrode or electrodes of interest. Although there are some important exceptions, the information gleaned in this way is generally not easy to relate to specific cognitive functions. A more revealing way of relating scalp electrical activity to cognitive function is to use **event-related potentials** (**ERPs**), which can be extracted from the EEG by time-locked averaging similar to the process (described earlier) used to generate single-unit peristimulus histograms.

ERPs are small voltage fluctuations in an ongoing EEG that are triggered by sensory and cognitive events; they reflect the summed electrical activity of neuronal populations specifically responding to those events (**Figure 3.5**). As such, they can provide high temporal resolution (milliseconds) of the neural processing underlying various cognitive functions. However, because ERPs are generally smaller (0.5–10 μV) than the raw EEG signal in which they are embedded (10–25 μV), it is necessary to average multiple trials to extract ERP signals from the background noise. As shown in Figure 3.5, ERPs are extracted by averaging those epochs of the EEG signal that are time-locked to repeated occurrences of a specific sensory, motor, or cognitive event. The ongoing EEG varies more or less

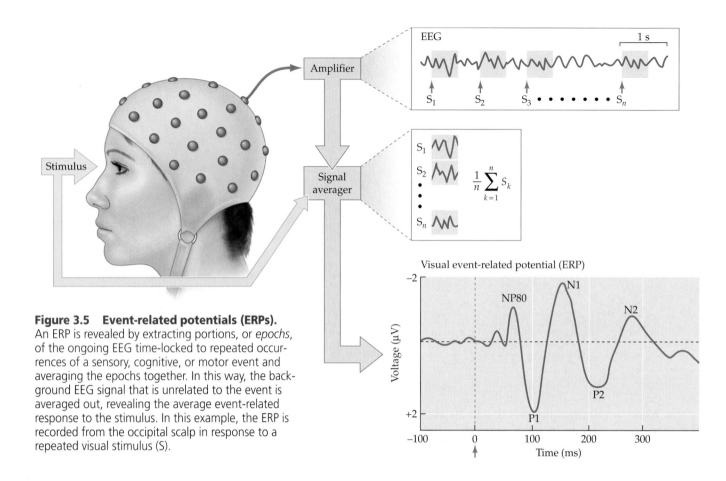

Figure 3.5 Event-related potentials (ERPs).
An ERP is revealed by extracting portions, or *epochs*, of the ongoing EEG time-locked to repeated occurrences of a sensory, cognitive, or motor event and averaging the epochs together. In this way, the background EEG signal that is unrelated to the event is averaged out, revealing the average event-related response to the stimulus. In this example, the ERP is recorded from the occipital scalp in response to a repeated visual stimulus (S).

randomly in amplitude relative to the timing of these events; these random fluctuations tend to average out, leaving only those voltage changes specifically associated with the processing of the event type of interest. An ERP obtained by such an averaging process is thus a measure of voltage changes over time, where time 0 is the time of occurrence of the event type.

The average trace obtained in this way typically comprises a series of negative and positive peaks that are named according to their *polarity* (N or P for negative or positive) and their *latency*; thus, for example, *N100* specifies a negative peak 100 milliseconds after the stimulus onset. Alternatively, and somewhat confusingly, the peaks are also named for their *order* in the sequence (thus the *N100* might also be referred to as the *N1*, due to it being the first major negative peak). To further confuse matters, for historical reasons ERP traces are typically plotted with scalp negativity upwards ("negative up"); however, some researchers prefer the opposite scheme ("negative down"), and thus the reader must always examine such plots for the indication of polarity. In addition, since the activity at *all* electrode sites is recorded, the experimenter must decide which set(s) of sites are important for the issue under study, and/or must use analyses that incorporate many or all of the sites. All these characteristics make EEG and ERP interpretation a rather complex business.

ERPs are thought to reflect the summed **dendritic field potentials** of the neuronal populations that are activated in relative synchrony in response to an event, rather than the action potentials reflected in single-unit recordings; the basis of these potentials is illustrated in **Figure 3.6**. The dendritic trees of the larger cortical neurons are generally oriented perpendicularly to the cortical surface. When, for example, there is excitatory synaptic input to the den-

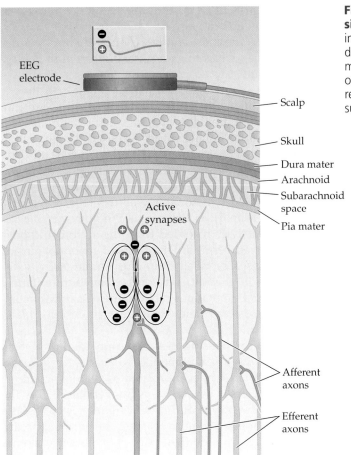

EEG electrode

Scalp

Skull

Dura mater

Arachnoid

Subarachnoid space

Pia mater

Active synapses

Afferent axons

Efferent axons

Figure 3.6 Electrophysiological basis of EEG and ERP signals. Fluctuating voltages are generated when synaptic input to a cortical area results in a voltage gradient along the dendritic trees of large pyramidal neurons that are oriented more or less perpendicular to the cortical surface. The electrode on the subject's scalp picks up the associated voltages from currents that are volume conducted through the skull and scalp tissues outside the neuronal dendrites.

drites near the cell body, the voltage within the underlying dendritic tree is depolarized (see the Appendix). A separation of charge is thus created along the length of the dendrite, which causes intracellular current flow along the dendrite, along with the return current being conducted through the tissue volume outside the dendrite. The scalp electrodes pick up the fluctuating voltages associated with these dynamically changing return volume currents. This interpretation of the basis of ERPs is well supported by other data, such as direct intracranial recordings in experimental animals of the local field potentials in and around the dendritic trees in the active neural tissue. The differences between the potentials arising from dendritic current flow and the activity measured by single-unit recordings of action potentials are important to keep in mind when relating findings from these two quite different measures of electrical brain activity.

ERPs are usually recorded while subjects are presented with various types of stimuli and are engaged in cognitive tasks related to the stimuli. Changes in the ERP responses as a function of stimulus type and task conditions are then used to infer something about the mechanisms underlying the cognitive process in question. Because the signals are electrical in nature, ERPs reflect neuronal activity with very high temporal resolution and are thus especially useful for studies in which the timing and sequence of functional brain activity are particularly important. For example, ERPs can indicate how early in the processing of auditory or visual stimuli attention can exert an influence (see Chapter 11), or at what point in language processing the semantic analysis of a word begins (see Chapter 21).

Although the major advantage of ERPs in studying cognitive processes is high temporal resolution, information can also be gained from the *spatial distribution* of the scalp recordings. The most common use of the topographic distribution of event-related potentials is to gain some understanding of the likely sources of the activity (**Figure 3.7**). For example, focal activation over the occipital scalp is likely to be coming from occipital cortex, and thus to entail visual processing (see Chapters 4 and 11). Coupled with their high temporal resolution, ERP recordings can provide a dynamic picture of brain activity over time. If many (e.g., 64 or more) electrodes are used, *source analysis algorithms* can be used to estimate the locations of the neural generators producing scalp-recorded ERPs. For simple distributions, such as ERP waves that reflect relatively early sensory processing activity (or the cognitive effects on such activity), this approach can work reasonably well. There is, however, a fundamental problem with such analyses, known as the *inverse problem*: a given distribution of electrical activity recorded from the scalp could have been produced by any one of a number of different sets of generators inside the head. Accordingly, such analyses, especially for more complex activity distributions and/or for studies without additional source-related information, must be viewed with caution. These limitations can to some degree be circumvented by combining ERP methods with other techniques, as described later in this chapter.

Although most cognitive research using electroencephalographic techniques has made use of ERP analyses using time-locked averaging, in recent years there has been increasing interest in event-related oscillatory activity in the EEG signal. This approach differs in several ways from earlier EEG analyses that focused on changes in the power of different frequency bands as a function of arousal, sleep stage, or other cognitive states. The newer approach extracts the average changes in amplitude (i.e., power) or phase coherence

Figure 3.7 Contour maps showing spatial-temporal patterns of ERP activity. The electrode locations where the ERP data were recorded are shown by the black dots; different colors correspond to different levels of voltage across the head, after interpolating the levels between the electrodes. The result is a topographic voltage map analogous to a geographic contour map. This example shows the response across time to a visual stimulus in the left visual field, a stimulus that activates the right occipital cortex.

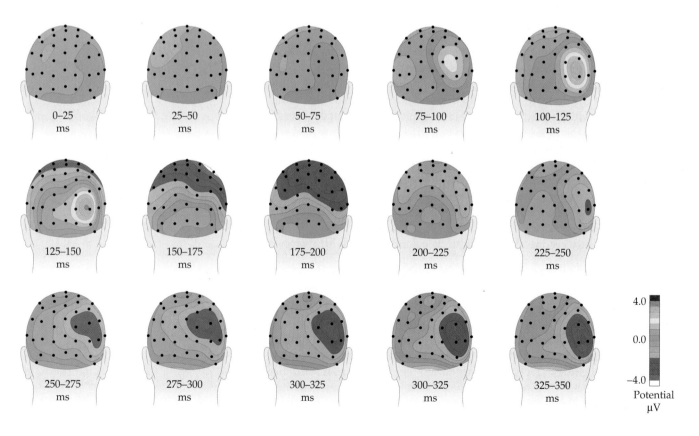

(i.e., synchronization) in specific frequency bands that occur following (or possible preceding) a specific type of cognitive event. The oscillatory activity observed, which has been investigated both in scalp EEG recordings in humans and intracranial recordings in animals, provides an additional window into the neural processes underlying cognitive functions. One such oscillatory phenomenon that has attracted much interest involves modulations of activity in the gamma frequency band (30–70 Hz) that have been proposed to reflect feature integration in perceptual processing (see Chapter 5). More generally, some investigators have proposed that time-varying oscillatory activity may modulate other stimulus-locked processes in a way that is relevant to cognitive functions.

Noninvasive neuromagnetic recording

Another way to measure electrophysiological brain activity noninvasively is to record the *magnetic* counterpart of the EEG, namely the **magnetoencephalograph**, or **MEG**. Much as one can extract ERPs from EEG recordings, this method can be used to extract time-locked responses, called **event-related magnetic field responses (ERFs)**, from MEG signals. The generation of MEG signals is closely related to that of ERP signals because both arise from current flow triggered by depolarization in the dendritic trees of cortical neurons oriented perpendicularly to the cortical surface. The key difference is that MEG measures the magnetic fields produced by these currents rather than the associated voltage fluctuations.

The principles of MEG are illustrated in Figure 3.8. When current flows in a wire or other conducting element, it produces a magnetic field in the volume surrounding the wire (**Figure 3.8A**). The configuration of the field follows the "right-hand rule" taught in introductory physics: if the right hand is made into a fist with the thumb pointing out and oriented in the direction of the current, then the field curves around the current in the orientation of the fingers. Thus, when synaptic activation causes currents to flow along the dendritic trees of a population of cortical neurons, a magnetic field is induced whose orientation is governed by the right-hand rule. This induced magnetic field "comes out of the head" on one side of the current source and "enters the head" on the other (**Figure 3.8B**). If the field strengths are measured at different points on the surface of the head with a magnetometer (**Figure 3.8C**), the distribution of these values over space and time can be obtained, including whether they are positive (coming out of the head) or negative (going into the head).

Although initially MEG recordings were made from only a few sites at a time, modern machines record fields from sites over the entire head. Based on the measured field distribution, it is possible to estimate the location and orientation of the underlying source, although the same general limitations imposed by the inverse problem for EEG recordings (see above) apply to MEG as well.

Although the MEG/ERF and EEG/ERP methodologies are related, they have practical as well as physical differences. One important difference concerns the brain areas that the two techniques can most successfully assess. MEG is mainly sensitive to neuronal activity in the cortical valleys or sulci; it is relatively insensitive to activity in gyri (see Figure 3.8B). The reason for this is found in the orientation of the electrical currents that generate the magnetic fields. As noted earlier, these currents arise from dendritic trees (see Figure 3.6). If the underlying electrical currents flowing along dendrites are in a sulcus, they produce fields that are either entering or exiting the head more or less orthogonally, as shown in Figure 3.8C, and are picked up well by the magnetometer. However, neuronal activity in a cortical gyrus produces currents that are mostly perpendicular to the surface of the head, inducing magnetic fields that are mostly parallel to the head surface and thus do not regis-

(A)

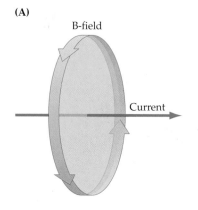

(B)

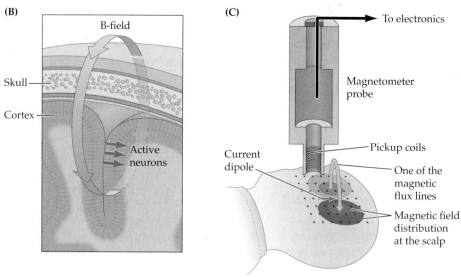

(C)

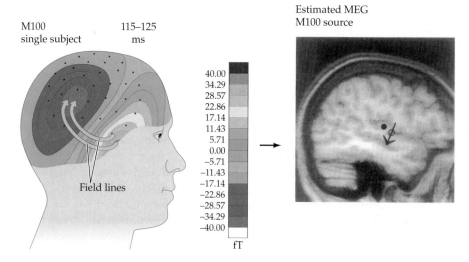

Figure 3.8 Magnetoencephalographic signals (MEG). (A) An electrical current in a wire creates a circular magnetic field. (B) Dendritic currents in cortex also produce circular magnetic fields, analogous to those produced by the current in a wire. Note that the fields most easily measured are generated in the sulci; this is because the sulcal fields enter and exit the scalp orthogonally, allowing them to be detected well by a magnetometer outside the head. Fields generated by neural activity in the gyri generally produce magnetic fields oriented parallel to the scalp, which are more difficult to detect. (C) Diagram of the field measurements by a magnetometer held adjacent to the surface of the head. (D) Distribution of the magnetic fields over the head of a normal subject (the M100 wave at 100 ms) induced by an auditory stimulus; MR image in the right panel shows the estimated location of the underlying source derived by dipole source analysis. fT = femtoTeslas. (D after Woldorff et al. 1999.)

ter well on the magnetometer. In contrast, the electrodes that pick up EEG and ERP signals detect voltage fluctuations produced by the return volume currents, which are not affected by this limitation. Accordingly, EEG picks up voltage fluctuations from sources in both cortical gyri and sulci, although this measure tends to be more sensitive to the former.

Although MEG's insensitivity to gyral sources renders it less complete than EEG methods, what MEG *does* pick up (i.e., mainly sulcal activity) is easier to localize. There are two main reasons for this. First, EEG currents suffer some distortion as they are conducted through the variable resistances of the skull and other tissues to reach the recording electrodes on the scalp. The magnetic fields in MEG recordings are much less affected by this problem. In addition, and probably more importantly, because MEG picks up mainly sulcal sources (and best from those nearer the magnetometer), the signal distributions it records tend to be less complex than those from ERP signals, thereby simplifying source estimation. Given their complementary sensitivities, recording MEG and EEG together can offer a more complete and effective way to estimate sources and study mechanisms than either method alone.

Noninvasive hemodynamically based functional brain imaging

Today, probably the most informative and popular techniques for assessing brain activity related to cognitive functions are those that rely on measuring changes in metabolism and blood flow to visualize active areas of the brain. The attractiveness of these **functional brain imaging** methods arises from several factors, but derives mainly from their ability to produce high-quality images that localize brain activity with high spatial resolution.

The brain utilizes a remarkably large fraction of the body's energy resources. About 20 percent of the glucose and oxygen used by the body is consumed by the brain, and at any given moment the most active nerve cells use more of these and other metabolites than relatively quiescent neurons. To meet the increased metabolic demands of particularly active neurons, the local flow of blood to the relevant brain area increases. Detecting and mapping these local changes in cerebral metabolism and blood flow is the hemodynamic basis of two functional imaging techniques that have been widely used: positron emission tomography (PET) and functional magnetic resonance imaging (fMRI). Because these techniques reveal patterns of activity in the intact brain with good spatial resolution, they have greatly advanced our ability to study cognitive functions and their neural underpinnings.

In **positron emission tomography**, or **PET**, unstable positron-emitting isotopes are synthesized in a cyclotron by bombarding elements such as oxygen, carbon, or fluorine with protons. Because of its short half-life, the isotope most commonly used for PET functional mapping is ^{15}O (half-life 2 min). Examples of other isotopes used as probes include ^{18}F (110 min) and ^{11}C (20 min). The labeled isotopes are incorporated into water, precursor molecules of specific neurotransmitters, or glucose or other metabolites. When the radiolabeled compounds are injected into the bloodstream, they distribute according to the physiological state of the brain, accumulating preferentially in more metabolically active areas. As the unstable isotope decays, the extra proton breaks down into a neutron and a positron. The emitted positron travels several millimeters, on average, until it collides with an electron. The collision of a positron with an electron destroys both particles, emitting two gamma rays going in opposite directions from the site of the collision. Gamma ray detectors placed around the subject's head are arranged to register a "hit" only when two detectors 180° apart react simultaneously (**Figures 3.9A,B**). By reconstructing the density of these collision lines using computer algorithms, the location of the active regions can be imaged.

Figure 3.9 Positron emission tomography (PET). (A) In PET, molecules labeled with radioactive probe atoms such as ^{15}O are injected into the bloodstream. These agents distribute preferentially to areas of increased neural activity because of increased metabolism and thus blood flow to those areas. Radioactive decay ultimately emits two "annihilation photons" (gamma rays) in opposite directions. (B) The annihilation photons are detected by sensors surrounding the head of the subject laying in the PET scanner. (C) A PET activation image overlain on a structural magnetic resonance image. (C courtesy of David Madden.)

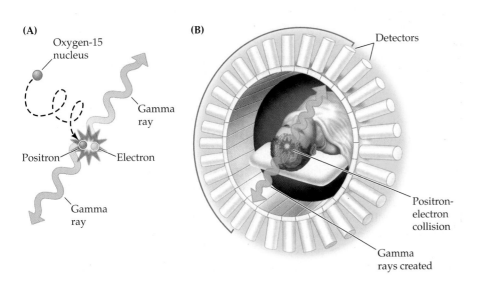

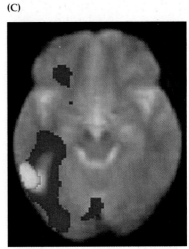

The mean distance that the positrons travel in brain tissue before the gamma-producing collision with an electron limits the theoretical resolution of PET scanning to several millimeters, although true resolution is typically somewhat less due to spatial smoothing, intrasubject averaging, and other steps in the analysis. A further limitation PET is the time required to accumulate an adequate signal (many seconds to a few minutes), which precludes its use in many cognitive paradigms (see below). Nonetheless, PET images can be superimposed onto magnetic resonance images from the same subject(s) to provide detailed spatial information about specific brain areas involved in a cognitive and other functions (**Figure 3.9C**). The limitations of PET (the short half-life of the reagents, the need for a nearby cyclotron to create the reagents, the use of radioactivity, and the very poor temporal resolution) have led to its replacement in most cognitive studies today by functional magnetic resonance imaging.

Functional magnetic resonance imaging (**fMRI**; **Figure 3.10A**) is based on the fact that oxyhemoglobin (hemoglobin carrying a bound oxygen molecule) has a different magnetic resonance signal than deoxyhemoglobin (the oxygen-depleted form of hemoglobin). As noted above, active brain areas use more oxygen than relatively inactive areas, and thus require more local blood flow. Within a second or two of an area being activated (by a specific cognitive task for example), the related microvasculature responds to the resulting local oxygen depletion by increasing the flow of arterial blood to the active area (**Figure 3.10B**). The relative concentration of deoxyhemoglobin decreases over the next few seconds, which leads to localized changes in the magnetic resonance signal from that part of the brain (**Figure 3.10C**). These MR changes, known as the **blood oxygenation level-dependent** (**BOLD**) signal, are the basis for most current forms of fMRI.

Functional MRI offers somewhat better spatial localization than PET (several millimeters compared to approximately a centimeter in PET), as well as much better temporal resolution (a few seconds compared to many seconds or minutes in PET). In addition, fMRI uses signals intrinsic to the brain rather than signals originating from exogenous, radioactive probes. But probably the greatest advantage of fMRI over PET for the study of cognitive processes is its higher temporal resolution.

Most PET imaging has a temporal resolution of the order of a minute or so (i.e., the signal to obtain a usable image must be compiled over this time frame), and therefore experiments using PET require the use of a **block design** (**Figure 3.11A**). In this design, the brain activity measure that is recorded reflects neural activity integrated over an extended period of time (a block) while the subject performs a task or is presented with a particular stimulus condition. The resulting activation pattern can then be compared to the brain activity recorded when the subject is not doing the task or is under a different stimulus or task condition. The need to integrate activity across time in this way limits the specificity with which brain activation can be associated with particular cognitive processes.

The initial fMRI studies in the 1990s followed the same block design as PET studies, although the blocks were only 20 seconds or so, and there was no need for a long waiting period between blocks (**Figure 3.11B**). However, investigators soon realized that fMRI had enough temporal resolution to allow a different sort of design. Today samples of fMRI activity throughout the whole brain can be acquired in a second or two, allowing the average fMRI hemodynamic response to a single stimulus or cognitive event to be captured. The fMRI response to a single event begins at around 1 to 2 seconds, peaks around 5 to 6 seconds, and returns to baseline at around 12 to 20 seconds (**Figure 3.11C**). Although this sequence is very slow relative to the millisecond resolution of electrophysiological methods such as EEG and MEG, it is fast enough

(A)

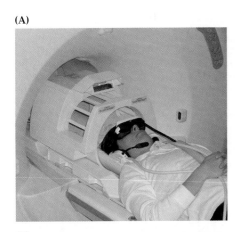

Figure 3.10 Functional magnetic resonance imaging (fMRI).   (A) A subject is moved into an fMRI scanner. The machine itself is not different from the scanner shown and described in Box 3A. The subject is wearing goggles in order to view visual stimuli for the experiment to be undertaken. (B) The blood oxygenation level-dependent (BOLD) signal. The vascular system supplies blood containing oxyhemoglobin to active region(s) of the brain. The influx of oxygenated blood to regions that becomes active reduces the local concentration of deoxyhemoglobin, which increases the BOLD signal; the difference in the signal provides a measure of local neuronal activity. (C) There are several ways to display functional MRI data on corresponding structural MRI scans, including overlaying onto an image slice; overlaying onto a 3-D image of the cortical surface extracted computationally from the MR structural image data; or overlaying onto the 3-D image of an extracted cortical surface that has been "inflated" by a computer algorithm. (B after Huettel et al. 2004.)

(C)

fMRI on MR slice

(B)

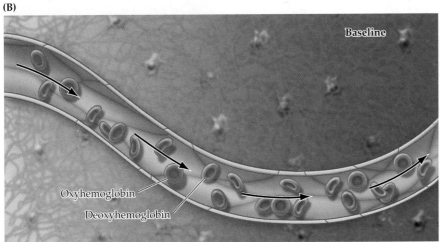

Baseline

Oxyhemoglobin
Deoxyhemoglobin

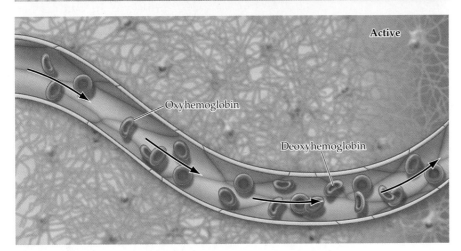

Active

Oxyhemoglobin

Deoxyhemoglobin

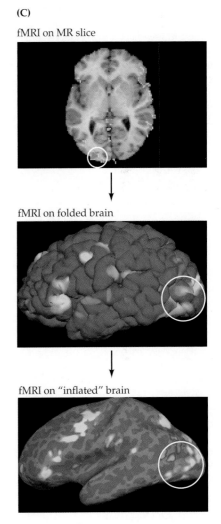

fMRI on folded brain

fMRI on "inflated" brain

to allow fMRI to be applied in an event-related manner, at least when using slower stimulus presentation rates. As shown in **Figure 3.11D**, this capability allows selective averaging of the responses to different event types *within* a run, much as is done with electrophysiological methods. Moreover, using temporal randomization of the stimulus or task events and modern signal processing algorithms that disentangle the overlapping responses from successive stimuli, it is now possible to present stimuli at even faster rates and still extract an event-related response (**Figure 3.12**).

Figure 3.11 Experimental designs in PET and fMRI studies. (A) In PET studies, the subject performs a cognitive task continuously over approximately 1 minute, with different tasks being performed in each block (in this example either task A or B, or, in the resting block, neither). Using ^{15}O-labeled water as a tracer, a 10-minute break between blocks is necessary to allow the radioactively labeled tracers to decay sufficiently before the next block. Accumulated activity for each block is then measured, and functional activity inferred by comparing the different blocks. (B) Block design for fMRI is similar, but with multiple samples of brain activity in each block, much shorter blocks, and without the need for a 10-minute break between blocks. (C) Because of the much faster activity sampling possible with fMRI (typically every 1.5 to 2 seconds), the fMRI responses to individual events can be captured in an event-related way. Shown is a representative fMRI response to a single event type (event type A). (D) This paradigm allows the time-locked responses to different event types within the same run to be selectively extracted (i.e., event types A and B).

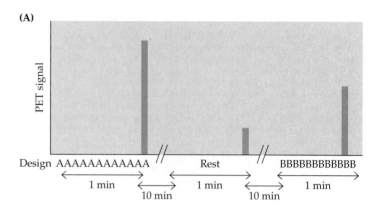

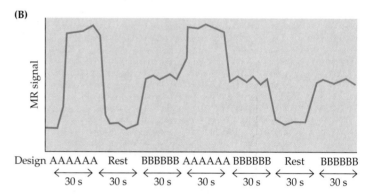

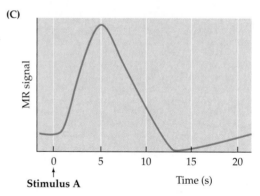

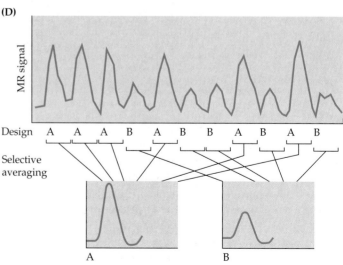

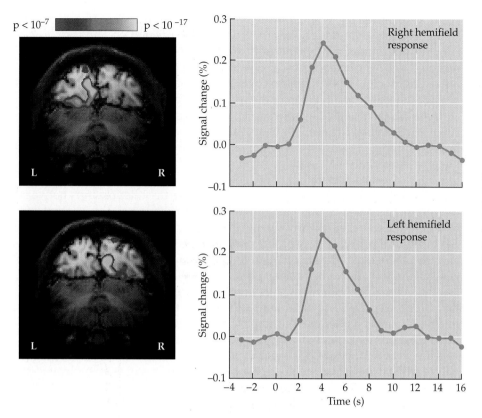

Figure 3.12 Event-related fMRI responses. Responses are from a visual stimulation paradigm obtained at fast stimulus rates (two events per second). Unilateral visual stimuli were presented in random order to the left and right visual fields at very fast stimulation rates (two events per second) while subjects fixated on a central cross. At this rate, there is severe overlap of the fMRI responses to successive stimuli in the sequence. This overlap was eliminated in this example by a subtraction technique, yielding clean average hemodynamic fMRI responses (right panels) in the visual sensory areas in contralateral occipital cortex (left panels). (From Burock et al. 1998.)

The development of event-related methods for fMRI was a highly significant advance, as it enabled many cognitive paradigms that could not be used in the early days of fMRI. The development of event-related paradigms using fMRI has also allowed researchers to compare result images with the activation patterns of high temporal resolution ERP and ERF responses to the same events. In addition, modern fMRI techniques allow the use of "hybrid" designs that have both block- and event-related experimental manipulations, the effects of which can be disentangled by appropriate analyses. Finally, the more rapid fMRI recording methods allow the tracking of activity variations in different brain areas across time; correlations of this data for co-activated brain areas provide additional information about the *functional connectivity* between areas.

As a result of its many advantages, fMRI has emerged as the dominant technology for imaging brain activity in studies of both normal and abnormal cognitive function.

Optical brain imaging

Another set of approaches to measuring neural activity in both animals and humans is based on **optical brain imaging** techniques. These approaches are based on the fact that active brain tissue transmits and/or reflects light differently than does inactive brain tissue, and these differences can be picked up and imaged by optical recording devices.

One prominent but invasive optical recording approach is, like fMRI, based on hemodynamic changes in response to neural activity. When populations of neurons become active, thereby inducing local hemodynamic changes, the amount of light reflected from the cortical surface changes as well. This optical signal, as with the BOLD signal in fMRI, is thought to arise from changes in the relative concentrations of oxyhemoglobin and deoxyhemoglobin that occur as neuronal activity varies in a given region in response to a stimulus. To detect these changes requires that the skull be opened up and the cortical surface illuminated with a red light in the 580–700 nanometer range. The reflected light is picked up by a sensitive video camera, and the changes in responses to stimulation averaged over a series of trials. The resultant images provide a highly detailed map of the cortical patterns of activity.

These hemodynamically based optical imaging approaches have been most successfully applied to study sensory map representations in the sensory cortices in animals, particularly in visual sensory cortex. For example, this type of imaging has produced highly detailed maps of the patterns of relative sensitivity across primary visual cortex to specific line orientations (see Chapter 5). These methods have also been useful in showing the relationships between the mapping configurations for different features, such as the relationship between orientation preference maps and ocular-dominance maps. Because the technique is invasive, it has mostly been used in experimental animals, and the results have thus far tended to be more informative in the context of neurobiology than cognitive neuroscience. Nonetheless, it has been used in a few circumstances in human patients undergoing neurosurgery (e.g., to map language areas). Because of its simplicity and relatively low cost, such optical imaging holds considerable promise for future studies of cognitive functions in both experimental animals and surgical patients.

Another recently developed technique known as **event-related optical signals** (**EROS**) uses optical methods based on a very different activity-dependent mechanism and can be applied noninvasively. When brain tissue is illuminated, even through the skull, the amount of light that is transmitted versus scattered varies as a function of whether or not the neuronal tissue is electrically active. This differential light diffusion is thought to be the result of changes that occur in and around the neuronal membranes during electrical activity (see Appendix). By shining light into the brain from a number of different sources around the head and measuring the intensity of the reflected light with multiple external sensors, these activity-dependent changes can be detected and imaged using three-dimensional, computer-assisted reconstruction algorithms.

Like ERPs, EROS has high temporal resolution but relatively low spatial resolution. However, the determination of the source of the activity monitored is not subject to the inverse problem inherent in EEG and MEG source analyses. Although the low signal-to-noise characteristics have limited the use of this method, EROS holds promise as a relatively inexpensive method for noninvasively imaging cortical activity.

Assembling Evidence and Delineating Mechanisms

A major goal in the quest to understand the neural bases of cognition is to establish links between localized brain structures and neural activity on the one hand, and cognitive functions or processes on the other. To establish these links and delineate underlying mechanisms, cognitive neuroscientists often must assemble evidence from multiple studies and from multiple methodologies. There are a number of ways to accomplish this.

Associations and dissociations

A fundamental approach to linking neuroscience and cognition has been apparent in the methods already discussed: to experimentally *associate* specific cognitive functions with the neural structures and/or local neural activity that underlie them. A complementary approach is to determine cognitive functions and neural processes that do *not* seem to be related—that is, that are *dissociated*. For example, if it is shown that damage to a particular brain area disrupts the performance of Task A but not Task B, then this establishes not only an **association** between the damaged area and Task A , but also a **dissociation** between the lesion and Task B (**Figure 3.13A**). An even firmer link between a specific cognitive function and a particular neural structure or process can be made by establishing a **double dissociation**. For example, say Task A is designed to engage mainly System A (say, the neural system for identifying a visually presented face), whereas Task B is designed to engage mainly System B (the neural system for identifying the emotional expression of a visually presented face). If Systems A and B are relatively distinct, one would expect to be able to find neurological patients with a particular brain lesion who are impaired in performing Task A (recognizing faces), but essentially normal when performing Task B (recognizing emotions), *and* to find patients with a lesion in a different brain region who showed the opposite pattern (normal performance on Task A but impaired performance on Task B). Such an inverting pattern of effects constitutes a classical double dissociation (**Figure 3.13B**).

The observation of double dissociations provides more definitive evidence for relatively separate mechanisms or functions than single dissociations do. This is because a single dissociation could arise from a general factor (such as the relative difficulty of the tasks) rather than from the physical engagement of separable functions. However, when another type of lesion produces the opposite characteristics, the case for the engagement of functionally distinct neural systems becomes much stronger. It often turns out, however, that the neural systems being examined are only partially separable; that is, performance on Task A for a certain patient group is seriously impaired, but performance on Task B is also disturbed to some degree (or vice versa). This situation would suggest that the functional systems in question interact to some degree—which of course is useful information as well.

Although these examples focus on establishing dissociations using brain lesions, double dissociations are also important in methods that measure brain activity during cognitive tasks (**Figure 3.13C**). For example, a neuro-

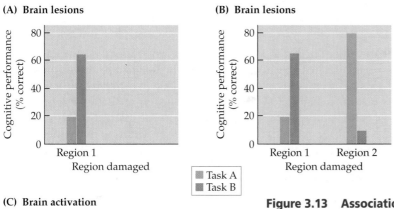

(A) Brain lesions

(B) Brain lesions

(C) Brain activation

Figure 3.13 Associations, dissociations, and double dissociations. (A) The relative performance on two tasks (A and B) for neurological patients with a common brain lesion in Region 1. Impairment in performing Task A but not Task B indicates an association between Region 1 and the neural basis for performing Task A, and a dissociation between this region and performing Task B. (B) Another group of patients, these with a lesion in a different brain region, shows the opposite pattern of impairment in the two tasks. The results from (A) and (B) taken together are a double dissociation providing strong evidence for the specific involvement of the two regions in the two different tasks. (C) Analogous double dissociation determined from brain activation data (e.g., from fMRI). In this case, subjects engaged in Task A show activation of Region 1 but not Region 2; during Task B this pattern is reversed.

■ **TABLE 3.1** **Summary of the Major Imaging Techniques Used in Cognitive Neuroscience**

Technique	Main Advantages	Main Disadvantages
Naturally occurring lesions	Can strongly implicate a region as being essential for a task Occur naturally	Still generally need double dissociation to strongly confirm selectivity of area Not specific to functional areas; variable in distribution and extent Does not identify a network No temporal resolution Relatively few available subjects; subjects often from heterogeneous groups Effects of recovery unknown or complex
Directed lesions	Can strongly implicate a region as being essential for a task Can be much more selective than naturally occurring lesions Can be timed (e.g., before or after training)	Can generally be done only in animals; ethical concerns Very limited temporal resolution
Intracranial stimulation	Can provide rather specific neural perturbation	Mostly limited to animals and rare clinical circumstances In humans, clinical concerns, limited locations that can be stimulated
Transcranial magnetic stimulation (TMS)	Advantages of lesions, but transient and noninvasive (or at least nonsurgical) With single-shot, can get some temporal resolution	Can mostly only do superficial cortex Not very focused; stimulates other areas nearby and above the target area Even for some superficial brain regions, is too uncomfortable Some safety issues, particularly for repetitive TMS (rTMS)
Single-unit recordings	High spatial and temporal resolution Very specific (single neurons)	Only picks up some neurons (typically larger ones) Very invasive; almost completely limited to animals Typically from only one brain area, thus does not identify a network or network interactions
Electroencephalogram (EEG)	Good temporal resolution Good for state effects (e.g., arousal, sleep stages) Noninvasive Inexpensive, fast, and easy recording procedures	Coarse or problematic spatial resolution Not very specific for information processing or cognitive function

imaging experiment might indicate that a specific brain area (say, Region 1) is *activated* during Task A but not during Task B. As with brain lesion studies, however, this neuroimaging pattern could be due to differing difficulty of the two tasks or to the degree to which a neural system is being engaged by the task. Thus, establishing a double dissociation in the context of neuroimaging is also important for more firmly linking specific brain activity measures to specific cognitive functions.

Multimethodological approaches

All of the individual methods described here provide a way of linking cognitive processes to underlying brain processes. Each has advantages and disadvantages. The spatial and temporal limitations of these approaches are depicted in **Figure 3.14**, and the most important advantages and disadvantages of each method are enumerated in **Table 3.1**.

Figure 3.14   Spatial and temporal resolution of the methods discussed in ▶
this chapter.   The methods for studying the neural bases of cognitive functions have widely varying spatial and temporal scales and capabilities. (After Churchland and Sejnowski 1998.)

■ **TABLE 3.1** *(continued)*

Technique	Main Advantages	Main Disadvantages
Event-related potentials (ERPs)	Very high temporal resolution Noninvasive Inexpensive, fast, and easy recording procedures	Coarse or problematic spatial resolution Difficult to disentangle multicomponent activity Activity may be associated with but not essential for the task
Magnetoencephalo-graph (MEG)	Very high temporal resolution Better localization than ERPs Noninvasive	Picks up mainly only sulcal activity Limited spatial localization Much more expensive than ERPs Recordings very susceptible to interfering noise Activity may be associated with but not essential for the task
Positron emission tomography (PET)	Good spatial resolution (three-dimensional) Identifies network of regions associated with task	No temporal resolution Cannot do event-related designs (block design only) Need cyclotron Need to inject radioactive molecules Indirect measurement of neuronal activity Activated areas may be associated with but not essential for the task
Functional magnetic resonance imaging (fMRI)	Very good spatial resolution Temporal resolution much better than PET Can do event-related designs Identifies network of regions associated with task Noninvasive	Spatial resolution still has limits (e.g., draining veins) Temporal resolution still very low (seconds) Indirect measurement of neuronal activity Activated areas may be associated with but not essential for the task
Optical imaging (hemodynamic)	High spatial resolution Temporal resolution a bit better than fMRI Can do event-related designs Can image all across a cortical area simultaneously	Almost exclusively limited to animals Temporal resolution still fairly low (hundreds of ms) Indirect measurement of neuronal activity Activated areas may be associated with but not essential for the task
Optical imaging (EROS)	Moderate spatial resolution Good temporal resolution Can do event-related designs Noninvasive	Low signal-to-noise ratio; may require multiple sessions or be able to image only limited brain regions Mainly sensitive to the more superficial cortical regions Activated areas may be associated with but not essential for the task

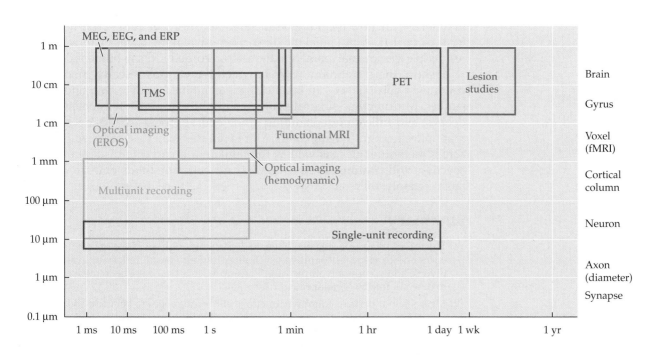

The different limitations of each of these methods, as well as their complementary scales, have led to a growing effort to combine approaches in the same or closely allied studies. For example, hemodynamic measures of brain activity like fMRI are very good at showing which areas of the brain are activated in a given cognitive task or type of event, but provide relatively limited temporal resolution (on the order of seconds). Since many cognitive operations occur on the order of tens or hundreds of milliseconds, fMRI cannot by itself indicate the timing or sequence of the underlying brain processes. ERPs and MEG, on the other hand, provide millisecond resolution of evoked brain activity, but can only coarsely localize that activity. Combining information derived from each of these methodologies with the goal of understanding both the temporal and spatial characteristics of the underlying brain activity makes good sense. Combining information gleaned from different methodologies can be done across studies to synthesize findings pertinent to particular functions, and can be done either retrospectively or prospectively. However, one can also directly combine information across methodologies within the same or linked studies.

An example of combining information derived from different methodologies is using data from PET or fMRI to help in the source analysis of ERP or MEG activity. Thus functional activation of specific brain areas during a task carried out in a functional imaging study indicates the areas that are likely sources of corresponding ERP or MEG activity in the same task. This information can be immediately valuable in associating specific ERP effects with fMRI or PET activations in parallel studies, but it can also be incorporated directly into source localization analyses and modeling as *a priori* "constraints," increasing the likelihood of obtaining accurate estimates of the ERP or MEG sources. In addition, since ERP/MEG activity derives mainly from neural current sources located within the cortex and oriented perpendicularly to the cortical surface, extracting the cortical surface from high-resolution structural MRI images can also provide useful anatomical constraints for source localization approaches.

Other useful ways to combine these approaches include linking functional imaging studies in normal individuals with similar studies in patients with brain lesions. Another example is to record both fMRI activity and single-unit activity in experimental animals (usually monkeys) engaged in the same cognitive task. Yet another is to pursue electrophysiological studies in monkeys and humans using parallel cognitive paradigms. Some electrophysiological studies in monkeys are now including intracranial recording of both single-units and local cortical field potentials, with the aim of making it easier to relate the results in experimental animals to the scalp-recorded ERPs in humans.

In short, there are many ways in which the various research methods of cognitive neuroscience can be effectively combined both within and across studies. Multimethodological syntheses hold the promise for achieving the deepest and fullest understanding of the neural processes and mechanisms that underlie cognitive functions. Moreover, the need to synthesize findings across methodologies, as well as to maintain a broad interdisciplinary perspective, will continue even as newer and better methods emerge, as they most certainly will.

Summary

1. The technical approaches that have made it increasingly possible to link the inferences and concepts of cognitive psychology to their neural underpinnings are diverse and continually improving. The approaches that have been most effective to date fall into two major categories.

2. Methods that perturb cognitive functions allow inferences to be made about the role of specific brain areas or systems in the cognitive function at issue. Approaches that entail perturbation include: the natural disturbances of brain function that

arise from trauma, stroke, or disease and affect one or more cognitive function; perturbations induced pharmacologically; and perturbations induced by electrical stimulation of relevant brain regions.

3. Methods that monitor and measure neural activity during cognitive tasks provide information about the specific neural activity patterns that are engaged during the processing of a stimulus or the performance of a cognitive task. The major activity measuring techniques associated with cognitive processes include: invasive electrical recording in experimental animals carrying out cognitive tasks; noninvasive electrical or magnetic recording in humans; and both noninvasive and invasive imaging methods that depend on altered metabolism and/or blood flow in active brain regions.

4. In single-unit electrophysiological recording, metal electrodes are inserted into the brain structures of experimental animals to measure the action potentials produced by individual neurons.

5. Electroencephalography (EEG) is a noninvasive method of recording the brain's electrical signals using electrodes fastened to the scalp. EEG and the event-related potentials (ERPs) that can be extracted from EEG data have been widely used in the study of human brain activity for many years.

6. EEG and ERPs have counterparts in the magnetoencephalograph (MEG) and event-related field responses (ERFs), which measure magnetic field fluctuations due to neuronal currents rather than the associated voltage fluctuations. These methods all have very high temporal resolution but coarse spatial.

7. Recently developed techniques of three-dimensional functional brain imaging have revolutionized cognitive neuroscience with their ability to visualize brain activity during cognitive task performance. Positron emission tomography (PET) requires the use of radioactive isotopes and has essentially no temporal resolution; for that and other reasons it has been largely supplanted in cognitive research by functional magnetic resonance imaging (fMRI), which has much higher temporal resolution (although still much lower than electrophysiological methods) and can be performed in an event-related way.

8. Optical brain imaging techniques are based on differences in light absorption and transmission in active brain areas that can be detected and imaged using optical recording devices.

9. With both brain perturbation studies and brain activity studies, the fundamental approach is to try to establish which cognitive functions are *associated* with certain neural structures or neural activity, and which are *dissociated*. This linkage of neural and cognitive processes is made even stronger by establishing double dissociations—that is, establishing that Task A is associated with neural region 1 but not with region 2 and that Task B is associated with region 2 but not with region 1.

10. Increasingly, the different methodologies are being combined in multimethodological approaches, providing insight into the neural basis of cognitive processes that until a few decades ago could only be inferred from indirect evidence.

Additional Reading

Reviews

CHURCHLAND, P. S. AND T. J. SEJNOWSKI (1988) Perspectives on cognitive neuroscience. *Science* 242: 741–745.

FOX, P. T. AND M. G. WOLDORFF (1994) Integrating human brain maps. *Curr. Opin. Neurobiol.* 4: 151–156.

HAMALAINEN, M., R. HARI, R. ILMONEIMI, J. KNUUTILA AND O. LOUNASMAA (1993) Magnetoencephalography: Theory, instrumentation, and applications to the noninvasive study of human brain function. *Rev. Modern Phys.* 65: 413–423.

HENSON, R. (2005) What can functional neuroimaging tell the experimental psychologist? *Q. J. Exp. Psychol.* 58A: 193–233.

RAICHLE, M. E. (1994) Images of the mind: Studies with modern imaging techniques. *Annu. Rev. Psychol.* 45: 333–356.

SUPER, H. AND P. R. ROELFSEMA (2005) Chronic multiunit recordings in behaving animals: Advantages and limitations. *Prog. Brain Res.* 147: 263–282.

Important Original Papers

BANDETTINI, P. A., E. C. WONG, R. S. HINKS, R. S. TIKOFSKY AND J. S. HYDE (1992) Time course EPI of human brain function during task activation. *Magn. Reson. Med.* 25: 390–397.

BERGER, H. (1929) Uber das Electroenkephalogram des Menschen. *Arch. Psychiatr. Nervenkr.* 87: 527–570.

BUROCK, M. A., R. L. BUCKNER, M. G. WOLDORFF, B. R. ROSEN AND A. M. DALE (1998) Randomized event-related experimental designs allow for extremely rapid presentation rates using functional MRI. *Neuroreport* 9: 3735–3739.

CATON, R. (1875) The electrical currents of the brain. *Brit. Med. J.* 2: 278.

Da Silva, F. H. and W. S. Van Leeuwen (1977) The cortical source of the alpha rhythm. *Neurosci. Lett.* 6: 237–241.

Dempsey, E. W. and R. S. Morrison (1943) The electrical activity of a thalamocortical relay system. *Am. J. Physiol.* 138: 283–296.

Fox, P. T. and M. E. Raichle (1986) Focal physiological uncoupling of cerebral blood flow and oxidative metabolism during somatosensory stimulation in human subjects. *Proc. Natl. Acad. Sci. USA* 83: 1140–1144.

Gratton, G. and 8 others (1997) Fast and localized event-related optical signals (EROS) in the human occipital cortex: Comparisons with the visual evoked potential and fMRI. *Neuroimage* 6: 168–180.

Grinwald, A., E. Lieke, R. D. Frostig, C. D. Gilbert and T. N. Wiesel (1991) Functional architecture of cortex revealed by optical imaging of intrinsic signals. *Nature* 324: 361–364.

Hubel, D. H. and T. N. Wiesel (1959) Receptive fields of single neurons in the cat's striate cortex. *J. Neurophysiol.* 148: 574–591.

Kwong, K. K. and 9 others (1992) Dynamic magnetic resonance imaging of human brain activity during primary sensory stimulation. *Proc. Natl. Acad. Sci. USA* 89: 5675–5679.

Logothetis, N. K., J. Pauls, M. Augath, T. Trinath and A. Oeltermann (2001) Neurophysiological investigation of the basis of the fMRI signal. *Nature* 412: 128–130.

Mountcastle, V. B., J. C. Lynch, A. Georgopoulos, H. Sakata and C. Acuna (1975) Posterior parietal association cortex of the monkey: Command functions for operations within extrapersonal space. *J. Neurophysiol.* 38: 871–908.

Ogawa, S. and 6 others (1992) Intrinsic signal changes accompanying sensory stimulation: Functional brain mapping with magnetic resonance imaging. *Proc. Natl. Acad. Sci. USA* 89: 5951–5955.

Petersen, S. E., P. T. Fox, A. Z. Snyder and M. E. Raichle (1990) Activation of extrastriate and frontal cortical areas by visual words and word-like stimuli. *Science* 249: 1041–1044.

Sereno, M. I. and 7 others (1995) Borders of multiple visual areas in humans revealed by functional magnetic resonance imaging. *Science* 268: 889–893.

Wurtz, R. H. and M. E. Goldberg (1971) Superior colliculus cell responses related to eye movements in awake monkeys. *Science* 171: 82–84.

Books

Huettel, S. A., A. W. Song and G. McCarthy (2004) *Functional Magnetic Resonance Imaging.* Sunderland, MA: Sinauer.

Luck, S. J. (2005) *An Introduction to the Event-Related Potential Technique.* Cambridge, MA: MIT Press.

Nuñez, P. L. R. and R. Srinivasan (2005) *Electric Fields of the Brain: The Neurophysics of EEG,* 2nd Ed. New York: Oxford University Press.

Raichle, M. E. and M. I. Posner (1994) *Images of Mind.* New York: Scientific American Library.

UNIT II

Principles of Sensory Processing and Perception

Understanding perception is, from any perspective, an intimidating challenge. The goal of this unit is to review the major sensory modalities, indicating what is known about how sensory systems generate the percepts we experience. For humans, these sensory modalities are *vision* (sight), *audition* (hearing), *somatic sensation* (touch, pressure, and pain), *olfaction* (smell), and *gustation* (taste). A good deal more is known about vision, audition, and somatic sensation than about olfaction and gustation—the *chemical senses*—and the first three have also figured more importantly in studies of human cognition. Thus the emphasis here is biased toward these modalities. Nonetheless, it is only by considering all of the sensory modalities that we come to appreciate how sensory processing and perception operate, the biological role that percepts play, and the deeper questions that perception raises for a variety of disciplines.

Considering sensory processing and perception as a series of separate modalities—a standard approach—is somewhat arbitrary, since in the normal course of events the sensory modalities operate together to guide behavior. By the same token, perception can only be divorced from the cognitive functions by convention; in fact, what we perceive is very much influenced by attention, memory, the emotional and motivational state of the perceiver, individual goals, and many other factors that are discussed in future units.

Finally, perception is not simply the end result of sensory processing. Other mental content that we are aware of—thoughts and feelings, most obviously—are also perceived, at least in the ordinary sense of this word. These aspects of perception are also taken up in other units and in Chapter 28, in which self-awareness and its bases are discussed. Indeed, perception and its neural foundations are pertinent to this entire book. ■

Overview of Sensory Processing

Introduction

The general role of sensory systems in the context of the overall organization of the human nervous system was introduced in Chapter 1. The aim of this chapter is to explain in more specific terms how the five major sensory systems—*vision* (sight), *audition* (sound), *somatic sensation* (touch, pressure, and pain), *olfaction* (smell), and *gustation* (taste)—give rise to successful behavior based on percepts generated by different forms of energy in the environment. This process begins when specialized *sensory receptor cells* initiate electrical activity in the peripheral neural circuitry of the relevant sensory system. This activity is then carried forward by *action potentials* to increasingly complex processing stations in the central nervous system, eventually reaching the *association cortices*, where many cognitive neuroscientists believe the neural representations of the percepts we experience are generated. Understanding how sensory processing works at these various levels has been and continues to be a major goal of contemporary neuroscience. Although each system is different in a variety of important ways, some general points apply to all five sensory modalities; the account here is intended to provide a broad sense of how sensory systems work in terms of these shared principles. Subsequent chapters take up the generation of the perceptual qualities that characterize specific sensory systems, illustrating both the advances and the many unsolved problems in this fascinating aspect of cognitive neuroscience.

Sensory Stimuli

Each of the sensory modalities in humans and other animals evolved to provide information derived from a particular form of energy in the ecological niche that the species in question occupies. Thus the human visual system processes neural activity generated by a specific spectrum of electromagnetic radiation in the terrestrial environment that humans inhabit, the auditory system processes activity generated by local pressure changes in the human auditory environment, the somatosensory system processes activity generated by the mechanical forces acting on the body, and so on. In each case, the end result of these **sensory stimuli** is useful percepts that guide and modify behavior in response to local environmental conditions. It should be noted from the outset, however, that sensory processing can lead to useful behavior even without generating percepts; indeed, the majority of behavioral responses occur without sensory processing ever reaching the level of subjective awareness.

Another general fact about sensory stimuli is that sensory systems respond to only a small subset of the full physical range of a given stimulus category. In vision, for example, the radiation energy (photons) to which the human eye is sensitive comprises only a minuscule fraction of the full electromagnetic spectrum. The human eye processes photons with wavelengths of from about 400 to about 700 nanometers; the full spectrum comprises wavelengths many orders of magnitude above and below this range. *Light* is therefore defined for us by the evolution of a human visual system that processes this particular spectral range, presumably driven by the fact the spectrum of sunlight at the surface of the Earth has a strong peak at about 550 nanometers. The same argument can be made for the sounds we hear, the forces we feel, and the molecules we smell and taste. In each domain, the sensations we experience are only a small fraction of what could be perceived, and we are aware of only a small amount of the energy that exists all around us (and which can be measured by other physical and chemical means).

Despite these limitations, human sensory systems respond to an extraordinary range of **stimulus intensities**. Visual percepts can be elicited by amounts of light ranging from values of a few tens of photons per mm^2 at the retinal surface to values a billion or more times greater. Humans process auditory percepts (sounds) ranging from minuscule pressure changes to those associated with an explosive force, and we can feel somatic percepts from the lightest touch to pain stimuli that do major physical damage to the body. The minimum stimulus intensity that elicits an appreciable percept in a given sensory system defines the **threshold stimulus value** for that system.

The great range of responsiveness of sensory systems, albeit limited in terms of the overall range of existing energies, allows us and other animals to function well in widely varying circumstances; we can see many objects in starlight as well as in the intense light of the midday sun, we can hear whispers as well as loud music, and we can respond appropriately to a feather's touch or to a hard tackle.

Initiation of Sensory Processing

Pre-neural stimulus enhancement

The sequence of events that leads to perception by any sensory system typically entails an elaborate **pre-neural apparatus** that collects, filters, and amplifies the relevant energy in the environment so that the energy can interact more effectively with the receptor cells. This general principle defines the onset of sensory processing in any modality. In the case of vision, this initial process entails image formation carried out by the optical elements of the eye: the cornea, lens, and ocular media that focus and filter light before it reaches the neural retina (**Figure 4.1A**). Similarly, auditory stimuli are filtered and amplified by the structure of the external ear, the ear canal, and the bones of the middle ear (**Figure 4.1B**). In the somatosensory system, mechanical forces acting on the body surface are modified by non-neural structures such as hairs or the dermal ridges on the fingertips (**Figure 4.1C**). The structure of the nose maximizes the interaction of volatile molecules in the air with receptors in the

(A) Human eye

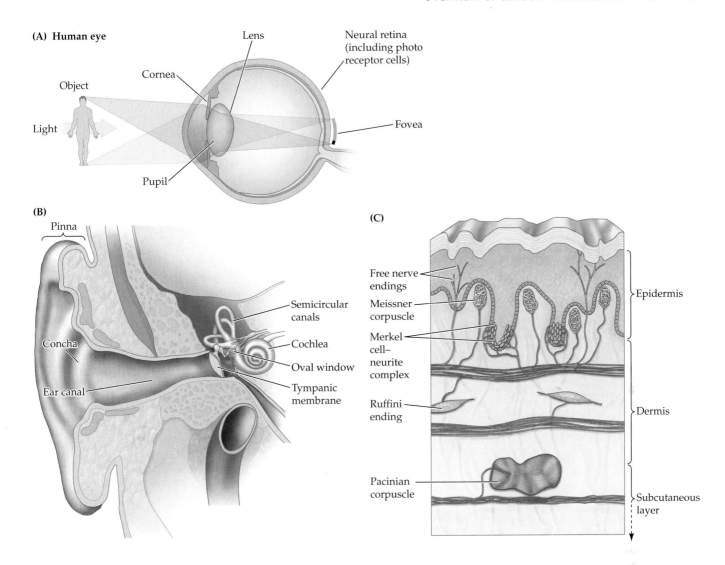

Lens

Cornea

Object

Light

Pupil

Neural retina
(including photo
receptor cells)

Fovea

(B)

Pinna

Concha

Ear canal

Semicircular
canals

Cochlea

Oval window

Tympanic
membrane

(C)

Free nerve
endings

Meissner
corpuscle

Merkel
cell–
neurite
complex

Ruffini
ending

Pacinian
corpuscle

Epidermis

Dermis

Subcutaneous
layer

olfactory mucosa when we sniff, and the structure of the taste buds on our tongue facilitates the exposure of soluble molecules to taste receptors.

Sensory transduction

The next step in sensory processing—and the first step that entails the nervous system—is the **transduction** of energy into neural signals by specialized **receptor cells**. In all the senses, the common denominator of this process is a *change in the membrane permeability* of the receptor cell produced by the effect of stimulus energy, which then *changes the membrane potential* of that receptor and ultimately *triggers action potentials* in afferent neurons that carry information toward the central nervous system. (Recall from Chapter 1 that changes in membrane potential of neurons are the basis for all neural signaling.) In the case of vision, transduction occurs when photons of the appropriate wavelength are absorbed by the pigment molecules in photoreceptor cells (**Figure 4.2A**). In audition, the energy produced by the movement of air molecules is transmitted to the fluid of the inner ear and moves receptors called hair cells (**Figure 4.2B**). Similarly, sensory nerve cell endings in the skin and subcuta-

Figure 4.1   Some pre-neural apparatus for processing sensation.   These structures filter and enhance stimulus energy before it reaches sensory receptor neurons. (A) The optical structures of the eye—the cornea, lens, and pupil—filter and focus the light energy that eventually reaches photoreceptor cells (rods and cones) in the retina. (B) The structures of the external ear (pinna and concha) collect and focus sound energy. The resonance properties of the ear canal and tympanic membrane further filter and amplify the sound energy that is particularly important to humans, and the bones of the middle ear (incus, malleus, and stapes) enhance the stimulus energy transmitted to the smaller surface area of the oval window in much the same way that pressure on the plunger of a syringe amplifies pressure at the smaller opening at the needle's end. (C) Structures on the surface of the skin, such as dermal ridges and hairs, act as levers. The intricate structure of the capsules of some of the subcutaneous mechanosensory organs act as filters to enhance and select types of mechanical energy before this energy acts on the receptors (nerve endings). (C after Johansson and Vallbo 1983.)

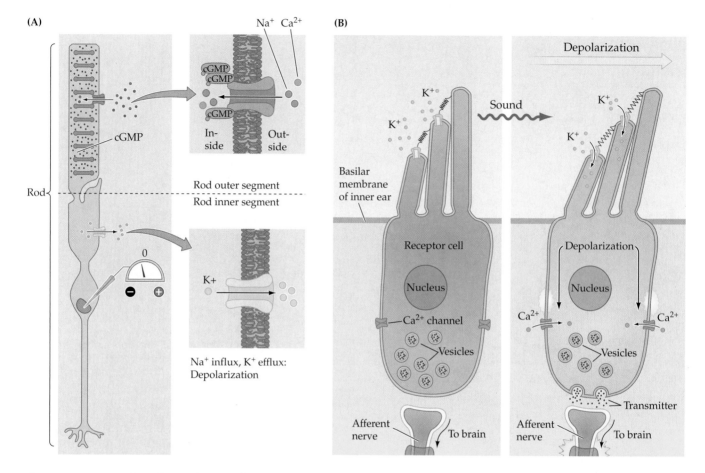

Figure 4.2 Examples of transduction by sensory receptor cells.
(A) Transduction of light energy by photoreceptor cells in the retina. Absorption of photons by pigments in a photoreceptor cell (here, a rod cell) changes the photoreceptor's membrane potential and initiates a neural signal that will eventually be conveyed to the rest of the visual system. (B) Transduction of atmospheric disturbances by receptor cells in the basilar membrane of the inner ear. Movement of hairs on the receptor cell changes the membrane potential, with the same ultimate effect of producing a neural signal that the brain will eventually interpret.

neous tissues undergo a change in membrane potential when various types of mechanical forces act on them (see Figure 4.1C). The same principles apply to the receptor cells for olfaction and taste in the nasal cavity and the mouth.

Adaptation to stimulus intensity

Another functional principle found in sensory systems at all levels of processing is **adaptation**. This term refers to a continual resetting of the sensitivity of the system according to ambient conditions. The primary purpose of adaptation is to ensure that, despite the signaling limitations of nerve cells, sensory processing occurs with maximum efficiency over the full range of environmental conditions that are biologically pertinent to the system and species in question.

The human visual system provides an especially well-studied example of adaptation to the ambient intensity of relevant stimuli, which entail an enormous range of light levels (**Figure 4.3A**). The need for resetting is apparent from the discrepancy between this range and the much more limited firing rate of visual sensory and other neurons. The firing rate, which conveys information about stimulus intensity (the more action potentials per unit time, the more intense the stimulus), has a maximum of only a few hundred action potentials per second (**Figure 4.3B**). A mere variation in firing rate is clearly inadequate to generate finely graded percepts that convey brightness values in response to a range of light intensities that spans 10 orders of magnitude or more. Thus the *sensitivity* of the system (i.e., the facility with which action potentials are generated in response to light stimuli) is continually re-set

(A)

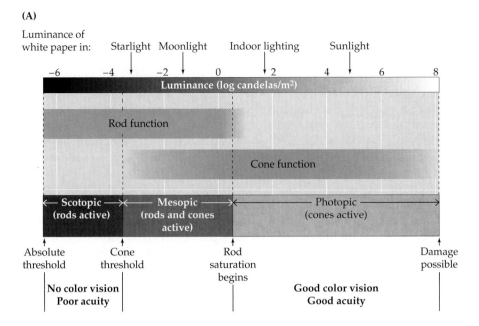

Luminance of white paper in:

Starlight   Moonlight   Indoor lighting   Sunlight

Luminance (log candelas/m²)

Rod function

Cone function

Scotopic (rods active) | **Mesopic (rods and cones active)** | **Photopic (cones active)**

Absolute threshold | Cone threshold | Rod saturation begins | Damage possible

No color vision Poor acuity | **Good color vision Good acuity**

(B)

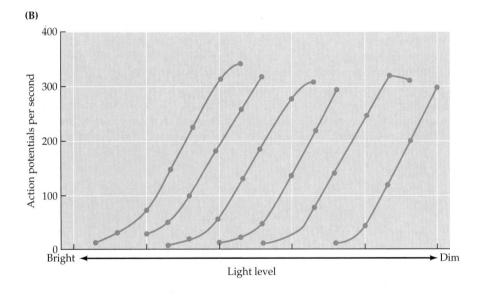

Action potentials per second

400

300

200

100

0

Bright ← Light level → Dim

Figure 4.3 The need for adaptation in sensory systems. This illustration uses vision as an example. (A) The light sensitivity of the human visual system, based on the rod and cone photoreceptor systems, spans more than 10 orders of magnitude. (B) To faithfully convey information about intensity over this broad range using the relatively small range of action potentials per second that neurons are capable of generating, the sensitivity of the system must continually adapt to ambient levels of light, so that the minimum and maximum firing rate of the relevant neurons reports light intensity over a new portion of the full range of sensitivity. In the experiment shown, the firing rate of retinal ganglion cells (the neurons that carry information from the eye to the processing centers in the brain) has been examined for six different levels of light intensity (luminance). The full range of neural signaling is apparent at each level as a result of adaptation. (After Sakman and Creutzfeldt 1969.)

(adapted) to match different levels of light intensity in the ambient environment, as shown by the experimental observations in Figure 4.3B.

Some aspects of adaptation are obvious. When we move from daylight into a darkened movie theater, for example, everything seems dark at first; the different light intensities inside the theater can't be easily distinguished. Over a few minutes, however, objects become increasingly visible as the visual system adapts to the much lower level of ambient light. Such **dark adaptation** when moving from *photopic* to *scotopic* conditions (see Figure 4.3A) takes 20 to 30 minutes to complete. The dark adaptation effect depends on restoring the biochemical integrity of the rod photoreceptor system, which is specialized for seeing in relative darkness (see Chapter 5). The rod system is degraded ("bleached") in daylight and takes many minutes to fully recover. The reverse phenomenon, **light adaptation**, is noticeable when you come out of the theater into daylight: the light outside seems much too bright until the visual system adapts to the increased light intensity. Light adaptation is much more rapid than dark adaptation, however, because the photoreceptor system responsible for seeing in daylight—the cone system—adapts more quickly to changes in illumination than the rod system does.

From a more general perspective, adaptation to ambient conditions is a broad challenge that involves not only the receptor mechanisms of the peripheral nervous system but the central stations (i.e., brain regions) of the visual and other sensory systems, which operating together determine the eventual perceptual experience. Adaptation is critical to all sensory functions, allowing useful percepts to be generated over a very large range of stimulus intensities.

Adaptation as a function of stimulus duration

One fundamental aspect of adaptation concerns changes in neuronal firing rate as a function of **stimulus duration**. In addition to the need to adjust to ongoing ambient conditions over minutes, the highly dynamic nature of stimuli on a shorter time scale (milliseconds to seconds) presents an opportunity for adjustments that provide useful information. Thus stimuli can be momentary or persistent, and we and other animals need to know when a stimulus stops or stops to generate appropriate behavior. Many studies have shown that some afferent neurons in sensory systems fire rapidly when a stimulus is first presented and then fall silent in the presence of continued stimulation; in this sense, they adapt to the stimulus on this shorter time scale (**Figure 4.4A**). Other sensory neurons, however, generate a sustained discharge in the presence of an ongoing stimulus (**Figure 4.4B**). Afferent neurons that initially fire in the presence of a stimulus and then become quiescent convey information about *changes* in stimulation, whereas those that fire continuously convey information about the *persistence* of a stimulus.

It would be wrong, however, to think that what we perceive is simply the result of action potential signals sent from the peripheral sensory receptors to the brain. Pursuing the example of the somatosensory system, even though

Stimulus

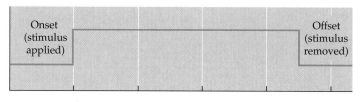

(A) Rapidly adapting

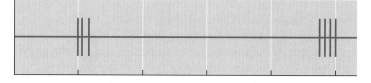

Figure 4.4 Rapidly and slowly adapting responses in sensory systems.   Here the example shown is somatic sensation. The upper panel indicates the application of a light touch stimulus to the skin. (A,B) Recordings of action potentials from two types of sensory neurons in response to the touch stimulus. (A) The rapidly adapting neuron fires only briefly when the stimulus is applied or removed, thus specifically reporting stimulus onset and offset. (B) The slowly adapting neuron continues to fire in the presence of the stimulus, and thus reports that the stimulus is ongoing.

(B) Slowly adapting

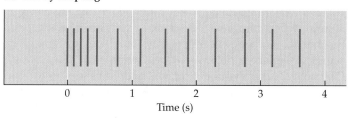

we spend most of the day wearing clothes, we are usually unaware of the ever-changing tactile stimulation resulting from the movement of clothes against the touch receptors in our skin. This and other examples described in the following chapters illustrate that what we end up perceiving is greatly influenced by attention, memory, emotional state, motivation, the context in which stimuli occur, and a long list of other factors. Thus higher order processing is at least as influential in perception as the signaling activity of sensory receptor cells.

Sensory acuity

Another shared property of perception generated by sensory systems is its precision, or **acuity**. *Acuity* is different from the sensitivity to stimulus intensity described in the preceding section. Rather than setting an appropriate level of amplification (gain) or determining the ability to accurately report stimulus onset and offset, the issue in acuity is the fineness of discrimination, as in distinguishing two points from each other in vision (the purpose of the standard eye chart used by optometrists), accurately determining the location of a sound source, or determining the position of a stimulus on the body surface (so we know just where to swat that mosquito).

The most obvious determinant of acuity is the density of peripheral receptors. Although applicable to all sensory systems, the influence of receptor density is particularly evident in vision and somatic sensation. In the visual and tactile sensory systems, the location of receptors on a two-dimensional sheet corresponds roughly to our perception of location in visual space or on the body surface, respectively. (Position on the receptor sheet is equally important in audition and the chemical senses, but in different ways that will be taken up in Chapters 6 and 7.)

In vision, acuity depends on the different distribution of receptors (and receptor types) across the retina. Although we seem to "see" the visual world quite clearly, visual acuity in humans actually falls off rapidly as a function of *eccentricity* (the distance in degrees of visual angle away from the line of sight; a degree is 1/360th of a circle drawn around the head and corresponds to about the width of the thumb held at arm's length). Consequently, vision beyond the central few degrees of the visual field is extremely poor; people without a normally functioning central retina (a deficiency all too common in the elderly as the result of a disease called *macular degeneration*), qualify as legally blind. "Legal blindness" is defined as uncorrected visual acuity of 20/200 or worse using the standard eye chart (i.e., being able to read correctly at a distance of 20 feet only the line on the chart that a normal individual would be able to read at a distance of 200 feet).

Lessened acuity outside the central retina means that a person must frequently move their eyes—and therefore the direction of their gaze—to different positions in visual space. Moving the eyes, which is of course what humans do during the normal inspection of a scene, is the only way to see objects in detail. Such eye movements are called **saccades** and they occur 3–4 times a second; this easily measured visual behavior has been widely used in cognitive studies described in later chapters.

The reason for this difference in acuity according to where an image falls on the retina is initiated by the distribution of photoreceptors (**Figure 4.5A**). Cones, which are responsible for detailed vision in daylight, greatly predominate in the central region of the retina, being most dense in a specialized region called the **fovea**. The fovea corresponds to the line of sight and the couple of degrees around it (see Figure 4.1A). The prevalence of cones falls off sharply in all directions as a function of distance from this locus; as a result, high-acuity vision is limited to the fovea and its immediate surround. Con-

Figure 4.5 The acuity of sensory systems is determined initially by the distribution of receptors. (A) Graph showing the density of rods (purple) and cones (green) as a function of distance from the cone-rich fovea. The poor resolution of vision a few degrees off the line of sight is a result of the relative paucity of cones at eccentricities greater than a few degrees. (B) Variation in two-point tactile discrimination as a function of the density of receptors in the skin. Perceptual acuity also varies according to the prevalence of the different touch receptor types in different regions of the body surface. (B after Weinstein 1968.)

(A)

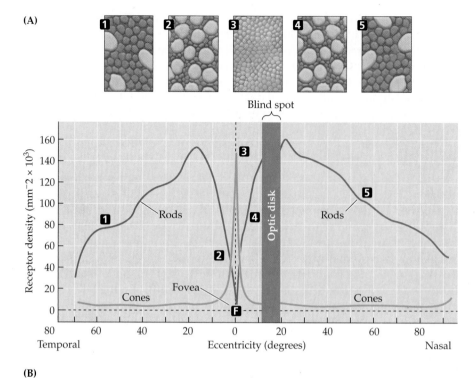

(B)

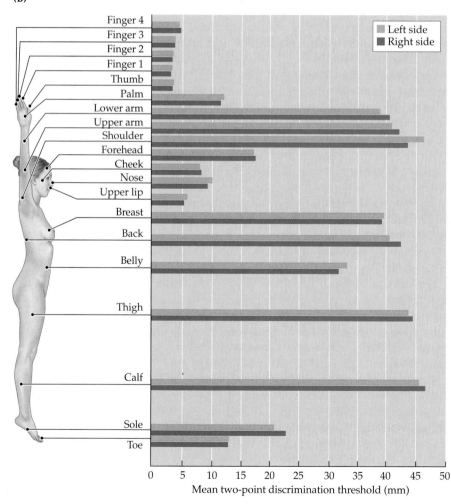

versely, rods, which lack the acuity of cones and are responsible for vision in dim light, are sparse in the fovea and absent altogether in the middle of it. In consequence, sensitivity to a dim stimulus is greater off the line of sight because of the paucity of rods in the fovea and their preponderance a few degrees away, even though acuity is less at this eccentricity. The reason people are generally unaware of the poor acuity of eccentric vision is simply because whenever it is important to see something clearly, the object of interest is brought onto the fovea by movements of the eyes, head, or body.

The same perceptual principle is apparent in the distribution of somatic sensory receptors at the body surface (**Figure 4.5B**). An experiment easily carried out with a friend is measurement of the distance apart two stimuli have to be on the skin to be perceived as separate. On the fingertips, this distance is only a few millimeters, whereas on the back it is a few tens of centimeters. This difference is due in part to the density of receptors; for good biological reasons, the relevant receptors are densely arrayed in the skin of the digital pads and are quite sparse on the skin of the back. And, just as in vision we align objects of interest with the fovea, when we want to make fine tactile discriminations we touch things with our fingertips. However, another key factor is the size of receptive fields of the relevant sensory neurons; the nature of this "cortical magnification" will be described in more detail later in the chapter.

Subcortical Processing

As already emphasized, it would be a mistake to imagine that percepts are determined solely by the peripheral sensory receptors: each level of each sensory modality has evolved to work with the other levels to serve the overall purpose of generating successful behavior. The peripheral initiation of sensory signals is only the beginning of a sequence of neural processing events that eventually determines subjective sensory awareness (bearing in mind that the majority of sensory stimulation never reaches the level of consciousness, despite its production of useful behavioral responses). This processing is the province of the central nervous system, and it occurs at a variety of anatomical levels that can be grossly divided into *subcortical* and *cortical* processing.

The processing of the information provided by receptor-initiated neural signals in virtually all sensory systems begins in stations of the central nervous system well before reaching the cerebral cortex, where perception is generally thought to occur. Such processing (and often the initial stages of cortical processing) is sometimes referred to as "low-level processing"—an unfortunate phrase because it falsely implies that these stages are somehow less complex or less important for perception than processing at "higher level" stations.

Feedforward, feedback, and lateral information processing

The most thoroughly studied examples of subcortical processing are in the visual system. In this system, much processing of the information transduced by photoreceptors is carried out in the retina by the cells that intervene between the rods and cones and the *retinal ganglion cells*, which are the output neurons of the eye (**Figure 4.6**). Although much is known about the connectivity and physiology of these intervening neurons (the relevant neuronal types are bipolar cells, horizontal cells, and amacrine cells), the purposes they serve are for the most part not well enough understood to summarize in this overview. In general, however, the lateral flow of information in the retinal circuitry modulates, often by *lateral inhibition*, the information that is eventually sent forward by retinal ganglion cells. The information passed on to the next stage of processing is often called **feedforward** information. This theme

(A)

Light

Optic nerve

(B) Section of retina

Light

Figure 4.6   The human retina.   The diagram shows some of the connectivity that mediates feedforward, feedback, and lateral information flow among the major neuronal types in this well-studied example of subcortical sensory processing. "Intervening" between the photoreceptors (rods and cones) that receive information and the retinal ganglion cells that transmit signals to the central nervous system are amacrine, horizontal, and bipolar cells that filter and process information, thus influencing the information that goes forward to higher processing stations.

(C)

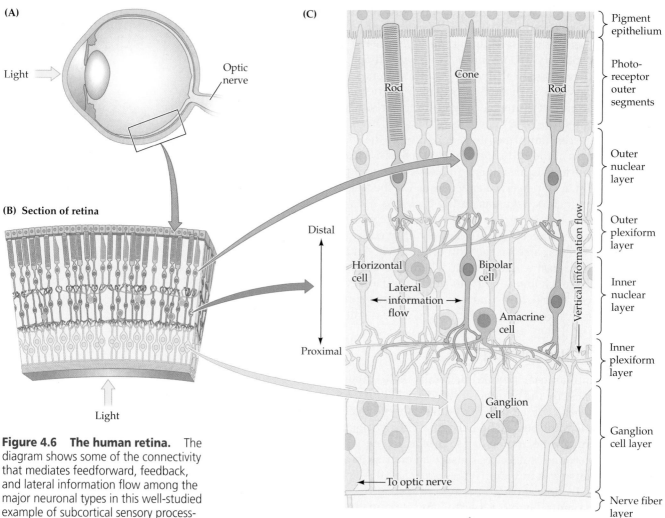

Pigment epithelium

Cone

Rod

Rod

Photo-receptor outer segments

Outer nuclear layer

Distal

Outer plexiform layer

Horizontal cell

Bipolar cell

Lateral information flow

Inner nuclear layer

Amacrine cell

Proximal

Inner plexiform layer

Ganglion cell

Ganglion cell layer

To optic nerve

Nerve fiber layer

Vertical information flow

Light

of *modulation of the information that goes forward in a sensory system by lateral connectivity* is a general one in sensory processing, and its presumed purpose is to filter or sharpen the information received by the next processing stage.

A second theme apparent in the organization of the retina and virtually all other sensory processing levels is **feedback** from one stage to another; the purpose of such feedback is presumed to be gating feedforward signals so that the next processing stage receives information that is particularly pertinent to its operational status at any given moment. The concepts of feedforward and feedback can be applied either within an anatomical level such as the retina, or between the anatomical levels, as between the retina and the thalamus (although the human retina is an exception in that it receives no feedback from the thalamus).

The thalamus: A subcortical processing and relay station

As described in Chapter 1, a major subcortical target for input from the retina and the other sensory systems (the olfactory system is an exception) is the **thalamus**, a walnut-sized complex of neuronal nuclei in the diencephalon of humans and other mammals (**Figure 4.7**). The thalamus, among many other

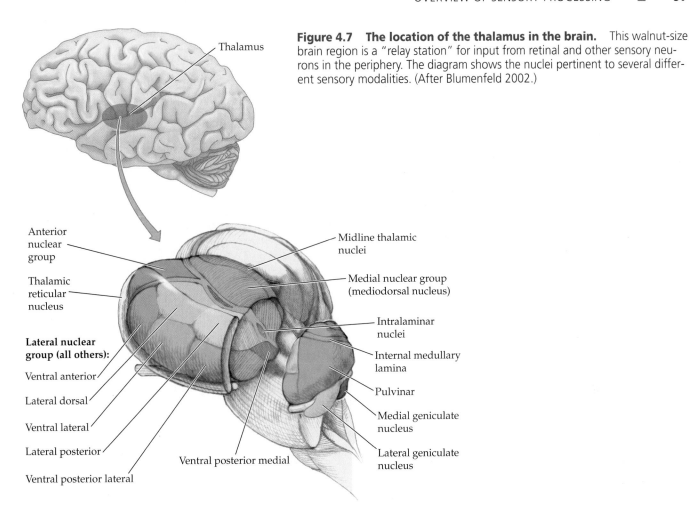

Figure 4.7 The location of the thalamus in the brain. This walnut-size brain region is a "relay station" for input from retinal and other sensory neurons in the periphery. The diagram shows the nuclei pertinent to several different sensory modalities. (After Blumenfeld 2002.)

Thalamus

Anterior nuclear group

Thalamic reticular nucleus

Lateral nuclear group (all others):

Ventral anterior

Lateral dorsal

Ventral lateral

Lateral posterior

Ventral posterior lateral

Ventral posterior medial

Midline thalamic nuclei

Medial nuclear group (mediodorsal nucleus)

Intralaminar nuclei

Internal medullary lamina

Pulvinar

Medial geniculate nucleus

Lateral geniculate nucleus

functions, relays sensory information from the output of peripheral sensory processing elements to the cerebral cortex. Each sensory system tracks a separate pathway through the thalamus within its own dedicated thalamic nuclei. In the visual pathway, the major target of the retinal ganglion cell axons that exit the eye is the *lateral geniculate nucleus*.

As described in the next chapter, information flow through the visual thalamus is highly organized, defining one **information stream** that is particularly sensitive to changes in the position of retinal images (i.e., motion), and a second stream that is primarily responsible for processing image detail and color information. This sort of parsing also occurs in the *medial geniculate nucleus* that processes auditory information in the thalamus, and in the *ventral posterior nuclear complex* that processes somatosensory information (including pain). Thus, within any given sensory modality, the segregation of information according to its type provides another general principle of sensory processing.

The processing that occurs in the diencephalon is not well understood, but clearly the thalamus is not simply a relay station for sensory information. In addition to extensive connections among thalamic neurons—neurons that presumably filter and sharpen the information to be fed forward from the thalamus to the cerebral cortex—each sensory nucleus in the thalamus is extensively innervated by **descending pathways** from the cortex and other brain regions. These descending pathways provide neural feedback that is generally assumed to mediate a variety of thalamic gating functions.

Although the thalamus is the first processing station after the retina in the visual pathway to the cortex, other sensory systems possess additional pro-

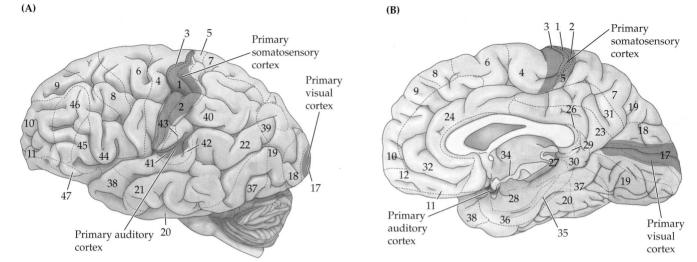

(A)

(B)

Figure 4.8 The primary cortices for the human sensory modalities.
(A) Lateral view. (B) Medial view. The pyriform cortex in the medial temporal lobe that receives olfactory input, and the insular cortex that receives input concerning taste, cannot be seen in these views of the brain. (Numbers indicate Brodmann's cytoarchitectonic areas; see Chapter 1.)

cessing stations that intervene between the periphery and the diencephalon. Thus in audition, somatic sensation, and taste, processing occurs in the brainstem nuclei pertinent to each of these systems, as will be described in Chapters 6 and 7. The scheme for all sensory systems is therefore more similar than the rather complicated anatomical differences among them suggest. Lateral processing in the retina and subcortical processing in the olfactory bulb can be thought of as providing the equivalent of the brainstem processing that takes place in the other three systems. In any event, each of the five sensory systems carries out extensive subcortical processing.

Cortical Processing

The primary sensory cortices

The initial target of the input to the cerebral cortex for any sensory modality is called the **primary sensory cortex** for that modality (**Figure 4.8**). In the case of the visual system, this region is located in the occipital lobe and is called the **primary visual cortex**, or **V1** (also called the *striate cortex* or *Brodmann area 17*). The **primary auditory cortex (A1)** is on the superior aspect of the temporal lobe and corresponds to Brodmann areas 41 and 42, and the **primary somatosensory cortex** is in the postcentral gyrus of the parietal lobe and corresponds to Brodmann areas 1, 2, and 3. The **primary olfactory cortex** is located in the medial temporal lobe and is also referred to as the *pyriform cortex*; the primary cortex of gustation is less well defined, but is at least in part located in the **insula** of the frontal lobe (see Figure 1.11C).

Higher-order cortical areas

The processing that goes on at the level of the primary sensory cortices in all sensory systems occurs in conjunction with processing in what, for lack of a better phrase, are usually referred to as "higher-order" cortical areas or, more formally, **cortical association areas** or **association cortices**. As is apparent in **Figure 4.9**, cortical association areas occupy the vast majority of the cortical surface, and together with their subcortical components are critical determinants of all of the perceptual qualities and cognitive functions discussed in subsequent chapters. Because such regions integrate the qualities of a given modality (e.g., color, brightness, and form in vision; loudness, pitch, and timbre in audition) as well as information from other sensory modalities and

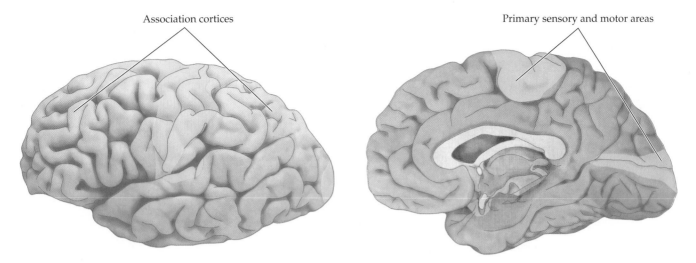

Association cortices

Primary sensory and motor areas

from brain regions carrying out other functions (e.g., attention and memory), the processing carried out by the association cortices is sometimes referred to as "top-down," to indicate that the influences of these areas on perception are broader than the influence of sensory processing per se.

With respect to percepts elicited more or less directly by sensory input, the relevant association cortices are typically adjacent to the primary sensory cortex and are extensively connected to it by feedforward and feedback neural circuitry. The most thoroughly studied examples of these higher order areas and their functional significance are in the visual system. A wealth of clinical and experimental evidence on the primary visual cortex (**V1** or **striate cortex**) has shown that several **extrastriate visual cortical areas** adjacent to V1 tend to process one or more of the qualities that define visual perception in specific ways. Thus in humans and non-human primates the area called **V4** is especially important in processing information pertinent to color vision, and areas **MT** (for *middle temporal*) and **MST** (for *middle superior temporal*) are especially important for the generation of motion percepts. Less well understood but analogous higher-order areas adjacent to other primary sensory cortices appear to follow this same general principle of integrating specialized information pertinent to the relevant perceptual qualities for a given system.

Some uncertainties notwithstanding, there is one further generalization about the organization of higher-order visual cortices about which there is broad agreement. Beginning with the work of Leslie Ungerleider and Mortimer Mishkin at the National Institutes of Health, a consensus emerged that the relevant extrastriate cortical areas in non-human primates are organized into two largely separate "streams" that feed information into cortical areas in the temporal and parietal lobes, respectively. A variety of evidence in humans indicates the same general organization (**Figure 4.10A**). One of these broad paths, called the **ventral stream** (the "what" pathway) leads from the striate cortex to the inferior part of the temporal lobe. Information carried in this pathway appears to be responsible for high-resolution *form vision* and *object recognition*, a finding that conforms with other evidence about functions of the temporal lobe discussed in later chapters. The **dorsal stream** (the "where" pathway) leads from striate cortex and other visual areas into the parietal lobe. This pathway appears to be responsible for *spatial aspects of vision*, such as the analysis of motion and positional relationships between objects. Melvyn Goodale at the University of Western Ontario and others who have worked on this issue have referred to these two streams as the "vision for perception" and "vision for action" pathways, respectively.

Figure 4.9 Higher-order cortical association areas indicated in lateral and medial views of the human brain. The extent of the association cortices are show in blue; the primary sensory and motor regions of the neocortex are shaded in yellow. Notice that the primary cortices occupy a relatively small fraction of the total area of the cortical mantle. The remainder of the neocortex—defined by exclusion as the association cortices—is the seat of human cognitive ability. The term *association* refers to the fact that these regions of the cortex integrate (associate) information derived from other brain regions.

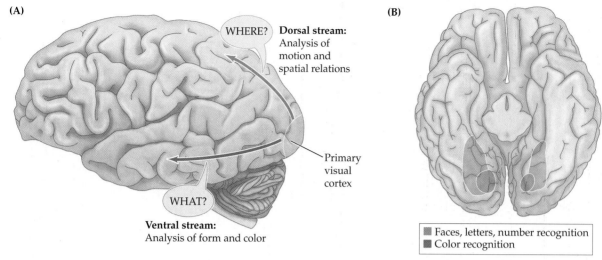

(A)

WHERE?

Dorsal stream:
Analysis of
motion and
spatial relations

Primary
visual
cortex

WHAT?

Ventral stream:
Analysis of form and color

(B)

■ Faces, letters, number recognition
■ Color recognition

Figure 4.10 The dorsal and ventral visual information streams. (A) These pathways have been well documented in the human brain with fMRI and other methods. They are often referred to as the "where" and "what" pathways. (B) The ventral pathway conveys information to regions of the inferior temporal lobe whose activity in fMRI studies indicates an important role in the recognition of objects, as further described in Chapter 5.

The functional significance of the ventral and dorsal streams is further supported by the response properties of neurons in these regions and by the effects of cortical lesions in the pathways. Electrophysiological recordings from neurons in the ventral stream tend to exhibit properties that are important for object recognition, such as selectivity for shape, color, and texture. At the highest levels in the ventral pathway, some neurons in the temporal lobe exhibit remarkable selectivity, responding preferentially to faces and object categories (**Figure 4.10B**). Conversely, neurons in the dorsal stream show selectivity for direction and speed of movement. In keeping with this finding, lesions of the parietal cortex severely impair the ability to distinguish the position of objects—or even their existence—while having little effect on the ability to perform object recognition tasks. Lesions of the inferotemporal cortex, on the other hand, produce profound impairments in the ability to perform recognition tasks but do not impair an individual's ability to carry out spatial tasks. Although the evidence is less clear in other sensory systems, it seems likely that they too will be found to send information pertinent to object recognition ventrally to the temporal lobe, and information pertinent to object location and motion to the parietal lobe.

Newer research, however, suggests that the segregation of visual information into ventral and dorsal streams should not be interpreted too rigidly: recent evidence indicates that there is a good deal of "crosstalk" between these broadly defined sensory pathways.

Multisensory integration

Evidence of sensory crosstalk is hardly surprising since, as already mentioned, integrating information among sensory modalities and incorporating the influence of non-sensory functions on perception is a key feature of the *association cortices*. As sensory information moves through the higher order processing areas, processing specific to a given sensation must be integrated with information being processed by the other sensory systems to improve the efficacy of behavior.

That such **multisensory integration** is ongoing during the processing of sensory information should be obvious: we hear a noise and immediately turn in the direction of the source to see what caused it; we feel something touch us unexpectedly and look to see what it is and what response is appropriate. Functional associations have many advantages, of which these simple examples of more or less sequential integration across sensory modalities are only one.

(A)

(B)

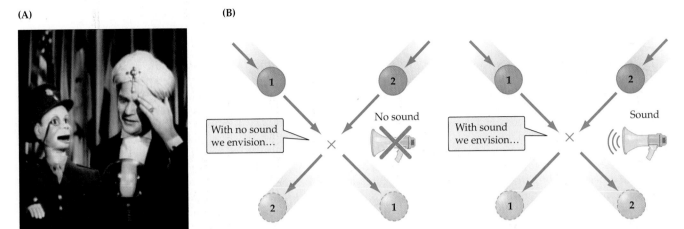

Figure 4.11 Examples of cross-modal (multisensory) influences on perception. (A) In the phenomenon of ventriloquism, what we see affects what we hear: because we see the dummy's mouth moving while the ventriloquist's lips are still, we perceive the sound as coming from the dummy's mouth. (B) What we hear also affects what we see. The apparent trajectory of moving balls is profoundly affected by what we hear, or do not hear. In the absence of a sound, the two balls appear to proceed past each other, as indicated; when a sound occurs coincident with the point at which they would collide, the balls seem to bounce off each other, as indicated.

As will be apparent in the following chapters, sensory integration has marked effects on perception. For example, what we see quite literally affects what we hear (**Figure 4.11A**), and what we hear affects what see (**Figure 4.11B**). Understanding how these effects are mediated is a difficult issue to which much effort in cognitive neuroscience is presently being devoted (**Box 4A**).

Organization of the Sensory Cortices

The sensory cortices devoted to the various modalities differ in a number of ways, but they do abide by some common principles. Although our understanding of them is far from complete, these principles include:

- The organization of sensory receptor cells in the peripheral nervous system corresponds topographically to the organization of those areas of the cortex and other central stations that process the input from the receptors.

- More complex neural processing requires more cortical (or subcortical) space relative to the amount of body area occupied by the peripheral sensory receptors. This phenomenon is known as *cortical magnification.*

- The primary sensory cortices (and some subcortical sensory stations) are organized into a repeating, often columnar pattern of neurons with similar functional properties. These iterated groups of cortical neurons are referred to as *modules.*

Mapping studies and topographical representation

One important rule relevant to perception concerns the relationship between the organization of the sensory receptors in the periphery and the organization of the corresponding sensory cortex and other central stations of each system. The most obvious feature of this relationship is that the organization of the peripheral receptors is reflected in the corresponding central stations. This relationship is particularly apparent in (but not limited to) the primary sensory cortices, and has been most thoroughly documented in the visual and somatic sensory systems, where the location of stimuli on the retinal surface or the body surface, respectively, is particularly important.

The general approach in such **mapping studies** is to stimulate a peripheral location while recording centrally to assess how the location of peripheral stimulation is reflected in the location of the corresponding central nervous system activity. The result for both vision and somatic sensation is that adja-

■ BOX 4A Synesthesia

An especially intriguing form of multisensory integration is the experience of certain individuals (estimates as to the number of people affected vary widely) who conflate experiences in one sensory domain with those in another, a phenomenon called **synesthesia**. Synesthesia was named and described by Francis Galton in the nineteenth century, and at that time the phenomenon received a good deal of attention among Galton's scientific circle in England. The term literally means "mixing of the senses," and its best understood expression is in persons who see different numerals, letters, or similar shapes printed in black and white as being differently colored; this condition is known specifically as *color-graphemic synesthesia*. Other fairly common synesthesias include the experience of colors in response to musical notes, and specific tastes elicited by certain words and/or numbers. The list of famous synesthetes includes painter David Hockney, novelist Vladimir Nabokov, composer and musician Duke Ellington, and physicist Richard Feynman.

The experience of synesthetes is not in any sense metaphorical or "abnormal"; it is simply the way these persons experience the world. Thus, color-grapheme synesthetes (the form of synesthesia that has been most thoroughly studied) actually see numbers printed in black and white as being differently colored; the reality of their ability has been demonstrated in a variety of psychophysical studies. They can segregate targets from backgrounds based on the synesthetic color (see figure), they can group targets in apparent motion displays, and they show the Stroop effect (i.e., the slowed reaction time that everyone exhibits when the printed ink and the spelling of a color word are at odds, as in yellow) based on the synesthetic colors they see. They are also subject to visual illusions such as color afterimages based on the synesthetic colors.

The basis of synesthesia is not known, but is clearly of considerable interest to researchers trying to sort out how information inputs from different sensory modalities are integrated. Synesthesia has attracted many cognitive neuroscientists to apply fMRI and other modern neuroscientific methods to this century-old phenomenon—so far without reaching any definite conclusions. Based on the influence of synesthetic color perception on the various psychophysical tasks mentioned earlier, it is clear that the mechanism is a central one: it is obvious that the conflated percepts arise at the level of the cerebral cortex. A number of neurobiological theories have been put forward, the most plausible of which entail some form of aberrant wiring during early development. It is noteworthy in this respect that the targets that are associated with some basic perceptual quality such as color or taste are learned though practice, often extensive, in childhood as a person learns numbers, words, letters, musical notes, and so on. Presumably a good deal of novel synaptic connectivity is required as a person becomes literate, numerate, or musically trained.

References

BARON-COHEN, S. AND J. E. HARRISON (1997) *Synesthesia: Classic and Contemporary Readings.* Malden, MA: Blackwell Scientific.

BLAKE, R., T. J. PALMIERI, R. MAROIS AND C.-Y. KIM (2005) On the perceptual reality of synesthetic color. In *Synesthesia*, L.C. Robertson and N. Sagiv (eds.). New York: Oxford University Press, pp. 47–73.

Improved performance on a visual search task by a color-grapheme synesthete, "subject W.O." (A) The physical stimulus exactly as presented to W.O. and to a non-synesthate control subject. The task is to find the numeral 2 among the multiple numeral 5's. (B) The same stimulus with synesthetic colors assigned to the two numbers tested, which presumably shows how W.O. perceives the physical stimulus. (C) The graph reveals that W.O.'s reaction time in the task is faster than that of the control subject. This improved performance is taken to occur because the "2" jumps out for W.O. because of its apparently different color, but not for the control subject. (After Blake et al. 2005.)

(A) Physical stimulus as presented

(B) Presumed synesthate perception

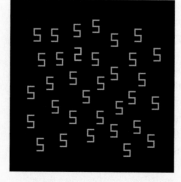

(C)

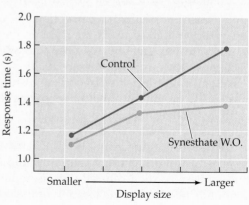

cent peripheral locations usually elicit activity in adjacent cortical locations. As described in Chapters 6 and 7, this sort of **topographical representation** is also apparent in some form in other sensory modalities, although in ways that are less obvious than in vision and somatic sensation.

In vision, topographical representation accords with the layout of the retinal projection of a scene. When electrophysiological recordings are made from neurons in the lateral geniculate nucleus of the thalamus (the thalamic nucleus that processes visual information en route to the cortex), activity at adjacent thalamic sites is elicited by stimulating adjacent retinal sites. Moreover, when a recording electrode is passed from one geniculate layer to another, the position on the retina (or in visual space) determined by recording in one layer is in exact register with the position determined from the neurons in the subjacent layer (see Chapter 5). The same phenomenon is apparent in electrophysiological mapping of the primary visual cortex. Clearly, and presumably importantly, the topography of the retina—and therefore the topography of the retinal image—is reestablished in both the thalamus and cortex (**Figure 4.12A**).

Several methods have allowed an anatomical comparison of the retinal image and its cortical representation. In experimental animals, these methods include the uptake of radiolabels such as 2-deoxyglucose by active neurons, and the optical imaging of the so-called "intrinsic signal" from active brain regions after surgical exposure of the cortex. In humans, functional magnetic resonance imaging (fMRI; see Chapter 3) is the most revealing technique, and many examples of cortical maps created using this method will be seen in later chapters. Each of these methods has confirmed the topographical arrangement of inputs to the primary visual cortex. Topographical maps can also be discerned in some adjacent secondary sensory cortices, but are generally less clear as a function of distance from the primary sensory cortex.

These studies notwithstanding, the ultimate reason for the topographical layout of the primary sensory cortices is not entirely clear. A simple intuition is that to perceive an integrated visual scene or impression of the body surface requires a cortical layout that corresponds to the peripheral layout of receptors. But this conclusion is unwarranted; as seen in **Box 4B**, unified percepts do not depend on cortical adjacency. It seems more likely that cortical topography has mainly to do with minimizing the "wiring" that is needed for maximally efficient processing, but this issue remains a matter of debate.

Cortical magnification

Figure 4.12A reveals an obvious distortion of the size of the peripheral receptor sheet in its representation at the level of the cortex. That is, a square degree of visual space in the foveal area of the human retina (which is concerned with visual detail and is greatly enriched in cone cells; see Figure 4.5A) is represented by proportionally more cortical area (and therefore more visual processing circuitry) than the same unit area in the peripheral retina. This disproportion is referred to as **cortical magnification**, and makes good sense: the visual detail that we perceive in response to stimulation of the fovea presumably requires more neuronal machinery in the cortex than do the less well resolved portions of the visual scene generated by stimulation of eccentric retinal regions.

Cortical magnification is also apparent in the somatic sensory system, where there is similar distortion accorded to cortical areas mapped to those areas of the body surface that process more detailed information (e.g., the lips and the fingers; **Figure 4.12B**). And once again, cortical magnification corresponds to the increased density of peripheral receptors in the hands and other cortically "overrepresented" regions. The idea that more complex neural pro-

Figure 4.12 Topographical representation and magnification of peripheral receptor surfaces.   The examples shown here are in the primary visual and somatosensory cortices. (A) The regions of the retina are color-coded to show their corresponding representation in the primary visual cortex. Notice that the area of central vision corresponding to the fovea is represented by much more cortical area than are the eccentric retinal regions. (B) Topographical mapping and magnification in the primary somatosensory cortex. As in the visual system, regions in which sensory receptors are densely arrayed (such as the hands) are allocated more cortical space in the topographic map. The human cartoon indicates this relative distortion in the cortical representation of different body parts.

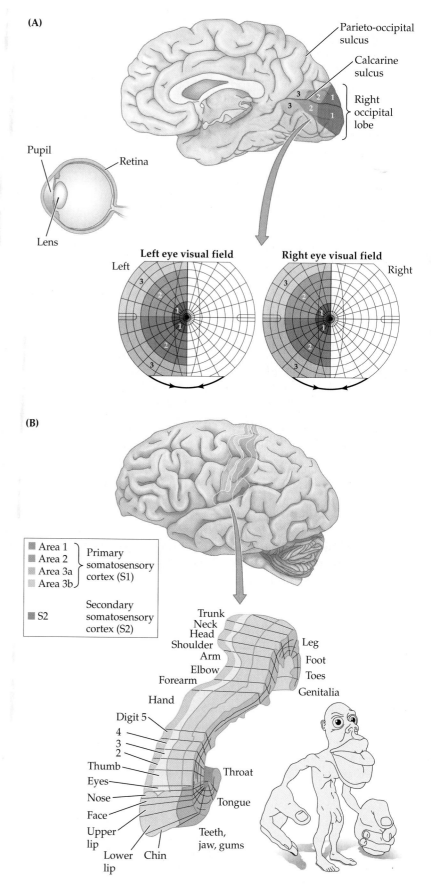

■ BOX 4B The Binding Problem

Given that we perceive objects as unitary entities characterized by a variety of attributes (size, weight, shape, color, texture, and so on), an issue that must concern anyone working on perception is how the sensory qualities we routinely experience are "brought together." This problem, generally referred to as the *binding problem*, applies not just to perception but to the conjunction of object features in memories, emotions, and other mental content.

There are several frameworks for thinking about a possible solution to the binding problem. One would be that the answer is fundamentally anatomical; in other words, the union of perceptual qualities is achieved by the convergence of information about various sensory properties in higher order neurons, whose activity would then represent a conjunction of the various qualities involved. This perspective is predicated on the idea that neurons representing percepts are at the apex of a sensory processing pyramid.

There are logical obstacles to this anatomical interpretation. For example, how could the activity of a given neuron represent the detailed experience of all the complex features that are routinely associated with objects? (See Chapter 28 for more on the inad-

equacy of this "grandmother cell" perspective.) Moreover, this type of solution would require a pattern of connectivity that does not conform with the organization of the brain as it is presently understood. These facts have led most neuroscientists to conclude that only the activity of a fairly large population of cells that is dispersed in different regions of the brain could accomplish this feat. But if a dispersed population is involved, then how does the activity of this cohort of nerve cells become associated with a specific object? In trying to answer this question, some researchers have hypothesized novel mechanisms such as synchronized oscillatory activity among the cortical neurons. The idea is that such activity, which is evident in electroencephalogram (EEG) recordings (see Chapter 3), might represent a coherence between the different properties of objects that need to be "bound" together by means of this sort of collective temporal identity. As described in Chapter 3, such activity at a variety of frequencies is characteristic of the brain, and thus this idea has appealed to a number of investigators.

Another proposed solution to the binding problem suggests a rapid transition of attention to the activity of

the various neurons representing different object qualities, with the perception of unity being a result of this rapid transitioning. A much more radical suggestion is that neither physiological nor anatomical union is necessary for unitary perception. In this view, whatever activity existed in the brain at a given moment of consciousness would constitutes a percept; binding would follow more or less automatically, without any special mechanism being required. At present, all of these possibilities remain potential solutions to the conceptual puzzle of how we bind diverse sensations in order to perceive a unitary object.

References

REVENOSO, A. AND J. NEWMAN (1999) Binding and consciousness. *Cognition and Consciousness* 8: 123–127.

ROSKIES, A. L. (1999) The binding problem. *Neuron* 24: 7–9. (This article is an introduction to a series of important reviews of the binding problem in this issue of the journal.)

TREISMAN, A. AND G. GELADE (1980) A feature integration theory of attention. *Cog. Psych.* 12: 97–136.

ZIMMER, H., A. MECKLINGER AND U. LINDENBERGER (EDS.) (2006) *Binding in Human Memory*. Oxford: Oxford University Press.

cessing requires more cortical (or subcortical) space is another general principle in the organization of sensory systems.

Modularity

Another organizational principle of primary sensory cortices, and some subcortical and higher order sensory stations as well, is their organization into iterated groups of neurons with similar functional properties (**Figure 4.13**). Each of these iterated units in the primary sensory cortices involves hundreds or thousands of nerve cells, and they are referred to generically as **cortical modules** or **cortical columns**. Their striking patterns are effectively superimposed on the topographical maps described in the previous section, and should not be confused with the much looser and ill-considered use of the term "modules" to refer to brain regions that carry out some nominally categorical function such as recognizing faces. As with cortical topography and magnification, cortical modules have been established in the visual, the somatic sensory, and to a lesser degree the auditory cortices; the cortices related to the chemical senses are less well understood.

(A)

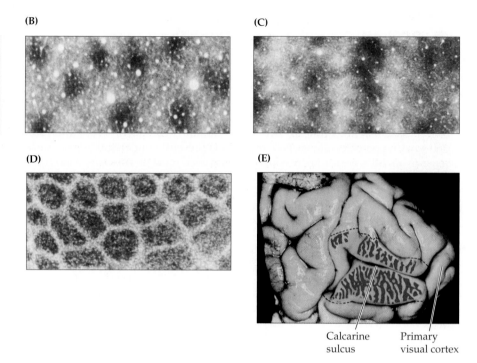

(B)

(C)

(D)

(E)

Calcarine
sulcus

Primary
visual cortex

Figure 4.13 Iterated, modular patterns in mammalian sensory cortices. All of these examples indicate that a relatively fine-grained modular organization is commonplace in sensory cortices. The patterns in each example have been revealed with one of several different histological techniques in sections in the plane of the cortical surface; the size of the units in each different pattern is on the order of several hundred μm across. (A) "Stripes" called ocular dominance columns in layer 4 of the primary visual (striate) cortex of a rhesus monkey. The cells in each column share a preference for stimuli presented to one eye or the other. (B) Repeating units, called "blobs," in layers 2 and 3 of the striate cortex of a squirrel monkey. (C) Repeating stripes in layers 2 and 3 in the extrastriate cortex of a squirrel monkey. (D) Repeating units, called "barrels," in layer 4 in the primary somatic sensory cortex of a rat. (E) Repeating stripes in the human primary visual cortex that share a preference for stimuli arising in either the left or right eye; they are similar to the monkey ocular dominance columns in (A); the columns have been overlain on the image of an intact brain. (A–D from Purves et al. 1992; E courtesy of Jonathan Horton.)

That sensory cortices comprise elementary functional units was first noted in the 1920s by the Spanish neuroanatomist Rafael Lorente de Nó. However, the potential importance of cortical modularity remained largely unexplored until the 1950s, when electrophysiological experiments indicated an arrangement of repeating units in cats and, later, in monkeys. Vernon Mountcastle, a neurophysiologist at Johns Hopkins University, found that vertical microelectrode penetrations in the primary somatic sensory cortex of these animals encountered cells that responded to the same sort of mechanical stimulus presented at the same location on the body surface. When Mountcastle moved the electrode to a nearby location he found the same similarity for the neurons along the vertical columns, but functional characteristics of the nerve cells were typically different from the properties of the neurons along the first track.

Soon after Mountcastle's pioneering work, David Hubel and Torsten Wiesel at Harvard Medical School discovered a similar arrangement in the cat primary visual cortex, which they later confirmed in monkeys. They found several features (e.g., response to stimulus orientation or to the eye in which stimulus was presented) that again indicated the presence of iterated vertical columns that shared the same functional characteristics. These and other observations led Mountcastle and others to the general view that "the elementary pattern of organization of the cerebral cortex is a vertically oriented column or cylinder of cells capable of input-output functions of considerable complexity." Since these discoveries in the late 1950s and early 1960s, the idea that modular units represent a fundamental feature of the mammalian cerebral cortex has gained wide acceptance, and many such entities have now been described in various cortical and subcortical regions using a range of methods, as indicated in Figure 4.13.

Despite its prevalence, there are problems with the view that modular units are pertinent to perception or other cognitive functions, or even that they are universally important in cortical function more generally. First, although modular circuits of a given class are readily apparent in the brains of some species, they have not been found in other, sometimes closely related, animals with similar cognitive and behavioral abilities. Second, not all regions of the mammalian cortex are organized in a modular fashion. And third, no clear and specific function of such modules has been discerned, much effort and speculation notwithstanding. This salient feature of the organization of the primary sensory cortices therefore remains a tantalizing puzzle, and, like topographical correspondence, may have more to do with the efficiency of wiring and the way that neuronal connections form during development than with cognitive processes. In any event, the advantage of iterated, modular patterns for brain function remains largely mysterious. Nevertheless, by providing detailed anatomical markers, such modules have provided scientists with much information about cortical connectivity and the mechanisms by which neural activity in early life influences brain development.

More Unresolved Issues in Sensory Processing

The previous section should have made it clear that despite enormous progress made in establishing the principles of sensory processing, fundamental uncertainties remain. One issue concerns the purpose of the anatomical features apparent in the primary sensory cortices; the inability to understand the purpose of iterated cortical columns or modules has already been mentioned. Another challenge alluded to earlier is the uncertainty surrounding the significance of topographical mapping in sensory systems. Two additional issues are understanding the relationship between primary and "higher order" sensory cortices and the question of *sensory coding*.

The relationship of primary and higher order sensory cortices

Is the relationship between the primary sensory cortex and the so-called higher order cortical regions hierarchical, as the terms applied to them implies, or is there another way of thinking about the organization of sensory systems? One puzzling aspect of this relationship can be appreciated in terms of the *receptive field* characteristics of individual nerve cells.

The **receptive field** of a sensory neuron is defined as the region of the receptor surface that, when stimulated, elicits a response in the neuron being examined. As described in Chapter 3, the relevant recordings from single cells are called **unit recordings** and are made with an extracellular microelectrode placed near the cell of interest to monitor its action potentials. Much of the relevant evidence has been collected in studies of the visual system. The receptive fields of visual neurons, whether in the retina, thalamus or cortex, are typically defined by the region of visual space (located and measured in degrees) that corresponds to the stimulated region of the retinal surface (**Figure 4.14**).

In addition to their responsiveness as measured in spatial terms, visual neurons are also sensitive to other characteristics of a stimulus. This further specificity is referred to as the **receptive field properties** of a neuron. In Figure 4.14, for example, the recorded neuron responds to a moving bar when the bar is oriented at some angles but not at others. By testing its responsiveness to a range of differently oriented stimuli, a sensory **tuning curve** can be defined that indicates the sort of stimulus to which the cell is maximally responsive. The receptive fields of cortical neurons serving foveal vision in the primary visual cortex generally measure less than a degree of visual angle, as do the receptive fields of the corresponding retinal ganglion cells and lateral geniculate neurons. Even for cells serving peripheral vision, the receptive fields in primary visual cortex measure only a few degrees. In extrastriate cortical areas (that is, those outside the primary visual cortex),

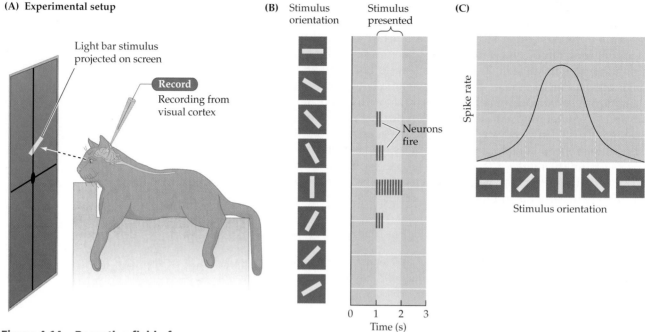

(A) Experimental setup

Light bar stimulus
projected on screen

Record

Recording from
visual cortex

(B) Stimulus
orientation

Stimulus
presented

Neurons
fire

0 1 2 3

Time (s)

(C)

Spike rate

Stimulus orientation

Figure 4.14 Receptive field of a neuron and its properties recorded in the primary visual cortex of a cat. (A) As different stimuli are presented in different locations, the neuron being recorded from fires in a variable way that defines both the location of the receptive field of the neuron and the properties of the stimulus. (B) In this instance, the neuron would not fire at all were the stimulus elsewhere on the scene, and even when it is in the appropriate location the stimulus activates the neuron only when it is presented in certain orientations. Although these factors are not shown here, direction of motion, which eye is stimulated, and other stimulus properties are also important. (C) Orientation tuning curve for the neuron illustrated in (B). In this example, the highest rate of action potential discharge occurs for vertical edges—the neuron's "preferred" orientation.

however, receptive fields often cover a substantial fraction of the entire visual field (which extends about 180° horizontally and 130° vertically). Clearly the location of retinal activity—and the corresponding topographical relationships in the primary visual pathway assumed to underlie the sense of where an object is in visual field—cannot be conveyed by neurons that respond to stimuli *anywhere* in such a large region of space, at least not in any simple way. In short, the topography that is apparent in the primary cortices breaks down in the higher order regions where, in traditional thinking, visual percepts are supposed to be generated. This relative mooting of retinal topography in higher order visual cortical areas (which presumably entails a correspondingly diminished ability to identify the location and qualities of visual stimuli) presents a problem for any rationalization of vision in terms of images and percepts based on image representation in higher order extrastriate cortices. Much the same general problem is apparent in the relationship of primary and secondary cortical regions in other sensory systems.

The underlying issue is really whether or not sensory processing is **hierarchical**. Up to the level of the primary visual cortex, to continue with this example, the organization of the visual system is hierarchical in the sense that lower order stations lead anatomically and functionally to higher order ones, albeit with much modulation and feedback at each stage. Thus at each of the initial stations in the primary visual pathway—the retina, the dorsal lateral geniculate nucleus, and the neurons in the primary visual cortex that receive thalamic input—the receptive field characteristics of the relevant neurons can be understood reasonably well in terms of the "lower order" cells that provide their input. Electrophysiological studies have shown that the responses of retinal ganglion cells can be rationalized on the basis of the rods and cones that supply information to them via the bipolar and other retinal cells, that geniculate cell responses can be understood in terms of the ganglion cells that innervate them, and that the responses of at least some lower order visual cortical neurons make sense in terms of their geniculate inputs. Beyond these initial levels, however, rationalizing the organization of the visual system in hierarchical terms—that is, in terms of lower order neurons shaping the response properties of higher order neurons—becomes increasingly difficult and perhaps impossible, because the cells in question are no longer being driven solely by visual input, but by a variety of other higher order neurons, including many conveying information that is not strictly visual.

The problem with the hierarchichal concept is not simply that it is hard to explain higher-order receptive field properties in terms of lower-order ones. A broader implication of hierarchy is that there is some *place* in the brain where the various qualities processed in the primary and more specialized areas of cortex are brought together (see Box 4B). This way of thinking has given rise to the idea that there are well-defined populations of cells whose activity corresponds more or less directly to the percepts we experience, and that a major goal of cognitive neuroscience should be to locate these cell populations. Given what is now understood about cortical function, this scenario seems implausible, but understanding the alternatives and how to test them depends on the outcome of current research.

Understanding the "neural code" in sensory systems

A final problem to be introduced here is the issue of **sensory coding**. Recall that whereas neuronal firing rate at the level of receptors in the peripheral nervous system is closely linked to the *intensity* of a stimulus, once the signal arrives in the central nervous system, even at the level of the primary sensory cortex, neuronal activity is tied much more specifically to *combinations* of stimulus properties. In Figure 4.14, for instance, not only stimulus intensity, but also stimulus orientation and direction of motion, along with other parameters such as which eye's input drives the neuron, all influence the response of the neuron being recorded from. These and other observations raise the question of what the basic scheme of sensory coding might be, if indeed there is a scheme that fits this rubric.

All parties are agreed that, as emphasized in Chapter 1 and the Appendix, the basis of neural signaling is action potentials traveling among the neurons in a sensory or any other system, and that a key determinant of the results of the information conveyed in this way is the anatomical starting point of the action potential (e.g., receptors in the retina versus receptors in the inner ear) and its terminus (e.g., the primary visual cortex versus the primary auditory cortex). This conclusion about connectivity gives rise to a **place coding** interpretation of the aspect of neural signaling that is determinative in neural processing.

Although the importance of place coding is not in dispute, the origin and destination of action potentials ignores the temporal characteristics of neural signaling, which also conveys information. The conventional wisdom has generally been that the firing rates of a neuron—or populations of neurons—conveys the time-dependent aspects of information about the stimulus features, as has already been introduced in the concept of stimulus intensity being encoded in the rate of action potential generation. Information conveyed in this way is called **rate coding**. Again, this idea is generally accepted. Another time-dependent concept of how action potentials convey information is that it is not simply the firing rate of neurons that is important, but their arrangement over time. A simple aspect of such **temporal coding** is information about the onset, offset and persistence action potential rate changes (see Figure 4.4). A more radical idea is that the precise order and interval between action potentials bears additional information, an idea that remains controversial.

Another aspect of neural coding concerns the inherently uncertain nature of stimulus information with respect to the "real-world" source that is generating the stimulus (this concept will be described further in Chapter 5). Scientists have known for several centuries that the action of a stimulus on neural receptors (e.g., an image on the retina) cannot directly represent the features of the "real" world (i.e., a two-dimensional image cannot directly represent a three-dimensional object). Neuroscientists have worried about this problem explicitly since the nineteenth century, the consensus being that neural activity must ultimately represent a probabilistic inference (otherwise known as a "good guess") about what a given stimulus represents, and thus what is actually present in the world. This idea has given rise to the overarching concept of **probabilistic coding**, also known as **empirical coding**.

Of course, these various coding schemes are not mutually exclusive, and it seems likely that all of them are used for different purposes in perceptual processing. Other points to bear in mind when thinking about coding are that information processing in sensory or other neural systems is not simply about neuronal excitation; inhibition is just as influential and at least as well represented in neural circuitry (see Chapter 1). In addition, we need to factor in the high baseline levels of activity that exist in sensory processing circuits even in the absence of explicit stimulation; this baseline activity must also figure into our understanding of the neural strategies that generate accurate perception and appropriate behaviors.

Summary

1. Sensory processing exhibits a number of principles that are apparent in all five modalities: vision, audition, somatic sensation, olfaction and taste. Each of these modalities has evolved to respond to a different type of energy in the human environment. Thus vision processes information about a particular bandwidth of the electromagnetic spectrum, audition a particular bandwidth of vibrational energy in the atmosphere, somatic sensation particular types of mechanical energy impinging on the body, and taste and olfaction particular categories of chemical energy.

2. Each form of stimulus energy is transformed (transduced) by a series of molecular mechanisms into changes in the membrane potentials of receptor cells. If changes in membrane potential reach threshold, they trigger action potentials; action potentials then convey information to subcortical and cortical sensory processing stations that make up the primary sensory pathway in each system.

3. Sensory processing at every station adapts to the stimulus levels that are most relevant in a given circumstance, thus maximizing the degree to which a limited range of nerve cell firing can convey information about environmental conditions that vary widely.

4. The organization of the primary sensory pathways is generally topographical, with a disproportionate representation in both the peripheral and central nervous systems of information that demands more detailed and complex processing because of its special importance to successful behavior.

5. Although broadly hierarchical at the input stages, the hierarchical arrangement of sensory processing tends to break down at higher cortical levels, making the concept of a pyramidal processing scheme with receptor cells at its base and perception at its apex untenable.

6. Despite great advances in discerning these and other principles of sensory processing over the last century, how neural events generate the perceptions we experience remains an extraordinarily challenging problem in cognitive neuroscience.

Additional Reading

Reviews

COURTNEY, S. M. AND L. G. UNGERLEIDER (1997) What fMRI has taught us about human vision. *Curr. Opin. Neurobiol.* 7: 554–561.

FELLEMAN, D. J. AND D. C. VAN ESSEN (1991) Distributed hierarchical processing in primate cerebral cortex. *Cerebral Cortex* 1: 1–47.

GOODALE, M. A. AND G. K. HUMPHREY (1998) The objects of action and perception. *Cognition* 67: 179–204.

HORTON, J. C. (1992) The central visual pathways. In *Alder's Physiology of the Eye*, W. M. Hart (ed.). St. Louis: Mosby Yearbook.

LIVINGSTONE, E. M. AND D. H. HUBEL (1988) Segregation of form, color, movement, and depth: Anatomy, physiology, and perception. *Science* 240: 740–749.

POUGET, A., P. DAYAN AND R. S. ZEMEL (2003) Inference and computation with population codes. *Annu. Rev. Neurosci.* 26: 381–401.

PURVES, D., D. RIDDLE AND A. LAMANTIA (1992) Iterated patterns of brain circuitry (or how the cortex gets its spots). *Trends Neurosci.* 15: 362–368.

UNGERLEIDER, J. G. AND M. MISHKIN (1982) Two cortical visual systems. In *Analysis of Visual Behavior*, D. J. Ingle, M. A. Goodale and R. J. W. Mansfield (eds.). Cambridge, MA: MIT Press, pp. 549–586.

Important Original Papers

HUBEL, D. H. AND T. N. WIESEL (1962) Receptive fields, binocular interaction, and functional architecture in the cat's visual cortex. *J. Physiol.* (Lond.) 160: 106–154.

HUBEL, D. H. AND T. N. WIESEL (1968) Receptive fields and functional architecture of monkey striate cortex. *J. Physiol.* (Lond.) 195: 215–243.

HUBEL, D. H. AND T. N. WIESEL (1977) Functional architecture of macaque monkey visual cortex. *Proc. R. Soc.* (Lond.) 198: 1–59.

MOUNTCASTLE, V. B. (1957) Modality and topographic properties of single neurons of cat's somatic sensory cortex. *J. Neurophysiol.* 20: 408–434.

SAKMANN, B. AND O. D. CREUTZFELDT (1969) Scotopic and mesopic light adaptation in the cat's retina. Abteilung für neurophysiologie. *Pflügers Arch.* 313: 168–184.

SERENO, M. I. AND 7 OTHERS (1995) Borders of multiple visual areas in humans revealed by functional magnetic resonance imaging. *Science* 268: 889–893.

WOOLSEY, T. A. AND H. VAN DER LOOS (1970) The structural organization of layer IV in the somatosensory region (SI) of mouse cerebral cortex. The description of a cortical field composed of discrete cytoarchitectonic units. *Brain Res.* 17: 205–242.

Books

ABBOTT, L. AND T. SEJNOWSKI, EDS. (1999) *Neural Codes and Distributed Representations: Foundations of Neural Computation.* Cambridge, MA: MIT Press.

BARLOW, H. B. AND J. D. MOLLON (1982) *The Senses.* London: Cambridge University Press.

HUBEL, D. H. (1988) *Eye, Brain, and Vision.* Scientific American Library Series. New York: W. H. Freeman.

KNILL, D. C. AND W. RICHARDS (1996) *Perception as Bayesian Inference.* New York: Cambridge University Press.

MOUNTCASTLE, V. B. (1998) *Perceptual Neuroscience: The Cerebral Cortex.* Cambridge, MA: Harvard University Press.

PURVES, D. AND R. B. LOTTO (2003) *Why We See What We Do: An Empirical Theory of Vision.* Sunderland, MA: Sinauer.

SEKULER, R. AND R. BLAKE (2002) *Perception*, 4th Ed. Boston: McGraw-Hill.

WANDELL, B. A. (1995) *Foundations of Vision.* Sunderland, MA: Sinauer Associates.

ZEKI, S. (1993) *A Vision of the Brain.* Oxford: Blackwell Scientific.

5

The Perception of Visual Stimuli

Introduction

The previous chapter introduced principles of sensory processing that are pertinent to all sensory modalities. The purpose of this and the following two chapters is to review the operation of the major human sensory systems, focusing on how each of them generates the perceptual qualities we routinely experience; a broader goal is to provide a basis for understanding the role of perception in other cognitive functions. Starting with a more detailed look at the visual system makes good sense, since vision is the sensory modality that has been most thoroughly studied in cognitive psychology, neuroscience, and most recently cognitive neuroscience. The chapter begins with an overview of the organization of the primary visual pathway, and then takes up in turn how—and why—we see the basic perceptual qualities that characterize vision: brightness, color, form, depth, and motion. The question then considered is how the visual system uses these qualities, or categories of information, to recognize and respond to complex visual objects and scenes. The discussion of visual object recognition also serves as an introduction to the way perception is affected by attention, memory, emotional, and motivational states as well as other cognitive factors discussed in the later units, including the more metaphysical question of exactly how we can be conscious of visual and other percepts. Indeed, visual perception and visual psychophysics are themes that permeate cognitive neuroscience.

Organization of the Visual System

The **primary visual pathway** refers to the major route from the retina of the eye to the primary visual cortex of the brain. The pathway conveys the information in light stimuli that we end up perceiving as objects (**Figure 5.1**; as indicated, there are also central retinal pathways that serve other functions).

Figure 5.1   The primary visual pathway.
The route (solid red and blue lines) that carries
information centrally from the retina to those
regions of the brain especially pertinent to what
we see comprises the optic nerves, the optic tracts,
the dorsal lateral geniculate nuclei in the thalamus,
the optic radiations, and the primary (striate) and
secondary (extrastriate) visual cortices in the occipital lobes. Note the partial crossing of the optic
nerve axons at the optic chiasm, which allows the
nasal and temporal halves of the retinas that
respectively see the right visual field (the temporal
half of the left retina and the nasal half of the
right) to send information to the left occipital lobe,
and conversely for the retinal halves that see the
left visual field. Other pathways to targets in the
brainstem (dashed red and blue lines) determine
the pupil's diameter as a function of retinal light
levels, help to organize and effect eye movements,
and influence circadian rhythms.

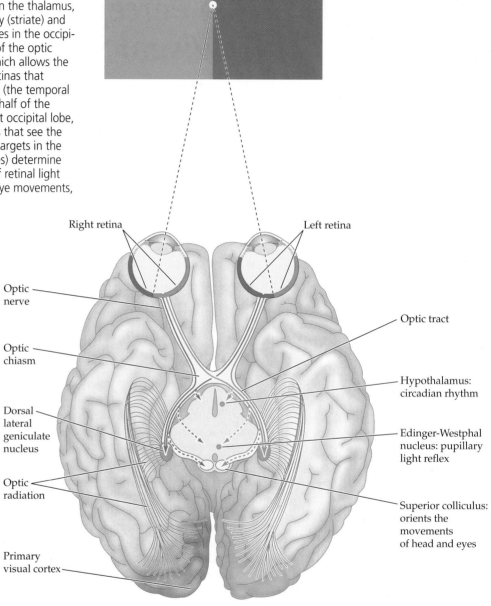

Right retina

Left retina

Optic nerve

Optic tract

Optic chiasm

Hypothalamus: circadian rhythm

Dorsal lateral geniculate nucleus

Edinger-Westphal nucleus: pupillary light reflex

Optic radiation

Superior colliculus: orients the movements of head and eyes

Primary visual cortex

Although several aspects of this primary pathway have already been touched
on, its components are reviewed here more specifically in relation to visual
perception.

The primary visual pathway begins in the retina with the transduction of
light energy by two types of receptor cells, **rods** and **cones**, which define two
overlapping but largely different light-level processing systems (see Figure
4.3A). The processing initiated by rods is primarily concerned with perception
at very low levels of light (the *scotopic* levels illustrated in Figure 4.3A); cones
only respond to greater light intensities (*photopic* levels) and are responsible
for the detail and color percepts that we normally think of vision. (Note that
mesopic levels of light engage both systems to some degree.)

(A)

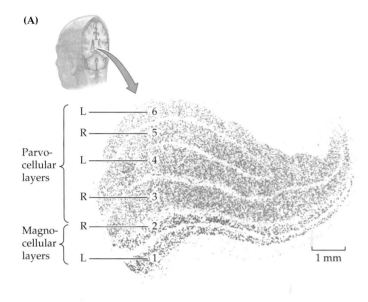

Parvocellular layers
Magnocellular layers

L — 6
R — 5
L — 4
R — 3
R — 2
L — 1

1 mm

Figure 5.2   The dorsal lateral geniculate nucleus of the thalamus.   (A) Cross section of the human thalamus showing the six layers of this distinctive nucleus. Each of the layers receives input from only one eye or the other (indicated by R or L, for right or left), and is further categorized by the size of the neurons it contains. The two layers shown in blue contain larger neurons and are therefore called the *magnocellular layers*; the four layers shown in green are the *parvocellular layers* because of their smaller constituent cells. (B) Tracings of representative magnocellular and parvocellular retinal ganglion cells, as seen in flat mounts of the retina after histological staining; these neurons innervate, respectively, the magno and parvo cells in the thalamus. (A after Andrews et al. 1997; B after Watanabe and Rodieck 1989.)

(B)

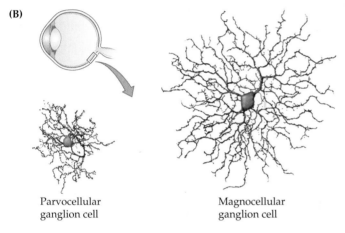

Parvocellular ganglion cell

Magnocellular ganglion cell

Subsequent to retinal processing, the information arising from both rods and cones converges onto retinal ganglion cells whose axons leave the retina via the optic nerve (see Figure 5.1). The major target of the retinal ganglion cells is the **dorsal lateral geniculate nucleus** in the thalamus (**Figure 5.2A**). Unlike other thalamic nuclei, the lateral geniculate is layered, consisting of two **magnocellular layers** (so named because the neurons that populate them are relatively large), and four **parvocellular layers** containing smaller neurons. The "parvo" and "magno" layers, as they are generally referred to, are innervated by distinct classes of retinal ganglion cells, as shown in **Figure 5.2B**.

The neuronal associations between specific classes of retinal ganglion cells and lateral geniculate neurons reflect different functions that have different perceptual consequences. The smaller P ganglion cells in the retina, and the related parvocellular neurons in the lateral geniculate nucleus, are primarily concerned with the spatially detailed visual information underlying the perception of form, and with processing that eventually leads to perceptions of brightness and color. The larger M retinal ganglion cells—and the magnocellular neurons they innervate in the thalamus—process information about changes in the stimulus—that is, motion percepts. Neurons in both the magno and parvo layers are extensively innervated by axons descending from the cortex and other brain regions, as well as from retinal ganglion cells. Although the function of this descending information is not known, the geniculate

(A) Lateral

(B) Medial

(C)

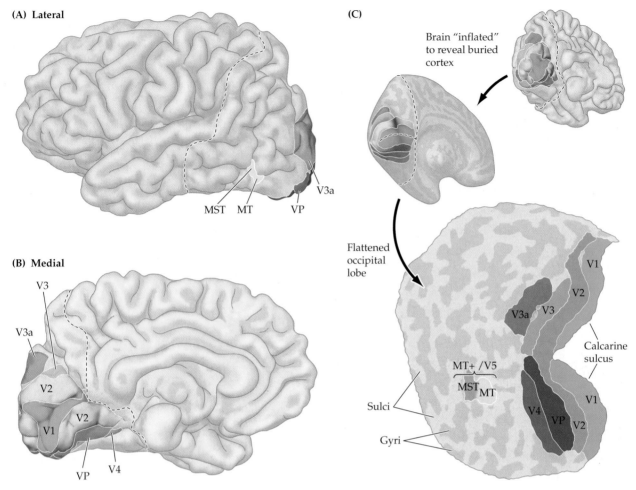

Figure 5.3 Localization of multiple visual areas in the brain using fMRI. (A,B) Lateral and medial views show the location of the primary visual cortex (V1) and additional visual areas V2, V3, VP (ventral posterior), V4, MT (middle temporal), and MST (medial superior temporal area). (C) Unfolded and computationally flattened view of the visual areas. Dark pink areas correspond to cortical regions that were buried in sulci; light regions correspond to regions that were located on the surface of gyri. (After Sereno et al. 1995.)

nucleus is clearly a station for processing visual information; it does not simply pass retinal output along to the cortex. The lateral geniculate neurons project to the **primary visual cortex**, also known as the **striate cortex*** or **V1**. The neurons in cortical layers 5 and 1 of the primary visual cortex project to **extrastriate visual cortical areas** in the occipital, parietal, and temporal lobes, as well as back to the thalamus (**Figure 5.3**; see Box 1B for a general description of canonical cortical organization, of which the visual cortex is a good example). Because of the increasing integration of information from other brain regions in extrastriate visual cortical regions, most investigators consider the primary visual cortex to be the terminus of the primary visual pathway, at least for descriptive purposes.

A wealth of clinical and experimental evidence indicates that both V1 and extrastriate cortical regions mediate key aspects of visual perception. As already mentioned, many V1 neurons process stimulus orientation and line length information (see Figure 4.14), many of the cells in the general area of **V4** process color information, and many neurons in the general area of **MT** and **MST** process responses to moving stimuli. MT stands for "medial temporal," and is adjacent to area MST, which stands for "medial superior temporal." Because

---

***Striate** is used to describe the primary visual cortex because this region is made apparent histologically by a stripe (*stria*) in cortical layer 4 that reflects the large number of myelinated axons in that layer. The generic term *extrastriate* refers to the fact that these additional visual regions lie outside the primary visual cortex.

areas MT and MST are not as clearly distinguished in humans as they are in monkeys (monkeys being the source of many of the foundational observations about vision), in humans they are usually lumped together under the rubric **MT+** or **V5**. The functional properties of visual neurons in these extrastriate cortical regions are determined in the main by lateral connections from other cortical regions rather than by ascending inputs per se. Indeed, even most V1 neurons are more strongly influenced by cortical than by thalamic innervation.

With this organizational information in mind, the following sections consider how visual perceptual qualities are generated. Understanding the basic perceptual qualities—brightness, color, form, depth, and motion—is fundamental to understanding more complex visual functions such as object recognition, visual attention, and visual memory.

The Perception of Brightness

A good place to begin a consideration of visual percepts is with **brightness**, the visual experience of light and dark elicited by different intensities of light.* Arguably, brightness is the most fundamental quality of human visual perception. Vision as we know it cannot occur without this perceptual quality, whereas some other qualities, such as color, are expendable—some animals have keen vision but little or no color vision. Like all percepts, brightness is not subject to direct measurement, and can only be evaluated indirectly by asking observers to report the appearance of one object or surface relative to that of another (**Box 5A**). The physical correlate of brightness is **luminance**, a physical measure of light intensity made by a photometer and expressed in units such candelas/m². As will be apparent in the following section, however, the relationship between luminance and brightness is odd indeed.

Some puzzling discrepancies between luminance and brightness

Given that brightness is the subjective experience of the intensity of a light stimulus, two logical assumptions would be, first, that luminance and brightness are directly proportional, since increasing the luminance of a stimulus increases the number of photons captured by photoreceptors; and, second, that two objects in a scene that return the same amount of light to the eye should appear equally bright. It has long been known, however, that perceptions of brightness fail to meet these seemingly simple expectations. Two patches returning equal amounts of light to the eye are perceived as looking differently bright when placed on backgrounds that have different luminances. Thus a patch on a background of relatively low luminance appears somewhat brighter than the same patch on a background of higher luminance, a phenomenon called **simultaneous brightness contrast** (**Figure 5.4A**). This effect becomes even more dramatic when the stimulus includes more information about the possible real-world conditions underlying the stimulus (**Figure 5.4B**).

Until relatively recently, the explanation of this effect was based on the properties of the neurons at the input level of the visual system (usually retinal ganglion cells) and the lateral interactions that occur in retinal processing. Presumably as a means of enhancing the detection of contrast boundaries (edges), the central region of the receptive fields of lower-order visual neurons has a surround of opposite functional polarity (**Figure 5.5**; see Chapter 4 for an explanation of neuronal receptive fields). The number of action potentials

---

*Technically, *brightness* refers the appearance of a light *source*, such as a light bulb, and *lightness* to the appearance of a surface such as a piece of paper; for present purposes, however, brightness is used in this more general inclusive sense.

Figure 5.4 Simultaneous brightness contrast. (A) Standard presentation of this effect; the two circular patches have exactly the same luminance (see the key), but the one in the dark surround looks somewhat brighter. (B) Simultaneous brightness contrast effects can be much greater when the scene is made more realistic, as it is here; as shown in the key, the patches that look very different in brightness again have the same luminance. Thus the amount of light returned to the eye is not a good predictor of the brightness seen. (B from Purves and Lotto 2003.)

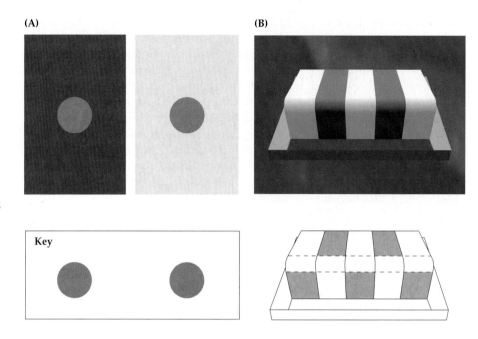

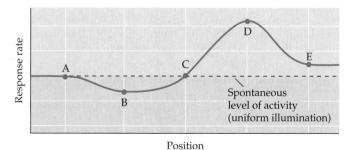

generated per unit time by neurons whose receptive fields intersect a contrast boundary will differ from the activity of neurons whose receptive fields fall entirely on one side of the boundary or the other. To illustrate, the neurons whose receptive field centers lie just within the target on the dark background in Figure 5.5 will fire at a *higher* rate than the neurons whose receptive field centers lie just within the target on the light background, because the former are less inhibited by their oppositely disposed receptive field surrounds than the latter. Many investigators thus supposed that the patch on the dark background looks brighter than the patch on the light background because of this difference in the retinal output.

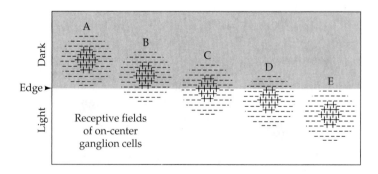

Figure 5.5 The effect of interactions mediated by retinal circuitry on retinal output. Diagram of the different firing rates of retinal ganglion cells as a function of their position with respect to a light-dark contrast boundary. See text for further explanation.

■ BOX 5A Measuring Visual or Other Sensory Percepts

The physical properties of stimuli can be measured with arbitrary precision. Measuring percepts, however, is quite another matter. The perceptual consequences of stimuli are subjective, and as such can't be measured in any direct way. They can, however, be reported in terms of thresholds, "least discernable differences," or other paradigms in which subjects state whether a percept is brighter or darker, larger or smaller, slower or faster than some standard of comparison. Such evaluations of perceptual responses are broadly referred to as *psychophysics*. The effort to make the analysis of percepts scientifically meaningful dates from 1860, when the German physicist and philosopher Gustav Fechner decided to pursue the connection between what he referred to as the "physical and psychological worlds" (thus the rather unfortunate word "psychophysics").

In practice, there are only a limited number of ways to carry out measurements of perception in relation to physical stimuli, although there are many permutations of the basic techniques. A conceptually straightforward but technically difficult measurement is to ascertain the least energetic stimulus that elicits a perceptual response in some sensory modality, such as the weakest retinal stimulation perceived as something seen by dark-adapted subjects. By varying the amount of energy delivered, a *psychophysical function* can be obtained that defines the *stimulus threshold value* (see Figure A). Since at threshold levels of stimulation subjects will have difficulty saying whether they saw something or not, such tests are usually carried out using a *forced choice paradigm* in which the observer must respond on each trial. Typically, a series of trials is presented in which stimuli of different energetic levels are randomly interspersed with trials that do not present a stimulus. Because 50 percent correct responses (i.e., saying "Yes, I saw something" or "No, I saw nothing" when a stimulus was or was not present, respectively) would be the average result obtained if the subject merely guessed on each trial, 75 percent correct responses is conventionally taken to be the criterion for establishing the threshold level of stimulus energy.

A technically easier and more generally applicable way of getting at the sensitivity of a sensory modality is to measure—at any level of stimulus intensity—how much physical change is needed to generate a perceptual change. Such functions, called *difference threshold functions*, have many practical implications. The *Weber-Fechner law* is a good example. The law states that the ability to notice a difference (called tests of *just-noticeable* or *equally noticeable differences*) is determined by a fixed proportion of the stimulus intensity, not an absolute difference. This proportion is referred to as the *Weber*

(Continued on next page)

Examples of psychophysical assessments. (A) The human luminosity function, determined by assessing the sensitivity of normal subjects to light as a function of stimulus wavelength. This determination can be made by measuring either threshold responses or just-noticeable differences at suprathreshold levels. The results show that humans are far more sensitive to stimuli in the middle of the light spectrum (i.e., between approximately 480 and 620 nm). (B) Magnitude scaling, showing that the relationship between a subject's perception of brightness and the intensity of a light stimulus is a nonlinear power function (the exponent in this case is approximately 0.5).

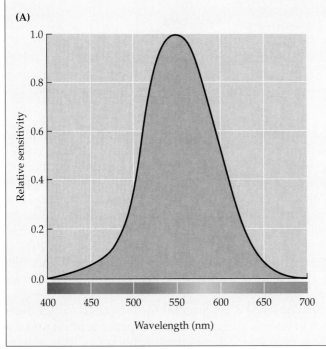

(A)

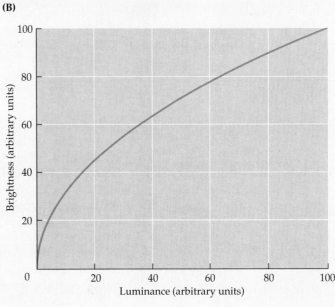

(B)

■ BOX 5A (continued)

fraction; if, for example, the Weber fraction is 1/10, then if a 1-g increment to 10-g weight can just be detected, 10 g will be the minimum detectable increment to a 100-g weight.

Based on what is now known about the physiology of sensory systems, the proportional relationship between just-noticeable differences and stimulus magnitude expressed by the Weber-Fechner law makes good sense. Recall from Chapter 4 that because neurons can generate only a limited number of action potentials per second, sensory systems must continually adjust their overall range of operation to provide subjects with information about the energy levels of, say, light, where those energy levels pertinent to humans span many or-

ders of magnitude. The Weber fraction thus provides an approximate measure of the *gain* of a sensory system under specified conditions.

Another psychophysical approach is called *magnitude scaling* and entails ordering percepts along an ordinal scale that covers the full range of some perceptual quality (brightness, for instance; see figure) The most extensive studies of this sort were carried out by the Harvard psychologist Stanley Stevens, who worked on this issue from about 1950 until 1975. To take a particular example, Stevens asked whether a light stimulus that is made progressively more intense elicits perceptions of brightness that linearly track the physical intensity. In making such determinations, Stevens simply

asked subjects to rate the relative intensities of a series of test stimuli on a number scale along which 0 represented the least intense stimulus and 100 the most intense (similar in principle to the common practice of rating pain on a scale of 1 to 10). In this manner, he determined that brightness scales as a *power function* with an exponent of approximately 0.5 under the standard conditions he used (Figure B). The power functions exhibited in such magnitude-scaling experiments are sometimes referred to as reflecting *Stevens's law*. Many people took these efforts to be misguided because of their obvious subjectivity, but data obtained using Stevens's law have been surprisingly useful. At the very least, rationalizing Stevens's results presents another challenge to theories seeking to explain the how visual and other sensory systems generate the percepts they do.

Finally, another staple of psychophysics entails measurements of *reaction time*. A logical assumption is that the more complex the neural processing entailed in performing a given task, the longer it will take to perform the task (Figure C). This simple paradigm is the basis of many studies in later chapters.

(C)

(C) A typical reaction-time task. Reaching a judgment about whether or not the object on the left is the same as the object on the right is a function of task difficulty; people make this judgment more quickly for objects that are closer to the same orientation in space (above) than for ones that are differently oriented (below).

Reference

STEVENS, S. S. (1975) *Psychophysics*. New York: John Wiley.

The percepts elicited by other stimulus patterns, however, undermine the idea that simultaneous brightness contrast effects are an incidental consequence of an anomalous retinal output in response to edges. In the pattern in **Figure 5.6**, for example, the target patches on the left are surrounded by a greater area of *higher* luminance (lighter) territory than lower luminance, and yet appear brighter than the targets on the right, which are surrounded by more *lower* luminance (darker) territory than higher. Although the average luminance values of the surrounds in Figure 5.6 are effectively opposite those in standard simultaneous brightness stimulus shown in Figure 5.4A, the brightness differences elicited are about the same in both direction and magnitude as in the standard presentation.

If the output of retinal neurons can't account for the relative brightness values seen in response to stimuli such as the simple patterns in Figures 5.4 and 5.6, what then *is* the explanation? An important clue is that the meaning

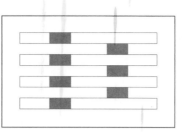

Figure 5.6 White's illusion.
This stimulus pattern elicits perceptual effects that cannot be explained in terms of sort of interactions arising from local contrast effects illustrated in Figure 5.5. The pattern and its perceptual consequences are called "White's illusion" after the psychologist who first described this stimulus more than 30 years ago. (After White 1979.)

of the luminance value in any part of a retinal image is uncertain in natural circumstances. An object's luminance is determined by three aspects of the physical world: the **illumination** of the object, the **reflectance** of the object's surfaces, and the **transmittance** of the space between the object and the observer. As indicated in **Figure 5.7**, these factors are inevitably conflated in the retinal image; thus an infinite number of different combinations of illumination, reflectance, and transmittance can give rise to the same value of luminance. There is no logical or direct way in which the visual system can determine how these three factors are in fact combined to generate a particular retinal luminance value (see also Box 5B). Since appropriate behavior requires responses that accord with the *physical source* of a stimulus, this uncertainty means that making brightness percepts directly proportional to

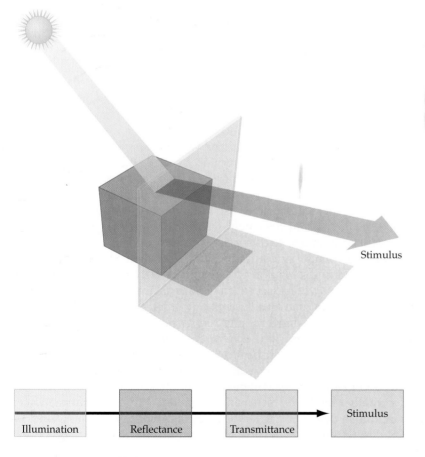

Figure 5.7 Conflation of illumination, reflectance, and transmittance in a light stimulus. An observer must parse these three factors—which the stimulus inevitably conflates—in order to respond appropriately to the pattern of luminance values in any visual stimulus.

luminance values in a stimulus would not provide a useful guide to success-ful behavior.

A more biologically useful approach to effectively perceiving brightness would be to determine the percepts empirically, according to past experience of success or failure in interacting with the different combinations of illumination, reflectance, and transmittance in natural scenes. In this framework, brightness should always correspond to the relative frequency with which different possible combinations have proved to be the source of the same or similar stimuli in the enormous number of visual scenes witnessed during the course of evolution, as well as by individual observers during their lifetimes. This general idea harks back to the nineteenth century, to visual scientist and polymath Hermann Helmholtz's suggestion that empirical information might be needed to augment what he took to be the more or less *veridical* ("true to life") information supplied by sensory mechanisms.

However, because retinal and other sensory receptors can't provide unambiguous information about the state of the world, the more radical idea now being examined by cognitive neuroscientists is that vision depends on a fundamentally statistical processing strategy. In this conception, the brightness values seen by an observer should accord with the empirical significance of the stimulus (i.e., what its behavioral significance has been in past experience), rather than with the physical intensities of light falling on the retina. The biological rationale for this way of seeing brightness is that by using the outcome of visual experiences accumulated both *phylogenetically* (as a species over evolutionary history) and *ontogenetically* (over the development and life of an individual), percepts—and, more importantly, visually guided behaviors—come to have an increasingly better chance of dealing successfully with the real-world sources of retinal images that are inherently ambiguous. Put another way, what *works* as a percept in eliciting a successful response to a given stimulus determines what we perceive. In fact, many peculiarities of brightness, including the percepts elicited by the stimuli in Figures 5.4 and 5.6, can be explained in this way.

The central processing of luminance

How and where in the central nervous system perceptions of brightness are generated is not yet understood. No cortical region appears to be specifically concerned with processing the luminance of stimuli in the way that some neurons in the general area of V4 are concerned with processing color, or neurons in the area of MT+ concerned with motion. Indeed, the close relationship between light intensity and the firing rate of retinal ganglion cells diminishes as neurons are tested in more central stations of the visual system. Although cells in the lateral geniculate nucleus respond in more or less the same way to intensity as retinal ganglion cells, neurons in the primary visual cortex and beyond respond only weakly to changes in stimulus intensity as such.

The observations made by neurophysiologists David Hubel and Torsten Wiesel working at Harvard Medical School in the 1960s showed that what central neurons care about with respect to luminance is not the intensity of a light stimulus, but the *contrast* between light and dark regions in the stimulus (see Figure 5.5). Thus central neurons are more concerned with the configuration of the stimuli encountered in nature—such as light/dark **edges**—than with illumination levels per se and, as described in Chapter 4, central responses become even more selective in higher-order extrastriate regions. This characteristic shift in selectivity accords with other evidence that central sensory neurons, whether in vision or another modality, increasingly combine empirical information to represent in human perception real-world objects whose properties cannot be appreciated directly simply by reporting image features such as luminance.

The Perception of Color

Recall that brightness is defined as the perceptual category elicited by the *overall amount* of light in a visual stimulus. **Color** is the perceptual category generated by the *distribution* of that amount of light across the visible spectrum—that is, the relative amount of light energy at short, middle, and long wavelengths in a given stimulus (**Figure 5.8A**).

The experience of color comprises three perceptual qualities:

■ **Hue,** which is the perception of the relative redness, blueness, greenness, or yellowness of a stimulus.

■ **Saturation,** which is the degree to which the percept approaches a neutral gray (e.g., a highly unsaturated red will appear gray, although with an appreciable reddish tinge).

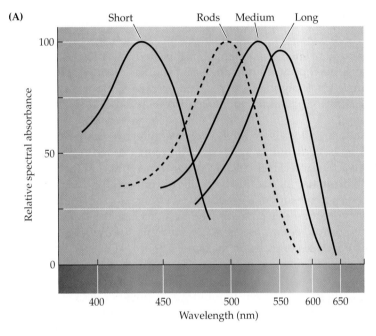

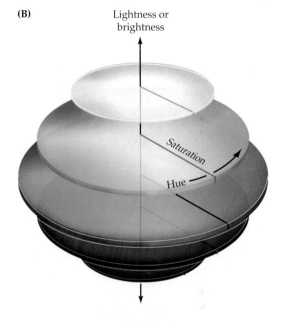

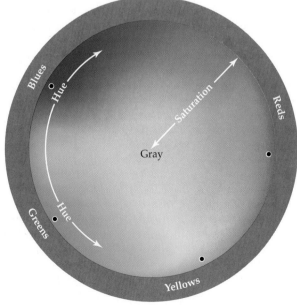

Figure 5.8 Color percepts.   (A) The solid curves indicate the absorption properties of the three cone types in the human retina, showing their differential sensitivity to short-, medium-, and long-wavelength light (the dashed curve shows rod absorption properties). (B) Perceptual "color space" for humans. At any particular level of light intensity (which evokes a sensation of *color brightness*), movements around the perimeter of the relevant plane, or "color circle," correspond to changes in *hue* (i.e., changes in the apparent contribution of red, green, blue, or yellow to the percept). Movements along the radial axis correspond to changes in *saturation* (i.e., changes in the approximation of the color to the perception of a neutral gray). Each of the four primary color categories (red, green, blue, and yellow) is characterized by a *unique hue* (indicated by dots) that has no apparent admixture of the other three (i.e., a color experience that cannot be seen or imagined as a mixture of any other colors). These four colors are considered *primary* due to their perceptual uniqueness, which has nothing to with "primary" paint colors talked about in art classes.

■ **Color brightness,** which is the perceptual category described in the previous section, but applied to a stimulus that elicits a discernible hue.

Taken together these three qualities describe a perceptual **color space** (**Figure 5.8B**). The ability to see colors has evolved in humans and many other mammals, presumably because perceiving spectral differences allows an observer to distinguish surfaces in the natural world more effectively than distinctions made solely on the basis of luminance.

The initiation of color vision

We see little or no color in dim light, a circumstance in which vision is predominantly mediated by rod photoreceptors. This is because all rod cells contain a single photopigment (*rhodopsin*), whereas each of three different cone types has a distinct photopigment (called a *cone opsin*). Each of these cone types has a different absorption spectrum, and thus responds best to a different portion of the visible light spectrum (roughly speaking, to long, middle, and short wavelengths, respectively; see Figure 5.8A). The different responsiveness of the three cone types thus allows cone cells to report information about the distribution of energy in a light stimulus, and this information eventually leads to our perception of hue and saturation as well as color brightness. With its single photopigment, the rod system can only report the overall amount of light captured and thus can generate only information pertinent to brightness.

The fact that human color vision is based on the different sensitivity of three cone types makes us **trichromats**; color vision in most other mammals that have significant color vision is based on only two cone types, and they are thus referred to as **dichromats**. A common disorder of human color perception is *anomalous color vision,* the result of a genetic defect in one (or sometimes more) of the three cone types, effectively creating human dichromats. The most common form of this sort of "color blindness" is deficiency of a single cone type and affects about 5 percent of males in the United States. The defective gene is located on the X chromosome, which explains the overwhelming preponderance of males among those with anomolous color vision. Although such individuals cannot distinguish between red and green hues (or, less commonly, between blue and yellow), for most this inability presents little practical difficulty in daily life. A far more severe but fortunately rare inherited defect entails the complete absence of cones, resulting not only in the loss of color vision but in a variety of other visual problems that result in extreme light sensitivity and very poor overall vision (as might be expected from the dependence of high-acuity central vision on foveal cones; see Figure 4.5A).

Central color processing

While successfully accounting for many aspects of color perception in the laboratory, explanations of color vision based on retinal output from the three human cone types have long been recognized to be inadequate, in much the same way that retinal output determined by luminance does not adequately explain the brightness values that people see. Indeed, as far back as the nineteenth century, Helmholtz's contemporary Ewald Hering pointed out that some aspects of color perception cannot be fully understood merely on the basis of three cone types. For example, humans with normal color vision perceive red to be an **opponent color** to green and blue to be an opponent color to yellow. Thus Hering emphasized that while observers can see and/or imagine a gradual transition from red to yellow through a series of intermediate colors (i.e., shades of orange), there is no parallel perception—or conception—of how to get from red to green or from blue to yellow, except through gray or through one of the other primary colors. Presumably as a corollary of these facts, humans perceive a particular hue of red, green, blue, or yellow to be *unique* in the sense of not being a mixture of any other colors (in contrast to seeing orange as a mixture of red and yellow, or purple as a mixture of blue and red; see Figure 5.8B). Since simply having three cone types offers no explanation of these perceptual phenomena, Hering argued correctly that the comparisons made by the three cone types provides only a partial account of the colors we end up seeing and therefore of how color sensations are generated. Clearly, central visual processing modulates the information generated by the retina to determine color percepts, just as central processing modulates luminance information to generate brightness.

The neural basis of opponent color percepts has been much advanced by modern electrophysiological studies of wavelength-sensitive neurons at different stations of the visual system in non-human primates and other experimental animals with color vision. The majority of color-sensitive neurons in the retina and the lateral geniculate nucleus of the thalamus have receptive fields that are organized in a color-opponent fashion. Such cells are excited by light of one wavelength (say, long wavelength or "red light") illuminating the center of their receptive field, and are inhibited (or "opposed") by another wavelength (such as middle wavelength or "green light") falling in the region surrounding the center of the receptive field. In macaque monkeys, which have color vision nearly identical to that of humans, most (but not all) color-opponent cells are antagonistic with respect to wavelengths that appear either red and green or blue and yellow.

In addition to red–green and blue–yellow classes of opponent cells, other neurons are insensitive to differences in wavelength. These cells are considered *white–black opponent* neurons. Thus the explanation usually given for the perceptual phenomena that Hering first noted is that perceptions of color are elicited by neurons comprising three color "channels" that operate in a push–pull fashion: when the neurons responsible for seeing red are excited, those responsible for green are inhibited, and vice versa. Even though the details and consequences of opponent color processing are not yet understood, Hering was clearly correct in surmising that color percepts arise from processing at higher levels in the brain and not just from the presence of three cone cell types.

Additional information about central color processing has come from other studies in non-human primates carried out preeminently by Semir Zeki and his colleagues at University College London. This work and related studies have suggested that area V4 (see Figure 5.3) is especially important in color processing. Particularly revealing have been neuropsychological and imaging studies of individuals suffering from a condition called **cerebral achromatopsia**. In effect, such individuals lose the ability to see the world in color, although other aspects of vision, such as brightness and form, remain intact. A striking example of cerebral achromatopsia has been presented by the neurologist and essayist Oliver Sacks. The case concerns an artist who described objects in visual scenes as all being "dirty" shades of gray. When asked to draw from memory, the patient had no difficulty reproducing relevant shapes or shading, but he was unable to appropriately color the objects he represented.

Patients with achromatopsia typically have damage to the extrastriate visual areas, with damage in the general area of V4 being the common denominator. As in any brain lesion study, however, some caution is warranted because of the great variability of cortical damage and uncertainty about the extent of neurological damage. A meta-analysis of a large number of cases of cerebral achromatopsia in the literature, carried out by Seth Bouvier and Stephen Engel at UCLA, shows that damage over a extensive region of the ventral

(A)

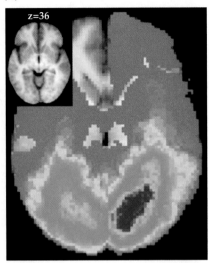

(B)

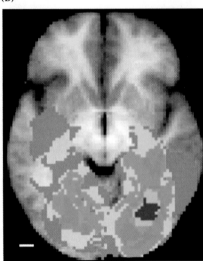

Figure 5.9 Damage to the ventral extrastriate occipital cortex affects color vision. A person with brain damage in this region (which includes visual cortical area V4) is often unable to perceive color (achromatopsia) despite being able to see brightness and form more or less normally. (A) Degree of overlap in the location of lesions in a series of 46 patients with achromatopsia who also had other cognitive problems, such as difficulty in face recognition. Given the anatomy of the primary visual pathway (see Figure 5.1), such patients are often blind to stimuli of any sort in the contralateral visual field. (B) Degree of overlap in 11 patients in this series with achromatopsia as the primary symptom. The narrower overlap in these patients is consistent with the conclusion that the integrity of the cortex in the general vicinity of V4 is important for some aspects of color vision. The inset shows the level of the horizontal sections shown. (From Bouvier and Engel 2006.)

Percent overlap

occipital cortex that included V4 could give rise to this condition, and that the region of injury typically affected other visual and cognitive functions (**Figure 5.9**). They concluded that, whereas V4 seems important to color vision, a number of related extrastriate areas probably participate in generating color percepts. Further support for the conclusion that V4 and surrounding regions of the extrastriate visual cortex are concerned with color processing comes from functional imaging studies in normal subjects, which show activation of these same regions when subjects undertake color processing tasks. Nonetheless, it is clearly not the case that V4 is simply a color processing area; neurons in this region respond to many other stimulus characteristics, and the function of V4 remains controversial.

Color contrast and constancy

Like our perceptions of brightness, the colors we see are strongly influenced by context. For example, a stimulus patch generating exactly the *same* distribution of light energy at various wavelengths can appear quite different in color depending on its surroundings, a phenomenon called **color contrast.** Conversely, patches in a scene returning *different* spectra to the eye can appear to be much the same color, an effect called **color constancy** (**Figure 5.10**). Although these phenomena were well known to psychologists and vision scientists in the late nineteenth and early twentieth centuries, they were not paid much attention until Edwin Land's work in the late 1950s. Land—an independent photochemist who among other achievements invented polarizing filters, instant photography, and founded the Polaroid Corporation—used three adjustable lights (generating short-, middle-, and long-wavelength light, respectively) to illuminate a collage of colored papers. Using three spectrophotometers, he showed that two patches that in white light appeared to be different colors (e. g., green and brown) continued to elicit these color percepts even when the three illuminators were adjusted so that the light being returned from the "green" surfaces produced exactly the same wavelength readings on the three spectrophotometers that had previously come from the "brown" surface—a striking demonstration of color constancy.

Color contrast and constancy effects present much the same problem for understanding color processing as do the contextual brightness effects described earlier. Together, these phenomena have led to a debate about brightness and color percepts that has lasted for more than a century. The key issue is how global information about the spectral context in scenes is integrated with local spectral information to produce color percepts. Land tried to explain such effects by postulating a series of algorithms that integrated the spectral returns of different regions over the entire scene (the implication being that color pro-

Figure 5.10 Color contrast and color constancy. (A) The four blue patches on the top surface of the cube in the left panel and the seven yellow patches on the cube in the right panel are actually identical gray patches. In this demonstration of *color contrast,* these identical stimulus patches are made to appear either blue or yellow by changing the spectral context in which they occur. (B) Patches that have very different spectra (see the different-colored patches on the left and right in the lower key) can be made to look more or less the same color (in this case, red) by contextual information, a phenomenon that demonstrates *color constancy.* (From Purves and Lotto 2003.)

(A)

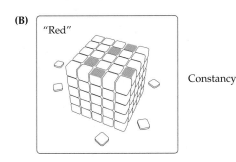

Contrast

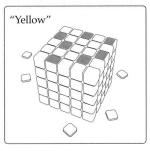

(B)

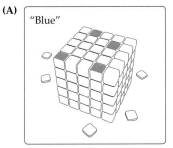

Constancy

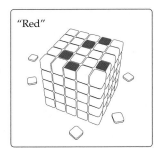

cessing in the visual system implemented these algorithms). It was recognized even before Land's death in 1991, however, that this so-called "retinex theory" did not hold true in all circumstances, and was in any event a description, not an explanation. Other vision scientists have emphasized the opponent receptive field properties of central neurons, **double opponent cells** in particular, as a possible neural substrate for such effects. Double opponent cells are neurons in which the activity of the surround is inhibited by activation of the receptive field center, and vice versa. Still other investigators have provided evidence that, like achromatic brightness, perceptions of hue, saturation and color brightness are generated according to the empirical significance of spectral stimuli in past experience. There is as yet no consensus about how central visual processing integrates local and global spectral information to produce the remarkable phenomenology of color perception.

The Perception of Form

A third fundamental quality of visual perception is **form**. In the simplest case, perceptions of form entail simple geometrical characteristics such as the length of lines, their apparent orientation, and the angles they make as they intersect with other lines. Understanding such stimuli is a first step in understanding how object shapes are perceived.

Seeing simple geometries

A starting point in exploring how the visual system generates perceptions of form is examining how we perceive the distance between two points in a visual stimulus, as in the perceived length of a line, or the dimensions (size) of a simple geometrical shape. It is logical to suppose that the perception of a line drawn on a piece of paper or on a computer screen should correspond more or less directly to the length we see. But, as in the case of brightness and color, perceptions of form do not correspond to physical reality.

A well-studied example of this discrepancy is the variation in the perceived length of a line as a function of its orientation (**Figure 5.11A**). As investigators have repeatedly shown over the last 150 years, a line oriented more or less vertically in the retinal image appears to be significantly longer than a horizontal line of exactly the same length—the maximum length being perceived, oddly enough, when the stimulus is oriented about 30° from vertical (**Figure 5.11B**). This effect is evidently a particular manifestation of a general tendency to perceive the extent of any spatial interval differently as a function of its orientation in the retinal image. For instance, as the psychologist Wilhelm Wundt first showed in 1862, the apparent distance between a pair of dots varies systematically with the orientation of an imaginary line between them, and a perfect square or circle appears to be slightly elongated along its vertical axis.

There is a rich literature on other perceptual distortions (or, as they are sometimes called, "geometrical illusions") elicited by simple stimuli, showing in each case that measurements made with instruments like rulers or protractors are often at odds with the corresponding percepts. Some of the most familiar geometrical illusions—and the ones whose etiology has been most hotly debated—are illustrated in **Figure 5.12**. Several of the stimuli shown in the figure are size contrast stimuli, similar in principle to brightness and color contrast stimuli: the same physical stimulus appears different when placed in different contexts.

Neural processing of form

Recall that all sensory neurons have receptive fields defined by their electrophysiological responses to stimuli; in vision, these stimuli are retinal images. Thus many vision scientists have been attracted to the idea that the neural activity of cells in visual cortex that respond to, for example, particular lengths or orientations leads directly to the perception of such features. As explained in

Figure 5.11 Variation in apparent line length as a function of its orientation. (A) The horizontal line in this figure looks significantly shorter than the vertical or oblique lines, despite the fact that all the lines are identical in length. (B) Quantitative assessment of the apparent length of a line reported by subjects as a function of its orientation in the retinal image (orientation is expressed as the angle between the line and the horizontal axis, 90° being vertical and 180° being horizontal). The maximum length seen by observers occurs when the line is oriented approximately 30° from vertical, at which point it appears 10–15 percent longer than the minimum length seen when the stimulus is horizontal. (In this graph the reference is the apparent length of the line when horizontal, which is plotted as 1.00.) (After Howe and Purves 2005.)

(A)

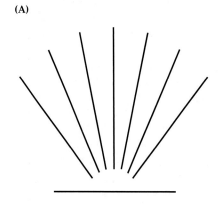

(B)

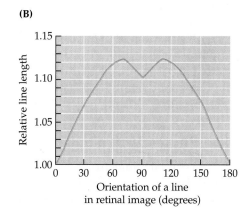

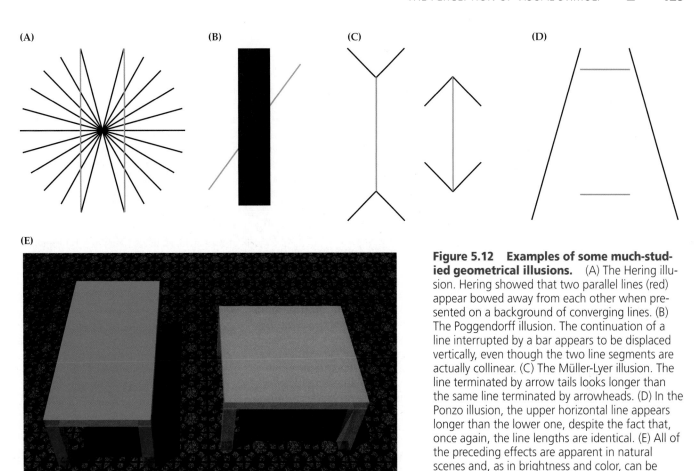

Figure 5.12 Examples of some much-studied geometrical illusions. (A) The Hering illusion. Hering showed that two parallel lines (red) appear bowed away from each other when presented on a background of converging lines. (B) The Poggendorff illusion. The continuation of a line interrupted by a bar appears to be displaced vertically, even though the two line segments are actually collinear. (C) The Müller-Lyer illusion. The line terminated by arrow tails looks longer than the same line terminated by arrowheads. (D) In the Ponzo illusion, the upper horizontal line appears longer than the lower one, despite the fact that, once again, the line lengths are identical. (E) All of the preceding effects are apparent in natural scenes and, as in brightness and color, can be enhanced by more complex contextual information. The table top illusion initially created by Stanford psychologist Roger Shepard is a good example. The two table tops are actually identical, as is apparent when the right top is rotated 90° (see inset). (After Purves and Lotto 2003.)

Chapter 4, however, there are a number of problems with this intuitively attractive view. The major obstacle is the uncertain relationship between retinal image features such as length and orientation and the length and orientation of objects in the real world (**Box 5B**). Given this "inverse problem," it seems unlikely that the receptive field properties relevant to form are engaged in a processing strategy whose aim is to produce veridical representations of image features. On the contrary, as described earlier, their contribution seems more likely to be directed to making an empirical link between inevitably ambiguous images and their underlying sources as a means of generating successful behavior. Studies that have used laser-scanning techniques to measure the geometry of scenes suggest that this may indeed be the case. Many of the classical geometrical illusions shown in Figure 5.12, for instance, can be explained in terms of the statistical distribution of the sources of such geometries in the natural scenes that humans have always been exposed to, consistent with empirical explanations of the generation of brightness and color percepts.

■ BOX 5B The Inverse Problem

A fundamental problem in understanding perception in any sensory modality is the indirect relationship between human perceptions and the physical world. The challenge presented by this relationship is especially evident in vision, where it was recognized as early as the start of the eighteenth century. The problem in this case is that images on the retina cannot, by their nature, uniquely specify the physical objects in a scene. Physical objects are of course three-dimensional, and what we see appears to be three-dimensional. But the retinal image is only *two*-dimensional. As a result of image projection, the actual size and arrangement of objects in real-world space cannot be specified by the retinal projection, and this information cannot be deduced by any logical operation on the image as such (see figure). The physical properties underlying the perceptual qualities of brightness, color, and form are, for these reasons, incapable of being specified by the information in the retinal image. This quandary in vision is referred to as the *inverse optics problem*, and a key question in visual perception is how the visual system solves it.

Beginning with the work of the brilliant physiologist and physicist Hermann von Helmholtz in the latter part of the nineteenth century, many vision scientists have supposed that the strategy for solving the inverse problem in perception is to make sensory systems depend in some degree on empirical information (i.e., information about the meaning of ambiguous stimuli based on past experience with what

the same or similar stimuli meant). In this way, Helmholtz proposed that the visual system might "disambiguate" images by an empirical boost that would help out their "interpretation." Only recently have vision scientists and others considered the possibility that percepts might be generated *entirely* on the basis of the empirical success or failure of visual experience in the pasts of both the species and the individual. If this scenario were true, then the purpose of visual processing would essentially be to determine relative probabilities of the possible sources of inherently uncertain stimuli rather than representing the "features" in the retinal projection.

As a result of these very different concepts of vision—seeing the "real world" by directly detecting its features versus seeing probable stimulus sources based on statistical evidence—there is considerable debate at present about what visual processing is actually doing and how best to interpret the wealth of information about the anatomy and physiology of visual neurons that modern neuroscience has provided over the last 50 years. One camp supposes that the way of resolving this debate in vision science is to continue obtaining more information about the receptive field properties of visual neurons, with the expectation that sooner or later it should be apparent how these properties give rise to visual perception. Another camp has tended to focus on visual percepts as such, asking whether what people actually see can tell us about the strategy of visual processing. In fact, both approaches make sense and will eventu-

ally need to come together to understand how percepts are generated. The central question in this prospective union is how the "nuts and bolts" of visual processing in the human brain instantiate the empirical probabilities that are needed to solve the inverse problem.

References

BERKELEY, G. (1709) *A New Theory of Vision*. Everyman's Library Edition, 1976.

HOWE, C. Q., R. B. LOTTO AND D. PURVES (2006) Empirical approaches to understanding visual perception. *J. Theor. Biol.* 241: 866–875.

KERSTEN, D. (2000) High-level vision as statistical inference. In *The New Cognitive Neurosciences*, M. S. Gazzaniga (ed.). Cambridge, MA: MIT Press, pp. 353–363.

MALONEY, L. T. (2002) Statistical decision theory and biological vision. In *Perception and the Physical World: Psychological and Philosophical Issues in Perception*, D. Heyer and R. Mausfeld (eds.). New York: John Wiley, pp. 145–189.

PURVES, D. AND R. B. LOTTO (2003) *Why We See What We Do: An Empirical Theory of Vision*. Sunderland, MA: Sinauer.

RAO, R. P. N., B. A. OLSHAUSEN AND M. S. LEWICKI, EDS. (2002) *Probabilistic Models of the Brain: Perception and Neural Function*. Cambridge, MA: MIT Press.

VON HELMHOLTZ, H. L. F. (1866) *Helmholtz's Treatise on Physiological Optics*. The Optical Society of America. Reprinted 1924.

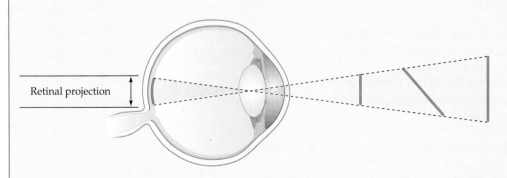

Retinal projection

The inverse optics problem. The inherent ambiguity of retinal stimuli is illustrated here in terms of the perception of objects in space. The same linear projection on the retina can derive from an infinite number of linear objects at different distances, of different sizes, and in different spatial orientations. As a result, a retinal image cannot specify its physical source. (See also Figure 5.7.)

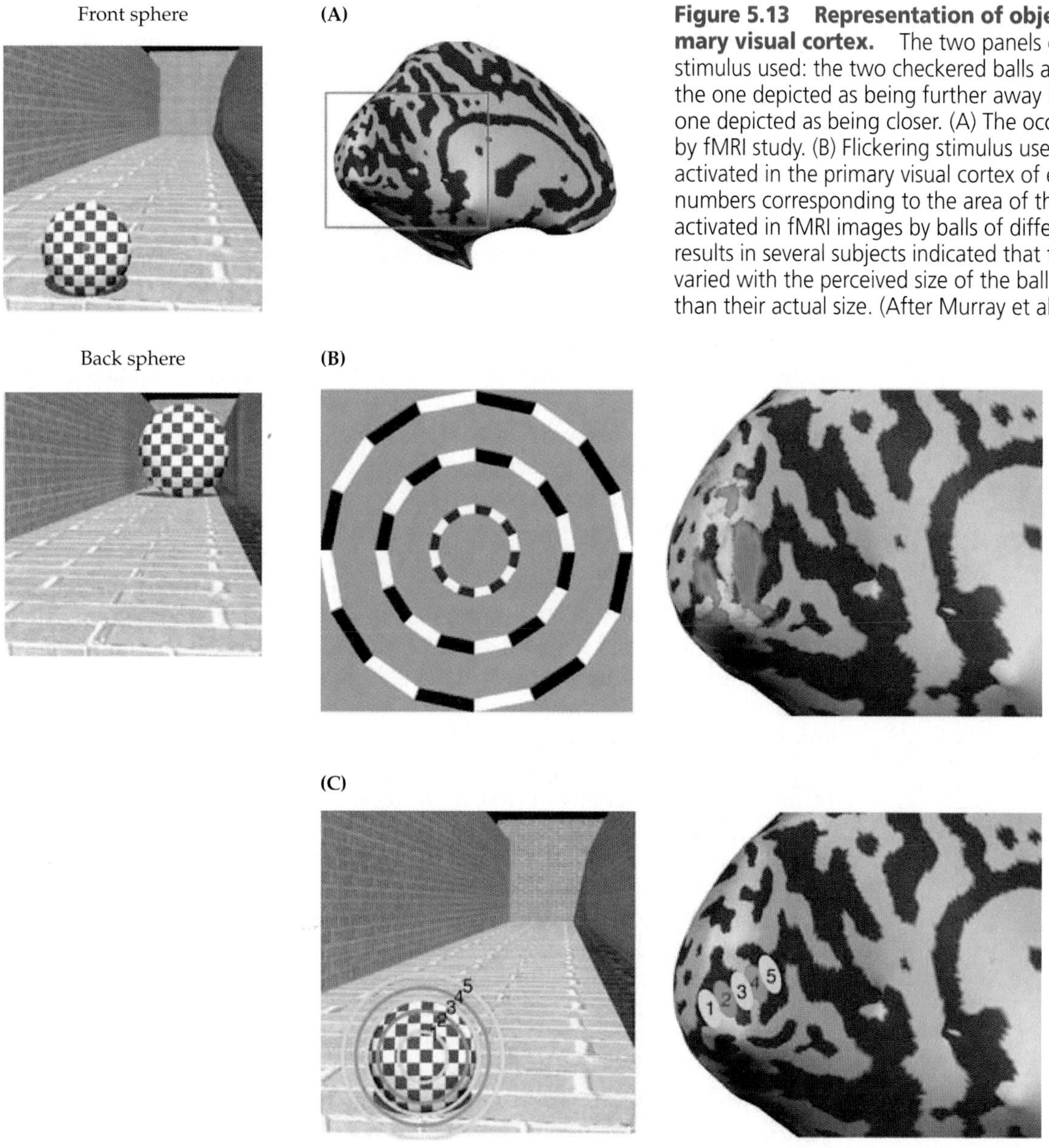

Front sphere

(A)

Back sphere

(B)

(C)

Figure 5.13 Representation of object size in the primary visual cortex.   The two panels on the left show the stimulus used: the two checkered balls are the same size, but the one depicted as being further away looks larger than the one depicted as being closer. (A) The occipital region examined by fMRI study. (B) Flickering stimulus used to define the region activated in the primary visual cortex of each subject. (C) The numbers corresponding to the area of the primary visual cortex activated in fMRI images by balls of different actual sizes. The results in several subjects indicated that the active region in V1 varied with the perceived size of the balls in the stimulus rather than their actual size. (After Murray et al. 2006.)

Recent observations made by Daniel Kersten and his colleagues at the University of Minnesota provide some insight into how the visual cortex may be dealing with the perception of size, using a classical size contrast stimulus (**Figure 5.13**). The investigators took advantage of the retinotopic organization of the primary visual cortex and used functional MRI to ask whether the area activated by a stimulus of a particular size corresponded to the *actual size* of the object in the retinal image or to its *perceived size*. Consistent with the idea that percepts do not derive from a direct representation of image features, the active area in V1 tracked perceived rather than actual size.

The Perception of Depth

A fourth basic quality of vision is the perception of depth; that is, the perception of a three-dimensional world from two-dimensional retinal images. Some aspects of depth are derived from information in the view of one eye alone, whereas another aspect is apparent only when both eyes are used. Thus depth perception is usually discussed in terms of **monocular** and **binocular** components.

Monocular depth perception

Monocular depth perception (the sense of three-dimensionality when looking at the world with one eye closed) is presumably learned—that is, it must largely derive from an individual's experience with the arrangement of objects in space. The most obvious fact we learn from such experience is the significance of **occlusion**: when a part of one object is obscured by another, then the obstructing object is always closer to the observer than is the obstructed object. Another universal experience pertinent to depth is the **relationship of size and distance**: as a result of projection onto an image plane, the same object occupies progressively less space on the retina the further away it is, thus providing additional information about depth (and defining *perspective*). Additional monocular depth comes from **motion parallax**. When the position of the observer changes (by moving the head from side to side, for instance), the position of the background with respect to an object in the foreground changes more for nearby objects than for distant ones. Finally, the fainter and fuzzier appearance of distant objects as a result of the Earth's atmosphere—referred to as **aerial perspective**—provides a further empirical indication of how far way things are. Moreover, because the atmosphere absorbs more long- than short-wavelength light (the interposed medium is effectively "sky"), distant objects look bluer compared to the same object's appearance when nearby, a fact landscape artists understand well.

That monocular information about depth is largely learned accords with the fact that infants do not at first appreciate depth (see Chapter 27). All of us gradually discover through experience that more distant objects are often occluded, are smaller in appearance, tend to change position less with respect to the background when we move, and look fainter, fuzzier, and bluer. Since we are only dimly aware of these issues (if aware at all), it follows that the incorporation of this sort of information is unconscious, in keeping with the general idea that percepts are continually shaped by feedback from "behaviors that work."

Binocular depth perception

A quite different sort of information about the arrangement of objects in space is available when scenes are viewed with both eyes. Binocular information about depth is called **stereopsis** and arises from the fact that the eyes are separated horizontally across the face by an average distance of 65 mm in adult humans; as a result, each eye has a slightly different view of the same nearby objects (**Figure 5.14A**). This difference in the two images is called **retinal disparity**. The behavioral significance of stereo vision can be appreciated by bringing the points of two pencils together from your left and right, respectively. Compare the difficulty of this task when using both eyes to when you try it with one eye closed. Making the tips of the pencils touch (to say nothing of performing more consequential tasks) is much easier in binocular view. Other animals with eyes in the front of their heads enjoy the same advantage in depth perception, and most mammals have some stereoscopic ability in the region of binocular overlap. Human binocular overlap, however, is about 140°, whereas wall-eyed animals like horses have only about 15° of overlap.

As the English physicist and vision scientist Charles Wheatstone showed with his invention of the **stereoscope** in the 1830s, the greater behavioral success with both eyes open in this and other tasks involving manipulation—and

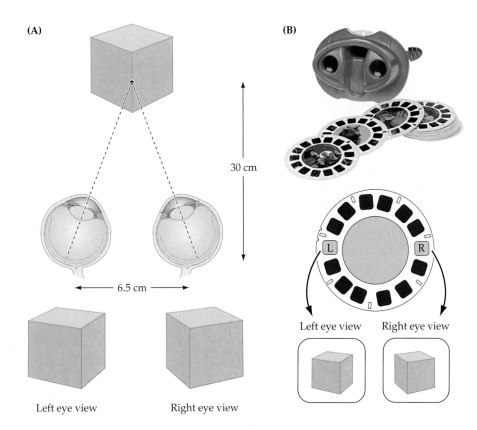

(A)

30 cm

6.5 cm

Left eye view

Right eye view

(B)

L R

Left eye view   Right eye view

Figure 5.14 The different views of the two eyes. (A) Viewing any nearby object with one eye and then the other makes the difference in the views of the two eyes obvious. (B) The consequences for generating sensations of depth can be demonstrated with a stereoscope. If two pictures of a scene are taken from slightly different angles, looking at the two-dimensional images binocularly produces a strong sensation of depth that is not present when the same images are viewed with one eye or the other, or identical images observed with both eyes.

the corresponding enrichment in the perceptual sense of depth—arises from a "fusion" in visual perception of the somewhat different views of the two eyes (**Figure 5.14B**; see also Box 5C). Wheatstone also pointed out that stereoscopic information is limited to viewing objects relatively close to the observer. The differences in the views of the right and the left eyes illustrated in Figure 5.14A decrease progressively as the lines of sight of the two eyes become increasingly parallel, causing the binocular disparity of objects in the image plane to eventually fall below the resolving power of the visual system. For all practical purposes, then, stereopsis adds little to the success of visually guided behavior for objects more than a few meters away, and presumably evolved because of its advantages in near tasks such as manipulation.

Binocular neural processing

The fact that stereopsis depends on retinal disparity implies that the visual system must in some way compare the loci on the two retinas that are stimulated by light rays arising from the same point in visual space. This idea is supported by the fact that many neurons in both the primary and extrastriate visual cortex of experimental animals have receptive fields that are "tuned" to specific disparities (**Figure 5.15**).

This evidence, together with the knowledge that stereopsis can be elicited by random dot stereograms (**Box 5C**) suggests that stereopsis is generated by neural computations of the disparity at corresponding retinal points. Although this explanation is eminently logical, understanding how the nervous system implements the postulated comparison of a stereo pair has been a difficult challenge. There is as yet no agreement about an algorithm that could accomplish this feat. Nor is it agreed whether this interpretation adequately explains two further aspects of binocular vision, cyclopean fusion and binocular rivalry.

Figure 5.15 Disparity tuning in visual cortical neurons. Electrophysiological recording of the activity of single neurons in cats and monkeys shows that many cells respond selectively to binocular stimuli that have different disparities, leading to the concept of "near" and "far" cells.

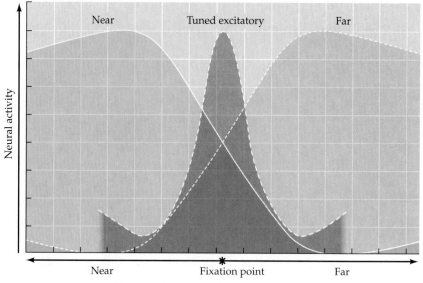

Although we normally view nearby objects with both eyes open—and thus process two appreciably different retinal images (see Figure 5.14A)—the perceived image of the nearby world is clearly a unified one (remember that for distant scenes the two retinal images are identical). Thus, what observers see in binocular view seems to have been generated by a single eye in the middle of the face, a subjective experience referred to as **cyclopean fusion**. This union of two quite different monocular views into a coherent cyclopean percept is taken for granted. Yet, like many other aspects of vision, it presents a deep puzzle: how are the two independent views of any nearby scene conjoined to create a single percept having qualities (including stereoscopic depth) that are not present in the view of either eye alone?

Most explanations of this puzzle depend on the fact that inputs from the two eyes converge on cortical neurons in the primary visual cortex (**Figure 5.16**). Although the inputs from the right and left eyes are kept apart in the thalamus and in cortical layer 4 (which receives the afferents from the lateral geniculate nucleus; see Chapter 4), many neurons in the deeper and more superficial cortical layers in the primary visual cortex of non-human primates (and presumably humans) are *binocularly* driven. The prevalence of binocular cells in the primate visual cortex thus suggests that cyclopean vision arises from this demonstrable conjunction of right and left eye inputs at the level of common target cells in the visual cortex.

Despite this attractive anatomical and physiological substrate for a perceptual union of the two monocular streams, the idea of "seeing" a cyclopean image by virtue of binocular neurons in the visual cortex, at least in any simple sense, is inconsistent with other evidence, the phenomenon of *binocular rivalry* in particular. **Binocular rivalry** refers to the fact that when a particular stimulus pattern (e.g., vertical stripes) is presented to one eye and a strongly discordant pattern (e.g., horizontal stripes) is presented to the other eye, the same region of visual space is perceived to be alternately occupied by vertical stripes or horizontal stripes, but rarely (and only transiently) by both (**Figure 5.17A**). If information from the two eyes were simply united in the visual cortex, the observer would presumably see some stable integration of vertical and horizontal stripes in response to such stimuli (a grid in the most simplistic interpretation). Moreover, work by Nikos Logothetis at the Max Planck Insti-

■ BOX 5C Random Dot Stereograms

Many studies of stereoscopic vision have made use of *random dot stereograms* (RDSs). In addition to their intrinsic interest, RDSs fascinate vision scientists because of basic issues they raise, in particular how locally random right and left eye information is put together by the brain. These intriguing stimuli were introduced about 50 years ago and adapted for experimental work in vision by the late psychologist Bela Julesz working at Bell Labs. Although the idea had been discovered some years earlier, the subject "took off" when Julesz showed how RDSs could be easily made and manipulated by a computer.

RDSs are essentially stereograms (see Figure 5.14B) of an object camouflaged so completely with respect to its background that the target can be seen *only* when the two monocular components of the random dot pair are viewed binocularly. Such stimuli thus eliminate all monocular depth cues (e.g., occlusion, perspective, motion parallax), and/or cognitive information (e.g., prior recognition of an object) that might surreptitiously affect neural processing specific to binocular

(Continued on next page)

Random dot stereograms and their construction. (A–C) Construction and perceptual result of shifting a set of random dots to the left in the view of the right eye. (D–F) Construction and perceptual result shifting a set of random dots to the left in the view of the left eye. The diagrams of the resulting percepts in (C) and (F) assume that the observer is fusing the images "divergently" (that is, by "looking through" the page or computer screen on which the stimuli are presented).

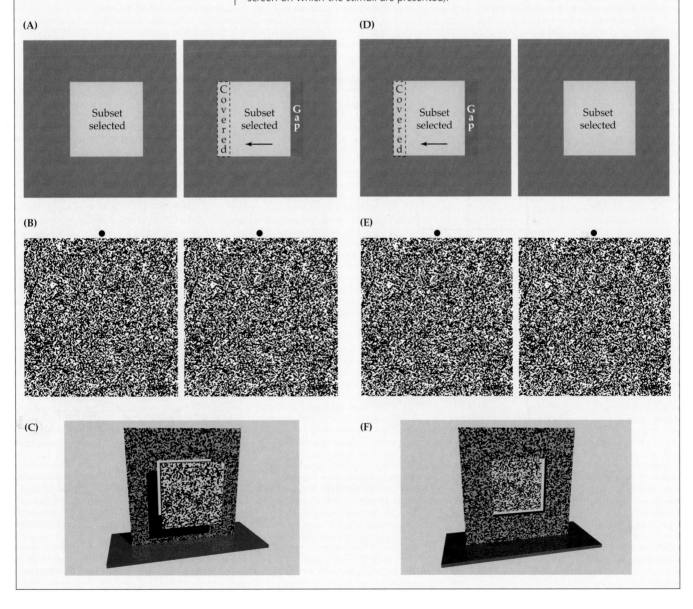

■ BOX 5C *(continued)*

depth perception. The accompanying figure shows how such stimuli are typically made. A target object (a square, in this case) within a field of randomly generated black and white "dots" (each comprising a few pixels on a computer screen) is selected and shifted a fraction of a degree over the background in the one member of the stereo pair; the corresponding set of dots in the view of the other eye remains in place. The gap created by the shifted set is then filled in with additional random dots; note also that another set on the other side of the shifted set has been "covered up" in this process. As a result of this manipula-

tion, the shifted square appears to be in front of or in back of the background array (depending on whether the shift was to the left or right) when the left and right random dot arrays are fused. Many people can, with a little practice, carry out such fusion by looking "through" the plane of the printed page. Alternatively, and perhaps more easily, the two components can be viewed in a stereoscope of the sort shown in Figure 5.14B, very inexpensive versions of which can be purchased on the Internet.

The perception of depth in response to an RDS is not as mysterious as it seems: the shifted pattern of dots

in the two eye views simply mimics what *would be seen* if an object in this spatial arrangement were perfectly camouflaged by the texture of the background; many natural situations approach this condition. The experience of looking at an RDS that lacks an obvious frame (as in the "autostereograms" found in popular books and posters of such stimuli) suggests that the visual system determines how to put the two eye views together by trial and error.

Reference

Julesz, B. (1995) *Dialogues on Perception.* Cambridge, MA: MIT Press.

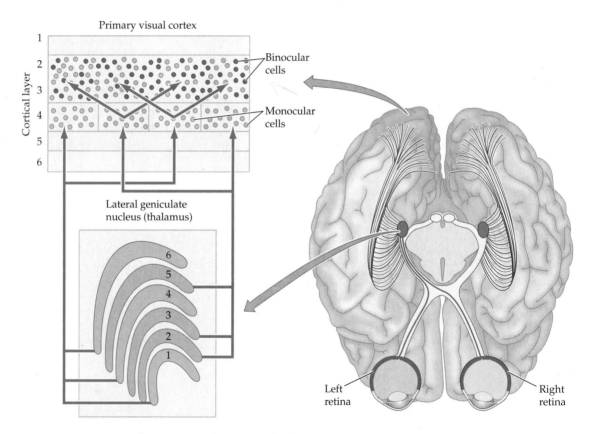

Figure 5.16   The anatomical conjunction of the two monocular streams of visual information.   Inputs related to the right and left eyes first come together in the primary visual cortex, where half or more of the neurons in rhesus monkeys can be activated by a stimulus presented to either the left or right eye. Note that the afferents related to the two eyes remain segregated at the level of the lateral geniculate nucleus in the thalamus and in the right eye/left eye cortical stripes in layer 4 that were described in Figure 4.13; binocularly driven cells are found above (and below; not shown) this thalamic input layer.

tute and Randolph Blake at Vanderbilt University has shown that it is not always the *images* on the two retinas that rival: at least in some circumstances, it is the percepts themselves that seem to be the source of the competition, consistent with the idea that cortical activity is more concerned with percepts than with image features (**Figure 5.17B**; see also Figure 5.13). As a result of this and other evidence, there has been no consensus about the basis of binocular fusion and rivalry; how the visual system processes and unites the views of the two eyes is not yet understood.

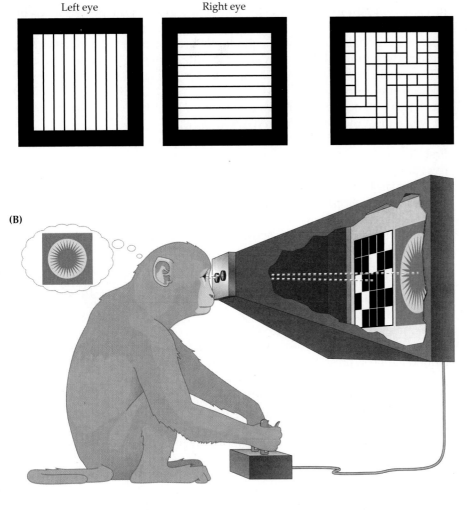

(A) Monocular stimuli   Binocular percept
Left eye   Right eye

(B)

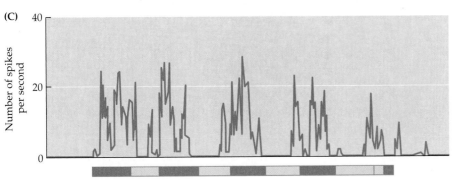

(C)

Number of spikes per second

40

20

0

Figure 5.17   Binocular rivalry.
(A) The perceptual phenomenon of binocular rivalry illustrated with vertical lines presented to the left eye and horizontal lines to the right eye. A grid pattern is not seen, indicating the views of the two eyes are not simply brought together in V1 by the activity of binocular neurons in the visual cortex. (B) Electrophysiological recordings from individual visual cortical neurons in a monkey trained to report whether he was aware of the left or right eye image in a rivalry paradigm. (C) The neuron shown in this example was active only when the monkey reported that the right eye view was perceived (red bars; yellow regions indicate perception of the other eye's view). This result indicates that percepts compete in binocular rivalry. (B,C after Blake and Logothetis 2002.)

The Perception of Motion

The final perceptual quality generated by visual processing considered here is **motion**, defined as the subjective experience elicited when a sequence of different but related images are presented to the retina over a brief span of time (physical motion can be either too fast or too slow to elicit the perception of motion; we don't see the trajectory of a bullet, nor can we see the hour hand move on a clock). Much as the perceptual category of color comprises perceptions of hue, saturation, and brightness, motion percepts have two components: a perception of speed and a perception of direction.

Evidence for dedicated motion processing areas

Just as overlapping but appreciably different regions of the posterior cerebral cortices emphasize the processing of color, so particular regions in the primate brain are especially concerned with motion processing. As mentioned earlier, these regions in monkeys are in an area of the posterior temporal lobe called MT (medial temporal) and MST (medial superior temporal; see Figure 5.3). Recall that the term MT+ is used for humans to indicate that these regions are much less well defined in humans than in monkeys, the experimental animals on which most motion studies have been done.

That the MT and MST regions are specialized for motion processing was first determined by experiments carried out in the 1970s using single-unit recording in monkeys. These investigations revealed that, compared with other visual cortical regions, many more cells within MT and MST are responsive to image *sequences*. Noninvasive brain imaging during the presentation of motion stimuli has shown that the same general areas are active in humans viewing motion stimuli. The neurons in MT and MST in monkeys receive input from motion-sensitive cells in V1 (a large majority) and are arranged in columnar modules that have the same preference for oriented-motion stimuli. As shown by John Allman and his colleagues at California Institute of Technology, these neurons respond to motion over large regions of a visual scene, a finding that accords with the large receptive field sizes of other neurons in extrastriate regions (see Chapter 4).

Evidence that the activity of MT neurons is related to the perception of motion has been provided by studies by neurophysiologist William Newsome and his collaborators at Stanford. Rhesus monkeys were shown a display of dots moving in different directions. If a sufficient proportion of the dots moved coherently, the monkeys (as would humans) perceived an overall direction of motion in the display (e.g., leftward). As indicated in **Figure 5.18A**, monkeys can be trained to move their eyes in the direction of the

Figure 5.18 Relating motion-sensitive neurons in MT to motion percepts. (A) In this experiment, a rhesus monkey was trained to report whether rightward or leftward motion was perceived in response to a pattern of moving dots. The monkey indicated the direction of perceived motion by shifting its eyes to either the green spot (for leftward) or red spot (for rightward) target. (B) By changing the amount of coherent motion in the moving dot pattern, a psychophysical function was obtained that plots perceptual accuracy against the amount of motion coherence among the dots. Electrical stimulation of small populations of MT neurons (not shown) can shift this curve in a systematic way, showing that the activity of these neurons influences motion perception. (After Sugrue et al. 2005.)

(A) Perceptual discrimination task

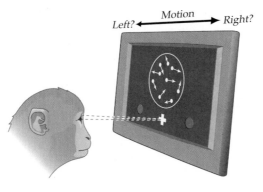

(B) Linking behavior to perception

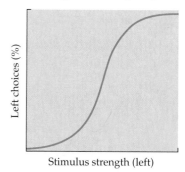

movement of the dots. While a monkey trained in this way performed the task, action potentials were recorded from neurons in MT. The recordings showed that the activity of single neurons was often correlated with the direction of dot motion (**Figure 5.18B**). Indeed, the activity of neurons in the population was sometimes a better predictor of the direction of dot motion than the behavior of the monkey (i.e., its eye movements).

To show that MT neurons play a causal role in such perceptual discriminations, it would be necessary to manipulate neuronal activity directly and then observe changes in behavior. To test this point, Newsome and colleagues identified neurons within MT that showed selective activity for a particular direction of motion. They then stimulated the neurons electrically. For about half of the electrode locations, microstimulation increased the probability that the monkeys would move their eyes in the direction consistent with the directionally selective receptive field properties of the stimulated neurons.

The importance of these extrastriate temporal areas for motion processing has been underscored by a "motion-blind" patient reported by the neuropsychologist Josef Zihl and his collaborators in Munich. The patient is a 43-year-old woman known as L.M., who suffered a vascular lesion that resulted in bilateral damage in the general region of the MT+ motion areas. Although the lesion resulted in several neurological problems, a striking feature of her case is difficulty perceiving motion. Thus when tea is poured, the liquid appears "frozen." She has difficulty following speech because she can't pick up mouth movement cues, and is hesitant when crossing a street because she can't judge the movement of cars. L.M. is nonetheless able to perceive certain kinds of motion. For instance, when lights are attached to the key joints of a person's body and their movements observed in the dark,* she can distinguish different types of common human movements such as walking. Consistent with this clinical evidence, transcranial magnetic stimulation (see Chapter 3) of the MT+ area in normal human subjects can also interfere with motion percepts.

Taken together, this evidence for specialized motion processing areas accords with the concept of a motion processing stream that conveys information from the magnocellular pathway that begins and the retina and is evident in the magnocellular layers of the thalamus and in V1. These areas are also components of the more broadly defined dorsal pathway concerned with object location and action, which contrasts to a broadly defined ventral pathway that is more concerned with object recognition (see Figure 4.10). It should be recognized, however, that these distinctions greatly oversimplify a more complex organization that is only beginning to be understood.

Some persistent problems

Despite advances, how motion percepts are generated by neural processing is far from understood. Because the movement of objects in three-dimensional space is projected onto the two-dimensional retinal surface, the changes in position that uniquely define motion in physical terms are always uncertain with respect to the possible sources of the retinal image sequence (see Box 5B). A much-studied example that makes this point is the perception of a rod seen through an aperture that renders its ends invisible. As illustrated in **Figure 5.19**, the combinations of speeds and directions in this situation that *could* have given rise to the sequence of images falling on the retina is infinite. The challenge of explaining how the visual system generates quite definite perceptions of speed and direction in response to such stimuli is called the **aperture problem**.

---

*Known as a *point-light walking display*, this is a popular method for studying biological movements; see Chapter 19.

Figure 5.19 The inherent ambiguity of motion stimuli.
The stimulus sequence elicited by an object like a rod moving
behind an aperture can be generated by an infinite number of
directions of physical motion, each associated with a different
speed. Imagine, for example, that the linear object in the aperture
is moving horizontally from left to right (yellow arrow). The same
stimulus sequence could have been generated by any of the directions of physical movement indicated by the other arrows around a
limiting hemisphere, each coupled with an appropriate speed. In
the absence of the aperture, such a line appears to be moving horizontally from left to right at a particular speed. The moment the
aperture is applied, however, the line appears to be moving downward and to the right at a slower speed.

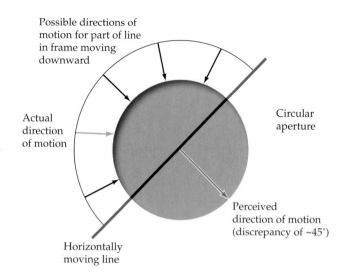

A further challenge in understanding motion percepts is the sense of entirely realistic motion generated from a series of *static images*, a phenomenon
called **apparent motion**. The simplest stimulus sequence that could be used to
study this phenomenon is the presentation of just two sequential "frames,"
which is what the German psychologist Max Wertheimer did nearly a century
ago (**Figure 5.20A**). For a spatial interval of one or a few degrees of visual
angle, Wertheimer found that if the temporal interval is less than 20 milliseconds or so, the two lights appear to come on *simultaneously* and no motion is
seen; at the other extreme, if the interval is greater than about 450 milliseconds, the two lights appear to come on *sequentially* and no motion is seen.
Between these limits subjects perceived some form of motion, the most "realistic" motion being in the middle of this range. The motion elicited by such
stimuli is the basis of movies and video. Static images are presented at 96
frames per second in movies (3 repetitions of 24 new images every second,
with each shift to a new image hidden by a "blanking frame"); in video the
idea is the same, although the frames are "refreshed" one line at a time such
that the whole picture changes approximately 30 times each second.

Other intriguing percepts occur if additional lights are added to the simple sort of pattern studied by Wertheimer. For instance, if instead of two
lights a quartet of lights is used, the apparent motion seen is horizontal and
not diagonal, even though there is no obvious prohibition against seeing
diagonal motion (**Figure 5.20B**). Explanations of apparent motion have tended to invoke rules or principles called *heuristics* that the visual system supposedly employs to guide perceptual "interpretations," an approach derived
from the school of Gestalt psychology that Wertheimer founded (see Chapter 2). The basis of apparent motion is, however, unresolved and raises the
broader issue of how the visual system (or the brain more generally) parses
time (see Chapter 22).

(A)

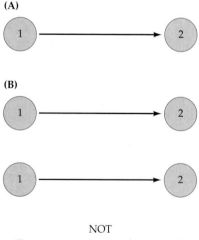

(B)

NOT

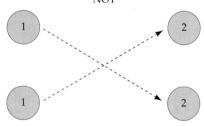

Figure 5.20 Apparent motion. (A) When two fixed lights separated by an appropriate distance are turned on and off at an interval greater than 20 milliseconds but less
than several hundred milliseconds, observers see the first light (1) moving to the position
of second light (2). (B) Manipulating these variables, and varying the number of lights
involved, elicits a variety of motion effects that are difficult to explain, such as why diagonal motion is not seen in this example.

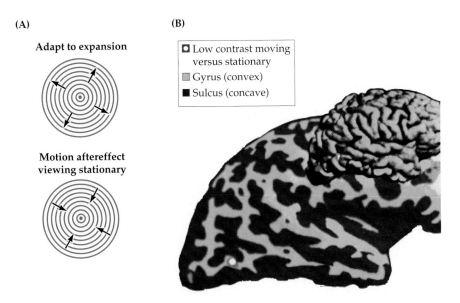

Figure 5.21 Activation of motion areas during the perception of motion aftereffects. (A) Upper diagram shows the stimulus used: an expanding ring that subjects viewed before looking at the static pattern below, thus eliciting a standard motion aftereffect. (B) Functional magnetic resonance imaging during the aftereffect showed activation of motion areas centered on MT (white dot; the brain has been computationally inflated, as in Figure 5.3). (From Tootell et al. 1995.)

Another puzzle is **motion aftereffects**. The most familiar of these phenomena is the so-called *waterfall effect*: After staring for many seconds at movement in a single direction (such as at falling water), one sees movement in the *opposite* direction when one looks away at a static part of the scene (say, at nearby rocks or trees; **Figure 5.21A**). The usual explanation is that prolonged exposure to a particular direction of motion causes the motion-activated neurons to adapt, such that when the motion stimulus is removed the nonadapted neurons involved in motion detection in other directions are relatively more active, leading to the illusion of motion in the opposite direction. (A similar explanation is given for the more familiar color aftereffects.) Using fMRI, Roger Tootell at Boston University and his colleagues have lent some support to this general concept by showing activation of motion (and other visual) areas following the cessation of prolonged motion stimuli (**Figure 5.21B**). Nonetheless, the neural basis of motion aftereffects is not settled.

The ongoing debate over how to rationalize perceived motion in the face of these problems is well beyond the scope of this chapter. In general, however, most theoretical explanations have been based on mathematical models of motion energy or on other nonlinear spatio-temporal filtering mechanisms. Another approach is to suppose that the perceived directions and speeds of moving objects are determined by the probability distributions of the possible sources of the inherently ambiguous stimuli. There is as yet no broad agreement about the strategy the visual system uses to generate the motion percepts that we depend on in daily life.

The Perception of Objects

The focus of the chapter has so far been on the basic *qualities* of visual perceptual qualities—brightness, color, form, depth, and motion. No understanding of complex visual percepts can emerge without understanding these fundamental characteristics of vision. It is obvious, however, that when we look at the world we don't see these qualities per se; what we see are *objects* that are defined by these qualities. Moreover, it is clear that some objects that have particular significance for our species—human faces, for instance—are much more carefully inspected and attended to than other classes of objects, as are meaningful symbols like letters and numbers for the cultures that use them. Although the recognition and processing of objects like faces and words are

(A)

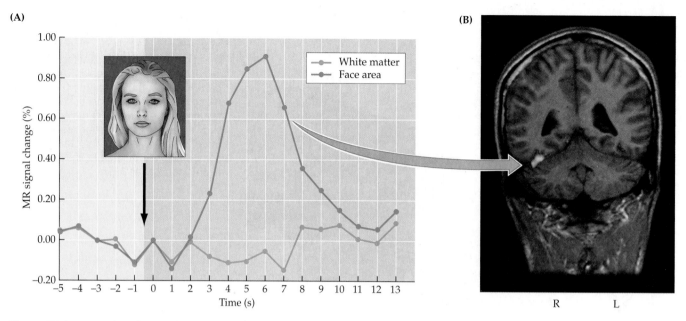

(B)

R   L

Figure 5.22 Functional MRI activation during a face recognition task.
(A) A face stimulus was presented to a normal subject at the time indicated by arrow. Graph shows activity change in the relevant area of the right temporal lobe. (B) Location of fMRI activity in right inferior frontal lobe. (Courtesy of Greg McCarthy.)

taken up specifically in a number of later chapters, some general points are worth emphasizing here.

As indicated in Chapter 4 and earlier in this chapter, the recognition of objects by means of vision involves the ventral visual processing stream that eventually leads to the temporal lobe (see Figure 4.10). The region of the temporal lobe that supports object recognition is not entirely uniform but, like other higher-order visual areas, is parsed in overlapping areas that are especially interested in broad but appreciably different object categories. The most thoroughly studied of these is relatively specific subdivision on the inferior aspect of the temporal lobe, called the *fusiform face area*. As the name suggests, many of the neurons in this region are responsive to faces (**Figure 5.22**; see Chapter 19 for a more detailed discussion). Another such subdivision is involved in processing information about animals; others are concerned with inanimate objects such as tools or houses, and still others are concerned with recognizing words. It is of course unlikely that every category of object we see has a dedicated area of temporal cortex; thus, how to think about this issue remains an active area of research and much controversy. Similarly, whether object recognition entails the appreciation of significant elements of the object (e.g., the eyes, nose, and mouth of a face), a more global integration, or some combination of these is much debated.

Perceiving Remembered Images

A final consideration in this overview of visual perception is the neural basis of images we can bring to mind that are not generated by retinal stimulation, but by **imaging** a remembered face, a special sunset, or some other memorable scene. A question of obvious interest is whether remembered images activate the same areas of brain as do retinally stimulated visual percepts. The experience of such "mental images" is clearly different in its immediacy, overall quality, and vividness compared to the image elicited by an actual scene being experienced; such differences pertain to all types of memories. Nonetheless, a number of studies have shown that when visual scenes are brought to mind, many regions of the visual cortex are activated. As shown in **Figure 5.23**, this reactivation can also be relatively specific to the category-specific processing

(A)

Perception

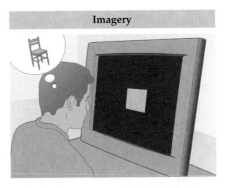

Imagery

(B)

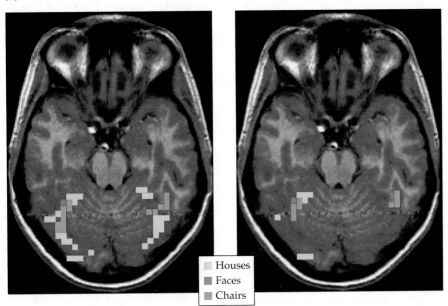

Houses
Faces
Chairs

Figure 5.23 Activation of the brain during remembered visual images. (A) In this experiment, subjects viewed images of objects in three different categories (left: houses, faces, or chairs), or were instructed to simply remember what they had been viewing in each of these categories (right). (B) The same general regions of the ventral temporal cortex were activated in both situations, and these regions tended to be category specific. (After Ishai et al. 2000.)

region in the temporal lobe relevant to type of visual objects being remembered. (The auditory cortices are activated in a similar manner when subjects remember auditory "scenes," such as a favorite song or a bit of dialog from a movie).

These observations are consistent with the idea that stored information is located in the regions of the brain that processed that information in the first place—an important issue in understanding memory, and a concept that is taken up in Chapters 13 and 14. The observations also accord with the evidence that motion aftereffects depend on ongoing activity in motion-selective processing areas (see Figure 5.21).

Summary

1. A great deal is now known about how information from photoreceptors is initiated and processed by neurons in the primary visual pathway, including the initial stages of processing in the primary visual cortex (V1).

2. How neural information is processed in the higher-order regions of the extrastriate visual cortices is less well understood, although a general theme is that activity in the cortex tends to track percepts, whereas neuronal activity in the retina, thalamus, and input layer of V1 is more closely tied to the actual properties of the stimulus.

3. A challenge to understanding the basic strategy of neural processing in the visual system is explaining how inherently uncertain retinal stimuli can give rise to definite percepts and generally successful visually guided behavior. For each of the basic visual qualities—brightness, color, form, depth, and motion—the perceptual evidence points to a strategy in which inevitably ambiguous images are empirically linked to sources as a means of contending with this inverse optics problem.

4. The idea that what we see in response to retinal stimuli is a manifestation of accumulated past experience rather than a logical analysis of the features of the retinal image runs counter to all our intuitions about vision. Nevertheless, the nature of the inverse problem and the phenomenology of what we actually see (e.g., the many discrepancies between visual percepts and physical reality) are difficult to explain in any other way.

5. The advantage of generating vision in this way is that over evolutionary time, percepts—and the visual circuitry that underlies them—progressively incorporate the vast amount information generated by the experience of both the species and the individual. How the receptive field properties of visual neurons might be understood in these terms is just beginning to be explored.

Additional Reading

Reviews

BLAKE, R. AND N. K. LOGOTHETIS (2002) Visual competition. *Nat. Rev. Neurosci.* 3: 1–11.

GERGENFURTNER, K. R. (2003) Cortical mechanisms of color vision. *Nat. Rev. Neurosci.* 4: 563–572.

GOODALE, M. A. AND G. K. HUMPHREY (1998) The objects of action and perception. *Cognition* 67: 179–205.

KANWISHER, N. (2006) What's in a face? *Science* 311: 617–618.

LAND, E. H. (1986) Recent advances in retinex theory. *Vision Research* 26: 7–21.

MOLLON, J. D. (1995) Seeing colour. In *Colour: Art and Science*, T. Lamb and J. Bourriau (eds.). Cambridge: Cambridge University Press, pp. 127–150.

PURVES, D., S. M. WILLIAMS, S. NUNDY AND R. B. LOTTO (2004) Perceiving the intensity of light. *Psych. Rev.* 111: 142–158.

SIMONCELLI, E. P. AND B. A. OLSHAUSEN (2001) Natural images statistics and neural representation. *Annu. Rev. Neurosci.* 24: 1193–1216.

SHIMOJO, S., M. PARADISO AND I. FUJITA (2001) What visual perception tells us about mind and brain. *Proc. Natl. Acad. Sci. USA* 98: 12340–12341.

SUGRUE, L. P., G. S. CORRADO AND W. T. NEWSOME (2005) Choosing the greater of two goods: Neural currencies for valuation and decision making. *Nat. Rev. Neurosci.* 6: 363–375.

UNDERLEIDER, L. G. AND J. V. HAXBY (1994) "What" and "where" in the human brain. *Curr. Opin. Neurobiol.* 4: 157–165.

ZEKI, S. (1989) A century of cerebral achromatopsia. *Brain* 113: 1721–1777.

Important original papers

BOUVIER, S. E. AND S. A. ENGEL (2006) Behavioral deficits and cortical damage in cerebral achromatopsia. *Cereb. Cortex* 16: 183–191.

MURRAY, S. O., H. BOYACI AND D. KERSTEN (2006) The representation of perceived angular size in primary visual cortex. *Nat. Neurosci.* 9: 429–434.

NEWSOME, W. T., K. H. BRITTEN AND J. A. MOVSHON (1989) Neuronal correlates of a perceptual decision. *Nature* 341: 52–54.

SALZMAN, C. D., K. H. BRITTEN AND W. T. NEWSOME (1990) Cortical microstimulation influences perceptual judgments of motion direction. *Nature* 346: 174–177.

SHEPARD, R. N. AND L. A. COOPER (1992) Representation of colors in the blind, color-blind, and normally sighted. *Psychol. Sci.* 3: 97–103.

TOOTELL, R. B. AND 6 OTHERS (1995) Visual motion aftereffect in human cortical area MT revealed by functional magnetic resonance imaging. *Nature* 375: 139–141.

WALLACH, H. (1935/1996) Über visuell wahrgenommene Bewegungsrichtung. *Psycholog. Forsch.* 20: 325–380. [On the visually perceived direction of motion by Hans Wallach: 60 years later, S. Wuerger, R. Shapley and N. Rubin (transl.). *Perception* 25: 1317–1367.]

WERTHEIMER, M. (1912/1950) Laws of organization in perceptual forms. In *A Sourcebook of Gestalt Psychology*, W. D. Ellis (ed. & trans.). New York: Humanities Press, pp. 71–88.

WHEATSTONE, C. (1838) Contributions to the physiology of vision. I. On some remarkable and hitherto unobserved phenomena of binocular vision. *Philos. Trans. Roy. Soc. B* 128: 371–394.

YANG, Z. AND D. PURVES (2004) The statistical structure of natural light patterns determines perceived light intensity. *Proc. Natl. Acad. Sci. USA* 101: 8745–8750.

ZEKI, S. M. (1983a) Colour coding in the cerebral cortex: The reaction of cells in monkey visual cortex to wavelengths and colours. *Neuroscience* 9: 741–766.

ZEKI, S. M. (1983b) Colour coding in the cerebral cortex: The responses of wavelength-selective and colour-coded cells in monkey visual cortex to changes in wavelength composition. *Neuroscience* 9: 767–781.

ZIHL, J., D. VON CRAMON AND N. MAI (1983) Selective disturbance of movement vision after bilateral brain damage. *Brain* 106: 313–340.

Books

CORNSWEET, T. N. (1970) *Visual Perception.* New York: Academic Press.

FARAH, M. J. (2000) *The Cognitive Neuroscience of Vision.* Oxford: Blackwell Scientific.

GIBSON, J. H. (1979) *The Ecological Approach to Visual Perception.* Hillsdale, NJ: Lawrence Erlbaum.

HOWARD, I. P. AND B. J. ROGERS (1995) *Binocular Vision and Stereopsis.* Oxford Psychology Series No. 29. New York: Clarendon Press.

HOWE, C. Q. AND D. PURVES (2005) *Perceiving Geometry: Geometrical Illusions Explained by Natural Scene Statistics.* New York: Springer.

HUBEL, D. H. (1988) *Eye, Brain and Vision.* New York: W. H. Freeman.

HUBEL, D. H. AND T. N. WIESEL (2006) *Brain and Visual Perception: The Story of a 25-Year Collaboration.* Oxford: Oxford University Press.

MARR, D. (1982) *Vision: A Computational Investigation into Human Representation and Processing of Visual Information.* San Francisco: W. H. Freeman.

MILNER, A. D. AND M. A. GOODALE (1995) *The Visual Brain in Action.* Oxford: Oxford University Press.

PURVES, D. AND R. B. LOTTO (2003) *Why We See What We Do: An Empirical Theory of Vision.* Sunderland, MA: Sinauer.

ROBINSON, J. O. (1998) *The Psychology of Visual Illusions.* New York: Dover. (Corrected republication of the 1972 edition published by Hutchinson & Co., England.)

ROCK, I. (1984, 1995) *Perception.* New York: W. H. Freeman.

The Perception of Auditory Stimuli

Introduction

Hearing is as important for humans as vision, and studies of audition have played a key role in cognitive neuroscience. The obvious importance of social communication by means of language and the prevalence of music in human cultures add to the great interest and importance of this sensory modality for understanding cognitive processes. This chapter reviews the principles of auditory perception as they have been discerned by a variety of approaches, ranging from acoustical physics to noninvasive brain imaging and neuropsychology. The account begins with a brief review of the organization of the auditory system and proceeds to consider sound stimuli, the perceptual qualities such stimuli elicit, and what is presently known about the generation of these percepts in the human brain. Of particular interest are the parallels with vision and other sensory systems at all these levels, which suggest similar solutions to basic problems in perception, despite the obvious differences between light and sound stimuli. These shared features underscore how much sensory processing has been influenced by the need to respond successfully to the sorts of natural stimuli in the human environment. Because of its special role in many human cognitive functions, the production and comprehension of speech and the neural basis of these abilities is taken up separately, in Chapters 20 and 21. However, some aspects of speech processing are introduced here, as is the perception of music.

The Human Auditory System

The ear

In humans and other mammals, the **auditory system** transforms (*transduces*) mechanical energy produced by the movement of air molecules into neural signals that ultimately give rise to the perceptual qualities of the sounds we hear. Auditory stimuli for humans arise from particular sorts of local pressure changes that form a subset of the pressure changes that normally occur in the auditory environment (much as the light stimuli that give rise to vision arise from a subset of electromagnetic waves in the terrestrial environment). In order to hear something, the variations in local pressure must fall within defined ranges of *frequency* and *absolute pressure* to activate the receptor cells of

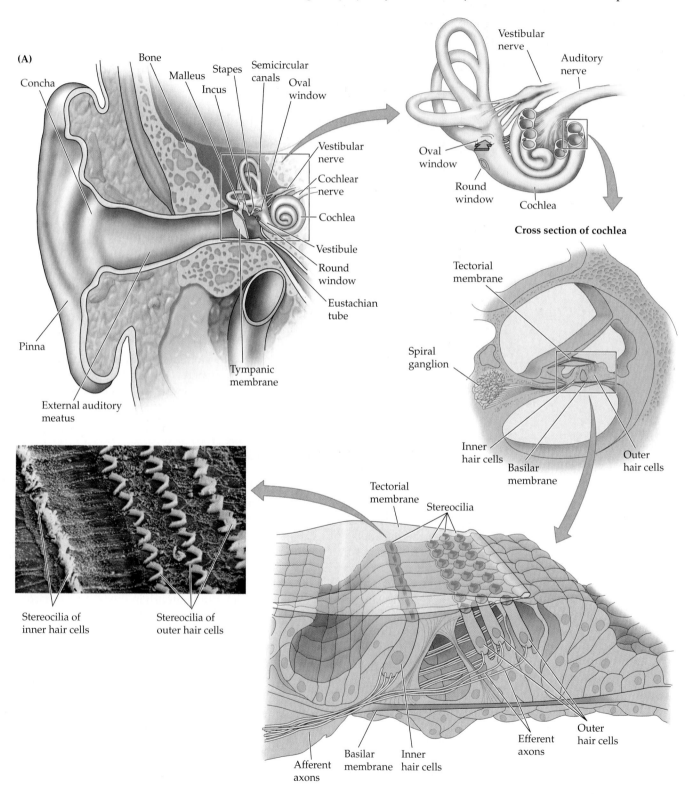

(A)

Concha
Bone
Malleus
Incus
Stapes
Semicircular canals
Oval window
Vestibular nerve
Cochlear nerve
Cochlea
Vestibule
Round window
Eustachian tube
Pinna
External auditory meatus
Tympanic membrane

Vestibular nerve
Auditory nerve
Oval window
Round window
Cochlea

Cross section of cochlea

Tectorial membrane
Spiral ganglion
Inner hair cells
Basilar membrane
Outer hair cells

Stereocilia of inner hair cells
Stereocilia of outer hair cells

Tectorial membrane
Stereocilia
Afferent axons
Basilar membrane
Inner hair cells
Efferent axons
Outer hair cells

the inner ear. Thus the local pressure changes produced by waving your hand back and forth beside your ear don't cause you hear anything; the absolute pressure of the air disturbance created by hand-waving is adequate, but the frequency of the changing pressure is too low for a human to hear. These sensitivities of auditory receptors to mechanical movement define the range of human hearing, just as the sensitivities of photoreceptors to light define the range of human vision.

The first stage of the transformation of local pressure changes into neural signals entails *pre-neural* effects produced by the **external ear** and the **middle ear** (**Figure 6.1A**). By virtue of their anatomical configuration and their resonance properties, these structures collect sound energy and amplify local pressure so that sound stimuli of particular ecological importance (e.g., speech stimuli) are transmitted with greater efficiency. Thus the odd-looking cartilaginous structures of the external ear, called the *concha* and *pinna*, function much like an old-fashioned "ear trumpet" to collect and focus sound energy, while the resonance of the ear canal helps filter out the less relevant aspects of sound stimuli. The three bones of the middle ear link the resulting deflections of the **tympanic membrane** (the eardrum) to the inner ear, further enhancing the stimulus energy transmitted to the **oval window.** This bony mechanism between the eardrum and oval window acts to enhance pressure in much the same way that a the pressure at the larger plunger of a syringe is greatly increased at the smaller, needle end.

The cochlea

The oval window marks the entry to the **cochlea,** which houses the neural receptor apparatus of the **inner ear** (Figure 6.1A, enlargements). The major features of the cochlea, so named because the overall shape of its bony shell is similar to the shell of a snail, are the **basilar membrane** and its embedded **receptor cells**, called **hair cells**. The movement of the oval window is transmitted to the fluid in the inner ear, which in turn moves protrusions on the tips of the hair cells called *stereocilia*. The movement of the stereocilia depolarizes the membrane of the hair cells, leading to the release of transmitter molecules from the basal portion of the cells, which in turn elicits synaptic potentials and, if these are sufficient, action potentials in the endings of the axons that form the **auditory nerve**. As shown in Figure 6.1A, the cell bodies of the bipolar neurons that give rise to these axons are in the nearby **spiral ganglion**. Action potentials in auditory nerve fibers convey information about the frequency, amplitude, and phase of sound stimuli to the auditory processing regions of the brain, leading eventually to the primary auditory cortex and higher-order auditory cortices.

Figure 6.1 The external, middle, and inner ear. (A) Overall view of the ear and its component parts. Blowups show the cochlea, the cochlea in cross-section, and a more detailed diagram of the basilar membrane and the receptor cells (*hair cells*) that initiate auditory processing and ultimately auditory perception. (B) The representation of frequencies along the length of the basilar membrane; 1 corresponds to the region nearest the middle ear that is activated by high frequencies, and 7 to the distal region that is activated by low frequencies. The differential responsiveness of the basilar membrane to stimulus frequency along its length (an arrangement referred to as *tonotopic* or *tonotopy*) is also evident in the central stations of the auditory system. (Micrograph from Kessel and Kardon 1979.)

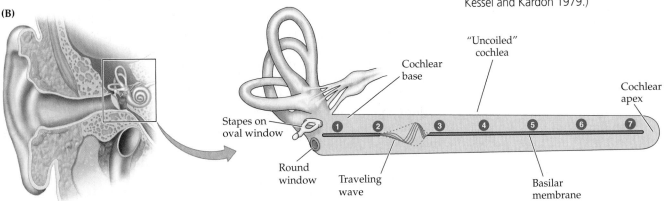

(B)

"Uncoiled" cochlea

Cochlear base

Cochlear apex

Stapes on oval window

Round window

Traveling wave

Basilar membrane

Using human cadavers, the Hungarian physiologist Georg von Bekesy working at Harvard Medical School in the 1950s showed that the *frequency* of a given sound stimulus is encoded by the region of the basilar membrane that is most deflected by a stimulus. The responses of the basilar membrane depend in turn on its mechanical properties: the stiffer portion near the oval window reacts to relatively high frequencies, while the more compliant portion at the cochlear apex reacts to low frequencies (**Figure 6.1B**). This **tonotopic organization** is an important feature that is apparent in the rest of the auditory system, as described below. The *amplitude* (intensity) of a stimulus is encoded in the number of action potentials per unit time in auditory nerve fibers, and *phase information* (see below) is encoded in the relative timing of the action potentials.

Central stations of the primary auditory pathway

The first stage of central auditory processing in the brain occurs in the **cochlear nucleus** in the rostral medulla of the brainstem, the initial target the auditory nerve axons that carry the information generated by the basilar membrane (**Figure 6.2**). From there, peripheral auditory information diverges into a number of parallel pathways that project to one of several targets:

■ The **superior olivary complex** is the first place that information from the two ears interacts, and is the site of the initial processing of the cues that allow listeners to localize sound in space.

■ Axons from the neurons of the cochlear nucleus project to the **inferior colliculus** in the midbrain, a major integrative center and the first place where auditory information interacts with the motor system to initiate auditory-guided behavior (e.g., turning the head toward a sound in order to see what caused it).

■ Cochlear nucleus neurons also send projections to the **nucleus of the lateral lemniscus** in the midbrain, whose neurons process temporal aspects of sound stimuli that are again critical to localization of the sound's source.

As in the case of the other sensory modalities (except olfaction), information processed in these stations in the brainstem and midbrain is sent is to the **thalamus**, where it is further processed and relayed to the **primary auditory cortex**, or **A1**. The relevant thalamic target in this case is the **medial geniculate nucleus**, a station homologous to the lateral geniculate nucleus in the primary visual pathway. This series of stations defines the **primary auditory pathway.**

The auditory cortices are located in the superior temporal and the adjacent regions of the parietal lobes. Like the visual cortex, auditory cortex is divided into primary and secondary regions (**Figure 6.3**). The primary auditory cortex includes Brodmann areas 41 and 42 and lies on the superior aspect of the temporal lobe (the specific region is along the *superior temporal gyrus*). Much as the primary visual cortex, it is defined by being the major cortical recipient of the thalamic projections for audition—in this case, projections arising from the medial geniculate nucleus. The adjoining areas of the temporal and parietal lobes comprise the **secondary auditory cortex**, or **A2**; the auditory cortical areas surrounding the primary auditory cortex are also referred to as *belt areas*. The secondary areas are regions where higher-order auditory processing occurs, including the processing germane to understanding speech and supporting the recognition and comprehension of words. These auditory areas are thus similar in principle to the extrastriate visual association areas where more complex and integrative processing of visual stimuli occurs.

A further comparison with the primary visual pathway concerns lateralization. Recall that information from the left and right eyes go to both hemispheres. This is also true for audition: information from both ears is processed

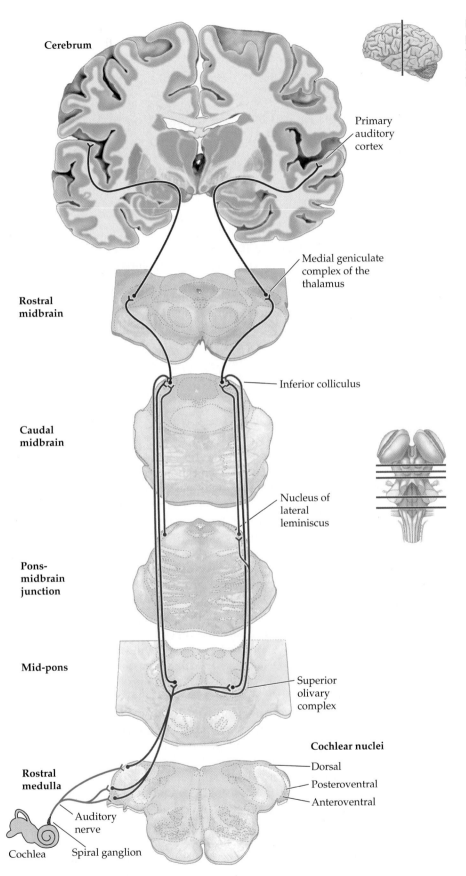

Cerebrum

Primary auditory cortex

Medial geniculate complex of the thalamus

Rostral midbrain

Inferior colliculus

Caudal midbrain

Nucleus of lateral leminiscus

Pons-midbrain junction

Mid-pons

Superior olivary complex

Cochlear nuclei

Rostral medulla

Dorsal

Posteroventral

Anteroventral

Auditory nerve

Cochlea

Spiral ganglion

Figure 6.2 The primary auditory pathway. The major anatomical features of the primary auditory pathway; insets show the levels at which the sections in the diagram are taken.

Figure 6.3 The primary and secondary (belt) auditory cortices.
A1 and the belt cortices are located in the superior and posterior temporal lobe; a retractor is shown pulling back the parietal lobe, since much of this cortex is buried in the lateral (Sylvian) sulcus. The tonotopy evident in the cochlea (see Figure 6.1B) is also evident in the primary auditory cortex (although not as precisely as implied by the demarcation lines in the blowup).

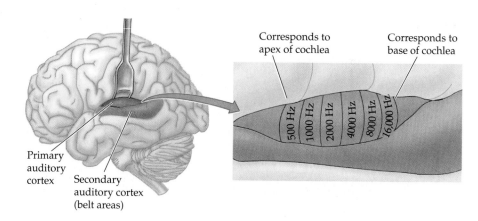

in both hemispheres, a fact that has been verified in humans by fMRI and magnetoencephalographic (MEG) studies (see Chapter 3). In the auditory system there is a slight tendency toward greater hemispheric processing of signals originating in the opposite ear. The bilateral processing in of both these systems contrasts with the arrangement of the somatic sensory system described in Chapter 7, in which processing of information arising from one side of the body is primarily processed in the contralateral hemisphere.

Additional aspects of cortical organization that have emerged from studies of the processing of different aspects of sound stimuli are taken up later in the chapter.

Sound Stimuli

The meaning of the word *sound* is ambiguous, since in common usage *sound* refers to both auditory stimuli (as in discussing the "speed of sound") and to the sensations that such stimuli elicit (as in "What was that sound I heard?"). Thus, to avoid confusion, it is best to use the phrase **sound stimuli** to designate the physical events that initiate audition, restricting use of the word *sound* to the perceptual consequence of those stimuli. A sound stimulus can be a brief change in local air pressure produced by the more or less instantaneous displacement of air molecules. Examples are breaking a twig or discharging a gun, and such stimuli elicit the perception of a *snap* or a *bang*. Many of the pressure changes that trigger human auditory responses, however, are caused by the ongoing movements of a *resonating body,* which provide stimuli that persist for hundreds of milliseconds or longer. **Resonance** refers to the tendency of strings, taut surfaces, columns of air confined in pipes, bells, and numerous other objects to vibrate in an ongoing manner determined by the details of their physical structure. Depending on the frequency components of these ongoing vibrations, longer-lasting stimuli can generate the perception of a **tone** if the vibrations are relatively coherent, but are perceived as **noise** if they incoherent. (*Pure tones* generated by a sinusoidal stimulus and *white noise* are the extremes of this continuum, as discussed below.) Whether the air pressure disturbance leads to the perception of a tone or noise, the relevant stimulus always propagates as a *front* of increased pressure immediately followed by *trough* of decreased pressure; this pressure variation is the basis of the frequency limitations of hearing, and is critical to the adequate stimulation of the hair cells.

When objects resonate (vibrate) as a result of being acted on by a force, the resulting compression and rarefaction of air molecules generates a **sound wave (Figure 6.4A)**. Sound waves are similar in principle to water waves, but are *longitudinal* (forward and back), whereas water waves are transverse (up and down). Although sound waves are typically introduced (as they are here)

(A)

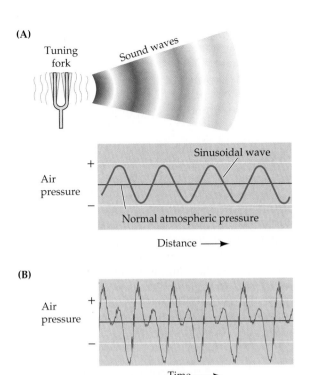

(B)

Figure 6.4 Sound stimuli. (A) The sine wave generated by a tuning fork. Although not found in nature, a sine wave stimulus is useful for demonstrating the basic features of sound waves. Like other wave phenomena, sound waves can be described in terms of four characteristics: *waveform* (whether the wave is simple or complex, as in B); *frequency* (expressed in cycles per second or hertz, Hz); *amplitude* (usually expressed in decibels, dB; see Box 6A); and *phase*. Because the frequency of sound waves is within the range of nerve cell signaling (at least at low frequencies), the auditory system can use this information directly in responding to sound stimuli; in vision, the frequencies of light waves are many orders of magnitude greater, and the response to frequency is only indirect via the energy content of different frequencies. (B) A naturally occurring periodic sound, the utterance of the vowel "ee" in this example, is complex in that the repeating period comprises a number of components. (C) A vibrating string and the resulting spectrum of sound energy. The illustration on the left indicates the multiple modes of vibration of a plucked string and the amplitudes of these excursions. The graph on the right shows the spectrum generated by such vibration, and the harmonic series determined by Fourier analysis (the numbers on the abscissa indicate each successive harmonic in the series; 1 indicates the fundamental frequency).

(C)

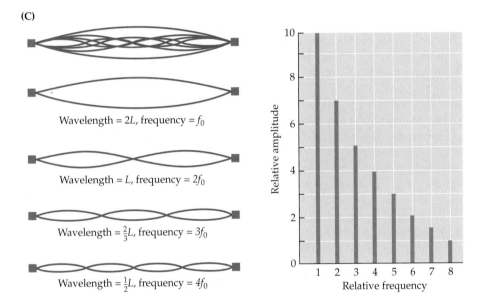

in terms of a *sine wave* to facilitate the appreciation of some general points about how sound waves are measured, the concept of sound waves as sinusoids is misleading; in fact, few if any natural sound stimuli have the simple repeating structure produced by a tuning fork, which generates only a single frequency. Indeed, relatively few natural sounds have the **periodicity** (i.e., a systematic repetition of a complex waveform over time) needed to generate the perception of a tone; most natural stimuli (rustling leaves, burbling brooks, buzzing insects, and so on) elicit perceptions that are closer to the noisy end of the sound stimulus continuum.

Although **periodic sound stimuli** are relatively rare in nature (and sinusoids virtually absent), such stimuli are especially important for humans because of their role in vocal communication, and are thus highly significant components of the human auditory environment (**Figure 6.4B**). Such stimuli are usually described in terms of the **harmonic series** that characterizes stimuli produced by systematically resonating objects. **Figure 6.4C** shows the **sound spectrum** (the distribution of the power as a function of frequency at a point in time) of a vibrating string; such spectra are determined by *Fourier analysis*, a widely used mathematical method for decomposing any sound stimulus into its frequency components.

When determined by Fourier analysis, the sound spectrum of a vibrating object such as a guitar string shows a series of power peaks at predictable frequencies. This regularity occurs because when a taut sting is plucked, a standing wave is generated that vibrates in a series of *modes*. The greatest up and down movement is over the full length of the string, and it is this mode of vibration that generates the most energetic component in the spectrum, called the **fundamental frequency**. The next most powerful vibratory mode is at half the length of the string, next at a third the length, the next at a quarter the length and so on. Since natural objects—including human vocal cords—also vibrate in this manner, the string and the harmonic series it produces is a much better paradigm for understanding the percepts elicited by natural periodic sound stimuli than a tuning fork. As will be apparent, these concepts are important in understanding auditory processing and ultimately perception.

Sensitivity and Range of Human Hearing

In audition, as in vision and other sensory modalities, different species are sensitive to widely different ranges and types of sound stimuli, depending on their ecological niches and needs. With respect to **sensitivity**, the human auditory system is capable of responding to levels of sound pressure changes that cover an enormous range. The rationale for this extensive range is to take advantage of as much ecologically relevant information as possible. At the low end of the range, the system can generate neural signals in response to air pressure changes that are on the order of a billionth of normal atmospheric pressure, and the hair cell displacements for such threshold stimuli are only about the diameter of a gold atom. However, the auditory system also responds to stimuli that are many orders of magnitude more intense, and continues to generate percepts up to the point where the stimulus energy becomes great enough to damage the hair cells.

With respect to the **frequency range** of human hearing, a child or young adult can process stimuli from about 20 Hz to about 20,000 Hz. In adults, this range diminishes at the high end of the frequency range; this deficiency is called *presbycusis* and is the most common type of hearing loss in people over 55. The typical complaint from those with presbycusis is difficulty understanding speech in venues such as a crowded restaurant, where the welter of low-frequency stimuli that can still be heard coupled with a loss of ability to distinguish high-frequency stimuli makes it difficult to understand what the person across the table is saying.

The frequency range of hearing is typically determined using sine wave stimuli (see Figure 6.4A). As the frequency of the sine tone stimulus approaches the lower end of the human range, the stimuli are perceived as increasingly "bumpy" and faint, and eventually can't be heard at all, although larger animals like whales and elephants can hear in this *infrasound range*. Similarly, humans cannot hear stimuli at frequencies higher than 20,000 Hz, although smaller animals can hear well into this so-called *ultrasound range*. Some bat species are sensitive to frequencies as high as 200,000 Hz and have a lower limit somewhere around the upper limit of human hearing. One reason for these differences across species is that small objects, including the auditory apparatus of smaller animals, vibrate at higher frequencies than larger objects, which largely explains why a violin has a higher frequency range than a cello, and a cello a higher range than a bass fiddle.

Sound Percepts

In vision, the basic qualities of perception are *brightness, color, form, depth,* and *motion.* The basic perceptual qualities generated by the human auditory system are *loudness, pitch,* and *timbre.* Some sequences of sound stimuli also generate a sense of *tempo* and *rhythm,* perceptions that are more or less comparable to the generation of motion by sequences of visual stimuli. In contrast to the extensive work on visual motion, however, rhythm and tempo are not yet well enough understood or studied to include in this introductory account, although they are clearly critical in understanding sound streams such as speech (see Chapters 20 and 21), as well as aspects of music and its appeal, as described later in the chapter. Finally, it is important to bear in mind that, just as what we see is experienced as visual scenes defined by recognizable objects, so what we hear is effectively an "auditory scene" defined by recognizable sounds. This section first considers the basic sound qualities and then the less well understood issue of auditory scene generation.

Loudness

Loudness is defined as the perception of sound intensity. In formal terms, *intensity* is measured as the *sound pressure level,* a physical parameter expressed in Newtons/m^2. For practical reasons, however, sound intensity is usually expressed in **decibels**, a physical unit of sound pressure level, but based on the *perceptual threshold* of human hearing, in much the same way measures of the intensity of visual stimuli are based on the sensitivity of the visual system. The use and importance of this unit in describing sound percepts is described in **Box 6A**.

As in the case of visual brightness, a commonsense expectation is that loudness should vary more or less directly with physical intensity. But like the perception of light intensity, things are not so simple. In fact, the human sense of loudness varies greatly as a function of stimulus frequency, bandwidth, duration, and other factors that influence what we actually hear in response to a given stimulus. Adding further to the problem of understanding the perception of sound stimulus intensity is the fact that the loudness of two equally intense sounds sums only if the stimuli are similar in other respects. An everyday example is when two people speak at once: two separate voices of normal loudness are heard; we don't hear one stimulus that is twice as loud, even though the intensity of the single sound stimulus at the ear is greatly changed. When studied with simple sine tones, how sound stimulus intensities sum depends on how far apart the frequencies of the stimuli are; summation does not occur unless the frequencies of the stimuli are about a quarter of an octave apart or more. Thus, perceptions of loudness are peculiar in that the subjective experience does not vary in any simple way with the physical measures of stimulus intensity.

The most thoroughly documented example of the nonlinear relation between the physical measurement of sound energy and the sound we perceive is the variation of loudness as a function of the frequency of a stimulus (**Figure 6.5**). If listeners in psychophysical experiments are asked to indicate the minimum sound intensity they can hear, it turns out that the detection threshold varies markedly with frequency (remember that the range of human hearing is from about 20 to 20,000 Hz). The human auditory system is least sensitive to intensity at the lower and higher frequencies, and most sensitive

◼ BOX 6A Measuring Loudness: The Decibel

Loudness is correlated with sound pressure level. Although local sound pressure at the ear can be measured in absolute physical terms that represent force per unit area (e.g., Newtons/m^2), it is typically measured in **decibels (dB)**, a relative unit defined by the sensitivity of human hearing. A sound-pressure level of 0 dB is the average threshold of human hearing, which is approximately 2×10^{-5} Newtons/m^2.

The device that measures loudness is called a sound pressure level meter, and is essentially a microphone, an amplifier, and a gauge. These devices are then calibrated (or "weighted") for a particular purposes. If the aim is specifically pertinent to human hearing and sound stimulus perception, the so-called "A-weighting" (dBA) is used, which mimics the frequency-dependent sensitivity of the human auditory system, much as photometers reflect the sensitivity of the human visual system (recall that luminance is a measure that is based on visual sensitivity). Settings with other weightings are used for other purposes such as monitoring very powerful sound stimuli. In these cases, the decibel scale is weighted somewhat differently and is so specified.

In thinking about the physical measurements pertinent to loudness, it is also important to distinguish measuring sound pressure at a particular point (e.g., the ear) from measuring the *overall power* of a source. Sound power per se reflects the energy of a source considered in *all directions*

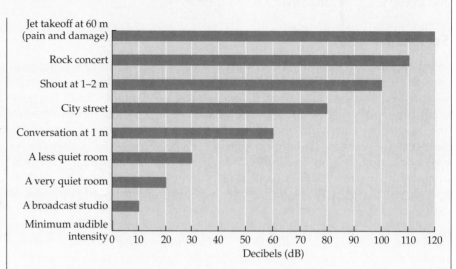

rather than at a single point such as the ear and, like the energy emitted by a light bulb, sound power is measured in watts. The reason for measuring sound pressure levels in decibels is that for most purposes cognitive neuroscientists are interested in issues related specifically to human audition, and not to physical absolutes.

Because humans can detect differences in the intensity of sound stimuli over pressures that cover a million-fold range or more, the decibel scale is logarithmic. Thus a small change in dB represents a large change in intensity; an increase in 6 dB represents a doubling the intensity a sound stimulus measured in terms of sound pressure level, with a (very) roughly commensurate effect on the subjective sense of loudness. The range of intensities for human hearing is about 120 dB (see fig-

ure), with sound pressure levels of about 120 dB being painful and damaging to the hair cells of the inner ear. Even levels of 85–90 dB (typical intensities when sitting relatively far from the speakers at rock concerts) can cause hair cell damage if the exposure is frequent; the resulting premature hearing loss for higher tones is now all too commonly found among younger adults.

Given these facts, an interesting question is why an operatic soprano who routinely practices high C—a note that generates 100–105 dB at the mouth—doesn't deafen herself over time. The answer is that the small muscles of the middle ear adjust their tension and damp the movement of the bones prior to our own vocalizations, and that the sound coming from a singer's mouth is directed away from her ears and is thus attenuated.

in the range of 500 to 5,000 Hz. Not surprisingly, the frequency range of the sound stimuli that are most important to human listeners (e.g., speech sounds) falls within this region of maximum sensitivity.

Most explanations of the variation of loudness as a function of stimulus frequency or other parameters of the stimulus (e.g., stimulus duration or bandwidth) have been **psychoacoustical models** based on the physiology of the input to the auditory system. In the case of the data presented in Figure 6.5, for instance, the resonance properties of the ear canal roughly coincide with the maximum sensitivity of the psychophysical functions, suggesting that stimuli at these frequencies are simply amplified and thus physically more intense before they reach the stage of neural processing. The problem with this seemingly sensible explanation is the many facts about what is actually heard do

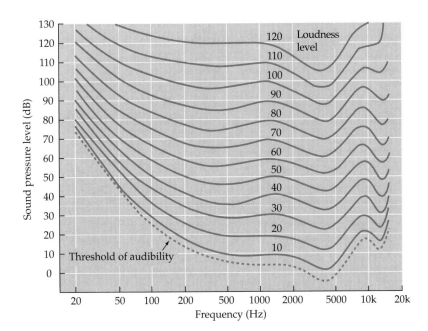

Figure 6.5 Variation in loudness as a function of frequency. Each blue curve indicates the intensities that were heard by normal listeners as equally loud when tested at different intensity levels and frequencies. The functions show that the sensitivity to sound stimuli is greatest in the range of about 500 to about 5000 Hz, which includes the range of speech sounds and music. The dotted line indicates the absolute threshold of human hearing.

not fit this interpretation. For example, psycholinguists Peter Ladefoged and Norris McKinney at UCLA measured the pressure in a speaker's vocal tract and the corresponding sound pressure levels of different vowel sounds at a listener's ear. When subjects were then asked to judge the loudness of the sounds, their judgments were better correlated with the measurements of the speaker's vocal pressure than with the measurements of sound pressure levels at the listener's ear. Moreover, models based on peripheral factors ignore the coordinated evolution of all levels of a sensory system to achieve the same ends—in this case, greater sensitivity to ecologically important sound stimuli.

Functional MRI studies have shown that more auditory cortex is activated by relatively more intense stimuli, and that louder sounds tend to mask weaker ones, but the reverse is not the case. Moreover, ERP and fMRI studies indicate that adaptation to sound stimuli occurs in the course of central processing (see Chapter 4 for an explanation of adaptation in sensory systems). However, much as in the visual system, no area specifically devoted to an analysis of stimulus intensity has been discovered, and neurons in the primary and higher-order auditory cortices are increasingly selective in the stimulus properties that activate them, as described in the following section.

What is clear is that loudness is not simply the brain's transformation of the physical intensity of an auditory signal. Perceived loudness depends on the context in which a given intensity occurs, the context being the other parameters of the sound stimulus, including frequency, duration, bandwidth and other characteristics of the sound signal being experienced. The biological rationale for this way of generating loudness, as in generating visual perceptions of brightness, is presumably a means of relating fundamentally ambiguous sensory stimuli to behaviorally relevant auditory sources.

Pitch

Pitch is defined as the ordered perception of higher or lower tones along a continuum of tonality that is closely related to, but not strictly defined by, the frequencies of sine wave stimuli and the more complex periodicities in natural sound stimuli (see above). This perception of tonality provides the basis for many aspects of speech (e.g., emotional coloring in all languages and semantic meaning in many; see Chapter 20) and the tonal relationships apparent in music. As in hearing loudness, however, what the listener experiences is only very roughly related to its physical basis, the basis in this case being the repetition rate of an acoustic waveform (see Figure 6.4A,B).

Several aspects of pitch perception have been particularly difficult to explain simply in terms of the sensory transduction of stimulus frequency or periodicity, including four significant observations:

1. The pitch heard in response to a harmonic series such as the one shown in Figure 6.4C corresponds to the lowest (first) harmonic (i.e., pitch corresponds to the fundamental frequency).

2. Oddly, the perception of the fundamental frequency persists even when there is no spectral energy in the stimulus at that frequency, a phenomenon referred to as *hearing the missing fundamental*.

3. When the frequencies of a set of successive harmonics such as those in Figure 6.4C are experimentally increased or decreased by a constant value such that they lack a common divisor, the pitch heard corresponds to neither the first harmonic nor to the frequency spacing between the harmonics, a phenomenon called the *pitch shift of the residue*.

4. When the frequencies of just *some* of the harmonics in a stimulus are experimentally increased or decreased by a constant proportion, the pitch heard corresponds to the fundamental of those harmonics that occupy a frequency band centered around 600 Hz, a phenomenon called *spectral dominance*.

Each of these observations indicates that pitch, like loudness, is not determined in any simple way by measurable qualities like frequency or repetition rate of the sound signal. An everyday demonstration of the human ability to hear pitches whose frequencies are not represented in the sound stimulus is the relatively normal-sounding voices we routinely hear over the telephone, which cuts off frequencies below ~500 Hz (the same limitation applies to low-quality portable radios or CD players whose speakers do not generate low frequencies).

The most completely studied and informative of these discrepancies between the physical characteristics of periodic sound stimuli and what is actually heard by listeners has been the phenomenon of the **missing fundamental**. Although this effect was known and used in the design of pipe organs much earlier as a means producing low tones with physically shorter and less cumbersome pipes, the mid-nineteenth century German physicist Thomas Seebeck was the first to demonstrate formally that the frequency of the pitch heard in response to a set of two or more adjacent harmonics corresponds to the greatest common divisor of the harmonic series (the fundamental frequency), even when there is no spectral energy at that frequency. As illustrated in **Figure 6.6**, listeners hear a pitch corresponding to the fundamental frequency of a harmonic series when any of a limited set of the higher harmonics is presented. Each of these stimuli sounds somewhat different in quality (e.g., the stimuli with only upper harmonics sound buzzy and artificial), but listeners typically match the *pitch* they hear to the fundamental frequency of the harmonic set.

A number of studies have provided some insight into the central processing of such stimuli. Studies using magnetoencephalography (MEG; see Chapter 3) were the first to show that pitch and frequency are processed differently in the auditory cortex, a finding consistent with clinical evidence that some patients with lesions in auditory cortex had more difficulty identifying pitch in response to complex tones than when they were presented with pure tones. Recent work carried out in non-human primates by Xiaoqin Wang and his group at Johns Hopkins have confirmed this distinction in much more detail. The investigators recorded responses from a large number of neurons in monkey auditory cortex, asking in each case whether the neurons responded to

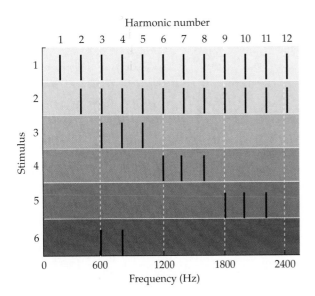

Figure 6.6 Hearing the missing fundamental. The first panel shows, in diagrammatic form, a complete harmonic series for a stimulus with a fundamental of 100 Hz (see Figure 6.4C); the subsequent panels illustrate presentations of subsets of the series with different upper harmonics removed. In each case, listeners judge the pitch of the sound stimulus to be the pitch of the fundamental frequency (i.e., a pitch corresponding to 100 Hz, the greatest common divisor of each series), even though there is no energy at 100 Hz in the stimulus spectra shown in the five lower panels.

both pure tones and to more complex harmonic stimuli in which the fundamental frequency was missing (much like the stimuli in Figure 6.5). One specific subset of the neurons they examined by electrophysiological recording responded to the missing fundamental as well as to the pure tone frequencies; these neurons were grouped together in a region at the anterior lateral boundary of the primary auditory cortex and higher-order auditory cortices (**Figure 6.7**). In contrast to these cells, however, neurons in the primary auditory cortex responded only to the pure tone stimuli.

As indicated in Figure 6.7, there is also more than one tonotopic map in the auditory cortex, much as there are multiple retinotopic maps in the visual cortex (see Chapter 5) and multiple maps of the body surface in the somatic sensory cortex (described in Chapter 7). Duplicated maps in regions with somewhat different functions are thus another general rule of cortical sensory processing.

Despite these advances achieved by more directly assessing the auditory processing of pitch, there is no general agreement about the rationale for the many discrepancies between the frequencies of sound stimuli and what the hearer perceives. A plausible interpretation is that the missing fundamental effect and other aspects of the pitch phenomenology, such as the pitch shift of the residue and spectral dominance (see above), are all consequences of the fact that pitch, like loudness, is determined by the context in which a given periodicity occurs to facilitate biologically useful behavioral responses. Thus in the case of the stimuli illustrated in Figure 6.6, the missing fundamental would be heard because the context provided by the higher harmonics in the series is associated with natural sources that would have contained the full set of harmonics (see Figure 2.2 for an example of such *filling-in* based on context). In any event, pitch percepts clearly correspond more closely to the periodicities of the natural sources with which they are normally associated than with the frequency characteristics of the stimuli as such, which may help explain why aural prostheses such as cochlear implants can be so effective in a selected group of hearing-deficient patients (**Box 6B**).

Timbre

Timbre (pronounced "tamber") is defined by default as the perceptual quality that allows listeners to detect differences between sound stimuli when loudness and pitch are identical. Thus, a clarinet and a bassoon playing the same

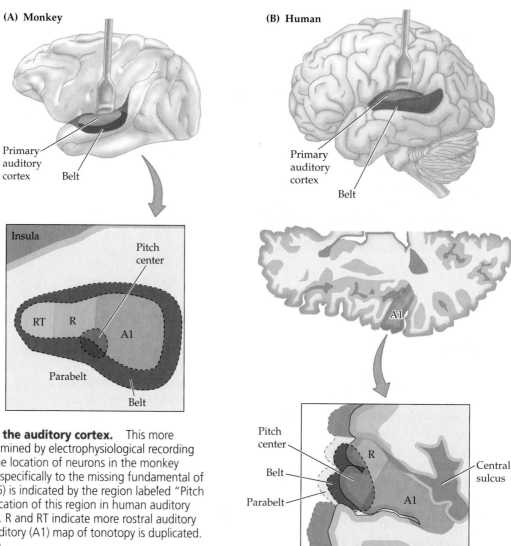

Figure 6.7 Organization of the auditory cortex. This more detailed presentation was determined by electrophysiological recording in a non-human primate. (A) The location of neurons in the monkey auditory cortex that responded specifically to the missing fundamental of a sound stimulus (see Figure 6.6) is indicated by the region labeled "Pitch center." (B) The approximate location of this region in human auditory cortex is shown for comparison. R and RT indicate more rostral auditory regions in which the primary auditory (A1) map of tonotopy is duplicated. (After Bendor and Wang 2006.)

note with the same physical power sound quite different, as do a soprano and a baritone singing the same note. Timbre has no units and is generally accepted as being "multidimensional," meaning that it arises from features of sound stimuli that do not fall into the categories of either intensity or frequency. These additional characteristics include the number of harmonics present (which explains why the presentations in Figure 6.6 sound different even though they are heard as having the same pitch), the amount and quality of noise in the stimulus (i.e., the nonperiodic information), and the temporal profile of the stimulus (e.g., the rate of attack and decay).

These and other factors underlying timbre are all relatively complex and difficult to assess. As a result timbre remains a poorly studied aspect of auditory perception and there is not much to be said about it here. Nonetheless, the characteristics included under this rubric are important, particularly in distinguishing various speech sounds, as described in Chapter 20. Indeed, insofar as the perception of any specific aspect of a stimulus such as loudness or pitch depends on context—as it seems to—the complex factors that timbre

■ BOX 6B The Remarkable Success of Cochlear Implants

An important clinical indication of the way that the frequencies of sound stimuli are related to auditory percepts comes from the success of *cochlear implants* in treating certain kinds of hearing loss. A cochlear implant consists of a peripherally mounted digital signal processor that transforms a sound stimulus into its individual frequency components, along with circuitry that uses this information to activate different combinations of contacts on a threadlike array of stimulating electrodes along the cochlea (see figure).

In a delicate surgical procedure, the electrode array is inserted into the cochlea through the round window of the ear and is positioned along the length of the basilar membrane. The auditory nerve can then be electrically stimulated in a manner that roughly mimics the tonotopic stimulation of the basilar membrane occurring in normal hearing (see Figure 6.1B), with the intensity of sound stimuli being conveyed by the intensity of the electrical stimulation.

Candidates for the procedure are individuals with profound hearing loss in both ears as a result of hair cell damage, but whose auditory nerve and central processing stations are fully intact. Many individuals qualify, including children as young as 2 years old; estimates are that, worldwide, more than 100,000 of these devices have been implanted. Cochlear implantation carries some risk (infection, for example) and works better in some patients than in others, but is now a fairly routine procedure in appropriate patients.

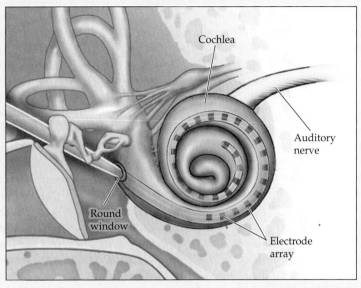

A cochlear implant device used in the treatment of some forms of deafness.

What is especially noteworthy in the present context is that using only a small number of different stimulation points (up to about two dozen), cochlear implants can restore auditory percepts that allow many patients to understand speech and other complex natural sounds quite well. Indeed, in the early days of this technology only a single stimulating electrode was used. Although patients with a single point of stimulation could not discriminate speech, even these individuals could become surprisingly adept at using the limited information from a single-point stimulus; the intensity, duration, and shape of the time "envelope" of the stimulus provided enough context to interpret many sounds in a useful manner.

The surprising success of the current generation of cochlear implants in understanding speech and other complex sound stimuli supports the idea that hearing does not depend on transformation of the physical characteristics of the stimulus as such, but on a more global strategy of perception that uses limited information to make associations between sound stimuli and their natural sources.

References

RAMSDEN, R. T. (2002) Cochlear implants and brain stem implants. *Brit. Med. Bull.* 63: 183–193.

RAUSCHECKER, J. P. AND R. V. SHANNON (2002) Sending sound to the brain. *Science* 295: 1025–1029.

entails are at least as important as the intensity of a stimulus or its frequency spectrum in determining what is actually heard.

Perceiving the Location of Sound Sources

A different aspect of auditory perception is how the human auditory system generates a sense of the *location* of sounds in space. Psychophysical studies show that humans can localize sound stimuli to within a degree or two in the horizontal axis (i.e., the left-to-right axis, also called the *azimuth*). We have a somewhat less accurate sense of sound location in the vertical axis, and relatively poor front-to-back localization. How, then, are these biologically important aspects of sound perception generated?

A series of experiments, mostly electrophysiological studies in experimental animals, have shown that two basic strategies are used to localize the horizontal position of sound sources, depending on the frequencies in the stimulus. For frequencies below 3 kHz, **interaural time differences** are used to localize the source; above these frequencies, **interaural intensity differences** are used. Distinct pathways originating from the cochlear nucleus to the primary auditory cortex and beyond serve these respective strategies for sound localization (see Figure 6.2 and below).

Using interaural time differences

Interaural time differences arise because of the distance between the two ears. Since the speed of sound is relatively slow (about 340 meters per second at sea level and 20°C), there is a significant interval between the time a stimulus arrives at one ear and then the other (**Figure 6.8**). The longest interaural time differences are produced by sounds arising directly lateral to one ear and are on the order of 700 microseconds (a value given by the width of the head divided by the speed of sound). Psychophysical experiments show that normal adults can detect interaural time differences as small as 10 microseconds, a sensitivity consistent with accurate sound localization to about 1° in the horizontal axis.

The neural circuitry that initiates the information about such tiny interaural time differences consists of binaural inputs to the medial superior olive component (the MSO) of the superior olivary complex indicated in Figure 6.2A; these inputs come from the left and right cochlear nuclei, thus allowing the MSO neurons to act as **coincidence detectors**. For a coincidence mechanism to be useful in localizing sound, different neurons must be sensitive to different time delays, a concept first suggested by psychologist and auditory physiologist Lloyd Jeffress in 1948. This feat is accomplished by having the axons that

Figure 6.8 Sound stimulus localization by virtue of interaural time differences. Neurons in the medial superior olive (MSO; see also Figure 6.2A) compute the location of sound stimulus sources by acting as coincidence detectors. The neurons respond most strongly when two inputs arrive simultaneously, as occurs when the contralateral and ipsilateral inputs precisely compensate via their different pathway lengths for differences in the time of arrival of a sound at the two ears. The systematic variation in the delay lengths of the two inputs effectively creates a map of sound location. In this diagrammatic example, neuron E would be most sensitive to sounds located to the left of the listener, and neuron A to sounds from the right; neuron C would respond best to sounds coming from directly in front of the listener.

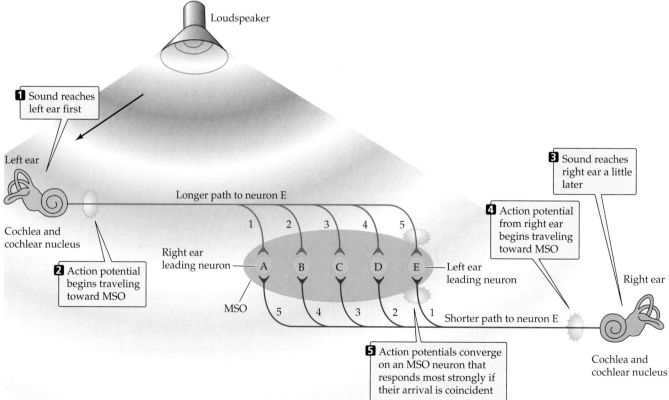

project from the cochlear nucleus vary systematically in length to create **delay lines** (the length of an axon multiplied by its conduction velocity equals the conduction time). These anatomical differences mean that action potential signals generated by different time intervals will arrive *simultaneously* at different MSO cells. The excitation of these neurons in response to the two inputs arriving at the same time will be maximal, thus providing information to the more central stations in the auditory pathway and the auditory cortex about stimuli arising from different locations.

Recent work has indicated that the central processing of information extracted and sent forward by the MSO may in fact depend more on the overall pattern of neuronal activity in the MSO than on the detection of coincidences as such (i.e., the firing of those neurons that are maximally activated by a stimulus in space). This caveat does not mean that the idea of coincidence detection is wrong, but underscores once again the idea that percepts are never simple translations of some physical stimulus parameter—interaural time differences in this instance. Such parameters only begin a complex process that transmutes and abstracts peripheral information for reasons that are only now beginning to be understood. In support of this last statement, there is abundant clinical evidence that lesions of the auditory cortices can lead to deficiencies of sound localization, indicating that the perception of where a sound is coming from is ultimately generated by cortical processing of the information the MSO supplies.

Using differences in sound intensity

In humans, sound localization perceived on the basis of interaural time differences applies to stimuli whose frequencies are below approximately 3 kHz. But it is clear that humans also are able to localize high frequency stimuli, meaning that another mechanism of sound localization must come into play. This additional mechanism takes advantage of the fact that that stimulus intensity at the two ears also varies as a function of the position of the source (**Figure 6.9**).

Figure 6.9 Sound stimulus localization by virtue of interaural intensity differences. (A) The head presents a physical obstacle whose mass diminishes stimulus intensity at the far ear for higher frequencies. Pathways to the lateral superior olive component of the olivary complex (LSO) and the medial nucleus of the trapezoid body (MNTB) are shown in the blowup cross section of the brainstem at the level of the mid-pons (see Figure 6.2A). (B) The output of the neurons in the lateral superior olive (i.e., the number of action potentials per second) reflects the relative intensity of the inputs to the two ears.

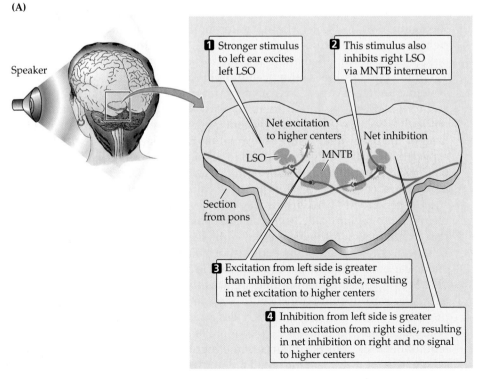

(A)

Speaker

1 Stronger stimulus to left ear excites left LSO

2 This stimulus also inhibits right LSO via MNTB interneuron

Net excitation to higher centers

Net inhibition

LSO

MNTB

Section from pons

3 Excitation from left side is greater than inhibition from right side, resulting in net excitation to higher centers

4 Inhibition from left side is greater than excitation from right side, resulting in net inhibition on right and no signal to higher centers

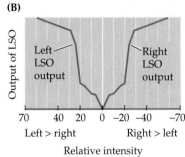

(B)

Output of LSO

Left LSO output

Right LSO output

70 40 20 0 −20 −40 −70

Left > right   Right > left

Relative intensity

Although sound stimulus intensity always falls off as function of distance, the separation of the two ears is too small for this aspect of sound physics to have much effect for relatively low-frequency sounds; because of their longer length, sound waves at lower frequencies are not affected by the presence of the head between the two ears. However, at frequencies above about 2 kHz, the head begins to act as an obstacle to sound waves. As a result, when high-frequency sounds are directed toward one side of the head, an acoustical "shadow" of lower intensity is created at the far ear. This difference allows the auditory system to assess the position of high-frequency sound sources on basis of relative intensities at each ear. The circuitry that carries out this processing is located in two other brainstem nuclei in the primary auditory pathway, the *lateral superior olive* and the *medial nucleus of the trapezoid body* (see Figure 6.9).

In summary, there are two pathways—and two separate mechanisms—for localizing sound at low and high frequencies. These pathways eventually merge in the inferior colliculus of the midbrain, consistent with the fact that these two ways of localizing sound stimuli are not perceptually distinguishable.

Other Aspects of Auditory Cortical Processing

Reviewing auditory processing in terms of the major auditory perceptual qualities—loudness, pitch, timbre, and sound location—necessarily omits some points about the organization and function of the auditory cortex that are pertinent to understanding auditory processing at this level. These points are also germane in comparisons with sensory processing in other modalities.

Iterated units within the primary auditory cortex

One point concerns the *iterated columns* (or *stripes*, or *modules*) that have been a focus of much research in the visual and somatic sensory systems (see Figure 4.13). In the visual system, different stimulus features preferentially activate iterated cortical regions within the primary visual cortex; these units, which are on the order of a millimeter or less in size, can be identified anatomically or electrophysiologically and indicate a strong tendency toward functional segregation on this scale. These iterated units in V1 include the alternating right- and left-eye stripes in cortical layer 4, the columnar organization for processing different orientations and the so-called blobs in layers 2 and 3.

On the basis of this anatomical and physiological evidence in the visual system, one might expect similar organizational features within the primary auditory cortices, but in fact there is relatively little evidence for such units within A1. Because the auditory system integrates binaural information at the level of the brainstem, distinct information from the two ears would not be expected to be distinctly represented in A1, and indeed it seems not to be. A1 neurons in experimental animals such as cats and monkeys respond to stimulation of either ear, and A1 thus lacks the equivalent of the left- and right-eye stripes seen in V1. There is, however, some evidence for some functional segregation into regions called *summation columns* and *suppression columns*. Neurons in summation columns respond with greater activity to the stimulation of either ear, whereas neurons in suppression columns are excited by stimulation of one ear but inhibited by stimulation of the other. This effect tends to subdivide the A1 cortex into areas that are sensitive to a given frequency, with a particular ear preference function. In any event, the segregation of functional properties in iterated units is much less apparent in A1 than in V1. Even in vision, such iterated units seem to be more of an epiphenomenon than a basic requirement for perception, since some highly visual primates do not show segregated modules such as ocular dominance stripes that are evident in closely related species. A prudent view would be the such modules are very useful clues about cortical organization, but are not essential to the successful operation of the primary sensory cortices or to perception.

Higher-order cortical processing

Another point concerns the comparison of audition and other sensory modalities with respect to the organization of cortical processing in the higher-order (*belt*) areas of auditory cortex. These areas correspond to extrastriate cortical regions in vision and to the secondary somatic sensory cortices described in the next chapter. As in the visual system, these higher-order auditory areas tend to be specialized for processing particular categories of sensory information of biological importance, as already implied by the discussion of pitch processing. As in vision, however, the degree of specialization and the underlying processing strategy remain quite controversial. The clearest evidence about the organization of these secondary areas in humans involves specialized areas devoted to speech processing; although this subject is covered in detail in Chapter 21, it is useful to briefly introduce some aspects of this and other related evidence about higher order auditory specialization here.

■ An area adjacent to A1 in the superior and posterior region of the temporal lobe (Brodmann area 22, also called **Wernicke's area**) is clearly important in linking speech sounds to their meanings (**Figure 6.10**). Patients with lesions in this area of the left hemisphere suffer a particular language deficiency called a *comprehension aphasia*, in which the affected individuals are able to produce speech, but unable to use words in a semantically correct way (i.e., the meanings are garbled).

■ There is some fMRI evidence for the existence of an area of auditory cortex that is particularly concerned with the motion of an auditory stimulus. This sort of specialization of auditory cortex for processing information about sound sequences in space is arguably similar to the specialization of some regions of extrastriate visual cortex for processing image sequences.

■ Animal studies support the implication that especially important natural sound stimuli are "overrepresented" in especially well-developed cortical areas in many species. In echolocating bats, for example, an extraordinarily large cortical region is devoted to the specific frequencies such bats use to catch prey by sonar. By analogy with the overrepresentation of the human fovea (see Chapter 4) in the primary visual cortex, this region of bat cortex has been referred to as an *auditory fovea*. In humans, it has been known for more than a century that the regions used to process speech sounds are not only overrepresented but lateralized as well. Thus, whereas speech sound processing is predominantly carried out in the left hemisphere, processing other environmental sound stimuli occurs in both hemispheres (**Figure 6.11**).

■ Extending this evidence for cortical specialization to the level of single cells, Joseph Raushecker and his group at the National Institutes of Health and others have shown that neurons in the auditory cortex of anesthetized monkeys are especially responsive to monkey vocalizations, and that in some instances are more responsive to one type of call than another (see Chapter 20).

■ In a similar vein, Michael Lewicki and his colleagues at Carnegie Mellon University have found that the tuning of auditory nerve axons encodes the sort of broadband stimuli characteristic of the sounds animals hear in nature more fully and efficiently than sound stimuli created in the laboratory. This bias towards efficient coding of natural stimuli accords with the sort of coding evident in the receptive field properties in studies of the visual system described in Chapter 5.

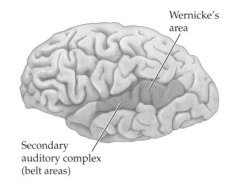

Figure 6.10   Specialized sound stimulus processing areas.   Some belt areas of auditory cortex are specialized for processing particularly important sound stimulus categories. Clinical evidence in patients, as well as numerous fMRI studies in normal individuals, show that Wernicke's area is specialized for processing and perceiving speech sounds and their meanings. However, as in the case of nominally specialized areas in the higher-order cortices of other sensory modalities, such regions are not sharply demarcated anatomically and entail a variety of additional processing functions that are not well understood.

Figure 6.11 Functional MRI evidence for a specialized speech processing area. Images from a normal subject compare the activity in auditory cortex elicited by speech sound stimuli and other (non-speech) environmental sound stimuli. The graphs below show the relative activation in the primary and secondary (belt) areas of auditory cortex in each hemisphere. Different categories of sound stimuli are processed in different degrees both within and between the two hemispheres. Thus, speech is more fully processed in the left belt areas, whereas non-speech environmental sounds are more fully processed in the belt areas of the right hemisphere. (Courtesy of Jagmeet Kanwal.)

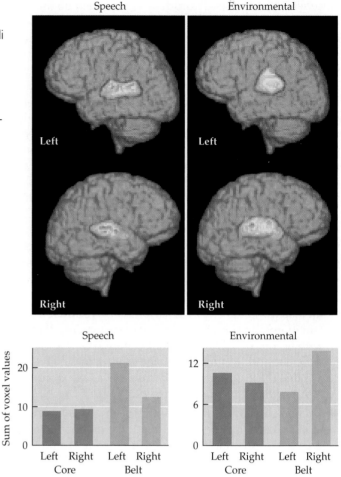

■ Finally, Norman Weinberger and his colleagues at Case Western Reserve have shown that the optimal frequency responses of neurons in the auditory cortex can be shifted to some degree by relatively brief training in a classical conditioning paradigm.

This range of evidence makes it clear that processing in the auditory cortex is strongly biased in favor of those stimuli whose perception is most relevant to successful behavior. Processing in these areas also seems particularly concerned with sorting out the implications of stimulus context. Finally, connectivity in these regions is in some degree malleable, presumably to allow experience to improve perceptual and ultimately behavioral responses.

Music and Its Esthetic Effects

Like speech sounds, music provides a fascinating stimulus category that has been of particular interest to cognitive neuroscientists. Why humans are so captivated by musical stimuli is a puzzling question, since unlike speech and other natural sounds, musical tones have no obvious ecological significance that would have driven the evolution of musical appreciation in our species. Studying music from this perspective also raises the more general question of why some stimuli are esthetically more appealing than others, a cognitive issue that has so far remained unresolved.

Definitions of music

Although everyone recognizes music when they hear it, its precise definition tends to be vague. The Oxford English Dictionary gives the primary definition of music as "The art or science of combining vocal or instrumental sounds with a view toward beauty or coherence of form and expression of emotion." The definition given in the glossary here is "Complex periodic sound stimuli produced by a variety of physical objects (including the human larynx) that are appreciated as pleasing to humans and that are implemented formally in the chromatic scale." An essential ingredient in both definitions is the esthetic pleasure and emotional stimulation humans derive from music.

The appeal of music to listeners entails all the major auditory perceptual categories discussed earlier in the chapter (i.e., loudness, pitch, and timbre). Rhythm, tempo, and meter are further aspects of music that link music to motor behavior and to the esthetic qualities of human movements, particularly dance. **Rhythm** refers to the accentuated beats in music (basically which beats correspond to a listener's tendency to tap their foot or clap), **tempo** to the rate beats occur in time (the number of beats per minute), and **meter** to the larger structure of the beats (how many beats per measure). However, the focus of interest over the centuries has been on the pitches and pitch relationships in music, which are generally referred to as *musical tones*. A sequence of such tones, formally notated as in **Figure 6.12A**, is the basis of musical **melody**, whereas combinations of tones played simultaneously are the basis of **harmony**. Evidence of musical instruments dating back tens of thousands of years indicates that these phenomena have existed since the dawn of human culture (**Figure 6.12B**).

Why do humans have a sense of tonality?

A starting point in thinking about the perceptual effects elicited by melodies and harmonies is understanding, in general terms, what the biological purpose of the human tonal sense might be, a question also pertinent to why a pitch center distinct from A1 might have evolved in the human brain (see Figure 6.7).

The brain presumably generates our sense of pitch or any other perceptual category because of the biological advantage that accrues from appreciating the information in the relevant aspect of the stimulus. In the case of tonality, the relevant information in the stimulus is, as already indicated, the *periodic repetition* of power peaks found some types of sound stimuli. The biologically important aspect of periodicity is the information it can provide about the natural sources of those stimuli. As mentioned earlier, periodic stimuli are rela-

(A)   Beethoven, Sonata for Piano, Op. 2, No. 1

(B)

Figure 6.12 Music. (A) The major characteristics of music and its formal representation. This small segment of a much longer musical score indicates the melodic line (notes played sequentially) and some harmony (the notes played simultaneously). The relative duration of notes (the quarter notes here) and the arrangement of the notes within each measure (signified by the vertical lines) reflect the intended rhythm and meter. "Allegro" alerts the performer to the composer's intent that this section be played brightly, at a rapid tempo. (B) This flute was discovered in an archeological site in France and has been determined to be about 32,000 years old. The distances between the holes in the flute suggest that the musical scales being played at that time were much like those in use today.

tively rare in nature, animal vocalizations being the most prevalent source (because their are few other objects that generate harmonic series; see Figure 6.4). The animal whose vocalizations are most pertinent to humans is of course other humans. The information embedded in the tonal characteristics of vocalizations include the probable size and gender of the speaker, his or her emotional state and a wealth of information particular to language (these characteristics, for example, are what enables us to differentiate vowel sounds from one another; see Chapter 20). Humans presumably evolved their sense of tonality to extract this information; it follows, then, that music and its cognitive effects are likely to be related to these general purposes, human vocalizations in particular.

What are the musical phenomena that need to be rationalized?

The aspect of musical tones that most begs explanation is the apparently universal tonal framework for composing and performing music. Nearly all cultures studied by musicologists use a subset of pitch intervals to divide an *octave* (i.e., a doubling of the fundamental frequency of a periodic stimulus) into a series of quite specific tones. In relatively simple ethnic music, the octave is divided into 5 tonal intervals, called a *pentatonic scale*. Western music of the last few centuries typically uses 7 divisions that define the *diatonic scale* (the familiar "do, re, mi…" scale). The complete set of musical notes that divides an octave entails the 12 notes of the **chromatic scale,** of which the scales just mentioned are subsets (although, as musicians will know, these 12 tones don't quite fit into an octave unless some ad hoc adjustments in tuning are made).

People from widely different cultures appreciate that some combinations of these chromatic scale tones are preferable to others when played together, thus defining musical **consonance.** The most compatible of these harmonically pleasing combinations are typically used to convey "resolution" at the end of a musical phrase or piece in a given key, whereas less compatible combinations are used to provide a sense of transition or tension in a chord or melodic sequence. Equally remarkable is the fact that all humans recognize tones separated by an octave as sounding musically the same (consider the "do" at the beginning and end of the diatonic scale).

These cross-cultural phenomena are deeply puzzling, since humans can discriminate many more intervals over an octave, and there is obvious reason why these specific tones and tone combinations should be so strongly preferred.

Some possible explanations

Despite the intense interest of musicians, philosophers, scientists, and entrepreneurs over the centuries, musical phenomena have no generally accepted explanation in either physical, psychological, or biological terms. Traditional approaches to rationalizing musical scales and consonance are based on the fact that the musical intervals corresponding to octaves, fifths, and fourths in modern musical terminology are produced by physical sources whose relative proportions (e.g., the relative lengths of two plucked strings or their fundamental frequencies) have ratios of 2:1, 3:2, or 4:3, respectively; see Figure 6.5).

This coincidence of numerical simplicity and perceptual effectiveness is so impressive that attempts to rationalize phenomena such as consonance and scale structure in terms of physical or mathematical relationships have tended to dominate the thinking about these issues. As a result, frameworks based on the physical overlap of the harmonics of two tones played together have been especially influential over the past century. For example, half of the harmonics in the two series generated by tones an octave apart overlap precisely, providing a compelling explanation of octave similarity. Other aspects of musical harmony, however, are difficult to explain in this way.

Another approach to understanding musical phenomena is based on the idea, preeminent throughout this unit, that audition is particularly geared to process natural sound stimuli that are behaviorally significant. From this perspective, the evolutionary forces that generated the human sense of tonality reflect the importance of gleaning social and other information from periodic stimuli, human vocalizations in particular. The fact that chromatic scale intervals are apparent in the spectra of speech—and that the pentatonic and diatonic intervals are the most salient of these—is consistent with the idea that musical scales derive from the acoustical characteristics of vocalizations. Investigators have also suggested that the esthetic responses to different musical scales (e.g., major versus minor scales) might derive from the acoustical similarity of musical tones in the scales and the tonal characteristics of speech uttered in different emotional states. In any event, it seems likely that the acoustical characteristics of speech will be relevant to understanding otherwise puzzling aspects of music.

The neural underpinnings of musical processing

How, then, does the brain process music, and is such processing distinct in any way from the processing of other sound stimuli? Since we know that speech processing is carried out by brain regions that are in some degree dedicated (see Figures 6.9 and 6.10), these questions are certainly plausible.

Whereas the lexical aspects of speech are processed predominantly in the belt areas of the primary auditory cortex in the left hemisphere, musical stimuli are processed more fully in the right hemisphere (**Figure 6.13**). This hemispheric distinction accords with the fact that the emotional qualities of speech (and emotion generally) are more strongly represented in the right hemisphere (see Chapters 18 and 21).

The connection between music and emotional feelings has been pursued by a variety of cognitive neuroscientists with musical backgrounds and interests. Mark Tramo at Harvard Medical School and others have shown that the areas in the right temporal and parietal cortices near the primary auditory cortex are particularly active in response to musical stimuli (although other regions are also involved), and that tones, melody, harmony, and rhythm are all influential in generating this activity (**Figure 6.14**). In agreement with this evidence, Anne Blood, Robert Zatorre, and other investigators at the Montreal Neurological Institute examined the aesthetic or emotional responses to music by asking what regions of the auditory brain are activated by music that elicits a "chills down the spine" response in normal subjects. Using PET imaging, they showed that pleasurable musical experiences of this sort are associated with increased activation in brain areas that mediate reward and motivation as well as overall level of arousal. These areas include the ventral striatum, midbrain, amygdala, orbitofrontal cortex, and ventral medial prefrontal cortex, all regions that are further discussed in the context of emotion, pleasure, and reward in Unit VI.

Auditory Objects and Auditory Scene Analysis

A key point in the discussion of auditory perception is that what a person actually hears is not loudness, tone, timbre, or sound location as such, but something more akin to the perception of visual objects—that is, percepts that are behaviorally useful as opposed to a collection of qualities. In vision, the groups of objects normally present in the environment give rise to "scenes." The parallel aspect of audition has led to the concept of *auditory scenes*, and an area of cognitive research referred to as **auditory scene analysis**.

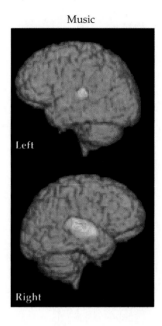

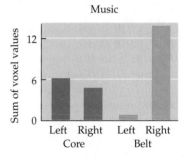

Figure 6.13 Functional MRI evidence for lateralization of musical sound processing. In most individuals, the processing of musical sounds occurs primarily in the auditory cortex (belt areas) of the right temporal lobe. The graph shows the relative activation in the primary and secondary areas of auditory cortex in each hemisphere in the subject studied, which contrasts with the predominantly left-hemisphere processing of speech sound stimuli (see Figure 6.11). (Courtesy of Jagmeet Kanwal).

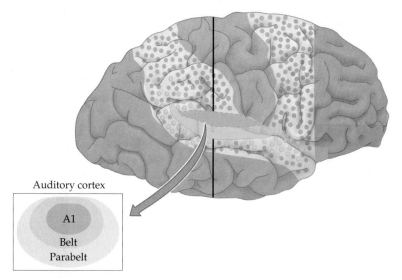

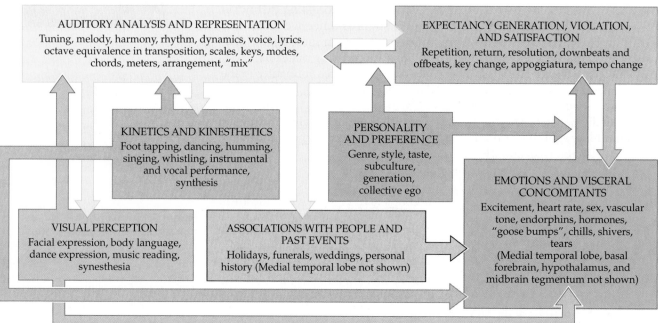

AUDITORY ANALYSIS AND REPRESENTATION
Tuning, melody, harmony, rhythm, dynamics, voice, lyrics, octave equivalence in transposition, scales, keys, modes, chords, meters, arrangement, "mix"

EXPECTANCY GENERATION, VIOLATION, AND SATISFACTION
Repetition, return, resolution, downbeats and offbeats, key change, appoggiatura, tempo change

KINETICS AND KINESTHETICS
Foot tapping, dancing, humming, singing, whistling, instrumental and vocal performance, synthesis

PERSONALITY AND PREFERENCE
Genre, style, taste, subculture, generation, collective ego

EMOTIONS AND VISCERAL CONCOMITANTS
Excitement, heart rate, sex, vascular tone, endorphins, hormones, "goose bumps", chills, shivers, tears
(Medial temporal lobe, basal forebrain, hypothalamus, and midbrain tegmentum not shown)

VISUAL PERCEPTION
Facial expression, body language, dance expression, music reading, synesthesia

ASSOCIATIONS WITH PEOPLE AND PAST EVENTS
Holidays, funerals, weddings, personal history (Medial temporal lobe not shown)

Figure 6.14 Regions of the right hemisphere activated by musical stimuli. This diagram is intended to convey the idea that musical stimuli can act on a wide variety of cognitive functions related to music appreciation and performance. Note that the primary auditory cortex (orange) is not visible in this view; see Figure 6.3. The inset shows the fMRI activation of the right auditory cortex in a normal subject listening to Beethoven's Seventh Symphony. (After Tramo 2001.)

Auditory scene analysis is to a considerable degree rooted in the heritage of Gestalt psychology (see Chapter 2). Researchers in this subfield, such as psychologist Albert Bregman at McGill University, have emphasized the importance of grouping and streaming in the perception of sound stimuli in natural circumstances. For example, we routinely "tune out" background noise as we listen to music, and we can follow the speech of a person we are talking with even if the conversation is taking place in a noisy environment (**Figure 6.15A**). In some sense, then, we have the ability to segregate a pertinent stream of stimuli from a welter of simultaneous auditory information and recognize that stream as an "auditory object." Many phenomena that depend on the larger-scale organization of auditory perceptual qualities have been described and the challenges of explaining them made clear.

It is possible to explore at least some aspects of these phenomena with more direct methods. For instance, studies using evoked response potentials (ERPs; see Chapter 3) have shown an enhanced component of subjects' responses to an unusual occurrence in a stream of stimuli that are otherwise related in an expected manner. This *mismatch negativity*, or "oddball effect," indicates a change in neural processing of auditory stimuli when a commonly experienced stimulus fails to conform to past experience. Claude Alain and his colleagues at Laval University have studied this phenomenon in situations in which the usually experienced form of a relatively simple stimulus is violated in one way or another. The example in **Figure 6.15B** shows that auditory cortical processing is altered when one component of a harmonic series is mistuned (see Figure 6.6). This effect presumably occurs because the usual presentation of the harmonic series is violated, requiring that additional processing circuitry be brought into play to sort out the possible meaning of the stimulus. Such observations are in keeping with much other evidence that auditory processing is strongly influenced by the typical significance of sound stimuli for human listeners.

(A)

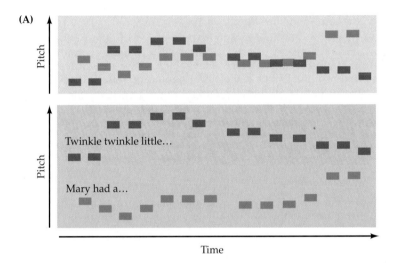

(B)

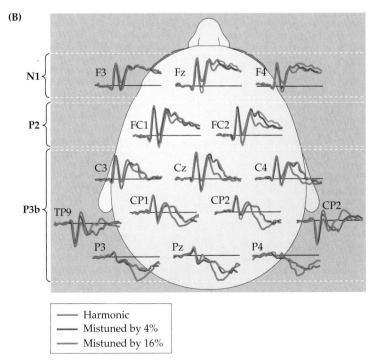

Figure 6.15 Auditory stream analysis. (A) When two streams of tones representing different familiar melodies are interspersed in the same frequency range (upper panel), listeners cannot distinguish them. If the streams are presented at frequency levels that elicit significantly different pitches, however, the two tunes are readily distinguished and tracked (lower panel). The two interspersed streams in the upper panel can also be distinguished if the intensity of one stream is made significantly different from the other. (B) Event-related potential (ERP) study showing differences in neural processing determined by this measure as a result of mistuning the second or the eighth harmonic of a stimulus (that is, a stimulus such as that shown in the top panel of Figure 6.6) by either 4 percent or 16 percent. The larger mistuning causes a significant "mismatch negativity" response. These examples indicate that we routinely use a variety of contextual information to group sound stimuli into useful streams according to what we have experienced in the past. (B after Alain et al. 2001.)

Summary

1. The primary auditory pathway begins with the receptors (hair cells) in the basilar membrane that respond to local pressure changes in the atmosphere within an appropriate range.

2. The information generated by the hair cells is processed in the cochlear nuclei, additional nuclei in the brainstem, the inferior colliculus in the midbrain, and in the medial geniculate nuclei of the thalamus before being sent on to the primary auditory cortex (A1).

3. A major feature of A1 is its tonotopic arrangement, which accords with the tonotopy of the basilar membrane; in both instances, the initial responses are predicated on stimulus frequency as such.

4. The major perceptual qualities in audition are pitch, loudness, and timbre. Pitch is the perception generated by periodic variations in the power of sound stimuli; loudness is the perception of sound intensity; and timbre is the perception of differences in the qualities of sound sources when their frequencies and intensities are the same.

5. None of these perceptual qualities are simply or directly related to the physical characteristics of the corresponding stimuli.

6. The higher-order processing of sound stimuli that gives rise to auditory percepts occurs in the belt areas of auditory cortex adjacent to A1, which are generally analogous to the extrastriate cortical areas in the visual system. These areas are especially responsive to auditory stimuli that have biological significance, such as speech.

7. Musical sounds stimuli also trigger strong auditory responses that are, like speech, associated with many other cognitive functions. Indeed, the appeal of music is probably related to the importance of tonality in speech.

Additional Reading

Reviews

ALAIN, C. AND S. R. ARNOTT (2000) Selectively attending to auditory objects. *Frontiers Biosci.* 5: 202–212.

BENDOR, D. AND X. WANG (2006) Cortical representations of pitch in monkeys and humans. *Curr. Opin. Neurobiol.* 16: 391–399

BURNS, E. M. (1999) Intervals, scales, and tuning. In *The Psychology of Music*, D. Deutsch (ed.). New York: Academic Press, pp. 215–264.

GRIFFITHS, D. G. AND J. D. WARREN (2004) What is an auditory object? *Nat. Rev. Neurosci.* 5: 887–892.

KAAS, J. H. AND T. A. HACKETT (2000) Subdivisions of auditory cortex and processing streams in primates. *Proc. Natl. Acad. Sci. USA* 97: 11793–11799.

NELKEN, I., A. FISHBACH, L. LAS, N. ULANOVSKY AND D. FARKAS (2003) Primary auditory cortex of cats: Feature detection or something else? *Biol. Cybernetics* 89: 397–406.

PLACK, C. J. AND R. P. CARLYON (1995) Loudness perception and intensity coding. In *Hearing*, B. C. J. Moore (ed.). New York: Academic Press, pp. 123–160.

RASCH, R. AND R. PLOMP (1999) The perception of musical tones. In *The Psychology of Music*, D. Deutsch (ed.). New York: Academic Press, pp. 89–112.

RAUSCHECKER, J. P. AND B. TIAN (2000) Mechanisms and streams for processing of "what" and "where" in auditory cortex. *Proc. Natl. Acad. Sci. USA* 97: 11800–11806.

READ, H. L., J. A. WINER AND C. E. SCHREINER (2002) Functional architecture of auditory cortex. *Curr. Opin. Neurobiol.* 12: 433–440.

SCHREINER, C. E., H. L. READ AND M. L. SUTTER (2000) Modular organization of frequency integration in primary auditory cortex. *Annu. Rev. Neurosci.* 23: 501–529.

SHEPARD, R. (1999) Pitch perception and measurement. In *Music, Cognition, and Computerized Sound: An Introduction to Psychoacoustics*, P. R. Cook (ed.). Cambridge, MA: MIT Press, pp. 149–166.

TRAMO, M. J. (2001) Biology and music: Music of the hemispheres. *Science* 291: 54–56.

WEINBERGER, N. M. (2004) Specific long-term memory traces in primary auditory cortex. *Nat. Rev. Neurosci.* 5: 279–290.

Important Original Papers

ALAIN, C., S. R. ARNOTT, S. HEVENOR, S. GRAHAM AND C. L. GRADY (2001) "What" and "where" in the human auditory system. *Proc. Natl. Acad. Sci. USA* 98: 12301–12306.

ALAIN, C., S. R. ARNOTT AND T. W. PICTON (2001) Bottom-up and top-down influences on auditory scene analysis: Evidence from event-related brain potentials. *J. Exp. Psych.: Human Perception and Performance* 27: 1072–1089.

BENDOR, D. AND X. WANG (2006) The neural representation of pitch in primate auditory cortex. *Nature* 436: 1161–1165.

BLOOD, A. J., R. J. ZATORRE, P. BERMUDEZ AND A. C. EVANS (1999) Emotional responses to pleasant and unpleasant music correlate with activity in paralimbic brain regions. *Nat. Neurosci.* 2: 382–387.

FLETCHER, H. AND W. A. MUNSON (1933) Loudness: Its definition, measurement, and calculation. *J. Acoust. Soc. Amer.* 5: 82–108.

GLAVE, R. D. AND A. C. M. RIETVELD (1975) Is the effort dependence of speech loudness explicable on the basis of acoustical cues? *J. Acoust. Soc. Amer.* 58: 875–879.

KANWAL, J. S., J. KIM AND K. KAMADA (2000) Separate distributed processing of environmental, speech, and musical sounds in the cerebral hemispheres. *J. Cogn. Neurosci.* (Suppl.) p. 32.

LADEFOGED, P. AND N. P. MCKINNEY (1963) Loudness, sound pressure, and sub-glottal pressure in speech. *J. Acoust. Soc. Amer.* 35: 454–460.

LEWICKI, M. (2002) Efficient coding of natural sounds. *Nat. Neurosci.* 5: 356–363.

MALMBERG, C. F. (1918) The perception of consonance and dissonance. *Psychol. Monogr.* 25: 93–133.

PANTEV, C., M. HOKE, B. LUTKENHONER AND K. LEHNERTZ (1989) Tonotopic organization of the auditory cortex: pitch versus frequency representation. *Science* 246: 486–488.

PIERCE, J. (1991) Periodicity and pitch perception. *J. Acoust. Soc. Amer.* 90: 1889–1893.

RITSMA, R. J. (1967) Frequencies dominant in the perception of the pitch of complex sounds. *J. Acoust. Soc. Amer.* 42: 191–198.

SCHOUTEN, J. F., R. J. RITSMA AND B. I. CARDOZO (1962) Pitch of the residue. *J. Acoust. Soc. Amer.* 34: 1418–1424.

SCHWARTZ, D. A. AND D. PURVES (2004) Pitch is determined by naturally occurring periodic sounds. *Hearing Res.* 194: 31–46.

SCHWARTZ, D., C. Q. HOWE AND D. PURVES (2003) The statistical structure of human speech sounds predicts musical universals. *J. Neurosci.* 23: 7160–7168.

SMITH, E. AND M. S. LEWICKI (2006) Efficient auditory coding. *Nature* 439: 978–982.

TERHARDT, E. (1974) Pitch, consonance, and harmony. *J. Acoust. Soc. Amer.* 55: 1061–1069.

ZAHORIK, P. AND F. L. WRIGHTMAN (2001) Loudness constancy varying with sound source distance. *Nat. Neurosci.* 4: 78–83

Books

BREGMAN, A. (1990) *Auditory Scene Analysis: The Perceptual Organization of Sound.* Cambridge, MA: MIT Press.

ISACOFF, S. (2001) *Temperament.* New York: Knopf.

LEVITAN, D. J. (2006) *This is Your Brain on Music.* New York: Dutton.

MOORE, B. C. J. (2003) *An Introduction to the Psychology of Hearing*, 5th Ed. London: Academic Press.

NEUHOFF, J. G. (2004) *Ecological Psychoacoustics.* San Diego: Elsevier.

PIERCE, J. R. (1992) *The Science of Musical Sound.* New York: W. H. Freeman.

PLOMP, R. (2002) *The Intelligent Ear: On the Nature of Sound Perception.* Mahwah, NJ: Lawrence Earlbaum.

ROSSING, T. D., R. F. MOORE AND P. A. WHEELER (2002) *The Science of Sound*, 3rd Ed. San Francisco: Addison-Wesley.

Mechanosensory and Chemosensory Perception

- ■ **The Mechanosensory Subsystems 175**
- ■ **The Chemosensory Modalities 187**
- ■ **Some Additional Questions about Sensory Systems 194**

Introduction

In addition to the percepts elicited by visual and auditory stimuli, two other major sensory categories remain to be considered: percepts produced by the mechanical forces acting on the body, and percepts elicited by chemical stimuli. The organization of the mechanosensory modalities is complex in that it includes several relatively distinct subsystems. One subsystem generates perceptions of touch, pressure, and vibration; another reports the position and status of the limbs and other body parts in space; still another subsystem generates perceptions of pain; and, finally, the vestibular system generates perceptions of body acceleration, dizziness, and the position of the head in space. Most of these somatic percepts are initiated by mechanoreceptors at or near the body surface, in muscles, in tendons, and in joints. The information from mechanoreceptors is processed and relayed by specific nuclei in the thalamus, further processed in the primary somatosensory cortex and ultimately in the secondary and higher-order somatosensory cortices. The organization of the chemical senses is also relatively complex. Olfaction (the sense of smell) generates perceptions of odors elicited by airborne chemicals that interact with receptors in the nasal epithelium and follows a unique pathway via the olfactory bulb to the pyriform cortex in the medial temporal lobe. The gustatory (taste) system generates perceptions in response to ingested substances that interact with receptors on the tongue; this information is processed in the insular cortex after peripheral and thalamic processing. The trigeminal chemosensory system gives rise to perceptions elicited by noxious substances that interact with receptors in and around the oral cavity and is effectively a specialized somatic sensory subsystem closely related to the generation of pain percepts. This chapter outlines the major features of each of these sensory systems, focusing on the perceptual consequences of the relevant stimuli and their significance for related cognitive functions.

The Mechanosensory Subsystems

Vision and audition are often seen as the pinnacles of human sensory abilities, but the other sensory modalities are at least as vital in neurobiological terms. We can survive reasonably well if blinded or deafened, but we could not live long without, for instance, the mechanosensory feedback that makes successful motor behavior possible. The sensory systems that provide information about mechanical stimuli acting on the body are usually considered in terms of four subsystems:

1. The **cutaneous/subcutaneous system** reports mechanical stimuli impinging on the body's surface; these stimuli give rise to the perceptions of touch, vibration, pressure, and cutaneous tension.

2. The **proprioceptive system** reports the mechanical forces acting on muscles, tendons, and joints, giving rise to perceptions of the position and status of the limbs and other body parts in space.

3. The **pain system** (also called the *nociceptive system*) warns of potentially harmful mechanical stimuli. In addition to perceptions of pain, this system is closely associated with perceptions of skin temperature; thus pain and temperature percepts are usually considered together.

4. The **vestibular system** reports the acceleration or deceleration of the body and, more specifically, the position of the head in space, which is importantly related to eye movements.

The key organizational aspects of each of these mechanosensory subsystems are outlined in the following sections.

The cutaneous/subcutaneous system

As described in Chapter 4, perceptions of touch, pressure, vibration, and cutaneous tension are initiated by sensory receptors associated with a variety of non-neural elements (hairs, dermal ridges, and various encapsulations of nerve endings) in the cutaneous and subcutaneous tissues (see Figure 4.1C). How these qualities are perceived (that is, what the stimulus is "like" and where it is coming from) is determined in the first instance—but only in the first instance—by the properties of the relevant receptors and the location of their ultimate targets in the cerebral cortex. As in vision and audition, the perceived intensity of a cutaneous/subcutaneous stimulus is determined, albeit in a complex and nonlinear way, by the rate of action potential discharge triggered by the peripheral receptors. The reason for adding these cautionary clauses should be clear from the preceding chapters: no perceptions can be understood as simple transformations of peripheral sensory input (**Box 7A**; also see Box 7B).

As is apparent from everyday experience, the accuracy with which mechanical stimuli can be perceived varies greatly from one region of the body to another (see Figure 4.5B). For example, the minimal separation of two stimuli simultaneously applied to the skin required to perceive them as distinct (e.g., the points of a caliper) is as little as 2 millimeters on a fingertip. In contrast, when such stimuli are applied to the forearm the two points are not distinct until the separation is at least 40 millimeters. Such regional differences in sensitivity are explained by the fact that the relevant mechanoreceptors are 3–4 times more densely distributed in the fingertips than in the forearm. It of course makes sense to concentrate receptors where they will be most useful in tactile discrimination, a principle already encountered in the concentration of retinal receptors in the human fovea, for example. As might be also be expected from a consideration of neural coverage, the sizes of the neuronal receptive fields vary in parallel with this variation in density (see Chapter 4 to review the concept of receptive fields; the receptive field of a somatic sensory neuron is the region of the skin from which a tactile stimulus evokes a sensory response in the associated nerve cell or its axon). If, for instance, the receptive fields of all the cutaneous receptor neurons in the fingertip covered the entire digital pad, it would be impossible to discriminate two spatially separate stimuli (since all the receptive fields would be returning the same spatial information to the brain). In fact, the receptive fields of mechanosensory neu-

▪ BOX 7B Phantom Limbs

Deeper insight into the nature of somatic sensory processing and pain comes from the extraordinary phenomenon of *phantom limb sensations*, a phrase coined by the American physician Silas Weir Mitchell in the late nineteenth century. Following the amputation of an extremity, nearly all patients feel that the missing limb is still present. Although this peculiar sense usually diminishes over time, it persists to some degree throughout the amputee's life and can be reactivated by injury to the stump or other perturbations near the amputation site.

Such phantom sensations are not limited to amputated limbs; phantom breasts following mastectomy, phantom genitalia following castration, and phantoms of the entire lower body following spinal cord transection have all been reported (Figure A). Phantoms are also common after local nerve block for surgery. During recovery from brachial plexus anesthesia, for example, it is not unusual for the patient to experience a phantom arm that is perceived as whole and intact, but displaced from the real arm. When the real arm is viewed, the phantom appears to "jump into" the arm and may emerge and reenter intermittently as the anesthesia wears off. Children born without limbs (from the effects of a mother having taken thalidomide during pregnancy, for example) have phantom sensations, despite the fact that the limb never developed.

Much like the somatic sensory illusions described in Box 7A, sensory phantoms indicate that the central stations for processing somatic sensory information are not simply passive recipients of peripheral signals arising from mechanical stimuli, but active participants in the generation of percepts. This evidence of the active, and to some degree independent, role of the central stations of sensory systems in the generation of percepts is consistant with evidence in vision and audition that percepts are not simply transforms of peripheral input.

Somatic sensory phantoms might simply be regarded as a provocative clue about the nature of higher-order somatic sensory processing were it not for the fact that a substantial number of amputees also develop *phantom pain*, which can be a very serious clinical problem. This unfortunate consequence of amputation is usually described as a tingling or burning sensation in the missing body part; such sensations are often merely an annoyance. Sometimes, however, the sensation is experienced as a stronger pain that patients find increasingly debilitating. Phantom pain is one of the more common causes of chronic pain syndromes, which are notoriously difficult to treat. Ablation of the ascending pathways, portions of the thalamus, or even primary sensory cortex does not generally relieve the discomfort felt by these patients.

A novel and imaginative cognitive approach to relieving phantom pain has been introduced by Vilayanur Ramachandran, a neurologist and cognitive neuroscientist at the University of California, San Diego. Using an apparatus that provides the patient with a mirror image of their intact limb in place of the amputated limb (Figure B), Ramachandran has been able to pro-

(Continued on next page)

(A) Some phantoms experienced by war veterans after limb amputations; the amputated areas are shown as dashed lines. The colored areas indicate the most vividly experienced regions. (B) Apparatus used by Ramachandran to relieve phantom pain by conflating normal and phantom sensory input. The patient shown has his amputated right limb in the right portion of the box, but sees the missing hand as being intact in the mirror image he perceives. When he moves his intact left hand he experiences movement of the phantom that corresponds to the mirror image; such training can sometimes alleviate phantom pain. (A after Solonen 1962.)

(A)

(B)

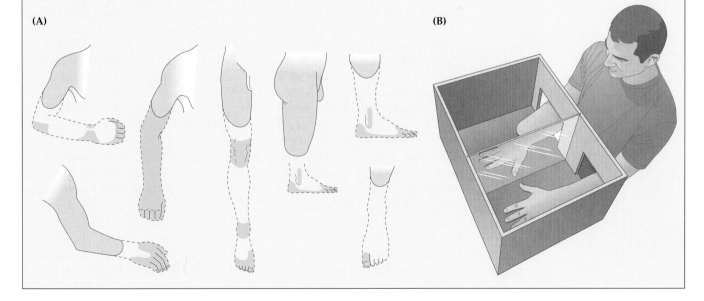

■ **BOX 7B** *(continued)*

vide some relief for a subset of these patients by having them perceptually associate the normal sensations with the intact mirror image that is seen in this circumstance as the missing limb. This therapeutic approach, odd though it may seem, shows again how readily our body image and the sensations related to it can be affected by the information arising from other sense modalities in unusual circumstances.

References

CRAIG, A. D., E. M. REIMAN, A. EVANS AND M. C. BUSHNELL (1996) Functional imaging of an illusion of pain. *Nature* 384: 258–260.

KOLB, L. C. (1954) *The Painful Phantom.* Springfield, IL: Charles C. Thomas.

MELZACK, R. (1989) Phantom limbs, the self and the brain: The D.O. Hebb Memorial Lecture. *Canad. Psychol.* 30: 1–14.

MELZACK, R. (1990) Phantom limbs and the concept of a neuromatrix. *Trends Neurosci.* 13: 88–92.

RAMACHANDRAN, V. S. AND S. BLAKESLEE (1998) *Phantoms in the Brain.* New York: William Morrow & Co.

SOLENEN, K. A. (1962) The phantom phenomenon in amputated Finnish war veterans. *Acta Orthop. Scand. Suppl.* 54: 1–37.

The best understood example of a proprioceptor and its operation is the so-called **muscle spindle**. These sensory specializations are present in all but a few skeletal muscles, and the rate at which they cause the associated sensory nerve endings to fire reports muscle length to the central nervous system (**Figure 7.2**; see Chapter 8 for further details). Much like receptors in the skin and subcutaneus tissues, the density of spindles in human muscles varies greatly. Large muscles that generate coarse movements have relatively few spindles, whereas the small muscles (like those in the hand) are richly supplied, reflecting the need to manipulate objects according to more precise information about the condition of these muscles at any moment.

Central processing of mechanosensory information

The pathways and central processing stations for information from cutaneous and subcutaneous receptors and proprioceptors are much the same and thus are considered together. Indeed, these two systems are often lumped together under the rubric **somatic sensory system** (or, as it is frequently called, the **somatosensory system**).

As indicated in **Figure 7.3**, the ascending pathways begin with the central processes of neurons in dorsal root ganglia (or the sensory ganglia of the cranial nerves), which enter the spinal cord (or brainstem) and run upwards to the thalamus via additional processing in nuclei at the rostral end of the spinal cord, in much the same way that visual and auditory pathways are relayed to the thalamus after much processing in the retina or cochlear nuclei, respectively. The **ventral posterior nuclear complex** of the thalamus is the main target of these ascending pathways. The axons arising from neurons in the thalamus project in turn to cortical neurons located primarily in layer 4 of the **primary somatosensory cortex**, or **S1** (**Figure 7.4A**). As in the visual and auditory pathways, the thalamus is not simply a relay but the site of further processing that includes extensive feedback from descending cortical input.

The primary somatosensory cortex is located in the parietal lobe just posterior to the central sulcus and comprises four distinct regions: Brodmann areas 3a, 3b, 1, and 2. Neurons in areas 3b and 1 respond primarily to cutaneous stimuli, whereas neurons in 3a respond mainly to stimulation of proprioceptors; neurons in area 2 process both tactile and proprioceptive stimuli. Map-

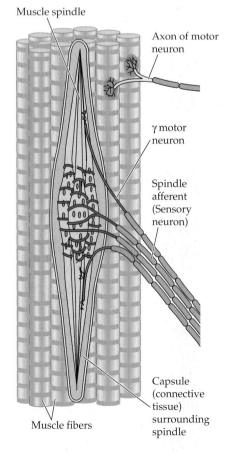

Muscle spindle

Axon of motor neuron

γ motor neuron

Spindle afferent (Sensory neuron)

Capsule (connective tissue) surrounding spindle

Muscle fibers

Figure 7.2 A muscle spindle. Because these receptors lie in parallel with the muscle fibers, they supply information about the *length* of skeletal muscles to the brain, which is crucial to the organization of motor behavior.

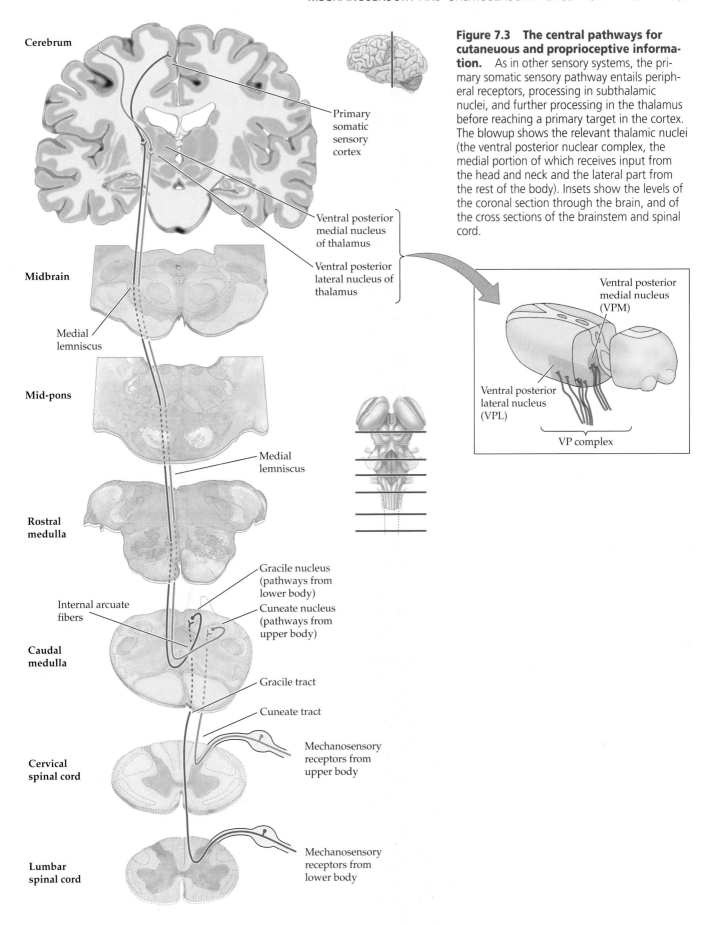

Cerebrum

Primary somatic sensory cortex

Ventral posterior medial nucleus of thalamus

Ventral posterior lateral nucleus of thalamus

Midbrain

Medial lemniscus

Mid-pons

Medial lemniscus

Rostral medulla

Gracile nucleus (pathways from lower body)

Cuneate nucleus (pathways from upper body)

Internal arcuate fibers

Caudal medulla

Gracile tract

Cuneate tract

Cervical spinal cord

Mechanosensory receptors from upper body

Lumbar spinal cord

Mechanosensory receptors from lower body

Ventral posterior medial nucleus (VPM)

Ventral posterior lateral nucleus (VPL)

VP complex

Figure 7.3   The central pathways for cutaneuous and proprioceptive information.   As in other sensory systems, the primary somatic sensory pathway entails peripheral receptors, processing in subthalamic nuclei, and further processing in the thalamus before reaching a primary target in the cortex. The blowup shows the relevant thalamic nuclei (the ventral posterior nuclear complex, the medial portion of which receives input from the head and neck and the lateral part from the rest of the body). Insets show the levels of the coronal section through the brain, and of the cross sections of the brainstem and spinal cord.

Figure 7.4 The somatosensory cortices. Location of the somatosensory regions in relation to other cortical structures; cross sectional blow-up shows the arrangement of the relevant Brodmann areas (i.e., the distinct cortical subregions that have been defined microscopically by differences in the number, size, and arrangements of their neurons). Note that Brodmann area 4, located on the anterior bank of the central sulcus, is the primary motor cortex.

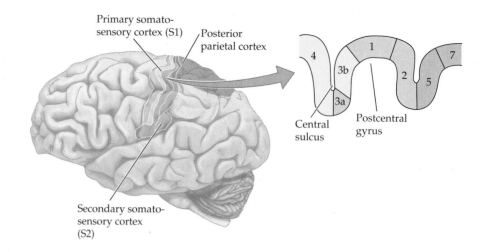

ping studies in both humans and non-human primates show further that each of these four cortical areas contains a separate and complete representation of the body (see Figure 4.12B). In these **somatotopic maps**, the genitals, foot, leg, trunk, forelimbs, and face are represented in a medial to lateral arrangement.

Similar to the distortions evident in the retinotopic and tonotopic cortical maps in the visual and auditory systems, the cortical maps for mechanosensroy information do not represent the body in actual proportion. Thus the **homunculus** ("little man") defined by such maps has an enlarged face and hands compared to the torso and proximal limbs (see Figure 4.12B). Like variable cortical magnification evident in other primary sensory cortices, these distortions reflect the fact that sensory feedback about manipulation, facial expression, and speaking are extraordinarily important for human cognitive functions, requiring more circuitry (both central and peripheral) in order to process relevant information.

Somatic sensory information, like information in other sensory modalities, is distributed from the primary somatosensory cortex to adjacent cortical regions that carry out further processing and integration with other information that is especially relevant to cognitive functions. Thus the **secondary somatosensory cortex (S2)** and other areas in the posterior parietal cortex (see Figure 7.4) receive convergent projections from the different submodalities in S1 and in turn send projections to limbic structures such as the amygdala and hippocampus (which are particularly concerned with emotional responses and memory, respectively). Neurons in motor cortical areas in the frontal lobe also receive information from these higher-order regions and provide feedback projections to most if not all cortical somatic sensory regions. These latter connections allow mechanosensory information to be integrated with motor information, an essential step in cognitive functions such as directing attention to stimulus sources—for example, moving the head and eyes to see what the source of a tactile stimulus might be.

The pain system

A third and quite different mechanosensory subsystem concerns the perception of **pain**, which is broadly defined as the sensations elicited by mechanical forces that are harmful to the body's integrity. Since alerting the brain to the dangers implied by noxious stimuli differs substantially from informing it about somatic sensory stimuli that are not in themselves harmful (though of course they may signify something in the environment that could be harmful), it makes sense that a special subsystem be devoted to the perception of dangerous mechanical forces (as well as thermal energy) acting on the body.

The perception of pain is initiated by *free nerve endings* in the skin and deeper tissues (see Figure 4.1C). These nerve endings are called **nociceptors**, from the Latin *nocere*, "hurt." Like other somatic sensory receptors, nociceptive nerve endings arise from cell bodies in dorsal root ganglia (or the analogous ganglia associated with the brainstem) that send one axonal process to the periphery and the other into the spinal cord or brainstem (**Figure 7.5**). The projections that carry information initiated by non-nociceptive temperature-sensitive neurons follow the same anatomical route to the central nervous system, and thus are typically included in a discussion of pain pathways.

The major targets of the ascending pain and temperature axons are, like the targets of other mechanosensory axons, in the ventral posterior nuclear complex of the thalamus (the inset in Figure 7.3). The subthalamic processing nuclei for pain lie in the dorsal horns of the spinal cord at or near the level entry rather than in the caudal medulla, and axons arising from these nuclei cross at the level of the cord rather than the medulla (compare Figures 7.5 and 7.3). The ventral posterior medial and ventral posterior lateral nuclei of the thalamus receive the bulk of these axons, and these neurons project in turn to Brodmann areas 3b and 1 in the primary somatosensory cortex. The generally similar cortical targets for noxious and other mechanosensory stimuli are presumably responsible for the ability to consciously locate painful stimuli and to judge their intensity. Parallel projections to the reticular formation of the medulla, pons, and midbrain are responsible for the strong but largely unconscious autonomic activation that pain elicits, and projections to other areas such as the anterior cingulate cortex mediate emotional reactions to pain, as might be expected from the role of this latter region in emotional processing (see Chapter 17).

The perceptual quality of pain is particularly important from a cognitive standpoint because it so clearly confirms the idea that somatic sensory percepts are mental constructs, not simply translations of stimuli per se or "features" of the "real world" (see Boxes 7B and 7C). Although all perceptual qualities are abstractions, it is easier to appreciate that there is nothing in the real world that corresponds to *pain*. Although we intuitively are inclined to think that objects can have properties that we describe as brightness or color, or that sounds qualities exist in sound stimuli in some objective sense, the idea that objects or the stimuli they produce are themselves imbued with pain makes no sense. A consideration of pain thus makes it easier to appreciate that although *objects* are tangible ("real"), *perceptual qualities*, painful or otherwise, exist only in our brains. Like pain, perceptual constructs such as color, brightness, loudness, and pitch have evolved in humans because they are biologically useful, allowing us generate behavior that is more successful than would be possible without these perceptual qualities.

Another aspect of pain that has great medical and economic importance is the underlying neuropharmacology. Analgesics, both prescribed and over-the-counter, are among the most widely used medications, and the relief of pain is one of the central goals of clinical practice. Although the rapidly evolving area of clinical pain research and its associated pharmacopoeia cannot be covered here, it is important to realize that the physiological, anatomical, and molecular bases of pain are now understood in some detail. Neurons in the regions of the dorsal horns and brainstem that process pain information (see Figure 7.5) have receptors for opioid analgesics (responding to drugs such as morphine), and other neurons in the primary pain pathway secrete endogenous opioids (i.e., morphine-like molecules produced by the body itself). These facts explain the efficacy of analgesic drugs that bind to opioid receptors, and the

Figure 7.5 The pain pathway. Like the mechanosensory subsystems for tactile and proprioceptive information, the primary pain pathway entails peripheral receptors, processing in subthalamic nuclei, and thalamic processing before reaching the primary somatosensory cortex.

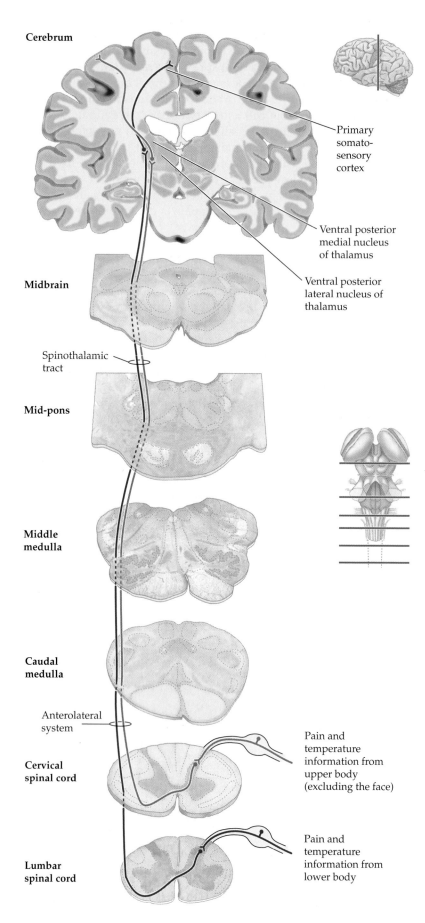

Cerebrum

Primary somatosensory cortex

Ventral posterior medial nucleus of thalamus

Ventral posterior lateral nucleus of thalamus

Midbrain

Spinothalamic tract

Mid-pons

Middle medulla

Caudal medulla

Anterolateral system

Cervical spinal cord

Pain and temperature information from upper body (excluding the face)

Lumbar spinal cord

Pain and temperature information from lower body

actions of opioid antagonists such as naloxone that are used to treat addiction to opioids such as heroin. This rapidly evolving knowledge of neuropharmacology and pain physiology also suggests possible explanations for the modulation of pain by hypnosis, acupuncture, and placebos (**Box 7C**). Cognitive processing elsewhere in the brain—including systems concerned with attention, memory, emotion, and reasoning—presumably affects these biochemical

■ BOX 7C The Placebo Effect

Physicians have long noted the difference between the objective reality of a painful stimulus and the subjective response to it. During World War II, the Harvard anesthesiologist Henry Beecher and his colleagues made a detailed study of this phenomenon. They found that soldiers suffering from severe battle wounds often experienced little or no pain; indeed, many of the wounded expressed surprise at this odd dissociation.

Beecher concluded that the perception of pain depends on the *context* in which potentially painful stimuli are experienced. Trauma to a soldier injured on the battlefield carries with it the benefit of being removed from further danger; a similar injury in a domestic setting presents quite a different set of circumstances (loss of work, financial liability, and so on). Such observations not only confirm that the perception of pain is a mental construct (see text), but that the constructs are subject to extraordinary modulation by other sensory and cognitive factors.

Of particular interest in this regard is the *placebo effect*, defined as a physiological response following the administration of a pharmacologically inert "remedy." The word *placebo* is Latin for "I will please," and the placebo effect has a long history of use (and abuse) in medicine. In one classic study of analgesia, fully 75 percent of patients suffering from postoperative wound pain reported relief after an injection of an inert saline solution. The researchers who carried out this work noted that the responders were indistinguishable from the nonresponders in both the apparent severity of their pain and in their psychological makeup.

(Continued on next page)

(A) Opioid analgesic

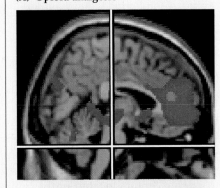
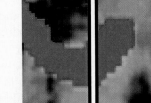
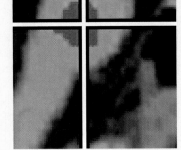

(B) Placebo

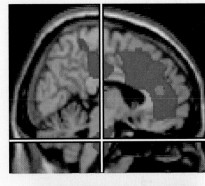
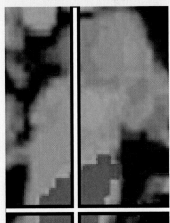
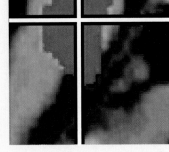

The regions activated in this fMRI study show that many of the same brain regions are active in response to (A) the administration of an opioid analgesic and (B) to the administration of a placebo, thus confirming the physiological basis of the placebo effect. The blue dot indicates the location of the anterior cingulate cortex. Cross-hairs identify the same region of the brainstem in all panels. (From Petrovic et al. 2002.)

■ BOX 7C *(continued)*

In another study, medical students were given one of two different pills, one said to be a sedative and the other a stimulant. In fact, both pills contained only inert ingredients. Of the students who received the "sedative," more than two-thirds reported that they felt drowsy, and students who took two such pills felt sleepier than those who had taken only one. Conversely, a large fraction of the students who took the "stimulant" reported that they felt less tired. About a third of the group also reported side effects ranging from headaches and dizziness to tingling extremities and a staggering gait! Only 3 of the 56 students studied reported that the pills had no appreciable effect.

A common misunderstanding about the placebo effect is that patients who respond to a therapeutically meaningless reagent are not really suffering pain, but are just "imagining" it. This is not the case. The placebo effect in postoperative patients suffering pain can be blocked by naloxone, a competitive antagonist of opiate receptors, illustrating a neuropharmacological basis for the pain relief experienced (see text). Moreover, recent neuroimaging studies show that the brain regions that are pharmacologically responsive to opioid analgesics (e.g., the anterior cingulate cortex and regions of the brainstem) are also active in response to a nominally analgesic placebo (see figure). Although

the mechanisms by which the perception of pain is modulated in this way are only beginning to be understood, the placebo effect is neither "magic" nor a sign of a suggestible intellect.

References

Beecher, H. K. (1946) Pain in men wounded in battle. *Ann. Surg.* 123: 96.

Blackwell, B., S. S. Bloomfield and C. R. Buncher (1972) Demonstration to medical students of placebo response and non-drug factors. *Lancet* 1: 1279–1282.

Petrovic, P., E. Kalso, K. M. Petersson and M. Ingvar (2002) Placebo and opioid analgesia: Imaging a shared neural network. *Science* 295: 1737–1740.

Skrabanek, P. and J. McCormick (1990) *Follies and Fallacies in Medicine.* New York: Prometheus Books.

interactions in the pain pathway, with marked consequences on the subjective experience of pain that follows.

The vestibular system

The last of the subsystems that provide information about the mechanical forces acting on the body is the **vestibular system**. The peripheral portion of the vestibular system is a part of the inner ear and functions as an accelerometer, continually reporting body (or head) motion and the effects of gravity to integrative centers located in the brainstem, cerebellum, and the somatosensory cortices.

Like much of the processing carried out by the proprioceptive system, we are normally unaware of the critical information the vestibular system provides and the ways it continually determines a variety of postural reflexes and eye movements. Despite its apparent remoteness from cognitive issues, the vestibular system is also critically important in understanding the behavioral responses elicited in several cognitive paradigms, including the studies of motor learning described in Chapter 9.

The main peripheral component of the vestibular system is the **labyrinth**, an elaborate set of interconnected canals that is continuous with the cochlea (**Figure 7.6A**). Like the auditory system, the vestibular system uses hair cells to transduce physical motion into neural impulses. The labyrinth (the name reflects the anatomical "maze" of these interconnected canals) consists of two **otolith organs** (the *utricle* and the *saccule*) and three **semicircular canals** (**Figure 7.6B**). The utricle and saccule respond to linear accelerations of the head and static head position. The semicircular canals, which are perpendicular to one another, are specialized for responding to rotational acceleration. The hair cells in each of these elements extend into the endolymph that fills the labyrinth, and their displacement generates membrane potential changes in the receptors that lead in turn to action potentials in the associated axons of the vestibular component of the eighth cranial nerve (see Figure 7.6A), the other component of this nerve being auditory.

(A)

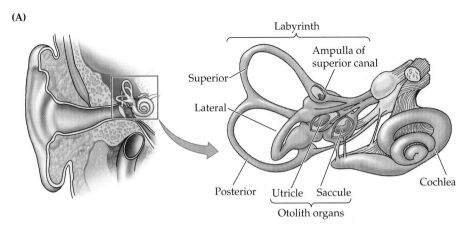

Figure 7.6 The vestibular system.
(A) The labyrinth of the inner ear houses the receptor cells of the vestibular system and is continuous with the cochlea (see Chapter 6). The blowup shows the locations of the organs that receive peripheral signal input: two otolith organs (utricle and saccule) and three semicircular canals. (B) The directions of the arrows indicate the orientation of hair cells in each of these receptor organs. Displacements from these orientations determine the information that the hair cells send centrally for eventual cortical processing.

(B)

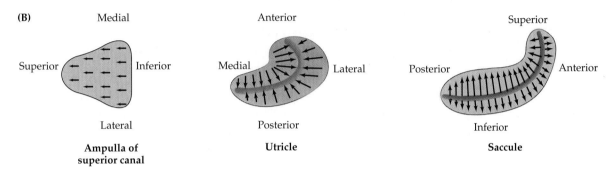

The neurons that innervate both the otolith organs and the semicircular canals originate from bipolar neurons in *Scarpa's ganglion*, which is analogous to the dorsal root or brainstem ganglia that innervate other mechanoreceptors. The central processes of these neurons project to the **vestibular nuclei**, which integrate information from the corresponding nuclei from the opposite side, as well as information from the cerebellum and from the visual and somatic sensory systems. The result of this integration is a variety of reflex postural and eye movements, the most thoroughly studied of which are the eye movements that maintain stable vision even as the body and head move (see Chapter 9).

The superior and lateral vestibular nuclei send axons to the ventral posterior nuclear complex of the thalamus, which in turn projects to the parietal cortex. A major cortical target is just posterior to the primary somatosensory cortex, near the representation of the face (see Figure 4.12B); another is at the transition between the somatosensory cortex and the motor cortex (Brodmann area 3a). These cortical regions are presumably responsible for our perceptions of body motion and orientation in extrapersonal space, and the integration of vestibulomotor information with that arising from other sensory systems.

The Chemosensory Modalities

Three sensory systems generate percepts in response to chemical stimuli: the **olfactory system**, the **gustatory system**, and the **trigeminal chemosensory system**. The olfactory system detects airborne molecules and generates the percepts generally called **odors**. The gustatory system responds to ingested (primarily water-soluble) molecules and generates the percepts we call **tastes**.

The trigeminal chemosensory system generates percepts elicited by noxious substances that come into contact with the skin or mucous membranes of the nose and mouth, e.g. the sensations elicited by chili peppers. These latter percepts have not been given a class name, but they are irritating sensations that in some cases can be quite strong, even painful.

In addition to perception as such, the importance of what we smell or taste to virtually all cognitive functions should be clear from everyday experience: these sensations can have dramatic effects on what we attend to, what we remember, our social interactions, our emotions, the decisions we make, and much more.

The olfactory system

The perception of odors begins in the **olfactory epithelium**, a sheet of **olfactory receptor neurons** and supporting cells that lines approximately half of the human nasal cavities (**Figure 7.7A**). Cellular processes called cilia extend from the receptor neurons into the layer of mucus that lines the nasal cavity, where they are exposed to odorant molecules in the air that dissolve in the mucus layer. The ability to detect particular odors is the result of **receptor proteins** in the membranes of cilia. Each receptor neuron expresses only a single receptor protein on its ciliary surfaces (out of an estimated total of 550–750 such proteins that are coded by the relevant gene family in humans). Olfaction is often considered the least acute of the human senses, and a number of animals are obviously superior to humans in this ability. This difference is presumably explained by the larger number of olfactory receptor neurons and different odorant receptor proteins in the olfactory epithelium in some other species, and the relatively larger number of neurons devoted to olfactory processing at all levels. For example, the surface area of the olfactory epithelium in a 70-kg human is approximately 10 cm^2; in contrast, a 3-kg cat has about 20 cm^2 of olfactory epithelium. And even a mouse expresses substantially more olfactory receptor proteins (an estimated 1000–1500) than humans.

Neurons that express the same receptor protein are distributed in a specific manner across in the olfactory epithelium, and their axons project via the olfactory nerve to specific subsets of neuronal clusters called **glomeruli** in the **olfactory bulb** (**Figure 7.7B**; see also **Box 7D**). As in other sensory systems, this topographical arrangement of central projections in the olfactory bulb is referred to as a *map*. The coding scheme for olfactory information also has a temporal dimension: sniffing, for example, is a periodic event that elicits trains of action potentials and synchronous activity in populations of neurons. As indicated in Figure 7.7B, the glomerular circuitry in the olfactory bulb processes olfactory information from the nasal receptors before relaying their output to the brain.

The axons arising from the bulb form a bundle called the **lateral olfactory tract** that projects to several central stations, including the olfactory tubercle, the entorhinal cortex, and portions of the amygdala (**Figure 7.7C**). The major target of the olfactory tract, however, is the three-layered **pyriform cortex** in the ventromedial aspect of the temporal lobe near the amygdala and the entorhinal cortex. The axons of neurons in the pyriform cortex project in turn to several thalamic and hypothalamic nuclei, to the hippocampus, and to the amygdala. Some neurons from the pyriform cortex also innervate a region in the orbitofrontal cortex. Thus information about odors readily reaches a variety of forebrain regions, allowing olfactory cues to influence involuntary visceral and homeostatic behaviors (i.e., behaviors that control body physiology), as well as the cognitive systems mediating emotion, attention, and memory, among others. The pyriform cortex is analogous to the primary sensory cortices in vision, audition and somatic sensation, and the adjacent areas indicat-

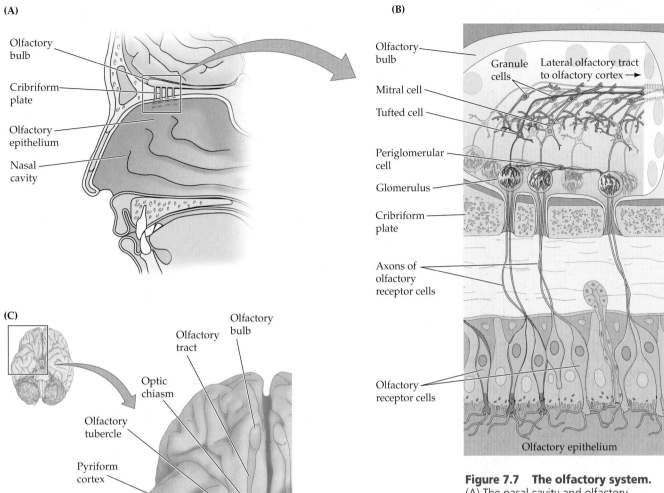

Figure 7.7 The olfactory system.
(A) The nasal cavity and olfactory epithelium. (B) Organization of the olfactory bulb and the formation of the olfactory tract in relation to the receptor cells in the olfactory epithelium. (C) Pathway from the bulb to the pyriform cortex, which is the primary target of the projections from the olfactory bulb. Note the close association of the pyriform cortex with the amygdala (a key structure in emotional processing) and the entorhinal cortex (a key structure in processing certain kinds of memory). The olfactory tract sends information to both of these structures, which can thus be affected by the processing that leads to the perception of odors.

ed in Figure 7.7C are analogous to the higher-order processing regions in these other systems.

Despite the olfactory superiority of many other species, humans can detect many substances at nanomolar concentrations or less. Moreover, minimal changes in molecular structure can lead to large perceptual differences when tested in the laboratory. The molecule D-carvone, for instance, smells like caraway seeds, whereas its stereoisomer L-carvone (a molecule identical except in its "handedness") smells like spearmint. Most naturally occurring odors are generated by several different odorant molecules, even though they are typically experienced as a single smell, such as the perceptions elicited by perfumes, or the bouquet of a wine.

Subliminal olfactory information can also be influential, suggesting that olfactory information could have subtle influences on cognitive processes of which we are unaware. Interest in this possibility was triggered by a study carried out several decades ago by behavioral psychologist Martha McClintock, then an undergraduate at Wellesley College. McClintock, now at the

■ BOX 7D Coding Chemosensory Information

One generally held idea about sensory coding in the nervous system is especially pertinent in chemosensory systems because of the detailed knowledge about the receptor molecules that has emerged over the last 15 years or so. Much of this thinking has focused on the idea that the peripheral receptors in olfaction are the starting point for specifically *labeled lines* (think of telephone lines) that carry through the central stations of the system, thus determining the basic strategies of central processing and the ensuing percepts.

A key advance came in the early 1990s with the discovery of genes that code for olfactory receptors. This research was pioneered by neuroscientists Richard Axel, Linda Buck, and other collaborators at several institutions. Subsequently Axel and Buck, among others, showed that receptor neurons expressing a particular receptor often project to specific glomeruli in the olfactory bulb of mice (see figure). More recently similar studies have been carried out identifying the genes and receptor proteins in the gustatory system. Might the relevant glomerulus then project in turn to a specific region of the pyriform cortex that would be responsible for perceiving the odor associated with the molecules that bound to the peripheral receptor?

Work pursuing this appealing possibility in the central olfactory and gustatory stations in the mouse brain have not supported a labeled line coding scheme. So far there is no evidence that the projections from specific glomeruli in the olfactory bulb have generated a correspondingly specific pattern in the pyriform cortex, and the nature of olfactory processing at this level remains unclear. From what is known from studies of processing in other primary sensory cortices (V1, A1, and S1), a labeled line strategy is also highly unlikely in these systems. In the primary visual cortex, for example, the same cortical neurons process information about a variety of stimulus features, and notions of labeled lines in V1 have long since been abandoned (although the broader concept of "channels" for different properties is still very much in play, as indicated in Chapters 4 and 5). It is equally clear that outside of the laboratory, olfactory percepts are rarely if ever generated by a single type of molecule. Whether the perfume of a flower or the repellent odor of decaying organic matter, olfactory percepts depend on complex mixtures of molecules that nonetheless elicit a unitary olfactory experience that signifies a rose, a dead animal, or any one of the other odors we are capable of sensing.

References

BUCK, L. B. (2000) The molecular architecture of odor and pheromone sensing in mammals. *Cell* 100: 611–617.

LAURENT, G. (1999) A systems perspective on early olfactory coding. *Science* 286: 723–727.

MOMBAERTS, P. AND 7 OTHERS (1996) Visualizing an olfactory sensory map. *Cell* 87: 675–686.

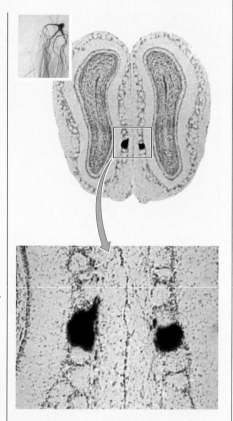

Specificity of neuronal connectivity at the initial level of olfactory processing. Inset at the upper left shows labeled axons from receptor neurons that express a single receptor protein converging to innervate glomeruli in the olfactory bulb. The associated micrographs show the location of the small bilaterally symmetrical subset of glomeruli innervated by this receptor type from among the approximately 1000 glomeruli in each mouse olfactory bulb. (From Mombaerts et al. 1996.)

University of Chicago, reported in her senior thesis that after several months of living together, the 135 women housed in her dormitory tended to have synchronized menstrual cycles. (This finding was later published as a report in the journal *Nature.*) McClintock went on to suggest that this effect is mediated by olfaction, since volunteers exposed the odorants in gauze pads from the underarms of women at different stages of their menstrual cycles also tended to have synchronized menses.

McClintock's work is often cited in discussions of the possible existence and nature of human pheromones. **Pheromones** are specific biochemical signals produced by various glands. They are used as a means of social communication in a number of non-human species. Reproductive and other behaviors in rodents and other animals clearly respond to pheromone signals; it is well

(A)

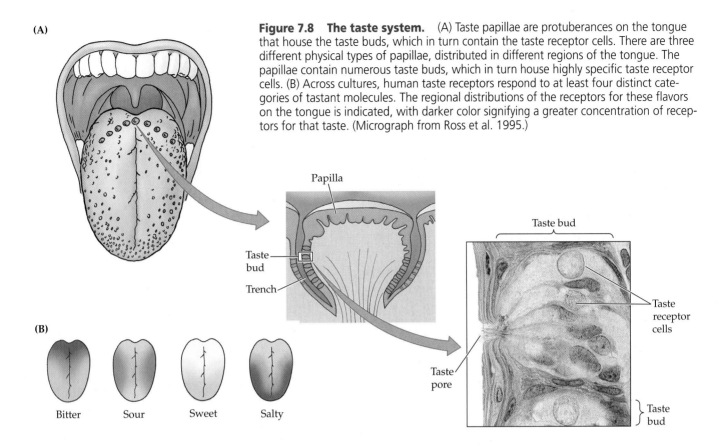

Figure 7.8 The taste system. (A) Taste papillae are protuberances on the tongue that house the taste buds, which in turn contain the taste receptor cells. There are three different physical types of papillae, distributed in different regions of the tongue. The papillae contain numerous taste buds, which in turn house highly specific taste receptor cells. (B) Across cultures, human taste receptors respond to at least four distinct categories of tastant molecules. The regional distributions of the receptors for these flavors on the tongue is indicated, with darker color signifying a greater concentration of receptors for that taste. (Micrograph from Ross et al. 1995.)

established, for example, that species-specific pheromones determine a variety of social, reproductive, and parenting behaviors in mice. The role of pheromones in human behavior, however, remains speculative and controversial.

The taste system

The **taste system** generates percepts derived for the most part from water-soluble molecular substances that interact with receptors in epithelial specializations on the tongue, called **taste buds** (**Figure 7.8A**). **Taste cells** embedded in the taste buds produce information about the identity, concentration, and pleasant or unpleasant (*hedonic*) quality of the substance—all pertinent to the cognitive determination of whether or not something should be eaten, and how pleasing the sensation will be if the item is consumed (**Figure 7.8B**). At a more basic physiological level, this information also prepares the gastrointestinal system to receive food by causing salivation and swallowing (or gagging and regurgitation if the substance is noxious). Information about the temperature and texture of food is relayed from the mouth and pharynx via sensory receptors from the trigeminal and other sensory cranial nerves to the thalamus and somatosensory cortices.

The innervation of taste cells arises from bipolar neurons in cranial nerve ganglia, as shown in **Figure 7.9**. The initial target of these axons is the **nucleus of the solitary tract** in the brainstem, which is also the main target of afferent visceral sensory information related to the sympathetic and parasympathetic divisions of the visceral motor system. Interneurons connecting the different regions of the nucleus integrate gustatory and visceral information. Such interactions make good sense, since humans and other animals must quickly recognize if they are eating something unpalatable, and respond accordingly by gagging and spitting it out.

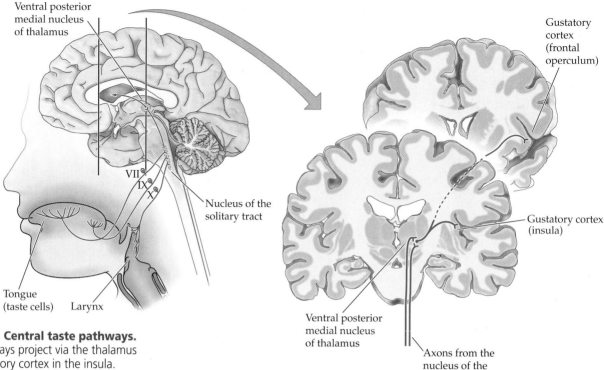

Figure 7.9 Central taste pathways. These pathways project via the thalamus to the gustatory cortex in the insula. Note the proximity of these cortical targets to the other structures related to olfaction (see Figure 7.7), to structures that mediate emotional responses (e.g., the amygdala), and to cortical regions that mediate some aspects of memory (medial temporal lobes). Although not shown, taste-system axons from the nucleus of the solitary tract also project to the hypothalamus, the key regulatory center for homeostatic functions.

Axons from the gustatory component of the solitary nucleus project to the ventral posterior complex of the thalamus, where they terminate in the medial half of the ventral posterior medial nucleus (see Figure 7.4). The primary cortical target of these neurons is the anterior *insula* in the temporal and the frontal lobes. As in other sensory systems, there is also a secondary taste area for higher-order cortical processing; this region is in the caudolateral orbitofrontal cortex, where neurons respond to combinations of visual, somatosensory, olfactory, and gustatory stimuli. When a given food is consumed to the point of satiety, some orbitofrontal neurons that have been studied in non-human primates diminish their activity to the tastant, suggesting that this cortical region is involved in the motivation to eat (or not to eat) particular foods. Finally, reciprocal projections connect the nucleus of the solitary tract to the hypothalamus and amygdala. These two-way projections presumably influence hunger, satiety, and other homeostatic states associated with eating. This overall arrangement is thus relevant to much the same range of cognitive functions as the olfactory system.

People perceive a wide variety of taste qualities, including sweet, salty, bitter, sour, astringent (cranberries and tea), pungent (spices such as ginger and curry), fat, starchy, and various metallic tastes, to name but a few. As in the case of odors, this superabundance of perceptual qualities has proved difficult to classify in the relatively simple way that the perceptual qualities in vision, audition, and somatic sensation have been categorized. As in olfaction, the sensory experiences engendered by the different tastes do not have a one-to-one correspondence with specific molecules. Tastes, like odors, typically derive from complex chemical mixtures. Moreover, quite different compounds can elicit the same general taste sensation. For instance, perceptions of sweet are elicited by molecules that include saccharides (glucose, sucrose, and fructose), organic anions (saccharin), amino acids (aspartame, or Nutrasweet®), L-phenylalanine methyl ester, and proteins (monellin and thaumatin).

To complicate matters even further, taste responses vary significantly among individuals. For example, 30 to 40 percent of the U.S. population cannot taste the bitter compound phenylthiocarbamide (PTC), but can taste molecules such as quinine and caffeine that also produce bitter sensations. This particular difference among individuals is the result of a single autosomal gene with a dominant (tasters) and a recessive (non-tasters) allele for the PTC receptor. People who are extremely sensitive to PTC and its analogues, called "supertasters," actually have more taste buds than normal and tend to avoid certain foods such as grapefruit, green tea, and broccoli, all of which contain bitter-tasting compounds.

These perceptual observations in olfaction and taste accord with evidence in other sensory systems that underscore the difficulty of relating subjective experiences to the physical characteristics of the relevant stimuli, the stimuli in this case being airborne or water-soluble molecules.

Trigeminal chemosensation

The third sensory system that responds to chemicals in the environment is the **trigeminal chemosensory system (Figure 7.10)**. The trigeminal system consists of nociceptive neurons and their axons in the trigeminal ganglion and its nerve (cranial nerve V) and, to a lesser degree, includes nociceptive neurons whose axons run in the glossopharyngeal and vagus nerves (cranial nerves IX and X; these latter two nerves are not shown in Figure 7.10). These neurons and their associated endings in the mouth, nasal cavity, and lips are activated by chemicals classified as irritants, including air pollutants (e.g., sulfur dioxide), ammonia ("smelling salts"), ethanol (liquor), acetic acid (vinegar), carbon dioxide (in soft drinks), menthol (in various inhalants), and capsaicin (the compound in chili peppers that elicits their characteristic "hot" sensation). The corresponding percepts alert the organism to potentially harmful chemical stimuli that have been ingested, respired, or come in contact with the face, and are thus closely tied to the pain system described earlier. As shown in Figure 7.10, trigeminal chemosensory information is carried centrally in the three major sensory branches of the trigeminal nerve.

The target of these afferent axons is the spinal component of the trigeminal nucleus in the brainstem, which relays this information to the ventral posterior medial nucleus of the thalamus, and from there to the primary somatosensory cortex and other cortical areas that process facial irritation and pain, as shown in Figure 7.5. The reflex responses mediated by the trigeminal chemosensory system include increased salivation, vasodilation, tearing, nasal secretion, sweating, decreased respiratory rate, and bronchoconstriction. All these reactions are protective in that they dilute the stimulus (tearing, salivation, sweating) and prevent inhaling or ingesting more of it (decreased respiratory rate, bronchoconstriction), and all can influence the full range of cognitive functions, as described for olfactory and taste percepts.

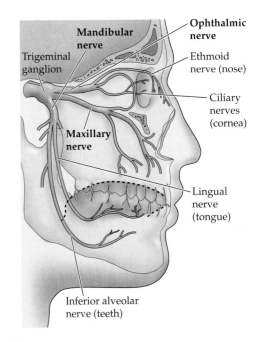

Figure 7.10 The trigeminal chemosensory system. The majority of the sensory input to this system arises from free nerve endings in the mouth, nose, and lips that respond to noxious chemical stimuli. Axons from these nerve endings travel in the three branches of the trigeminal nerve (boldface labels) to the trigeminal nucleus in the brainstem, which sends the relevant information to the thalamus and ultimately to the somatosensory and other cortical regions, much the same pathway as that taken by pain information arising from cutaneous stimulation of the head and neck.

Some Additional Questions about Sensory Systems

Having reviewed in the preceding three chapters the generation of percepts by the major sensory systems and some of the ways these percepts influence other cognitive functions, it is useful to add some unresolved issues to those already alluded to in Chapter 4. Chapter 4 touched on questions concerning the uncertain relationship between primary and higher-order sensory cortical areas, and the question of how neural information is encoded in the nervous system. The issues considered here include the extent to which sensory circuitry is malleable; the role in cognitive functions of conscious versus unconscious sensory experience; and the question of how percepts are ultimately represented in sensory systems.

The malleability of sensory circuitry

An issue of obvious importance in cognitive neuroscience as well as clinical practice is the *malleability*, or plasticity, of the neural circuitry in sensory systems. When some region of a cortical sensory map is destroyed following a stroke, for instance, to what extent can another region be expected to "take over" the missing function? Conversely, when a normal individual uses some portion of their sensory cortex to an unusual degree (such as becoming a highly trained musician or learning a second language), what changes in cortical organization occur as a result? Although aspects of these and related questions are taken up in more detail elsewhere (the neuronal basis of learning is discussed in Chapter 13, plasticity as a function of development in Chapter 27, and issues of second-language acquisition in Chapters 20 and 21), an introduction to **sensory plasticity** and some puzzling aspects of this subject is appropriate here.

A series of highly influential experiments on the plasticity of the visual system was carried out by neurophysiologists David Hubel and Torsten Wiesel at Harvard Medical School in the 1960s and 1970s. Their results indicated what appeared to be relatively little plasticity of connections in the primary visual cortex of cats and monkeys after the earliest weeks or months of life. If, for example, they removed one eye from a newborn kitten (or sutured one eye shut at birth), substantial rearrangement of cortical connections was apparent in both anatomical assessments of connectivity and in the receptive field properties of the affected cortical neurons. However, when the same procedures were carried out in adult animals there was little evidence of reorganization, in keeping with the clinical observation that when the equivalent of this sort of deprivation occurs in human infants (e.g., neonatal cataracts, in which the lenses of a newborn's eyes are opaque and "milky") and is not corrected early in life, later correction fails to prevent a permanent visual deficit. (These sorts experiments are discussed in Chapter 27.)

It was therefore surprising when Michael Merzenich and his colleagues at the University of California at San Francisco reported experiments in the somatic sensory system of adult monkeys that gave a different result. When a digit was amputated in an adult monkey, recordings from the relevant cortical region showed that the neurons that would normally have been responsive only to the amputated digit could now be activated by tactile stimuli applied to the adjacent fingers (**Figure 7.11A**). Moreover, augmented use of a given set of digits over a period of several months in a normal monkey caused the topographically related areas of the primary somatosensory cortex to expand significantly when mapped in the same way (**Figure 7.11B**). Observations of this sort are not possible in humans for obvious reasons, but studies of individuals with a particular sensory skill obtained through years of practice appear to confirm such neural plasticity. Accomplished musicians, for example, show

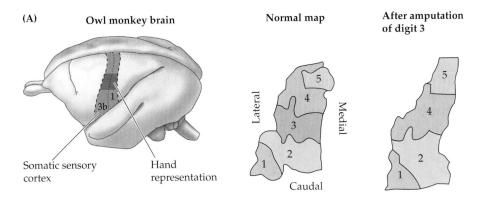

(A)

Owl monkey brain

Somatic sensory cortex

Hand representation

Normal map

Lateral

Medial

Caudal

After amputation of digit 3

Figure 7.11 Plasticity of the somatic sensory cortex. (A) Reorganization of the primary somatic sensory map in a monkey following amputation of a digit several weeks earlier. Numbers in the cortical maps correspond to the areas activated by stimulation of the indicated digits. (B) Expansion of the regions of the map representing digits 2–4 following several months of augmented activity of these digits by a specific task that required their use. (After Jenkins et al. 1990.)

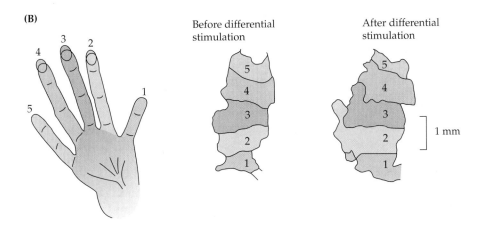

(B)

Before differential stimulation

After differential stimulation

1 mm

greater activation of the relevant regions of the right hemisphere than musically naïve subjects.

Given these seeming differences between the malleability of the visual versus the somatic sensory system, visual physiologist Charles Gilbert and his group at Rockefeller University reexamined the plasticity of the visual system using experimental methods that were more like those Merzenich used to study the somatic sensory system. They destroyed small regions of the retina in a cat or monkey using a laser beam, a lesion similar in principle to the amputation of a digit. Much like the results in the primary somatosensory cortex, the topographical cortical region that would normally have responded to the damaged area of retina now responded to stimulation of adjacent retinal regions, a change similar to the effect illustrated in Figure 7.11B.

The most reasonable conclusion based on this and much other evidence is that sensory cortices are capable of a great deal of reorganization in early life, when neural connections must adapt to a body that is changing rapidly as a result of postnatal growth and learning abilities are maximal. Plasticity diminishes with maturation, but is not lost altogether. Thus, the effects of damage (e.g., an amputation) will cause some changes in functional connectivity, and extraordinary practice of a specific skill will be apparent in the greater overall activation of the region of cortex habitually stimulated in the practiced individual. Much clinical evidence, however, together with the classic experiments of Hubel and Wiesel (and now many others), make equally plain that cortical plasticity in adults is relatively limited, leading to permanent deficits after brain damage and progressively less facility learning new skills as humans and other animals age (as adults struggling to learn music for the first time or a second language know all too well).

Awareness of sensory stimuli

Another unresolved issue in sensory perception in any modality is how to think about stimuli that lead to behavioral responses even though they do not generate percepts that we are aware of. Examples in this chapter are the changes in body posture based on proprioceptive stimuli, the eye movements elicited by vestibular stimuli, and the complex gastrointestinal responses elicited by olfactory or gustatory stimuli. The sensory processing of such stimuli is influential, indeed vital, but the concept of "unconscious percepts" is a contradiction in terms.

One approach to this problem is to dismiss these behavioral responses as "simple reflexes" that are in some sense different from or less important than the behavioral responses correlated with sensory percepts, which are by definition conscious. This tack, however, is unwarranted by what we now know about neuroscience. The relevant stimulus-response pathways are no more or less "simple" by anatomical or physiological criteria than those pathways and processing stages that generate conscious experiences. In fact, the same pathways and central processing stations are involved. These facts have led to an effort to define the so-called "neural correlates of consciousness," a field of cognitive neuroscience taken up in Chapter 28. For the moment, it is enough to point out that sensory processing does not necessarily lead to percepts, which are far less important in determining the vast majority of human behaviors than most of us assume.

The representation of sensory percepts

A final question is how sensory percepts are represented in the brain. That is, exactly what *are* sensory percepts in neurobiological terms? Although the answer is a matter of ongoing debate, there is consensus on at least some general points. First, there is widespread agreement that percepts are represented by the activity of *populations* of sensory neurons in the relevant regions of the cortex. Indeed, there seems to be no real alternative to this conclusion, although as discussed in Box 4B, the concept of convergence of information onto one or a few cells that stand at the apex of a hierarchy and whose activity corresponds to a percept does have a history in the field. Second, it is apparent from much of the evidence covered in this unit that individual neurons respond to multiple stimulus attributes; thus there can be no simple linkage between stimulus features and the activity of particular neurons. And third, it is equally evident that the responsiveness of cortical sensory neurons and the resulting perceptual qualities are related to stimulus properties in a highly nonlinear and counterintuitive way.

None of this evidence is consistent with the intuition that percepts are generated by neurons that simply encode the absolute features or properties of objects, or that their purpose is to represent the world in the veridical way that the measuring instruments of physics and chemistry do. A reasonable guess, based on present evidence, is that the neuronal population activity underlying percepts reflects the statistical relationship of stimulus attributes to the objects and conditions in the world, and that these relationships have been instantiated in sensory processing circuitry according to the success or failure of human behavior over evolutionary time. In this conception, the processing circuits that generated successful behavior by better reflecting these statistical relationships in the diverse progeny in each generation increased in prevalence in the sensory systems of our ancestors, whereas those that failed to generate successful behavior did not. This empirical interpretation of sensory processing and its consequences is just beginning to be explored.

Summary

1. The responses to mechanical forces acting on the body are generated by four relatively distinct subsystems.

2. The first of these is the somatic sensory system, which generates the perceptions of touch, pressure, and vibration that arise from mechanical stimulation of receptors in the cutaneous and subcutaneous tissues.

3. The second is the proprioceptive system, which informs the brain about forces that act on mechanoreceptors in the muscles and joints of the body. In general, this processing does not reach the level of awareness, and is thus not perceived.

4. The third mechanosensory system is the pain system; free nerve endings called nociceptors generate highly unpleasant perceptions that alert us to mechanical or thermal stimuli that are potentially harmful.

5. Finally, the vestibular system associated with the inner ear informs the brain about the acceleration or deceleration of the body and the position of the head.

6. Responses to biologically relevant chemicals in the environment are generated by three subsystems: the olfactory system, the gustatory system, and the trigeminal system.

7. Olfaction involves responses to airborne molecules that interact with receptors in the nasal cavities, leading to the perception of odors. Gustation results when soluble molecules interact with receptors primarily on the tongue, leading to the perception of tastes. The trigeminal system responds to noxious chemicals that find their way into the nose and mouth, generating percepts usually described as irritating; the trigeminal system is closely related to the pain system.

8. All three chemosensory systems ultimately provide information to regions of the brain that are closely tied to autonomic and emotional responses, such the reticular formation, the entorhinal cortex, the insula, and the amygdala.

9. Among the many unanswered questions raised by studies of the human sensory modalities is the degree to which the underlying neural circuitry can change in response to experience or injury; how to think about unconscious sensory-motor responses in relation to percepts; and how percepts are ultimately represented in the brain.

Additional Reading

Reviews

BRANDT, T. (1991) Man in motion: Historical and clinical aspects of vestibular function. *Brain* 114: 2159–2174.

BUCK, L. B. (2000) The molecular architecture of odor and pheromone sensing in mammals. *Cell* 100: 611–618.

DARIAN-SMITH, I. (1982) Touch in primates. *Annu. Rev. Psychol.* 33: 155–194.

DUBNER, R. AND M. S. GOLD (1999) The neurobiology of pain. *Proc. Natl. Acad. Sci. USA* 96: 7627–7630.

FIELDS, H. L. AND A. I. BASBAUM (1978) Brain stem control of spinal pain transmission neurons. *Annu. Rev. Physiol.* 40: 217–248.

GOLDBERG, J. M. AND C. FERNANDEZ (1984) The vestibular system. In *Handbook of Physiology*, Section 1: *The Nervous System*, Volume III: *Sensory Processes, Part II*, J. M. Brookhart, V. B. Mountcastle, I. Darian-Smith and S. R. Geiger (eds.).

Bethesda, MD: American Physiological Society, pp. 977–1022.

KAAS, J. H. (1990) Somatosensory system. In *The Human Nervous System*, G. Paxinos (ed.). San Diego: Academic Press, pp. 813–844.

LAURENT, G. (1999) A systems perspective on early olfactory coding. *Science* 286: 723–728.

MERZENICH, M. M., G. H. RECANZONE, W. M. JENKINS AND K. A. GRAJSKI (1990) Adaptive mechanisms in cortical networks underlying cortical contributions to learning and nondeclarative memory. *Cold Spring Harbor Symp. Quant. Biol.* 55: 873–887.

MOORE, C. I., S. B. NELSON AND M. SUR (1999) Dynamics of neuronal processing in rat somatosensory cortex. *Trends Neurosci.* 22: 513–520.

LINDEMANN, B. (1996) Taste reception. *Physiol Rev.* 76: 719–766.

Important Original Papers

BEECHER, H. K. (1946) Pain in men wounded in battle. *Ann. Surg.* 123: 96.

BUCK, L. AND R. AXEL (1991) A novel multigene family may encode odorant receptors: A molecular basis for odor recognition. *Cell* 65: 175–187.

GILBERT, C. D. AND T. N. WIESEL (1992) Receptive field dynamics in adult primary visual cortex. *Nature* 356: 150–152.

HUBEL, D. H. AND T. N. WIESEL (1970) The period of susceptibility to the physiological effects of unilateral eye closure in kittens. *J. Physiol.* 206: 419–436.

HUBEL, D. H., T. N. WIESEL AND S. LEVAY (1977) Plasticity of ocular dominance columns in monkey striate cortex. *Philos. Trans. R. Soc. Lond. B* 278: 377–409.

JENKINS, W. M., M. M. MERZENICH, M. T. OCHS, E. ALLARD AND T. GUIC-ROBLES (1990) Functional reorganization of the primary somatosensory cortex of owl monkeys after behaviorally controlled tactile stimulation. *J. Neurophysiol.* 63: 82–104.

JOHANSSON, R. S. (1978) Tactile sensibility of the human hand: Receptive field characteristics of mechanoreceptive units in the glabrous skin. *J. Physiol.* (Lond.) 281: 101–123.

MALNIC, B., J. HIRONO, T. SATO AND L. B. BUCK (1999) Combinatorial receptor codes for odors. *Cell* 96: 713–723.

MERZENICH, M. M., R. J. NELSON, M. P. STRYKER, M. S. CYNADER, A. SCHOPPMANN AND J. M. ZOOK (1984) Somatosensory cortical map changes following digit amputation in adult monkeys. *J. Comp. Neurol.* 224: 591–605.

MOMBAERTS, P. AND 7 OTHERS (1996) Visualizing an olfactory sensory map. *Cell* 87: 675–686.

VASSAR, R., S. K. CHAO, R. SITCHERAN, J. M. NUNEZ, L. B. VOSSHALL AND R. AXEL (1994) Topographic organization of sensory projections to the olfactory bulb. *Cell* 79: 981–991.

WALL, P. D. AND W. NOORDENHOS (1977) Sensory functions which remain in man after complete transection of dorsal columns. *Brain* 100: 641–653.

WIESEL, T. N. AND D. H. HUBEL (1965) Comparison of the effects of unilateral and bilateral eye closure on cortical unit responses in kittens. *J. Neurophysiol.* 28: 1029–1040.

Books

BARLOW, H. B. AND J. D. MOLLON (1989) *The Senses.* Cambridge: Cambridge University Press, Chapters 17–19.

DOTY, R. L., ED. (1995) *Handbook of Olfaction and Gustation.* New York: Marcel Dekker.

FIELDS, H. L. (1987) *Pain.* New York: McGraw-Hill.

SIMON, S. A. AND S. D. ROPER (1993) *Mechanisms of Taste Transduction.* Boca Raton, FL: CRC Press, Chapters 2, 6, 9, 10, 12, 13, and 14.

WALL, P. D. AND R. MELZACK (1989) *Textbook of Pain.* New York: Churchill Livingstone.

UNIT III

Principles of Motor Processing and Motor Behavior

The ultimate goal of all mental processes—including perception, attention, memory, emotional and social influences, executive control, and decision making—is to produce appropriate voluntary and involuntary motor actions. Thus, to understand how and why the human brain mediates cognitive functions, one must first understand how it generates action. This unit considers the central nervous system circuitry that makes complex movements possible.

The most obvious aspect of behavior is the movement of body parts produced by the skeletal motor system. Skeletal muscles contract in response to the activation of lower motor neurons in the spinal cord and brainstem that directly innervate skeletal muscle fibers. The activity of lower motor neurons is coordinated by neuronal circuitry within the spinal cord and brainstem that modulates sensory reflexes and sustains complex rhythmic movements. Lower motor neurons in the spinal cord and brainstem are under the control of the upper motor neurons of the brainstem and cerebral cortex. Upper motor neurons indirectly influence movement via descending projections to local circuits in the brainstem and spinal cord or, more rarely, to lower motor neurons themselves. These upper motor neuron centers enable the planning, coordination, and initiation of complex sequences of movements. Additional circuitry in the basal ganglia and cerebellum modulates signals generated by upper motor neurons, thus adapting movements to ongoing changes in both internal and external environments.

Equally important in understanding key aspects of cognition—emotion in particular—is the behavior generated by activity in the autonomic motor system that causes contraction of the smooth muscles found in most organs of the body. The neurons that innervate smooth muscle fibers are located in ganglia outside the central nervous system, which are coordinated and modulated by higher-order neurons in the spinal cord, brainstem, and most especially the hypothalamus. ■

Motor Systems and Motor Control

Introduction

Sensory systems provide the initial inputs to cognitive processes, and motor systems deliver the physical behavioral output that expresses cognitive goals. Thus, understanding the organization of the body's motor systems is essential for understanding the organization of cognitive systems, which ultimately manifest functions such as perception, attention, emotion, and the consequences of decisions in motor behavior. All body movements are generated by the stimulation of skeletal muscle fibers by the lower motor neurons—neurons whose cell bodies are located in the brainstem and spinal cord. The activation of lower motor neurons is coordinated by local circuits consisting of interneurons, also located in the spinal cord and brainstem. Complex reflexes and rhythmic locomotor movements can be generated and sustained by the coordinated activation of such local circuits in the absence of inputs from higher motor centers. Although local circuits can produce simple movements in the absence of higher-order control, their activity is also controlled by descending projections from upper motor neurons in the cerebral cortex and brainstem. These descending influences modulate the activity of local circuits to produce and coordinate complex sequences of movements that comprise the purposeful, goal-directed actions characteristic of human behavior. This higher-order control of movement is mediated by upper motor neurons in the primary motor cortex and other premotor areas of the frontal and parietal lobes. Damage to upper or lower motor neurons produces distinct motor deficits, whose clinical characteristics offer clues to the location and nature of the underlying neurological problem. Whereas all movements of the skeleton are produced by the contraction of muscle fibers controlled by the skeletal motor system, movements critical to the functions of body organs (which are intimately tied to emotion) are generated by muscles controlled by the autonomic motor system.

Motor Control Is Hierarchical

Behavioral and theoretical studies of motor control strongly support a hierarchical model of the neural systems that organize movement. The notion of hierarchical organization is vividly illustrated by the observation that complex movements, such as signing one's name, preserve distinctive features such as shape and style even when performed by different muscle groups. For example, the Russian physiologist Nikolai Bernstein asked people to sign their name with a pen held in the dominant (usually right) hand, and then with the pen attached near the wrist, elbow, or shoulder; with the pen attached to the right shoe; and even with the pen held in the mouth. Although penmanship was clearly sloppier and larger in scale under these decidedly unnatural conditions, the signature remained remarkably similar in overall form (**Figure 8.1**).

Such observations support the notion that complex behaviors are organized at several levels. At the highest level are **motor programs**, which are sets of commands to initiate a sequence of movements. Such motor programs are distinguished by the fact that they are more or less ballistic, in the sense that they are not strictly dependent on incoming sensory information. Moreover, as demonstrated by Bernstein's handwriting experiment, motor programs are independent of the actual muscle groups used to carry them out. Finally, motor programs originate within the central nervous system itself rather than arising directly from sensory signals from the periphery.

By contrast, at the lowest level of the motor control hierarchy are elementary behavioral units that directly activate muscles. As described in the remainder of this chapter, as well as in Chapter 9, a variety of intermediate processing levels intervene between motor programs and the elementary units of motor control. Such intermediate processing in the motor system

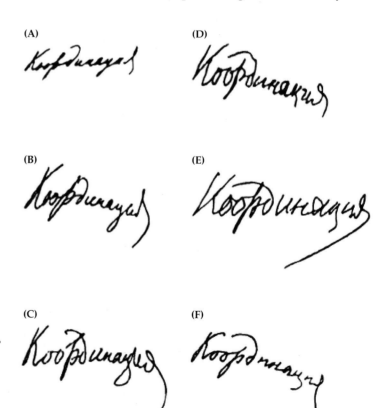

Figure 8.1 Behavioral evidence for motor programs. These signatures were made with a pen held in the right hand (A), attached at the right wrist (B), attached at the elbow (C), attached at the shoulder (D), attached to the right shoe (E), and held in the teeth (F). Note the remarkable similarity in form retained by all the signatures. (From Bernstein 1947.)

translates motor programs into the precisely coordinated sequences of motor neuron activation and suppression that are needed to generate the patterns of muscle contraction and relaxation responsible for complex behavior.

Organization of the skeletal motor system

Hierarchical models of motor control can be loosely mapped onto neuroanatomically and neurophysiologically distinct elements of the central nervous system. At a broad level, the neural circuits controlling skeletal movements can be thought of as being made up of four distinct but interacting subsystems: lower motor neurons in the spinal cord and brainstem; upper motor neurons in the cortex and brainstem; the cerebellum; and basal ganglia (**Figure 8.2**).

At the lowest level are local circuits within the spinal cord and brainstem, composed of **lower motor neurons** and **local circuit neurons**. Lower motor neurons in the gray matter of the spinal cord and brainstem send axons out of the central nervous system to directly innervate skeletal muscle fibers, and they can be considered synonymous with the elementary behavioral units already mentioned (see Chapter 1). Local circuit neurons, on the other hand, provide synaptic input to lower motor neurons and contribute to the local coordination of lower motor neuron activity.

At higher levels of the motor system, **upper motor neurons** in the cerebral cortex and brainstem provide descending control of local circuitry in the spinal cord and brainstem. The other two components of the motor system—the cerebellum and basal ganglia—modulate the activity of upper motor neurons in order to make "online" corrections in response to perturbations in ongoing movements and to help initiate goal-directed movements, respectively. The cerebellum and basal ganglia are discussed in more detail in Chapter 9. The localization of motor programs remains an active area of investigation.

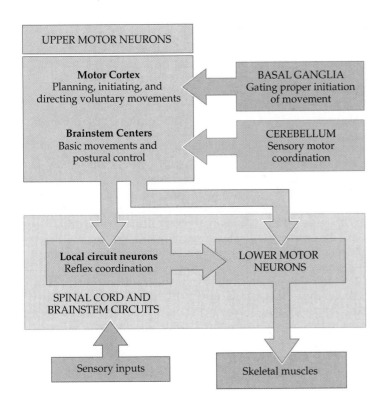

Figure 8.2 The overall organization of the human motor system. Four systems—upper motor neurons in the cortex and brainstem (blue), lower motor neurons in the spinal cord and brainstem (red), the cerebellum (green), and basal ganglia (brown)—make essential and distinct contributions to motor control.

Motor neurons and muscle fibers

Any neurobiological account of how higher-order motor circuits enable voluntary and even thoughtful behavior must begin by considering how lower motor neurons interact with the muscles they innervate, since these neurons constitute the final common pathway for movement.

During either voluntary or reflexive movement, **skeletal** (*striated*) **muscle** contracts when it is excited by lower motor neurons located in the spinal cord and brainstem (skeletal muscles are called *striated muscles* because of the appearance of their fibers in the microscope; smooth muscle fibers lack these striations). The cell bodies of the lower motor neurons reside in the **ventral** (*anterior*) **horn** of the spinal cord and in the analogous cranial nerve nuclei in the brainstem. Upper motor neurons, on the other hand, have cell bodies that reside in the cerebral cortex or brainstem. The axons of upper motor neurons synapse on the cell bodies of lower motor neurons or local circuit neurons, which in turn innervate lower motor neurons in the brainstem or spinal cord. Damage to upper or lower motor neurons produces distinct motor deficits that indicate the location and nature of the underlying physical problem (**Box 8A**).

Individual muscles are made up of dozens to thousands of cells called **muscle fibers**. Each fiber is capable of generating force through contraction caused by the calcium-mediated interaction of actin and myosin molecules in the fiber. These molecular events are set in motion when the muscle fiber is excited by neurotransmitter released from the terminal of a lower motor neu-

■ BOX 8A Motor Neuron Syndromes

When the lower motor neurons themselves become damaged or diseased, a characteristic suite of motor problems—known as *lower motor neuron syndrome*—ensues. The main deficit in this syndrome is loss of movement—that is, paralysis or weakness of the affected muscles. In addition, such damage usually weakens or abolishes reflexes involving the affected lower motor neurons, and reduces or eliminates the tone (the normal resting tension) in the affected muscles. The affected muscle may also exhibit fibrillations and fasciculations, spontaneous contractions resulting from a loss of normal innervation.

Lower motor neuron syndrome can be caused by local damage to the gray matter in the spinal cord or brainstem that destroys lower motor neurons, or by damage to the peripheral nerves or cranial nerves carrying efferent (motor) output to the muscles. The presence and nature of such damage can be diagnosed by the characteristic pattern of paralysis, paresis, and loss of reflexes, and the damage can be localized within the central nervous system by knowledge of the topographic organization of motor units in the brainstem and spinal cord. For example, loss of the knee-jerk (stretch) reflex on the right side might indicate damage to the spinal cord gray matter on the right side or damage to a segmental nerve leading to the right leg, depending on the extent of the symptoms; and an inability to look rightward with the right eye would indicate damage to the brainstem nucleus controlling the lateral rectus muscle of the eye on the right side.

When the upper motor neurons in the motor cortex or their axons in descending tracts are damaged or destroyed, motor control is disrupted quite differently. The set of deficits observed is known as *upper motor neuron syndrome* and is distinct from lower motor neuron syndrome. Upper motor neuron syndrome is characterized by an initial paralysis of the affected motor structures, particularly for upper motor neurons involved in limb control. After this initial period, spinal cord and brainstem circuits again assert local control of reflexes, but now independent of the missing higher control centers. This lack of control results in a condition known as *hyperreflexia*, in which sensory-motor reflexes are much more active than normal.

Clinicians often test for upper motor neuron syndrome by stroking the bottom of the foot from heel to toe with a stiff object. In normal subjects, the toes flex downward, but in a patient with upper motor neuron syndrome the toes fan outward and upward. In addition to hyperreflexia, upper motor neuron syndrome presents as an increase in muscle tone, known as *spasticity*, as well as rigidity. Spasticity is caused by a loss of descending inhibitory influences on the vestibulospinal and reticulospinal circuits that mediate unconscious postural control. Thus, a physician can effectively use the severity and pattern of motor deficits displayed by a patient to identify and localize the underlying physiological cause of the problem.

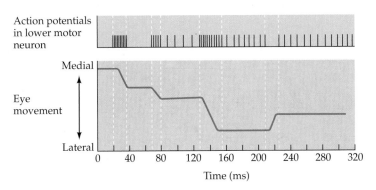

Figure 8.3 Activity of lower motor neurons predicts muscle contraction and ultimately movement. In the example here, the upper trace shows a recording from a lower motor neuron that innervates one of the eye muscles, causing the eye to rotate laterally. Note that the rate of action potentials is directly correlated with the amplitude and direction of the eye movement. (After Fuchs 1967.)

ron following a volley of action potentials conducted down its axon. Each muscle fiber is typically contacted, or *innervated*, by only a single motor neuron; each motor neuron, on the other hand, innervates from several dozen to several thousand muscle fibers.

Lower motor neurons begin to fire action potentials immediately preceding contraction of the muscles they innervate; thus, their activity is directly correlated with the movement of the relevant body part (**Figure 8.3**). Motor neurons involved in fine motor control, such as those used to move the fingers or control the position of the eyes, innervate far fewer muscle fibers than do motor neurons involved in gross movements of larger muscles, such as those used to move the legs when walking and running.

Lower motor neuron pools

For lower motor neurons located within the spinal cord, the axons that contact the muscle fibers themselves exit the spinal cord via the **ventral spinal roots** and then enter segmental nerves, and the axons of motor neurons located within the brainstem exit the skull via analogous **cranial nerves**. Each lower motor neuron innervates muscle fibers within a single muscle, and the population of lower motor neurons innervating a single muscle is called the **motor neuron pool** for that muscle. The motor neuron pool for a given muscle can be identified by injecting the muscle with dyes that are transported back along the axons of the motor neurons innervating the muscle. Such labeling shows that the cell bodies of neurons in each pool are aggregated into clusters running lengthwise within the spinal cord, or into similar nuclear clusters within the brainstem (**Figure 8.4**).

Motor neuron pools are also organized topographically within the spinal cord and brainstem. Thus, motor neuron pools that innervate more proximal muscles, such as those that move the torso or shoulders, lie more medially within the ventral-horn gray matter in the spinal cord. Motor neurons that innervate more distal muscles, such as those that move the fingers or toes, lie more laterally (**Figure 8.5**). The motor neuron pools within the brainstem are also organized topographically, although in a somewhat more complex way. In the longitudinal axis of the cord, the greater number of motor neuron pools innervating muscles in the upper and lower extremities, compared to the relatively meager musculature of the trunk, causes prominent enlargements in the

Dye injected into

| Gastrocnemius muscle | Soleus muscle |

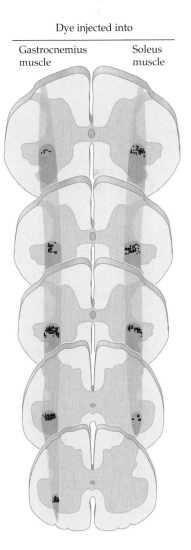

Figure 8.4 Organization of lower motor neurons in the ventral horn of the spinal cord. The cell bodies of motor neurons show up in black following labeling by injection of a retrograde dye into individual muscles. Cross sections from the spinal cord illustrate the overall distribution of motor neurons innervating individual skeletal muscles—the gastrocnemius and soleus muscles in the lower leg, in this example—in both axes of the spinal cord. (After Burke et al. 1977.)

Figure 8.5 Topographic organization of the lower motor neurons in a cross section of the cervical spinal cord. Motor neurons innervating proximal muscles (i.e., those closest to the shoulder) are located medially (close to the midline); those innervating distal muscles (toward the digits) are located laterally (to the right or left).

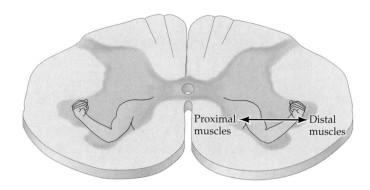

cervical and lumbar cord that are visible on gross inspection. This overrepresentation is thus analogous to the greater amount of neural circuitry devoted to especially important body regions in sensory systems (described in Unit II).

Regulation of Muscle Force

Each lower motor neuron and the set of muscle fibers it innervates are together called a **motor unit**, the fundamental organizational element of the motor system (**Figure 8.6**). The muscle fibers innervated by any particular motor neuron are distributed throughout a muscle, thereby ensuring integrated movement of the muscle during contraction. The linkage of a motor neuron to each of the muscle fibers within a motor unit is typically all or none. Thus, activation of the motor neuron usually causes contraction of all the muscle fibers that it contacts. This one-to-one coupling means that a motor unit—that is, a single motor neuron and all the muscle fibers it contacts—constitutes the smallest unit of force that can be activated to produce movement. Because every action potential generated by a motor neuron results in a muscle fiber contraction, repeated activity of a motor neuron produces sustained contraction of the muscle fibers that it innervates.

The amount of force generated by a muscle is therefore determined by the number and frequency of motor neuron action potentials during a given movement and by the number of muscle fibers in the muscle's motor units (**Figure 8.7**). In general, smaller lower motor neurons innervate relatively small numbers of muscle fibers and are involved in fine motor control, and larger motor neurons innervate larger numbers of fibers and are involved in controlling coarse movements of large muscles. Thus, when small motor units are activated, smaller, more finely graded forces are generated. The force generated by a muscle can also be enhanced by an increase in the number of motor neurons and thus the number of motor units activated; this increase activates more muscle fibers (Figure 8.7A). Especially forceful muscle contractions are generated by an increase in the firing rate of all the relevant motor neurons to a maximal level (Figure 8.7B).

The pattern of motor unit recruitment has important implications for motor control. During voluntary movement, the central nervous system recruits smaller motor neurons (and thus smaller motor units) first. Larger motor neurons are sequentially recruited only after smaller ones have already been activated. The orderly recruitment of motor units as a function of their size is known as the **size principle**. Because motor units are recruited in order of size, small muscle forces needed to generate fine movements involve only small motor neurons innervating small numbers of muscle fibers. When more forceful muscle contractions are needed, however, as in the explosive movements used in running and jumping, both small and large motor neurons are

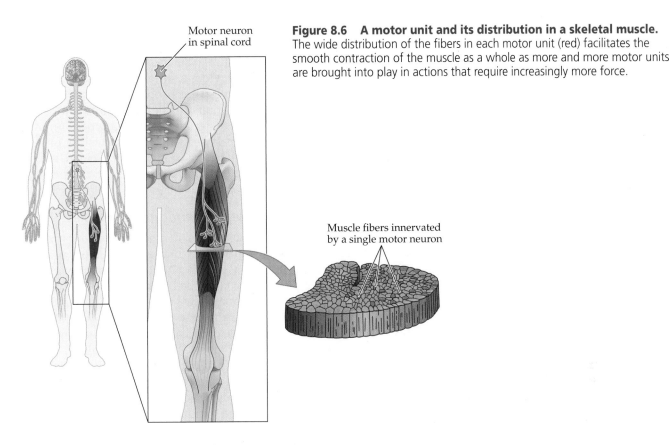

Figure 8.6   A motor unit and its distribution in a skeletal muscle. The wide distribution of the fibers in each motor unit (red) facilitates the smooth contraction of the muscle as a whole as more and more motor units are brought into play in actions that require increasingly more force.

Motor neuron in spinal cord

Muscle fibers innervated by a single motor neuron

recruited, thereby activating all the muscle fibers within a given muscle (see Figure 8.7).

This pattern of motor unit recruitment explains why it is more difficult to type on a manual typewriter, which requires forceful keystrokes, than it is to type on a computer keyboard. Generating the higher forces needed to strike the paper on a manual typewriter recruits a larger number of motor units, and a larger number of muscle fibers, than are recruited for typing on an electronic keyboard. Thus, although all typing requires highly accurate movement selec-

Figure 8.7   Different ways of increasing the force generated by a muscle. (A) The recruitment of motor units in the leg muscle of a cat during different behaviors. As the force needed for different movements increases, more motor units are recruited. (B) Motor units recorded from a muscle of the human hand as the amount of voluntary force is progressively increased. The firing rate increases for each unit as the subject generates more force. (A after Walmsley et al. 1978; B after Monster and Chan 1977.)

(A)

Jump
Gallop
Run
Walk
Stand

Maximum force (%) vs. Motor neuron pool recruited (%)

(B)

Unit firing rate (Hz) vs. Voluntary force (g)

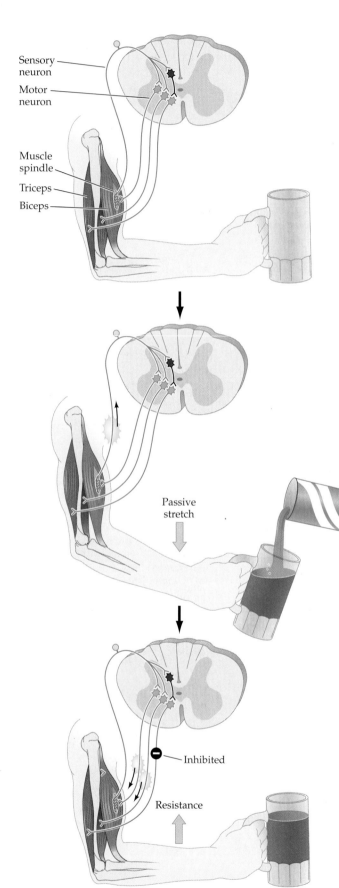

Sensory neuron

Motor neuron

Muscle spindle

Triceps

Biceps

Passive stretch

Inhibited

Resistance

tion, manual typing recruits a broader, less precisely tuned array of motor units, thus increasing the need for attention, concentration, and practice to be effective.

The size principle provides a simple solution to the need for graded muscle forces; the problem is solved by the recruitment of combinations of motor units tuned to the range of forces needed to generate different types of movement. The physiological mechanisms responsible for the precise recruitment of motor units are embedded within local circuits in the spinal cord and brainstem that are discussed later in this chapter.

Muscle sensory receptors and simple reflexes

As described in Chapters 1 and 7, specialized sensory receptors called **muscle spindles**, which are embedded in muscles, provide sensory feedback about the amount of stretch that is being experienced by the parent muscle. Themselves made up of a small number of specialized muscle fibers, muscle spindles are arranged in parallel with skeletal muscle fibers. As the capsule of the spindle is stretched by external forces acting on the muscle, action potentials are set up in afferent nerves leading from the spindle to the spinal cord (**Figure 8.8**). Spindle fibers also receive their own innervation from a small, highly specialized population of motor neurons. These so-called **gamma motor neurons** adjust the length of the spindles, allowing them to signal effectively over the full range of lengths of the parent muscle (**alpha motor neurons** are the name given to the neurons that innervate skeletal muscle fibers).

The importance of muscle spindles for behavior is evident in **stretch reflexes**, also known as *deep tendon reflexes* or *myotatic reflexes*. In Figure 8.8, stretching of the biceps muscle resulting from the increased weight in the mug causes the muscle spindles to be briefly stretched as well. As a result, action potentials are generated in the sensory receptor endings and then along the afferent sensory nerve axons to the spinal cord. The nerve enters the spinal cord via the **dorsal spinal root** and synapses directly on the cell bodies of motor neurons innervating the biceps and other flexor muscles. In addition, the afferents synapse onto local interneurons within the spinal cord, which inhibit the activity of motor neurons innervating opposing muscles at the back of the upper arm. Called **reciprocal innervation**, this pattern of connectivity coordinates the contraction and

Figure 8.8 A stretch reflex. Stretching a muscle like the biceps elicits receptor potentials in muscle spindles. Afferents from the muscle spindle travel to the spinal cord, where they directly excite motor neurons activating the muscle, as well as other synergistic flexors. In addition, the activity of the muscle sensory receptors stimulates inhibitory interneurons in the spinal cord, which in turn inhibit the activity of a motor neuron driving the antagonistic extensor muscle (the triceps muscle in this example). The net activation of this reflex arc results in flexion of the arm, which is a useful reflex behavior under these conditions.

relaxation of opposing muscles. Such reflexes are in continual operation to defend posture in the face of unexpected perturbations.

Sensory feedback from muscles may have an important influence on the cognitive processes underlying some very basic social interactions. Nearly everyone has witnessed how physical conflicts escalate in children. Each child retaliates against a punch from the other with increasing force (this pattern of force escalation is not uncommon in other sorts of conflicts as well, including those between nations). Mismatched sensory-motor feedback may be critical for such force escalation.

To investigate this idea, Daniel Wolpert and his colleagues at University College London asked human adults to match the amount of force they perceived being applied to one hand by squeezing a force transducer with the other. These researchers found that subjects exerted much more force than they received, suggesting that self-generated forces are perceived as weaker than externally generated forces of equal magnitude. The researchers went on to speculate that suppressing feedback from self-generated forces may help enhance the perception of externally generated sensations, thereby promoting behavioral responses to stimuli affecting the body. This example demonstrates the relevance of basic motor control processes to understanding complex behaviors.

Reflex pathways governing more complex movements

An example of a more complex spinal reflex is the *cutaneous withdrawal reflex*, a type of **flexion reflex** (**Figure 8.9**). Unlike reflexes that result from sensory stimulation originating within the muscle itself, this reflex circuit enables withdrawal of a limb from a noxious or painful stimulus sensed by receptors in the skin, such as the prick from stepping on a tack. Even though the behavioral outcome of this reflex is generated very quickly, the flexion reflex actually involves several synaptic connections. The afferent pain fibers synapse on local circuit neurons in the spinal cord. Activation of this circuitry leads in turn to flexion of the stimulated limb via excitation of the ipsilateral flexor muscles and reciprocal inhibition of the ipsilateral extensor muscles. Although important in withdrawing the affected limb from a potentially harmful event, the flexion reflex creates a secondary problem in maintaining upright posture on the remaining leg. To counteract the sudden shift in weight balance caused by the flexion reflex, the other limb is extended by an opposite set of mechanisms, known as the **crossed extension reflex**, that activate the contralateral extensor muscles and reciprocally inhibit the contralateral flexors, thereby maintaining postural support.

The local circuitry involved in the flexion and crossed extension reflexes receives modulatory inputs from several sources, including upper motor neuron pathways and other spinal cord interneurons. When these inputs are damaged or destroyed, the affected reflexes can be activated by relatively benign stimuli that would not normally activate them. Thus, the relative sensitivity of these local circuits is under the control of descending projections to the spinal cord from various upper motor neuron pathways.

Central pattern generators and locomotion

The reflexes just described, as well as others like them, show that circuits connecting the muscles to the spinal cord and then back to the muscles provide simple yet powerful mechanisms for controlling basic behavior. Key components of these circuits are local circuit neurons within the spinal cord that help connect incoming sensory information to appropriate motor neurons that enable movement. In fact, activation of the appropriate sets of local circuit neurons can generate complex patterns of muscle contraction and relaxation

Figure 8.9 The spinal cord circuitry responsible for a flexion reflex. Stimulation of pain receptors in the foot activates spinal cord local circuits that withdraw (flex) the stimulated limb. In what is known as the *crossed extension reflex*, these circuits also extend the opposite limb to maintain support.

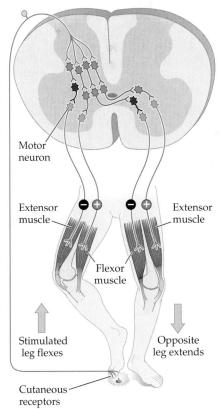

Pain afferent

Motor neuron

Extensor muscle

Extensor muscle

Flexor muscle

Stimulated leg flexes

Opposite leg extends

Cutaneous receptors

that result in rather sophisticated behavior. For example, the spinal cord (and brainstem) contains circuits capable of producing coordinated movements of the limbs with no input from the brain. Not surprisingly, these local circuits can also produce and sustain even more complex movements that are not simply reflexive responses to sensory inputs. Experimental work in a variety of animals has shown that rhythmic movements such as locomotion and swimming are actually produced by local spinal cord circuits known as **central pattern generators**.

Walking, to take a specific example, is a rhythmic behavior in which each foot moves from the stance phase, where it is in contact with the ground, to the swing phase, in which it is lifted and brought forward to begin the next stance phase. These phases of locomotion are associated with bursts of activity in extensor muscles during the stance phase and in flexor muscles during the swing phase (**Figure 8.10A**). Cats that have undergone surgical transection of the spinal cord anterior to the motor neurons controlling the hind limbs can nonetheless walk relatively normally on a treadmill. Their gait continues to follow the normal stance-swing-stance pattern, and the extensor and flexor muscles show coordinated bursts of activity typically associated with the stance and swing phases in normal animals (**Figure 8.10B**). Remarkably, cats with transected spinal cords can also adjust their walking speed when the treadmill is sped up or slowed down. When the sensory fibers entering the spinal cord via the dorsal roots are cut, however, the cat can continue to walk on the treadmill but can no longer adjust its gait or avoid obstacles.

(A)

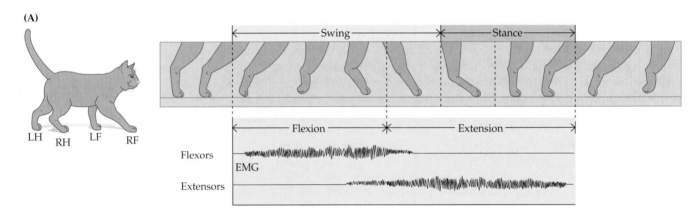

(B)

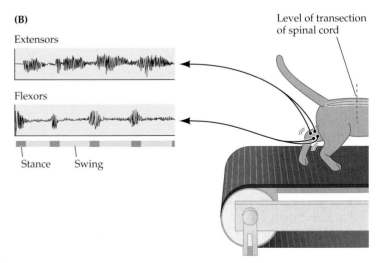

Figure 8.10 A central pattern generator in the spinal cord. (A) Electrical recordings from muscles in the legs of a cat show the relations of stance (foot planted), swing (foot lifted), and stance phases of locomotion. (B) After spinal cord transection, the hind limbs are still able to walk on a treadmill, and the reciprocal bursts of action potentials in the flexors and extensors during swing and stance phases are still evident. (After Pearson 1976.)

These experiments, and others like them, demonstrate that the spinal cord and brainstem contain circuitry capable of controlling the timing and coordination of multiple muscles to produce complex rhythmic movements, that these circuits can respond to variations in the local physical environment such as obstacles, and that the needed processing can be performed in the absence of any input from higher brain centers. Unfortunately for human victims of spinal cord injury, central pattern generators in the spinal cord that control locomotion are under strong control of descending upper motor neuron pathways and are thus much less effective in generating walking in humans than in animals like the cat.

Once evolution has generated a neural solution to a particular motor problem, the same mechanisms are often applied in new contexts to solve similar problems. Thus, central pattern generators, which evolved originally to mediate basic rhythmic functions such as swimming, walking, or swallowing, serve important roles in more complex, often cognitive, motor behaviors. For example, spoken language is arguably the most complex cognitive behavior generated by the brain, yet all human languages rely on the same basic motor processes for generating meaningful utterances (see Chapters 20 and 21). Verbal sequencing, much like the sequencing of other complex movement patterns, appears to rely on endogenous central pattern generators instantiated in feedback loops between the cortex and basal ganglia, as will be described in Chapter 9. Sequential patterning in these loops is quite similar to the sequences of neuronal activation in the spinal cord and brainstem central pattern generators considered here.

Coordination of Movement by the Brainstem

Both evolutionarily and developmentally, the brainstem can be considered an anatomical and physiological extension of the spinal cord, which is devoted to sensory-motor functions of the face, head, and neck. Nonetheless, motor neuron pools in the brainstem are also important in cognitive functions (**Box 8B**). These motor neurons are influenced by additional local circuit neurons that coordinate reflexes among these muscle groups, contributing to more complex coordination of reflexive and rhythmic movements controlled by local circuits in the spinal cord and brainstem. Many of these local circuits reside in the brainstem **reticular formation**, so called because it consists of loose, ribbon-like aggregations of neurons rather than discrete clusters or nuclei. This formation extends throughout the brainstem and contributes to a variety of functions, including cardiovascular and respiratory control, organization and control of eye movements, and regulation of sleep and wakefulness.

Particularly relevant to understanding cognitive functions such as attention (see Unit IV) is an area of the reticular formation in the medial pons known as the **paramedian pontine reticular formation** (**PPRF**), which coordinates movements of the two eyes in response to descending projections from upper motor neurons (**Figure 8.11**). Binocular vision requires alignment of the visual axes of the two eyes, so the six ocular muscles controlling the position of each eye must be coordinated to produce conjugate gaze shifts. The complex patterns of neural activity needed to coordinate the sequence of extraocular muscle contractions underlying gaze shifts are controlled by the PPRF. Unilateral damage to the reticular formation, as might be caused by a stroke in the caudomedial pons, abolishes the ability to shift gaze to the affected side. Similar circuitry within the reticular formation contributes to coordinated, multijoint movements of the muscles of facial expression (see Box 8B), mastication, and vocalization.

Figure 8.11 Circuitry controlling eye movements. The paramedian pontine reticular formation (PPRF) in the pons contains neurons that organize and coordinate the activity of lower motor neurons in the abducens nucleus and oculomotor nucleus, whose activation determines the contractile state of the extraocular muscles, and therefore the position of the eye. The medial longitudinal fasciculus is a fiber bundle connecting the abducens nuclei and the oculomotor nuclei. (After Blumenfeld 2002.)

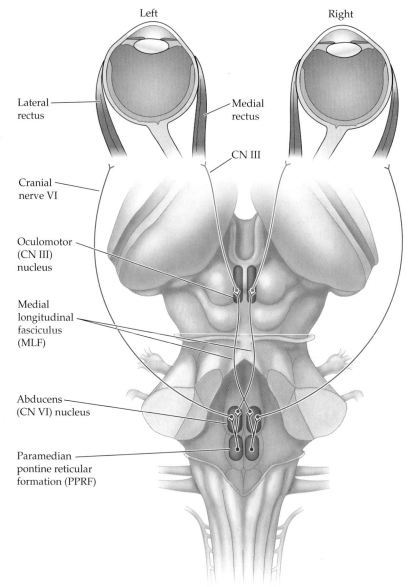

Activation of the reticular formation thus enables fast and efficient coordination of the lower motor neuron activity necessary for initiating and generating coordinated movements of multiple muscles, and it is important for cognitive behaviors such as visual attention. Typically we shift our gaze to salient objects in a visual scene (see Chapter 9). Because the reticular formation coordinates lower motor neuron activity underlying such movements, attentional systems, like higher motor systems, need only issue "commands" to move the eyes to a particular position. Such commands ultimately reach the reticular formation, where they are "read out" by neurons projecting to the brainstem and spinal cord. Covert attending without moving the eyes may be mediated by the issuing of such commands at strengths below threshold for initiating overt eye movements. In partial support of this idea, Tirin Moore and colleagues at Stanford have demonstrated that weak electrical stimulation of saccade-related neurons in the frontal cortex (see the next section), some of which project directly to the PPRF, enhances attention to stimuli within the contralateral visual field—without overt movements of the eyes.

■ BOX 8B Motor Control of Facial Expressions

The neural control of facial expressions provides a fascinating and instructive example of how upper and lower motor neurons are coordinated to generate useful behavior, and how some aspects of emotion play into the generation of facial movements. The muscles of facial expression, including those that elevate the corners of the lips in a smile and raise the eyebrows in surprise, are under the direct control of lower motor neurons in the facial nerve nucleus in the pons. The projections of these lower motor neurons to the fa-cial muscles via cranial nerve VII are strictly unilateral. Thus, damage to upper motor neurons in the facial nucleus or to the nerve itself causes uni-lateral paralysis of the muscles of facial expression on that side (Figure A). In contrast, the upper motor neurons that initiate and coordinate voluntary facial expressions reside in the primary motor cortex.

A particularly common, and usually reversible, form of such facial paralysis known as *Bell's palsy* occurs following inflammation of the facial nerve. Notably, the upper motor neu-rons controlling the inferior facial muscles project to the contralateral pons, and the upper motor neurons controlling the superior facial muscles project bilaterally. Thus, damage to the portion of the primary motor cortex corresponding to movements of the face result in weakness of the inferior facial muscles on the opposite side, but movements of the superior facial muscles are spared.

A second motor pathway more closely linked to emotion contributes to largely involuntary facial expressions. This pathway originates in pre-motor areas in the prefrontal cortex and basal ganglia, projects to the hy-pothalamus, and then continues to the brainstem reticular formation, ulti-mately targeting the facial motor nuclei in the pons. Activation of this pathway by an emotional experience evokes involuntary facial expression, such as the smile produced upon hear-ing a joke. Damage to this multisynap-tic "extrapyramidal" pathway (the voluntary pathway is referred to as the *pyramidal pathway* because it travels in the pyramids in the caudal medulla) renders patients unable to sponta-neously express emotions in the face, although they can still produce sym-metrical voluntary facial expressions (Figure B). Conversely, patients with damage to upper motor neuron path-ways have difficulty voluntarily mov-ing the muscles of the lower part of the contralateral face but nonetheless can smile, frown, or cry normally in response to emotional stimulation.

These distinctions between the pathway for voluntary facial expres-sion and spontaneous, emotional fa-cial expression were first described by

(Continued on next page)

(A)

Voluntary and emotional control of facial expression. (A) Anatomical circuit control-ling voluntary facial expression. Lower motor neurons in the pons project to the muscles of the upper and lower face. Upper motor neurons projecting to the pons are unilateral for the lower face, but bilateral for the upper face. A unilateral lesion to the facial nucleus in the pons results in complete paralysis of the face on the same side, whereas a unilateral lesion in the lateral part of the primary motor cor-tex results in paresis of the lower face on the opposite side due to bilateral projec-tions serving the upper facial muscles.

BOX 8B *(continued)*

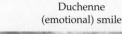

(B)

Pyramidal (volitional) smile

Duchenne (emotional) smile

Volitional facial paresis

Emotional facial paresis

(B) Voluntary and emotional paresis of the face. Lesions to the face representation in primary motor cortex lead to unilateral weakness in smiling on command (left). Lesions to the emotional pathway for facial expression lead to an inability to smile in response to a joke, while voluntary smiling remains intact (right). (C) Duchenne de Boulogne's pioneering study of "faradization," or electrical stimulation, of the facial muscles. The patient in the photographs had lost sensation in the face and thus did not feel the effects of stimulation. Compare the stimulated "smile" (second from left) with the emotional smile (third from left).

(C)

   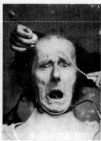

strained and unnatural. The distinctions between voluntary and emotional facial expression pathways are often painfully obvious in the contrived facial expressions worn when we are less than sincere.

References

BLUMENFELD, H. (2002) *Neuroanatomy through Clinical Cases.* Sunderland, MA: Sinauer.

DARWIN, C. R. (1872) *The Expression of the Emotions in Man and Animals.* London: Murray.

DUCHENNE DE BOULOGNE, G. B. (1862) *Mécanisme de la Physionomie Humaine.* Cambridge: Cambridge University Press.

the French neurologist and physiologist Duchenne de Boulogne, who photographed subjects producing facial expressions in response to direct electrical stimulation of the muscles and in response to emotional stimulation (Figure C). Duchenne demonstrated

that some facial muscle groups, such as the orbicularis oculi, can be activated involuntarily only by subjective emotional experience, an expression known as the *Duchenne smile*. A forced or voluntary smile does not activate this muscle group, thus appearing

Cortical Pathways for Motor Control

As we have seen in the preceding discussion, the spinal cord and brainstem contain circuitry capable of generating an array of complex motor behavior. These subcortical systems serve animals with limited behavioral repertoires quite well, but in primates and other animals in which evolution has favored more demanding behaviors, the brain has evolved correspondingly complex higher motor centers capable of initiating and coordinating the local circuits and lower motor neurons that generate movements more directly.

Descending projections from the cerebral cortex to brainstem and spinal cord originate from upper motor neurons within the **primary motor cortex** and the adjacent **premotor cortical areas**, including the **premotor cortex** and **supplementary motor cortex**, in the frontal lobes (**Figure 8.12**; see also Chapter 1). The upper motor neurons whose axons form these descending projections are large pyramidal neurons mostly in layer 5 of the primary motor cortex (**Figure 8.13A**), although a smaller number of these cells also reside in

(A) Lateral view

Premotor cortex | Supplementary motor cortex | Primary motor cortex

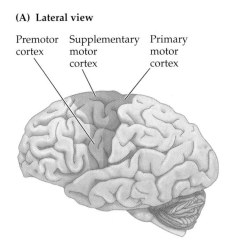

(B) Medial view

Supplementary motor cortex | Primary motor cortex

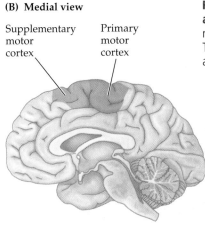

Figure 8.12 The primary motor cortex and premotor cortical areas. The primary motor cortex is located in the precentral gyrus. The motor and supplemental premotor areas are more rostral in the frontal lobe.

layer 5 of the parietal, somatosensory, and cingulate cortices. The primary motor cortex lies just anterior to the central sulcus in the precentral gyrus, and it is distinguished by the size, shape, and packing density of neurons that define this area cytoarchitectonically (the primary motor cortex is also called *Brodmann area 4*). In addition to having anatomical differences, the primary motor cortex is distinguished from other premotor areas by the very low intensity of current needed to evoke movements by electrical stimulation. The fact that low electrical current intensities applied to primary motor cortex can evoke movements indicates that the upper motor neurons of this area have relatively direct access to local circuit neurons and lower motor neurons in the brainstem and spinal cord.

The axons of the upper motor neurons in the primary motor cortex descend in the corticobulbar (terminating in the pons) and corticospinal (terminating in the spinal cord) tracts into the cerebral peduncle at the base of the midbrain (**Figure 8.13B**). Axons that innervate neurons in the brainstem branch off at appropriate levels, and those continuing to the spinal cord coalesce and descend through the **medullary pyramids** (so named for their triangular appearance) in the pyramidal tract alluded to earlier. The majority of corticospinal fibers cross the midline, or *decussate*, at the caudal end of the medulla and enter the lateral corticospinal tracts in the spinal cord (see Figure 8.13B); they terminate within the gray matter of the cord at levels appropriate to the distal muscles that they serve. A small minority of corticospinal fibers remain uncrossed, forming the medial or ventral corticospinal tract; these axons terminate within the medial spinal cord gray matter on both sides (after crossing through the spinal cord commissure). These medial corticospinal projections, as suggested by the loci of their targets, are involved in control of the midline (proximal) musculature (see Figure 8.5).

Organization of the primary motor cortex

It has been known since the late nineteenth century that electrical stimulation of the primary motor cortex in the precentral gyrus on one side of the primate brain evokes muscle contractions on the opposite side of the body. At about the same time, the British neurologist John Hughlings Jackson noted that epileptic seizures often advanced systematically from one part of the body to another, beginning locally and spreading until the entire body was enveloped in a grand mal seizure. This "Jacksonian march" of seizure activity across the body surface suggested a systematic topography in the representation of the body's musculature in the brain.

Figure 8.13 Descending pathways from the primary motor cortex. (A) Pathway to the spinal cord. (B) The lateral corticospinal tract in cross section.

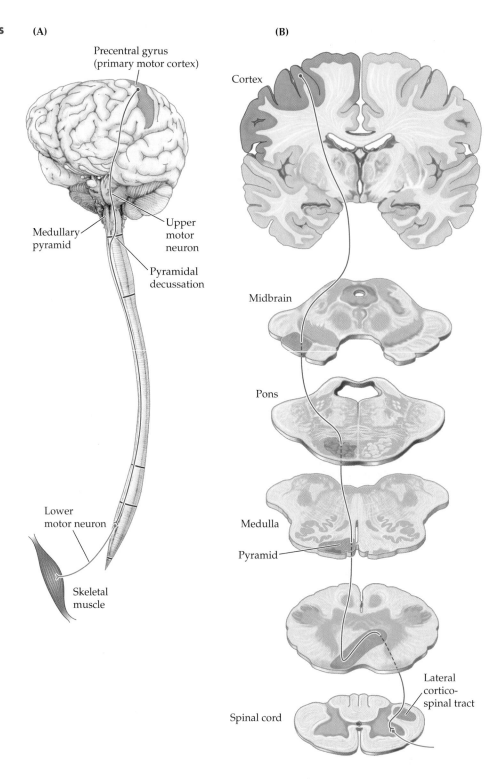

This apparently topographic organization of the primary motor cortex was confirmed shortly after the start of the twentieth century by Charles Sherrington, who showed that stimulating adjacent regions of the precentral gyrus in great apes elicited movements of adjacent contralateral body parts. The presence of a topographic map of body musculature in primary motor cortex was further verified in humans by Sherrington's student Wilder Penfield, who, as a neurosurgeon in the 1930s, systematically stimulated different brain regions

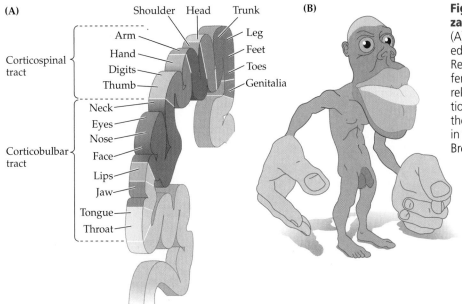

(A)

Corticospinal tract

Shoulder Head Trunk
Arm
Hand
Digits
Thumb

Leg
Feet
Toes
Genitalia

Corticobulbar tract

Neck
Eyes
Nose
Face
Lips
Jaw
Tongue
Throat

(B)

Figure 8.14 The topographic organization of the primary motor cortex. (A) The primary motor cortex (M1) is located just in front of the brain's central sulcus. Regions controlling motor responses in different parts of the body are shown here in relative size and sequence. (B) The proportions of the homunculus show the parts of the body relative to their represented size in the primary motor cortex. (After Breedlove et al. 2007.)

in human patients (see Chapter 7 for the similar results that he defined in the primary somatosensory cortex).

As in the sensory maps described in Unit II, these motor maps define a distorted representation of the body. A disproportionately large area of the lateral primary motor cortex was devoted to the lips, tongue, and hands; and a much smaller area of the dorsal and medial primary motor cortex was devoted to the lower extremities and genitalia (**Figure 8.14**). Thus, the amount of cortical space devoted to motor function corresponds to the capability of that area to exercise fine motor control, and it underscores the principle that more sophisticated processing is always reflected in a greater allocation of cortical space (see Chapters 4 and 26).

Movement maps in primary motor cortex

An issue especially pertinent to understanding how cognitive functions relate to the generation of motor behavior is the long-standing debate about exactly what is represented in these motor maps. Early studies in monkeys carried out by Hiroshi Asanuma and his colleagues at Rockefeller University using low-intensity electrical stimulation suggested that primary motor cortex might contain a map of muscles as such. However, later electrical stimulation studies in monkeys by Michael Graziano and Charles Gross at Princeton University confirmed earlier reports by Penfield and Sherrington that activation of some portions of the primary motor cortex evokes coordinated, multijoint movements (**Figure 8.15**). This observation is what would be expected, given that descending projections from primary motor cortex primarily target local circuits in the brainstem and spinal cord rather than the lower motor neurons themselves.

Electrophysiological recordings from single neurons in the primary motor cortex of monkeys have largely supported the conclusion that movements and not muscles are represented in motor maps. In the late 1960s, Edward Evarts and his group at the National Institutes of Health pioneered the technique of implanting electrodes in the motor cortex of monkeys that had been trained to reach to "cued" targets in order to receive rewards (**Figure 8.16A**). The electrical signals generated by neurons were then compared to the muscle fiber action potentials recorded from the arm muscles, as well as to recordings of

Figure 8.15 Complex movements evoked by stimulation of primary motor cortex in the monkey. Each drawing represents the animal's posture at the end of the stimulation. (A) Defensive-like posture of face. (B) Hand to mouth. (C) Manipulation-like shaping of fingers and movement of hand. (D) Outward reach with hand open, as if shaping to grasp. (E) Climbing- or leaping-like posture involving all four limbs. (After Graziano 2006.)

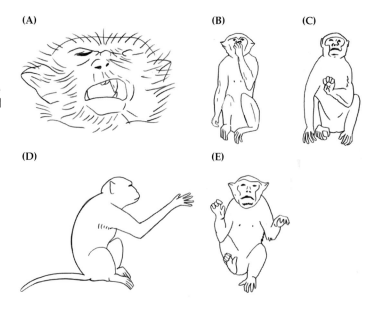

Figure 8.16 Determining the role of cortical motor neurons in generating movements. (A) Experimental setup for recording from monkey primary motor cortex neurons in relationship to reaching. (B) Neurons in the primary motor cortex fire before movements occur. Movement onset is defined by the increase in activity of the muscles in the electromyograph. (A after Evarts 1981; B after Porter and Lemon 1993.)

the direction and force generated by the arm during movement (**Figure 8.16B**). Evarts' group found that most neurons in primary motor cortex fired action potentials in relation to a subset of movements, and that firing rate corresponded to the changes in force generated by the muscles during movement. Moreover, many of these neurons began to discharge before the movements themselves were initiated, suggesting that their activation did not cause movement directly.

Commands to move the eyes are generated in a similar set of circuits comprising the **frontal eye fields** in the cortex and superior colliculus in the midbrain, which then project to the brainstem reticular formation that organizes

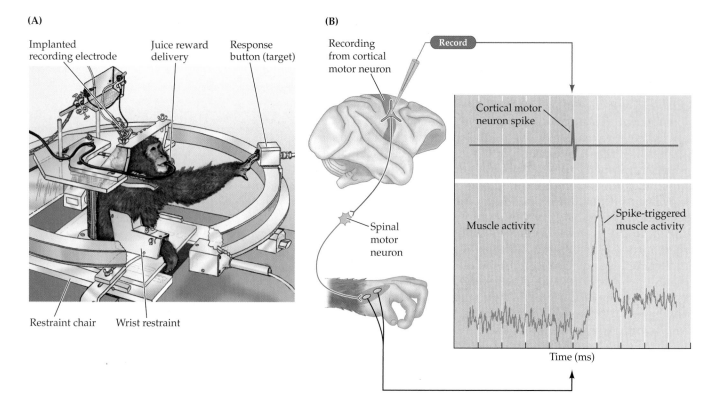

and coordinates activation of the extraocular muscles by lower motor neurons in the brainstem (as discussed earlier). These and other observations are all consistent with the idea that higher motor centers, including the primary motor cortex and the frontal eye fields, provide motor command signals that engage lower-level circuits to produce coordinated movements.

Coding Movements by the Activity of Neuronal Populations

The somatotopic motor maps discussed in the previous section are essentially gross anatomical descriptions of how the motor system at higher levels is organized, but how these maps are related to coordinated movements as such is not entirely clear. The relatively coarse tuning of neurons in the primary motor cortex and other higher movement centers presents a problem for understanding how the brain generates a particular movement. Although the work by Evarts, Graziano, and others described in the previous section provided evidence that maps represent movements and not muscles, the direction and amplitude of a movement cannot be predicted with any precision from the activity of single neurons, which are often activated during a wide array of different movements.

To address this problem, David Sparks and his colleagues at the University of Pennsylvania suggested that the activity of hundreds or perhaps thousands of neurons is averaged in computing the desired movement vector (**Figure 8.17**). Sparks focused on maps of eye movements because the oculomotor system, by virtue of its simplicity, is a useful model for sorting out the principles governing more complex movements. Movements of the eyes are also under the control of higher movement centers, although the organization of these pathways is distinct from higher pathways controlling limb movements.

Studying eye movements is facilitated by the fact that the local circuits in the brainstem coordinating eye movements are under the direct control of

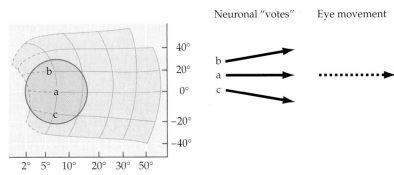

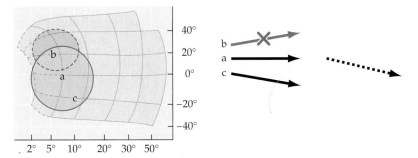

Figure 8.17 Population coding in the superior colliculus in an experimental monkey. (A) Topographic map showing eye movements in the superior colliculus. Movement amplitude is coded in increasing steps from left to right, and movement direction is coded on the vertical axis. The light gray region is the zone of neurons activated preceding a movement 5 degrees to the right of the zone marked "a." (B) Pharmacological inactivation of the zone centered on "b" (red circle) results in a shift in the weighted average of collicular activity, as well as the endpoint of the eye movement. (After Lee et al. 1988.)

neurons in the **superior colliculus**, an easily accessible layered structure in the midbrain (see Figure 8.17). Electrical stimulation in the intermediate and deep layers of the superior colliculus in monkeys produces coordinated gaze shifts, and single neurons in these layers fire action potentials just prior to the onset of the rapid, ballistic eye movements known as **saccades**. Moreover, electrical stimulation at any site evokes a saccade with a particular direction and amplitude, whereas stimulation at nearby sites evokes saccades with slightly different vectors. Thus, the superior colliculus contains a topographic map of eye movements, much like the topographic maps of skeletal movements in the primary motor cortex (see Figure 8.17A).

Sparks and colleagues supposed that each superior colliculus neuron "voted" for its range of movements, and that the weight of the vote cast was determined by how strongly the neuron fired. The weighted votes would then be averaged across the population to arrive at the vector for the desired movement. To test this idea, Sparks and his group reversibly inactivated small portions of the map of eye movements in the superior colliculus of monkeys trained to look to visual targets for fruit juice rewards. They found that eye movements were systematically biased away from the inactivated portion of the collicular map, as would be expected if movements were specified by the weighted average of the activity of all the neurons in the superior colliculus (see Figure 8.17B). This experiment provided the first functional support for the notion that the brain achieves precise movements by averaging together the activation of large populations of coarsely tuned neurons.

The idea that precise movements are encoded by averaging the activity of large numbers of coarsely tuned neurons has also been applied to the primary motor cortex by Apostolos Georgopolous and colleagues at the University of Minnesota. They recorded action potentials from neurons in this area in monkeys trained to push a joystick to lighted targets in order to receive rewards. The results showed that neurons of the primary motor cortex are broadly tuned to generate a range of movement directions and amplitudes, firing strongly for some movements but weakly or not at all for others.

Georgopolous and his group then computed a vector representing the weighted average of activity across the population of neurons in motor cortex and plotted this vector as a function of time (**Figure 8.18**). They found that when monkeys were forced to delay a planned movement, the **population vector** indicated the impending movement well in advance of any activity in the muscles. This observation supports the idea that the primary motor cortex encodes intended movements by the vector average of activity across the active neuronal population. The emergence of the population vector in the activity of neurons in motor cortex before movement is initiated may prepare local circuit neurons in the spinal cord, as well as reticular formation circuits

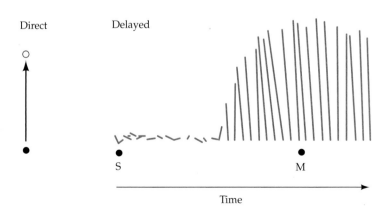

Figure 8.18 Population vectors in the primary motor cortex. Each line indicates the direction and amplitude of an arm movement decoded from the activity of a population of neurons recorded in primary motor cortex. The time of the trials goes from left to right; S indicates the cue for movement, and M indicates the onset of movement. Movement in direct response to a cue results in immediate generation of a population vector specifying the movement. Delayed movement evokes a population vector specifying the movement hundreds of milliseconds before movement onset. (After Georgopolous et al. 1986.)

involved in anticipatory postural adjustments (see the next section), for the upcoming movement.

Anticipatory Postural Adjustment and Coordination by the Brainstem

To be effective, voluntary movements also depend on unconscious coordination and adjustment of muscles involved in postural control. Consider the importance of postural adjustments when we walk on uneven ground or ice. In the absence of rapid postural adjustments to unanticipated trips or slips, it would be difficult to avoid falling. In more routine circumstances, movement commands from the motor cortex are always setting the appropriate postural tone to permit the effective performance of desired actions.

This essential postural control is provided by descending circuits originating in the brainstem. One key pathway relies on inertial guidance for postural control. As described in Chapter 7, the **vestibular system** senses changes in angular velocity of the head, and some neurons within the vestibular nuclei send axonal projections down to local circuits in the spinal cord gray matter (**Figure 8.19A**). The **medial vestibulospinal pathway** projects to medial zones within the spinal cord gray matter and helps coordinate movements of the trunk; the **lateral vestibulospinal pathway** projects to lateral zones within the spinal cord gray matter and activates extensor muscles of the limbs. The lateral vestibulospinal pathway is responsible for extending the limbs when a person slips and is about to fall.

A second set of pathways originating in the brainstem that contributes to postural maintenance arises from the reticular formation, forming the **reticulospinal tract** (**Figure 8.19B**). Upper motor neurons in the reticular formation receive motor commands issued by other upper motor neurons in the motor

Figure 8.19 Motor systems controlling posture.   (A) Lateral and medial vestibulospinal tracts initiate postural changes in response to inertial signals arising in the vestibular system. (B) Reticulospinal tracts generate anticipatory postural adjustments needed to maintain balance when the body's center of gravity is shifted voluntarily. (C) Posture adjusts automatically during a biceps curl. Flexion of the arm muscles is preceded by increased tone in the leg muscles to maintain posture.

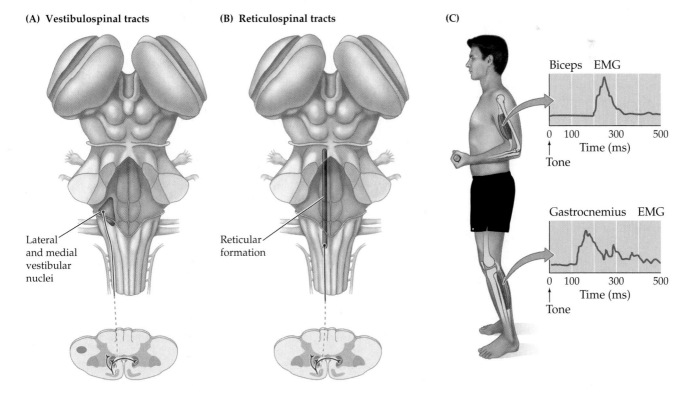

(A) Vestibulospinal tracts

(B) Reticulospinal tracts

(C)

Lateral and medial vestibular nuclei

Reticular formation

Biceps   EMG

0   100   300   500
Time (ms)
Tone

Gastrocnemius   EMG

0   100   300   500
Time (ms)
Tone

cortex and brainstem, and thus they initiate anticipatory movements that stabilize posture during movements of the limbs. The importance of these anticipatory postural adjustments is obvious in a weight lifter performing a heavy dumbbell curl (**Figure 8.19C**). The voluntary action of pulling the weight up to the chest requires a compensatory unconscious contraction of the muscles on the back of the leg to keep the weight lifter from falling forward. As suggested by the example of the weight lifter contracting the extensor muscles of the leg during the biceps curl, muscle recordings in human experimental subjects show that the gastrocnemius muscles begin to contract about 100 milliseconds prior to voluntary contraction in the biceps during lifting.

Organization of the Autonomic Motor System

Just as important as understanding the behaviors elicited by skeletal muscles and the neural systems that control them (and just as influential in cognitive and emotional functions) is understanding the motor activity generated by **smooth muscles**. The smooth muscles found in nearly all the organs of the body (and the special cardiac muscle fibers of the heart) are governed by the **autonomic** (or *visceral*) **motor system**. This system therefore controls a vast array of involuntary motor behaviors, including cardiac rhythm and blood pressure, aspects of respiration, bladder control, pupil dilation and constriction, and reproductive behavior (**Figure 8.20**).

The autonomic motor system comprises two major independent but complementary subsystems: the **sympathetic** and **parasympathetic divisions**. These two subsystems are sometimes referred to as the "fight or flight" and "rest and digest" systems, respectively. The sympathetic division marshals bodily resources in the face of various challenges (fight or flight); the parasympathetic division restores bodily resources under more peaceful circumstances (rest and digest).

Like somatic motor neurons, lower motor neurons in the autonomic motor system reside in the brainstem and spinal cord. Rather than projecting directly to the muscles, however, these neurons project to visceral motor neurons in peripheral **ganglia**, which then innervate smooth muscle fibers in the viscera and glands. Autonomic motor neurons in the spinal cord and brainstem are under the higher control of local circuits in the brainstem and spinal cord, which are in turn under the descending control of neurons in the hypothalamus (see Chapter 17 for further discussion of the links between the hypothalamus and cognitive functions mediated by the cerebral cortex).

As in the somatic motor system, the autonomic motor system includes simple reflex arcs that connect afferent sensory information about the status of organs and glands to efferent motor responses. For example, light entering the eye stimulates a subcortical visual pathway that stimulates parasympathetic neurons in the Edinger-Westphal nucleus in the midbrain, which in turn activate neurons in the ciliary ganglion of the eye and thus cause pupillary constriction. This light reflex controls the amount of light entering the eye, which facilitates photoreceptor operation in different amounts of ambient illumination (see Chapter 5). Similar reflex arcs modulate respiration rate in response

Figure 8.20 The autonomic motor system. The diagram shows many of the ▶ organs innervated by this system's sympathetic and parasympathetic components. The sympathetic system (left) ultimately targets organs using the neurotransmitter norepinephrine. The parasympathetic system (right) targets organs using the neurotransmitter acetylcholine. These two systems have broadly opposing actions on organs such as those indicated in the figure.

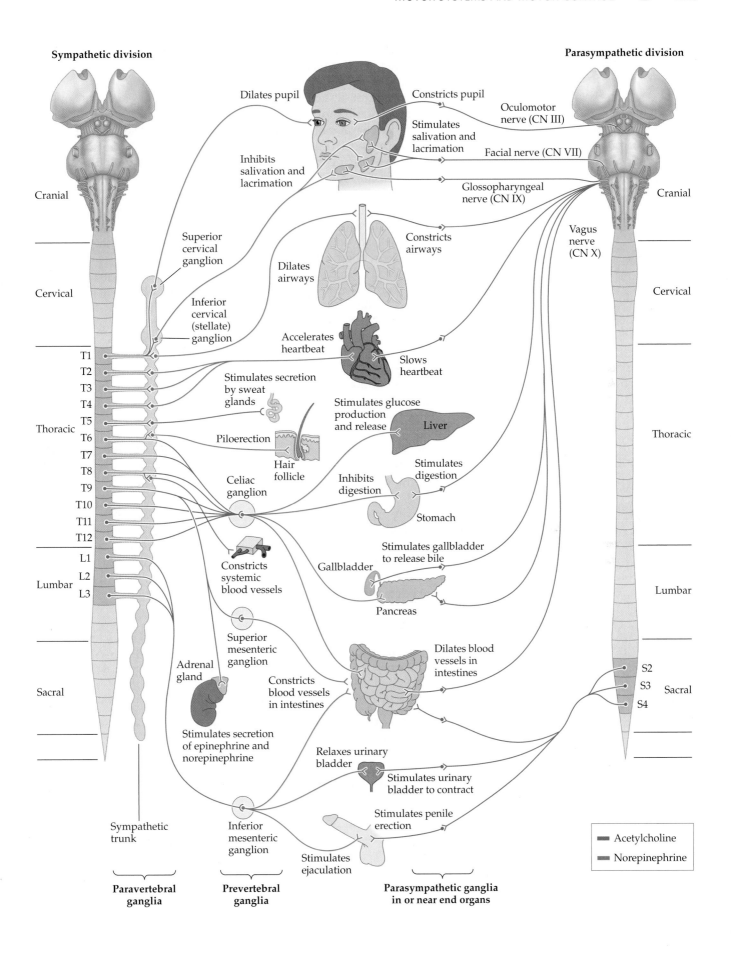

Sympathetic division

Parasympathetic division

Dilates pupil

Constricts pupil

Oculomotor nerve (CN III)

Stimulates salivation and lacrimation

Facial nerve (CN VII)

Inhibits salivation and lacrimation

Glossopharyngeal nerve (CN IX)

Cranial

Superior cervical ganglion

Vagus nerve (CN X)

Cranial

Cervical

Inferior cervical (stellate) ganglion

Constricts airways

Cervical

Dilates airways

Accelerates heartbeat

Slows heartbeat

Stimulates secretion by sweat glands

Stimulates glucose production and release

Liver

Thoracic

Piloerection

Stimulates digestion

Hair follicle

Celiac ganglion

Inhibits digestion

Stomach

Stimulates gallbladder to release bile

Gallbladder

Constricts systemic blood vessels

Lumbar

Pancreas

Superior mesenteric ganglion

Dilates blood vessels in intestines

Adrenal gland

Constricts blood vessels in intestines

Sacral

Stimulates secretion of epinephrine and norepinephrine

Relaxes urinary bladder

Stimulates urinary bladder to contract

Stimulates penile erection

Sympathetic trunk

Inferior mesenteric ganglion

Stimulates ejaculation

	Acetylcholine
	Norepinephrine

Paravertebral ganglia

Prevertebral ganglia

Parasympathetic ganglia in or near end organs

Cranial

Cervical

Thoracic

Lumbar

Sacral

T1
T2
T3
T4
T5
T6
T7
T8
T9
T10
T11
T12
L1
L2
L3

S2
S3
S4

to oxygen and carbon dioxide levels in the blood, cardiac output in response to blood pressure, and numerous other **homeostatic functions** (a term that refers to all the functions that are basic to the maintenance of the body's essential metabolic and physiological needs).

The visceral motor system, however, is equally involved in more complex behaviors, particularly those related to emotions, as described in Chapter 17. Unconscious peripheral motor responses to emotional experience, such as pallor and increased heart rate in response to fearful stimuli, or blushing in response to embarrassing circumstances, are also mediated by the autonomic motor system. Such responses depend on the integration of a variety of sensory information, contextual information, and past experience, thus ultimately involving many cortical regions. A complex network of brain areas and nuclei, including the insular and medial prefrontal cortex, amygdala, visceral sensory nuclei in the brainstem, and hypothalamus, mediates this integration and generates visceral motor responses.

Activation of the autonomic motor system by emotionally arousing stimuli can have far-reaching cognitive consequences. For example, when the sympathetic division of the autonomic motor system is activated by an emotionally significant experience such as the announcement of a pop quiz, the level of adrenaline in the blood, as well as the level of noradrenaline in the central nervous system, goes up as a result of sympathetic activity. This change increases heart rate and blood pressure, among other visceral motor consequences, and modulates ongoing cognitive processing through the associated emotional effects on perception, attention, and memory. Indeed, when the action of the sympathetic system is blocked by propranolol, a drug widely prescribed to lower blood pressure, memory for emotionally charged events is somewhat impaired. This effect may reflect the reduction of the visceral sensory information normally associated with emotionally arousing events, which the brain presumably uses as an indicator of the current emotional context.

In short, the autonomic motor system, which originally evolved for somatic homeostasis, also contributes to "cognitive homeostasis"—that is, matching the internal state of information processing in the brain to the current state of the internal and external environments. The autonomic motor system is thus just as important as the more obvious musculoskeletal system in expressing and indeed determining aspects of normal cognitive function.

Summary

1. Lower motor neurons in the spinal cord and brainstem are the final common pathway for the motor commands that determine behaviors arising from skeletal muscle movements, and are thus the effectors for many cognitive processes.

2. Local circuits governing the activation of lower motor neurons are influenced by descending projections from upper motor neurons in the cerebral cortex and brainstem, which are themselves modulated by neurons in the cerebellum and basal ganglia, as will be described in Chapter 9.

3. Lower motor neurons directly contact skeletal muscle fibers. A single motor neuron and the muscle fibers it innervates define the functional units generating muscular force. Graded muscle forces are produced by the systematic recruitment of motor units according to their size, as well as by the systematic modulation of their rate of firing.

4. Motor behaviors are organized into reflex arcs. Such arcs maintain appropriate postures and protect against the effects of excessive or unexpected forces. Other reflex circuits mediate rapid withdrawal from painful stimuli.

5. At a more complex level, central pattern generators in the spinal cord and brainstem produce the spatiotemporal patterns of motor neuron activation needed for coordinated, rhythmic movements such as locomotion. Other motor centers in the

brainstem—the vestibular complex and reticular formation—provide descending control of the spinal circuitry that mediates anticipatory postural adjustments needed to maintain balance during movement.

6. At higher levels still, upper motor neurons in the primary motor cortex and cortical premotor areas issue motor commands that activate local circuits and lower motor neuron pools to achieve more specific behavioral goals.

7. The autonomic motor system controls visceral motor functions and is intimately tied to the generation of emotions, which in turn influence perception, attention, memory, and other cognitive functions.

Additional Reading

Reviews

BURKE, R. E. (1981) Motor units: Anatomy, physiology, and functional organization. In *Handbook of Physiology*, Section 1: *The Nervous System*, Vol. 2, Part 1, V. B. Brooks (ed.). Bethesda, MD: American Physiological Society, pp. 345–422.

DUM, R. P. AND P. L. STRICK (2002) Motor areas in the frontal lobe of the primate. *Physiol. Behav.* 77: 677–682.

GAHERY, Y. AND J. MASSION (1981) Coordination between posture and movement. *Trends Neurosci.* 4: 199–202.

GEORGOPOULOS, A. P., M. TAIRA AND A. LUKASHIN (1993) Cognitive neurophysiology of the motor cortex. *Science* 260: 47–52.

GRILLNER, S. AND P. WALLEN (1985) Central pattern generators for locomotion, with special reference to vertebrates. *Annu. Rev. Neurosci.* 8: 233–261.

HENNEMAN, E. AND L. M. MENDELL (1981) Functional organization of the motoneuron pool and its inputs. In *Handbook of Physiology*, Section 1: *The Nervous System*. Vol. 2, Part 1, V. B. Brooks (ed.). Bethesda, MD: American Physiological Society, pp. 423–507.

PEARSON, K. (1976) The control of walking. *Sci. Am.* 235 (December): 72–86.

Important Original Papers

BURKE, R. E., D. N. LEVINE, M. SALCMAN AND P. TSAIRES (1974) Motor units in cat soleus muscle: Physiological, histo-chemical, and morphological characteristics. *J. Physiol.* (Lond.) 238: 503–514.

COSTA, M. AND S. J. H. BROOKES (1994) The enteric nervous system. *Am. J. Gastroenterol.* 89: S129–S137.

EVARTS, E. V. (1981) Functional studies of the motor cortex. In *The Organization of the Cerebral Cortex*, F. O. Schmitt, F. G. Worden, G. Adelman and S. G. Dennis (eds.). Cambridge, MA: MIT Press, pp. 199–236.

FETZ, E. E. AND P. D. CHENEY (1978) Muscle fields of primate corticomotoneuronal cells. *J. Physiol.* (Paris) 74: 239–245.

GEORGOPOLOUS, A. P., A. B. SCHWARTZ AND R. E. KETTNER (1986) Neuronal population coding of movement direction. *Science* 233: 1416–1418.

GRAZIANO, M. S., C. C. TAYLOR, T. MOORE AND D. F. COOKE (2002) The cortical control of movement revisited. *Neuron* 36: 349–362.

HENNEMAN, E., E. SOMJEN AND D. O. CARPENTER (1965) Excitability and inhibitability of motoneurons of different sizes. *J. Neurophysiol.* 28: 599–620.

HUNT, C. C. AND S. W. KUFFLER (1951) Stretch receptor discharges during muscle contraction. *J. Physiol.* (Lond.) 113: 298–315.

JANSEN, A. S. P., X. V. NGUYEN, V. KARPITSKIY, T. C. METTENLEITER AND A. D. LOEWY (1995) Central command neurons of the sympathetic nervous system: Basis of the fight or flight response. *Science* 270: 644–646.

LEE, D. L., W. H. ROHRER AND D. L. SPARKS (1988) Population coding of saccadic eye movements by neurons in the superior colliculus. *Nature* 332: 357–360.

LIDDELL, E. G. T. AND C. S. SHERRINGTON (1925) Recruitment and some other factors of reflex inhibition. *Proc. R. Soc. Lond.* 97: 488–518.

WALMSLEY, B., J. A. HODGSON AND R. E. BURKE (1978) Forces produced by medial gastrocnemius and soleus muscles during locomotion in freely moving cats. *J. Neurophysiol.* 41: 1203–1215.

Books

ASANUMA, H. (1989) *The Motor Cortex.* New York: Raven.

BLESSING, W. W. (1997) *The Lower Brainstem and Bodily Homeostasis.* New York: Oxford University Press.

BRODAL, A. (1981) *Neurological Anatomy in Relation to Clinical Medicine*, 3rd Ed. New York: Oxford University Press.

GABELLA, G. (1976) *Structure of the Autonomic Nervous System.* London: Chapman and Hall.

PENFIELD, W. AND T. RASMUSSEN (1950) *The Cerebral Cortex of Man: A Clinical Study of Localization of Function.* New York: Macmillan.

SHERRINGTON, C. (1947) *The Integrative Action of the Nervous System*, 2nd Ed. New Haven, CT: Yale University Press.

Computation and Cognition in the Motor System

Introduction

Neurons in motor cortex and premotor areas of the prefrontal and parietal cortex contribute critically to cognitive functions such as the planning and initiation of complex sequences of movements, the selection of behavioral goals for movement, and learning and remembering new movement sequences. Thus, higher motor areas enhance the complexity and efficacy of behavior and, in so doing, enhance survival and reproductive success. All of these higher motor areas themselves are monitored and modulated by two other key motor systems not described in Chapter 8: the cerebellum and the basal ganglia. A major function of the cerebellum is to correct errors in ongoing movements; a major function of some components of the basal ganglia is to gate motor commands. As will be apparent, the complex neural processing carried out by the basal ganglia and cerebellum also influence cognitive functions that are not directly expressed in motor activity.

Motor Planning

Although many movements are more or less automatic in response to a sensory stimulus, other actions are planned in advance and their initiation withheld until the circumstances are appropriate for their execution. For example, when monkeys are cued to reach to a target but are forced to delay initiation of the reach, neurons in the primary motor cortex become active before the movement is initiated. Anticipatory activation of neurons during arm movement planning has been observed in a number of premotor areas as well, including the premotor, supplementary motor, dorsolateral prefrontal, and parietal cortices (see Chapter 8).

In the case of visual orienting movements, such activity is seen in the frontal and supplementary eye fields, and in the dorsolateral prefrontal and lateral parietal cortices. Planning-related activity in premotor areas typically persists when movement cues are removed and ceases when monkeys are cued to stop planning the movement, thus suggesting a role in intention (**Figure 9.1**). One indication of the functional role of these premotor areas is that

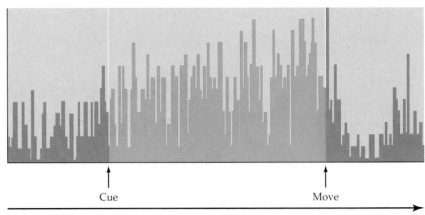

Cue   Move

Time

Figure 9.1 Evidence of anticipatory activity as a correlate of movement intention in premotor cortex. The histogram shows neuronal firing as a function of time in a monkey cued to reach toward a target after a delay (red). Neuronal activity continues from the cue until the movement, suggesting a neural correlate of the intention to reach toward the target.

planning-related neuronal activity typically begins even earlier in these areas than in the primary motor cortex (or the superior colliculus for saccades).

These observations support the idea that motor areas are hierarchically organized, with premotor areas providing more abstract planning information related to behavioral goals, which is then translated into the intention to perform specific movements in the primary motor cortex (and the superior colliculus for visual orienting movements). Thus, higher motor areas appear to serve a functional role in specifying the motor program discussed in Chapter 8. Motor intention signals in the primary motor cortex are then translated by downstream local circuits in the brainstem and spinal cord into neural activity that specifies the patterns of muscle contraction necessary to accomplish the intended movements.

Scalp recordings from humans (see Chapter 3) have tended to confirm this hierarchical organization of movement planning. When subjects are asked to voluntarily generate a movement—for example, lifting a finger at a time of their choosing—EEG recordings from medial frontal electrodes show a pronounced negative wave that begins up to several seconds in advance of the actual movement. This **readiness potential** initially begins bilaterally over premotor areas, but later becomes enhanced over the primary motor cortex contralateral to the finger movement (**Figure 9.2**). Neuroimaging studies have identified the readiness potential with activation in premotor areas, particularly the supplementary motor areas. Interestingly, when premotor areas are damaged along with the primary motor cortex, patients are unaware of (or even deny) their inability to move—a phenomenon known as **anosognosia**, meaning "loss of awareness." This clinical observation provides further evidence that the premotor cortex is the source of motor planning and intentional awareness.

The readiness potential also provides a means of further exploring the role of awareness in motor planning. In a famous but controversial study several decades ago by Benjamin Libet, who was then a physiologist at the University of San Francisco, subjects were asked to produce an uncued voluntary movement and then estimate (from a clock display) the time at which they became aware of the intention to move. EEG recordings indicated, not surprisingly, that estimates of the intention to move preceded the movement itself by about 200 milliseconds. However, readiness potentials over premotor areas clearly preceded subjects' awareness of when they intended to move. Although this study has a number of possible confounding factors, it implies that conscious awareness actually follows the intention to move rather than preceding and thus causing it. The puzzle of conscious awareness and its role in cognitive functions is taken up in Chapter 28.

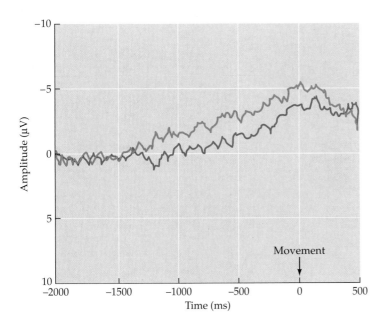

Figure 9.2   Readiness potential.   These EEG recordings were taken from scalp electrodes over premotor and supplementary motor cortices in human subjects asked to voluntarily move a finger. EEG amplitude when subjects attend to their own movement (blue) increases several seconds in advance of the actual movement. EEG amplitude when subjects attend to the urge to move, the readiness potential (red), is enhanced relative to the movement potential. Readiness potentials begin later in the contralateral primary motor cortex, consistent with a hierarchical progression of motor intention. (After Eagleman 2004.)

Goal selection

At any given moment, several competing or alternative behavioral goals might be options for motor planning. For example, on approaching a stoplight that just turned yellow, a driver might either slow to stop, or accelerate to get through the intersection before the light turns red. The neural processes responsible for selecting a course of action to reach a goal (e.g., getting to the destination faster) and generating the relevant movement have come under increasing scrutiny as researchers have realized the importance of cognitive contexts for motor behaviors. Most such studies have focused on the processes that link sensory information to motor output.

Early electrophysiological studies in monkeys demonstrated that neurons in a variety of premotor areas where planning-related activity occurs respond to sensory cues used to guide movements. Moreover, these responses to sensory cues can be enhanced or diminished if the stimulus is made more or less likely to be the target of a movement. For example, Jeffrey Schall and his colleagues at Vanderbilt University trained monkeys to shift their gaze from a central light to an "oddball" visual target within a ring of identical visual distracters. The monkeys became proficient at this task but sometimes made errors. The results showed that neurons in the frontal eye fields responded more strongly to a visual stimulus when it was an oddball and therefore more likely to be the target of a saccade. Neuronal activity was strongest when the monkey successfully identified and shifted gaze to the oddball target, suggesting further that the active neurons played a role in linking sensory information to the intention to move the eyes. Similar studies in humans using fMRI have also shown oddball-related activation in the prefrontal and parietal cortices.

Subsequent work showed that such sensory-motor linkage is graded by the quality of information guiding the movement integrated over time. For instance, William Newsome at Stanford University and Michael Shadlen at the University of Washington provided evidence that neuronal responses in a number of premotor areas involved in saccadic eye movements are systematically related to the weight of sensory evidence favoring a particular movement. In these experiments, monkeys were trained to judge the net direction of motion in a field of moving dots and report this evaluation by shifting their gaze to a specific target if they judged the motion to be in one direction and a

(A)

Fixation

Targets

Motion

Delay

Go

T2   T1

RF

(B)

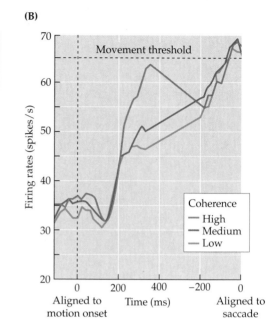

Figure 9.3 Dependence of a motor response on the weight of evidence. (A) Monkeys performed a visual discrimination task in which, by moving their eyes, they reported the direction of motion in a field of randomly moving dots. One target was in the response field (*RF*) of a neuron in the posterior parietal cortex; the other was in the opposite visual field. (B) The firing rate of neurons in posterior parietal cortex increased when monkeys viewed dots moving toward the target in the *RF*. The rate of increase over time was directly proportional to motion coherence, or the weight of evidence favoring an eye movement to the *RF* target. The relation between firing rate as a function of motion coherence reflects the integration of motion over time. (After Shadlen and Newsome 1996.)

different target if they saw motion in the opposite direction (**Figure 9.3**). Newsome and Shadlen systematically manipulated the quality of the evidence favoring responses to each target by changing the fraction of dots moving coherently in one direction or another. Thus, when about 50 percent of the dots moved in one direction, monkeys were nearly always correct in their responses; their performance fell to chance levels, however, when less than 5 percent of the dots moved coherently.

The responses of neurons in the posterior parietal cortex, frontal eye fields, supplementary eye fields, dorsolateral prefrontal cortex, and even superior colliculus were all found to be modulated by the strength of the motion stimulus favoring a particular eye movement response. When monkeys were permitted to move their eyes as soon as they had made a decision, the speed with which neuronal activity in the parietal cortex increased matched the speed of the monkeys' eye movement responses. Similar graded responses as a function of stimulus quality have been reported in the higher-order somatosensory cortex and premotor areas in monkeys trained to report the frequency of vibration applied to the forearm by pushing a button.

Taken together, these studies imply that neurons in a number of premotor areas specify movements in a graded manner as sensory evidence is accumulated. This hypothesis was tested directly by Shadlen and Josh Gold, who applied microstimulation to the frontal eye fields while monkeys performed the dot discrimination task illustrated in Figure 9.3A. Stimulation in this area evoked saccadic eye movements at short latencies, but the endpoints of the movements were systematically biased by the pattern of motion that the monkeys saw (**Figure 9.4A**). Moreover, the amount of bias gradually increased as monkeys viewed the motion longer, as well as when the fraction of coherently moving dots was gradually increased (**Figure 9.4B**). When the locations of the movement targets were not revealed in advance of the dot stimulus, however, dot motion had very little effect on stimulation-evoked saccades.

All told, a variety of observations support the conclusion that motor preparation is a dynamic, competitive process linking sensory information to the intention to move, and that such processing entails the graded activation of neurons in a variety of higher-order premotor cortical (and subcortical) areas.

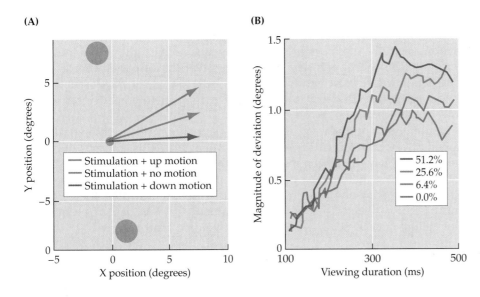

Figure 9.4 Graded conversion of sensory percepts into action. (A) Monkeys were trained to fixate centrally while observing motion stimuli that were moving either up or down, or that had no net motion. Microstimulation of the frontal eye fields evoked eye movements that were systematically biased by the direction of viewed motion, thus indicating that ongoing motor planning in this area is influenced by gradually accumulating motion information. (B) The magnitude of the deviation in stimulation-induced eye movements depended on both motion coherence of the stimuli and viewing duration. With higher motion coherence, the rate of deviation in eye position as a function of time increased, implying that the integration of sensory evidence over time favors a particular motor response. Each curve represents a particular percentage of dots moving coherently. (After Gold and Shadlen 2002.)

Motivational control of goal selection

Although sensory stimulation often indicates which movement should be produced (e.g., the response to the yellow light in the driving example described in the previous section), people must often select a goal primarily on the basis of additional, far more complex stimuli, as well as stored information about the likely state of the environment (in the yellow-light example, the factors indicating the relative need to get to the destination quickly that influence the significance of the stimulus). Indeed, when monkeys performed the moving-dot task illustrated in Figure 9.3, they reported their judgments not because of the stimulus per se, but because if they responded, they would receive squirts of fruit juice—highly desirable treats. To ensure that monkeys are willing to work hard in such experiments, their access to water is often limited before the trials so that they will be strongly motivated and thus respond more readily to the stimuli.

Although behavior is typically directed toward acquiring rewards and avoiding punishments, insofar as doing so improves the chances of individual as well as kin survival and reproductive success, very little is understood about the mechanisms that guide the motor system to select goals that satisfy biological motivations. This question was tackled directly in a series of studies by Paul Glimcher and Michael Platt, then at New York University, designed to understand how internal motivations shape the responses of neurons in posterior parietal cortex (**Figure 9.5**). They trained monkeys to choose

Figure 9.5 The sensitivity of premotor neurons to the value of movements. (A) Monkeys choose to spend time looking at a target in direct proportion to its relative reward value. (B) Neurons in posterior parietal cortex respond in direct proportion to the relative reward value associated with an eye movement. (After Platt and Glimcher 1999.)

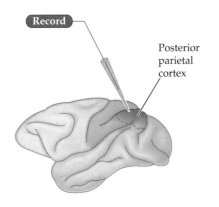

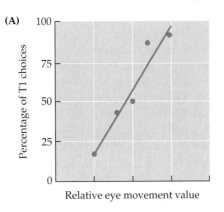

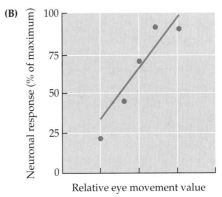

between looking at two visually identical lights and then, across a series of trials, systematically varied either the probability or the amount of fruit juice reinforcement the monkeys received for looking at one light versus the other. Platt and Glimcher found that neurons in the posterior parietal cortex were sensitive to the **reward value** of shifting gaze to a particular target, which depended on both the probability and the magnitude of juice reinforcement associated with that target.

Neurons in a number of premotor areas, including the dorsolateral prefrontal cortex, supplementary eye fields, frontal eye fields, and posterior cingulate cortex have also been found to be sensitive to movement value. These studies suggest that selecting a movement goal involves scaling neuronal responses associated with each possible movement by its value, thereby biasing the motor system to produce a movement that best satisfies biological motivations such as acquiring rewards or avoiding punishments.

Sequential Movements and the Supplementary Motor Areas

The discussion so far has focused on the selection and planning of a *single* movement. Clearly, however, the behavioral repertoire of humans and other animals normally consists of *sequences* of movements that together comprise meaningful behaviors that satisfy specific goals. Not surprisingly, regions of the frontal cortex are specialized to support the production of movement sequences. As a rule, the **supplementary motor area** (Brodmann area 6) is crucial for generating movements in the absence of explicit sensory cues, and the premotor cortex is especially important for the production of cued movements. When the supplementary motor area is ablated, monkeys can no longer perform well-learned movements and must instead rely on external cues indicating which movement should be performed. The reverse is true for lesions of the premotor cortex, which selectively disrupt visually guided movements but do not affect well-learned responses that can be made in the absence of any sensory cues. These results suggest a functional dissociation between premotor cortex and supplementary cortex for producing cued and uncued movements, respectively.

A similar logic applies to the production of movement sequences, which requires the ability to generate action in the absence of external cues specifying each individual movement. In an important and revealing experiment, Jun Tanji and his colleagues at the Tohoku University School of Medicine trained monkeys to make a sequence of arm movements based on a visual cue. For example, a red light might mean "push, pull, turn," whereas a green light might mean "turn, push, pull." Note that the visual cues specify which sequence of movements to make rather than cuing any single movement directly. Tanji and his group then recorded from neurons in the supplementary motor area while monkeys performed this sequence generation task.

Tanji's group found that many neurons in the supplementary motor area were selectively activated when a particular action embedded within a sequence was performed (**Figure 9.6A**). Moreover, many neurons responded only for a particular action sequence, irrespective of the type of movement (**Figure 9.6B**). For example, some neurons responded to the second movement in the sequence, whereas others responded to the third. These observations suggest that neurons in the supplementary motor area convey information needed to guide the production of a sequence of reaching movements. This supposition was confirmed when Tanji and colleagues reversibly deactivated the supplementary motor area by injecting the GABA agonist muscimol, thus enhancing local inhibitory connections and silencing the output neurons.

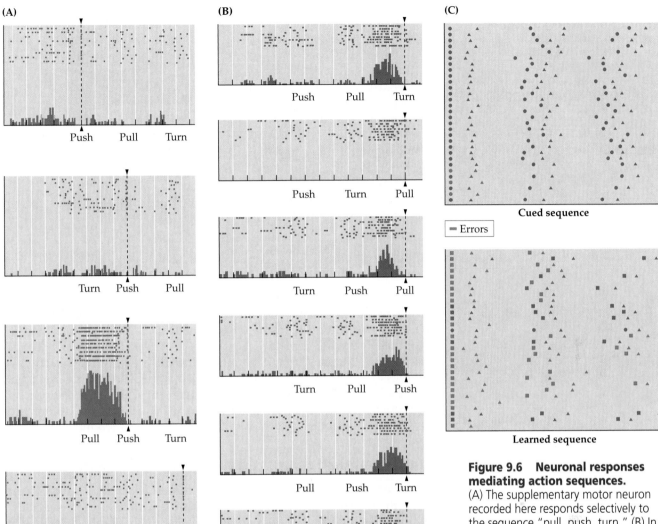

Figure 9.6 Neuronal responses mediating action sequences.
(A) The supplementary motor neuron recorded here responds selectively to the sequence "pull, push, turn." (B) In this case, the supplementary motor neuron responds selectively to the last movement in a sequence, independent of the type of movement required. (C) Pharmacological inactivation of supplementary motor cortex causes errors in producing learned sequences but not explicitly cued sequences of movements. (After Tanji and Shima 1994.)

When the supplementary motor area was silenced in this way, monkeys were unable to perform sequences from memory (**Figure 9.6C**). Transcranial magnetic stimulation applied over the supplementary motor cortex in humans (see Chapter 3) also disrupts the production of manual sequences, in accord with the results in monkeys.

Similar sequence-related neurons have been reported in the supplementary eye fields in monkeys trained to produce sequences of saccades. A subsequent study by Ann Graybiel and colleagues at MIT demonstrated that some neurons in the dorsolateral prefrontal cortex signal the beginning and end of a sequence of eye movements (**Figure 9.7**). The prefrontal cortex provides inputs to the supplementary eye fields and supplementary cortex, thus suggesting a hierarchical organization for the production of movement sequences.

Activation of supplementary motor neurons in monkeys by internally generated sequences of action are supported by recent neuroimaging studies in humans demonstrating preferential activation of the supplementary motor cortex during self-initiated finger movements, compared with visually trig-

Figure 9.7 Signals marking the beginning and ending of sequences of eye movements. Monkeys were trained to perform a sequence of eye movements, and each colored line indicates neuronal activity during a different sequence produced in response to a visual cue. Neuronal responses in the dorsolaterial prefrontal cortex were strongest at the beginning and end of the sequence, irrespective of which movement or which sequence was produced. (After Fujii and Graybiel 2003.)

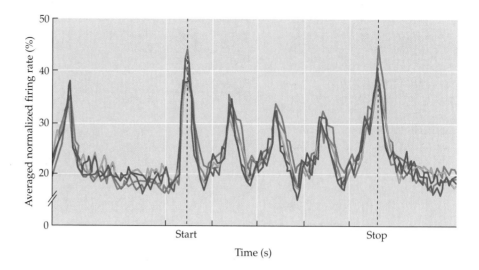

gered movements; moreover, such modulations were even stronger when subjects generated sequences of movements rather than repeating the same movement over and over (**Figure 9.8**). Together, these observations support the conclusion that the supplementary motor area provides relatively abstract motor intention signals that control the internally guided production of sequences of actions, whereas the prefrontal cortex plays a more important role in the initiation and termination of movement sequences. The primary motor cortex then issues sequences of commands that activate pools of motor units in the brainstem and spinal cord to produce the desired movements.

Reference Frames and Coordinate Transformations

Another key issue in understanding motor control concerns frames of reference for the transformations needed to translate information from one behavioral context to another. For example, shifting gaze to a visual target is a relatively trivial computational problem, mainly because the vector representing the locus of retinal stimulation relative to the fovea is aligned with the vector representing the amplitude and direction of an eye movement that directs the fovea to the target. This happy marriage of sensory and motor coordinates does not, however, apply to other sensory-guided movements. Thus, reaching toward a visible target such as a cup of coffee requires translating the retinal location of the target into a location anchored to the position of the hand.

To do this, the retinal vector must in some way be combined with information about the position of the eye in the head, the head's position with respect to the rest of the body, and the hand and arm relative to everything else! Similarly complex coordinate transformations are needed in order to look accu-

Figure 9.8 Activation of human supplementary motor cortex when subjects generate sequences of finger movements from internal intentions. These fMRI data were gathered from a single human subject asked to repeatedly touch index finger to thumb (A) or generate a learned sequence of finger-to-thumb movements (B), cued either internally (SI) or by a visual stimulus (VT). (From Deiber et al. 1999.)

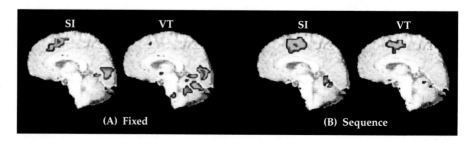

rately in the direction of an auditory stimulus, scratch an itch, walk to a geographically challenging destination, or undertake innumerable other routine challenges that require translations from one or more frameworks to another. Thus, in addition to selecting, planning, and initiating a movement, neural mechanisms must translate sensory information into appropriate coordinates for guiding movement.

The processes underlying sensory-motor coordinate transformation have been investigated by several groups. David Sparks and his colleagues demonstrated that neurons in the superior colliculus encode sensory information in coordinates anchored to the eyes. Thus, whether monkeys look toward visible targets, sounds, or stimulation of the skin, neurons in the superior colliculus respond to these events as a function of the eye movement necessary to bring them onto the fovea. Richard Andersen and his collaborators at Caltech have also explored the spatial coordinates in which eye movement and arm movement information are represented in the parietal cortex. Distinct cortical areas within the parietal lobe are dedicated to planning and initiating arm movements and eye movements. Nonetheless, neurons in both of these areas appear to encode sensory information in relation to the eyes, regardless of whether the stimuli are visual or auditory. Andersen has argued that this makes sense, since vision provides a uniquely precise channel for localizing targets for movement, and that other information is thus more accurately represented relative to the eyes.

In partial support of this idea, damage to the parietal cortex in humans can disrupt both reaching and saccades—a clinical syndrome known as **optic ataxia**. The spatial errors that arise from this condition reveal a failure to correctly integrate information about the location of the eye, hand, and target. Disruptions in sensory-motor integration are also manifest when patients with parietal lesions attempt to grasp objects (**Figure 9.9**). Compared to control subjects without lesions, such patients fail to grasp objects accurately across their centers of mass. Such errors invariably lead to difficulties in actually picking up objects—a deficit also found in monkeys following pharmacological inactivation of the parietal cortex.

In sum, electrophysiological evidence in monkeys and lesion data from human patients support the idea that the parietal cortex is a critical locus supporting the integration of visual, eye position, and limb position data necessary to produce coordinated movements of the eyes and hands. Note, however, that complex computations like transforming retinal coordinates into object-centered coordinates may not be made explicitly. Because the circuitry that enables complex motor behavior has evolved simply to associate complex inputs with complex outputs based on evolutionary success, neuronal computations such as those underlying coordinate transformations may never be understood explicitly.

(A)

(B)

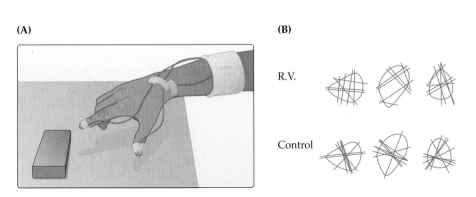

R.V.

Control

Figure 9.9 Deficits in visually guided reaching and grasping caused by parietal lesions.
(A) The reaching and grasping of objects is measured by electrodes hooked up to the subject's finger, thumb, and wrist. (B) Lines connect the precision grip made with thumb and forefinger for a patient with parietal lesion (R.V.) and a control subject. The optimal grasp crosses the center of mass of the object. (A from Goodale, Web page; B after Milner and Goodale 1995.)

Initiation of Movement by the Basal Ganglia

Motor cortex (and the superior colliculus for eye movements) comprises a more or less hierarchical set of circuits responsible for selecting, planning, and initiating sequences of movements that satisfy goals. At the same time, an important set of subcortical circuits in the **basal ganglia** appears to serve as a **gating** mechanism, inhibiting potential movements until they are fully appropriate for the circumstances in which they are to be executed.

The basal ganglia are made up of three principal nuclei: the *caudate* and *putamen*, known collectively as the **striatum**, and the *globus pallidus* (**Figure 9.10A**). In addition, two other nuclei—the subthalamic nucleus and substantia nigra pars compacta—contribute importantly to basal ganglia function. Nearly all cortical areas project to the basal ganglia, principally through the caudate and putamen. The globus pallidus is the output nucleus of the basal ganglia and modulates the activity of cortical neurons via a relay through the thalamus. Activation of the caudate and putamen inhibits the globus pallidus, thereby releasing the thalamus and its cortical targets from tonic inhibition (**Figure 9.10B**).

The net effect of basal ganglia activation through this so-called **direct pathway** is thus excitation of cortical neurons. The subthalamic nucleus, on the other hand, forms part of an internal loop within the basal ganglia that, via excitation of a portion of the globus pallidus, has a net inhibitory effect on cortical neurons via the so-called **indirect pathway**. The balance of excitatory and inhibitory effects of the basal ganglia releases and coordinates desired movements. Circuits projecting through the caudate to the **substantia nigra pars reticulata** (**SNr**) and on to the superior colliculus serve a similar braking function for saccades.

Figure 9.10   The basal ganglia "loop" that starts and stops movements.   (A) Coronal section through the human forebrain showing the principal components of the basal ganglia. The caudate and putamen (orange) comprise the main inputs to the basal ganglia. The globus pallidus (purple) provides the principal output, which projects to the ventral anterior and ventral lateral (VA/VL) nuclear complex of the thalamus, which in turn projects to the motor cortex. The substantia nigra pars reticulata in the midbrain serves as the output nucleus for the basal ganglia circuits controlling eye movements. (B) Projections from the cortex excite neurons in the caudate and putamen, which then inhibit neurons in the globus pallidus and substantia nigra pars reticulata. This effect suppresses tonic inhibition of the thalamus by the globus pallidus, thereby further exciting the cortex. The substantia nigra pars compacta provides modulatory dopaminergic inputs to the basal ganglia, and a circuit through the subthalamic nucleus serves a secondary role in releasing movement.

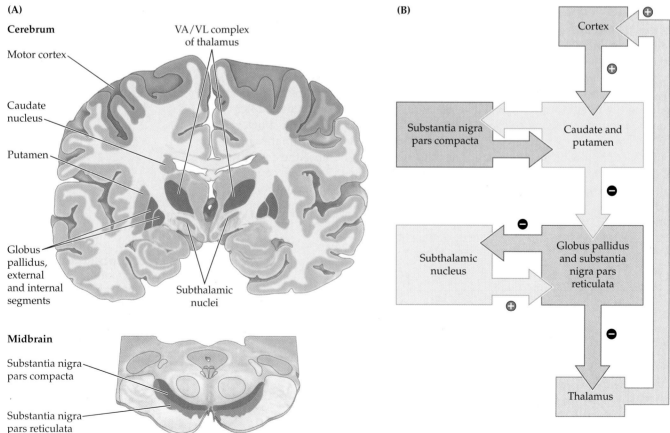

(A)

Cerebrum

Motor cortex

VA/VL complex of thalamus

Caudate nucleus

Putamen

Globus pallidus, external and internal segments

Subthalamic nuclei

Midbrain

Substantia nigra pars compacta

Substantia nigra pars reticulata

(B)

Cortex

Substantia nigra pars compacta

Caudate and putamen

Subthalamic nucleus

Globus pallidus and substantia nigra pars reticulata

Thalamus

The role of the basal ganglia in movement inhibition and initiation was examined by Okihide Hikosaka and Robert Wurtz at the National Institutes of Health. They trained monkeys to make eye movements to visible and remembered targets while recording from neurons in the SNr, the analogue of the globus pallidus output circuit for eye movements. They found that SNr neurons fired tonically at about 50 to 100 hertz until just before saccade onset, when they abruptly ceased firing for the duration of the movement (**Figure 9.11**). At about the same time, neurons in the superior colliculus associated with the saccade began firing action potentials.

When Hikosaka and Wurtz studied the effects of releasing the superior colliculus from tonic inhibition by injecting the GABA agonist muscimol into the SNr, monkeys could not suppress unwanted saccades. These results indicate that one important function of the basal ganglia is to inhibit undesired move-

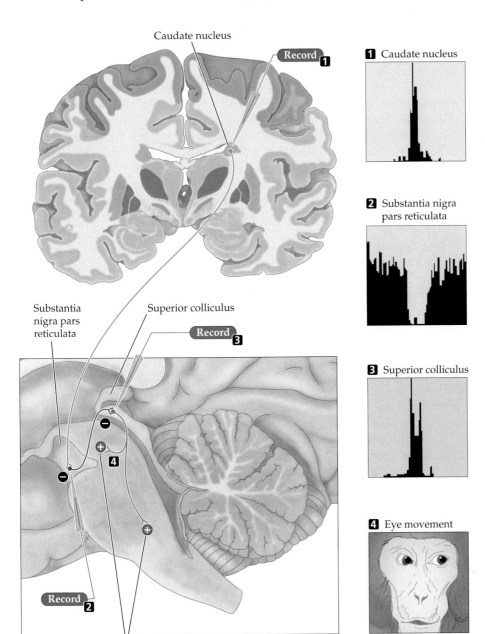

Figure 9.11 The relationship between superior colliculus and basal ganglia. Neurons in the caudate nucleus fire bursts of action potentials just before eye movement initiation (1). Immediately thereafter, neurons in the substantia nigra pars reticulata shut down (2), resulting in a burst of action potentials in the superior colliculus (3) and the production of an eye movement (4). (After Hikosaka and Wurtz 1989.)

ments and permit desired ones. More recent work, however, has suggested that this "braking function" is not all or none. When the rewards delivered for successful saccade performance are varied, neurons in the caudate nucleus show graded changes in firing rate that correspond to reward size. Similar reward-dependent modulations are apparent in the firing rates of SNr neurons. Thus, graded changes in the net activation of basal ganglia circuits may help ensure that biologically valuable movements are produced.

The importance of the basal ganglia for motor control and initiation is vividly evident in two relatively common neurological disorders: Parkinson's disease and Huntington's disease. In **Parkinson's disease**, the selective death of neurons in the substantia nigra pars compacta that use the neurotransmitter dopamine increases the excitatory tone of the direct pathway through the basal ganglia. Patients with Parkinson's show a marked disruption in the ability to initiate voluntary movement. In addition to the tremor at rest that is characteristic of this disease, these patients have difficulty generating purposeful movements and often show a slow, shuffling gait as a result. By contrast, when their movements are guided by more immediate sensory stimuli such as marks on the floor that the patient is asked to step over, gait appears relatively normal. A primary treatment for Parkinson's disease remains supplementation of dopamine levels with L-dopa, a synthetic precursor to dopamine. This augmentation of dopamine function helps restore the ability of the basal ganglia to release tonic inhibition from the thalamus, thereby enhancing motor cortex excitability and improving motor function. Chronic treatment with the drug, however, can lead to cognitive problems.

In contrast to Parkinson's disease, **Huntington's disease** involves hereditary atrophy of the caudate nucleus. Patients with Huntington's typically have signs and symptoms that are the opposite of those seen in Parkinson's patients. They exhibit **choreiform** (dancelike) **movements** of the trunk and extremities that they are unable to control. They also suffer a gradual onset of psychotic thought patterns and eventually dementia. We can understand these symptoms by considering the net inhibitory effect of caudate projections through the indirect pathway described already. Damage to this pathway releases potential movements from inhibition, thus resulting in the production of unwanted actions.

Another basal ganglia syndrome, **hemiballismus**, ensues from unilateral damage to the subthalamic nucleus. This neurological insult causes similar choreiform movements of the contralateral limbs. Thus, electrophysiological, pharmacological, and neurological patient data all support the idea that a main function of the basal ganglia is to gate the production of movements directed to specific goals.

In addition to releasing movements in a goal- and context-appropriate manner, the basal ganglia contribute to motor learning. The ability to produce learned sequences of movements is disrupted in patients with damage to the basal ganglia, and this disruption is evident in both Parkinson's disease and Huntington's disease. Neuroimaging studies have confirmed that the basal ganglia are activated when human subjects learn new movement sequences. Moreover, recent neuroimaging studies demonstrate that the basal ganglia are specifically activated during motor learning.

In one typical study, Ravi Menon and colleagues at the University of Western Ontario asked subjects to perform a task in which they were required to manipulate a joystick with the right hand (**Figure 9.12A**). During some blocks of trials, the mapping between the joystick movement and the direction of movement of a target cursor on a computer screen was shifted by 90 degrees. When brain activity was compared between blocks of trials requiring such motor adaptation and blocks of trials in which movements were produced

(A)

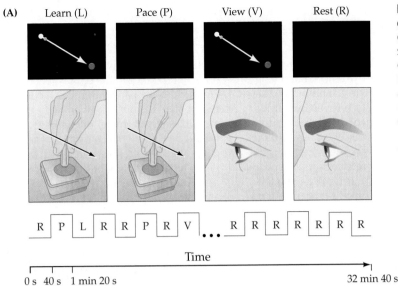

Figure 9.12 The contribution of the basal ganglia to motor learning. (A) Human subjects grasped a joystick to move a cursor on a computer screen. In some blocks of trials (Learn), the direction of cursor movement and the direction of joystick movement were offset by 90 degrees. In other blocks of trials, subjects simply moved the cursor without feedback (Pace), watched the cursor move by itself (View), or rested (Rest). (B) Functional MRI activation during motor learning was strongest in the putamen (circled). (After Graydon et al. 2005.)

(B)

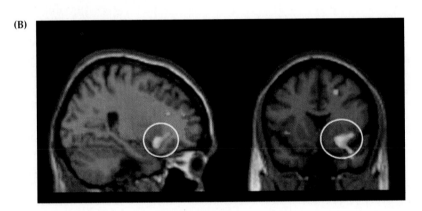

without visual feedback, the putamen was selectively activated (**Figure 9.12B**). These observations, and others like them, endorse the idea that the basal ganglia play a broad role in linking sensory events and motor actions, in addition to helping to suppress undesirable movements and to initiate movements that satisfy goals. As implied by some of the more subtle problems in basal ganglia disorders and their treatment, these structures also appear to be important in cognitive functions that are not closely tied to overt movement (**Box 9A**).

Coordination of Movement by the Cerebellum

As discussed in Chapter 8, circuits within the brainstem help coordinate lower-level reflex circuits in the spinal cord and brainstem motor nuclei to make the anticipatory postural adjustments needed to accommodate movements, correct posture for ongoing changes in balance, and coordinate more complex multijoint movements. In addition to the brainstem circuits mediating these aspects of motor coordination, another specialized set of neural circuitry has evolved to provide additional control of sensory-motor interactions. The key component at the center of this circuitry is the **cerebellum**, a large, foliated structure that sits atop the pons in the brainstem (**Figure 9.13**). The cerebellum is responsible for online error corrections necessary to produce smoothly coordinated skilled movements.

■ BOX 9A Cognitive Functions of the Basal Ganglia

The motor deficits associated with basal ganglia dysfunction, tragically evident in Parkinson's and Huntington's diseases, lead inexorably to the conclusion that these structures play a critical role in gating movement. Some of the problems with these diseases and their treatment, however, seem explicitly cognitive, and recent neurophysiological and neuroimaging findings appear to confirm this implication. Anatomical studies have also demonstrated the existence of several nonmotor pathways through the basal ganglia, including a limbic or emotional channel and an associative or cognitive channel (Figures A–C).

Henry Yin and Barbara Knowlton at UCLA, among others, have argued that these separate pathways serve distinct but related functions in emotion and cognition, and that these roles are especially prominent in humans and other primates. According to this view, the same principles governing movement disinhibition in the motor pathway apply to emotional or cognitive processing in the limbic and associative channels. Each channel thus comprises a feedback loop beginning in the cortex, projecting through the basal ganglia, and ultimately providing excitatory feedback to the cortex. In this model, cortical inputs to the basal ganglia serve as a source of potential variability in behavior, and the basal ganglia themselves contribute to the selection of behavior on the basis of prior outcomes.

Anne Graybiel at MIT has likened the nonmotor functions of the basal ganglia to a "cognitive pattern generator"—a reference to the pattern generators in the brainstem and spinal cord that sustain rhythmic movements such as walking, swimming, or chewing (see Chapter 8). Such cognitive pattern generators would presumably select, refine, and automate the production of action sequences leading to reward and avoiding punishment.

This framework helps explain some of the nonmotor consequences of basal ganglia dysfunction. For example, animals with lesions of the basal ganglia, particularly the caudate and putamen, can perform movements but cannot

The motor model of basal ganglia contributions to emotion and cognition. (A) The basal ganglia influence movement via a sensory-motor network from cortex, through the basal ganglia and thalamus, and back to the cortex. This network disinhibits desired movements. (B) The basal ganglia contribute to emotional function via an analogous limbic network, beginning in orbital and ventral prefrontal cortex, projecting through the ventral or limbic striatum, through the thalamus, and back to cortex. (C) The basal ganglia may contribute to cognitive function via a similar associative feedback loop between association cortex and the basal ganglia. The action of all three networks is enhanced by projections from midbrain dopamine neurons. (After Yin and Knowlton 2006.)

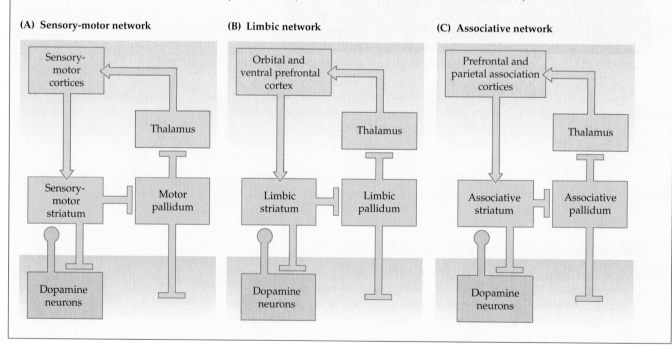

(A) Sensory-motor network

Sensory-motor cortices

Thalamus

Sensory-motor striatum

Motor pallidum

Dopamine neurons

(B) Limbic network

Orbital and ventral prefrontal cortex

Thalamus

Limbic striatum

Limbic pallidum

Dopamine neurons

(C) Associative network

Prefrontal and parietal association cortices

Thalamus

Associative striatum

Associative pallidum

Dopamine neurons

The cerebellum is organized into an outer cortex of cells, deep nuclei containing output neurons, and white matter fiber tracts along which inputs and outputs course. The cerebellum receives both ascending projections from the spinal cord and brainstem and descending projections originating in the

perform or learn new actions to acquire rewards or avoid punishments. Patients with Parkinson's disease, who exhibit diminished basal ganglia functioning due to dopaminergic dysfunction, also show impairments in probabilistic classification tasks that require subjects to make predictions based on a series of cues. Similar impairments in learning and memory follow damage to prefrontal regions projecting to the associative basal ganglia pathway, and, as noted, one of the hallmarks of Huntington's disease is psychotic thought processes.

Neurophysiological studies in animals, as well as neuroimaging in humans, have also demonstrated that basal ganglia neurons are modulated by the anticipation of reward, thus linking this network to the adaptive modification of behavior based on outcomes. Such studies suggest that addictive behavior could reflect the "hijacking" of this basal ganglia system by chemicals that activate receptors associated with reward. Specifically, cue-induced craving could ensue from the unconscious association of environmental cues present during drug con-

sumption with pathological reward modulation of basal ganglia cognitive pattern generators. In any event, these and other studies hint at the powerful influence of the basal ganglia on a wide range of cognitive behavior.

References

PLATT, M. L. (2002) Caudate clues to rewarding cues. *Neuron* 33: 316–318.

YIN, H. H. AND B. J. KNOWLTON (2006) The role of the basal ganglia in habit formation. *Nat. Rev. Neurosci.* 7: 464–476.

frontal motor and parietal cortices (**Figure 9.14A**). Spinal cord inputs come mainly from muscle proprioceptors and convey information about ongoing muscular activity and the position of the joints in space directly to the medial portions of the cerebellar cortex (also known as the **spinocerebellum**, because of its inputs) via the inferior cerebellar peduncle (see Figure 9.13B). The medial part of the spinocerebellum, known as the **vermis**, contributes to the coordination of axial musculature and also regulates eye movements. The more lateral part of the spinocerebellum mediates coordination of the distal muscles, especially during locomotion. In addition to the ascending spinal inputs, the vestibular nuclei project to specialized lobes at the base of the cerebellum, and circuits in these structures are principally involved in regulating movements controlling posture and balance.

Signals arising in the spinocerebellum are relayed via the deep interposed nuclei and descend to local circuits in the ipsilateral spinal

Figure 9.13 Organization of the cerebellum. (A) The cerebellum consists of an outer cortex of neurons, deep nuclei, and large fiber tracts, known as *peduncles*, coursing in and out. Inputs to the cerebellum arrive via the middle and superior cerebellar peduncles, and the deep nuclei project out of the cerebellum via the inferior and superior cerebellar peduncles. (B) The cerebellar cortex can be divided into the spinocerebellum, which receives inputs from the spinal cord; the cerebrocerebellum, which receives inputs from the cerebral cortex via the pons; and the vestibulocerebellum, consisting of the flocculus and nodulus, which receives inputs from the vestibular nuclei. The spinocerebellum is organized topographically according to inputs from spinal cord neurons carrying proprioceptive information. In contrast with upper motor neurons of the cortex and basal ganglia, cerebellar circuits mediate movements of the ipsilateral musculature.

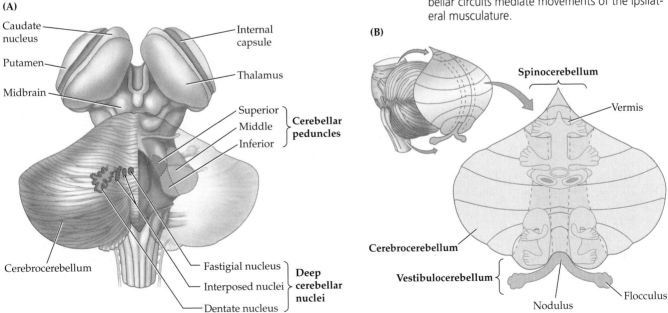

(A)

Caudate nucleus
Putamen
Midbrain
Internal capsule
Thalamus
Superior
Middle
Inferior
} **Cerebellar peduncles**
Cerebrocerebellum
Fastigial nucleus
Interposed nuclei
Dentate nucleus
} **Deep cerebellar nuclei**

(B)

Spinocerebellum
Vermis
Cerebrocerebellum
Vestibulocerebellum {
Nodulus
Flocculus

Figure 9.14 Inputs and major outputs of the cerebellum. (A) Functional organization of the inputs into the cerebellum. (B) The major outputs that affect upper motor neurons in the cerebral cortex. The axons of the deep cerebellar nuclei cross the midline of the brain before reaching the thalamus.

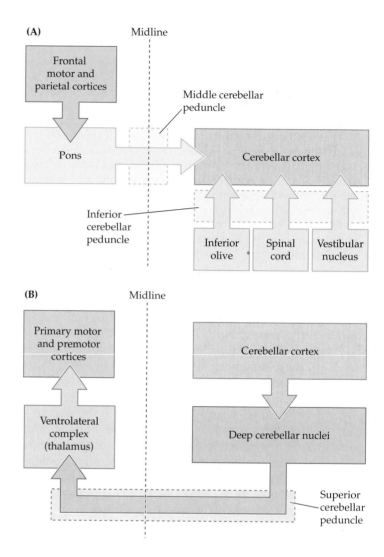

cord, whereas signals arising in the **vestibulocerebellum** are relayed via the deep fastigial nucleus. Descending projections to the cerebellum originating in the frontal and parietal cortices first relay on neurons within the pons aggregated in structures called the *pontine nuclei*. Axons from neurons in the pontine nuclei cross the midline and enter the lateral zones of the contralateral cerebellar hemisphere, or **cerebrocerebellum** (see Figure 9.13B).

Exquisitely organized circuits of specialized neurons within the cerebellar cortex appear to compute the net error between ongoing motor commands issued by the motor cortex and the actual movements being produced. These error signals are relayed back to the frontal and parietal cortices via projections from the dentate nucleus, the deep nuclear output structure for the cerebrocerebellum, to the ventrolateral complex of the thalamus (**Figure 9.14B**). As a result, damage to the cerebellum causes an inability to perform smooth movements.

Lesions of the medial cerebellar vermis result in a condition known as *truncal ataxia* (uncoordinated, disorganized movement), which is characterized by a wide-based, unsteady gait similar to that of someone who has had too much alcohol to drink. In fact, the stumbling movements seen in people who have drunk too much are due to the depressive effects of alcohol on cerebellar function. Damage to the lateral cerebellum, on the other hand, disrupts the sensory coordination of limb movements and is known as *appendicular ataxia*. A use-

(A)

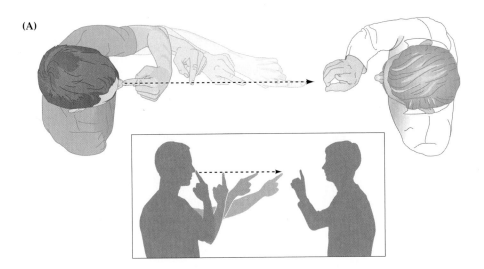

(B)

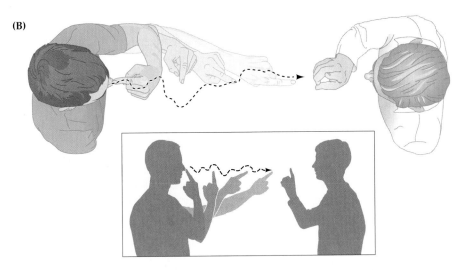

Figure 9.15 Cerebellar ataxia.
The patient is asked to point rapidly from the clinician's finger to his nose and back again. (A) Normal subjects point smoothly and rapidly from nose to finger and back again. (B) Patients with cerebellar ataxia produce irregular, jerky movements, known as *intention tremor*, when reaching from nose to finger and back again. (After Blumenfeld 2002.)

ful clinical test thus requires patients to point from their nose to the clinician's finger and back again (**Figure 9.15**). Patients with damage to the ipsilateral cerebellum show halting, uncoordinated movements of the hand and arm; this deficit is called **intention tremor** because it is evident only during voluntary movements. The jerky movements of appendicular ataxia appear to result from disruptions in the normal smooth compensation for ongoing errors in finger trajectory.

In addition to its role in movement coordination, the cerebellum is important for setting the *gain* of sensory-guided motor responses during learning. For example, the **vestibulo-ocular reflex** (**VOR**) normally produces eye movements that compensate for changes in head position, thus maintaining a stable image on the retina. When the relationship between retinal image size or orientation and the size of head or body movements is altered by prisms, the size of compensatory eye movements rapidly adapts to match changes in the retinal image. This ability to change the gain of the vestibulo-ocular reflex is vital to anyone who puts on a pair of vision-correcting glasses or contact lenses. The gain-setting functions of the cerebellum have been studied in monkeys, who also show adaptation of the VOR when wearing prism goggles (**Figure 9.16**). When the cerebellum is removed or damaged, the ability of the VOR to adapt is abolished.

(A) Normal VOR

(B) VOR out of register

(C) VOR gain reset

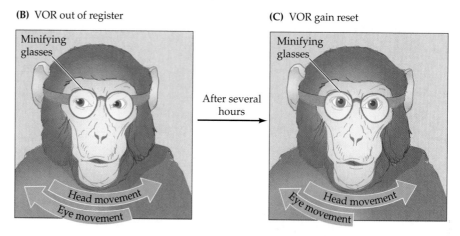

After several hours

Figure 9.16 Cerebellar contributions to motor adaptation. (A) The vestibulo-ocular reflex (VOR) rotates the eyes to counter head rotation. (B) After the experimental monkey is outfitted with lenses that make the visual scene smaller, VOR-induced eye movements overshoot the extent of head rotation. (C) After several hours, the VOR adapts to the distorted visual inputs. Damage to the cerebellum prevents such VOR adaptation.

In addition to setting the gain of the VOR, the cerebellum contributes to other types of motor learning and is vital for the production of learned movements like those involved in playing the piano. In short, lesions that damage the cerebellum disrupt the ability to learn new motor skills. Moreover, the cerebellum is activated during motor learning. When subjects are asked to track a target on a computer screen and the target randomly jumps to another position at the end of each trial, motor error during tracking is initially quite large but improves with practice (**Figure 9.17**). Activation in the cerebellum parallels this change in performance, peaking during initial learning and declining with improvement in performance. Although the evidence is less clear, the canonical circuitry of the cerebellum has also been implicated in a variety of other cognitive functions, as outlined in **Box 9B**.

Figure 9.17 Changes in the cerebellum during motor adaptation. (A) Subjects tracked a target on a computer screen using a mouse. During test sessions, the cursor was rotated 120 degrees about the center of the screen, thus requiring motor learning. In baseline sessions, the cursor remained unrotated. Improvements in the average performance of subjects over time in test sessions indicate motor learning. (B) The corresponding brain activation maps show significant activation in test sessions (increasing from left to right) relative to baseline during learning. Activity in the cerebellum decreased with motor learning. (After Imamizu et al. 2000.)

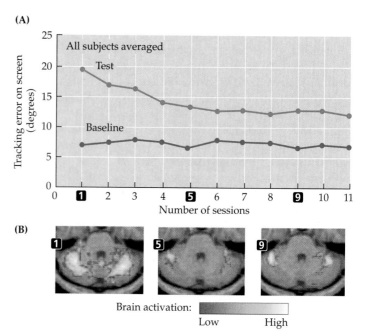

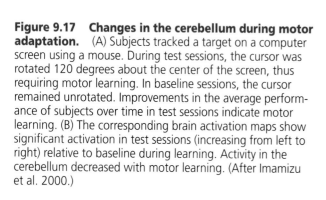

Brain activation: Low — High

■ BOX 9B Canonical Cerebellar Circuitry and Its Role in Cognitive Functions

Traditionally, the cerebellum and its canonical circuitry (Figure A) have been considered a strictly motor structure providing error correction during motor acts and motor learning. With the advent of modern neuroimaging, however, it has become increasingly clear that the cerebellum contributes to cognitive processing as well. Thus, portions of the cerebellum are activated during non-motor learning, attention, timing, and verbal working memory tasks. Furthermore, recent neuropsychological studies of patients with cerebellar damage have reported deficits in speech, learning rates, timing, and working memory. Problems in orienting attention in autistic individuals have also been linked to abnormalities in the cerebellum.

Despite this evidence, it is not clear how or why the cerebellum participates in cognitive functions. One proposal is that the computational power of the cerebellum as an efficient and accurate error correction device has simply been harnessed to serve cognitive functions that also require error correction. This model assumes that the cellular architecture repeated throughout the cerebellum can be used to perform the same computation on any set of inputs. For the motor system, these inputs would arise in the primary and premotor cortices, and the output would be a feedforward prediction of the sensory consequences of the impending movement. For cognitive tasks, the inputs would arise in the prefrontal cortex and specify intended cognitive operations, and the output would be the predicted cognitive consequences of the operation. Such predictions would then be compared against actual cognitive consequences, and the resulting

(Continued on next page)

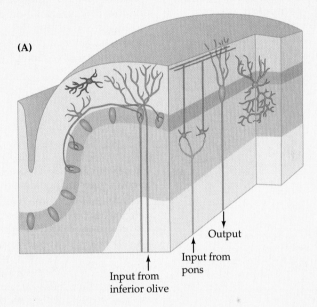

Model of cerebellar contributions to cognition. (A) The canonical circuitry of the cerebellar cortex. Inputs to the cerebellar cortex arrive from the pons and inferior olive, a brainstem relay nucleus. (B) Model of cerebellar feedforward simulation and error correction of motor commands. The cerebellum computes the predicted sensory consequences of movement. The error between the predicted and actual consequences of movement is then fed back into the cerebellum to update future predictions. (C) The same model applied to cognitive processing. The cerebellum computes the predicted cognitive consequences of cognitive operations, and the error between predicted and actual cognitive outcomes is used to refine future predictions. (After Ramnani 2006.)

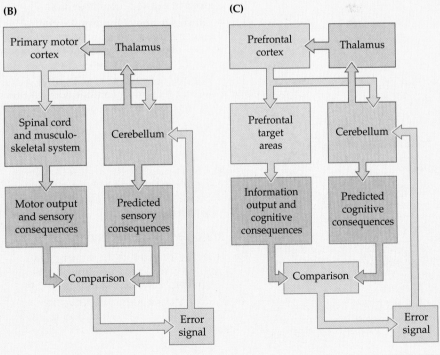

■ **BOX 9B** *(continued)*

error signals would be used to update both future cognitive operations and the internal models of their outcomes.

Support for this general class of models comes from the observation that, in addition to the heavy inputs from the motor and premotor cortices, the prefrontal cortex has massive connections to the cerebellum via the pontine nuclei. In fact, prefrontal inputs to the cerebellum in humans are at least as prominent as inputs from motor and premotor cortex. Moreover, prefrontal inputs to the cerebellum are more developed in humans than in

non-human primates, and these differences parallel differences in cognitive complexity across species (see Chapter 26). Cognitive operations instantiated in prefrontal circuits feeding to the cerebellum might rely on the highly stereotyped cellular architecture of the cerebellum to provide fast, accurate, and automatic "simulations" of the output of these cognitive operations. This conjecture is supported by the observation that prefrontal circuits show reduced activation during the course of learning, whereas cerebellar circuits become more active. The cerebellum

may thus provide another example in which neural circuitry originally adapted to one purpose is co-opted for another; that is, the circuitry for motor control (Figure B) is co-opted for use in cognitive information processing (Figure C).

References

FIEZ, J. A. (1996) Cerebellar contributions to cognition. *Neuron* 16: 13–15.

RAMNANI, N. (2006) The primate cortico-cerebellar system: Anatomy and function. *Nat. Rev. Neurosci.* 7: 511–522.

Summary

1. Descending pathways from the motor and premotor cortices are important in planning and initiating voluntary, goal-directed sequences of movement, especially for learned motor skills. Of special relevance here, these circuits are sensitive to motivational goals that guide movement selection.

2. The motor and premotor cortices are under the modulatory influence of the basal ganglia and cerebellum. The basal ganglia control the initiation and stopping of movements and contribute to motor skill learning, the production of movement sequences, and the selection of movements that satisfy behavioral goals. The cerebellum acts further to coordinate movements by correcting unanticipated errors in ongoing motor processing in the motor and premotor cortices.

3. Acting together, these various motor circuits mediate production of the complex intrinsic and learned sequences of movement characteristic of human motor behaviors that express cognitive goals.

4. Damage to any of these motor control circuits results in specific disruptions in movement planning, initiation, or coordination, and damage to some of these circuits—the basal ganglia and cerebellum in particular—also causes deficits in a variety of cognitive functions.

5. This body of evidence underscores the general point introduced in Chapter 8—namely, that understanding cognitive functions demands understanding the generation, monitoring, and ongoing modulation of motor behavior.

Additional Reading

Reviews

COHEN, Y. E. AND R. A. ANDERSEN (2002) A common reference frame for movement plans in the posterior parietal cortex. *Nature Rev. Neurosci.* 3: 553–562.

HIKOSAKA, O. (1991) Basal ganglia: Possible role in motor coordination and learning. *Curr. Opin. Neurobiol.* 1: 638–643.

RAMNANI, N. (2006) The primate cortico-cerebellar system: Anatomy and function. *Nature Rev. Neurosci.* 7: 511–522.

YIN, H. H. AND B. J. KNOWLTON (2006) The role of the basal ganglia in habit formation. *Nature Rev. Neurosci.* 7: 464–476.

Important Original Papers

PLATT, M. L. AND P. W. GLIMCHER (1999) Neural correlates of decision variables in parietal cortex. *Nature* 400: 233–238.

SHADLEN, M. N. AND W. T. NEWSOME (1996) Motion perception: Seeing and deciding. *Proc. Natl. Acad. Sci. USA* 93: 628–633.

TANJI, J. AND K. SHIMA (1994) Role for supplementary motor area cells in planning several movements ahead. *Nature* 371: 413–416.

Books

GLIMCHER, P. W. (2004) *Decision, Uncertainty, and the Brain: The Science of Neuroeconomics.* Cambridge, MA: MIT Press/Bradford Books.

PURVES, D. AND 6 OTHERS (2008) *Neuroscience*, 4th Ed. Sunderland, MA: Sinauer.

UNIT IV
Principles of Attention

During every waking moment, humans and other animals are bombarded with stimuli arriving from multiple directions and through the various modalities described in Unit II. At the same time, we are inundated by information from non-sensory sources, including ongoing and planned motor behavior, emotions, memories, and trains of thought that arise as problems are encountered, solutions imagined, and decisions made. To succeed in the real world, the neural processing resources available in a brain with finite capabilities must be efficiently directed to the aspects of this overwhelming information load that are likely to matter most in a given situation. Without such allocation, behavioral performance would be far less effective than it typically is. *Attention* is the name given to this broad cognitive function, which plays a fundamental role in virtually everything we do.

Historically, most studies of attention have sought to understand how and why various sensory events or other inputs are selected and passed on to higher levels of neural processing, how the processing of attended information compares to the processing of information that is not attended, and what mechanisms determine this differential processing. A variety of methods have been used in this quest, including behavioral measures, clinical studies of the behavioral deficits of patients with neurological lesions, noninvasive electrophysiological approaches (EEG and MEG recording), hemodynamically based functional brain imaging methods (PET and fMRI), and recording from individual neurons in experimental animals (e.g., awake, behaving monkeys with implanted electrodes).

The following chapters explore the ways in which attentional processes have been studied and the major conclusions that have been drawn from those studies. Chapter 10 provides an overview of the field, focusing on behavioral approaches that have characterized attention and the limits of attentional capacity. Chapter 11 covers the relatively recent, neurally based approaches that have studied the influence of attention on sensory and perceptual processing, and Chapter 12 considers the mechanisms and neural systems concerned with the organization and control of attentional processes. ■

10

Overview of Attention

Introduction

Attention is an essential neurobiological function that allows humans and other animals to continually and dynamically select the most important and/or interesting stimuli in the external or internal environment so that greater neural processing resources can be directed to their analysis. Before the development of modern methods for directly measuring brain activity, studies of attention were largely limited to the behavioral measures traditionally used in cognitive psychology. Nonetheless, by manipulating aspects of stimulus presentation and task instructions and then measuring behavioral response characteristics, such as reaction time and performance accuracy, researchers were able to learn a great deal about attentional processing and the limits of attentional capacity. These observations led to the development of theoretical models of attention that remain influential today. Much more has been learned about the neural mechanisms of attention in the last few decades using modern methods of cognitive neuroscience. This chapter presents an overview of attentional phenomena, including the major paradigms that have been used in psychological studies of attention and the key findings and models that have been derived from those studies. It also introduces a framework for studying the neural bases of attention.

The Concept of Attention

Global states and attention

The word **attention** is used in several ways in everyday discourse, as well as more formally in cognitive psychology and cognitive neuroscience. To complicate matters further, *attention* must be distinguished from other brain-related terms that are related to it but not synonymous. A key distinction is the relationship between attention and **arousal** (**Figure 10.1**). From a neural standpoint, the term *level of arousal* describes a global state of the brain. The broadest categorization of arousal is whether an individual is awake or

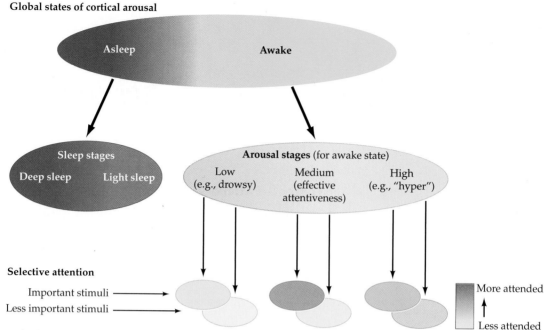

Figure 10.1 Relationships between attentional concepts and general states of arousal. The top row of the diagram indicates global states of cortical arousal, from sleep through wakefulness. The second row shows ranges within these global states. The bottom row shows the selectivity of attentional focus at the different arousal levels (for the awake state). At low levels of arousal, neither important nor unimportant stimulus input is given much processing (yellow ovals). At medium levels of alertness, attention can be selectively focused on the important information in the environment (red oval versus yellow oval). At very high arousal levels, attention may boost responses to stimulus input, but not in a very focused or effective manner (orange ovals).

asleep, although it may be more accurate to view neural arousal as falling along a continuum whose extremes are deep sleep and maximum wakefulness (see Chapter 28). Both subjective experience and behavioral studies make it clear that an individual who is asleep is not only less aroused than someone who is awake, but also much less attentive and reactive to external stimuli and events.

Even individuals who are awake, however, can clearly be operating at different levels of arousal; or, in terms of how individuals interact with the world around them, at different levels of "alertness" (see Figure 10.1). Describing someone as *alert* typically means that the person is fully awake, generally vigilant, and attending intently to the local environment. In contrast, when people are drowsy, they are less attentive to the events going on around them than when they are alert. This conclusion is both intuitively clear and readily supported by behavioral testing data, which show slowed reaction times and reduced performance accuracy in cognitive tasks.

How, then, do attention and arousal relate to one another? First, whereas arousal is a state of the brain that can range from very low to very high, attention generally refers to the selective allocation of neural processing resources to important information, at any level of arousal (with the exception of sleep). Second, the relationship between arousal and the ability to focus attention effectively is not linear; rather, arousal and attentional effectiveness are roughly related as an inverted *U*-shaped function, with low arousal levels generally being associated with inattentiveness, mid-arousal levels with the ability to focus attention effectively, and extremely high arousal levels with ineffective attention (e.g., highly aroused people are too "hyper" to effectively focus their attention).

The selective nature of attention

A key distinction between arousal and attention is that attention can be selectively focused. **Selective attention** refers to the allocation of processing resources to the analysis of certain stimuli or aspects in the environment, generally at the expense of resources allocated to other stimuli or aspects. Understanding how attention can be selectively focused on specific aspects of the environment can be traced back to the late-nineteenth-century psychologist William James, who summed up this quality of attention as follows:

> Everyone knows what attention is. It is the taking possession of the mind, in clear and vivid form, of one out of what seem several simultaneously possible objects or trains of thought … It implies withdrawal from some things in order to deal effectively with others.
>
> *William James, 1890 (Principles of Psychology, Vol. 1, pp. 403–404)*

As a result of this insight, most research in the cognitive psychology and cognitive neuroscience of attention has been devoted to the study of selective attention, typically in the context of sensory processing.

A particularly well studied example of selective attention in the auditory modality is the **cocktail party effect**. This term refers to the situation in which multiple conversations and other sounds are occurring simultaneously but a listener can selectively focus on one voice or conversation and effectively "tune out" the others. Although this ability is facilitated by looking at the speaker, it is also possible to attend one voice in a cocktail party situation without looking at the speaker.

Another example of selective attention is **visual spatial attention (Figure 10.2)**, a phenomenon first described in studies carried out by the German physicist and vision scientist Hermann von Helmholtz at the end of the nineteenth century. In particular, Helmholtz observed that if a subject steadily fixated gaze on a particular point in the visual field but attended covertly to another region (without moving the eyes), then the stimuli presented in the covertly attended location could be reported much better than stimuli in the rest of the field. Thus, attention to particular aspects of the environment generally leads to improved processing of the attended stimuli, typically at the expense of the processing of other simultaneously presented information.

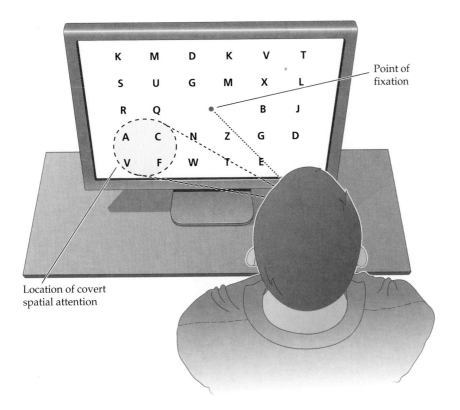

Figure 10.2 Studying visual spatial attention.   Selective attention to a subset of a visual scene enhances the processing of information from the attended portion at the expense of processing information from the rest of the scene. In the original experiment by Hermann von Helmholtz, subjects were briefly presented with an array of letters and asked afterward to recall the letters that they had seen. Helmholtz observed that if a subject were asked to covertly attend to a certain area of the visual field away from fixation, then the items in the attended portion of the letter array could be accurately reported, whereas items in unattended locations could not be.

Behavioral Studies of Processing-Capacity Limitations and Attention

Historical background

As noted in Chapter 2, psychology in the first half of the twentieth century was dominated by the behaviorist approach. By the 1950s, however, an information-processing approach was taking root, providing a framework that allowed researchers to think of attention as adaptively maximizing the utility of limited processing resources. This way of thinking led to a series of experiments that investigated attentional capacity and its limits by testing the comprehension or retention of information by subjects placed in attentionally demanding situations.

A particularly influential experiment of this sort was carried out by psychologist Colin Cherry, working at Imperial College London in the early 1950s (**Figure 10.3**). In this study, two different channels of auditory information (two voices, each speaking a different verbal passage) were presented to the left and right ears, respectively. The subject was instructed to attend to one of these inputs, immediately repeating its content (a task called *shadowing*). Such shadowing is demanding, requiring that subjects attend closely to one input while ignoring another.

After the subjects had performed this task, Cherry tested them on their ability to report the content of the two vocal inputs. He found that they could accurately report the content of the attended channel, but could report very little information from the unattended stream. Indeed, the only feature of the unattended channel that most subjects could accurately report was whether the speaker was male or female. This sort of observation was interpreted as indicating that unattended inputs are filtered out at fairly low levels of perceptual processing on the basis of a basic physical characteristic. Moreover, this type of study made clear that subjects cannot attend effectively to two input streams at the same time, illustrating a fundamental limitation of attentional processing capacity.

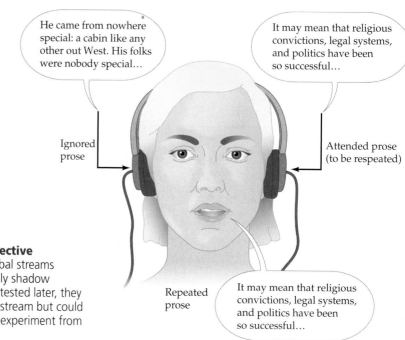

Figure 10.3   Auditory shadowing study of selective attention.   Subjects were presented with two verbal streams simultaneously, one to each ear, and asked to verbally shadow (i.e., immediately repeat) one of the streams. When tested later, they could accurately report the content of the attended stream but could report little of the unattended stream. (Depiction of experiment from Cherry 1953.)

Other studies that followed, however, cast doubt on the strength of these conclusions. For instance, a study by Neville Moray at the University of Sheffield showed that subjects noticed when their name was mentioned in an unattended auditory channel. Indeed, most of us have had the experience of attending to one conversation while ignoring other simultaneous conversations, and suddenly noticing that our name (or another key word or phrase) is mentioned in one of those other conversations. Such observations indicate that at least some information in an unattended channel is being processed up to the level of semantic meaning, and is not completely filtered out at a lower level.

Determining the level at which attention exerts its influence

These and other observations led researchers to propose various models that might account for the cognitive architecture underlying attentional phenomena. A key aspect of such models concerned the level at which attention affects the processing of sensory input. During the development of these ideas, models of attention were traditionally divided into those proposing early levels of attentional selection and those proposing later levels. Models of **early selection** postulated that there is a low-level gating mechanism that can filter out or attenuate irrelevant information before the completion of sensory and perceptual analysis. In contrast, theories of **late selection**, at least the strong versions, proposed that all stimuli are processed through the completion of sensory and perceptual processing before any selection occurs.

In the late 1950s, in an important step for the development of early-selection theories, Donald Broadbent at the University of Cambridge published a paper in which he asserted that attentional selection can occur very early in processing. More specifically, he proposed that sensory input can be gated at early sensory-processing stages on the basis of fundamental physical characteristics of the stimuli (e.g., color, sound frequency, location, and so on), thereby determining which information proceeds to higher levels of analysis (**Figure 10.4A**).

The need to modify this simple gating model became apparent shortly thereafter because of Moray's finding that some information in an unattended channel can reach the level of semantic analysis (see the previous section). These findings led some researchers in the early 1960s—most notably J. Anthony Deutsch and Diana Deutsch at Stanford—to propose a late-selection model, in which attentional filtering occurs relatively late in stimulus processing. According to such theories, all sensory stimuli are fully processed, in terms of both their physical characteristics and their possible higher-level meaning. Thus, in this view, not until after this higher-level processing was complete could attention exert its influence and determine what input information entered consciousness or influenced behavior.

In the 1960s Anne Treisman, then working at Oxford University, proposed another solution. She altered Broadbent's concept of a gate that is simply open or closed to be a more adaptable filtering system that could attenuate the inputs from concurrent sensory channels in a flexible manner (**Figure 10.4B**). This model allows some unattended semantic information through to higher levels, although it might be heavily attenuated. Accordingly, in an unattended channel only especially salient information (e.g., one's own name) would pass the threshold to be selected, reach conscious awareness, and be reportable by the individual.

In the 1970s, other researchers concluded that an even better model to explain the various findings was one in which incoming information could be filtered at various levels of processing, depending on the needs for a particular task or set of circumstances (**Figure 10.4C**). These models proposed that sensory information might be filtered out or selected at relatively early pro-

Figure 10.4 Information-processing models of selective attention. (A) In the model proposed by Broadbent, a gating mechanism under top-down control determines what information is passed on for higher-level analysis. (B) Treisman's model is based on attenuation and/or modulation rather than all-or-none gating. (C) More recent models incorporated the possibility of selection at early, middle, or later stages of stimulus processing, depending on the circumstances. (A after Broadbent 1958; B after Treisman 1960.)

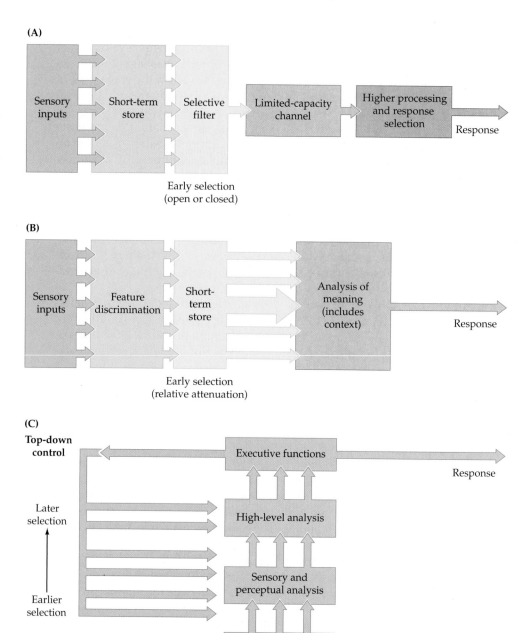

cessing stages according to basic physical characteristics such as color or pitch. Depending on the circumstances, however, more complex aspects of the information in a stimulus, such as its semantic content, would be required to make the selection, which would then occur at a later stage.

In the 1990s, other researchers, most notably Nilli Lavie and her colleagues at University College London, modified attentional theories still further by focusing on the consequences of the **perceptual load** imposed by a task. The perceptual load of a task would vary according to characteristics of the task-relevant stimuli to be processed, such as how complex they were, how degraded they were, or how rapidly they were presented. Tests of this idea supported the conclusion that if the perceptual load for the task to be performed on the input channel of interest is high, then the amount and level of processing afforded other simultaneous inputs is relatively low. In such cases, early-selection mechanisms filter out the unattended input information at low levels of processing. If, on the other hand, the perceptual load in the input channel of interest were low, then more processing would be available for other input information, allowing it to reach higher processing levels wherein later attentional selection mechanisms could exert their influence.

As noted earlier, one way that researchers used behavioral measures to assess the level of stimulus processing at which attention exerted its influence was verbal report—that is, how well and what aspects of an unattended input subjects could report later, relative to what they could report about the attended input. One criticism of this approach is that an accurate report depends on the ability of the subject not only to perform the processing to a certain level during stimulus presentation, but also to encode it into memory and then retrieve it for the later report. Thus, it could be the case that all stimulus input is processed up to the level at which meaning can be extracted (e.g., semantic content), but that unattended information is not consolidated and stored well enough to retrieve at the time reporting is required.

Accordingly, another behavioral approach that researchers have used to assess the level at which attentional influences occur is derived from information theory. In any detection or discrimination task, the numbers of correctly detected/discriminated targets (hits), missed targets (misses), and nontargets that were incorrectly identified as targets (false alarms) can be analyzed to yield two key values about the processing system involved: **d-prime** and **beta**. The d-prime value is theoretically a measure of the discriminability of a sensory stimulus by the relevant processing system for a given subject. In contrast, any response biases (i.e., being likely to press the response button even when very unsure versus only when very sure) is captured by the beta value.

Researchers have used this methodology to infer the level of processing of attentional influence by, for example, using a paradigm in which one stimulus channel is strongly attended and a second one only weakly attended. The assumption is that a change in d-prime implies that the attentional influence was at an early sensory level, with no change in d-prime implying influence at a higher, later level. In general, researchers have found that selective attention does indeed tend to influence d-prime values, at least in some tasks. Accordingly, attention in those tasks was inferred to be affecting processing at a relatively early level of sensory analysis.

In most of these psychological theories of attentional function, the concepts of "early" and "late" refer to time, with the more basic sensory analyses (e.g., analyses of the physical characteristics of stimuli) presumably being done early in the processing sequence and the more complex analyses (e.g., of stimulus meaning) not occurring until later stages. Some of these psychological theories also tend to imply a rough mapping of these processing stages onto the brain, with early processing presumably corresponding to basic analyses in the brainstem and low-level sensory cortices, and late processing occurring in higher-level association cortices. Behavioral testing, however, cannot provide direct or compelling evidence for such ideas. These problems will be taken up in Chapter 11, which describes how newer cognitive neuroscience approaches have helped settle these questions concerning the levels and timing of attentional influence on stimulus processing, the neuroanatomical foci of such influence, and the circumstances under which it takes place.

The psychological refractory period and response selection

The studies described in the previous section have made clear that the processing of multiple inputs of sensory stimuli has capacity limitations and that attention is invoked to select the stimulus input to which processing resources should be most heavily directed. In contrast to such studies of attentional capacity limitations and stimulus selection, other research has examined capacity limitations related to **response selection**, the selection of a behavioral response to a stimulus. Much of this research has focused on a phenomenon termed the **psychological refractory period (PRP)**, defined as the time interval during which the selection and implementation of one response precludes the selection and implementation of another (**Figure 10.5**).

Suppose, for example, that a subject is instructed to press a button when one type of stimulus appears (e.g., a letter on a screen), and to step on a pedal when another type of stimulus occurs (e.g., a tone). These are both easy tasks, and when either stimulus is presented alone, it takes the subject only about 400 milliseconds to respond appropriately. If, however, the second stimulus occurs soon after the first (e.g., the tone follows the letter by 100 milliseconds or so), then the response to the second stimulus is slowed substantially, especially if the subject is not well practiced at the task.

Such results have led some psychologists to propose a three-stage model of processing that entails a perception phase, a response-selection phase, and a response-production phase (see Figure 10.5B). This theory postulates that the response-selection phase presents a sort of bottleneck, in that a person can select a response for only one task or target at a time. Thus, during the

---

■ BOX 10A Attention and Stimulus Conflict

During selective attention to a specific stimulus or task, concurrent stimuli can generate conflicting information. Another important cognitive function in which attention has been thought to play a role is dealing with conflicting information from irrelevant stimuli that would interfere with an intended or appropriate behavior.

A well-known paradigm for studying such conflict is the so-called **Stroop task**, developed by John Ridley Stroop in 1935 as part of his dissertation at George Peabody College in Nashville (see also Chapter 23). In the standard version of this paradigm, a color word stimulus (e.g., *red*) is presented either in the font color that the word describes (congruent) or in a different color (incongruent), and the subject must verbally report or otherwise discriminate the color of the font (Figure A). Although the meaning of the color word is irrelevant for this task, subjects are typically slower at naming the font color when the word stimulus is incongruent, presumably because reading the incongruent word is so automatic that it leads to interfer-

ence at some level of processing. It has been postulated that attentional mechanisms need to be invoked in such circumstances to suppress or otherwise manage the conflicting information from the word stimulus meaning, or to relatively enhance the processing of its color. Thus, another function of attention may be resolving competition between stimuli that tend to direct behavior in different directions.

Variations of the Stroop task have been developed that show incongruency effects in other realms. In the *emotional Stroop task*, for example, subjects are slower to name the colors of words with strong emotional valences (e.g., *beheaded*) versus those with neutral valence (e.g., *automobile*). In this case, there is no conflict between a word meaning and the font color, but rather the emotionality of the word meaning appears to capture attention, distracting the subject and slowing the subject's response time. The emotional Stroop task has been used in clinical studies in which emotional words are related to specific problem areas for individuals, such as alcohol-related words for someone who suffers from

alcoholism, or words involving a particular phobia for someone with anxiety or phobic disorders.

In another variation of the Stroop paradigm, the *number Stroop task*, subjects are presented with several identical number words (e.g., *two*) and asked to identify the number of presented items. Subjects are slower to respond if the number of items and the number word meaning do not match (i.e., they are incongruent, as in three *twos*) than if they match (two *twos*). In all of these tasks, subjects must suppress the processing of, or responses associated with, distracting or conflicting word information while selectively maintaining attention on another aspect of the stimuli to perform the designated task.

Another paradigm that has been used to study the cognitive aspects of stimulus conflict is the **flanker task** developed in the 1970s by Charles Eriksen and colleagues at the University of Illinois. In a typical version of this task (Figure B), subjects are presented with a series of stimulus trials, each consisting of a horizontal row of five letters. The task is to discriminate

(A) Paradigm

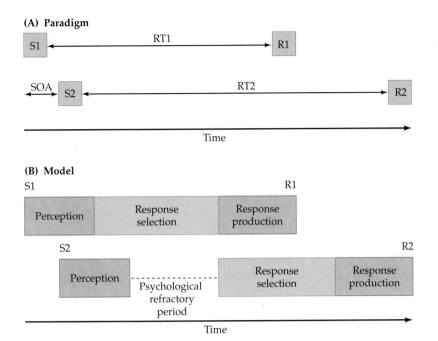

(B) Model

Figure 10.5 The psychological refractory period. (A) This basic paradigm, consisting of two successively presented stimuli each requiring a response, is designed to demonstrate and analyze the psychological refractory period. (B) A model illustrating the putative information-processing stages of perception, response selection, and response production. The model posits that a central bottleneck impedes response selection for Stimulus 2 (S2), in that it cannot begin until the response-selection process for Stimulus 1 (S1) is completed. R1, Response 1; R2, Response 2; RT1, Response Time 1; RT2, Response Time 2; SOA, Stimulus Onset Asynchrony. (After Pashler 1994.)

(A) Task: What is the ink color of the word?

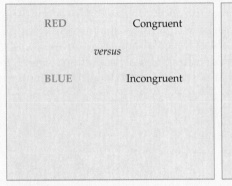

(B) Task: Is the middle letter A or E?

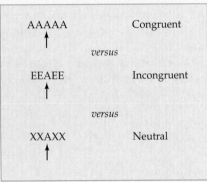

Paradigms used for studying the role of attention in dealing with stimulus conflict. (A) The Stroop paradigm. Color word stimuli are presented in different font colors, the subject's task being to name or otherwise discriminate the font color. Subjects are slower to respond if the color of the font and the word meaning are incongruent versus congruent. (B) The flanker paradigm. A series of letter sets is presented sequentially, the task being to discriminate whether the central letter of each set is one of two possibilities. In this example, subjects are required to discriminate whether the central letter is an *A* or an *E*. Subjects are faster to respond on congruent trials, in which the flanking letters are the same as the central target letter (e.g., an *A* surrounded by *A*s) than on incongruent trials (e.g., an *A* surrounded by *E*s). Subjects have intermediate response times on neutral trials, in which the surrounding flankers are different from the central target letter but are not mapped to an instructed response.

central target letter and thus associated with the same button press), incongruent (not the same as the central target letter and thus associated with the other possible response), or neutral (different from the central target letter but not mapped to any response).

The behavioral finding, reflecting the influence of conflict, is that reaction times are faster on trials with congruent flankers compared to trials with incongruent flankers, reaction times in trials with neutral flankers being intermediate. As with the Stroop task, it is generally thought that attention is invoked in the flanker task as the means of filtering out or suppressing the processing of concurrent information when it is incongruent, or in conflict with, the task to be performed.

References

ERIKSEN, B. A. AND C. W. ERIKSEN (1974) Effects of noise letters upon identification of a target letter in a nonsearch task. *Percept. Psychophys.* 16: 143–149.

MACLEOD, C. M. (1991) Half a century of research on the Stroop effect: An integrative review. *Psychol. Bull.* 109: 163–203.

STROOP, J. R. (1935) Studies of interference in serial verbal reactions. *J. Exp. Psychol.* 18: 643–662.

between two possibilities for the center letter (e.g., *A* versus *E*), the flanking letters being task-irrelevant distracters. The two possibilities for the central target are mapped to different responses (in Figure B, for example, one button if the central letter is an *A*, another if it is an *E*). The key manipulation is that the flanker letters can either be congruent (the same as the

response-selection phase for the first target, a subject cannot perform the response selection for a second target, or at least cannot do so as efficiently. This bottleneck would explain why the reaction time to the second target is delayed. That the putative bottleneck is at the response-selection level rather than in the perceptual processing phase suggests that the mechanism involves a form of late attentional selection following a stimulus, rather than one occurring at an early level.

Late-selection processes also appear to be involved in resolving situations in which irrelevant stimuli in the environment conflict on a higher level of processing with the relevant stimuli or task. The idea is that once the conflicting aspect of the irrelevant stimulus is detected at the level of its meaning, selective attention is invoked to help filter it out (**Box 10A**).

Attentional blink

Other evidence for attention-related bottlenecks in processing sensory input has come from studies of a phenomenon that has been called the **attentional blink**. This phenomenon was discovered through use of a paradigm developed in the early 1990s by Jane Raymond and colleagues at the University of Wales at Bangor. Stimuli are presented in rapid sequence in a single stream, typically about eight or nine per second, the task being to detect occasional targets in the stream (e.g., a digit among a series of letters). This paradigm is called **rapid serial visual presentation (RSVP)**.

The main behavioral finding is that shortly after detecting a target, which a subject might signal by pressing a button, the subject's ability to detect a second target is reduced. By varying the lag times of the second target relative to the first, experimenters have shown that the ability to detect the second target is reduced for about 150 to 450 milliseconds after the initial target is detected (**Figure 10.6**). This effect was termed *attentional blink* because it seemed to suggest that while someone is engaged in detecting or discriminating a target, for a brief period of time, there is a deficit in the ability to devote sufficient pro-

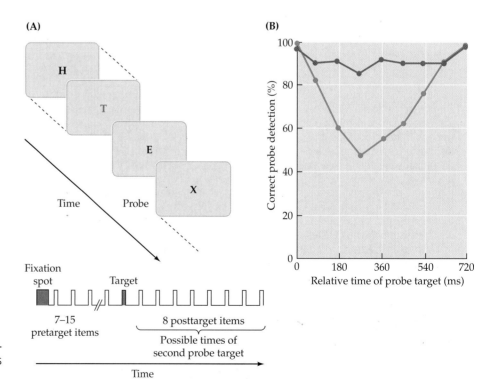

Figure 10.6 Behavioral measures of attentional blink. (A) Stimuli are presented in a rapid stream (here, 11 per second) in which occasional target stimuli (T) are to be detected. (B) When one target (blue line) follows another within approximately 150 to 450 milliseconds, the ability to report the occurrence of the second target (green line) is reduced. (After Raymond et al. 1992.)

cessing resources to detect a second target, presumably because of attentional capacity limitations.

This temporary deficiency has parallels to the psychological refractory period, but in this case the paradigm places the processing bottleneck within stimulus detection rather than in the selection of a response. It is also different from the limitations indicated during the stimulus selection processes described earlier. In the previous cases of stimulus selection, attention was focused on particular speakers, spatial locations, or stimulus features, which then resulted in a reduced allocation of attention to other inputs, locations, or features. In the case of the attentional blink there is only one stream of stimuli, and all the stimuli in that stream occur in a spatially attended location, are relevant, and are attended. The phenomenon of attentional blink nonetheless adds to the evidence that attending to one thing—whether a target in a stream of stimuli, the selection of a response, or a particular location or source—impedes the ability to attend to something else at the same time.

Thus, all these phenomena underscore that attentional resources are fundamentally limited. In light of these intrinsic capacity limitations, however, the ability to selectively focus attention has a generally positive consequence for the animal. Attending assiduously to one type of stimulus, source, or response and temporarily ignoring less important information or alternatives allows behavior to be more efficiently directed to dealing with the most important aspects of the environment at any moment.

Behavioral Studies of Directing and Focusing Selective Attention

Many of the behavioral observations described in the preceding sections entail *voluntary* attentional tasks. That is, to follow the instruction of an experimenter or to fulfill an intrinsic desire, subjects consciously direct attention to a particular aspect of the environment, such as to a specific voice or to a particular location in visual space. This type of attention is called **endogenous attention**. In contrast, numerous stimuli arising from events or conditions in our everyday environment attract attention automatically; such attention is called **exogenous**, or *reflexive*, **attention**. A major distinction that has been made in attention research is between these two ways in which processing resources are induced to be directed toward items in the environment. This section first examines the characteristics of these two categories of attention, and then considers some of the particular ways in which they have been studied.

Endogenous attention

Endogenous attention refers to a person's ability to voluntarily direct attention to specific aspects of the environment, typically based on an individual's goals, expectations, and/or knowledge. A good example is the ability to voluntarily direct visual attention to specific locations in the visual field (as described earlier; see Figure 10.2). To study such spatial attention, researchers have often used a paradigm in which subjects receive advance cues as to where in the visual field a visual stimulus is most likely to occur. The general finding has been that stimuli occurring in the cued location are processed faster and/or more completely and accurately than are stimuli that occur elsewhere, even when subjects don't move their eyes to the stimulus location, but only attend to it covertly.

These cuing paradigms, developed by Michael Posner and colleagues in the late 1970s at the University of Oregon, enabled the relative facilitation of processing due to attention to be characterized and quantified. In the standard version of this paradigm, subjects maintain visual fixation on a central point during a series of trials (**Figure 10.7A**). Each trial begins with a centrally pre-

Figure 10.7 A cuing paradigm for studying endogenous visual spatial attention.   (A) In this paradigm, a centrally presented instructional cue indicates where a target will most likely be presented. (B) Typical results show the benefits and costs in the reaction time for target detection after valid and invalid cuing, relative to the neutral-cue condition that provides no information as to the likely target location. (After Posner et al. 1980.)

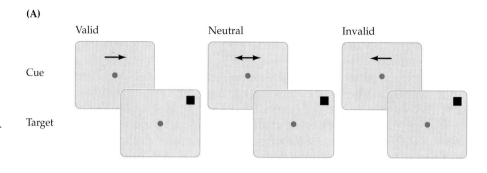

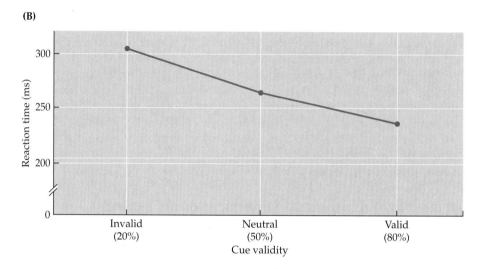

sented cue, such as an arrow pointing to the left or the right, or a letter or word cue, indicating where an upcoming target stimulus is most likely to occur. When the target appears, regardless of whether it occurs in the cued location, the subject must detect it or perform a discrimination task related to it, such as deciding whether it is a circle or an oval. In most of the trials (e.g., 80 percent of the time) the target is presented at the validly cued location, but sometimes it is presented at the other (invalidly cued) location. In addition, some trials may have neutral cues (e.g., a double arrow or a neutral letter) that provide no information about the likely location.

Figure 10.7B shows the typical results obtained in such cuing studies. Subjects are faster to respond to validly cued targets than to invalidly cued targets. In addition, relative to the neutral-cue condition, subjects respond more quickly to validly cued targets and more slowly to invalidly cued targets. In reports of these differences relative to the neutral-cue condition, the faster reaction times for validly cued trials are often described as reflecting the *benefits* of attention having been directed to the location where the target occurs and the slower reaction times for invalidly cued trials as reflecting the *costs* of attention having been directed to another location. Although the cue-to-target interval in such experiments is typically 800 milliseconds or so, varying the target occurrence time has shown that these effects can begin by about 300 milliseconds after the cue and can last for seconds afterwards.

The general view that has emerged from this sort of work is that the behavioral effects observed reflect the influence of attention on the processing of targets in the cued location. This facilitation is further assumed to arise from attentional modulation of the relevant sensory processing, in accord with early-selection models of attention (discussed earlier).

Exogenous attention

Although we voluntarily direct attention to events that interest us because of behavioral goals and other intrinsic factors, it is more often the case that stimuli arising from the environment attract our attention involuntarily. These involuntary shifts of attention, which define *exogenous attention*, occur continuously during our waking lives as we attend to different aspects of an ever-changing environment. Particularly salient stimuli, such as a loud noise, a flash of light, or a quick movement, typically trump whatever we happen to be attending to at the moment, but we are always attending to *something* (externally or internally) while we are awake, and all manner of stimulus characteristics and combinations can determine what attracts our attention at any given moment.

Like endogenous attention, exogenous attention has been studied in a variety of behavioral experiments. One commonly used approach has also employed a cuing paradigm, but one in which a sensory cue such as a flash of light is presented at a particular location shortly before a target stimulus is presented either in that location or elsewhere (**Figure 10.8**). In such circumstances, subjects are again quicker to respond to a target presented in the cued location compared to the uncued location. Subjects are also faster to respond to validly cued targets than to those following a neutral cue (e.g., when the light flash cues occur at both the target location and the other location), and slower to respond to targets at invalidly cued locations than in the neutral-cue condition. As in the example described in the previous section, these effects can be conceptualized in terms of benefits and costs.

On the face of it, this sort of paradigm and the behavioral effects observed are similar to studies of endogenous cuing. In both instances, a cue induces a shift in the focus of attention that facilitates the sensory processing of stimuli in the attended region, and diminishes the efficacy of processing elsewhere. Despite these similarities, however, endogenous and exogenous cuing have important functional differences. In endogenous cuing, information about the likelihood that the target stimulus will occur in the cued location is provided by prior knowledge (i.e., being informed that, or figuring out that, the target is likely to occur at the location indicated by the instructional cue). If an instructional cue provides no information about the likely location of the target, there is no behavioral enhancement. In contrast, exogenous attention is not driven by any explicit information about a likely target location. That is, even if an exogenous cue (e.g., a flash) is presented randomly in the two possible locations from trial to trial, and has no predictive value for where a tar-

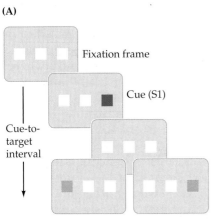

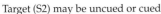

Target (S2) may be uncued or cued

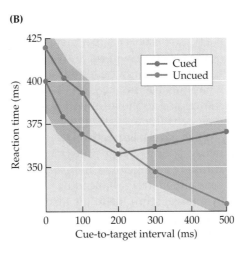

Figure 10.8 Exogenously triggered (reflexive) attention. (A) In this paradigm a brief flash is presented in one of two possible target locations, serving as an exogenous cue for a target that might follow at that location or at the other location. The occurrence of a target at the cued versus uncued location is random, with the probability at each location being 50 percent. (B) Shortly after the exogenous cue (green-shaded time period), stimulus processing at that location is facilitated, as indicated by faster response times to cued relative to uncued targets. At longer intervals (red-shaded time period), however, there is a decrement in performance for the cued targets, known as *inhibition of return*. (After Klein 2000; data from Posner and Cohen 1984.)

get will occur, the processing of a target in the cued location is nonetheless facilitated, presumably because the flash preceding the appearance of a target automatically draws attention to the cued location.

Endogenous and exogenous attentional cuing also differ in the time course of the modulation of target processing. For endogenously cued conditions, the improved processing of a validly cued target, as mentioned, begins about 300 milliseconds after the cue and can last for seconds afterward—in practice, for as long as subjects maintain their focus of attention on the instructed location. In contrast, exogenous cuing starts earlier and is short-lived, beginning by about 100 milliseconds after the cue and lasting only a few hundred milliseconds or so (see Figure 10.8). Moreover, at still longer intervals (about 400–800 milliseconds), the effect of the target validity reverses. That is, subjects are actually slower at responding to targets in the cued location compared to the uncued location—a phenomenon known as **inhibition of return** (**IOR**). Although the cause of this phenomenon is not understood, it has been suggested that IOR promotes exploration of new, previously unattended places or objects in the environment by slowing the return of attention to recently attended ones.

Despite these differences, some researchers take the view that endogenous and exogenous attention are not fundamentally different, but simply are different ways that attention can be used to biological advantage. For example, one could take the perspective that a shift of attention is always in response to a stimulus of some sort, whether the stimulus is an obvious change in the external environment, an instructional cue, or a series of internal thought processes related to behavioral goals. Thus, regardless of whether the attentional shift is due to endogenous or exogenous factors, the neurobiological mechanisms might be the same.

Arguing against this view as an adequate explanation of all the data are the different functional characteristics and time courses of effects on behavioral performance observed in exogenous and endogenous attentional shifts, which imply that at least some aspects of the attentional mechanisms in the two cases are not the same. A prudent view might be that these two types of attentional processes probably share some underlying neural components and mechanisms, while also possessing some unique ones. Moreover, even if some of the neural mechanisms are shared, they may be invoked somewhat differently, depending on the significance and context of the circumstances. In any event, these issues will arise again in the next two chapters.

Gaze-triggered shifts of attention

Some forms of exogenous cuing are particularly significant in everyday life and have thus been considered as important research topics in their own right. One such topic is the way attentional shifts can be triggered by social cues, such as by the gaze shifts observed in another individual. For example, if a person is observing a friend who suddenly looks to the right, the attention of the observer will be drawn in that direction, such that the observer may well turn his or her eyes to look in that direction as well, presumably to see what the friend may have noticed there. The biological advantages of responding to the information that others have gleaned and are revealing by their behavior are intuitively clear.

Such **gaze-triggered shifts of attention** have been studied recently in laboratory settings using cuing paradigms similar to those already described for studying endogenous and exogenous attention. For instance, a face with the gaze either straight ahead or to one side can be presented as a cue, followed by a target stimulus to the left or the right that subjects have been instructed to detect without moving their eyes from a central fixation point. As reported by Alan Kingstone at the University of British Columbia and Jon Driver at

University College London, subjects respond faster to targets on the side toward which the presented eye gaze was directed (validly cued trials). Subjects respond fastest on validly cued trials, slowest on invalidly cued trials, and at an intermediate level on neutral cues (e.g., when the presented gaze is straight ahead), thus showing both benefits and costs. Such gaze-based cuing of attention is also amenable to studies in monkeys, who show similar behavioral enhancement effects, as recently reported by Michael Platt and his colleagues at Duke.

Although gaze cues can lead to behavioral effects on target detection, revealing both costs and benefits relative to a neutral cue, the functional characteristics of the gaze-cued effects do not quite match those of either endogenous or exogenous cuing. In particular, the gaze-cue effects happen almost as quickly as with more conventional exogenous cues (e.g., a flash of light at a location), and are likewise relatively automatic or reflexive (i.e., they do not depend on providing any probability information). However, gaze-triggered effects do not show the same inhibition of return that characterizes exogenous cuing, and they tend to persist longer, as is the case with endogenously induced shifts of attention.

These additional observations again raise the idea that different types of attentional shifts may share some of the same basic neural mechanisms but are executed in different ways under circumstances that have different biological significance. In this case, observing the gaze shift of another human is likely to indicate something important enough to attend to quickly, for more time, and with less inhibition of return, as compared to something cued by a non-human stimulus.

Visual search

Another domain of attentional studies that has become a research topic in its own right is **visual search**. Often in everyday life we search the environment for something of particular interest by sequentially shifting our attention. For example, we may be looking for a friend in a crowd of people and having a tough time finding that person. Then we remember that our friend is wearing a green sweater, and we facilitate our search by looking around for green things, in particular for people in green sweaters or jackets. If only a few people are wearing green, the friend might easily be found by this search for green. But if a lot of people are wearing green (e.g., if it is St. Patrick's Day in Boston), we might need a different strategy.

The processes underlying visual search were studied in pioneering experiments carried out by Anne Treisman and colleagues beginning in the 1980s and have been examined by many others since. Such experiments typically employ a paradigm in which an array of multiple items is presented, and, like the example of the friend in the crowd, subjects are asked to find a particular item in the array. The item being searched for is the target; the other items in the array are called *distracters*. Manipulating the defining characteristics of the target and distracters allows the strategies used in visual search to be identified. For example, the array presented to subjects might consist of Ts and Os, each of which could be green or orange. If the task is to detect a green item and all the rest of the items are orange, the search is easy and the target is found quickly. Indeed, the target appears to "pop out" of the array (**Figure 10.9A**). Detecting a T in an array of Os is similarly easy and fast.

In these sorts of searches it does not seem to matter much how many distracters are in the array. Indeed, if the reaction times of detection are plotted against the number of distracters, the resulting function is essentially flat. Such results suggest that the detection of pop-out items does not require sequential shifts of attention to individual items, but rather that the task is

(A) Pop-out search

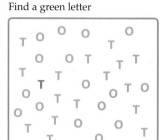

Find a green letter

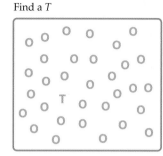

Find a *T*

(B) Conjunction search

Find a green *T*

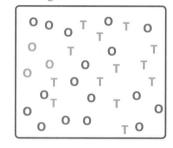

(C)

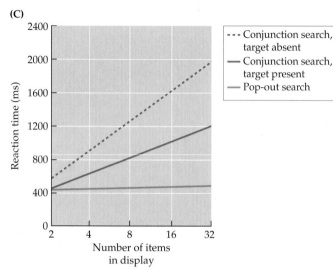

Figure 10.9 Attention in visual search paradigms.
(A) Each of these two examples of search arrays contains a pop-out target (one green item among orange items on the left, one *T* among *O*s on the right). (B) In this search array the target (a green *T*) is defined by a conjunction of two features (being green and being a *T*), each of which is present separately in various of the distracters but not together in any of them. (C) This idealized plot shows response times as a function of the number of distracters in a pop-out search as in (A), or a conjunction search as in (B). Pop-out searches are quick, and the reaction times do not vary with the number of distracters, suggesting that the search is done in a parallel fashion by taking in the array as a whole. In contrast, conjunction searches are slower, and the reaction time increases linearly as a function of the number of distracters, suggesting a serial search process. In accord with this interpretation, a conjunction search in which the target is absent (and the subject presses the appropriate button to note its absence) takes substantially longer. (After Treisman and Gelade 1980.)

accomplished by taking in the whole array more or less at once and processing all the items in parallel. In this sense, the salient nature of the pop-out target, like an exogenous cue, tends to attract attention to that location and item more or less automatically.

In contrast to pop-out stimuli, detection of a target item defined by a *conjunction* of features shows quite different characteristics. For example, consider trying to find a green *T* in a display like the one shown in **Figure 10.9B**, which contains both *T*s and *O*s and both green and orange items. Even if the display contains only one target (e.g., only one green *T*), that target is neither the only green item among orange ones nor the only *T* among *O*s. Thus, it does not pop out and is not easily or quickly found. Moreover, whereas detection time for a pop-out target is not influenced by how many distracters are in the display, the speed of finding a conjunction target is clearly influenced by the number of distracters, increasing linearly as more distracter items are added to the display (**Figure 10.9C**).

This behavioral pattern in visual searches for conjunction targets suggests that a focused form of attention is required to find the target. As common sense suggests, finding the target in this circumstance requires that attention be serially directed to the various items individually to determine which has the feature combination of interest. Thus, the increased reaction time as a function of the number of distracter items is presumably due to the time required to perform this process for more individual items. Moreover, when subjects have to press one button when the target is present in a display and another when the target is absent, the slope of the search function is greatly increased, differing by about a factor of two (see Figure 10.9C). One explanation proposes that on target-absent trials, attention has to be explicitly directed to every item in the display to determine that none have the right conjunction of features. In contrast, in target-present trials, on average, only half of the items will need to be scrutinized before the target is found, thereby yielding a search function with roughly half the slope of the function in the target-absent trials.

These sorts of results led Treisman and Garry Gelade at the University of British Columbia to develop a model of visual attention known as **feature integration theory**. The model proposes that the perceptual system is organized as a set of feature maps. In vision, these maps would represent characteristics such as color, form, motion, or texture—each map providing information about the locations in the visual field of that particular feature. According to this theory, the processing in these feature maps is done early and in parallel, consistent with the fact that searches for an item with a unique feature are not influenced by the number of distracters. In contrast, in conjunction searches information from separate feature maps must be compared or combined in some way, consistent with the fact that this type of search takes longer and requires that focused attention be shifted in a serial manner across the array.

In addition, Treisman and colleagues proposed that the focusing of attention is also important in **binding** perceptual features into coherent representations of objects (see Chapter 4). This view is supported by studies of the tendency of subjects to report **illusory conjunctions** of features in a display. For example, subjects might report seeing a red *O* in a briefly displayed multi-item array containing red items and *O*-shaped items but not actually any red *O*s. The key finding is that subjects are more likely to report illusory conjunctions among unattended items than among attended ones. This result accords with the idea that focused attention is required to find conjunction items in an array and thus must be shifted serially to each item in turn, as well as the idea that such focused attention helps bind the different features of an object into a coherent whole.

An important caveat about these models of visual search is that they suggest a dichotomy between the search characteristics for detecting stimuli that pop out (flat search functions and parallel sensory processing of the display items across the display) and stimuli that do not (positive-slope search functions, serial attentional shifts, and serial sensory processing of the display items). However, other research has indicated that there is not such a clear dichotomy in processing visual search stimuli. Thus, for some stimulus features the search functions have a quite shallow slope but are not completely flat, indicating a modest dependence on the number of distracter items. In addition, searches for certain types of target items in displays can initially require a degree of serial attention and serial processing, but after extensive training they show relatively flat search functions characteristic of pop-out. In short, the data accumulated in visual search studies suggests a more complex situation in which attention and its influence on sensory processing are more flexible than these initial models implied.

Other models of search have been proposed to deal with some of the limitations of the feature integration theory, in particular the fact that a conjunction search is often more efficient than this theory would predict. One such model, proposed by Jeremy Wolfe while at Harvard Medical School, is known as **guided search**. In this scheme, two basic components determine the allocation of attention: an activation map driven by stimulus factors, and an activation map driven by top-down influence from higher-level factors and behavioral goals. In this conception, visual inputs are first filtered by different feature-tuned subsystems to generate the sorts of maps suggested in Treisman and Gelade's feature integration theory. The activation intensity of items within each stimulus-driven feature map is proposed to depend on the local difference of the item in that feature dimension relative to neighboring areas in the visual field—a concept similar to what have been termed **saliency maps** in other models. The intensity associated with each item in the various top-down activation maps is further postulated to depend on prior knowledge; items that share more similar feature values to the target to be searched for will thus be more strongly activated. The summed effect of the bottom-up and top-down activation maps forms a general activation map that reflects the probability of the target presence across the search space. The combined map then "guides" the search, in that attention is first allocated to the highest value within the general activation map, then reallocated to the second highest activation value if the highest value is not the target, and so on. This allocation and reallocation of attention is imagined to continue until the target is found (or it is determined that a target is not present).

Whatever the validity of these several models of visual search is, they emphasize that attention can be directed and allocated in different ways, employed in a flexible manner according to the circumstances and experience of the individual. Equally clear is that the conclusions that can be drawn from behavior alone are inevitably limited. Many of these concepts and controversies will be considered further in the following chapters in the context of how brain-based methods have helped clarify these issues.

Covert versus overt visual attention

Many studies of visual spatial attention considered earlier in the chapter have focused on the processes related to **covert attention**—that is, attending to, or shifting attention to, a location in the visual field different from where the eyes are fixated. One of the major reasons for the widespread use of this paradigm is technical. If a subject fixates on a central location and stimuli are presented elsewhere in the visual field, the experimenter can compare the behavioral responses to attended and unattended stimuli with no confounding change in the physical stimulation received by the subject. If the eyes are moved around while the stimuli are being presented, it is not possible to maintain control over the exact stimulus input that a subject will be processing.

Although people often practice covert attention to locations or items in the environment, we typically move our eyes to look directly at objects of interest; that is, we make shifts in **overt attention**. How, then, are covert attention and this more overt form of attention related? One possibility is that overt shifts of attention are preceded by covert attentional shifts to that location; however, clear evidence for this idea has been hard to obtain. Nonetheless, covert attentional shifts are generally believed to be closely related to overt shifts. Indeed, it has been proposed that covert visual attention coevolved with the gaze control system in humans and other primates, perhaps because of the resultant advantages for such social species (e.g., observing a potential mate or competitor without looking at them directly). In any event, the relationship between overt and covert attention will be considered further in Chapters 11 and 12, which describe studies of the neurobiological underpinnings of attention.

Attentional Systems in the Brain

Cognitive psychologists have schematically represented the cognitive architecture of attention generally along the lines depicted in Figure 10.4C, at least in regard to its role in allocating resources for sensory and perceptual processing. In this conception, "higher" levels of the system are able to modulate stimulus processing at various possible lower levels. In translating such a scheme to a neuroscience perspective, the study of attention can be approached from two major directions: (1) investigating the ways in which the neural processing of stimuli are modulated by attention under different circumstances, and (2) determining the sets of higher-level control regions of the brain that coordinate this modulation, and the mechanisms by which they do so. Most brain-based studies of attention tend to roughly follow this general distinction, as summarized in the following sections.

Studying the effects of attention on stimulus processing

Much of attention research has focused on the first of the two main aspects just noted—namely, assessing the effects of attention on stimulus processing. It is logical to hypothesize that attentional modulation of stimulus processing would be reflected in dynamic alterations in the neural activity evoked by stimuli in particular regions of the brain. For sensory systems, this means modulation at one or more levels of the sensory processing streams described in Unit II and represented generically by the yellow arrows in **Figure 10.10**.

If such modulation happened at a relatively early stage in a sensory processing pathway, this effect would presumably be apparent in the modulation of activity in the brainstem, thalamus, or primary and secondary sensory cortices, and it would occur relatively early in the sequence of electrophysiological activity initiated by the presentation of a stimulus. The occurrence of attentional influence at a later stage would presumably be reflected by altered activity in the higher-order association cortices somewhat later in the processing sequence. Of course, other patterns of altered activity in time might be observed—for example, effects of attention occurring later but at lower-level brain regions—but most work has been predicated on these general expectations.

As described earlier in the chapter, studies of attention using behavioral measures have provided insight into many attentional phenomena, in particular the role of attention in controlling the degree to which sensory events are ultimately processed, as well as some of the limitations of processing capacity. These studies have also provided some insight into the levels at which attention can affect stimulus processing. Behavioral studies, however, have depended on relatively indirect approaches, such as the types of interactions that are observed during dual task paradigms or the level of knowledge that subjects can later report concerning the content of the information in unattended channels.

As described in Chapter 3, the ability to measure brain activity while subjects (human or animal) are engaged in cognitive tasks has evolved rapidly in recent years. The methods now available provide an unprecedented ability to directly assess the influence of attention on sensory and perceptual processing by monitoring neural activity in increasingly accurate ways. These method-

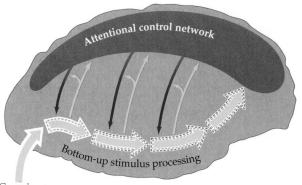

Generic
sensory input

Figure 10.10 Attentional functions in the brain. In this schematic representation, the yellow arrows indicate a generic sensory input and processing system, and the blue region and arrows represent an attentional control network—broadly construed—and the associated control signals. The dotted orange and red lines around the yellow processing arrows are meant to indicate modulation of the stimulus processing stream by the putative control network. The yellow and blue vertical arrows indicate interactions between the sensory processing and control networks at various levels.

ologies now provide the ability to delineate the timing, brain areas, and level at which these influences can occur under different circumstances. Moreover, these approaches can also reveal something about the neurobiological mechanisms of attentional effects on stimulus processing. For example, if attention affects processing of a stimulus in the relevant sensory cortex, does it do so by enhancing the gain of the evoked response, by extending the duration of its processing in an area, or by narrowing the tuning curves of the neurons involved?

By the same token, approaches that measure brain activity can directly assess the characteristics of the neural activity elicited by stimuli that are unattended and task-irrelevant, even when no behavioral response is required or given for them. In any case, all these modulatory effects on stimulus processing presumably underlie the effects of attention on performance observed in behavioral studies (e.g., altered reaction times or altered ability to report stimulus content later). The investigation of the effects of attention on the processing of stimuli using these neurally based techniques is the subject of Chapter 11.

Studying the control of attention in the brain

The other major goal in studies of attention using more direct, brain-based methods is to understand the mechanisms by which these attentional modulations of stimulus processing are brought about and coordinated in the brain and to examine the idea that specific sets of brain regions might define an attentional control network (see Figure 10.10). As described in Chapter 12, these studies have indicated that some higher-level brain areas are indeed involved in attentional control, including relatively specific regions in the frontal and parietal cortices. For example, patients with brain damage in parietal cortex, particularly in the right hemisphere, show major deficiencies in the control of attention. In accord with these brain lesion findings, neuroimaging studies have indicated that various regions of the frontal and parietal cortex are activated during tasks involving attentional control. Finally, single-unit recording studies in awake, behaving animals have also implicated these regions in the control and maintenance of attention. Taken together, these studies suggest that a network of frontal and parietal regions is involved in attentional control of sensory processing and perception, presumably by regulating stimulus processing at various levels in the sensory and association cortices.

In addition to descending modulatory influences directed from higher-order to relatively lower-order brain areas, other attentional mechanisms have been proposed for the control of stimulus processing, such as those involving dynamic interactions between different brain regions related to the importance or salience of stimuli arising from the environment. These other proposed mechanisms for managing our attentional resources within a limited-capacity processing system are also taken up in Chapter 12.

A More General View of Attention

This overview has considered attention mainly in terms of the allocation of processing resources to different stimuli in the environment, reflecting the fact that most work on attention to date has focused on the role of attention in sensory and perceptual processing. The role of attention in stimulus processing is thus the major focus of this unit. From a broader perspective, however, attention can be viewed as determining the allocation of processing resources for whatever cognitive functions are needed from one moment to the next. For example, in one circumstance we might need to direct attention to performing a motor action—especially one that is not well practiced—in order to perform it properly. In other circumstances we might need to attend to retrieving the memory of a specific event or to manipulating a sequence in working memory, or we might need to attend to an emotional feeling or state, to an ethical decision, or to the nature of an abstract problem in algebra.

All these routine circumstances can be viewed as requiring attention to focus limited cognitive resources selectively to accomplish our behavioral goals. Thus, attention is pertinent to the organization and control of motor functions described in Unit III, to key aspects of memory discussed in Unit V, to the executive functions reviewed in Unit VIII, and in some way to the topics covered in virtually every other unit in this book. The reason for the limited discussion of the role of attention in these other domains is that they have been much less studied thus far.

Summary

1. Attention is a fundamental cognitive function familiar to everyone in daily experience. The nature of attention in more formal terms was initially explored by cognitive psychologists using behavioral measures such as reaction time, discrimination accuracy, and the ability to report the content of attended versus unattended stimulus streams.

2. Early work quantitatively established that attention is limited in its capacity, confirming the commonsense intuition that it is difficult to attend to more than one thing at a time, and that if one is asked to do so, performance deteriorates. Other studies have investigated the different ways that attention is induced to shift to new locations or stimulus streams in the environment, and the behavioral consequences of attention being focused on specific locations or stimuli.

3. The ability to ascertain how, when, and where attention operates in the central nervous system is rather limited when using studies based on behavioral measures alone. Understanding of both the psychological and the neural mechanisms of attention has been greatly advanced in recent years by adding to behavioral approaches the various cognitive neuroscience methods now available, including the direct recording of brain activity while human subjects or other animals are engaged in attentional tasks. In addition, important insights about attentional mechanisms have been provided by the effects of specific types of brain lesions studied in patients.

Additional Reading

Reviews

KAHNEMAN, D. AND A. TREISMAN (1984) Changing views of attention and automaticity. In *Varieties of Attention*, R. Parasuraman and D. R. Davies (eds.). New York: Academic Press, pp. 29–61.

KLEIN, R. M. (2000) Inhibition of return. *Trends Cogn. Sci.* 4: 138–147.

LOGAN, G. (2004) Cumulative progress in formal theories of attention. *Annu. Rev. Psychol.* 55: 207–234.

Important Original Papers

CHERRY, E. C. (1953) Some experiments on the recognition of speech, with one and with two ears. *J. Acoust. Soc. Am.* 25: 975–979.

DEANER, R. O. AND M. L. PLATT (2003) Reflexive social attention in monkeys and humans. *Curr. Biol.* 13: 1609–1613.

DEUTSCH, J. A. AND D. DEUTSCH (1963) Attention: Some theoretical considerations. *Psychol. Rev.* 70: 80–90.

DRIVER, J., G. DAVIS, P. RICCIARDELLI, P. KIDD, E. MAXWELL AND S. BARON-COHEN (1999) Gaze perception triggers reflexive visuospatial orienting. *Vis. Cogn.* 6: 509–540.

ERIKSEN, B. A. AND C. W. ERIKSEN (1974) Effects of noise letters upon the identification of a target letter in a nonsearch task. *Percept. Psychophys.* 16: 143–149.

FRIESEN, C. K. AND A. KINGSTONE (1998) The eyes have it! Reflexive orienting is triggered by nonpredictive gaze. *Psychon. Bull. Rev.* 5: 490–495.

LAVIE, N. (1995) Perceptual load as a necessary condition for selective attention. *J. Exp. Psychol. Hum. Percept. Perform.* 21: 451–468.

MORAY, N. (1959) Attention in dichotic listening: Affective cues and the influence of instructions. *Q. J. Exp. Psychol.* 11: 56–60.

PASHLER, H. (1994) Overlapping mental operations in serial performance with preview. *Q. J. Exp. Psychol.* 47: 161–191.

POSNER, M. I. AND Y. COHEN (1984) Components of visual orienting. In *Attention and Performance*, Vol. 10: *Control of Language Processes*, H. Bouma and D. Bouwhuis (eds.). London: Erlbaum, pp. 531–556.

POSNER, M. I., C. R. R. SNYDER AND B. J. DAVIDSON (1980) Attention and the detection of signals. *J. Exp. Psychol. Gen.* 109: 160–174.

RAYMOND, J. E., K. L. SHAPIRO AND K. M. ARNELL (1992) Temporary suppression of visual processing in an RSVP task: An attentional blink? *J. Exp. Psychol. Hum. Percept. Perform.* 18: 849–860.

TREISMAN, A. (1960) Contextual cues in selective listening. *Q. J. Exp. Psychol.* 12: 242–248.

TREISMAN, A. AND G. GELADE (1980) A feature integration theory of attention. *Cogn. Psychol.* 12: 97–136.

WELFORD, A. T. (1952) The "psychological refractory period" and the timing of high speed performance: A review and a theory. *Br. J. Psychol.* 43: 2–19.

WOLFE, J. (1994) Guided search 2.0: A revised model of visual search. *Psychol. Bull. Rev.* 1: 202–238.

YANTIS, S. AND J. JONIDES (1990) Abrupt visual onsets and selective attention: Voluntary versus automatic allocation. *J. Exp. Psychol. Hum. Percept. Perform.* 16: 121–134.

Books

BROADBENT, D. E. (1958) *Perception and Communication.* London: Pergamon.

JAMES, W. (1890) *Principles of Psychology,* Vol. 1. New York: Holt.

PASHLER, H., ED. (1998) *Attention.* East Sussex, UK: Psychology Press.

POSNER, M. I. (1978) *Chronometric Explorations of Mind.* Hillsdale; NJ: Lawrence Erlbaum.

11

Effects of Attention on Stimulus Processing

Introduction

As described in the previous chapter, studies using measures of behavioral performance such as reaction time and accuracy have investigated the brain's limited capacity to process information, as well as the role of attention in selectively allocating these limited processing resources. Some of the major questions in such studies concerned the level at which attention affects stimulus processing, and the type of information that attentional selection affects. Behavioral studies, however, provide only indirect insights into these issues. As described in Chapter 3, the ability to measure brain activity directly while humans or experimental animals are engaged in cognitive tasks has greatly enhanced the amount and quality of evidence that can be brought to bear in answering such questions. As a result, much more can now be said about the timing and anatomical sites at which attentional influences on stimulus processing occur under different circumstances, as well as about the specific modulatory mechanisms themselves.

Historically, brain-based studies have focused on the effects of attention on the processing of sensory stimuli, in particular in the auditory and visual modalities. Keep in mind, however, that the role of attention in directing cognitive resources is not limited to stimulus processing; we can and do routinely attend to motor processes, to memories, and to internally generated neural processes such as trains of thought. However, what has been determined in the studies of attention in the processing of sensory stimuli is likely to represent principles that apply to these other domains as well. Regardless, these investigations of attention to sensory stimuli can be broadly divided into studies of the effects of spatial and nonspatial attention. The chapter begins with an examination of the effects of auditory spatial attention on auditory stimulus processing, followed by a parallel discussion of the effects of visual spatial attention on visual stimulus processing. Next the discussion turns to the effects of specifically attending to nonspatial stimulus attributes, and finally to the effects of attention across sensory modalities.

The Effects of Auditory Spatial Attention

As discussed in Chapter 10, *auditory selective attention* is invoked when two or more streams of auditory information are occurring simultaneously and processing resources need to be selectively focused on one of them. In most natural circumstances, streams of auditory stimuli—such as verbal streams coming from different people in a room—are differentiated by the fact that the sources are separated spatially, as well as by physical qualities such as pitch or timbre. In the laboratory, experimenters can simulate such circumstances by presenting sound stimuli from two or more speakers at different locations around a subject, whose task is to direct attention to one source in particular. In most studies of auditory attention, however, the two streams of auditory stimuli have been spatially segregated by being delivered separately to the two ears, as described in Chapter 10.

The relatively few studies in which auditory attention has been directed toward locations in space have generally shown similar effects on stimulus-evoked neural activity as those involving attention to one ear versus the other (although future research is likely to show some differences in mechanisms). Thus, for present purposes these studies are grouped together as forms of auditory attention that are predominantly spatial.

Electrophysiological studies of the effects of auditory spatial attention

A major question raised in Chapter 10 concerned the stage (or stages) of stimulus processing at which attentional mechanisms come into play. Event-related potentials (ERPs) that extract specific responses from the ongoing scalp EEG by time-locked averaging have been particularly informative in addressing this question because of their temporal precision. Figure 11.1 shows a typical ERP response to a tone stimulus, which can be broken down into three main phases.

During the first 10 milliseconds after onset of the tone, a number of small wavelets known as the **brainstem-evoked responses** are observed (**Figure 11.1A**); these wavelets reflect activity in the auditory brainstem nuclei as the sound stimulus information reaches them via the auditory afferent pathway (see Chapter 6). The next phase (10–50 ms), the so-called **midlatency responses** (**Figure 11.1B**), is thought to reflect mainly the early evoked activity in auditory cortex, as indicated by intracranial recordings and ERP source analysis (see Chapter 3). This activity is followed by a series of longer-latency waves, sometimes called the *late waves*, which continue for several hundred milliseconds (**Figure 11.1C**). Late waves are thought to reflect longer-latency activity in the secondary and association auditory cortices. Recording these responses while subjects are engaged in attentional tasks can provide a good idea of the timing and level at which attention affects auditory stimulus processing.

Analyzing the responses to spatially segregated auditory stimulus streams that are selectively attended (**Figure 11.2A**) reveals the usefulness of this approach. In this paradigm, monaural tone pips are delivered to the left and right ears in random order, with an occasional deviant tone (e.g., slightly fainter or of a slightly different pitch) in each stream. On half of the trial blocks, the task is to attend closely to all the sounds in one ear in order to detect the occasional deviant stimulus in that ear, while ignoring all sounds presented to the other ear. In the other half of the trial blocks the subjects attend to the other ear to detect targets in that ear. In this **attentional stream paradigm**, introduced by Steve Hillyard and his colleagues at UC San Diego in the early 1970s, the stimuli are identical in both attention conditions; the only difference is the covert focusing of attention toward either one input

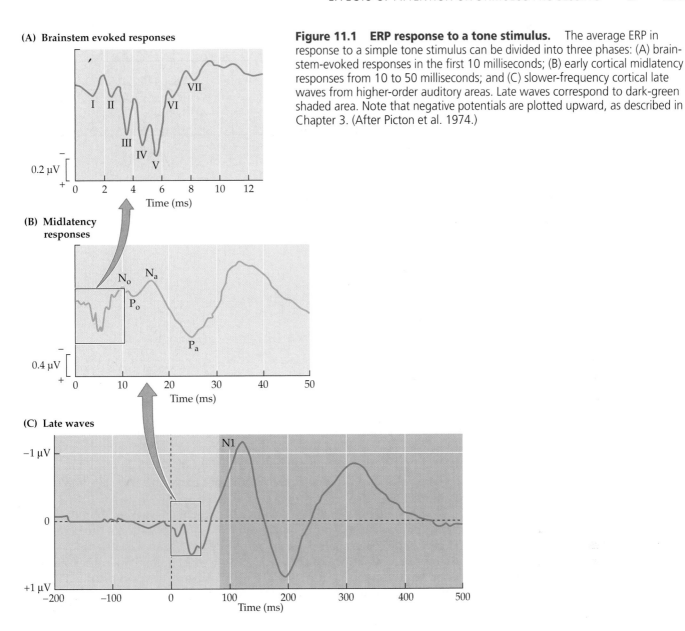

(A) Brainstem evoked responses

(B) Midlatency responses

(C) Late waves

Figure 11.1 ERP response to a tone stimulus. The average ERP in response to a simple tone stimulus can be divided into three phases: (A) brainstem-evoked responses in the first 10 milliseconds; (B) early cortical midlatency responses from 10 to 50 milliseconds; and (C) slower-frequency cortical late waves from higher-order auditory areas. Late waves correspond to dark-green shaded area. Note that negative potentials are plotted upward, as described in Chapter 3. (After Picton et al. 1974.)

channel or the other. The ERP responses to the same physical stimulus when it was attended versus when it was unattended can then be compared.

Using this paradigm, Hillyard's group showed that a specific ERP component known as the **auditory N1** (a negative-polarity sensory wave occurring about 100 milliseconds after a sound) was larger when the tone stimulus was attended (**Figure 11.2B**). This increase of the N1 with attention was observed for *all* stimuli in the attended ear (i.e., for both the nontarget stimuli and the deviant target stimuli). On the basis of its relatively early timing, the investigators concluded that this effect provided neural evidence for an early-selection mechanism of attention (see Chapter 10).

In addition to eliciting an enhanced N1, the detected deviant targets in the attended ear elicited a large, longer-latency, positive wave known as the **P300**, peaking at about 300 to 400 milliseconds over posterior parietal areas (**Figure 11.2C**). This later separation of activity within the attended channel between the target and nontarget responses—the so-called **P300** (or **P3**) **effect**—was proposed to reflect the late selection of the target occurring at longer latencies.

Figure 11.2 Early and late selection during auditory attention. (A) The auditory attentional stream paradigm is a means for studying the mechanisms of auditory selective attention. Asterisks indicate tones that deviate slightly from the rest of the stimuli in that stream in some feature, such as loudness or pitch. (B) The effect of auditory attention on the N1 wave at 100 milliseconds in the auditory ERP is thought to reflect a relatively early attentional selection. (C) The P300 effect elicited only by detected targets in the attended channel is thought to reflect a late-selection process to distinct elements within the attended channel. (B,C after Hillyard et al. 1973.)

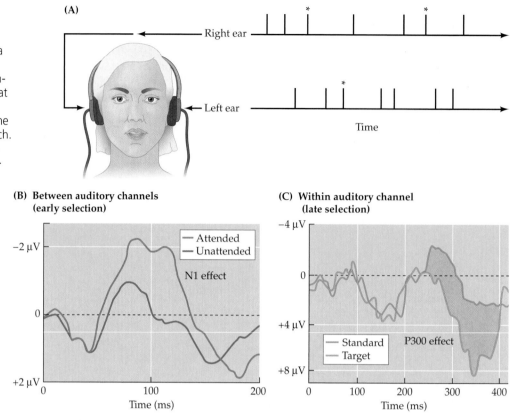

These results thus provide evidence for both early and late selection during auditory attention.

The N1 enhancement just described can begin as early as 70 milliseconds after stimulus onset. Intracranial studies in human patients during neurosurgery and source analysis of human ERPs have shown that sensory signals reach primary auditory cortex as early as 15 to 20 milliseconds after stimulus onset (see Chapter 6). Thus, the lack of an attentional effect prior to 70 milliseconds suggested that all the sensory processing prior to about 70 milliseconds after stimulus onset, including cortical processing from 20 to 70 milliseconds, is immune to attentional influence.

To address the question of early attentional influences more closely, Marty Woldorff, Hillyard, and colleagues at UC San Diego used a modified version of the auditory stream paradigm that required subjects to attend more strongly. In particular, they presented stimuli at substantially faster rates (making it extremely difficult to attend to both channels), and they made the deviant discrimination task in the attended channel more demanding. Despite these greater demands on attention, the brainstem-evoked responses remained unaffected (**Figure 11.3A**), thus arguing against any brainstem-level gating as a mechanism of selective auditory attention (**Box 11A**). However, a slightly later effect was observed—an enhanced positive wave at 20 to 50 milliseconds for the attended compared to the unattended stimuli, which was then followed by the longer-latency N1 attention effect (**Figure 11.3B**). Because the latency of this **P20–50 attention effect** coincides with the onset of the initial activity in auditory sensory cortex, this result provided strong neural evidence that early attentional selection can occur at this stage of sensory processing.

Although these studies demonstrated early effects of attention on sensory processing, the precise neuroanatomical sources of these effects were not

(A) No effect on attention on BERs

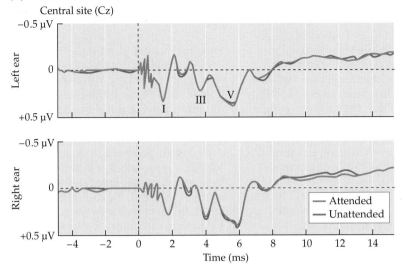

(B) P20–50 attention effect (20–50 ms)

Event-related potentials

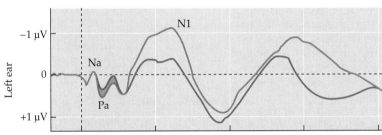

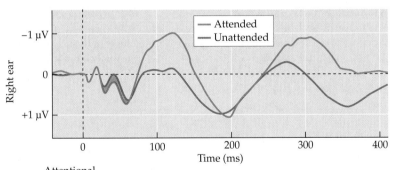

Attentional difference waves (attended minus unattended)

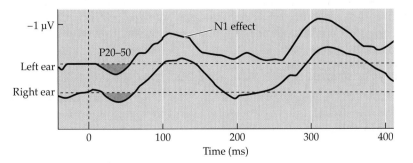

(C) MEG localization of P20–50 attention effect

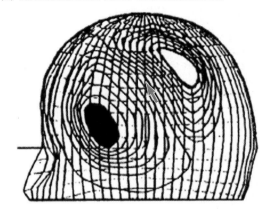

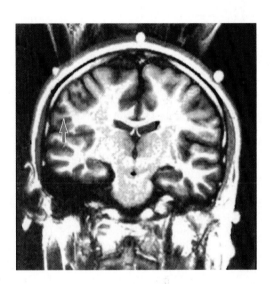

Figure 11.3 Early auditory attention effects during a dichotic listening experiment. (A) Even during very strongly focused auditory spatial attention, no modulation of the brainstem-evoked potentials (BERs) in the first 10 milliseconds is observed. (B) However, an early cortical effect is reflected as enhanced activity from 20 to 50 milliseconds for attended relative to unattended tones (the P20–50 attention effect). (C) Using MEG, the P20–50 effect was indeed localized as a local dipolar source (red arrow) in primary auditory cortical areas on the lower bank of the Sylvian fissure. (A,B after Woldorff et al. 1987; C after Woldorff et al. 1993.)

◼ BOX 11A Peripheral Gating

In terms of neural mechanisms, the most extreme form that early attentional selection could take is termed *peripheral gating*, in which top-down neural influences can gate or attenuate sensory input at the earliest levels of a sensory system, including the level of the sensory receptors. The possibility that attention can affect stimulus processing at such an early level seems particularly plausible in the auditory system because of well-established descending pathways that could, in principle, mediate such early effects. In particular, the auditory system has a descending pathway that parallels the ascending pathways all the way to the cochlea. (Note that in the visual system, by contrast, the descending pathways from higher centers run only as far peripherally as the thalamus.) The last component of this descending pathway, the *olivo-cochlear bundle* (*OCB*), runs from the superior olivary complex in the brainstem to both the cochlea and the cochlear nucleus (the first relay center in the auditory afferent pathway; see Chapter 6).

Robert Galambos, working at Walter Reed Hospital in Washington DC, showed in the 1950s that stimulation of the OCB has an inhibitory influence on the stimulus-evoked activity of the ascending auditory nerves from the cochlea carrying auditory sensory in-

formation. Moreover, electrical stimulation in secondary auditory cortex can activate the descending pathway, including structures as peripheral as the OCB. Thus, the auditory system has a set of neural substrates by which higher levels of the brain could, in principle, modulate sensory input at the level of the sensory receptors themselves.

Following the discovery of this descending auditory pathway, early animal experiments in the 1950s tested whether there might be a peripheral gating mechanism during auditory attention. In one such experiment, the attentional state of a cat was manipulated while neural activity in response to auditory stimulation was recorded from the cochlear nucleus. The neural responses to the sounds were substantially smaller when the cat was attending visually to a mouselike doll, relative to the responses when the mouse stimulus was absent and the cat was simply relaxing.

Although this result appeared to provide evidence for peripheral gating, subsequent work showed the study to be flawed. In particular, when the cat was visually attending to the dangling mouse, the ears (which cats can move to better capture sound stimuli coming from different directions) were directed toward the mouse

and thus away from the auditory test stimuli, resulting in a reduction of the sound input intensity. With proper controls that eliminated this confounding factor, the effect was also eliminated. Since this false start in the 1950s, numerous other attempts to demonstrate peripheral gating as a mechanism for selective attention have also generally failed. As described in the text, the earliest effect of auditory attention reliably observed has been at the level of the initial activity in primary auditory cortex. The descending OCB influence seems likely to serve mainly as a mechanism for modulating the dynamic range of the cochlear responses, rather than for purposes related to selective attention.

References

GALAMBOS, R. (1956) Suppression of auditory nerve activity by stimulation of efferent fibers to cochlea. *J. Neurophysiol.* 19: 424–437.

HERNANDEZ-PEON, R., H. SCHERRER AND M. JOUVET (1956) Modification of electric activity in cochlear nucleus during attention in unanesthetized cats. *Science* 123: 331–332.

WORDEN, F. G. (1966) Attention and auditory electrophysiology. In *Progress in Physiological Psychology*, Vol. 1, F. Stellar and J. M. Sprague (eds.). New York: Academic Press, pp. 45–116.

clear. Follow-up studies by these researchers using MEG indicated that the magnetic counterparts of the P20–50 and the N1 attention effects both derived from low-level auditory cortical areas on the lower bank of the Sylvian fissure, with the P20–50 effect likely arising from primary auditory cortex (**Figure 11.3C**) and the N1 effect from nearby secondary auditory cortex. In any event, this combination of results strongly supported the view that attention can affect stimulus processing in the sensory cortices very early in the auditory input stream.

Neuroimaging studies of the effects of auditory spatial attention

Compared to electrophysiological techniques, functional neuroimaging has been used far less for studies of auditory attention in humans. Several PET studies in the 1990s showed that attending versus not attending to auditory stimuli resulted in overall enhanced activity in the auditory cortical regions on the lower bank of the Sylvian fissure. Other studies using dichotic listening paradigms similar to the ones described in the preceding section showed that attending to input to one ear versus the other enhanced activity more in contralateral than in ipsilateral auditory cortex. Both of these results accord with the ERP and MEG studies already discussed in showing that auditory attention influences sensory processing activity in low-level auditory cortex.

The use of fMRI to study auditory attention has also been limited, especially compared with its more extensive use in studies of visual attention. A major reason is that the rapid switching of the magnetic-field gradients in magnetic resonance imaging is acoustically noisy, thus tending to interfere with the auditory stimuli of the study. However, improvements in fMRI methodology have enabled its more effective use for auditory studies, thus allowing its higher spatial resolution to be brought to bear on mechanisms of auditory attention.

For example, an fMRI study by Christopher Petkov, David Woods, and colleagues at UC Davis showed that attention tends to modulate activity in specific regions of the auditory cortex. In particular, attention had relatively little effect on stimulus processing in primary auditory cortex, the neuroimaging effects appearing to reflect mainly the modulation of activity in the surrounding auditory belt areas (**Figure 11.4**). The effect in the secondary auditory cortex areas most likely corresponds to the large N1 effect, described earlier, that is often observed in auditory attention studies. The considerably smaller P20–50, which is likely to derive from primary auditory cortex, may not last long enough or be large enough to produce a good fMRI signal.

Animal studies of the effects of auditory spatial attention

Relatively little neurally based research on auditory attention has been carried out in experimental animals, especially compared to studies of visual attention in animals, which will be described shortly. The reason for this deficiency is that such research must be performed in awake, behaving animals—typically monkeys—and it is considerably harder to train them to carry out auditory attention tasks than visual ones. The research that has been done, however, supports the conclusions drawn from the ERP and imaging work, suggesting

(A) Stimulus-dependent activation

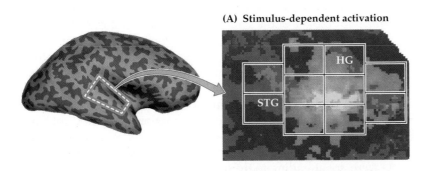

(B) Attention-related modulation

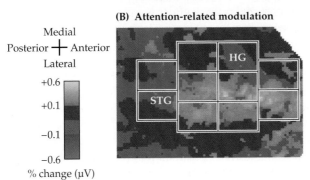

Figure 11.4 Effects of auditory attention on processing in the auditory cortical regions. In this fMRI study, the effects of attention were seen mainly in the auditory belt areas surrounding the primary auditory cortex. (A) Stimulus-dependent activation is observed in both the primary auditory cortex in Heschl's gyrus (HG) and the more lateral auditory belt areas in the superior temporal gyrus (STG). (B) Attention-related modulations were seen mainly in the more lateral belt areas and not in the primary auditory cortex. (From Petkov et al. 2004.)

that the same attentional effects occur across species, and that they can also be observed at the level of (single) neurons. An early electrophysiological study of auditory attention in monkeys in a simplified dichotic listening paradigm indicated that attended stimuli produced larger single-unit responses in auditory cortex as early as 20 milliseconds after stimulus onset. These results fit well with the P20–50 electrophysiological effects described earlier in this chapter in human dichotic listening studies. Concordantly, more recent studies have shown that localizing sound, compared to simply detecting it, results in enhanced firing of single units in auditory cortex.

The effects of auditory spatial attention on auditory feature processing

Although these results demonstrated that attention to a spatially segregated auditory stimulus stream can increase the amplitude of evoked neural activity early in auditory processing, another question concerns the consequences of such enhancement for later processing stages. For example, does this early enhancement lead to an improved ability to perform sensory discrimination of the auditory features within the attended channel? If so, one would predict a greater differentiation in neural processing between stimulus types having different feature characteristics in an attended versus an unattended auditory channel.

In pursuing this issue in a dichotic listening paradigm with occasional deviant stimuli, another ERP component, called the **mismatch negativity** (**MMN**), has been especially useful. Deviant auditory stimuli in a stream of otherwise identical sounds produce a negative wave peaking at about 150 to 200 milliseconds after the deviant stimulus occurs. This MMN effect, first noted by Risto Näätänen and colleagues at Helsinki University in the late 1970s, is elicited by deviations in any basic auditory feature (e.g., pitch, intensity, location), and source analysis has confirmed that it derives mainly from auditory cortex. Moreover, the MMN becomes larger as the feature deviation increases, and the threshold of deviation that produces this neural response is about the same as the perceptual threshold at which subjects discriminate the deviant stimulus.

Näätänen theorized that this response reflects the outcome of a series of processes in which a template of the standard repeated stimulus, including all its features, is established and stored in the brain. Each auditory stimulus is automatically compared to this template; if it doesn't match the template in any of its fundamental sensory features, a mismatch response is triggered and reflected in the MMN wave. Accordingly, the MMN has been used as a marker of auditory feature analysis, with its amplitude reflecting the extent or quality of the feature discrimination (i.e., the discrimination of the deviant from the standard stimuli).

Early studies by Näätänen's group reported that the MMN was elicited when subjects were not attending to the auditory stimuli, and that the amplitude of this feature deviance effect was not affected by attention. These observations were interpreted as suggesting that the processes causing the MMN (auditory feature analysis, template making, comparison processes, and ultimately the mismatch activity) were all automatic and not subject to attentional influence. However, later ERP and MEG studies by Woldorff and colleagues, generating more focused attention, showed that the amplitude of the MMN was actually substantially suppressed within an unattended channel relative to an attended channel (**Figure 11.5**). Moreover, this modulation of activity elicited by feature deviance in an attended versus an unattended auditory channel occurs even if the deviant is not task-relevant (i.e., not a target to be detected).

Figure 11.5 Effects of attention on the mismatch negativity to deviant auditory stimuli. (A) Overlays of the ERP elicited by the deviant and standard (nondeviant) stimuli in the attended and unattended auditory streams show that the mismatch negativity (MMN), which typically appears as increased negative-wave activity between 150 and 225 milliseconds, is significantly larger in the attended condition. (B) The overlay of deviance-related difference waves (deviant ERP minus nondeviant ERP for the two attention conditions) shows strong effects of auditory attention on the MMN, and thus on auditory feature discrimination. (After Woldorff et al. 1991.)

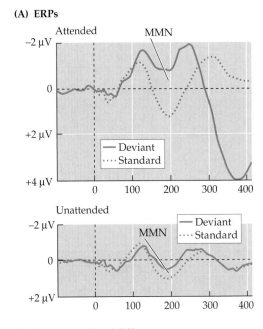

(A) ERPs

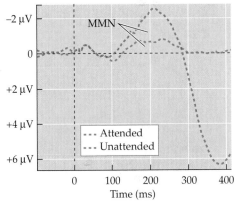

(B) Deviance-related difference waves

These results indicate not only that attention can modulate the overall gain of early neural activity elicited by auditory stimuli, but also that this early modulation leads to a large later effect on auditory feature analysis. On the other hand, some MMN is elicited in even a strongly ignored auditory channel, indicating that some feature analysis is automatically performed for all auditory input, as proposed by Näätänen. This evidence accords with the commonsense idea that although it is valuable to allocate more processing resources to sensory input of greatest interest at each moment, it would be ill advised to completely turn off the processing of other inputs that might indicate the sudden occurrence of a new, biologically important stimulus elsewhere.

Figure 11.6 summarizes the main ERP effects of auditory attention, along with the various corresponding ERP effects of visual attention that will be discussed next.

The Effects of Visual Spatial Attention

As in audition, brain activity can be recorded in different states of attention in visual tasks to ask how attention influences stimulus processing in the visual system. Historically, studies of visual attention have also concentrated on spatial paradigms, reflecting the fact that vision is highly spatial.

Figure 11.6 Summary. The major effects of auditory and visual attention on various ERP components.

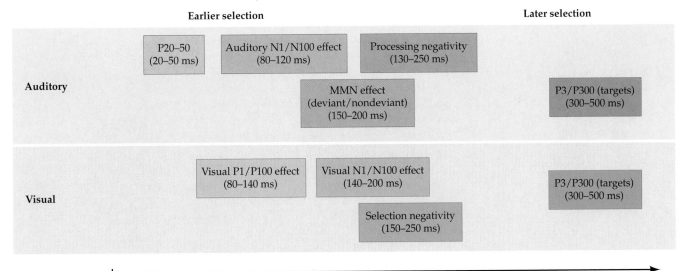

Electrophysiological studies of the effects of visual spatial attention

As in audition, ERPs in response to visual stimuli are especially informative about the timing of attentional effects. **Figure 11.7A** shows a typical averaged visual ERP response to a stimulus in one visual field (the right in this example), recorded from a site over the left occipital cortex. The first prominent wave is the **visual P1**, or *P100 wave*, a positive wave that begins about 60 to 70

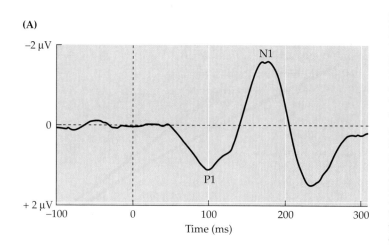

(A)

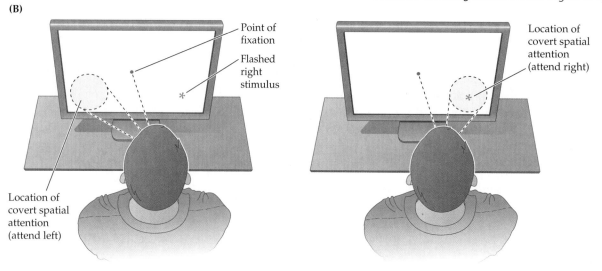

Figure 11.7 Effects of visual spatial attention on ERP responses to visual stimuli. (A) Recorded over the left occipital lobe to a light flash in the right visual hemifield, this ERP shows the P1 and N1 components peaking at 100 and 180 milliseconds, respectively. (B) In this paradigm for investigating the effects of visual spatial attention, the subject is attending to a location either in the right visual field or in the left visual field for visual flash stimuli, and ignoring stimuli on the other side. (C) Representative ERPs elicited by right-field stimuli when attended versus unattended are shown here along with the corresponding topographic distributions on the scalp at the latency of the P1 peak. Attention enhances the amplitude of the sensory P1 component, with little change in waveform or scalp distribution. Such an effect is consistent with the conclusion that attention induces a gain enhancement in the responses to stimuli occurring in an attended region of space.

(B)

(C) Right stimulus ERPs

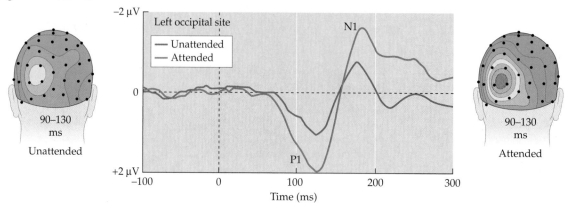

milliseconds after stimulus onset and peaks at about 100 milliseconds over occipital sites contralateral to the visual field of the stimulus (consistent with the crossing of the visual pathways on the way to visual cortex; see Chapter 4). Visual-evoked cortical activity begins somewhat later than the auditory response because of an initial 30- to 40-millisecond processing delay in the retina that has no counterpart in the cochlea. The visual P1 derives mainly from neural activity in the low-level extrastriate visual cortical areas (V2, V3, V4), with some contribution on its ascending phase from the primary visual cortex (V1). The P1 wave is followed by the **visual N1** (or *N100 wave*) component of the ERP, which peaks about 180 milliseconds after the stimulus and is thought to reflect sensory processing activity in a combination of extrastriate and parietal visual areas.

In a manner analogous to the dichotic listening experiments described earlier, streams of visual stimuli can be presented to two (or more) locations in the visual field. In this sort of paradigm subjects typically attend to the stream of stimuli at one location or another to detect occasional target stimuli in that stream (**Figure 11.7B**). Evoked brain activity to the same physical stimuli can then be analyzed for differences as a function of whether the stimuli were attended or unattended.

Like the auditory stream paradigm, the visual analogue has several strengths. One advantage is that responses such as pushing a button are required from only a small percentage of all the stimuli presented (the targets in the attended channel). Nonetheless, the subject must selectively focus on all the stimuli in the attended channel to detect those targets, while ignoring all the stimuli in the other channel. This approach thus allows an assessment of the effects of attention on the processing of stimuli to which the subject need not respond (i.e., all the nontargets in the streams). Moreover, this paradigm allows direct assessment of the processing of unattended stimuli without the subject having to perform a secondary task on those stimuli.

ERP studies of visual spatial attention using such a visual stream paradigm, carried out by George R. Mangun (now at UC Davis), Steve Hillyard, and others beginning in the 1980s, have shown distinctive effects of visual spatial attention on early visual ERP components. The hallmark of visual spatial attention is an enhanced occipital P1 component at about 100 milliseconds, often followed by an enhanced occipital N1 at about 180 milliseconds (**Figure 11.7C**).

For a unilateral visual stimulus, the P1 attention effect typically appears as a simple enhancement of amplitude (i.e., a larger positive wave), with little change in wave shape or distribution on the scalp. Thus, this effect appears to reflect a change in the "gain" of the underlying sensory processing activity; that is, the same neural areas are activated, but more strongly. This effect has been interpreted as reflecting an early-selection mechanism that boosts the early activity elicited by attended stimuli in the visual sensory cortices. Additional studies have indicated that these effects reflect an enhancement of activity specifically in extrastriate visual cortex rather than in primary visual cortex (see the next section).

Mangun and others also applied ERPs in endogenously cued attention paradigms to examine brain activity elicited by targets as a function of whether they were validly or invalidly cued (see Chapter 10). The electrophysiological effects observed were similar to those in visual stream experiments, with validly cued targets (which are presumably more attended) producing larger P1 and N1 responses relative to invalidly cued targets, thus correlating with the faster behavioral responses. Similarly, Joseph Hopfinger at the University of North Carolina used ERPs to study the neural effects of exogenously cued attention and showed that the enhanced processing of validly cued targets (again as reflected in faster reaction times) at very short cue-target intervals

■ BOX 11B Evidence for Late Attentional Selection

The studies described in the text show that attention can affect stimulus processing at relatively early stages and anatomically low levels of the sensory pathways. However, other studies have indicated that, in some circumstances, attentional selection happens at later times and at higher anatomical levels. An example of such higher-level late selection comes from the attentional blink paradigm described in Chapter 10. Recall that in this paradigm a stream of visual stimuli is presented at a rapid rate (say, 9 stimuli per second) at or near the point of visual fixation, and the task is to detect designated target stimuli embedded in the stream, such as occasional digits among letters. The behavioral result is that if a second target follows a first one by about 150 to 450 milliseconds, the ability to detect and/or report that second target is reduced (see Figure 10.6).

To understand the level of processing reached by the second target, Steve Luck and his colleagues at the University of Iowa designed a series of experiments that looked at the components of ERPs elicited by the second target when it occurred at different lag times relative to the first target. In particular, they analyzed the ERPs elicited by the second target when it occurred in the "blink" period after the first target and could not be reported, compared to the ERPs elicited when the second target occurred at the nonblink lag times and thus could be reported. The results showed that the sensory components elicited by the second target—the P1 at 100 milliseconds and N1 at 180 milliseconds—did not differ as a function of whether the target occurred during the blink period (see the figure). This observation is in sharp contrast to studies of visual spatial attention, in which attention strongly modulates the P1 and N1 amplitudes.

Next, Luck's group structured an experiment to ask whether the second unreported target elicited a semantically related wave, known as the *N400*, that is generated when subjects attend to and process words, occurring at about 300 to 500 milliseconds. When the second target occurred during the blink period and could not be reported, it nonetheless elicited a robust N400 similar to that elicited by target words occurring outside the blink period. Thus, even when the second target could not be reported, the information in the stimulus had nevertheless been processed up through the level of semantic analysis.

Taken together, these findings demonstrate that, under circumstances involving the rapid processing demands of the attentional blink paradigm, selection can occur quite late in processing. In particular, selection appears to occur after semantic analysis but prior to a stage of conscious awareness, or at least prior to a stage of encoding and storage that would enable later verbal reporting.

References

LUCK, S. J., E. K. VOGEL AND K. L. SHAPIRO (1996) Word meanings can be accessed but not reported during the attentional blink. *Nature* 383: 616–618.

RAYMOND, J. E., K. L. SHAPIRO AND K. M. ARNELL (1992) Temporary suppression of visual processing in an RSVP task: An attentional blink? *J. Exp. Psychol. Hum. Percept. Perform.* 18: 849–860.

VOGEL, E. K., S. J. LUCK AND K. L. SHAPIRO (1998) Electrophysiological evidence for a postperceptual locus of suppression during the attentional blink. *J. Exp. Psychol. Hum. Percept. Perform.* 24: 1656–1674.

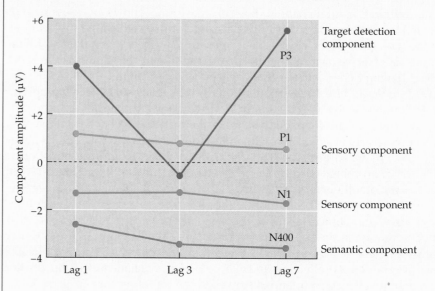

ERP activity elicited by target stimuli during the attentional blink paradigm. Visual stimuli are presented in rapid sequence while the subject attempts to detect occasional target stimuli in the sequence. In this situation the detection of a second target following a first by 150 to 450 milliseconds is impaired. The figure plots the amplitudes for several ERP components elicited by the second target when it occurred during the blink period following the first target and thus could not be reported (Lag 3 = 270 milliseconds) and when it occurred at nonblink lag times and thus could be later reported (Lags 1 and 7). Neither the P1 nor N1 sensory component elicited by the second target—nor the longer-latency semantically related N400 wave—differed as a function of whether the target occurred during the blink period. The only component affected was the even later P3 wave associated with conscious detection. Thus, the second target was processed up through the level of semantic analysis, even when it could not be detected or reported. (From Vogel et al. 1998).

were also associated with enhanced P1 and N1 components. Moreover, the slower response times for validly cued stimuli at longer latencies (the inhibition of return described in Chapter 10) were associated with *smaller* P1s and N1s. Thus, although there may be differences in the mechanisms and timing factors leading up to these sensory processing effects for endogenously and exogenously cued visual spatial attention, in both cases the effects on the sensory pathways appear to entail a modulation of relatively early sensory processing activity in visual sensory cortex.

These early attentional influences on stimulus processing in the sensory pathways are most typically observed during spatial attention. Some studies have indicated, however, that during other circumstances the attentional selection and influence can occur at much later stages of processing (**Box 11B**).

Neuroimaging studies of the effects of visual spatial attention

The effects of visual spatial attention have also been extensively studied with hemodynamically based functional neuroimaging techniques. One of the earliest such studies was carried out by Hans-Jochen Heinze and colleagues in the early 1990s at the University of Magdeburg, using a combined PET/ERP approach and a stream paradigm much like that described in the previous section. Subjects were presented with bilateral stimuli in the upper visual field and asked to attend to either the left or the right half of the stimuli for the occurrence of occasional targets on that side. Given the crossed anatomical organization of the human visual system, if visual attention affected stimulus processing at early sensory levels, then the effects of attention should also follow this organization. That is, relative to passively viewing bilateral stimuli, attending to the left side of the stimuli should cause increased activity in right occipital cortex, whereas attending to the right side should increase activity in the left occipital cortex. As **Figure 11.8** shows, this is exactly the pattern that was found.

Recall from Chapter 4 that the low-level visual cortical regions are retinotopically organized. The upper visual fields are represented in ventral contralateral occipital cortex inferior to the calcarine sulcus, whereas the lower visual fields are represented in contralateral dorsal occipital cortex, superior to the calcarine sulcus. In Heinze's study, the attention-related enhancement of neural activity occurred in ventral occipital regions, in agreement with the attention being directed to the stimuli in the upper visual field. In later studies, Roger Tootell and others more precisely demonstrated this retinotopic organization of the effects of spatial attention by mapping the early visual areas using an fMRI mapping technique before performing a visual spatial attention study in the same subjects. This approach allowed these and other researchers to show that visual spatial attention directly enhances stimulus processing in the specific portions of the low-level visual sensory areas that represent the attended region of space (**Figure 11.9**).

In agreement with the ERP observations discussed in the previous section, the neuroimaging studies just described found robust effects of visual attention on stimulus processing in relatively low-level extrastriate visual cortical areas (e.g., V2, V3, V4) but did not observe significant effects in primary visual cortex (V1). However, more recent imaging studies have shown that strongly focused visual attention can also influence stimulus processing at the level of V1, although typically less strongly. Moreover, in accordance with these effects, other fMRI studies have shown that the trial-to-trial variations in activity in V1 evoked by a visual stimulus during a difficult visual detection task correlated with the likelihood of detecting and/or perceiving the visual stimulus on each trial.

Neuroimaging studies have also reported effects of visual spatial attention on stimulus processing at even lower anatomical levels of the visual system. A recent fMRI study found enhanced stimulus-evoked activity due to spatial

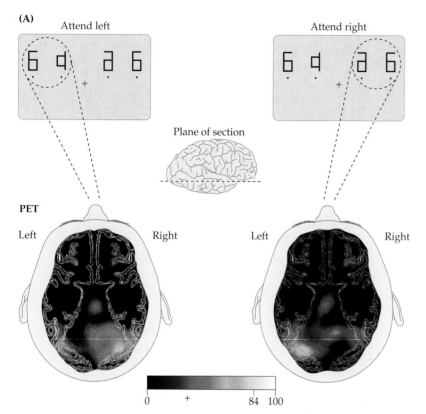

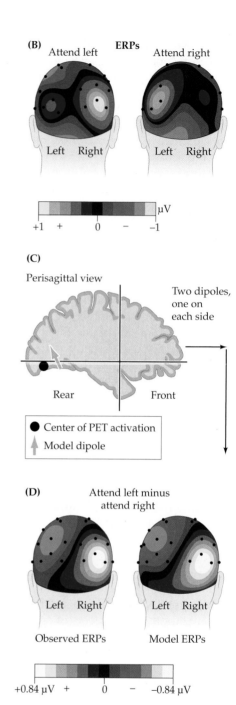

Figure 11.8 Effects of attention in the occipital cortices. In studies using PET and ERP recordings, subjects were presented with bilateral stimuli in the upper visual field. In different trials they attended to either the left or the right side of the screen (or, as a control, viewed the stimuli passively). (A) PET images show that the lateralized spatial attention enhanced activity in the contralateral ventral occipital cortex. (B) Corresponding ERP effects on the P1 at 100 milliseconds show enhanced activity over contralateral occipital scalp. (C,D) Source analysis of the P1 attention effect, facilitated by the combining of the PET and ERP data, indicates that model dipoles in the locations of the PET activation foci fit the observed ERP distributions quite closely. (From Heinze et al. 1994.)

attention in the lateral geniculate nucleus, the main thalamic relay station in the primary visual pathway from retina to visual cortex (see Chapter 4). Note, however, that fMRI alone cannot determine the timing of any of these effects, whether in thalamus, V1, or extrastriate regions. Resolving this issue using noninvasive brain activity measures generally requires a combination of methods, as described in the next section.

Other neuroimaging studies have investigated the influence of visual spatial attention on processing a stimulus when it occurs by itself compared to being presented in the context of distracting stimuli. Sabine Kastner and colleagues at Princeton and the National Institutes of Health (NIH) used fMRI to show that when multiple stimuli are presented simultaneously in the visual field, their cortical representations in the areas concerned with object recogni-

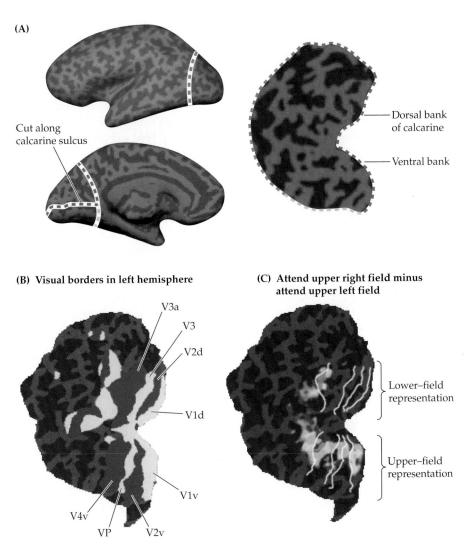

(A)

Cut along
calcarine sulcus

Dorsal bank
of calcarine

Ventral bank

(B) Visual borders in left hemisphere

V3a
V3
V2d

V1d

V1v

V4v
VP   V2v

**(C) Attend upper right field minus
attend upper left field**

Lower–field
representation

Upper–field
representation

**Figure 11.9 Retinotopic organiza-
tion of spatial attention effects.**
An example of an fMRI study showing
the location of attention effects with
respect to the retinotopic organization
of low-level areas of visual cortex. (A)
MRI scans were used to create a model
of the cortex as a convoluted surface;
from this model the occipital lobe was
separated from the rest of the cortex by
computer analyses and "cut" along the
calcarine sulcus so that it could be laid
flat with minimal distortion. (B) An fMRI
mapping technique was used to identify
the low-level sensory areas of visual cortex, as shown by the alternating colors.
v, ventral; d, dorsal. (C) Attending to the
right side of bilateral stimuli presented
in the upper visual field produces attention-related enhancements in the low-
level visual cortical region in left ventral
occipital cortex. (From Noesselt et al.
2002.)

tion in the temporal lobe interact in a competitive, mutually suppressive fashion. Directing attention to one of the stimuli, however, counteracts the suppressive influence of nearby stimuli, and thus may serve as a mechanism for
filtering out irrelevant information in cluttered visual scenes.

In related studies, other investigators at the National Institutes of Health
found that selective lesions to these object recognition areas in the visual cortex of monkeys impaired their ability to discriminate targets in the presence of
nearby distracters. Such results suggest that these higher-order sensory processing areas must be intact in order for competing but irrelevant stimuli to be
effectively filtered out by attention. These sorts of mutual interactions
between competing stimuli, along with the role that attention plays to bias
processing toward one or the other of them, has been termed **biased competition**—a theoretical model originally proposed based on findings from single-
unit recording studies.

Combining electrophysiological and neuroimaging studies of
visual spatial attention effects

The PET and fMRI studies described in the previous section have shown the
areas of visual cortex, and thus the *anatomical levels* in the visual system at
which the processing of visual stimuli is influenced by visual spatial attention.

Because of the sluggishness of hemodynamically based imaging signals, however, these methods do not provide information on the timing of these effects. Both EEG and MEG techniques provide timing information but have substantially coarser spatial resolution. Thus, effective combining of these methods has obvious advantages. Consider, for example, the visual attention study by Heinze's group that combined PET and ERPs. In addition to showing enhanced PET activation in the expected regions of visual cortex (described in the previous section; also see Figure 11.8A), these researchers recorded an enhanced P1 component at 100 milliseconds in the ERP responses over occipital scalp contralateral to the direction of attention (see Figure 11.8B). Moreover, dipole source analysis of the P1 enhancement placed it close to the focus of the PET activation in contralateral ventral occipital cortex (see Figure 11.8C,D). Later, combined-methodology studies of visual spatial attention by other investigators in which attention was directed toward stimuli in the *lower* visual field showed that both the PET attention effect and the source of the P1 attention effect were in the contralateral *dorsal* occipital cortex, thus both following the retinotopic organization of the visual sensory pathways. This pattern of results therefore supports the view that visual spatial attention affects the sensory processing of visual stimuli not only in low-level visual cortical areas, but also early in the processing sequence.

Other studies, however, have indicated that attention can also have an affect at *longer* latencies on low-level sensory activity evoked by stimuli. The pattern of these effects suggests a **reentrant** process, in which there is a return of attention-related activity to the same low-level sensory areas that were activated in the ascending pathways, presumably reflecting enhanced late processing of the stimulus information in those areas (**Box 11C**.)

Animal studies of the effects of visual spatial attention

Visual attention has also been studied to great advantage in awake, behaving animals with single-unit recording techniques. The findings, mostly in macaque monkeys, provide details on the effects of attention in the visual cortices at the local circuit level that are not possible with scalp recording or noninvasive brain imaging. As described in Chapters 3 and 4, the key information derived from such studies is typically related to the neuronal receptive fields. In general, visual cortical neurons fire strongly only if a stimulus is presented within the cell's receptive field, and if the stimulus has the specific characteristics to which the cell is tuned (a particular orientation, direction of movement, color, etc.). Once a sensory neuron is located for recording and its receptive field characterized, the animal's attention can be manipulated to investigate the effects on the neuron's firing rate and pattern in response to stimuli.

Jeff Moran and Robert Desimone working at the National Institutes of Health more than 20 years ago reported that spatial attention could indeed modulate neuronal responses in visual cortex, and that the influence observed depended on how the attended location, the stimulus features, and the cell's receptive field were related (**Figure 11.10**). Recall from Chapter 4 that sensory neurons are typically rather selective about the stimuli to which they respond. Certain stimuli (i.e., those with particular features—e.g., horizontal bars) are especially effective at activating a visual sensory neuron when they fall within its receptive field, whereas other stimuli without that feature (e.g., vertical bars) are rather ineffective.

In this study, monkeys were trained to attend to stimuli at one location in the visual field and ignore stimuli at another while the activity of single cells was recorded from visual area V4. Before a block of trials, the monkeys were cued where to attend—an approach similar to paradigms in human studies described earlier in the chapter. When an effective sensory stimulus and an

■ BOX 11C Attention-Related "Reentrant" Activity

As noted in the text, studies have provided evidence of effects of spatial attention that are temporally early in the processing stream, as well as in anatomically "early" (i.e., low-level) cortical regions in the sensory systems. One example is the extrastriate P1 effect during visual spatial attention. Such effects can be explained in terms of attention modulating the activity evoked in these sensory cortices during the initial ascending flow of sensory information. Spatial attention can also enhance later stimulus-evoked activity, at about 250 milliseconds, however, with a similar overall scalp distribution but of opposite polarity than the P1 (see the figure). This "N2 effect" localizes to the same occipital cortical regions that are activated and enhanced with attention in the P1 latency. These observations

(Continued on next page)

Modulation of reentrant sensory processing by attention. Subjects were presented with bilateral stimuli, and the task was to covertly attend to either the left or the right side of the stimuli. These topographic maps reveal the time sequence of differential ERP activity from 0 to 400 milliseconds for attending to the left versus attending to the right of the bilateral stimuli. The subtraction shows that the enhanced activity contralateral to the direction of attention occurs in two phases: an early phase at about 100 milliseconds (the "P1 effect," described earlier) and a later phase at about 250 milliseconds (an "N2 effect"). Both of these attention effects were localized to extrastriate areas in contralateral dorsal occipital cortex identified in a matching PET study (corresponding to the visual cortical representation of the lower visual field). The late effect presumably reflects the reentrance of attention-related activity to the same early visual areas that are also modulated by attention early in processing. (From Woldorff et al. 2002.)

Attending left minus attending right: 0–400 ms in 20-ms intervals

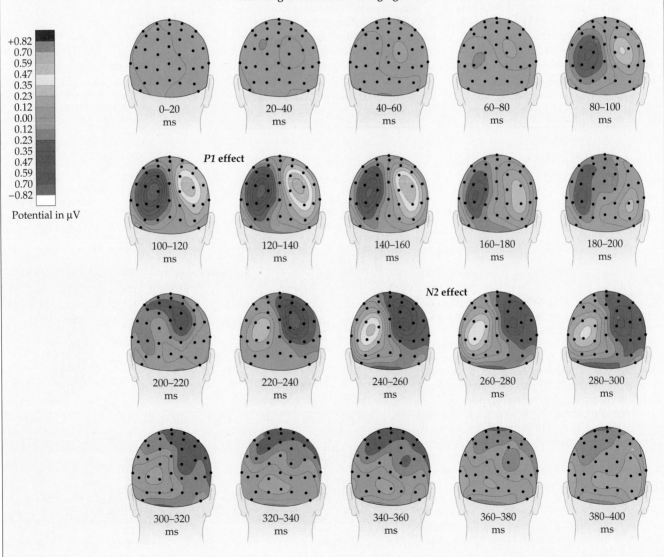

■ BOX 11C (continued)

suggest attention-related *reentrant* processes in which there is a "return" of attention-related activity to the same low-level sensory cortical areas, but at longer latencies.

Whereas the N2 late reentrant effects of attention occur in extrastriate visual cortex, fMRI studies have also shown attention effects in V1. On the other hand, there has been little evidence of early-latency effects of attention in V1 observed with ERPs, the earliest being the P1 effect described in the text. This pattern of findings led to the hypothesis that the fMRI attentional enhancement in V1 may reflect a longer-latency reentrant effect that is not picked up by ERP recording. In agreement with this idea, a later study by Tomme Noesselt and colleagues at the University of Magdeburg provided MEG evidence for longer-latency attentional effects in V1 occurring at about 200 to 250 milliseconds.

Single-unit recording studies in monkeys have also shown late attention-related activity in early visual areas, including V1. For example, in a study of the effects of attention on stimulus processing in visual cortex by Ashesh Mehta and colleagues at the Nathan Kline Institute in New York, effects were found at the level of V1, as well as in extrastriate visual cortex. Importantly, the V1 attention effects were relatively late (after 300 milliseconds), following those in V2 and V4, and well past the initial feedforward activation of V1. Thus, these results fit well with the attention-related reentrant effects in the human electrophysiological studies.

The functional role of such attention-related feedback in low-level sensory regions is not clear. One possibility is that the first ascending volley through the system, even when enhanced by prestimulus focused attention, may provide only a relatively coarse first "look" at the stimulus input. The reentrant activity would presumably enable more finely tuned analyses after some interaction with higher brain areas. The reason that late attention effects might extend back to V1 in some cases and not others could be the greater need to extract more detailed information for tasks that are more demanding, such as when stimuli are closely spaced.

References

MARTÍNEZ, M. AND 9 OTHERS (1999) Involvement of striate and extrastriate visual cortical areas in spatial attention. *Nat. Neurosci.* 2: 364–369.

MEHTA, A. D., I. ULBERT AND C. E. SCHROEDER (2000) Intermodal selective attention in monkeys. I: Distribution and timing of effects across visual areas. *Cereb. Cortex* 10: 343–358.

NOESSELT, T. AND 8 OTHERS (2002) Delayed striate cortical activation during spatial attention. *Neuron* 35: 575–587.

WOLDORFF, M. G., M. LIOTTI, M. SEABOLT, L. BUSSE, J. L. LANCASTER AND P. T. FOX (2002) Temporal dynamics of the effects in occipital cortex of visual-spatial selective attention. *Cogn. Brain Res.* 15: 1–15.

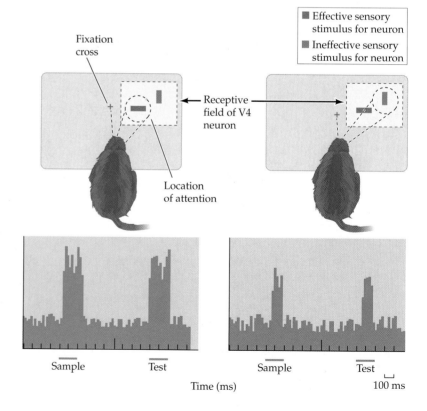

Figure 11.10 Effects of spatial attention on the firing rate of single neurons in area V4. At the attended location (circled), two stimuli—sample (S) and test (T)—were presented sequentially; the monkey had to discriminate whether they were the same or different. Irrelevant stimuli were presented simultaneously with the sample and test but at a separate location in the receptive field. Stimuli could either be effective stimuli for the neuron (red bars in this example) or ineffective stimuli (green bars; see Chapter 4). When both an effective stimulus and an ineffective stimulus were presented within the receptive field and the monkey attended to the effective stimulus, the responses were robust. When the monkey attended to the ineffective stimulus, however, the responses were much reduced, despite the presence of an effective stimulus in the receptive field. (After Moran and Desimone 1985.)

ineffective sensory stimulus were both presented within a cell's receptive field, and the effective stimulus was attended, the cell fired strongly. If the ineffective sensory stimulus was attended, however, the cell gave a much weaker response, even though the effective stimulus was also being presented within its receptive field. This result indicated that neuronal responses depend on the locus of attention *within* the receptive field, at least in V4.

Importantly, when attention was directed to a location outside (versus inside) the receptive field of the cell, the response to the effective stimulus within the receptive field was not modulated. In the later stages of visual processing in the ventral pathway—that is, in inferior temporal cortex—the pattern was different. At this higher-order level of processing, attention modulated the neuronal responses even if the ignored stimulus was far away from the attended one, presumably because at this level the receptive fields are much larger.

In contrast to the modulations observed in extrastriate cortical regions, Moran and Desimone found no effects on stimulus processing in the primary visual cortex (V1). However, subsequent studies showed that this lack of a V1 effect may have been due to the small size of the receptive field of V1 relative to the size of the stimuli used. Accordingly, attentional modulations of V1 responses could be observed when relevant and distracting stimuli were placed very close to one another.

In another later study, by Carrie McAdams and John Maunsel at Baylor College of Medicine, the orientation tuning curves of neurons in both V4 and V1 were assessed as a function of whether the stimuli were presented in a spatially attended location. Enhanced activity with attention was observed in both areas, although the enhancement was substantially larger in V4. However, the stimulus selectivity, as measured by the width of the orientation tuning curve, was not systematically altered by attention (**Figure 11.11**). These results were interpreted to mean that the modulatory effects of spatial attention consisted of a multiplicative scaling (i.e., simple gain modulation) of the driven response to all stimulus orientations.

Another important effect shown at the neuronal level is that spatial attention increases contrast sensitivity (**Figure 11.12**). In this study, luminance-modulated gratings were presented inside the receptive field at different values of contrast spanning the dynamic range of each neuron while monkeys attended to a location either within the receptive field or outside of it. The largest increases in firing rate were in response to contrasts in the lower and middle portions of the dynamic range of the neuron, where amplification would be more useful. Moreover, attention increased the likelihood of eliciting a neuronal response near threshold. Recent studies using fMRI have shown similar results.

Other work has focused on the influence of attention on oscillatory electrical activity in the brain, and the mechanisms that such influences may reflect. In one such study by Pascal Fries and colleagues at the National Institutes of Health, neuronal activity was recorded in V4 while monkeys directed their spatial attention to behaviorally relevant visual stimuli and ignored nearby distracters. Neurons responding to the attended stimulus showed increased synchronization of oscillatory activity in the gamma-band range (35–70 Hz; see Chapter 3), but reduced synchronization at lower frequencies (<17 Hz).

It has been hypothesized that increased gamma-band synchronization may amplify cortical responses to behaviorally relevant signals during visual selective attention. In line with this hypothesis, later studies have shown that behavioral responses are faster when there is strong gamma-band synchronization in the neurons activated by the relevant stimulus, and slower when there is strong gamma-band synchronization among the neurons sensitive to

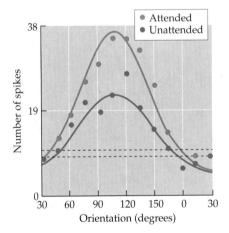

Figure 11.11 Effects of attention on the tuning curves of single neurons. Attention has no effect on the width or shape of the tuning curve, but rather enhances responses to all stimulus orientations, consistent with a multiplicative scaling mechanism. (From McAdams and Maunsell 1999b.)

Figure 11.12 Spatial attention increases contrast sensitivity of V4 neurons. The influence of attention on neuronal responses in monkey V4 was plotted as a function of contrast of the stimulus in the receptive field. Contrast was varied across a wide range while attention was directed to either the location of the stimulus inside the receptive field (red line) or a location outside the receptive field (blue line). The monkey's task was to detect a target grating at the attended location. Spatial attention increased the neuronal responses, but more strongly at lower and middle contrast levels, where it would presumably be more useful. The percentage change of this attentional manipulation is shown in the green line. (After Reynolds et al. 2000.)

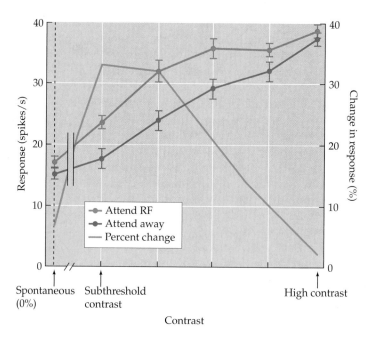

distracters, suggesting that these neural oscillatory effects are related to successful selection of the relevant stimulus.

In sum, the results from single-unit and local field potential studies in experimental animals underscore the influence of visual spatial attention on the sensory processing of stimuli at low levels of the system, at the same time providing important details about the characteristics of these effects at the neuronal and local circuit level.

The effects of visual spatial attention on visual feature processing

Just as the processing of auditory features in a spatially unattended channel can be studied using the mismatch negativity as a measure, the processing of the visual features of a stimulus occurring at an unattended visual location can also be examined using brain activity measures. For instance, as described in Chapter 5, area MT+ in the lateral occipital lobe is a key brain region for processing the motion of visual stimuli. Using fMRI activity in this region as a gauge, Geraint Rees, Nilli Lavie, and colleagues at University College London investigated motion feature processing at an unattended visual location, while also examining processing-capacity limitations (**Figure 11.13**). In particular, the perceptual load of a task (see Chapter 10) in the center of the visual field was manipulated (easy versus hard task) while task-irrelevant motion stimuli were presented in the peripheral visual field. The key finding was that more activity was elicited in area MT+ during the easy central-vision task compared to the difficult one.

This result was interpreted to mean that, when subjects had only an easy task to attend to in one spatial location, more processing capacity was available for stimuli in unattended locations, leading to fuller processing of the stimulus features of those unattended-location stimuli (in this case, motion-related features). In contrast, when the foveal task was more difficult, fewer resources were available for the concurrent stimuli, resulting in less processing of the sensory features of those other stimuli. These results again underscore the capacity limitations for processing sensory stimuli and the role of attention in allocating those resources.

(A)

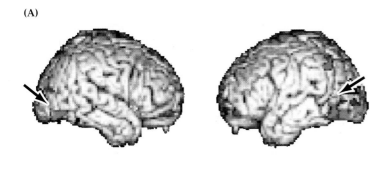

(B)

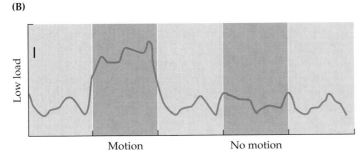

(C)

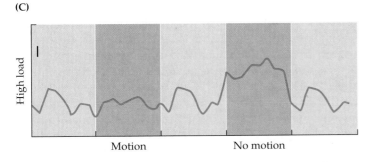

Figure 11.13 Effects of attention on visual feature processing at unattended locations.
In this fMRI study, subjects performed either an easy (low-load) or a difficult (high-load) task in central vision while task-irrelevant motion stimuli either were or were not presented peripherally. (A) These functional images show the enhanced activity in motion-processing area MT+ (arrows) due to the irrelevant peripheral motion during the low- versus high-load central-task condition. (B,C) Time courses of the average activity levels in MT+ in the different load conditions show greater activity to the irrelevant peripheral motion during the low-load central task. The small black vertical bar on the left side of each graph indicates a 0.1 percent fMRI signal change. (After Rees et al. 1997.)

The Effects of Attention to Nonspatial Stimulus Attributes

The studies of attention effects discussed so far have focused on paradigms in which attention is directed to different locations in visual space or to spatially segregated auditory input streams, although it is clear that spatial attention can influence the feature processing of stimuli (e.g., enhancing feature processing in the spatially attended versus spatially unattended locations, as discussed in the previous section). In contrast, the work described in this section focuses on the effects on stimulus-evoked neural processing when attention is specifically directed toward the nonspatial attributes of stimuli, such as the pitch of auditory stimuli, or the color or motion of visual stimuli.

The effects of attention to nonspatial auditory features

In audition, an obvious nonspatial quality that might be attended is pitch (see Chapter 6). Attending to this aspect of sound stimuli is biologically useful because pitch in vocalizations provides information on body size, gender, emotional state, and, in many languages, the meanings of words (see Chapter 20). By the same token, attending selectively to pitch is also useful in discriminating auditory streams, either for speech sources or for other circumstances.

Studies of attention to auditory features such as pitch have been carried out using streams of auditory stimuli of different pitches presented in random order while brain activity is measured with ERPs. Instead of attending to stimuli in one ear or one spatial location, subjects attend to a stream of stimuli of a particular pitch (e.g., high tones in a randomly presented sequence of high and low tones) to detect an infrequent deviant sound in the attended stream (e.g., a slightly fainter high tone). The ERPs to the sounds are then compared on the basis of whether they were in the attended pitch stream or not.

One effect of attention observed in this paradigm is a prolonged negative wave over frontal and frontocentral scalp regions that begins sometime after the N1 component, which peaks at about 100 milliseconds. Thus, the effects of feature-based auditory attention on stimulus processing generally start later than those observed in studies of spatial auditory attention, and do not include an enhancement of the N1 sensory component, or the earlier P20–50 wave. Such effects fit into the concept of a **processing negativity** proposed by Näätänen: the size of the negative-wave activity reflects the degree to which each stimulus matches an attentional "template."

Functional neuroimaging has also been used to study featural auditory attention, such as attending to tonal versus linguistic features of speech sounds. For example, Robert Zatorre and colleagues at McGill University in Montreal had subjects attend to streams of speech sounds to perform either a phonetic comparison (comparing the vowels in two consonant-vowel-consonant nonwords) or a tonal comparison (comparing the pitches of the same nonword stimuli). Whereas attending to the phonetic comparison resulted in greater activation of left frontal parietal areas associated with language processing, attending to the tonal comparison resulted in greater activity in right frontal regions (**Figure 11.14**). These results are in line with neuropsychological studies showing that left-hemisphere lesions impair semantic processing, whereas right-hemisphere lesions impair the ability to extract tonal information that helps define a speaker's emotional state (see Chapter 21). Thus, these results indicate that attending to an auditory feature enhances activity in the brain areas that normally process that feature.

Figure 11.14   Effects of attention to auditory features.   Averaged PET subtraction images superimposed upon averaged MRI horizontal slices, showing significant focal cerebral blood flow increases between conditions. (A) Passive listening to noise minus a baseline condition of silence yielded significant activations bilaterally in Heschl's gyri (Talairach atlas z height of slice = +10 mm). (B,C) Passive listening to speech minus passive listening to noise in these slices show significant bilateral activation in the superior temporal gyrus anterior to Heschl's gyri (B), in the left inferior frontal cortex (B and C), and in the left posterior temporal area (C). (D and E) Phonetic task versus passive listening to speech in these slices show activation increases in the superior portion of Broca's area in the left frontal lobe (D) and within the left superior parietal lobe (E). (F) Pitch task versus passive listening to speech produced significant activity in the right prefrontal cortex.

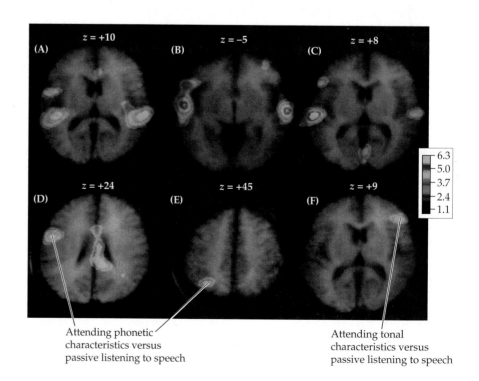

Attending phonetic characteristics versus passive listening to speech

Attending tonal characteristics versus passive listening to speech

The effects of attention to nonspatial visual features

The neural effects of attending to specific nonspatial features of visual stimuli have also been studied in some detail. For example, visual streams that differ in a single feature (e.g., red versus blue) can be presented in random order at a single spatial location, the task being to attend to only those stimuli with a certain feature value (e.g., red) to detect occasional targets among them. ERPs elicited by the nontarget stimuli when they are attended can then be compared to the ERPs elicited by the same stimuli when a different color is attended. The hallmark of these feature attention effects is a sustained negative wave, called a **selection negativity**, over posterior (parieto-occipital) cortex beginning about 150 milliseconds after the stimulus. This effect thus begins later than the effects observed in visual spatial attention, and it does not include an enhancement of the sensory-evoked P1 and N1 occipital components (the modulations of which appear to be specific for spatial attention).

Attention to nonspatial visual stimulus attributes has also been examined using functional neuroimaging. A PET study by Maurizio Corbetta and colleagues at Washington University in St. Louis in the early 1990s had subjects attend to the form, color, or motion of visual stimuli. Subjects were presented with a series of trials, each containing two stimuli—a reference stimulus followed by a test stimulus. The task was to compare the reference and test stimuli and decide whether they differed in these various feature characteristics. On some runs, subjects had to attend to all of the features and decide whether the reference and test stimuli differed on any of them. On other runs the participants focused attention on a particular feature.

In the focused versus divided attention conditions, enhanced activity was seen in regions of visual cortex that corresponded to the feature selectively attended. That is, attending to the color of the stimuli enhanced activity in regions associated with color processing (V4), attending to the stimulus motion activated the motion-processing area MT+, and attending to the stimulus form activated lateral occipital areas associated with form processing (see Chapter 4). Studies using fMRI have confirmed and extended these findings (**Figure 11.15**). Therefore, as in spatial attention studies in which attending to specific locations in the visual field enhanced activity in the regions of visual sensory cortex that represent that location in space, attention to stimulus fea-

Figure 11.15 Effects of attention to a visual feature. In this fMRI study, subjects were presented with superimposed patterns of stationary dots and moving dots, and the task was to attend to either the stationary or the moving dot pattern (A). Attending to the moving dot patterns enhanced activity in motion-processing area MT+ (B). (From O'Craven et al. 1997.)

(A)

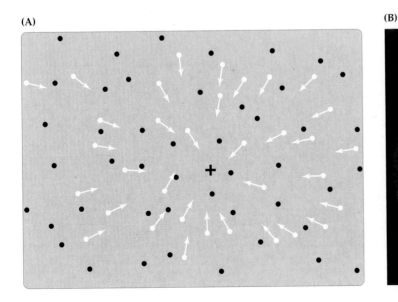

(B)

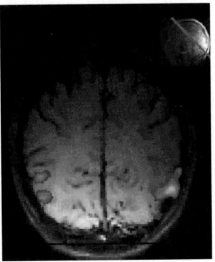

tures enhances activity in the regions of visual cortex that specifically process the feature being attended.

Single-unit recordings in monkeys have also contributed to understanding this aspect of attention. Stefan Treue and Julio Martinez-Trujillo at the University of Tübingen performed an important study of feature attention in monkeys in which they recorded from motion area MT+ (**Figure 11.16**). Visual dot patterns moving in either one direction or the opposite direction were presented in two different locations on the screen (see Figure 11.16A); the task was to detect and report changes in the motion direction or speed. The stimulus inside the receptive field of the recorded cell always moved in that cell's preferred direction, whereas the stimulus outside the receptive field moved in either the same or the opposite direction.

The key finding was that attending to the preferred motion outside the cell's receptive field increased the neuron's firing compared to attending to the non-preferred motion outside the field. Because the stimulation inside the receptive field and the location of spatial attention were kept constant, the researchers could attribute this enhanced firing to the manipulation of feature attention *outside* the receptive field. This feature-based attention enhanced the amplitude of the tuning curve in a multiplicative way (modulating the gain), without affecting its width, similar to the effects described earlier for spatial attention.

Because of the similarity of these multiplicative scaling effects in both spatial and feature attention, Treue and Martinez-Trujillo proposed that these effects can be unified in a **feature similarity gain model**. In this model, the attentional modulation of the amplitude (gain) of a sensory neuron's response depends on the similarity of the features of the currently relevant target and the feature preferences of that neuron (recall from Chapter 5 that all visual neurons have such preferences, including spatial location and nonspatial features such as motion or color). These results also suggested that neural representations of stimuli in parts of the visual field with no relevance to the task can be modulated by feature-based attention. Such influence of feature attention broadly across the visual field in turn suggests that this mechanism could be useful in visual search tasks. Recent studies using fMRI have also provided evidence in support of this theory.

The effects of attention to objects

Just as attention to stimulus features such as color, form, or motion modulates sensory processing in the regions of visual cortex that process those features, attention to objects has been shown to modulate stimulus processing in the

Figure 11.16 Feature attention in monkeys.   (A) The stimulus in the receptive field of the neuron that was recorded from (dashed circle) always moved in the cell's preferred direction (motion c), whereas the stimulus outside the field could move in either the same direction (*b*) or the opposite direction (*a*). Monkeys attended to either *a* or *b* motion to detect changes in speed or direction. (B) Attending *outside* the receptive field to motion in the *preferred* direction of the cell (*b*, in this example) enhanced the firing rate relative to attending to motion *outside* the field in the *nonpreferred* direction (*a*). More specifically, the histogram categorizes 131 recorded cells as a function of an attentional index, for which positive values reflect increased responses when the attended stimulus moved in the preferred direction of the cell. The histogram is shifted to the right, indicating an increased response when the attended stimulus outside the receptive field moved in the cell's preferred direction. (C) In addition, spatial attention—attending to a preferred stimulus *within* the receptive field versus attending to a nonpreferred stimulus outside the receptive field—shifts the histogram even farther to the right, reflecting additional enhancement of the firing rate. (After Treue and Martinez-Trujillo 1999.)

(A)

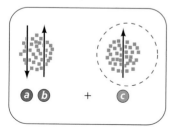

(B) Featural attentional modulation

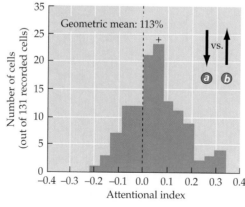

(C) Spatial + feature attentional modulation

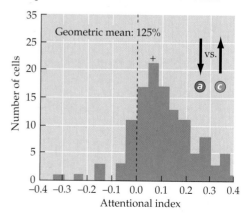

regions of visual cortex that process information about those objects as categorical entities. As described in Chapter 5, different regions of higher-level visual cortex along the fusiform gyrus in the inferior occipital and temporal lobes are relatively specialized for processing faces, whereas a more medial and anterior area is relatively specialized for the processing of houses and buildings.

In an fMRI study of object-based attention, Kathleen O'Craven and colleagues working at MIT showed that when overlapping, partially transparent faces and houses were presented and attention was directed to the faces, activity increased in the face-sensitive areas of cortex. Conversely, attending to the houses increased activity in the house-sensitive area of the gyrus. Note that spatially overlapping object stimuli were used in the study so that attention to location could not be used to separate the objects, thus allowing the effects to be validly attributed to object-based attention.

Object-based attention has been investigated further in studies asking how attention increases the efficiency of information processing. For instance, in addition to causing increased neural firing rates (as mentioned already), attention could increase the selectivity of the neural population representing an object stimulus. Knowing that the human lateral occipital complex is heavily involved in object analysis, investigators have used fMRI to measure the influence of attention on the selectivity in this region as a function of the angle at which an object is viewed. Attention to objects increased not only the neural response overall in the lateral occipital complex, but also the selectivity of the responses as a function of the viewing angle, suggesting that attention increases the specificity of the neural population representing an attended object. This result would appear to be at odds with the study by McAdams and Maunsell described earlier, which indicated that the feature selectivity of individual neurons does not narrow or otherwise change with attention. The reason for this discrepancy is not yet clear.

Object-based attention has also been studied in the context of how image features are bound together (see Box 4B for discussion of the binding problem). For example, in a recent combined MEG-fMRI study by Ariel Schoenfeld and colleagues at the University of Magdeberg in Germany, subjects attended to one of two superimposed transparent surfaces composed of dot arrays moving in opposite directions. When the surface moving in the attended direction displayed an irrelevant color feature change, neural activity localized to a color-selective region of visual cortex increased rapidly. Such an increase did not occur, however, when the irrelevant color change was in the unattended surface. This effect suggests that when an object is attended for certain of its features, the attentional enhancement can extend across the object's features to encompass even those features that are task-irrelevant.

The Effects of Attention across Sensory Modalities

Studies of attention have typically been carried out within a single sensory modality. However, sensory stimuli arising from natural objects typically have features of several sensory modalities. Thus, attention is presumably continually active in allocating resources to the stimulus information in the sensory modality or combination of modalities that are especially important in a given circumstance. In recent years, studies have increasingly focused on how attention operates in the context of multisensory stimulation.

In some multisensory situations it may be important for attention to be directed specifically to the stimulus features of one modality, while potentially distracting stimuli in another modality are relatively "tuned out." This function is referred to as **intermodal attention**. As expected from the studies already described, attention can enhance the neural processing of stimuli in the relevant modality and suppress processing in irrelevant ones. As with attention to different locations or aspects of stimuli in a single modality, these effects are evident at relatively low-level sensory processing stations, and at fairly early latencies.

Other studies have provided evidence for **supramodal attention** in certain circumstances, such as within the domain of spatial attention. The term *supramodal* refers to processes that are invoked jointly or in a common way across modalities (in contrast to **modality-specific**, which refers to a process that is unique for one specific modality). Consider, for example, what happens to auditory processing when visual attention is directed to a particular location in space to facilitate processing of the visual stimuli presented there. ERP studies have shown that the sensory components elicited by auditory stimuli are enhanced when they occur in a visually attended location, even when they are task-irrelevant. By the same token, the sensory ERP responses to task-irrelevant visual stimuli are enhanced when they occur in a location being attended for auditory stimuli.

Complementary studies using fMRI have indicated that these enhanced responses to stimuli in the task-irrelevant modality include increased activity at relatively low-level processing areas in the sensory cortices. These results imply that supramodal mechanisms are invoked during spatial attention. The biological value of this linkage is easily appreciated; if important stimuli pertinent to one modality arise from a particular location, stimulus information from another modality arising from the same location is also quite likely to be important.

Similarly, tactile stimuli occurring simultaneously in the same location as an attended visual stimulus improve the processing of the visual stimuli—a behavioral result proposed to be related to cross-modal links in spatial attention. In an fMRI study related to this finding, Emiliano Macaluso and colleagues working at University College London found that when irrelevant tactile stimuli occurred synchronously with attended visual stimuli and were spatially congruent, activity was enhanced not only in cortical areas where information from different sensory modalities is brought together (e.g., in the parietal cortex), but also in areas of visual sensory cortex that are generally considered unimodal. These effects are also interpreted as reflecting enhancement due to supramodal attentional mechanisms.

Finally, another influence of attention in multisensory contexts concerns the integration of sensory information from different modalities when an entire multisensory phenomenon is relevant and attended. In the real world, many objects and events are fundamentally multisensory, and the information from across the modalities needs to be integrated perceptually into more or less coherent multisensory wholes (e.g., a barking dog, a talking person, a bouncing ball). The predominant view until recently was that such **multisensory integration** is mostly preattentive and relatively automatic. However, recent studies indicate that most multisensory integration effects in the brain, including those that occur relatively early in processing and within low-level sensory cortices, are enhanced when the entire event or object is attended. In sum, attention has an extensive reach, affecting the neural processing of stimuli at multiple levels and in a variety of ways, including the integration of stimulus features that cross modality boundaries.

Summary

1. Attention has most often been studied in the context of stimulus processing, where it is fundamental in determining the extent to which different incoming stimulus information is processed. Studies using ERPs, MEG, functional neuroimaging, and single-unit recording have been useful in delineating when and where these effects occur in the nervous system, as well as the general form they take.

2. Electrophysiological studies in both humans and experimental animals have shown that the effects of auditory and visual *spatial* attention on stimulus processing can begin at the early cortical processing stages in the ascending sensory pathways. In humans, auditory spatial attention can affect stimulus processing starting at 20 millisecond poststimulus in primary auditory cortex, and visual spatial attention beginning at 70 milliseconds in extrastriate visual cortex. Corresponding neuroimaging studies have been especially informative about the precise locations of these effects, including showing that spatial attention specifically enhances stimulus processing activity in the sensory cortical areas that process the attended region of space. Other studies have shown that spatial attention, both auditory and visual, enhances feature analysis of stimuli in an attended spatial location relative to in an unattended location.

3. Attention can also be directed toward *nonspatial* attributes of stimuli, such as their feature attributes (e.g., pitch or color) or their object characteristics. Such nonspatial attention tends to influence stimulus processing activity somewhat later in time than does spatial attention. However, just as spatial attention enhances stimulus processing in cortical regions specific to the attended location in space, feature and object attention has been shown to enhance stimulus-evoked activity in the sensory cortical regions specifically involved in the processing of that particular stimulus attribute.

4. Under some circumstances, such as during the attentional blink, attention influences stimulus processing only at later stages involving higher levels of analysis in non-sensory cortical regions. Attention effects can also occur at later phases of processing in a *reentrant* way, influencing stimulus-evoked activity at later stages but in low-level sensory cortical regions.

5. Single-unit studies in experimental animals have provided insight into the details of attentional effects on stimulus processing at the cellular level. These studies have shown that neurons fire at higher rates when the stimulus attributes to which they are tuned (both spatial and nonspatial) are attended, with little effect on the breadth of their tuning curves. Studies also have shown that attention to a feature in one location tends to enhance the processing of that feature for all stimuli across the visual field, a mechanism that might play a role in attentional processes during visual search.

6. Recent studies have increasingly focused on how attention operates in multisensory contexts, rather than just within a single sensory modality. These studies have shown that in some situations attention can be directed intermodally, enhancing stimulus processing within one modality relative to another. Under other circumstances, attention can be directed supramodally (i.e., across modalities), and its influence can begin early in processing and facilitate the integration of stimulus information from several modalities into a multisensory perceptual whole.

Additional Reading

Reviews

Desimone, R. and J. Duncan (1995) Neural mechanisms of selective visual attention. *Annu. Rev. Neurosci.* 18: 193–222.

Driver, J. (2001) A selective review of selective attention research from the past century. *Br. J. Psychol.* 92: 53–78.

Kastner, S. and L. G. Ungerleider (2000) Mechanisms of visual attention in the human cortex. *Annu. Rev. Neurosci.* 23: 315–341.

Luck, S. J., G. F. Woodman and E. K. Vogel (2000) Event-related potential studies of attention. *Trends Cogn. Sci.* 4: 432–440.

Mangun, G. R. (1995) Neural mechanisms of visual selective attention. *Psychophysiology* 32: 4–18.

Maunsell, J. H. R. and S. Treue (2006) Feature-based attention in visual cortex. *Trends Neurosci.* 29: 317–322.

Reynolds, J. H. and L. Chelazzi (2004) Attentional modulation of visual processing. *Annu. Rev. Neurosci.* 27: 611–647.

Important Original Papers

Beck, D. M. and S. Kastner (2005) Stimulus context modulates competition in human extrastriate cortex. *Nat. Neurosci.* 8: 1110–1116.

Corbetta, M., F. M. Miezin, S. Dobmeyer, G. L. Shulman and S. E. Petersen (1991) Selective and divided attention during visual discriminations of shape, color, and speed: Functional anatomy by positron emission tomography. *J. Neurosci.* 11: 2383–2402.

De Weerd, P., M. R. Peralta III, R. Desimone and L. G. Ungerleider (1999) Loss of attentional stimulus selection after extrastriate cortical lesions in macaques. *Nat. Neurosci.* 2: 753–758.

Fries, P., J. H. Reynolds, A. E. Rorie and R. Desimone (2001) Modulation of oscillatory neuronal synchronization by selective visual attention. *Science* 291: 1560–1563.

Heinze, H. J. and 11 others (1994) Combined spatial and temporal imaging of brain activity during visual selective attention in humans. *Nature* 372: 543–546.

HILLYARD, S. A., R. F. HINK, V. L. SCHWENT AND T. W. PICTON (1973) Electrical signs of selective attention in the human brain. *Science* 182: 177–180.

HOPFINGER, J. B. AND G. R. MANGUN (2001) Tracking the influence of reflexive attention on sensory and cognitive processing. *Cogn. Affect. Behav. Neurosci.* 1: 56–65.

KASTNER, S., P. DE WEERD, R. DESIMONE AND L. G. UNGERLEIDER (1998) Mechanisms of directed attention in the human extrastriate cortex as revealed by functional MRI. *Science* 282: 108–111.

MACALUSO, E., C. D. FRITH AND J. DRIVER (2000) Modulation of human visual cortex by crossmodal spatial attention. *Science* 289: 1206–1208.

MCADAMS, C. J. AND J. H. R. MAUNSELL (1999a) Effects of attention on orientation-tuning functions of single neurons in macaque cortical area V4. *J. Neurosci.* 19: 431–441.

MCADAMS, C. J. AND J. H. R. MAUNSELL (1999b) Effects of attention on reliability of individual neurons in monkey visual cortex. *Neuron* 23: 765–773.

MORAN, J. AND R. DESIMONE (1985) Selective attention gates visual processing in the extrastriate cortex. *Science* 229: 782–784.

MOTTER, B. C. (1993) Focal attention produces spatially selective processing in visual cortical areas V1, V2, and V4 in the presence of competing stimuli. *J. Neurophysiol.* 70: 909–919.

O'CRAVEN, K. M., P. E. DOWNING AND N. KANWISHER (1999) fMRI evidence for objects as the units of attentional selection. *Nature* 401: 584–587.

PETKOV, C. I., X. KANG, K. ALHO, O. BERTRAND, E. W. YUND AND D. L. WOODS (2004) Attentional modulation of human auditory cortex. *Nat. Neurosci.* 7: 658–663.

REES, G., C. D. FRITH AND N. LAVIE (1997) Modulating irrelevant motion perception by varying attentional load in an unrelated task. *Science* 278: 1616–1619.

REYNOLDS, J. H., T. PASTERNAK AND R. DESIMONE (2000) Attention increases sensitivity of V4 neurons. *Neuron* 26: 703–714.

SAENZ, M., G. T. BURACAS AND G. M. BOYNTON (2002) Global effects of feature-based attention in human visual cortex. *Nat. Neurosci.* 5: 631–632.

SCHOENFELD, M. A. AND 6 OTHERS (2003) Dynamics of feature binding during object selective attention. *Proc. Natl. Acad. Sci. USA* 100: 11806–11811.

TOOTELL, R. B. AND 6 OTHERS (1998) The retinotopy of visual spatial attention. *Neuron* 21: 1409–1422.

TREUE, S. AND J. C. MARTINEZ TRUJILLO (1999) Feature-based attention influences motion processing gain in macaque visual cortex. *Nature* 399: 575–579.

WOLDORFF, M. G., S. A. HACKLEY AND S. A. HILLYARD (1991) The effects of channel-selective attention on the mismatch negativity wave elicited by deviant tones. *Psychophysiology* 28: 30–42.

WOLDORFF, M. G. AND 6 OTHERS (1993) Modulation of early sensory processing in human auditory cortex during auditory selective attention. *Proc. Natl. Acad. Sci. USA* 90: 8722–8726.

ZATORRE, R. J., A. C. EVANS, E. MEYER AND A. GJEDDE (1992) Lateralization of phonetic and pitch discrimination in speech processing. *Science* 256: 846–849.

Books

HUMPHREYS, G., J. DUNCAN AND A. TREISMAN, EDS. (1999) *Attention, Space and Action: Studies in Cognitive Neuroscience.* Oxford: Oxford University Press.

NÄÄTÄNEN, R. (1992) *Attention and Brain Function.* Hillsdale, NJ: Lawrence Erlbaum.

PARASURAMAN, R., ED. (1998) *The Attentive Brain.* Cambridge, MA: MIT Press.

12

Attentional Control and Attentional Systems

Introduction

The previous chapter described how attention affects the neural processing of sensory stimuli. The evidence outlined indicated that often attention can influence stimulus processing early in the sensory pathways, but sometimes attentional influences can occur only later and at anatomically higher levels of processing. This chapter focuses on the processes and mechanisms by which these modulatory effects on stimulus processing are controlled, examining in particular the evidence for an overarching system or set of systems that coordinates attention more generally. Like most other cognitive functions, the relevant insights have come from complementary studies of the effects of specific brain lesions and measures of functional brain activity. The findings from clinical observations suggest a preeminent role of the parietal and frontal cortices in attentional control. The findings determined by monitoring brain activity in normal subjects and animals carrying out attentional tasks confirm the importance of these regions and suggest how the control of attention is exercised. The various empirical findings have led to the development of some major models of attentional control, all of which have proposed that this function is accomplished via networks of interacting brain areas. Further experimental studies testing the between-area interactions that are predicted by these models have provided support for some of their basic tenets.

Brain Lesions That Impair Attentional Control

Well before the advent of modern techniques that can measure brain activity directly during attentional tasks, clinical data from patients showed that when certain areas in the parietal and frontal cortices are damaged, the ability to direct attention is markedly compromised. The characteristics of these remarkable and well-documented syndromes suggest that these areas are involved in the control of attention.

Neglect syndrome

A relatively common brain lesion that results in striking attentional deficits arises from strokes, tumors, or traumatic injury to the right inferior parietal lobe (**Figure 12.1**). Such lesions, as first described in the 1940s by the British

Figure 12.1 Left hemispatial neglect syndrome.
This composite diagram shows the distribution of right-hemisphere damage in eight patients with left hemispatial neglect. The degree of overlap of damaged brain areas across patients is indicated by shading level. Although some of the lesions include parietal and frontal lobes, as well as parts of the temporal lobe, the region most commonly affected is in the right inferior parietal lobe (dashed line). (After Heilman and Valenstein 1985.)

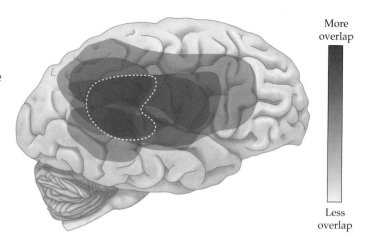

More overlap

Less overlap

neurologist Russell Brain, cause deficits in spatial attention to the left side of personal and extrapersonal space (i.e., the side contralateral to the lesion). The most obvious characteristic of patients with right parietal lesions is that they tend to ignore stimuli in their left visual field. For example, a patient with such a **hemispatial neglect** syndrome may fail to notice another person if that person approaches the patient from the left, although the patient notices when the person approaches from the right. Similarly, when shown a picture with three horizontally aligned objects (on the left, middle, and right) and asked how many objects they see, such patients typically fail to report the object on the left.

Depending on the extent and severity of the lesion, when an object in the left visual field is specifically pointed out to some patients, they may then report being able to see it. Thus, the impairments in neglect syndrome are quite different from the visual deficit that follows a lesion in the visual cortex. Patients with visual cortical lesions are effectively blind in specific corresponding parts of the contralateral visual field (the blind area of the visual field is called a *scotoma*). In contrast, the underlying problem in neglect syndrome appears to be more of an attentional deficit, not a sensory one; the patients can apparently *see* stimuli in the left visual field, but they tend not to notice them or be able to orient their attention to them very effectively.

The left-sided neglect evident in these patients is often demonstrated clinically by one of several classic tests. In the single-line bisection test in **Figure 12.2A**, patients are asked to mark the center of a horizontal line. Patients with neglect tend to discount the left side of the line and thus their estimate of the center is displaced to the right. In the line cancellation test (**Figure 12.2B**), the patient is asked to draw a line through each of a number of lines scattered across a page; in this test patients cancel lines mainly on the right side of the page. In addition, the left-sided neglect is not limited to just ignoring objects in left hemispace; patients with this syndrome also tend to ignore the left sides of objects wherever they are in visual space. For example, if asked to draw a copy of an object, these patients tend to draw only its right side (**Figure 12.2C**).

Such patients even ignore the left side of their visual imagery. So, if asked to draw a clock from memory, they are likely to draw half a clock, sometimes remembering to include all 12 numbers in the drawing, but placing all of the numbers to the right (**Figure 12.2D**). Some studies have suggested that the lesion in patients with neglect symptoms that are more globally spatial (as reflected by the line cancellation test) may be in a somewhat different brain location than the lesion leading to more object-related manifestations (as reflected by the line bisection or picture-copying tests), but this idea remains to be fully documented.

(A) "Bisect the line"

(B) "Cancel the lines"

(C) "Copy this picture of a house"

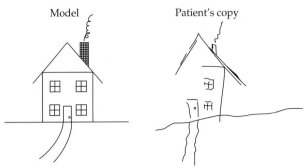

Model   Patient's copy

(D) "Draw a clock"

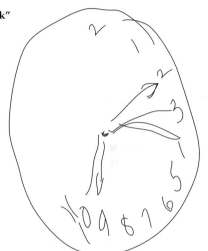

Figure 12.2 Clinical tests of neglect caused by damage to the right inferior parietal lobe. The performance in the single-line bisection test (A) and the line cancellation test (B) shown here is characteristic of neglect patients. (C) A right-parietal neglect patient drew the copy of the visual object shown here. (D) A neglect patient made this drawing of a clock face from memory. (A,C from Posner and Raichle 1994; B from Blumenfeld 2002; D from Grabowecky et al.,1993.)

Although attentional neglect is typically most obvious in vision, the deficit can also be observed in other sensory modalities. For example, many patients seem to be less aware of the left side of their own body. This deficit is reflected by the tendency of such patients to shave or apply makeup on only the right side of the face, or to be concerned about aspects of their clothes only on the right side of their body (an impairment called *dressing apraxia*). Thus, the attentional deficits in right parietal neglect appear to involve supramodal attentional mechanisms (see Chapter 11), although the degree to which these deficits are manifest across sensory modalities also varies across subjects.

Another hallmark of neglect syndrome is **extinction**. This phenomenon is revealed when the neurologist stands in front of the patient with arms outstretched and moves a finger on either the right or the left hand. If a finger on either side is moved by itself, the patient generally reports the presence of the moving finger correctly. If both fingers are moved at the same time, however, the patient typically reports seeing only the one on the right. Such effects suggest that there normally is a relatively symmetrical competition between the stimulus inputs from the two sides, but in these patients the stimulus input from the right dominates, "extinguishing" the input from the left. Extinction emphasizes again that the underlying problem is an attentional deficit, not a sensory one. In accord with the supramodal character of the deficit, a similar sort of extinction is evident if the neurologist touches the patient on the right and left arm instead of using visual stimuli.

For cognitive neuroscience models of attention, this clinical evidence implies that the right parietal cortex is involved in attentional control. An obvious question, however, is why the neglect exhibited in such patients is generally limited to lesions in the right parietal lobe. Why don't left parietal lesions cause analogous neglect in the right hemispace? The answer is that, at least in humans, the right parietal lobe appears to play a more important role in attentional control than does the left parietal lobe. Evidently the right parietal lobe controls attention to both left and right hemispaces, whereas the left parietal lobe controls attention mainly on the right. Accordingly, attention to the right side of personal or extrapersonal space is controlled by both parietal lobes, whereas attention to the left is controlled primarily by the right parietal lobe. This asymmetry would explain why loss of function in the right parietal lobe, but not generally the left, results in a contralateral attentional deficit. Interestingly, at least some non-human primates do not show this right-sided asymmetry; rather, damage to either side of the inferior parietal lobe induces neglect symptoms in the contralateral hemispace.

Although damage to the parietal lobe has been most clearly associated with neglect syndrome, lesions in regions of frontal cortex that are heavily connected with the parietal regions can also cause attention deficits. In particular, lesions to the frontal eye fields disrupt the ability both to initiate eye movements to targets in the contralesional visual field and to direct attention toward that side. As a general rule, unilateral frontal lesions tend to have a greater effect on the more motor-related aspects of attention, compromising the ability to direct eye or limb movements toward the contralateral hemispace or to initiate movements of the contralesional limbs to that region of space. These observations suggest that the frontal lobes also play a role in attentional control.

If hemispatial neglect is produced by a stroke (which is the most common cause), the attentional deficits are particularly apparent immediately afterward. Typically the effects tend to substantially resolve over a few weeks or months, although with extensive lesions they may be permanent. The reason is generally thought to be that the affected cortical region was only marginally or transiently damaged and it regains enough blood supply over time to resume more or less normal function, or that the function is partially taken over by other brain areas.

Balint's syndrome

Another brain lesion that has marked effects on attention is bilateral damage to the posterior parietal and lateral occipital cortex (**Figure 12.3**). Damage of this sort presents a quite different clinical picture and causes an even more debilitating deficit called **Balint's syndrome**. First characterized by the Hungarian physician Rezso Balint, the signature of this syndrome is threefold: (1)

Figure 12.3   Balint's syndrome.
The lesion in Balint's syndrome is typically located in posterior parietal and lateral occipital cortex bilaterally. (From Friedman-Hill et al. 1995.)

Lateral views

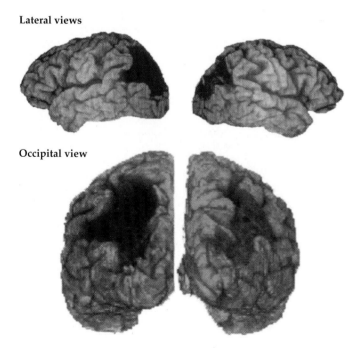

Occipital view

Coronal MRI

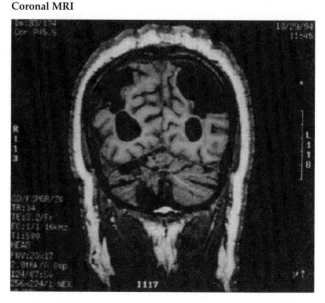

simultanagnosia, the inability to attend to and/or perceive more than one visual object at a time; (2) **optic ataxia**, the impaired ability to reach for or point to an object in space under visual guidance; and (3) **oculomotor apraxia**, difficulty voluntarily directing the eye gaze toward objects in the visual field with a saccade.

Simultanagnosia is the sign most closely associated with the syndrome. For example, if the neurologist holds up two different objects and asks Balint's patients what they see, they report seeing only one object or the other but not both, even if the objects are right next to each other. If the unseen object is jiggled to attract attention, patients may say they see it, but then they lose the perception of the first object. Moreover, when patients with Balint's syndrome are presented with an array of randomly distributed objects, half of which are one color and half another, they report seeing just one color or the other, but not both (**Figure 12.4A**). But if the differently colored items are attached so that each object contains both colors, patients then report seeing both colors in the array.

Similarly, these patients have trouble perceiving and comparing the lengths of two nearby rectangular bars unless they are connected as parts of the same overall object (**Figure 12.4B**). Thus, Balint's patients can attend to more than one stimulus quality or stimulus part, but only when the parts are embodied in the same object. Why bilateral damage to the posterior parietal and lateral occipital cortex causes these curious deficits is not yet understood.

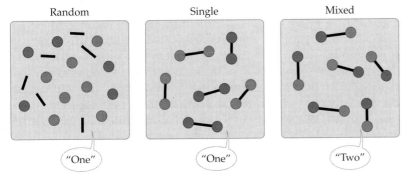

(A) "How many colors do you see?"

Random · Single · Mixed

"One" · "One" · "Two"

(B) "Are the two projections the same height?"

Condition	Unequal length	Equal length	Percent correct
1. Complete			84%*
2. Separate			54%
3. Occluder present			48%
4. Collinear			86%*

Figure 12.4 Simultanagnosia in Balint's syndrome. (A) The inability of Balint's patients to perceive or attend to more than one object at a time prevents them from noticing more than one color in the displays shown in the left and middle panels. If the blue and red circles are connected to form single objects (right panel), however, the patient is able to report both colors, indicating that the deficit lies in the inability to attend to multiple objects rather than in a failure to attend to multiple qualities. (B) Similarly, if patients are asked to compare the lengths of two nearby rectangles, their performance is near chance (50 percent correct) if the objects are separated, whereas they perform much better when the components are connected as part of the same object. The asterisk denotes performance statistically better than chance. (A after Humphreys and Riddoch 1993; B after Cooper and Humphreys 2000.)

Brain Activity Related to the Control of Endogenous Attention

The clinical observations described in the previous sections imply that the deficits from damage to parietal and frontal regions are related more to attentional control than to sensory processing. Accordingly, tasks involving attentional orienting and control in normal subjects would be expected to elicit changes in neural activity in these areas. Both imaging and electrophysiological studies have shown that this is indeed the case, providing additional insight into the cortical regions involved in the control of attention.

Activation in frontal and parietal cortex during endogenous attentional tasks

In its discussion of numerous studies in which subjects were asked to attend to specific aspects of their environment (e.g., locations, features, objects) while their brain activity was recorded, Chapter 11 focused on the effects of attention on the stimulus-evoked neural activity in the sensory cortices. In these studies of voluntary attention, however, other brain areas were necessarily also activated by the attentional manipulation, including areas that presumably were controlling the orienting and sustaining of attention. For example, in block-design neuroimaging studies comparing attending to visual stimuli (either at certain spatial locations or with certain features) and simply passively viewing the stimuli, not only were modulatory effects of attention observed in the sensory cortices, but enhanced activity in frontal and parietal regions was seen as well.

Because clinical studies of the sort described earlier in this chapter indicate that damage in these regions causes deficits in attentional orienting (as opposed to the blindness within a scotoma caused by lesions in visual cortex), it has been generally assumed that these activations in frontal and parietal brain areas probably reflect processes related to the control and maintenance of attention rather than the effects of attention on stimulus processing. Without an explicit experimental manipulation to isolate attentional control, however, it was difficult to assess whether this interpretation is correct.

One of the first functional neuroimaging studies that specifically investigated the voluntary orienting of attention was a PET experiment carried out in the early 1990s by Maurizio Corbetta and colleagues at Washington University in St. Louis. Subjects were required to switch attention repeatedly from one location to another in either the left or the right visual field to detect a target. Relative to a baseline task in which attention was maintained but not switched, the attentional shifting elicited enhanced activity in regions of posterior parietal and superior frontal cortex. Other studies confirmed that tasks that involve the voluntary orienting of attention, relative to baseline tasks that do not, typically activate regions of a frontoparietal network, as well as regions of the insular cortex and the anterior cingulate cortex, consistent with the view that these regions play a role in attentional control.

A limitation of early neuroimaging studies for studying attentional control, however, derived from their dependence on block designs (see Chapter 3). Applying block designs to the study of attention requires subjects to attend to one stimulus location or feature during one block, and another location or feature in other blocks (or perhaps just to passively view the stimuli). The neuroimaging measures of brain activity in the two different types of blocks are then compared. As a result, the activity in a block related to the initiation, control, and maintenance of an attentional change is inevitably conflated with other processes, including differential stimulus processing due to the between-block attentional manipulation and the processes related to the detection of target stimuli and motor responses. Block designs thus limit the ability to identify brain activity specifically associated with attentional control.

Event-related cuing paradigms and the attentional control network

A particularly useful approach for distinguishing brain activity specifically related to attentional control from activity related to other processing is a cued-attention event-related design. As discussed previously, the standard cuing paradigm contains an instructional cue followed shortly after (typically about 1 second later) by a target stimulus (see Figure 10.7). Behavioral studies have shown that targets at validly cued locations versus invalidly cued locations are detected faster and more accurately (see Chapter 10), and neurophysiological studies have demonstrated corresponding enhancements of the early sensory responses (see Chapter 11).

An advantage of the cuing paradigm for studying attentional control is that it separates the point in time at which subjects are instructed by the cue to direct their attention to a specific spatial location or sensory feature from the point in time at which the target stimulus occurs (and thus the point at which the allocation of attention may affect the processing of the target). By measuring the brain responses specifically associated with the cue, which presumably triggers the orienting of attention to a specific stimulus location or feature, researchers can differentiate the neural activity related to attentional control from other processes.

Because of their high temporal resolution, ERPs are well suited for studying the time course of cue-related versus target-related processes in cued-attention paradigms. Such studies have shown that attention-directing cues elicit a slow negative wave termed the *contingent negative variation* (CNV), as well as several other ERP components associated with expecting or anticipating a possible stimulus. However, the neural sources underlying these orienting-related ERP measures are difficult to delineate using ERPs alone, probably because they derive from multiple generators in the brain. On the other hand, applying hemodynamic imaging approaches, even event-related ones, to the cued-attention paradigm is difficult because the sluggishness of the hemodynamic response results in substantial overlap of the cue and target responses.

One of the first ways that researchers got around this problem was just to slow down the entire cued visual attention paradigm. For example, Joseph Hopfinger and colleagues working at UC Davis cued subjects with a central arrow to attend to either the left or the right side of a computer screen for an upcoming bilateral target display. To address the overlap of the cue and target fMRI responses, most trials had a rather long cue-target interval (about 8 to 9 seconds) and the research focused on only those trials. Thus the investigators were able to extract and compare the event-related fMRI responses to the cues and to the targets (**Figure 12.5**). Cue-triggered activations, which included activity related to attentional control, occurred in the dorsal lateral prefrontal cortex, inferior parietal cortex, medial frontal cortex, and a part of the posterior cingulate cortex. In contrast, activity time-locked to the targets was found in the visual cortex and motor-related processing areas in the frontal lobe.

Although this study allowed separation of cue-related and target-related processing, the slow rate used to mitigate response overlap introduced some other limitations, such as leading subjects not to orient as fully and to invoke increased working memory processes (see Chapter 16). Such slow rates also made it difficult to directly compare the results to most behavioral and/or ERP cued-attention studies. Accordingly, other studies pioneered by Corbetta and Gordon Shulman at Washington University used faster rates and a combination of special trial types and signal-processing techniques to separate the cue-related and target-related activity. These studies also demonstrated the

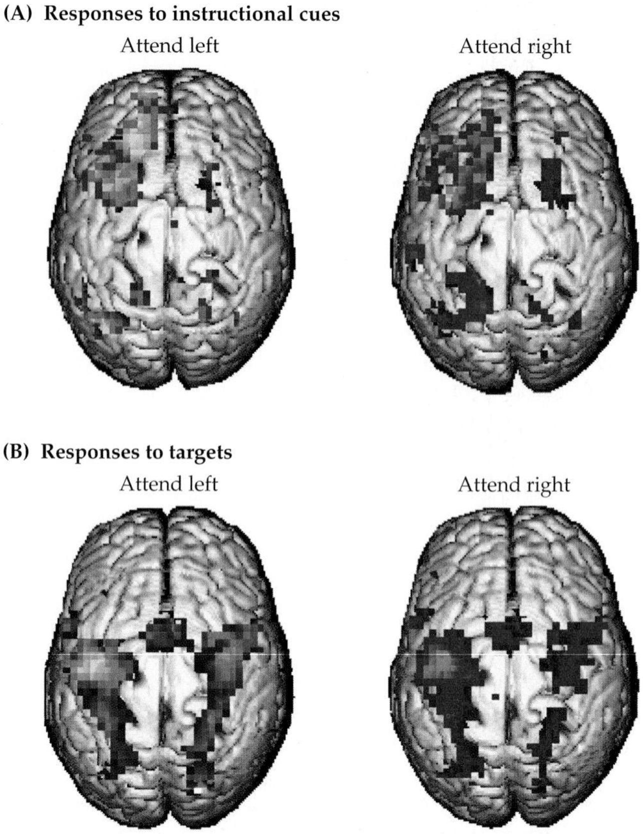

Figure 12.5 Dissociation of cue- and target-triggered responses in a slow-rate spatial cued-attention paradigm. Subjects in this fMRI study were presented with central instructional cues instructing them to attend to a location in the left or the right visual field to discriminate a target stimulus that would follow. On most trials, the cue-target interval was about 9 seconds, thus reducing the overlap of the cue and target event-related fMRI responses and allowing the responses to be separately extracted and compared. (From Hopfinger et al. 2000.)

(A) Responses to instructional cues

Attend left   Attend right

(B) Responses to targets

Attend left   Attend right

cue-triggered activation of frontal and parietal cortical regions in response to attentional orienting, although with less activation of the anterior frontal cortex, presumably because of the need for less working memory at faster rates.

Other studies have further delineated the functional roles of different portions of the frontoparietal network and neighboring regions. For example, Steve Yantis and colleagues at Johns Hopkins University used a different sort of cuing paradigm, in which subjects attended to one of two simultaneously presented streams of stimuli; the occurrence of specific cues within the attended stream signaled the subjects either to switch attention to the other stream or continue attending to the same stream. A comparison of the event-related response to "switch" versus "stay" cue events also activated regions mainly in the parietal portions of the frontoparietal network (**Figure 12.6A**), with less contribution from the frontal regions compared to the central-cuing experiments already described. The reason for the reduced frontal activity may be that both switch and stay conditions involve a continued or reinstantiated orienting of attention that includes a frontal component; the frontal component would thus be subtracted in the comparison.

Other studies using this sort of paradigm showed that parietal regions near those activated during switching of visual spatial attention are also activated when switching nonspatial attention, such as between streams of auditory stimuli or between different stimulus features. In these cases the switch-specific activations tended to be closer to the midline than in the studies of visual spatial attention (**Figure 12.6B**).

Although these event-related fMRI cuing paradigms enabled the identification of some putative components of an attentional control system, fMRI provides little information about the timing and sequence of the activations of

(A) Switching attention between different visual features (switch versus stay)

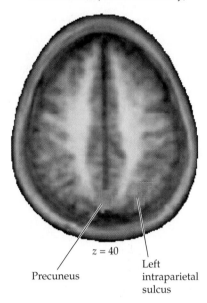

z = 40

Precuneus

Left intraparietal sulcus

(B) Switching attention between different object catagories (switch versus stay)

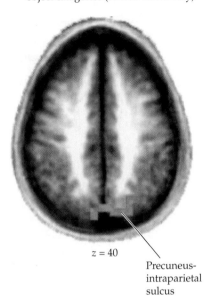

z = 40

Precuneus-intraparietal sulcus

Figure 12.6 Nonspatial switching of attention. Subjects in fMRI studies were presented with two streams of stimuli while they attended to one stream or the other. Cuing stimuli embedded in the stream indicated a switch point at which the subject either continued to attend to that stream ("stay") or switched to attend to the other stream ("switch"), depending on the embedded cue. In (A), subjects switched attention between features (color versus motion direction). In (B), subjects switched attention between object categories (faces versus houses). (A from Liu et al. 2003; B from Serences et al. 2004.)

these regions, again because of the sluggishness of the fMRI signals. To investigate the temporal characteristics of activity in these components, Tineke Grent-'t-Jong and Marty Woldorff at Duke combined data from parallel ERP and fMRI studies using identical visual spatial attentional cuing paradigms. In addition, they included control trials with cues that instructed subjects *not* to shift attention on a particular trial, thereby enabling better delineation of the activity specific for attentional orienting. As **Figure 12.7A** shows, the ERPs indicated that the attention-directing cues and the control cues elicited similar activity in the first 350 milliseconds, presumably reflecting general processing and interpretation of the cue, which the fMRI showed to be associated with the more lateral portions of the frontoparietal network.

Subsequently, the attention-directing cues (but not the control cues) elicited a sustained, orienting-specific ERP wave that could be linked to fMRI activity in the more medial portions of the frontoparietal network. Moreover, analyses of this orienting-specific activity indicated an earlier contribution from the medial frontal sources than from the medial parietal sources (**Figure 12.7B**). The initiation of the orienting-specific activity by the medial frontal regions is consistent with a role proposed more generally for the frontal cortex of keeping track of task goals and controlling and coordinating other regions to help accomplish those goals (see Chapter 23).

Single-unit activity in frontal and parietal attentional control areas

Studies of single-unit activity in frontal and parietal areas in non-human primates have provided a more detailed view of attentional control processes at the neuronal level. A number of electrophysiological studies of attention in monkeys have focused on recordings from neurons in an area in the posterior parietal cortex called the *lateral intraparietal (LIP) area* and in the *frontal eye fields (FEFs)* in the frontal cortex. These two regions in the monkey are assumed to correspond functionally with the parietal and frontal areas in humans where damage causes neglect symptoms, and where neuroimaging studies have shown activity related to attentional control, although the exact correspondence between the relevant human and monkey areas is not clear.

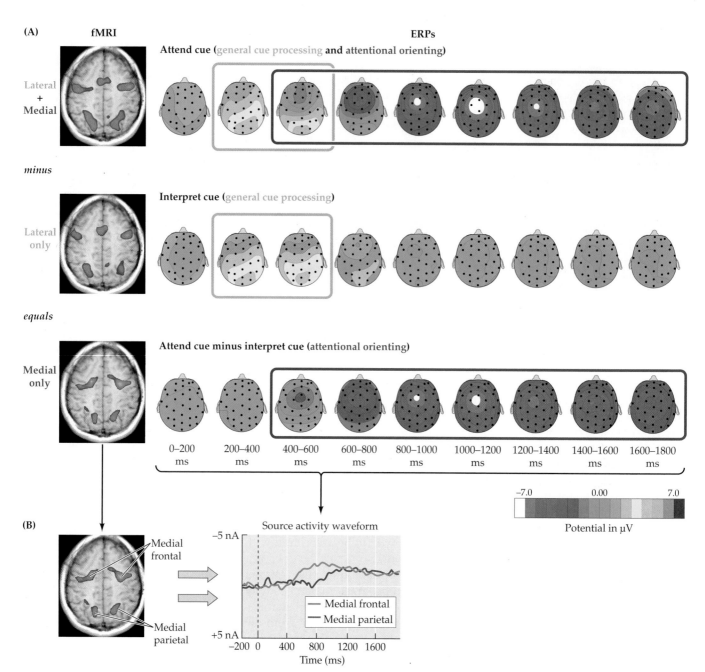

Figure 12.7 Temporal dynamics of cue-triggered activity in the frontoparietal control network.   In this combined fMRI-ERP study, subjects were given a centrally presented instructional cue to shift attention to the left or right ("attend cue") to detect a possible upcoming target there, or a cue indicating that no shift of attention was required on that trial ("interpret cue"). (A) In the fMRI study, a contrast between the interpret-cue responses (second row) and the attend-cue responses (first row) revealed that the more medial portions of the frontoparietal cortex were more specifically involved in attentional orienting, and the more lateral areas with general cue processing. Corresponding contrasts of the ERP data show that attend cues and interpret cues elicited similar general cue-processing activity in the first 350 milliseconds, followed by a sustained negative wave over frontal, central, and parietal scalp lasting hundreds of milliseconds that was associated with attend cues only. (B) Using the fMRI activations to facilitate the analyses, source modeling of the ERP orienting-specific control activity showed that the frontal regions of the medial orienting network were activated 200–300 milliseconds earlier than the parietal regions. nA = nanoamperes. (After Woldorff et al. 2004; Grent-'t-Jong and Woldorff 2007.)

Neuronal firing patterns in the LIP area have implicated this region in planning a saccade to a relevant target in the visual field, and in the covert focusing of attention toward that location (**Figure 12.8**). For example, the response amplitude (in terms of action potentials per second) of some LIP neurons to a stimulus in their receptive field is greater when the task is to make a saccade to a specified location than when it is a simple fixation task. However, the neuronal response is also enhanced when the monkey attends to the stimulus but does not make a saccade, or when the saccade is delayed. These results have been interpreted to mean that the enhancement is not due to saccade preparation per se, but rather to the allocation of attention to the spatial location of the target in the neuron's receptive field.

Similar increases of neuronal activity occur in the LIP area during fixation tasks in which the monkey can predict the onset of a behaviorally significant stimulus; these increased levels of background firing during the period before stimulus onset are analogous to the cue-triggered activity seen in the human neuroimaging and electrophysiology studies described in previous sections. Thus, the activity of LIP neurons is modulated by factors that are not necessarily associated with sensory processing or motor planning, but are more related to attentional or other cognitive factors.

Other studies have suggested that overall stimulus salience is the key determinant of this enhanced activity observed in LIP neurons. The salience could derive from stimulus-driven factors (e.g., the sudden onset of a stimulus) or relevance to a specific behavioral goal. Indeed, it has been suggested (but not yet confirmed) that the LIP area has a topographically organized salience map of the environment that is influenced by both stimulus-driven and endogenous factors.

The frontal eye fields, located in dorsal frontal cortex, are also known to be involved in the control of saccades. Indeed, the links to saccade production are particularly strong in the FEF as microstimulation of specific regions in

Figure 12.8 Attentional influence on neuronal activity. In this study, an electrode was placed into the lateral intraparietal (LIP) area of a macaque monkey and used to record action potentials from single neurons, shown here as peristimulus histograms aligned with stimulus onset (see Figure 3.3). (A) Neuronal firing was recorded in response to a stimulus occurring in the receptive field of the neuron while the monkey was engaged in a fixation task. (B) Covertly attending to the stimulus resulted in an increase in the firing rate of the neuron in response to the stimulus occurrence relative to the rate in the fixation task. (C) When the monkey needed to respond to the target by making a delayed saccade to the target location according to memory of that location, there was an additional increase in firing rate just before the saccade. FP, fixation point; H, horizontal eye channel; RF, receptive field; V, vertical eye channel. (After Colby et al. 1996.)

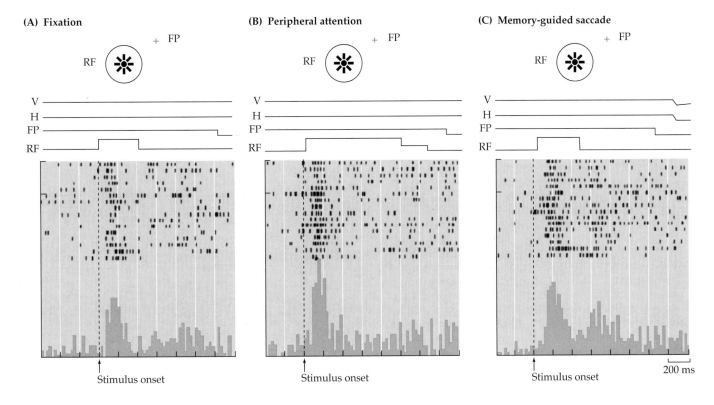

FEF triggers saccades to specific locations in the visual field. Saccade-related activity in this area has provided evidence for the **premotor theory of attention**, which posits that shifts of attention and preparation of goal-directed action are closely linked because they are controlled by shared sensory-motor mechanisms.

This theory also claims that the saccade-related circuitry mediates covert visual spatial attention. Nonetheless, the FEF may have attentional control functions that are distinguishable from saccade-planning processes. For example, like LIP neurons, recordings in FEF show enhanced activity not only when the monkey is about to make a saccade to a neuron's saccade movement field, but also when an attended or otherwise relevant target stimulus appears at that location. Moreover, both visually responsive and saccade-related movement neurons have been found in the FEF, and the activity of these neurons has been examined during tasks in which the response is a lever press rather than a saccade. The results have indicated that when attention is allocated to a visual target under these circumstances, enhanced activity is observed in the visually responsive neurons, but not in the non-visually responsive, saccade-related neurons (**Figure 12.9**).

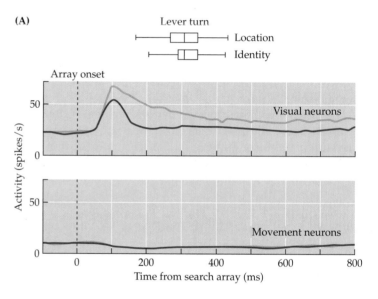

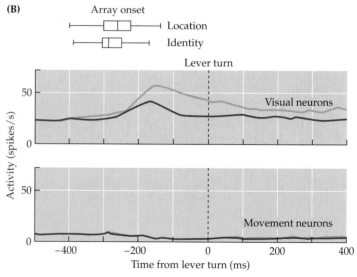

Figure 12.9 Attention-related activity in frontal eye field neurons. Average activity from FEF neurons was recorded during search tasks involving a manual response. (A) Neuronal activity aligned with the time of the search array presentation. (B) The same data aligned with the time of the manual lever response. The responses of target-selective visually responsive neurons and the responses of movement (i.e., saccade-related) neurons are shown separately. Orange lines plot the average activity on trials in which the target landed in the response field; purple lines, the activity on trials in which only distracters landed in the response field. For the visually responsive neurons there is a clear target-related effect; for the movement neurons, however, the target-related and distracter-related activity levels were nearly identical. (After Thompson et al. 2005.)

Such results support the hypothesis that FEF neurons give rise to some attentional control signals that are independent of explicit saccade-command or saccade-preparation activity. On the other hand, the occurrence of saccade-independent and saccade-dependent shift-related activity in the same area of frontal cortex suggests that there are nevertheless important links between covert and overt shifts of visual spatial attention.

Biasing of sensory cortices by higher-level regions

Although frontal and parietal regions are consistently activated during attentional tasks, an important question is how activity in these higher-level regions could lead to enhanced stimulus processing in the sensory cortices. Some insight into this issue has also been provided by cued-attention fMRI studies. In a study by Sabine Kastner and colleagues working at the National Institutes of Health, when subjects directed sustained attention to a particular visual-field location while expecting the onset of a visual stimulus there, not only did activity in the frontal and parietal cortices increase, but so did activity in the extrastriate cortex. These researchers theorized that the increased activity in visual cortex in the absence of visual stimulation reflects a "preparatory bias" due to top-down neural signals from the frontoparietal network that favor the attended location.

This idea was extended in the cued-attention study by Hopfinger and colleagues described in an earlier section. **Figure 12.10A** (bottom) shows the contralateral attention-related enhancement of the bilateral target processing in that study, similar to the sensory processing enhancement described in Chapter 11. However, these same regions showed enhanced contralateral activation in response to the instructional cues *before* the targets actually appeared (Figure 12.10A, top). Thus, although this enhanced activity is in sensory cortex, it does not reflect attentional effects on target stimulus processing, because the stimulus has not occurred yet. Rather, it appears to reflect a priming or biasing of visual sensory areas due to top-down influences from the frontoparietal cortices during visual spatial attention, which then leads to a modulation of the stimulus-evoked activity when the expected stimulus input appears. A simple but intuitive metaphor for this prestimulus biasing process might be turning up the volume on the radio because an important announcement is expected, such that when the announcement is delivered, it is louder than it would have been, facilitating interpretation of the message.

Electrophysiological studies have also supported this concept of biasing. For example, in a single-unit recording study in monkeys, Steve Luck and colleagues at the University of Iowa and the National Institutes of Health developed a visual spatial attention task in awake, behaving monkeys that was structured like those used in human visual attention studies. They found a sustained level of enhanced background firing rates in neurons in the extrastriate visual cortex that process the stimuli to be attended. This enhanced background firing was separable from the attention-related enhancement of the transient responses evoked by attended stimuli, but presumably helped lead to the evoked-response enhancement for the attended stimuli when they occurred (**Figure 12.10B**). ERP studies in humans also support attention-related pretarget biasing of activity in the sensory cortical regions (**Figure 12.10C**).

Other neural activity changes that have been observed in the sensory cortices following an instructional cue are changes in oscillatory brain activity. For example, during cued visual attention tasks similar to those described earlier in the chapter, oscillatory EEG activity (see Chapter 3) in the alpha band (8–12 Hz) is reduced over occipital cortex contralateral to the direction of attention, sometimes with corresponding increases observed over ipsilateral occipital cortex. These changes have also been interpreted as reflecting

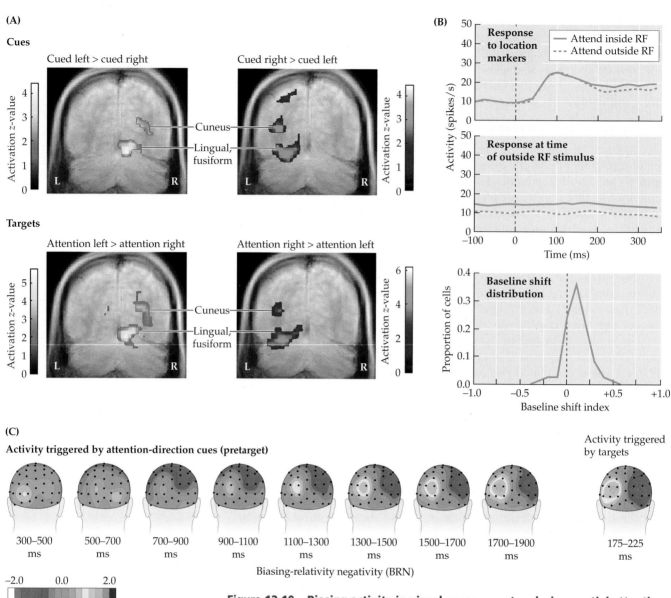

Figure 12.10 Biasing activity in visual sensory cortex during spatial attention tasks. (A) This fMRI study of humans performing visual spatial attention tasks shows that engaging the attentional control network by attention-directing cues leads to enhanced activity in contralateral visual sensory cortex prior to—or even in the absence of—a visual target. The sensory cortex activity elicited by the targets themselves closely corresponds to the pretarget biasing activity elicited by the cues. (B) Single-unit recordings in awake, behaving monkeys show that attention to a location in space increases the background firing of V4 neurons that have receptive fields in that location. (C) Pretarget biasing of sensory cortex triggered by attention-directing cues is also seen with ERPs (a negative-polarity wave termed *biasing-related negativity*), which also provide timing information for this effect in humans. (A from Hopfinger et al. 2000; B after Luck et al. 1997; C after Grent-'t-Jong and Woldorff 2007.)

preparatory activity in specific areas of sensory cortex for the processing of upcoming stimulus information, with decreased alpha power contralaterally reflecting increased excitability of occipital areas specific to the target location, and increased alpha power ipsilaterally reflecting active inhibition of nonrelevant areas. Other electrophysiological studies, both of scalp-recorded EEG and MEG activity in humans and of intracranial local field potential activity in non-human primates, have shown cue-triggered changes in other frequency bands, which also seem likely to be related to preparatory processes induced in the sensory cortices by attention.

Brain Activity Related to the Control of Exogenous Attention

Attentional shifts triggered by sudden stimulus onsets

Most experimental work on attention control has focused on endogenous attention employing instructional cues in the laboratory. However, attentional shifts are often triggered exogenously by stimuli in the environment that happen suddenly or are otherwise salient, such as a loud sound or the sudden movement of an object. As described in Chapter 10, such stimulus-driven shifts of attention also result in enhanced detection or discrimination of stimuli that occur shortly afterward at the same location as the cuing stimulus. In this case, the shifts occur reflexively, being triggered even if the cuing stimulus does not predict a subsequent stimulus occurring at that location. In addition, as described in Chapter 11, exogenously triggered shifts of attention, particularly to a specific location in space, result in enhanced activity in the corresponding regions of sensory cortex in response to stimuli that occur shortly afterward in that location.

The control mechanisms for these exogenously triggered attentional shifts have also been studied using approaches in which brain activity associated with the triggered orienting of attention is recorded, although there have been far fewer such studies. It is generally more difficult to distinguish the brain activity specifically involved in the control of such attentional shifts from brain activity reflecting the stimulus processing of the exogenous cue (which occurs at the same location as the target). Nevertheless, the results suggest that some of the same frontal and parietal control regions implicated in the control of endogenous attention are also activated by exogenous attention. Other brain areas, however, appear to be involved in the triggering of these dorsal frontal and parietal regions during exogenous attention, as described in the following section.

Attentional reorienting activates a right-sided ventral system

In studies of mainly endogenous attentional orienting, Corbetta and colleagues concluded that some of the observed brain activity appeared to be closely related to the exogenous triggering of attentional shifts. In particular, although the studies were aimed mainly at the mechanisms of endogenously cued attention, areas in more inferior regions of the right hemisphere, near the right temporoparietal junction (TPJ), were more strongly activated by invalidly than validly cued targets (**Figure 12.11**). The investigators reasoned that on invalidly cued trials, subjects first oriented their attention to the cued location but then had to reorient attention to another location when the target appeared there. Accordingly, when the target occurred in this new location, it acted as an exogenous cue to trigger a shift of attention to that spot. The increased activity in the right TPJ was interpreted as reflecting this stimulus-triggered shift of attention. Corbetta and colleagues reasoned further that if these TPJ areas were involved in responding to shifts of attention toward new stimuli in the environment, they would also be activated by infrequent targets in a stream or by other novel stimuli. Both of these predictions were borne out by empirical studies, further supporting the role of the right TPJ, along with similarly behaving areas in the right ventral frontal lobe, in the triggering of stim-

(A)

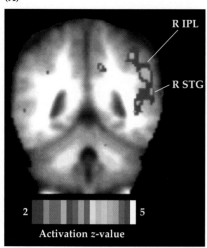

Figure 12.11 Activation of the right temporoparietal junction during reorienting of attention. In an event-related fMRI study of visual spatial attention, subjects were presented with cues instructing them to shift attention to a location on a particular side of the screen to detect a target that was more likely to occur there (80 percent chance; validly cued) versus the other side (20 percent chance; invalidly cued). (A) The functional map comparing the fMRI responses to invalidly and validly cued targets shows greater activity in the right TPJ for invalidly cued targets, suggesting involvement of this area in the reorienting of attention to unexpected events. (B) The event-related fMRI response waveforms show that this increased activity is elicited for both left and right invalidly cued targets. R IPL, right inferior parietal lobule; R STG, right superior temporal gyrus. (After Corbetta et al. 2000.)

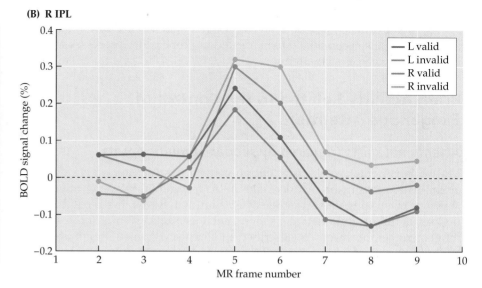

ulus-driven shifts of attention. As described in more detail in the next section, these areas might be activated first in detecting a novel or salient stimulus, which would then invoke control activity in the more dorsal frontoparietal control network.

Single-unit recording studies in non-human primates have provided additional support for these ideas. The TPJ in humans is located near the intraparietal lobule (IPL) and near a region of somatosensory association cortex referred to in monkeys as Brodmann area 7a (although the original Brodmann cytoarchitectonic areas referred specifically to humans, analogous identifiers were given to corresponding areas in the macaque brain by later anatomists). Recordings from this location show neurons responding more strongly for "task-relevant" stimuli occurring at unattended than at attended locations, mirroring the neuroimaging findings. In addition, neurons in this area appear to encode the location of distinctive stimuli that differ from the background (e.g., the pop-out stimuli described in Chapter 10), responding strongly to particularly salient stimuli in the environment.

Attentional Control as a System of Interacting Brain Areas

These studies make clear that, like other complex cognitive functions, attentional control is mediated by a large network of brain regions and not by a single control region. Accordingly, it is useful to look at these areas as components of a system that work together, with different parts being recruited for the different types of attentional functions under different circumstances. Various models of interacting brain areas in the control of attention have been proposed over the last couple of decades. Several of the most influential are briefly described in this section.

Initial models of attentional control

Clinical evidence from neglect syndromes and findings from single-unit studies in non-human primates led Marcel Mesulam, working in the early 1980s at Harvard Medical School, to propose a large-scale brain network for the control and coordination of attention that included regions in frontal and parietal cortex. His model included a frontal component (the frontal eye fields, premotor cortex, and prefrontal cortex), a parietal component (superior parietal lobe, especially areas around the intraparietal sulcus), and a limbic component (cingulate cortex). The frontal component was proposed to convert strategies for attentional shifting into specific motor acts; the parietal component, to provide a dynamic representation of salient events in multiple frames of references and to compute strategies for attentional shifting; and the limbic component, to compute the "motivational relevance" of external events and maintain the "level of effort" of executing attentional tasks. Mesulam's model also identified the reticular activating system as important in modulating overall arousal (see Chapters 10 and 28).

In the early 1990s, Michael Posner and Steve Petersen at Washington University in St. Louis proposed that attentional control in the brain can be divided into two main subsystems: an anterior attentional system and a posterior attentional system. The anterior system, in which the anterior cingulate played a key role, was taken to be important for monitoring the environment and detecting the occurrences of target stimuli, largely because of PET studies associating anterior cingulate activity with such processes. The posterior system, comprising the posterior parietal lobe, the superior colliculus in the midbrain, and the lateral pulvinar in the thalamus, was proposed to be involved in orienting to visual locations.

More recent versions of this model describe three systems: (1) an "alerting system" associated with frontal and parietal regions, particularly in the right hemisphere, which may be due in part to the cortical distribution of the brain's norepinephrine system; (2) an "orienting system" associated with the superior parietal and frontal regions and the temporoparietal junction, along with the superior colliculus and pulvinar, modulated mostly by the neurotransmitter acetylcholine; and (3) an "executive system" associated with superior midline frontal areas (the anterior cingulate) and lateral prefrontal cortex, characterized by dopaminergic activity. In these and other recent models, the anterior cingulate, especially the dorsal part, has been proposed to also play a key role in signaling and helping to resolve conflicting stimulus information from the environment that would interfere with an intended or appropriate behavior (see Box 10A).

A dorsal endogenous system and a right ventral exogenous system

Incorporating findings from more recent neuroimaging studies, Corbetta and Shulman proposed that the cortical control of attention can be divided into two main systems that carry out different functions but interact extensively (**Figure 12.12**). One system, consisting of parts of the intraparietal cortex and superior frontal cortex, was taken to be involved in preparing and applying goal-directed (endogenous) selection of relevant stimuli and responses. As already noted, a number of cuing studies using neuroimaging have implicated these areas in endogenous attentional control. The other system, consisting mainly of the temporoparietal junction and ventral frontal cortex in the right hemisphere, was proposed to be specialized for the detection of behaviorally relevant stimuli, particularly unexpected or highly salient stimuli that trigger attentional orienting in a more exogenous way. Moreover, after detection of such events, these areas were proposed to act as an alerting system or "circuit breaker" to signal and recruit activity in more dorsal frontal and parietal regions to direct neural processing resources to these novel triggering events or to the location in which they occurred. Thus, this proposal incorporates interactions between stimulus-driven and endogenous mechanisms of attentional control. Similar interactive models have been proposed to describe the mechanisms underlying the coordination of visual search (**Box 12A**).

One view of this model is that the actual attentional orienting and shifting processes are generally accomplished by the more dorsal and frontal regions typically implicated in endogenous attentional studies, although activation of these dorsal areas can be initiated in different ways. In exogenously triggered

Figure 12.12 A combined endogenous-exogenous model of attentional control. (A) The attentional control network in this model is functionally segregated into two interacting systems. The left panel shows a dorsal frontoparietal network controlling endogenous shifts of attention (blue), and a right ventral system responsible for reorienting and the exogenous capture of attention (orange). The right panel indicates the areas that cause neglect syndrome when damaged, which are proposed to match the ventral network better. (B) In this model, the dorsal IPS-FEF network is proposed to be involved in the top-down control of visual processing (blue arrows), and the TPJ-VFC network to be more involved in stimulus-driven control (orange arrows). The IPS and FEF are also modulated by stimulus-driven control. Connections between the TPJ and IPS can interrupt ongoing top-down control when unattended salient stimuli are detected. FEF, frontal eye field; IFG/MFG, inferior frontal gyrus/middle frontal gyrus); IPS/SPL, intraparietal sulcus/superior parietal lobule; IPL/STG, inferior parietal lobule/superior temporal gyrus; TPJ, temporoparietal junction; VFC, ventral frontal cortex. (After Corbetta and Shulman 2002.)

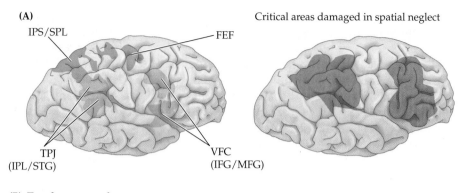

(A)

IPS/SPL
FEF

TPJ
(IPL/STG)
VFC
(IFG/MFG)

Critical areas damaged in spatial neglect

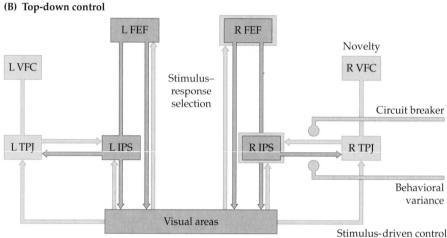

(B) Top-down control

L FEF   R FEF

L VFC   Novelty   R VFC

Stimulus–response selection   Circuit breaker

L TPJ   L IPS   R IPS   R TPJ

Behavioral variance

Visual areas

Stimulus-driven control

attention, activation would be initiated by signaling from the right-sided regions in the right temporoparietal junction and ventral frontal cortex. During endogenous attentional shifting in response to an instructional cue or another event preceding a goal-directed shift of attention, the processing is presumably funneled in from other higher-level brain regions. For example, the processing flow could come from the more lateral regions of the dorsal frontoparietal network (see Figure 12.7A), which may be more involved in either interpreting the meaning of an instructional cue or making a decision on the basis of a complex set of external or internal processes. In these cases, these other regions may induce activation in the more medial areas of the dorsal frontoparietal network, which then initiate and coordinate the orienting of attention to relevant facets of the environment. Regardless of how the medial regions of the frontoparietal network are activated, the system would work by sending signals to appropriately bias or otherwise prepare the sensory cortical regions that need to process the upcoming (or ongoing) stimuli. This biasing would result in enhanced processing activity of those stimuli in the pertinent sensory regions, leading to corresponding enhancements in behavioral performance.

Corbetta and Shulman also proposed that the deficits seen in neglect syndrome are more related to the right-sided exogenous system than to the more dorsal system. One reason for this proposal is that neglect, at least in humans, is due to right-sided lesions, and activation of the ventral system is apparent predominantly on the right. Moreover, although initial studies suggested that the lesions causing hemispatial neglect were located in the right parietal lobe, more recent studies have suggested that the area of damage that most consistently leads to neglect is actually somewhat more inferior, quite close to the right temporoparietal junction, which is the region implicated during exoge-

■ BOX 12A Neural Processes Related to the Coordination of Visual Search

As described in the text, models of attentional control have proposed interacting systems in which stimulus-driven and top-down mechanisms interact. Another realm of attention in which such interactions have been proposed is visual search. For example, if one is searching for a salient stimulus (e.g., a red item among green ones, or a friend wearing a red sweater in a crowd; see Chapter 10), the cognitive processes at play entail both stimulus-driven and endogenous factors. In particular, the stimulus itself (the presence of a distinctive popout color) presumably serves as a bottom-up trigger to drive the attentional shifts. On the other hand, if there are multiple possibilities (e.g., a red item and a blue item among mostly green items) and a subject is specifically searching for only one of these (e.g., a red item), it is that item to which attention is shifted. Thus, behavioral goals come into play, effectively setting priorities that help establish a *salience map*, as discussed in Chapter 10. Moreover, when attention must be shifted serially to find a conjunction of features, neural processes must be involved in the shifting processes as well.

Some studies have investigated the brain events underlying visual search. For example, event-related fMRI has shown that most of the areas of dorsal frontal and parietal cortex implicated in endogenous attentional control are also active during visual search. Moreover, the activity in these areas falls off after visual search is terminated (e.g., after a target is found), further suggesting that these areas play a role in these search processes. Single-unit recordings in monkeys have shown further that neurons in the inferior parietal cortex near the temporoparietal junction appear to code the location of distinctive (popout) stimuli in the visual field, consistent with the fMRI activation findings. In addition, during visual search tasks aimed at finding a popout target in an array, the frontal eye field neurons appear to discriminate between targets and distracters, regardless of whether the monkey makes a saccade to the target or just shifts attention covertly. Moreover, distracter stimuli have been shown to produce larger responses in FEF neurons when they are more similar to the current target.

These findings thus also suggest interactions between more dorsal brain regions (FEFs) and more ventral ones (monkey area 7a or the human TPJ) during visual search, thus suggesting that these interactions may in part reflect the neural implementation of so-called salience maps that have been proposed on the basis of behavioral studies. Finally, it has been shown that neurons in the ventral occipitotemporal cortex are also active during visual search, although this activity may

(Continued on next page)

(A) Pop-out condition

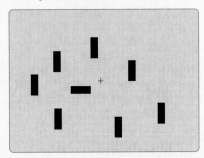

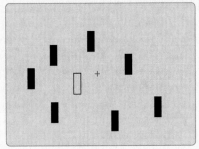

(B)
Target

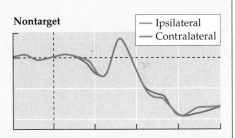

Nontarget

— Ipsilateral
— Contralateral

Difference waves

3.0 µV

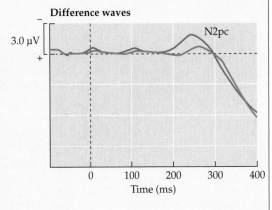

The N2pc ERP response to target pop-out stimuli in a visual array. The detection of a pop-out target in an array (A) elicits an enhanced negative wave over contralateral parietal and occipital scalp regions (B), reflecting the shift of attention to that location. The top panel shows the contralateral and ipsilateral ERP responses when the popout was the target to be directed, the middle panel shows the corresponding ERPs when the popout was not the target, and the bottom panel shows the difference waves between these. In the term N2pc, N stands for "negative," 2 for the second large negative peak, *p* for "posterior," and c for "contralateral." (After Luck et al. 1994.)

■ **BOX 12A** *(continued)*

reflect an effect of the attention shifting rather than the control process per se.

The neural underpinnings of visual search have also been studied with ERPs and MEG. When an array of stimuli is presented containing a feature popout item as a target to be detected, a negative wave peaking at about 250 milliseconds is evoked over parietal and occipital regions contralateral to the popout location (see the figure). This so-called **N2pc wave**, first discovered by Steve Luck and Steven Hillyard working at UC San Diego, has been used in numerous experiments to study the temporal characteristics of attentional shifting during visual search tasks.

Some of these studies have included determining the speed of attentional shifting during visual search. In one study, for example, subjects needed to

detect and shift attention first to a popout of one color on one side of the visual field, and then to a popout of a different color on the other side. These processes were reflected by first an increased negative wave (an N2pc) peaking at 250 milliseconds contralateral to the first popout, followed shortly after (100 milliseconds later) by an increased negative wave on the other side, presumably reflecting the temporal characteristics of these switching processes.

Source analyses of the N2pc activity have indicated that it derives from a combination of activity in the contralateral parietal and ventral occipitotemporal cortex. Thus, this activity may include both the control processes for the shifting of attention (e.g., processing in the parietal cortex) and the ramifications of that switch on processing in the contralateral visual sensory cortex. Other findings, however, have suggested that this activity may reflect filtering of the surrounding distracter stimuli in the array, rather than the shifting process itself. In any event, this neural activity provides a useful marker for studying mechanisms of attentional shifting in complex visual scenes.

References

Luck, S. J. and S. A. Hillyard (1994) Spatial filtering during visual search: Evidence from human electrophysiology. *J. Exp. Psychol. Hum. Percept. Perform.* 20: 1000–1014.

Woodman, G. F. and S. J. Luck (1999) Electrophysiological measurement of rapid shifts of attention during visual search. *Nature* 400: 867–869.

---

nously triggered reorienting of attention in neuroimaging studies, as just described (see Figure 12.11). On the other hand, the right TPJ and right ventral frontal cortex are activated by sudden stimuli in both visual fields. Why damage to these areas does not cause orienting problems for stimuli in *both* visual fields is not explained by this model.

Nevertheless, other findings have supported the idea of interactions between exogenous and endogenous attentional systems. A neuroimaging study by John Serences and colleagues at Johns Hopkins University focused on the capture of visual attention by nontarget stimulus items that, although task-irrelevant, nonetheless shared a defining feature of the relevant target. Such attentional capture seems to be reflexive (i.e., automatic) and stimulus-driven; on the other hand, setting the target features as a priority in the first place is a top-down process based on behavioral and task goals. The findings indicated that these distracting nontarget items also activated the right TPJ and ventral frontal cortex, despite being task-irrelevant. These results were interpreted as indicating that the right TPJ and ventral frontal cortex may play a role in detecting and signaling the need to switch attention to any stimulus with a target-defining feature. Thus, attentional control in these circumstances would presumably also require a dynamic interplay between the dorsal and ventral systems.

Interactions of components of the attentional systems

The view that attentional control depends on networks of brain regions that work together as interacting systems to enhance neural processing in sensory and other brain regions is supported by studies that have investigated the relationships between these areas. For example, the temporal activation sequence described earlier for the shifting of endogenous visual attention (see Figure 12.7) indicates that cue interpretation and decision processes are first performed in the lateral frontoparietal regions of the dorsal network, which may then funnel information into the more medial portions of the network that more specifically underlie the attentional orienting. Within the medial network, attentional orienting appears to be initiated by the medial dorsal frontal regions, joined shortly later by activity in the medial dorsal parietal regions, which together then lead to biasing in the appropriate sensory cortices (see Figure 12.10).

It is not clear whether, during exogenously triggered attention, a similar sequence of activity occurs in these medial regions (i.e., medial frontal, then medial parietal, and then sensory cortical biasing). Considering the speed with which exogenous attentional shifts are implemented (less than 100 milliseconds), and the fact that an initial period of enhancement is followed by inhibition of return (see Chapter 10), the temporal characteristics of activity in the dorsal control regions triggered during exogenous attention seem likely to be rather different from those during endogenous attention. Regardless, the timing sequence during exogenous attention presumably involves the right-sided TPJ and ventral frontal regions before engagement of the medial portions of the dorsal frontal and parietal network, although this speculation has not yet been demonstrated.

In addition to these temporal-sequence findings, other data provide more direct evidence for causal links between the components of these systems. For example, Robert Knight and colleagues at the University of California showed that, during auditory selective attention, patients with damage to one side of the prefrontal cortex had reduced attention-related modulations of the early sensory processing for auditory stimuli received by the contralateral ear. These results suggest that the frontal cortex is required for such attention-related modulations in the sensory cortex, in accord with the view that the frontal cortex provides the signal that helps accomplish the observed modulations of sensory activity.

Similarly, transcranial magnetic stimulation (TMS; see Chapter 3) of the frontal cortex on one side increases activity in the visual cortex ipsilateral to the stimulated frontal lobe and modulates behavioral performance in discriminating stimuli in the contralateral visual hemifield. Finally, a TMS pulse applied to the right parietal lobe produces neglect-like symptoms in normal subjects. Again, these findings support the idea that regions in a frontoparietal network are critical for coordinating and modulating the sensory cortices to process stimulus input optimally (or at least more efficiently).

Related work in non-human primates is consistent with this interpretation. Tirin Moore and Katherine Armstrong at Princeton applied microstimulation to specific areas of the frontal eye fields in macaque monkeys while visual responses were being recorded from single units in area V4 (**Figure 12.13A–C**). Low-level microstimulation in the FEF (i.e., below the level of stimulation that produces saccades) resulted in enhanced visual responses of single neurons in the corresponding areas of V4 (see Chapter 5). Microstimulation of noncorresponding areas of the FEF, on the other hand, suppressed V4 responses. Moreover, a related study showed that subthreshold stimulation in FEF also improved target discrimination performance of attended targets in the relevant spatial location in the visual field (**Figure 12.13D–F**). These findings support the view that the dorsal frontoparietal network exerts modulatory control over stimulus processing in the sensory cortices, and thus over corresponding behavioral performance.

Further support for the interactive roles proposed for these various components of the attentional control systems is provided by a recent fMRI study by Daniel Weissman and colleagues at Duke investigating dynamic changes in the level of attention across time. In this study, trial-by-trial variations in reaction time during a visual attention task (which were assumed to reflect, at least in part, variations in attentional focus) were correlated with variations in the fMRI activity in the brain regions of the attentional control systems discussed in this chapter.

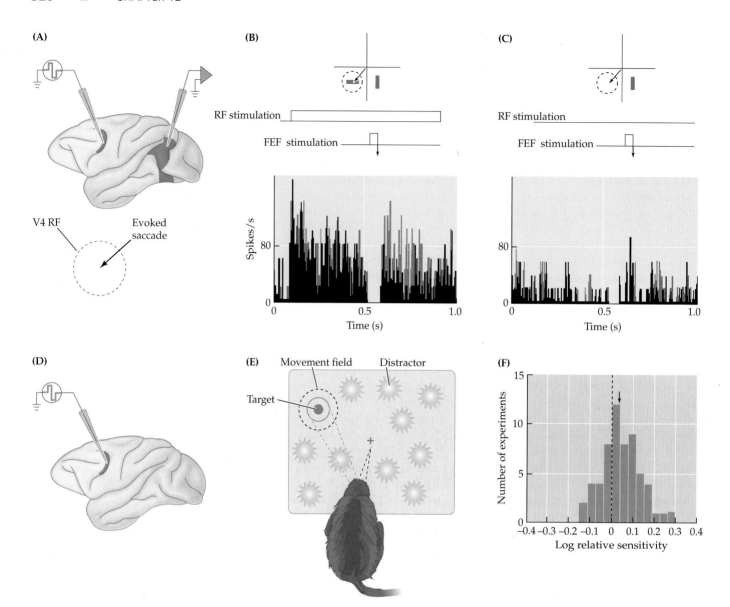

Figure 12.13 Effects of frontal eye field microstimulation on neuronal responses in V4 and on covert attention.   (A–C) Microstimulation of sites within the FEF, below the threshold for eliciting a saccade, was carried out while the visual stimulus responses of single V4 neurons were recorded in monkeys performing a fixation task. (A) The stimulating electrode was positioned so that suprathreshold stimulation would evoke a saccade into the receptive field (RF) of the V4 cell under study. (B) This example shows the effect of sub-threshold FEF microstimulation on the response of a single V4 neuron to an oriented bar presented in the cell's receptive field. The mean response during control trials is shown in black; the enhanced response arising from the FEF microstimulation, in red. (C) In contrast, on trials in which the visual stimulus was presented outside the receptive field of the V4 neuron, no enhancement is seen. (D–F) In another study, subthreshold microstimulation in FEF was carried out while the monkey's performance in a covert attention task was measured. (D) To study the effects on covert attention, a microelectrode was positioned in the FEF to evoke saccades to a fixed location with respect to the center of gaze ("movement field"). (E) Monkeys performed an attention task in which they had to detect the transient dimming of a visual stimulus (target) at the movement field location corresponding to the FEF microstimulation site. The attention task was performed with and without subthreshold stimulation of the FEF site just prior to dimming of the target stimulus. (F) Subthreshold microstimulation increased the monkey's sensitivity to the target change (i.e., the relative sensitivity distribution was shifted to right). This effect was observed only when the target was within the movement field of the cells being recorded. (After Moore et al. 2003.)

First, attentional lapses (trials with slower reaction times) began with reduced activity *prior* to the stimulus trial in the dorsal anterior cingulate and dorsal prefrontal regions that have been implicated in controlling attention. This pretrial decrease in frontal activity was followed after the stimulus occurrence by reduced evoked activity in the relevant areas of visual cortex. This temporal sequence supports the hypothesis that regions of the dorsal frontoparietal network, including the dorsal anterior cingulate, regulate attention and performance from moment to moment by modulating processing in the appropriate task-relevant sensory cortical regions. Attentional lapses were also characterized by concurrent increases in activity in a complementary **default-mode network** that becomes more active when someone is *not* engaged in an attentionally demanding task (**Box 12B**).

Finally, increased stimulus-evoked activity in the right inferior frontal gyrus and the right temporoparietal junction in a trial predicted better performance on the *next* trial. This effect could reflect stimulus-triggered reorienting activity in the right-sided ventral exogenous system proposed by Corbetta and Shulman, possibly providing the hypothesized interrupt signal for the dorsal system and a mechanism for recovery from a transient waning of attentional focus. In any event, patterns of activation across the brain as a dynamic function of attention and performance endorse the view that attentional control is mediated by these several interacting brain networks.

■ BOX 12B A Default-Mode Network

On the basis of neuroimaging studies, Marcus Raichle and colleagues at Washington University in St. Louis proposed that there is a *default* level of activity in many regions of the brain, a baseline level from which cognitive tasks induce increases of activity. Moreover, studies by this group and other researchers indicate that certain brain regions, including the posterior cingulate cortex, the ventral anterior cingulate cortex, and the medial prefrontal cortex, consistently show *greater* activity during resting states than during the processing of specific cognitive tasks. When the activity during a baseline or rest condition is subtracted from the activity during cognitive tasks, relative decreases of activity (generally called *deactivations*) are observed in these areas. Because cognitive tasks induce activation increases in other brain areas carrying out the relevant processing, this finding led to the proposal that these regions constitute a network supporting a default mode of brain function that is engaged in the *absence* of any particular cognitive task. Supporting the hypothesis that these areas constitute a network, analysis of the functional connectivity of these areas (i.e., how much their activity covaries) has shown strong coupling during the resting state.

From the standpoint of understanding attentional control, analyses of the functional connectivity between the components of this default-mode network and the components of the frontoparietal network activated during attentional tasks (see text) found significant *inverse* correlations of activity during rest. Such results suggest that these may be complementary networks—the attentional control systems being activated for demanding cognitive tasks, and the default-mode network being activated when the brain is "idling."

A central question is what purpose neural activity in a default-mode network would serve (i.e., why should these regions be active if and when the brain is doing nothing in particular?). Although the default-mode network activity might be related to the mind's simply idling, another possibility is that this network is activated when attention is inwardly focused, the "standard" attentional control system being activated primarily when a subject is focused on events and stimuli in the external environment. Whereas sorting out the functions of these postulated networks will require a good deal more work, the inverse relationship of activity in the default network and activity in the dorsal frontoparietal attentional control network during focused attention suggests that these complementary systems play an overarching role in systemwide brain function related to attentional and cognitive control.

References

McKiernan, K. A., J. N. Kaufman, J. Kucera-Thompson and J. R. Binder (2003) A parametric manipulation of factors affecting task-induced deactivation in functional neuroimaging. *J. Cogn. Neurosci.* 15: 394–408.

Raichle, M. E., A. M. MacLeod, A. Z. Snyder, W. J. Powers, D. A. Gusnard and G. L. Shulman (2001) A default mode of brain function. *Proc. Natl. Acad. Sci. USA* 98: 676–682.

Generality of the attentional control systems

An important basic question about attentional systems and attentional control concerns their generality. For example, are the same dorsal frontal and parietal regions that are widely implicated in visual attentional control also used for attentional orienting in other sensory modalities? And are the control regions that shift visual attention to features or objects the same as those invoked for visual spatial attention? Even more generally, do these regions, or at least some of them, reflect a central executive control system that directs attentional resources throughout the brain? And finally, do these same regions control attention directed to mental processes such as thoughts, feelings, desires, and plans that are not directly related to environmental stimuli?

Neuroimaging studies thus far have suggested a provisional answer to some of these questions. For instance, current evidence suggests that some portions of these attentional control circuits are rather general and others more specific. Thus, many of the same regions of dorsal frontal and parietal cortex implicated in visual spatial attention are also active in auditory attentional orienting or switching tasks, although the locus of the neural activation for the latter tasks appears to be somewhat more medial and dorsal. In addition, greater activity is elicited in inferior frontal regions and nearby regions of the insular cortex for auditory attentional orienting than for visual. Other findings have indicated that switching attention between different object types also elicits activity near or in some of the same medial regions in parietal cortex implicated in other switching tasks (see Figure 12.6).

In a review of studies of the parietal cortex and its role in attention and cognitive processes, Eva Wojciulik and Nancy Kanwisher working at MIT presented evidence for the generality of the role of parietal cortex in a number of different kinds of attentional and executive control tasks. Similarly, numerous studies have shown activation of portions of the FEF and other nearby frontal cortical regions during a variety of attentional and cognitive control tasks, in accord with the view that the frontal cortex is a key player in executive control more generally, such as keeping track of task goals and coordinating processes in other brain areas (see Chapter 23). Relatively few studies, however, have examined attentional control in the context of non-sensory processing, and thus this aspect of the question remains open.

Finally, the consensus about the generality of attentional control networks is, to a considerable degree, based on studies of covert attention, most often in the context of vision—that is, paradigms in which the subject attends to a particular region of the visual field but without moving the eyes to fixate that location (see Chapter 10). In the real world, however, we usually move our eyes to the location or the object that interests us or that has otherwise attracted our attention. The control of overt attention shifts seems likely to be closely related to the covert attentional control systems, but the evidence for this view is thus far relatively limited.

In support of the idea that covert and overt attention share the same neural bases, the control circuits for saccadic eye movements and overt attention shifting show considerable overlap with the control circuits for covert attention (**Figure 12.14**). Indeed, these data have been used to support the *premotor theory of attention* mentioned earlier, which postulates that saccade planning in the FEF and other oculomotor structures provides the basis for covert attentional orienting. Moreover, it has been hypothesized that the covert visual attention control system evolved as an adjunct to the system already in place underlying the control of eye movements.

In short, the evidence to date indicates that attentional control systems make use of many brain areas for the same general purposes, although, as might be expected, specific patterns of activation vary as a function of the task at hand, the sensory modalities used, and the degree to which attention is

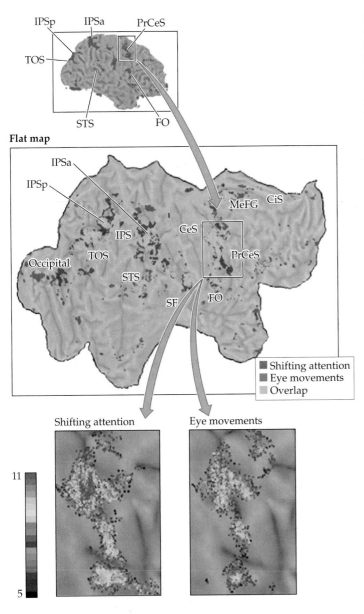

Figure 12.14   Covert versus overt attentional networks. Functional MRI activation during covert attentional (red) and overt eye movement (green) shifts to different stimulus locations is shown for one subject. The functional data are projected onto both a three-dimensional and a flattened two-dimensional representation of the subject's brain. The inset shows the activity in cortical regions in and around the precentral sulcus (PrCeS). Considerable overlap (shown in yellow) is observed in frontal, parietal, and temporal regions, indicating a close functional relationship between the neural systems for shifting attention and for shifting eye gaze to spatial locations. It has been suggested that this overlap might reflect a covert attentional system that, during the course of evolution, co-opted the circuits already in place for saccadic eye movement control. CeS, central sulcus; CiS, cingulate sulcus; FO, frontal operculum; IPS, intraparietal sulcus; IPSa, anterior intraparietal sulcus; IPSp, posterior intraparietal sulcus; MeFG, medial frontal gyrus; SF, Sylvian fissure; STS, superior temporal sulcus; TOS, transverse occipital sulcus. (From Corbetta et al. 1998.)

directed externally to the environment or internally to thoughts, desires, or other subjective concerns.

Summary

1. Given that paying attention elicits changes at many levels of the nervous system, an obvious question is whether there is an overarching control system (or systems) for the attentional effects that are apparent in patients described by clinicians, or in explicit studies of attention in normal subjects using electrophysiological or brain imaging methods.

2. Most studies of attentional control systems have been carried out on subjects who are given specific task instructions about what to attend to, which they then implement voluntarily. These studies have yielded abundant evidence that the orienting of attention to locations or stimuli in the external environment elicits activity in several regions of the dorsal frontal and parietal cortices.

3. In contrast, exogenously induced attention, such as the reorienting of attention to salient and unexpected events, triggers increased activity in cortical regions near the right temporoparietal junction and right ventral frontal cortex, which may in turn trigger the involvement of portions of this same dorsal frontoparietal network.

4. In both endogenously and exogenously induced attention, the dorsal frontoparietal network, once activated, appears to operate as a control system that sends a priming or biasing signal to the relevant sensory cortices to increase the baseline activity, thus facilitating stimulus processing in those cortices (or other pertinent brain regions). This scheme is consistent with the enhanced sensory activity elicited by attended stimuli, and with the associated improvement in behavioral performance in tasks involving these stimuli.

Additional Reading

Reviews

CORBETTA, M. AND G. L. SHULMAN (2002) Control of goal-directed and stimulus-driven attention in the brain. *Nat. Rev. Neurosci.* 3: 201–215.

HUSAIN, M. AND C. RORDEN (2003) Non-spatially lateralized mechanisms in hemispatial neglect. *Nat. Rev. Neurosci.* 4: 26–36.

KANWISHER, N. AND E. WOJCIULIK (2000) Visual attention: Insights from brain imaging. *Nat. Rev. Neurosci.* 1: 91–100.

MILLER, E. K. AND J. D. COHEN (2001) An integrative theory of prefrontal cortex function. *Annu. Rev. Neurosci.* 24: 167–202.

MOORE, T., K. M. ARMSTRONG AND M. FALLAH (2003) Visuomotor origins of covert spatial attention. *Neuron* 40: 671–683.

POSNER, M. I. AND S. E. PETERSEN (1990) The attention system of the human brain. *Annu. Rev. Neurosci.* 13: 25–42.

Important Original Papers

BISIACH, E. AND C. LUZZATTI (1978) Unilateral neglect of representational space. *Cortex* 14: 129–133.

BRAIN, W. R. (1941) Visual disorientation with special reference to lesions of the right cerebral hemisphere. *Brain* 64: 244–272.

COLBY, C. L., J. R. DUHAMEL AND M. E. GOLDBERG (1996) Visual, presaccadic, and cognitive activation of single neurons in monkey lateral intraparietal area. *J. Neurophysiol.* 76: 2841–2852.

COOPER, A. A. AND G. W. HUMPHREYS (2000) Coding space within but not between objects: Evidence from Balint's syndrome. *Neuropsychologia* 38: 723–733.

CORBETTA, M., J. M. KINCADE, J. M. OLLINGER, M. P. MCAVOY AND G. L. SHULMAN (2000) Voluntary orienting is dissociated from target detection in human posterior parietal cortex. *Nat. Neurosci.* 3: 292–297.

CORBETTA, M., F. M. MIEZIN, G. L. SHULMAN AND S. E. PETERSEN (1993) A PET study of visuospatial attention. *J. Neurosci.* 13: 1202–1226.

CORBETTA, M., AND 10 OTHERS (1998) A common network of functional areas for attention and eye movements. *Neuron* 21: 761–773.

FRIEDMAN-HILL, S. R., L. C. ROBERTSON AND A. TREISMAN (1995) Parietal contributions to visual feature binding: Evidence from a patient with bilateral lesions. *Science* 269: 853–855.

GRENT-'T-JONG, T. AND M. G. WOLDORFF (2007) Timing and sequence of brain activity in top-down control of visual-spatial attention. *PLoS Biol.* 5: 114–126.

HOPFINGER, J. B., M. H. BUONOCORE AND G. R. MANGUN (2000) The neural mechanisms of top-down attentional control. *Nat. Neurosci.* 3: 284–291.

KASTNER, S., M. A. PINSK, P. DE WEERD, R. DESIMONE AND L. G. UNGERLEIDER (1999) Increased activity in human visual cortex during directed attention in the absence of visual stimulation. *Neuron* 22: 751–761.

KNIGHT, R. T., S. A. HILLYARD, D. L. WOODS AND H. J. NEVILLE (1981) The effects of frontal cortex lesions on event-related potentials during auditory selective attention. *Electroencephalogr. Clin. Neurophysiol.* 52: 571–582.

LIU, T., S. D. SLOTNICK, J. T. SERENCES AND S. YANTIS (2003) Cortical mechanisms of feature-based attentional control. *Cereb. Cortex* 13: 1334–1343.

LUCK, S. J., L. CHELAZZI, S. A. HILLYARD AND R. DESIMONE (1997) Neural mechanisms of spatial selective attention in areas V1, V2, and V4 of macaque visual cortex. *J. Neurophysiol.* 77: 24–42.

MESULAM, M. M. (1981) A cortical network for directed attention and unilateral neglect. *Ann. Neurol.* 10: 309–325.

MOORE, T. AND K. M. ARMSTRONG (2003) Selective gating of visual signals by microstimulation of frontal cortex. *Nature* 421: 370–373.

RAICHLE, M. E., A. M. MACLEOD, A. Z. SNYDER, W. J. POWERS, D. A. GUSNARD AND G. L. SHULMAN (2001) A default mode of brain function. *Proc. Natl. Acad. Sci. USA* 98: 676–682.

RIHS, T. A., C. M. MICHEL AND G. THUT (2007) Mechanisms of selective inhibition in visual spatial attention are indexed by alpha-band EEG synchronization. *Eur. J. Neurosci.* 25: 603–610.

SERENCES, J. T., J. SCHWARTBACH, S. M. COURTNEY, X. COLAY AND S. YANTIS (2004) Control of object-based attention in human cortex. *Cereb. Cortex* 14: 1346–1357.

SERENCES, J. T., S. SHOMSTEIN, A. B. LEBER, X. GOLAY, H. E. EGETH AND S. YANTIS (2005) Coordination of voluntary and stimulus-driven attentional control in human cortex. *Psychol. Sci.* 16: 114–122.

STEINMETZ, M. A. AND C. CONSTANTINIDIS (1995) Neurophysiological evidence for a role of posterior parietal cortex in redirecting visual attention. *Cereb. Cortex* 5: 448–456.

THOMPSON, K. G., K. L. BISCOE AND T. R. SATO (2005) Neuronal basis of covert spatial attention in the frontal eye field. *J. Neurosci.* 25: 9479–9487.

WEISSMAN, D. H., K. C. ROBERTS, K. M. VISSCHER AND M. G. WOLDORFF (2006) The neural bases of momentary lapses in attention. *Nat. Neurosci.* 9: 971–978.

WOJCIULIK, E. AND N. KANWISHER (1999) The generality of parietal involvement in visual attention. *Neuron* 23: 747–764.

WOLDORFF, M. G., C. J. HAZLETT, H. M. FICHTENHOLTZ, D. H. WEISSMAN, A. M. DALE AND A. W. SONG (2004) Functional parcellation of attentional control regions of the brain. *J. Cogn. Neurosci.* 16: 149–165.

WORDEN, M. S., J. J. FOXE, N. WANG AND G. V. SIMPSON (2000) Anticipatory biasing of visuospatial attention indexed by retinotopically specific alpha-band electroencephalography increases over occipital cortex. *J. Neurosci.* 20: 1–6.

YANTIS, S. AND 6 OTHERS (2002) Transient neural activity in human parietal cortex during spatial attention shifts. *Nat. Neurosci.* 5: 995–1002.

Books

ITTI, L., G. REES AND J. K. TSOTSOS, EDS. (2005) *Neurobiology of Attention.* Amsterdam: Elsevier.

UNIT V

Principles of Memory

Memory allows us to learn from the past, to understand the present, and to plan for the future. All cognitive abilities depend on memory to one degree or another. Thus perception depends on the interaction between sensory stimuli and stored knowledge about objects in the world, and this knowledge is critical for attentional processes. Emotions are influenced by past experiences, and language depends on concepts and grammatical rules stored in memory. Even our sense of self is based on accumulated memories.

Memory involves the creation, stabilization, persistence, and recovery of the traces left in neural circuitry by experience. These processes are respectively called encoding (also referred to as learning), consolidation, storage, and retrieval. At the cellular and molecular levels, "memory traces" are believed to involve changes in the synaptic connections between neurons.

Memory is not a unitary phenomenon. In terms of *duration*, researchers distinguish between the maintenance and manipulation of information for brief periods (working memory) and the acquisition and recovery of information over longer periods (long-term memory). In terms of *quality*, one can distinguish between memory for events and facts (declarative memory) and memories that are expressed through task performance (nondeclarative memory). Although working memory, declarative memory, and nondeclarative memory involve similar mechanisms of synaptic plasticity, they differ at the systems level. In particular, declarative memory depends on the anatomical and functional integrity of the medial temporal lobes of the brain, whereas nondeclarative memory and working memory do not. Other brain regions are critical for different forms of nondeclarative memory and working memory.

The chapters in this unit are an overview of research on the neural basis of memory. Chapter 13 describes memory mechanisms at the cellular level and explains the distinctions among the different types of memory. Chapter 14 focuses on declarative memory. Chapter 15 focuses on nondeclarative memory. Chapter 16 focuses on working memory. However, the impact of memory on virtually all of our cognitive abilities is evident throughout this book. ■

13

Memory and the Brain: From Cells to Systems

Introduction

Recall from Unit I that the goal of cognitive neuroscience is to investigate the neural correlates of cognitive processes by integrating the domains of cognitive psychology and neuroscience. Understanding memory provides a good example of this integration in that there is a long tradition of memory studies and theories in both these domains. In general, cognitive neuroscientists have sought to link psychological theories regarding memory representations, memory processes, and memory systems to neural phenomena at both cellular and system levels of analysis. At the cellular level, researchers investigate molecular and morphological changes within and between neurons that appear to underlie the formation and persistence of memory traces. Researchers working at the systems level study the roles of different brain regions in different forms of memory. Although cellular and systemic analyses have often proceeded independently, they are intimately related and are both essential for a complete understanding of the neural mechanisms of memory. This chapter offers a brief summary of memory research at both levels and considers various models of integrating this research.

Memory at the Cellular Level

In Chapter 2, *memory* was broadly defined as the mechanism whereby past experiences alter present behavior. The link between past experiences and present behavior is assumed to be physical and biochemical changes in the brain. In the early 1900s, the pioneering German student of memory Richard Semon referred to these changes as **engrams**; they can be thought of as **memory traces** in the brain. Two related questions about engrams, or memory traces, have fascinated memory researchers ever since: *where* are they located in the brain, and *how,* in neurobiological terms, are they formed?

Early contributions

With respect to the question of *where*, the notion that memory traces are distributed over the cortex and other brain structures is now generally accepted This was not always the case, however. Early in the 1900s, the success of Pavlovian conditioning led to the idea that engrams might be specific to pathways connecting sensory and motor regions (sometimes called the *switchboard metaphor*). To test this idea, the American neuroscientist Karl Lashley undertook a series of experiments that began in the 1920s. Lashley's approach was to make knife cuts in the cortex of a rat's brain that would disconnect the sensory regions from the motor regions of the cortex. He performed this procedure either before or after the rats had learned to run mazes of varying difficulty (**Figure 13.1A,B**). When the cuts he made failed to show much effect, he went on to remove parts of the cortex of varying size and location. Lashley found that in fact the location of the lesions did not matter much—only the extent of the tissue destruction and difficulty of the task seemed consequential (**Figure 13.1C**). These findings were clearly inconsistent with the switchboard metaphor.

Lashley then conceptualized his findings in terms of a **mass action principle**, which states that the reduction in learning is proportional to the amount of tissue destroyed, and that the more complex the learning task, the more disruptive the lesion. The mass action principle resembles a property of *graceful degradation* seen in parallel distributed, or *connectionist*, neural network mod-

Figure 13.1 Lashley's experiments in search of the engram. (A) Lesions of varying size and location were made in rat brains before or after maze learning. (B) Three levels of maze difficulty. (C) The reduction in learning observed is proportional to the amount of tissue destroyed; the more complex the learning task, the more disruptive the lesions. (University of Rome, Psychology Lab Website.)

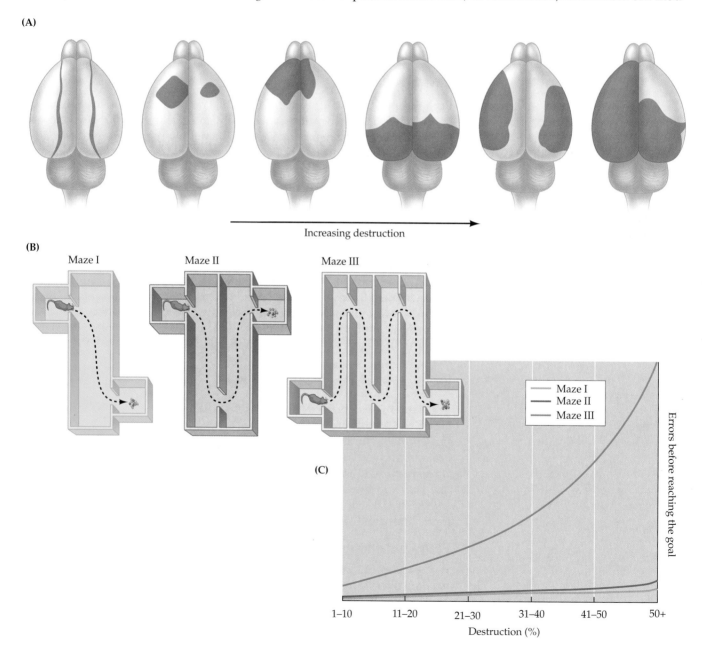

(A)

Increasing destruction

(B)

Maze I   Maze II   Maze III

Maze I
Maze II
Maze III

(C)

Destruction (%)

1–10   11–20   21–30   31–40   41–50   50+

Errors before reaching the goal

els (see Box 2B). Unlike serial processing models, in parallel distributed neural processing, damage to a few processing components does not produce a major disruption of function. Only when the damage is widespread does network performance show a significant decline. Thus, a cortical engram can be considered a parallel distributed network that is seriously impaired only when a large number of nodes are destroyed or disconnected.

The idea that engrams are distributed throughout the brain does not imply that individual memory traces span the whole brain, or that engrams are randomly distributed over the cortex. The modern view is that memories are stored primarily within the brain regions originally involved in processing each kind of information. That is, memory traces for visual information are stored in the striate and extrastriate visual cortices, those for auditory information in auditory cortices, and so on. Some researchers believe that engrams are distributed according to "knowledge domains," citing as evidence cases of brain-damaged patients who are impaired in very specific semantic or object categories, such as information about animals (see Chapters 5 and 14). Finally, some forms of learning have been associated with memory mechanisms in restricted brain regions, such as the localization of eye-blink conditioning in the cerebellum (see Chapter 15), or the amygdala as the site of fear conditioning (see Chapter 18).

This general answer to the *where* question suggested an answer to the *how* question. If an engram is mediated by a network of neurons, then creating an engram should be the process whereby neurons that once functioned independently start working together as a network. This broad answer to how engrams might be formed was first proposed in 1949 by the Canadian psychologist Donald Hebb, who hypothesized that memories are stored in the brain in the form of networks of neurons that he called **cell assemblies**. His idea was that through experience (i.e., learning), these assemblies gradually come to represent specific objects and concepts. To explain how the relevant neurons come to be linked, Hebb further proposed a cellular mechanism known today as **Hebbian learning**. His hypothesis was that when presynaptic and postsynaptic neurons fire action potentials together (see the Appendix), the strength of the synaptic connections between them are enhanced—in other words, the strength of the connections between neurons is increased when these nerve cells are simultaneously active. As a result, synaptic associations would grow stronger and tend to persist. This mechanism is captured in the adage "cells that *fire* together, *wire* together."

Even though they were articulated more than 50 years ago, the gist of Hebb's proposals remains the basis for understanding memory in cellular terms. Only in the last few decades have neuroscientists begun to understand some of the cellular and molecular mechanisms that allow a strengthening of synaptic connectivity as a result of conjoint neural activity.

Habituation and sensitization

One of the main difficulties in investigating the cellular bases of memory is the sheer complexity of neuronal circuits. One way to simplify this problem is to investigate information storage as a function of experience in a simple organism—one with few neurons and a limited behavioral repertoire. Eric Kandel and his colleagues at Columbia University pioneered this approach when, beginning in the late 1960s, they carried out studies using the sea slug *Aplysia californica*. The ganglia which comprise the nervous system in this animal contain only a few thousand neurons, many of which are large and individually identifiable. Despite the simplicity of its nervous system, the sea slug shows rudimentary learning abilities, which Kandel and his group measured in terms of changes in a *withdrawal reflex*. A sea slug withdraws its gill when its siphon is lightly touched, presumably as a defensive maneuver, and this simple reflex

Figure 13.2 Two forms of learning in the sea slug *Aplysia*. The simple neuronal circuit in the abdominal ganglion of the sea slug is used in studies of habituation and sensitization. Touching the animal's siphon elicits withdrawal of the gill. When the siphon is repeatedly touched, this response progressively decreases (habituation). Conversely, a shock to the tail enhances the habituated gill withdrawal response (sensitization). (After Squire and Kandel 1999.)

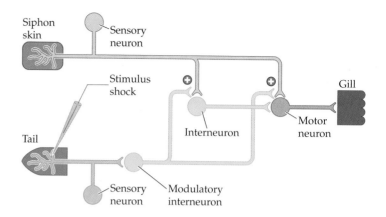

demonstrates two forms of learning that occur in many animals, including humans: **habituation** and **sensitization**. *Habituation* refers to a reduced response when the same stimulus is repeated over and over, whereas *sensitization* refers to an increased response to the habituated stimulus when it is paired with an aversive stimulus such as a shock to the animal's tail (**Figure 13.2**). Touching the siphon skin stimulates sensory neurons, which in turn excite interneurons and motor neurons; the excited motor neurons then elicit the withdrawal of the gill. Electrical recordings show that habituation involves a *decrease* in neurotransmitter release at the sensory neuron-motor neuron synapse. Sensitization involves an *increase* in neurotransmitter release, but depends on the activity of additional neurons. A tail shock excites different sensory neurons, which in turn excite modulatory interneurons that increase neurotransmitter release from the siphon sensory neurons, enhancing gill withdrawal.

Both habituation and sensitization are simple forms of memory. In particular, the modulatory effect of tail shock on the gill withdrawal reflex lasts a matter of minutes, and can thus be regarded as a model for short-term memory in this system. Moreover, repeated tail shocks over longer periods trigger gene expression, new protein synthesis, and the formation of new synaptic connections, all of which result in enhancement of the gill withdrawal reflex that can last weeks—a model of long-term memory.

Long-term potentiation and depression

A second major advance in understanding the cellular mechanisms of memory was made in the early 1970s by Terje Lømo and Timothy Bliss working in the laboratory of Per Anderson at the University of Oslo. While studying rabbit hippocampus, they found that a high-frequency train of electrical stimuli enhanced postsynaptic potentials elicited by subsequent stimuli for the stimulated pathway, but not for other pathways (**Figure 13.3**). Because this focal enhancement was long-lasting, they called the phenomenon **long-term potentiation** (**LTP**). Although LTP was first localized in the hippocampus, subsequent research showed that it occurs in many other brain regions, including the cortex, the amygdala, the basal ganglia, and the cerebellum. Depending on the locus and stimulation paradigm, LTP can last minutes, hours, or much longer.

The discovery of LTP provided another good candidate for the sort of cellular mechanism that could underlie the storage of memories. LTP can be induced by a single high-frequency stimulus; since some memories are often established by a single experience, LTP is a good candidate mechanism for memories of this sort. And since LTP can last for days or even weeks, it also provides a neural mechanism supporting long-term memories. As implied by the work in *Aplysia*, however, maintaining memories for longer periods pre-

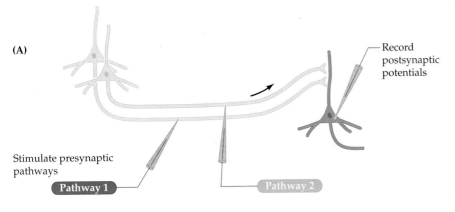

(A)

Record postsynaptic potentials

Stimulate presynaptic pathways

Pathway 1

Pathway 2

Figure 13.3 Long-term potentiation.
(A) Two pathways in the hippocampus that can be stimulated independently. (B) Following high-frequency stimulation (not shown), the postsynaptic potential elicited by a single stimulus is enhanced, but only for the stimulated pathway. (After Malinow et al. 1989.)

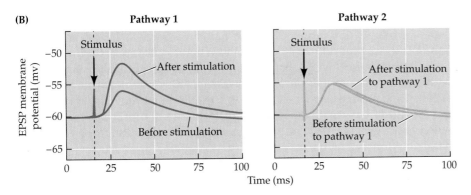

(B)

Pathway 1

Stimulus

After stimulation

Before stimulation

Pathway 2

Stimulus

After stimulation to pathway 1

Before stimulation to pathway 1

EPSP membrane potential (mv)

Time (ms)

sumably requires changes in gene expression and ultimately changes in synaptic connectivity; we will describe such changes further in a subsequent section.

LTP has two further properties that are critical for explaining the phenomenology of memory storage: **specificity** and **associativity**. *Specificity* refers to the fact that only those synapses activated during stimulation are enhanced; other synapses—even other synapses on the same neuron—are not affected (**Figure 13.4A**; see also Figure 13.3). This property accords with the specificity of memories (i.e., the fact that memories are often highly particular). Thus, although we have thousands of memories of eating with other people, we

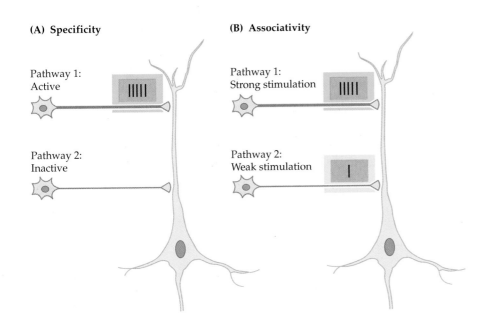

(A) Specificity

Pathway 1: Active

Pathway 2: Inactive

(B) Associativity

Pathway 1: Strong stimulation

Pathway 2: Weak stimulation

Figure 13.4 Features shared by long-term potentiation and the phenomenology of memory.
(A) *Specificity* refers to the fact that only those synapses activated during stimulation are enhanced in LTP. (B) *Associativity* refers to the finding that if one pathway is weakly activated at the same time that another pathway to the same neuron is strongly activated, then both pathways show LTP.

may still remember a particularly special lunch we had with a friend several years ago. Specificity accords with the extraordinary capacity of memory, so that the pianist's repertoire can be expanded indefinitely.

Associativity refers to the finding that if one pathway is weakly activated at the same time that another pathway to the same neuron is strongly activated, then both pathways show LTP (**Figure 13.4B**). By spreading synaptic potentiation over many weakly activated pathways, associativity can increase the chances of the simultaneous pre- and postsynaptic firing, thus enhancing learning of sort envisioned by Hebb (see above).

As suggested by the phenomenon of habituation, synaptic *weakening* is equally a part of learning and memory. If synapses continued to increase in strength due to LTP, they would eventually reach some maximum. It makes sense, therefore, for synaptic potentiation to be counterbalanced by a mechanism of synaptic inhibition. Such a mechanism, known as **long-term depression** (**LTD**), was found in the late 1970s. Whereas LTP occurs with high-frequency stimulation over a brief period, LTD is elicited by low-frequency stimulation over a longer period (**Box 13A**). LTD can also last several hours and is specific to activated synapses. As might be expected, LTD can counteract LTP, and vice versa. There is also some evidence that LTD can enhance LTP in neighboring synapses, and that it can block the formation of associations that do not follow Hebb's rule.

■ BOX 13A Molecular mechanisms of LTP and LTD

An enormous amount of work in recent years has been devoted to sorting out the molecular mechanisms of long-term potentiation and long-term depression. The molecular mechanism behind the standard form of LTP involves the neurotransmitter **glutamate** and two types of glutamate receptors: AMPA and NMDA receptors. The acronyms stand for α-amino-3-hydroxyl-5-methyl-4-isoxazole propionate and *N*-methyl-D-aspartate, respectively (these two chemicals are the antagonists of these two receptor types).

Whereas AMPA receptors mediate normal synaptic transmission in the hippocampus, NMDA receptors play a special role in LTP. Unlike AMPA receptors, the operation of NMDA receptors depends on the state of the postsynaptic cell (Figure A). When the postsynaptic cell is resting, NMDA receptors are blocked by magnesium ions (Mg^{2+}). But when the postsynaptic cell is depolarized, magnesium is expelled from NMDA receptors, allowing calcium ions (Ca^{2+}) to pass through the receptor pore into the postsynaptic cell (right panel in Figure

A). The entry of Ca^{2+} into the postsynaptic cell triggers LTP. Thus, NMDA receptors behave like a molecular "and" gate: only when glutamate is bound to these receptors *and* the postsynaptic cell is depolarized is calcium

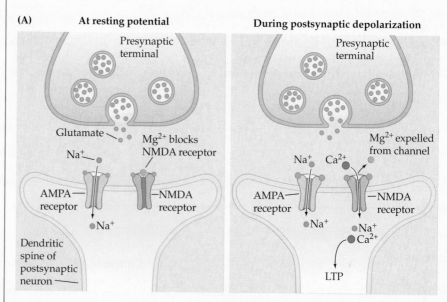

(A) Molecular mechanisms of LTP induction. The neurotransmitter glutamate acts on two types of receptors, AMPA and NMDA. When the postsynaptic cell is resting, NMDA receptors are blocked by magnesium ions (Mg^{2+}), but when the postsynaptic cell is depolarized, magnesium is expelled and calcium ions (Ca^{2+}) flow into the postsynaptic cell. The entry of Ca^{2+} into the postsynaptic cell is the trigger for LTP.

Linking LTP to memory performance

Although LTP has many of the properties required for memory storage and behavior (e.g. specificity and associativity), it is a phenomenon so far elicited only in vitro, and thus may or may not be related to memory in behaving animals. To directly link LTP and memory performance has been a major research effort in recent years.

One approach to this question has been to find evidence of **behavioral LTP**—that is, a demonstrated change in synaptic efficacy similar to LTP that follows a natural learning experience. In this there has been some success. For example, rats raised in an enriched stimulatory environment show enhanced postsynaptic potentials similar to those observed after LTP when compared to rats raised in an environment impoverished in stimulation and learning experiences. The enhancement disappears within a few weeks if the "enriched" rats are placed in the impoverished environment. In addition, changes in synaptic efficacy lasting about 30 minutes have been observed in the rat hippocampus following the exploration of a novel environment. Although these changes could reflect a variety of factors, they could be indicative of learning and memory storage. There is also evidence that inducing LTP in sensory pathways can enhance synaptic responses to natural sensory stimulation, and that learning experiences can lead to long-term increases in correlated firing among hippocampal neurons that were active during learning (thus showing associativity).

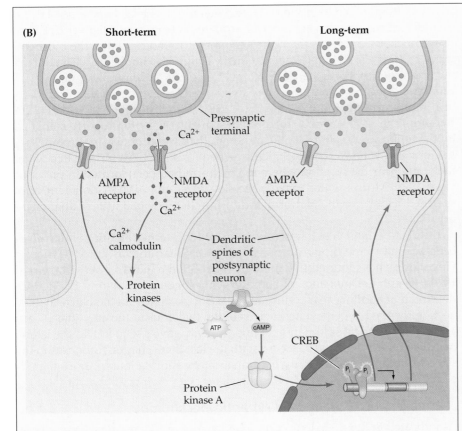

(B) Molecular mechanisms of short-term and long-term processes following LTP induction. The increase in Ca^{2+} activates protein kinases such as calmodulin, leading to the activation and creation of AMPA receptors (left). Long-term processes include protein kinases that activate the transcriptional regulator CREB, which turns on the expression of a number of genes. Gene expression leads to the synthesis of new proteins and can eventually cause long-lasting changes in synaptic morphology and connectivity.

allowed to flow into the postsynaptic cell to initiate LTP.

These properties of NMDA receptors account for both the specificity and associative properties of LTP. Thus LTP is limited to active synapses where glutamate has been released (specificity), and can occur at synapses where a weak stimulus is not enough to depolarize the postsynaptic cell when the membrane is depolarized by a simultaneously occurring strong stimulus at synapses nearby (associativity).

The mechanisms that maintain LTP are less well understood. The dominant theory is that Ca^{2+} activates protein kinases that in turn may activate already-present AMPA receptors and/or add new ones, resulting in a long-lasting enhancement of synaptic transmission (Figure B). In addition to this kind of protein modification, the maintenance of LTP also depends on changes in gene expression and protein synthesis, and eventually on changes in synaptic morphology.

Figure 13.5 Genetic impact on learning the water maze task.
(A) The landscape shows that control mice focused their search in the trained area, resulting in a high total occupancy peak (yellow) in the old platform position, which they apparently remembered. (B) Laboratory mice in which the gene for certain receptors was eliminated ("knocked out") in the hippocampus navigated more or less randomly over the full area of the pool, apparently failing to have learned where the platform should be located. (From Tsien et al. 1996.)

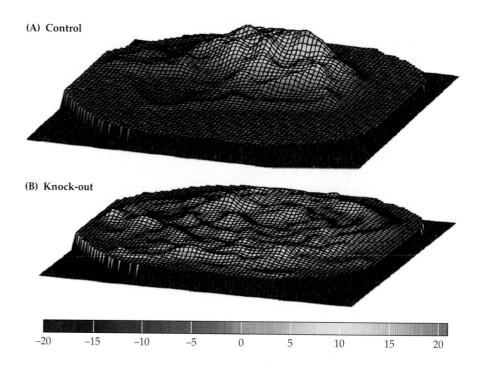

(A) Control

(B) Knock-out

Another approach to linking LTP and memory has been to *prevent* LTP and then determine whether memory is impaired. One way to disrupt LTP is to use "knockout" mice in which the gene for a protein crucial to the biochemistry of LTP is eliminated ("knocked out") using biotechnological ("gene splicing") techniques. For instance, Susumu Tonegawa and his colleagues at MIT produced a strain of laboratory mice that lacked the gene for NMDA receptors in hippocampal region CA1 (see Box 13B). The adult mice lacked NMDA receptors and were severely impaired in spatial learning (a property mediated by the hippocampus in rodents), although they were unimpaired in nonspatial learning. Whereas control mice searched for a platform hidden in a water tank only near the location where the platform had been located in previous trials (the "Morris water maze"; see Box 14A), the NMDA-deficient mice searched widely for the platform, indicating that they had little spatial memory (**Figure 13.5**).

Efforts to establish behaviorally relevant long-term potentiation have not been limited to the hippocampus or to spatial learning; as noted earlier, in vitro studies have located LTP in many other brain regions as well. In the mid 1990s, Joseph LeDoux and collaborators investigated behavioral LTP within the circuit of auditory fear conditioning, particularly within the pathway connecting the medial geniculate nucleus of the thalamus to the amygdala. They found that electrical stimulation of this pathway gave rise to LTP in the lateral nucleus of the amygdala, in accord with the fact that synaptic responses in the same nucleus are enhanced by natural auditory stimulation. In short, there is accumulating evidence that LTP is correlated with memory behavior.

Learning-related changes in synaptic morphology

As indicated in Box 13A, long-term maintenance of LTP requires gene expression and the synthesis of new proteins. Among other effects, these changes can, and in some cases do, lead to long-lasting structural alternations in synapses. These morphological changes in neuronal connectivity can be considered the culmination of a process called *synaptic consolidation* (discussed later in this chapter).

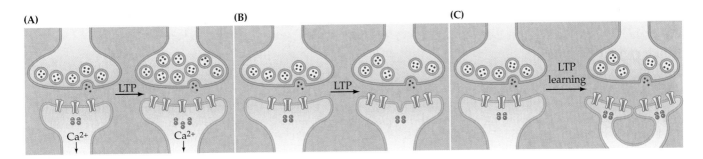

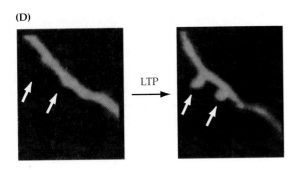

Figure 13.6   Morphological changes in dendritic spines associated with the maintenance of LTP.   (A) Synapses may increase in number of presynaptic vesicles, postsynaptic receptors, and ribosomes (red circles). (B) Synapses may develop separate synaptic zones divided by a wall or a cleft (perforated synapses) in the spine. (C) A single spine may divide in two. (D) New dendritic spines (white arrows) appear approximately 1 hour after a stimulus that induces LTP. (A–C after Lamprecht and LeDoux 2004; D from Engert and Bonhoeffer 1999.)

For many neurons, learning-related alterations in synaptic morphology involve **dendritic spines**—small, mushroom-shaped protrusions from dendritic branches that receive synaptic terminals from other neurons. Many cortical neurons do not have these protuberances, and the rationale for dendritic spines is not well understood. However, their prominence on some neurons and the ease with which their number and shape can be quantified have made them favored targets for the study of structural synaptic change.

Four sorts of morphological change of dendritic spine structure in response to LTP have been described; the simplest is an *increase in the size* of the spine (**Figure 13.6A**). This growth allows an increase in the number of presynaptic vesicles, vesicle release sites, and postsynaptic receptors on a given spine. Spines may also develop separate synaptic zones divided by a wall or a cleft to form what are known as *perforated synapses* (**Figure 13.6B**). Alternatively, a spine may *split completely* into two separate spines (**Figure 13.6C**). Finally, new spines can emerge from the shaft of the dendrite, thereby *increasing the number* of spines and synapses (**Figure 13.6D**). All such changes arguably support the long-term maintenance of LTP.

These four types of change in dendritic spines may occur in sequence. In this scenario, AMPA receptors (see Box 13A) are phosphorylated and their conductance increases within minutes of LTP induction. The size of the spines increases and AMPA receptors are inserted into the postsynaptic membrane. This membrane insertion leads to the production of perforated synapses within 30 minutes or so. After about an hour, some synapses become multispine synapses, and at still longer times the total number of synapses increases further by the emergence of new spines. Whether this "sequence scenario" is realistic and general, however, remains to be seen.

The cellular basis of memory: A summary

The physical representations of memories (engrams) are assumed to be functional and structural changes in synaptic connections among neurons that strengthen the connections between some neurons and weaken other connections. The cellular and molecular mechanisms underlying these changes have been most completely studied in simple nervous systems such as the abdomi-

■ BOX 13B Organization of the Medial Temporal Lobe Memory System

The medial temporal lobe memory system consists of the hippocampus and the surrounding rhinal cortex and parahippocampal cortex (Figure A). The amygdala is located in the anterior part of the medial temporal lobe; although it modulates declarative memory processing (see Chapter 18), the amygdala is not considered a memory region per se.

The main output of the hippocampus is the *fornix*, a tract that connects the hippocampus to the mammillary bodies, the mammillary bodies in turn project to the anterior nucleus of the thalamus. The rhinal cortex consists of the entorhinal cortex medially, and the perirhinal cortex laterally (Figure B). Taken together, the entorhinal,

perirhinal, and parahippocampal cortices constitute the parahippocampal gyrus. (The *parahippocampal gyrus* should not be confused with the *parahippocampal cortex,* which represents only the posterior half of the gyrus.) The perirhinal and parahippocampal cortices receive inputs from association areas in frontal, parietal, temporal, and cingulate cortices (Figure C). In humans and other primates, the perirhinal and parahippocampal cortices project to the entorhinal cortex, which provides the predominant cortical input to the hippocampus.

Of these regions of the medial temporal lobe, the one that has received

the most attention is the hippocampus (a name derived of its seahorse-like shape). The hippocampus is not a homogeneous structure but consists of several interconnected subregions, including the *dentate gyrus*, the *cornus Ammon* (Latin for "horn of Ammon," and often referred to by its abbreviation, "CA"), and the *subiculum* (Figure D). Input from the entorhinal cortex reaches all three hippocampal subregions. There are also several internal "loops" that connect the dentate gyrus to the CA3 and CA1 regions, to the subiculum, and then back to entorhinal cortex (Figure E).

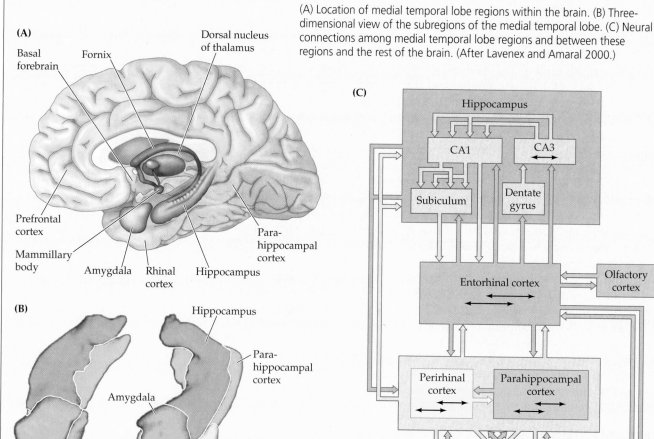

(A) Location of medial temporal lobe regions within the brain. (B) Three-dimensional view of the subregions of the medial temporal lobe. (C) Neural connections among medial temporal lobe regions and between these regions and the rest of the brain. (After Lavenex and Amaral 2000.)

(A)

Basal forebrain
Fornix
Dorsal nucleus of thalamus
Prefrontal cortex
Mammillary body
Amygdala
Rhinal cortex
Hippocampus
Para-hippocampal cortex

(B)

Hippocampus
Para-hippocampal cortex
Amygdala
Entorhinal cortex
Perirhinal cortex

(C)

Hippocampus
CA1
CA3
Subiculum
Dentate gyrus
Entorhinal cortex
Olfactory cortex
Perirhinal cortex
Parahippocampal cortex
Unimodal association areas
Polymodal association areas

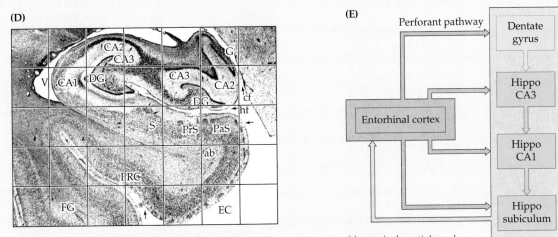

(D) Nissl-stained coronal section of the hippocampus. The 4-mm squares (the typical spatial resolution of fMRI studies) illustrate the difficulty of distinguishing medial temporal lobe subregions using functional neuroimaging. *, collateral sulcus; DG, dentate gyrus; EC, entorhinal cortex; FG, fusiform gyrus; hf, hippocampal fissure; PRC, perirhinal cortex; PaS, parasubiculum; PrS, presubiculum; S, subiculum. (E) Connections within subregions of the hippocampus, including the entorhinal-dentate-CA-subiculum-entorhinal loop. (D from Amaral 1999.)

Thus, as described here, the organization of the medial temporal lobe can be thought of as a hierarchical sequence in which information is processed through perirhinal, parahippocampal, and entorhinal cortices, finally reaching the hippocampus. It is clear, however, that the cortices of the parahippocampal gyrus do not simply funnel information to the hippocampus. On the contrary, each of these cortices consists of several subregions that are densely associated by reciprocal connections and clearly carry out extensive processing in their own right. Moreover, these different cortices are linked to each other by rich intrinsic connections, and hence collaborate in processing incoming information before it reaches the hippocampus.

References

AMARAL, D. G. (1999) Introduction: What is where in the medial temporal lobe? *Hippocampus* 9: 1–6.

LAVENEX, P. AND D. G. AMARAL (2000) Hippocampal-neocortical interaction: A hierarchy of associativity. *Hippocampus* 10: 420–430.

nal ganglion circuitry of *Aplysia*, and in mammalian brain circuits such as region CA1 of the hippocampus, where long-term potentiation and long-term depression are especially evident in laboratory studies. Even though LTP has so far been demonstrated conclusively only in laboratory procedures, it shows properties of memory such as specificity and associativity, and has been reasonably well linked to memory effects in behaving animals. Long-term maintenance of LTP and other memory mechanisms presumably requires changes in gene expression and the synthesis of new proteins that eventually lead to structural alternations in synaptic morphology and neuronal connectivity.

Memory at the Brain Systems Level

When Karl Lashley discovered that memory deficits following brain damage are a function of the size of the lesions rather than their location, he concluded that memory traces were found throughout the brain and that no single brain region had a privileged role in memory. Yet data from a large number clinical cases have shown clearly that different brain regions play different and often quite special roles in different kinds of memory and different stages of memory processing. The medial temporal lobes, for instance, are critically important in encoding and consolidating the sorts of memories that are accessible to consciousness and can thus be reported (**Box 13B**). At the same time, it has become apparent that this region does not permanently store such conscious memories, nor is it necessary for encoding and consolidating other sorts of memories. These observations over the least 50 years or more have led to the now generally accepted idea of different forms of memory and related memory systems. Lashley was not wrong in his view that the features of a memory trace are widely distributed and involve many brain regions; but his experiments were too crude to reveal the far more subtle organization of memory systems. The case of patient H.M., first described in the 1950s, was a landmark in our current understanding of human memory.

The case of H.M.

One of the most consequential discoveries in the history of memory research was serendipitous, resulting from the unexpected side effects of a neurosurgical procedure performed in 1953. Patient H.M. was a 27-year-old man who suffered from medically intractable epilepsy that left him unable to work and severely debilitated. With the intent of relieving H.M.'s frequent generalized seizures, William Scoville, a neurosurgeon in Hartford, Connecticut, removed much of the patient's temporal lobes on both sides, including the amygdala, the entorhinal cortex, and about two-thirds of the hippocampus (**Figure 13.7**; also see Box 13B). Prior to the surgery, H.M. was experiencing about 10 minor seizures every day, with a major seizure every few days. The source was assumed to be in the medial temporal lobes. Consistent with this assumption,

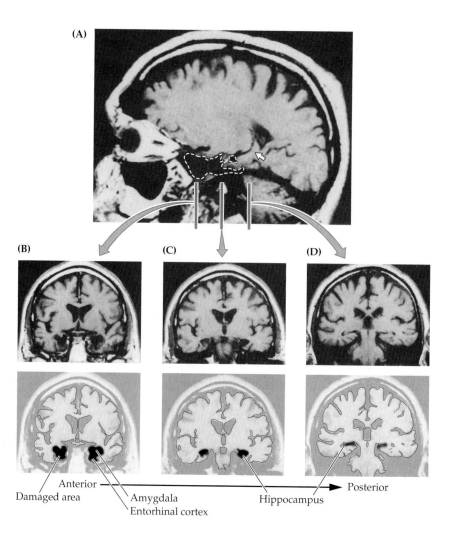

Figure 13.7   MRI images of H.M.'s brain.   (A) The area of H.M.'s anterior temporal lobe destroyed by surgery is indicated by the white dotted line. The intact posterior hippocampus is the banana-shaped object indicated by the white arrow. (This sagittal view shows the right hemisphere; H.M.'s lesions were in fact bilateral.) (B–D) Coronal sections at approximately the levels indicated by the red lines in (A). Image (B) is the most rostral and is at the level of the amygdala. The amygdala and the associated cortex are entirely missing. Image (C) is at the level of the rostral hippocampus; again, this structure and the associated cortex have been removed. Image (D) is at the caudal level of the hippocampus; the posterior hippocampus appears intact, although shrunken. The outlines below indicate the areas of H.M.'s brain that were destroyed (black shading). (From Corkin et al. 1997.)

the surgery was successful in relieving his epilepsy. Unfortunately, the bilateral removal of these structures had an unforeseen consequence: after the surgery, H.M. was unable to form certain types of new memories.

Since the original report of his memory loss, which Scoville and neuropsychologist Brenda Milner published in 1957, more than a hundred researchers have tested H.M.'s cognitive deficits using a variety of tasks, making him the best-known of a long list of patients with brain lesions who have contributed greatly to the understanding memory and other cognitive functions. The main reason of the importance of H.M.'s case is the purity of his memory deficit, which shows the major features of amnesia (the broad term for memory loss) that are often present in other cases, but seldom with the same degree of clarity.

First, although H.M. is severely impaired in memory functions, he has little or no difficulty in other cognitive domains. He has some olfactory deficits (possibly due to pyriform cortex damage; see Chapter 7), but his sensory and perceptual functions are remarkably normal. Nor did the surgery impair H.M.'s intelligence. On the contrary, his IQ improved a bit following surgery, perhaps due to the relief from seizures. Moreover, he has no deficit in executive functions, including performance on tasks assumed to measure frontal-lobe function (see Chapter 23). Thus, H.M. has a selective memory deficit rather than a perceptual or intellectual problem.

A second important feature of H.M.'s clinical picture is that he can remember events that happened up until a few years before the surgery reasonably well, but cannot remember events that happened after the surgery. These intact memories from his earlier life include language, faces, songs, public events, and what he learned in school—in short, the complete set of memories that a 27-year-old would be expected to have. His postsurgical memories, however, are minimal, a condition that is unfortunately as debilitating as his epilepsy was. For instance, when he meets new people, including investigators who have tested him numerous times, he forgets them almost immediately after they leave the room. Thus, H.M. is mainly impaired in learning new information rather than in retrieving well-established memories. This problem is known **anterograde amnesia** because it primarily affects memory of events that occurred *after* the onset of some brain disorder. In contrast, **retrograde amnesia** affects memory of events that happened *before* the lesion (**Figure 13.8**).

A third characteristic is that H.M.'s memory is impaired independently of the nature of the information or sensory modality involved. He can remember neither verbal stimuli, such as new names and words, nor nonverbal stimuli, such as faces and spatial layouts. He has a severe memory deficit regardless of whether the information to be learned or the questions posed are presented visually, auditorily, or in another sensory modality. Thus, H.M.'s memory

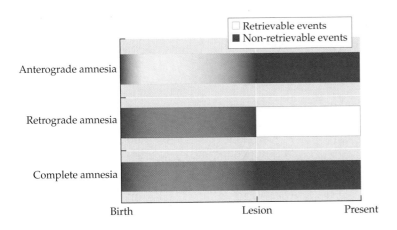

Figure 13.8 Types of amnesia. The diagram shows the lifetime periods for retrievable and nonretrievable events in anterograde, retrograde, and complete amnesia. The early nonretrievable period corresponds to events before 3–5 years of age, known as *childhood amnesia*. For most individuals, these events are difficult or impossible to remember.

deficit is pervasive and generalizes to different kinds of information and sensory modalities, affecting all memories that can be explicitly called into consciousness.

Fourth, although H.M.'s long-term memory is severely impaired, his ability to retain information for brief periods of time, or **working memory**, is intact. To measure working memory, neuropsychologists often use the **digit-span task**. The experimenter reads a list of digits (numbers), and the patient or subject repeats them back immediately. The number of digits is increased until the individual starts making errors. The number of digits repeated without error is known as *digit span* and is 7–9 digits (about the length of a phone number) in normal subjects. H.M.'s digit span is normal and he shows normal working memory for pictorial material.

Finally, and perhaps most important, H.M.'s long-term memory deficits are limited to tasks that require the retrieval of events and facts; his problems do not affect memories that are expressed through performance, such as motor skills. An example is H.M.'s performance in the **mirror drawing task**, which involves tracing geometric figures that can be seen only via a mirror (**Figure 13.9**). H.M. shows normal learning ability in daily improvements in doing this and many other difficult procedural tasks, and his learning of such skills persists in much the same way as in normal subjects.

(A)

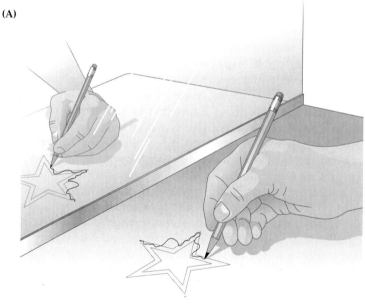

(B)

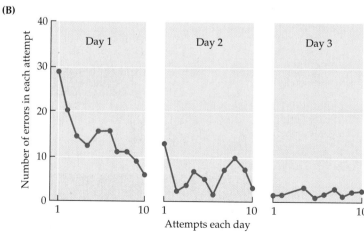

Figure 13.9   Normal skill learning in patient H.M. (A) The mirror drawing test involves tracing geometric figures seen through a mirror. (B) H.M. shows evidence of learning (errors drop during the first session), which persists normally across time (errors start at a lower level the second day). (After Milner et al. 1968.)

In sum, the case of H.M. made clear for the first time the critical importance of the medial temporal regions in certain types of human memory. Indeed, the key features of his memory deficits provide important information regarding the specific role of these regions. The implications of H.M.'s case, along with a series of other cases of patients with amnesia following damage to medial temporal lobes, make the following points about this brain region's role in human memory:

- The medial temporal lobes are necessary for certain memory functions, but not for perceptual, intellectual, and executive functions.

- These regions are necessary for remembering recent events but are not needed for the memory of remote events.

- They are necessary for explicit memory functions regardless of the sensory modality (vision, hearing, touch, etc.) involved.

- They are necessary for transferring events and facts into long-term memory storage, but they are not necessary for the current retention of information "online" (i.e., working memory).

- Although necessary for remembering events and facts, the medial temporal lobes are not needed for memories expressed through performance, such as motor and other skills.

A Taxonomy of Memory Systems

The cases of H.M. and other patients with medial temporal lobe amnesia imply the existence of different memory systems. Nonetheless, categorizing memory systems has been a difficult and sometimes contentious issue. In considering the evidence for distinct memory systems, it is important to begin with the basic distinctions among types or categories of memory illustrated in **Figure 13.10**.

There are two major distinctions in this taxonomy, which has been advocated by memory researchers Larry Squire, Endel Tulving, and others. The first is based on the *duration* of the memories. Whereas **working memory** refers to the maintenance and manipulation of information for brief periods of time, **long-term memory** refers to the acquisition and recovery of information over longer periods. The term *working memory* subsumes the term short-term memory, which most investigators take to be only one component of the broader con-

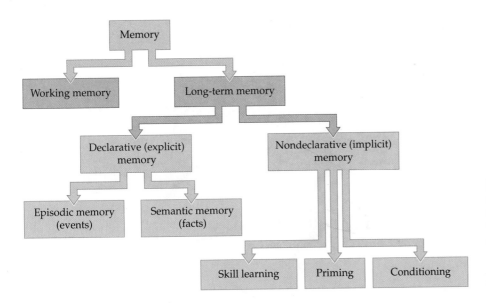

Figure 13.10 A general taxonomy of memory systems. The two major distinctions are based on memory duration (working, or short-term, memory; and long-term memory). Long-term memory can be further subdivided based on the characteristics, or qualities, of the different types of memory.

cept of working memory. As illustrated by H.M., medial temporal lobe damage impairs the formation of long-term memories but has no apparent effect on working memory. Completing a double dissociation of these categories, other forms of brain damage impair working memory but not long-term memory.

The second major distinction is based on the *quality* or character of different memories. This parsing applies mainly to long-term memory, and has already been raised indirectly in discussing H.M. **Declarative memory** refers to remembering of events and facts, and thus memories that (for humans, at least) can be reported verbally—that is, memories that can be "declared." **Nondeclarative memory** refers to memories expressed through performance. In humans, declarative memory is assumed to depend on conscious awareness (and thus is also referred to as **explicit memory**), whereas nondeclarative memory is assumed to operate unconsciously (and is referred to as **implicit memory**). As described in the context of amnesic subjects such as H.M., declarative memory depends on the integrity of medial temporal lobe structures, whereas nondeclarative memory does not.

As indicated in Figure 13.10, declarative memory and nondeclarative memory can be further subdivided. Declarative memory includes **episodic memory**, which refers to memory for personally experienced past events, and **semantic memory**, which refers to general knowledge about the world. Nondeclarative memory includes *priming, skill learning,* and *conditioning.* **Priming** refers to facilitated processing of a particular stimulus based on previous encounters with the same or a related stimulus. **Skill learning** refers to a gradual improvement in performance as a result of practicing a motor or cognitive task. **Conditioning** refers to the formation of simple associations between different stimuli and between stimuli and responses. These subdivisions are specifically considered later in Chapters 14 (declarative memory) and 15 (nondeclarative memory). The following sections focus on evidence supporting the major distinctions between working memory and long-term memory, and between declarative and nondeclarative memory.

Working memory versus long-term memory

A standard way of making the functional distinction between working and long-term memory is evident in *word list free-recall* studies (**Figure 13.11**). When participants study a list of words and recall them immediately, they

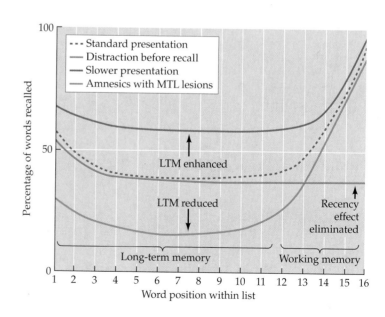

Figure 13.11   Free recall of a word as a function of its position within a list.   Normally, the last few words of the list are recalled better than the rest of the list (the *recency effect*). Distraction eliminates the recency effect (i.e., distraction disrupts working memory) but does not affect recall of the rest of the list (long-term memory, LTM). Slower presentation of the list at the time of study enhances long-term recall except for the recency portion of the list. Amnesic patients are impaired in list free-recall except for the recency portion of the list.

typically remember words presented at the end of the list with better fidelity, an effect known as a **recency effect** (the dashed line in Figure 13.11; note, however, that the beginning of the list is also remembered better). The recency effect presumably occurs because the last few words are still active in working memory when participants start to recall the list. In contrast, previous words are no longer in working memory and must be retrieved from long-term memory. The recency portion of the list and the rest of the list reflect working memory and long-term memory, respectively. Variables that differentially affect these two components suggest dissociations between these two forms of memory. For example, the data in Figure 13.11 show that introducing a 30-second distraction between the last word on the list and the recall test eliminates the recency effect (the distraction impairs working memory) but does not affect recall of the rest of the list (it spares long-term memory). In contrast, a slower presentation rate enhances recall of most of the list (improves long-term memory) but does not alter the recency effect (does not affect working memory). Medial temporal lobe lesions like the one affecting H.M. impair recall of most of the list without altering the recency effect (green curve in Figure 13.11). Thus, as noted in discussing H.M., medial temporal lobe damage impairs long-term but not working memory.

The effects of medial temporal lobe damage in which a lesion to a given brain region impairs one task (task A) but not another (task B) provide a *single dissociation*, which is not enough evidence to claim the existence of separate systems (see Chapter 3). To support such a claim, it is critical to have a *double dissociation*—to demonstrate that another sort of lesion impairs performance of task B but not A. In other words, there should be patients with damage in a region other than the medial temporal lobes who are impaired in working memory but not in long-term memory. Such patients have indeed been identified, and the damage to their brains is typically in left temporoparietal regions.

Elizabeth Warrington and Tim Shallice described the case of patient K.F., whose digit span was strikingly small: he could only hold about two digits in memory, compared to the normal seven or eight. K.F. also failed to show a recency effect. However, his long-term memory performance was normal—even slightly better than normal. Although his ability to immediately recall a list of four words was very poor, he needed fewer repetitions than normal participants to learn longer lists, and he remembered them for long periods (**Figure 13.12A**). This pattern contrasts with the one typically displayed by amnesic patients, who are impaired in long-term memory but not in working memory (**Figure 13.12B**). Since the Warrington and Shallice report, several other patients have been described with damage of left temporo-parietal areas and similar memory deficits. Thus, it appears that medial temporal lobe lesions tend to impair long-term but not working memory, whereas left perisylvian lesions tend to yield the opposite pattern of memory deficits. This double dissociation provides support for the idea that working memory and long-term memories depend on largely different anatomical substrates.

Declarative versus nondeclarative memory

Although H.M. is severely impaired in declarative memory, his performance of many nondeclarative memory tasks (including skill learning, priming, and conditioning tasks) is normal. This evidence supports the conclusion that some or all of the structures in the medial temporal lobe are necessary for declarative memory but not for nondeclarative memory. This idea has been supported by many studies with amnesic patients with similar damage. For example, in a study in the 1980s by Graf and colleagues, amnesic and control participants studied a list of words, and at test they were provided with

Figure 13.12 Evidence for different anatomical substrates of working and long-term memory. (A) Patient K.F. was impaired in immediate word recall, but he needed fewer repetitions than control subjects to remember word lists for longer periods of time. (B) In contrast, amnesic patients such as M.H. tend to show intact working memory but impaired long-term memory. (A after Warrington and Shallice 1969; B after Drachman and Arbit 1966.)

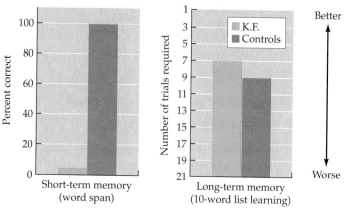

(A) Patient K.F.: Impaired STM versus preserved LTM

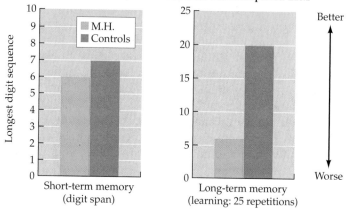

(B) Patient M.H. (amnesic): Preserved STM versus impaired LTM

words stems (**Figure 13.13A**). In a declarative (explicit) version of this test, participants were asked to complete the stems with studied words, whereas in a nondeclarative (implicit) version, they were asked to complete them with the first word that came to mind.

In the case of the implicit stem completion task, *priming* is measured as an increase in the probability of completing stems with target words when these words were previously encountered in the experiment than when they were not. Thus, priming makes it more likely that a target word will be generated in response to the stem, even though participants are asked to complete the stem with any word and are not asked to remember the study episode. The results yielded a clear dissociation: amnesic patients were impaired in the declarative version of the task but not in the nondeclarative version of the test (**Figure 13.13B**). This result is impressive because the two tests employed the same targets and retrieval cues, differing only in the explicit versus implicit nature of the instructions.

However, as in the case of the working versus long-term memory distinction, it is not enough to find single dissociations. For a long time, no double dissociation of declarative memory and priming was forthcoming. Although there were many reports of brain lesions, drugs, and developmental changes that affected declarative memory but not priming, there was no clear evidence of a situation in which priming was impaired but declarative memory was not. Such evidence eventually was reported in 1995, when John Gabrieli and his collaborators at Stanford University published studies of patient M.S. Like H.M., M.S. had had surgery to attenuate intractable epileptic seizures; but

(A)

	Study	Test
	ABSENT	ABS _ _ _
	INCOME	INC _ _ _
	FILLY	FIL _ _
	DISCUSS	DIS _ _ _ _
	CHEESE	CHE _ _ _
	ELEMENT	ELE _ _ _ _

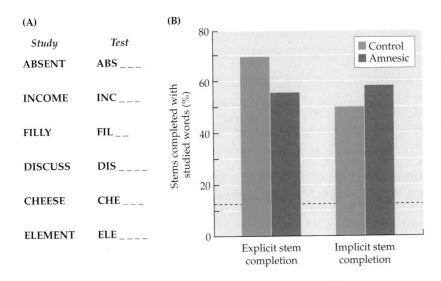

(B)

Figure 13.13 Effects of amnesia on declarative and nondeclarative memory. Participants studied words and were subsequently tested with word stems. (A) In a declarative (explicit) version of the test, participants were asked to complete the stems with studied words, whereas in a nondeclarative (implicit) version they were asked to complete them with the first word that came to mind. (B) Proportion of stems completed with studied words. The dashed line indicates the probability of completing the stems with target when they were not studied (baseline). In the implicit test, the difference between the completion rate and the baseline indicates *priming*—the facilitated processing of a stimulus based on previous encounters with similar stimuli. Amnesic participants are impaired in the explicit test but showed normal priming in the implicit test. (From Graf et al. 1984.)

unlike H.M., the brain regions removed were not the medial temporal lobes, but right occipital regions, including the primary and much of the secondary visual cortex (**Figure 13.14A**). As a result of the surgery, M.S. became blind in his left visual field, but aside from his vision deficits, he is in good health and shows normal performance on standardized tests of attention, memory, language, perception, and reasoning. Gabrieli and colleagues compared M.S. to a group of healthy controls and a group of amnesic patients using an implicit test in which each word was presented for increasing periods until it was identified correctly. Half the words had been seen in a previous session and half were presented for the first time. As illustrated in **Figure 13.14B**, control and amnesic subjects identified previously seen words after shorter presentations, thus demonstrating priming. Despite good word identification performance, M.S. showed no priming effect in this task. In contrast, in an explicit recognition test, his performance was normal, whereas amnesic subjects were impaired (**Figure 13.14C**). Thus, M.S. was impaired in implicit but not in explicit memory, whereas

Figure 13.14 Double dissociation of working and long-term memory in patient M.S. (A) The surgery performed on M.S. removed the right occipital regions of his brain, including the primary and much of the secondary visual cortex (light area). He is blind in the left eye, but otherwise is healthy and, on the basis of standard tests, his memory does not appear to be impaired. (B,C) M.S. and a group of amnesic patients show a double dissociation between implicit and explicit memory. (B) In an implicit word identification test, M.S. shows impaired priming whereas amnesic patients show normal priming. (C) In an explicit recognition test, M.S. shows normal performance but amnesic patients show impaired performance. (After Gabrieli et al. 1995.)

(A)

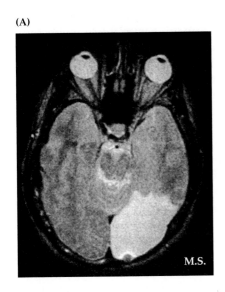

(B)

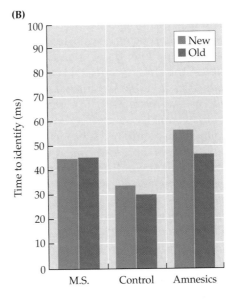

(C)

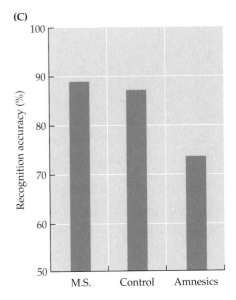

amnesic patients showed the opposite pattern. M.S.'s priming deficits cannot be attributed to his visual impairment: he is blind only in the left visual field and, as mentioned, his performance on the (visually mediated) word identification test was normal.

These results support the conclusion that whereas the medial temporal lobe is critical for declarative memory, the occipital cortex is critical for some forms of nondeclarative memory—visual perceptual priming in this instance. This double dissociation has been confirmed by functional neuroimaging studies that associated declarative memory performance with changes in medial temporal lobe activity (see Chapter 14) and perceptual priming with changes in visual cortex activity (see Chapter 15).

In sum, the distinction between working and long-term memory systems and the distinction between declarative and nondeclarative memory systems have now been supported by a good deal of evidence. Whereas medial temporal lobe damage impairs long-term but not working memory, left perisylvian damage disrupts working but not long-term memory. Within the domain of long-term memory, medial temporal lobe damage impairs declarative memory as evidenced by performance on recall and recognition tests, but not nondeclarative memory functions such as priming. In contrast, occipital lobe damage impairs some forms of priming without altering declarative memory performance. There are, however, some complicating factors that are more obvious in considering memory systems than other neural systems (e.g., the visual system or the auditory system). Although some brain regions are differentially involved in working memory, declarative long-term memory, or nondeclarative long-term memory, these functions also overlap. As emphasized throughout this unit, many brain regions contribute to more than one memory system. For example, the frontal lobes contribute to both short- and long-term memory, and to both declarative and nondeclarative memory. Moreover, all forms of memory presumably depend on similar cellular and molecular mechanisms.

Linking the Cellular and Systems Levels of Memory

Whereas research at the cellular level has revealed memory mechanisms that are common across brain regions and presumably support all forms of memory by altering the strength of synaptic connections, research at the systems level has shown certain brain regions that are critical for some forms of memory but not others. These findings are in no way inconsistent; mechanistic homogeneity at the cellular level is not incompatible with functional heterogeneity at the systems level. To illustrate this point by analogy, organs such as the heart and liver depend on the same cellular mechanisms for metabolism, but use the energy acquired by metabolism to carry out very different functions. As suggested by this analogy, it will require an understanding of both cellular- and systems-level mechanisms for a fully integrated picture of memory to eventually emerge.

One way of linking heterogeneity at the system level with homogeneity at the cellular level is in terms of the three main phases of memory: encoding, storage, and retrieval. **Encoding** refers to the creation of memory traces. **Storage** is the persistence of memory traces over time, and **retrieval** is the ability to access these traces. Differences among the various memory systems are primarily in encoding and retrieval; storage processes appear to entail common cellular mechanisms (**Figure 13.15**). In terms of information storage, for example, both declarative memory and priming are assumed to depend on the cellular mechanisms of altered synaptic strength in the neocortex described earlier in the chapter. Thus the conclusion that declarative memory depends on

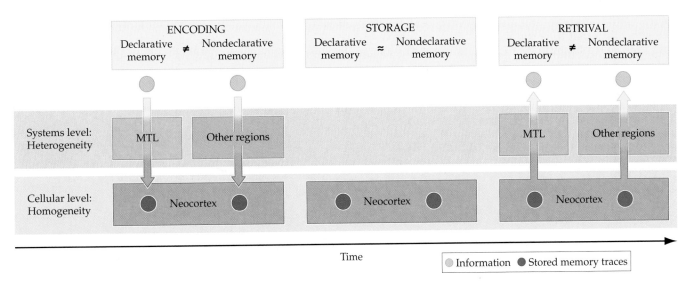

Figure 13.15 System-level heterogeneity is harmonious with cellular-level homogeneity. In this simple model, different forms of memory depend on different brain regions during encoding and retrieval (system-level heterogeneity). However, all forms of memory depend on the same cellular mechanisms of synaptic change to effect information storage (cellular-level homogeneity).

the medial temporal lobes whereas priming does not applies largely to encoding and retrieval phases, not to storage.

Of course the relation between systems and cellular phenomena is not as simple as this scheme implies. Memory traces are not created instantly during encoding, nor do they remain immutable during storage, as suggested in Figure 13.15. Thus, a more accurate description of the relationship between systems and cellular levels requires an examination of how memory traces change across time, that is, an examination of *consolidation* processes.

Consolidation at cellular and system levels

The term **consolidation** (from the Latin for "to make firm") refers to the progressive stabilization of long-term memory that follows the initial encoding of memory traces. To demonstrate consolidation, one must show that after encoding is completed, an amnesic agent (e.g., a drug, a lesion, or a behavioral manipulation) impairs memory to a greater extent during an early time window (that is, before consolidation) than during a later window (after consolidation). If the effects of the agent are constant across time, then any observed effect is presumably on storage or retrieval processes rather than on consolidation.

Consolidation processes occur at both cellular and systems levels, known respectively as *synaptic consolidation* and *system consolidation*. **Synaptic consolidation** is accomplished within a few minutes to hours after encoding. It is assumed to involve changes in gene expression, protein synthesis, and synaptic plasticity that allow the persistence of memory traces at the cellular level, as described earlier. In all species studied, synaptic consolidation occurs in the brain regions pertinent to long-term memory tasks. One way of disrupting synaptic consolidation is by administering *protein-synthesis inhibitors*. These drugs block changes in synaptic morphology but do not impair the perceptual and motor processes required for task performance. In the example shown in **Figure 13.16A**, protein-synthesis inhibitors disrupted nondeclarative memory when administered during the first hour after training but not thereafter, indicating that synaptic consolidation was completed within this time frame.

In contrast, **system consolidation** can take days, months, or even years, and involves a reorganization of the brain regions that support the memory in question. System consolidation is said to occur when a particular brain region that was necessary for post-encoding memory performance is no longer required, or when it can be demonstrated that another brain region is now needed to preserve the memory. Although system consolidation applies to

Figure 13.16 Synaptic- and system-level consolidation show different time courses. (A) Synaptic consolidation was demonstrated in this example by administering a protein synthesis inhibitor to goldfish at different times following shuttle-box learning. Sensitivity to the drug lasted for about an hour. (B) System consolidation has been demonstrated by damaging the hippocampus of rats at different times following contextual fear conditioning. Sensitivity to the lesion lasts about a month. (After Dudai 2004; A data from Agranoff et al. 1966 and B from Kim and Fanselow 1992.)

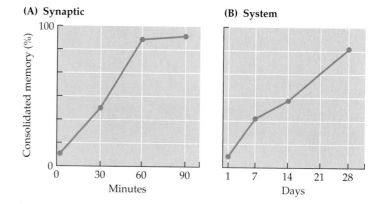

both declarative and nondeclarative memory and can be observed even in invertebrates, this term is typically used to describe changes in the role of the medial temporal lobe regions in declarative memory.

System consolidation was first described in 1982 by the French psychologist Théodule Ribot, who noted that memory loss following brain damage affects recent memories to a greater extent than remote memories; this temporal gradient became known as *Ribot's Law*. Indeed, the medial temporal lobe amnesia displayed by H.M. and similar patients shows such a temporal gradient. Studies on human patients are limited, however, because the locations of the lesions cannot be controlled and the assessment of memory must rely on retrospective measures, such as memory for news events and the like. In contrast, animal studies can selectively damage a region assumed to be critical for system consolidation at different times after encoding. For example, hippocampal lesions in rats impaired declarative memory during the first month after encoding but not thereafter (**Figure 13.16B**).

Theories of declarative memory system consolidation

There are two main theories of declarative system consolidation. According to the **standard consolidation theory**, the hippocampus rapidly encodes an integrated representation of an event or concept, which is then slowly transferred to the cortex and eventually becomes independent of the hippocampus. Given that memory traces consist of connections among neurons, the word "transfer" means that indirect connections via the hippocampus are gradually replaced by direct connections among the neocortical neurons relevant to the memory (**Figure 13.17**). When consolidation is complete, cortical neurons hold the unified memory and connections with the hippocampus are no longer necessary.

Figure 13.17 The standard model of declarative system consolidation. (A) Declarative memories are initially stored as a pattern of connections between hippocampal neurons and cortical neurons. (B) As the memory is repeatedly reactivated during conscious remembering, or perhaps during sleep, the connections supporting the memory are established among cortical neurons themselves. (C) Eventually, cortical neurons hold a unified representation of the memory and connections with the hippocampus become unnecessary. (After Frankland and Bontempi 2005.)

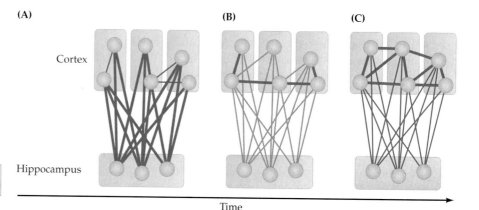

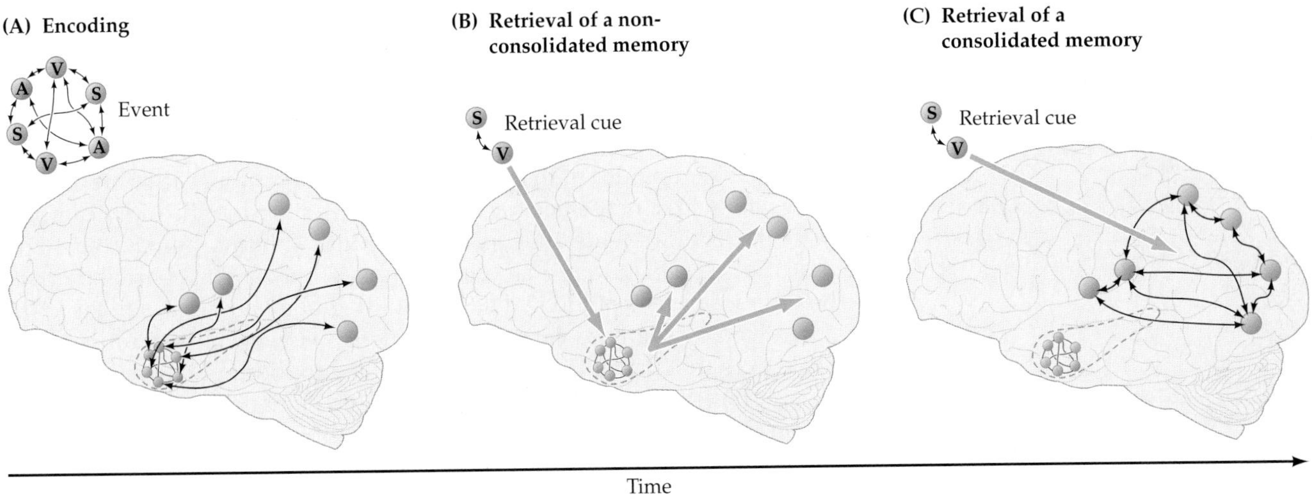

(A) Encoding

Event

(B) Retrieval of a non-consolidated memory

Retrieval cue

(C) Retrieval of a consolidated memory

Retrieval cue

Time

Figure 13.18 Retrieval of consolidated and nonconsolidated declarative memories.   (A) Event information is distributed over the cortex within the regions involved in processing each category of information (visual information in visual cortex [V], auditory information in auditory cortex [A], spatial information in parietal cortex [S]). An integrated representation of the event with pointers to the cortical engrams (called the hippocampal index) is stored in the hippocampus. (B) When a retrieval cue (i.e., a stimulus that elicits recall) is encountered, the hippocampal index for the event is accessed, which leads to the reactivation of the corresponding traces on the cortex. (C) After the traces have been fully consolidated in the neocortex, they can be accessed directly so that the hippocampus is no longer necessary.

The explanation in this theory of why the hippocampus is needed during an early stage of memory consolidation is that memory traces are distributed across several regions, each of which processed different aspects of the original event. For example, memory traces from a birthday party would include information about the color of the balloons, stored in visual cortex; about the music, stored in auditory cortex; about the spatial layout of the party room, stored in parietal cortex; and so forth (**Figure 13.18A**). Because memory traces are distributed, it seems critical to have a region in the brain, such as the hippocampus and related temporal lobe structures, that holds a unified representation of the whole event, along with pointers to the locations of distributed traces. This hypothesis explains why medial temporal damage has such a devastating effect on declarative memory. Nonconsolidated declarative memories can only be accessed via the hippocampus (**Figure 13.18B**); hence damage to this region impairs the person's ability to store new memories and to access recent memories. In contrast, nondeclarative memory tests, such as priming tests, do not require an integrated representation of the event that is available for reporting. The presumption is that nondeclarative memory can directly access partial features of an object or event stored in the cortex or other brain regions.

In this conception, consolidation occurs when a memory is repeatedly reactivated, which can happen during conscious remembering or, as recent evidence suggests, during sleep. Memory reactivation leads to the creation of direct connections among distributed cortical traces, and thence to the formation of an integrated representation in the neocortex. As a result of neocortical integration, cortical traces can be directly accessed and the integrated representation in the hippocampus is no longer needed (**Figure 13.18C**). This hypothesis would explain why there is often a temporal gradient in retrograde amnesia: remote memories have been fully consolidated and can be retrieved without the hippocampus, whereas recent memories have not been consolidated and cannot be retrieved.

In 1997, Lynn Nadel at the University of Arizona and Morris Moscovitch at the University of Toronto pointed out problems with this standard consolidation theory. One of the problems they noted is that in patients with medial temporal lobe amnesia, retrograde amnesia for autobiographical (episodic) memory information is often quite extensive, sometimes spanning almost the entire life of the individual. If interpreted according to standard consolidation theory, this observation would suggest that the consolidation process may take more than 40 years—as long as the average human lifespan throughout much of history. To explain this and other phenomena, Nadel and Moscovitch proposed an alternative, called the **multiple-trace theory**, in which episodic memories, consolidated or otherwise, are always dependent on the hippocampus. In this account, the temporal gradient found in some amnesic patients is not due to transfer to the cortex, but to the *number* of traces stored in the hippocampus. A central idea of the multiple-trace theory is that each time a memory is reactivated, a new trace for the memory is stored in the hippocampus. As a result, remote events are encoded by multiple hippocampal traces and become more resistant to partial hippocampal damage. Thus partial damage of the hippocampus would yield a temporally graded amnesia, similar to the one predicted by standard consolidation theory. However, the multiple trace theory makes the further prediction that when hippocampal damage is complete, the gradient for episodic memories should be flat or nonexistent. As for semantic memories, the theory postulates that they are gradually extracted from repeated episodes and are stored in the cortex independently of the hippocampus. At present, there is evidence for both the standard and multiple-trace theories, and their respective strengths and weaknesses are the topic of much debate.

An assumption shared by both standard and multiple-trace theories is that hippocampal storage occurs very fast whereas cortical storage occurs only slowly. Both models agree that the hippocampus can encode declarative information in a single trial, whereas the cortex requires many reactivations of the memory. In the standard model, these reactivations lead to a transfer of declarative memories from the hippocampus to the cortex, whereas in multiple-trace theory, they lead to the creation of separate semantic traces in the cortex with the further idea that hippocampal traces are always necessary for episodic memory. Despite these differences, both models see the hippocampus as a "fast learner" and the cortex as a slow one.

The reason for these different learning rates is unclear. One possibility suggested by a computational memory model proposed by James McClelland and collaborators at Carnegie Mellon University is that the cortex acquires information through a process of **interleaved learning**, in which a particular item is not learned all at once but through a series of presentations intermixed with exposure to other examples of the same general domain. This arrangement would allow the cortex to extract invariant relationships among concepts, and to form the categorical organization that characterizes semantic knowledge. Computer simulations show that if one attempts to incorporate new information in a semantic network too fast, the structure of the whole network destabilizes. (This phenomenon is known as *catastrophic interference*.) Thus, in the interleaved learning scenario, the hippocampus and the neocortex are seen as complementary learning systems, one rapidly acquiring novel information and the other slowly learning invariant relationships among various pertinent bodies of information (e.g., words, persons, locations, and concepts) to weave long-lasting and usefully accessible memories.

Summary

1. Memory must be considered at both the cellular/molecular and systems levels.

2. At the cellular level, memories are transiently stored as changes in the efficacy of existing synaptic connections between assemblies of neurons. Longer lasting memories require more permanent changes in gene expression, protein synthesis, and morphological changes, including the formation of novel synaptic connections.

3. There is a generally accepted taxonomy of memory systems that distinguishes among three major memory systems: declarative memory (Chapter 14), nondeclarative memory (Chapter 15), and working memory (Chapter 16).

4. At the systems level, a variety of converging evidence has shown that the several memory systems differ in terms of the duration of the memories they hold (working memory versus long-term memory) and/or in terms of the quality of the information they process (declarative memory versus nondeclarative memory). Thus, whereas at the cellular level memory mechanisms are relatively homogeneous, memory processing at the systems level can be relatively heterogeneous.

5. These concepts can be integrated by postulating that memory systems tend to differ in the strategies they use during encoding and retrieval, but share the cellular mechanisms of memory storage.

6. Encoding is not completed immediately but requires a process of synaptic consolidation.

7. Storage is not a constant state but involves a process of system consolidation. According to the "standard" model, system consolidation involves a transfer of memory traces from the hippocampus to the cortex; the "multiple-trace" model proposes that consolidation involves the iteration of episodic memory traces in the hippocampus and the creation of semantic memory traces in the cortex. Both these models, as well as computational models, hold that the hippocampus learns rapidly and the cortex more slowly.

Additional Reading

Reviews

DUDAI, Y. (2004) The neurobiology of consolidations, or, how stable is the engram? *Annu. Rev. Psychol.* 55: 51–86.

GABRIELI, J. D. E. (1998) Cognitive neuroscience of human memory. *Annu. Rev. Psychol.* 49: 87–115.

LAMPRECHT, R, AND J. LEDOUX (2004) Structural plasticity and memory. *Nat. Rev. Neurosci.* 5: 45–54.

MILNER, B., L. R. SQUIRE AND E. R. KANDEL (1998) Cognitive neuroscience and the study of memory. *Neuron* 20: 445–468.

SQUIRE, L. R., C. E. STARK AND R. E. CLARK (2004) The medial temporal lobe. *Annu. Rev. Neurosci.* 27: 279–306.

TULVING, E. (1995) Organization of memory: Quo vadis? In *The Cognitive Neurosciences*, M. S. Gazzaniga (ed.). Cambridge, MA: MIT Press, pp. 839–847.

Important Original Papers

BLISS, T. V. AND T. LOMO (1973) Long-lasting potentiation of synaptic transmission in the dentate area of the anaesthetized rabbit following stimulation of the perforant path. *J. Physiol.* 232: 331–356.

COHEN, N. J. AND L. R. SQUIRE (1980) Preserved learning and retention of pattern-analyzing skill in amnesia: Dissociation of knowing how and knowing that. *Science* 210: 207–210.

GABRIELI, J. D. E., D. A. FLEISHMAN, M. M. KEANE, S. L. REMINGER AND F. MORRELL (1995) Double dissociation between memory systems underlying explicit and implicit memory in the human brain. *Psychol. Sci.* 6: 76–82.

GRAF, P., L. R. SQUIRE AND R. MANDLER (1984). The information that amnesic patients do not forget. *J. Exp. Psychol.: Learning, Memory and Cognition* 10: 164–178.

MCCLELLAND, J. L., B. L. MCNAUGHTON AND R. C. O'REILLY (1995). Why there are complementary learning systems in the hippocampus and neocortex: Insights from the successes and failures of connectionist models of learning and memory. *Psychol. Rev.* 102: 419–457.

MOSCOVITCH, M. (1992) Memory and working-with-memory: A component process model based on modules and central systems. *J. Cognitive Neurosci.* 4: 257–267.

SCOVILLE, W. B. AND B. MILNER (1957) Loss of recent memory after bilateral hippocampal lesions. *J. Neurol. Neurosurg. Psychiat.* 20: 11–21.

TULVING, E. AND D. L. SCHACTER (1990) Priming and human memory systems. *Science* 247: 301–305.

Books

EICHENBAUM, H. AND N. J. COHEN (2001) *From Conditioning to Conscious Recollection: Memory Systems of the Brain*. New York: Oxford University Press.

SCHACTER, D. L. AND E. TULVING (1994) *Memory Systems*. Cambridge, MA: MIT Press.

SQUIRE, L. R. AND E. R. KANDEL (1999) *Memory: From Mind to Molecules*. New York: Holt.

14 *Declarative Memory*

Introduction

Declarative memory refers to remembering personal events, cultural history, semantic information, and other facts that we can be explicitly aware of and thus report, or "declare," either verbally or nonverbally (as when pressing a button in a test paradigm). Even though non-human primates and other animals are incapable of verbal reports, what is taken to be the equivalent of human declarative memories can be reported nonverbally; thus monkeys can indicate mental content by bar presses, eye movements, or other gestures, and rodents effectively report what they do or do not remember by their behavioral choices in mazes or other paradigms. As emphasized in the discussion of H.M. and other amnesic subjects in the previous chapter, declarative memory in humans is critically dependent on the integrity of the medial temporal lobes. Indeed, the link between declarative memory and medial temporal lobe function is so strong that this brain region is sometimes taken to define declarative memory. Thus, when verbal reports are not available (as in the case of young children and non-human animals), memory tasks are often classified as declarative if there is evidence that they are sensitive to medial temporal lobe lesions. Although the medial temporal lobes are necessary for normal declarative memory, much of the evidence described here shows that this region is not by itself a sufficient basis for its operation. Declarative memory involves many other brain regions, including the prefrontal cortex, lateral and medial parietal regions, and the occipito-temporal cortices. This chapter reviews the functions of both the medial temporal lobes and the additional regions that support the encoding, consolidation, and retrieval of declarative memories, and considers the various ways that investigators have tried to rationalize the complex interactions among these regions that result in functioning declarative memory.

Subcategories of Declarative Memory

Working at the University of Toronto in the early 1970s, psychologist Endel Tulving introduced a distinction between two basic forms of declarative

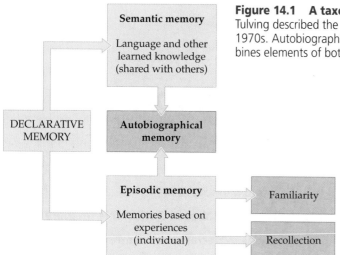

Figure 14.1   A taxonomy of declarative memory functions.   Psychologist Endel Tulving described the distinction between episodic and semantic memory in the early 1970s. Autobiographical memory—an individual's memory of his or her own life—combines elements of both forms of memory. Episodic memory has further subdivisions.

memory that he named *episodic* and *semantic* (**Figure 14.1**). **Episodic memory** refers to memory of events that an individual has experienced personally in a specific place and at a particular time; in contrast, **semantic memory** refers to knowledge about the world that individuals share with other members of their culture, including the knowledge of a native language and facts learned in school. For example, remembering being in your living room listening to reggae music last Sunday evening is an episodic memory, whereas knowing that reggae is a popular style of Jamaican music characterized by syncopated rhythm and lyrics that often entail social protest is a semantic memory.

In the laboratory, episodic memory is sometimes defined as memories created during the experiment, such as memory of a list of words participants were asked to study; semantic memory, on the other hand, is defined as information that the participants had stored before the experiment started (**Box 14A**). In life, episodic and semantic memories interact and to some degree overlap. In fact, memory for the events of our own lives, called **autobiographical memory**, is a complex mixture of episodic and semantic memories. For example, the semantic knowledge that the river Seine runs through Paris, that the Louvre is a famous museum in that city, and that long lines are frequent at famous museums may affect our reconstruction of episodic memories of a particular day actually spent in Paris. Complicating this distinction further, things learned in school can also be remembered as episodes (e.g., the day in French class when Paris was the topic of discussion).

Episodic memory is typically subdivided into two further categories, *recollection* and *familiarity*. **Recollection** refers to memories of a past event that include specific associations and contextual details, whereas **familiarity** refers to the sense that we experienced an event at some point in the past, even though no specific associations or contextual details come to mind. An example of familiarity without recollection is seeing a person's face and knowing that we have seen that person before, but being unable to remember any specific previous encounter or information about the person, such as their name. Again, these distinctions are somewhat fuzzy, and it has been argued that familiarity is more closely related to semantic memory or even to priming than it is to episodic memory.

The Role of the Medial Temporal Lobes in Declarative Memory

Given the dramatic effects of medial temporal lobe damage in human and non-human animals described in the last chapter, there is no doubt that the medial temporal lobes play a fundamental role in declarative memory. However, memory processing in this region and the specific contributions of various medial temporal lobe components to declarative memory and its subcategories are not well understood. Several different theories have been proposed regarding the role of this brain region (the hippocampus in particular) in declarative memory.

■ BOX 14A Declarative Memory Tests for Humans

Tests of episodic memory can be divided into recall or recognition types based on the nature of the cues or information provided.

In *recall tests*, participants are provided with a partial description of the targets (i.e., the information to be retrieved) and are then asked to generate the targets. For example, in a *word list free-recall test* participants may be asked to generate all the words on a list that was presented at the beginning of the experiment.

In *recognition tests*, participants are provided with targets intermixed with nontargets and are asked to distinguish the targets. Recognition does not require the generation of targets as such, but depends on the ability to discriminate targets (studied, or "old" items) and nontargets (nonstudied, or "new" items). Thus there are four possible outcomes in a recognition test: target items may be classified correctly as old ("hits") or incorrectly as new ("misses"); and nontarget items may be classified correctly as new ("correct rejections") or incorrectly as old ("false alarms"). If a subject responds "old" to all trials, he or she maximizes the number of hits but at the expense of increasing the number of false alarms. Thus, in order to evaluate memory performance, the experimenter must consider both correct and incorrect responses, so memory researchers use a *corrected recognition score* calculated by subtracting false alarms from hits.

Different episodic memory tests discriminate according to the type of information targeted. When we remember past events, we usually remember not only what happened (*item information*) but also where, when, and how it happened (*context information*). Although item and context information tend to be intermixed in natural retrieval situations, in the laboratory it is possible to examine each kind of information separately. Thus, in *item memory tests* participants are asked to retrieve the core elements or content of an event, such as the words in a list. In *context memory tests*, however, subjects are asked to retrieve the context associated with each item. For example, participants might be asked if a particular word presented during the study phase was on the left side or the right side of the screen (*spatial memory*); if the word was included in the first or the second list of words (*temporal order memory*) or if a male or a female speaker presented the word (*source memory*). Context memory tests are primarily sensitive to recollection, whereas item memory tests entail both recollection and familiarity. Both lesion studies and functional neuroimaging suggest that context memory is more dependent on hippocampal and prefrontal cortex functions than item memory.

Semantic memory tests include measures of the meaning of words (e.g., an elephant is an animal), factual knowledge (e.g., elephants are native to Africa and Asia), and the properties of objects (e.g., elephants are large and have trunks). As with episodic memory tests, semantic memory tests involve recall (e.g., *What is the capital of Turkey?*) or recognition (e.g., *Is Ankara the capital of Turkey?*). Studies with brain-damaged patients often test the ability to generate words that start with a certain letter or belong to a certain category (*verbal fluency tests*), the ability to define the meaning of difficult words (*vocabulary tests*), or the ability to name objects presented visually (*picture-naming tests*). Visual semantic memory can be further tested by asking participants to recognize photos of celebrities or famous buildings, and spatial semantic information can be tested by asking subjects to estimate the relative locations of cities in a country, or to draw a map of a well-known neighborhood or of their house.

Cognitive map theory

The **cognitive map theory** was originally proposed in 1978 by John O'Keefe at University College London and Lynn Nadel at the University of Arizona. In their view, the hippocampus mediates memory for spatial relations among objects in the environment. The strongest evidence for this idea is the existence of **place cells** in the rodent hippocampus (**Figure 14.2A**). These neurons become active only when the animal is in a particular spatial location in its local environment. The existence of place cells in the human hippocampus is less clear, but studies in which epileptic patients with implanted electrodes played a "taxi driver" computer game that involved driving passengers to target locations within a virtual town suggests that they do (**Figure 14.2B**). As in rats, some neurons of the hippocampus were active only when the "taxi" passed through a specific locale.

The fact that cells in the hippocampus fire when patients drive a virtual taxi through specific locations reinforces studies by Eleanor Maguire and collaborators at the University College London that reveal taxi drivers to have significant changes in the gross anatomy of this region of the brain. The investigators found that in London cab drivers with years of experience, the size of

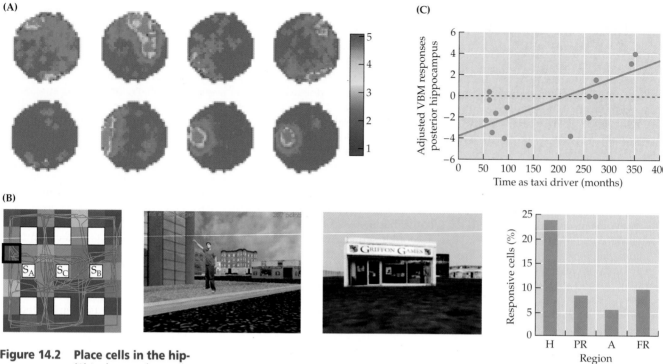

Figure 14.2 Place cells in the hippocampus. (A) In the rat, place cells fire when the animal is in a specific location of an open circular cage. The color code in this illustration shows the firing pattern of eight different place cells, with red indicating intense activity. Note that each cell being recorded from is active only when the rat is in a particular position in its environment (shown here as if looking down on the circular arena the animal is exploring). The color scale shows cell firing rate in Hz. (B) A neuron in the human hippocampus was active only when the subject was in a specific location (red square) of a virtual town (red lines indicate the trajectory of the "taxi"). Lettered squares are store locations, and white squares are nontarget buildings. Although most place cells in humans were found in the hippocampus (H), some were also found in the parahippocampal region (PR), the amygdala (A), and the frontal lobes (FR). (C) In this study, the size of the posterior hippocampus in London taxi drivers was found to be positively correlated with the number of years the subject had worked in this profession. (B from Ekstrom et al. 2003; C after Maguire 2000.)

the posterior hippocampus was significantly larger than in controls. Moreover, this effect was positively correlated with the number of years the subjects had worked as cab drivers (**Figure 14.2C**). Although these findings in a single such study must be interpreted with caution, they suggest that the circuitry in hippocampus gradually increases in complexity as a function of navigational experience.

Relational memory theory

Rather than contest the substantial evidence that the hippocampus is involved in spatial aspects of declarative memory, Howard Eichenbaum at Boston University and Neal Cohen at the University of Illinois proposed a more general theory of hippocampal function. Their theory, put forth in the early 1990s, incorporates spatial memory but also attempts to explain the role of the hippocampus in other aspects of declarative memory. According to this **relational memory theory**, the hippocampus does not mediate a representation of space as such (**Figure 14.3A**), but rather a *memory space*, in which relationships are coded by the conjunction of overlapping cues (**Figure 14.3B**). Consistent with this idea, there is evidence that place cells in rodents do not represent a global topology of the environment, but the *spatial relationships among subsets of cues*. Furthermore, the firing of place cells is also affected by nonspatial variables, such as the speed with which the rat moves and the presence of particular stimuli or rewards in environment. Thus the relational memory theory holds that the hippocampus actually mediates associations among spatial cues, temporal cues, rewards, and perhaps other factors as well.

An example of how the hippocampus is involved in remembering overlapping associations is seen in a study that tested rats using an odor association task (**Box 14B**). By hiding treats such as Fruit Loops cereal in cups of differently odorized sand, rats were trained to prefer odor A over odor B, odor B over odor C, and so on. The trained rats later showed that they remembered not only each paired relationship (e.g., A > B, B > C), but also more complex rela-

■ BOX 14B Investigating Declarative Memory in Non-Human Animals

The most obvious challenge to investigating declarative memory in non-human animals is that they cannot follow verbal instructions or "declare" their memories verbally. However, there are ways of measuring declarative memory in such circumstances.

One such method used in studies on non-human primates is known as a *delayed nonmatch-to-sample task* (Figure A). A typical trial in this paradigm has three phases. During the *sample phase*, a monkey is shown a single stimulus (e.g., a white cross) above a well containing a food reward; during the *delay phase*, a door is lowered so the monkey can no longer see the stimulus and reward; and during the *choice phase*, the monkey is presented with the previously rewarded stimulus (the white cross) along with a new stimulus (e.g., a black rectangle). This time the animal must select the new (nonmatching) stimulus in order to obtain the reward. (There is also a matching version of this task, discussed in Box 16A, but monkeys learn the non-matching rule faster because they have a natural tendency to manipulate novel objects.) Using nonmatch-to-sample tasks, David Gaffan at Oxford University and Mortimer Mishkin at the National Institutes of Health

(Continued on next page)

(A) Delayed nonmatch-to-sample task. Declarative memory is indexed by the ability to choose the novel stimulus. (B) The Morris water maze. Declarative memory is indexed by the ability to find the hidden platform.

(A)

Food reward

Right

Wrong

Sample phase　　　　Delay phase　　　　Choice phase

(B)

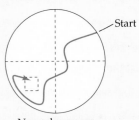
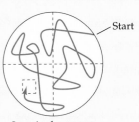

Start

Normal memory

Start

Impaired memory

■ BOX 14B *(continued)*

showed that lesions of the medial temporal lobe severely impair memory in monkeys, thus providing the first animal model of the human amnesic syndrome described in Chapter 13.

Such studies can also be done using rodents—a particularly important advance because the use of rodents allows us to examine the genetic basis of behavior in these animals. The most popular "declarative" memory task for rodents is the *Morris water maze*, pioneered by Richard Morris and his

group at the University of Edinburgh. The animal's task is to swim to a small platform hidden just beneath the surface in a circular tank filled with murky water, which then provides a safe haven (Figure B). Once the animal has learned where to find the platform, the experimenter can assess memory by measuring how long the rat takes to find the platform again, or how much time it spends within the quadrant that contains the platform compared to the other three quadrants

of the tank. Given that the murky water means the animal's view of the tank is the same in all directions, remembered cues from objects in the room (e.g., windows, a large wall clock) are presumably used to locate the platform.

The Morris water maze measures spatial memory; however, it is also possible to measure nonspatial forms of declarative memory in rodents in paradigms such as the odor association task described in the text and Figure 14.4.

---

tionships *among the elements of the pairs* (A > B > C > D > E; **Figure 14.4**). In contrast, animals with lesions that disrupted the output of the hippocampus could remember the individual paired relationships they were trained on, but could not express memories of the overlapping relationships.

Episodic memory theory

Whereas the cognitive map and relational memory theories were originally inspired by research with non-human animals, a further issue in humans is

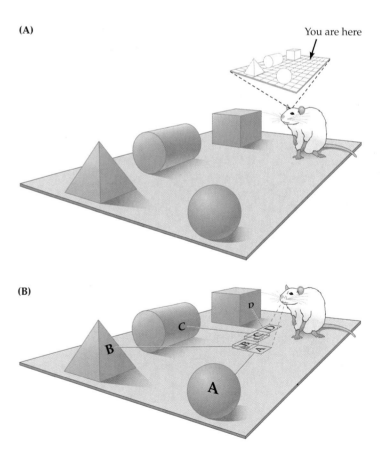

Figure 14.3 Comparing the cognitive map and relational memory theories of hippocampal function. (A) According to cognitive map theory, the hippocampus holds a spatial map of the environment. (B) According to relational memory theory, the hippocampus stores a set of overlapping associations (A/B, B/C, etc.) that are not necessarily or even primarily spatial. (After Eichenbaum et al. 1999.)

(A)

(B)

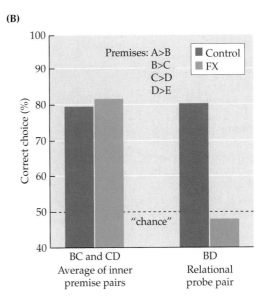

Figure 14.4 Odor association task. (A) In this paradigm, declarative memory is indexed by a rat's ability to choose cups associated with a series of odors that have been differentially rewarded. (B) Rats with fornix (FX) lesions that disrupt hippocampal output can remember their choices that entail individual odor pairs (B > C and C > D), but fail to show memories for the relationships among the elements of different pairs (B > D). (After Dusek and Eichenbaum 1997.)

whether the hippocampus contributes equally to episodic and to semantic memory. According to the **episodic memory theory**, supported by Endel Tulving, Morris Moscovitch, and other researchers, the hippocampus is critical for episodic memory but is not required for semantic memory.

The episodic memory theory is supported by several pieces of evidence. First, retrograde memory deficits following hippocampal damage are more pronounced for episodic than for semantic information. An example is K.C., an amnesic patient investigated by Tulving and other memory researchers at the University of Toronto. K.C. had a motorcycle accident in which he sustained damage to several brain regions, including the hippocampus (**Figure 14.5**). As with patient H.M., K.C.'s intellectual abilities were well preserved: he is able to read, write and play chess at much the same level as before his accident. However, both his anterograde and retrograde episodic memory are severely impaired.

Unlike H.M., K.C.'s retrograde amnesia covers his whole life, and for all intents and purposes he cannot remember any personal history. In contrast, his memory for semantic information acquired before the accident is intact. He has a good vocabulary, and his knowledge of subjects such as mathematics, history, and geography is not greatly different than that of others with his educational background. Thus, medial temporal lobe damage can in at least some cases impair retrograde episodic memory while sparing retrograde semantic memory. It could be argued that K.C.'s general knowledge was acquired earlier than the episodic memories tested and hence was more consolidated and less dependent on the hippocampus (see Chapter 13). However, K.C. can readily retrieve semantic information he acquired while working as a machinist, such as the meaning of technical terms like *spiral mandrel* and *keyway shank*, whereas he fails to remember events that happened in the factory during the same time period.

A second line of evidence supporting the episodic memory theory is that anterograde memory deficits following hippocampal damage can spare new

(A)

(B)

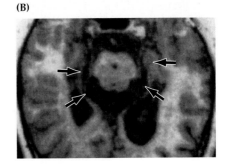

Figure 14.5 Amnesic patient K.C. (A) K.C.'s ability to play chess was not affected by his brain lesions. (B) Sagittal MRI slice showing K.C.'s bilateral hippocampal and parahippocampal damage. (A from Tulving 2002; B from Rosenbaum et al. 2000.)

Figure 14.6 Hippocampal lesions in young children can result in developmental amnesia.
(A,B) Compared to control subjects, developmental amnesic children Beth, Jon, and Kate are impaired in episodic but not in working memory tasks for both verbal and nonverbal stimuli. (C,D) The three children show normal reading ability, as indicated by similar actual and expected scores on the basis of their IQs. (After Vargha-Khadem et al. 1997.)

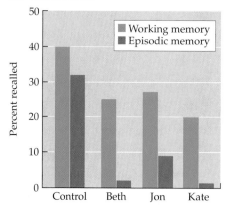

(A) Verbal stimuli

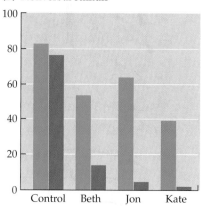

(B) Nonverbal stimuli

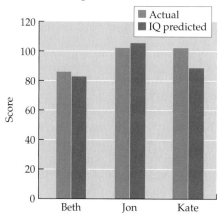

(C) Basic reading

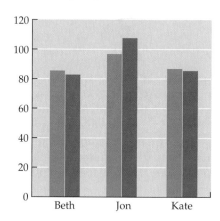

(D) Reading comprehension

semantic learning to certain degree. Several studies have shown that adult patients with anterograde amnesia (including K.C.) can in fact learn new vocabulary and facts, albeit slowly. Preserved semantic learning also is seen in children who suffer selective hippocampal lesions due to anoxic accidents at an early age, usually through complications at birth. Faraneh Vargha-Khadem and her collaborators at University College London have shown that these cases of **developmental amnesia** have severe difficulties in remembering personal occurrences and perform poorly on tests of episodic memory (**Figure 14.6A,B**). Nonetheless, they make normal or near-normal progress in school, and acquire semantic knowledge about the world more or less normally (**Figure 14.6C,D**).

Finally, a double dissociation supports this distinction of hippocampal function in declarative memory within the temporal lobes. Whereas hippocampal lesions affect episodic more than semantic memory, left-lateralized damage to anterior temporal cortex tends to affect semantic more than episodic memory. The latter pattern is displayed by patients with the progressive disorder known as **semantic dementia** (**Figure 14.7A**). An example is A.M., a patient investigated by Kim Graham and John Hodges at Cambridge University. A.M. first sought medical attention because he had difficulty finding the right words to name things (*anomia*). Otherwise his speech was fluent. His episodic memory was also good, and he could relate—albeit with severe difficulty finding the right words—the details of recent holidays and golfing achievements. Neuropsychological testing showed a dissociation between semantic and episodic memory deficits: A.M. was severely impaired in

(A)

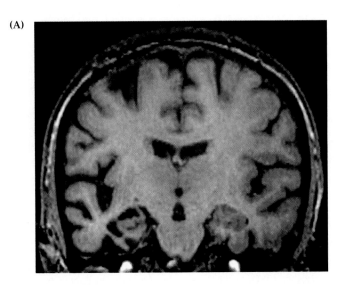

(B)

(C)

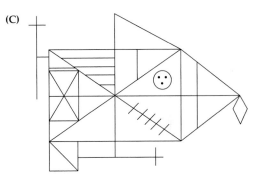

Figure 14.7 Semantic dementia.   (A) Coronal-section MRI of A.M., a patient with semantic dementia, showing left-lateralized atrophy of the anterior temporal lobes. The left hippocampus is mildly atrophied. (B) Subjects suffering from semantic dementia perform poorly on tests of semantic knowledge such as the "pyramid and palm trees" test. Here participants are asked to indicate which of the bottom two images fit better the top image. (C) Example of a nonverbal episodic test. Semantic dementia spares those brain regions necessary for normal performance on tests such as the Rey complex figure test, in which participants copy and then draw from memory an intricate geometric figure.

semantic knowledge tests (e.g., the "pyramid and palm trees" test shown in **Figure 14.7B**) but performed normally on nonverbal episodic memory tasks (e.g., the Rey complex figure test, **Figure 14.7C**). Thus, whereas amnesic patients with hippocampal lesions may be impaired in episodic but not in semantic memory, semantic dementia patients with left anterior temporal damage tend to be impaired in semantic more than in episodic memory.

Evidence supporting both relational and episodic memory theories

Evidence linking the hippocampus to recollection is consistent with both the relational and the episodic memory theories. *Recollection* involves relational memory and is the prototypical form of episodic memory; thus a number of investigators have sought to show that the hippocampus is more concerned with processing recollection than in providing a sense of familiarity.

Several methods have been used to distinguish recollection from familiarity. In one method, participants are asked to use introspection to distinguish between recognition responses based on recollection ("remember" responses) and those based on familiarity ("know" responses). Supporting the validity of both the relational and episodic memory theories, fMRI studies show that "remember" responses elicit greater hippocampal activity than "know" responses (**Figure 14.8A**).

Another method is to measure participants' ability to encode and retrieve specific associations between items, or between items and contexts. For instance, another fMRI study found that the left hippocampus was associated with both successful encoding and successful retrieval of semantic and perceptual associations (**Figure 14.8B**). Finally, estimates of recollection and familiarity can be calculated on the basis of the proportion of hits and false alarms. A study that used this method to assess memory for odors in rats found that

(A) Left hippocampus

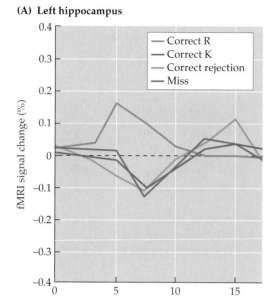

(B)

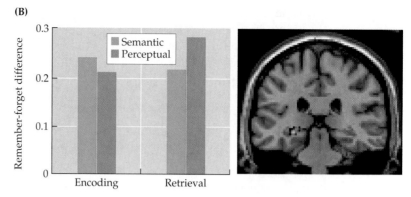

(C)

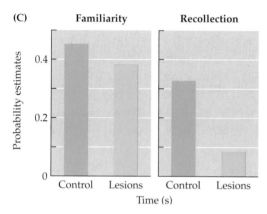

Figure 14.8 Evidence for a greater hippocampal role in recollection than in familiarity. (A) In this study, the hippocampus in participants was activated during recognition responses based on recollection ("remember"; R responses) but not during recognition responses based on familiarity ("know"; K responses). (B) During both encoding and retrieval, activity in the left hippocampus was associated with successful memory for both semantic and perceptual associations. (C) Compared to controls, rats with selective hippocampal lesions are impaired in recollection but not in familiarity. (A after Eldridge et al. 2000; B after Prince et al. 2005; C after Yonelinas et al. 2002.)

selective hippocampal lesions impaired recollection but not familiarity estimates (**Figure 14.8C**). In sum, several lines of evidence indicate a strong link between the hippocampus and recollection, implying a key role for this structure in episodic memory.

Declarative memory theory

The **declarative memory theory** supported by Larry Squire and his collaborators at the University of California at San Diego argues that the hippocampus mediates *all* declarative memories, regardless of whether they are spatial or nonspatial, relational or nonrelational, episodic or semantic. Supporting this view, studies of patients with hippocampal lesions have shown that some amnesic individuals are impaired to about the same extent in item- and context-memory tasks. Furthermore, several functional neuroimaging studies have shown that, under certain conditions, the hippocampus is similarly activated in normal subjects carrying out these tasks. The reasons why these studies failed to observe the differences reported in other patient and functional neuroimaging studies remain uncertain, emphasizing the difficulty of decisively delineating medial temporal lobe functions with the research methods currently available.

Integrating theories of hippocampal memory function

Given that all four of these theories about hippocampal functions—cognitive map, relational, episodic, and declarative memory—are supported by substantial evidence, a reasonable view at present is that all of them are correct in some measure. Thus, rather than seeing these ideas as competitors, it makes sense to integrate them. For example, the cognitive map and relational memory theories could be integrated by assuming that they apply to different regions of the hippocampus. Indeed, it been suggested that spatial memory functions are more pronounced in the *right* hippocampus, whereas general relational functions are more the province of the *left* hippocampus. Another proposal is that spatial memory functions depend primarily on *posterior* hippocampal regions, whereas general relational memory functions depend primarily on *anterior* hippocampal regions.

Moreover, the relational memory and episodic theories are already closely related. As noted already, both views are consistent with evidence linking the hippocampus to recollection. These two theories could be further integrated with the declarative memory theory by postulating that the distinctions between relational and item memory and between episodic and semantic memory are not clear-cut but a continuum, as indeed seems likely.

Distinguishing the functions of different medial temporal lobe subregions

An issue of obvious importance is how hippocampal functions—however one interprets them—are related to the functions of other structures in the medial temporal lobes, the surrounding perirhinal and parahippocampal cortices in particular (see Box 13B). Several ideas about functional differences between the hippocampus and the other medial temporal lobe structures have been proposed.

According to a **hippocampal-perirhinal theory** put forward by Malcolm Brown and John Aggleton at Bristol University, England, the hippocampus processes information relatively slowly and is associational and spatial, whereas the *perirhinal cortex* processes information more rapidly and is item-based. In this conception, neurons in the hippocampus signal information about spatial positions or associations between items (i.e., recollection), whereas neurons in the perirhinal cortex signal information about the novelty of individual items (i.e., familiarity). Consistent with the latter hypothesis, single-cell recordings in experimental animals have shown that perirhinal neurons do indeed show a stronger response when an item is first presented than when the same item is shown again (**Figure 14.9A**). Functional neuroimaging

Figure 14.9 Evidence for complementary hippocampal and perirhinal systems. (A) Neurons in the perirhinal cortex show a strong response when an item is first presented but not when the item is repeated. (B) Functional MRIs show that activity in the hippocampus increases sharply for items recognized as "definitely old," whereas activity in rhinal cortex decreases gradually as items becomes more familiar. (A from Xiang and Brown 1998; B from Daselaar et al. 2006.)

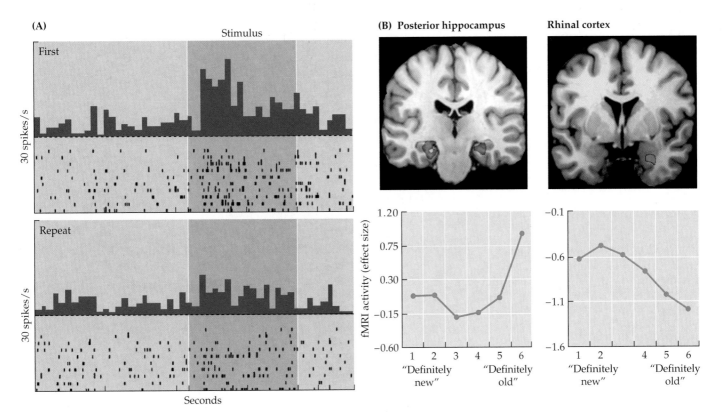

studies also suggest that the hippocampus and the perirhinal cortex make different contributions to recollection. For example, the hippocampus shows a sharp increase in activity when participants are sure they have encountered an item before ("definitely old"), consistent with its putative role in recollection. Activity in perirhinal cortex, on the other hand, decreases gradually as items are regarded as more and more familiar, consistent with a greater role in familiarity than recollection (**Figure 14.9B**). It is unclear, however, whether the decrease in perirhinal activity measured with fMRI reflects the reduction in firing rate measured with single-cell recording studies seen in Figure 14.9A.

As discussed Chapter 15, a reduction in neural response as a function of repetition has also been proposed as a mechanism for priming (see also the discussion of habituation in Chapter 13). Also pertinent to this and other theories about different regional functions in the medial temporal lobe are the different connections of the hippocampus and perirhinal cortex to the thalamus. Whereas the hippocampus is connected to the anterior nucleus of the thalamus via the fornix and the mammillary bodies (see Box 13B), the perirhinal cortex are connected to the medial dorsal nucleus of the thalamus. It seems likely, then, that these thalamic regions also play some role in declarative memory.

A different conception is the **item-in-context theory** proposed by Howard Eichenbaum at Boston University in collaboration with Andrew Yonelinas and Charan Ranganath at the University of California at Davis. They proposed that the perirhinal cortex and associated lateral entorhinal cortex are concerned with *memory for items*, whereas the parahippocampal cortex and associated medial entorhinal cortex are involved in *memory for context*. In this view, the hippocampus interacts with *both* regions and is thus involved in memory for the *item in context* (**Figure 14.10**).

This three-process theory has several strengths. First, it accounts for evidence linking the perirhinal cortex to familiarity and the hippocampus to recollection. Second, the distinction between perirhinal and parahippocampal

Figure 14.10 The item-in-context theory of medial temporal lobe memory functions. The perirhinal cortex and associated lateral entorhinal cortex are taken to be concerned with memory for items, whereas the parahippocampal cortex and associated medial entorhinal cortex are involved in memory for context. In this theory, the hippocampus interacts with both regions to produce item-in-context memories. (After Eichenbaum et al. 2007.)

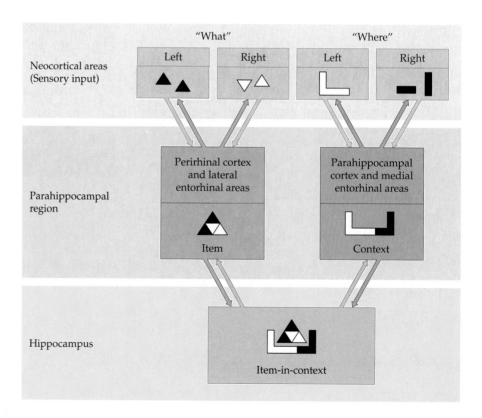

functions fits well with anatomical, lesion, and functional neuroimaging evidence. The perirhinal cortex receives most of its visual input from the ventral ("what") pathway, whereas the parahippocampal cortex receives most of its visual input from the dorsal ("where") pathway (see Figure 14.10 and Chapter 4). In monkeys, perirhinal lesions tend to impair object memory rather than spatial memory, whereas parahippocampal lesions yield the opposite pattern. In humans, functional neuroimaging studies have repeatedly shown that a parahippocampal region known as *parahippocampal place area* is consistently activated during perception and memory of spatial layouts. Finally, the notion of item-in-context memory accommodates both the role of the hippocampus in spatial memory (the cognitive map theory) and its more general role in context memory and recollection (the relational and episodic theories). Despite these strengths, however, this newer model has not yet been well tested.

In sum, there are several theories about the relative contributions of the hippocampus and other medial temporal lobe regions to declarative memory, All the theories linking the hippocampus and associated structures in the medial temporal lobe to spatial memory, relational memory, and episodic memory are supported by empirical evidence and are likely to be at least partially correct. A full-fledged theory of declarative memory, however, will need to consider not only medial temporal lobe functions but also the role of other brain regions, the frontal lobes in particular.

The Role of the Frontal Lobes in Declarative Memory

Effects of frontal lobe damage

Whereas medial temporal lobe lesions are associated with a devastating amnesic syndrome, frontal lesions typically cause only mild declarative memory deficits, and only in certain tasks. In general, the effects of frontal damage on declarative memory appear to be a function of the strategic demands of the task. In the case of episodic memory, for example, recall and context memory tests, which are more dependent on strategic control processes (see Box 14A), are more affected by frontal lesions than recognition memory tests are. The importance of frontal regions in context memory has been known for some time.

In 1971, Brenda Milner reported that patients with frontal lobe damage were more impaired in temporal-order memory (a form of context memory) than on simple recognition memory tests. This finding was later supported by parallel studies in monkeys, and in humans was extended to other forms of context memory, such as memory for source of information. For example, in one study, patients with frontal lobe damage, age-matched controls, and younger controls were presented a series of facts that previous testing indicated they had not known prior to the study; after a delay, their memory for these facts was tested. When a test question was answered correctly, participants were asked whether they had learned the fact during the experiment or whether they had known it all along (the latter being an incorrect answer). Although the three groups performed at about the same level in recall and recognition, frontally damaged patients made many more errors in identifying the source of the memory than the two control groups (**Figure 14.11**).

Declarative memory deficits following brain lesions may reflect difficulties during encoding, difficulties during retrieval, or both. Thus, one of the great advantages of using functional neuroimaging to investigate declarative memory is that it provides separate measures of encoding and retrieval. The next two sections review functional neuroimaging studies investigating each of these two phases of declarative memory.

Figure 14.11 Recall, recognition, and source memory in patients with frontal lobe damage. Patients were compared with age-matched controls and with younger control subjects. (A) Performance on tests of fact recall and recognition was similar across all three groups. (B) Source memory was significantly impaired in patients with frontal lobe damage. F = frontal lobe damage patients; O = age-matched controls; Y = young controls. (After Janowsky et al. 1989.)

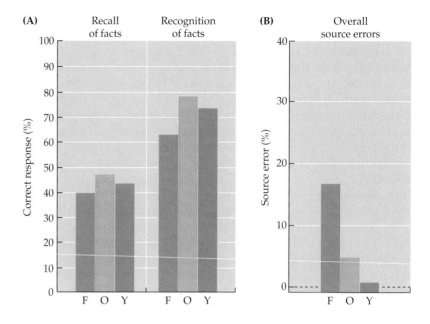

Functional neuroimaging of episodic encoding and semantic retrieval

The rationale for considering episodic encoding and semantic retrieval together is that these two processes are closely related; they are often considered to be two sides of the same coin. For example, thinking about the meaning of a piece of information (semantic retrieval) normally leads to the storage of this information in episodic memory (episodic encoding). Conversely, the attempt to learn new information (episodic encoding) usually involves semantic processing (semantic retrieval). It is therefore not surprising that in functional neuroimaging studies, episodic encoding and semantic retrieval tasks activate many of the same brain regions.

The most prominent of these shared regions is the left inferior frontal gyrus. In the 1990s, the first functional neuroimaging study of episodic encoding found that the left inferior frontal gyrus showed greater activity when participants processed the meaning of words than when they processed their orthography (e.g., does the word contain the letter *o*?) (**Figure 14.12A**). Given that subsequent memory for words was much better for semantic than for perceptual processing (the *levels of processing* effect mentioned in Chapter 2), these researchers attributed the left prefrontal activation not only to semantic retrieval but also to episodic encoding. The role of left inferior frontal gyrus in successful episodic encoding was later confirmed by Anthony Wagner (then at Harvard University) and his collaborators using the *subsequent memory paradigm* (**Box 14C**). As illustrated in **Figure 14.12B**, the left inferior frontal gyrus showed greater encoding activity for words that were subsequently remembered than for words that were subsequently forgotten. Greater activity for subsequently remembered than forgotten words (the "difference in memory" or Dm effects described in Box 14C) was also found in the left medial temporal lobe region. In general, the Dm effects in the left inferior frontal gyrus tended to occur in the left hemisphere for verbal stimuli, and bilaterally for visual stimuli.

As already mentioned, the role of left inferior frontal gyrus in encoding is likely to reflect semantic processing. However, not all parts of this gyrus mediate semantic processing. In fact, studies with *aphasic* patients (patients with language deficits; see Chapter 21) and studies of working memory using

(A)

(B)

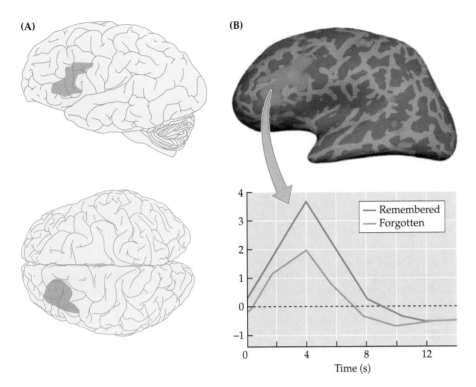

Figure 14.12 Frontal lobe activity during encoding of declarative information. (A) Greater left ventrolateral prefrontal activity is seen for words encoded during a semantic task (here, attending to whether the words referred to living or nonliving things) than during a perceptual processing task (attending to whether the words contained the letter "a"). (B) Greater encoding activity is seen in the left inferior frontal gyrus for words that were subsequently remembered than for words that were subsequently forgotten. This is the difference-in-memory, or Dm effect. (A after Kapur et al. 1994; B after Paller et al. 2002.)

functional neuroimaging (see Chapter 16) have linked the posterior part of the left inferior frontal gyrus, known as *Broca's area*, to phonological processing. (Another view, discussed in Chapter 16, suggests that the general function of Broca's area is to provide inhibitory control processes.) This functional subdivision of the left inferior frontal gyrus has been confirmed by fMRI studies that manipulated and compared semantic (meaning) to phonological (sound) processing. These studies have shown that the anterior part of the left inferior frontal gyrus (Brodmann areas 45/47) is more activated during semantic processing, whereas the posterior portion of this gyrus (areas 44/46) is more activated during phonological processing (**Figure 14.13**).

Dm effects, in contrast, are usually found in the *inferior* frontal gyrus (ventrolateral prefrontal cortex; **Figure 14.14A**) but rarely in the *middle* frontal

Semantic versus baseline

Phonological versus baseline

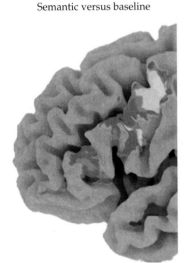

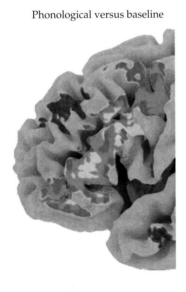

Figure 14.13 Word processing in Broca's area. Semantic processing of words activates both anterior and posterior regions of the left inferior frontal gyrus, whereas phonological processing of words activates mainly the posterior region. (From McDermott et al. 2003.)

■ BOX 14C Functional Neuroimaging Methods to Study Episodic Memory

As described in Chapter 3, functional neuroimaging provides a powerful method to investigate the neural correlates of cognitive functions. With respect to episodic memory, these methods are especially useful in that they can distinguish between memory encoding and retrieval. When studying brain-damaged patients who are impaired in episodic memory, it is difficult or impossible to know whether the impairment reflects encoding deficits, retrieval deficits, or both. Functional neuroimaging studies of normal subjects, however, have identified differences in the involvement of several brain regions in encoding versus retrieval.

In working to isolate activity specifically associated with successful encoding or retrieval operations, the event-related potential (ERP) designs described in Chapter 3 are well suited to this purpose because they allow a direct comparison between successful and unsuccessful trials during encoding and/or retrieval. When applied to encoding, this method is known as the *subsequent memory paradigm* and involves four steps (Figure A, left panel).

In Step 1, participants study a series of items (*a,b,c…*) while their brain activity is recorded. Step 2 requires that they perform encoding trials, remembering some of the studied items and forgetting others. On the basis of retrieval performance, in Step 3 the encoding trials are coded as subsequently remembered or subsequently forgotten; activity during these two types of encoding trials is compared in Step 4. Greater activity for subsequently remembered than forgotten trials is assumed to reflect successful encoding processes, and is known as *subsequent memory effects* or **difference-in-memory (Dm) effects.**

Although only recently adapted to fMRI studies, the subsequent memory paradigm has been used in ERP studies since the early 1980s by Kenneth Paller (now at Northwestern University) and other researchers. In ERP studies, Dm effects tend to be seen over frontoparietal scalp regions. Although the neural generators of scalp ERPs are uncertain, this method has the ad-

vantage of providing fine temporal resolution. As an example, Figure B, which measures Dm effects during the encoding of faces, shows that ERPs for later-remembered and forgotten faces start to diverge around 300 ms after stimulus onset, a distinction that persists until about 800 ms. This time window provides a useful limit on speculation about the cognitive processes supporting successful face encoding.

As illustrated by the right panel in Figure A, successful versus unsuccessful trials (i.e., hits versus misses) can also be compared during retrieval. An alternative approach to isolating activity associated with retrieval success is to compare hits to correct rejections of new items. An important advantage of the hit versus miss contrast is that the same set of items is compared as in the subsequent memory paradigm (e.g., *a,b,e,h…* versus *c,d,f,g…* in Figure A). An advantage of the hit versus correct rejection comparison is that it is based on correct responses, and hence not

(A) Methods for comparing successful and unsuccessful trials during encoding and retrieval.

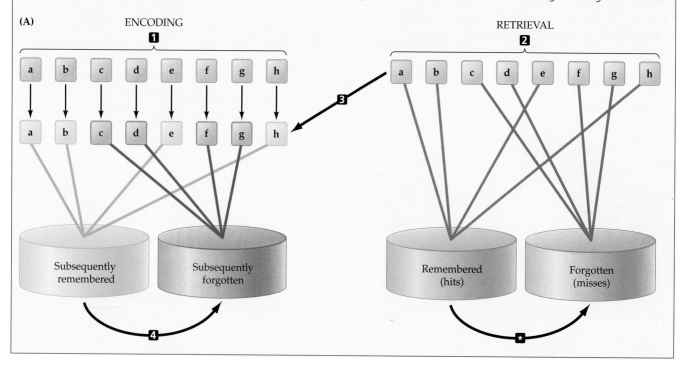

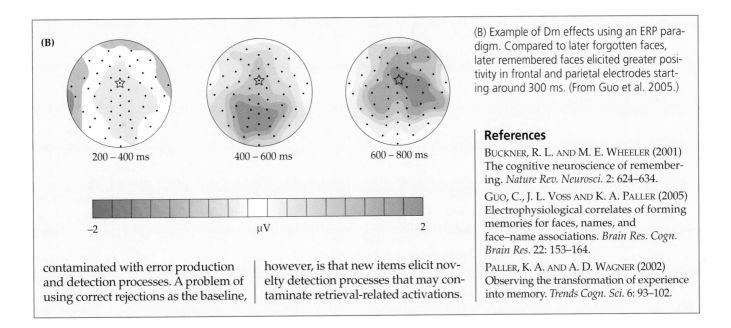

(B) Example of Dm effects using an ERP paradigm. Compared to later forgotten faces, later remembered faces elicited greater positivity in frontal and parietal electrodes starting around 300 ms. (From Guo et al. 2005.)

200–400 ms 400–600 ms 600–800 ms

−2 µV 2

References

BUCKNER, R. L. AND M. E. WHEELER (2001) The cognitive neuroscience of remembering. *Nature Rev. Neurosci.* 2: 624–634.

GUO, C., J. L. VOSS AND K. A. PALLER (2005) Electrophysiological correlates of forming memories for faces, names, and face–name associations. *Brain Res. Cogn. Brain Res.* 22: 153–164.

PALLER, K. A. AND A. D. WAGNER (2002) Observing the transformation of experience into memory. *Trends Cogn. Sci.* 6: 93–102.

contaminated with error production and detection processes. A problem of using correct rejections as the baseline, however, is that new items elicit novelty detection processes that may contaminate retrieval-related activations.

gyrus (dorsolateral prefrontal cortex). This pattern may reflect the simple nature of stimuli used in Dm studies, which may not require the organizing functions attributed to dorsolateral prefrontal regions. To investigate this idea, a recent fMRI study scanned participants while they were reordering or

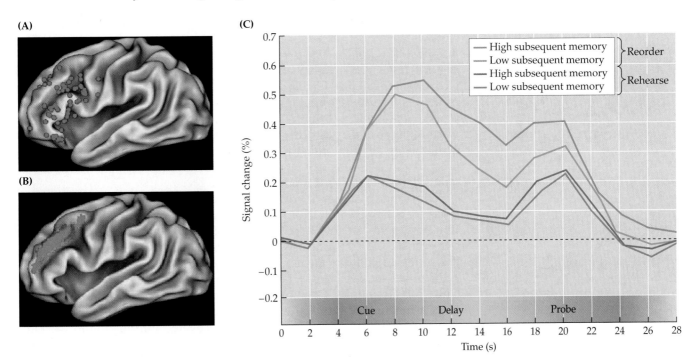

Figure 14.14 Dm effects in the inferior vs. middle frontal gyri. (A) Greater activity for subsequently remembered than forgotten items (the Dm effect) is typically found in the inferior frontal gyrus (green dots), but rarely in the middle frontal gyrus (red dots). (B) When the encoding task requires organizing information within working memory, the middle frontal gyrus (shown in red) shows significant Dm effects. (C) This region showed a significant Dm effect during the delay period of a working memory task when participants reordered words during this period, but not when they just rehearsed them. (After Blumenfeld and Ranganath 2006.)

rehearsing words in working memory; the participants' memory was later tested for the words outside the scanner. As shown in **Figure 14.14B,C**, the left dorsolateral prefrontal region showed a significant Dm effect, but only for the reorder condition. This finding suggests that the dorsolateral prefrontal region contributes to successful episodic encoding through its role in organizing information within working memory.

In sum, episodic encoding and semantic retrieval are associated with activation of the left inferior frontal gyrus. Dm effects, on the other hand, are usually left-lateralized for verbal stimuli and bilateral for pictorial stimuli. The anterior part of the left inferior frontal gyrus has been associated to semantic processing, and the posterior part with phonological processing. Finally, dorsolateral prefrontal regions may also show Dm effects when stimuli are more complex and require organization of the information in working memory to facilitate subsequent memory retrieval.

Episodic memory retrieval

Consider trying to remember what you had for breakfast the day before yesterday. The train of thought elicited by this challenge might go something like this:

> Hmm… the day before yesterday I had a class in the morning and I didn't have much time for breakfast. I think I just grabbed something in the kitchen. I made coffee, which I always have in the morning, and I probably had a piece of toast. No… I didn't have toast because I was in a hurry. Now, I remember… I spread peanut butter on a slice of bread and ate it while I drank some coffee and browsed through a clothing catalog. I drank the rest of the coffee in the car…

This example illustrates typical components of episodic memory retrieval. A **retrieval cue** (the question about breakfast) triggers a **memory search** that narrows the focus to a particular time and place (the day before yesterday, in the kitchen), which leads to the **recovery** of increasingly specific stored memory traces (*coffee, toast, peanut butter, browsing a clothing catalog*). The information recovered is evaluated by a **monitoring process** that can reject inappropriate memories (e.g., *toast*), leading to further refinement. While these various processes are being performed, attention remains focused on a particular place and time in the past. This sustained mental state, which is assumed to be qualitatively different from the mental states associated with other cognitive processes such as semantic memory retrieval, is known as **episodic retrieval mode**, or simply **retrieval mode**.

To investigate the neural correlates of the components of episodic retrieval, researchers have manipulated different variables in neuroimaging studies. One important variable is the amount of valid information recovered, or **retrieval success**. Retrieval success can be measured by comparing conditions in which studied items are remembered well or poorly; by comparing recognition of old and new items; or by comparing correct and incorrect recognition ("hits" versus "misses"; see Box 14C). Brain regions in which activity increases as a function of retrieval success are likely to be involved in recovery processes, or in processes that maintain recovered information in working memory. In contrast, brain regions that are more active when recovery is low, which indexes **retrieval effort**, are likely to be involved in more demanding search or monitoring processes. Retrieval mode is assumed to reflect a *qualitative* aspect of episodic retrieval, and hence to be relatively immune to variations in retrieval success or effort. Thus, regions that show similar activity for old and new items, such as anterior right prefrontal regions, have been associated with the retrieval mode.

Retrieval processes also differ in their temporal characteristics. In a typical episodic retrieval test that includes several items from the same past event (e.g., a study list), recovery and monitoring processes are assumed to vary from trial to trial, and to dissipate during the intertrial interval. Retrieval mode, however, is assumed be sustained throughout the task, including the interval between the trials. One way of distinguishing sustained from transient activations is to use the hybrid block/event-related designs described in Chapter 3.

The first hybrid-design study of episodic retrieval measured slow and fast changes on scalp electrical activity. As illustrated in **Figure 14.15A**, electrical activity over right frontopolar regions showed not only transient changes associated with the retrieval of each item (every 2 seconds), but a slower, positive-going drift across the whole retrieval block (10 seconds). This right-lateralized drift occurred for episodic but not for semantic retrieval, consistent with the notion of episodic retrieval mode. Subsequent fMRI studies using hybrid designs confirmed that right anterior prefrontal regions show sustained activity during episodic retrieval (**Figure 14.15B**). This sustained right anterior prefrontal activation thus links this region to involvement in the retrieval mode.

Turning to transient prefrontal activations detected with event-related fMRI designs, transient activation in the left hemisphere has been associated with recollection, whereas transient activity in the right hemisphere is better associated with familiarity. For example, a study investigating the "remember/ know" paradigm (see previous discussion) found that left dorsolateral prefrontal cortex was more strongly activated for recollection-based than for

(A) Right frontopolar electrode

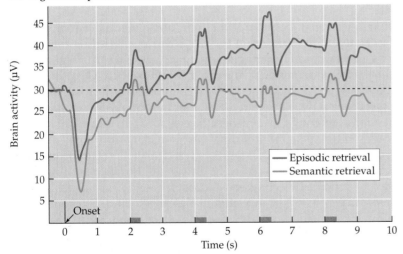

(B) Right frontopolar cortex

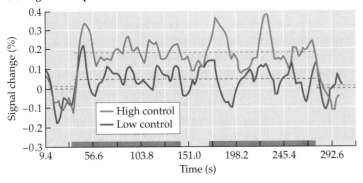

Figure 14.15 Evidence of sustained activity in right frontopolar cortex associated with retrieval. (A) Electrical activity in a right frontopolar electrode during a 10-second block consisting of the block instruction (onset, indicated by the arrow) and four items presented at 2-second intervals (gray bars). In addition to transient item-related activity every 2 seconds, there is a slow, positive-direction drift that lasts throughout the entire block. (B) Similar finding in a hybrid blocked/event-related fMRI study. The right frontopolar cortex showed sustained activity during an episodic retrieval task. Dashed lines indicate average activity and show differences during the block (gray bars) but not during the interblock intervals. (A after Düzel et al. 1999; B after Velanova et al. 2003.)

Figure 14.16 Transient prefrontal activation differentially associated with recollection and familiarity. (A) Left prefrontal cortex shows greater activity for "remember" responses (recollection) than for "know" responses (familiarity), whereas right prefrontal cortex shows the opposite effect. (B) A context memory task (recollection) engaged left dorsolateral regions more than right dorsolateral regions, whereas a recency task (familiarity) yielded the opposite pattern. (A from Henson et al. 1999; B after Dobbins et al. 2003).

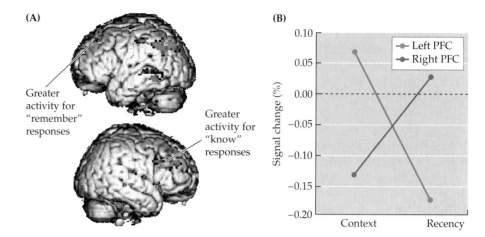

familiarity-based recognition responses; the right dorsolateral cortex showed the opposite pattern (**Figure 14.16A**). A similar dissociation was found in a study that compared a context memory task that was dependent on recollection to a recency discrimination task assumed to be more dependent on familiarity (**Figure 14.16B**). Besides differentiating recollection versus familiarity, these double dissociations fit well with other distinctions. For instance, Marcia Johnson and collaborators have proposed that left prefrontal regions mediate **systematic processes** (such as detailed, deliberate analyses of activated information), and that right prefrontal regions mediate **heuristic processes** (such as simple contrasts between the activated information and a decision criterion).

In addition to its role in familiarity, the right dorsolateral prefrontal cortex has been associated with monitoring processes during retrieval. This idea is supported by functional neuroimaging evidence showing this region to be activated during more demanding retrieval conditions (**Box 14D**). For example, in a study in which participants made recognition memory decisions followed by confidence ratings, right dorsolateral prefrontal activity was greater for low- than for high-confidence recognition responses (**Figure 14.17A**). The link between right dorsolateral prefrontal cortex and monitoring is also supported by brain-lesion evidence. Daniel Schacter's group at Harvard reported a patient (patient B.G.) with a large right dorsolateral prefrontal lesion who showed a severe deficit in rejecting nonstudied distractors among the studied items in a recognition test. As illustrated in **Figure 14.17B**, B.G. produced an abnormally high proportion of "old" responses to nonstudied items ("false alarms"), many of which he classified as "remember" rather than "know." This sort of impairment suggests a monitoring deficit, although since the study used only behavioral methods, it is impossible to determine if impairments reflect encoding or retrieval deficits.

In short, retrieval of episodic memories has been associated with both sustained and transient activations of the prefrontal cortex. Sustained activation has been linked to the qualitative mental state accompanying episodic retrieval (i.e., retrieval mode), and tends to occur in right anterior prefrontal regions. In contrast, transient activation of the left dorsolateral regions has been associated more specifically with recollection or the attempt to recollect, whereas transient activation in right dorsolateral regions is more strongly associated with familiarity or monitoring. The role of left prefrontal cortex in recollection and right prefrontal in familiarity is also supported by lesion evidence. Although left prefrontal lesions do not usually impair semantic memo-

(A)

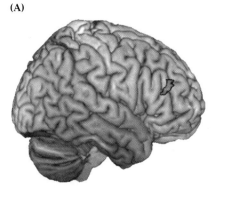

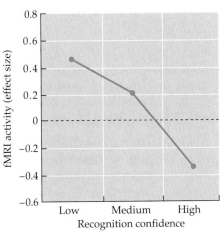

(B)

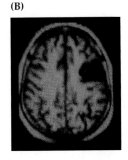

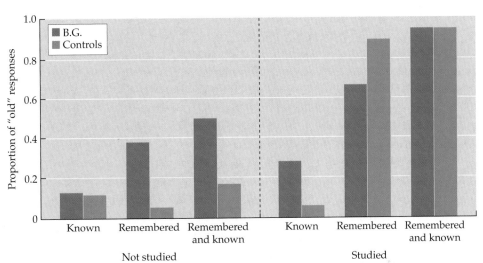

Not studied   Studied

Figure 14.17 Role of frontal brain regions in monitoring remembered information.   (A) This study showed right dorsolateral prefrontal activity to be greater for low- than for high-confidence recognition responses, supporting the hypothesis that this brain region is involved in monitoring retrieval output. (B) Patient B.G., who has a large lesion of the right dorsolateral prefrontal cortex, is impaired in memory monitoring. He shows a very high false-alarm rate for nonstudied words, many of which he classified as remembered rather than known. (A after Fleck et al. 2006; B after Schacter et al. 1996.)

ry retrieval, the apparent inconsistency with functional neuroimaging findings may be explained by some degree of functional reorganization following brain damage. Thus, the evidence to date generally supports an important role for the frontal cortices in declarative memory.

The Role of the Parietal and Posterior Midline Regions in Declarative Memory

In addition to the medial temporal and prefrontal regions, episodic memory retrieval has also been associated with parietal regions. The contribution of parietal regions was first revealed by ERP studies (see Box 14D), and later confirmed by PET and fMRI. The functional imaging studies identified not only lateral posterior parietal regions, but several posterior midline regions as well, including the precuneus, the posterior cingulate cortices, and the retrosplenial cortices. A hypothesis about the role of the precuneus in episodic retrieval was proposed by Paul Fletcher (now at Cambridge University), who suggested that this region is involved in visual imagery. This idea could account for the neuroimaging evidence that the precuneus is more active during the retrieval of words that elicit a visual image (e.g., *house, dog*) than ones that don't (e.g., *true, false*). However, the precuneus is also active in conditions with no obvious visual imagery component. In general, activity in the precuneus and other pos-

■ BOX 14D ERP Studies of Episodic Retrieval

Studies of episodic memory retrieval using event-related potentials have identified three consistent differences between recalling old and new items. First, some 300–500 milliseconds after a stimulus has been presented, new items tend to elicit greater negative voltage over mid-frontal regions than old items do. This *frontal negativity (FN) effect* has been called **FN400 effect** to distinguish it from the central parietal N400 effect typically associated with semantic processing (see Chapter 21). The FN400 effect responds similarly to studied items and to new items that appear familiar, and to both deeply and shallowly encoded items (see figure). Because of these and other findings, the FN400 effect has been attributed to familiarity.

Second, 400–800 milliseconds after the stimulus, old items tend to elicit more positive voltage over parietal electrodes than new items do. This effect is typically left-lateralized for verbal materials, and is known as the **left-parietal effect**. This phenomenon tends to be more pronounced when higher (more complex) levels of recollection are required. For example, the effect tends to be greater for deeply encoded items than for shallowly encoded items (see figure); for words judged as "remembered" rather than "known"; and for words accompanied by successful rather than unsuccessful source retrieval. The source of

the left-parietal effect is most likely the left posterior parietal region in that it is typically activated during PET and fMRI studies of episodic retrieval and is strongly associated with retrieval success.

Finally, at 600–1200 milliseconds poststimulus, old items sometimes elicit a more positive response over right frontal regions than do new items; this is known as the **right-frontal effect**. The right-frontal effect is usually apparent during tasks that entail demanding source memory decisions and is assumed to reflect postretrieval operations. This idea fits the extended time-course of the right-frontal effect, and is consistent with functional neuroimaging and lesion

evidence linking the right prefrontal cortex to monitoring.

References

CURRAN, T., K. L. TEPE AND C. PIATT (2006). ERP explorations of dual processes in recognition memory. In *Binding in Human Memory: A Neurocognitive Approach*, H. D. Zimmer, A. Mecklinger and U. Lindenberger (eds.). Oxford: Oxford University Press, pp. 467–492.

RUGG, M. D. (2004). Retrieval processing in human memory: Electrophysiological and fMRI evidence. In *The Cognitive Neurosciences*, 3rd ed., M. S. Gazzaniga (ed.). Cambridge, MA: MIT Press.

RUGG, M. D. AND A. P. YONELINAS (2003) Human recognition memory: A cognitive neuroscience perspective. *Trends Cogn. Sci.* 7: 313–319.

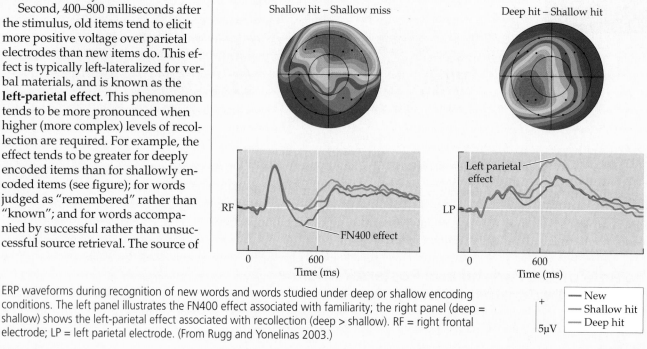

ERP waveforms during recognition of new words and words studied under deep or shallow encoding conditions. The left panel illustrates the FN400 effect associated with familiarity; the right panel (deep = shallow) shows the left-parietal effect associated with recollection (deep > shallow). RF = right frontal electrode; LP = left parietal electrode. (From Rugg and Yonelinas 2003.)

terior midline and lateral parietal regions increases as a function of retrieval success. These regions usually show greater activity during correct recognition of old items ("hits") than for correct recognition of new items ("misses").

An aspect of the role of the lateral posterior parietal and posterior midline regions in episodic retrieval is the contrast with their role during encoding. During retrieval, these regions are typically activated with respect to the baseline levels, and tend to show more activity for successful than for unsuccess-

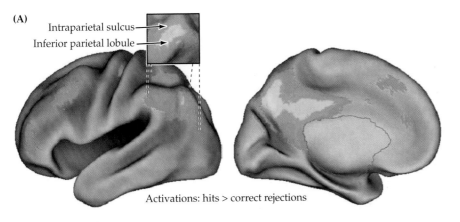

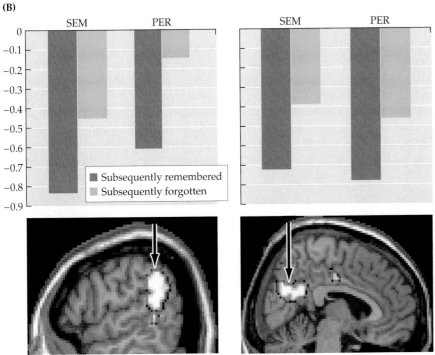

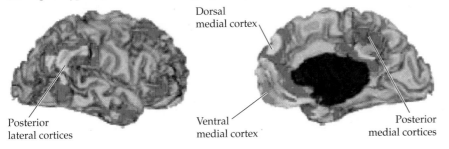

(C) **Regions typically deactivated during cognitive performance**

Figure 14.18 Posterior parietal and dorsal midline activity during declarative memory tasks.
(A) Brain regions that typically show greater activity for correct recognition of old items ("hits") than for correct recognition of new items ("correct rejections"). (B) These same regions are deactivated during encoding, and to a greater extent for items that are subsequently remembered than for items that are subsequently forgotten. (C) Posterior parietal and posterior midline regions are part of a set of brain areas that are typically deactivated during demanding cognitive tasks, possibly because they support processes during resting conscious state, or default mode.
(A after Wagner et al. 2005; B after Daselaar et al. 2004; C after Gusnard and Raichle 2001.)

ful trials (**Figure 14.18A**). During encoding, however, these regions are usually *de*activated with respect to the baseline, and tend to show *less* activity for successful than for unsuccessful trials (i.e., a "reverse Dm" effect; **Figure 14.18B**). The finding that these regions are deactivated during encoding makes some sense in light of the fact these same regions are part of a group of regions that are typically deactivated during cognitive performance (**Figure 14.18C**).

According to Marcus Raichle and his collaborators at Washington University, these typically deactivated brain areas are involved in processes that occur normally during resting but nonetheless conscious brain states, which these researchers have called the **default mode**. In their view, the default mode must be "turned off" during cognitive performance. Episodic retrieval seems to be an exception to the rule, because it is associated with activation rather than deactivation of these regions. One hypothesis is that episodic retrieval is part of the default mode of the brain, and hence disengagement of these regions during episodic retrieval tasks is not required. Although much more work will be needed to sort out these speculations, these regions do show a dissociation between encoding and retrieval, which constrains possible accounts of their functions.

The Role of Sensory Cortices in Declarative Memory

As described in Chapter 13, most memory researchers believe that memory traces, or *engrams*, are stored in or near the cortical regions originally involved in processing each aspect of a complex event (i.e., visual information is stored in visual cortex, auditory information in auditory cortex, and so on). More abstract memory representations such as concepts are thought to be stored in association areas of the ventral and lateral temporal cortices. Thus an important question regarding the role of occipital and temporal cortices in declarative memory is how such knowledge is organized. This issue is discussed in the chapters on vision (Chapter 5) and on the neural correlates of language (Chapter 21).

(A) Encoding

Image > Read

Read > Image

Parahippocampal

Premotor/prefrontal

(B) Retrieval

Hits with recollection

Parahippocampal

False alarms

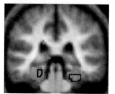

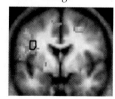

"Imagined"   "Read"

Premotor/prefrontal

"Imagined"   "Read"

Figure 14.19 Recapitulation during retrieval of episodic memories. (A) During encoding, a parahippocampal region was more active in the "image" than in the "read" condition, whereas a left premotor/prefrontal region showed the reverse pattern. (B) During retrieval, these two regions were both activated when participants correctly or incorrectly assigned words to these conditions. (After Kahn et al. 2004.)

The idea that memory traces are stored in the regions originally involved in encoding an event predicts that those same regions should be reactivated when the memory of that event is retrieved, in some sense *recapitulating* the original experience. Functional neuroimaging data have generally supported this idea. In one such study, Lars Nyberg at Umeå University, Sweden, and his collaborators at the University of Toronto had participants memorize visually presented words (e.g., *dog*, *drill*), some of which were presented alone and some of which were accompanied by a matching sound (e.g., a barking sound or the whirring of a drill). Later the subjects were scanned while retrieving the words. The words accompanied by sounds during the initial exposure elicited greater auditory cortex activity than those presented alone, implying that recapitulation is indeed elicited when multiple aspects of the original event are presented.

Complementing these findings, fMRI studies carried out by Randy Buckner (now at Harvard University) and John Gabrieli (now at MIT) and their collaborators showed greater visual cortex activity for written words that were encoded as pictures than for words presented alone. In another fMRI study, participants encoded words by making mental images (image encoding) or by thinking about the sound of words (read encoding). The parahippocampal region was more active in the image- than in the read-encoding condition, whereas a left premotor/prefrontal region showed the reverse pattern (**Figure 14.19A**). During retrieval, these two regions were activated when participants correctly or incorrectly assigned words to these conditions (**Figure 14.19B**). The fact that these regions are activated during incorrect source assignments suggests further that the reactivation during retrieval of encoding regions does not necessarily reflect stored memory traces. Again, some further effort will be required to sort out this interesting issue.

Summary

1. Declarative memory functions are strongly associated with the neural processing in the medial temporal lobes, and also with regions of the frontal and parietal lobes, as well as with sensory regions throughout the brain.

2. Within the medial temporal lobes, the key structure is the hippocampus. The functions of the hippocampus in declarative memory are not fully settled, but normal hippocampal operation is clearly important for encoding spatial, relational, and episodic memories. Other medial temporal structures, adjacent to the hippocampus and richly connected to it, are also critical for the normal operation of declarative memory.

3. Whereas the hippocampus appears to be particularly important for successfully establishing memory for items in a context, the perirhinal cortices influence both memory for items as such and memory of context.

4. With respect to the frontal lobes, different regions of the prefrontal cortex have been specifically implicated in the retrieval of different types of declarative memory. Thus episodic retrieval is associated with neural activity in anterior prefrontal regions, recollection with activity in the left dorsolateral prefrontal regions, and familiarity/monitoring with activation of the right dorsolateral prefrontal regions.

5. Other frontal lobe regions are active in semantic retrieval, and these are strongly linked to the language areas in the left inferior frontal gyrus. Posterior lateral parietal and posterior midline regions are also involved in episodic retrieval, but are usually deactivated during episodic encoding.

6. The primary sensory and sensory association cortices, which are the presumed loci of the stored memory traces that entail perceptual qualities, appear to be reactivated during retrieval as a function of the quality of the information that was stored during encoding. Accordingly, sensory regions of the brain are also necessary for the storage and retrieval of many sorts of declarative memories.

7. More abstract information involves still other regions of the brain. The interaction of many different brain regions is needed to successfully encode, store, and retrieve the memories that we and other animals are explicitly aware of and can in one way or another report to ourselves and to others.

Additional Reading

Reviews

BROWN, M. W. AND J. P. AGGLETON (2001) Recognition memory: What are the roles of the perirhinal cortex and hippocampus? *Nat. Rev. Neurosci.* 2: 51–61.

EICHENBAUM, H. (2000) A cortical–hippocampal system for declarative memory. *Nat. Rev. Neurosci.* 1: 41–50.

EICHENBAUM, H., A. R. YONELINAS AND C. RANGANATH (2007) The medial temporal lobe and recognition memory. *Annu. Rev. Neurosci.* 30: 123–152.

RUGG, M. D. AND A. P. YONELINAS (2003) Human recognition memory: A cognitive neuroscience perspective. *Trends Cogn. Sci.* 7: 313–319.

SQUIRE, L. R., C. E. STARK AND R. E. CLARK (2004) The medial temporal lobe. *Annu. Rev. Neurosci.* 27: 279–306.

WHEELER, M. A., D. T. STUSS AND E. TULVING (1995) Frontal lobe damage produces episodic memory impairment. *J. Internatl. Neuropsychol. Soc.* 1: 525–536.

YONELINAS, A. P. (2002) The nature of recollection and familiarity: A review of 30 years of research. *Memory and Language* 46: 441–517.

Important Original Papers

BUCKNER, R. L., S. E. PETERSEN, J. G. OJEMANN, F. M. MIEZIN, L. R. SQUIRE AND M. E. RAICHLE (1995) Functional anatomical studies of explicit and implicit memory retrieval tasks. *J. Neurosci.* 15: 12–29.

ELDRIDGE, L. L., B. J. KNOWLTON, C. S. FURMANSKI, S. Y. BOOKHEIMER AND S. A. ENGLE (2000) Remembering episodes: A selective role for the hippocampus during retrieval. *Nature Neurosci.* 3: 1149–1152.

JANOWSKY, J. S., A. P. SHIMAMURA, M. KRITCHEVSKY AND L. R. SQUIRE (1989) Cognitive impairment following frontal lobe damage and its relevance to human amnesia. *Behav. Neurosci.* 103: 548–560.

WAGNER, A. D. AND 7 OTHERS (1998) Building memories: remembering and forgetting of verbal experiences as predicted by brain activity. *Science* 281: 1188–1191.

ZOLAMORGAN, S., L. R. SQUIRE AND D. G. AMARAL (1986) Human amnesia and the medial temporal region: Enduring memory impairment following a bilateral lesion limited to field CA1 of the hippocampus. *J. Neurosci.* 6: 2950–2967.

Books

BADDELEY, A., M. A. CONWAY AND J. P. AGGLETON (EDS.) (2002) *Episodic Memory: New Directions in Research.* Oxford: Oxford University Press.

O'KEEFE, J. A. AND L. NADEL (1978) *The Hippocampus as a Cognitive Map.* Oxford: Oxford University Press.

TULVING, E. (1983) *Elements of Episodic Memory.* Oxford: Oxford University Press.

15

Nondeclarative Memory

Introduction

Nondeclarative memory is a heterogeneous category that covers several different forms of memory that, in contrast to declarative memory, are expressed through performance without the requirement of conscious content. For this reason, nondeclarative memories are referred to as *implicit*, whereas declarative memories are *explicit*. Major forms of nondeclarative memories fall into three broad categories: priming, skill learning, and conditioning. These three forms of nondeclarative memory depend on different brain regions; the main characteristic they have in common is that they are all independent of the medial temporal lobe, which is the most critical region for declarative memory. At the same time, nondeclarative memories are likely to depend on the same cellular and molecular mechanisms (described in Chapter 13) that support declarative memory. This chapter focuses on the neural bases of nondeclarative memory, and considers in turn priming, skill learning, and conditioning. Although the emphasis is on research at the systems level, theories regarding the cellular bases of priming are also reviewed.

Priming

Why is it so easy to recognize objects and people we know well, even if we see only a small part of them—a pair of scissors partially hidden under a book, or a friend we see only from the back? And why does a whole string of related stories come to mind when we are engaged in an interesting conversation? These are examples of the numerous cognitive phenomena in which *priming* plays a role.

Roughly speaking, **priming** is the alteration of performance (or neural processing) as a result of preceding experience; a more formal definition is given below at the end of this section. Priming affects everything we do from the time we wake up until the time we go back to sleep; even then it may affect our dreams. Despite its prevalence, we seldom notice the effects of priming, because it occurs automatically and unconsciously, without attention or other cognitive resources. Priming is also resistant to brain damage, aging, and dementia. As a result, its contributions are less obvious (and less easily studied) than other forms of memory that are compromised by specific brain insults, such as impaired declarative memory following damage to the medial temporal lobes. For all these reasons, it was not until the late

1970s that memory researchers turned to studies of priming. Since then, however, the situation has changed dramatically, and priming is now a major topic in memory research.

Before defining priming more explicitly, it is useful to describe one of the methods used to measure this phenomenon in the laboratory (**Figure 15.1A**). At Time 1, participants are asked to read a list of words (e.g., List A in the figure). To reduce the chances of participants employing explicit memory strategies (**Box 15A**), they are not told that their memory for these words will be tested later. On the contrary, they are usually told a cover story that conceals this fact; for example, they may be told that the experimenter is studying "how words are read."

At Time 2 (which may happen during the same experimental session or days or weeks later), participants are given a list of word stems and asked to complete each of them with the first word that comes to mind. This challenge is known as the *word-stem completion test*. Importantly, no reference is made the reading task performed at Time 1, and efforts are made to reduce the chances that participants will notice any relation. Unbeknownst to the participants, half of the stems can be completed with words from the list they read (List A in this example), and the other half can be completed with words from another list (List B in Figure 15.1A) that participants did not read in the context of the experiment. To control for potential differences between the two lists, half of the participants read List A at Time 1 with List B as the unknown factor, whereas for the other half this is reversed, with List B being read at Time 1.

After participants finish the test, the percentage of stems completed with list words is calculated for List A and List B, respectively. If the percentage is greater for the list that was read than for the list that was not read, it is reasonable to conclude that reading the words at Time 1 enhanced (*primed*) the completion of the stems at Time 2. The amount of priming is typically measured as the difference between completion performance in the two lists (e.g., 65% − 40% = 25% priming; **Figure 15.1B**).

The example in Figure 15.1 is only one of many ways priming can be observed and investigated. Thus, to arrive to a general definition of priming, it is important to consider the full breadth of the priming phenomena. In the foregoing example the stimulus that generated the priming effect (e.g., the

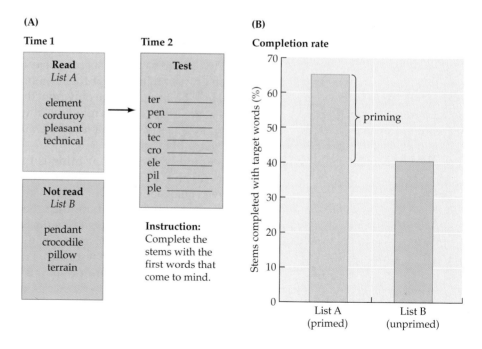

Figure 15.1 A test for priming effects. (A) In a commonly used test, the subject is presented at Time 1 with a list of words to study (List A), and is later tested using a word-stem completion test (Time 2). The stems could also be completed from List B, which the subject did not see during the study session. (B) Subjects typically complete the stems with about 25 percent more studied than unstudied words; this percentage represents the priming effect.

■ BOX 15A Explicit Memory Contamination

A potential problem in interpreting the results of implicit memory tests is *explicit memory contamination*, which occurs when participants realize that some of the test cues match the studied items and start relying on episodic memory to perform the test. For example, while completing the stem WIN____ with the word "window," a participant may spontaneously remember that this word was part of a word list previously read, and may try to recall other words from the list to complete the remaining word stems. If this happens for a significant fraction of the test items, it becomes a test of episodic rather than implicit memory.

Several methods have been developed to contend with this problem. An experimenter can reduce the likelihood that participants will notice the presence of old items by using convincing "cover stories" when presenting the study list and the test; a perceptual rather than semantic encoding task may be used; there may be a large proportion of new items in the test, and/or a long interval between study and later testing.

A more drastic method to control for spontaneous awareness is to present the primes *subliminally* (e.g., masked), so that participants are not consciously aware of the priming stimuli. Another approach is to use priming tests that require very rapid responses, in which participants don't have enough time to access episodic retrieval. Participants can also be specifically told not to use studied words when completing word fragments or stems. Thus, if a studied word is generated in spite of that direction, the experimenter can presume with some confidence that the participant did not consciously remember its occurrence in the studied list.

Finally, to check that explicit memory contamination did not take place, experiments can measure both priming and episodic memory and manipulate variables known to affect only one of these two forms of memory. Most priming studies use one or more of these control methods.

References

ROEDIGER, H. L. AND K. B. MCDERMOTT (1993) Implicit memory in normal human subjects. In *Handbook of Neuropsychology,* Vol. 8, F. Boller and J. Grafman (eds.). Amsterdam: Elsevier.

SCHACTER, D. L., J. BOWERS AND J. BOOKER (1989) Intention, awareness, and implicit memory: The retrieval intentionality criterion. In *Implicit Memory: Theoretical Issues,* S. Lewandowsky, J. C. Dunn and K. Kirsner (eds.). Hillsdale, NJ: Lawrence Erlbaum, pp. 47–65.

---

word *element* read) and the stimulus that reveals the priming effect (the word *element* generated) involves the same stimulus, but this is not always case; the two stimuli may be different, although they need to be related in some way. Furthermore, although priming usually enhances performance, it may also hinder performance in some circumstances. Thus, priming is better thought of as causing a change in performance rather than as simply enhancing performance. Finally, priming can be measured in many different ways. In the word-stem completion test, it is observed as a change in the probability of generating a particular sort of response, but in other paradigms it is measured as a change in the speed of identifying a stimulus, or as a change in eye movement pattern.

Priming thus reflects a change in neural processing that is evident in many contexts. Given this perspective, **priming** can be defined formally as a change in the processing of a stimulus due to a previous encounter with the same or a related stimulus, in the absence of conscious awareness of the original encounter. The last condition is critical for distinguishing priming from declarative memory, as explained in Box 15A.

Main forms of priming

Of the many different forms of priming, only a few of the more important ones are considered here. The major categories are illustrated in **Figure 15.2**. The broadest distinction of these phenomena is *direct* versus *indirect* priming and is based on the relation between the stimulus that generates the priming effect, known as the *prime*, and the subsequent stimulus used to test the effect, sometimes called the *target*. In **direct priming**, also called *repetition priming*, the prime and the target stimulus are the same (e.g., ENVELOPE and ENVELOPE). In **indirect priming**, the stimuli are different (e.g., ENVELOPE and LETTER).

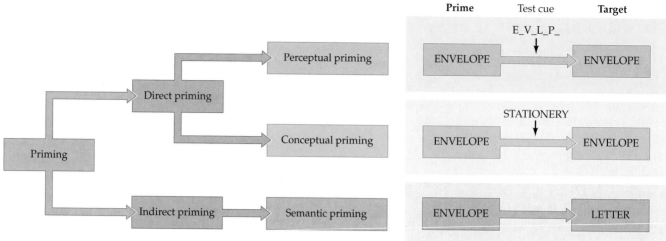

Figure 15.2 The major forms of priming. The left-hand portion of the diagram is a hierarchy of the major types of priming. On the right is an illustration of the nature of the primes, test cues, and targets to distinguish between perceptual, conceptual, and semantic priming.

A second categorical distinction only applies to direct priming and concerns the relation between the test cue, which stimulates the participants' responses at the time of testing (e.g., a word stem), and the target (i.e., the related word that was initially studied). In **perceptual priming**, the test cue and the target are perceptually related, whereas in **conceptual priming**, they are semantically or associatively related. An example of a perceptual priming test is the *word fragment completion test*; in the instance illustrated in Figure 15.2, the test cue E_V_L_P_ is perceptually related to target ENVELOPE. An example of a conceptual priming test is the *category association test*; in the instance illustrated the test cue STATIONERY is semantically related to the target ENVELOPE. (You should bear in mind that memory tests are never pure measures of a single form of memory, and tests of implicit memory are no exception.)

The most important form of *indirect* priming is **semantic priming**, which occurs when the prime and the target are semantically related (e.g., ENVELOPE and LETTER). (Don't confuse semantic priming with conceptual priming. In conceptual priming, the prime and target are the same, and it is the *test cue*, not the prime, that is semantically related to the target; see Figure 15.2.) A behavioral difference evident in tests of semantic priming compared with direct priming is that semantic priming is usually short-lived; hence it must be studied using continuous tasks in which the prime and target stimuli are adjacent or close to each other in time.

The following sections expand on some of these distinctions and consider the neural correlates of perceptual priming, conceptual priming, and semantic priming.

Perceptual priming

The assumption that perceptual priming does not depend on the same brain regions as declarative memory is supported by dissociation studies (see Chapter 3). Such studies provide clues regarding the neural mechanisms supporting this form of nondeclarative memory. Although perceptual priming has been dissociated from both episodic and semantic memory (the major forms of declarative memory), this section focuses on dissociations between priming and episodic memory. Dissociations of perceptual priming and declarative memory have been shown in *functional*, *developmental*, and *pathological* contexts.

Functional dissociations refer to differential effects of experimental factors manipulated in the laboratory. For example, manipulations that affect the subject's processing of a stimulus' meaning tend to affect episodic memory but

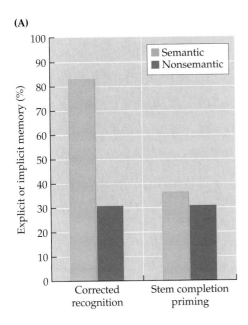

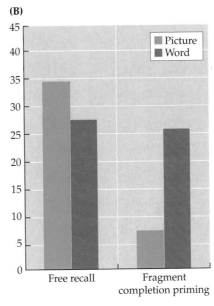

Figure 15.3 Functional dissociations between episodic memory and perceptual priming. (A) Recognition is better for words encoded under semantic than nonsemantic study conditions, whereas stem completion priming is similar across these conditions. (B) Verbal free recall is as good for items studied as words as for items studied as pictures, whereas word-fragment completion priming is much greater for items studied as words than for items studied as pictures. (A after Graf and Mandler 1984; B after Weldon and Roediger 1987.)

not perceptual priming, whereas manipulations that affect processing of the physical features of a stimulus tend to produce the opposite effect. Thus episodic memory is typically better for items encoded under semantic rather than nonsemantic study tasks, whereas perceptual priming is usually insensitive to this manipulation (**Figure 15.3A**). This finding suggests that perceptual priming is *presemantic* and *automatic*.

Conversely, changing the physical format of stimuli between study and test produces little or no effect on episodic memory, but markedly attenuates perceptual priming (**Figure 15.3B**). Episodic memory is flexible and can be applied even when the physical features of the information differ between the time of encoding and the time of retrieval. For instance, a student can write out the answer to an exam question (visual retrieval), even if the target information was something the student heard during a lecture (auditory encoding). In contrast, perceptual priming is impaired by study-to-test perceptual shifts. In general, the greater the *perceptual* difference between study items and test items, the greater the reduction in priming. A change in surface format (e.g., from one font to another, or from handwritten to typewritten) reduces priming by approximately 15 percent. A change in sensory modality (e.g., from auditory to visual) reduces priming by about 50 percent, and a change in symbol type (e.g., from picture to words) reduces it by about 75 percent. These findings suggests that perceptual priming is mediated by brain areas that are very sensitive to the physical properties of stimuli, such as sensory regions of the cortex. In short, these studies reveal a double dissociation of episodic memory and perceptual priming.

Developmental dissociations refer to different rates of cognitive and neural changes during childhood and adult aging. In a developmental study, for example, picture *recognition* priming was much better in young adults than in 3-year-olds, whereas picture *identification* priming was about the same in the two groups (**Figure 15.4A**). At the other end of the life span, older adults tend to be impaired in episodic memory but not in perceptual priming. For example, word-stem cued recall (an explicit memory version of the word-stem completion test) was significantly worse in older than in young adults, whereas word-stem completion priming was similar across the groups (**Figure 15.4B**). Thus, while episodic memory shows pronounced developmental

Figure 15.4 Changes in declarative and nondeclarative memory over the human life span. (A) Comparison between young children and young adults. Explicit picture recognition (declarative memory) increases dramatically from childhood to young adulthood (red trace); however, priming effects in picture identification (nondeclarative memory) are largely unchanged during childhood development (blue trace). (B) Comparison between older and younger adults in the proportion correct between stems that could be completed with studied (old) versus nonstudied (new) words when participants were given implicit instructions (word-stem completion) or explicit instructions (word-stem cued recall). Word-recall performance (red trace) declines markedly with aging, while word-stem priming (blue trace) is largely preserved in older adults. Older adults showed as much priming as young adults, but significantly reduced episodic memory. Taken together, these results indicate that declarative memory is very sensitive to life-span development, whereas nondeclarative memory is not. (A after Parkin and Streete 1988; B after Light and Singh 1987.)

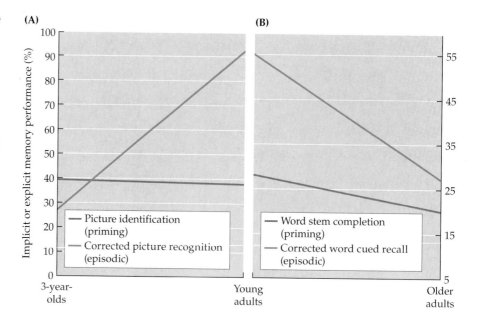

changes, perceptual priming is quite stable across the human life span. This pattern suggest that that episodic memory depends on brain regions that mature slowly during childhood and decline rapidly during aging, such as hippocampal and prefrontal regions. Conversely, perceptual priming depends on brain regions that mature early and are well preserved in old age, such as sensory regions of the neocortex.

Finally, **pathological dissociations** refer to differential effects observed in patients with brain lesions or from perturbations of brain function induced, for example, by drugs or transcranial magnetic stimulation (TMS; see Figure 3.2). As reviewed in Chapter 13, medial temporal lobe damage tends to impair episodic memory but not perceptual priming. Patients such as H.M. and other amnesics in whom declarative memory is severely impaired show normal perceptual priming in tasks that include word fragment completion, word identification, picture identification, and picture naming. Conversely, the case of patient M.S. described in Chapter 13 showed that occipital damage impairs visual perceptual priming but not episodic memory.

In sum, these several dissociations indicate that, unlike episodic memory, perceptual priming is affected by perceptual but not by conceptual manipulations, is relatively stable across the life span, and is sensitive to lesions of sensory cortex but not to lesions in the medial temporal lobes. These differences support the conclusion that perceptual priming depends on changes in neural function in the sensory cortices.

Although the nature of these neural changes in sensory cortices is not known, one way researchers have thought about the genesis of perceptual priming is in terms of a reduction in neural responses. Neurons that fire in response to the initial presentation of a stimulus often show decreased response when the stimulus is repeated. For example, Robert Desimone and collaborators at the National Institutes of Health found that neurons in the inferior temporal cortex showed a decreased level of firing when a novel stimulus was repeated. The term **repetition suppression** has been used to describe a similar and presumably related phenomenon observed in functional neuroimaging studies in which previously encountered (primed) stimuli result in smaller hemodynamic responses in frontal and posterior brain regions than novel (unprimed) stimuli (**Box 15B**). These reduced responses occur even if

■ BOX 15B Repetition Suppression as a Tool: Adaptation in fMRI Studies

The phenomenon of repetition suppression is widely used as an fMRI tool for investigating the function of different brain regions, particularly sensory regions. The method most commonly used is known as *fMRI adaptation (fMRI-A)*, and was applied in block designs by Kalamit Grill-Spector and Rafael Malach at the Weizmann Institute, and in event-related designs by Zoe Kourtzi and Nancy Kanwisher at MIT.

The fMRI-A method is based on the assumption that if a brain region shows repetition suppression for a particular prime–target combination, then the two stimuli share a process supported by the region. Thus, by manipulating the relationship between primes and targets, it is possible to constrain hypotheses regarding the function of a particular brain region. For example, Kourtzi and Kanwisher found that a brain region known as *lateral occipital complex* showed repetition suppression for repeated objects (e.g. "table") even when the two stimuli were presented in different formats (e.g., as a drawing versus as a photo). This finding suggests that the lateral occipital complex is concerned with processing an object's abstract properties rather than its sensory features.

In some instances, fMRI-A appears to yield greater functional resolution (known as "hyper-resolution") than standard fMRI methods. One possible explanation is that in conventional fMRI, comparing two stimulus conditions A and B may fail to find differences between conditions because the populations of neurons sensitive to these conditions are mixed within the same brain region being sampled (Figure A). In contrast, in the fMRI-A paradigm, the subpopulations of neurons sensitive to stimulus A adapt when this stimulus is repeated, giving rise to a lower (and thus more distinctive) fMRI signal than that elicited for stimulus B (Figure B).

References

GRILL-SPECTOR, K., T. KUSHNIR, S. EDELMAN, G. AVIDAN, Y. ITZCHAK AND R. MALACH (1999) Differential processing of objects under various viewing conditions in the human lateral occipital complex. *Neuron* 24: 187–203.

KOURTZI, Z. AND K. GRILL-SPECTOR (2005) fMRI adaptation: A tool for studying visual representations in the primate brain. In *Fitting the Mind into the World: Adaptation and After-Effects in High-Level Vision*, G. Rhodes and C. Clifford (eds.). New York: Oxford University Press.

KOURTZI, Z. AND N. KANWISHER (2001) Representation of perceived object shape by the human lateral occipital complex. *Science* 293: 1506–1509.

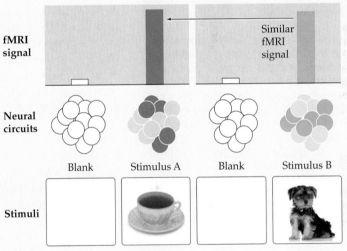

(A) Standard fMRI experiment

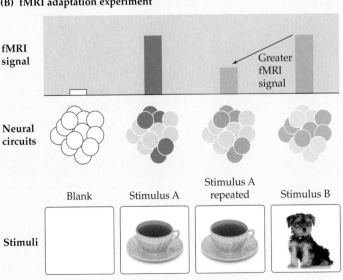

(B) fMRI adaptation experiment

Hyper-resolution in adaptive fMRI studies. (A) A conventional fMRI experiment may fail to distinguish between stimulus A and stimulus B because the two stimuli activate different populations of neurons (orange versus blue in the figure) within the same brain region sampled; hence the total fMRI signal may be similar. (B) An adaptive fMRI (fMRI-A) experiment may detect a difference in fMRI signal within a brain region. When the subpopulation of neurons sensitive to stimulus A adapt, the signal is weak for stimulus A but strong for stimulus B. (After Kourtzi and Grill-Spector 2005.)

(A) Word-stem completion

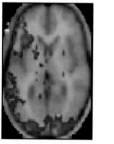 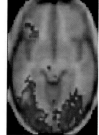

(B) Priming

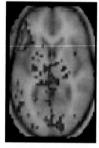 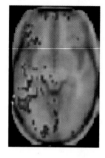

Figure 15.5 Repetition suppression and the brain regions involved in priming. (A) Word-stem completion activates several brain regions, including the left ventrolateral prefrontal cortex (left) and ventral occipitotemporal cortex (right). (B) Priming reduced activity in both of these regions, a phenomenon called repetition suppression. (From Buckner et al. 2000.)

prime and target stimuli are separated by several intervening stimuli, indicating that relatively long-term memory representations are required.

Randy Buckner and collaborators at Harvard University measured brain activity while participants completed word stems that matched (primed stems) or did not match (unprimed stems) words read before testing. Word-stem completion performance activated a distributed network of brain regions (**Figure 15.5A**), and repetition suppression was found in several of these regions, including ventrolateral prefrontal and ventral occipitotemporal cortex (**Figure 15.5B**). The fact that the priming-related activity reductions occurred in several regions activated by the task suggests that perceptual priming enhances the cognitive operations normally required by a task rather than recruiting additional processes. The further fact that several brain regions showed repetition suppression suggests that priming may facilitate several stages of stimulus processing.

As already mentioned, perceptual priming is markedly reduced by changes in perceptual format between study and test, such as modality shifts. The amount of priming that remains across these changes is assumed to reflect more abstract representations, and perhaps conceptual priming. In functional neuroimaging studies, brain regions mediating form-specific versus abstract forms of priming can be distinguished by determining whether or not study-to-test perceptual shifts attenuate repetition suppression effects (see Box 15B). For example, the lateralization of repetition suppression in ventral temporal cortex differs depending on whether the prime and target objects are the same or are different exemplars of the same object (**Figure 15.6A**). A right fusiform brain region showed repetition suppression only in the "same" condition, whereas a left fusiform region showed repetition suppression in both conditions (**Figure 15.6B**).

It could be argued that the priming across different exemplars reflects a contamination by explicit strategies (see Box 15A). However, the hemispheric asymmetry in ventral occipitotemporal regions was also found using a technique known as **masked priming**, whereby conscious awareness of the prime is prevented by an interfering noise, or **mask**, that follows shortly after the prime. In this study, the prime and the target could be either in the same case or in a different case (**Figure 15.6C**). Repetition suppression was found in right occipital for case-specific priming, but in left fusiform cortex for case-independent priming (**Figure 15.6D**). The hemispheric asymmetry found in these two and other priming studies is consistent with evidence linking the right hemisphere to nonverbal and pictorial processes and the left hemisphere to verbal and other semantic processes.

Conceptual priming

Whereas perceptual priming reflects prior processing of the perceptual aspects of a stimulus, conceptual priming reflects prior processing of the conceptual aspects. The phenomenon is best understood in terms of the ways it is tested. In addition to the category association test described earlier, another popular conceptual priming test is the *general knowledge test*, in which participants answer trivia-type questions such as "What is the fastest land animal?" Having seen the word *cheetah* in the study phase increases the chances of answering this question correctly, even if the participant is not aware of the previous encounter with this word when answering.

Unlike perceptual priming—but similarly to episodic memory—conceptual priming is sensitive to conceptual manipulations but not to perceptual manipulations. However, conceptual priming and declarative memory are clearly distinguished by pathological dissociations. Like perceptual prim-

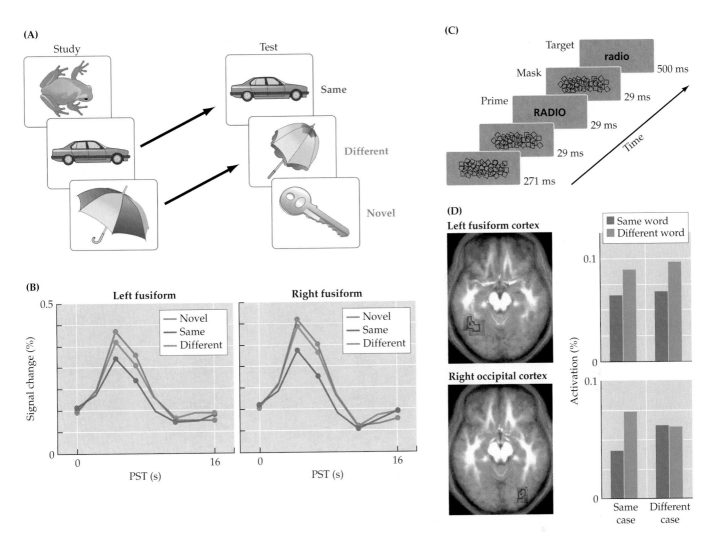

Figure 15.6 Hemispheric asymmetries in perceptual priming.
(A) In this case, the study and test objects were identical ("same" condition) or were different exemplars of the same object ("different" condition). (B) The left fusiform cortex showed repetition suppression in both conditions, whereas the right fusiform cortex showed it only in the "same" condition. (C) In this study, the prime word (masked) and the target word were either in the same or in a different case (i.e., capitals or lowercase). (D) Repetition suppression in the left fusiform gyrus was case-independent, whereas repetition suppression in right occipital cortex was case-specific. (A,B after Koutstaal et al. 2001; C,D from Dehaene et al. 2001.)

ing—and unlike episodic memory—conceptual priming does not depend on conscious awareness, and is preserved in amnesic patients with medial temporal lobe damage. Chandan Vaidya (now at Georgetown University), John Gabrieli (now at MIT), and their collaborators found memory performance in amnesic patients to be impaired in both perceptual and conceptual memory tests when the tests were explicit (word-fragment and word-associated cued recall tests), but performance was normal when the tests were implicit (word fragment completion and word association tests). Thus, despite their functional differences, both perceptual and conceptual priming operate independently of the neural circuitry in the medial temporal lobes.

Nonetheless, given their contrasting properties, perceptual and conceptual priming are likely to depend on different brain regions. Early evidence supporting this idea was provided by research with Alzheimer's patients, who showed impaired conceptual priming but intact perceptual priming in visual tasks. One explanation of this dissociation is that conceptual priming is more dependent on the frontal, parietal, and temporal cortices, which are more affected by Alzheimer's disease, whereas visual perceptual priming is more dependent on visual cortex, which is relatively spared. In functional neuroimaging studies, perceptual priming is usually associated with repetition suppression in occipitotemporal and prefrontal regions, whereas conceptual priming tends to be associated with repetition suppression in lateral temporal and prefrontal regions.

Figure 15.7 Brain regions underlying conceptual priming and their functional differences. This neuroimaging study showed that although an anterior region of the left inferior frontal gyrus shows repetition suppression only when semantic processing is reinstated (within-task condition), a posterior region of left of the gyrus shows priming whenever the word is repeated (both within- and across-task conditions). (A,B from Wagner et al. 2000.)

(A) Left inferior frontal gyrus

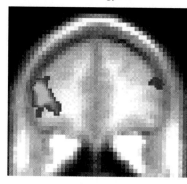

Anterior

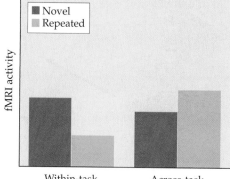

(B)

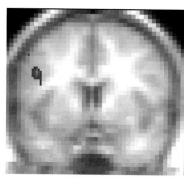

Posterior

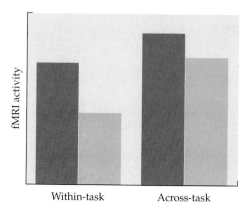

Within the prefrontal cortex, conceptual priming has been linked to the anterior portion of the left inferior prefrontal gyrus, an area strongly associated with semantic processing (see Chapters 14 and 21). In an fMRI study carried out by Anthony Wagner and his collaborators at MIT and Stanford, participants classified words as abstract (e.g., *honesty*) or concrete (e.g., *table*), or as uppercase versus lowercase. They subsequently repeated the abstract versus concrete classification task, which this time included words previously encountered in the experiment, either during the abstract/concrete task (*within-task condition*), or during the uppercase/lowercase task (*across-task condition*). The study indicated a dissociation within the left inferior frontal gyrus: whereas an anterior region showed repetition suppression only in the within-task condition, a posterior region showed it in both the within- and across-task conditions (**Figure 15.7**). These results suggest that repetition suppression in the anterior region reflects an influence on semantic processes (conceptual priming), whereas repetition suppression in the posterior region reflects an influence on nonsemantic processes (e.g., processing word sounds).

Semantic priming

In both perceptual and conceptual priming, the prime and target stimuli have the same name (e.g., *cheetah* in the example above). In **semantic priming**, however, the prime and target are different although semantically related. In a typical paradigm, participants make simple decisions about each word in a sequence, and response times are faster for words (e.g., *nurse*) that were preceded by a semantically related word (e.g., *doctor*). Whereas perceptual priming can

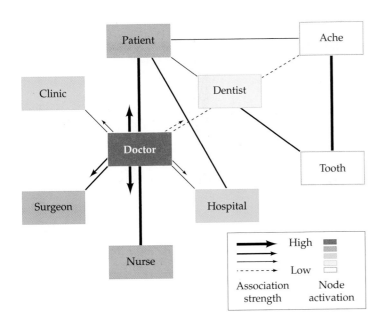

Figure 15.8 Portion of a semantic memory network. The example shows the spread of activation from the node "doctor" to associated nodes (e.g., nurse).

last for months and conceptual priming can persist for days, semantic priming lasts only a few seconds (or a few intervening items in a continuous test).

The most popular theoretical account of semantic priming is based on the assumption that semantic memory is organized as a *network* in which each *node* corresponds to a concept and each *link*, to an association between two concepts (**Figure 15.8**; see also Chapter 20). When a node is accessed it becomes *activated*, so the argument goes, and activation spreads through the network according to the strength of the associations between neurons encoding the concepts. The concept of **spreading activation** has been used to rationalize many semantic memory phenomena, including semantic priming. When a word such as *doctor* is presented, the presumption is that activation spreads to the neural circuits encoding other concepts (*nurse*) according to the strength of the associations (presumably the strength of the relevant synaptic connections). If a word referring to one of these associated concepts is presented before the activation dissipates, the word is processed faster than if the corresponding node was not activated.

In this view, the neural mechanisms of semantic priming should involve brain regions associated with the storage of semantic knowledge, such as left anterior temporal cortical regions. As mentioned in Chapter 14, these regions show relatively more atrophy than other brain regions in dementia patients impaired in accessing semantic knowledge. To further investigate the neural correlates of semantic priming, event-related fMRI (see Chapter 3) can be used in normal subjects to compare sequentially presented pairs of words, either related or unrelated (**Figure 15.9A**). Consistent with semantic dementia evidence, the only region that shows less activity in the related than in the unrelated condition is the left anterior temporal cortex (**Figure 15.9B**). In the same study, semantic priming was associated with a reduction in the N400 ERP component associated with semantic processing demands. Thus semantic priming reduces semantic processing demands and activity in left anterior temporal cortex.

What then could be the purpose of semantic priming? Presumably, it contributes to all sorts of cognitive tasks in everyday life, including helping us remember a word based on contextual cues, reading speed and comprehension, and abstract-problem solving. For example, semantic priming may auto-

(A)

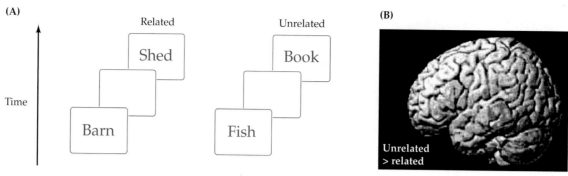

Time

Related

Shed

Barn

Unrelated

Book

Fish

(B)

Unrelated
> related

Figure 15.9   Location of neural activation related to semantic priming.   (A) This functional neuro-imaging study of semantic priming compared sequentially presented word pairs that were related or unrelated. (B) Left anterior temporal cortex showed less activity in the related than in the unrelated condition, thereby linking this region to semantic priming. (From Rossell et al. 2003.)

matically activate related but not consciously considered ideas when solving a problem, the ideas seeming to simply "pop into our heads" to give an unexpected solution (see Chapter 25).

Priming mechanisms: Some theories

Like any form of memory, priming requires an enduring change in the nervous system (i.e., an *memory trace* or *engram*; see Chapter 13). In terms of memory representations, there are two different ways of conceptualizing engrams that could mediate priming. According to the **modification theory**, priming reflects an alteration in preexisting memory representations. For example, activation models assume that when a word is encountered, the corresponding node in the semantic network is activated (see Figure 15.8); residual activity of the node would then account for enhanced processing of the word when it is encountered again. In contrast, the **acquisition theory** posits that priming entails the creation of new representations.

Evidence supporting the existence of both mechanisms in the same brain region in an fMRI study was reported by Richard Henson (now at Cambridge University) and his collaborators. The researchers compared priming of familiar faces (Marilyn Monroe is the example used here), which have preexisting memory representations, to priming of unfamiliar faces, which do not (**Figure 15.10A**). As illustrated by **Figure 15.10B**, the repetition of familiar faces in the right fusiform gyrus was associated with repetition suppression (F1 > F2), whereas the repetition of unfamiliar faces was associated with **repetition enhancement** (U1 < U2)—that is, an increase rather than a decrease in activity. Whereas repetition suppression, as discussed earlier, may reflect access to a partially activated preexisting representation, repetition enhancement is more likely to reflect the retrieval of a new memory representation. The latter idea fits with the fact that episodic retrieval, which is generally assumed to involve the recovery of new memory traces, is associated with increases rather than with decreases in brain activity.

Focusing on the phenomenon of repetition suppression, Kalamit Grill-Spector, Richard Henson, and Alex Martin distinguished three factors that could account for the various aspects of priming: *fatigue*, *sharpening*, and *facilitation* (**Figure 15.11**). According to the **fatigue model**, when a stimulus is repeated, all of the initially responsive neurons show a proportionally equivalent reduction in their response. Thus, the mean response of the population is reduced, but distribution of responses across neurons is not affected. This general "fatigue effect" could reflect firing-rate adaptation or synaptic depression. One limitation of the fatigue model is that it is unclear how reduced firing rate can account for behavioral priming effects like increased speed and accuracy.

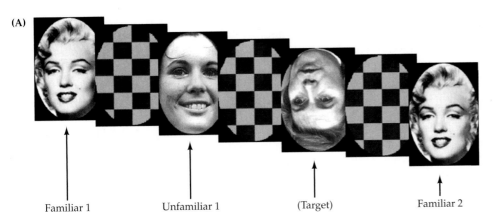

(A)

Familiar 1   Unfamiliar 1   (Target)   Familiar 2

Figure 15.10   Priming-related decreases and increases in brain activity.   (A) Familiar and unfamiliar faces were presented twice in this paradigm. (B) The right fusiform gyrus showed repetition suppression (Familiar 2 < Familiar 1) for the familiar stimuli, but repetition enhancement for the unfamiliar stimuli (Unfamiliar 2 > Unfamiliar 1). (From Henson et al. 2000.)

(B)

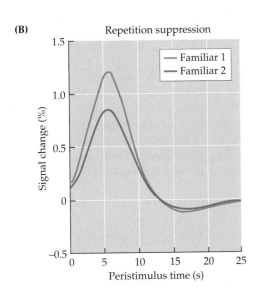

Repetition suppression — Familiar 1, Familiar 2; Signal change (%) vs. Peristimulus time (s)

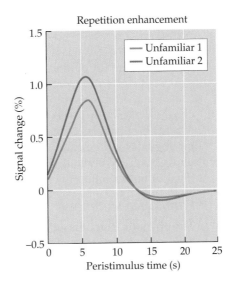

Repetition enhancement — Unfamiliar 1, Unfamiliar 2; Signal change (%) vs. Peristimulus time (s)

Figure 15.11   How priming and repetition suppression might be generated at the neuronal level.   (A) The circles represent neural networks with three hierarchical layers (input layer at the bottom, higher-order processing at the top). The graphs indicate firing rate as a function of time for the most responsive neurons in each layer (black). (B) All three models predict reduced fMRI signal for repeated presentations, but for different reasons. In the fatigue model, all initially responsive neurons show a proportional reduction in response. In the sharpening model, the maximally active neurons respond as strongly during the repeated presentation as during the first presentation, but the less active neurons drop out. In the facilitation model, firing rate is unaffected, but the neurons respond faster and/or for a shorter period of time. (After Grill-Spector et al. 2006.)

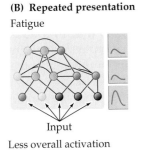

(A) First presentation

Input

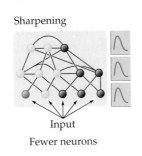
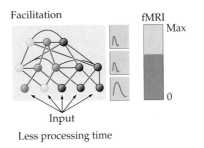

(B) Repeated presentation

Fatigue — Input — Less overall activation

Sharpening — Input — Fewer neurons

Facilitation — Input — Less processing time

Other aspects of priming can be accounted for in a **sharpening model**. When a stimulus is repeated, neurons that carry critical information about the stimulus continue to fire vigorously, whereas neurons that are not essential for processing the stimulus respond less and less, leading to reduced hemodynamic responses. Thus, whereas the fatigue model assumes a reduction of firing in all neurons, the sharpening model assumes a reduction only in noncritical neurons. This "drop-out" of noncritical neurons is assumed to yield a cortical representation that is both smaller (fewer neurons) and more selective (only critical neurons). This "sharpened" representation could explain behavioral priming effects. A mechanism that could suppress noncritical neurons is *lateral inhibition*, a phenomenon that clearly exists in neocortex and influences many functions.

Finally, according to the **facilitation model**, priming via repetition suppression reflects faster processing of stimuli due to shorter latencies and/or shorter duration of neural firing. When integrated over several seconds, these effects could result in reduced hemodynamic responses. The idea of faster processing fits well with evidence that repetition may lead to faster peaks, or to faster decay following the peak.

A challenge for all these models is the heterogeneity of repetition suppression: some repetition suppression effects are transient, others are long-lasting; thus some effects require prolonged adaptation to emerge, whereas others occur after a single presentation. Moreover, there is some evidence of different repetition suppression mechanisms in lower- and higher-level visual processing regions (e.g., primary visual cortex compared to the MT region; see Chapter 4). It may be that all three models are pertinent to the mechanism of priming, but under different conditions.

Priming: In summary

The phenomenon of nondeclarative memory known as priming has three subtypes: perceptual, conceptual, and semantic priming. All three forms are independent of conscious awareness or the integrity of the medial temporal lobes; rather, they depend on altered activity in different neocortical regions. In functional neuroimaging studies, primed stimuli have been associated with a reduction in neuronal activity known as repetition suppression; these studies have resulted in a focus on repetition suppression as a clue to priming mechanisms. Perceptual priming is characterized by repetition suppression in posterior cortical regions, conceptual priming by suppression in anterior left inferior prefrontal cortex, and semantic priming by suppression in left anterior temporal cortex. Whereas repetition suppression fits with the idea of a modification in a preexisting representation, priming for novel stimuli may involve creating new representations and an increase in activity (known as repetition enhancement). Three different theories of repetition suppression, based respectively on fatigue, sharpening, and facilitation, may account for different aspects of priming.

Skill Learning

Skill learning refers to the forms of nondeclarative memory that, in contrast to priming, depend on more extensive experience, as in learning a language, or to play a musical instrument, or to throw a baseball, or innumerable other skills that take practice over time. The requirements of experience and practice distinguish skill learning from priming, which can result from a single exposure to a stimulus. A further distinction is that, whereas priming is largely neocortical in origin, skill learning also depends on structures such as the basal ganglia and cerebellum.

Like other forms of nondeclarative memory, skill learning is preserved in amnesic patients such as H.M., indicating that skill learning does not depend on the medial temporal lobe. Skilled performance requires both efficient processing sensory stimuli (perceptual operations) and fast and accurate responses (motor operations). In some instances cognitive operations may help associate stimuli and the most useful responses (e.g., the emotional meaning in expressing a particular piece of music). Learning a musical instrument provides an especially good example of how closely the sensory, motor, and cognitive aspects of skilled performance are intertwined. Although learning a skill tends to progress concurrently in all three of these domains, some tasks nevertheless emphasize one more than the others. Accordingly, the following sections consider the neural correlates and testing methods of skill learning for tasks that emphasize motor, perceptual, or cognitive operations.

Motor skill learning

Several tasks have been widely used to test motor skill learning; one of the simplest is the *serial reaction time task*. A typical version of this task involves four screen locations and four spatially mapped response keys (**Figure 15.12A**). On each trial, a stimulus appears in one of the locations and the participant presses the corresponding key. Unbeknownst to the subjects, the order of the stimulus location follows a repeated sequence, typically one that is 10 to 12 units long. The results of such tests show that even though participants are completely unaware that there *is* a sequence, the sequence repetition leads to faster reaction times as the test progresses. Such *implicit learning of sequence* can be detected by interposing a block of trials in which the order of the stimulus locations is completely random (e.g., Block 6 in **Figure 15.12B**); note that reaction times during this block are significantly slower than in neighboring blocks (e.g., Blocks 5 and 7).

Another commonly used motor learning paradigm is the *rotary pursuit task*, in which participants try to keep a hand-held stylus in continuous contact with a small metal disk on a rotating turntable. Learning is evident in the increased proportion of time the stylus is in contact with the disk.

These and other types of skill learning are preserved in patients with medial temporal lobe damage but are impaired in those with basal ganglia disor-

Figure 15.12 Testing motor skill learning.   (A) In serial reaction time paradigms, participants press keys corresponding to the locations in which stimuli are presented. (B) When the order of locations follows a repeated sequence, response times decline, even if participants are unaware of the sequence. This improvement in performance reflects implicit learning of the sequence. R, random; S, sequence.

(A)

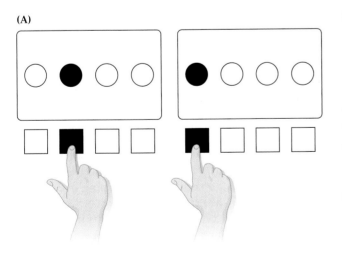

(B)

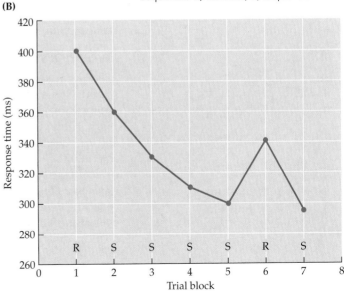

ders, such as the neural degeneration that occurs in Parkinson's or Huntington's diseases (see Chapter 9). Thus serial reaction time learning, rotary pursuit learning, and learning in tasks such as mirror writing are all preserved in patients with medial temporal lobe damage, but impaired in patients with basal ganglia deficits. Consistent with this evidence, functional neuroimaging of implicit learning in normal subjects shows activation in the *striatum*, the portion of the basal ganglia that includes the caudate and putamen nuclei.

Activation in the posterior parietal cortex, supplementary motor area, cingulate cortex, and cerebellum are also apparent during motor skill learning. Posterior parietal activation has been linked to spatial processing, consistent with a PET study carried out by Scott Grafton and colleagues at Dartmouth, who showed that changing from a smaller to a larger keyboard affected sensorimotor activity but not parietal activity. This observation suggests that the parietal cortex codes for abstract, effector-independent spatial locations. Similarly, the supplementary motor area has been linked to motor preparation, and the cingulate cortex to sequence prediction (see Chapters 8 and 9). Consistent with the latter idea, Scott Huettel at Duke found that anterior cingulate activity is sensitive to violations in repeating patterns.

To investigate motor learning in the context of challenges that require novel visual-motor associations, the experimenter may ask participants to follow a moving dot on a screen with a cursor controlled by a joystick until they master this skill The experimenter then has the subjects wear *prism spectacles* that systematically shift the visual image either horizontally or vertically; alternatively, the experimenter may alter the computer program so that joystick movements produce different or even opposite effects. After such manipulations, tracking is initially inaccurate but improves rapidly with practice. Functional neuroimaging studies have associated adaptation to novel sensory-motor relationships with activity changes in the posterior parietal cortex. Transcranial magnetic stimulation (TMS) of this cortical region, which produces transient disruption of neural processing, also impedes adaptation and motor learning. In one TMS study, participants moved a handle attached to a metal arm to specific points in space. Torque motors were then used to create a force field that disturbs the normal movement of the handle (**Figure 15.13A**). TMS on occipital cortex regions did not disrupt the normal adaptation process: when the force field was introduced, arm trajectories were initially distorted, but as participants learn to counteract the force field, trajectories become straight again. In contrast (**Figure 15.13B**), TMS on posterior parietal regions interfered with normal adaptation: although trajectories improved with practice, they never became completely straight.

Perceptual skill learning

Perceptual skill learning refers to improvements in processing perceptual stimuli, whether fully familiar, familiar but with some transformations, or entirely novel. Perceptual skill learning is essential in everyday life. For example, it is this type of skill learning that underlies our ability to understand spoken and written language. Language comprehension based solely on declarative memory is slow and laborious, as anybody who has tried to learn a foreign language can confirm. However, perceptual skill learning eventually enables us to understand strings of words effortlessly, without the need to consciously retrieve the meaning of individual words or the rules of grammar every time we converse.

In language processing, the neural correlates of perceptual skill learning include all the brain regions involved in language comprehension regions, which are reviewed in Chapter 21. Perceptual skill learning plays an equally a critical role in processing music (see Chapter 6), and there is some evidence

(A)

(B)

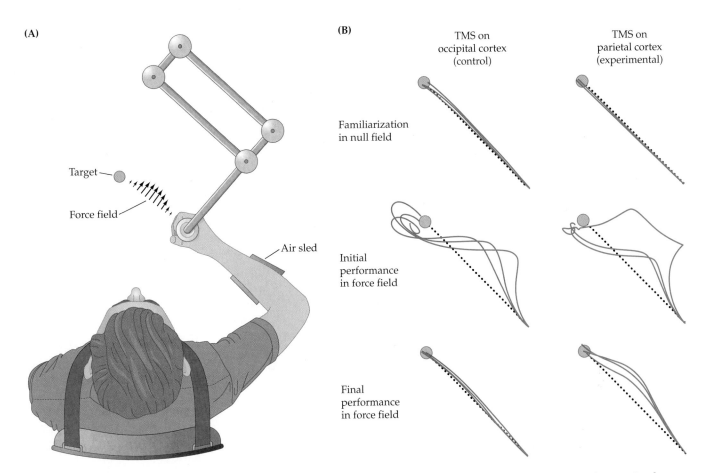

TMS on occipital cortex (control)

TMS on parietal cortex (experimental)

Target

Force field

Air sled

Familiarization in null field

Initial performance in force field

Final performance in force field

Figure 15.13 Testing motor learning and its basis in paradigms that alter sensory-motor relationships. (A) This method of investigating motor learning measures how people learn to adapt their movements to compensate for a force field applied to a handle. (B) TMS interference of posterior parietal cortex disrupts motor adaptation. (After Della-Maggiore et al. 2004.)

that trained musicians may co-opt language brain regions for the symbolic learning aspects this task. Perceptual skill learning in the visual domain plays an obvious role in may other circumstances where improved perceptual performance is valued. Radiologists, for example, gradually learn to identify subtle differences in X-ray, CAT, MRI, and other images.

Perceptual skill learning can be studied in the laboratory using simple sensory discrimination tasks. A popular test of this sort is the *mirror-reading task*, in which subjects learn to read geometrically altered text. Like many other skill learning tasks, mirror reading is learned normally in patients with medial temporal lobe damage, but impaired in conditions that affect the basal ganglia (see Chapter 9). Functional neuroimaging studies show that, compared to normal reading, mirror reading elicits activation in occipitotemporal and parietal regions (i.e., in both ventral and dorsal pathways), as well as the striatum.

Another way to examine perceptual skill learning is to train participants to recognize meaningless three-dimensional objects known as "Greebles" (**Figure 15.14A**). Isabelle Gauthier, Michael Tarr, and collaborators at Brown University found that expertise in classifying and identifying Greebles is associated with increased activity in the right fusiform region known as the *fusiform face area*, or FFA (**Figure 15.14B**). This observation suggests that rather than being a face-specific module, the function of the FFA is related to visual expertise (see Chapter 5). It has been argued that Greebles activate the FFA because they have features that resemble faces. However, a further fMRI study by the Brown University group found that the FFA of car experts is more readily acti-

Figure 15.14 Perceptual skill learning. (A) Examples of meaningless three-dimensional objects known as Greebles. (B) Expertise in classifying and identifying Greebles is associated with increased activity in the face fusiform area (FFA; boxed areas), suggesting that this region is not specific to faces. (C) In car experts, the FFA is more strongly activated by pictures of cars than of birds, whereas in bird experts, the opposite pattern is seen. (A courtesy of Isabel Gauthier; B from Gauthier et al. 1999; C from Gauthier et al. 2000.)

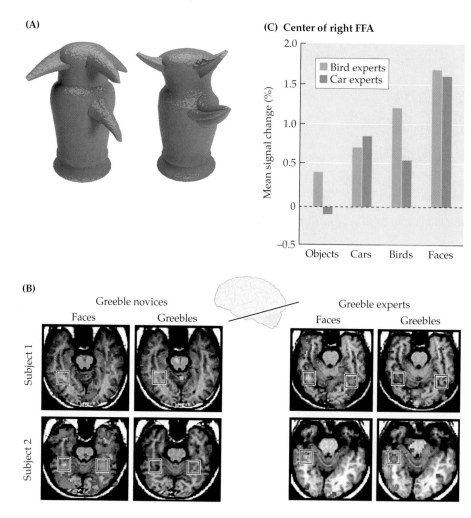

(A)

(C) Center of right FFA

(B)

Greeble novices — Faces — Greebles

Greeble experts — Faces — Greebles

Subject 1

Subject 2

vated by picture of cars than of birds, whereas in bird experts the region is more readily activated by picture of birds than of cars (**Figure 15.14C**). Nonetheless, the interpretation of these observations remains a matter of some controversy.

Although motor and perceptual skill learning are described separately in most accounts, acquiring skills typically involves both forms of learning. Moreover, skill learning often involves a shift from perceptual to motor processes. For example, someone learning to drive devotes much visual attention to relevant visual cues and the appropriate motor responses (think of the challenge involved in learning to parallel park). Eventually these stimuli become automatically linked to appropriate motor responses, and thus no longer require conscious mediation. An fMRI study of this shift in perceptual-to-motor learning used a simple task in which participants decided whether or not a pair of geometrical figures matched. The attentional demands for analyzing feature differences in this task are initially high, but as memory templates for each figure pair are created, visual attention decreases and the role of automatic motor associations increases. Consistent with this interpretation, learning in this task is associated with a shift from activation in a region associated with visual attention (the intraparietal sulcus; **Figure 15.15A**) to regions associated with motor processing (hand areas in motor and sensory cortices; **Figure 15.15B**).

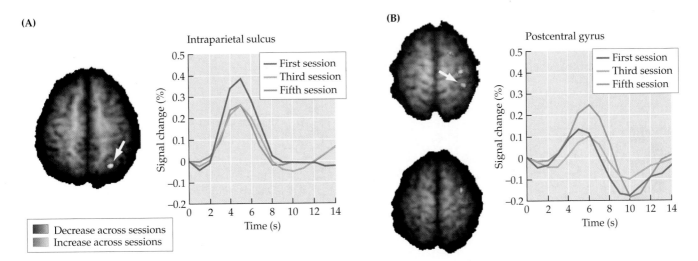

Figure 15.15 Shift of activity from attention to motor-related brain areas during visual learning. (A) Participants decided in each trial whether or not a pair of geometrical figures matched. During early learning, attentional demands for analyzing feature differences elicited greater activity in the intraparietal sulcus, but this activity decreased across sessions (Session 1 > Sessions 3 and 5). (B) As participants learned to associate each figure pair with a motor response, activity increased in hand areas in motor and sensory cortices (Session 5 > Sessions 1 and 3). Arrows indicate activations from which the data in the graphs were extracted. (After Pollmann and Maertens 2005.)

Cognitive skill learning

Cognitive skill learning refers to problem-solving tasks in which subjects are required to use (at least nominally) various cognitive skills to solve a task. (Problem solving is taken up in detail in Chapter 25.) An example of this sort of task is **probabilistic classification learning,** in which participants learn to classify stimuli on the basis of statistical information. In a paradigm called the *weather prediction task*, participants look at four cards in each trial with geometric shapes that predict whether it will rain or not (**Figure 15.16A**). The subjects must then say what they think, based on the cards' prediction, the weather will be (in the game, not in real life!). After each decision they are informed whether the prediction was correct. The critical feature of this task is that each of the cards is only *probabilistically* related to the two possible weather outcomes (e.g., a certain card may be associated with rain only 70 percent of the time); thus, an explicit rule is difficult to infer. Nevertheless, the participants implicitly learn to use the probabilistic information (that is, they come to associate certain card combinations with an increased probability of rain), and over many trials the accuracy of their predictions slowly improves.

Barbara Knowlton (now at UCLA) and her collaborators found a significant difference in performance in the weather prediction task between amnesic patients who had medial temporal lobe damage, and Parkinson's patients, who had impaired basal ganglia function. Although amnesic patients improved somewhat more slowly than controls, they eventually learned the task as well as controls. In contrast, Parkinson's patients never learned the task (**Figure 15.16B**). When these groups of patients were tested in an episodic memory test, the opposite result was found: amnesic patients were impaired compared to controls, whereas Parkinson's patients were not (**Figure 15.16C**). Thus, the study yielded a clear double dissociation between the memory functions of the basal ganglia and the medial temporal lobe: damage of the basal ganglia in Parkinson's patients impaired skill learning but not declarative

(A) Weather prediction task

In this learning game, you are the weather forecaster. You will learn how to predict rain or shine using a deck of four cards:

Examples of probabilistic relations

Predicts rain 80% of the time

Predicts rain 40% of the time

(B) Weather prediction task

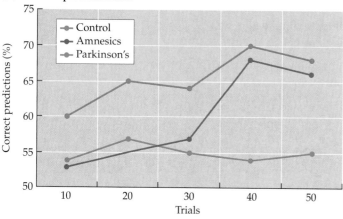

(C) Episodic memory recall

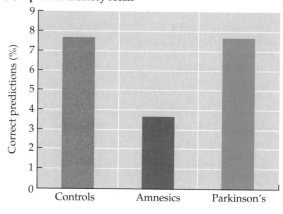

Figure 15.16 Probabilistic classification learning in Parkinson's and amnesic patients. (A) The weather prediction task. In each trial, participants are asked to guess whether the set of four cards predicts rain or shine, and they are given feedback as to whether their response was correct or incorrect. Even though the relation between each card and the two outcomes is only probabilistic and participants cannot consciously abstract a simple rule, the accuracy of the predictions increases over many trials. (B) Comparison of the performance of amnesic (medial temporal lobe damage) and Parkinson's (basal ganglia deficits) patients in the weather prediction task. Amnesic subjects are slow to learn but eventually reach the same level of performance as controls do; in contrast, the performance of Parkinson's patients never improves. (C) Performance of the same three groups in an episodic memory task (declarative memory). In sharp contrast with probabilistic learning performance, amnesic patients are markedly impaired, whereas Parkinson's patients perform as well as controls. Taken together, the results presented here constitute a double dissociation between the memory functions of the basal ganglia (critical for implicit skill learning but not for episodic memory) and those of the medial temporal lobes (critical for episodic memory but not for implicit skill learning). (After Knowlton et al. 1996.)

memory, whereas damage of the medial temporal lobes in amnesic patients impaired declarative memory but not skill learning.

These observations are once again consistent with the idea that episodic memory depends on medial temporal lobe structures, whereas cognitive skill learning is at least to some degree dependent on the integrity of the basal ganglia.

This conclusion about cognitive skill learning is further supported by a functional neuroimaging study done by Russell Poldrack and colleagues at UCLA. Normal participants were scanned while they carried out a simplified version of the weather prediction task (**Figure 15.17A**). Consistent with patient studies, the medial temporal lobe was more activated in the paired-association task than in the weather prediction task, whereas the striatum showed the opposite pattern (**Figure 15.17B**). Early trials in this task presumably have a significant episodic memory component that reflects explicitly learning the symbol cards needed to make the prediction. This interpretation would also explain why amnesic patients are a bit slower than controls in learning the weather prediction task. Consistent with this idea, the medial temporal lobe was activated during initial trials in Poldrack's study, but deactivated during most of the learning phase; the striatum showed the opposite temporal pattern (**Figure 15.17C, D**). These contrasting temporal patterns imply an opposing relationship between medial temporal and the striatum. One possible explanation is a competition between medial temporal lobe-based and striatal-based memory systems reflecting the need

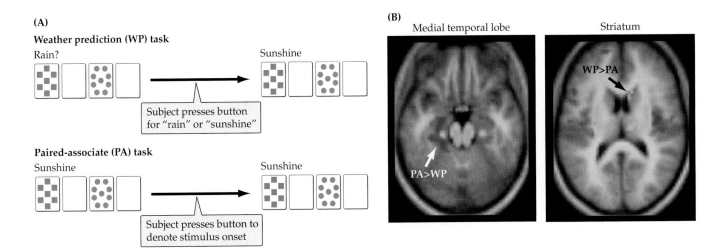

(A)

Weather prediction (WP) task

Rain?

Subject presses button for "rain" or "sunshine"

Sunshine

Paired-associate (PA) task

Sunshine

Subject presses button to denote stimulus onset

Sunshine

(B)

Medial temporal lobe

Striatum

PA>WP

WP>PA

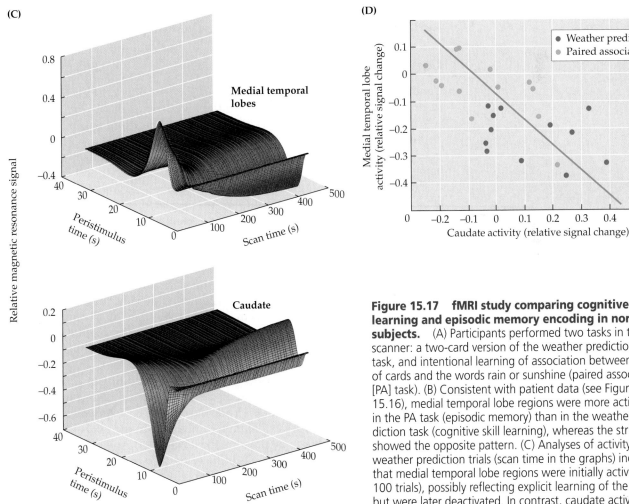

(C)

Relative magnetic resonance signal

Medial temporal lobes

Peristimulus time (s)

Scan time (s)

Caudate

Peristimulus time (s)

Scan time (s)

(D)

Medial temporal lobe activity (relative signal change)

Caudate activity (relative signal change)

● Weather prediction
● Paired associate

Figure 15.17 fMRI study comparing cognitive skill learning and episodic memory encoding in normal subjects. (A) Participants performed two tasks in the scanner: a two-card version of the weather prediction (WP) task, and intentional learning of association between pairs of cards and the words rain or sunshine (paired associate [PA] task). (B) Consistent with patient data (see Figure 15.16), medial temporal lobe regions were more activated in the PA task (episodic memory) than in the weather prediction task (cognitive skill learning), whereas the striatum showed the opposite pattern. (C) Analyses of activity across weather prediction trials (scan time in the graphs) indicated that medial temporal lobe regions were initially active (first 100 trials), possibly reflecting explicit learning of the cards, but were later deactivated. In contrast, caudate activity was originally deactivated and became activated as implicit learning increased over trials. These results suggest an opposing relationship between the medial temporal lobes and striatum. (D) Consistent with this idea, a negative correlation was found between medial temporal and caudate activations. (Images from Poldrack et al. 2001.)

for accessible knowledge (the medial temporal lobe) versus the need to learn fast, automatic responses in specific situations (the striatum).

In sum, there is abundant evidence that skill learning depends on the integrity of the basal ganglia. Patients with basal ganglia disorders, such as Parkinson's and Huntington's diseases, are impaired in motor skill learning tasks such as the serial reaction time task; in perceptual skill learning tasks such as the mirror-reading task; and in cognitive skill learning tasks such as probabilistic classification learning.

In addition to the basal ganglia, however, skill learning involves other brain regions that vary depending on the task. Motor skill learning has been associated with activation of the posterior parietal, supplementary motor area, cingulate cortex, and cerebellum. Perceptual skill learning involves activation of sensory cortices and higher order regions in the association cortices such as in the fusiform gyrus when the learned skills are visually based. Finally, complex cognitive skill learning involves medial temporal regions initially when the explicit components and rules of the task are being acquired, but these regions are not necessary for subsequent learning of implicit rules as demonstrated by preserved probabilistic classification learning in amnesic patients. Implicit cognitive learning, like other learned skills, depends on the striatum and the regions of neocortex relevant to the particular cognitive domain.

Conditioning

Conditioning, considered last here, is in fact the type of nondeclarative memory that has been most intensively studied over the past century, from both psychological and neurobiological perspectives. **Conditioning** can be defined as the generation of a novel response that is gradually elicited by repeatedly pairing a novel stimulus with a stimulus that normally elicits the response being studied. There are two broad forms, *classical* and *operant* conditioning.

Classical conditioning occurs when an innate reflex is modified by associating its normal triggering stimulus and an unrelated stimulus; the unrelated stimulus eventually will trigger the original response by virtue of this repeated association. This type of conditioning was famously demonstrated by the Russian psychologist Ivan Pavlov's experiments with dogs, carried out early in the twentieth century. The dogs' innate reflex was salivation (the **unconditioned response**, or **UR**) in response to the sight and/or smell of food (the **unconditioned stimulus, US**). The association was elicited in the animals by repeatedly pairing the sight/smell of food with the sound of a bell (the **conditioned stimulus, CS**). Such conditioning, also called the *conditioned reflex*, was considered established when the CS (i.e., the sound of the bell) by itself elicited salivation (the **conditioned response, CR**).

Operant conditioning refers to the altered probability of a behavioral response engendered by associating the response with a reward (or in some instances a punishment). In Edward Thorndike's original experiments, carried out as part of his thesis work at Columbia University in the 1890s, cats learned to escape from a puzzle box by pressing the lever that opened the trap door to get a food reward. Although the cats initially pressed the lever only occasionally—and more or less by chance—the probability of their doing so increased sharply as the animals associated this action with escape and reward. In Frederick Skinner's far more complete and better-known experiments (performed a few decades later at Harvard) pigeons or rats learned to associate pressing a lever with receiving a food pellet in a widely used device that came to be known as a **Skinner box**.

In both classical and operant conditioning, it takes a number of trials for the conditioning to become established, a process called **acquisition**. Furthermore, if the conditioned animal performs the critical response but the reward

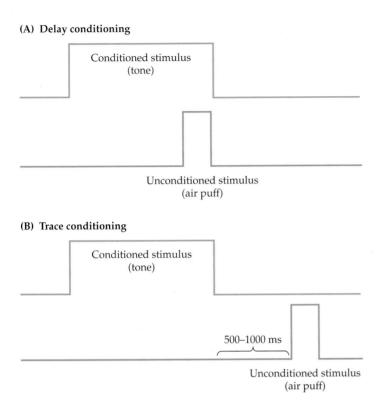

(A) Delay conditioning

Conditioned stimulus
(tone)

Unconditioned stimulus
(air puff)

(B) Trace conditioning

Conditioned stimulus
(tone)

500–1000 ms

Unconditioned stimulus
(air puff)

Figure 15.18 Two classical conditioning paradigms illustrated using an eye-blink paradigm. (A) In delay conditioning, the conditioned stimulus (CS) starts before the unconditioned stimulus (US), but is ongoing when the US starts. (B) In trace conditioning, the CS is over before the US starts, leaving a time interval between the two stimuli.

is no longer provided, the conditioning gradually disappears, a phenomenon called **extinction**.

Neural mechanisms of classical conditioning

The neural correlates of fear conditioning, as well as those of reward- or punishment-based operant conditioning, are considered with other forms of emotional learning in Unit VI. In considering the neural basis of classical conditioning, we focus here on classical conditioning carried out in paradigms that are emotionally neutral. In this context, it is important to distinguish between *delay* and *trace* conditioning. Figure 15.18 illustrates the difference between these two variants of classical conditioning using *eye-blink conditioning* as an example.

In **eye-blink conditioning**, a puff of air, which elicits a reflexive (automatic) blink, is repeatedly paired with a tone until the tone by itself elicits blinking. In both delay and trace conditioning, the tone (the conditioned stimulus) starts before the air puff (the unconditioned stimulus). The difference is that in **delay conditioning**, the CS is still present when the US starts, and both terminate at the same time (**Figure 15.18A**); in **trace conditioning**, however, there is a brief time interval between the end of the CS and the start of the US (**Figure 15.18B**). Thus, in trace conditioning the CS must leave some kind of memory "trace" in the nervous system in order for a CS-US association to be established, whereas this is not the case in delay conditioning. Although the difference between delay and trace conditioning may seem trivial, these different forms of classical conditioning are now known to have different neural correlates. Delay conditioning has the further advantage for some studies of being able to control the moment when the conditioned response will occur.

Delay conditioning is primarily dependent on the cerebellum, in particular the interpositus nucleus and the cerebellar cortex. Both of these structures receive information about the tone (CS) from the auditory system and information about the air puff (US) from the visual and somatic sensory systems. Supporting the critical role of the interpositus nucleus, lesions or transient disruption of this structure lead to deficits in the acquisition and retention of delay eye-blink conditioning. Supporting the role of the cerebellar cortex, mutant mice deficient in Purkinje cells (the output neurons of the cerebellar cortex) are impaired in eye-blink conditioning. As both the interpositus nucleus and the cerebellar cortex receive information about the CS and the US, both structures are potentially capable of supporting CS–US associations.

The major difference between the neural correlates of delay and trace conditioning is the role of the hippocampus. Although electrophysiological studies using the eye-blink paradigm in rabbits show the hippocampus to be involved in delay conditioning, damage to the hippocampus does not impair delay conditioning. In contrast, damage to the hippocampus impairs trace conditioning in both experimental animals and human patients.

The finding that trace conditioning depends on the hippocampus creates a problem for the standard taxonomy of memory systems. On one hand, trace conditioning is a quintessential form of nondeclarative memory. On the other hand, it depends on the integrity of the hippocampus, which is the defining neural correlate of *declarative* memory in the double dissociation studies described in Chapters 13 and 14. Is trace conditioning truly a form of nondeclarative memory, then, or is it a form of declarative memory?

A possible solution to this puzzle was provided by Robert Clark and Larry Squire at the University of California, San Diego. These researchers investigated delay and trace eye-blink conditioning in amnesic patients with hippocampal damage and in control participants. The conditioning took place while both groups were also watching a silent movie. Immediately after conditioning, participants completed a questionnaire that included a number of questions about their awareness of CS–US contingencies. They were asked, for example, whether the statements "I believe the air puff usually came immediately before the tone" and "I believe the tone predicted when the air puff would come" were true or false. Those whose number of correct responses to such questions were significantly above chance were designated as *aware* of the relationships among the stimuli; those who did not meet this criteria were designated *unaware*.

The results showed that none of the amnesic patients were aware of CS–US contingencies. Nonetheless, all the participants showed delay conditioning (**Figure 15.19A**). This outcome is consistent with the idea that the

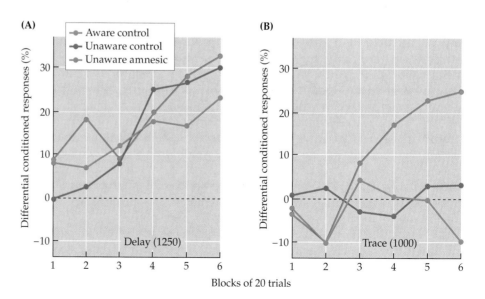

Figure 15.19 Delay and trace eye-blink conditioning in humans. Test results for amnesic patients versus controls indicate an underlying difference between delay and trace conditioning. Graphs plot the percentage of differential conditioned eye-blink (CR – CS/CR × 100). (A) All groups showed delay conditioning. (B) Only the control group was aware of the relationship of the tone and the air puff, and only this group showed trace conditioning. These results indicate that trace conditioning depends on awareness of CS/US contingencies and therefore imply that it is a form of declarative memory.

delay form of nondeclarative memory is independent of conscious awareness and the hippocampus. In contrast, only the aware control participants showed trace conditioning (**Figure 15.19B**). Thus trace conditioning depends on awareness of temporal contingencies among stimuli and is effectively a form of declarative rather nondeclarative memory. Thus, at the systems level, nondeclarative memory can be distinguished from declarative memory. As noted in Chapter 13, however, declarative and nondeclarative memory presumably depend on the same neural mechanisms at the cellular and molecular levels. This same conclusion applies to working memory, which is the subject of the next chapter.

Summary

1. Nondeclarative memory is a heterogeneous category defined largely by its differences from declarative memory: it includes all those forms of memory that are independent of consciousness and the integrity of the medial temporal lobes.

2. Here we recognize three main forms of nondeclarative memory: priming, skill learning, and conditioning.

3. Priming is defined as a change in processing a stimulus due to a previous encounter with the same or a related stimulus in the absence of conscious awareness of the original encounter.

4. The neural correlates of priming include neocortical regions that vary with the type of priming: perceptual priming is associated with altered activity in the occipitotemporal areas, conceptual priming with anterior left inferior prefrontal areas, and semantic priming with left anterior temporal areas. In functional neuroimaging studies of priming, these regions typically show a reduction in activity known as repetition suppression.

5. Skill learning is dependent on the basal ganglia, as well as being associated with cortical regions that depend on the type of skill learning (parietal regions for motor learning, the temporal fusiform regions for perceptual learning, and so on).

6. Conditioning refers to the altered probability of a behavioral response engendered by associating with response with a reward. This emotionally neutral conditioning has been linked to circuits in the cerebellum. A form known as trace conditioning is also dependent on the medial temporal lobes, and may better be thought of as a component of declarative memory.

Additional Reading

Reviews

GRILL-SPECTOR, K., R. HENSON AND A. MARTIN (2006) Repetition and the brain: Neural models of stimulus-specific effects. *Trends Cogn. Sci.* 10: 14–23.

KOURTZI, Z. AND K. GRILL-SPECTOR (2005) fMRI adaptation: A tool for studying visual representations in the primate brain. In *Fitting the Mind into the World: Adaptation and After-Effects in High Level Vision*, G. Rhodes and C. Clifford (eds.). Oxford: Oxford University Press.

POLDRACK, R. A. AND D. T. WILLINGHAM (2006) Functional neuroimaging of skill learning. In *Handbook of Functional Neuroimaging of Cognition*, 2nd Ed., R. Cabeza and A. Kingstone (eds.). Cambridge, MA: MIT Press.

SANES, J. N. (2003) Neocortical mechanisms in motor learning. *Curr. Opin. Neurobiol.* 13: 225–231.

THOMPSON, R. E. (2005) In search of memory traces. *Annu. Rev. Psychol.* 56: 1–23.

Important Original Papers

BUCKNER, R. L., S. E. PETERSEN, J. G. OJEMANN, F. M. MIEZIN, L. R. SQUIRE AND M. E. RAICHLE (1995) Functional anatomical studies of explicit and implicit memory retrieval tasks. *J. Neurosci.* 15: 12–29.

CLARK, R. E. AND L. R. SQUIRE (1998) Classical conditioning and brain systems: The role of awareness. *Science* 280: 77–81.

GRILL-SPECTOR, K., T. KUSHNIR, S. EDELMAN, Y. ITZCHAK AND R. MALACH (1998) Cue-invariant activation in object-related areas of the human occipital lobe. *Neuron* 21: 191–202.

HENSON, R., T. SHALLICE AND R. DOLAN (2000) Neuroimaging evidence for dissociable forms of repetition priming. *Science* 287: 1269–1272.

KNOWLTON, B. J., J. A. MANGELS AND L. R. SQUIRE (1996) A neostriatal habit learning system in humans. *Science* 262: 1747–1749.

POLDRACK, R. A. AND 7 OTHERS (2001) Interactive memory systems in the human brain. *Nature* 414: 546–550.

TULVING, E. AND D. L. SCHACTER (1990) Priming and human memory systems. *Science* 247: 301–305.

Books

FOSTER, J. K. AND M. JELICIC (1999) *Memory: Systems, Process, or Function?* Oxford: Oxford University Press.

16

Working Memory

Introduction

Imagine looking around the house for a lost item, say, car keys. To do so efficiently, you must keep the goal (finding the keys) active in short-term memory while continuously updating a mental list of the places you have already searched. This is a simple example of the many everyday activities that depend on working memory, generally defined as the temporary maintenance and manipulation of information not currently available to the senses but necessary for successfully achieving short-term behavioral objectives. Working memory interacts closely with other cognitive functions; for instance, it is intimately linked to perception and long-term memory, which provide most of its input and content. Working memory also has a direct connection with motor and premotor systems, since it holds not only information about the past but also information about immediate goals and possible actions that will achieve them. Working memory is also closely related to attention, and in fact is sometimes considered to be a special category of attention that operates on internal representations rather than on the perceptual input. Working memory is also essential for language comprehension and production, and in turn, language enhances the capability of working memory (imagine the mental conversation that might accompany looking for your lost keys). Finally, working memory and its neural underpinnings include more complex executive functions that overlap to some degree with reasoning and problem solving, as the example of searching for a lost item again makes plain. Thus, working memory influences and is influenced by all the other cognitive systems in the brain, and understanding it is a topic of much interest in cognitive neuroscience.

Properties of Working Memory

Although there are different theories about working memory, several properties of this phenomenon are generally accepted. One shared assumption is that a central function of working memory is the maintenance of information in an

Figure 16.1 Juggling as a metaphor of working memory. The balls in the air represent working memory representations and the throws the ability to keep them in the air—i.e., the maintenance process. Changing the number of balls used could be viewed as analogous to working memory manipulation.

active state for a relatively brief time, in order to achieve specific goals. This **working memory maintenance** function corresponds to what traditional memory models call *short-term memory* (see Chapter 2). Beyond a few seconds, however, memory maintenance requires reactivating information held in working memory. Reactivation can be as simple as briefly thinking about a piece of information, a process known as **refreshing**, or it may involve the more laborious iterative process of **rehearsal**. An example of rehearsal is maintaining a phone number in working memory by repeating the number over and over.

It is also generally accepted that working memory is limited in both duration and capacity. Thus many working memory representations persist for only a few seconds—say 20 seconds or so; they are forgotten unless they are continuously reactivated by explicit refreshing or rehearsal. It is unclear, however, if such forgetting is due to simple *decay* as a function of time, or to *interference* resulting from new information entering working memory. The capacity of working memory is relatively small (generally speaking, about 4–9 items; think of the phone number example), which contrasts with the enormous capacity of long-term memory. The number of items held in working memory at one time is known as the **working memory load**.

Another general property of working memory is that in addition to its maintenance function, it is assumed to perform **manipulations**, that is, operations that organize, associate, and transform the representations held in working memory. For example, whereas the simple rehearsal process of "holding on to" a phone number illustrates maintenance, the steps involved in mentally calculating 26×37 are examples of working memory manipulation. Manipulation may also be evident in **chunking**, which refers to "packing" more information into each "item" within working memory, thereby increasing its capacity. For instance, although we may only be able hold 7 random numbers or letters in working memory, we can easily hold 12 items (e.g., U, I, S, A, B, N, M, F, P, D, L, F) if we reorder them into meaningful chunks (USA, IBM, NFL, PDF).

A useful metaphor for these several properties of working memory is juggling. Imagine a juggler keeping a number of balls in the air (**Figure 16.1**). The balls correspond to working memory representations, the number of balls in the air to the working memory load, and the maximum number of balls a particular individual can juggle to that person's working memory capacity. The force of gravity that causes the balls to fall down corresponds to decay, and the sequence of upward throws that keep balls in the air to the process of rehearsal. To explain chunking in these terms, one can imagine a juggler who glues several balls together, thus increasing the total number of objects that can be kept in the air. Finally, the juggler metaphor illustrates the maintenance-manipulation distinction: if maintenance corresponds to the throws of the juggler, manipulation corresponds to the ability to add or subtract balls from the group.

Working Memory Models

The first widely influential model of working memory was proposed by psychologist Alan Baddeley working at the University of York during the 1970s. In its more recent version, the **Baddeley model** consists of three capacity-limited *memory buffers* and a *control system* (**Figure 16.2**). Each memory buffer maintains a different kind of representation. The *phonological loop* holds phonological (sound-based) representations, the *visuospatial sketchpad* holds visuospatial representations, and the *episodic buffer* contains integrated, multimodal representations. Each buffer interacts closely with different long-term memory representations: the phonological loop with language knowledge, the visuospatial with visual semantics, and the episodic buffer with episodic

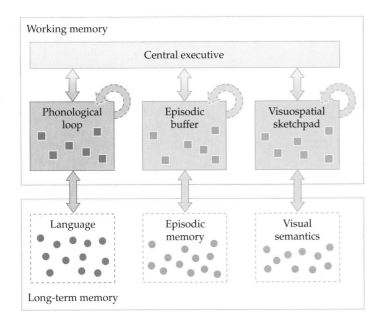

Figure 16.2   The Baddeley model of working memory.   Separate memory buffers hold phonological, visuospatial, and integrated multimodal information (the episodic buffer). The operation of the three buffers is taken to be controlled by a central executive. Dashed arrows associated with each buffer represent rehearsal. (After Baddeley 2003.)

memory. The control system in the model, which Baddeley called the *central executive*, is assumed to allocate attentional resources to the memory buffers and to perform manipulations.

In further tenets of this model, each memory buffer has two components: a *store* that holds information briefly, and a *rehearsal mechanism* that reactivates this information before it dissipates (see Figure 16.2). In the case of the phonological loop, these two components are respectively known as *phonological store* and *articulatory rehearsal*. Baddeley conceived of the articulatory rehearsal process as analogous to subvocal speech, that is, the "inner voice" that we sometimes "hear" while reading or counting. In the case of the visuospatial sketchpad, the store and rehearsal mechanism were called *visual cache* and *inner scribe*, respectively.

Whereas Baddeley's model assumes that working memory and long-term memory involve different representations (indicated diagrammatically by the squares and circles in Figure 16.2), other working memory models posit that working memory and long-term memory depend on the same memory representations. For example, Nelson Cowan at the University of Missouri proposed a model in which working memory is organized in two embedded levels (**Figure 16.3**). In the **Cowan model**, the first level of working memory consists of long-term memory representations in an "activated state" (the filled circles in Figure 16.3). There is no fixed limit on the number of long-term memories that can be activated at one time, but activation decays rapidly unless it is rehearsed. Unlike Baddeley's model, working memory representations for different types of information (verbal, visual, and so on) are all held in the same long-term memory store rather than in separate working memory stores (the different colored circles in Figure 16.3).

The second level of working memory in Cowan's model consists of activated representations that fall within the focus of attention (the "illuminated"

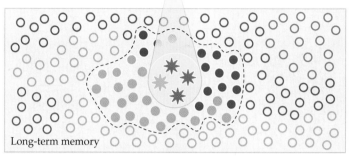

Figure 16.3 The Cowan working memory model. Different types of memory representations (open circles) are held within the same long-term memory store. Working memory consists of a subset of these representations in an activated state (filled circles). Only a few of these activated representations (stars) fall within the focus of attention (yellow "illuminated area"), which is controlled by the central executive. (After Cowan 1998.)

yellow area in the figure). The focus of attention can hold up to four items at one time. Thus, the capacity limitation of working memory is in the focus of attention, not in the number of activated long-term representations, which as noted above has no fixed limit. As in Baddeley's model, Cowan's model assumes that the allocation of attention to a particular set of representations is under the control of a central executive component.

These two models of working memory provide a useful framework for organizing the presentation of this chapter. Although both models were developed to account for behavioral findings, each has somewhat different neural implications that can be tested. The Baddeley model suggests that the regions actively storing working memory representations are different from those storing long-term memories. Cowan's model, on the other hand, suggests that both regions are the same. Given that long-term memory representations of sensory information are stored in the sensory and association cortices pertinent to each type of stimulus information (see Chapters 13 and 14), Cowan's model suggests that working memory maintenance should be associated with sustained activity in these regions.

Another difference is that Baddeley's model suggests that the "store" and "rehearsal" components of each buffer (e.g., phonological store versus articulatory rehearsal, in the case of the phonological loop) depend on different brain regions, whereas Cowan's model does not. Given that top-down control processes are generally attributed to the dorsolateral prefrontal cortex, both models imply that this brain region controls working memory processes in posterior brain regions. Neuroscientific evidence pertinent to the relative validity of each of these models emerges in the rest of this chapter, and ultimately indicates that both perspectives have some merit.

Working Memory and Brain Activity

Much of the evidence on regarding the neural correlates of working memory has been provided by measures of ongoing brain activity, such as single-unit electrophysiological recordings, ERPs, and event-related fMRI. Each of these methods has enough temporal resolution to distinguish brain activity during

(A) Single-cell recordings

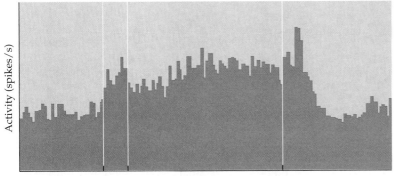

Figure 16.4 Phases of working memory.
Neuromonitoring methods can distinguish activity during encoding, delay, and response phases of working memory tasks. (A) Single-cell recordings measure changes in firing rates during each phase of working memory. (B) In event-related fMRI studies, the hemodynamic response is delayed and sluggish compared to unit responses, but different activity levels during the three phases can nevertheless be distinguished.

(B) Event-related fMRI

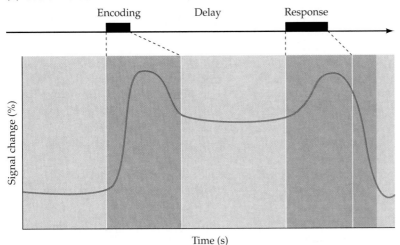

three phases: encoding, delay, and response. During the **encoding phase**, one or more items of information are incorporated into working memory. During the **delay phase**, the encoded information is maintained in working memory for several seconds. Finally, during the **response phase**, an action is executed on the basis of the maintained information.

The single-unit recording studies in **Figure 16.4A** measure changes in neuronal firing rate during each of the three phases. Even though the hemodynamic response is much more sluggish than neuronal responses, event-related fMRI studies can also distinguish activity in the three phases, as indicated in **Figure 16.4B**. We will return to these findings later in the chapter; the focus here is on the interpretation of the delay-period activity. Both types of studies have demonstrated sustained delay-period activity in several brain regions, including dorsolateral prefrontal, premotor, parietal, and temporal regions.

Sustained delay-period activity is generally attributed to the active maintenance of information within working memory. This interpretation is supported by several findings. First of all, neuroimaging studies show that delay-period activity in the brain usually persists for the entire length of the delay period (e.g., as long as 24 seconds) of the delayed-response or match-to-sample behavioral tasks (**Box 16A**). Moreover, delay-period brain activity tends to increase as a function of the working memory load. For example, an fMRI study found greater delay-period activity when information about five faces was maintained compared to information about three faces. This load effect is found in several brain regions, including the dorsolateral prefrontal cortex

■ BOX 16A Working Memory Tasks

As described in the text, most working memory tests consist of three phases: encoding, delay, and response. There are many variations, however, in the type of information presented during the encoding phase (e.g., spatial, verbal); the duration and manipulations during the interval (e.g., presentation of distractors); and the nature of the response (decision required or not required, motor versus verbal output, and so on). Working memory tasks also differ regarding overlap of the three phases across trials. In one sort of task, each trial has its own encoding, delay, and response phases, whereas in other tasks these phases may overlap across trials. The delayed response and delayed match-to-sam-

ple tasks considered here belong to the former group, and the *N*-back tasks described belong to the latter.

In **delayed response tasks**, the response to the stimulus is made only after the delay period. For example, in the *oculomotor delayed response task* often used with monkeys (Figure A), the monkey views a stimulus indicating a screen location (the encoding phase) and holds this location in spatial working memory (the delay phase). When a signal is presented, the monkey makes a saccade to the target location (the response phase). Thus the action to be made is "known" during the delay period.

Delayed match-to-sample tasks (also known as **delayed recognition tasks**) are similar to delayed response

tasks, but in this case the response requires the subject to make a choice based on the contents of working memory (Figure B). During the encoding phase, one or more items are presented. These items, called the *memory set*, can be alphanumeric characters (verbal working memory), shapes (object working memory), or locations (spatial working memory). During the delay phase, the memory set is maintained in working memory. As noted in the text, the number of items maintained is known as working memory *load*. During the response phase, a *probe* is presented and subjects must indicate whether or not the probe matches an item in the memory set. Therefore, the action to be made during the response phase is not known during the delay period.

(A) Delayed-response task

(A) Delayed response task. The monkey holds information about where to make a saccade (eye movement) in working memory during the delay period prior to the response phase. (B) Delayed match-to-sample tasks. Participants decide whether or not the stimulus presented during retrieval matches one of the stimuli held in working memory. (C) *N*-back tasks. In each trial, participants indicate by their response whether the stimulus matches one presented *N* number of trials back in the stimulus series.

(B) Delayed match-to-sample tasks

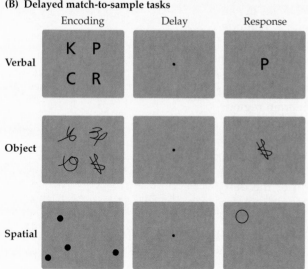

(C) *N*-back tasks

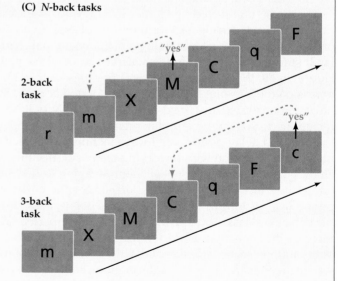

In *N*-back tasks, subjects must indicate whether each item in a continuous stream matches an item presented one, two, or more items "back" in the series (e.g., "2 back," "3 back"; Figure C). Functional neuroimaging studies have compared 1-, 2-, and 3-back tasks to measure the effects of memory load on brain activity (although increasing load may also lead to changes in strategies).

Unlike delayed response and match-to-sample tasks, *N*-back tasks do not provide separate measures of encoding, delay, and response phases, because these phases overlap across trials. Compared to simple delayed response and recognition tasks, *N*-back tasks are assumed to be more dependent on modification of the working memory store. With each new item presented, participants must incorporate the new item into working memory and drop an older item. This *updating* process is thus a form of the working memory *manipulation* mentioned in the text.

(**Figure 16.5A**). Increases in delay-period activity have also been associated with better working memory performance. For instance, delay-period activity in several frontal and parietal regions is greater for correct than incorrect trials (**Figure 16.5B, left panel**). Indeed, the effect of delay-period activity and performance is apparent even in individual trials (**Figure 16.5B, right panel**).

Load effects and direct links to working memory performance, however, do not exclude other possible interpretations of delay-period activity. For example, this activity could reflect encoding processes that continue beyond the encoding phase, or response processes that start before the response phase. In delayed recognition tasks (see Box 16A), the contribution of response processes to delay-period activity is minimized because the appropriate response is unknown until the probe is presented. One could nonetheless argue that load effects reflect the deployment of greater attentional resources in preparation for a more difficult decision.

(A) Load effect

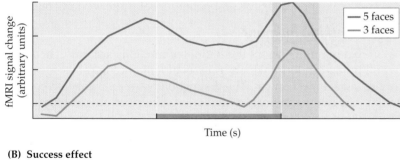

(B) Success effect

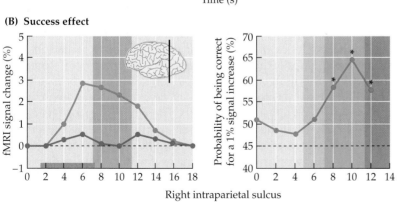

Right intraparietal sulcus

— Correct trials
— Incorrect trials

Figure 16.5 Delay-period activity and working memory maintenance.
(A) As shown by fMRI studies, delay-period (gray bar) activity in dorsolateral prefrontal cortex was greater during maintenance of five faces than when the subject was asked to maintain three faces in working memory. (B) In this study, delay-period activity in right intraparietal sulcus was greater for correct than for incorrect trials. The gray bar indicates the delay period (dark green area shows delay period shifted forward to account for the hemodynamic delay). The graph on the right shows the link between fMRI signal amplitude and behavioral performance. Light, medium, and dark green areas correspond to encoding, delay, and response phases, respectively; asterisks indicate significant effects. (A after Leung et al. 2002; B after Pessoa et al. 2002.)

Even if one accepts that delay-period activity reflects maintenance rather than encoding- or response-related processes, the understanding and interpretation of maintenance processes is difficult. For example, a brain region may show delay-period activity because it is actually holding memory representations, because it is mediating rehearsal, or because it is involved in high-level control processes in a central executive function. All these scenarios predict significant load effects and an association with successful performance.

Furthermore, even if the delay-period activity in a particular brain region reflects the continued reactivation of working memory representations, it is not clear whether the representations concern the stimuli perceived during the encoding phase (a *retrospective code*) or the action to be made during the response phase (a *prospective code*). This issue is especially important in delayed response tasks, in which the appropriate response is known during the delay phase (see Box 16A and below).

In summary, ongoing activity during the delay period provides a neural basis for working memory maintenance, but this fact must be interpreted with caution in relation to the specific demands of each task employed. This issue applies to all forms of working memory, including verbal, spatial, and object working memory, which are considered in more detail in the subsequent sections.

Verbal Working Memory

Maintaining verbal information in working memory is essential for language comprehension and production; absent this ability we would be unable to link the subject and the verb of the sentences we hear or read, and hence we would not understand their meaning. Likewise, we would not be able to organize words into the sentences we speak or write. As described in Chapter 22, verbal working memory is used to manipulate numbers and other symbolic representations. Because the maintenance of verbal information is fundamental to human cognition, working memory has been much studied in this context, typically in terms of either phonological, graphemic, or semantic working memory.

Phonological working memory

Recall that verbal maintenance in the Baddeley model is accomplished by a postulated phonological loop, which consists of a phonological store and an articulatory rehearsal mechanism. The distinction between these two components can explain two behavioral phenomena: the phonological similarity effect, and the word length effect.

The **phonological similarity effect** refers to the fact that working memory for letters is worse when the letters sound similar to each other (e.g., P, B, V) than when they sound different (e.g., X, K, R). The phonological similarity effect suggests the existence of a store that maintains representations in a phonological format, supporting the concept of a phonological store. The **word length effect** refers to the fact that people can hold more words in working memory when the words are short (e.g., *cup, luck, hear*) than when they are long (e.g., *desperation, porcupine, phonological*). The word length effect can be explained by assuming that there is indeed an articulatory rehearsal process and that this process is slowed down by more complex words that take longer to rehearse—given that working memory traces decay rapidly, more words are lost before they can be rehearsed.

Neuropsychological evidence from brain-damaged patients has linked the phonological store to the left inferior parietal cortex (Brodmann area 40), and the articulatory rehearsal process to the posterior part of the left inferior frontal gyrus, which corresponds to Broca's area (Brodmann area 44). As

(A) Left inferior parietal (Brodmann Area 40)

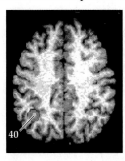

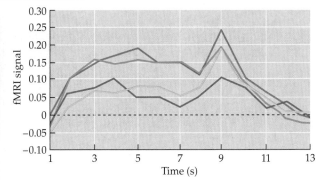

(B) Left inferior frontal (Brodmann Area 44)

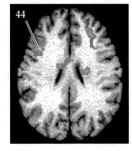

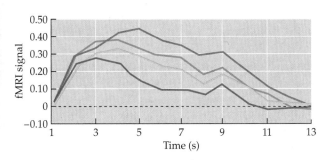

— 1–syllable distinct words
— 3–syllable words
— 1–syllable phonologically
      similar words
— 1–syllable pseudowords

Figure 16.6 Regions involved in phonological working memory. (A) In an event-related fMRI study, the left inferior parietal cortex (Brodmann area 40) was activated for phonologically similar words but not for distinct words, consistent with the presumed role of this region in phonological storage. Pseudowords also activated these regions, possibly because they depend on phonological storage. (B) The posterior part of the left inferior frontal gyrus (Broca's area, Brodmann area 44) showed greater activity for three-syllable than for one-syllable words, consistent with greater demands on the articulatory rehearsal process. (From Chein and Fiez 2001.)

described in Chapter 13, lesions in the left inferior parietal cortex have been shown to impair working memory but not long-term memory. These patients have a normal capacity to articulate, but when words are presented visually, they fail to show the phonological similarity effect. This finding suggests that these patients avoid using an impaired phonological store. In contrast, the articulatory rehearsal process associated with Broca's area would explain why patients with lesions in this area have deficits in language production and word articulation (Broca's aphasia; see Chapter 21).

The distinction between the roles of the left inferior parietal cortex and Broca's area in phonological working memory is further supported by functional neuroimaging evidence, such as an fMRI study that investigated the phonological similarity and word length effects. Participants were scanned while maintaining distinct one-syllable words (e.g., *pit, stem*); phonologically similar one-syllable words (*fight, height*); distinct three-syllable words (*telescope, computer*); and one-syllable pseudowords (*blick, rame*). The left inferior parietal cortex was activated for phonologically similar words but not for distinct words (**Figure 16.6A**), consistent with idea that the phonologically similar words place greater demands on the phonological store. This same region was also activated by pseudowords, which may be more dependent on phonological storage given that they lack semantic representations. Broca's area showed greater activity for three-syllable than for one-syllable words (**Figure 16.6B**), consistent with greater demands on the articulatory rehearsal process. These results are consistent with the idea that the phonological store is mediated by left inferior cortex, while articulatory rehearsal is mediated by Broca's area.

Graphemic working memory

In addition to distinct brain regions that process the phonological properties of spoken words, there are also distinct regions that support processing of the

(A)

(B)

(C)

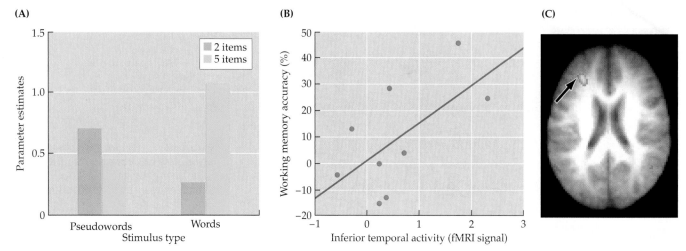

Figure 16.7 Regions involved in working memory for written words. (A) Activity in a left inferior temporal region shows a load effect (5 > 2) in delay-period activity for words but not for pseudowords. (B) This load effect is correlated with the load effect in working memory accuracy. (C) Delay-period activity in the left inferior temporal area is correlated with delay-period activity in left prefrontal cortex. (From Fiebach et al. 2006.)

visual properties of written words in working memory. An event-related fMRI study identified a left inferior temporal region that showed greater activity for words than for than for symbol strings, using the effects load on delay-period activity during word maintenance. Participants were presented with a set of either two or five words that they maintained during a 10-second delay before comparing the word set to a probe. In this study, the left inferior temporal region showed load effects (5 > 2) in delay-period activity for words, but not for pseudowords (**Figure 16.7A**). Confirming a contribution to delay-period activity, the load effect on brain activation was also correlated with the load effect in working memory accuracy (**Figure 16.7B**). Finally, delay-period activity in the left inferior temporal area was correlated with delay-period activity in left prefrontal cortex for words but not for pseudowords (**Figure 16.7C**), a finding consistent with the implication of Cowan's idea that sustained activity in sensory regions is controlled by a top-down processes mediated by the prefrontal cortex. Thus, available evidence suggests that verbal working memory representations are held in the left inferior *parietal* cortex in the case of phonological properties, but in the left inferior *temporal* cortex in the case of graphemic (visual word) properties.

Semantic working memory

Although phonological working memory and semantic working memory are assumed to be intimately related, they depend on overlapping but significantly different brain regions. Thus Randy Martin and collaborators at Rice University reported one patient who is more impaired in semantic than phonological working memory, and another patient who displayed the opposite pattern—a double dissociation (see Chapter 3). Even if the lesions in these patients were not selective enough to accurately localize the exact regions involved in semantic compared to phonological working memory, these observations imply that different regions are indeed involved.

To further define these regions, Geeta Shivde and Sharon Thompson-Schill at the University of Pennsylvania conducted an fMRI study that directly compared semantic and phonological versions of a modified delayed match-to-sample task (see Box 16A). In each trial, subjects saw a single word (e.g., *buy*) during the encoding phase, and after a 10-second delay compared the word to a second word in either meaning or phonology. In the semantic condition, subjects maintained the meaning of the first word during the delay, and during the response phase they decided whether or not the first word was a synonym of the second word (e.g., *purchase*). In the phonological condition, subjects repeated the word silently and decided whether it shared a vowel sound with a nonsense word (e.g., *kine*).

Regions showing greater delay-period activity in the semantic than in the phonological condition included the anterior portion of the left inferior frontal gyrus (Brodmann areas 45/47) and the left lateral temporal cortex (**Figure 16.8**). As mentioned in Chapter 14, the anterior left inferior frontal gyrus has been strongly associated with the control of semantic processing and retrieval. Thus this region is likely to mediate the rehearsal of semantic representations. In contrast, the left lateral temporal cortex is likely to be involved in storage rather than rehearsal. Damage to left temporal cortex often leads to knowledge loss for specific semantic categories (i.e., *agnosias*). This loss of knowledge is independent of input or output modalities, suggesting it reflects loss of memory representations.

In summary, phonological working memory has been associated mainly with Broca's area (which is assumed to mediate the articulatory rehearsal process) and with left inferior parietal cortex (which is assumed to store phonological representations). In contrast, the region that holds working memory representations of written words is in left inferior temporal cortex. Finally, semantic working memory is associated with delay-period activity in anterior left inferior frontal cortex and left lateral temporal cortex, which may mediate rehearsal and storage processes.

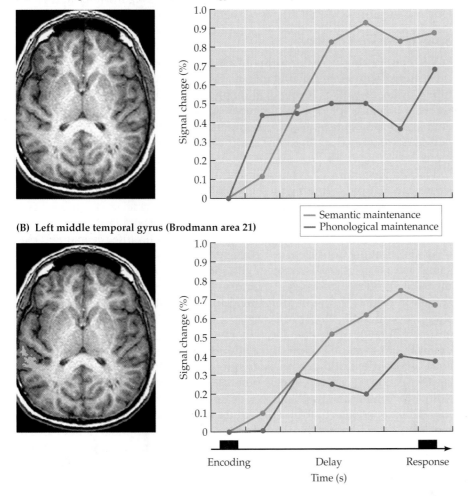

(A) Anterior portion of left inferior frontal gyrus (Brodmann area 45/47)

(B) Left middle temporal gyrus (Brodmann area 21)

— Semantic maintenance
— Phonological maintenance

Signal change (%)

Encoding   Delay   Response

Time (s)

Figure 16.8 Brain regions associated with semantic working memory. The anterior portion of the left inferior frontal gyrus (A) and the left middle temporal gyrus (B) showed greater delay-period activity when participants maintained the meaning of words than whey they maintained their phonology. (From Shivde and Thompson-Schill 2004.)

These findings are generally consistent with *both* Baddeley's and Cowan's models. In agreement with Baddeley's model, the rehearsal and storage components of working memory depend on different brain regions. Although this model does not postulate a specialized semantic memory buffer with its own rehearsal and storage components, such a buffer could easily be added to the model to account for semantic working memory findings. At the same time, the association of semantic working memory with left lateral temporal cortex—a region assumed to store long-term semantic knowledge—fits Cowan's model. The involvement of inferior temporal regions in working memory for written words, but not for pseudowords, also fits Cowan's model, given that the former have preexistent long-term memory representations and the latter do not.

Although both models do a reasonable job of accounting for the available data, Baddeley's model provides a better account of the dissociations between rehearsal and storage components, and Cowan's model a better account of delay-period activity in posterior regions associated with long-term memory storage.

Visual Working Memory

Working memory in the visual sensory system can be divided into working memory for spatial locations and working memory for object features. Consistent with studies of visual perception (see Chapter 5), the neural bases of spatial and object working memory are to some degree dissociable. The following sections consider the neural correlates of spatial working memory and object working memory, and the differences between them.

Spatial working memory

While maintaining verbal information is critical for language and symbolic processing, maintaining spatial information is essential for processing visual information, as well as for navigation and other motor tasks. Unlike verbal working memory, spatial working memory can be investigated in non-human animals. In fact, some of the earliest and most important studies regarding the neural correlates of spatial working memory used single-cell recording in monkeys.

Joaquin Fuster at UCLA and Patricia Goldman-Rakic at Yale established a strong link between working memory maintenance and the firing of neurons in the prefrontal cortex of monkeys. In the oculomotor delayed response task (see Box 16A), for example, neurons in dorsal prefrontal cortex tended to fire continuously during the delay period, presumably reflecting the maintenance of spatial location. Consistent with this interpretation, delay-period activity in some neurons is indeed associated with specific spatial locations, which Goldman-Rakic referred to as the "memory fields" of the cells in question. As shown in **Figure 16.9**, a neuron tuned to an orientation of 135° would not show delay-period activity to targets presented at 270°. Goldman-Rakic suggested that neurons such as these that encode spatial location are more frequent in dorsolateral region of the prefrontal cortex, and that neurons that code object information are more frequent in ventrolateral region (although see the section on content- versus process-based models, below).

In addition to this single-cell evidence, fMRI studies in humans have also found delay-period activity in the both the frontal eye fields (in humans, this is the dorsal frontal region in or near Brodmann area 8) and the intraparietal sulcus. One such study distinguished the contributions of these two regions to spatial working memory using a human version of oculomotor delayed response task. In one condition, participants knew the direction of the impend-

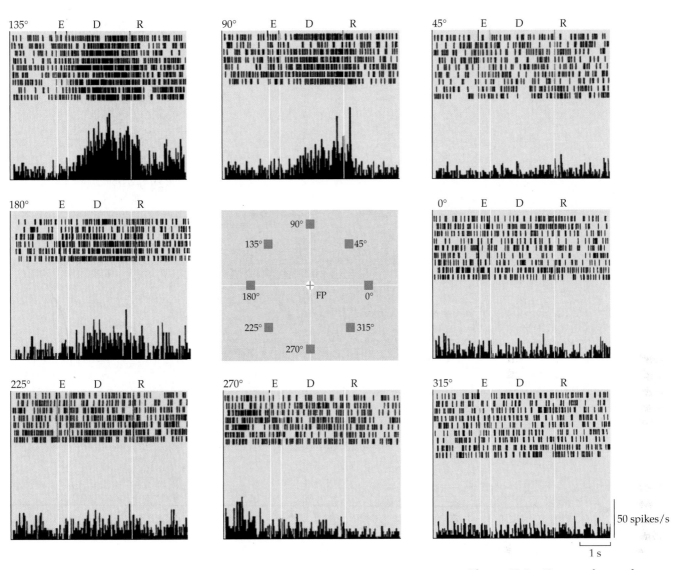

Figure 16.9 Neurons in monkey prefrontal cortex have a tuned "memory field." The neuron tuned to an orientation of 135° showed delay-period activity to targets presented at this orientation, but not to targets at 270°. E, encoding; D, delay; R, response. (From Funahashi et al. 1989.)

ing saccade (eye movement) during the delay period, whereas in another con-dition the direction of the necessary saccade was unknown until the end of the delay period. As might be expected, the frontal eye field showed greater delay-period activity in the former condition than in the latter (**Figure 16.10A**), while the intraparietal sulcus showed the opposite pattern (**Figure 16.10B**). These results link the frontal eye fields to the maintenance of oculomotor information, and the intraparietal sulcus area to the maintenance of spatial locations. The idea that the frontal eye field activity maintains accurate oculo-motor coordinates during the delay period was confirmed by a correlation between delay-period frontal eye field activity and accuracy of the subsequent saccade (**Figure 16.10C**).

In short, spatial working memory, like verbal working memory, involves both frontal and posterior brain regions. Frontal regions include dorsolateral regions and frontal eye fields; the posterior regions are in the intraparietal sul-cus. Whereas the frontal eye fields appear to maintain oculomotor coordinates, the intraparietal sulcus appears to maintain spatial locations. This last finding is also consistent with either the Baddeley or the Cowan model. In terms of Baddeley's model, the frontal eye fields and the intraparietal sulcus can be attributed to the rehearsal and storage components of spatial working memo-

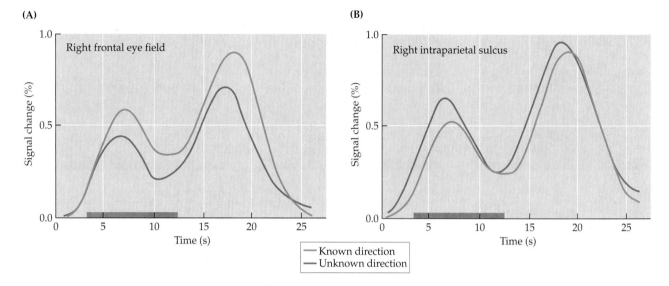

(A) Right frontal eye field

(B) Right intraparietal sulcus

— Known direction
— Unknown direction

Figure 16.10   Neural correlates of visual spatial working memory.   (A) During the delay period (gray bar) of this fMRI study, the right frontal eye field was more active when the direction of the impending saccade was known than when it was not. (B) The right intraparietal sulcus showed the opposite pattern. (C) Frontal eye field activity during the delay period predicted the accuracy of the subsequent saccade. (After Curtis et al. 2004.)

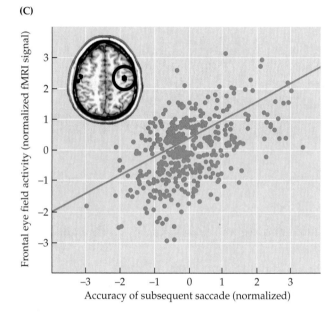

ry, respectively, much like Broca's area and the left inferior parietal cortex can be attributed to the rehearsal and storage components of verbal working memory. In terms of Cowan's model, both the frontal eye fields and the intraparietal sulcus could be regions holding long-term memory representations, either oculomotor or spatial, which are activated during working memory.

Object working memory

While the maintenance of spatial information is associated with the parietal cortex, maintenance of object information is associated mainly with occipital and temporal cortices. Joaquin Fuster and John Jervey found that monkeys performing a delayed response task involving color recognition showed increased firing of some neurons in the lower bank of the superior temporal sulcus during the delay period in response to some colors but not others (**Figure 16.11A,B**). They proposed that these neurons mediated the retention of color information during the delay period. Some neurons also show delay-period activity for more complex stimuli. For example, some neurons in ante-

(A)

(B)

(C)

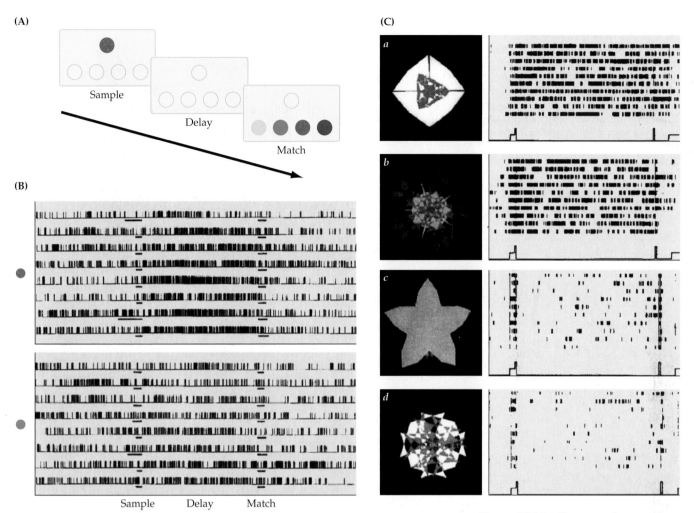

Sample

Delay

Match

Sample   Delay   Match

a

b

c

d

Figure 16.11 Neurons show maintenance of object information. (A) The delayed color-response task presented to monkeys. (B) During the delay period, some neurons fired specifically in response to specific colors. (C) Neuronal activity in another region of the temporal cortex showed maintained activity to patterns *a* and *b*, but not to patterns *c* and *d* (A,B from Fuster and Jervey 1982; C from Miyashita and Chang 1988.)

rior ventral temporal cortex showed delay-period activity for some kaleidoscopic patterns but not others (**Figure 16.11C**).

Functional neuroimaging studies in humans have generally confirmed these findings by showing that delay-period activity in temporal cortex is category-specific. Functional MRI work by Susan Courtney and her collaborators at Johns Hopkins found that the medial fusiform gyrus in the temporal lobe showed greater delay-period activity for subjects viewing houses than for those looking at faces, whereas the lateral fusiform gyrus showed the opposite effect (**Figure 16.12A**). The link between these ventral temporal regions and category-specific object working memory is also supported by responses to imagined visual scenes. For instance, another study found that scans of participants asked to envision mental images of houses yielded greater activity in the medial fusiform gyrus, whereas conjuring mental images of faces yielded greater activity in the lateral fusiform gyrus (**Figure 16.12B**; see also Chapter 5).

Demonstrating delay-period or imagery-related activity in particular brain regions, however, does not show conclusively that such activity is actually necessary for successful working memory. Resolving this issue depends on studies of patients, or on other methods such as transcranial magnetic stimulation (TMS; see Chapter 3). With respect to clinical information, Martha Farah (now at the University of Pennsylvania) and her collaborators described a patient who had deficits not only in perceiving faces (*prosopagnosia*) and colors (*achro-*

Figure 16.12 Maintenance-related activity in temporal regions may be category-specific. (A) In a delayed response fMRI study, delay-period activity was found in medial fusiform gyrus (MedFus) for subjects viewing images of houses, but in lateral fusiform gyrus (LatFus) for those looking at faces. (B) A similar dissociation was found for imagined scenes: house imagery was associated with medial fusiform gyrus activity, and face imagery with lateral fusiform gyrus activity. Activity in the inferior temporal gyrus is also shown. (A from Sala et al. 2003; B after Ishai et al. 2000.)

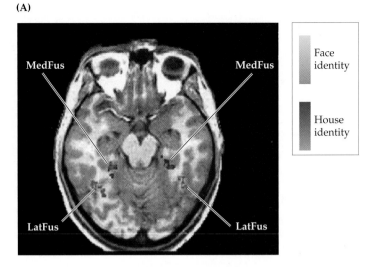

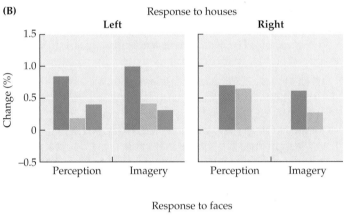

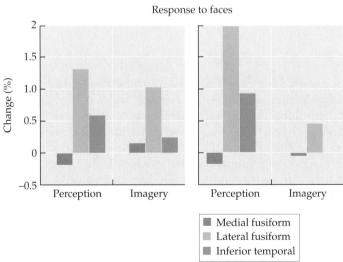

matopsia), but also in describing faces and the colors of objects from memory. Thus, as described in Chapter 5, the regions that are necessary for perception also seem to be necessary for **imagery** (i.e., the mental representation of an image without the physical presence of sensory stimuli).

A more specific study of maintained activity in working memory was carried out by Stephen Kosslyn and colleagues at Harvard using combined PET and TMS. Participants were scanned with their eyes closed while they mentally envisioned and compared four previously memorized quadrants contain-

(A)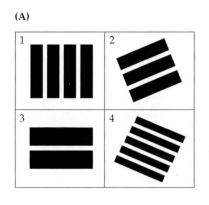

(B)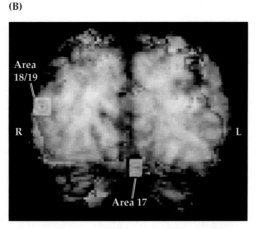

Figure 16.13 Occipitotemporal activity may be causally involved in working memory of visual information. (A) Participants memorized stripe patterns and were then scanned with PET while comparing remembered images of those patterns. (B) The imagery task activated primary and secondary visual cortices. (C) TMS disrupting visual cortex functions slowed down response times in the imagery task. (From Kosslyn et al. 1999.)

(C)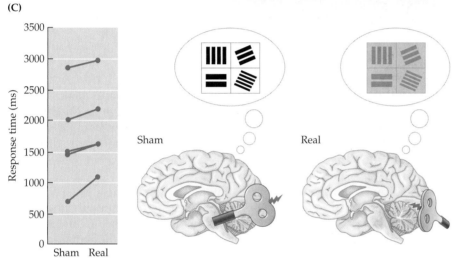

ing patterns of stripes that differed in length and width (**Figure 16.13A**). In each trial, participants heard two numbers and a word (e.g., *one, two*; *length*) indicating the two quadrants and dimension to be compared. As expected, this imagery task activated the primary visual cortex and right lateral occipital cortex (**Figure 16.13B**). To ask whether these regions played a causal role in working memory, the same task was investigated under real and sham TMS conditions. Compared to the sham condition, transient TMS interference with processing in the occipital cortex slowed down reaction times in the imagery task (**Figure 16.13C**). This observation implies that activity in visual cortex is necessary not only for perceiving visual stimuli, but for maintaining visual images active in working memory.

Differences between spatial and object working memory

Although Baddeley's original model of working memory attributed the maintenance of visual object and spatial information to a single working memory component (the "visuospatial sketchpad"), it is now clear that object and spatial maintenance mechanisms are dissociable at both the behavioral and neural levels. For instance, one behavioral study found different patterns of interference in object and spatial span tasks. In the *object span task*, participants were asked to remember an object matrix (**Figure 16.14A**), whereas in the *spatial span task* they were asked to remember the sequence in which a series of blocks were tapped (**Figure 16.14B**). In both tasks, working memory load (size of the matrix or

Figure 16.14 Distinction of spatial and object working memory in behavioral tests. (A) In the object span task, a matrix with half of its cells filled in is briefly presented. Participants must then mark in an empty matrix the cells they remember as being filled. (B) In a spatial span task, the experimenter taps a sequence of blocks, and the participants must imitate the sequence. (C) Object interference impaired the object span task more than it did the spatial span, whereas spatial interference produced the opposite pattern. (After Baddeley 2003.)

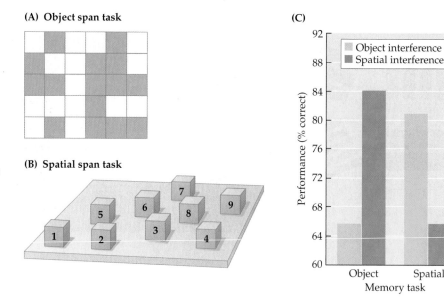

length of the sequence) was progressively increased until performance deteriorated. During the delay period, participants performed either an *object interference task* (viewing abstract paintings) or a *spatial interference task* (individually touching a series of pegs). The results showed that object interference disrupted visual working memory more than the spatial working memory, whereas spatial interference yielded the opposite effect (**Figure 16.14C**).

Dissociations between object and spatial working memory have been also reported in clinical, functional neuroimaging, and TMS studies. Farah and collaborators described a patient who had difficulty describing spatial relations from memory but showed no problems in object imagery; they contrasted this case with another patient who had deficits in face and color imagery, but not in spatial imagery. In confirmation of this distinction, a PET study by Courtney and collaborators found that occipitotemporal regions were more activated during maintenance of faces than maintenance of spatial locations, whereas occipitoparietal regions showed the opposite pattern (**Figure 16.15A**). Another study found that TMS applied over parietal regions selectively slowed down reaction times in a spatial working memory task, whereas TMS

Figure 16.15 Dorsal and ventral pathways process spatial and object working memory, respectively. Functional imaging offers evidence for this distinction between the two pathways. (A) The parietal regions in a PET study performed during working memory tasks showed greater activity for locations than for faces, whereas occipitotemporal regions showed the reverse pattern. (B) In this study, TMS over parietal cortex slowed completion of a spatial working memory task to a greater extent than it slowed an object working memory task. TMS over temporal cortex produced the opposite effect. (A after Courtney et al. 1997; B after Harris et al. 2002.)

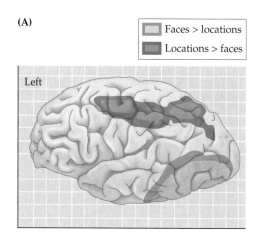

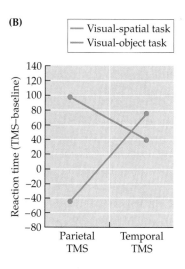

over temporal cortex regions slowed down a visual-object working memory task (**Figure 16.15B**). Thus the distinction described in Chapter 4 between a ventral pathway for object processing and a dorsal pathway for spatial processing also applies to working memory.

Working Memory in Other Modalities

Although most studies of working memory have been done using visual stimuli (either words or nonverbal representations such as pictures), there has been some investigation of working memory in other modalities. From a theoretical viewpoint, these other studies are important because they test the generalizability of Cowan's notion that working memory is supported by neural activity in the sensory cortices. Recall that the Cowan model assumes working memory to consist of activated long-term memory representations stored in sensory cortices. Selective attention to these activations is attributed to higher-level control processes that depend on prefrontal cortical regions. How well does this conception hold up when auditory and somatic sensory modalities are examined?

Auditory working memory

Imagery is a form of working memory, and a number of functional neuroimaging studies have focused on auditory imagery. Consistent with the assumption that the neural correlates of imagery overlap with those of perception, auditory imagery elicits activity in auditory cortex. In one such study participants listened to familiar songs with lyrics (e.g., the Rolling Stones classic "Satisfaction"); equally familiar compositions without lyrics (e.g., the theme from "The Pink Panther"); and unfamiliar music of both kinds. In each presentation, short (2–5 seconds) sections of the music were silenced. As you might expect, participants reported that during these silent periods, they could still "hear" the familiar music; however, they could not image the unfamiliar music in the same way. Thus researchers were able to study brain activity associated with auditory imagery of music with and without lyrics. Auditory imagery for both types of music activated secondary auditory cortex. However, imagining music without lyrics also activated primary auditory cortex, possibly because greater attention is focused on tonality rather than the simultaneous semantic content (**Figure 16.16**).

Somatosensory working memory

Studies of the somatic sensory system have led to the same general conclusion (i.e., that this sensory modality also plays an important role in working memory). Transcranial magnetic stimulation was also used to investigate the role of primary somatosensory cortex in maintaining sensory information. Participants in a delay-period activity study were asked to maintain information in working memory about the specific frequency of a vibration delivered to a finger, and to compare this memory to another vibration administered at the end of the delay period. Single-pulse TMS was then delivered to the ipsilateral or contralateral primary somatosensory cortex at different times during the delay period.

As illustrated by the graph in **Figure 16.17**, contralateral TMS impaired working memory performance more than did ipsilateral TMS when the pulse was

Figure 16.16 Auditory working memory. Participants listened to music (both with and without lyrics) in which 2–5-second-long sections were replaced with silence. During these gaps, secondary auditory cortex (SAC) activity was greater for familiar than for unfamiliar music, reflecting auditory imagery. Imagery of instrumental melodies activated primary auditory cortex (PAC) as well, possibly reflecting auditory imagining with greater tonal detail. (From Kraemer et al. 2005.)

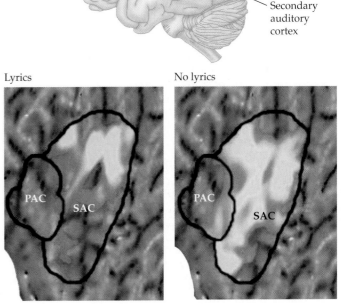

(A) Somatosensory working memory

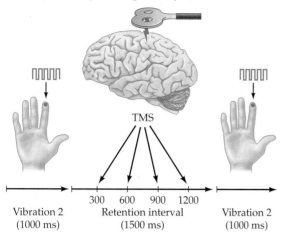

Vibration 2 (1000 ms) Retention interval (1500 ms) Vibration 2 (1000 ms)

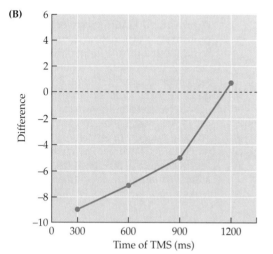

Figure 16.17 Somatosensory working memory. (A) Subjects felt two 1-second vibrations separated by 1.5 seconds; a single pulse of TMS was delivered to the ipsilateral or contralateral primary somatosensory cortices at different times during this delay. (B) Compared to ipsilateral TMS, contralateral TMS impaired working memory when delivered during the first half of the delay. (After Harris et al. 2002.)

delivered during the first half of the delay period. The investigators concluded that the pulse had interfered with the memory trace for the first vibration, stored in contralateral primary somatosensory cortex. The fact that the effect occurred only during the first second of the delay period suggested that the perceptual record after this time is held in higher-order processing areas, possibly secondary somatosensory cortex. Single-cell recording studies in monkeys have failed to find sustained activity in primary somatosensory cortex, but this apparent contradiction may simply reflect the prolonged training required when animals are the study subjects; such training could lead to faster transfer of working memory information to higher-order cortical areas.

In addition to work on auditory and somatic sensory working memory, attentional modulation can affect activity in primary olfactory cortex (see Chapters 10 and 11). In sum, when taken together, studies on working memory in nonvisual modalities support the idea that sensory cortices play an important role in maintaining working memory representations.

The Role of Dorsolateral Prefrontal Cortex

The roles of several prefrontal regions associated with the rehearsal of different kinds of information have been mentioned in earlier sections. Thus Broca's area (Brodmann area 44 in the left hemisphere) was linked to articulatory rehearsal of phonological information during verbal working memory tasks; the frontal eye fields (Brodmann area 8 bilaterally) with the rehearsal of oculomotor codes during spatial working memory; and the right ventrolateral prefrontal regions (Brodmann area 45/47) with the rehearsal of visual images during object working memory tasks.

There is some evidence that dorsolateral prefrontal cortex also participates in working memory. Damage to this region impairs delayed response performance in monkeys, and the observation that the degree of impairment increases as a function of the delay's duration is consistent with this idea. However, exactly what part this region plays in working memory remains unclear. One issue is whether the contribution of dorsolateral prefrontal cortex to working memory depends on the *content* of working memory information or on the *type of process* involved. Another question concerns the type of process supported by dorsolateral prefrontal cortex, and whether this process is specific to working memory. These two issues are considered in the following sections.

Content-based versus process-based models

There has been a heated debate between two different models of prefrontal cortex organization. Both models postulate that ventrolateral prefrontal cortex regions (Brodmann area 45/47) and dorsolateral regions (areas 9 and 46) play different roles in working memory. The models differ, however, in their views of the nature of this distinction (**Figure 16.18**). According to the **content-based model** (originally proposed by Patricia Goldman-Rakic and later supported by Susan Courtney and others), ventrolateral regions are primarily involved in *object* working memory, whereas dorsolateral regions are more involved in *spatial* working memory. According to the **process-based model** (originally proposed by Michael Petrides at McGill University and later advocated by a number of other investigators), ventrolateral regions are primarily involved in simple maintenance operations, whereas dorsolateral regions are involved in

Figure 16.18 Content- and process-based models of prefrontal cortex function in working memory. The content-based model proposes that ventrolateral regions of the prefrontal cortex are mostly involved in object working memory, whereas dorsolateral regions are more involved in spatial working memory. According to the process-based model, however, ventrolateral regions are involved in simple maintenance operations while dorsolateral regions are involved in monitoring and manipulating information.

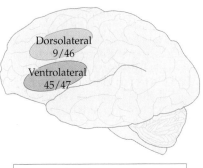

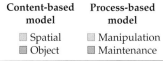

more complex processes involving monitoring and manipulating information within working memory.

The content-based model is consistent with evidence that the ventral pathway for object processing (see above and Chapter 4) projects mainly to ventrolateral prefrontal regions, whereas the dorsal pathway for spatial processing projects primarily to dorsolateral prefrontal regions. Ventrolateral prefrontal regions can thus be seen as the anterior terminus of the object processing pathway, and dorsolateral prefrontal regions as the terminus of the dorsal pathway for spatial processing. Consistent with this interpretation, single-cell recordings in monkeys have found that some ventral prefrontal neurons show delay-period firing for objects but not for spatial locations, whereas dorsal neurons tend to show delay-period firing for spatial locations but not for objects.

Other evidence, however, is inconsistent with a content-based model. For example, single-cell studies in monkeys have also found mixed populations of object and spatial neurons throughout the lateral prefrontal cortex. Moreover, dorsolateral lesions in monkeys can impair object working memory, and ventrolateral lesions can affect spatial working memory. Several functional neuroimaging studies have also failed to find ventral–dorsal differences in comparing activity in these regions elicited by object and spatial working memory tasks.

Other observations have tended to support the process-based model, including lesion studies in monkeys and functional neuroimaging in human subjects. As an example of the latter type of study, Mark D'Esposito and his group (then at the University of Pennsylvania) compared a "forward condition," in which participants *maintained* an ordered sequence of letters in working memory, to an "alphabetize condition," in which participants *manipulated* the letters by rearranging them in alphabetical order during the delay period. Delay-period activity was found in both ventrolateral and dorsolateral prefrontal cortex regions, but dorsolateral prefrontal cortex activity was greater in the alphabetize condition than the forward condition (**Figure 16.19**). These results suggest that dorsolateral prefrontal cortex is involved in working memory only when operations more complex than simple maintenance are required.

Although this debate continues, it seems likely that elements of both models will turn out to have merit. For example, ventrolateral regions could be involved both in object working memory and maintenance, while dorsolateral regions could be more involved in spatial working memory and manipulation. Another possibility is that different subregions within ventrolateral and dorsolateral cortices are sensitive to the object–spatial dimension and the maintenance–manipulation dimension. Finally, different populations of neurons within these areas may be involved in both dimensions.

The nature and specificity of dorsolateral prefrontal contributions

Whatever the outcome of this debate, it is clear that the contribution of the dorsolateral prefrontal cortex to working memory goes well beyond simple maintenance. The nature and specificity of the working memory processes mediated by this region remain open questions.

Figure 16.19 Evidence for the process-based model. In an fMRI study, delay-period activity (gray bar) was found in both ventrolateral and dorsolateral prefrontal cortex regions, but dorsolateral prefrontal cortex activity was greater when the test condition involved manipulation ("alphabetize") than in a condition involving only maintenance ("forward"). (After D'Esposito et al. 2000.)

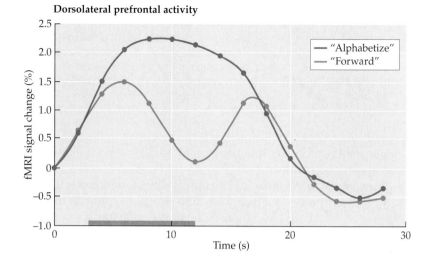

Dorsolateral prefrontal activity

One idea that could account for both the alphabetization effect shown in Figure 16.19 and the contributions of dorsolateral prefrontal cortex to episodic memory encoding (see Chapter 14) is that delay-period activity in this region reflects the *organization* of information within working memory. Consistent with this idea, dorsolateral prefrontal delay-period activity makes working memory more resistant to the effects of distraction. In addition to the standard encoding, delay, and response phase, the paradigm used to show this involved a distraction phase inserted between the delay and the response phases (**Figure 16.20A**). As indicated in **Figure 16.20B**, dorsolateral prefrontal cortex (Brodmann area 46) showed greater delay-period activity for trials that later survived the effect of distraction (i.e., correct trials) than for those that did not (incorrect trials). In contrast, delay-period activity in the frontal eye fields and the intraparietal sulcus did not differ between correct and incorrect trials (**Figure 16.20C**).

The organization hypothesis could also explain why dorsolateral prefrontal activity tends to be greater for structured than for unstructured sequences of spatial locations or numbers, even though working memory load is greater for unstructured than for structured sequences.

This conception of prefrontal organization, however, is too broad to account for the involvement of dorsolateral prefrontal cortex in working memory tasks that do not involve interference or chunking, or for its involvement in other cognitive tasks. One possibility is that the functional organization involves the repeated execution of a simpler process. James Rowe, Richard Passingham, and their collaborators at the Institute of Neurology in London suggested that the key functional role of dorsolateral prefrontal cortex is to select from working memory those representations that are appropriate for guiding a specific action. This idea was supported by an fMRI study of spatial working memory in which selection demands were eliminated from the delay phase by making selection completely dependent on information presented during the response phase.

As illustrated in **Figure 16.21A**, participants viewed three red dots during the encoding (stimulus) phase; they maintained this image in spatial working memory during a delay of varying length. Importantly, the participants did not know during the delay which of the three locations would have to be selected to guide future action. After the delay, a line was briefly presented. The line crossed only one of the locations being maintained in working memory, which was selected for the subsequent response. Finally, a central dot appeared and participants moved it to the selected location using a joystick. A right dorsolateral prefrontal region (Brodmann area 46) was not activated *dur-*

(A) Paradigm

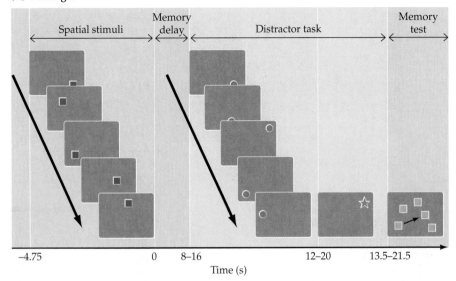

(B) Dorsolateral PFC (Brodmann area 46)

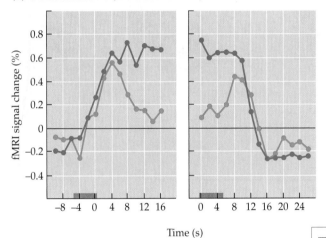

(C) Intraparietal sulcus

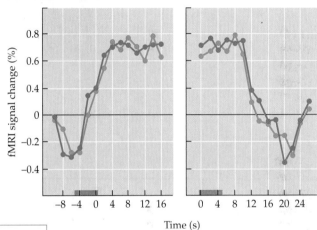

— Correct trials
— Error trials

Figure 16.20 Delay-period dorsolateral prefrontal activity may protect working memory from the effects of interference. (A) During the encoding phase, participants viewed the location of five purple squares. After a delay of 8–16 seconds, they performed a distractor task in which they had to remember the location of five red dots and decide if a red star matched one of their locations. Finally, they viewed five boxes in the locations of the purple targets with an arrow between two boxes, and reported whether or not the arrow matched the order of the boxes in the sequence. (B) Delay-period activity (gray bar) in dorsolateral prefrontal cortex was greater for correct trials than incorrect trials. (C) Delay-period activity (gray bar) in the intraparietal sulcus did not distinguish correct and incorrect trials. (After Sakai et al. 2002.)

ing the delay phase, but only *after* the delay phase—that is, during the selection period (**Figure 16.21B**). This result suggests that dorsolateral prefrontal cortex is specifically involved in the selection of working memory representations in order to make an appropriate response rather than in the maintenance of representations. Thus it could be argued that the activity of this region during the delay phase of tasks involving interference and chunking is due to the fact that these processes involve repeated selection processes.

Figure 16.21 Dorsolateral prefrontal cortex may be involved in selecting working memory representations to guide actions.
(A) Participants maintained three locations in working memory but did not know which had to be selected until after the delay phase (see text). (B) The right dorsolateral prefrontal cortex showed greater activity during the selection period. (C) This region was not activated during the delay phase, as indicated by trials sorted according to delay duration. (From Rowe et al. 2000.)

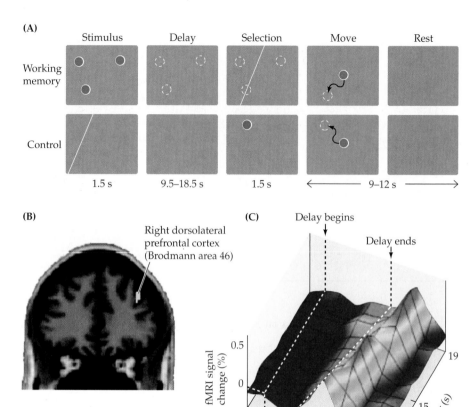

SUMMARY
Organizational features of working memory. In this diagram summarizing the main points discussed in the chapter, the two hemispheres of the brain are shown separately to indicate those working memory functions that tend to be lateralized, as well as their different anterior-posterior distributions.

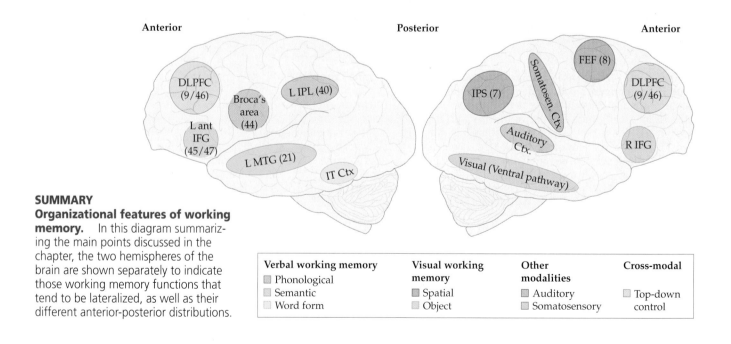

Summary

1. Working memory refers to the maintenance and manipulation of information that is no longer directly available to the senses. Neurologically speaking, the most general feature of working memory is that the maintenance of sensory information depends on sustained neural activity in posterior cortical regions, whereas working memory control of these posterior regions is exerted by prefrontal cortical regions.

2. Which particular brain regions are actively involved in working memory depends on the type of information being maintained and manipulated. The regions involved in verbal working memory tend to be left-lateralized. Posterior regions assumed to store verbal representations include left inferior parietal cortex (area 40) for phonological information, left middle temporal gyrus (area 21) for semantic information, and left inferior temporal cortex for word form information.

3. Regions associated with verbal rehearsal processes include Broca's area for phonological information and the anterior portion of the left inferior frontal gyrus (areas 45/47).

4. Regions involved in nonverbal visual working memory tend to be right-lateralized and differ for spatial and object working memory.

5. Visuospatial working memory involves a network that includes intraparietal sulcus (area 7) and the frontal eye fields (area 8), the former associated with spatial representation and the latter with oculomotor coding.

6. Visual object working memory has been related to sustained activity in occipito-temporal regions, with different subregions supporting the maintenance of different object categories, such as faces and houses. The control of object maintenance involves the right inferior frontal regions.

7. As in the case of visual working memory, working memory in other modalities tend to involve unimodal sensory regions, such as auditory cortex for auditory working memory and somatosensory cortex for somatic sensory working memory.

8. Dorsolateral prefrontal regions are assumed to mediate general control over working memory operations for all modalities.

Additional Reading

Reviews

BADDELEY, A. (2003) Working memory: Looking back and looking forward. *Nat. Rev. Neurosci.* 4: 829–839.

CURTIS, C. E. AND M. D'ESPOSITO (2006) Functional neuroimaging of working memory. In *Handbook of Functional Neuroimaging of Cognition,* 2nd Ed., R. Cabeza and A. Kingstone (eds.). Cambridge, MA: MIT Press, pp 269–306.

GOLDMAN-RAKIC, P. S. (1995) Architecture of the prefrontal cortex and the central executive. *Ann. NY Acad. Sci.* 769: 71–83.

WAGER, T. D. AND E. E. SMITH (2003) Neuroimaging studies of working memory: A meta-analysis. *Cogn. Affect Behav. Neurosci.* 3: 255–274.

Important Original Papers

COURTNEY, S. M., L. PETIT, J. M. MAISOG, L. G. UNGERLEIDER AND J. V. HAXBY (1998) An area specialized for spatial working memory in human frontal cortex. *Science* 279: 1347–1351.

D'ESPOSITO, M., B. R. POSTLE, D. BALLARD AND J. LEASE (1999) Maintenance versus manipulation of information held in working memory: An event-related fMRI study. *Brain and Cognition* 41: 66–86.

FUSTER, J. M. AND J. P. JERVEY (1981) Inferotemporal neurons distinguish and retain behaviorally relevant features of visual stimuli. *Science* 212: 952–955.

MIYASHITA, Y. AND H. S. CHANG (1988) Neuronal correlate of pictorial short-term memory in the primate temporal cortex. *Nature* 331: 68–70.

PAULESU, E., C. D. FRITH AND R. S. J. FRACKOWIAK (1993) The neural correlates of the verbal component of working memory. *Nature* 362: 342–345.

ROWE, J. B., I. TONI, O. JOSEPHS, R. S. J. FRACKOWIAK AND R. E. PASSINGHAM (2000) The prefrontal cortex: Response selection or maintenance within working memory? *Science* 288: 1656–1660.

SAKAI, K., J. B. ROWE AND R. E. PASSINGHAM (2002) Active maintenance in prefrontal area 46 creates distractor-resistant memory. *Nat. Neurosci.* 5: 479–484.

WILSON, F. A. W., S. P. O'SCALAIDHE AND P. S. GOLDMAN-RAKIC (1993) Dissociation of object and spatial processing domains in primate prefrontal cortex. *Science* 260: 1955–1958.

Books

MIYAKE, A. AND P. SHAH (2001) *Models of Working Memory*. Cambridge: Cambridge University Press.

FUSTER J. M. (2003) *Cortex and Mind: Unifying Cognition*. New York: Oxford University Press.

UNIT VI

Principles of Emotion and Social Cognition

Our discussion of cognitive functions has so far largely neglected the question of how behavior is shaped by an individual's emotions, motivation, and the social context that necessarily accompanies any human activity. However, the emotional, social, and cognitive aspects of brain function are central factors in mobilizing bodily resources appropriate to circumstances, to evaluating goals, to setting priorities for action based on conscious and unconscious goals, and for interacting appropriately with others. From a purely biological perspective, emotions and an appreciation of social contexts help humans and other animals survive and reproduce successfully. Although neuroscience has sometimes neglected these complex influences on what we think and do in favor of issues that can be more readily understood in reductionist terms, it has become increasingly clear that emotional and social influences are amenable to the same conceptual and methodological approaches that have been used to successfully study other cognitive functions.

Accordingly, this unit reviews the history, cognitive psychology, and neural substrates of social and emotional processes and their interactions with other cognitive systems. Historically, studies of emotion have often been framed in a psychosomatic tradition that attempted to understand how bodily reactions are linked to brain function. This work ultimately led to the so-called visceral-brain hypothesis in the mid twentieth century; because of the brain regions involved, this perspective became known as the *limbic system theory of emotion*.

Although investigators have long since recognized that a broader perspective is required to bring together the many neural systems involved, at present there is no agreed-upon neurobiological account of how visceral (autonomic), emotional, and social information interacts. Nonetheless, there is much to say about emotions and how they influence other cognitive and social functions, as the following chapters make plain. Despite the absence of a unified theory of emotion and social behavior, these topics remain very much in the forefront of contemporary cognitive neuroscience. ■

17

Overview of Emotions

Introduction

Echoing Plato, the eighteenth-century philosopher Immanuel Kant stated that "there are three absolutely irreducible faculties of the mind, namely *knowledge, feeling*, and *desire.*" In today's scientific parlance, the terms for this mental trilogy would be *cognition, emotion*, and *motivation*. Of these faculties, emotional aspects of brain function have proved especially difficult to study and, until recently, were relatively ignored. Behaviorism in the early twentieth century focused on quantifiable behavioral observations and laws governing stimulus-response relations. Harvard psychologist B. Frederick Skinner went so far as to argue that the "private events" of emotion are outside the realm of objective assessment. Skinner's pessimism arose from the historical idea that emotions were merely subjective reflections of the bodily states elicited by stimuli. Because feelings require introspection and verbal articulation, their investigation was taken to be impossible in non-human animals and prelingual infants. The mid-twentieth-century cognitive revolution in psychology moved researchers even further from the study of emotion and motivation (see Chapter 2). Around the same time, the advent of the computer as a metaphor for the rational mind led others to view emotions as entirely cognitive constructs! Despite these various impediments, a great deal of progress has been made in recent decades in understanding how emotions are organized in psychological terms, and how they are represented in the brain. This chapter outlines this history and defines the terms and modern approaches being used in the rapidly growing field of affective neuroscience.

What Is an Emotion?

Psychologists tend to define **emotion** in terms of conscious feelings, like love, jealousy, contempt, anger, and despair. Because consciousness itself defies clear neurobiological explanation (see Chapter 28), defining emotions merely in terms of conscious states is problematic. Among other difficulties,

Figure 17.1 The components of emotions. Emotions can be broken down into three components, each of which can be studied independently: behavioral action (a motor output, such as social approach); conscious experience (a subjective feeling, such as love); and physiological expression (autonomic activity, such as increased heart rate). In emotional health, these components are generally integrated into a coherent pattern that defines particular emotions and leads to the facilitation of biologically useful responses. In various forms of psychopathology, however, these normal patterns are discordant. For example, patients who suffer from schizophrenia often show increased autonomic arousal despite reduced motor output. Consequently, it is sometimes difficult to understand why patients with schizophrenia react to situations by observation of their behavior alone.

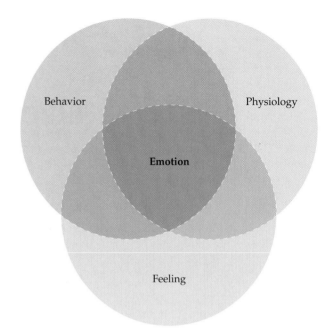

such a definition implies that organisms with less self-awareness do not experience emotional feelings to the degree that humans do. Yet, as Charles Darwin noted in the late nineteenth century, many non-human animal species produce affective displays during predator-prey interactions, sex and mating, and maternal care of the young that are similar to those observed in humans. Researchers now conceptualize emotion as a composite of *feelings*, *expressive behavior*, and *physiological changes* (**Figure 17.1**).

Emotions are neurally based dispositions that facilitate appropriate reactions to events of biological significance, thus achieving better outcomes that ultimately influence evolutionary success. To illustrate, a basic emotion like fear at the sight of a predator engages defensive behavior that prepares the organism either to fight or to flee, by redistributing blood flow from internal organs to peripheral muscle fibers, releasing stress hormones, increasing sensory vigilance, facilitating startle reflexes, and altering breathing, heart rate, and blood pressure. As described in Chapter 18, this physiological repertoire can be elicited by otherwise innocuous sensory stimuli through the principles of classical conditioning, thus enabling appropriate behavior through mechanisms of learning and memory. In some individuals, such learned associations may also contribute to the development of phobias and other affective disorders.

Comparing patterns of behavior and physiology to common elicitors across species makes the study of specific emotions like fear tractable in experimental animals. Examining *emotion families* (like fear, anxiety, terror, horror) in different species also permits inferences about the shared neural substrates of similar emotions. In addition, comparative studies provide insight into how emotional systems break down in various mood and anxiety disorders. This expanded view of emotion has thus opened the door to developing animal models essential for understanding the neurobiological basis of emotions in health and disease.

Accordingly, emotions are defined here as sets of physiological responses, action tendencies, and subjective feelings that adaptively engage humans and other animals to react to events of biological and/or individual significance.

This definition has several corollaries. First, emotions are typically triggered by a specific event in the local environment, although in humans spontaneous thoughts or memories can also trigger emotions. Second, emotions include behavioral and physiological changes that may not be accessible to conscious awareness but are nonetheless amenable to scientific investigation. Third, emotions specifically facilitate social interactions that are beneficial to individual survival and propagation of the species. By investigating emotional reactions in individuals, across cultures and species, it is possible to determine the neurophysiological signatures of specific emotions and, in humans, to relate them to self-reported feelings.

Mood, Affect, and Motivation

To be adaptive in continually changing circumstances, emotions must be (and are) relatively short-lived. The physiological changes elicited by emotion-inducing stimuli typically develop and dissipate on the order of seconds to minutes. Emotional states that endure for longer periods are called **moods**. Moods engage other cognitive operations, such as working memory, to sustain the internal state in the absence of an eliciting stimulus. Unlike emotions, moods are often triggered without a clear antecedent event or thought. Moods have been studied largely within the context of disorders such as clinical depression, although some work has characterized the effects of experimentally manipulated mood on cognitive abilities, including memory (see Chapter 18).

The term **affect** is often used as a synonym for *emotion*, although most clinicians think of affect as the outward expression of emotion, which usually reflects an internal feeling. Affective displays include changes in facial expression, vocal inflection (*prosody*), posture, gestures, or the physiological end products of autonomic activity (e.g., production of tears). *Affect intensity* refers to the degree to which an individual experiences and expresses emotions. Someone who displays a "flat" affect is relatively unemotional in response to life's ups and downs. In contrast, someone who is emotionally labile exhibits large swings in affect.

Whereas *affect* usually describes an individual's current state, **temperament** refers to an individual's general predisposition to experience events as pleasant or unpleasant. For example, some individuals tend to react with rage to confrontational situations, whereas others keep their cool. Temperament depends on both experiential and genetic factors and is a component of an individual's personality. In other circumstances, affective displays do not match internal states. For instance, when intentionally deceiving others or in some social contexts, an outward affective display may mask an underlying feeling. Such display rules for emotion vary considerably across cultures according to norms of decorum and social status.

Motives are defined as basic needs or desires that cause a person to act and thereby determine goal-oriented behavior. At a basic physiological level, motivated behavior is driven by homeostatic mechanisms like thirst, hunger, and sleep, which serve as incentives for action to reduce drives, in addition to those related to emotion specifically. Of course, many complex cognitive and social factors influence an individual's motives. Whereas the circumstances that elicit emotion are most often immediate (e.g., receiving a bad grade on an exam), motivational drives are typically less immediate (e.g., setting an academic achievement goal).

In many cases, however, emotion and **motivation** are closely intertwined; emotions are often evoked when motives are achieved or thwarted, and thus they can be indicators of an underlying motivational state. Conversely, emotions influence motives by activating approach or withdrawal behaviors. For instance, a student who wants to graduate with high honors is highly motivated to study. After receiving a bad grade, however, the student's emotional response (say, anger or dejection) may lead to behavior (not studying) that reduces the likelihood of attaining the goal. As this example illustrates, reward and punishment contingencies are important regulators of both emotion and motivation.

Methodological Issues in Emotion Research

Workers in the field of emotion research are confronted not only with ethical issues of the sort described in **Box 17A** but with a host of methodological problems as well. One set of such issues concerns the difficulty of obtaining the needed neurobiological measurements. As described later in the chapter, many emotional functions are mediated by subcortical structures deep within the brain, such as the amygdala and the hypothalamus. Unfortunately, methods that measure or perturb predominantly cortical activity (EEG recordings from the scalp, transcranial magnetic stimulation) are relatively insensitive to activity changes in such structures; and other techniques, such as fMRI and PET imaging, also have problems extracting signals from deep brain struc-

---

■ BOX 17A Ethical Issues in Emotion Research: The Case of Traumatic Memories

A specific example that underscores ethical issues in emotion research is the condition known as *posttraumatic stress disorder* (*PTSD*). PTSD emerges following exposure to a traumatic stressor that elicits fear, horror, or helplessness and involves bodily injury or threat of death to oneself or another person. Community-based studies in the United States estimate that 50 percent of people will have a traumatic experience during their lifetime, but only about 5 percent of men and 10 percent of women will develop PTSD. Diagnostic symptoms include persistently reexperiencing the traumatic event, avoiding reminders of the event, numbed responsiveness, and heightened arousal.

Researchers and clinicians interested in studying and treating patients who suffer from PTSD face many challenges. Since it is generally considered unethical to induce physical or psychological trauma in the laboratory, how should the topic be approached scientifically? For instance, is it ethical to have PTSD patients relive their painful past experiences for the purpose of evoking emotions in the labo-

ratory? As new treatments develop, additional dilemmas emerge. If a pharmacological agent selectively blocks emotional memories, should it be administered to all rape victims? Finally, if a genetic variant of a molecular marker is discovered to be a risk factor for developing PTSD, should military recruits be screened for it? Researchers must carefully consider how potential adverse outcomes of their experiments can be minimized and how their findings should be applied in clinical contexts.

Thus, the study of emotion, more than other domains of cognitive neuroscience, raises special ethical concerns. On the one hand, a primary goal of emotion research is to improve the human condition and alleviate the suffering of patients afflicted with affective disorders. It is therefore incumbent on researchers to study emotional phenomena that mimic or reactivate the emotions associated with the disorder of interest. If emotions are evoked only weakly in the laboratory, the mechanisms uncovered may bear little resemblance to those that operate in the real world.

On the other hand, there is always a concern for causing harm to a study volunteer. As with all other scientific research, a balance must be struck between the risks posed to an individual participant and the ultimate benefit to society as a whole.

There are no clear-cut answers to the questions posed here. As technology enables more detailed probing of the emotional brain, researchers must always establish and update acceptable practices according to institutional standards and the standards of the community at large.

References
GLANNON, W. (2006) Neuroethics. *Bioethics* 20: 37–52.

CANLI, T. AND Z. AMIN (2002) Neuroimaging of emotion and personality: Scientific evidence and ethical considerations. *Brain Cogn.* 50: 414–431.

KESSLER, R. C., A. SONNEGA, E. BROMET, M. HUGHES AND C. B. NELSON (1995) Posttraumatic stress disorder in the National Comorbidity Survey. *Arch. Gen. Psychiatry* 52: 1048–1060.

tures (see Chapter 3). Nonetheless, technical advances have enabled useful studies of the neural basis of emotions both in healthy individuals and in patients with brain lesions that affect emotional behavior.

A second set of problems arises from the fact that these subcortical structures exert emotional influences on cortical processing both directly via neural connections and indirectly by hormonal actions. The hormones of interest (such as adrenal corticoids) are secreted peripherally as a result of subcortical processing and subsequently influence cortical neurons that express hormone receptor molecules. Monitoring such changes requires the ability to observe activity simultaneously in cortical and subcortical brain regions. In experimental animals, this simultaneous observation can be accomplished by multi-unit electrode recording; in humans, by brain imaging techniques such as PET. However, the longer time courses of hormonal actions and the enduring quality of moods are difficult to assess with techniques that basically capture snapshots of mental activity. Combining information from multiple methodologies is thus necessary to understand how emotional information processing is integrated across subcortical to cortical levels, and across central and peripheral actions.

A third set of methodological issues relates to the behavioral quantification and analysis of emotion. In recent years, the development of tests of emotional function has advanced greatly, but assessment is still complicated by the subjective nature of emotional experience and the reliance on introspection. Self-reporting inventories are commonly used by clinicians to assess personality traits such as extroversion and emotional status such as anxiety level. However, these measures are susceptible to factors that are difficult to control, including daily fluctuations in the circumstances of a person's life, and social factors such as the presence of an examiner. Despite these difficulties, objective test batteries and emotional-stimulus databases have been validated and norms established across different cultural, age, gender, and socioeconomic groups for at least some aspects of emotion (see the example in **Box 17B**).

A final problem to consider concerns the variability of emotional expression both within and across individuals, which can mask brain-behavior relationships when data analysis techniques rely on averaging across trials and subjects. For instance, ERP or fMRI activity in various brain regions in response to sad music may differ according to the current mood of each participant in the study. Consequently, averaging the data across all the individuals in the study may give an unclear or even false picture of the neural correlates of the affective perceptions elicited by music. Many researchers have taken advantage of the **individual difference** approach to characterize how variability in emotional behavior systematically relates to brain function. In the example just given, a researcher can correlate an index of brain activity, such as the hemodynamic response of primary auditory cortex, with scores on a self-report inventory of current mood in individual participants. Clinically, this approach is useful for determining how brain activity in psychiatric patients varies as a function of treatment, since cognitive or drug therapies can be more or less successful in particular individuals.

Psychological Theories of Emotional Organization

Theories about how emotions are organized and related to one another have evolved greatly over the years. This section describes the major psychological perspectives on these issues, and the following section indicates how these ideas have been informed and refined as newer methods have examined and clarified the neural bases of emotional behavior.

■ BOX 17B Standardized Tests and Stimulus Databases for Studying Depression and Facial Expression

Many neuropsychological batteries that test for emotional functions rely on self-reports of individuals (or, for some patients, their caregivers) to provide information about their emotional behavior or feelings. Such tests often take the form of a checklist of possible symptoms or a series of statements that serve as indicators of a person's current emotional status or general temperament. For example, in the 1960s psychologist Aaron Beck of the University of Pennsylvania created the *Beck Depression Inventory* (*BDI*) to screen for the presence of depressive symptoms. The BDI, which has been revised and is still in common use today, is a 21-item, 4-choice checklist of statements that probe various features of depression, including sadness, suicidal ideation, social withdrawal, and loss of appetite.

The BDI has a standard set of instructions to ensure uniform administration, and it assesses symptoms occurring within the 7 days prior to the date of testing. The level of depression is determined by summing the individual's scores across the items. As with all other neuropsychological batteries, the BDI has been tested for its *validity* (its ability to measure depression in terms of its cognitive and somatic features) and its *reliability* (the repeatability of the scores for an individual participant). The BDI was not designed for children or the elderly, for whom other tests, such as the Children's Depression Inventory and the Geriatric Depression Scale, are available. The BDI does not measure frequency or duration of depressive states and naturally is of no use in individuals who simply deny their symptoms. Such neuropsychological test batteries must always be interpreted in the context of a broader clinical evaluation and professional judgment.

In addition to standardized neuropsychological tests, research on emotion has benefited from the development of stimulus databases and data-coding systems. In the 1970s, Paul Ekman, working at UC San Francisco (UCSF), compiled a series of photographs of Caucasian and Asian adult faces expressing the basic emotions of fear, anger, sadness, happiness, surprise, and disgust (see Figure 17.2). To validate the photographs of facial affect, participants from various cultures were asked to identify the emotions expressed by the actors in the photos. Even preliterate tribes in New Guinea and Borneo were able to do this effectively.

This sort of universal recognition provides further evidence for Darwin's contention that emotions have a common, inherited form of expression. Some researchers have criticized the methods that Ekman used for cross-cultural validation in that subjects had to choose among certain emotional labels and match these to facial expressions. Recent work using unconstrained emotion recognition questions, however, has largely con-

Categorical theories

Categorical theories regard each emotion as a discrete entity and typically distinguish a small set of basic emotions from a larger pool of complex emotions. **Basic emotions** are taken to be innate, pan-cultural, evolutionarily old, shared with other species, and expressed by particular physiological patterns and facial configurations. In contrast, **complex emotions** are learned, socially and culturally shaped, evolutionarily new, most evident in humans, and typically expressed by combinations of the response patterns that characterize the basic emotions. Complex emotions are influenced by language use and emerge later in development. Researchers interested in distinguishing and classifying basic and complex emotions use techniques that monitor physiological responses, as well as techniques for coding and analyzing facial or vocal expressions (see Figure 17.2 and Box 17B). Because basic emotions can be studied readily in non-human animals, the biology of this set of emotions has been the best characterized to date.

Nonetheless, researchers still debate about which emotions are basic. Although the list of basic emotions ranges from 4 to about 10 items in different theories, fear, anger, surprise, sadness (distress), happiness (joy), and disgust are included in most schemes (**Figure 17.2**). Even basic emotions like disgust take on nuanced forms and expanded functions in humans. Paul Rozin and his colleagues at the University of Pennsylvania showed that moral disgust is elicited by acts that violate an individual's innocence or integrity, such as rape. The facial expression of moral disgust emphasizes the upper lip curl-

firmed the original findings. The Ekman facial affect series remains one of the best characterized to date and is widely used, although more modern databases with a wider variety of facial stimuli are being developed.

Developing stimulus sets of facial affect is challenging because not all actors pose expressions with the same intensity or using exactly the same alterations of facial musculature (called *physiognomy*). Exemplars of facial-affect photographs must be rated by a large sample of individuals across cultures and races to establish norms in determining which featural changes prototypically indicate a given expression. To provide an objective tool for analyzing facial movements, including those elicited by particular emotions, Ekman, along with his UCSF colleague Wallace Friesen, subsequently developed a *facial-action coding system* (*FACS*). FACS is an anatomy-based system for coding 44 visible facial-action units controlled by specific facial muscles. Because each muscle may control more than one movement, action units rather than muscle movements are counted. Intensity of change

in each action unit is coded on a five-point scale, and the relative timing of each action unit can be indicated.

FACS coding has been widely applied to quantify the facial movements present in recorded video images of spontaneous and posed facial expressions of emotion. In fact, Lisa Parr and her colleagues, working at the Yerkes National Primate Research Center at Emory University, have developed an analogous coding system for chimpanzees. Not surprisingly, assessments of facial movement are difficult and time-consuming, and those who evaluate such data must pass a certification test to use the coding system. Data obtained from a certified FACS coder can be compared to a computerized Affect Interpretation Database to determine whether the coded action units match the expression of particular emotions. Electromyographic recording from facial muscles during emotional expression has also verified aspects of the coding system.

Nevertheless, behavioral and physiological measures do not always provide identical information, because electrical changes do not necessarily

yield observable actions, and electrical recordings can sum activity across more than one muscle. This line of work has extended findings compiled by the nineteenth-century neurologist G.-B. Duchenne de Boulogne, who used electrical stimulation to elicit the contraction of specific facial muscles in studies of facial affect (see Chapter 8). This approach to emotional expression emphasizes changes in specific facial features. However, it is the combination of features that yields unique emotional expressions, and holistic (synthetic) analysis of facial configurations is just as important as, if not more important than, feature-based analyses when the emotional states of others are interpreted from their facial displays.

References

BECK, A. T. (1970) *Depression: Causes and Treatment.* Philadelphia: University of Pennsylvania Press.

EKMAN, P. AND W. V. FRIESEN (1976) *Unmasking the Face: A Guide to Recognizing Emotions from Facial Clues.* Englewood Cliffs, NJ: Prentice-Hall.

Anger

Sadness

Happiness

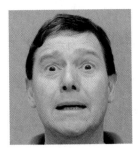

Fear

Disgust

Surprise

Figure 17.2 Categorical theories of emotion. Posed facial expressions are taken to exemplify discrete emotion categories. Emotions typically classified as *basic* are depicted and include (from left to right and top to bottom) anger, sadness, happiness, fear, disgust, and surprise. Note that most of the basic emotions are unpleasant in valence.

ing over the wrinkled nose that accompanies disgust in response to a bad taste or smell.

As an indicator of the sorts of problems that these more subtle distinctions raise, the distinction between disgust and contempt is continually debated. Contempt is another emotion (considered to be basic in some theories) that reflects reactions to violations of community standards, such as defrauding poor individuals with financial scams. Contempt is expressed by a modified disgust facial display that is often restricted to one side of the face and lacking tongue protrusion. The common linguistic use of the word *disgust* to indicate contempt sometimes confuses the issue, contributing to the difficulty of sorting out these emotional categories.

As one might expect, not only are complex emotions more difficult than basic emotions to categorize, but they are also more difficult to study for several reasons. First, the external features of expression are more subtle; second, context varies more; and finally, cross-cultural differences are more prominent. Take the emotion pride as an example. Pride is elicited when a person takes credit for achieving a positive outcome on a personal accomplishment that boosts self-esteem, such as winning a marathon or a chess tournament. This response to success following challenging circumstances is expressed by a modest smile combined with erect postural gestures of dominance (shoulders back, chin up, arms raised). The unique body profile, which is harder to quantify than facial expression, tends to distinguish pride from other positive emotions. There are also wide variations in the circumstances and frequency with which pride is expressed in social settings, because of individual value systems (e.g., people may feel quite differently about how boastful to be in the presence of authority figures). A cross-cultural complication is that some Asian cultures promote an expanded concept of self that includes relatives or the larger community. In these cultures, expressions of pride arising from one's own accomplishments may be viewed negatively and are often curtailed.

Dimensional theories

In contrast to categorical theories, **dimensional theories** consider each emotion a point on a continuum that varies along two or more fundamental axes. Most researchers consider **arousal** (the physiological and/or subjective intensity of the emotion) and **valence** (its relative pleasantness or unpleasantness) to be critical dimensions. Researchers in this tradition use techniques that enable analyses on ordinal scales. For instance, subjects might be asked to rate movie clips that vary in emotional content on nine-point valence scales ranging from "very unpleasant" to "very pleasant." Two models of this sort have been proposed.

One way to represent emotions dimensionally is to use **vector models**. Vector models tend to order emotions along axes of positive and negative valence that are oriented at 90 degrees and meet at a common neutral endpoint, forming a boomerang shape (**Figure 17.3A**). In these models, arousal is represented according to the distance from the neutral endpoint along each arm of the boomerang and is functionally equivalent to increases in valence. Alternatively, the motivational concepts of approach (activation) and avoidance (inhibition) can be used as the axes. Vector models have been supported by experimental studies that ask participants to rate the emotional properties of pictures, sounds, and/or memories.

In contrast to vector models, **circumplex models** order emotions around the circumference of a circle centered at the intersection of two orthogonal axes of arousal and valence (**Figure 17.3B**). The arousal dimension varies from low (calm) to high (excited), and the valence dimension varies from unpleasant to pleasant, with neutral in the middle. Emotions that cluster together in the resulting graph are taken to be similar in their dimensional features. Stud-

(A) Vector model

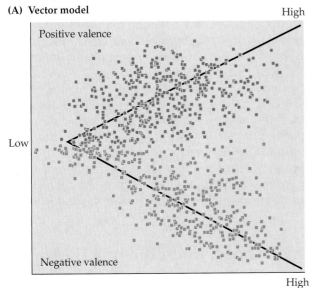

(B) Circumplex model

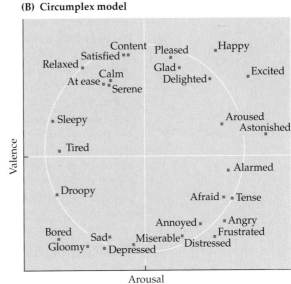

Figure 17.3 Dimensional theories of emotion: the vector and circumplex models. (A) Vector models are supported by studies in which participants rate pictures on ordinal scales of arousal and valence. The ratings are then plotted on two co-terminating axes that reflect unipolar dimensions of positive and negative valence. Plotting the mean ratings by a large number of individuals to hundreds of pictures results in a boomerang shape in which the most arousing stimuli of each valence are plotted the farthest away from the neutral endpoint that joins the two axes. Individual pictures that are rated similarly cluster together on the boomerang. (B) Circumplex models are supported by studies in which participants rate words on ordinal scales of arousal and valence. The ratings are then plotted on orthogonal axes of arousal (activation) and valence (pleasantness) that intersect in the middle of the scales. Words that represent similar emotions cluster together along the circumference of the circle. (A after Lang et al. 1993; B after Russell 1980.)

ies that ask participants to rate the emotional properties of words, facial expressions, and music tend to support the validity of this class of models. Dimensional models are also tested with psychophysiological measures that index arousal and valence, as described in **Box 17C**.

Either circumplex or vector dimensional models can represent individual emotions. However, the genesis of individual emotions is accounted for simply by their position along valence-arousal or approach-avoidance axes. As a result, dimensional theorists don't look for discrete neural systems underlying each emotion but argue that seeking the neural correlates of the dimensional axes will be more fruitful.

Component process theories

Newer psychological approaches to emotion are based on **component process theories** (**Table 17.1**). Rather than viewing emotions as fixed states, component process theories attempt to capture the fluid nature of emotions, which

■ **TABLE 17.1 Component Processes That Invoke Appraisal Mechanisms Shared by Some Emotions and Not Others**

Appraisal criterion	Joy	Anger	Fear	Sadness
Novelty	High	High	High	Low
Pleasantness	High	Open	Low	Open
Goal significance				
Outcome certainty	High	Very high	High	Very high
Conduciveness	Conducive	Obstructive	Obstructive	Obstructive
Urgency	Low	High	Very high	Low
Coping potential				
Agency	Self/other	Other	Other	Open
Control	High	High	Open	Very low
Power	High	High	Very low	Very low
Adjustment	High	High	Low	Medium

require flexible interactions of multiple component processes. These theories emphasize the role of cognitive appraisal in evaluating the emotional meaning of events, as well as the link between the appraisal outcome and a behavioral and physiological response. In this view, emotions are related according to the similarity of the appraisal processes engaged.

Klaus Scherer of the University of Geneva has argued that important appraisals include the sense of urgency for action in response to the elicitor, how well a person can cope with the presence of the elicitor, and whether the elicitor facilitates or impedes progress toward a goal. Emotions are thus organized in the brain according to their overlap in recruiting specific appraisal mechanisms, which may vary across individuals according to social and cultural influences. So far, component process models have not been extensively tested with the neuroscience methods that have been applied to other models.

The Generation of Emotions: Neurobiological Ideas

The generation of emotions can be characterized in terms of three processing stages: (1) the *evaluation* of sensory input; (2) the conscious (or unconscious) *experience* of a feeling; and (3) the *expression* of behavioral and physiological responses. Neurobiological accounts have differed over the years in how these stages are related to one another conceptually, anatomically, and temporally.

The James-Lange feedback theory

The late-nineteenth-century psychologist William James posed the following question about emotion: "Do we run from a bear because we are afraid, or are we afraid because we run?" Although most of us would submit that the act of running from a bear is initiated by a fearful feeling, James took the opposite stance. For him, the act of running itself (combined with increased sweating, rapid breathing, increased heart rate, and other physiological manifestations) generates the fear. Thus, for James (and for others like James's contemporary Duchenne, the French neurologist mentioned in Box 17B), the experience of an emotion depended on a prior set of changes in the body that feeds back onto the brain (**Figure 17.4**).

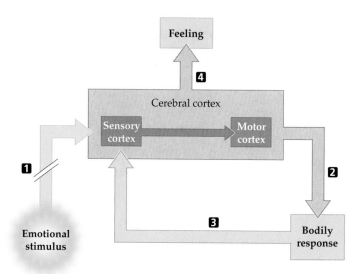

Figure 17.4 The James-Lange feedback theory of emotion. An eliciting stimulus (1) directly causes a bodily reaction (2), which feeds back into the brain (3) to generate an emotional feeling (4). According to this theory, no specialized brain region for processing emotion exists, and bodily reactions and feelings have a one-to-one functional correspondence.

This theory rests on two assumptions: first, that a deterministic relationship exists between bodily reactions and emotions; and second, that no emotions are felt in the absence of bodily reactions, since those reactions are causal. James did allow for individual differences in emotion and acknowledged that situational context may alter the response profile. Nonetheless, in this view the physiological pattern for each emotion must be reasonably consistent among individuals.

The Danish physiologist Carl Lange also proposed a feedback theory at about the same time. Although James accommodated other bodily feedback signals, such as those arising from the facial musculature (as emphasized by Duchenne), Lange postulated that cardiac function was most relevant for emotion. Lange was less concerned about explaining conscious awareness of emotion (which is not surprising, given that, unlike James, he was a physiologist). Despite differences in theoretical orientation, these early feedback ideas of emotion are referred to as the **James-Lange theory**.

James did not postulate dedicated neural structures for emotional processing, but Lange felt that brainstem nuclei that control cardiac function were important. Lange believed that specific feelings emerged directly from the pattern of feedback obtained from the periphery onto diffuse cortical sites. This theory nevertheless highlighted the relationship between brain activity and physiological reactions—an idea that was further developed in the early twentieth century by a wealth of information about the functions and anatomy of the autonomic nervous system.

The Cannon-Bard theory

A generation after James and Lange, Harvard physiologist Walter Cannon and his student Philip Bard challenged their theory. Cannon and Bard argued that responses of the **autonomic nervous system** (see Chapter 8) were too undifferentiated to yield the variety of emotional states that we experience. For example, flushing of the skin increases during embarrassment, anger, and sexual arousal. Therefore, the presence of a specific peripheral response could not uniquely determine which emotion would be felt. Cannon and Bard further argued that neurohormonal feedback from the body's endocrine organs to the brain would take too long to account for the abrupt onset of emotions (although feedback from the facial musculature potentially could).

Finally, hormonal feedback was shown to be insufficient to generate emotions; systemic injection of hormones, such as norepinephrine (which stimulates a variety of sympathetic responses associated with emotions such as fear and anger) does not consistently result in a particular emotional state. Cannon and Bard instead suggested that the autonomic nervous system coordinates the body's general *fight-or-flight* response, which mobilizes the body's resources in preparation for appropriate action in an emotional conflict. This view is more aligned with the arousal-activation axis proposed by dimensional theories of emotion.

Cannon and Bard investigated the effects of surgically disconnecting the cerebral cortex from the brainstem and other subcortical nuclei in experimental animals (**Figure 17.5**). They found that decorticate animals could exhibit

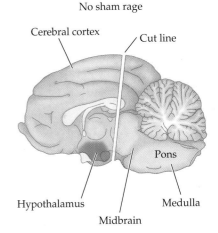

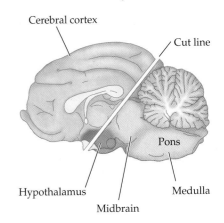

Figure 17.5 Emotions in decorticate animals. Transection experiments show that decorticate animals can express an integrated emotional reaction such as sham rage, but only if the neural pathways are interrupted above the level of the diencephalon. Cuts below the diencephalon disconnect the forebrain from the rest of the body and preclude centrally generated autonomic and motor control.

■ BOX 17C Psychophysiological Indices of Emotional Arousal and Valence

Psychophysiology is a scientific discipline that relates psychological constructs such as emotion to measurable changes in the body. Two indices that have been particularly useful for distinguishing emotions along the dimensions of arousal and valence are *skin conductance* and *startle responses*. The **skin conductance response (SCR)** is an index of electrodermal activity taken from electrodes placed over the palmar surface of the hands and feet. At these locations, eccrine sweat glands are highly concentrated (about 1000 glands/cm²; glands of another class—the apocrine glands—are located in the armpit and pubic regions). Activity of the sweat glands during emotional arousal, as is commonly experienced during public speaking, increases the electrical conductance of the skin surface. The biological benefits of this response are not entirely clear, but arguably they include grip strength, protection against wounds, improved tactile discrimination, and heat reduction via evaporation. Eccrine sweat gland activity as a result of arousal is mediated solely by the sympathetic nervous system; thus, skin conductance is a good measure of

the sympathetic response to arousing circumstances, and by the same token a good indicator of the arousal levels associated with specific emotions.

Several different aspects of the skin conductance response can be assessed. The average skin conductance level over time is a measure of the basal (tonic) level of arousal. Spontaneous fluctuations in the baseline level are taken as measures of anxiety or contextual fear because they occur in the absence of a particular sensory stimulus. Finally, phasic skin conductance responses are amplitude modulations that have a characteristic time course and profile time-locked to the onset of a sensory stimulus (Figure A). The fact that the temporal profile of this response is similar to that of the hemodynamic response measured with fMRI conveniently facilitates the design of studies that combine the two techniques.

Because fear and anxiety are linked to high arousal states, the skin conductance response is a good measure of these emotions, and it is widely used in "lie detector" (polygraph) tests in criminal cases. However, skin conductance is modulated by other emotions, such as sexual arousal and orienting responses to novel stimuli, complicating the interpretation of polygraph tests. Skin conductance has also been used to identify stimulus-evoked arousal responses that arise unconsciously. For instance, patients with prosopagnosia (see Chapter 19) often show skin conductance responses to pictures of family members, despite being unable to consciously recognize the individuals by sight.

The **startle response** is a protective reflex elicited by intense and unexpected sensory stimuli (e.g., a flash of light or a loud noise). Such stimuli interrupt ongoing thoughts and behav-

Psychophysiological measures of emotional states in humans. (A) Skin conductance level (SCL) is typically recorded from the second and third digits of the hand, although it can be recorded from the palm or the bottom of the foot as well. If the task requires a motor response from the hand, to avoid movement artifacts the nondominant hand is used for recording. The skin conductance change in response to a stimulus (i.e., the skin conductance response, or SCR), measured in microsiemens (μS), has a characteristic onset latency (usually 1–2 seconds after stimulus onset) and peak latency (usually 1–4 seconds later) before decaying back to baseline levels.

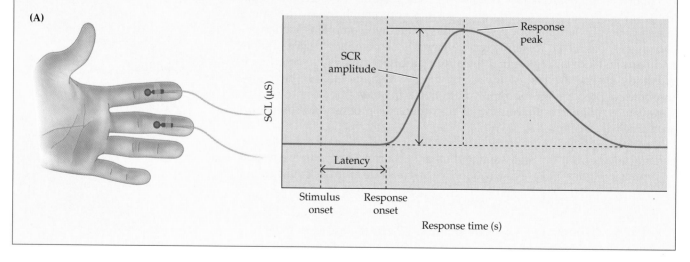

(A)

(B)

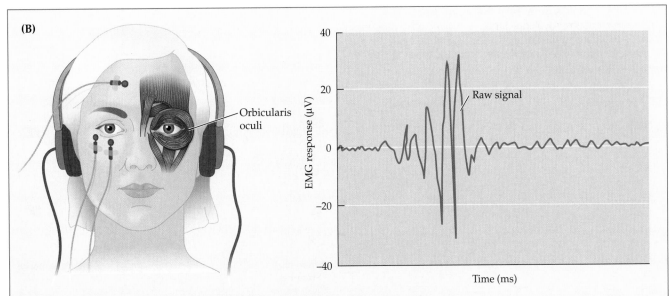

Orbicularis oculi

Raw signal

(B) The eye-blink component of the startle response can be measured by electrodes over the obicularis oculi muscle (a ground electrode is typically placed on the forehead). The electromyographic response has a rapid onset (<50 milliseconds) and a brief duration (<100 milliseconds).

ior to evaluate the location and significance of sensory input. The startle response is mediated by subcortical neural circuitry that includes the brainstem reticular formation, which plays a key role in arousal and interfaces with sensory and motor functions. This complex set of nuclei is modulated by descending corticolimbic projections, including projections from the amygdala.

A component of the startle response that is readily measured in both humans and experimental animals is the eye-blink reflex, which helps protect the eye from unexpected noxious stimuli. Eye-blink startle is measured either by electromyographic recordings of activity in the obicularis oculi muscle or by infrared monitoring of eyelid closure (Figure B). Several measures can be extracted from such recordings, including the probability of blinking in response to a stimulus, the magnitude of the blink, and its latency after the stimulus.

Startle responses are influenced by attention; for instance, when we attend to visual stimuli, startle responses to an auditory stimulus are attenuated, and vice versa. Thus, startle can be used to determine the relative allocation of sensory or other processing resources to a particular aspect of the environment. This attentional influence is modulated by emotion. Thus, in circumstances that generate fear (e.g., walking down a dark alley at night), startle responses are potentiated; a sudden noise or touch will elicit a larger startle response than in the circumstance of walking down a well-populated street during the day.

Fear-potentiated startle has been particularly beneficial in the development of animal models of anxiety disorders. In contrast, circumstances that generate positive emotions or moods reduce startle amplitude relative to baseline conditions, although this effect is generally less robust than is startle potentiation by negative emotions.

Measures such as the skin conductance and startle responses can be combined to provide powerful physiological indices of the two fundamental dimensions of emotion space: arousal and valence.

References

AMELI, R., C. IP AND C. GRILLON (2001) Contextual fear-potentiated startle conditioning in humans: Replication and extension. *Psychophysiology* 38: 383–390.

CRITCHLEY, H. D., R. ELLIOTT, C. J. MATHIAS AND R. J. DOLAN (2000) Neural activity relating to generation and representation of galvanic skin conductance responses: A functional magnetic resonance imaging study. *J. Neurosci.* 20: 3033–3040.

DAVIS, M., J. M. HITCHCOCK AND J. B. ROSEN (1991) Neural mechanisms of fear conditioning measured with the acoustic startle reflex. In *Neurobiology of Learning, Emotion, and Affect*, J. I. Madden (ed.). New York: Raven, pp. 67–96.

HUGDAHL, K. (1995) *Psychophysiology: The Mind-Body Perspective*. Cambridge, MA: Harvard University Press.

LANG, P. J., M. M. BRADLEY AND B. N. CUTHBERT (1990) Emotion, attention, and the startle reflex. *Psychol. Rev.* 97: 377–395.

ÖHMAN, A. AND J. J. SOARES (1993) On the automatic nature of phobic fear: Conditioned electrodermal responses to masked fear-relevant stimuli. *J. Abnorm. Psychol.* 102: 121–132.

Figure 17.6 The Cannon-Bard theory of emotion.
Input from emotion-provoking stimuli (1) is directed in parallel from the thalamus to the cortex directly (2b) or indirectly (2a,3b) for the generation of feelings (4), and from the thalamus to the hypothalamus (2a) for bodily expression (3a).

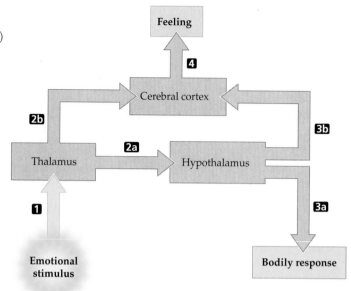

integrated emotional reactions, such as defensive behavior, only if the transection occurred above the level of the diencephalon (**hypothalamus** and **thalamus**). These findings were bolstered by the studies of Walter Hess, a contemporary who showed further that electrical stimulation of the hypothalamus elicited emotional reactions in the cat, including **sham rage**, in which hissing, growling, and attack behaviors were directed randomly toward innocuous targets.

Cannon and Bard thus proposed that when an emotional stimulus was processed by the diencephalon, it was directed simultaneously to the neocortex for the generation of emotional feelings, and to the periphery for the expression of emotional reactions (**Figure 17.6**). This theory is known as the **Cannon-Bard theory** (or *diencephalic theory*) of emotion, and it represents one of the first parallel-processing models of brain function—a theme in brain organization that appears in many contexts in cognitive neuroscience (see Chapters 2 and 5). This theory's focus on the hypothalamus emphasizes the key relationship between emotional information processing in the brain and the activity of the autonomic nervous system. It also paved the way for more elaborate parallel-processing models of emotion.

Early ideas about the limbic forebrain

Working at Cornell University in the late 1930s, neuroanatomist James Papez described a circuit for emotion in the medial wall of the forebrain. This brain region, which the French neuroanatomist Paul Broca had earlier called *la grande lobe limbique* (the Latin word *limbus* means "rim" or "border"), is evolutionarily older than the neocortex. Structures contained within Papez's circuit straddle the diencephalon and forebrain, and include the anterior thalamus, hypothalamus, hippocampus, and cingulate gyrus (see Figure 17.10). Papez's rationale in identifying this complex was based on brain structures monosynaptically connected with the hypothalamus, the locus most central to the Cannon-Bard theory.

Papez further extended the Cannon-Bard theory by proposing that the cingulate gyrus mediated emotional feelings (**Figure 17.7**). According to his parallel-processing model of emotion, the cingulate cortex could accomplish this in two ways. The *stream of thought* (what he referred to as the "cortical route")

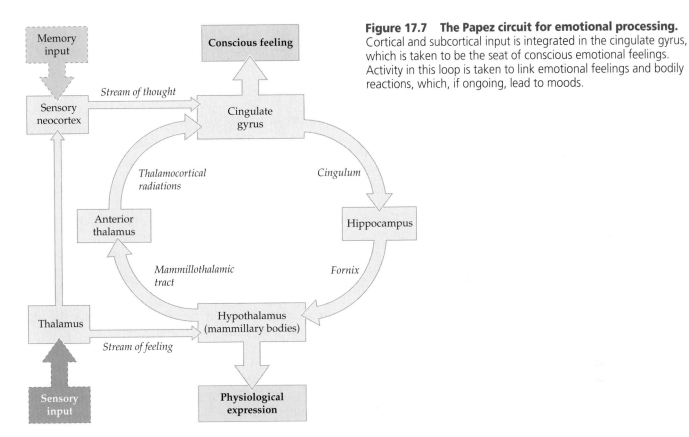

Figure 17.7   The Papez circuit for emotional processing.
Cortical and subcortical input is integrated in the cingulate gyrus, which is taken to be the seat of conscious emotional feelings. Activity in this loop is taken to link emotional feelings and bodily reactions, which, if ongoing, lead to moods.

carried sensory input from the thalamus to the sensory neocortex and on to the **cingulate gyrus**. Papez also envisioned activation of the cingulate by memories stored in the neocortex. The *stream of feeling* (subcortical route) in Papez's view carried sensory input from the thalamus to the mammillary bodies of the hypothalamus, which projects to the cingulate gyrus via the anterior thalamus. To close the loop, neurons in the cingulate gyrus project back down to the hypothalamus by way of the hippocampus via the white matter tracts that form the fornix. For Papez, then, the cingulate gyrus was the center in the brain that integrated subcortical and cortical emotional processing; reverberation of activity in this circuit thus provided a substrate for the reciprocal influence of emotional feelings and bodily reactions.

About the same time that Papez was carrying out this anatomical research, Heinrich Klüver and Paul Bucy at the University of Chicago were investigating the effects of mescaline on the brain. They hypothesized that the temporal lobes were important in the mastication behaviors that accompany mescaline use, which resemble those seen in some patients with temporal lobe epilepsy. By surgically removing the temporal lobes in a rhesus monkey, they made the following remarkable (and quite serendipitous) observations:

> The animal does not exhibit the reactions generally associated with anger and fear. It approaches humans and animals, animate as well as inanimate objects, without hesitation, and although there are no motor deficits, tends to examine them by mouth rather than by use of the hands … Various tests do not show any impairment in visual acuity or in the ability to localize visually the position of objects in space. However, the monkey seems to be unable to recognize objects by the sense of sight. The hungry animal, if confronted with a variety of objects, will, for example, indiscriminately pick up a comb, a bakelite knob, a sunflower seed, a screw, a stick, a piece of apple, a live snake, a piece of

banana, and a live rat. Each object is transferred to the mouth and then discarded if not edible.

H. Klüver and P. Bucy, 1939

Although these observations did not lead to insights into mastication effects of mescaline, a new behavioral syndrome was discovered that included loss of fear, visual agnosia, hyperorality, altered food preferences, hypersexuality, and increased exploratory behaviors. This constellation of behavioral changes is now known as **Klüver-Bucy syndrome**. The major hallmark of this disorder is the inability to evaluate the emotional and motivational significance of objects in the environment, particularly by the sense of sight. Because the brain ablation in these monkeys included the hippocampus (the only component of the Papez circuit that resides in the temporal lobe), damage to this structure was hypothesized to underlie the behavioral deficits.

Subsequent studies have shown this speculation to be incorrect, because selective neurotoxic damage to the hippocampus yields few, if any, signs of Klüver-Bucy syndrome. Regardless, Klüver and Bucy's dramatic behavioral descriptions, combined with Papez's neuroanatomical circuit, provided the backdrop for the further refinement of emotion theory that dominated the rest of the twentieth century—namely, the **limbic system theory**.

The limbic system theory

As a clinician in the tradition of psychosomatic medicine, Paul MacLean, working at Yale University in the 1940s through the 1970s, offered a compelling neurobiological account of emotion that integrated the ideas of Cannon and Bard, Klüver and Bucy, Papez, and even Freud. MacLean's work combined clinical case reports of patients with known brain damage, animal studies, and psychiatric insights. MacLean argued that evolutionarily older (three-layered) cortex in the medial wall of the forebrain (as well as the underlying subcortical structures) played a general role in bodily functions related to survival. He renamed what had been called the **rhinencephalon** (or "smell brain," because of its prominent olfactory connections) the *visceral brain*. The visceral brain included structures in the Papez circuit (thalamus, hypothalamus, cingulate gyrus, hippocampus), Broca's limbic lobe (including pyriform, rhinal, subcallosal, and parasplenial cortices), and subcortical nuclei like the septum and portions of the basal ganglia (**Figure 17.8**). Later, MacLean added

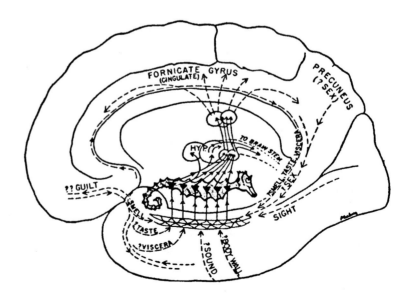

Figure 17.8 Components of the limbic system and their connections. MacLean's original 1949 drawing of the visceral brain is reproduced here. In MacLean's interpretation, the cornerstone of this system was the hippocampus ("seahorse") and its connections to the hypothalamus. (From MacLean 1949.)

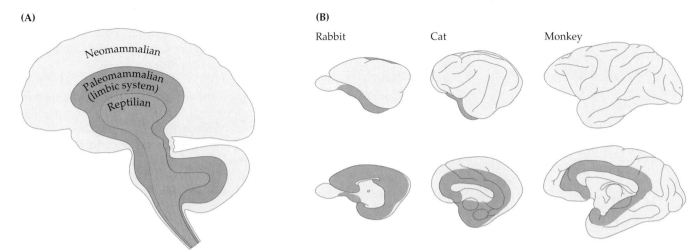

Figure 17.9 The triune brain theory. (A) MacLean theorized that the brain had evolved in three major stages: a reptilian brain (brainstem), a paleomammalian brain (limbic system), and a neomammalian brain (neocortex). (B) Comparative anatomical diagrams of the brain showing the relative ratio of limbic cortex (shaded) to neocortex across various species of mammals. (After MacLean 1970.)

the **amygdala** and **orbitofrontal cortex** to the visceral brain and called this set of structures the **limbic system**.

The centerpiece of the limbic system concept is the **hippocampus**, which contains an orderly array of pyramidal neurons that MacLean thought of as a "keyboard" upon which the emotions played. In this conceptualization, the hippocampus was the seat of emotional feelings and the integrator of emotional reactions. In the 1970s, MacLean broadened his ideas to describe how the brain had evolved more generally. He referred to the **triune brain** as having a core reptilian component (the brainstem) that provided basic mechanisms for survival, a paleomammalian component (the limbic system) that afforded greater environmental interactions, and a neomammalian component (the neocortex) that developed flexibility in thought and executive control (**Figure 17.9**).

Although the term *limbic* describes the rim structures that form the medial wall of the forebrain, the limbic system theory can be considered to distinguish and link brain regions concerned primarily with the internal milieu (visceral systems) to those primarily concerned with the external environment (sensory systems), leading to visceromotor responses to stimuli arising from the world. The functions of the system thus link together Papez's stream of thought (cognition) and stream of feeling (emotion). Damage to components of this system yield clinical affective syndromes, which also link the medical disciplines of neurology and psychiatry.

Finally, the limbic system theory was proposed at a juncture in the history of psychology that marked the transition from behaviorism to cognitivism, which fundamentally changed the nature of theorizing about emotion. Each of these facets of the limbic system theory has contributed to its long-standing appeal as an account of emotional processing in the brain.

Contemporary Approaches to the Neurobiology of Emotion

The limbic system theory, revised

In recent decades, the limbic system theory has been considerably revised, and in some quarters challenged in a more basic way. As Joseph LeDoux at New York University has argued, there are no independent anatomical criteria for defining which regions should be contained within the system and which should not. Although the limbic system theory grew out of Papez's circuit model of hypothalamic connectivity, many brainstem nuclei that are connected directly to the hypothalamus were not included. Similarly, on functional grounds, many brainstem nuclei are directly involved in autonomic regulation yet are curiously absent from the visceral-brain concept.

In other words, MacLean's collection of brain areas is not organized, either functionally or structurally, as clearly as are other systems in the brain, such as sensory or motor systems. In addition, several limbic system structures are now known to have primarily cognitive rather than emotional or visceral functions. Most importantly, selective damage to the hippocampus, the cornerstone of the limbic system theory, yields declarative memory and spatial cognition deficits (see Chapters 13 and 14), but has little impact on emotion. Finally, the concept of the triune brain is widely considered too simplistic an account of brain evolution (see Chapter 26).

Nonetheless, MacLean's concept of the limbic system has had a lasting impact, perhaps because it includes a number of brain regions whose emotional functions have stood the test of time (including the amygdala, orbitofrontal cortex, hypothalamus, and ventral anterior cingulate gyrus). Moreover, evidence has continued to accumulate that damage to the emotion-related limbic forebrain areas can produce some (but rarely all) of the signs and symptoms originally described by Klüver and Bucy.

More recent conceptualizations of the limbic system further suggested a functional subdivision between a ventral belt that is more involved in olfactory and emotional functions, and a dorsal belt that is more involved in cognitive and executive functions (**Figure 17.10**). This idea is similar to dorsal and ventral processing streams in sensory systems. As will be discussed in Chapter 18, brain structures in these belts work together to integrate emotional and cognitive functions. Given the abundant evidence in earlier chapters that brain regions rarely, if ever, have a single function, a monolithic system is unlikely to be responsible for all aspects of emotional processing.

Beyond these anatomical revisions, some investigators have taken the more radical position that the limbic system theory should be abandoned altogether, arguing that a better strategy might be to decompose the overarching concept of emotion into constituent parts to look for more specific emotion systems in the brain (the discussion of memory in Unit V provides an example of

Figure 17.10 The current conception of the limbic system.   Following his original description, MacLean added the amygdala, the orbitofrontal cortex, and the ventromedial prefrontal cortex to the list of included structures. More recent conceptualizations further propose a division of the limbic system into a dorsal cognitive belt (blue) and a ventral emotional belt (green).

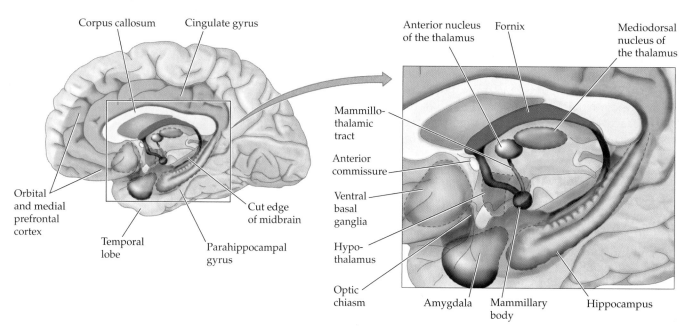

this approach). Although psychological theorists disagree on whether or how such efforts might proceed (see Table 17.1, as well as Figures 17.2 and 17.3), researchers have made advances by probing the limbic forebrain and other areas related to emotion with imaging and electrophysiological methods, as described in the next section and in the following chapters.

Studies in humans lend some support to the idea of neural specialization for discrete emotions in limbic brain regions. For instance, the insula appears to be important for the emotion disgust, which is related to its role in gustatory processing (see Chapter 7). As Figure 17.2 shows, facial reactions of disgust, which curl the upper lip, wrinkle the nose, and protrude the tongue, have evolved in part for the physical ejection of toxic substances from the oral cavity. Consistent with this idea, disgust is associated with the parasympathetic circuitry that mediates feelings of nausea and the vomiting reflex.

Some neurological patients with damage to the insula are impaired in their ability to recognize facial and vocal expressions of disgust compared to other basic emotions. Functional neuroimaging studies have confirmed involvement of the insula (and other brain areas) in disgust, including the recognition of someone else reacting to a disgusting situation. Other emotions, however, are not so easily segregated with respect to regional brain activity, and the concept of emotional subsystems remains a matter of considerable debate.

Hemispheric-asymmetry hypotheses of emotion

The marked expansion of neocortex in primate evolution affords complexity and flexibility not only in cognitive and executive functions but also in social and emotional behavior (see Chapters 26 and 27). The limbic system theory largely ignores the important contributions of the neocortex to emotional behavior. As lateralization of cortical function has become a focus of investigation in recent decades, researchers have applied EEG, imaging, clinical correlations in patients, and lesion methods in experimental animals to examine the contributions of the right and left cerebral hemispheres to emotional processing.

Studies of neurological patients with unilateral damage to the neocortex suggest that the right cerebral hemisphere is specialized for processing many aspects of emotion (**right-hemisphere hypothesis**). Patients with right-hemisphere damage tend to have more difficulty than patients with left-hemisphere damage in emotion perception tasks in visual and auditory domains, as well as in the production of emotion in facial expression and speech prosody (**Figure 17.11**; see Chapters 20 and 21 for evidence specifically related to language).

Elliott Ross of the University of Pennsylvania has proposed that the right hemisphere is organized for speech **prosody** (the term for the inflections, rhythm, and stress in vocal sounds) in a way that parallels left-hemisphere organization for analysis of the content of speech. Consistent with these find-

Figure 17.11 Lateralization of affective aspects of sound stimuli. Neuropsychological studies reveal right-hemisphere lateralization of affective aspects of speech and other sound stimuli, such as music. (A) Anterior areas, centered near the right hemisphere (the homologue of Broca's area), are important for generating prosody in one's own speech. (B) Posterior areas, centered near the right-hemisphere homologue of Wernicke's area, are important for perceiving and evaluating prosody in someone else's voice. (C) Patients with widespread damage to the right hemisphere lack both functions; they are unable to interpret affective intonation of the speech of others, and they speak in a flat affective tone themselves. (After Ross 1997.)

(A) Motor

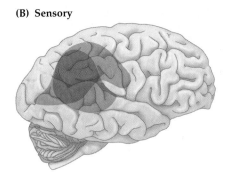

(B) Sensory

(C) Global

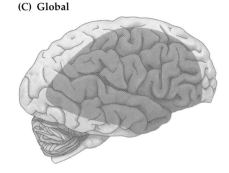

ings, healthy individuals are better able to discriminate vocal and facial affect when stimuli are presented to the left ear or left visual field and thus processed by the right hemisphere (but recall from Chapter 6 that lateralized processing in audition is not absolute). The left half of the face also tends to be more spontaneously expressive than the right, although this effect varies among individuals. Given that the right hemisphere has been associated with visuospatial and synthetic processing strategies (see Chapter 21), some of these findings may reflect lateralization of more basic functions that are only indirectly recruited during emotional processing.

A different lateralization model—the **valence hypothesis**—posits that the left and right hemispheres are specialized for positive and negative emotions, respectively. According to this hypothesis, positive emotions serve more linguistic and social functions (e.g., expressing romantic love, friendly affection, or pride) than do negative emotions, which tend to be reactive and survival-related. In this scheme, the left hemisphere is more adept at implementing the social display rules of positive emotions and linking them with communicative functions. A more recent incarnation of the valence hypothesis restricts the hemispheric asymmetries to the experience and expression stages of emotional processing. According to this hybrid model, right posterior sensory regions are dominant for the *evaluation* of all emotions. However, the *experience* and *expression* of emotions is postulated to be asymmetrical, such that left frontal regions are dominant for positive emotions and right frontal regions for negative emotions.

Scalp EEG studies have provided evidence for the valence hypothesis of emotion asymmetry. Power in the alpha band (8–13 hertz) of the EEG recorded over the prefrontal cortex tends to exhibit a leftward asymmetry in response to stimuli with positive valences and a rightward asymmetry in response to negative stimuli. However, the emotion-related prefrontal asymmetry across the hemispheres varies considerably across individuals. This intersubject variability extends to baseline (resting) activity when no emotional stimuli are presented.

Most individuals exhibit a symmetrical response and report having a more evenhanded affective disposition (being neither strongly optimistic nor strongly pessimistic, for example). Nonetheless, when it is found, the pattern of asymmetry is stable across individuals over testing sessions. The asymmetry is thought to predispose an individual to react emotionally in a positive or negative way, given an appropriate elicitor. In depression, a reduction of the leftward prefrontal asymmetry has been related to the **anhedonia** present in the illness, whereby patients are unable to experience positive affect as intensely as healthy individuals do. Since the asymmetry does not remit with treatment, it may serve as a trait marker of depression.

Because alpha-band EEG activity over the prefrontal cortex during resting conditions is relatively easy to measure in children, this neural index has also been used in developmental studies of temperament (**Figure 17.12A**). As explained earlier, the term *temperament* refers to a habitual emotional response tendency that characterizes aspects of an individual's personality. Consistent with its role in social emotions, the degree of leftward prefrontal asymmetry predicts the extent to which toddlers engage in play behavior with novel toys and other children. Conversely, the degree of rightward prefrontal asymmetry predicts crying behavior when infants are separated from their mothers for a short period of time. In infant monkeys, the degree of rightward prefrontal asymmetry correlates with the degree of baseline stress hormone levels present during the morning diurnal peak in cortisol release (**Figure 17.12B**). Rightward EEG asymmetry in preschoolers also predicts later development of anti-

(A)

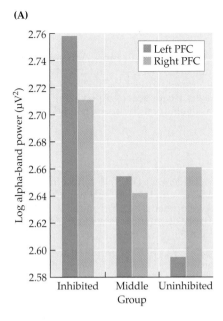

(B)

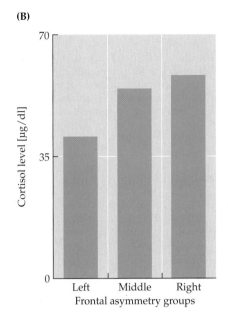

Figure 17.12 Emotional reactivity predicted by hemispheric asymmetries in EEG activity. (A) Socially engaged (uninhibited) children show a leftward asymmetry in resting EEG activity of the prefrontal cortex. Socially inhibited children show a reversal of this asymmetry. In alpha-band power EEG studies, lower numbers represent more activity. (B) In 1-year-old rhesus monkeys, basal stress hormone (cortisol) levels are positively correlated with the degree of rightward prefrontal EEG asymmetry. (A after Davidson 1995; B after Kalin et al. 1998.)

social behavior in grade school, suggesting some value of this neural marker as an index of temperament across developmental stages.

Studies by Eddie Harmon-Jones of Texas A&M University have indicated that the prefrontal EEG asymmetry in the alpha band may reflect motivational tendencies of approach and avoidance rather than simply positive and negative valence. Whereas most positive emotions are associated with approach behavior, most negative emotions are associated with avoidance behavior. The emotion anger is an exception to this general rule. In offensive anger, one feels a sense of control over the outcome of the conflict and approaches the offender. Offensive anger is accompanied by a leftward prefrontal EEG asymmetry. This asymmetry is reduced if one feels empathic toward the offender, which reduces approach tendencies and hostile attitudes. In contrast, rightward EEG asymmetry is found during defensive anger, when one feels a sense of helplessness over the conflict and there is a tendency to avoid the offender.

Summary

1. Emotion is a complex set of regulatory and cognitive functions defined by related changes in physiology, behavior, and feelings that helps humans and other animals respond flexibly to biologically significant stimuli. By focusing on aspects of emotion that are amenable to neurobiological investigation, researchers have begun to identify the neural circuits and systems involved in emotional evaluation, expression, and experience.

2. Structures in the limbic forebrain have long been known to be critical for emotional information processing, in part because of their rich anatomical connections with both sensory and visceral motor regions.

3. The original limbic system theory put forward in the 1940s has been repeatedly revised to acknowledge the contributions of additional brain areas, along with the fact that some medial forebrain structures, such as the hippocampus, also participate in functions that are not primarily emotional. The involvement of these brain regions in emotion—including the amygdala, insula, orbitofrontal cortex, and ventral anterior cingulate gyrus—has now been confirmed with modern techniques in humans and other species. Such studies have further identified hemispheric asymmetry in aspects of emotional processing, including a right-hemisphere dominance for affective prosody, and prefrontal asymmetry in processing emotional valence.

4. Recent advances in brain imaging techniques have also yielded more nuanced views of earlier findings by demonstrating overlapping systems for several emotions.

5. Because emotional processing is so important to human health and well-being, and to understanding and treating common disorders like depression and anxiety, this area of cognitive neuroscience research will continue to grow rapidly. The following chapters review much of what has been learned in recent years, emphasizing links to other cognitive systems and the implications of emotions for social behavior.

Additional Reading

Reviews

BOROD, J. C., R. L. BLOOM, A. M. BRICK-MAN, L. NAKHUTINA AND E. A. CURKO (2002) Emotional processing deficits in individuals with unilateral brain damage. *Appl. Neuropsychol.* 9: 23–36.

DAVIDSON, R. J. AND W. IRWIN (1999) The functional neuroanatomy of emotion and affective style. *Trends Cogn. Sci.* 3: 11–21.

LEDOUX, J. E. (1991) The limbic system concept. *Concepts Neurosci.* 2: 169–199.

ROSS, E. D. (1997) The aprosodias. In *Behavioral Neurology and Neuropsychology*, T. E. Feinberg and M. J. Farah (eds.). New York: McGraw-Hill, pp. 699–710.

Important Original Papers

BARD, P. (1928) A diencephalic mechanism for the expression of rage with special reference to the sympathetic nervous system. *Am. J. Physiol.* 84: 490–515.

KALIN, N. H., C. LARSON, S. E. SHELTON AND R. J. DAVIDSON (1998) Asymmetric frontal brain activity, cortisol, and behavior associated with fearful temperament in rhesus monkeys. *Behav. Neurosci.* 112: 286–292.

KLÜVER, H. AND P. C. BUCY (1939) Preliminary analysis of functions of the temporal lobes in monkeys. *Arch. Neurol. Psychiatry* 42: 979–1000.

LANG, P. J., M. K. GREENWALD, M. M. BRADLEY AND A. O. HAMM (1993) Looking at pictures: Affective, facial, visceral, and behavioral reactions. *Psychophysiology* 30: 261–273.

MACLEAN, P. D. (1949) Psychosomatic disease and the "visceral brain": Recent developments bearing on the Papez theory of emotion. *Psychosom. Med.* 11: 338–353.

PAPEZ, J. W. (1937) A proposed mechanism for emotion. *Arch. Neurol. Psychiatry* 38: 725–743.

RUSSELL, J. A. (1980) A circumplex model of affect. *J. Pers. Soc. Psychol.* 39: 1161–1178.

Books

EKMAN, P. AND R. J. DAVIDSON (1994) *The Nature of Emotions.* New York: Oxford University Press.

PANKSEPP, J. (1998) *Affective Neuroscience: The Foundations of Human and Animal Emotions.* New York: Oxford University Press.

18

Emotional Influences on Cognitive Functions

Introduction

Previous chapters of this book have not explicitly considered how emotion influences cognitive functions. However, virtually any cognitive performance is affected by a person's emotional status, and neural processing resources are preferentially allocated to events that have emotional significance. For instance, athletes perform better when they are "in the zone" or "feeling it," anxiety impairs a student's recall of material for a final exam, and authority figures speak in heated tones to command attention. This chapter describes how internally and externally triggered emotions modulate information processing in brain regions that mediate various cognitive functions, focusing on perception and attention, learning and memory, and decision making (the topics that have been most thoroughly studied in this context). From an evolutionary standpoint, neural systems that support thinking developed in part to solve problems that were made salient by emotional considerations, so it is not surprising that emotion is intimately intertwined with higher cortical functions. Thus, information processing always occurs amid a backdrop of emotional states, social goals, and motivational incentives. Understanding, in neural terms, how cognitive processes are shaped by these influences will greatly broaden thinking about how the brain works.

The Integrative and Iterative Nature of Emotional Processing

As indicated in Chapter 17, emotional feelings arise from internal sources (e.g., visceral signals associated with various moods or with anxiety) as well as from external sources that signify potentially rewarding or punishing circumstances or events in the environment. The limbic regions of the forebrain are in an anatomical position to integrate information from both the internal milieu and the external world, and indeed these structures combine information from parallel cortical and subcortical processing pathways (**Figure 18.1**).

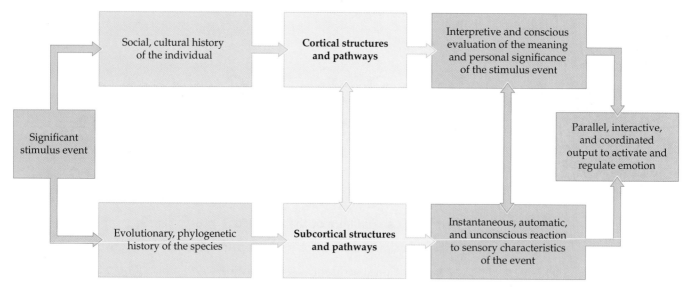

Figure 18.1 Emotion pathways.
Subcortical and cortical routes of information processing converge to generate an emotional response. (After Buck 1984.)

Subcortical afferent pathways that carry information about sensory features of the world and visceral activity can rapidly initiate emotional reactions. Cortical pathways simultaneously elaborate the meaning of such input and compare it to stored knowledge and prior experiences with similar behavioral significance. Afferent sensory pathways converge on particular forebrain structures—including the amygdala, insula, anterior cingulate cortex, and orbitofrontal cortex—and the processing in these regions integrates the relevant information and signals the executive control and premotor regions of the brain to select appropriate behavioral responses. These forebrain structures also send projections back to the sensory and association cortices involved in pertinent cognitive functions.

This interplay between cognitive and emotional-motivational functions is thus a dynamic process. For example, sensory pathways may detect the slithering movements of a snake, but defensive reactions may cease upon realization that the snake is a plastic toy. Knowledge gained from this episode may then contextually constrain the generation of emotional reactions in the future. As Yale psychologist Marcia Johnson has put it,

> Feelings are critical for defining motives and agendas; they signal the potential importance of events; they activate related knowledge … Their functional role in perception and thought must be enormous, whether we think of them as "first" or "later" or "immersed" in the cognitive stream … Their profound functional importance may arise not because they come first, but because they act iteratively.

M. K. Johnson and C. Weisz, 1994, p. 161

The Central Role of the Amygdala

Among the key forebrain structures that mediate emotions, the **amygdala** has been a special focus of research on emotion-cognition interactions because of its widespread anatomical connections to subcortical structures that control autonomic functions and to cortical areas involved in processing cognitive and emotional information. From estimates of the number of primary, secondary, and tertiary cortical projections in macaque monkeys, Malcolm Young of Newcastle University concluded that the amygdala is the most densely interconnected structure in the primate forebrain. To rapidly detect threats and other emotionally pertinent sensory stimuli, the amygdala gets direct input from the thalamus that bypasses the primary sensory cortical reception areas. In addition, it has direct input from the olfactory bulb, which may partly explain why smells often evoke strong emotional responses.

This fast input route to the amygdala is capable of only crude sensory discrimination, however, and, as already implied, more sophisticated perceptual analysis reaches the amygdala somewhat later than cortical inputs. The rapid subcortical pathway may prime the amygdala to more effectively process the additional information that follows from the slower cortical pathway after the initial detection of a potentially significant stimulus arising from the environment. This parallel anatomical arrangement may have evolved because of the advantages of triggering emotional responses more quickly than if information were processed solely by cortical sensory pathways. Studies in rodents indicate that activation of the rapid subcortical pathway is sufficient to evoke fear reactions to simple stimuli, but the extent to which this pathway contributes to emotions in primates, including humans, remains unclear.

The amygdala can obtain additional sensory information as needed to process emotional stimuli through extensive feedback projections. In primates, these connections have been best described in vision, which has an asymmetrical pattern of connectivity. Whereas the amygdala receives input from only late stages of visual processing in the inferotemporal cortex, it has feedback connections to most stations along the ventral visual stream, all the way back to the primary visual (striate) cortex itself (**Figure 18.2**; see Chapter 5). Note that other emotion-related forebrain structures also have close contact with sensory areas. For example, the orbitofrontal cortex includes a portion of primary olfactory cortex, and the insular cortex includes a portion of primary gustatory (taste) cortex.

The amygdala also has extensive interconnections with medial temporal and ventral frontal lobe structures that provide a substrate for emotional enhancement of memory, and indirect connections with the dorsal frontoparietal attentional control network via prefrontal cortex (PFC) interfaces, including the anterior cingulate, ventromedial PFC, ventrolateral PFC, and orbitofrontal cortex. The amygdala can thus be thought of as a center that shuttles information back and forth from subcortical and cortical pathways to initiate and coordinate emotional reactions, including output to the hypothalamus and brainstem autonomic control centers that modulate the visceral changes accompanying various emotional states.

In sum, in conjunction with other limbic and paralimbic structures, the amygdala modulates activity in specific sensory and higher-order cognitive

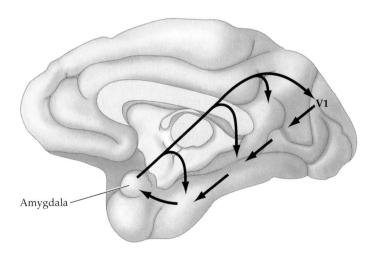

Amygdala

V1

Figure 18.2 Bidirectional communication between the amygdala and the ventral visual processing stream. This drawing illustrates the macaque brain, but the same arrangement is assumed to occur in humans. The amygdala receives input from late stages along this cortical pathway. However, it feeds back to multiple stages of the pathway, including the earliest stage of visual input, the primary visual cortex (V1). Such feedback projections provide a means for emotional states to access and tune perceptual representations.

sectors of the cortex in response to biologically significant events that often have emotional consequences. The discussion that follows describes how emotion influences several domains of cognition, from the perception and evaluation of sensory input to the selection of actions that direct behavior to agents and objects in the world.

Emotional Influences on Perception

Processing sensory information that has potential emotional significance takes priority over processing inconsequential sensory information. Such emotional prioritization is accomplished either by automatic (involuntary) detection of salient features in crowded environments, such as the presence of a gun at a crime scene, or by a voluntary attentional bias to process such emotional features, as often happens in anxiety disorders to sources of threat. Therefore, it is important to distinguish the direct influence of emotion on perception from that occurring through the engagement of voluntary attention or other executive functions. Another challenge is that individuals interpret sensory stimuli in different ways, and emotional responses can be elicited to stimuli that are themselves relatively innocuous, as readily demonstrated by the placebo effect (see Chapter 7). For these reasons, researchers interested in studying emotional influences on perception often present stimuli briefly and mask the stimuli to limit awareness or present the stimuli in situations where attentional resources are highly taxed. Although some have argued that these manipulations don't completely eliminate awareness or attention, the more automatic effects of emotion on sensory processing are nonetheless emphasized while the impact of contributing higher-order influences related to subjective stimulus interpretation and engagement of attentional control systems may be minimized.

Experiments of this type typically investigate whether masked visual or auditory emotional stimuli elicit autonomic responses, modulate early ERP components, or elicit hemodynamic responses in sensory and limbic brain areas. Of all the emotions, fear has received the most attention because threat in the environment must be detected quickly for **defensive reflexes** to be effective. Indeed, images of biologically relevant stimuli that have high threat value, such as spiders or fearful facial expressions, elicit amygdala activity and the skin conductance response—a measure of sympathetic arousal that is part of the defensive response to threat, even when the participant is not consciously aware of the nature of the stimulus being presented (**Figure 18.3**).

Other evidence indicates that the amygdala tends to signal fear preferentially over other emotions in facial displays when they are presented supraliminally. However, when the ability to extract information about fear is limited (e.g., by visual masking of the expression), the amygdala's response is broadened to include a wider variety of expressions. This change in perceptual tuning may be behaviorally adaptive when the immediate emotional meaning of the stimulus is less clear.

In patients with specific phobias and posttraumatic stress disorder, these patterns of autonomic and brain activity elicited by fear-inducing stimuli are exaggerated, particularly for threatening stimuli relevant to the individual's traumatic experience or fear. Apparently the emotional consequences of unconscious threat processing become maladaptive at some point. In sum, masking paradigms have been useful for understanding how emotional reactions are elicited by threat cues even when participants do not report the presence of the threat, underscoring the potential contribution of covert perceptual processes to anxiety disorders.

Perceptual awareness can also be limited by *rapid serial visual presentation* (*RSVP*). Recall from Chapter 10 that when two target words are embedded in

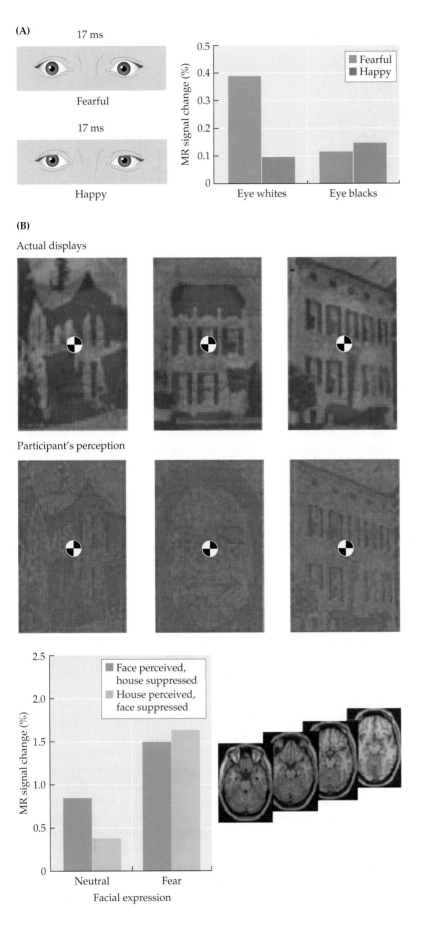

Figure 18.3 Perception of fear without awareness.   (A) The amygdala signals visually fearful facial expressions, even when stimuli are presented briefly (17 milliseconds) and masked to limit conscious awareness. In these stimuli, fear is conveyed solely by the whites of the eyes (the exposed area of which increases during fear as a result of sympathetically mediated contraction of the subcutaneous muscles in the skin surrounding the eye). (B) In this experiment, participants were shown images of a face projected to one eye and a house to the other eye, creating binocular rivalry (see Chapters 5 and 28). Participants indicated on each trial whether they perceived a face or a house. The amygdala exhibited greater activity for fearful than for neutral facial expressions, even when participants reported seeing only the house (i.e., when the fearful face was presumably processed only subcortically as a result of rivalry). (A after Whalen et al. 2004; B from Williams et al. 2004).

Figure 18.4 Emotional content improves processing pertinent to target detection. (A) When target words (green) are embedded in a rapid stream of nontarget distracters, detection of the second target (T2) is impaired at short lag times. If the second target has emotional content, however, detection is facilitated. (B) A patient with bilateral amygdala damage (blue) does not show this effect. (After Anderson and Phelps 2001.)

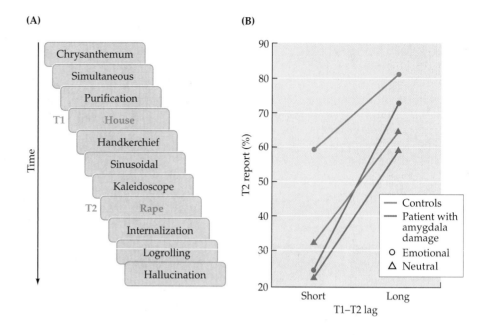

a rapidly presented stream of stimuli, reporting of the second stimulus is impaired, presumably because attention was still focused on the first one when the second one appeared (**Figure 18.4**). If only the second word in the pair is emotionally arousing, it can be detected at shorter lag times relative to neutral words. Importantly, this emotion-related improvement in performance is not found in patients with left-sided or bilateral lesions of the amygdala. The amygdala evidently overrides a capacity-limited perceptual encoding mechanism that allows emotional stimuli to reach awareness more readily.

Patients who suffer from **blindsight** provide another opportunity to examine emotional processing in circumstances that are not confounded by conscious awareness (see Chapter 28). Studies of one patient with blindsight showed that he could correctly guess which emotional expressions were presented in his blind hemifield when forced to make a discrimination, despite being consciously unaware of their presence. These findings have been interpreted to support the idea that some aspects of emotional evaluation operate on perceptual input arising from subcortical visual pathways that bypass the primary visual system. This notion is appealing but continues to be debated because the evidence to date has been indirect.

The anatomical connections between the amygdala and sensory cortices provide one avenue by which emotion might influence perception (see Figure 18.2). Patrik Vuilleumier and his colleagues at University College London tested whether damage to the amygdala in patients with medial temporal lobe epilepsy influenced extrastriate fMRI activity in response to fearful facial expressions. They found that, although patients with hippocampal lesions and healthy controls showed enhanced activity in the fusiform gyrus and occipital cortex for fearful facial expressions relative to neutral expressions, the patients with lesions of the amygdala did not. Furthermore, the amount of amygdala damage in the patients was correlated with the level of fusiform gyrus activity in response to fearful faces. These results provide compelling evidence that the amygdala exerts a remote influence over perceptual processing in sensory regions, consistent with emotional feedback. Moreover, the anatomical connections are known to exist in the monkey brain. However, these data alone cannot determine whether the emotional effects in humans are mediated by a direct or an indirect feedback route.

Emotional Influences on Attention

Even though emotional stimuli may initially elicit autonomic and neural responses relatively quickly and automatically, attentional and other cognitive functions are recruited to further evaluate the stimulus and initiate appropriate behavioral reactions. A first step in the allocation of attention is to alert and orient an individual to the emotional trigger. As already described, one way this is accomplished is to arrest ongoing behavior by engaging the autonomic nervous system. Doing so reallocates attention by virtue of the accompanying emotion. One consequence of the orienting response is to redirect visual and auditory attention to the spatial location of the relevant stimulus. For example, in crowded visual scenes or when multiple visual stimuli compete for attention, emotional stimuli bias both the initial direction of eye movements (overt attentional orienting) and the distribution of eye movements over time (sustained attention) (**Figure 18.5**). These changes in visuospatial exploration ensure that the stimuli of greatest importance at any particular time are preferentially processed.

Furthermore, when one is searching for an emotional item in a crowded display, emotional stimuli can "pop out," especially when the search is for a particular threat signal among multiple nonthreatening distracters. **Pop-out effects** indicate a parallel search mechanism that rapidly signals the presence of a target item irrespective of the number of distracting stimuli. For example, depictions of snakes and spiders pop out when presented against a crowded background of innocuous stimuli such as flowers or mushrooms (the *snake-in-the-grass effect*). However, the reverse does not hold; searching for an individual flower against a background of snakes depicted with similar features, such as color, does not yield a visual pop-out effect. Similarly, searching for an

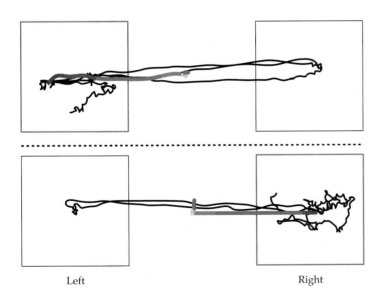

Left   Right

Figure 18.5 Eye tracking reveals emotional biases in both attentional orienting and sustained attention.   When participants view two scenes simultaneously on a computer screen, their initial eye movement (colored line segment) away from central fixation is directed toward the emotional scene (red box) in the pair instead of the neutral scene (black box). In addition, they spend more time scanning the emotional scene relative to the neutral scene over a 10-second viewing period (compare the lengths of the black line segments over the two boxes), even when the scenes are equated for visual complexity. (From LaBar et al. 2000.)

Figure 18.6 The face-in-a-crowd effect.
Searching for an angry face among a crowd of
happy faces (left) tends to generate a pop-out
effect—rapid detection irrespective of the number
of distracters. However, searching for a happy face
among a crowd of angry ones (right) tends to
require a serial search and hence greater reaction
times as the number of distracters increases. Numbers at the top of the bars indicate the number of
distracters. (Data hypothetical.)

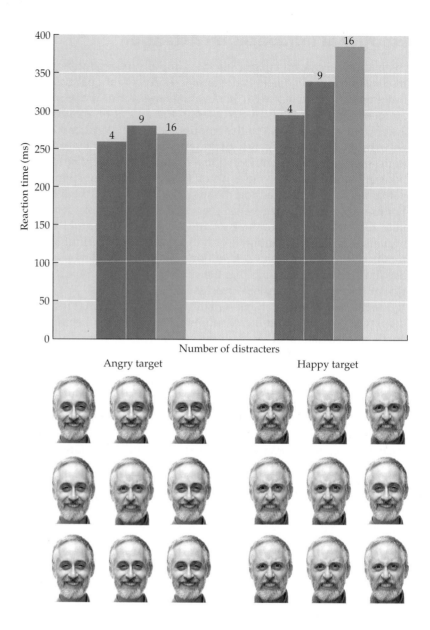

angry face embedded in a display of happy faces tends to produce a pop-out
effect, but the reverse is not so true (the *face-in-a-crowd effect*; **Figure 18.6**).
Although these effects are small and the mechanisms are probably similar to
other visual pop-out effects, the asymmetry in pop-out as a function of emotional content indicates that threatening signals attract attention reflexively.

Dichotic listening studies have shown similar effects of emotion on attention in the auditory domain. In these studies, emotional words or words
associated with aversive outcomes presented in an unattended audio stream
trigger autonomic responses. Consistent with hemispheric-dominance theories of emotion (see Chapter 17), such effects are more reliable when the emotional stimuli are presented to the left ear. Occasionally the auditory processing of unattended emotional words captures attention sufficiently to shift a
participant's focus from the attended to the unattended auditory stream. This
phenomenon is commonly observed in crowded social settings, where attention can be captured, for instance, when someone from across the room utters
an obscenity or the listener's name. In this way, potentially significant emo-

tional auditory information can call attention to previously ignored stimulus locations.

There is no consensus about how emotion influences attentional functions in neurobiological terms, although the attentional control systems discussed in Chapter 12 are obviously pertinent to consider. Automatic effects of stimuli with content that can elicit emotional responses may be implemented directly in the subcortical and ventral cortical pathways connecting sensory and limbic regions, without engagement of the dorsal attentional control network (see Figure 18.2). Indirect support for this idea comes from the hemineglect syndrome arising from unilateral damage to the attentional control network described in Chapter 12.

Although these patients tend to neglect stimuli in the contralesional visual field when the stimuli compete with similar stimuli in the intact hemifield, this effect is reduced when social or predatory threats are presented in the neglected hemifield. In other words, the patients' attention is reflexively drawn toward emotional stimulus features presented in the neglected field, despite the impaired functioning of the frontoparietal attentional control system. Neuroimaging studies show more directly that emotion can enhance activity in the ventral visual stream and limbic forebrain, without necessarily eliciting concomitant changes in dorsal frontoparietal regions.

In addition to these automatic influences, limbic regions involved in emotional evaluation (the amygdala, insula, etc.) have several means by which they can influence goal-directed attentional processing. Indirectly, these regions can activate systems that broadly facilitate cortical activity. For instance, the amygdala can prompt the release of acetylcholine from the nucleus basalis of Meynert in the basal forebrain, as well as the release of dopamine from the substantia nigra. Peter Holland and Michela Gallagher of Johns Hopkins University have shown that these modulatory actions of the amygdala boost various aspects of attention that contribute to appetitive conditioning in rodents and presumably serve similar functions in humans.

Also having an influence are the prefrontal cortex and anterior cingulate interfaces that link the amygdala, insula, and other limbic areas to the dorsal frontoparietal attentional network. Helen Mayberg, now working at Emory University, has theorized that the anterior cingulate and related regions in the medial and orbital PFC maintain a balance between ventral emotional and dorsal attentional functions in normal **mood regulation**. According to Mayberg, these activity patterns become skewed in mood disorders such that there is too much emphasis on somatic-emotional processing at the expense of cognitive-attentional operations. Consequently, individuals suffering from depression devote greater-than-normal resources to mulling over sad and stressful experiences, and they have difficulty refocusing attention on short-term behavioral goals.

In support of this hypothesis, neuroimaging studies of healthy individuals have shown how top-down attentional demands interact with emotional information processing to enhance activity in the anterior cingulate and medial PFC. For example, in the **emotional oddball task**, participants are asked to detect attentional targets (e.g., circles) that appear rarely among a stream of frequent stimuli (e.g., squares). While performing the task, participants are distracted by intermittently presented pictures that are either emotionally arousing or neutral (**Figure 18.7**). The attentional targets activate the dorsal processing stream, including the frontoparietal network; and the arousing distracters activate the ventral processing stream, including the amygdala and inferior PFC. The dual streams of processing are integrated in the anterior cingulate, which responds to both attentional targets and emotional distracters.

Interestingly, the PFC shows a mirror effect on this task. Whereas dorsal PFC activity increases to attentional targets and decreases to emotional dis-

Figure 18.7 The emotional oddball task.
(A) Participants try to detect rare circles interspersed among a stream of squares while distracting emotional and neutral scenes are intermittently presented. (B) Attentional targets (circles) engage the dorsal processing stream; emotional distracters engage the ventral processing stream. (C) The anterior cingulate responds to both attentional targets and emotional distracters (left). When the circles are the distracters and the emotional pictures are the targets (right), anterior cingulate activity increases in response to the emotional pictures but is negligible in response to the circles. (After Yamasaki et al. 2002 and Fichtenholtz et al. 2004.)

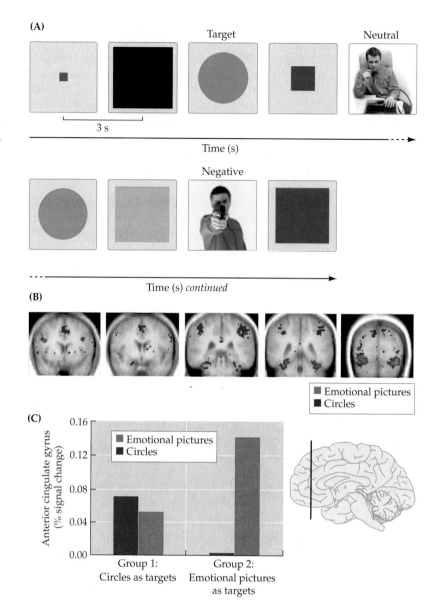

tracters, ventral PFC shows the opposite pattern. In other words, attentional control regions are suppressed when emotional stimuli unexpectedly appear, and emotional regions are suppressed when task-relevant attentional targets are processed. These findings dovetail with other evidence showing reciprocal engagement of dorsal and ventral sectors of PFC for attentional and emotional functions, respectively. If the task instructions are switched such that the emotional stimuli become the attentional targets (the circles thereby becoming task-irrelevant), activity in the anterior cingulate doubles in response to the emotional pictures (see Figure 18.7C), suggesting a convergence of attentional and emotional processing.

Emotional Influences on Memory

When we reflect on our lives, we tend to recall events that are personally meaningful and emotionally salient. These markers of life's ups and downs are often shared by family members and close friends, and thus become the fabric of shared memories that facilitate social bonds. In some cases, unexpected tragedies experienced by individuals or communities leave long-lasting emotional traces that William James called "scars on the mind." In 1977, Roger Brown and James Kulik introduced the term **flashbulb memory** to refer to all the vivid details of an emotionally fraught episode that are registered graphically in the mind's eye. Although this camera analogy in the relatively literal terms in which it was originally proposed has not held up, salient experiences (both positive and negative) do tend to leave a lasting impression in memory relative to more mundane events. The psychologist Daniel Schacter at Harvard University has called such emotional persistence one of the seven "sins" of memory, meaning that classic accounts of memory function fail to describe the neurobehavioral impact of emotion.

Emotions associated with events or circumstances may have different consequences at different stages of memory processing, including encoding, consolidation, and retrieval. Each emotional dimension (e.g., along the axes of arousal or valence; see Figure 17.3) or emotion category (e.g., contempt, surprise, elation) can drive distinct aspects of memory processing. Also, emotions do not always facilitate memory encoding, storage, or retrieval. For example, high stress can impair memory retrieval, as anyone who has given a public speech can attest. From an evolutionary perspective, we and other animals should preferentially retain information about environmental events and social interactions that cause emotional reactions so that they can be reexperienced if they proved ecologically beneficial, or avoided if they proved detrimental. Accordingly, several neural and psychological mechanisms promote the persistence of emotional memories.

James McGaugh, working at UC Irvine, has argued that emotionally arousing events enhance memory by engaging systems that regulate the storage of newly acquired information. His **memory modulation hypothesis** emphasizes the role of the amygdala in enhancing consolidation processes in other regions of the brain after an emotional episode has occurred. For declarative memory, these regions include structures in the medial temporal lobe and the dorsolateral and ventrolateral PFC, among others. McGaugh takes the arousal dimension of emotion to be the primary force behind the neuromodulatory influences of the amygdala. The amygdala's influence on the relevant brain areas is both direct by virtue of axonal projections, and indirect through the release of hormones into the bloodstream that have effects on the brain.

Although many neurotransmitters alter memory function, central to the hypothesis are the actions of the catecholamine hormones **epinephrine** and **norepinephrine** and the corticosteroid hormone **cortisol** (called *corticosterone* in rodents). These **stress hormones** are secreted from the adrenal gland when stimulated by its sympathetic innervation (**Box 18A**). Although cortisol can cross the blood-brain barrier and act on central receptor sites (including those on neurons in the amygdala, hippocampus, and PFC), epinephrine and norepinephrine activate β-adrenergic receptors on visceral sensory endings in the periphery. Activation of the peripheral receptors initiates afferent signals that are carried centrally in the vagus and glossopharyngeal nerves. This information is then integrated in the nucleus of the solitary tract in the brainstem, which in turn influences the activity in the amygdala, as well as the hypothalamus and other central autonomic targets relevant for generating emotional feelings and expression.

The influence of these two stress hormone systems in the basolateral amygdala is critical for modulating memory storage in the cortex in response to emotional events (**Figure 18.8**). Because the neuromodulatory action of stress hormones is relatively slow compared to neural signaling, such effects are maximal during a period of memory consolidation, after the actual events have already occurred. The impact of the stress hormones thus reinforces whichever aspects

■ BOX 18A Stress and the Hypothalamic-Pituitary-Adrenal Axis

Stress is a complex term referring to the psychological and physiological changes that occur in response to a real or perceived threat to homeostasis. When encountering an aversive stimulus that is interpreted as potentially harmful to the individual (a *stressor*), the body initiates a complex pattern of endocrine, neural, and immunological activity (the *stress response*) in an attempt to cope with the elicitor and restore homeostatic balance. This *allostasis* (literally, "achieving stability through change") affects many bodily processes, including changes in cardiovascular function, respiration, glucose metabolism, muscle tension, and digestion.

Although the stress response evolved to handle physical threats such as extreme temperature changes or the appearance of a predator, psychosocial threats elicit similar response profiles. In the short term, the stress response is beneficial in that it mobilizes the body's resources to facilitate chances of survival. However, repeated or long-term stress increases the risk of developing a variety of physical and mental health problems, including peptic ulcers, hypertension, suppressed immune function, neuronal degeneration, reduced synaptic plasticity, cognitive impairment, obesity, and mood and anxiety disorders. Neuroscientist Bruce McEwen of Rockefeller University has coined the term *allostatic overload* to refer to the body's cumulative wear and tear that results from either too much stress or inefficient management of it over time.

The principal stress response is mediated by a trio of organs—the paraventricular nucleus of the hypothalamus, the anterior lobe of the pituitary gland, and the cortex of the adrenal gland—that are commonly referred to as the **hypothalamic-pituitary-adrenal (HPA) axis** (see the figure). Neurons in the paraventricular hypothalamus synthesize corticotropin-releasing factor (CRF) and vasopressin (AVP). In response to stress, CRF is released into hypophyseal portal vessels and binds to receptors in the anterior pituitary

gland. Consequently, adrenocorticotropic hormone (ACTH) is released into the peripheral circulation (an action that is independently facilitated by AVP), which stimulates the synthesis and release of glucocorticoid steroid hormones (called *corticosterone* in rodents and *cortisol* in humans) in the adrenal cortex.

Glucocorticoids, in turn, regulate the downstream physiological changes associated with the stress response and have an inhibitory feedback action on the hypothalamus and pituitary gland to prevent further engagement of the HPA axis. Glucocorticoid hormones bind to two different receptor subtypes—the mineralocorticoid and glucocorticoid receptors—but have a lower affinity for the latter subtype, which is more implicated in the stress response. In contrast, mineralocorti-

coid receptors are occupied primarily during nonstressful states, and their activity regulates the basal tone of the system, which is highest upon waking and gradually decreases over the day's activity cycle. The HPA axis is further modulated centrally and peripherally by neuropeptides (including substance P, neuropeptide Y, and galanin), serotonin, the catecholamines epinephrine and norepinephrine, and parasympathetic engagement.

Regions in the limbic forebrain and brainstem are important regulators of the HPA axis and are also targets of the long-term neurocognitive consequences of stress. The nucleus of the solitary tract in the brainstem integrates information from limbic and visceral sources to regulate CRF release in the hypothalamus through adrenergic and neuropeptide receptor-de-

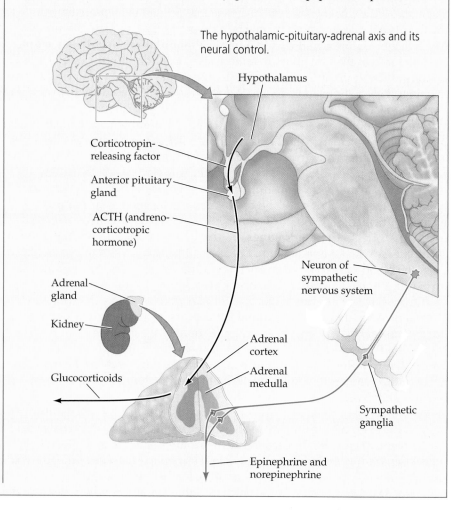

The hypothalamic-pituitary-adrenal axis and its neural control.

Hypothalamus

Corticotropin-releasing factor

Anterior pituitary gland

ACTH (adrenocorticotropic hormone)

Adrenal gland

Kidney

Glucocorticoids

Adrenal cortex

Adrenal medulla

Neuron of sympathetic nervous system

Sympathetic ganglia

Epinephrine and norepinephrine

pendent mechanisms. The amygdala, particularly its central and medial nuclei, is sensitive to circulating glucocorticoids and initiates a positive feedback loop of HPA activation that promotes stress via connections with the bed nucleus of the stria terminalis, nucleus of the solitary tract, and hypothalamus. In contrast, the hippocampus and medial PFC exert inhibitory influences over the HPA axis through a similar set of anatomical intermediaries.

Interestingly, chronic stress treatments and/or glucocorticoid manipulations induce different cellular effects in these structures. Chronic restraint (immobilization) stress in a rat induces dendritic atrophy and reduces synaptic plasticity in the hippocampus and medial PFC, which are associated with impaired memory and fear extinction, respectively. But the same stressor will increase dendritic arborization and glutamatergic transmission in the amygdala, which is associated with greater fear conditioning. Deleterious

effects of chronic stress on hippocampal volume and function in humans are especially pronounced in depression, posttraumatic stress disorder, development, and aging; and they are associated with low socioeconomic status (as well as subordinate status in monkey dominance hierarchies).

Individuals differ widely in their stress tolerance (which is, in part, genetically influenced) and in the range of stimuli that they interpret as being stressful. A key variable in coping with stress is the perceived control of the situation. When aversive stimuli are perceived as uncontrollable, stress effects are exacerbated, and over the long haul, feelings of helplessness may emerge. The impact of stress on behavior and cognitive function also varies by sex and is related in part to the modulatory influence of oxytocin and estrogen on brain regions that regulate the HPA axis. Understanding how such individual differences translate into risk factors for stress-

induced disease is an important area of ongoing research.

References

BALE, T. L. (2006) Stress sensitivity and the development of affective disorders. *Horm. Behav.* 50: 529–533.

MACHER, J. P. AND M. A. CROCQ, EDS. (2006) Special issue on Stress. *Dialogues Clin. Neurosci.* 8: 361–484.

MCEWEN, B. S. AND R. M. SAPOLSKY (1995) Stress and cognitive function. *Curr. Opin. Neurobiol.* 5: 205–216.

SAPOLSKY, R. M. (2005) The influence of social hierarchy on primate health. *Science* 308: 648–652.

SHORS, T. J. (1998) Stress and sex effects on associative learning: For better or for worse. *Neuroscientist* 4: 353–364.

TAYLOR, S. E., L. C. KLEIN, B. P. LEWIS, T. L. GREUENEWALK, R. A. R. GURUNG AND J. A. UPDEGRAFF (2000) Biobehavioral responses to stress in females: Tend-and-befriend, not fight-or-flight. *Psychol. Rev.* 107: 411–429.

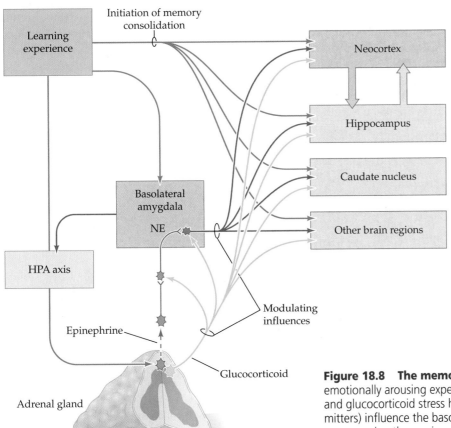

Figure 18.8 The memory modulation hypothesis. As an emotionally arousing experience is being consolidated, catecholamine and glucocorticoid stress hormone systems (along with other transmitters) influence the basolateral amygdala to enhance storage processes in other regions of the brain.

of the episode are being consolidated in the relevant cortical storage sites. These hormonal influences may also explain why moderate stress is beneficial to learning and the encoding of new memories. Using passive avoidance and other conditioning paradigms in rodents, McGaugh and his colleagues have amassed an impressive amount of experimental support for the hypothesis.

This line of work has recently been extended to study the relevant pathways in humans. Three lines of research support the memory modulation hypothesis in humans: (1) stress hormone manipulations; (2) observations of patients with amygdala damage; and (3) neuroimaging studies of amygdala interactions with other medial temporal lobe (MTL) regions.

With regard to stress hormones, acute administration of cortisol or induction of psychosocial stress (e.g., public speaking) or cold pressor stress (e.g., immersing the hand in a bucket of ice) generally enhances the retention of emotional memory, although this effect usually generalizes to non-emotional material as well. Because basal cortisol levels normally fluctuate during the day, influence a variety of receptor subtypes, and vary according to gender and other factors, the effects of cortisol on emotional memory have been somewhat inconsistent. A more striking effect on emotional memory is found in healthy participants who are administered the β-adrenergic blocker **propranolol** before being exposed to an audiovisual narrative with emotional content (**Figure 18.9**). These participants remember fewer details of the emotional portion of the narrative than do placebo controls when memory is tested several weeks later. Interestingly, recognition memory for the neutral portions of the narrative is unaffected by blocking the adrenergic effects, implying that the catecholamine hormones have a selective effect on emotional memory.

Patients with lesions of the amygdala exhibit similar selective deficits, supporting the view that these effects in normal subjects are mediated by the amygdala. The difference in memory for arousing material when amygdala-lesioned patients and controls are compared is larger after a delay than immediately after encoding, consistent with a memory consolidation interpretation. Administering propranolol to subjects being scanned during emotional memory tasks is a way to provide more direct fMRI evidence for mediation by the amygdala. Although the results suggest a possible pharmacological treatment for posttraumatic stress disorder (ethical issues associated with such interventions are discussed in Box 17A), propranolol has not proved to be an effective

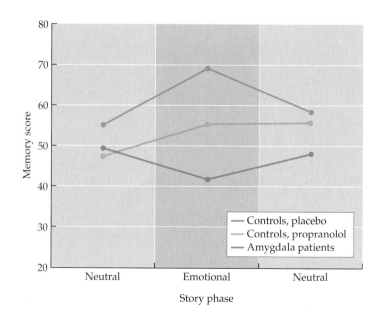

Figure 18.9 Pharmacological intervention blocks the effects of emotional arousal on memory. Participants are presented with an audiovisual narrative that contains three parts: the first and last parts of the story are emotionally neutral; the middle part of the story is emotionally arousing (describing a car accident). Healthy adults show long-term memory enhancement for the emotionally arousing (middle) portion of the story. This advantage is eliminated when propranolol, a β-adrenergic blocker, is administered to healthy adults before they hear the story, or to patients with bilateral amygdala damage. (After LaBar and Cabeza 2006.)

treatment to date, perhaps because of the chronic and severe nature of this problem compared to acute experimental manipulations on healthy subjects.

Further support of the memory modulation hypothesis comes from fMRI studies employing emotional versions of the *subsequent memory paradigm* (see Chapter 14). In this paradigm, participants undergo brain scanning while viewing words or pictures that vary in emotional content. Memory is tested later, outside of the scanning environment. Recall that by comparing fMRI scans for items that are subsequently remembered versus forgotten, one can identify brain regions that engage in successful encoding operations (called the *difference-in-memory*, or *Dm effect*). Such effects are larger for emotional than for neutral material when activation is examined in the amygdala, hippocampus, entorhinal cortex, and ventrolateral and dorsolateral PFC, among other regions.

Emotional Dm effects in the amygdala and other MTL structures are highly correlated, and this correlation is not found during the encoding of neutral stimuli (**Figure 18.10**). Patients with MTL damage show reductions in hippocampal fMRI activity as a function of the extent of damage to the amygdala

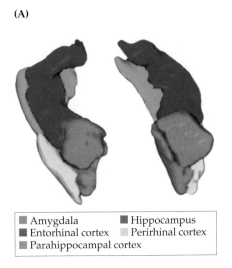

(A)

Legend:
- ■ Amygdala
- ■ Entorhinal cortex
- ■ Parahippocampal cortex
- ■ Hippocampus
- ■ Perirhinal cortex

Figure 18.10 Interactions between the amygdala and memory-related regions of the medial temporal lobe. These structures appear to be functionally coupled during the successful encoding of emotional memories. (A) Anatomical reconstruction of the medial temporal lobe in one participant. (B) Activity in the amygdala, hippocampus, and entorhinal cortex is greater for emotional pictures that are subsequently remembered than for those that are forgotten. (C) In individual participants, successful encoding activity is correlated in the amygdala and entorhinal cortex for emotional stimuli, but not for neutral stimuli (similar effects occur in the hippocampus but are not shown). (After Dolcos et al. 2004.)

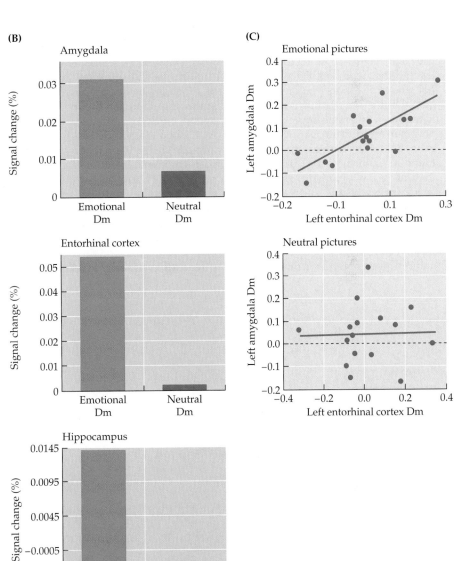

■ BOX 18B Mood and Memory

Most research on emotional memory emphasizes the transient influence of emotional stimulus content on autonomic physiology, brain activity, and behavior that has consequences on memory performance. As introduced in Chapter 17, however, prolonged and diffuse moods can also influence cognitive abilities, although the mechanisms associated with these effects are not well understood. Two related concepts that are relevant for understanding mood effects on memory are mood-congruent memory and mood-dependent memory.

Mood-congruent memory refers to the phenomenon whereby one's current mood biases the encoding and retrieval of events according to the valence of the mood. For instance, a runner who experiences a euphoric mood after winning a marathon is more likely to form a favorable impression of a newspaper reporter covering the event than if she had lost the marathon, and she is also more likely to recall prior joyful than sad experiences during the interview.

Mood-dependent memory refers to the phenomenon whereby material is remembered better when there is a match between the mood at encoding and the mood at retrieval than when

mood differs across these two memory stages. For instance, one is better able to recall details of a pleasant summer vacation when in a happy mood than when in a brooding mood. In this case, the prevailing mood reinstates the internal context associated with the events, which benefits retrieval according to Tulving's encoding specificity principle. It follows that mood effects should be more pronounced for explicit (declarative) rather than implicit (nondeclarative) memory because explicit memory is more sensitive to context manipulations, and indeed experimental work bears out this prediction.

To provide a general framework for understanding these phenomena, psychologist Gordon Bower, working at Stanford University, proposed a **spreading activation theory** of mood and memory. According to this theory, each mood is associated with particular nodes in the brain that represent basic emotional categories (anger, surprise, etc.). Experiences or stimuli that share the emotions affiliated with the mood become linked to these nodes. When a given mood is experienced, the emotion nodes associated with it become activated, and this activation spreads automatically to related mem-

ories and concepts according to the strength of the association between them and the particular emotion node (Figure A). Moreover, emotion nodes that are not connected to the current mood are inhibited such that the summation of activity across the nodes yields a net activation signature of the current mood. The associative network architecture of this theory accounts for mood-congruent memory effects because events and memories that are causally linked to the current mood become activated automatically.

Now consider how the theory accounts for mood-dependent memory. Suppose that in an experiment you are asked to generate personal associations to a list of cue words, including the word *church*. If your mood at the time of encoding is sad, you will be more likely to generate an association of the word *church* with a funeral memory because of spreading activation of the mood to the cue word (Figure B). If you are later asked to retrieve the words on the list but you are now in a pleasant mood, you will be at a disadvantage to remember the word *church* because the happy emotion node associated with your current mood has no connection to the contextual cue that you used to generate associations while encoding the list of words.

Although some researchers have questioned the reliability of such

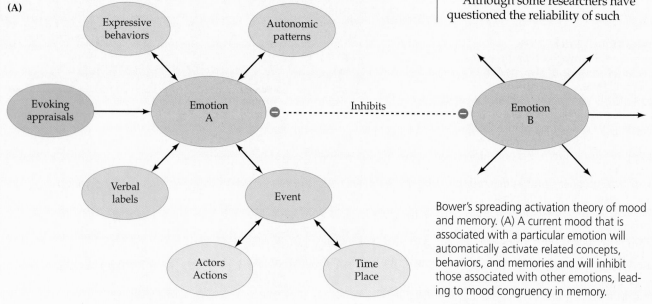

(A)

Bower's spreading activation theory of mood and memory. (A) A current mood that is associated with a particular emotion will automatically activate related concepts, behaviors, and memories and will inhibit those associated with other emotions, leading to mood congruency in memory.

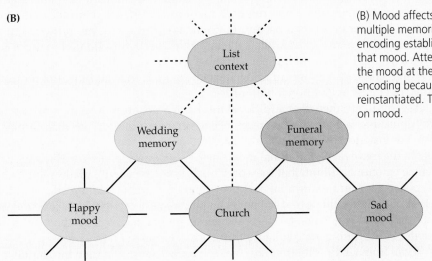

(B) Mood affects how a word on a list that is associated with multiple memories is encoded. A person's mood at the time of encoding establishes a bias toward experiences consistent with that mood. Attempts to retrieve the word later are facilitated if the mood at the time of retrieval is the same as that during encoding because the internal context of encoding is then reinstantiated. These findings indicate that memory depends on mood.

mood influences, other researchers have shown that mood effects on memory are consistent when the moods induced are strong, when free recall rather than recognition memory is used as the dependent measure, and when the material is self-relevant. Although Bower did not specify particular brain substrates for the nodes in the network, his theory relies on a categorical representation of emotions in the brain, which, as discussed in Chapter 17, is not well established. Because mood effects are valence-specific, they cannot be readily explained by the memory modulation hypothesis discussed in the text, which instead emphasizes the influence of the arousal dimension of emotion on memory consolidation.

Perhaps the best evidence for mood effects on memory comes from studies of patients suffering from clinical de-pression. Depressed individuals show a strong bias to retrieve personal memories that are negative rather than positive in valence. The bias is particularly strong for depression-related triggers and self-concepts. Interestingly, most healthy individuals show a positive valence bias in autobiographical memory (called the *Pollyanna effect*), and less severely depressed individuals show a more evenhanded recall pattern as a function of valence, indicating an intermediate pattern. Positive life memories retrieved by depressed patients tend to be less detailed and specific than in healthy individuals, and sometimes they are blends of multiple events—a phenomenon called *overgeneral memory*.

Unfortunately, the repeated recall of sad or stressful life experiences tends to reinforce and prolong the sad mood, contributing to the cycle of de-pression. When the depression remits, the negative memory biases are reduced, indicating that the mnemonic effects are related to the current mood and are not simply a trait that is characteristic of depression. Cognitive-behavioral therapies are targeted at helping depressed patients avoid ruminative, negative self-reflection to break the cycle of depression through distraction, cognitive reappraisal (see Box 18C), or other techniques.

References

BOWER, G. H. (1981) Mood and memory. *Am. Psychol.* 36: 129–148.

BOWER, G. H. AND J. P. FORGAS (2000) Affect, memory, and social cognition. In *Cognition and Emotion*, E. Eich, J. F. Kihlstrom, G. H. Bower, J. P. Forgas and P. M. Niedenthal (eds.). New York: Oxford University Press, pp. 19–189.

EICH, E. AND D. MCCAULEY (2000) Fundamental factors in mood dependent memory. In *The Role of Affect in Social Cognition*, J. P. Forgas (ed.). New York: Cambridge University Press, pp. 109–130.

MINEKA, S. AND K. NUGENT (1995) Mood-congruent memory biases in anxiety and depression. In *Memory Distortion: How Minds, Brains, and Societies Reconstruct the Past*, D. L. Schacter (ed.). Cambridge, MA: Harvard University Press, pp. 173–193.

(and reductions in amygdala fMRI activity as a function of the extent of damage to the hippocampus) during the encoding of emotional items. Taken together, these results indicate that the amygdala and adjacent MTL memory-processing regions are functionally coupled during the encoding of emotional items that are later remembered, as predicted by the memory modulation hypothesis.

Other aspects of emotional memory are not directly addressed by the memory modulation hypothesis. For instance, the hypothesis emphasizes the consolidation stage of memory and does not consider how emotional arousal affects the retrieval stage of memory. Moreover, because the hypothesis emphasizes arousal-mediated effects, it does not consider how emotional valence affects memory in the absence of high arousal (see **Box 18B** for a discussion of valence-dependent effects of mood on memory). Recent work in rodents also suggests that, for simple forms of fear memory, the amygdala may be a storage site for the relevant memories rather than a modulator of storage in other brain regions, and that when fearful events are retrieved, the memory trace returns to a labile state and must be reconsolidated in order to have a lasting behavioral impact. Although controversial, these findings suggest that the memory modulation hypothesis does not account for the full range of effects in emotional memory.

It seems likely, then, that additional mechanisms contribute to the retrieval of emotional information from memory. Some evidence accords with this supposition. For instance, fMRI studies indicate that the amygdala and MTL also play a role in the retrieval of emotional memories. When participants are asked to recognize emotional stimuli that they previously studied, activity in the amygdala, hippocampus, and entorhinal cortex is greater for items that are successfully retrieved than for those that are not. This difference in activity as a function of successful retrieval is greater in these regions for emotional items than for neutral items, indicating a modulatory influence of emotion on this process.

Recall from Chapter 14 that retrieval can be further subdivided into familiarity- and recollection-based responses. Behavioral studies have shown that emotional memories are more likely to be accompanied by a sense of recollection than of familiarity (presumably because of their rich contextual detail). This feeling of recollection during emotional retrieval is also linked to the degree of activity in the amygdala and hippocampus. Activity in these regions is also enhanced during the successful retrieval of neutral items that were previously encoded in emotional contexts relative to those encoded in neutral contexts. Therefore, interactions between the amygdala and MTL extend to the retrieval stage of memory, are enhanced by specific retrieval operations, and can be generalized to the retrieval of both emotional items and emotional contexts.

As with memory encoding, the amygdala and MTL do not act in isolation during the retrieval of emotional episodes. Hans Markowitsch of Bielefeld University in Germany has proposed that retrieving remote events from one's personal past (which are typically emotional in nature) involves interactions between these MTL structures and the inferior PFC. Damage to the uncinate fasciculus that connects these regions, particularly in the right hemisphere, causes dense amnesia for remote autobiographical events. Neuroimaging studies have supported this hypothesis by showing activity in the right inferior PFC, amygdala, and hippocampus during autobiographical retrieval. These regions also exhibit greater correlated activity (functional coupling) during the retrieval of autobiographical episodes than during the retrieval of semantic facts. The activity of these regions also depends on how emotionally intensely the autobiographical recollection is experienced.

Emotional Influences on Learning

Learning from emotional experiences is fundamental to well-being and survival. It is important not only to retain information about emotional events themselves, but also to determine which features of the environment predict desired (or undesired) emotional outcomes. As introduced in Chapter 15, the principles of classical and operant conditioning can explain in part how animals extract regularities that indicate when and where something positively or negatively reinforcing is likely to occur. Unlike the gradual acquisition of habits or motor skills, the conditioning of responses that entail emotion, particularly responses to fear, can be quite rapid. Understanding the mechanisms that mediate the acquisition and extinction of fear in response to sensory cues has important implications for the treatment of anxiety disorders and is taken up here. Reward learning is considered in Chapter 24.

The neural basis of fear acquisition

Studies in rodents by Michael Davis, Michael Fanselow, Joseph LeDoux, and others have established a detailed understanding of the neuroanatomy, neurophysiology, and molecular signaling that underlies the acquisition of fear elicited by relevant cues and contexts. In a typical paradigm, rats are presented with an auditory conditioned stimulus (CS) that predicts the occurrence of a mild foot shock, which is the unconditioned stimulus (US). The testing chamber where conditioning occurs is the context. After a few CS-US pairings, rats exhibit a constellation of changes in physiology and behavior to the CS (the tone presented alone) that are adaptive in the sense of preparing the animal to deal with the impending threat. These changes indicate a state of fear and include potentiation of startle reflexes, a cessation of exploratory behavior (freezing), and engagement of the sympathetic **fight-or-flight response** (pilo-erection, pupillary dilation, increased blood pressure, increased heart and breathing rate; see Chapters 8 and 17 for a review of the visceral motor system). The conditioned response is elicited not only to the presence of the CS itself (cued fear) but also to features of the environment (the testing chamber) where the conditioning episode took place (contextual fear).

The acquisition and expression of conditioned fear require the integrity of the amygdala (**Figure 18.11**). Rats with bilateral lesions to the lateral and central nuclei of the amygdala are dramatically impaired in acquiring conditioned fear responses to both cues and contexts. Electrophysiological recordings from lateral amygdala neurons show conditioned increases in firing rates that occur within 15 milliseconds of CS onset in some cells, implying mediation via the direct thalamo-amygdala pathway. Long-term potentiation (LTP), a potential electrophysiological signature of learning (see Chapter 13),

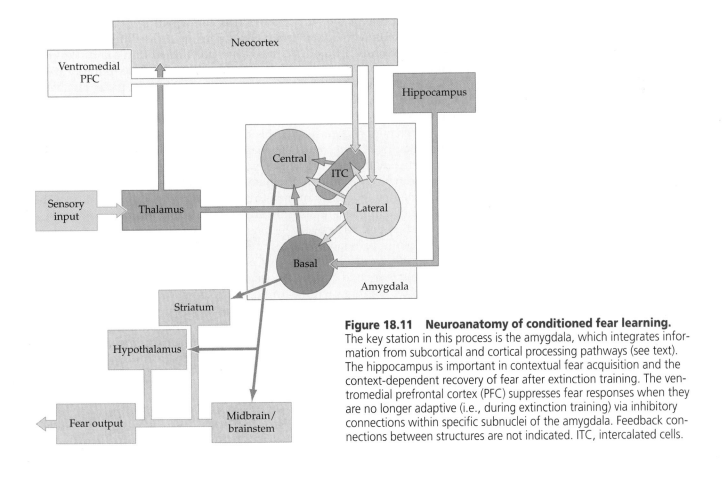

Figure 18.11 Neuroanatomy of conditioned fear learning. The key station in this process is the amygdala, which integrates information from subcortical and cortical processing pathways (see text). The hippocampus is important in contextual fear acquisition and the context-dependent recovery of fear after extinction training. The ventromedial prefrontal cortex (PFC) suppresses fear responses when they are no longer adaptive (i.e., during extinction training) via inhibitory connections within specific subnuclei of the amygdala. Feedback connections between structures are not indicated. ITC, intercalated cells.

Figure 18.12 Double dissociation of declarative memory and conditioned fear learning. (A) Patient S.M., who has bilateral amygdala damage, shows intact factual knowledge of the predictive relationship between the conditioned stimulus (CS) and the unconditioned stimulus (US) but fails to exhibit conditioned skin conductance responses (SCRs). (B) In contrast, patient W.C. has bilateral hippocampal damage and shows the opposite pattern—that is, intact SCRs to conditioned fear cues but no factual knowledge about the predictive relationship between the CS and the US. The results are consistent across visual and auditory CS modalities. (After Bechara et al. 1995.)

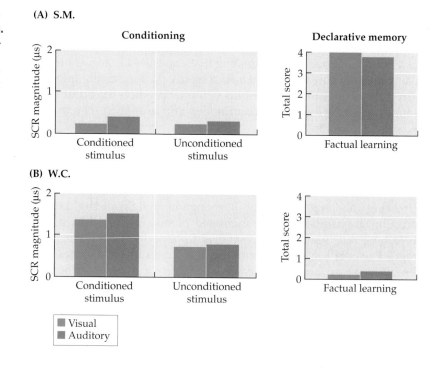

is also observed in this afferent pathway. Alterations in gene expression and protein synthesis further strengthen synaptic connections related to this sort of conditioning as a means of consolidating memories of the associations that elicit fear.

The critical role of the amygdala in **fear conditioning** is also evident in humans. Patients with bilateral amygdala damage show diminished conditioned fear responses, including reduced fear-potentiated startle and **skin conductance responses** (**SCRs**; see Box 17C for a detailed description of these physiological measures). These deficits persist even when the patient is able to state the predictive properties of the CS, indicating that declarative knowledge about the learning parameters is not by itself sufficient to generate appropriate defensive behavior (**Figure 18.12**). This evidence suggests that simple forms of fear conditioning can be partly dissociated from declarative memory—a finding supported by the fact that fear-relevant stimuli (e.g., angry facial displays, or snakes) can be conditioned subliminally in normal participants.

Neuroimaging studies in humans also show activity in the vicinity of the thalamus and amygdala (among other regions) during the acquisition phase of fear conditioning. Moreover, the degree of amygdala activation in individual participants correlates with the magnitude of fear learning expressed physiologically (usually in terms of SCR amplitude). Other brain regions activated during fear conditioning, such as the anterior cingulate gyrus, do not show a strong coupling with learning, and they may index other cognitive processes (e.g., attention) that are recruited at various points during training. Taken together, these findings provide strong evidence for the importance of the amygdala and related structures in warning animals of impending danger by associating the emotion of fear with potentially threatening circumstances.

The neural basis of fear extinction

Just as fear mandates changes in emotional response, it is also important to revise emotional responses when experience indicates that potentially threatening circumstances are no longer threatening. Indeed, persistent fear responses to stimuli that are no longer real threats are a hallmark of anxiety disorders, including phobias and posttraumatic stress disorder. This unwarranted persistence of fear has been termed **emotional perseveration** and is analogous to the continued deployment of cognitive strategies when they are no longer appropriate in problem-solving tasks (see Chapter 25). In fear-conditioning protocols, the fear value of a CS can be changed simply by removal of the negative reinforcer during the ongoing training. Through repeated presentation of the CS without the US (e.g., foot shock), the animal learns that the meaning of the CS has changed. The conditioned fear responses then subside in a process called **fear extinction**.

Extinction appears to depend on the integrity of the ventromedial prefrontal cortex (VMPFC). Thus rats with damage to the VMPFC, while able to acquire fear normally, take much longer to extinguish a conditioned fear response than do controls. As noted earlier, the VMPFC influences the activity of neurons in the amygdala, and stimulation of this pathway in conjunction with presentation of a CS is sufficient to suppress amygdala responses and reduce conditioned fear behavior. In humans, VMPFC damage leads to difficulty reversing stimulus-reinforcer relationships, and fMRI activity in this region correlates with the retention of extinction behavior. Because of the important implications of these PFC-amygdala interactions for the suppression of irrelevant fears, clinicians have had a keen interest in targeting pharmacological agents to mimic or augment these effects in patients with anxiety disorders. The regulatory influence of the PFC over emotional processing in the amygdala and related limbic regions is a general theme in neurobiological studies of the cognitive control of emotion, a topic explored further in **Box 18C**.

The neural basis of contextual fear

Fears are elicited not only by discrete cues but also by certain places or other contextual information in the environment. Walking down a dark alley is likely to induce more fearful and defensive behavior than would walking along a brightly lit street, and fear responses to a stimulus such as a bear may be more appropriate when encountered in some situations (the woods) than others (the zoo). We and other animals must therefore learn when and where fear reactions are useful and when and where they are not.

Given its role in spatial processing and declarative memory (see Chapter 14), the hippocampus is a likely site for the mediation of some aspects of **contextual fear conditioning**. Indeed, rats with hippocampal lesions can be conditioned normally to discrete cues but fail to generalize and retain fear responses to the context in which the training took place. Similarly, amnesic patients with hippocampal damage exhibit conditioned SCRs to a discrete CS that predicts shock delivery, but they do not retain information about the contextual details of the conditioning episode (see Figure 18.12). Evidently the hippocampus makes similar contributions to both emotional and non-emotional forms of learning and memory that depend on associating pertinent information with the contexts in which the learning occurs. In this regard it would be inappropriate to consider the hippocampus a structure specifically dedicated to emotional processing—an idea previously emphasized in the limbic system theory of emotion (see Chapter 17).

Emotional Influences on Decision Making

Philosophical accounts of behavior have sometimes maligned the emotions (passions) as impediments to rational thinking and decision making. However, researchers now acknowledge that social and emotional factors not only contribute to the types of decisions that humans and other animals make on a

■ BOX 18C Emotion Regulation

The ability to regulate emotions in response to routine stressors is central to mental health. Transient emotional episodes are often healthy responses that permit adaptive behavioral actions when environmental situations demand. However, emotions that are socially inappropriate, displaced to irrelevant targets, or excessively prolonged, intense, or variable can lead to personal distress and interfere with daily activities; and in extreme cases they are hallmarks of psychopathology.

Psychological studies of emotion regulation have revealed many ways in which individuals consciously and unconsciously attempt to influence the intensity, duration, or quality of the emotions they feel. Some of these strategies are more effective than others. Central to this research is the fact that emotions are not experienced passively in response to elicitors but instead are active, subjective processes in humans (and most likely other animals). Therefore, cognitive-behavioral interventions are targeted at training

individuals to generate new, adaptive responses to emotion elicitors; to modify existing reactions as they unfold; or to be accepting (mindful) of their reactions and then let them go to avoid emotional perseveration (see the text). Although much research has focused on dampening negative affect, researchers are also examining the potentially beneficial effects of enhancing positive affect.

Stanford University psychologist James Gross has classified emotion regulation into different strategies ac-cording to the time course of their engagement (e.g., preceding or following elicitation of an emotional response) and the regulatory target (e.g., controlling physiological expression or cognitive interpretations of the elicitor). At one extreme, individuals change their activity patterns beforehand to avoid the emotional encounter altogether (*situation selection*), as when a person who is afraid of flying chooses to travel by train.

In a less extreme strategy, individuals engage in *cognitive reappraisal* to at-

Cognitive reappraisal of negative emotion. In this experiment, participants were instructed either to decrease negative emotions elicited by the presentation of aversive pictures or to passively look at them. Participants decreased emotions by cognitively reappraising the stimulus either to imagine that things get better in the depicted scene (situation-focused reappraisal) or to cognitively distance themselves from the picture by viewing it from a detached third-person perspective (self-focused reappraisal). Either way, when participants attempted to decrease their negative emotions, activity increased in the dorsal frontoparietal attentional network (relative to passive viewing), as well as other regions in the inferior PFC and anterior cingulate (A). In contrast, decreasing negative emotion reduced activity in the amygdala from the passive look condition, making it more similar to that observed for passively looking at neutral pictures (B). These patterns suggest that frontoparietal regions implement the regulatory strategy and the amygdala is a target of the regulatory action on emotion generation. The instructions were effective in decreasing emotion associated with the pictures, as indicated by reduced subjective reports of negative affect in response to the pictures (C). (After Ochsner et al. 2004.)

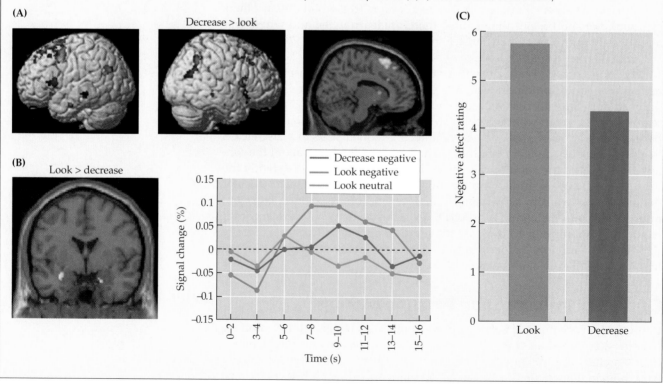

(A) Decrease > look

(B) Look > decrease

Signal change (%)

Time (s)

Decrease negative
Look negative
Look neutral

(C) Negative affect rating

Look   Decrease

tend to or interpret the meaning of an elicitor in such a way as to alter its emotional impact. One way that cognitive reappraisal is investigated in the laboratory is to have participants use imagery to generate alternate hypothetical outcomes of emotional scenarios. For instance, when presented with pictures of combat, participants may be instructed to reinterpret the pictures to decrease the negative affect associated with viewing the picture, such as imagining that a wounded soldier depicted will return home soon and get well. Reappraisal strategies are generally beneficial in reducing physiological arousal associated with the emotional elicitor and can facilitate explicit memory for the episode.

In contrast, response-focused strategies in which individuals actively mask their facial expressions and associated feelings in response to emotion elicitors (*expressive suppression*) tend to be maladaptive in that sympathetic arousal is inadvertently increased, unpleasant feelings are sometimes unaffected, and memory is worsened. Although these strategies are often studied individually, it is well recognized that people use a variety of interacting schemes selected according to the constraints of the particular socioemotional context, although some individuals tend to engage in certain strategies over others (*affective style*).

Neuroimaging studies have detailed some of the ways in which conscious attempts to change emotional experience affect activity in the relevant frontolimbic structures. When individuals engage in cognitive reappraisal of negative emotional stimuli, activity increases in the dorsal frontoparietal network, as well as in other prefrontal regions, including the dorsal anterior cingulate cortex, ventrolateral PFC, and orbitofrontal cortex (see the figure). Interestingly, some of these areas are responsive whether the regulatory goal is to increase or to decrease affect, suggesting that they are involved in selecting and applying the cognitive strategy. By contrast, other regions, including the amygdala and insula, are targets of prefrontal modulation; accordingly, their activity is sensitive to the regulatory goal (e.g., increasing when negative affect is enhanced and decreasing when negative affect is dampened). Thus, attempts to cognitively alter emotional experience involve interactions between dorsal executive control and ventral emotion-processing regions of the brain.

Although much of this chapter describes how emotions influence cognitive functions, studies of emotion regulation provide an excellent example of the opposite case. They illustrate how higher-order executive processing regions of the brain are recruited to modify emotional experience directly or indirectly through alterations in other cognitive functions, including thinking, visual imagery, behavioral inhibition, and selection of information in working memory. Research in this area holds considerable promise for understanding individual differences in regulatory abilities, responsiveness to cognitive-behavioral therapy, and resilience to developing psychopathology following traumatic experiences.

References

DAVIDSON, R. J., K. M. PUTNAM AND C. L. LARSON (2000) Dysfunction in the neural circuitry of emotion regulation—A possible prelude to violence. *Science* 289: 591–594.

GROSS, J. J. (1998) The emerging field of emotion regulation: An integrative review. *Rev. Gen. Psychol.* 2: 271–299.

LAZARUS, R. S. AND E. ALFERT (1964) Short-circuiting of threat by experimentally altering cognitive appraisal. *J. Abnorm. Soc. Psychol.* 69: 195–205.

OCHSNER, K. N. AND J. J. GROSS (2005) The cognitive control of emotion. *Trends Cogn. Sci.* 9: 242–249.

OCHSNER, K. N. AND 6 OTHERS (2004) For better or for worse: Neural systems supporting the cognitive down- and up-regulation of negative emotion. *Neuroimage* 23: 483–499.

---

daily basis, but also often improve the decisions made (e.g., fear may wisely lead a person to take a somewhat longer route via a well-lit street rather than cut through a dark alley). As discussed in Chapter 24, normative models of decision making based solely on mathematical and economic principles fail to account for the ways decisions are made in the real world. The major reason is that decision making is influenced heavily by emotion and other factors that don't follow the rules of logic but are instead accumulated by information acquired through phylogenetic and ontogenetic experience.

Three categories of emotions—anticipatory, expected, and immediate—can act on decision making. *Anticipatory emotions* occur prior to the decision and can help guide decision making by influencing risk and reward valuation. For instance, during "last call" at a bar, a patron might decide to have one more drink because of an emotional anticipation of the immediately rewarding properties of alcohol, despite the increased risk of causing an accident while driving home.

In contrast, *expected emotions* result from the outcomes of decisions, leading to future expectations of feelings based on responses to similar outcomes. The decision to break up with a romantic partner because of job relocation might elicit feelings of regret as the person ponders how things "might have been" if he or she had not taken the job.

Finally, *immediate emotions* influence decision making simply because they occur at the same time the decision is being made, even though they are not relevant from a more objective perspective. For example, a high school student's visit to a college campus might be tainted if the weather is particularly miserable on the day of the visit, and the negative mood induced could generate a more pessimistic view of that college than is warranted. Mechanisms of mood congruency that apply to declarative memory play a similar role in decisions affected by immediate emotions (see Box 18B). Studies of these three sorts of emotional influences on decisions have focused on anticipatory emotions and have culminated in the so-called somatic marker hypothesis described next.

The somatic marker hypothesis

Patients with damage to the VMPFC have particular deficits in decision making and long-term planning in real-world settings. As described in Chapter 23, such individuals often make poor judgments about interpersonal relationships, business relationships, or other matters that can lead to social estrangement, financial loss, and other negative consequences. From observations of such patients in studies conducted at the University of Iowa, Antonio Damasio proposed the **somatic marker hypothesis**, a scheme by which bioregulatory processes, including those related to emotion, influence reasoning in complex circumstances.

The somatic markers in question are internal representations of bodily states that indicate the personal consequences of actions associated with particular situations. In this view, the history of one's emotional responses to action outcomes triggered by similar situations is represented by somatic states, including the associated autonomic (visceral) and skeletomuscular responses; and these emotional responses are stored as long-term dispositions or biases. According to this theory, the VMPFC is instrumental in learning and retaining these associations between environmental events and the somatic states based on prior experience. When contemplating potential actions in response to novel exemplars in the same event category, the VMPFC reactivates the relevant somatic states by engaging cortical and subcortical structures, including the insula, somatosensory cortex, and amygdala. Consequently, the current body state matches the stored emotional associations to the event, which are then used to determine whether contemplated action will be beneficial or detrimental to achieving one's goals in the situation at hand.

According to Damasio, somatic states can be reactivated either consciously or unconsciously, via a *body loop* or an *as-if loop*. In the body loop scenario, the VMPFC engages corticolimbic structures that induce actual motoric and visceral changes that are fed back to the somatosensory and insular cortices. Alternatively, somatic states can be reactivated through an as-if loop in which the VMPFC influences somatosensory cortices while bypassing the body proper (either by direct neural connections or by indirect neuromodulatory actions in the brain). Either way, activation of somatosensory cortices is the final common pathway to the explicit or implicit "recalling" of somatic states associated with particular event outcomes.

For example, suppose a student is deciding whether to attend an 8:00 AM class following a long night of socializing. Upon waking, the student recalls the pertinent information about the schedule via cortical association networks that activate semantic representations and sensory images relative to the decision. The VMPFC concurrently calls up dispositional linkages between this factual knowledge and somatic states as the student considers what action to take. Perhaps the decision to skip class in the past elicited guilt, which is associated with a particular somatic state. Alternatively, decisions to attend this class in the past may have led to learning something interesting and may have been socially rewarding, eliciting another somatic state. The decision of whether to attend class on a particular day will thus be guided by somatic markers that facilitate the decision process by reinstating bodily states useful in making the best choice. In this way, emotion constrains possible decisions and facilitates reasoning about goal-directed behavior.

From the historical perspective outlined in Chapter 17, the somatic marker hypothesis is neo-Jamesian in that it emphasizes the role of feedback from the periphery in determining how emotional states influence behavior. The as-if loop postulated by Damasio softens the James-Lange claim about the necessity of peripheral feedback. On the other hand, some have argued that this caveat makes the somatic marker hypothesis untestable. Because the hypothesis doesn't predict *how* specific emotional representations differ from others, it is not a theory about emotion per se. In any event, the somatic marker hypothesis is a good example of how modern-day theorists are applying emotion-related concepts to explain specific aspects of complex behavior observed in the real world. Chapter 24 presents additional experimental support for the somatic marker hypothesis generated in the context of gambling tasks.

Summary

1. One goal of the nascent field of affective neuroscience is to describe how emotions systematically influence other cognitive functions.

2. Several brain regions are clearly implicated in emotional processing, including the amygdala, anterior cingulate, insula, and the ventral, medial, and orbital prefrontal cortex. These brain areas are effectively nodes connecting regions that mediate emotional functions with brain regions that mediate other cognitive functions. The resulting interactions ultimately guide behavior.

3. Features of the environment that elicit emotional responses receive priority in perception and attention; the rapidity of such prioritization in some paradigms suggests subcortical as well as cortical processing. Attention to emotional stimuli in other instances requires cognitive influences arising from dorsal frontoparietal regions, and in these circumstances the anterior cingulate and ventral sectors of the prefrontal cortex are key interfaces.

4. Both reflexive and voluntary attentional effects enhance the encoding of emotional material in memory. Arousal also enhances memory consolidation and retrieval by way of the stress response systems, which interact with the amygdala and with memory-processing regions of the prefrontal cortex and the medial temporal lobe, including the hippocampus.

5. In addition to facilitating the retention of information about emotional events, the amygdala detects regularities in the environment that predict aversive and appetitive outcomes, as exemplified by fear conditioning. The association of conditioned fears with environmental contexts requires the hippocampus as well. The extinction of conditioned fear involves inhibitory interactions between the ventromedial prefrontal cortex and the amygdala.

6. Somatic states elicited by fear and other emotions are represented in the insula and somatosensory cortices, regions that interact with the orbital and ventromedial prefrontal cortex and other executive control regions to guide decision making.

7. Contemporary theories, including McGaugh's memory modulation hypothesis and Damasio's somatic marker hypothesis, may help explain specific influences of emotion on cognitive functions. Understanding the neural architecture and pharmacological substrates of such influences provides potential targets for the treatment of affective disorders.

Additional Reading

Reviews

DOLAN, R. J. (2002) Emotion, cognition, and behavior. *Science* 298: 1191–1194.

HOLLAND, P. C. AND M. GALLAGHER (1999) Amygdala circuitry in attentional and representational processes. *Trends Cogn. Sci.* 3: 65–73.

JOHNSON, M. K. AND C. WEISZ (1994) Comments on unconscious processing: Finding emotion in the cognitive stream. In *The Heart's Eye: Emotional Influences in Perception and Attention*, P. M. Neidenthal and S. Kitayama (eds.). San Diego: Academic Press, pp. 145–164.

LABAR, K. S. AND R. CABEZA (2006) Cognitive neuroscience of emotional memory. *Nat. Rev. Neurosci.* 7: 54–64.

MCGAUGH, J. L. (2004) The amygdala modulates the consolidation of memories of emotionally arousing experiences. *Annu. Rev. Neurosci.* 27: 1–28.

MAYBERG, H. S. (1997) Limbic-cortical dysregulation: A proposed model of depression. *J. Neuropsychiatry Clin. Neurosci.* 9: 471–481.

PESSOA, L. (2005) To what extent are emotional visual stimuli processed without attention and awareness? *Curr. Opin. Neurobiol.* 15: 188–196.

Important Original Papers

ANDERSON, A. K. AND E. A. PHELPS (2001) Lesions of the human amygdala impair enhanced perception of emotionally salient events. *Nature* 411: 305–309.

BECHARA, A., D. TRANEL, H. DAMASIO, R. ADOLPHS, C. ROCKLAND AND A. R. DAMASIO (1995) Double dissociation of conditioning and declarative knowledge relative to the amygdala and hippocampus in humans. *Science* 269: 1115–1118.

CAHILL, L., B. PRINS, M. WEBER AND J. L. MCGAUGH (1994) Beta-adrenergic activation and memory for emotional events. *Nature* 371: 702–704.

DE GELDER, B., J. VROOMEN, G. POURTOIS AND L. WEISKRANTZ (1999) Non-conscious recognition of affect in the absence of striate cortex. *Neuroreport* 10: 3759–3763.

DOLCOS, F., K. S. LABAR AND R. CABEZA (2004) Interaction between the amygdala and the medial temporal lobe memory system predicts better memory for emotional events. *Neuron* 42: 855–863.

LABAR, K. S., M. M. MESULAM, D. R. GITELMAN AND S. WEINTRAUB (2000) Emotional curiosity: Arousal modulation of visuospatial attention is preserved in aging and early-stage Alzheimer's disease. *Neuropsychologia* 38: 1734–1740.

WHALEN, P. J. AND 10 OTHERS (2004) Human amygdala responsivity to masked fearful eye whites. *Science* 306: 2061.

WILLIAMS, M. A., A. P. MORRIS, F. MCGLONE, D. F. ABBOTT AND J. B. MATTINGLEY (2004) Amygdala responses to fearful and happy facial expressions under conditions of binocular suppression. *J. Neurosci.* 24: 2898–2904.

YAMASAKI, H., K. S. LABAR AND G. MCCARTHY (2002) Dissociable prefrontal brain systems for attention and emotion. *Proc. Natl. Acad. Sci. USA* 99: 11447–11451.

Books

BUCK, R. (1984) *The Communication of Emotion.* New York: Guilford.

DALGLEISH, T. AND M. J. POWER, EDS. (1999) *The Handbook of Cognition and Emotion.* Chichester, England: Wiley.

DAMASIO, A. R. (1994) *Descartes' Error.* New York: Putnam.

NIEDENTHAL, P. M. AND S. KITAYAMA (1994) *The Heart's Eye: Emotional Influences in Perception and Attention.* San Diego: Academic Press.

UTTL, B., N. OHTA AND A. L. SIEGENTHALER (2006) *Memory and Emotion: Interdisciplinary Perspectives.* Malden, MA: Blackwell Scientific.

19

Social Cognition

Introduction

A major goal of cognitive neuroscience as applied to social interactions is to identify the neural underpinnings of the processes by which individuals understand themselves and their relationships to others. This subfield builds on the developments in affective neuroscience described in Chapters 17 and 18—in particular, the evidence that emotions serve important social functions. Indeed, emotions evident in facial expressions, body language, and speech are a means by which we communicate our intentions to others, and by which we interpret the actions of others. Humans and other species that live in social groups have evolved neural mechanisms for establishing hierarchies among members, for building kinship and other social bonds, and for setting acceptable norms of behavior. In many animals the basis for social behaviors is determined genetically, with individual experience playing a relatively minor role. In humans, however, culture, customs, and learning from others clearly influence what we become over the course of development and the behavior that characterizes us as adults. Because social psychologists and neuroscientists have joined forces only recently, many issues and observations in this field are contentious, and the answers to many questions remain open. This chapter summarizes some of the advances that have been made to date, drawing upon four domains of research: self-referential processing, perception of social cues gleaned from observing others, social categorization, and theory of mind. Social communication by means of language is taken up specifically in Chapters 20 and 21, and aspects of social influences on decision making are discussed in Chapter 24.

The Self

Distinguishing oneself from others is a necessary first step in establishing fluent social interactions. Understanding the nature of the self has long perplexed philosophers, psychologists, and laypeople alike. In his treatise on psychology written at the end of the nineteenth century, William James described the self in the following way (italics in original):

> Whatever I may be thinking of, I am always at the same time more or less aware of *myself*, of my *personal existence*. At the same time it is *I* who am

aware; so that the total self of me, being as it were duplex, partly known and partly knower, partly object and partly subject, must have two aspects discriminated in it.

W. James, 1890, Psychology: Briefer Course, p. 176

Despite the conceptual difficulties in defining what constitutes the entity we all consider **self**, a core cognitive ability described by James is the ability to consider one's own being as an object, and thus subject to consideration in objective terms. This ability is called **self-reflexive thought**.

Non-human animals presumably possess a rudimentary ability to distinguish themselves from other animals because of its obvious biological value, but at the same time it seems unlikely that all but perhaps advanced non-human primates are capable of self-reflexive thought and actions determined in this way. The ability to think of oneself in abstract and even symbolic terms, including creating a mental avatar of oneself to imagine alternative outcomes in complex social situations, depends on the sort of self-awareness that defines consciousness as we know it in ourselves.

As described in Chapter 28, the capacity for self-awareness has probably evolved gradually in mammals and other animals in conjunction with related social, emotional, and cognitive skills. Rodents, for example, can navigate in their environment using either egocentric or allocentric frames of reference. Evidently they can deal with the world either in terms of their own place in it, or simply in terms of external cues. Animals with smaller brains and less complex nervous systems seem to operate primarily on external cues. In arboreal primates, an awareness of the body and its abilities may facilitate the difficult task of swinging from tree to tree, because landing on a branch that would be insufficient to support the body could be fatal. And, as described in Chapter 28, some non-human animals can recognize themselves in a mirror. Nonetheless, self-recognition and self-reflexive thought are clearly much better developed in humans than in other animals. Indeed, the archaeological record suggests that the rapid development of culture with a focus on the importance of individuals (and thus the self) emerged in the evolution of humans approximately 50,000 years ago.

The value of symbolic self-reflexive thought is not difficult to imagine. This ability enables an appraisal of one's personality traits, strengths, and weaknesses in comparison to others and to cultural norms. Such evaluation is essential to successful social behavior by generating self-esteem and self-regulation. The importance of these cognitive functions is evident in pathologies in which they are compromised. Whereas most humans possess a sense of a unitary self across both time and space, the stable concept of the self breaks down in some clinical disorders. For example, **fugue states** are defined as transient states of confusion in which self-relevant knowledge is temporarily unavailable to consciousness and uncharacteristic and often self-destructive behaviors ensue.

Self-reflection

The techniques used today in cognitive neuroscience have only recently been brought to bear on these philosophical, practical, and clinical concerns, by identifying brain areas that mediate self-reflexive thoughts and feelings; but in that short time some important observations have been made.

Self-reflection requires an initial redirection of attentional focus from sensory events to internal thoughts, memories, feelings, and visceral sensations. As introduced in Chapter 3, neuroimaging studies have identified brain areas that are active in the absence of explicit stimulation from or attention to the extrapersonal environment. The activity of these regions *decreases* during tasks that require attention to stimuli in extrapersonal space. Although the evidence is still sparse, this **default mode** activity provides a basis for beginning to understand the brain regions that mediate focusing attention on the self. This spontaneous, coordinated activity occurs in the dorsal and ventromedial prefrontal cortex (PFC), posterior cingulate, and medial and lateral parietal cortex; and it is correlated with EEG power in the beta band. These observations have been interpreted by some to reflect an ongoing stream of consciousness. The same brain regions are sensitive to variations in the level of consciousness associated with different levels of self-awareness (e.g., stages of sleep, the effects of anesthesia, or vegetative states).

Building on these observations of resting-state activity, researchers have directed participants to explicitly engage in self-reflection during brain scanning. For instance, participants are asked to indicate how well adjectives referring to personal traits (e.g., *ambitious*) and sentences (e.g., "I tend to worry a lot") describe them, or to compare their personality traits with those of famous people or individuals they know well. Activity changes in the medial PFC and parietal regions have been consistently reported. Moreover, TMS applied to the medial parietal cortex temporarily blocks the retrieval of some self-relevant knowledge.

The degree of medial PFC activity in response to specific trait words during self-endorsement tasks also predicts subsequent memory for the words. That is, when rating trait words for their self-relevance, the degree of activity in the medial PFC in response to the words predicts which ones are remembered later. Because this finding does not generalize to nonsocial encoding tasks, such as those involving perceptual, semantic, or emotional processing (see Chapters 14 and 18), a specific neural signature of self-referential memory encoding is implicated. However, because of the variety of cognitive processes that contribute to self-referential encoding, additional supporting evidence is warranted.

These studies revealed significant overlap in medial PFC and parietal regions for attributions of characteristics to oneself compared to attributions to other people. Some clarification has come in further work by Todd Heatherton, William Kelly, and their colleagues at Dartmouth, who have shown that a region of medial PFC (Brodmann area 10) is recruited more strongly for judgments focused on oneself than on others (**Figure 19.1**). Furthermore, a specific role for the medial PFC in self-referential processing has been suggested in studies of autobiographical memory retrieval. For example, successful memory retrieval for spatial landmarks cued by photos taken by the subject elicits greater medial PFC activity than does successful retrieval cued by photos of the same landmark that were previously studied but taken by others. As discussed in Chapters 14 and 16, the medial PFC has been implicated more generally in mental processes needed to reflect on autobiographical memories, and in generating the mental imagery required in working memory tasks that project actions of the self into the future.

Other work has focused more specifically on the subjective feelings and the sorts of visceral changes that accompany emotional or painful stimuli. These studies have implicated not only the brain regions involved in self-reflexive thought, but also the orbitofrontal cortex, anterior cingulate, and insula. Richard Lane at the University of Arizona found that when participants view emotionally aversive scenes, an explicit focus on subjective arousal response elicits greater activity in the rostral anterior cingulate than does an explicit focus on the spatial layout of the scenes, which instead elicits greater activity in the posterior parietal cortex.

Anterior cingulate responses to emotional stimuli and emotional memories are further modulated by individual differences in performance on Lane's Levels of Emotional Awareness Scale, which attempts to measure how deeply

Figure 19.1 Role of the medial prefrontal cortex in self-referential processing. (A) Greater activity in Brodmann area 10 (yellow circle) is found when participants make trait judgments about themselves relative to trait judgments of a best friend, or perceptual judgments of the appearance of the trait word (i.e., whether it is upper or lower case). (B) Activity in the same brain area during autobiographical memory retrieval. College students were instructed to take pictures of campus landmarks; they then viewed these photos and pictures of the same landmarks taken by other people. Successful recollection of photos taken by the participants was associated with greater activity in the medial PFC than was successful recollection of photos taken by others. Note that in both (A) and (B), a self-referential effect is inferred from the lack of deactivation from baseline, since this region is tonically active in the absence of external stimulation (see text). (A from Heatherton et al. 2006; B from Cabeza et al. 2004.)

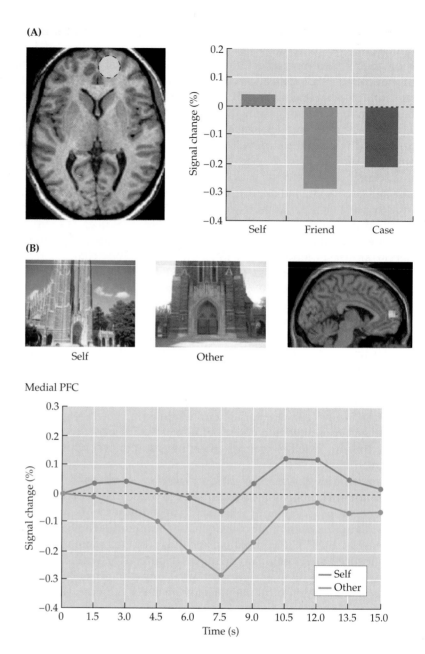

and complexly emotions are being experienced. Anterior cingulate activity scales with autonomic measures of arousal and the subjective experience of the unpleasantness of pain, and is implicated in the regulation of pain modulation. This work further reinforces the idea that the anterior cingulate integrates attentional and emotional functions (see Chapter 18), but with the more specific goal of directing attention to one's own emotional reactions.

In contrast, the anterior **insula** signals awareness of bodily sensations (called *interoception*), such as alterations in respiration and heart rate during arousing states. The posterior and mid insula are part of a visceral processing network that includes brainstem autonomic centers, the hypothalamus, the mediodorsal and ventromedial thalamus, and the anterior cingulate. Multiple afferent pathways converge on the anterior insula, particularly in the right hemisphere, which, in turn, projects to the orbitofrontal cortex. The neocortical components of this hierarchy are hypothesized to represent bodily state in an integrated way. Thus, neuroimaging studies have shown that anterior insula activity is sensitive to individual differences in the ability to detect one's own heartbeat as well as the personality trait of neuroticism, which is associated with a heightened tendency to experience negative affect. An awareness of bodily states signaled by these cortical regions presumably provides a basis for self-reflective feelings that entail this component of self-awareness.

Embodiment

Embodiment refers to the sense of being localized within the body. Several phenomenological aspects of the sense of self relate to embodiment, including *self-location* (the feeling of being at a particular location in space) and *egocentric frame of reference* (navigating in the world with reference to the location of oneself and one's own viewpoint). Although most individuals experience a spatial unity of self and body, in certain conditions individuals lose this routine sense. As described in Chapter 12, individuals with right parietal damage may ignore or deny the existence of the left side of their body (called *neglect syndrome*). Others experience sensations from an amputated body part (*phantom limb sensations*; see Box 7B). Still other patients deny that their body is suffering from a particular ailment (*agnosognosia*) or may experience a feeling of being dislocated outside their body (called *disembodiment*).

The ability of humans to use symbolic analogues or avatars of themselves permits mental imagery of the body from a non-egocentric frame of reference (e.g., imaging the view of oneself from behind). In dreams and memories, experiences are sometimes transformed from a first-person to a third-person (observer) perspective, and some memories, such as the memory of giving a public address, tend to have a canonical third-person perspective.

Two brain regions have been implicated in body representations and disembodied phenomena. A region of extrastriate visual cortex, sometimes called the *extrastriate body area*, is engaged when individuals visually process human bodies or body parts, imagine changes in the position of a body part, or are asked to adopt a third-person perspective for visualizing their own body (**Figure 19.2A**). In addition, out-of-body experiences have been linked to the **temporoparietal junction**, a multisensory area at the border between the temporal and parietal lobes and surrounding the posterior terminus of the Sylvian fissure (**Figure 19.2B**).

The Swiss neurologist Olaf Blake has examined these phenomena in epileptic patients undergoing neurosurgery, as well as in healthy adults during mental imagery tasks. One patient reported out-of-body experiences, illusory changes in arm and leg position, and whole-body displacements following stimulation of the right angular gyrus in the vicinity of the temporoparietal junction. Another patient was asked to mentally rotate her body to mimic the viewpoint of her seizure-induced out-of-body experience, and in this case electrical activity was noted near the seizure focus at the left temporoparietal junction. Similarly, healthy adults who imagine rotations of their body axis show enhanced event-related potentials localized by source modeling to the temporoparietal junction bilaterally, but with a right-sided bias.

When TMS is applied to this region, there is a selective response to making judgments of body rotations, but not to making judgments of mentally rotated objects (see Figure 19.2B). Recall that the temporoparietal junction in the right hemisphere has also been implicated in neglect syndrome (see Chapter 12), and it may integrate visual attention with vestibular and somatosensory information to track body positions in space, establish an egocentric visual perspective, and create a spatial unity of self and body.

In summary, focusing on oneself relies on processing in particular brain areas. The midline PFC, cingulate, and parietal regions contribute to aspects of

(A)

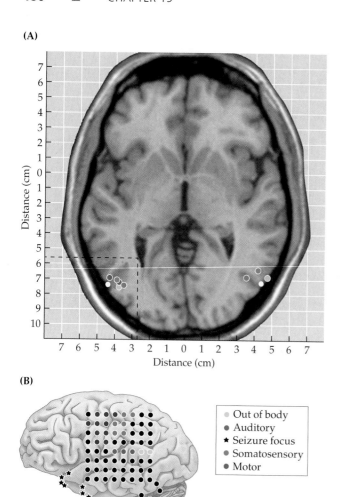

(B)

- ○ Out of body
- ● Auditory
- ★ Seizure focus
- ● Somatosensory
- ● Motor

(C)

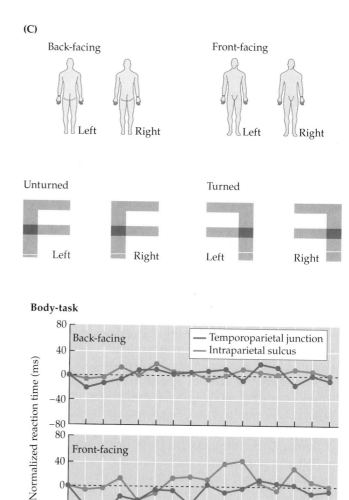

Back-facing   Front-facing

Left   Right   Left   Right

Unturned   Turned

Left   Right   Left   Right

Body-task

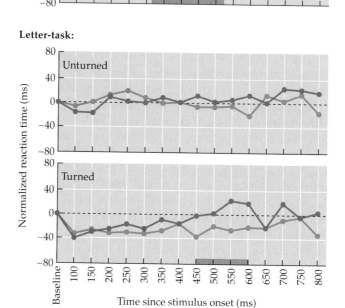

Back-facing
— Temporoparietal junction
— Intraparietal sulcus

Front-facing

Letter-task:

Unturned

Turned

Time since stimulus onset (ms)

Figure 19.2 Brain regions implicated in body perception and imagery tasks. (A) A region of visual association cortex is sensitive to visual features of body parts and is active during the genesis of body imagery. Each dot represents the peak activation from a different functional imaging study. (B) The temporoparietal junction is implicated in body illusions and mental transformations of body position. Cortical stimulation sites are centered on the right angular gyrus of a patient with epilepsy. Stimulation at these sites reliably elicited illusions of body movement and out-of-body experiences. (C) In healthy adults, TMS applied over the right temporoparietal junction 350 to 550 milliseconds after stimulus onset (gray bar) produced slower reaction times in making judgments of hand location (red wrists) using a mentally rotated body frame of reference, but not when making similar dot location judgments on rotated letters. TMS applied over the intraparietal sulcus 450 to 600 milliseconds after stimulus onset (gray bar) impairs performance in the letter rotation task, demonstrating a double dissociation between the brain areas underlying body and object mental rotation tasks. (A from Arzy et al. 2006; B from Blanke et al. 2005.)

self-reflexive thought; the orbitofrontal cortex, insula, and anterior cingulate contribute to the representation of central feelings, visceral sensations, and autonomic arousal; and the sense of embodiment relies on visual processing in the extrastriate visual processing areas and on multisensory integration in the region of the temporoparietal junction. Other aspects of the self, including a first-person perspective during social interactions, a capacity for self-regulatory control, and the experience of ownership of intentional actions (agency), evidently build on these basic processes that mediate focusing on the self and on a bodily representation of the self.

Perception of Social Cues Evident in the Face and Body

In primates, nonverbal cues in facial expressions and body language provide an abundance of information that influences interpersonal exchanges. Consider your reaction to greeting an acquaintance who fails to make eye contact, whose head and shoulders are turned down, and who appears uninterested in what you have to say. Many attributes about the personality, mood, and intentionality of others can be inferred from such cues, even unconsciously. Comparisons of these cues with cultural schemas pertinent to social contexts and prior encounters with the same individual are used to infer the appropriateness of behavior, to detect changes in comportment, and thus to evaluate appropriate responses to the situation at hand. Specific perceptual mechanisms have evolved to decode the nuances of these social signals, for an inability to extract such information can cause debilitating deficits (**Box 19A**).

Perception and recognition of faces

Human faces are particularly salient and complex social cues that we use to infer the mental states of others (a receptive function) and to influence someone else's thoughts and behavior (a communicative function). Most psychological models of face perception postulate an initial visual processing stage that encodes the physical structure of faces to distinguish faces from other objects and to individuate people from each other.

As introduced in Chapter 5, a region in the fusiform gyrus called the **fusiform face area** is at least to some degree specialized for encoding information about faces, although activity in this general region is also modulated by tasks that involve processing other objects. Following initial encoding, different aspects of face processing proceed in parallel.

One pathway appears to form the basis for **person recognition**, processing invariant facial features and linking face representations with semantic knowledge about individuals and their names. This pathway connects the fusiform gyrus with the lateral temporal neocortex, the temporal pole, and the hippocampus, where biographical information is presumably accessed and names are retrieved. Another pathway is thought to process dynamic facial features, such as emotional expression, mouth movements, and gaze direction. This pathway includes the superior temporal sulcus, amygdala, and other limbic forebrain structures (**Figure 19.3A**). The two pathways must interact (e.g., detecting someone's quirky smile can facilitate person recognition), and later processing stations are assumed to feed back onto earlier ones to enhance attention to particular facial features as necessary (e.g., to distinguish facial expressions that are ambiguous).

Evidence for the partial independence of invariant and dynamic featural processing of faces comes from studies of **prosopagnosic** patients who have suffered damage to ventral regions of the temporal lobe. These patients have difficulty recognizing individuals according to their facial features, but they often evaluate facial expressions correctly. In contrast, patients with damage

■ BOX 19A Social and Emotional Deficits in Autism

utism refers to a spectrum of neurodevelopmental disorders characterized by functional deficits in communication and social interactions, and by repetitive, stereotyped behaviors. Originally described by psychiatrist Leo Kanner at Johns Hopkins University in 1943, autism is distinguished from other neuropsychiatric disorders by having social deficits as a core symptom. For this reason, researchers have been greatly interested in studying autistic individuals to gain insight into brain regions specialized for social cognitive functions. Because autism is often accompanied by mental retardation, neuroscientific studies have tended to focus on high-functioning individuals (those with an IQ of 70 or higher).

Autistic individuals typically have difficulty processing faces, emotional expressions, and biological motion. Studies using eye-tracking techniques show that people with autism allocate their attention to noncanonical facial features, such as the forehead, cheeks, or other features located near the face (e.g., earrings). In contrast, normal subjects scan faces in a characteristic triangular pattern, looking back and forth between the two eyes and the mouth—the regions that convey the dynamic information used in social and emotional communication (see the figure). Moreover, when making social judgments about others from facial features alone, autistics tend to rate more favorably faces that are judged by controls to be untrustworthy, and they exhibit other deficits in the perception of facial affect as well.

Functional neuroimaging studies show that, relative to control subjects, autistics show activity reductions in the fusiform gyrus, inferior temporal gyrus, superior temporal sulcus, and amygdala when viewing faces. The activity decrements in the fusiform gyrus

and amygdala correspond to a reduction in attentional allocation to the faces as measured by eye fixations. Autistic individuals also do not exhibit the normal enhanced activity in these brain regions when the faces that they are viewing express emotions. Finally, unlike controls, autistics do not show modulation of activity in the superior temporal sulcus when viewing goal-directed biological motion, such as when viewing avatars whose gaze shifts are either directed or misdirected at peripheral targets. Rehabilitative training of autistic individuals attempts to use such tasks to facilitate directing attention to socially relevant cues. The extent to which the oculographic and fMRI activation patterns normalize in response to treatment indicates the suc-

cess of such training. Humans and non-human primates with lesions of the relevant brain regions also exhibit some of the deficits that characterize autistic individuals, confirming the role of those regions in the processing of social and emotional cues.

Thus, functional impairments in autism are most likely a result of altered processing and/or connectivity among these and other interacting brain regions that form networks mediating social cognition, communication, and executive-motor functions. Consistent with this idea, autistics sometimes have extraordinary talent in restricted domains like mental calculation, historical facts, or art—a phenomenon sometimes referred to as the *savant syndrome*. At the same time, they lack the ability

(A)

Control group   Autistic group

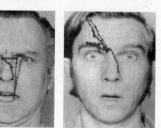

(B)

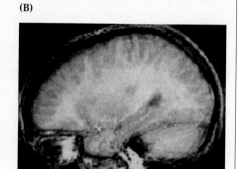

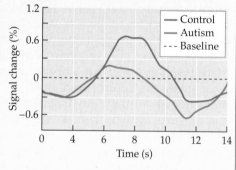

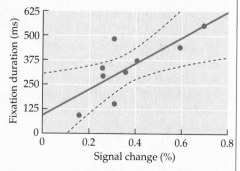

Face processing deficits in autism. (A) In contrast to control subjects (left), autistic individuals (right) tend to focus on features of faces that are not critical for socioemotional communication, as the lines tracing eye movement in these photos indicate. (B) Faces elicit greater fMRI activity in the fusiform gyrus (indicated in the scan and graph on the top) in controls than in autistics. The bottom plot shows that, in autistic individuals, fusiform activity is positively correlated with the duration of eye fixations on the face. (A from Pelphrey et al. 2002; B after Dalton et al. 2005.)

to integrate parts into wholes, or to synthesize information across domains (called *central coherence*)—skills that require the normal operation of other large-scale networks. However, the precise etiology of autism and its manifestation during pre- and postnatal development is not yet understood.

References

DALTON, K. M. AND 7 OTHERS (2005) Gaze fixation and the neural circuitry of face processing in autism. *Nat. Neurosci.* 8: 519–526.

DiCICCO-BLOOM, E. AND 8 OTHERS (2006) The developmental neurobiology of autism spectrum disorder. *J. Neurosci.* 26: 6897–6906.

KANNER, L. (1943) Autistic disturbances of affective contact. *Nerv. Child* 2: 217–250.

MOLDIN, S. O. AND J. L. R. RUBENSTEIN, EDS. (2006) *Understanding Autism: From Basic Neuroscience to Treatment.* Boca Raton, FL: CRC Press.

PELPHREY, K. A., N. J. SASSON, J. S. REZNICK, G. PAUL, B. D. GOLDMAN AND J. PIVEN (2002) Visual scanning of faces in autism. *J. Autism Dev. Disord.* 32: 249–261.

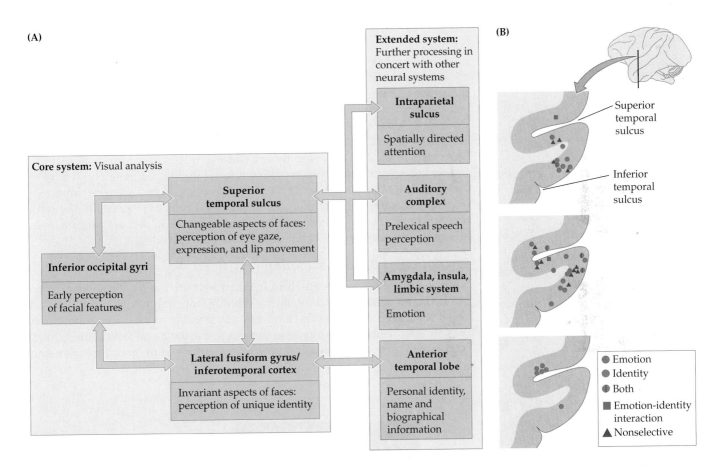

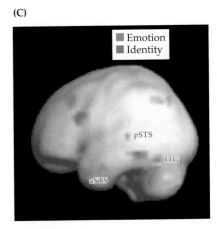

Figure 19.3 Postulated pathways for face processing in the temporal lobe. (A) According to a model proposed by James Haxby and colleagues at the National Institute of Mental Health, visual information flows along an inferior temporal-hippocampal route for facial identity, person recognition, and name retrieval. In contrast, a superior temporal-amygdala route processes dynamic feature encoding of facial information, including analysis of eye gaze and emotional expression. (B) Single neurons in the monkey temporal lobe code for facial expression and identity. Macaque monkeys were shown three faces of conspecifics that expressed three different emotions. Recordings were obtained from 45 neurons that showed selective responses to faces relative to other objects. Whereas most emotion-selective neurons were located in the superior temporal sulcus, most identity-selective neurons were located in the inferotemporal cortex. (C) Similar dorsal-ventral dissociations in the temporal lobe are apparent in human subjects when participants are presented with dynamic changes in facial expression and identity induced through stimulus morphing techniques. aSTS, anterior superior temporal sulcus; ITG, inferior temporal gyrus; pSTS, posterior superior temporal sulcus. (A after Haxby et al. 2000; B from Hasselmo et al. 1989; C from LaBar et al. 2003.)

to the amygdala or superior temporal sulcus have difficulty evaluating emotional expression and/or eye gaze direction, but they can recognize and name individuals normally. Electrophysiological recordings from neurons in the temporal lobe in non-human primates confirm that different populations of cells are specialized for signaling facial identity versus facial expression (**Figure 19.3B**), in accord with neuroimaging observations in healthy humans (**Figure 19.3C**).

Evidence for the integration of dynamic social information in faces has also come from electrophysiological studies of non-human primates. When monkeys watch images of conspecifics, neurons of the superior temporal sulcus tend to increase their firing rate when there is a correspondence between the direction of head movement and the direction of eye gaze, suggesting a preference for a spatial alignment of these two signals (e.g., face forward with eye contact, or both face and eyes averted). In the human amygdala, activity in response to facial expressions also varies according to whether the direction of gaze is forward or averted (**Figure 19.4**). Responses in both of these regions are enhanced in response to stimuli that present dynamic shifts in facial configurations compared to static displays.

Decoding rapid changes in facial movements facilitates quick reactions during personal interactions and helps predict the impending actions of others. Extracting signals from the position of the eyes in higher primates may have been helped by an evolutionary change in the color of the sclera, from the darker color in non-human primates to white in hominids. The whites of the eyes allow better analysis of the direction of gaze, and they are important in detecting a person's emotional state. For example, in response to the sympathetic nervous system activity elicited by fear, the palpebral fissure widens markedly, showing more scleral white, and the pupils dilate.

Perception of biological motion

Social communication is much more than just analyzing faces; as already implied, analyzing body language is equally important. Visual information about the position and status of other body parts is relayed in parallel from the primary visual and extrastriate cortices to the temporal lobe in the "what" pathway for visual information processing. Information about location and

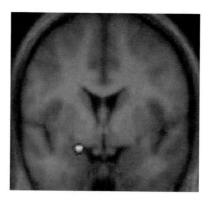
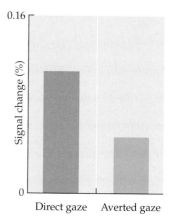

Figure 19.4 The importance of eye features in socioemotional communication. The amygdala responds with more vigorous fMRI activation to threatening faces when eye gaze is direct compared to when it is averted. (From Adams et al. 2003.)

motion is relayed primarily to the parietal lobe in the more dorsal "where" pathway (see Chapter 4).

Neuroimaging studies of hand gestures and ambulation using point-light walking displays or animated avatars show that the superior temporal sulcus, particularly in the right hemisphere, discriminates biologically plausible from implausible motion (**Figure 19.5**). Responses of the superior temporal sulcus are greater to human and robotic walking relative to either coherent mechanical motion, such as pendulum swings, or fragmented biological motion, such as moving but detached body parts. This area also responds to human walking even when body parts are partially occluded, which is important for tracking biological motion in natural circumstances.

Furthermore, the superior temporal sulcus preferentially signals body actions that are meaningful and goal-directed. For instance, hand and arm gestures that complete intentional action sequences, such as grabbing a coffee cup and lifting it to the lips, are signaled more robustly than are meaningless

(A)

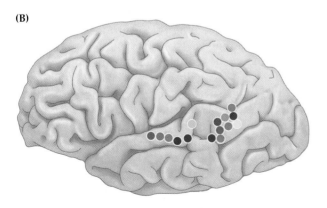

(B)

Figure 19.5 Perception of biological motion activates neurons in the superior temporal sulcus (STS).   (A) Intracranial recording from an epilepsy patient with electrodes implanted in the temporal lobe to monitor seizures (arrow) shows a strong response to stimuli that show movements of the mouth (red line) and smaller responses to shifts in gaze direction (blue and green lines) relative to a static, neutral control face (top left). ERPs recorded from the scalp of a healthy participant over the temporal lobes indicate a similar pattern of response arising from a source in the vicinity of the STS. (B) A meta-analysis of neuroimaging studies of biological motion reveals a focus of activity in the STS and adjacent cortical surface. Each colored dot represents a different experiment. (From Allison et al. 2000.)

or scrambled action sequences. In accord with this observation, sign language gestures that complete grammatically appropriate sentences engage this region more in studies of congenitally deaf individuals than do nonsense gestures. As described in Unit IV, the output of the superior temporal sulcus is conveyed to frontoparietal cortices for attentional modulation and action planning, as well as to limbic forebrain structures for further interpretation of the emotional and motivational significance of the motion patterns.

Interpersonal attention and action direction

In social groups, changes in body posture, head orientation, direction of gaze, and facial expression are combined with vocalizations to communicate the attitudes of individuals toward one another, social hierarchies, and the presence of significant stimuli in the environment. How these cues are used to interpersonally direct attention and action has been investigated in studies of social referencing and shared attention.

Social referencing is the ability of a person, often an infant or child, to interpret the body gestures and facial and vocal expressions of others (often parents) to determine how to deal with an ambiguous or novel situation. For instance, when confronted by a visual cliff apparatus that gives the illusion of a sudden drop in height, 10- to 12-month-old infants will cross the cliff only if encouraged by positive emotions and encouraging gestures expressed by the parent (see also Chapter 27). In this case, emotional expression communicates to the child whether approach or withdrawal behavior is appropriate in a given context. Note that the communication of emotions is used in this setting to direct the actions of the infant rather than to express the internal state of the parent. Although extensively studied developmentally, social referencing is obviously used in a variety of interpersonal contexts across the human life span to glean information from others to help select appropriate actions.

Shared attention is the allocation of processing resources toward an object or region of space cued by another individual. Gaze direction, head orientation, and body and trunk position all indicate where an individual is focusing attention, making it easy for others to take advantage of this information, particularly to make inferences about relevant features of the environment that have been ignored or are out of one's own field of view. Higher primates can also exploit shared attention through deception, presenting misleading displays to others and then directing their own actions elsewhere. Good examples are pickpockets, magicians, and athletes, who "fake" an intended action to succeed in making a different one.

Electrophysiological studies of the monkey superior temporal sulcus show that some neurons are tuned to multiple body features to signal the information conveyed by the orientation of a conspecific animal. For example, a neuron might fire in much the same way in response to the downward deflection of the eyes, head, or a crouched body position of another monkey, all of which indicate the other animal's attention to something on the ground.

A variant of the Posner attentional cuing task (see Chapter 10) has been used to investigate how gaze shifts direct visuospatial attention in monkeys and humans. The position of the eyes in a face stimulus serves as a salient cue about where a face is looking. The subject's task is to respond to a subsequent target that appears either in a location cued by the gaze of the face (valid trials) or in the opposite hemifield (invalid trials; **Figure 19.6**). The subject's reaction time to detect or discriminate the target is then compared for validly cued and invalidly cued trials to quantify whether the gaze shift was attended by the participant (who is given no other explicit instruction about where to attend).

Validly cued targets improve performance and elicit larger-amplitude early ERP components (P1 and N1), implying attentional modulation of visual pro-

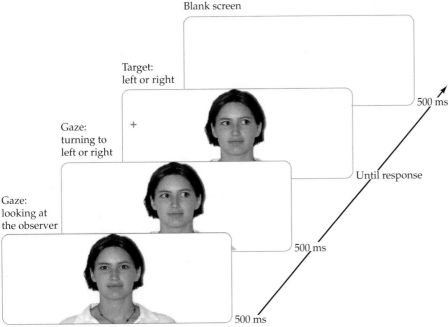

Figure 19.6 Modulation of attentional orienting by gaze cuing. Participants view a face stimulus with a sudden onset of a particular direction of gaze. Targets subsequently appear in the location at which gaze is directed (valid trials) or in the opposite visual field (invalid trials). Reaction times are faster in valid trials, and ERPs show a facilitation of early potentials (P1 and N1) that indicate attentional enhancements in extrastriate cortex. (After Schuller and Roisson 2001.)

cessing in extrastriate regions of cortex (see Chapters 10 and 11). Invalidly cued targets slow reaction times and elicit later enhancement of a P300 component, suggesting a need to update working memory processes because the target appears in an unexpected location. Violations of expectancy based on gaze direction also modulate fMRI activity in the superior temporal sulcus, further supporting the importance of biological motion cues in the signaling of contexts and goals.

Social Categorization

The perception of people's identifying features is used to form impressions and place individuals into social categories. Both automatic and controlled processes are used for categorizing individuals, and this categorization is influenced by cultural norms, personal beliefs, and social attitudes generally. Because personal biases toward social groups are often expressed implicitly and can be consciously suppressed in most circumstances, investigators have turned to neuroimaging techniques combined with some ingenious behavioral paradigms to uncover automatic evaluative responses to people as a function of their gender, race, age, and other personal attributes.

From an evolutionary perspective, social categorization serves important survival functions in defending territories from invading groups, identifying and protecting kin, and selecting mates. In human cultures, however, it is all too clear that prejudicial reactions based on categorizing individuals can and do lead to social injustice. As a result, there is much interest in using neuroscientific approaches to inform theories and identify mechanisms of stereotyping, and to determine the extent to which these phenomena can be voluntarily regulated and changed by experience.

Perception of social category information

Research using electroencephalography has begun to identify the earliest stages of neural processing that are influenced by social category information. For example, Tiffany Ito of the University of Colorado asked participants (mostly Caucasian) to make gender or racial category judgments in response to faces that varied in gender and race. Effects attributed to social categorization appeared within 200 milliseconds of stimulus onset and were characterized by larger frontocentral P200 amplitudes for Asian and African American faces than for Caucasian faces, as well as for male faces than for female faces. Later these effects were somewhat reversed, such that enhanced frontocentral N200 responses were observed to Caucasian and female faces, perhaps indicating a shift toward greater individuation of the faces. Automatic influences of social category were also reflected in amplitude enhancements of a subsequent parietal P300 component when task-irrelevant social category information changed from the preceding stimulus (e.g., when a male face was followed by a female face while race judgments were being made).

Importantly, these effects occurred irrespective of the gender of the participant and the nature of the categorization task. Other studies have replicated these findings using tasks known to reduce stereotyping effects, such as detecting a particular visual feature in the stimulus or judging whether the person depicted was likely to be introverted or to exhibit a particular food preference. The impact of social category on early ERP amplitudes is also greater when viewing racially unambiguous relative to ambiguous (biracial) faces, and when viewing faces relative to other body parts.

Reasons for these initial attentional biases toward out-group and male faces are not yet clear. Nonetheless, the results indicate that social category information extracted from faces is processed rapidly and automatically when we encounter new people, even when that information is not critical to the context of the social interaction.

Automatic and controlled racial biases

In addition to the analysis of perceptual features that indicate social category membership, interpersonal exchanges can be affected by stereotypical beliefs, prejudicial emotional responses, and, ultimately, overt discrimination. In racially biased individuals, executive processing resources are often recruited in an effort to control the expression of automatic negative attitudes toward out-group members. Even in individuals who espouse more egalitarian social views, automatic activation of familiar cultural stereotypes must be overcome to guide social behavior according to one's own beliefs. Building on a foundation of research on emotion processing (Chapter 17), emotion regulation (Chapter 18), and cognitive control (Chapter 23), researchers have begun to identify brain regions whose activity varies as a function of performance on racism scales, and during simulated or staged interracial interactions.

It should go without saying that such endeavors present numerous ethical and experimental challenges, and the results must be interpreted cautiously. For instance, functional brain imaging is inherently correlational, and the causal role of brain activity in a given region and behavior as complex as social biases can only be suggestive. Thus, an individual brain scan cannot indicate whether someone is racially biased, whether the activity patterns represent a source or a consequence of behavior, or whether the activity has been shaped by prior exposure to stereotyped messages or personal experiences. Moreover, brain imaging provides only a snapshot of activity in an experimental setting during the performance of a particular cognitive task, and the results may not generalize to real-world social exchanges. These caveats notwithstanding, some progress has been made in detailing the relationship between behavioral indices of racial bias and patterns of fMRI and ERP activity.

Elizabeth Phelps and her colleagues at Yale reported a correlation in Caucasian participants between amygdala activity to unfamiliar African American faces and two implicit indices of racial bias: the Implicit Association Test (IAT) and startle eye-blink responses (**Figure 19.7**). Because potentiated eye-blink responses are indicative of negatively valenced evaluations (see Box 17C), this study provided additional validation of the IAT as a measure of implicit racial attitudes. The results did not extend to explicit measures of racial bias as assessed by the Modern Racism Scale (**Box 19B**), implying that the brain imaging findings may be more specifically associated with implicit racial biases. Subsequent research has shown that psychophysiological and amygdala responses to African American faces in Caucasian participants are attenuated when the faces are familiar, when the task emphasizes individuated rather than categorical processing of people, when the faces are shown for prolonged durations, and when the faces are explicitly verbally labeled.

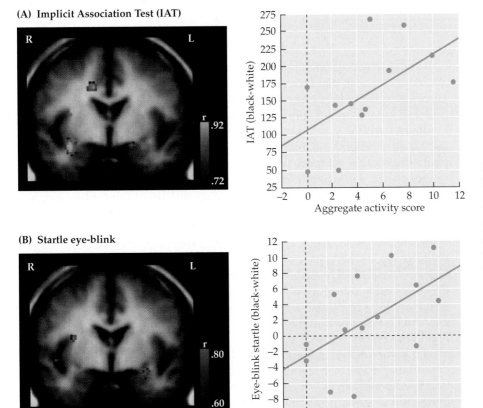

Figure 19.7 Amygdala activity and racial bias. Amygdala activity in response to novel African American faces correlates with implicit measures of racial bias in Caucasian participants. Although the amygdala did not exhibit an overall difference between African American and Caucasian faces when averaged across all participants, the degree to which the amygdala differentiated African American and Caucasian faces in individual participants is correlated with (A) Implicit Association Test performance and (B) differential startle eye-blink responses obtained outside the scanning environment. Correlation coefficients are displayed in the fMRI scans (left), and aggregate scores of significant activity are displayed in the graphs (right). (From Phelps et al. 2000.)

■ BOX 19B Ways of Measuring Implicit and Explicit Racial Attitudes

To measure implicit racial attitudes, investigators commonly use the *Implicit Association Test* (*IAT*) developed by social psychologist Anthony Greenwald and his colleagues at the University of Washington. In one version of this test, participants are presented with a series of faces (either African American or Caucasian) intermixed with positively and negatively valenced words that represent good or bad concepts (e.g., *friend*, *enemy*). One set of trials requires the same button-press response for both African American faces and negative words, whereas another response is given for both Caucasian faces and positive words. The response requirements are then reversed so that participants make the same button-press response for both African American faces and positive words, and another response for both Caucasian faces and negative words. Participants are instructed to respond as quickly as possible.

Implicit racial biases are quantified as a difference in reaction time for the second condition compared to the first, such that higher scores reflect greater difficulty (response cost) when pairing African American faces with positive words and Caucasian faces with negative words than the reverse. Alternate versions assess attitudes toward other social groups (readers can test themselves at www.implicit.harvard.edu).

Although the reasons for the reaction-time costs are debated (including suggestions that they reflect knowledge of cultural stereotypes rather than personal attitudes), the IAT has good test reliability. Furthermore, the IAT has been validated with a psychophysiological index of evaluative emotional responding (see the text). Performance on this test is compared to other paper-and-pencil assessments that test racial attitudes explicitly, such as the Modern Racism Scale. Other tests determine if subjects are motivated to respond to out-groups in a way that appears more socially appropriate to others. Often, IAT performance reveals biases in processing that are not captured by the explicit measures.

References

CUNNINGHAM, W. A., K. J. PREACHER AND M. R. BANAJI (2001) Implicit attitude measures: Consistency, stability, and convergent validity. *Psychol. Sci.* 12: 163–170.

GEHRING, W. J., A. KARPINSKI AND J. L. HILTON (2003) Thinking about interracial relations. *Nat. Neurosci.* 6: 1241–1243.

GREENWALD, A. G., D. E. MCGHEE AND J. K. L. SCHWARTZ (1998) Measuring individual differences in implicit cognition: The Implicit Association Test. *J. Pers. Soc. Psychol.* 74: 1464–1480.

MCCONAHAY, J. B. (1986) Modern racism, ambivalence, and the Modern Racism Scale. In *Prejudice, Discrimination, and Racism*, J. Dovidio and S. Gaertner (eds.). Orlando, FL: Academic Press, pp. 91–125.

PLANT, E. A. AND P. G. DEVINE (1998) Internal and external motivation to respond without prejudice. *J. Pers. Soc. Psychol.* 69: 811–832.

Although less research has been conducted on other racial groups, some evidence suggests that face-processing regions of the fusiform gyrus show enhanced activity for faces of one's own race in both African American and Caucasian participants, perhaps because of greater individuation and/or familiarity with in-group members. Amygdala activation to African American faces is generally similar in African American and Caucasian participants, but there is evidence for faster habituation effects in the amygdala for in-group than out-group faces. Together these findings highlight the plasticity, contextual modulation, and regional specificity of neurophysiological signatures of automatic evaluations to members of stigmatized cultural groups.

Additional work has focused on neural mechanisms that are engaged when group stereotypes induce response conflicts and thus a need for voluntary control. A two-stage model of cognitive control put forward by Matt Botvinick and colleagues at Princeton supposes (1) that anterior cingulate activity reflects continual monitoring of conflict during information processing, and (2) that prefrontal regions are subsequently recruited to implement regulatory responses once a need for conflict resolution is detected.

The **error-related negativity** (**ERN**) is a component of event-related potentials (ERPs) that is sensitive to information-processing conflicts that lead to response errors. The ERN has been localized to the anterior cingulate gyrus and offers a potential neural index of ongoing conflict monitoring that can be applied to studying personal interactions that lead to self-regulation failures.

Research by David Amodio at New York University has capitalized on this use of the ERN to investigate conflict monitoring of racial stereotypes on a weapons identification task. In this rapid classification task, Caucasian participants had to decide whether briefly presented pictures of objects on a computer screen were weapons or tools. Prior to each presentation, an African American or Caucasian face was flashed on the screen. Priming of objects by African American faces tended to facilitate detection of weapons and impair detection of tools, whereas priming by Caucasian faces had no differential effect. The ERN time-locked to the response showed not only sensitivity to performance (larger for errors than for correct object classifications) but also stereotype incongruity on error trials (larger for tools primed by African American faces than for the other face-object combinations).

The ERN stereotyping effects were larger in individuals who characterized themselves as being primarily internally motivated to regulate prejudiced reactions than in those who acknowledge avoidance of social disapproval as part of the motivation to regulate their reactions. This finding suggests that internally motivated individuals exhibit greater online monitoring of stereotype conflict as a potentially biased response is generated. Because the behavioral and ERN results occur in individuals with low levels of racial bias, they implicate a Stroop-like response conflict due to automatic activation of learned cultural stereotypes in relation to aggression and hostility.

Functional MRI studies have also examined the impact of racial out-group processing on hemodynamic responses in brain regions associated with cognitive control. For instance, a study done by William Cunningham, Mahzarin Banaji, and their colleagues at Yale, found differences in the balance between amygdala and prefrontal cortical activity in response to African American faces in Caucasian participants as a function of viewing time. When the faces were presented so briefly that they were subliminal, the amygdala showed greater activity in response to African American than Caucasian faces, presumably reflecting automatic evaluative processes. When the faces were presented supraliminally, the same contrast yielded greater activity in the anterior cingulate and the ventrolateral and dorsolateral sectors of the prefrontal cortex. The degree of dorsolateral prefrontal engagement in the supraliminal condition across participants predicted the reduction of amygdala activity from the subliminal to the supraliminal condition. Although indirect, these findings suggest controlled modulation of subcortical responses to out-group faces, given sufficient processing time.

Prefrontal responses to out-group faces may also mediate the relationship between implicit racial attitudes and cognitive consequences following an interracial encounter. Researchers at Dartmouth College gave Caucasian participants the IAT test followed by a staged encounter with either an African American or a Caucasian experimenter, who asked them to comment on social topics of racial profiling and the college fraternity system. A classic Stroop color-naming interference task (see Chapters 5 and 23) was then administered. In a separate session, the participants underwent fMRI scanning while being presented with either African American or Caucasian faces. Performance on the Stroop task was quantified as a function of implicit racial attitudes and the race of the experimenter in the social encounter, and compared with the fMRI activity to out-group faces.

As **Figure 19.8** shows, individuals who were characterized by implicit racial biases based on IAT performance exhibited greater Stroop interference following the interracial encounter but not following the encounter with an in-group member. Functional MRI analyses revealed a positive correlation between performance on the IAT test and activity in the anterior cingulate and dorsolateral prefrontal cortex (DLPFC) to African American faces relative to

(A)

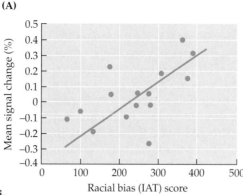

(B)

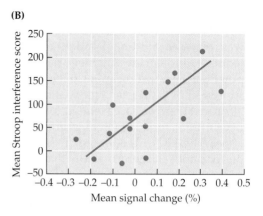

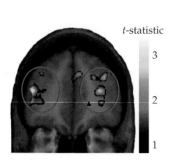

Figure 19.8 Implicit racial attitudes and cognitive performance. (A) Individuals who had greater dorsolateral prefrontal cortex activity in response to out-group faces also had greater implicit racial biases as assessed by the IAT. (B) The same individuals exhibited a strong relationship between right dorsolateral prefrontal cortex activity and Stroop task interference following an interracial encounter. (After Richeson et al. 2003.)

Caucasian faces. The magnitude of DLPFC activity also predicted the relationship between IAT and Stroop task performance. These results suggest that individuals with implicit racial biases exert greater effort in controlling reactions to out-group members in part through engaging prefrontal circuitry.

In sum, an initial body of neuroscientific research has laid the groundwork for discovering the relationships between social behavior and brain correlates of the psychological constructs underlying racial bias. Although many issues raised by these studies remain to be sorted out and confirmed, such endeavors already inform debates about the genesis of racial, gender-based, and other social prejudices.

Impression formation and trust

In addition to gender and race, other personal attributes are readily judged from physical features and inferred from nonverbal behaviors to form general impressions of individuals. One personality trait that has received much attention is *trustworthiness*. Patients with damage to the orbitofrontal cortex, elderly adults, and many others end up in bankruptcy because they are susceptible to deceptive financial scams. One common denominator of people who find themselves in this predicament is an inability to evaluate the trustworthiness of those who are trying to get their money.

Neuroimaging studies have found that assessment of the trustworthiness of individuals based on facial appearance alone is associated with activity in brain regions involved in other aspects of social cognition and emotional evaluation. In particular, enhanced activity is observed in the amygdala and insula when participants are shown faces of individuals whom others have judged to have an untrustworthy appearance, and enhanced activity is observed in the orbitofrontal cortex for faces deemed trustworthy. These patterns are evident even when the faces are not explicitly appraised for trust, implicating an automatic evaluative mechanism.

Explicit judgments of trustworthiness recruit additional processing in the superior temporal sulcus. As mentioned in Box 19A, judgments of trustworthiness are impaired in autistic individuals and in patients with selective amygdala damage, providing converging evidence for the neuroimaging findings. Behavioral studies have shown that judgments of trustworthiness are related to facial attractiveness—a fact exploited by Hollywood casting agents and by those who hire salespeople. Analysis of shifts in eye gaze also contributes to trustworthiness appraisals in that individuals who are "shifty-eyed" are rated as less trustworthy than those whose gaze reliably tracks targets in a goal-oriented fashion. These findings show how the basic building blocks of social perception, which are based on nonverbal cues related to gaze analysis, shared attention, and emotional evaluation, can be combined to infer attributes of the personality of others. Studies of trust in economic game paradigms are described in Chapter 24.

Understanding the Actions and Emotions of Others

Successful social interactions require that individuals map perception to action in order to interpret and predict the behavior of others and respond appropriately. This ability ranges from mere mimicry of motoric and emotional gestures to complex goal-directed modulation of imitation behavior, and ultimately to absorbing cultural information by explicit learning from mentors. In humans, social competence is further facilitated by inferring unobservable mental states in others and attributing actions of others to their beliefs, goals, desires, and feelings. This multifaceted capacity is called **mentalizing** or *theory of mind*.

There is much debate about whether mentalizing occurs though simulation of the behaviors and internal states of others (e.g., mentally representing potential actions, feelings, or thoughts of others as if they were one's own) or by the building of theories (scripts) of how others typically behave in particular contexts. The philosopher Daniel Dennett, of Tufts University, suggested that social interactions benefit when one adopts an *intentional stance*—that is, assuming that others are agents motivated to behave in a way that is consistent with their current mental state, which may differ from one's own mental states and/or the reality of the situation. As detailed in the discussion that follows, coding and interpreting the actions and mental states of others are complex processes involving both dedicated neural systems and the co-opting of domain-general functions like working memory and symbolic representation.

Mirror neurons

To interpret behaviors meaningfully, it is useful to code actions performed by others in a way that is related to how similar actions are performed by oneself. As the philosopher David Hume wrote, "Our minds mirror each other." In the 1990s, the discovery of **mirror neurons** in the premotor cortex of the macaque brain sparked much interest and debate about possible neural mechanisms underlying action representation. Working at the University of Parma, Giacomo Rizzolatti and his colleagues described populations of neurons in and around the inferior frontal gyrus (area F5, presumably similar to the inferior frontal convexity in humans) that increase their activity not only when a grasping action is selected and performed, but also when that or a related action is passively viewed while it is being performed by another animal (**Figure 19.9**).

These neurons respond more robustly when another monkey performs the observed action, but they are also activated when a human experimenter performs the action. Such mirror responses are more responsive to observing goal-directed biological actions compared to non-goal-directed biological actions (mimes) or goal-directed mechanical actions (e.g., a hammer hitting a nail). A smaller proportion of F5 neurons respond to both visual and auditory features of a unique goal-directed biological action (e.g., ringing a bell).

Mirror neurons have also been found in a region of rostral inferior parietal cortex that projects to premotor area F5, implicating an interconnected frontoparietal mirror system. Some neurons in this circuit also exhibit context specificity of the action sequences (e.g., selectively responding to grasping actions that lead to eating rather than actions that simply move an object from one place to another). Evidently the neurons in the superior temporal sulcus relay perceptual information about biological motion to the parietal component of this system, but do not exhibit mirroring responses themselves.

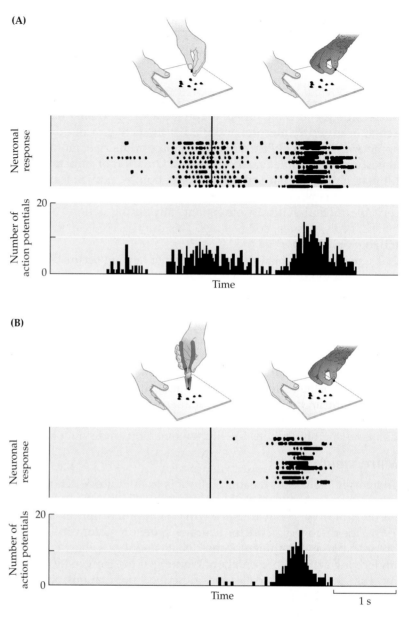

Figure 19.9   A mirror neuron in the premotor cortex of a monkey.   (A) The experimenter is shown placing and removing a food morsel from a tray while the monkey watches. The raster plot shows the neuronal responses, which are compiled in the histograms below. The neuron is activated as the monkey watches passively (left panels; the vertical line indicates the time the morsel was placed on the tray), and when the monkey itself retrieves the morsel (right panels). (B) The same neuron shows no response when the morsel is placed on the tray in a different manner (with pliers; left panels). The same activity occurs in both instances when the monkey itself retrieves the morsel (right panels). (After Rizzolatti et al. 1996.)

Because the observation of actions does not automatically elicit an analogous motor response in the monkey, activity in this premotor circuit is arguably inhibited to prevent obligatory copying behavior.

Not surprisingly, a number of investigators have used this neurophysiological evidence to speculate about the importance of these areas of the primate brain in generating an understanding of the intentions of others, language acquisition, and empathy (discussed shortly), as well as the functional deficits apparent in behavioral disorders such as autism (see Box 19A). Whether these implications will be validated remains to be seen, and some caution is warranted. For one thing, adult monkeys do not learn much by direct imitation—a fact that undermines what would perhaps be the simplest interpretation of the role of mirror neurons. And in humans, where these speculations are most pertinent, the evidence for mirror neurons is suggestive but does not correspond directly to the anatomical or functional properties observed in monkeys. For instance, cortical activity detected with fMRI in response to similar paradigms in humans is widely distributed in the motor system and superior temporal sulcus; moreover, much the same activity occurs when people mime. Whatever the correct interpretation, these observations indicate that passively viewing actions pertinent to particular behavioral goals influences the activity of some frontoparietal neurons.

Perspective taking and mental-state attribution

Although mirroring functions may help establish shared representations used for understanding actions, by definition they do not distinguish well the execution of one's own actions from the observation of similar actions executed by others. Moreover, actions do not map onto intentions in a one-to-one manner. In short, differentiating one's actions from those of others and understanding the reasons behind others' actions clearly require cognitive abilities and mechanisms that go far beyond mirroring.

Key among these is the ability to flexibly adopt the perspective of another individual (third-person perspective) and distinguish that viewpoint from one's own (first-person perspective). Because an egocentric view of the world is part of a default mode of information processing (see the earlier discussion of the self), adopting other people's perspectives and inferring their beliefs, motives, or feelings requires a disengagement of self-directed thoughts, a redirection of attention to the mental and physical states of others, and a decoupling of knowledge of the actual unfolding of events from other people's perceptions of those events. Memory is also important in this process because prior knowledge about the personality traits and response patterns of others in similar contexts will refine one's own interpretation of the current social context and the possible responses to it.

Neuroimaging studies have contributed to understanding the brain regions involved by comparing first- and third-person **perspective taking** across different cognitive, emotional, and motoric domains. For instance, participants might imagine themselves or someone else performing specific actions (e.g., dialing a phone number), responding to a painful stimulus, reacting to an emotional scenario (including those that violate social norms), or judging the persuasiveness of advertising messages. Other studies of mental-state attributions have asked participants to consider the viewpoint of different characters in stories or cartoons, to guess what an opponent might do during an interactive game, or to judge whether historical figures have access to knowledge about specific artifacts.

In all these domains, taking the perspective of others and inferring their mental states elicit activity in a distributed network that includes the frontopolar cortex, medial prefrontal cortex (most consistently the paracingulate cortex, Brodmann area 32), temporal polar cortex, right inferior parietal cortex, temporoparietal junction, and superior temporal sulcus (**Figure 19.10**). Because of the complexity of the mentalizing construct, heterogeneity of tasks involved, and variety of control conditions employed, it is difficult to ascribe specific functions to these network components. In particular, it is not clear whether they contribute the domain-specific mentalizing functions required or simply the supporting cognitive operations needed to solve the tasks (the functions needed to retrieve memories or semantic knowledge, reallocate attentional resources, manipulate internal representations, etc.). Despite these uncertainties, the neural circuitry that underlies perspective taking and other mentalizing tasks is beginning to emerge.

Theory of mind in children and apes

In the late 1970s, David Premack and Guy Woodruff, working at the University of Pennsylvania, raised the question of whether chimpanzees and other great apes have the capacity to represent and understand the mental states of conspecifics in the same general way that humans do. Observations of great apes in the wild indicate that they engage in deception (to hoard food sources, for example), which requires at least some understanding of where conspecifics are orienting their attention and what they expect to happen in a given social context (see Box 19C for other examples of social insight and competence in non-human animals).

However, the acid test for the presence of a theory of mind is the capacity to predict others' behavior according to *false beliefs* that they hold. Understanding the false beliefs of others requires making a distinction between knowledge about a true state of affairs from what another individual falsely believes to be true. False-belief tasks come in two major flavors: location-

(A) Temporal pole

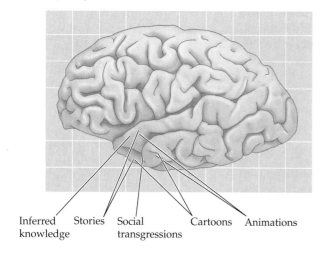

Inferred knowledge Stories Social transgressions Cartoons Animations

(B) Superior temporal sulcus

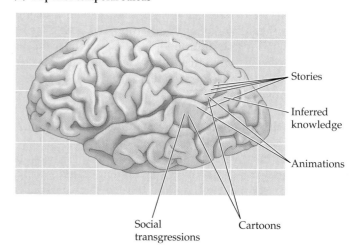

Stories
Inferred knowledge
Animations
Social transgressions Cartoons

(C) Paracingulate cortex

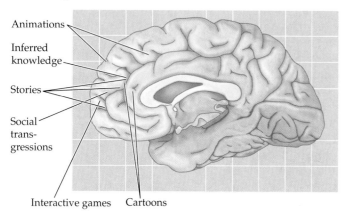

Animations
Inferred knowledge
Stories
Social transgressions
Interactive games Cartoons

Figure 19.10 Brain regions implicated in mentalizing tasks. Across various domains, activity in the temporal pole (A), superior temporal sulcus (B), and paracingulate cortex (C) is elicited when participants adopt the perspectives of other individuals and infer their mental states. (From Frith and Frith 2003.)

change tasks and unexpected-contents tasks. In *location-change tasks*, an object is placed in one location and, unbeknownst to a third party, the position of the object is switched to an alternate location. The participant then must indicate where the third party would look for the object (its true location or the location where the third party last viewed the object). In *unexpected-contents tasks*, an object is placed in a container and, unbeknownst to a third party, the object is replaced by another one. The participant must then indicate which object the third party thinks is in the container.

Research by Brian Hare and his colleagues at the Max Planck Institute for Evolutionary Anthropology in Leipzig used an ecologically valid task to ask whether chimpanzees have basic mentalizing abilities (**Figure 19.11**). In these tests, a subordinate chimpanzee was paired with a dominant chimp. The subordinate chimp was shown food items that the dominant chimp could either see or not see, or was shown that the location of a food item had or had not been switched out of view of the dominant chimp. In either case, the subordinate chimp showed a preference for moving toward food items about which the dominant chimp had no knowledge, or could be assumed to hold a false belief about its location. Such behavior clearly imparts an advantage to the subordinate chimp in the context of competition for food with a dominant conspecific, and it could be interpreted as relying on some degree of mentalizing.

Humans develop false-belief attributions to characters in animated vignettes by about 4 years of age (see Chapter 27). However, because these tasks require complex narrative and action sequence comprehension, working memory, and inhibition of rapid responses, there is some debate about the specificity of the findings. Some investigators have proposed that children between 3 and 4 years old simply learn to select the correct responses in the task rather than develop theory-of-mind abilities. Nonetheless, children of this age routinely use words like *pretend*, *think*, *know*, *want*, and *like*, implying some knowledge about mental states. In contrast, autistic children (and autistic adults) generally fail false-belief tests, although some investigators find the evidence to be equivocal because of the potentially confounding deficits in language abilities and executive function present in the disorder.

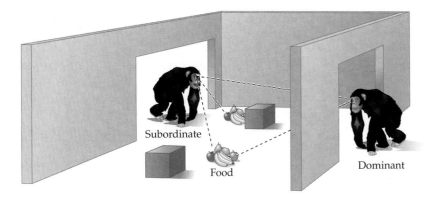

Figure 19.11 Mentalizing ability in chimpanzees. This socially competitive paradigm tests what chimpanzees know about the viewpoint of a conspecific. A subordinate chimp is shown multiple food caches that are either out of the view or in the view of a dominant chimp. Subordinate chimps prefer to move toward the food cache that is out of view of the dominant chimp, conferring a behavioral advantage. Chimps exhibit similar behavior when a food cache is switched to a different location, again unbeknownst to a dominant chimp. These observations imply that, in socially competitive situations, chimps have rudimentary mentalizing abilities. (From Hare et al. 2001.)

Given the controversy over whether children and chimpanzees possess theory-of-mind abilities, some investigators have turned to the distinction made in memory research between implicit and explicit processes. Most researchers believe that young children and great apes can implicitly (i.e., unconsciously) track another individual's mental state. However, they also admit that there is currently no convincing evidence that young children and apes can explicitly represent the mental contents of another individual, as in the ability to have thoughts such as "I know my friend thinks that the food is in location A when I know it is really at B." This ability to abstract the elements of a social situation, also called *metarepresentation*, presumably requires further development that allows the symbolic representation of mental states and is unlikely in young children, let alone non-human primates.

Empathy, sympathy, and prosocial behavior

Understanding another individual's beliefs, goals, and intentions also extends to emotion. Although sometimes incorporated into the concept of theory of mind, understanding others' emotional states recruits brain regions that are not necessarily used to make inferences about other mental states. A better descriptor of emotion understanding is *empathy*. **Empathy** is the capacity to comprehend and resonate with another individual's emotional experience, which leads to a sharing of that person's feelings. Once an empathic feeling arises, individuals must distinguish their own emotional response from that of the other individual and regulate their responses accordingly.

Rather than exemplifying a specific emotion, empathy can be considered a process by which any emotion is shared according to the social context. For instance, having a conversation about a friend's nervousness before a job interview may lead to shared feelings of anxiety; when the conversation shifts to the outcome of the interview, feelings of disappointment may be shared upon hearing that the job was not obtained. Eliciting empathy is critical for effective storytelling and for advertising. Across these and other domains, empathy has proved to be particularly challenging to elicit from animated characters and robots.

Empathy differs from **sympathy** in that a sympathetic reaction does not entail a sharing of emotional experience. Rather, a person who is sympathetic may feel concerned or sorry for the plight of another person but not feel the actual emotion felt by the other. In the job interview example, for instance, one may feel sympathetic toward a friend's situation without actually experiencing anxiety or disappointment of one's own.

Empathy has both automatic and controlled components and builds on basic social cognitive and emotional processing mechanisms. Early in development, human infants will cry in reaction to another infant's cry and will mimic basic facial emotions expressed by a parent. At about 2 years of age, when self-versus-other distinctions and social emotions begin to emerge, children will express sympathetic concern, such as gestures of consolation to family members in distress. Although initially such gestures are egocentric (e.g., offering a gift such as a doll to an adult whom the child likes), the offerings gradually become other-focused (e.g., offering a gift that the adult family member likes). With increased cognitive and emotional capacities for perspective taking later in childhood, more complex forms of empathy are conveyed. Forms of empathy observed in apes presumably rely on more automatic aspects of emotion interpretation and somatic activation, which contribute to helping behavior, cooperation, and reciprocity (**Box 19C**).

Jean Decety of the University of Chicago developed a model of empathy that encompasses several of the social and emotional processes, as well as the

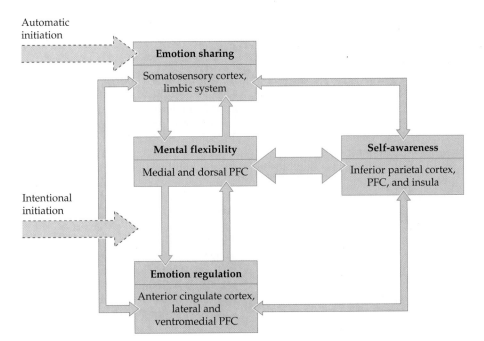

Figure 19.12 A proposed component process model of empathy. A full empathic response to another individual is thought to depend on brain regions involved in sharing somatic and emotional responses, self-awareness and maintaining distinctions between self and other, perspective taking (mental flexibility), and emotion regulation. PFC, prefrontal cortex.

concepts of mental representation, discussed earlier (**Figure 19.12**). The model has four primary components:

1. *Emotion sharing* between individuals is based on automatic perception-action coupling and shared somatic-emotional representations that rely on processing in the somatosensory cortex and limbic forebrain regions. It is unclear whether mirror neurons like those found in the inferior prefrontal and parietal cortices that are arguably related to action understanding are involved in the sharing of emotional responses. But there is evidence for insula involvement in both the observation and experience of disgust, and the anterior cingulate is involved in both the observation and experience of pain.

2. *Self-awareness* and the distinction between self and other are also thought to entail processing in the parietal lobes, prefrontal cortex, and insula.

3. *Mental flexibility.* Neural interactions provide the mental flexibility to adopt the perspective of another individual, which recruits medial and dorsolateral prefrontal regions, among others.

4. *Emotion regulation* (see Box 18C) operates on the emotional and somatic states generated by engaging executive control mechanisms in the anterior cingulate and lateral and ventromedial prefrontal cortex.

According to Decety, a full empathic response, which can be initiated either automatically or voluntarily, requires the coordinated operation of all four of these component systems.

Although it is generally assumed that empathy leads to helping others and altruistic actions, additional factors influence such behaviors (which are referred to as *prosocial*). For instance, high levels of arousal associated with observing another's troubled emotional state can lead to personal distress, a lack of emotion regulation, and thus an inability to take actions other than to alleviate one's own distress. Prosocial behaviors are more likely when an individual is in a positive mood, when the action required is not unpleasant or onerous, and when the person to be helped is not a direct competitor. Adults (but not young children) may also engage in helpful behaviors to repair sad moods, because

■ BOX 19C Social Skills in Non-Human Animals

Ethological and comparative studies reveal an impressive variety of social skills in non-human animals that facilitate behaviors matched to the specific needs and characteristics of their social groups. A variety of studies have shown that olfactory, visual, and auditory cues are used to help identify kin, social rank, and mates in many non-human species.

The most intensively studied of these behaviors concern mating and kinship. Some primate species analyze secondary sex coloration in the face and anogenital regions to select mates. Female rhesus monkeys prefer looking at males whose faces are redder, and this coloration is in turn related to the amount of circulating testosterone in males during the mating season. In mandrills, a male's social dominance rank is accompanied by continually updated changes in secondary sexual characteristics such as testicular volume and reddening of anogenital skin. Many primates, particularly arboreal species, distinguish kin from non-kin by vocal characteristics alone (see the figure). Female vervet monkeys distinguish the cries of juvenile monkeys in their troop. A mother vervet will respond selectively to the cry of her own infant and will look preferentially at other mothers in the troop when their own infants cry. Auditory characteristics of primate calls, such as the acoustic structure and number of vocalizations, are also used to indicate social rank and physical health.

In rodents, social behaviors are especially dependent on olfactory cues. Thus, detection of novel pheromones signals an intruder in a colony. Rats administered vasopressin show increased social recognition abilities by olfactory cues, as measured by habituation in sniffing behavior toward a recently introduced partner. Vasopressin and oxytocin knockout mice exhibit a form of social amnesia in which they fail to habituate to the presence of a recently introduced partner, despite normal habituation to the repeated presentation of other odorants. These social recognition abilities in rodents have been linked to activity in mesolimbic structures, including the amygdala and septum.

Pair bonding in prairie voles has also been studied extensively, primarily as a model system for monogamous partner preferences. In this species, a breeding pair shares the same nest, intruders of either sex are rejected, and males contribute to care of the young. Even following death, a new mate is accepted by either sex only rarely (about 20 percent of the time). Offspring remain sexually immature until they leave the natal group, and females undergo puberty only when exposed to the urine of an unrelated male, at which time they mate repeatedly with the same male and form a selective and long-lasting pair bond. During mating, oxytocin and vasopressin are released in mesolimbic pathways, including the nucleus accumbens, where they interact with the

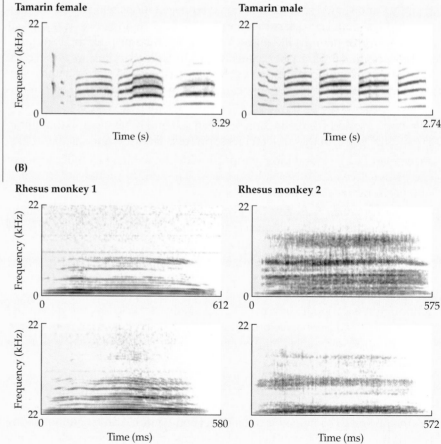

Primate vocalizations are used to characterize sex and individual identity. (A) These spectrograms show recordings of long calls produced by a female and a male tamarin when they are separated from members of the group. Analyzing the different frequencies present in the calls can identify the sex of the caller, in part because of sex differences in the vocal apparatus. (B) Two coos from two rhesus monkeys show more between-subject than within-subject variation in the spectral frequencies present. Extracting distinguishing features of an individual's coos can facilitate social recognition by auditory information alone. (From Ghazanfar and Santos 2004.)

dopaminergic reward system (see Chapter 24). This neurochemical interaction presumably links social information of the partner with reward circuits to reinforce the sexual preference and solidify the social bond.

Another domain of social skills studied in non-human animals is competition for food resources. A variety of other species, including animals as diverse as apes and birds, engage in deception and occasionally cooperation to obtain food caches. Captive chimpanzees can learn from others to use particular tools to retrieve inaccessible food rewards, and they cooperate to operate machinery to obtain food

that would be unattainable otherwise. They also keep track of partners who have been helpful in this regard. Even captive scrub jays will move food stashes to hide them from potential competitors according to their social dominance, expending more effort in response to the thieves that are most likely to be successful.

Importantly, in many of these studies of social skills the experimental approach is aligned with the natural abilities and ecologically relevant purposes of social behavior in the species investigated. Such endeavors continue to reveal impressive social skills in a variety of non-human animals.

References

EMERY, N. AND N. CLAYTON (2004) The mentality of crows: Convergent evolution of intelligence in corvids and apes. *Science* 306: 1903.

GHAZANFAR, A. A. AND L. R. SANTOS (2004) Primate brains in the wild: The sensory bases for social interactions. *Nat. Rev. Neurosci.* 5: 203–216.

INSEL, T. R. AND R. D. FERNALD (2004) How the brain processes social information: Searching for the social brain. *Annu. Rev. Neurosci.* 27: 697–722.

SEARCY, W. A. AND S. NOWICKI (2006) *The Evolution of Animal Communication: Reliability and Deception in Signalling Systems.* Princeton, NJ: Princeton University Press.

they understand the social rewards associated with the actions. Nonetheless, in some circumstances empathy can lead to antisocial behavior, as when an accomplice is empathic toward the actions and motives of a fellow criminal.

Summary

1. Whether social interactions are an emergent property of all of the domains of cognitive neuroscience described in other chapters or constitute a core set of specialized representations, brain structures, and processes has been widely debated. Probably both domain-specific and domain-general factors contribute to social cognition.

2. The findings to date suggest that social interactions engage a distributed set of brain regions involved in self-referential processing, perception of biologically relevant cues and their motion, social categorization, and action and emotion interpretation.

3. The ability to think reflexively about the self and our sense of embodiment depends on processing in the temporoparietal junction, medial parietal, and prefrontal cortical regions, and specialized sectors of visual association cortex.

4. The perception of socially relevant cues arising from the faces and bodies of others depends critically on the fusiform gyrus, superior temporal sulcus, amygdala, and orbitofrontal cortex.

5. The categorization of individuals as members of social groups occurs quickly (even if not relevant to the social context) and depends in part on evaluative processes in the amygdala. Automatic influences of social stereotypes engage conflict-monitoring and self-regulation functions of the anterior cingulate gyrus and dorsolateral PFC.

6. Theory-of-mind abilities, though present implicitly in great apes and young children, increase in complexity in late human development and depend on processing in the frontopolar cortex, medial PFC, temporal polar cortex, inferior parietal cortex, temporoparietal junction, and superior temporal sulcus, as well as areas that mediate symbolic representation more broadly.

7. Empathizing with the emotional state of others involves regions implicated in somatic and emotional state representation (including the insula and orbitofrontal cortex), self-awareness, perspective taking, and emotion regulation.

8. Insights into the ways we perceive and make inferences from social cues are also leading to new developments in the treatment of diseases such as autism, as well as in the domains of computer animation and artificial intelligence. Of particular interest are the ways in which avatars communicate and interpret socioemotional signals—an issue that will facilitate human-machine interactions.

Additional Reading

Reviews

ALLISON, T., A. PUCE AND G. MCCARTHY (2000) Social perception from visual cues: Role of the superior temporal sulcus region. *Trends Cogn. Sci.* 4: 267–278.

BROTHERS, L. (1990) The social brain: A project for integrating primate behavior and neurophysiology in a new domain. *Concepts Neurosci.* 1: 27–51.

GALLESE, V., C. KEYSERS AND G. RIZZOLATTI (2004) A unifying view of the basis of social cognition. *Trends Cogn. Sci.* 8: 396–403.

HAXBY, J. V., E. A. HOFFMAN AND I. GOBBINI (2000) The distributed human neural system for face perception. *Trends Cogn. Sci.* 4: 223–233.

NORTHOFF, G. AND F. BERMPOHL (2004) Cortical midline structures and the self. *Trends Cogn. Sci.* 8: 102–107.

RIZZOLATTI, G. AND L. CRAIGHERO (2004) The mirror neuron system. *Annu. Rev. Neurosci.* 27: 169–192.

Important Original Papers

ADAMS, R. B., JR., H. L. GORDON, A. A. BAIRD, N. AMBADY AND R. E. KLECK (2003) Effects of gaze on amygdala sensitivity to anger and fear faces. *Science* 300: 1536.

BLANKE, O., S. ORTIGUE, T. LANDIS AND M. SEECK (2002) Stimulating illusory own-body perceptions. *Nature* 419: 269–270.

BLANKE, O. AND 7 OTHERS (2005) Linking out-of-body experience and self processing to mental own-body imagery at the temporoparietal junction. *J. Neurosci.* 25: 550–557.

BRUCE, V. AND A. YOUNG (1986) Understanding face recognition. *Br. J. Psychol.* 77: 305–327.

HASSELMO, M. E., E. T. ROLLS AND G. C. BAYLIS (1989) The role of expression and identity in the face-selective responses of neurons in the temporal visual cortex of the monkey. *Behav. Brain Res.* 32: 203–218.

LABAR, K. S., M. J. CRUPAIN, J. B. VOYVODIC AND G. MCCARTHY (2003) Dynamic perception of facial affect and identity in the human brain. *Cereb. Cortex* 13: 1023–1033.

PERRETT, D. I., J. K. HIETANEN, M. W. ORAM AND P. J. BENSON (1992) Organization and functions of cells responsive to faces in the temporal cortex. *Philos. Trans. R. Soc. Lond. B.* 335: 23–30.

PHELPS, E. A. AND 6 OTHERS (2000) Performance on indirect measures of race evaluation predicts amygdala activation. *J. Cogn. Neurosci.* 12: 729–738.

RICHESON, J. A. AND 6 OTHERS (2003) An fMRI investigation of the impact of interracial contact on executive function. *Nat. Neurosci.* 6: 1323–1328.

RIZZOLATTI, G., L. FADIGA, V. GALLESE AND L. FOGASSI (1996) Premotor cortex and the recognition of motor actions. *Cogn. Brain Res.* 3: 131–141.

SCHULLER, A. M. AND B. ROSSION (2001) Spatial attention triggered by eye gaze increases and speeds up early visual activity. *Neuroreport* 12: 2381–2386.

Books

CACCIOPPO, J. T., P. S. VISSER AND C. L. PICKETT, EDS. (2006) *Social Neuroscience: People Thinking about Thinking People.* Cambridge, MA: MIT Press.

HARMON-JONES, E. AND P. WINKIELMAN, EDS. (2007) *Social Neuroscience: Integrating Biological and Psychological Explanations of Social Behavior.* New York: Guilford.

JAMES, W. (1890) *Psychology: Briefer Course.* New York: Holt.

UNIT VII

Principles of Symbolic Representation

erhaps the most sophisticated cognitive behaviors are those that use *symbols*, meaning tokens (loosely called *representations*) that stand for something more concrete or immediate in the world. The most obvious manifestation of such symbolism is human language. All humans communicate with one another by stringing together spoken words that convey meaningful statements or other kinds of thoughts. By convention, the spoken words in any given language are agreed to stand for the various objects, concepts, conditions, and other categories that are important to the population in question. Because of their preeminence in human culture, speech and language have been the focus of most theoretical and practical work on symbolic representation, and indeed they receive the lion's share of the coverage in this unit.

There are, however, other cognitive domains in which we and other animals have evolved representational schemas. The most significant of these are representations of the passage of time and representations of quantity. In societies like ours, time and number are expressed in words and written symbols, but these graphical tokens are not central to the mental processes involving time and number, any more than vocabulary and writing are core issues in understanding the basis of language. In fact, all mammals and many other species have neural mechanisms for representing time and number, although these representations are, like the symbolic bases of social communication, far more developed in humans. Thus, like the cognitive abilities considered in earlier chapters, symbolic representations are widely manifest in animal brains, presumably because of the advantages conferred in generating successful behavior. ■

20

Overview of Speech and Language

Introduction

The production and comprehension of speech are highly specialized cognitive abilities that have been a fundamental factor, arguably the key factor, in the evolution of human culture. A standard dictionary definition of *language* is "the particular form of speech of a group of people." For cognitive neuroscience, however, a better definition of human language is "a symbolic system used to communicate concrete or abstract meanings, irrespective of the sensory modality employed or the particular means of expression." This broader definition includes spoken and heard language, language communicated in written form, and sign (gestural) language. Because of their enormous importance in all human societies, speech and language have been intensively studied by linguists, philologists, anthropologists, sociologists, psychologists, neurologists, and of course, cognitive neuroscientists. Although speech differs widely in the approximately 6000 languages used in the world today, any given language includes a vocabulary, a grammar, and rules of syntax. For a minority of languages (only about 200 out of 6000) speech has been translated into writing, and how the brain processes this visual form of a subset of languages has also been of interest. Finally, vocal and auditory communication systems in non-human primates and other animals have been intensively examined to explore the fascinating question of how these systems compare with human language, and what present evidence implies about the origins of language. This chapter reviews what is known (or hypothesized) about speech and language as such; Chapter 21 then examines the neural bases of language abilities. Although some aspects of the evolution and development of speech and language are mentioned here, these issues are taken up in more detail in Chapters 26 and 27.

Producing Speech Sounds

Speech depends on a variety of vocal sounds whose intensity, timbre, and tonal qualities convey semantic and other biologically useful information, such as the size, gender, and emotional state of the speaker. It is thus important to understand some basic facts about speech sound stimuli.

Basic facts about speech sounds and the vocal apparatus

The usual presentation of sound physics in terms of tuning forks and the simple sinusoidal stimuli they produce is both useful and conventional (see Chapter 6), but in nature such stimuli are rare, and certainly not characteristic of speech sounds. A more useful framework for understanding speech sounds is the **resonance** of a vibrating object such as a taut string. As **Figure 20.1A** illustrates, a plucked string vibrates at a particular frequency determined by its length, tension, density, and a variety of other physical factors. However, rather than vibrating at a single frequency like a tuning fork, such objects vibrate at a set of frequencies, or *vibratory modes*.

In the case of the string, the greatest vibration corresponds to the full length of the string; this mode is called the **fundamental frequency** (f_0). The next most powerful vibration is at ½ the length, and this mode is called the first **harmonic**, or f_1. The next most powerful vibratory mode is at ⅓ the length (the second harmonic, f_2); the next at ¼ the length (the third harmonic, f_3); and so on (**Figure 20.1B**). In most natural circumstances, vibrating objects are physically attached to other objects that modulate the original vibrations, enhancing some modes and damping others (**Figure 20.1C**). The reason for belaboring these points is that the human **vocal cords** (also called *vocal folds*) are analogous to vibrating strings, and the **vocal tract** is analogous to the filtering effects of the attached body of a stringed instrument like a guitar or violin. Speech sounds are thus produced in much the same way as musical sounds.

The vocal tract includes the entire vocal apparatus from larynx to lips (**Figure 20.2**). The air expelled from the lungs streams through the opening between the vocal cords in the **larynx** (the *glottis*). As the airstream accelerates through this narrowing, the decreased pressure that results causes the cords to

Figure 20.1 Natural resonances and their modulation. (A) A vibrating string illustrates the different modes of vibration that characterize resonating objects. *L* = length of the string, f_0 = fundamental frequency of vibration. (B) The spectrum (power, or amplitude, versus frequency) generated by the string is characterized by a series of frequency peaks called a *harmonic series*, each peak corresponding to a different mode of vibration. (C) The associated structure, such as the body of a guitar, modulates the natural resonances of the strings by virtue of its own resonance frequencies, giving the sound stimulus specific characteristics that depend on the detailed construction of any particular guitar. The resonance characteristics of the guitar body are demonstrated here as they would be seen by holographic interference photography.

(A)

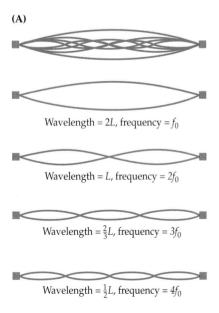

Wavelength = 2*L*, frequency = f_0

Wavelength = *L*, frequency = $2f_0$

Wavelength = $\frac{2}{3}L$, frequency = $3f_0$

Wavelength = $\frac{1}{2}L$, frequency = $4f_0$

(B)

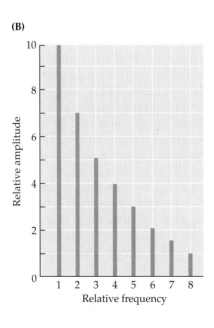

Relative amplitude

Relative frequency

(C)

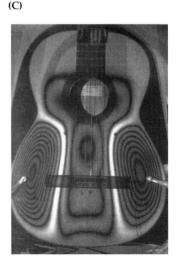

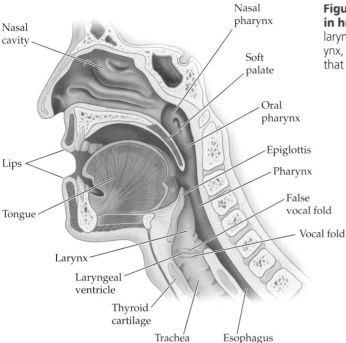

Nasal cavity

Lips

Tongue

Larynx

Laryngeal ventricle

Thyroid cartilage

Trachea

Esophagus

Nasal pharynx

Soft palate

Oral pharynx

Epiglottis

Pharynx

False vocal fold

Vocal fold

Figure 20.2 Structures that determine speech sound stimuli in humans. The vocal tract includes the vocal apparatus from the larynx to the lips. The structures above the larynx, including the pharynx, soft palate, and nasal cavity, shape and filter the harmonic series that are generated by the vocal chords when they vibrate.

come together until the pressure buildup in the lungs forces them open again (the physical principle involved is what generates the lift given an airplane by the faster movement of air over the top surface of the wings; it is called *Bernoulli's principle*). This process thus gives rise to a vibration whose frequency is determined primarily by the muscles that control the tension of the vocal cords. The fundamental frequency of these oscillations ranges from about 100 to 400 hertz, depending on the gender and size of the speaker. The rest of the vocal tract is effectively an attached resonating body. Much like the body of the guitar in Figure 20.1C, the vocal tract above the larynx shapes and filters the power in harmonic series produced by vibration of the vocal cords.

This **source-filter model** of speech was first proposed in the nineteenth century by the German anatomist and physiologist Johannes Müller and has been generally accepted ever since (**Figure 20.3**). The lungs serve as a reservoir of air, and the muscles of the diaphragm and chest wall provide the motive force. The vocal cords then provide the periodic vibration that characterizes **voiced** (tonal) sounds such as those made when vowels are spoken. The pharynx, oral and nasal cavities, and their included structures (e.g., tongue, teeth, and lips) are the filter. These dynamically changing spaces and their natural resonances modify the periodic energy generated by the laryngeal source, thus determining speech sounds that eventually emanate from the speaker. Of course, not all human vocalizations are speech, and, as described in **Box 20A**, nonspeech vocalizations are important in their own right.

The natural resonances of the vocal tract that filter the sound pressure oscillations generated by the larynx produce speech **formants**, defined as the peaks of power that are produced by this source-filter mechanism (see Figure 20.3). To generate different speech sounds, the shape of the vocal tract is actively changed by the musculature of the pharynx, tongue, and lips, in this way producing different natural resonances, and thus different formant frequencies. The relative frequencies of the formants create the variety of voiced speech sound stimuli that humans routinely produce in their native language.

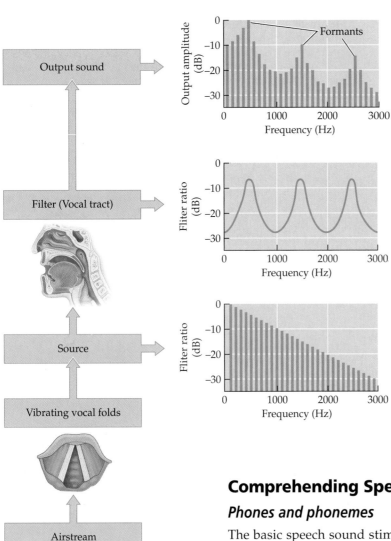

Figure 20.3 The source-filter model of speech sound production. Using air expelled by the lungs, the vocal cords of the larynx are the source of the vibrations that become speech stimuli. Other components of vocal tract, including the pharynx and the structures of the oral and nasal cavities, filter the laryngeal harmonics by the superposition of their own resonances, thus creating the speech sound stimuli that we ultimately hear. (After Miller 1991.)

Comprehending Speech Sounds

Phones and phonemes

The basic speech sound stimuli in any language are called **phones**, and the perceptions they elicit are called **phonemes**. One or more phones make up *syllables* in speech, which in turn make up *words*, which ultimately make up *sentences*. Considering languages worldwide, most linguists estimate the number of phones (and phonemes) to be about 200, of which roughly 30 to 100 are used in any given language. The use of different subsets of these speech sound stimuli in different languages helps explain why people have trouble learning a new language (they have to produce and comprehend unfamiliar phones), and why they retain accents characteristic of their native language (the familiar ways of producing phones and hearing phonemes are deeply entrenched in the organization of the adult brain).

Phones can be divided into **vowel** and **consonant** speech sound stimuli. The approximately 40 phones that characterize English are nearly equally divided between vowels and consonants, but other languages vary greatly in this respect. Vowel sounds comprise most of the voiced elements of speech—the elemental speech sounds that are generated by oscillations of the vocal cords in any language (see the preceding section). Because these oscillations are periodic, vowel sounds have a **tonal** quality, eliciting the perception of pitch in both speech and song. The majority of the acoustic power in speech is in the vowel sounds.

Consonant sound stimuli are phones that begin and/or end syllables, in contrast to vowel phones, which typically form the nucleus of each syllable. Consonant sounds are typically briefer than vowel sounds, involve more

■ BOX 20A Human Vocalizations That Are Not Speech

Not all vocal sound stimuli produced by humans are speech sounds in the usual sense of uttering words, phrases, or sentences that have semantic content. Sounds such as cries, grunts, screams, laughter, and humming; interjections and fillers such as "ah" or "uh" (or even the ubiquitous "like"); and singing without words (e.g., "la-la-la") are all examples of vocalizations that are not strictly speech. Nonetheless, they are clearly important in our system of vocal communication.

As might be imagined, nonspeech vocal sounds have been much less studied than semantic speech. Perhaps the category that has received the most attention over the years is laughter. Although philosophers and theorists including Plato, Kant, Bergson, and others have speculated about humor and the genesis of laughter in centuries past, a few contemporary cognitive neuroscientists have had the temerity to take on laughter as a subject for serious inquiry. An example is the neuroscientist and psychologist Robert Provine at the University of Maryland. Taking what he has called an "etholog-

ical approach," Provine recorded 1200 episodes of natural laughter in a variety of settings to examine when and why laughter occurs, and how it is used as a paralinguistic form of social communication. From these data he determined that (1) laughing almost never occurs without an audience; (2) speakers laugh more than their listeners; (3) women laugh more than men; and (4) men elicit more laughter by what they say than women do.

When Provine examined the acoustics of laughter, the individual elements (the "ha," "he," or "ho" components) typically occurred at a rate of about five per second and lasted about 150 milliseconds each—roughly the same duration as the utterance of a verbal syllable. The fundamental frequency (pitch) of these units was about twice that of syllables in normal speaking, and typically occurred with diminishing loudness (i.e., a *decrescendo*). He also found that laughter in his database was produced in a highly formulaic manner, with common variations and possible sequences that were never produced (Figure A).

Although the interpretation of these facts is debated, laughter is not limited to humans and thus provides insight into the evolution of language discussed later in this chapter and in Chapter 26. As Charles Darwin noted in *The Expression of Emotion in Man and Animals*—and as other ethologists have confirmed since—great apes produce laughlike vocalizations, and chimps laugh when tickled, much as humans do (see Figure B). However, these rhythmic sounds are pantlike when produced by chimps, almost always associated with physical play, and clearly not used in the variety of ways that humans use laughter (we use laughter not just to respond to something that is funny or playful, but to express friendliness, enthusiasm, sarcasm, derision, and even evil intentions, as in the wicked laughter of fictional witches).

Arguably, chimp laughter provides a good example of what the antecedents of human laughter may have been, and thus how vocal sounds began to be carriers of nonverbal meanings that eventually evolved semantic meanings. Although linguists have understandably chosen to focus on the speech sounds, insight into the nature and origins of speech can also arise from studies of nonspeech that are rich in significance, even though their meanings are not found in any dictionary.

(A)

Common laugh variants

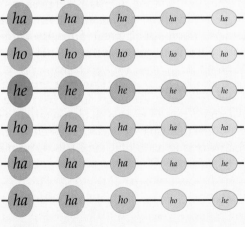

Forbidden laugh variants

Aspects of laughter in humans and a non-human primate. (A) Variations of a five-element laugh showing common and forbidden element sequences. (B) The "play face" of a chimp that typically accompanies pantlike laugher. (A after Provine 2000; B photograph by Frans de Waal, from de Waal 2003.)

(B)

References

BACHOROWSKI, J.-A. AND M. J. OWREN (2003) Sounds of emotion: The production and perception of affect-related vocal acoustics. *Ann. N. Y. Acad. Sci.* 1000: 244–265.

BERGSON, H. (1911) *Laughter: An Essay on the Meaning of the Comic.* (Translated by C. Bereton and F. Rothwell.) New York: Macmillan.

DARWIN, C. (1872) *The Expression of Emotion in Man and Animals.* Reprint, Chicago: University of Chicago Press, 1965.

PROVINE, R. R. (2000) *Laughter: A Scientific Investigation.* New York: Penguin.

rapid changes in sound energy over time, and are acoustically more complex. Consonants are categorized according to the site in the vocal tract that determines them (the *place of articulation*), or the physical way they are generated (the *manner of articulation*). The "click languages" of southern Africa, of which about 30 survive today, show another variation in the production of consonants. Each of these languages has four or five different click sounds that are double consonants (the consonant equivalent of diphthongs) made by sucking the tongue down from the roof of the mouth (everyone can make such sounds, but they are rarely incorporated in speech). Somewhat surprisingly, consonants are the main carriers of information in speech. Thus, in interpreting spoken sentences from which either the vowels or the consonant sounds have been artificially removed, it is much easier to understand utterances without vowels than without consonants.

Interpreting speech sounds

Although our impression is that speech is physically divided into words, syllables, and phones—and, by implication, that the neural analysis of speech operates on these elements as such—this expectation is clearly not met. Recordings of speech, such as the example in **Figure 20.4**, show that the sense we have that speech comprises a string of discrete words is false, at least in acoustic terms. Although this is the way we *hear* speech, our perception is at odds with the lack of any physical distinction or breaks between different syllables or even words. Thus, we cannot decipher what a speaker has said simply by looking at recordings of speech.

The neural processing—and ultimately cognitive understanding—of speech evidently proceeds in a much more holistic way. This idea is confirmed by the fact that listeners generally do not notice short bursts of noise that interrupt speech sounds 10 to 15 times per second. Consistent with the generation of other classes of percepts described in Unit II, this so-called **continuity effect**, or *filling in*, implies that speech percepts are actively created by the human auditory and language processing systems, and are not simply neural translations or representations of physical stimuli at the ear. Underscoring this general point, studies of eye movements as people read a text indicate that syllables, words, and even distinct phrases are not the elements being processed during normal reading. The eyes fixate sequentially on portions of a line of text that do not follow these written distinctions (i.e., the included segments are not defined by syllabic or word boundaries). Thus, the formal elements of a language, whether in spoken or written form, are not natural units of speech production or processing.

These facts present an additional challenge to understanding the neural underpinnings of language comprehension. How and why do we hear speech sounds in ways that bear little resemblance to the physical characteristics of the stimuli? One approach to resolving this puzzle was suggested by the speech psychologist Alvin Liberman working at Yale in the 1970s. Liberman

Figure 20.4 Recording of the spoken sentence "This is a glad time indeed." The intensity of the sound signal is plotted against time, with the elements of the sentence indicated on the time axis (which represents about 2 seconds). Such recordings of human speech show no clear or consistent physical distinction between the various components of speech (phones, syllables, and words), as might be assumed by the discrete way we seem to hear these components of speech. (From Schwartz et al. 2003.)

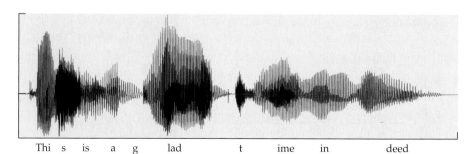

proposed that what we perceive in speech sounds are what he called the underlying "vocal gestures." By this he meant that what we hear corresponds much more closely to what the vocal tract is doing as speech is uttered than to the acoustic signal as such (see Figure 20.4).

This perspective cannot, however, be taken too literally. One problem is that vocal-tract changes during speech overlap in time and influence one another—a phenomenon called **coarticulation**. Another problem is that the acoustic characteristics of the phones associated with different vocal gestures overlap in the natural speech of men, women, and children, making it difficult to imagine how sound stimuli could be unambiguously associated with configurations of the vocal tract. Nonetheless, Liberman's idea seems to point in the right direction, implying that what we hear in speech is more closely related to vocal intention and contextual meaning than to the acoustics of the signal as such.

In any event, these and other facts about speech undermine any strictly syllabic or phonic approach to rationalizing its comprehension. Indeed, studies of illiterates suggest that syllabic and phonic distinctions emphasized in most systems of formal education are more a product of the way we learn to read and spell than of the neurobiology of speech processing.

Sentences, grammar, and syntax

Words are combined in most forms of speech to make **sentences**, defined as sequences of words that express a complete and meaningful thought. The organization of speech at this level is described in terms of grammar and syntax. **Grammar** is the system of rules by which words are properly formed and combined in any given language. **Syntax** refers to the more general set of rules describing the combinations of grammatically correct words and phases that can, in turn, be used to make meaningful sentences.

Surprising as it may seem, given the time devoted to it in most systems of education, the rules of grammar and syntax are arbitrary conventions that change continually over the history of any language. As a result, grammar and syntax vary enormously among languages, as well as over the history of a language, as anyone who has struggled to read Chaucer will know. English speakers today use the word order subject-verb-object (e.g., "The boy threw the ball") and might well imagine that this seemingly natural and logical order is characteristic of all languages. In fact, all possible arrangements are found among the world's languages, and more languages today use the order subject-object-verb than the order familiar in English. The intuition that grammar and syntax must be logical is simply not supported by the reality of languages, despite the effort imposed on students to learn these "rules" in school. Grammatical and syntactical conventions change continually, often quite radically, and the rules taught for any language today are presumably no less in flux than ever.

At the most basic level, of course, some aspects of grammar and syntax are more or less common to all languages. For instance, meaningful sentences in all languages use words, and these can be broadly categorized as object words, action words, and concept words. Whether or not such common features support the idea of a "universal grammar" is discussed later in the chapter in the context of language theories. This issue is clearly an important one because any universal characteristics of the world's languages would provide powerful clues about the neural strategies of language processing.

The importance of context in comprehending speech

The meanings of phones, syllables, words, phrases, and sentences, even when used with grammatical and syntactical correctness, are fraught with ambiguity. In addition to the acoustic ambiguity of phones already alluded to, this uncertainty raises challenges for understanding how speech is comprehended. Consider, for example, the prevalence in any language of homonyms and homophones. **Homonyms** are words represented by the same spelling and sound stimulus that have multiple meanings; the word *bank*, for example, has several meanings as both a noun and a verb. **Homophones** are words that are also represented by the same sound stimulus, but have different meanings and spellings—the words *kernel* and *colonel*, for instance. As a result of these additional ambiguities, understanding the meaning of a given word in speech is deeply dependent on context. Because these disambiguating contexts must be learned, the comprehension of speech—and the underlying neural processing—necessarily relies on the accumulated experience of the listener.

The early-twentieth-century American teacher and educator William Bagley was one of the first investigators to carry out experimental work on the importance of context in understanding speech. By cutting up and rearranging words (an approach he referred to as "word mutilation"), Bagley showed that correctly identifying and understanding syllables depend critically on the acoustic characteristics of their immediate surroundings in a word or sentence. Indeed, a familiar experience is misunderstanding a spoken or written word in an unexpected context (deciphering newspaper headlines provides good examples of how an odd or limited context can lead to misunderstanding). Much work since has shown that words are easier to recognize in sentences than in isolation, and that the ability to recognize words increases monotonically with their frequency of use in the relevant language, confirming the conclusion that familiarity based on past experience is how speech is disambiguated.

A different sort of demonstration of the importance of context in understanding speech is the **McGurk effect**. More than 30 years ago, psychologists Harry McGurk and John McDonald showed that the speech sounds we hear are strongly influenced by what we see. As illustrated in **Figure 20.5**, the effect arises when subjects see movements of a speaker's lips and tongue that have been experimentally changed so that they do not accord with the speech sound stimuli that are heard simultaneously. Such experiments reinforce the conclusion that what a listener hears is not simply determined by the sound signal processed by the auditory system, but a more complex construct elaborated by language-processing regions of the brain. Such constructs are based

Figure 20.5 What we see influences what we hear.   This phenomenon, known as the McGurk effect, was demonstrated in studies that presented videos of a person's face while speaking coupled with speech sound stimuli controlled by the experimenter. Here the position and visibility of the lips, teeth, and tongue are those that would normally accompany the sound /ga/; however, the synchronized sound was /ba/. When looking at a video of the speaker in these circumstances, most people hear /da/, a speech sound that, in visual terms, lies more or less between the visible vocal-tract configurations for the sounds /ga/ and /ba/. This type of altered perception is known as the *fused response*. When observers close their eyes, however, they hear /ba/, the stimulus that is actually being presented to the ears.

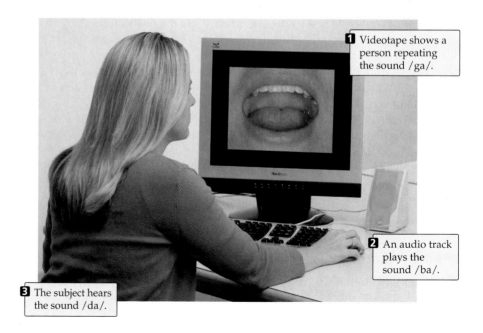

1 Videotape shows a person repeating the sound /ga/.

2 An audio track plays the sound /ba/.

3 The subject hears the sound /da/.

on a range of sensory and experiential information—in the case of the McGurk effect, both auditory and visual.

The simplest interpretation of these several lines of evidence is that speech perception is based on the *empirical significance* of speech sounds derived from the broader context of the speech signal, whether considered in terms of phonemes, syllables, words, phrases, sentences, or even entire passages. Indeed, the importance of context and the consequences for the empirical meaning of a stimulus apply not only to speech sounds, but to sound stimuli generally (see Chapter 6). Given this range of complexities, it is interesting to consider the recent success of computational systems now widely used for recognizing and producing speech (**Box 20B**).

Representing Speech Sounds in Written Form

As mentioned in the introduction to this chapter, only about 200 of the 6000 extant languages have systems of representing speech sounds visually, as writing. Writing is thus a specialized adjunct to a language, and it is certainly

---

■ BOX 20B Automated Speech Recognition

Nearly everyone by now is familiar with the annoying but useful automated interrogatories to which we are subjected when seeking the arrival time of a flight, renewing a prescription at the drugstore, or checking a bank account balance over the phone. Embedded in these automated exchanges is the production of speech asking various questions or indicating a next step in the sequence, along with an automated system for understanding your verbal response. The component for artificial speech *production* presents no great mystery, in that the enunciation of actual words by a human speaker are strung together in phrases appropriate to the various circumstances that arise in these relatively simple "conversations." In light of the enormous complexity of human speech comprehension, however, automated digital systems for *recognizing* speech, even in stereotypical conditions, are truly remarkable. How is this recognition possible, and what do speech recognition systems indicate about human language and the way the brain comprehends speech?

Surprisingly inexpensive software programs are now available for translating speech into type, which, if properly used, reach a level of accuracy of about 95 percent or more. The key to the success if such systems is the use of a *hidden Markov model* algorithm that estimates the probability that small sequential windows (tens of milliseconds) of the speech signal represent a particular phoneme. Each word in a vocabulary list is specified in phonetic terms pertinent to the speaker, and a statistical search procedure then determines the relationship of the phoneme sequence to the possible words spoken. The word in the vocabulary list that corresponds most closely to a phoneme sequence detected is then typed. Versions of such systems in use just a few years ago had to be extensively and specifically trained on the voice and vocabulary of each user to incorporate particular ways of speaking and words used. During this training, each error that the system made was corrected manually such that it gradually improved by taking into account the idiosyncratic nature of any individual user's speech. Current versions, however, work remarkably well with little or no training.

Impressive though these systems are, they accomplish only a small part of what happens in human conversations. Even young children not only recognize words, but also understand what they mean and can generalize those meanings. Automated speech recognition systems, of course, have no knowledge of what is being said. Nonetheless, the success of such systems provides a powerful indication of how some aspects of speech recognition are likely to be carried out by the human brain. The strategy of both the child and an artificial speech recognition system is to accumulate an ever-increasing amount of information that allows a word spoken in a variety of specific ways to be associated with the correct archetype on a statistical basis.

Speech recognition devices at present are really more akin to a camera that correctly converts stimuli (light versus sound) into a useful form (a photograph versus printed text), but leaves any interpretation to the viewer—or to the listener, as the case may be. From this perspective, automated speech recognition is a very long way indeed from the human recognition of speech as meaningful information.

References

The best way to explore this rapidly evolving technology is to browse the many Internet sites on this subject.

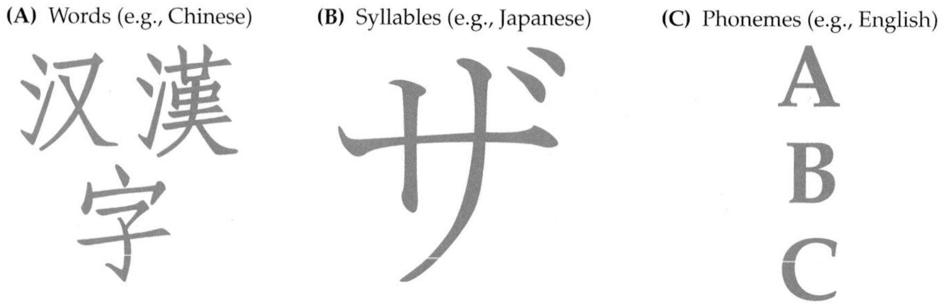

Figure 20.6 The three major ways of representing speech visually with graphemes. (A) Representing entire words (Chinese; each of the three symbols here is a different word). (B) Representing syllables (Japanese). (C) Representing phonemes (English).

(A) Words (e.g., Chinese)   **(B)** Syllables (e.g., Japanese)   **(C)** Phonemes (e.g., English)

汉漢
字

ザ

A
B
C

not equivalent in importance to speech. Nonetheless, the responses to written language are commonly used in cognitive neuroscience paradigms. Whether written or presented as gestures in sign language, this information is processed by brain regions different from those used to process speech, as will be described in Chapter 21.

Among the approximately 200 written forms of language, three major types of graphical systems have been used to represent speech symbolically (**Figure 20.6**): symbols that represent *words*, symbols that represent *syllables*, and symbols that represent *phonemes*. Taken together, these visual tokens are called *graphemes*. Chinese *logograms* are examples of graphemes that represent words (in some cases with features that are visually similar to an object word). This is a difficult system from a practical perspective; Chinese children must learn about 8000 graphemes to be fully literate, and knowledge of at least 2000 is the definition of literacy in China. This system has presumably persisted because Chinese words are generally monosyllabic. In any event, this system obviously has worked for a significant fraction of the world's population for thousands of years.

Egyptian *hieroglyphs* evidently began as logograms but eventually came to correspond to syllables. Representing syllables in writing is still evident in modern languages like Japanese. The most flexible system, however, is representing phonemes—the basic heard sounds of speech. The phonetic system arose in the Semitic languages of the early Phoenicians, Arabs, and Hebrews; the English alphabet is effectively one of the progeny of this symbolic approach. There is, however, no one-to-one correlation between the letters of a phonetic alphabet (e.g., the graphemes in English) and phonemes, just as there is no one-to-one correlation of phonemes to the acoustic stimuli (phones) underlying the heard sounds in language.

Acquiring Language

Learning a vocabulary

Learning any one of the thousands of human languages is obviously a remarkable feat. There is, first of all, the need to know the meanings of a significant number of words—that is, the acquisition of a **vocabulary**. About 500,000 words are included in the current edition of the *Oxford English Dictionary* (OED), a monumental project that began in the mid nineteenth century (there are many prior dictionaries of English, the most famous of which are those produced by Samuel Johnson and Noah Webster in 1755 and 1806, respectively).

The compilation of a dictionary is bedeviled by the fact that vocabulary, like grammar and syntax, is in continuous flux, with words being lost and added at a prodigious rate. Think, for instance, of all the words now in use that have been generated by the rapid rise of digital computation in the last few decades (*byte*, *Web site*, *laptop*, *blog*, and *wiki*, to name just a few). Think, too, of all the obscure words in the dictionary that are, for all intents and purposes, extinct and will eventually be dropped, although they were once used and are still included for reasons of completeness and etymology (much to the delight of Scrabble® players and crossword puzzle addicts).

A highly verbal person with a college-level education knows perhaps 100,000 of the words in the OED, although many fewer (approximately 10,000) are used in ordinary discourse. The challenge of learning a language, however, is not just acquiring an adequate vocabulary. Speakers must also learn grammar and syntax—tasks that are greatly complicated by the importance of context in speech, as just discussed. This wealth of linguistic information is normally learned through an enormous amount of trial and error in infancy and childhood—a process that continues to some degree throughout life.

The shaping of phonemes and phones during language acquisition

Much research in linguistics and cognitive neuroscience has shown that the speech sounds that an infant hears begin to shape and indeed to limit the child's perception and production of speech from the earliest days of postnatal life. As already mentioned, the various languages that exist today use quite different subsets of the approximately 200 phones that humans employ to produce speech of languages worldwide. Infants can initially perceive and discriminate among all these speech sounds and are not innately biased toward any particular phonemes, as the fact that an infant can become fluent in any language indicates. However, this ability at birth to appreciate and then produce the full range of human phones does not persist, eventually giving rise to the difficulties that older children and adults have in perceiving and uttering the phones that are not used in their native language.

One of the most thoroughly studied examples of this phenomenon concerns the phonetic differences between Japanese and English. Native Japanese speakers cannot reliably tell the difference between the /r/ and /l/ sounds in English because this phonetic distinction is not made or used in Japanese. Nonetheless, 4-month-old Japanese infants can make this discrimination as reliably as 4-month-old babies raised in English-speaking households can. As described in Chapter 27, researchers can make these inferences about what infants perceive by measuring sucking frequency on a pacifier or the duration of looking at a stimulus source. Sucking rate and eye fixation time increase in the presence of a novel stimulus and can thus indicate whether an infant perceives two speech stimuli as the same or different. By 6 months of age, infants already show preferences for phonemes in their native language compared to those in foreign languages, and by the end of the first year they no longer respond to phonetic elements peculiar to a non-native language.

Interestingly, the "baby talk" that adults instinctively use when speaking to very young children (sometimes called *motherese*) emphasizes the phonetic distinctions in a language to a greater degree than normal speech among adults does, presumably helping the infant hear the phonetic characteristics of the language that it is struggling to learn. Moreover, losing the ability to discriminate these acoustic differences is specifically related to speech sounds; adult Japanese and Americans are equally good at discriminating nonspeech sounds that include the acoustic characteristics of the phones that give them so much trouble in the context of language.

Critical period for language acquisition

Although a maturing child begins to lose the ability to hear non-native phonetic distinctions at a remarkably early age, the ability to learn another language fluently persists for some years. As is apparent from the experience of learning a new language in school or from watching friends and family who began learning a second language at various ages, becoming fluent nevertheless requires linguistic experience relatively early in life. This fact reflects a broader generalization about neural development—namely, that neural circuitry is especially susceptible to modification during early development, and that this malleability gradually diminishes with maturation (see Chapter 27). The window for extensive neural modification supporting a behavior is referred to as the **critical period** (also called the *sensitive period*), and is evident in the acquisition of language, as it is in many other cognitive behaviors.

Psycholinguists Jacqueline Johnson and Elissa Newport at the University of Rochester undertook a detailed study of this aspect of language learning, examining the critical period for the acquisition of a second language in Asian Americans who had come to the United States at various ages (**Figure 20.7A**). Using a battery of grammatical and other tests of fluency, they found that learning a second language before about age 7 results in adult performance that is indistinguishable from that of native speakers. However, fluency declined progressively as a function of people's age at first exposure.

The requirement for experience during a critical period is also apparent in studies of language acquisition in children who become deaf at different ages. The effects on language skills are marked when the onset of deafness occurs early in life, but are much less when the onset occurs later in childhood or in adult life. Younger children who have acquired some speech but then lose their hearing suffer a substantial decline in spoken language because they are unable to hear themselves speak and thus cannot refine their initial efforts at speech by testing the relative adequacy of what they are trying to say through auditory feedback. Differences in brain activation observed in children and adults doing language-based tasks provide some indication of the neural regions pertinent to diminished language-learning skills in adults (**Figure 20.7B**). However, the significance of these differences for understanding the critical period for language acquisition is not yet clear.

In sum, the normal acquisition of human language is subject to a critical period of approximately a decade; exposure and practice must occur within this time for a person to achieve full fluency. Of course, some ability to learn language persists into adulthood, but at a reduced level of efficiency and ultimate performance. This generalization is consistent with much other evidence from neural development that underscores the special importance of early experience in the full development of cognitive abilities (see Chapter 27).

Figure 20.7 The critical period for language learning. (A) The critical period for fully fluent language learning is apparent in studies of the fluency of Chinese-Americans as a function of the age of their arrival in the United States, marking the onset of significant exposure to English. Ultimate fluency begins to drop off when language learning begins after about age 7. (B) Areas in the brains of children and adults that are differently active during language-based tasks are shown in yellow. These differences provide a possible neural basis for the diminishing ability to learn a new language with increasing age, although more specific interpretation of this evidence is not yet possible. (A from Johnson and Newport 1989; B from Brown et al. 2005.)

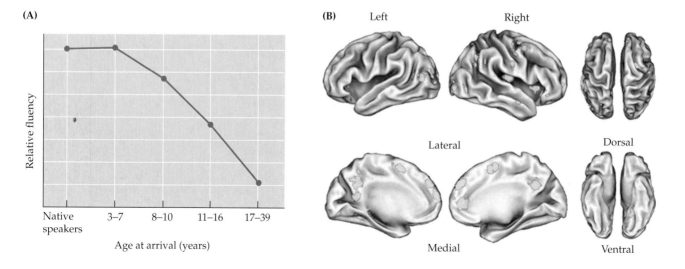

Mechanisms of language learning

The most obvious aspect of the biological mechanisms that underlie language learning is extensive exposure and *practice*. Like other complex skills, language proficiency requires repeated activation of the relevant neural circuits, presumably because of the neural associations made by altering the relative strengths of synaptic connections (see Chapter 13). Many neurobiological studies in simple model systems suggest that exposure and practice would selectively preserve and strengthen the brain circuits pertinent to phonetic distinctions in the language in which a child is immersed daily. At the same time, the absence of exposure to non-native phones would presumably result in a gradual weakening of the connections representing sound stimuli that are not heard and practiced, which would in turn be reflected in a declining ability to distinguish and enunciate these phones correctly.

In this conception, the language circuitry that is used is retained, whereas circuits that are unused weaken and, after some years, cease to be functional or are perhaps lost altogether. Given what is known about developmental neurobiology more generally, these changes presumably arise from the influence of neural activity or the lack of it on the cellular and molecular mechanisms that regulate the strength and prevalence of synaptic connections. That is not to say, however, that all language learning is necessarily based on extensive repetition. Psychologist Paul Bloom at Yale and others have suggested that children are also capable of "fast mapping" new words with only a few exposures or even just one. Although this issue is currently being debated, Bloom has proposed that this rapid acquisition is the result of fitting a new word into an existing schema of language associations that makes use of the full range of cognitive information that the child is learning.

Some more detailed insight into speech sound learning has emerged from work by Patricia Kuhl and her colleagues at the University of Washington. Her studies show that adults have a strong tendency to group speech sounds. For example, when asked to categorize a continuous spectrum of artificially constructed phones between /r/ and /l/, native English speakers tend to perceive the intermediate stimuli as all sounding like either /r/ or /l/. These perceptions are based on core phonemic preferences in different languages—a phenomenon that Kuhl has likened to a **perceptual magnet**. A similar effect is apparent in developing infants, as illustrated in **Figure 20.8**; infants only 6 months old tend to group phones according to the biases in their native lan-

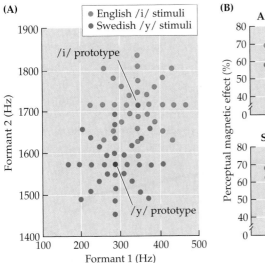
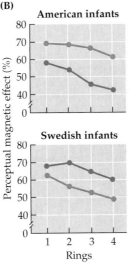

Figure 20.8 The "perceptual magnet" concept of phonemic grouping. (A) Formant frequencies associated with a prototypical American English /i/ are shown in red; those with a Swedish /y/ prototype, in blue. (B) Six-month-old American and Swedish babies show greater generalization for the speech sound stimulus to which they have been exposed in their native language than to the foreign phone when tested with the range of stimuli in (A), supporting the perceptual magnet idea. ("Rings" refers to areas included in the prototype regions in [A]). (From Kuhl et al. 1992.)

guage. The implication is that by means of such grouping, related but acoustically different sounds are eventually perceived as representing the routine variations of the phones and phonemes in the language to which the learner is being exposed (see also Figure 2.9).

Effects of language deprivation

An issue complementary to normal language learning concerns the effects of **language deprivation**, a topic already touched on in the earlier consideration of the deterioration of language in hearing-deficient individuals as a function of age. A broader question, asked since antiquity, is what would happen if an otherwise normal child were *never* exposed to language. Would the child remain mute, or could it develop some ability to speak and, if so, what sort of language would it have?

The closest approximation to a realization of this sort of "thought experiment" is a handful of unfortunate cases in which children have been deprived of significant language exposure as a result of having been raised by deranged parents. In the most fully documented case, a girl in a Los Angeles suburb was raised from infancy until age 13 under conditions of almost total language deprivation (she is known in the literature as *Genie*). Genie was brought to the attention of social workers in 1970, who found her locked in a small room, where she had been isolated and allegedly beaten if she made any noise. She was removed from these desperate conditions and taken to the children's hospital at UCLA, where she was found to be in adequate general health.

Given these highly unusual circumstances, a team of psychologists and linguists at UCLA studied Genie's language and other cognitive skills during the subsequent five years. Although Genie had little or no language ability initially, the investigators found no evidence of brain damage or mental retardation in the usual sense, and they described her overall personality as rather docile and generally pleasant. As might be expected, Genie also received extensive remedial training to teach her the language skills that she had never learned as a child. Despite these efforts, as well as daily life in more or less normal conditions in foster homes, Genie never acquired more than rudimentary language skills. Although she eventually learned a reasonable vocabulary, she could not put words together grammatically, saying things like, "Applesauce buy store?" when she wanted to ask whether she might buy some applesauce at the store.

Genie's case and a few similar examples starkly define the importance of adequate early experience for successfully learning any language, in accord with the more abundant evidence of a critical period for learning a second language.

Theories of Language

Given the enormous diversity of speech sounds, grammar, and syntax among the world's 6000 spoken languages and the profound dependence of speech comprehension on context in any language, the idea of an encompassing "theory of language" would seem a daunting if not impossible goal. Nevertheless, some important theoretical generalizations about languages have received much attention over the years and are useful to consider.

The question of a universal grammar

Beginning with the MIT linguist Noam Chomsky and his students in the 1950s, many investigators have explored the idea that all languages must share some basic rules—a concept referred to as a **universal grammar**. Chomsky argued that all languages must have "deep structures" that are "transformed" into the "surface structures" of particular languages as expressed in speech.

Finding a universal grammar, if indeed there is one, proved elusive in the decades that followed Chomsky's introduction of this idea. From what has already been said, any such structures would have to be deeply buried indeed, since fundamental grammatical features such as subject-verb-object order; the use of past, present, and future verb tenses; and every other structural feature that has been examined vary widely across languages. Nonetheless, the neurobiological evidence that has accumulated over the last half century supports the idea that human infants (as well as the young of other vertebrate species) come into the world with a great deal of preprogrammed circuitry pertinent to social communication, including, in the case of humans, a very strong predisposition to learn a language using the particular regions of the brain described in Chapter 21.

In addition, studies of congenitally deaf individuals living in relatively isolated communities have shown that idiosyncratic sign languages that allow the affected children to communicate with their families emerge quickly and spontaneously. This preparation of neural circuitry for language in specialized brain regions implies a basis for the deep structures that Chomsky imagined, but no one has so far been able to say much about these preparatory circuits, let alone translate their organization into grammatical or syntactical terms. As a result, the gulf between the neurobiology of language and what linguists think of as a universal grammar remains wide.

Connectionist theory

Another general approach to understanding language across the idiosyncrasies of particular languages has focused on its associational character. When someone is presented with any word (e.g., *chair*), other words automatically come to mind (e.g., *table*)—some far more frequently than others (**Table 20.1**). This sort of word association is the basis of various psychological tests described in previous chapters, whether predicated on the Freudian supposition of unconscious influences welling up from the "id," or simply on the statistical co-occurrence of words in normal speech and language-based thought (the latter is presumably the primary reason that *table* pops to mind in response to *chair*).

Whatever the focus of psychological interest, the associative nature of language indicates something fundamentally important about the underlying neural basis of languages—namely, that they entail linkages that must depend on the relative strength of synaptic connections in the relevant parts of the brain. In this conception, words like *table* and *chair* are associated because their common co-occurrence in language use has strengthened the neuronal circuitry between their respective representations in the language areas of the cortex. A more specific extension of this general idea about the organization of language in associational networks is a broadly hierarchical cascade of related categories. Such associations can diverge in very different directions, as illustrated for the category "chair" in **Figure 20.9A**, presumably accounting for some of the odder associations in Table 20.1.

■ **TABLE 20.1 Frequency of Words Associated with the Probe Word *Chair***

Response to probe word *chair*	Frequency[a]
Table	191
Seat	127
Sit	107
Furniture	83
Sitting	56
Wood	49
Rest	45
Stool	38
Comfort	21
Rocker	17
Rocking	15
Bench	13
Cushion	12
Legs	11
Floor	10
Desk; room	9
Comfortable	8
Ease; leg	7
Easy; sofa; wooden	6
Couch; hard; Morris; seated; soft	5
Arm; article; brown; high	4

Source: KENT, G. H. AND A. J. ROSANOFF (1910) A study of association in insanity. *J. Insanity* Jul/Oct: 37–96.

[a]Number of times the probe word elicited the response indicated, based on a survey of 1000 men and women.

Figure 20.9 A connectionist framework for the organization of words in the mental lexicon. (A) A hierarchical concept of the word associations, illustrated here in terms of the hierarchy of concepts that might underlie the organization of language related to the word *chair*. (B) A typical neural network. If the weights between neural nodes are changed according to feedback from performance (i.e., experience contending with a given problem), the associativity of an artificial neural network is changed, thus changing its function. Such networks provide a plausible way of modeling the acquisition of word associations during development and their subsequent expression in maturity.

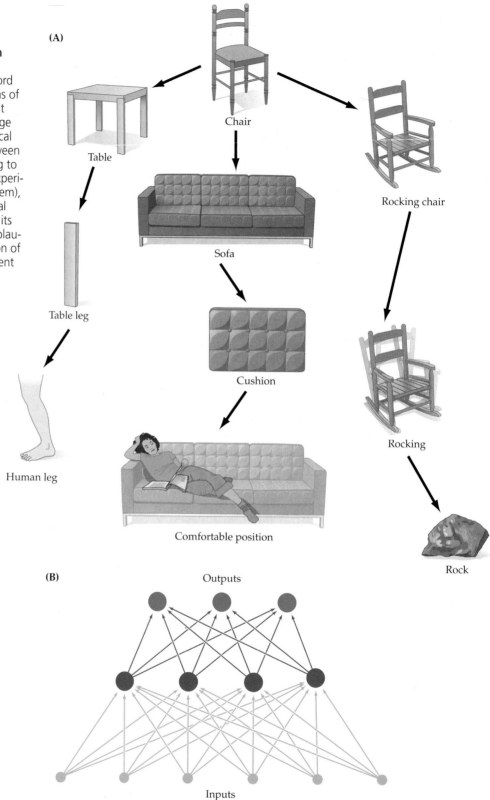

(A)

Chair

Table

Table leg

Human leg

Sofa

Cushion

Comfortable position

Rocking chair

Rocking

Rock

(B)

Outputs

Inputs

This general idea of associational linkages as a model for the lexical aspects of language (and many other cognitive functions) has found more specific expression in **connectionist** theories (see Box 2B) of how such associations might work, and their simulation in artificial **neural networks** whose properties are changed by alteration of the weightings (*synaptic connections*, in biological terms) of the relevant nodes (neurons) in such networks (**Figure 20.9B**). Although the history of neural networks goes back to the 1940s, the major figures in the modern connectionist approach are David Rumelhart and James McClelland, who began this work at Carnegie Mellon University in the 1970s. A particular attraction of a connectionist view of language organization is its foundation in statistical association—a powerful mechanism that accords with neural mechanisms for encoding and storing information discussed in several other chapters (e.g., Chapters 5 and 13). Connectionist theory does not, however, give much insight into other key aspects of language, such as grammar and syntax.

Is Human Language Unique?

Over the centuries, theologians, natural philosophers, and a good many neuroscientists have argued that language is uniquely human; in this view, human language sets us apart from our fellow animals. However, evidence of sophisticated forms of vocal or other symbolic communication in species as diverse as bees, birds, monkeys, and whales has made this point of view untenable, at least in a broad sense.

Nonetheless, some aspects of human language appear to have no equivalent in the communication systems of other animals. One such aspect is that, whereas other animals have only a limited repertoire of vocal sounds whose acoustic patterns have specific and fixed meanings, humans arbitrarily link phones to an indefinitely large set of meaningful words. By the same token, only human language has appeared to use a **recursive grammar**. By this, linguists and others mean the ability to embed clauses meaningfully in sentences, and to iterate these additions ad infinitum (in principle) in a manner that still makes sense. For example, for any particular sentence of the type "Jane knows cognitive neuroscience," it is possible to embed another similar phrase to make a meaningful sentence, such as "Bob knows that Jane knows cognitive neuroscience," and to embed the same sort of phrase yet again to make something like "Bill knows that Bob knows that Jane knows cognitive neuroscience," and so on. Humans routinely use recursion and easily recognize the meaning of such constructions. The progressive addition and back-referencing is why such embedment is called *recursive*, a term borrowed from logic.

This sort of grammar is referred to as a **context-free grammar** by linguists because the addition of "Z knows that …" to "X knows Y" will work for any specific terms X and Y. A context-free grammar is thus distinct from a **finite-state grammar**, in which the pattern as such determines the significance of the stimulus. In general, communication among non-human animals has long been thought to depend on this simpler finite-state grammar. In the dance of the honeybee, for example, each symbolic movement made by a foraging bee that returns to the hive encodes only a single meaning, whose expression and interpretation has been hardwired into the nervous system of the actor and the respondents. The same general point has long been made for birdsong, in which vocal stimuli are presumably attached to a fixed biological meaning (e.g., "I own this territory" or "Here I am, if you are looking for a mate"; **Box 20C**).

Several recent studies have explored the apparent absence of recursive grammatical abilities in other species more directly. Cognitive neuroscientist Marc Hauser, working with Tecumseh Fitch at Harvard, asked whether a primate (the cotton-tailed tamarin monkey in this case) could distinguish recursive grammatical structures of the form $a^n b^n$ from nonrecursive grammatical structures of the form $(ab)^n$ (**Figure 20.10**). The test was a habituation discrimination paradigm without any training, and the stimuli used were simple human speech sounds rather than monkey vocalizations, strung together in

Figure 20.10 Structures used for testing the uniqueness of human language. These finite-state (A) and recursive grammatical (B) structures have been used to test the uniqueness of human language in non-human primates and birds. (After Gentner used for testing et al. 2006.)

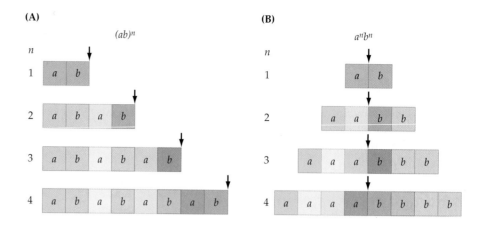

either recursive or nonrecursive form. The monkeys consistently failed this test; they could recognize when an *ababab* pattern was disrupted by an extra element, but they could not tell the difference when an *aabbaabb* pattern was changed in this same way. Not surprisingly, college students readily recog-

---

■ BOX 20C Learned Vocal Communication in Non-Human Species

Humans are not the only animals that learn to communicate during a critical period of development, and studies of non-human species have added greatly to a better understanding of social communication by vocalization. Many animal vocalizations are innate in the sense that they require no experience to be correctly produced and interpreted. For example, quails raised in isolation or deafened at hatching so that they never hear conspecific vocal stimuli nonetheless produce the full repertoire of species-specific vocalizations. Some species of birds, however, *learn* to communicate by vocal sounds, a process that is in some respects similar to the way humans learn language. Particularly well characterized is vocal learning in song sparrows, canaries, and finches. These and other bird species use songs to define their territory and attract mates (Figures A and B).

As with human language, early sensory exposure and practice are key determinants of subsequent perceptual and behavioral capabilities. Furthermore, the developmental period for learning these vocal behaviors, as for learning language, is restricted to early life. (Canaries are exceptional in that

they continue to build their song repertoire from season to season, which is one reason these birds have been such popular pets over the centuries.) Song learning in these species entails an initial stage of *sensory acquisition*, when the juvenile bird listens to and memorizes the song of an adult male "tutor" of its own species. This period is followed by a stage of vocal learning through practice, when the young bird matches its song to the memorized tutor model by auditory feedback. This *sensory-motor learning* stage ends with the onset of sexual maturity, when songs become acoustically stable (called *crystallized song*; Figure C).

In the species typically studied, young birds are especially impressionable during the first two months after hatching and become refractory to further exposure to tutor songs as they age, thus defining a critical (or sensitive) period for song learning. The early exposure to the tutor (typically the father) generates a memory that can remain intact for months (or longer) in some species before the onset of the vocal practice phase. Moreover, juveniles need to hear the tutor song only 10 to 20 times to vocal-

ly mimic it months later, and exposure to other songs after the sensory acquisition period does not affect this memory. The songs heard during this time, but not later, are the only ones that the young bird mimics. Songbirds also exhibit learned regional dialects, much as human infants learn the language characteristic of the region in which they are raised.

Other studies indicate that birds have a strong intrinsic predisposition to learning the song of their own species. Thus, when presented during maturation with a variety of recorded songs that include their own species' song, together with that of other species, juvenile birds preferentially learn the song of their own species. This observation shows that juveniles are not really naive, but are innately biased to learn the songs of their own species in preference to those of other species. Indeed, some evidence suggests that songbirds have a very rough template of their species song that is expressed in the absence of any exposure to that song or any other. Thus, birds raised in isolation produce highly abnormal "isolate" songs that have some characteristics of the song they would normally have learned (unlike

nized this difference between patterns, consistent with the idea that only humans routinely process and distinguish recursive forms.

It was thus of considerable interest when Timothy Gentner and his colleagues at UC San Diego and the University of Chicago examined this issue in a songbird (the European starling) and found a different result. They took advantage of the fact that the starling song has two components—a rattle and a warble—both of which occur in the starling's song motifs (see Figure B in Box 20C for an example of motifs in birdsong). Gentner and collaborators could thus synthesize recursive $a^n b^n$ vocal stimulus forms such as *ab* (rattle, warble), *aabb* (rattle, rattle; warble, warble), *aaabbb* (rattle, rattle, rattle; warble, warble, warble), and so on, as well as nonrecursive $(ab)^n$ forms such as *ab* (rattle, warble), *abab* (rattle, warble; rattle, warble), *ababab* (rattle, warble; rattle, warble; rattle, warble), and so on. They found that, after a great deal of training, most of the birds tested could reliably distinguish the two forms in an operant-conditioning paradigm in which only the recursive grammatical form was rewarded. Although starlings presumably make no use of this ability in vocal communication, the researchers concluded that the rudiments of the ability to use recursive grammars are present in some non-human animals.

Genie in the comparable human example). Such songs, however, are biologically ineffective in that they fail to attract mates.

In sum, the vocally relevant parts of the bird brain are already prepared during early life to learn the specific vocal sounds of the species, much as the brains of human infants are prepared at birth to learn language. Although the similarities with human language acquisition can be exaggerated, at least some aspects of human language have analogues in the vocal communicative abilities of other animals.

References

DOUPE, A. AND P. KUHL (1999) Birdsong and human speech: Common themes and mechanisms. *Annu. Rev. Neurosci.* 22: 567–631.

(A)

(B)

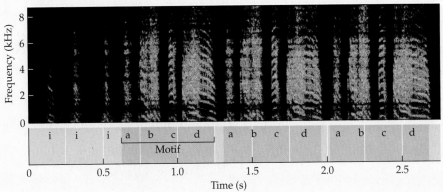

Birdsong learning. The spectrogram in (B) shows the song of an adult male zebra finch—the bird on the right in (A)—that is used in courting the female (as a general rule, only male songbirds sing). The recording plots the frequency of the song against time, showing the syllables and motifs that characterize the song of this species. Color indicates the intensity of the vocal signal, with red representing higher intensity and blue lower. (C) The stages of song learning in the zebra finch (0 indicates the time of hatching). (Courtesy of Rich Mooney.)

(C)

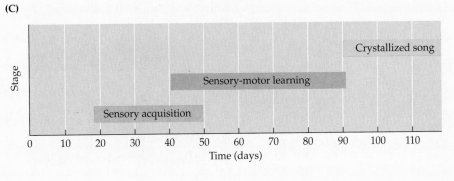

This and other evidence does not, of course, settle the centuries-old debate about the uniqueness of human language. However, it challenges those who want to claim that human speech and language are fundamentally different from vocal communication in other species.

The Origins of Human Language

The fact that human language is similar in a number of ways to systems of vocal communication in some other species raises the question of how human language originated. Although it should be clear that no one knows the answer, some clues are worth considering.

Field studies in a variety of non-human primate species have shown a surprising degree of vocal communication that seems a plausible antecedent for human speech. One well-studied example is the alarm calls of vervet monkeys, which differ according to the nature of the perceived threat. Ethologists Dorothy Cheney and Robert Seyfarth at the University of Pennsylvania found that a specific alarm call uttered when a leopard had been spotted by one animal caused other nearby monkeys to climb a tree. In contrast, the different alarm call given when a monkey saw an eagle caused the other members of the group to look skyward.

This work has now been augmented by detailed studies of the vocalizations of rhesus monkeys carried out by Asif Ghazanfar (now at Princeton) and Nikos Logothetis at the Max Planck Institute in Tübingen, as well as related work by Hauser. These animals utter at least five food-related vocalizations that are referred to respectively as *warble, harmonic arch, chirp, coo,* and *grunt,* as well as a threat call (**Figure 20.11**). Ghazanfar and Logothetis showed that different vocalizations had appreciably different effects on the monkeys who were listening (assessed, for example, by the degree to which other monkeys turned toward the monkey uttering a particular call). They also showed that the animals integrated visual and auditory information in doing so, much as humans

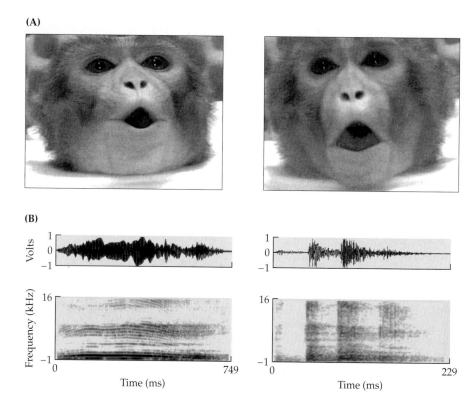

Figure 20.11 Rhesus monkey calls. The *coo* call (A) is relatively long and drawn out, as indicated by the sound signal and spectrographic recordings. It is quite different from the more pulsatile *threat* call (B). (From Ghazanfar and Logothetis 2003.)

Symbols

Meanings

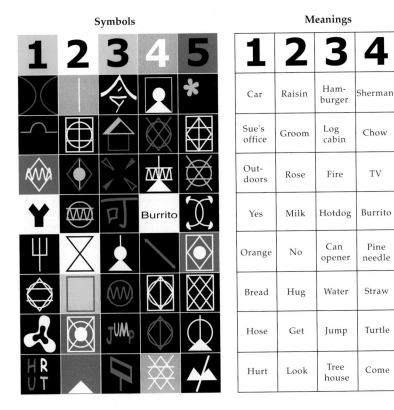

Figure 20.12 Abstract symbols used to assess the ability of chimpanzees to communicate. The animals are trained to manipulate tiles (left) with symbols that represent words and syntactic constructs (right) in order to communicate demands, questions, and even spontaneous expressions. (From Savage-Rumbaugh et al. 1998.)

do (see Figure 20.5). Moreover, studies in the field indicated that the different vocalizations are specifically related to the motivational state of the monkey uttering the call, as well as to the affective state and even to the particular qualities of food that had been discovered by the "speaker" during foraging.

More controversial studies in great apes going back several decades have sought to show more directly that the rudiments of the abstract symbolic communication are present, or at least latent, in our closest relatives. Although techniques have varied, most such studies have used some form of manipulable symbols that can be arranged to express ideas in an interpretable manner. For example, chimpanzees have been trained to manipulate tiles to represent words and syntactic constructs, allowing them to communicate simple expressions (**Figure 20.12**). With extensive training, chimps can choose from as many as 400 different symbols to construct what appear to be meaningful statements or questions. The more accomplished of these animals are alleged to have "vocabularies" of several thousand words or phrases. Compared to a child, however, the way chimps use these words is far less impressive; moreover, children can learn new words and how to use them very rapidly (see earlier). Indeed, whether the chimps are using symbols in the same way that humans use words as tokens is much debated, and many cognitive neuroscientists remain skeptical of how analogous such usage is to human language.

Summary

1. The human vocal tract and its controlling neural apparatus have become highly specialized over evolutionary time, allowing this system to produce approximately 200 distinct speech sounds (phones), which produce corresponding auditory percepts (phonemes). A few tens of these speech sounds are used in any given language to produce the syllables, words, phrases, sentences, and ultimately the narratives that humans use to communicate verbal information.

2. Language must be learned in early life, and if such experience does not occur for any reason, then a person's linguistic ability is severely and permanently limited. Nonetheless, the infant brain, like the vocally relevant brain regions of some other species, is already prepared to incorporate the speech information that an infant hears.

3. Although phenomenally well developed in humans compared to other animals, language has many basic similarities with systems of social communication in other species, which appear to entail the same general scheme of constructing acquired neural associations within a framework of dedicated brain circuitry that has already been put in place by inherited developmental programs.

4. Whether the differences between human language and vocal communication in some other social species are a matter of quality or simply quantity remains hotly debated. It is clear, however, that what other animals do in a limited way to meet their ecological needs, humans have refined and extended to an extraordinary degree, driven by the biological advantages afforded by the acquisition, storage, and transmission of the cultural information that language enables.

Additional Reading

Reviews

DOUPE, A. AND P. KUHL (1999) Birdsong and human speech: Common themes and mechanisms. *Annu. Rev. Neurosci.* 22: 567–631.

HAUSER, M. D. (2001) The sound and the fury: Primate vocalizations as reflections of emotion and thought. In *The Origins of Music*, N. L. Wallin, B. Merker and S. Brown (eds.). Cambridge, MA: MIT Press, pp. 77–102.

HAUSER, M. D., N. CHOMSKY AND W. T. FITCH (2002) The faculty of language: What is it, who has it, and how did it evolve? *Science* 298: 1569–1579.

KUHL, P. K. (2000) A new view of language acquisition. *Proc. Natl. Acad. Sci. USA* 97: 11850–11857.

MILES, H. L. W. AND S. E. HARPER (1994) "Ape language" studies and the study of human language origins. In *Hominid Culture in Primate Perspective*, D. Quiatt and J. Itani (eds.). Niwot: University Press of Colorado, pp. 253–278.

POLLICK, A. S. AND DE WAAL, F. B. M. (2007) Ape gestures and language evolution. *Proc. Natl. Acad. Sci. USA* 104: 8184–8189.

SEYFARTH, D. M. AND D. I. CHENEY (1984) The natural vocalizations of non-human primates. *Trends Neurosci.* 7: 66–73.

Important Original Papers

BAGLEY, W. C. (1900–1901) The apperception of the spoken sentence: A study in the psychology of language. *Am. J. Psychol.* 12: 80–130.

BROWN, T. T., H. M. LUGAR, R. S. COALSON, F. M. MIEZIN, S. E. PETERESEN AND B. L. SCHLAGGAR (2005) Developmental changes in human cerebral functional organization for word generation. *Cereb. Cortex* 15: 275–290.

FROMKIN, V., S. KRASHEN, S. CURTIS, D. RIGLER AND M. RIGLER (1974) The development of language in Genie: A case of language acquisition beyond the "critical period." *Brain Lang.* 1: 81–107.

GENTNER, T. Q., K. M. FENN, D. MARGOLIASH AND H. C. NUSBAUM (2006) Recursive syntactic pattern learning by songbirds. *Nature* 440: 1204–1207.

GHAZANFAR, A. A. AND N. LOGOTHETIS (2003) Facial expressions linked to monkey calls. *Nature* 423: 937.

JOHNSON, J. S. AND E. L. NEWPORT (1989) Critical period effects in second language learning: The influence of maturational state on the acquisition of English as a second language. *Cogn. Psychol.* 21: 60–99.

KUHL, P. K., B. T. CONBOY, D. PADDEN, T. NELSON AND J. PRUITT (2005) Early speech perception and later language development: Implications for the "critical period." *Lang. Learn. Dev.* 1: 237–264.

KUHL, P. K., K. A. WILLIAMS, F. LACERDA, K. N. STEVENS AND B. LINDBLOM (1992) Linguistic experience alters phonetic perception in infants 6 months of age. *Science* 255: 606–608.

MILLER, G. A. AND J. C. R. LICKLIDER (1950) The intelligibility of interrupted speech. *J. Acoust. Soc. Am.* 22: 167–173.

SCHLAGGAR, B. L., T. T. BROWN, H. M. LUGAR, K. M. VISSCHER, F. M. MIEZIN AND S. E. PETERSEN (2002) Functional neuroanatomical differences between adults and school-age children in the processing of single words. *Science* 296: 1476–1479.

TOMASELLO, M. (2004) What kind of evidence could refute the UG hypothesis? *Stud. Lang.* 28: 642–644.

WHITEN, A. AND 8 OTHERS (1999) Cultures in chimpanzees. *Nature* 399: 682–685.

Books

BLOOM, P. (2002) *How Children Learn the Meanings of Words.* Cambridge, MA: MIT Press.

CHOMSKY, N. (1957) *Syntactic Structures.* The Hague: Elsevier.

GOODALL, J. (1990) *Through a Window: My Thirty Years with the Chimpanzees of Gombe.* Boston: Houghton Mifflin.

GRIFFIN, D. R. (1992) *Animal Minds.* Chicago: University of Chicago Press.

HAUSER, M. (1996) *The Evolution of Communication.* Cambridge MA: MIT Press.

LIBERMAN, A. M. (1996) *Speech: A Special Code.* Cambridge, MA: MIT Press.

LENNEBERG, E. (1967) *The Biological Foundations of Language.* New York: Wiley.

McNEIL, D. (2000) *Language and Gesture.* Cambridge: Cambridge University Press.

MILLER, G. A. (1991) *The Science of Words.* New York: Scientific American Library.

PLOMP, R. (2002) *The Intelligent Ear: On the Nature of Sound Perception.* Mahwah, NJ: Erlbaum.

ROGERS, T. T. AND J. L. McCLELLAND (2004) *Semantic Cognition: A Parallel Distributed Processing Approach.* Cambridge, MA: MIT Press.

SAVAGE-RUMBAUGH, S., S. G. SHANKER AND T. J. TAYLOR (1998) *Apes, Language, and the Human Mind.* New York: Oxford University Press.

VON FRISCH, K. (1993) *The Dance Language and Orientation of Bees.* (Translated by Leigh E. Chadwick.) Cambridge, MA: Harvard University Press.

WINCHESTER, S. (2003) *The Meaning of Everything: The Story of the Oxford English Dictionary.* Oxford: Oxford University Press.

21

The Neural Bases of Language

Introduction

The approach to understanding the substrates of language in terms of brain anatomy and physiology dates back as far as the nineteenth century, when physicians documented the clinical-pathological correlations in patients who had suffered brain damage that resulted in some form of language disability. When such patients died, postmortem examination of their brains in light of these correlations could indicate which regions were specifically involved in language and, more specifically, which regions were involved in the production of speech and which in its comprehension. As in many other areas of cognitive neuroscience, such correlative studies have now been augmented by a variety of more direct approaches. Particularly important in the history of understanding language have been "split-brain" studies of patients whose cerebral hemispheres were surgically disconnected as a treatment for epilepsy, as well as electrophysiological mapping studies of cortical language areas as an adjunct to various neurosurgical procedures—a technique pioneered in the 1930s. More recently, noninvasive brain imaging, electroencephalography, and other methods have added much information about the neural bases of language. The purpose of this chapter is to review the major conclusions gleaned in these ways, pointing out the areas—and there are many—in which questions remain.

The Relation of Language to the Auditory and Motor Systems

As might be expected, the regions of the brain that support language are closely related to the sensory and motor areas that process nonspeech sounds and that generate the non-speech-based motor behaviors (see Chapter 6 for a more general review of the auditory system, and Chapters 8 and 9 for a review of motor systems). The most general features of the language regions described in the following sections are their broad division into regions in the frontal lobe (where other motor functions are carried out) that have become specialized for the *production* of speech, and regions in the temporal lobe (where other auditory functions are carried out) that are specialized for its *comprehension*.

Another key generalization is that, despite the presence of basic motor and auditory functions in both hemispheres, in the vast majority of people the regions pertinent to language in the two hemispheres are significantly different. The left hemisphere supports primarily the lexical and syntactical functions that we ordinarily think of as forming the core of language abilities. The corresponding regions of the right hemisphere also contribute to language, but in more subtle ways, as described later in the chapter. Although the following account focuses on the cerebral cortices, it should also be apparent from earlier chapters (e.g., Chapters 8 and 9) that subcortical structures such as the basal ganglia and cerebellum serve the same role for language functions that they serve in the gating and ongoing control of any other cortical processes.

Neural Bases for Producing Language

The initial evidence that the production and comprehension of language are localized to significantly different regions of the brain was provided by *clinical-pathological correlations* (see Chapter 3). Such studies were first reported in the late 1800s, by the French anatomist and neurologist Paul Broca and the German neurologist and psychiatrist Carl Wernicke—both of whom made many basic contributions to understanding the relationship of a variety of neurological lesions and their clinical consequences. Broca and Wernicke examined the brains of patients who had suffered brain damage (typically from a stroke or a tumor), had difficulty with language as a result, and later died (Broca's most famous patient actually suffered from a tertiary syphilitic lesion, a common neurological problem in the days before penicillin and other antibiotics). The term given to such problems with language is **aphasia**, which describes difficulty producing and/or comprehending speech, even though the vocal apparatus and hearing mechanisms are intact (difficulty speaking because of a lesion involving an aspect of the vocal control apparatus is called *dysarthria*).

Correlating the clinical picture and the site of brain damage in his patients, Broca concluded that loss of the ability to produce meaningful sentences arose from damage to the ventral posterior region of the frontal lobe (**Figure 21.1**). Equally important, he observed that this sort of aphasia is typically associated with damage to the *left* hemisphere. The preponderance of aphasic syndromes associated with damage to various parts of the left hemisphere noted by neurologists ever since has supported Broca's nineteenth-century claim that "one speaks with the left hemisphere."

Patients with classic **Broca's aphasia** (caused by damage to the ventral posterior region of the frontal lobe, which is also called **Broca's area**), cannot express thoughts appropriately, because the rules of grammar and syntax have been disrupted by the lesion in the frontal lobe. These rules of language are closely related to the overall organization of other motor behaviors that depend on the general region of the frontal cortex anterior to the primary motor cortex in the prefrontal gyrus (the *premotor cortex*; see Chapter 9). The typical effects of damage in this area are evident in the following example reported by the neurologist Howard Gardner (who is the author in the passage quoted). The patient was a 39-year-old Coast Guard radio operator named Ford, who had suffered a stroke that affected his left posterior frontal lobe.

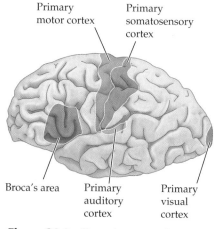

Primary motor cortex

Primary somatosensory cortex

Broca's area   Primary auditory cortex   Primary visual cortex

Figure 21.1 Broca's area. Broca took this region of the brain to be the basis for the production of language. The primary sensory, auditory, visual, and motor cortices are indicated to show the relation of Broca's area in the left hemisphere to these other areas that are necessarily involved in the production and comprehension of speech, albeit in a less specialized way. Broca's area includes Brodmann areas 44 and 45.

"I am a sig … no … man … uh, well, … again." These words were emitted slowly, and with great effort. The sounds were not clearly articulated; each syllable was uttered harshly, explosively, in a throaty voice. With practice, it was possible to understand him, but at first I encountered considerable difficulty in this. "Let me help you," I interjected. "You were a signal …" "A sig-nal man … right," Ford completed my phrase triumphantly. "Were you in the Coast Guard?" "No, er, yes, yes, … ship … Massachu … chusetts … Coastguard … years." He raised his hands twice, indicating the number nineteen. "Oh, you were in the Coast Guard for nineteen years." "Oh … boy … right … right," he replied. "Why are you in the hospital, Mr. Ford?" Ford looked at me strangely, as if to say, Isn't it patently obvious? He pointed to his paralyzed arm and said, "Arm no good," then to his mouth and said, "Speech … can't say … talk, you see."

HOWARD GARDNER, 1974
The Shattered Mind: The Person after Brain Damage,
pp. 60–61

Despite the structural disorder of the patient's speech, a listener would be impressed that this individual knew what he was trying to say. The lack of ability to organize and/or control the linguistic content of their utterances suggests a lack of language comprehension in patients with damage to the posterior and inferior regions of the left frontal lobe. In fact, however, they continue to comprehend language and know what they want to say. Even though they produce nonsense syllables, transpose words, and generally utter structurally incorrect utterances, some sensible meaning can still be discerned in what they are saying. Thus, this type of aphasia is also called *production aphasia* or *motor aphasia*.

Neural Bases for Comprehending Language

Broca was basically correct in his assertion about the location and laterality of the lexical and syntactical aspects of language. Modern studies have confirmed that damage in the vicinity of Broca's area is indeed responsible for many production aphasias, and that about 97 percent of individuals have the circuitry for both the production and comprehension of the lexical and semantic aspects of language primarily in the left cerebral hemisphere. However, he was off the mark in implying that language is a unitary function whose neural infrastructure is limited to a single brain region, or even a single hemisphere for that matter. As will be evident in the discussion that follows, laterality is a far more complicated phenomenon than Broca imagined. It was Carl Wernicke who first made clear that the instantiation of language in the brain is indeed more complex. Wernicke distinguished between the locations of lesions in patients who had lost the ability to *produce* language and locations in those who could no longer *comprehend* language.

From his own clinical observations, Wernicke concluded that some aphasic patients retain the ability to produce utterances with appropriate grammar and syntax but don't understand what is being said to them (or what they read). In addition, they generate utterances that, although structurally coherent, convey little or no meaning. In general, the patients that fit Wernicke's description are found at autopsy to have lesions of the posterior and superior temporal lobe, almost always on the left side (**Figure 21.2**). These findings have led to the generalization that damage to the posterior and superior regions of the temporal lobe on the left causes a deficiency referred to as *sensory*, or *receptive*, *aphasia*. (Deficits of reading and writing—*alexias* and *agraphias*—are related disorders that can arise from damage to other brain areas; most aphasics, however, also have difficulty with these closely linked

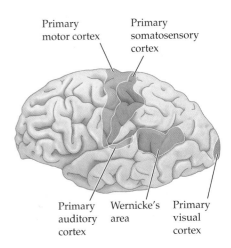

Primary motor cortex

Primary somatosensory cortex

Primary auditory cortex

Wernicke's area

Primary visual cortex

Figure 21.2 Wernicke's area.
The brain area described by Wernicke defines a major part of the neural substrate for the comprehension of language and includes Brodmann area 22.

■ TABLE 21.1 Characteristics of Broca's and Wernicke's Aphasias

Broca's aphasia[a]	Wernicke's aphasia[b]
Halting speech	Fluent speech
Tendency to repeat phrases or words (perseveration)	Little spontaneous repetition
Disordered syntax	Syntax adequate
Disordered grammar	Grammar adequate
Disordered structure of individual words	Contrived or inappropriate words
Comprehension intact	Comprehension not intact

[a]Also called motor, expressive, or production aphasia.
[b]Also called sensory or receptive aphasia.

abilities if the language that they speak has a written form.) This region is referred to as **Wernicke's area** in honor of its discoverer, and the corresponding deficiency is also called **Wernicke's aphasia**.

In contrast to a production (Broca's) aphasia, the major difficulty in a sensory (Wernicke's) aphasia is putting together objects or ideas and the words that signify them and subjectively comprehending this relationship. Thus, in a sensory aphasia, speech is superficially fluent and well structured but makes little or no sense because words and meanings are not correctly linked, as is apparent in the following example. The patient in this case (again from Gardner) was a 72-year-old retired man who had suffered a stroke affecting his left posterior temporal lobe.

> Boy, I'm sweating, I'm awful nervous, you know, once in a while I get caught up, I can't get caught up, I can't mention the tarripoi, a month ago, quite a little, I've done a lot well, I impose a lot, while, on the other hand, you know what I mean, I have to run around, look it over, trebbin and all that sort of stuff. Oh sure, go ahead, any old think you want. If I could I would. Oh, I'm taking the word the wrong way to say, all of the barbers here whenever they stop you it's going around and around, if you know what I mean, that is tying and tying for repucer, repuceration, well, we were trying the best that we could while another time it was with the beds over there the same thing.

Gardner 1974, p. 68

Unlike the example of a Broca's aphasia, this example would cause a listener to conclude that the patient had little understanding of what he was trying to say. **Table 21.1** summarizes the primary differences between these major sorts of aphasias.

A final general category of aphasic syndromes is called *conduction aphasia.* Conduction aphasias arise from lesions to the pathways connecting the relevant temporal and frontal regions, and they can lead to an inability to produce appropriate responses to heard communication, even though the communication is understood by the speaker.

Additional Evidence from Neurosurgical Procedures

This more or less classical description of the localization and lateralization of language functions might give the impression that two well-defined regions of the brain are responsible for language production and comprehension, and that these regions are in the left hemisphere. Not surprisingly, matters are a good deal more complex. During the 1950s and early 1960s, Harvard neurologist Norman Geschwind undertook a major effort to refine the earlier categorization of aphasias. Clinical and anatomical data from a large number of patients, along with a better understanding of cortical connectivity gleaned by that time from animal studies, led Geschwind to conclude that several other regions of the parietal, temporal, and frontal cortices are involved in human language abilities. A variety of subsequent studies using a range of approaches have confirmed that many additional regions of the brain in both hemispheres contribute to language.

Studies of divided brains

The most dramatic additional evidence about the organization of language and other brain functions has come from ongoing studies of patients in whom the connections between the two hemispheres have been severed during neurosurgery to relieve intractable epileptic seizures. Interrupting these connections is an effective way of treating epilepsy in a small minority of patients who are refractory to conventional medical treatments of this common disorder. This surgical treatment is used less today than it was several decades ago; the procedure is now done only in patients who suffer frequent seizures that cause a sudden loss of consciousness and are thus quite dangerous.

In patients whose hemispheres have been surgically separated by cutting the corpus callosum and the related structures that normally connect the right and left hemispheres, the function of the two cerebral hemispheres can be assessed independently in a variety of ingenious ways. The first studies of these so-called **split-brain patients**, carried out by Roger Sperry and his colleagues at Caltech in the 1960s and 1970s, established the hemispheric lateralization of language beyond any doubt. This work also gave much insight into the role of the *right* hemisphere in language and demonstrated many other functional differences between the left and right hemispheres. Sperry's studies continue to stand as an extraordinary contribution to understanding the cognitive organization of the brain, not least the relative roles of the two hemispheres in language.

To evaluate the range of cognitive and other functions of each hemisphere in split-brain patients, it is essential to provide information to one side of the brain only. Sperry, his student Michael Gazzaniga, and others devised several ways to do this. The simplest method was to ask the subject to use each hand independently to identify objects without visual assistance (**Figure 21.3A**). Recall that somatosensory information from the right hand is processed by the left hemisphere, and vice versa (see Chapters 1 and 7). By asking the subject to describe an item being manipulated by one hand or the other, researchers were able to examine the language capacity of the relevant hemisphere. Such testing showed that the two hemispheres indeed differ in their language ability, as expected from the postmortem correlations described earlier. Using the left hemisphere, split-brain patients were able to name objects held in the right hand without difficulty. Using the right hemisphere, however, most subjects could produce only an indirect description of the object that relied on rudimentary words and phrases rather than the precise lexical tokens for the object (e.g., "a round thing" instead of "a ball"), and some could not provide any verbal account of what they held in their left hand.

Observations using special techniques to present visual information to the hemispheres independently (a method called *tachistoscopic presentation*) showed further that the right hemisphere can respond to nonverbal stimuli such as pictorial instructions to carry out an action or, in some cases, to rudimentary written commands (**Figure 21.3B**). One interesting patient who could not verbalize a response could nonetheless spell out a simple answer such as "yes" or "no" with Scrabble® tiles!

(A)

Figure 21.3 Hemispheric specialization of language. Such specialization has been confirmed by studies of patients in whom the connections between the right and left hemispheres have been surgically severed. (A) The task of recognizing shapes using one hand hidden from view can be used to evaluate the language capabilities of each hemisphere. Split-brain subjects are unable to name objects that they identify by feeling with the left hand. The right hand provides somatosensory information to the left hemisphere, and thus objects felt with the right hand are easily named. Objects held in the left hand, however, cannot generally be named accurately, because the tactile information processed in the right hemisphere cannot access the language areas in the left hemisphere, and the relevant language areas in the right hemisphere do not have this ability. (B) Visual stimuli or simple instructions can be given independently to the right or left hemisphere in normal and split-brain individuals. Since the left visual field is perceived by the right hemisphere (and vice versa), a briefly presented (tachistoscopic) instruction in the left visual field is appreciated only by the right brain (assuming that the individual maintains fixation on a mark in the center of the viewing screen). In normal subjects, activation of the right visual cortex leads to hemispheric transfer of visual information via the corpus callosum to the left hemisphere. In split-brain patients, information presented to the left visual field cannot reach the left hemisphere, and patients are unable to produce a verbal report regarding the stimuli. However, such patients *are* able to provide a verbal report of stimuli presented to the right visual field. A wide range of hemispheric functions can be evaluated using this tachistoscopic method, even in normal subjects.

(B)

Normal individual

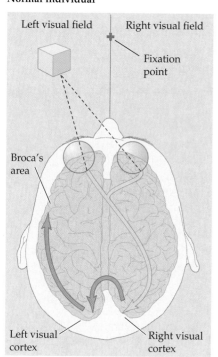

Split-brain individual

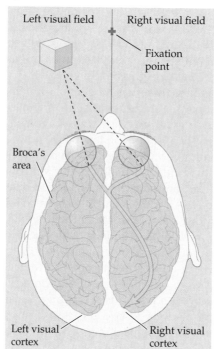

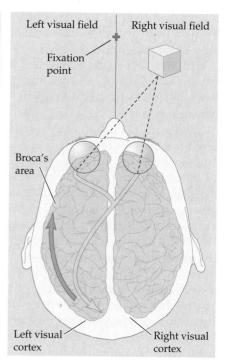

Table 21.2 summarizes the major functional differences between the cerebral hemispheres determined in split-brain studies. These distinctions in the language abilities of the two hemispheres appear to reflect broader hemispheric differences summarized by the statement that the left hemisphere in most humans is specialized for (among other things) the more explicit aspects of the verbal and symbolic processing that is important in communication, whereas the right hemisphere is specialized for (among other things) processing visuospatial and, as described in the following section, emotional information (see also Chapter 17). **Box 21A** makes the additional point that this detailed evidence

■ **TABLE 21.2 Major Distinctions between the Language and Other Functions of the Left and Right Hemispheres**

Left-hemisphere functions	Right-hemisphere functions
Analysis of right visual field	Analysis of left visual field
Stereognosis (right hand)	Stereognosis (left hand)
Lexical and syntactic language	Emotional coloring of language
Writing	Spatial abilities
Speech	Rudimentary speech

for lateralization of function does not support the pop psychology notion that one hemisphere "dominates" the other in any simple sense. The hemispheres are simply dedicated to significantly different but complementary functions.

One particular patient in Sperry's original split-brain series also gives some insight into the latent potential of the right hemisphere for language processing. L.P., as he is known in the literature, was highly exceptional in that, as the result of an unusual congenital anomaly, he had never developed a corpus callosum—a defect that had been discovered incidentally. Unlike the patients

■ **BOX 21A Cerebral Dominance**

The evidence that language and some other cognitive functions are strongly lateralized has led to the popular idea that the left cerebral hemisphere is "dominant" over the right. In addition, clinicians refer to the hemisphere that serves as the substrate for the explicitly verbal aspects of language as the "dominant hemisphere." Another factor underlying the idea of a dominant hemisphere is handedness. Approximately 9 out of 10 people are right-handed in all human cultures. A superficial implication of the predominance of right-handedness is that the left hemisphere, which controls the right hand, is "stronger" or "better" than the right.

This unwarranted bias spills over into the sense many people have that being left-handed is somehow less "good" than being right-handed. A century ago, many parents in the United States routinely tried to discourage emerging left-handed behavior in children. In most countries, however, such attempts to change a child's natural behavior have waned, largely in response to the empirical evidence that being left-handed is a disadvantage

only in that many objects have been created for the right-handed majority (e.g., scissors, guitars, manual can openers, and so on). However, four out of five U.S. presidents by the end of the twentieth century were left-handed, and recent evidence indicates that, on average, left-handers actually do somewhat better in school than right-handers do. Being left-handed is also an advantage in sports like fencing (because opponents are less practiced in dealing with the thrusts and parries of left-handers).

Speculation notwithstanding, the reason that the semantic and lexical aspects of language and handedness are typically represented in the left hemisphere is not that the left half of the brain is in any sense superior. Indeed, there is no evidence for a deep link between the lateralization of language and handedness. Consider, for example, the results obtained over many years from the so-called *Wada test*, in which a short-acting anesthetic is injected into one of the carotid arteries to determine the hemisphere in which language function is primarily located (the patient will become tran-

siently mute if language function is in the anesthetized hemisphere). The large number of such tests carried out for clinical purposes has shown that, in the vast majority of humans—including a large majority of left-handers—major language functions are in the left hemisphere. Because most left-handers have language function on the side of the brain opposite the right hemispheric control of their preferred left hand, there is clearly no strict relationship between these two lateralized functions (although language in the right hemisphere is more common among left-handers).

The lateralization of language and hand preference is presumably a result of the advantage of having any highly specialized function on one side of the brain or the other to make the most efficient use of the neural circuitry available for cognitive and other functions in a brain of limited size. A belief that the neural circuitry on the one side of the brain is less well developed, less useful, or less effective than the cerebral circuitry on the other is simply unwarranted.

who had undergone surgery in maturity, L.P. was shown to have good bilateral language function, indicating that the right hemisphere in such circumstances is fully capable of producing and comprehending language. This indication that the right hemisphere can do the same job as the left under some conditions is, of course, supported by the 3 percent of people who, for reasons that are not understood, normally have the major language functions in the right hemisphere (see Box 21A). This observation also agrees with the fact that children who have undergone left hemispherectomy at an early age for a rare form of intractable and life-threatening epilepsy can also develop right-sided verbal skills, as can children who, during the perinatal period, have a large left-hemisphere stroke that includes the language areas. In adults, such insults would be permanently crippling to language and many other functions, in keeping with much other evidence that neural plasticity decreases progressively with age (see Chapter 27).

Given the radical nature of split-brain surgery, it is not surprising that the inability of the two halves of the brain to communicate also has significant, if subtle, effects on the overall cognitive functioning of these individuals. Split-brain subjects are reported to be less efficient than control subjects in carrying out coordinated bimanual tasks (threading a needle or playing the guitar, for example), and they have been described by Sperry and others as being less able to generate imaginative ideas and express them verbally. Although these latter observations are more difficult to document, they support the idea that communication between the hemispheres is important for the fullest expression of language and language-based thought.

More detailed mapping of language functions

Further insight into the ways language is organized in the brain has come from the detailed mapping of language areas that has long been carried out in patients undergoing surgical procedures that involve (or are simply near) the language areas of the brain. Neurosurgeons typically map language functions by electrically stimulating the cortex during surgery to refine their approach to the problem at hand. In removing a brain tumor or an epileptic focus, for instance, the surgeon must make sure exactly where the language (and other) regions in a patient are located so that the procedure causes minimal subsequent impairment. Because the brain has no pain receptors, such surgery can be done under local anesthesia (i.e., with the patient awake and conscious), allowing the surgeon to assess the location of sites that cause interference with speech when stimulated.

The legendary neurosurgeon Wilder Penfield and his colleagues at the Montreal Neurological Institute initiated this approach in the 1930s. Using electrical mapping techniques adapted from work that had been done since the late nineteenth century in experimental animals, Penfield specifically delineated the language areas of the cortex (among many other functional regions) before removing diseased brain tissue (**Figure 21.4A**). This general approach has been employed ever since, with increasingly sophisticated stimulation and recording methods, to guarantee that the effects of surgery will not be worse than the effects of the disorder being treated. Over the years this neurosurgical safeguard has yielded a wealth of additional information about the organization of language.

Penfield's observations, together with more recent studies performed by George Ojemann and his group at the University of Washington and others, have amply confirmed that large regions of the perisylvian frontal, temporal, and parietal cortices in the left hemisphere are involved in language production and comprehension. A surprise, however, has been the variability in language localization from patient to patient in such studies (**Figure 21.4B**). Oje-

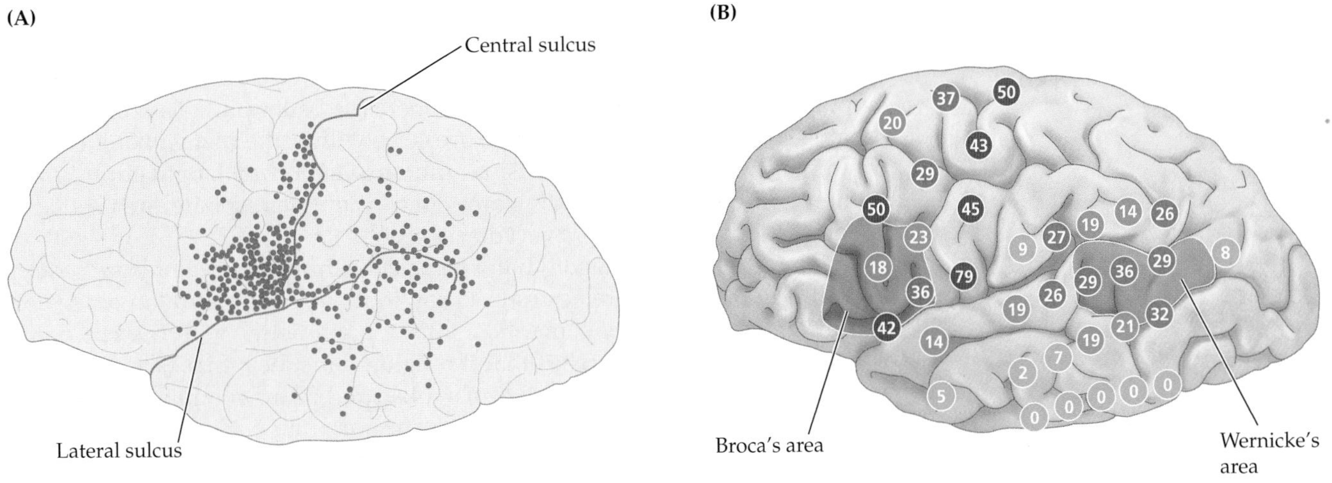

(A)

Central sulcus

Lateral sulcus

(B)

Broca's area

Wernicke's area

Figure 21.4 Cortical mapping of language areas in the left cerebral cortex. (A) The red dots indicate sites of stimulation that caused interference with speech in Penfield's original study, based on neurosurgeries performed in the 1930s. (B) More recent evidence for the variability of language representation among individuals. This diagram summarizes data from 117 patients whose language areas were mapped by electrical recording at the time of surgery by Ojemann and his colleagues. The number in each circle indicates the percentage of the patients who showed interference with language in response to stimulation at that site. Note both that the percentages vary considerably, and that many of the sites that elicited interference in both Penfield's and Ojemann's series fall outside the classic language areas described by Broca and Wernicke. (A after Penfield and Roberts 1959; B after Ojemann et al. 1989.)

mann and his colleagues found that the cortical regions involved in language are only approximately those indicated by most textbook treatments of the "classic" language areas (see Figures 21.1 and 21.2)—the exact locations differing widely among individuals.

Equally unexpectedly, bilingual patients do not necessarily use the same region of cortex for storing the names of the same objects in two different languages. Moreover, although neurons in the temporal cortex in and around Wernicke's area respond preferentially to spoken words, they do not show preferences for a particular word. Rather, a wide range of words can elicit a response in any given cortical location. All these observations have broadened classical and simpler concepts of language organization in the brain.

Contributions of the Right Hemisphere to Language

Although split-brain studies, mapping at neurosurgery, and other evidence have shown unequivocally that the left hemisphere in most individuals is the major seat of semantic and lexical language functions, it would be wrong to suppose that the right hemisphere has little or no importance for language. As already described, the right hemisphere in some split-brain individuals can produce rudimentary words and phrases. More significantly, clinical and other observations have long suggested that the right hemisphere is normally the source of the emotional coloring of language, an idea already introduced in Unit VI. This evidence is also consistent with the studies described in Chapter 6 showing that the right hemisphere is also primarily responsible for the processing of musical information and its emotional effects.

It should not be surprising, then, that language deficits of a different and more subtle sort are apparent following damage to the right hemisphere. The clearest effect of such lesions is a deficit in the emotional and tonal components of language—called its **prosodic** elements—which normally impart additional meaning to verbal expression. This emotional coloring of speech is a critical component of the message conveyed, and in most languages it is used to modulate the significance of the words or phrases uttered (think of the variety of inflections commonly used in English to distinguish questions, statements, demands, and the emotional state of the speaker).

These deficiencies, referred to as **aprosodias**, are generally associated with right-hemisphere damage to the cortical regions that roughly correspond to Broca's and Wernicke's areas in the left hemisphere. The aprosodias are characterized by monotonic, or "robotic," speech that listeners find hard to interpret from the perspective of understanding the speaker's emotional state and intentions. Imagine the loss of meaning when statements such as "I love you!" are uttered in a monotone. These deficits following right-hemisphere damage emphasize that, although the left hemisphere (or, better put, relatively distinct regions specialized for language processing within the hemisphere) figures prominently in the comprehension and production of language for most humans, other regions, including areas in the right hemisphere, are needed to generate the full richness of everyday speech.

In sum, Broca's conclusion that we speak with the left brain is not strictly correct. It would be more accurate to say that we understand language and communicate its explicit semantic content much better with the left hemisphere than with the right, but that the right hemisphere makes a major contribution to the overall significance of spoken and heard communication. Language processing in both hemispheres supports the overall goals of social communication, but in different ways.

Noninvasive Studies of Language Organization

For many decades, the bulk of the evidence about the organization of language in the brain came from neurologists and neurosurgeons, as described in the previous section. The advent of noninvasive brain imaging in the late 1970s and ongoing improvements in recording event-related potentials, however, opened the door to studies of the neural organization of language in normal subjects.

Evidence for the importance of context in the neural processing of language

Prior to the functional neuroimaging revolution, noninvasive studies of the neural processing of language were limited to electroencephalography. Recall from Chapter 3 that the temporal resolution of this technique is one of its major advantages. Thus, recording event-related potentials (ERPs) is especially useful in exploring how the language areas of the brain respond to semantic stimuli, where words and meanings normally follow each other in quick succession.

Marta Kutas and Steven Hillyard at UC San Diego pioneered such language studies. In a paper published in 1980, they showed that when people read sentences, ERP responses vary quite strikingly as a function of the nature of the semantic material (**Figure 21.5**). In particular, they found that the N400 component of the response to a word in a sentence read silently was enhanced if the word was semantically inappropriate, and thus unfamiliar or unexpected (e.g., "The *table* chased the cat"; recall from Chapter 11 that the N400 is the "mismatch negativity" observed in response to unexpected events like this). This effect was not seen, however, if the test word was printed in a different font, showing that this ERP response is specific to language anomalies and not simply a reflection of anything unusual in the material being read. On the basis of these and other observations, Kutas and Hillyard suggested that the N400 wave reflects a sort of "stumbling over" and reprocessing of language information that does not make sense in comparison to the semantic flow that is usually experienced.

Kutas and Cyma Van Petten went on to show that words used frequently in speech elicit *smaller* N400 waves than uncommon words do, suggesting that processing familiar language information requires less neural engagement (or more distributed neural processing) than more difficult material does—a finding that also holds for processing sentences and more complex material. A related finding is that homonyms (e.g., words like *bank* that have multiple meanings; see Chapter 20) elicit a smaller N400 wave when embedded in a sentence that clarifies the intended meaning compared to a context that does not (e.g., "She was waiting for money at the bank" versus "She was waiting for someone near the bank").

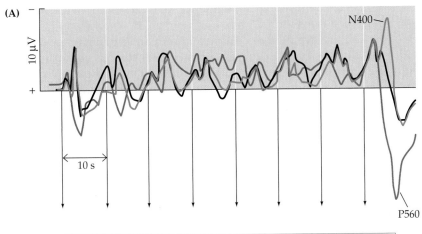

(A)

	IT	WAS	HIS	FIRST	DAY	AT	WORK
——	HE	SPREAD	THE	WARM	BREAD	WITH	SOCKS
——	SHE	PUT	ON	HER	HIGH	HEELED	**SHOES**

Figure 21.5 Semantic processing.
(A) ERP recordings show the average responses of subjects to silent reading of the three sentences indicated. The seventh words in the first two sentences are semantically sensible and nonsensical, respectively; in the third sentence, the seventh word is printed in a larger font, providing a nonsemantic anomaly as a control. The N400 wave in the ERP response is increased by the nonsensical word, but not by the larger font. (B–D) These graphs show average responses to moderate violation of semantic expectation (B), strong semantic violation (C), and a physical rather than semantic violation (D). Note the absence of an N400 response in (D). (After Kutas and Hillyard 1980.)

(B) Semantic (moderate)

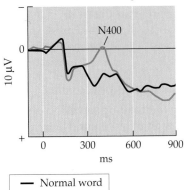

(C) Semantic (strong)

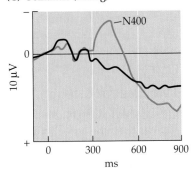

(D) Physical (nonsemantic, font-based)

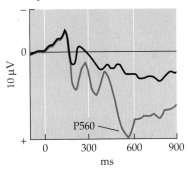

—— Normal word
═══ Deviant word

Thus, language processing in the relevant cortical regions appears to depend on an individual's prior experience with word frequencies and contextual meanings. This evidence accords with the conclusions reached on other grounds in Chapter 20—that is, that the strategies of language processing are fundamentally associational, and that probabilities conveyed by contextual information are used to disambiguate the inherently uncertain information in speech sound stimuli.

Further evidence for the involvement of many cortical areas in language

Although ERP approaches to language continue to be used by many investigators, such work has increasingly turned to imaging techniques. The initial brain imaging studies of language were based on PET—many carried out by Marc Raichle, Steve Petersen, and their colleagues at Washington University in St. Louis. These investigators provided results that, like the mapping studies done during neurosurgery, challenged older concepts about the representation of language in the brain. Although high levels of activity were found in the expected regions, large areas of both hemispheres were activated in various language tasks, indicating that language processing involves far more of the brain than was initially supposed (**Figure 21.6**)—a result that accords with

Passively viewing words

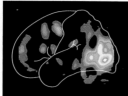

Listening to words

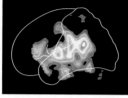

Speaking words

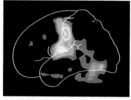

Generating word associations

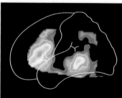

Figure 21.6 Language-related regions of the left hemisphere mapped by positron emission tomography. In human subjects, language tasks such as listening to words and generating words elicit activity in Broca's and Wernicke's areas, as expected. However, primary and association sensory and motor areas are also activated in both the active and passive language tasks. These observations indicate that language processing involves many cortical regions in addition to the classic language areas. (From Posner and Raichle 1994.)

the electrophysiological evidence derived from neurosurgical mapping (see Figure 21.4).

The involvement of additional brain areas in language-related tasks can be even broader in special circumstances. For instance, in blind individuals reading Braille, Harold Burton, Raichle, and colleagues showed extensive activation of the visual cortex with fMRI, implying that nonlanguage regions can be brought into play when needed, and that these regions may normally be involved in some aspects of language and reading (again, in accord with evidence, mentioned earlier in the chapter, that the right hemisphere can develop language capabilities in cases of callosal agenesis or hemispherectomy in young children).

Transcranial magnetic stimulation (TMS; see Chapter 3) has also made a contribution to this broader picture of the way language is processed. An example is the work of Alvaro Pascual-Leone and his collaborators at Harvard Medical School. These investigators showed that TMS can suppress the function of various language regions, thus providing a less invasive way of determining language laterality than the Wada test mentioned in Box 21A, which carries a significant mortality rate. In keeping with other evidence that language is more broadly supported in the brain than was thought in earlier decades, TMS causes significant interference with language processing when processing in either hemisphere is disrupted in this way.

Evidence for categorization in language processing

Other studies using noninvasive brain imaging have focused on the categorization of words and meanings by neural networks in the temporal lobes, showing that some lexical and conceptual categories activate overlapping but appreciably different cortical regions within the areas of the brain that mediate these aspects of language (i.e., Wernicke's area and surrounding regions). For instance, Hanna Damasio and her co-workers, then at the University of Iowa—and now others—have shown in PET studies that distinct regions of the temporal cortex are activated by tasks in which subjects are asked to name particular people, animals, or tools. This work has been extended using fMRI by Alex Martin and his colleagues at the National Institute of Mental Health, who found that category-specific patterns of activity were elicited in the temporal cortices when subjects viewed, named, or read category-specific material (**Figure 21.7**).

These studies are consistent with Ojemann's electrophysiological studies, which also suggest that language is organized according to categories of meaning rather than individual words, and with the work described in Chapter 5 indicating that visual objects are represented in overlapping but distinguishable areas of the temporal lobe (see Figure 5.23). With respect to language, this evidence for a more specific organization by categories within the general cortical region first described by Wernicke helps explain the clinical finding that, when a relatively limited region of the temporal lobe is damaged (usually by a stroke on the left side), language deficits are sometimes limited to particular sorts of objects. For instance, some patients show impaired knowledge for animals but normal knowledge for nonliving objects such as tools. The reverse pattern has also been described but is much less frequent.

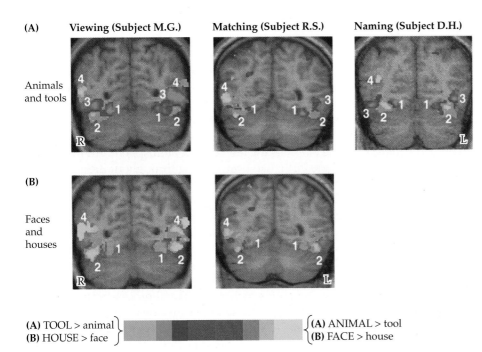

(A) Viewing (Subject M.G.) Matching (Subject R.S.) Naming (Subject D.H.)

Animals and tools

(B)

Faces and houses

(A) TOOL > animal
(B) HOUSE > face

(A) ANIMAL > tool
(B) FACE > house

Figure 21.7 Lexical and conceptual categories activate overlapping but different cortical regions. Functional MRIs show activation of different regions in the temporal lobe in three normal subjects during viewing, matching, and naming tasks that involved different object categories—either animals and tools (A) or faces and houses (B). The color code at the bottom indicates the category-specific activations; numbers indicate anatomical regions: 1, medial fusiform gyrus; 2, lateral fusiform; 3, middle and inferior temporal; 4, superior temporal sulcus. Notice that the activity elicited is bilateral, implying a significant role for both right and left temporal lobes in this aspect of language processing. (From Chao et al. 1999.)

Although the location of the damage in these conditions is variable and somewhat controversial, deficits in animate knowledge are more often associated with lesions of the temporal cortex, and deficits in inanimate knowledge, with left-sided damage that is more anterior, extending into the parietal and frontal lobes.

Some researchers have attempted to rationalize this evidence about categorization in various theoretical frameworks. One theory, proposed by Elizabeth Warrington and collaborators at University College London, suggests that conceptual or category knowledge is organized according to *sensory* features such as form, motion, and color, as well as according to *functional* properties such as the motion and/or the location of objects. Another idea, advocated by Alfonzo Caramazza and his collaborators at Harvard, entails a *domain-specific* theory, which argues that ecological relevance has led to the evolution of specialized brain mechanisms for processing classes of objects. The fact that activation patterns for different stimulus categories are distributed and overlapping (see Figures 21.7 and 5.23) is more easily reconciled with property-based theories because the regions involved in processing different properties are distributed and thus shared across categories. However, since both lesion and functional neuroimaging results allow different interpretations of the categories represented and the degree to which they are really separate, this controversy about the basis of categorization is ongoing.

In any event, these studies leave little doubt that the temporal cortices (and very likely other cortical regions) include overlapping neural networks that represent various objects and concepts, or at least aspects of them, and that these areas are not exclusively devoted to categorizing language.

Evidence that the neural basis of language is fundamentally symbolic

Another informative approach to understanding what the language areas in the brain actually do has been to examine the neural substrate of **sign language** in congenitally deaf individuals. The basic question asked in this work is whether the major language areas in the brain are devoted specifically to processing speech sounds, or are more generally concerned with symbolic processing (see also Chapter 22).

American Sign Language has all the elements—vocabulary, grammar, and syntax—of spoken and heard language, and it clearly serves the same purposes of social communication. Moreover, signers can express emotional coloring and most, if not all, of the nuances that are conveyed by speech. In an important addition to work on sign language, Ursula Bellugi and her colleagues at the Salk Institute examined the cortical localization of signing abilities in patients who had suffered lesions of either the left or right hemisphere. All these individuals had been deaf since birth, had been signing throughout their lives, had deaf spouses, were members of the deaf community, and were right-handed.

The patients with left-hemisphere lesions, which in each case involved the language areas of the frontal and/or temporal lobes, had measurable deficits in sign production and comprehension when compared to normal signers of similar age (**Figure 21.8**). In contrast, the patients with lesions in approximately the same areas in the right hemisphere did not have signing "aphasias." Instead, as might be expected from evidence in hearing patients with similar lesions, right-hemisphere language functions such as emotional processing and expression were impaired in the signing of these individuals. Although the number of subjects studied was necessarily small (deaf signers with lesions of the language areas are difficult to find), the capacity for signed and seen communication is evidently represented predominantly in the left hemisphere, in much the same areas as spoken language. This evidence indicates that the language regions of the brain are specialized for the representation of social communication by means of *symbols*, rather than for heard and spoken language per se.

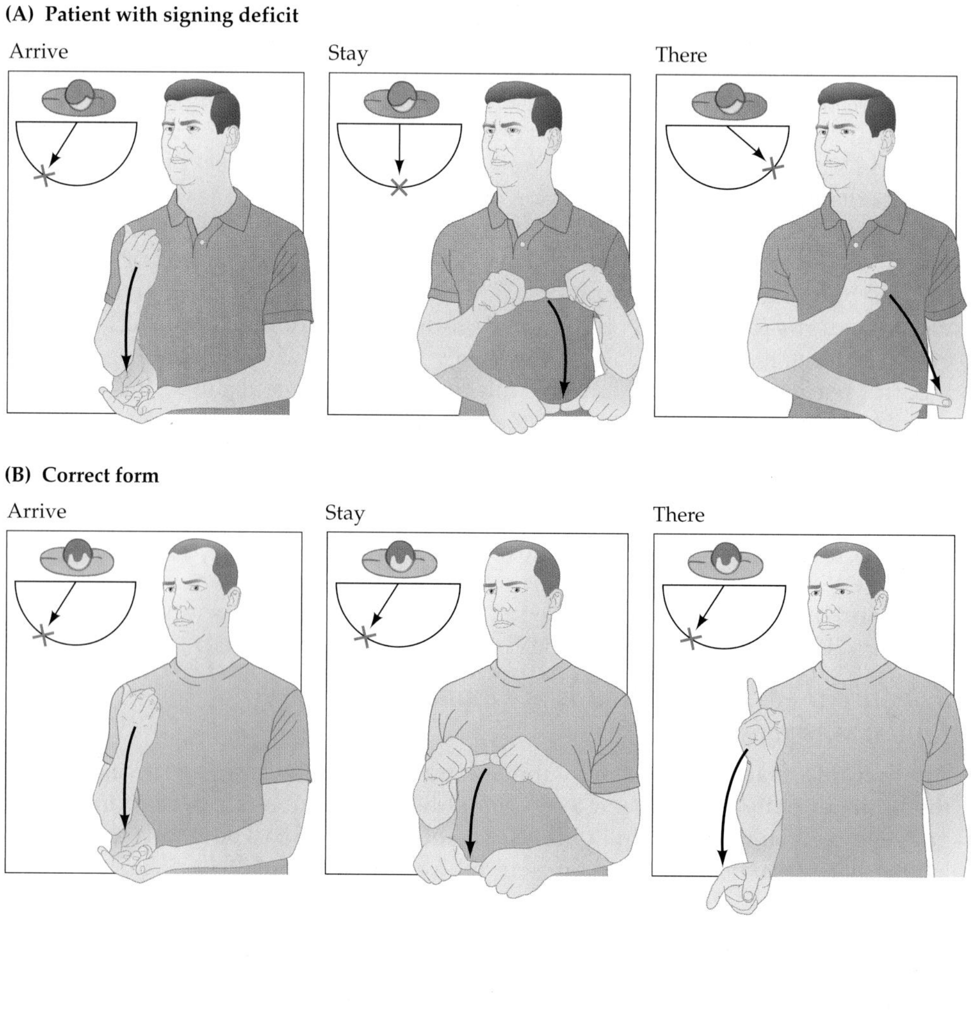

Figure 21.8 Signing "aphasia." Signing deficits are seen in congenitally deaf individuals who learned sign language from birth and later suffered lesions of the left-hemisphere language areas. Left-hemisphere damage produced signing problems in these patients analogous to the aphasias seen after comparable lesions in hearing, speaking patients. In this example, the patient (A) is expressing the sentence "We arrived in Jerusalem and stayed there." Compared to a control subject (B), he cannot properly control the spatial orientation of the signs. The direction of the correct signs and the aberrant direction of the "aphasic" signs are indicated in the upper-left corner of each panel. (After Bellugi et al. 1989.)

(A) Patient with signing deficit

Arrive   Stay   There

(B) Correct form

Arrive   Stay   There

In line with this conclusion, the capacity for seen and signed communication, like that for spoken language, emerges in early infancy. As discussed in Chapter 20, observations of early language practice (called *babbling*) in hearing and eventually speaking infants shows the production of a predictable pattern of sounds related to the ultimate acquisition of fluent language. Thus, babbling prefigures mature language. The congenitally deaf offspring of deaf, signing parents "babble" with their hands in gestures that are evidently the forerunners of fluently expressed signs. Like verbal babbling, the amount of manual babbling increases with age until the child begins to form accurate, meaningful signs. These observations imply that the strategy for acquiring the rudiments of symbolic communication from parental or other social cues—regardless of the means of expression—is similar in deaf and hearing individuals.

These developmental facts are also pertinent to the possible antecedents of language in the nonverbal communication of other animals, and they suggest a continuum across species between spoken language and other symbols or tokens of meaning, such as gestures, facial expressions, and body language. Despite this contentious question, the organization of language areas in the brain does not simply reflect specializations for hearing and speaking; rather, these areas are more broadly organized for processing the variety of symbols pertinent to social communication. This conclusion again emphasizes that the brain areas supporting the production and comprehension of speech are by no means exclusively dedicated to these cognitive tasks.

Brain Activity Elicited by Vocalizations in Non-Human Primates

An additional question related to the conclusion that the language areas of the brain are more broadly constructed to process nonverbal symbolic information pertinent to social communication concerns the function of the homologues of human language areas in non-human primates. Do the regions in the non-human primate brain activated by vocalizations carry out functions that are, in some sense, similar to those of the regions activated by speech processing in humans?

Although the answer is not yet clear, studies using modern techniques have begun to explore this issue. For instance, a PET study in rhesus monkeys has recently led to the claim that the vocal calls of these animals (see Chapter 20) do indeed activate cortical regions homologous to Broca's and Wernicke's areas in humans, and that this activity is limited to conspecific vocalizations and is not simply elicited by any acoustic stimulus (**Figure 21.9**). The activity elicited was not lateralized, however, and other researchers have raised methodological objections to the study. Given the importance of the question and the availability of the means now of carrying out such studies by noninvasive imaging in non-human primates, it should be possible to resolve this issue.

General Theories about Hemispheric Differences

A number of theories have been proposed over the years to explain the hemispheric differences in language and other functions on the basis of a more general difference between neural processing in the right and left brains. Some investigators, for example, have argued that the left hemisphere is specialized for analytic and sequential processing, and that the right hemisphere is concerned with spatial and synthetic processing. Others have suggested that the left hemisphere is specialized mainly for voluntary motor functions (including speech production). Still others have offered the idea that the left hemisphere is specialized for rapid information processing and the right

Figure 21.9 Language areas in the brains of non-human primates? The figure shows PET activation in three different rhesus monkeys in response to the vocalizations that these animals use in social communication. The areas activated are arguably similar to the major language areas on the human brain. Whether this activity is comparable to the activity elicited by speech in the human brain remains a matter of active investigation and some dispute at present. (The letters A, B, and C in the inset identify the levels of the brain sections shown.) (From Gil-da-Costa et al. 2006.)

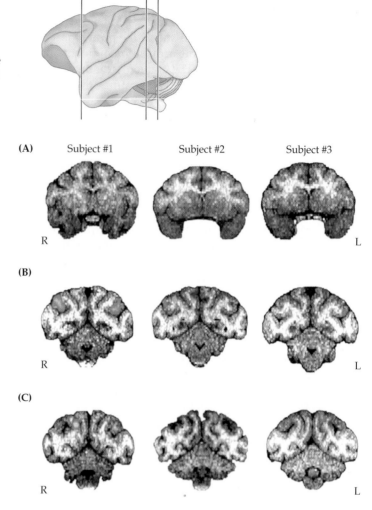

hemisphere for slower processing. In this view the left hemisphere is more adept at the rapid associations involved in lexical and syntactical processing; and the right, in the somewhat less time-dependent emotional features of speech.

Not surprisingly, there is no consensus about such speculations and their significance for language. It seems unlikely on the face of it that there any general hemispheric differences of this sort, simply because both hemispheres carry out so many of the same functions using the same neuronal types, neural transmitters, and elemental neural circuits.

Genetic Determination of Language Functions

Evidence that human language processing is essentially symbolic in nature and that other animals share some of the same processing abilities and neural substrates raises questions about the genetic basis of these functions. Indeed, the search for the genetic contribution to cognitive functions and their disorders is an endeavor being pursued in many contexts. Because the propensity for language and its neural bases are inherited by all humans, exploring the genes involved is plausible, at least in principle. The occurrence of language and/or reading problems that run in families makes plain that genetic anomalies can play a role in the normal development of these cognitive functions, as in any other. The most common of these disorders is **dyslexia**. Dyslexia tends to run in families (up to 50 percent of the children of dyslexic parents are affected) and has been associated with anomalies of particular genes (**Box 21B**).

Another inherited but quite rare disorder has more specifically raised the question of the genetic determination of language and, in popular accounts, whether there might be a "language gene." The gene of interest, called *FOXP2*, is located on human chromosome 7. It was discovered in 1990 in a family in which about half the members are afflicted. The affected individuals in the pedigree, known in the literature as the K.E. family, are unable to fluently select the movements of the vocal apparatus needed to make appropriate speech sounds. Thus, what they try to say is largely incomprehensible. The impairment, which is caused by a single autosomal recessive mutation, is thus one of motor organization as it pertains to speech rather than one of comprehension. The afflicted family members, however, also have lower IQs than their unafflicted relatives, indicating that the defect is not specific for language.

The mechanism by which the gene defect exerts these effects is not known, but the protein that it encodes is a transcription factor, meaning that the gene

■ BOX 21B Dyslexia

Dyslexia is a surprisingly common problem that specifically affects a child's ability to read. Despite having normal or above-normal levels of intelligence, dyslexics are poor readers and have difficulty more generally in processing speech sounds and translating visual to verbal information, and vice versa. Thus, in addition to suffering reading problems, people with dyslexia often have difficulty writing, are poor spellers, and are prone to errors arising from letter transposition. Because there is no specific diagnostic criterion, estimates of the prevalence of dyslexia vary widely; figures of from 5 to 15 percent of children are usually given, with roughly equal occurrence in boys and girls. The incidence of attention deficit hyperactivity disorder is also higher among dyslexic individuals.

Although dyslexia is generally accepted as a learning disability, its cause is unclear, and some investigators have argued that this disorder is simply the lower tail of the distribution of performance in learning to read. There is, however, a strong tendency for the problem to run in families, and anomalies of chromosomes 1 and 6 have been implicated. These genetic findings do not necessarily negate the argument that dyslexia is just the tail of the distribution of reading skill in children, since virtually any cognitive attribute is a product of both nature and nurture. Because reading is a recent development in human history and even today exists in only a minority of languages (about 3 percent; see Chapter 20), dyslexia would presumably have had little selective significance.

Many treatments for dyslexia have been advocated, but there is no generally accepted therapy. Most investigators agree, however, that identifying the problem early and implementing early remediation through extra training and effort is helpful, as would be expected for improving the performance of any learned task. One prominent theory is that dyslexics are deficient in "phonological awareness," meaning that they have difficulty breaking down speech sounds into their phonetic components. Recall from Chapter 20, however, that speech is not physically divided into separate vocal phones, and thus how a normal child learns to parse speech sounds (or to read) is unclear. Brain imaging studies of dyslexics show much more brain activity during reading tasks than in control children, but this observation probably indicates only that dyslexics struggle more with such tasks than normal readers do; in general, much more brain activity is elicited when tasks are being learned than when they become automatic after practice.

In summary, dyslexia is not well understood, and it is likely to remain so until much more is known about how speech is normally comprehended from written symbols, and how vision and hearing interact in this complex process.

References

GALABURDA, A. M. (1994) Developmental dyslexia and animal studies: At the interface between cognition and neurology. *Cognition* 50: 133–149.

GALABURDA, A. M., J. LOTURCO, F. RAMUS, R. H. FITCH AND G. D. ROSEN (2006) From genes to behavior in developmental dyslexia. *Nat. Neurosci.* 9: 1213–1217.

GRIGORGENKO, E. L. (2001) Developmental dyslexia: An update on genes, brains and environment. *J. Child Psychol. Psychiatry* 42: 91–125.

SHAYWITZ, S. E. (1998) Dyslexia. *New Engl. J. Med.* 338: 307–312.

TALLAL, P., R. L. SAINBURG AND T. JERNIGAN (1991) The neuropathology of developmental dysphasia: Behavioral, morphological, and physiological evidence for a pervasive temporal processing disorder. *Read. Writ.* 3: 363–377.

product is an agent that binds to the promoter regions of other genes to control their expression. The *FOXP2* gene is strongly expressed in other animals, including mice, where it affects many aspects of development, including the ultrasonic vocalization of these animals.

Interesting though this gene may be, reports about the discovery of a "language gene" were clearly unwarranted. Because it encodes a transcription factor, *FOXP2* affects many other genes with a range of developmental consequences, some evidently influencing the mechanisms that generate neural circuits in those parts of the brain that support the organization and expression of language. Supposing that this or any cognitive function is directly related to a gene is misleading; the relation of genes to cognitive functions and behavior is widely misunderstood.

Summary

1. Work on the neural basis of language over the last century or more has established many basic points about the physiology and anatomy of this remarkable aspect of human cognition.

2. Virtually all researchers studying the neural bases of language are now agreed that most of the semantic, grammatical, and syntactical processing of language comprehension and expression resides in a number of interconnected regions of the left frontal, temporal, and parietal cortices in the majority of humans. Nevertheless, there is a great deal of individual variation, including variation in the degree of lateralization and the location of the relevant areas.

3. Most researchers also agree that the corresponding cortical regions in the right hemisphere contribute importantly to language by adding the emotional coloring evident in speech prosody, and presumably by interpreting this and other nonverbal aspects of language. The right hemisphere also has the rudiments of the processing abilities that exist in the left hemisphere, as evidenced by split-brain patients, again with wide variation among individuals.

4. The use of electrophysiological recording, brain imaging, and other techniques has gradually made clear that the language-processing areas initially identified by clinical-pathological correlations are components of a widely distributed set of brain regions that allow humans to communicate effectively by means of tokens that can be attached ad infinitum to objects, concepts, and feelings that humans deem important, and that these same areas are involved in other functions.

5. Comparison of the neural substrates of sign language in congenitally deaf individuals shows further that the cortical representation of language is independent of the means of its expression and perception (spoken and heard versus gestured and seen). Thus, the neural bases of language represent a system for symbolic processing that transcends verbal expression as such.

Additional Reading

Reviews

BELIN, P., S. FECTEAU AND C. BEDARD (2004) Thinking the voice: Neural correlates of voice perception. *Trends Cogn. Sci.* 8: 129–135.

BELLUGI, U., H. POIZNER AND E. S. KLIMA (1989) Language, modality, and the brain. *Trends Neurosci.* 12: 380–388.

DAMASIO, A. R. (1992) Aphasia. *New Engl. J. Med.* 326: 531–539.

DAMASIO, A. R. AND N. GESCHWIND (1984) The neural basis of language. *Annu. Rev. Neurosci.* 7: 127–147.

GAZZANIGA, M. S. (1998) The split brain revisited. *Sci. Am.* 279 (1): 50–55.

GAZZANIGA, M. S. AND R. W. SPERRY (1967) Language after section of the cerebral commissures. *Brain* 90: 131–147.

GHAZANFAR, A. A. AND M. D. HAUSER (2001) The auditory behavior of primates: A neuroethological perspective. *Curr. Opin. Neurobiol.* 11: 712–720.

KUTAS, M., C. K. VAN PETTEN AND R. KLUENDER (2006) Psycholinguistics electrified II (1924–2005). In *Handbook of Psycholinguistics*, 2nd Ed., M. A. Gernsbacher and M. Traxler (eds.). New York: Elsevier, pp. 659–724.

OJEMANN, G. A. (1983) The intrahemispheric organization of human language, derived with electrical stimulation techniques. *Trends Neurosci.* 4: 184–189.

ZUBERBUHLER, K. (2005) Linguistic prerequisites in the primate lineage. In *Language Origins: Perspectives on Evolution*, M. Tallerman (ed.). New York: Oxford University Press, pp. 262–282.

Important Original Papers

CHAO, L. L., J. V. HAXBY AND A. MARTIN (1999) Attribute-based neural substrates in temporal cortex for perceiving and knowing about objects. *Nat. Neurosci.* 2: 913–919.

DeLONG, K., T. URBACH AND M. KUTAS (2005) Probabilistic word pre-activation during language comprehension inferred from electrical brain activity. *Nat. Neurosci.* 8: 1117–1121.

GIL-DA-COSTA, R., A. MARTIN, M. A. LOPES, M. MUNOZ, J. FRITZ AND A. R.

BRAUN (2006) Species-specific calls activate homologs of Broca's and Wernicke's areas in the macaque. *Nat. Neurosci.* 9: 1064–1070.

KUTAS, M. AND S. A. HILLYARD (1980) Reading senseless sentences: Brain potentials reflect semantic incongruity. *Science* 207: 203–205.

OJEMANN, G. A. AND H. A. WHITAKER (1978) The bilingual brain. *Arch. Neurol.* 35: 409–412.

SHULMAN, G. L., J. M. OLLINGER, M. LINENWEBER, S. E. PETERSEN AND M.

CORBETTA (2001) Multiple neural correlates of detection in the human brain. *Proc. Natl. Acad. Sci. USA* 98: 313–318.

Books

GARDNER, H. (1974) *The Shattered Mind: The Person after Brain Damage.* New York: Vintage.

LENNEBERG, E. (1967) *The Biological Foundations of Language.* New York: Wiley.

POSNER, M. I. AND M. E. RAICHLE (1994) *Images of Mind.* New York: Scientific American Library.

Representation of Time and Number

Introduction

The representation of time and number are conceptual domains that, on the face of it, appear to be rooted in language. We think of time in seconds, minutes, hours, or other tokens of duration; and the numbers that we use routinely in arithmetic tasks such as making change or calculating a tip also rely on arbitrary symbols. The everyday human use of explicit verbal or written symbols in communicating about time and number is, however, misleading. The evidence described in this chapter shows that nonverbal representations of time and number underlie conventional, symbolic notation, and that these abilities are shared with non-human animals. This evidence underscores the point made in earlier chapters that the vast majority of human cognitive processing does not depend on language or conscious thought, but stems from a deeper link between biologically useful percepts and adaptive behavior. The behavioral utility of representing time and number presumably derives from the enormous advantages that animals gain from tracking the duration and expected occurrence of events and the quantity of items, whether food, mates, predators, or other objects of interest. Although time and number can be represented independently of human language, speech and writing allow both time and number to be conceptualized and expressed precisely rather than approximately, with obvious advantages for human culture.

Representing Time

Representing time is essential for many aspects of behavior and critically linked to survival. It is thus not surprising that multiple biological mechanisms allow animals to track time over different scales. Circadian rhythms control sleep-wake cycles over the 24-hour light-dark cycle, foraging and decision making involve timing on the order of seconds to minutes, and coordinating the fine motor movements used in innumerable daily tasks requires timing intervals in the millisecond range. This section describes some of the key features of temporal processing and what is known about how timing is implemented in the brain.

Circadian rhythms

Many physiological processes in mammals and other animals show patterns of regulated change, called **circadian rhythms**, that vary systematically over the 24-hour cycle of light and darkness (the word *circadian* means "about a day"). Examples of processes that exhibit such rhythms include body temperature, circulating hormone levels, urine production, blood pressure, levels of neural activity that control homeostatic functions, and of course the familiar sleep-wake cycle (see Chapter 28). When animals are kept in environments without external cues to the day, or light-dark, cycle, they still maintain a circadian rhythm, demonstrating an internal oscillator that works independently. Humans typically revert to a rhythm that is slightly longer than 24 hours (about 25–26 hours); some other species (e.g., mice) have rhythms that are slightly less than 24 hours.

Although the "biological clocks" that control these functions are extraordinarily complex, ranging from molecular clocks that control the circadian activity of individual cells to complex neural circuits, in mammals a key control center is the **suprachiasmatic nucleus (SCN)** of the hypothalamus (**Figure 22.1A**). Lesions of the SCN can destroy circadian rhythms, and grafting a suprachiasmatic nucleus from one animal into another animal whose SCN was ablated restores the 24-hour activity-rest cycle.

The SCN receives information about the daily light-dark cycle from the eye, using a novel class of photoreceptors that was only recently discovered. This information reaches the SCN by way of axons that extend from the eye through the retinothalamic tract to the hypothalamus. The SCN projects to autonomic neurons in the spinal cord that modulate many bodily functions, including the pineal gland's release of melatonin, a hormone that modulates the sleep-wake cycle (**Figure 22.1B**). Measurements of electrical and metabolic

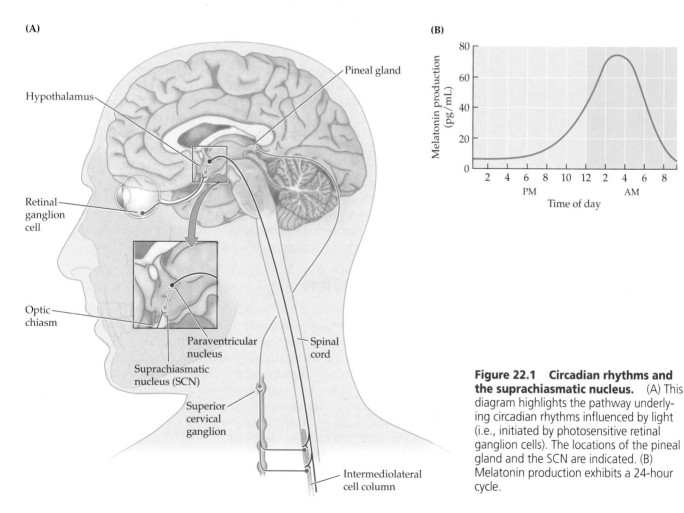

Figure 22.1 Circadian rhythms and the suprachiasmatic nucleus. (A) This diagram highlights the pathway underlying circadian rhythms influenced by light (i.e., initiated by photosensitive retinal ganglion cells). The locations of the pineal gland and the SCN are indicated. (B) Melatonin production exhibits a 24-hour cycle.

activity of neurons in slices taken from the SCN have shown that these neurons possess intrinsic circadian oscillators that enable them to continue to cycle even without light-dark stimulation. This ability to perpetuate a rhythm even when the usual stimulus is absent may serve as a backup system that maintains the responsiveness of the SCN neurons to light, mediated by the pathway illustrated in Figure 22.1A.

Although such daily rhythms may seem remote from human cognition, virtually all cognitive functions are influenced by the physiological functions that vary with the time of day. A familiar example is the greater facility that people experience carrying out many mental operations when they are relatively refreshed earlier in the day than when they are tired and ready for sleep at night. Broadly speaking, these cognitive differences are the result of circadian rhythms that alter body and brain physiology over the 24-hour day.

Interval timing in human experience

In addition to the overall ability of the brain to adjust numerous functions to daily cycles of light and dark, it is essential for humans and other animals to keep time on much shorter timescales, allowing them to anticipate predictable events that have biologically important consequences. **Interval timing** refers to the ability to keep track of time on the order of seconds to minutes, and nearly all aspects of human behavior require this sort of temporal judgment. Changing lanes on a highway, catching a ball, cooking an omelet, playing a musical instrument, and telling a joke all require accurate tracking of temporal intervals.

One question in seeking to understand interval timing is how the subjective representation of time relates to real time. If real time were represented perfectly, our ability to discriminate two intervals would be flawless. However, it is clear that we don't often represent time with clocklike accuracy; most durations are monitored in a more approximate fashion, although the intervals for many motor actions (e.g., successfully catching a ball) are normally quite precise. Generally, the standard deviation of an interval that is tracked cognitively is proportional to the mean of the interval, and this relationship is referred to as **scalar variability**.

For example, when asked to hold a button down for 5 seconds over and over again, subjects hold it down for approximately 5 seconds each time, within a range of error that is typically about 20 percent (i.e., plus or minus about a second). If asked to hold the button down for 50 seconds, a subject would thus depress the button about 40 or 60 seconds. Temporal estimates vary in proportion to the magnitude of the interval that a subject is attempting to track, following **Weber's law** (see Box 5A; remember that Weber's law states that the change in a stimulus needed for perceptual detection, divided by the stimulus magnitude, is a constant). As will be apparent later in the chapter, Weber's law predicts duration discrimination in a wide array of species across many different timing tasks.

Attention is also a critical factor in time perception and provides additional insight into how the brain parses time. Everyone has experienced the feeling that the hour will never pass when listening to a boring talk, or conversely, that time passes more quickly than usual when engrossed in conversation. The idiom "a watched pot never boils" illustrates the conclusion that paying close attention to the apparent passage of time makes the time seem longer. A host of experiments show that when subjects are engaged in concurrent processing while attempting to time an interval, their subjective estimates of duration are shorter than when they allocate undivided attention to the timing task. Furthermore, the easier the distracting task is, the more subjects tend to overestimate the interval that they are timing. These findings suggest that when subjects are unable to attend to cues that indicate the passage of time, they underestimate physical duration.

Another important aspect of interval timing is the fact that perceived duration is lengthened as a function of the amount of information in an elapsing interval. Thus, the number of stimuli in an interval (and their complexity) is positively correlated with estimates of duration. For example, highly salient events, such as getting mugged or being in a car accident, are often perceived as lasting much longer than they actually do. Another temporal illusion occurs at the interface between the perception of causality and the time perception. An event that one perceives as being caused by one's own actions is judged as having occurred earlier compared to an event caused by someone else's actions. For example, imagine an experiment in which pressing a button causes a red square—and occasionally at the same time, a noncontingent blue circle—to appear on a monitor. Participants in such experiments typically perceive the red square to have preceded the appearance of the blue circle, even though when both are presented, the two stimuli appear simultaneously.

In short, these examples show that, in keeping with other perceptual categories described in Unit II, temporal perceptions are often quite different from reality.

Interval timing in non-human animals

Not surprisingly, interval timing is equally important for non-human animals. For instance, this ability plays an essential role in foraging behaviors. The best-studied examples of interval timing in non-human animals concern the optimal intervals before returning to a food source. For example, European starlings calculate the amount of food they find in a given period in a given patch of space (rate of prey capture) and use this information to decide how long to stay in one patch and when to move on to another patch. Similarly, hummingbirds return sooner to flower species that replenish their nectar in 10 minutes than to flowers that replenish this nutrient only after 20 minutes (**Figure 22.2**).

In experimental settings, birds can be trained to find food at particular intervals, to make one versus two discrete responses when exposed to each of two distinct temporal intervals, or to choose between tokens that indicate different delays to reward. For example, garden warblers rapidly learn which of four feeding rooms is available at different times of the day. Similarly, pigeons can learn to switch every 15 minutes from pecking on one key to pecking on another. Thus, animals readily learn to make simple duration discriminations and can readily predict the timing of important events in their environment.

A task known as the *bisection procedure* has been widely used to explore how time is represented in non-human animals (as well as in humans). Subjects are trained to make one response after a short signal and another response after a long signal. Responses are highly accurate when the short and long signals are distinct. For example, when rats are required to classify signals that are 2 and 8 seconds in duration, they can easily reach 90 percent accuracy after about 10 sessions. When intermediate values (e.g., 3–7 seconds) are then introduced in unreinforced trials, the probability of classifying a signal as long, as opposed to short, increases with signal duration. Thus, animals are more likely to classify a 7-second, compared to a 3-second, inter-

(A)

(B)

Figure 22.2 Timing optimal intervals for obtaining food. (A) This hummingbird is feeding from an experimental flower. (B) These plots show median postreinforcement pauses for three different birds over 12 experimental days. Birds wait longer to revisit flowers that replenish their nectar every 20 minutes compared to flowers that replenish every 10 minutes. (From Henderson et al. 2006.)

mediate duration as long if they choose the icon previously associated with 8 seconds.

An important property of the psychophysical function relating response probability to duration is the **point of subjective equality**—the value for which animals are equally likely to classify an intermediate signal as long or short. Tests in rats and other animals show that this point is close to the geometric mean of the anchor values—that is, $\sqrt{2 \times 8} = 4$. The fact that the psychological midpoint between two values is the geometric mean rather than the arithmetic mean—that is, $(2 + 8)/2 = 5$—again indicates that subjective time is not linearly related to real time. There remains some debate, however, as to whether subjective time is logarithmically organized or linearly spaced, with the variance in the remembered distributions for temporal intervals simply increasing with the mean value being represented.

The fact that time is not represented veridically is also apparent in tasks that require non-human animals or humans to indicate the end of a temporal interval. In the *peak-interval procedure*, a visual or auditory stimulus is presented for a fixed time, and after that time has elapsed a subsequent response is rewarded. Occasional "empty" probe trials are inserted in which the stimulus persists past the time at which responses should have elicited a reward, but no reward is in fact given. As **Figure 22.3A** shows, on these empty trials a normal distribution in the rate of responding is observed, with the modal value

(A)

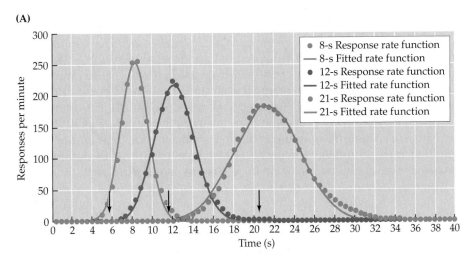

(B)

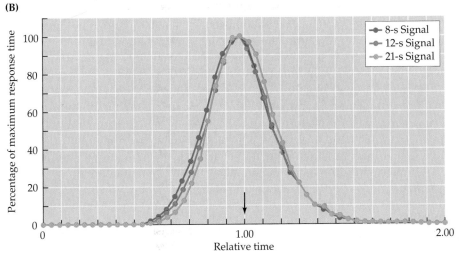

Figure 22.3 Scalar timing revealed in the peak-interval procedure.
(A) Mean response rate in responses per minute as a function of signal duration for human participants tested in three conditions (8, 12, and 21 seconds). (B) Data from (A) are replotted as the mean percentage of maximum response rate as a function of relative time, then superimposed as predicted by scalar expectancy theory. (After Rakitin et al. 1998.)

occurring at the time the reward should have been obtained. Scalar variance in the peak-interval procedure is apparent when the variability of the response distributions increases with the remembered duration. Furthermore, when the response distributions are plotted in relative time, the functions are superimposed (**Figure 22.3B**). The superimposition of the curves when plotted in relative coordinates indicates that the variance associated with temporal representations increases in proportion to the magnitude of the durations remembered.

Models of interval timing

Models of interval timing can be distinguished on the basis of whether they propose one (or more) internal clock that functions as a pacemaker or they attempt to account for interval timing without an internal clock. An internal clock might function like a stopwatch, stopping and restarting at time intervals. The most influential clock-based model is the **scalar timing theory**, proposed by John Gibbon at Columbia University, Russell Church at Brown, and Warren Meck at Duke. Scalar timing theory can be thought of as an information-processing model comprising clock, memory, and decision stages (**Figure 22.4**).

The clock is taken to be a pacemaker that emits pulses of some sort. When a switch that links the pacemaker to an accumulator is closed, pulses from the pacemaker flow into the accumulator. The switch closes at the onset of any event that is to be timed, and it opens again at the offset of such an event. In the memory stage of the model, the accumulated pulses are stored in working memory (see Chapter 16). Accumulator values are transferred directly into reference memory or via working memory. Finally, in the decision stage of the model, the value stored in the accumulator is compared to a sample value taken from a distribution of values stored in reference memory. A ratio comparison rule is used to determine whether the value in the accumulator is close enough to the reference value to warrant a positive response. If the current accumulator value is close to the reference value, the current value is added to the memory distribution, thus affecting future judgments.

Although this information-processing model is not biologically based, pharmacological manipulations provide some support for the general idea that separate clock and memory stages are involved in interval timing. For

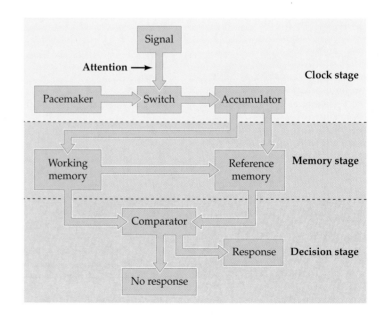

Figure 22.4 An information-processing model of interval timing. Pulses are imagined to be emitted at a constant rate from a pacemaker and transmitted via a switch into an accumulator. See text for explanation. (After Gibbon et al. 1984.)

example, when rats are given dopamine agonists such as methamphetamine or cocaine, tests show that the animals' subjective time is lengthened relative to actual time. Evidence comes from the bisection procedure described in the previous section. The point of subjective equality in such tests is shifted to the left under the influence of dopamine agonists, suggesting that actual durations are experienced as being subjectively longer. This result could be explained if dopamine agonists caused the postulated pulses to be emitted from the pacemaker at a higher rate, allowing more to accumulate than under normal circumstances and thus imparting the sense that more time had elapsed than really had. In contrast, a dopamine antagonist such as haloperidol causes rats to exhibit a rightward shift of the point of subjective equality, as if the rate at which pulses were emitted were slowed down.

Recently Matthew Mattell and Meck have proposed a variation on this theory of interval timing: the *striatal-beat frequency model*. This theory also relies on a pacemaker, but it is more biologically realistic in that it depends on the coincidental activation of medium spiny neurons in the basal ganglia driven by neural oscillators in the neocortex (see Chapter 28). In this conception, synchronized cortical oscillations are assumed to reflect the onset of an event that is to be timed, oscillating at a constant frequency during the interval that is being timed for the purpose of obtaining a food or other reward.

Through experience, striatal neurons learn the pattern of cortical activation associated with the time of reward. Ensemble recordings from rats trained in interval-timing tasks offer some support for this idea by showing that the firing rate of some striatal neurons increases as the time for the reinforcement approaches. In this model the basal ganglia are thought to monitor activity in thalamo-cortico-striatal circuits and act as a coincidence detector that signals particular patterns of oscillatory activity.

A second family of models entails *state-dependent networks*. These theories do not invoke a specific pacemaker or internal clock, but propose that all neural circuits are inherently capable of temporal processing. Thus, networks with different properties are thought to emerge from the natural complexity of cortical circuits combined with neuronal properties that are time-dependent.

One such model, proposed by Dean Buonomano and colleagues at UCLA, successfully explains human timing in the millisecond range. In this case a given temporal interval is represented as a specific state of a neural network that reflects stimulus intervals experienced earlier, as well as the current interval. This model accounts for the relevant psychophysical data well, perhaps explaining why interval discrimination in this range is impaired by a distracter interval that appears at unpredictable times, as discussed earlier.

Although the model is useful for explaining millisecond-range timing, the facts that time perception depends on the initial state and preceding intervals, and that the model results in a nonlinear metric of subjective time, make it a poor candidate for timing longer intervals. In any event, all of these models are highly speculative, and there may well be several separate and perhaps overlapping ways to time intervals of different durations, each with different biological purposes.

The neural basis of interval timing

Both non-human animal research and human neuroimaging studies indicate that interval timing depends in some way on the basal ganglia, and on the circuitry that links the frontal cortex and the striatum. Lesions of the basal ganglia (the substantia nigra, caudate, and putamen in particular) disrupt interval timing in rats. Patients with damage to the basal ganglia (e.g., in Huntington's or Parkinson's disease) show increased variability in timing tasks in both millisecond and second ranges. Patients with right prefrontal lesions have also

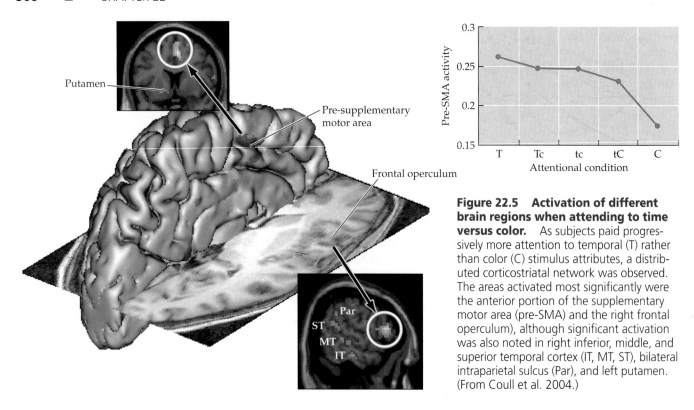

Figure 22.5   Activation of different brain regions when attending to time versus color.   As subjects paid progressively more attention to temporal (T) rather than color (C) stimulus attributes, a distributed corticostriatal network was observed. The areas activated most significantly were the anterior portion of the supplementary motor area (pre-SMA) and the right frontal operculum), although significant activation was also noted in right inferior, middle, and superior temporal cortex (IT, MT, ST), bilateral intraparietal sulcus (Par), and left putamen. (From Coull et al. 2004.)

shown timing deficits, supporting the idea that memory and timing are critically related.

In keeping with this evidence, when human subjects are instructed about the amount of attention they should allocate to the duration versus the color of a stimulus, different brain regions are recruited depending on the feature being attended. As **Figure 22.5** illustrates, attending to time activates the pre-supplementary motor area, dorsal premotor cortex, putamen, and frontal operculum, and the strength of activation increases as the amount of attention paid to time increases.

Neuroimaging studies have further supported a link between interval timing and working memory. A recent meta-analysis showed that the right dorsolateral prefrontal cortex, an area implicated in working memory, is recruited in consciously mediated timing tasks to a greater degree than in more automatic timing tasks. Moreover, when subjects are required to perform two tasks at once, this working memory overload interferes with success on an interval-timing task. A final piece of circumstantial evidence that interval timing and working memory are linked is that both are modulated by dopamine receptor agonists and antagonists.

Other brain regions also appear to be involved in timing. Richard Ivry of UC Berkeley and Steven Keele of the University of Oregon observed that patients with cerebellar damage performed various time production and discrimination tasks poorly when they receive no feedback about the accuracy of their responses. On the basis of this result, they suggested that one of the functions of the cerebellum is to serve as a supplemental biological clock. Ivry went on to propose that the cerebellum is critical for timing in the millisecond range, whereas the basal ganglia would support timing functions in the range of a second or so. However, a recent PET study that monitored cerebellar activity when subjects were asked to reproduce different intervals found activation associated with both long and short timing judgments, leaving the role of the cerebellum up in the air at this point. Some evidence also suggests involvement of the hippocampus and perhaps other medial temporal lobe structures in interval timing.

In sum, interval timing involves a number of brain regions, preeminently the basal ganglia, the prefrontal cortex, and the cerebellum. Exactly what these several regions do to support timing judgments and how they interact are not yet understood.

Representing Number

The representation of number is fundamentally important for successful behavior in humans and other animals. We routinely use numbers to make judgments about sets of items, to measure continuous quantities, to order priorities by rank, and more generally to label objects in the world around us. Culturally specific ways of using arbitrary symbols to represent number depend on language as another means of symbolic communication (see Chapter 20), and this ability is thus especially germane to humans. In addition to language-dependent numerical systems, however, we possess an ability to represent number in ways that are independent of language. This nonverbal system represents number in terms of continuous, analog values and is shared by many non-human animals.

Number representation in humans

Many forms of number use in humans—such as the arithmetic and higher math that we learn in school—depend on explicit symbols and words used to describe them. To solve even a simple problem, such as determining the sum of 17 + 12, requires a good deal of cognitive processing. Those seeking the answer must understand the meaning of the symbol for addition and the meaning of the arbitrary symbols that represent number. They must then retrieve or calculate the answer, using either declarative memory systems if the answer has been worked out earlier and is remembered, or working memory if it the answer must be calculated de novo.

However, humans also possess an ability to represent number that presumably evolved well before any sophisticated language numbers or schooling in arithmetic existed. Even in the absence of explicit symbols for numbers, humans represent quantity approximately as imprecise **mental magnitudes**. Whereas numbers are discrete and used in this way to make useful judgments (3 shoes, 16 marbles, 23 grains of sand), nonverbal mental representations of number are continuous. The basic idea is that, although we can enumerate only discrete entities, we can also represent number in terms of magnitudes that are proportional to the actual number of elements represented.

Evidence for the routine use of such nonverbal mental magnitudes is apparent when adults are given pairs of numbers and asked to choose the symbol that represents the larger magnitude (**Figure 22.6A**). Accuracy increases and latency decreases with increasing numerical distance—a phenomenon referred to as the **numerical distance effect** (**Figure 22.6B**). For example, people take more time to indicate that 5 is larger than 3 than to indicate that 8 is larger than 3. Furthermore, when numerical distance is held constant, performance decreases with increasing numerical magnitude—a phenomenon referred to as the **numerical size effect** (**Figure 22.6C**). In this case, people take more time to indicate that 9 is larger than 7 than to indicate that 7 is larger than 5.

These distance and size effects indicate that accuracy and latency are modulated by the *ratio* of the quantities that the numerals represent. The effects have been replicated in many languages and cultures, with different representational formats, with double-digit stimuli, and in children as young as 5

(A)

Which is larger?

2 or 8

(B)

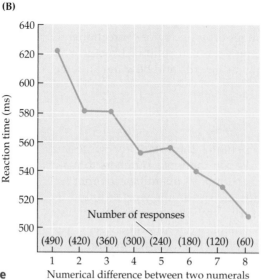

(C)

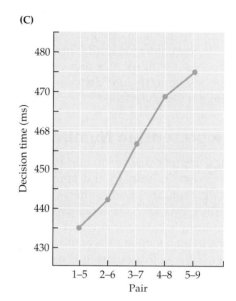

Figure 22.6 Numerical distance and size effects. (A) In experiments designed to measure numerical distance and size effects, subjects are posed questions like the one illustrated here. (B) The time taken to choose the larger of two numerical symbols is a function of the numerical distance between them. (C) Reaction time when the task is to choose the larger of two numerical symbols increases as a function of numerical size when the numerical distance is held constant. (B after Moyer and Landauer 1967; C after Moyer and Dumais 1978.)

years old. Ratio dependence means that numerical discrimination, like time discrimination, follows Weber's law. For example, if a subject required a 3:4 ratio to discriminate a value from 12 (e.g., could differentiate 12 from 16 but not 12 from 14), then if presented with a larger value (such as 24), the subject would be able to differentiate it from 32 but not from 28, even though 24 and 28 have the same linear difference as 12 and 16 have.

Further evidence that humans can represent number without number words comes from studies of indigenous cultures with languages that have few number words and no formal counting system. Two tribes in the Amazon region of Brazil (the Piraha and Munduruku) do not use number words to count or tally objects, and they have very few number words in their vocabularies. Nevertheless they use nonverbal number representations that obey Weber's law. For example, when Munduruku subjects were asked to compare arrays that contained anywhere from 20 to 80 dots whose surface area, perimeter, and density were carefully controlled, their accuracy decreased as the ratio between the two values (larger to smaller number) increased (**Figure 22.7**).

This finding shows that even with little or no experience with verbal counting and symbolic number representation, humans have a capacity for nonsymbolic number representation that is ratio-dependent. In fact, Munduruku performance on the number comparison task was much the same as that of educated French-speaking control subjects who were told to respond rapidly and refrain from verbal counting. Despite the culturally specific and linguistically mediated system of representing number and making calculations that is acquired in developed countries, all normal people also continue to represent number imprecisely in this way.

Another aspect of number representation in humans is how numbers are organized. For instance, most of us have a sense that numbers are mentally organized along a number line from small to large. Reaction-time data for number judgment tasks suggest that we do, in fact, possess such a **mental number line**. In Western cultures in which individuals read from left to right, the mental number line places small values on the left side of space and large values on the right side. Furthermore, when subjects are required to make an odd-even parity judgment with the left or right hand, they are faster at responding to small values with the left hand and larger values with the right hand. This phenomenon, sometimes called the **spatial-numerical association**

(A)

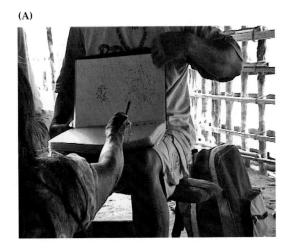

(B)

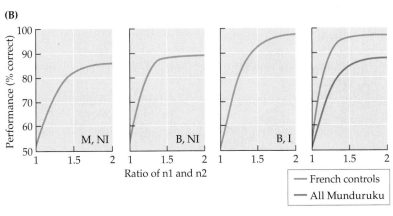

Performance (% correct)

Ratio of n1 and n2

— French controls
— All Munduruku

Figure 22.7 Ratio-dependent number judgments made by people whose language has no counting words. (A) This Munduruku participant is being tested in a numerical comparison task. (B) The fraction of correct choices is plotted here as a function of the ratio of the two numerical values (n1 and n2) being compared (larger/smaller) for each group tested. M, monolinguals who speak only Munduruku; B, bilinguals who speak Munduruku and French; NI, subjects given no explicit instruction on how to solve the task; I, subjects given explicit instruction on how to solve the task. (After Pica et al. 2004.)

of response codes, is greatly influenced by experience. For example, whereas the Western mental number line runs from left to right, in Iran, where text is read from right to left, people represent the mental number line with small numbers on the right side of space.

Taken together, these various observations show that even though numbers describe sets of discrete entities and can be mentally represented in this way in carrying out arithmetic, the mental representation of number can also be in a continuous analog format that follows Weber's law, as in perceptual discriminations of other continua.

Number representation in non-human animals

A German circus trainer operating more than a century ago claimed that a horse named Clever Hans could solve mathematical problems by tapping its hoof a certain number of times to give the answer. Not surprisingly, it was eventually discovered that the horse was not really doing arithmetic, but was responding to subtle cues from the trainer in giving the answers. Despite the skepticism generated by this and other bogus feats of animal skill in math and logic (people are still bamboozled at fairs today by the challenge of playing tic-tac-toe against a chicken that, unknown to the human player, has simply been trained to peck a lighted key that has been programmed to win the game), many non-human animals do in fact represent the numerical attributes of stimuli. Furthermore, although only an adult human with number words and concepts can represent large quantities with precision, precursors of human mathematical abilities are present in animals.

The value of such skills is not hard to imagine, since a change in number is often biologically relevant. However, sorting out the importance of number from other variables can be experimentally challenging. For example, 10 seeds are more numerous than 5 seeds, but they also weigh more and have greater surface area. Three alarm calls emitted in sequence are more numerous than two, but they are also longer in overall duration and cumulatively contain more sound energy. Nevertheless, it is possible to show that some non-human animals represent number independently of other physical dimensions.

Elizabeth Brannon and her colleagues at Duke University have trained monkeys to choose the numerically smaller or larger of two arrays via a touch screen to obtain a juice reward, and several monkey species have been trained to order visual arrays according to number while ignoring other features (**Figure 22.8**). By varying non-numerical stimulus features such as color, shape, surface area, and density of the arrays, the researchers could show that mon-

(A)

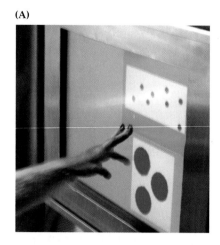

(B)

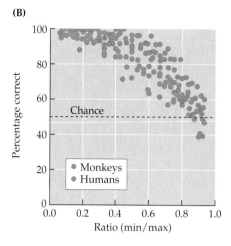

(C)

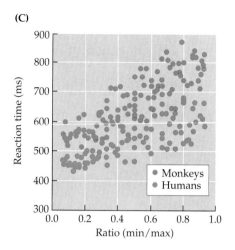

Figure 22.8 Human and monkey numerical distance effects. (A) This monkey is engaging in a numerical ordering task using a touch screen. (B) Monkey and human performance in the numerical ordering task is plotted as a function of the ratio between the two numerical values being compared. (C) Response time is plotted here as a function of the ratio between the two numerical values being compared for monkeys and human college students. (After Cantlon and Brannon 2006.)

keys are able to order stimuli on the basis of number alone. Indeed, monkeys and humans tested in the same ordinal comparison task have strikingly similar response times and show much the same ratio-dependent accuracy.

The remarkable overlap in humans and monkeys of reaction time and accuracy in numerical distance or numerical ratio tasks implies a common nonverbal representational scheme. A parallel has also been shown between humans and rats when tested in a paradigm that requires the production of a certain number of responses of lever pressing (**Figure 22.9**). Both rats and humans show response distributions centered on the

(A) Rats

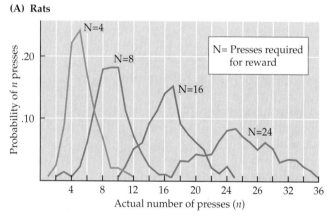

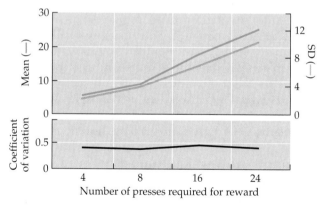

(B) Humans

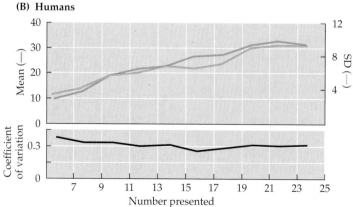

Figure 22.9 Performance of rats and humans tested on a similar number discrimination task. (A) The probability that a rat will make a particular number of responses is plotted as a function of the number of responses required to obtain a reward in a lever-pressing task. The number of responses made was normally distributed around the required number. Data from (A) are replotted in the graph on the right to show that the standard deviation (SD) of the response distributions increased linearly with the mean number of presses required. (B) Human subjects were shown an Arabic numeral between 7 and 25 and required to press a key that number of times as fast as they could without counting. As in the rat study, the coefficient of variation was approximately constant. (A after Platt and Johnson 1971; B after Whalen et al. 1999.)

required number of responses with a variance that increases proportionally to the required number of bar presses in a comparable paradigm. Ratio-dependent number discrimination is not limited to animals that have had extensive laboratory training. Marc Hauser and his colleagues at Harvard found that tamarin monkeys familiarized to sequences with a given number of sounds spontaneously oriented to sequences of sounds that differed in number, but only when the ratio between the familiar and novel numbers was sufficiently large.

Models of Numerical Representation

Imagine looking at a collection of 57 peanuts and attempting to identify the number of nuts in the set. There are two possible strategies: *counting* the actual number of peanuts or, alternatively, simply *estimating* the size of the set. Given this particular challenge, most people would estimate the set size unless instructed to count. An adult would probably give a number somewhere between 40 and 60 peanuts, and a guess of, say, 10 or 100 would be very unlikely. When shown a small collection of 2 or 3 peanuts, however, the same person would be able give the correct number without having to count verbally. This automatic, rapid, and precise labeling of small sets is called **subitizing**. What, then, are the cognitive processes that underlie counting, estimating, and subitizing?

Psychologists Rochel Gelman and Charles Gallistel, now at Rutgers University, have provided a useful definition of counting in cognitive terms. Counting, in their conception, is based on three principles:

1. The **stable order principle** states that the person (or animal) doing the counting must possess a stably ordered set of labels. In English our labels are "one," "two," "three," and so on. One cannot count 1-2-3 sometimes and 2-3-1 at other times; the counter must use a list that is the same from one counting episode to the next.

2. The **one-to-one correspondence principle** states that a counter must apply the labels from the stably ordered sequence in correspondence to the objects that are being counted. In other words, the person counting cannot apply two counting symbols or representations to one object or skip another object altogether.

3. The **cardinal principle** states that the final label applied to an object to be counted in a set represents the numerical value of the set.

Gelman and Gallistel further argued that although verbal symbols such as "one," "two," and "three" serve well as labels, nonverbal symbols, or **numerons**, could also be used both by humans and by other animals. The essence of counting defined by these principles is thus a process whereby each element in a set is serially labeled up to a clear endpoint. Whether any of the impressive numerosity discriminations that animals make spontaneously or after extensive training in the laboratory actually meet Gelman and Gallistel's counting criteria is still debated.

Evidence for a distinction between counting and subitizing has come from reaction-time patterns as adults enumerate items in a set. When asked to identify the number of elements in a random dot pattern, for instance, subjects show responses that are rapid and constant for small values but begin to increase steadily for sets larger than four or five. The "elbow" in the reaction-time function at about 4 or 5 suggests that two distinct enumeration processes may underlie the evaluation of small and large numbers. People apparently subitize small sets by simply taking the number in "at a glance," but to be accurate with larger sets requires actually counting the items, which entails a constant increment of about 250 milliseconds per item counted.

■ BOX 22A Possible Relationship between the Representation of Time and Number

About 25 years ago Meck and Church proposed the idea that time and number are represented by the same representational currency. Several lines of evidence support this claim, primarily from studies in rats. First, when number and time co-vary such that one dimension could be used alone, evidence suggests that animals sometimes automatically encode both the temporal and numerical attributes of stimuli such that when they are decoupled, either attribute controls responding. Second, the midpoint between two anchor values (e.g., 2 seconds versus 8 seconds, and 2 versus 8 items) is at the geometric mean for both time and number (see the figure). Third, when rats are given a dopamine agonist that speeds up the pacemaker, they behave as if both the timing and number tasks required fewer counts and shorter durations to classify a stimulus as long or many. Finally, rats trained to classify a single tone as short or long transferred this time discrimination to number (few

versus many), as if a count were equivalent to about 200 milliseconds.

Consistent with this idea, time and number share a representational currency in humans. Thus, a 1:2 ratio is required for a 6-month-old infant to discriminate two numerical values or two temporal intervals. Within a few months, however, infants become capable of discriminating a 2:3 ratio in

duration or number, suggesting a common developmental trajectory for time and number discrimination.

Despite the evidence that time and number discrimination have these parallels, other work implies that timing may be more important than counting in some nonverbal animals. In one study, one color cued pigeons that a reward would be available after

(A)

(D)

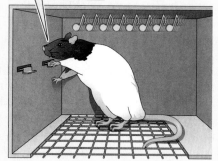

(B) Training stimuli

⎍⎍⎍_ 2 s

⎍⎍⎍⎍⎍⎍⎍⎍ 8 s

(C)

Test for number

Number of cycles	Duration (s)	Stimulus	Reinforced response
2	4		Lever 1
3	4		- - - -
4	4		- - - -
5	4		- - - -
6	4		- - - -
8	4		Lever 2

Test for time

Number of cycles	Duration (s)	Stimulus	Reinforced response
4	2		Lever 1
4	3		- - - -
4	4		- - - -
4	5		- - - -
4	6		- - - -
4	8		Lever 2

Procedure used to study time and number representation in experimental animals. (A) Rats were tested in chambers that provided a choice of one of two levers. (B) Training stimuli consisted of 2-second (2-cycle) stimuli and 8-second (8-cycle) stimuli in which each cycle contained a 0.5-second tone followed by 0.5 second of silence. (C) Half of the test stimuli were of a constant duration of 4 seconds, with the number of cycles (i.e., tone on/tone off) varying from 2 to 8; the other half of the test stimuli always contained 4 cycles, but the cycles varied in duration from 2 to 8 seconds. (D) The probability of classifying a stimulus as many cycles (e.g., 8) or long (e.g., 8 seconds) varied as a function of the duration when number was held constant, and as a function of number when duration was held constant. The point of subjective equality is the value that is classified as long or many on 50 percent of trials and is equal to the geometric mean of the two anchor values. (After Meck and Church 1983.)

<table>
<tbody>
<tr><td>

a fixed number of flashes, and a second color cued that the reward would be available after a fixed duration. Midway through a trial the experimenters changed the cue and found that when the pigeons had originally been cued to count, they had also kept track of time; when cued to time, however, the pigeons had apparently not counted. Thus, timing may be more automatic than counting in pigeons. It

</td><td>

is possible that species differences will be found in the relative salience of number and time and that differences may reflect the biological importance of assessing duration versus quantity in the biological niches occupied by different species.

References

BREUKELAAR, J. W. C. AND J. C. DALRYMPLE-ALFORD (1998) Timing ability and numeri-

</td><td>

cal competence in rats. *J. Exp. Psychol. Anim. Behav. Process.* 24: 84–97.

MECK, W. H. AND R. M. CHURCH (1983) A mode control model of counting and timing processes. *J. Exp. Psychol. Anim. Behav. Process.* 9: 320–334.

ROBERTS, W., S. ROBERTS AND K. A. KIT (2002) Pigeons presented with sequences of false flashes use behavior to count but not to time. *J. Exp. Psychol. Anim. Behav. Process.* 28: 137–150.

</td></tr>
</tbody>
</table>

The fact that non-human animals can represent number raises an important question about how this feat is achieved in the absence of number words. Three different ideas have been proposed that would work for both humans and other animals with or without language. In one approach to the problem, Meck and Church adapted the scalar expectancy model of timing behavior described earlier to postulate what they refer to as the **mode control model**. In this conception, the pulses from the pacemaker (see Figure 22.4) can be gated into the accumulator by different switches to determine whether the animal is representing number or time. If the switch is operating in the *event mode*, the gate is closed for a given duration for each element to be enumerated. In this way, the system yields an accumulation proportional to the number of events. In contrast, if the switch is operating in the *run mode*, the gate opens at the onset of a sequence of events to be timed and closes when the sequence is complete. The accumulator value in this condition indicates the duration of the whole sequence. **Box 22A** describes related evidence that time and number are represented by a single mechanism, at least in rodents.

A second idea about how number could be represented nonverbally is the **neural network model** proposed by Stanislas Dehaene and Pierre Changeux at the Pasteur Institute. These investigators posited "numerosity detectors" that represent the number of objects independent of their specific size and configuration (**Figure 22.10**). The model has three "layers": a sensory input (referred to as a "retina"), a map of object locations, and an array of numerosity detectors. The map of object locations converts stimuli from the retina to a representation of each stimulus irrespective of object size (an auditory memory also allows the system to enumerate sounds). The location map sends its output to numerosity detectors, which consist of summation units and numerosity units. Each summation unit has a set threshold value. When the total activity from the output of the location map (which is proportional to numerosity) exceeds the summation unit's threshold, the output is activated. These units differ from the *event mode* of the mode control model in that they

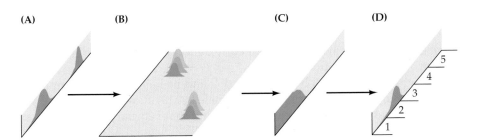

Figure 22.10 A neural network model of number representation. Objects of diverse size and shape (A) are normalized by a location map (B) and then summed by summation units (C). If a given threshold of summation units is activated, a numerosity unit (D) is activated. See text for further explanation. (After Dehaene and Changeux 1993.)

(A) Analog magnitude representations

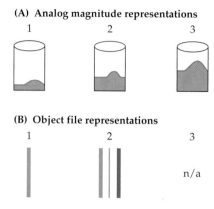

(B) Object file representations

Figure 22.11 Possible formats of nonverbal number representation. (A) Analog magnitude codes, which could result from the mode control model or the neural network model, represent the numerosity of a set as a continuous amount and have no upper limit on the number of elements that can be represented. (B) Object files are used to represent each individual in a set, and only a limited number of files is available at any given time.

are active only when the number of events exceeds a specific level (greater than or equal to 3, for example). Finally, the summation clusters project to numerosity clusters, which represent numerosities 1 through 5. A given numerosity cluster will be activated if the corresponding summation cluster is active (e.g., 3), but those representing higher values (e.g., 4 and 5) are not. Therefore, presentation of stimuli with the same numerosity despite differences in size, location, and modality results in activation of the same numerosity detectors.

Importantly, the mode control model and the neural network model both generate analog representations of number as shown in **Figure 22.11A** and predict that numerical discrimination should follow Weber's law. The models differ, however, in the process by which they achieve numerical representations. The neural network model implies that nonverbal number representation is not a serial counting process, whereas the mode control model follows the counting principles proposed by Gelman and Gallistel and can thus be thought of as a nonverbal counting algorithm. Another distinction is that the mode control model predicts that number and time are represented by a single currency, whereas the neural network model does not.

A third proposal for how number could be represented nonverbally is the **object file model** (**Figure 22.11B**). This model proposes that an "object file" is opened for each element in a visual array, and that the number of object files available at any given time is limited. Thus, if the only means of representing number were object files, an observer could represent only small sets of objects, explaining some of the behavioral phenomenology described in adult humans under the rubric of subitizing (described earlier).

This model has also been invoked to explain why, under some circumstances, human infants are able to represent sets of only up to three objects (see earlier discussion and Chapter 27). An important feature of the object file model is that the numerosity of a set is represented with no explicit symbol. Instead, each element is represented by an individual file that is stripped of features such as color, shape, or size. Although the object file system can represent only a few objects at a time, it may be faster and/or more accurate than other enumeration strategies, and may therefore allow humans and other animals to track small numbers of objects efficiently.

This section has described the prominent models proposed to account for nonverbal numerical processing. Of course, human numerical cognition also includes verbally mediated computations that rely on a more diffuse set of neural substrates, including language areas of the brain. **Box 22B** describes a handful of models that have been proposed to account for how verbal and nonverbal numerical processing interact.

Neuropsychological studies of numerical cognition

Patient studies suggest that the semantics of number words are separable from the semantics of other verbal categories, in that some patients comprehend number words but not other word categories. Dehaene and Laurent Cohen compared patients who had selectively lost the ability to semantically represent number in an approximate way with patients who retained this sort of semantic number representation but had lost the ability to remember precise numerical facts and algorithms. Their patient M.A.R., for example, had damage to the right inferior parietal cortex and had no difficulty retrieving memorized multiplication facts (e.g., 5 × 6 = 30). However, he could not decide which number fell between 2 and 4, and he had difficulty comparing the relative magnitude of numbers. Nonetheless, M.A.R. was able to make the judgments that C comes between B and D, and that February comes between January and March.

■ BOX 22B Models of Human Arithmetic Abilities

In addition to representing number as mental magnitudes (see the text), modern humans rely on various symbolic codes to represent number. Given a standard education, children quickly come to represent numbers verbally as spoken words, as written words, and as strings of numerals in one form or another, depending on the culture. There is controversy, however, over how these different forms of number processing fit together, and how the symbolic systems map onto mental magnitudes. Michael McCloskey of Johns Hopkins University has argued for what he calls the *abstract code model*, which posits that all numerical inputs (Arabic, verbal, etc.) are translated into an abstract representation of number, and that all mental calculations are then performed using this abstract code (Figure A). A production system then converts the abstract code into output in a specific format. This model implies that input format should have no influence on the computation stage of processing.

Unlike the abstract code model, the *triple code model* suggested by Stanislas Dehaene and Laurent Cohen working at Inserm in Paris proposes that numbers are mentally represented in three different codes, and that these codes can be activated independently of each other (Figure B). In the visual Arabic code, numbers are manipulated as numerals, presumably on a spatially formed number line. In the analog magnitude code, number is represented in terms of mental magnitudes that obey Weber's law. Numbers can also be represented in an auditory verbal code that is language-dependent and allows numbers to be represented in written or spoken format. Translation "paths" allow representations in any format to be converted to any other format. A feature of this model is that each numerical procedure requires a specific input format. Thus, all numerical values are ultimately converted to an auditory verbal code for expressing arithmetic facts (e.g., $2 \times 4 = 8$).

References

DEHAENE, S. (1992) Varieties of numerical abilities. *Cognition* 44: 1–42.

DEHAENE, S., M. PIAZZA, P. PINEL AND L. COHEN (2003) Three parietal circuits for number processing. *Cogn. Neuropsychol.* 20: 487–506.

MCCLOSKEY, M. (1992) Cognitive mechanisms in numerical processing: Evidence from acquired dyscalculia. *Cognition* 44: 107–157.

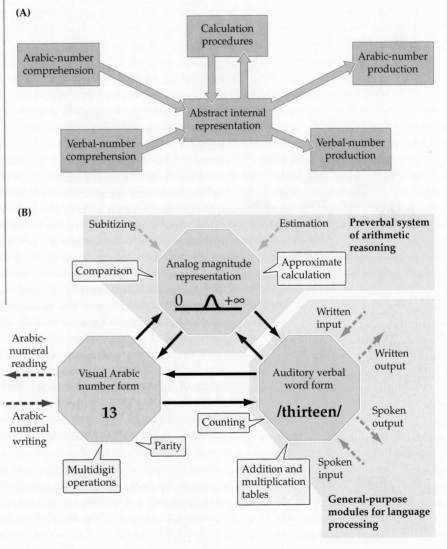

Schematic models of how arithmetic might be processed. (A) According to McCloskey's abstract code model, all representations are translated into an abstract code, and all mathematical calculations are performed using this code. (B) Dehaene's triple code model posits that number is represented in one of three codes (analog magnitude representation, visual Arabic number form, or auditory verbal word form), and that each mathematical operation requires number to be represented in a specific code. (After Dehaene 1992.)

A second patient, Mr. N, with diffuse cerebral damage that spared the parietal lobe, retained an approximate semantic representation of number, but had lost the ability to make exact calculations or retrieve exact calculation facts. For example, when presented with the problem 2 + 2 = ? he would answer 3, 4, or 5 but never 10. He was unable to read digits and had to use special strategies to access number words for answers he knew. When asked his daughter's age, he was unable to answer "seven" without counting from 1 to 7. In contrast to M.A.R., Mr. N had no difficulty comparing the relative magnitude of two numbers; nonetheless he described a year as having 5 seasons, a month as having 15 or 20 days, and a dozen as having 6 or 10 eggs.

Rosemary Varley, Michael Siegal, and their colleagues at the University of Sheffield described a related dissociation between grammatical and mathematical syntax in three patients with diffuse damage to the left perisylvian language area. As expected, all three showed acute aphasia resulting in severe grammatical comprehension and production difficulties (see Chapter 21). However, the patients retained proficiency in mathematical syntax, despite being unable to fluently express or comprehend analogous spoken or written syntax. For example, although the patients understood the words *John, Mary,* and *hit,* they were unable to differentiate between "Mary hit John" and "John hit Mary." They were nevertheless unimpaired at solving mathematical operations of this same sort—easily comprehending, for instance, the difference between 52 – 11 and 11 – 52.

Clinical evidence for the importance of the parietal cortex in number processing comes from a handful of studies that have looked at the neural correlates of **developmental dyscalculia**, a disorder in children defined as a severe impairment in the ability to perform mathematical calculations, despite having a normal IQ. Although studies disagree as to the lateralization of the parietal abnormalities, there is consensus that parietal activity in one or both hemispheres in such patients differs from controls when subjects engage in math problems. In addition, a genetic anomaly known as *Turner's syndrome* has been linked to poor math achievement and may shed light on genetic influences in dyscalculia. Turner's syndrome is a relatively common sex chromosome abnormality in females, occurring in about one in 2500 female births, arising when one (or part of one) of the two X chromosomes normally present in females is missing. Children with Turner's syndrome usually have average intelligence but poor math skills. This poor performance is apparently due to structural and functional abnormalities in the inferior parietal sulcus (**Figure 22.12**). A similar pattern of difficulty with math and abnormalities in this same general brain area has been reported in patients with fragile X syndrome, a much less common genetic disorder characterized by mental retardation and other abnormalities.

Clinical studies also suggest that the mental number line may be more than a metaphor. When patients with unilateral neglect syndrome arising from a lesion of right parietal cortex (see Chapter 12) are tested in a number bisection task (e.g., what is the midpoint of the number interval between 2 and 6?), their answers are significantly right-shifted, as is the case for line bisection (see Figure 12.2A). This parallel between neglect of the left side of space and neglect

(A) Reduced size of the right IPS in TS subjects

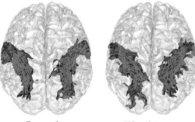

Controls   TS subjects

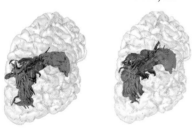

(B) Posterior displacement of central sulcus in TS

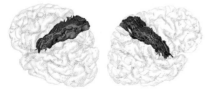

Figure 22.12 Intraparietal sulcus abnormalities in Turner's syndrome. (A) The left and right sulci are smaller and less symmetrical in patients with Turner's syndrome (TS) compared to control subjects. (B) The central sulci (red) in subjects with Turner's syndrome are more posterior than in control subjects (blue). The difference in position may be due to bilateral parietal atrophy. (From Molko et al. 2003.)

of the lower values along a number continuum implies that the mental number line is spatially mapped.

This brief summary of patient studies shows that the parietal cortex is involved in number representation—a conclusion supported by the imaging studies in normal subjects described in the following section.

Neuroimaging studies in normal individuals

As described in several preceding chapters, knowledge about different semantic categories appears to be stored in overlapping but at least partly distinct brain regions. Consistent with this evidence, PET and fMRI studies in normal subjects suggest that parietal regions are recruited for semantic processing of numbers, regardless of the specific number task. For example, when subjects classify a number as odd or even, compare the magnitude of a number to a standard value, or perform numerical subtraction, regions in the left and right intraparietal sulci become active. In contrast, the inferior temporal gyrus is activated when subjects decide whether animals are mammals (see Chapter 21). This result is consistent with studies of patients who have impaired knowledge in different semantic domains, but intact numerical knowledge (discussed earlier).

Neuroimaging studies also show that parietal areas (the horizontal segment of the intraparietal sulcus and/or the posterior superior parietal sulcus) are more active in both hemispheres in estimation and approximation tasks compared to exact calculation tasks, which are associated with activity in the left angular gyrus. The intraparietal sulcus (IPS) is activated by ordinal numerical comparisons or any kind of mental calculation that requires accessing the semantics of numbers. The IPS also shows greater activation for subtraction than for multiplication and addition, consistent with the idea that multiplication and addition facts are more often memorized and therefore more likely to be language-dependent; subtraction, on the other hand, relies more heavily on quantitative calculations.

Neuroimaging studies also show that the IPS represents number irrespective of sensory modality or notational format. For example, Evelyn Eger and colleagues working at Inserm in Paris used an event-related fMRI study and had subjects respond when a target letter, color, or numeral was visually presented (e.g., 2, *B*, or a red square) or when they heard the word for that color, letter, or number (e.g., "two," "be," or "red"). The six targets were presented randomly intermixed with other exemplars of each of the six categories, and neural activity to the targets was assessed. Numbers compared with letters or colors elicited activity bilaterally in the horizontal segment of the IPS. Importantly, there was no difference in IPS activation when numbers were presented visually or as spoken words.

Similarly, another study used an event-related adaptation paradigm to show that the IPS is sensitive to the numerical magnitude of the stimulus represented (e.g., number word or Arabic numeral) but insensitive to notational format. Subjects were required to indicate whether an Arabic numeral or number word represented a value greater or smaller than 5, and they were primed with a symbol in the same or a different format that represented the same or a different value. IPS activity was reduced when the prime was the same magnitude as the target regardless of whether the stimuli were presented in the same or a different format.

Although most research on the neural bases of number representation has examined verbal and symbolic number notations, some recent studies have investigated how the brain encodes numerical magnitude. Manuella Piazza and her colleagues at Inserm found that the horizontal segment of the intraparietal

Figure 22.13 Activity in the intra-parietal sulcus linked with process-ing of numerical quantity. (A) In this fMRI study, these stimuli were used to adapt the brain's response to a given numerosity. On one of every eight trials, deviant stimuli were presented that dif-fered in number from the standard stim-ulus by a ratio of 1.25, 1.5, or 2. (B) Shown in red are the brain regions that responded to these number changes. (C) Brain activation elicited by a change in number was systematically related to the degree to which the novel value deviated from the habituated value. (After Piazza et al. 2004.)

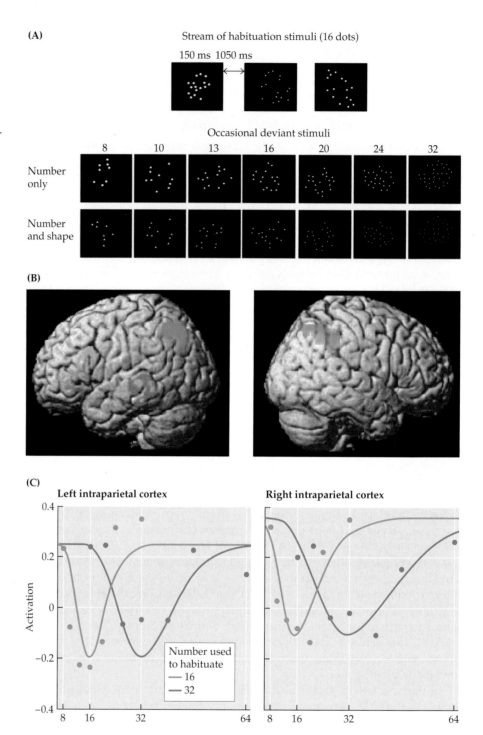

sulcus habituates to a given numerosity, and that recovery of brain activation is modulated by numerical distance from the habituated value (**Figure 22.13**).

Subjects were shown visual arrays that contained a standard number of ele-ments but occasionally presented a deviant number. Activity in the intrapari-etal sulcus decreased with repeated presentation of the standard numerosity. Moreover, recovery of the signal was proportional to the numerical distance between the habituated and deviant numerosity. ERP and fMRI studies indi-cate that by 4 or 5 years of age, children already show neural responses to deviations in number similar to those of adults.

Animal studies of the neural bases of numerical cognition

Until recently, almost nothing was known about the neural basis of numerical ability in non-human animals. In the 1970s, an intriguing report described number-related neural activity in the association cortex of the anesthetized cat, showing that a few neurons fired preferentially in response to a particular ordinal position in a sequence of lights or tones. More recently, Andreas Nieder working at the University of Tübingen and Earl Miller at MIT isolated cells in both the prefrontal cortex and the intraparietal sulcus of macaque monkeys whose activity was associated with the number of elements in a visual display. The monkeys they studied were trained to match two physically different stimuli based on number values of 1 through 5 (**Figure 22.14**).

Cells were maximally responsive to a given numerosity; moreover, the firing rate to other numerosities decreased with numerical distance. Numerical selectivity was also broader for larger numbers, suggesting a possible mechanism for the numerical distance and magnitude effects in behavioral tests described earlier in the chapter. Importantly, parietal neurons were selective for number slightly earlier than were prefrontal neurons, supporting the idea that parietal cortex is the primary region for number processing.

Another type of numerosity neuron has been found in the lateral intraparietal (LIP) region of the macaque monkey by Jamie Roitman and colleagues at Duke University. Rather than responding maximally to specific numerical val-

Figure 22.14 Evidence for number cells in the parietal cortex of the monkey brain. (A) Stimuli like these were used in the task structure illustrated here to test macaques during electrophysiological recording. Monkeys viewed sample arrays and after a short delay were required to release a bar when the test array matched the sample array in number. (B) This lateral view of a monkey brain shows recording sites. Color coding indicates the relative proportion of number-selective cells. AS, arcuate sulcus; CS, central sulcus; IPS, intraparietal sulcus; LF, lateral fissure; LS, lunate sulcus; PS, principal sulcus; STS, superior temporal sulcus. (C) Firing rate is plotted as a function of sample numerosity during the sample period (blue region) for a neuron that was maximally responsive to one item, the numeral 1. (D) Here firing rate is plotted as a function of sample numerosity during the delay period (blue region) for a neuron that was maximally responsive to four items. (After Nieder and Miller 2004.)

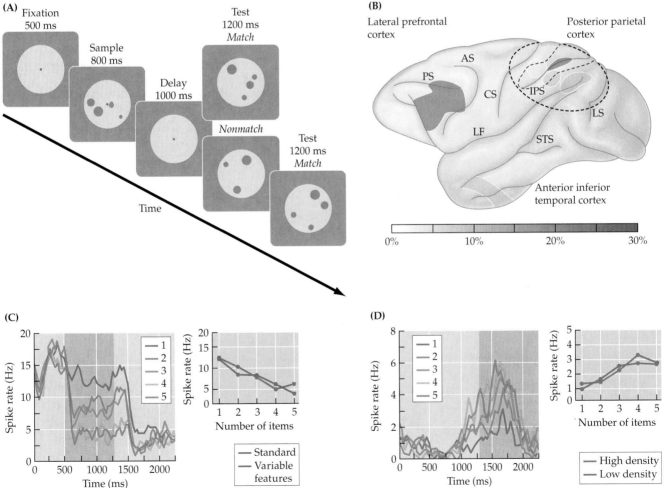

ues, these LIP neurons responded maximally to small or large values and they increased or decreased firing rate with number. Monkeys in this experiment were not trained to make a numerical discrimination. Instead they performed a simple eye movement task while arrays of between 2 and 32 dots were presented briefly in the receptive field of a given LIP neuron. Despite the lack of numerical training, neurons fired monotonically with increasing or decreasing number, and the population was evenly split between neurons that preferred small or large values. One possibility is that LIP neurons function as a spatial integrator for number, numerically summing elements over space and representing number in an ordinal manner.

Summary

1. People and many non-human animal species possess circadian timing mechanisms that operate over the 24-hour light dark cycle and other mechanisms that allow us to track intervals in the milliseconds and seconds to minutes range.

2. While the biological bases of circadian timing are relatively well understood and critically depend on the suprachiasmatic nucleus, the biological basis of interval timing is less well-understood and is currently the subject of much research. The basal ganglia, cerebellum, and prefrontal cortex are all likely key players in interval timing.

3. Adult humans employ explicit language-based algorithms to represent numbers symbolically and to calculate. However, humans also share with many other species a nonverbal system for representing time and number in approximate but highly useful ways.

4. A signature of nonverbal number discrimination in non-human animals and humans is that it is dependent on the ratio between values to be differentiated. Thus an animal that can successfully discriminate 8 versus 12 dots should also easily discriminate 12 versus 18, but not necessarily 12 versus 16 dots.

5. Neuropsychological, neuroimaging, and electrophysiological studies in experimental animals all point to the intraparietal sulcus as a major locus of nonverbal number processing. Many other regions of cortex, such as the angular gyrus, are involved in verbally mediated mathematics. The parietal cortex may also be involved to some degree in timing, although this relationship is less clear.

Additional Reading

Reviews

Brannon, E. M. (2006) The representation of numerical magnitude. *Curr. Opin. Neurobiol.* 16: 222–229.

Buhusi, C. V. and W. H. Meck (2005) What makes us tick? Functional and neural mechanisms of interval timing. *Nat. Rev. Neurosci.* 6: 755–765.

Dehaene, S., N. Molko, L. Cohen and A. J. Wilson (2004) Arithmetic and the brain. *Curr. Opin. Neurobiol.* 14: 218–224.

Feigenson, L., S. Dehaene and E. Spelke (2004) Core systems of number. *Trends Cogn. Sci.* 8: 307–314.

Gelman, R. and B. Butterworth (2005) Number and language: How are they related? *Trends Cogn. Sci.* 9: 6–10.

Gibbon, J., C. Malapani, C. L. Dale and C. R. Gallistel (1997) Toward a neuro-

biology of temporal cognition: Advances and challenges. *Curr. Opin. Neurobiol.* 7: 170–184.

Ivry, R. B. (1996) The representation of temporal information in perception and motor control. *Curr. Opin. Neurobiol.* 6: 851–857.

Piazza, M. and S. Dehaene (2004) From number neurons to mental arithmetic: The cognitive neuroscience of number sense. In *The Cognitive Neurosciences*, 3rd Ed., M. S. E. Gazzaniga (ed.). Cambridge, MA: MIT Press, pp. 865–875.

Spelke, E. S. (2003) What makes us smart? Core knowledge and natural language. In *Language in Mind: Advances in the Study of Language and Thought*, Vol. 8, M. S. E. Gazzaniga (ed.). Cambridge, MA: MIT Press, pp. 277–311.

Important Original Papers

Brannon, E. M. and H. S. Terrace (1998) Ordering of the numerosities 1 to 9 by monkeys. *Science* 282: 746–749.

Buonomano, D. V. and M. M. Merzenich (1995) Temporal information transformed into a spatial code by a neural network with realistic properties. *Science* 267: 1028–1030.

Cantlon, J. and E. M. Brannon (2006) Shared system for ordering small and large numbers in monkeys and humans. *Psychol. Sci.* 17: 401–406.

Eger, E., P. Sterzer, M. O. Russ, A. Giraud and A. Kleinschmidt (2003) A supramodal representation in human intraparietal cortex. *Neuron* 37: 719–726.

Hauser, M. D., P. MacNeilage and M. Ware (1996) Numerical representations in primates. *Proc. Natl. Acad. Sci. USA* 93: 1514–1517.

MECK, W. H. AND R. M. CHURCH (1983) A mode control model of counting and timing processes. *J. Exp. Psychol. Anim. Behav. Process.* 9: 320–334.

MOYER, R. S. AND T. K. LANDAUER (1967) Time required for judgements of numerical inequality. *Nature* 215: 1519–1520.

NIEDER, A. AND E. K. MILLER (2004) A parieto-frontal network for visual numerical information in the monkey. *Proc. Natl. Acad. Sci. USA* 101: 7457–7462.

PIAZZA, M., V. IZARD, P. PINEL, D. LE BIHAN AND S. DEHAENE (2004) Tuning curves for approximate numerosity in the human intraparietal sulcus. *Neuron* 44: 547–555.

PICA, P., C. LEMER, W. IZARD AND S. DEHAENE (2004) Exact and approximate arithmetic in an Amazonian indigene group. *Science* 306: 499–503.

ROITMAN, J., E. M. BRANNON AND M. L. PLATT (2007) Monotonic coding of numerosity in macaque lateral intraparietal area. *PLoS Biol.* 5: e208.

WYNN, K. (1992) Addition and subtraction by human infants. *Nature* 358: 749–750.

XU, F. AND E. SPELKE (2000) Large number discrimination in 6-month-old infants. *Cognition* 74: B1–B11.

Books

BUTTERWORTH, B. (1996) *Mathematical Cognition*, Vol. 1. East Sussex, UK: Psychology Press.

CAMPBELL, J. I. D. (2005) *Handbook of Mathematical Cognition.* New York: Psychology Press.

DEHAENE, S. (1997) *The Number Sense: How the Mind Creates Mathematics.* New York: Oxford University Press.

DUNLAP, J. C., J. J. LOROS AND P. J. DeCOURSEY (2004) *Chronobiology: Biological Timekeeping.* Sunderland, MA: Sinauer.

GELMAN, R. AND C. GALLISTEL (1978) *The Child's Understanding of Number.* Cambridge, MA: Harvard University Press.

MECK, W. H. (2003) *Functional and Neural Mechanisms of Interval Timing.* Boca Raton, FL: CRC Press.

MOORE-EDE, M. C., F. M. SULZMAN AND C. A. FULLER (1982) *The Clocks That Time Us.* Cambridge, MA: Harvard University Press.

UNIT VIII

Principles of Executive Processing

A driver on a dark road slams on his brakes as a deer darts out of the woods. A shopper considers whether to buy a fuel-efficient sedan or a flashy sports car. A player stares across a chessboard at an opponent, anticipating the next move. Though drawn from very different domains of human activity, these examples all reflect the aspect of cognition known as *executive processing*. As the name implies, executive processes perform supervisory or regulatory roles; that is, they modulate the activity of other cognitive processes in a flexible and goal-directed manner.

Executive processes may operate rapidly and largely unconsciously to guide the flow of sensory information or to initiate a motor action, as when a driver encounters an unexpected obstacle. They may require assessing the advantages and disadvantages of different options, as when we decide which car to buy. Or they may involve measured and thoughtful processing, as when we mentally simulate an opponent's strategies in a complex game. Because these control processes often lead to explicit or implicit decisions, the topics of decision making and reasoning are also considered in this unit.

Executive processes are diverse and difficult to categorize. Moreover, they raise broader philosophical questions about what determines human behavior. Half a century ago, these concepts were given relatively short shrift in psychology textbooks, typically being discussed as aspects of "thinking." Over the past two decades, however, executive processes have become recognized as central to many unconscious as well as conscious aspects of cognition, and research into the brain mechanisms underlying executive control has become one of the most active areas of cognitive neuroscience. ■

23

Executive Control Systems

Introduction

Like a busy business executive, the human brain must perform a broad array of complex oversight functions, such as deciding among alternative courses of action, inhibiting irrelevant information while focusing on things of importance, reasoning through complex problems, spurring different components of the whole into action, and planning for the future. However, no single part of the brain—no "homunculus"—can be identified as the neural equivalent of a chief executive. Instead, several interrelated brain systems combine to support flexible and goal-directed control of behavior. Primary among these are regions within the prefrontal cortex. Patients with prefrontal damage are often superficially normal; they can identify objects and sounds, can comprehend and carry on conversations, and can perform motor tasks with dexterity. Yet when faced with real-world challenges, they do poorly. Depending on the location of the damage, they are apathetic and/or lack insight into the consequences of their actions. Although the prefrontal cortex has long been considered critical for executive control, recent studies implicate other brain regions as well, including the posterior parietal cortex and the basal ganglia. Functional neuroimaging, in particular, has provided new information about how different parts of the brain contribute to different aspects of executive control. This chapter presents a general account of executive control and its neural underpinnings; the following two chapters consider more specific applications of executive control—to decision making and reasoning, respectively.

What Is Executive Control?

Central to nearly all definitions of **executive control** is a single idea: that control processes are important for overcoming behaviors that would otherwise be carried out more or less automatically. To use the terminology advanced by neurologist Marsel Mesulam at Northwestern University, in the absence of control processes, behavior is determined by a **default mode** of brain operation; that is, responses are made more or less reflexively to a stimulus or series of stimuli. (Note that the term *default mode* has also been used by Marcus Raichle and his colleagues at Washington University, St. Louis, to describe brain activation that occurs in the absence of an experimental task. Although these two senses of this term are related, the former sense is the focus here.)

Automaticity does not, of course, preclude complexity; for example, we and other animals can learn to execute a complex series of behaviors following a single command (such as "When the conductor gestures, perform Mozart's Piano Concerto No. 20"). Nevertheless, such behavioral series are relatively inflexible, thus, as any music student knows, it is far harder to begin playing a piece in the middle than at the beginning, presumably because the starting context is now less familiar. This default mode of behavior is thought to predominate in animals with limited prefrontal cortices, in human infants with immature frontal lobes, and in adults with prefrontal damage. Similarly, behaviors that entail only well-learned responses can be carried out in the default mode. To overcome the limitations of the default mode, we and many other animals have evolved executive control processes that allow more flexible and dynamic relationships between stimuli and behaviors.

To overcome more automatic processing, several general types of control processes are especially important. The first is **inhibition**, the suppression of an automatic or potentiated behavior that is not appropriate in the current context. Once the automatic behavior is inhibited, other processes may facilitate the selection of and transition to another, more appropriate behavior. For example, when the deer mentioned in the unit introduction appears in the road, the driver must not only inhibit an ongoing behavior but also must engage a new behavior (e.g., braking or swerving). This latter process is called **task switching** (or, when contrasted with inhibition, **initiation**).

Depending on the situation, the person may need to evaluate the relative value of several possible actions, and complex situations often require more than just consideration of past consequences. Thus, the process of **simulation** allows us and other animals to test out courses of actions without suffering their consequences. If simulation suggests that an action would be ineffective or maladaptive, the action can be avoided without its consequences being incurred. As is emphasized throughout this chapter, the prefrontal cortex supports these and related control processes.

Also important for successful behavior is learning what stimuli provide signals to switch from more automatic to controlled processing. Brain systems for reward evaluation (see Chapter 24) track the consequences of behavior to determine which actions lead to desired outcomes. Animals use information about rewards to set goals and to plan for the future. Structures within the **midbrain** and the **basal ganglia** have been implicated in reward evaluation, along with some basic control processes (e.g., building associations between specific stimuli and reward outcomes). Regions along the medial surface of the frontal lobe, most notably the **anterior cingulate cortex** (**ACC**), have been implicated in matching the allocation of control processes to meet current environmental demands. In circumstances that require more control—whether because of new information about rewards or because the task becomes more challenging—activity in this region tends to increase.

Although this perspective on executive control may seem to confound executive control processes with processes associated with other cognitive functions, such as attention and conscious awareness, there are some clear dis-

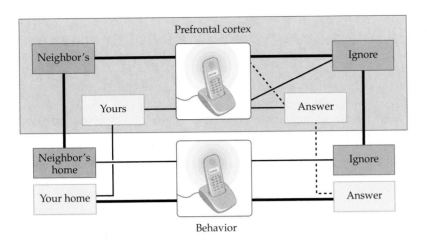

Prefrontal cortex

Neighbor's — Yours — Ignore — Answer

Neighbor's home — Your home — Ignore — Answer

Behavior

Figure 23.1 A general scheme for prefrontal control. In the framework advanced by Miller and Cohen, control processes in prefrontal cortex inhibit or strengthen processing pathways elsewhere in the brain. Thus, when a person hears a phone ringing, there is a strong tendency (indicated here by the thick connections) to answer it, especially at home. However, this behavior is inappropriate in other contexts, such as at a neighbor's house. The prefrontal cortex is postulated to model the current context and possible actions, so that the necessary action can be potentiated (thick lines) and undesirable actions can be inhibited (dashed lines). In this conception, the prefrontal cortex allows information to flow along some paths but not others to facilitate effective behavior. (After Miller and Cohen 2001.)

tinctions. Like attention, control implies directed influence—enhancing neural activity in some brain regions while weakening it in others. However, processes mediating attention act on incoming sensory information or internal representations, whereas executive control processes act on plans for behavior. A useful metaphor for executive control introduced by the neuroscientists Earl Miller at MIT and Jonathan Cohen at Princeton is that of a switch operator who controls the pattern of tracks in a busy railroad yard (**Figure 23.1**). In many circumstances, especially when a single train travels along frequently used tracks, no action from the operator is required. But when two trains are on a collision course, the operator must set up a new pattern of tracks to maximize the efficiency and success of what might follow. Miller and Cohen suggest that executive control processes in prefrontal cortex bias patterns of information flow in other brain regions, in order to meet immediate demands and achieve future goals.

Note that nothing in this metaphor or in any other description of control requires that control be exerted consciously. Of course, some aspects of executive control, such as reasoning, entail conscious experience by definition, but most control processes, even some that are quite complex, occur unconsciously.

Early Evidence for the Importance of Prefrontal Cortex in Executive Control

The localization of executive control systems in the brain has a checkered history. At the beginning of the nineteenth century, many scientists believed that the frontal lobes were critical for controlling behavior and for higher cognitive functions generally. However, such beliefs were based on very limited evidence, such as the gross anatomical fact that the frontal lobes are far more developed in humans and great apes than in other mammals (**Box 23A**).

By studying the skulls of different species and individual humans, the German physician and anatomist Franz Gall went even further, speculating that the brain comprised 27 different faculties, or "organs," that could be discerned by the way they had shaped the surface features of the skull—a theoretical framework called **phrenology**. Although these ideas were widely popular at the time, they raised immediate skepticism from many of Gall's scientific contemporaries. These speculations did, however, have two salutary effects. They encouraged exploration of how different cognitive processes are localized in the brain and suggested that higher cognitive functions might be specifically localized in the frontal lobes.

■ BOX 23A Comparative Anatomy of the Prefrontal Cortex

Despite some unsavory uses, the measurement of brain size across species remains an important tool in cognitive neuroscience. Investigators recognized early on that overall brain size is a poor index of intelligence or other cognitive functions. The average adult human brain, for example, is only about a fourth as large as the brain of an adult elephant, and the brains of orangutans and cows are of roughly similar size. Most research has thus focused on the relative size of specific regions. With respect to the prefrontal cortex, there are clear differences across a range of mammals. The early-twentieth-century German physiologist and anatomist Korbinian Brodmann estimated that only 7 percent of the dog's cortex, and less than 4 percent of the cat's, is prefrontal. In contrast, Brodmann found that the prefrontal cortex constitutes about 10 percent of total brain volume in monkeys (e.g., gibbon, macaque), 20 percent in the great apes (e.g., chimpanzee), and 30 percent in humans.

Although this ranking is plausible, given what is known about the relative capabilities of these species, contemporary researchers have modified Brodmann's original estimates. The neuroanatomist Katerina Semendeferi and her colleagues at UC San Diego and at the University of Iowa used structural MRI to measure the frontal lobes in a wide variety of primate species. They found that the proportional size of the frontal lobes in humans is actually about the same as that in great apes, occupying about 35 percent of the brain volume. Nor were there any significant differences between humans and other great apes in the extent of the prefrontal cortex, defined as the cortex anterior to the precentral sulcus. In all the species tested, the prefrontal cortex was 26 to

(A) Comparative anatomy of the prefrontal cortex. Not only is absolute brain size relatively greater in primates compared to other mammals, but there is also a disproportionate increase in the size of the prefrontal cortex (blue). The porpoise brain is provided for size comparison; its prefrontal cortex is not indicated because there are no clear homologies between the prefrontal cortices of primates and cetaceans.

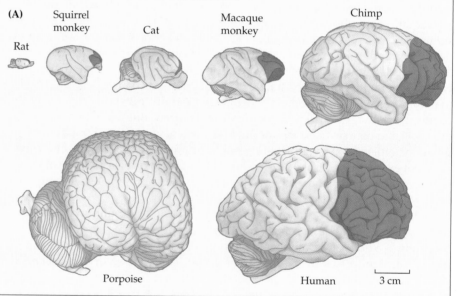

As described in Chapter 21, the seminal work on cortical localization came from the human clinical-pathological correlations made by neurologists such as Broca and Wernicke. At about the same time, however, experimental physiologists began to study cortical localization with direct methods in animals. The first studies of the frontal lobes in an animal were conducted by the German physiologist Eduard Hitzig and his colleague Gustav Fritsch in the late 1860s and provided conclusive evidence that the more posterior portions of the frontal lobes are associated with motor function. When these regions were stimulated electrically in a dog, the animal moved its limbs on the opposite side.

These investigators also found that damage to the posterior frontal lobe led to a lack of control over motor movements. Animals with such damage could walk normally, but they had reduced voluntary control over their movements. In contrast, damage to the anterior frontal lobes caused neither paralysis nor any obvious sensory deficits; moreover, electrical stimulation evoked no spontaneous activity. Hitzig and Fritsch therefore speculated that the anterior frontal lobes are associated with higher cognition rather than sensation or

(B) Prefrontal cortex scaling according to Brodmann (1912)

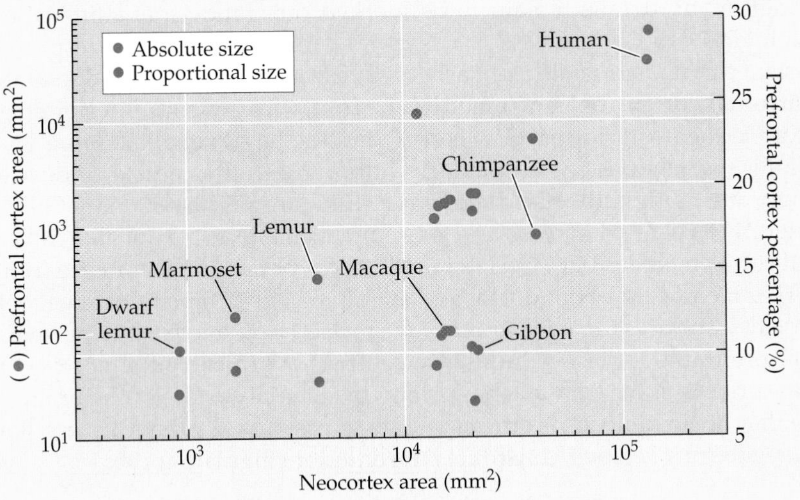

Absolute size
Proportional size
Human
Chimpanzee
Lemur
Marmoset
Macaque
Dwarf lemur
Gibbon
(●) Prefrontal cortex area (mm²)
Neocortex area (mm²)
Prefrontal cortex percentage (%)

(C) Frontal lobe scaling according to Semendeferi et al. (1997, 2002)

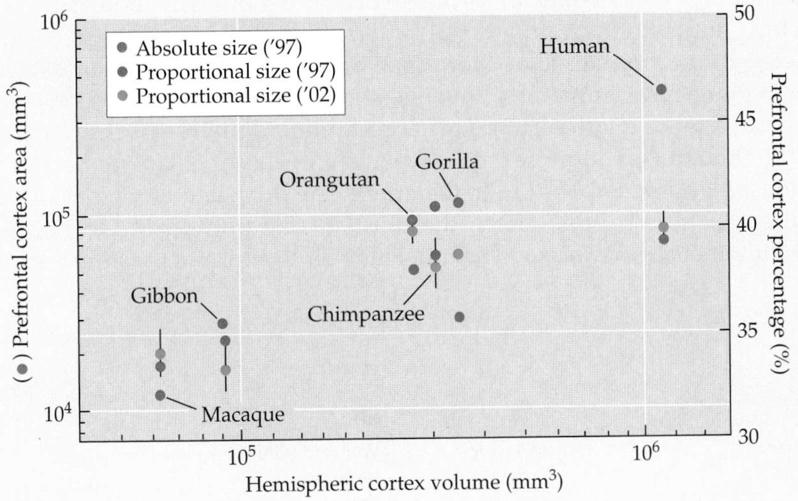

Absolute size ('97)
Proportional size ('97)
Proportional size ('02)
Human
Gorilla
Orangutan
Gibbon
Chimpanzee
Macaque
(●) Prefrontal cortex area (mm³)
Hemispheric cortex volume (mm³)
Prefrontal cortex percentage (%)

(B) The prefrontal cortex is particularly well developed in primates. Largely because of Brodmann's work, it was thought that the proportional size of the prefrontal cortex was greater in humans than in other great apes. (C) More recent studies indicate that the frontal lobes and the prefrontal cortex occupy about the same proportion of overall brain volume in great apes and humans. (B after Brodmann 1912; C after Semendeferi et al. 1997, 2002.)

33 percent of total brain volume. Although the proportion of prefrontal cortex generally tracks cognitive competence across mammals, these modern results indicate that the relative size of the frontal lobes does not, by itself, explain the different cognitive capabilities of humans and other great apes.

References

Brodmann, K. (1912) Neue Ergebnisse über die vergleichende histologische Lokalisation der Grosshirnrinde mit besonderer Berücksichtigung des Stirnhirns. *Anat. Anzeiger* 41: 157–216.

Semendeferi, K., H. Damasio, R. Frank and G. W. Van Hoesen (1997) The evolution of the frontal lobes: A volumetric analysis based on three-dimensional reconstructions of magnetic resonance scans of human and ape brains. *J. Hum. Evol.* 32: 375–388.

Semendeferi, K., A. Lu, N. Schenker and H. Damasio (2002) Humans and great apes share a large frontal cortex. *Nat. Neurosci.* 5: 272–276.

Striedter, G. F. (2005) *Principles of Brain Evolution.* Sunderland, MA: Sinauer.

motor control. This suggestion was confirmed in the 1870s by the British physiologist David Ferrier, who achieved similar results by removing the anterior frontal lobe in monkeys.

This experimental approach was extended and refined by the Italian physiologist Leonardo Bianchi around the start of the twentieth century. Bianchi created various prefrontal lesions and followed up with careful observations of behavior. He found that bilateral prefrontal damage caused a failure to recognize known objects, an inability to use past experience to guide behavior, deficits in initiative, loss of higher emotions, and a lack of coherent behavior. He also made the important observation that unilateral damage was insufficient to cause these behavioral changes. These and other early studies provided the first clear evidence that the executive control of behavior is supported primarily by the prefrontal cortex—that is, by those parts of the frontal lobes anterior to the motor and premotor regions. Although the early observations of Hitzig, Fritsch, Ferrier, and Bianchi remain valid today, more recent research has shown that other brain regions play an important part in executive control.

A Modern Anatomy of Executive Control

Although many details remain to be worked out, modern anatomical and physiological studies indicate that several brain structures are especially important for mediating different aspects of executive control: the **dorsolateral prefrontal cortex**, the **ventromedial prefrontal cortex**, the anterior cingulate cortex, the **posterior parietal cortex**, and the basal ganglia (**Figure 23.2**). The latter two regions are particularly important in the context of decision making; thus, although introduced here, they are discussed more fully in Chapter 24. As defined in these and subsequent chapters, the dorsolateral prefrontal cortex includes both the lateral and the superior surfaces of the frontal lobes (i.e., it comprises both dorsal and lateral regions). Some researchers refer to these two surfaces together as *lateral prefrontal cortex*. In contrast, the ventromedial prefrontal cortex includes the ventral (or **orbitofrontal cortex**) and medial surfaces of the frontal lobes. Along the medial surface of the brain just above the corpus callosum is the cingulate gyrus, whose anterior part, along with neighboring regions, constitutes the anterior cingulate cortex.

Connectivity of executive control systems

The anatomical connections of various cortical regions are good (although imperfect) indicators of functional interactions—a rule that is clearly expressed in the frontal lobes. More than any other part of the cortex, prefrontal regions have numerous, diverse, and bidirectional connections with other brain regions (**Figure 23.3**). The largest input to prefrontal cortex comes from the **thalamus**, and more than 80 percent of these thalamic fibers arise from the *mediodorsal nucleus* of the thalamus. The dorsolateral regions of prefrontal cortex receive input from the most medial portion of the nucleus, called the *pars magnocellularis*. This nucleus relays information from various

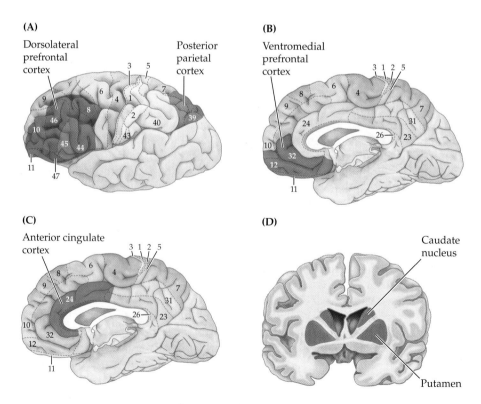

Figure 23.2 Major brain regions that support executive control. The brain regions that mediate executive control are (A) the dorsolateral prefrontal cortex and posterior parietal cortex; (B) the ventromedial prefrontal cortex; (C) the anterior cingulate cortex; and (D) the basal ganglia. Corresponding Brodmann areas are indicated by numbers.

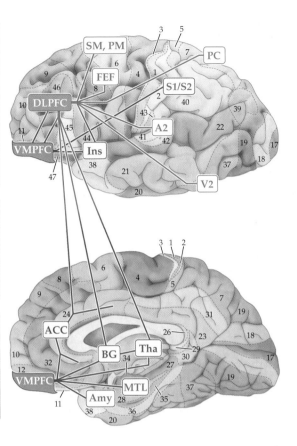

Dorsolateral Prefrontal Cortex	
SM:	Supplementary motor cortex
PM:	Premotor cortex
FEF:	Frontal eye fields
PC:	Parietal cortex
V2:	Secondary visual cortex
A2:	Secondary auditory cortex

Ventromedial Prefrontal Cortex	
Amy:	Amygdala
MTL:	Medial temporal lobe
S1/S2:	Primary and secondary somatosensory cortices

Shared Regions of Connectivity	
Tha:	Thalamus
BG:	Basal ganglia
ACC:	Anterior cingulate cortex
Ins:	Insular cortex

Figure 23.3 Connectivity of the prefrontal cortex. Neurons in the prefrontal cortex project to and receive input from secondary sensory cortices, motor preparatory structures, and the parietal cortex. This schematic diagram shows some of the major connections for dorsolateral prefrontal cortex (DLPFC) and ventromedial prefrontal cortex (VMPFC). All indicated connections are bidirectional, with the important exception of a unidirectional projection from DLPFC to the basal ganglia (which projects back to DLPFC via the thalamus).

parts of the brain, including the substantia nigra, cerebellum, globus pallidus, and ventral tegmental area—all regions that are important for motor control and reward (see Chapter 24). Ventromedial regions of prefrontal cortex receive input from the *pars parvocellularis* of the mediodorsal nucleus, which receives input from brain regions associated with arousal and emotion, including the amygdala. A third, much smaller and more lateral part of the mediodorsal nucleus, called the *pars paralamellaris*, projects to the frontal eye fields (see Chapter 9), which are not usually considered part of the prefrontal cortex. A final source of thalamic input to prefrontal cortex is the pulvinar, a nucleus that also has prominent projections to parietal cortex.

In addition to these direct projections from (and indirect projections via) the thalamus, prefrontal cortex is a target of fibers from many other cortical and subcortical regions. The main sources of these projections are the secondary rather than primary sensory cortices. For example, the inferior temporal cortex, which supports higher-level object processing (see Chapter 5), projects to Brodmann area 46 within the dorsolateral prefrontal cortex. The primary visual cortex, in contrast, has no direct projections to prefrontal cortex. The one notable exception to the rule that prefrontal cortex receives projections from only secondary sensory cortices is the orbitofrontal cortex, which receives projections from primary taste, olfactory, and somatosensory cortices. Other sources of projections include the posterior parietal cortex, which is heavily interconnected with dorsolateral prefrontal cortex; the hippocampus, which projects throughout prefrontal cortex; the amygdala, which projects primarily to ventromedial prefrontal regions; and the ventral tegmental area of the midbrain, which also projects primarily to ventromedial regions.

Like many other regions of cortex, the prefrontal cortex sends efferent fibers to many of the same regions from which it receives afferents. Thus, secondary (but not primary) sensory regions receive substantial prefrontal input. The amygdala and other limbic areas are other targets of prefrontal projections, especially from ventromedial prefrontal regions. The prefrontal cortex is also notable because it is the only region of the cerebral cortex that has direct projections to the hypothalamus. Although there are few direct projections from prefrontal cortex to the hippocampus, there are substantial indirect projections to that region via the neighboring entorhinal cortex. Exceptions to this bidirectionality are the basal ganglia, which are a target of prefrontal cortex but connect back to the prefrontal cortex only indirectly via the substantia nigra and thalamus. This arrangement may reflect the role of the basal ganglia in the control of motor output, since it is similar to the pathways from prefrontal cortex to premotor regions (see Chapter 9). The prefrontal cortex does not have significant projections to primary motor cortex.

In summary, the broad interconnectivity of executive control systems is consistent with the diversity of processes that such control requires. Understanding how these regions interact to guide complex behaviors remains a major challenge. The following sections consider in turn how these different brain regions contribute to specific aspects of executive control.

Dorsolateral Prefrontal Control Systems

Evidence about the specific role of the dorsolateral part of the prefrontal cortex in executive control comes from both patient and neuroimaging studies in normal subjects. Together, these studies indicate that the dorsolateral prefrontal cortex supports at least three executive control processes: (1) initiating and shifting behavior; (2) inhibiting behavior; and (3) simulating behavioral consequences. None of these processes, however, are exclusive to this region. Inhibition, in particular, seems to be a general function of all prefrontal cortical areas. Nor are these processes necessarily unitary. Simulation, for instance, may include both creating mental models for future events and abstracting core meanings from complex situations. Such caveats notwithstanding, these three control processes rely heavily on dorsolateral prefrontal cortex.

Initiating and shifting behavior

Damage to the lateral frontal lobes typically impairs the ability of an individual to initiate and change actions, motor movements, and mental plans. A visible consequence of initiation impairments is *apathy*; like Hitzig's dogs and Ferrier's monkeys, human patients with lateral prefrontal damage lose interest in the world around them. Typically they show little spontaneity of thought or action, even if verbal and motor abilities are spared; and they may withdraw from society, losing contact with friends and family. This reclusiveness is the result of not only blunted affect, but also a loss of interest in maintaining social relationships. Furthermore, when questioned about these changes in personality and lifestyle, patients with lateral prefrontal damage show little concern. They may know that they should feel sad following the loss of a job or of a loved one, but they do not experience the corresponding emotion. Together, this constellation of deficits and symptoms is called the *dorsolateral prefrontal syndrome* or **frontal dysexecutive syndrome**.

Of course, different individuals may exhibit some but not all of these impairments. For example, motor deficits are characteristic in the clinical condition known as **abulia**, which is characterized by lethargy and quiet withdrawal. Abulia can result from strokes or lesions that damage lateral aspects of the frontal lobes but spare ventromedial aspects. Patients with this condition can perform movements or answer questions in response to commands, but they act slowly and are easily distracted. They also have difficulty sustaining attention or continuing a motor action for an extended period of time (e.g., dealing with the instruction to "stick out your tongue for 20 seconds"). As in the more general dysexecutive syndrome, patients with abulia are apathetic about the surrounding environment and about their future.

Neuroimaging studies have also implicated the dorsolateral prefrontal cortex in the selection of an appropriate action in response to a stimulus. In particular, two sites on the surface of the lateral frontal lobe are activated in such circumstances—one anterior and one posterior (**Figure 23.4**). The anterior middle frontal gyrus (Brodmann area 46) is activated when subjects must initiate or shift behavior (activation in this region is also found when subjects must inhibit a prepotent response, as described in the following section). A second site at the intersection of the inferior frontal sulcus and the inferior precentral sulcus has been implicated in establishing mappings between sensory stimuli and the required tasks (i.e., task-specific preparation for behavior). One common paradigm in cognitive studies is task switching, in which the rules for behavior change in the middle of the experiment. Neuroimaging studies that involve task switching often are associated with activation in the dorsolateral prefrontal cortex, typically lateralized to the right hemisphere. Confirming these results, damage to dorsolateral prefrontal cortex impairs task switching, with performance worsening as the extent of damage increases.

Even these simple processes, however, involve brain regions other than and in addition to the dorsolateral prefrontal cortex. For example, when an experimental task involves initiating or shifting behavior, neuroimaging data often reveal coactivation of dorsolateral prefrontal and posterior parietal cortices.

Inhibiting behavior

Although discussed separately, initiation and inhibition are really complementary aspects of executive control. *Initiation* is the selection of desired information or behavior; *inhibition* is the suppression of unimportant or distracting information or behavior. In both cases, the strength of some processes is altered relative to others in order to effect change. Behavioral research suggests that there are at least three forms of inhibition: (1) restraining potentiated behaviors; (2) preventing irrelevant information from interfering with other processing; and (3) removing irrelevant information from working memory.

In keeping with these ideas about inhibition, a widely used test of executive function is the **Wisconsin Card Sorting Test**. The test requires participants to learn rules for classifying a deck of cards, and then to inhibit those rules when the evidence for the validity of the rules unexpectedly changes (**Figure 23.5**). Each card in the deck contains one to four simple shapes (e.g., circles, stars, triangles, or crosses), all of the same color (e.g., red, green, yellow, or blue). The subject's task is to sort the cards into piles according to one of the three stimulus attributes—number, shape, or color. For example, suppose that the first card in the deck has one yellow star. The subject might sort it according to its shape (the star). If feedback reveals that sorting to be incorrect, the participant might try to sort the next card according to its color. Using trial and error, subjects can determine the correct rule and begin to sort the cards correctly. Unbeknownst to the subject, however, after a predetermined number of consecutive correctly sorted cards, the sorting rule changes. Individuals with an intact prefrontal cortex quickly recognize this change and adjust their sorting to the new rule.

As first reported by the Canadian neuropsychologist Brenda Milner in 1963, patients with prefrontal damage continue to use the previously valid rule, despite receiving negative feedback. This persistence of behavior is known as **perseveration**, which is considered a hallmark of impaired prefrontal function. Perseveration does not simply reflect an inability to switch between behavioral

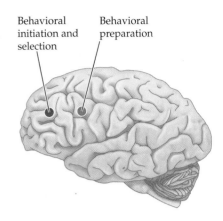

Figure 23.4 Activation of the dorsolateral prefrontal cortex in the initiation and selection of behavior. Many fMRI studies have found that preparation behaviors and initiation/selection behaviors are supported by distinct regions within dorsolateral prefrontal cortex.

Figure 23.5 The Wisconsin Card Sorting Test. This test uses a deck of cards whose faces differ in color, shape, and number of the symbols depicted. On each trial, the subject is given a "rule" by which they sort each card into one of four piles. The correct rule periodically changes without warning during the course of the trial, and patients with prefrontal damage are often poor at inhibiting the previously valid rule.

rules; if the previously valid rule is unavailable—for example, if all the cards now share the same color—prefrontal patients learn the new rule at the same rate as neurologically normal individuals. Thus, perseveration reflects difficulty inhibiting the previous rule, even when it is no longer valid.

Although perseverative behavior is the most frequently discussed consequence of prefrontal damage in this paradigm, it is not the only effect. Prefrontal patients also make more random errors on the Wisconsin Card Sorting Test (i.e., not using either the previous or current response rules), presumably because of an increased susceptibility to distraction. Furthermore, some studies suggest that damage to other brain regions, including the medial prefrontal cortex and the temporal lobe, can also cause perseverative behavior.

Using both electrophysiological and behavioral methods, Robert Knight and colleagues at UC Berkeley have confirmed that patients with dorsolateral prefrontal damage have difficulty inhibiting task-irrelevant sensory information. At early stages of neural processing, this deficiency is evident as increased amplitude—or **disinhibition**—of evoked scalp potentials generated by the primary sensory cortices. One consequence of sensory disinhibition may be that irrelevant information is not effectively filtered, impairing the ability of prefrontal patients to keep information "online" in the presence of distraction. The importance of prefrontal cortex for suppressing distracting information is also apparent in a delayed match-to-sample task (see Box 16A for a discussion of this paradigm). In control trials carried out by Knight's group, each subject heard a single tone, maintained that tone in working memory over a delay of a few seconds, and then indicated whether a second tone matched the first. Despite having normal working memory, prefrontal patients make many more errors when the delay includes distracting auditory stimuli than when no distraction is present; they are also more impaired by distraction than are patients with damage in other brain regions.

Functional neuroimaging studies also show that dorsolateral prefrontal cortex is activated when people must unexpectedly inhibit a previously potentiated behavior (**Figure 23.6**). For example, in the oddball task, subjects attend to a continuous sequence of stimuli, most of which require one response (e.g., pressing a button with the left hand). On a fraction of trials, typically about 5 to 10 percent, a target stimulus appears that requires inhibition of the standard response and selection of a different response (e.g., pressing a button with the right hand). As shown first by Gregory McCarthy and his colleagues at Yale University using fMRI, the oddball stimuli evoke activation in dorsolateral prefrontal cortex, typically in Brodmann area 46, as well as in the parietal cortex.

Figure 23.6 Dorsolateral prefrontal activation when subjects must inhibit a potentiated response. Subjects were presented with a random sequence of two stimuli, each requiring a different response; short-term patterns in that sequence influence behavior and brain activation. (A) For the sample sequence shown here, subjects were instructed to press one button when a circle was presented and a second button when a square was presented. (B,C) Regions within lateral prefrontal cortex were more active in response to events in the sequence that violated repeating patterns (B) and even to events that violated alternating patterns (C). This outcome demonstrates the effect of context on control processes in prefrontal cortex. (From Huettel et al. 2002.)

(A)

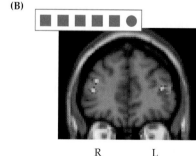

(B)

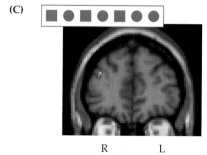

(C)

The converse of the oddball task is the go/no-go task, which requires subjects to respond to most stimuli ("go"), but to inhibit responding to particular infrequently presented stimuli ("no go"). Like the target stimuli in the oddball task, the no-go stimuli evoke activation in the dorsolateral prefrontal and parietal cortices. Some brain disorders are associated with deficits in this form of inhibitory control. In particular, patients with **schizophrenia** perform normally on go trials, but are greatly impaired on no-go trials. These behavioral impairments are accompanied by abnormal ERP and fMRI responses, suggesting a frontal lobe deficit in schizophrenia. In a *stop-signal task*, participants respond to stimuli whenever they are presented but must inhibit those responses when a signal to stop is presented shortly thereafter. Patients with damage to the posterior inferior frontal cortex (Brodmann area 44) in the right hemisphere, but not those with damage to other prefrontal regions, have difficulty inhibiting their responses following the signal to stop. Similar problems are observed in patients with impulse control disorders, such as **attention deficit hyperactivity disorder** (**ADHD**).

Simulating behavioral consequences

The ability to create mental models of the world around us has long been championed as fundamental (and potentially unique) to human cognition. The German neuropsychologist Kurt Goldstein argued in the early twentieth century that this process, which he called **abstraction**, is the fundamental phenomenon in executive control. Writing with Martin Scheerer, Goldstein noted that the loss of abstraction causes a variety of deficits in executive control:

> What [frontal damage] affects and modifies is the *way of manipulating and operating with ideas and thoughts*. Thoughts do, however, arise but can become effective only in a concrete way. Just as the patient cannot deal with outer world objects in an abstract manner, he has to deal with ideas simply as "things" … This lack of abstract frame of reference holds also for the patient's inner experiences; it manifests itself in his inability to arouse and organize, to direct and hold in check ideas or feelings by conscious volition.
>
> K. GOLDSTEIN AND M. SCHEERER (1941)
> (EMPHASIS IN ORIGINAL)

The force of this argument is apparent in the abstraction deficits seen in many patients with prefrontal damage. For example, Goldstein describes a patient who is asked simply to repeat the sentence "The snow is black." The patient tells the interviewer that he cannot repeat that sentence, because it is untrue. Only after the experimenter explains that sentences can be spoken even if false does the patient repeat the sentence but the sentence is immediately followed by the disclaimer "No, the snow is white." The same patient would not repeat the phrase "the sun is shining" when the sun was hidden behind clouds. More generally, when presented with pictures that tell a story, patients with prefrontal damage are often unable to describe what is represented. They also give literal responses when asked to interpret simple proverbs. For instance, when given the proverb "People who live in glass houses should not throw stones," one frontal lobe patient explained the sense of the metaphor to be "Otherwise they will break the walls around them."

Simulation deficits are also evident in tasks that require planning or processing the future consequences of actions. Commonly used to test this aspect of executive function are the Tower of London and Tower of Hanoi manipulation puzzles (**Figure 23.7**). In these puzzles, subjects view a starting configuration of balls stacked on rods and must move one ball at a time to reach a goal configuration. To solve the puzzle efficiently, the subject must simulate the consequences of a series of moves: "If I move the red ball to the right pole, then I will be able to

Figure 23.7 Testing executive function with the Tower of London puzzle. (A) In this puzzle, subjects must determine mentally the fewest number of moves required to transform one arrangement of colored elements (e.g., all stacked on one of a set of posts, as above) to a different arrangement (below). (B) Patients with damage to the left anterior frontal lobe perform much more poorly at this task than normal subjects do, especially when the puzzles are more complex. (After Shallice 1982.)

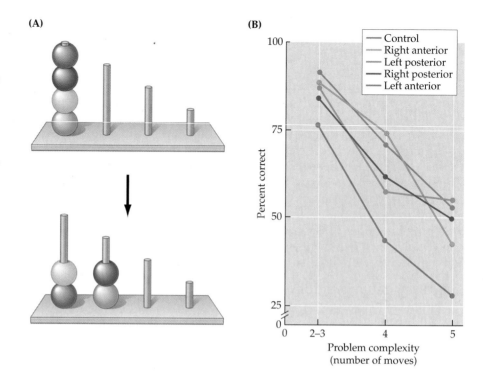

move the green ball to the center pole. That will free up the blue ball …" As Timothy Shallice and his colleagues at University College London have shown, patients with prefrontal damage—especially of the left hemisphere—have difficulty with these puzzles, reflecting their deficits in planning into the future.

A central feature of abstraction is the ability to recognize and create rules for behavior that generalize across a range of triggering stimuli. Single-unit electrophysiology in non-human primates has provided evidence that prefrontal cortex neurons may encode such abstract rules. In one such study, Jonathan Wallis, Earl Miller, and their colleagues trained monkeys to associate sets of cues with particular behavioral rules (**Figure 23.8**). On each trial, a visual stimulus and a cue (e.g., an auditory tone) were presented simultaneously. The cue indicated whether a matching or a nonmatching rule was active on that trial. About 2 seconds later a second stimulus was presented. If the second stimulus was consistent with the rule, then the monkey had been trained to respond; if not, the monkey was trained to respond to a third stimulus presented immediately afterward. The result was that neurons in prefrontal cortex behaved as if they were selective for particular rules, independent of the cues signaling which rule to follow and of the stimuli on which the rules acted.

Rule-selective neurons were found throughout prefrontal cortex, most prevalently along the principal sulcus in lateral prefrontal cortex. Other studies indicated that neurons in premotor cortex (see Chapter 9) also exhibit rule selectivity, and they do so even earlier after cue presentation. These basic findings have since been replicated with fMRI in human subjects. Prefrontal and premotor regions may thus act together to support the coding and execution of behavioral rules.

In sum, the abilities to simulate the consequences of future actions and to abstract rules for actions allow behavior to be modified flexibly depending on context. This flexibility is mediated, in large part, by dorsolateral prefrontal cortex. As discussed in Chapter 25, other aspects of abstract thought are specifically supported by the most anterior part of the frontal lobes, the **frontopolar cortex**.

(A) Matching rule

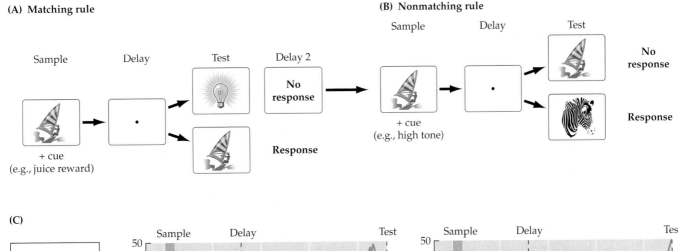

(B) Nonmatching rule

(C)

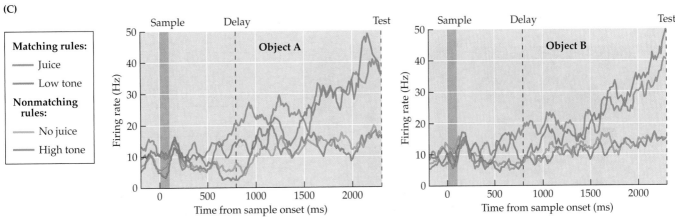

Matching rules:
—— Juice
—— Low tone
Nonmatching rules:
—— No juice
—— High tone

Figure 23.8 Evidence for rule specificity in prefrontal cortex. Monkeys were trained to follow particular rules—either matching rules (A) or nonmatching rules (B)—that varied according to a sensory cue (e.g., a juice reward). The experimenters recorded from neurons in the lateral prefrontal cortex. Some neurons exhibited increased activity to particular rules, regardless of what picture was presented as the sample or what cue was used to signify the rule. (C) Data from a neuron whose firing rate increased when the cue indicated a match-to-sample trial, but whose firing rate remained low on non-match-to-sample trials. Each line indicates a different rule cue. (After Wallis et al. 2001.)

Ventromedial Prefrontal Control Systems

In contrast to the dorsolateral prefrontal cortex, ventromedial prefrontal cortex is important for adhering to rules of behavior—in particular, those that indicate how to interact appropriately with others and with objects in the environment. The most salient ventromedial control process is inhibition, especially in the adherence to well-learned rules for behavior. Thus, the absence of ventromedial control often results in socially inappropriate behavior and/or dependency on information from the immediate sensory environment (**Box 23B**). Ventromedial prefrontal cortex is also important for linking behaviors to consequential rewards or punishments.

Inhibition of socially inappropriate behavior

Bilateral damage to ventral and medial portions of the frontal lobe gives rise to what has been termed **frontal disinhibition syndrome**. Patients with this syndrome, like dysexecutive syndrome patients, perform normally on many neuropsychological tests. Moreover, they tend to perform normally on tests of response selection and working memory (unlike dysexecutive syndrome patients). Nonetheless, their lives outside of the laboratory are often chaotic. Patients with disinhibition syndrome often exhibit constant movement not channeled toward productive activities, and they may be euphoric or manic with an abnormal sense of humor. They may laugh at inappropriate times in simple social situations, fail to respond to normal social cues, or reveal embarrassing personal information. Their outward expressiveness stands in sharp contrast to the quietness and apathy associated with dorsolateral prefrontal damage.

■ BOX 23B Environmental Dependency Syndrome

In the mid 1980s, the French neurologist François Lhermitte identified a set of behaviors associated with damage to the ventromedial prefrontal cortex, especially the anterior and medial parts of the frontal lobe. Lhermitte was an unusual clinician in that he made a point of observing his patients in complex, open-ended interviews and real-world situations. He found that patients with ventromedial prefrontal damage, but not those with damage to other brain regions, behaved as if they were driven primarily by the external social and other stimuli that were immediately available.

Two types of atypical behaviors were apparent in Lhermitte's patients, whom he described as having an *environmental dependency syndrome*. The first was *imitation behavior*. If, for example, the interviewer unexpectedly touched his nose with his thumb, the patients did the same, touching their own noses. Imitation was evident both for physical movements such as common hand gestures or changes in body posture, and for actions with objects, such as drawing, combing hair, or chewing on a pencil. Imitation also extended to vocalizations like singing or speaking simple phrases. Most such patients imitated the interviewer from the outset, and continued to do so even after being told to stop. When their behavior was questioned, patients reported feeling compelled to imitate. Lhermitte tested many neurologically normal subjects in a

(A)

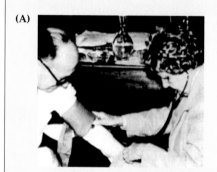

Overdependence on immediate sensory cues to guide behavior after damage to the ventromedial prefrontal lobe. The patient in (A) was brought into a room where several pieces of medical equipment lay on a table. Without prompting, she picked up the equipment and began examining the doctor.

Underlying this behavior is a generalized failure to appreciate how one's own actions are viewed by other people. In severe cases, patients with disinhibition syndrome can be argumentative, profane, aggressive, violent, and/or unable to control sexual impulses. Their behavior becomes self-indulgent and directed toward the desires of the moment, even as family responsibilities, work demands, and future plans languish. All the while, these patients show a lack of insight. Even when they recognize that their behavior is self-destructive, they are neither concerned about its consequences nor motivated to seek a solution.

Antonio Damasio and his co-workers, formerly at the University of Iowa, have called the most severe form of frontal disinhibition syndrome **acquired sociopathy**. Like congenital sociopathy (now part of antisocial personality disorder in the standard manual of psychiatric diagnosis, the DSM-IV), people with acquired sociopathy have blunted emotional affect punctuated by extreme emotional outbursts; make poor decisions, especially in social situations; and have difficulty interacting with others. However, there are differences between acquired and congenital sociopathy. Patients with acquired sociopathy can state the rules for reasonable behavior and can distinguish good actions from bad, even if their impulsivity leads them to select the latter. Similarly, they feel remorse for their actions, although that remorse may not be followed by behavioral change. Patients with congenital sociopathy, in contrast, have difficulty expressing the reasoning behind social rules, and they rationalize the consequences of their actions (especially the consequences for others); moreover, their behavior is goal-directed rather than impulsive, and they are rarely remorseful.

One explanation of these differences is that ventromedial prefrontal damage impairs social behavior, but not necessarily the cognitive appreciation of rules

(B)

When on a social visit to the apartment of his doctor, the patient in (B) encountered a picture that was lying on the floor unhung. He grabbed a nearby hammer and nailed a bracket into the wall to hang the painting. (Photos from Lhermitte 1986.)

similar fashion, who, not surprisingly, showed no such imitation (although many were amused by his actions).

The second aspect of the environmental dependency syndrome observed by Lhermitte was what he called *utilization behavior*, referring to an abnormal reliance on immediate environmental stimuli to trigger behavior (see examples in Figures A and B). For instance, if a glass and pitcher were placed on a table, patients might repeatedly pour water into the glass and drink it, whether or not they were thirsty. Utilization behavior was present in about half of the patients with imitation behavior, and can be considered a more severe expression of the same underlying deficit.

Patients with environmental dependency syndrome, like those with other frontal lobe syndromes, lack insight into the causes and consequences of their actions. Lhermitte suggested that, because such patients do not initiate actions of their own accord, their behavior is excessively determined by social or environmental cues. The patients simply perform whatever actions are most strongly associated with an object or stimulus in the local environment, much like the patient shown in Figure B who, when he sees a hammer, drives a nail.

References

LHERMITTE, F., B. PILLON AND M. SERDARU (1986) Human autonomy and the frontal lobes. Part I: Imitation and utilization behavior: A neuropsychological study of 75 patients. *Ann. Neurol.* 19: 326–334.

LHERMITTE, F. (1986) Human autonomy and the frontal lobes. Part II: Patient behavior in complex and social situations: The "environmental dependency syndrome." *Ann. Neurol.* 19: 335–343.

---

for behavior that were established during development. Clinical and neuropsychological studies of young adult patients who have suffered damage to ventromedial prefrontal cortex in infancy are particularly revealing. These patients have troubled histories that include habitual misbehavior, shunning by peers, problems maintaining employment and living independently, risky sexual behavior, and minor criminal activity. Importantly, such patients are similar to those with congenital sociopathy in their inability to comprehend social rules (although their impulsivity differs from the goal-directedness of those with congenital sociopathy); and they are impaired in moral reasoning tasks, treating social dilemmas in a superficial and self-centered manner.

Sensitivity to the consequences of actions

The ventromedial prefrontal cortex, especially the lateral parts of orbitofrontal cortex, is thought to be important in establishing links between stimuli or actions and the rewards or punishments that follow (see Chapter 24 for evidence from the domain of decision making). The orbitofrontal cortex is heavily interconnected with sensory regions (including primary taste, olfactory, and somatosensory cortices) and the inferior temporal areas in the visual stream, consistent with the receipt of information about the physical consequences of actions. On this basis, Damasio and colleagues proposed what they have termed the **somatic marker hypothesis**, which postulates that behavior is guided by representations of bodily states that in turn indicate the potential consequences of actions (see Chapter 18).

In support of this framework, damage to the orbitofrontal cortex causes impairments in learning the relationship of stimuli and rewards. This kind of deficit is particularly apparent in **discrimination reversal learning** tasks. Animals with orbitofrontal lesions learn stimulus-reward contingencies (e.g., a bright light predicts food, whereas a dim light predicts no food) about as well as control animals do. When stimulus contingencies are unexpectedly reversed, however, the lesioned animals are slower to learn the new relationships. Neuroimaging studies have also found that orbitofrontal cortex is activated when neurologically normal subjects switch to a new stimulus-reward contingency. Conversely, patients with damage to orbitofrontal cortex are impaired in reversal learning tasks, frequently switching their responses following large rewards, while not switching responses following losses.

Although some patients with dorsolateral prefrontal damage are similarly impaired, this deficit is caused by a problem with task compliance (i.e., they fail to remain engaged in the task) that is distinct from the evaluation of rewards. As long as dorsolateral prefrontal patients attend to the feedback from the response in each trial, performance is normal. The impairment in reversal learning is reminiscent of the perseverative behavior seen in the Wisconsin Card Sorting Task. In both cases, prefrontal damage leads to an inability to recognize a context change, and thus to the inappropriate persistence of a previously relevant behavior. The two prefrontal syndromes differ, however, in that the perseveration following dorsolateral damage lies in the inability to modify arbitrary response rules, whereas the persistence following ventromedial damage lies in the inability to modify expectations about stimulus-reward links within a given perceptual domain.

Parietal Control Systems

In many neuroimaging studies of executive control, activation of the dorsolateral prefrontal cortex is accompanied by activation in the posterior parietal cortex. These two regions have strong and bidirectional connections, as revealed both by classical anatomical studies and by modern diffusion tensor imaging (see Box 3A). Further complicating matters, the parietal cortex plays a critical role in the allocation of attention (see Chapter 12). These interrelations can make it difficult to distinguish the functions of prefrontal and parietal cortices. Nevertheless, the parietal cortex makes a contribution to executive control.

Like the prefrontal cortex, the parietal lobes have been labeled historically as *association cortex*, meaning that they neither process sensory input nor generate motor output, acting to form associations between sensation and action. This idea was supported by the pioneering work of the physiologist Vernon Mountcastle and his colleagues at Johns Hopkins, who collected some of the earliest single-unit recording data from awake, behaving monkeys. In the 1970s, Mountcastle verified that neurons in the posterior parietal cortex respond to the behavioral actions associated with the stimuli rather than to the stimuli per se. He therefore argued that the activity of these neurons represented a *command signal*, a term with unequivocal executive connotations.

The question of whether parietal cortex (in particular, posterior parietal cortex) plays a role in volitional behavior was debated for much of the following two decades, with some researchers suggesting that parietal cortex supports intentionality and others favoring a simpler explanation in terms of visual attention. More recent results from primate electrophysiology and human neuroimaging argue for a more integrative perspective. As discussed in Chapter 24, studies of decision making in primates have indicated that neurons along the intraparietal sulcus (called the **lateral intraparietal area**, or *area LIP*) encode the expected value of possible actions. Likewise, fMRI research has found that the parietal cortex is activated when subjects create and maintain the set of possible behaviors that might be required in a given situation.

Thus, the coactivation of parietal and prefrontal cortices may reflect two ongoing but distinct processes: for parietal cortex, creating and updating a set of stimulus-response associations; and for prefrontal cortex, generating an appropriate motor behavior in response to a given stimulus.

Cingulate Control Systems

A general question about executive control is what triggers the brain to engage particular control processes. For example, what determines whether automatic stimulus-response contingencies are sufficient for a task, or whether increased control is needed to achieve a goal? Control processes carry a cost, in that they can slow down or disrupt automatic processing—a problem familiar to athletes, musicians, or other skilled performers. For control processes to be implemented efficiently, the brain must spend resources to monitor the success of behavioral actions and resolve conflicts between actions that might be taken.

The brain region most closely associated with engaging and disengaging control processes is the anterior cingulate cortex, especially its dorsal aspect. Understanding the contribution of this brain region to cognition has long been an important question in cognitive neuroscience, and data from functional neuroimaging, electrophysiology, and lesion studies have not yet converged on a clear answer. Although the anterior cingulate cortex is on the medial surface of the frontal lobe, it is spatially and cytoarchitectonically distinct from the ventromedial prefrontal cortex. This region contains portions of two Brodmann areas. The portion of the cingulate gyrus closest to the corpus callosum is area 24, which wraps around the genu (the frontal horn of the corpus callosum) anteriorly and extends to the parietal lobe boundary posteriorly. Surrounding the cingulate gyrus is area 32, which has a roughly similar extent. The anterior cingulate cortex can itself be separated into ventral and dorsal components, supporting emotional and monitoring processes, respectively (see Chapter 17). The connectivity of these subregions is consistent with this distinction. The ventral ACC is connected to the ventromedial prefrontal cortex, insular cortex, and limbic subcortical regions. Dorsal subregions are connected to dorsolateral prefrontal cortex, parietal cortex, and supplementary motor cortices. Despite the focus here on the anterior cingulate cortex, other parts of the medial frontal lobe have been implicated in performance monitoring—most notably, Brodmann areas 6 and 8.

The conflict-monitoring model

An early perspective on cingulate cortex function was introduced in 1990 by Michael Posner at the University of Oregon and Steven Petersen at Washington University, St. Louis. As part of their theory of attentional control, Posner and Petersen hypothesized the existence of three general systems: one for maintaining alertness/vigilance; one for orienting to sensory stimuli; and one for detecting and identifying events that require additional resources for their processing (see Chapter 10). The last of these systems was postulated to depend on the anterior cingulate cortex. Evidence in support of this conjecture came from PET studies showing that activation in the anterior cingulate increased under conditions of high conflict between responses (**Figure 23.9**). **Response conflict** arises when information that points to an incorrect response is available earlier than or simultaneously with information indicating the correct response. The **Stroop task** (see Chapters 5 and 10) is a good example of a paradigm that generates such conflicts. Because reading words is so much faster than naming ink colors, the irrelevant color words automatically evoke a response that interferes with production of the correct ink name.

Figure 23.9 The Stroop effect on the anterior cingulate cortex.
(A) Subjects are able to read color words very fast, and their speed does not depend on whether the color words are printed in black or in incongruent ink colors. But when asked to name the color of the ink in which the word is printed, subjects are slower when the ink color is incongruent with the printed word than when the ink color is congruent or the word is neutral. (B) Neuroimaging studies that use Stroop tasks show increased activation in anterior cingulate cortex on incongruent trials. (C) Meta-analysis shows that the dorsal part of the ACC responds to cognitive control demands, while more ventral regions support emotional processing. Numbers along the axes represent the distance, in millimeters, from the origin of a stereotactic space centered on the anterior commissure. CC, corpus callosum. (B after Bush et al. 1998; C after Bush et al. 2000.)

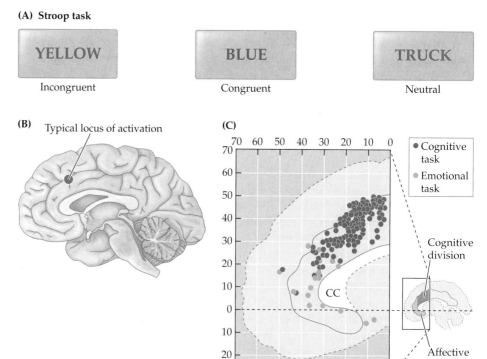

When such a conflict is present, control processes are thought to be necessary for its resolution.

Over the past decade, numerous functional neuroimaging studies using the Stroop task, as well as other paradigms, have implicated the medial prefrontal cortex in monitoring and allocating resources for cognitive control. Jonathan Cohen at Princeton, Cameron Carter now at UC Davis, and their colleagues have elucidated the conditions under which control processes are invoked. For example, they found that activation of the anterior cingulate cortex during a Stroop task was greater in response to incongruent trials than in congruent trials (**Figure 23.10**). Furthermore, this activation is greater when the previous trial is a congruent trial rather than an incongruent trial, indicating conflict monitoring rather than behavioral selection. Increased activation in the anterior cingulate cortex on one trial results in increased activation in the dorsolateral prefrontal cortex on the next trial, supporting the idea of an interaction between cingulate and dorsolateral control systems.

Electrophysiological recordings have provided further evidence for the role of anterior cingulate cortex in monitoring behavior, notably in the processing of feedback. William Gehring and co-workers at the University of Michigan examined the **error-related negativity**, a negative-polarity scalp electrical potential that occurs about 100 milliseconds after the onset of a motor movement that a subject realizes is incorrect. Gehring's group and others found that the amplitude of this potential was positively correlated with response time on the subsequent trial, suggesting that executive control processes had been engaged. Gehring speculated that the error signal was generated by neurons in the anterior cingulate cortex, an idea later confirmed by fMRI. Gehring and colleagues also identified a similar electrophysiological response—also thought to be localized to the anterior cingulate cortex—following feedback about a monetary loss in a gambling paradigm.

Challenges to the conflict-monitoring model

Although the idea that the anterior cingulate cortex mediates the monitoring and resolution of conflict has substantial support, recent studies have raised challenges. One open question is what sort of monitoring occurs. Whereas the majority of neuroimaging tasks that elicit ACC activation have required subjects to monitor response conflict, some studies require subjects to monitor response outcomes at a later stage. In these latter studies, feedback about correct responses or other rewarding outcomes often evoked ACC activation. Conflict monitoring might also occur at processing stages earlier than that underlying the response itself. These observations suggest that the medial prefrontal cortex may monitor forms of conflict at stages of processing other than response generation.

Another open question is whether the increased activation on error trials has to do with errors themselves or another process. Recent neuroimaging data indicate that, when subjects are allowed to choose whether to guess on a trial of a visual search task, ACC activation is greatest when the subjects choose not to guess, but it does not differ between correct and error trials. This observation suggests that, when cognitive control processes are dissociated from error monitoring, the anterior cingulate supports the avoidance of mistakes, not the detection of errors.

Data from electrophysiological and lesion studies have also been difficult to reconcile with a conflict-monitoring explanation for ACC activation. When monkeys are trained to perform a stop-signal task of the sort described earlier in the chapter, the activity of ACC neurons does not increase when the animals must stop a previously initiated movement (i.e., the condition in which maximal response conflict would be expected). Another paradigm used cue-induced conflict: a cue that signaled whether to move the eyes to the left or right was sometimes presented on the same side of the display as the cued direction (low conflict) or on the opposite side of the display (high conflict). Again, no conflict-related signals were observed in neurons within the anterior cingulate cortex.

Likewise, patients with damage to the dorsal anterior cingulate cortex (**Figure 23.11**) perform normally on tasks involving response conflict, despite having significant damage to the region that is most frequently activated in neuroimaging studies of conflict. These patients have normal conflict-related adjustments of performance in both the Stroop and the go/no-go tasks. This finding suggests that the monitoring/control role of the cingulate cortex might be linked to aspects of motivation. Similarly, in a recent study of macaque monkeys, lesions to the cingulate cortex did not influence their abilities to detect errors or to modify their behaviors in response to those errors. Instead, the monkeys had difficulty learning the optimal behaviors in response to a series of rewards. Thus, although there is strong evidence that the anterior cingulate cortex plays a role in executive control, the specific processes that it supports remain a subject of considerable controversy.

Basal Ganglia Control Systems

Among subcortical structures, the basal ganglia are particularly important for the control of behavior (see Chapter 9). As Figure 23.3 shows, the basal ganglia receive input from the frontal lobes and send extensive projections to the thalamus and to motor cortex. It is well established that the basal ganglia contribute greatly to motor control, consistent with this pattern of connectivity (**Figure 23.12A**). For example, individuals with **Parkinson's disease** have difficulty controlling and planning movements. Some patients with this disorder

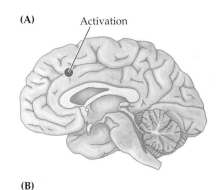

(A) Activation

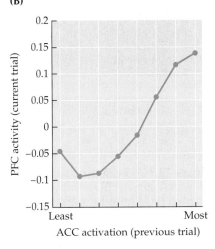

(B)

Figure 23.10 Interactions between anterior cingulate cortex and dorsolateral prefrontal cortex. (A) The same region (colored red here) of anterior cingulate cortex (ACC) is active when subjects are faced with conflicting responses and when they make errors. (B) When ACC activation is high on one trial, activation in the lateral prefrontal cortex increases on the next trial. (After Kerns et al. 2004.)

(A)

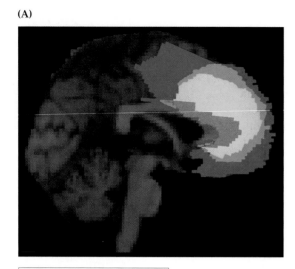

(B)

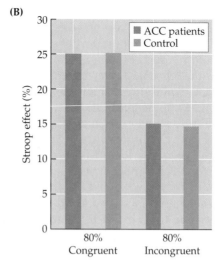

Number of patients who have damage in the indicated part of the brain:

■ 4   ■ 3   ■ 2   ■ 1

Figure 23.11 Evidence against the idea that conflict monitoring is attributed to anterior cingulate cortex.   The information here is based on a study of patients with damage to the ACC. (A) Color maps indicate the areas of lesion overlap. All patients had damage to the dorsal aspect of the cingulate cortex. (B) Although patients with ACC damage responded more slowly than neurologically normal control subjects, the magnitude of the Stroop effect (incongruent > congruent) was similar. This similarity was present in both congruent and incongruent trials. These results suggest that an intact anterior cingulate cortex is not necessary for normal interference effects in the Stroop task, at least under the conditions tested. (After Fellows and Farah 2005.)

exhibited continual and disordered movements; others are rigid and unable to initiate behavior. Parkinson's disease has been associated with damage to dopaminergic neurons within the basal ganglia. Importantly for the issues under consideration here, there is now growing evidence that the basal ganglia also support nonmotor cognitive functions.

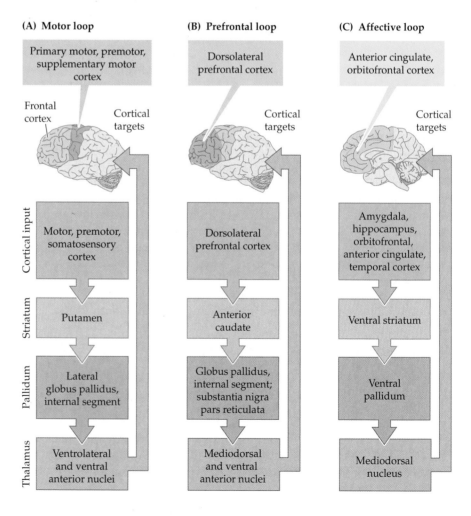

Figure 23.12 Basal ganglia control of behavior.   (A) Inputs to and projections from basal ganglia contribute greatly to motor control. (B,C) Basal ganglia loops in the prefrontal cortex affect nonmotor behavior and support particular forms of cognitive control.

The basal ganglia apparently interact with prefrontal control systems to support particular forms of cognitive control (**Figure 23.12B,C**). In category learning tasks, for example, subjects must use abstract rules to match stimuli to responses. As described earlier, neurons in the prefrontal cortex respond preferentially to particular rules, indicating that they code such abstractions. In contrast, both fMRI and lesion studies indicate that the basal ganglia are important for the creation of links between specific stimuli and specific responses (**Figure 23.13**). When the rule for mapping a stimulus onto a response changes, activation of the basal ganglia increases. When the abstract rules change, however, but the specific stimulus-response mappings do not, activation does not increase. Thus, the basal ganglia may play a complementary role to the prefrontal cortex in executive control, through their support of direct links between stimuli and behavior. This conception of basal ganglia function will be revisited in Chapter 24 in the context of learning associations between stimuli and rewards.

(A)

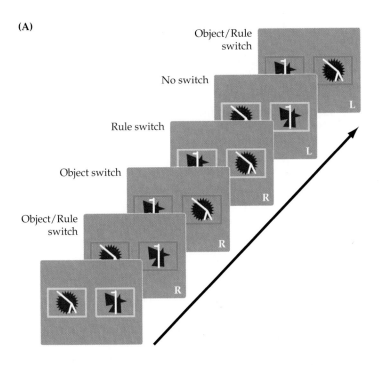

(B)

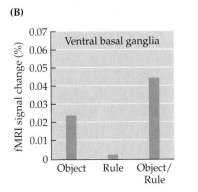
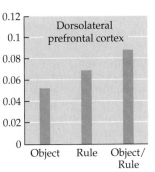

Figure 23.13 The different contributions of basal ganglia and prefrontal systems to executive control. (A) Subjects were shown pairs of complex, difficult-to-name objects, each surrounded by a box. If the boxes were outlined in yellow, the subject was to choose the same object as they chose on the previous trial and hold it in working memory. If the boxes were outlined in blue, the subject was to choose the other object and hold it in working memory instead. Thus, each trial could involve no switch at all; a switch in rule but not object; a switch in object but not rule; or a switch in both object and rule. The correct responses—left (L) or right (R)—are indicated at the lower right of each display. (B) Signal change in each switch condition is compared here to trials with no switching at all. The key finding was that the basal ganglia were activated only for object switches and not for rule switches. In contrast, the dorsolateral prefrontal cortex was activated for all types of switches. (After Cools et al. 2004.)

Summary

1. Executive control processes play a supervisory role in cognitive functions, allowing behavior to be modified flexibly to attain a wide variety of explicit or implicit goals. These processes may be conscious or nonconscious, depending on the circumstances in which they are evoked.

2. Several brain systems interact to support executive control, including the dorsolateral prefrontal cortex, the ventromedial prefrontal cortex, the posterior parietal cortex, the anterior cingulate cortex, and the basal ganglia.

3. The prefrontal cortex receives much of its input from the secondary sensory cortices and is richly interconnected with the parietal cortex, as well as locally. Projections from the prefrontal cortex extend primarily to the basal ganglia and the cortical motor systems.

4. In general, the dorsolateral prefrontal cortex supports the selection, inhibition, and abstraction of novel rules for behavior. In contrast, the ventromedial prefrontal cortex facilitates behavioral control in situations with well-established behavioral rules, as in social situations or in interaction with objects in the environment.

5. Damage to the prefrontal cortex causes selective deficits in executive control whose specific characteristics depend on the region affected.

6. The parietal cortex is implicated in control processes, although its specific contribution remains unclear.

7. The anterior cingulate cortex monitors behavior and signals the need for the increased allocation of executive control. The basal ganglia initiate and gate at least some cognitive functions, similar to the role they play in initiating and gating motor acts. Together, these executive control systems allow behavior to transcend simple stimulus-response associations, providing a foundation for many complex aspects of human activity.

Additional Reading

Reviews

KNIGHT, R. T. AND D. T. STUSS (2002) Prefrontal cortex: The present and the future. In *Principles of Frontal Lobe Function*, D. T. Stuss and R. T. Knight (eds.). New York: Oxford University Press, pp. 573–597.

MILLER, E. K. AND J. D. COHEN (2001) An integrative theory of prefrontal cortex function. *Annu. Rev. Neurosci.* 24: 167–202.

RIDDERINKHOF, K. R., M. ULLSPERGER, E. A. CRONE AND S. NIEUWENHUIS (2004) The role of the medial frontal cortex in cognitive control. *Science* 306: 443–447.

Important Original Papers

ANDERSON, S. W., A. BECHARA, H. DAMASIO, D. TRANEL AND A. R. DAMASIO (1999) Impairment of social and moral behavior related to early damage in human prefrontal cortex. *Nat. Neurosci.* 2: 1032–1037.

BOTVINICK, M., L. E. NYSTROM, K. FISSELL, C. S. CARTER AND J. D. COHEN (1999) Conflict monitoring versus selection-for-action in anterior cingulate cortex. *Nature* 402: 179–181.

CHAO, L. L. AND R. T. KNIGHT (1995) Human prefrontal lesions increase distractibility to irrelevant sensory inputs. *NeuroReport* 6: 1605–1610.

COOLS, R., L. CLARK AND T. W. ROBBINS (2004) Differential responses in human striatum and prefrontal cortex to changes in object and rule relevance. *J. Neurosci.* 24: 1129–1135.

FELLOWS, L. K. AND M. J. FARAH (2005) Is anterior cingulate cortex necessary for cognitive control? *Brain* 128: 788–796.

GOLDMAN-RAKIC, P. S. AND L. J. PORRINO (1985) The primate mediodorsal (MD) nucleus and its projection to the frontal lobe. *J. Comp. Neurol.* 242: 535–560.

GOLDSTEIN , K. AND M. SCHEERER (1941) Abstract and Concrete Behavior; An Experimental Study with Special Tests. Psychological Monographs, Vol. 53, No. 2. Evanston, IL: American Psychological Association.

HUETTEL, S. A., P. B. MACK AND G. McCARTHY (2002) Perceiving patterns in random series: Dynamic processing of sequence in prefrontal cortex. *Nat. Neurosci.* 5: 485–490.

KENNERLEY, S. W., M. E. WALTON, T. E. BEHRENS, M. J. BUCKLEY AND M. F. RUSHWORTH (2006) Optimal decision making and the anterior cingulate cortex. *Nat. Neurosci.* 9: 940–947.

KERNS, J. G., J. D. COHEN, A. W. MacDONALD, III, R. Y. CHO, V. A. STENGER AND C. S. CARTER (2004) Anterior cingulate conflict monitoring and adjustments in control. *Science* 303: 1023–1026.

McCARTHY, G., M. LUBY, J. GORE AND P. GOLDMAN-RAKIC (1997) Infrequent events transiently activate human prefrontal and parietal cortex as measured by functional MRI. *J. Neurophysiol.* 77: 1630–1634.

MILNER, B. (1963) Effects of different brain lesions on card sorting. *Arch. Neurol.* 9: 90–100.

STROOP, J. R. (1935) Studies of interference in serial verbal reactions. *J. Exp. Psychol.* 18: 643–662.

WALLIS, J. D., K. C. ANDERSON AND E. K. MILLER (2001) Single neurons in prefrontal cortex encode abstract rules. *Nature* 411: 953–956.

Books

FINGER, S. (1994) *Origins of Neuroscience.* New York: Oxford University Press.

FUSTER, J. (1997) *The Prefrontal Cortex: Anatomy, Physiology, and Neuropsychology of the Frontal Lobe.* Philadelphia: Lippincott-Raven.

MACMILLAN, M. (2000) *An Odd Kind of Fame: Stories of Phineas Gage.* Cambridge, MA: MIT Press.

STUSS, D. T. AND R. T. KNIGHT (2002) *Principles of Frontal Lobe Function.* New York: Oxford University Press.

24 *Decision Making*

Introduction

Decisions are defined by three conditions: (1) at least two possible choices are in some sense known; (2) expectations can be formed about the potential outcomes of each choice; and (3) the values of the potential outcomes can be assessed at some level. Although these terms imply awareness of the conditions, this tripartite framework applies equally to decisions that are made unconsciously. In this view, decisions, whether they are made consciously or unconsciously, rely heavily on neural processes that entail selection, inhibition, planning, and other aspects of executive control. People are continually faced with opportunities for an enormous variety of decisions: whether to brake or speed up while driving, whether to walk on the left or the right of an oncoming pedestrian, whether or not to meet the gaze of a partner in conversation. These and innumerable other routine choices require doing one thing or another. All of these examples meet the criteria for decision making, and all occur frequently in the absence of any explicit sense that we are making decisions. The approaches to understanding the neural bases of decisions have been diverse. Some researchers have focused on simple and rapid perceptual-motor decisions made by humans and other animals; others have investigated more reflective, social, and interactive types of decisions. As will be apparent in the discussion that follows, work on these issues has borrowed much from cognitive psychology, probability theory, game theory, and economics, as well as from neuroscience, using a wide range of methods.

The Phenomenology of Decision Making

Normative theories

Early theories of decision making were developed in response to largely practical concerns—for instance, how to make good bets and fairly divide betting stakes in the context of gambling. The conception of probability as the likelihood of future events was first articulated in the mid seventeenth century by the French polymath Blaise Pascal. Pascal demonstrated that the relative probabilities of events could be determined by calculating the number of positive outcomes (e.g., winning rolls of dice) divided by the total number of possible outcomes (e.g., all potential rolls of dice). This insight led to the concept of **expected value**, derived by multiplying the probability of each possible outcome by its associated reward. For example, imagine being given the opportunity to roll a standard six-sided die, for which you would earn $1 times the number of spots rolled (e.g., a five leads to $5). The expected value of this gamble can be calculated to be $3.50, so it would seem wise to pay $3 to roll the die once, but unwise to pay $4. The simplest **normative theory** of decision making—that is, a theory of how people *should* make decisions—is to select the option with the highest expected value.

Expected value is an extraordinarily powerful concept, but it has clear limitations. Suppose a player in a coin-flipping game receives $2 if the coin comes up heads, but $0 for tails. A person who had to decide between playing the game or receiving a sure $0.90 might do a quick expected-value calculation and choose to play. But what if the stakes were increased by a factor of 10,000? Most people, when faced with such decisions, prefer a sure smaller gain ($9,000) to a risky larger gain (a one-in-two chance of $20,000). In fact, non-human animals often show a similar pattern of risk aversion when faced with choices about food quantities. Such biases show that expected value alone cannot account for decision making.

An important factor omitted from calculations of expected value is the degree of *risk*, as was recognized by the Swiss mathematician Daniel Bernoulli in 1738. Bernoulli noted that in the coin flip game, most individuals prefer the sure $9,000 (in his case in ducats, not dollars), although very rich individuals might consider the coin flip a reasonable investment. Bernoulli explained this result by introducing the concept of **utility**, which reflects the *psychological* (as opposed to *economic*) value assigned to an outcome (**Figure 24.1**). He argued that the concept of expected value should be replaced by a new quantity: **expected utility**. Bernoulli pointed out that the utility of a small increase in wealth is inversely proportional to a person's current wealth. For example, the utility difference between $0 and $1,000 is much larger than the utility difference between $100,000 and $101,000.

The perception of monetary value has been postulated to mirror that of many other quantities in that the perceived utility of a change in wealth depends on the starting point. Most people are risk-averse, preferring a sure reward to a risky gamble with identical expected value. Though they are uncommon, some people are risk seekers, preferring risky situations to sure

Figure 24.1 The relation between value and utility. (A) For most people, the utility of money is a diminishing function. Doubling the amount of money to be gained, for example, results in less than a doubling of utility, as indicated in this graph of utility plotted against monetary value. Note that utility is an abstract quantity that can be expressed only in arbitrary units. Also, the specific shape of the utility curve differs across individuals. (B) People generally make decisions on the basis of expected utility, not expected value. If faced with a choice between the two options here, each presented as a "wheel of fortune," most people would choose the option on the left, even though it has a much lower expected value.

(A)

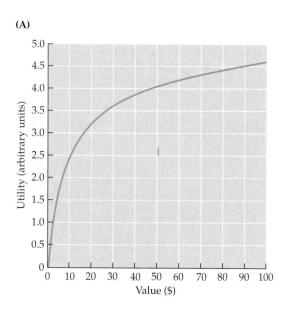

(B)

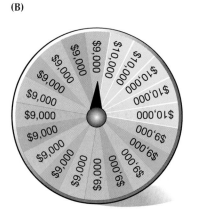

Look carefully at the two wheels. Which wheel would you spin?

rewards; such individuals are exemplified by the maladaptive risk-seeking behavior that is apparent in problem gamblers and other sorts of addicts (**Box 24A**).

Expected-utility theory and its variants have proved remarkably useful as a description of economic decision making for more than two centuries. One result of this history is that the concept of **rationality** has come to dominate many accounts of decision making. Although there is no single agreed-upon definition of *rationality*, the term is used to connote consistency in decisions based on a conscious evaluation of the circumstances. Accordingly, rational decisions are characterized by preferences and decision rules that do not change in different contexts (e.g., the **framing effects** introduced in Chapter 2 and illustrated in **Figure 24.2**), and that are immune to whim or cognitive limitations.

Rationality does not, in itself, imply particular preferences. Preferring to spend a day reading in the library to relaxing at the beach, assuming that neither carries any cost, is not irrational. If there were a $20 charge for each activity, however, the library might seem much less attractive because people are more used to paying for beaches than for libraries. No purely rational decision maker would change from preferring the library to the beach; because both have the same $20 charge, that cost should be irrelevant to the decision. Rational decision makers also assume (by definition) that others will behave in a similarly rational manner; this assumption is important for understanding how people behave in interactive situations like bargaining, negotiating, and games.

Descriptive theories

Despite their intuitive attraction, normative models often fail to describe real-world behavior (see Figure 24.2). For example, people pay to avoid risk when they buy insurance, but many of the same people pay to take on risk by buying lottery tickets for more than their expected value. By the same token, gamblers believe that they are more likely to win when on a "hot streak" and people tend to keep losing stocks too long and sell winning stocks too soon. Economists Daniel Kahneman and Amos Tversky, along with their colleagues at Princeton, developed a new approach to solving these behavioral puzzles, which they called **prospect theory**. The term *prospect* refers to any decision option whose rewards and probabilities are known or can be estimated.

Figure 24.2 Examples of "irrational" decision making. (A) Framing effects. Suppose you are a physician trying to halt the spread of a fatal disease with two vaccines: a proven one that will save 200 of 600 villagers (Vaccine A), and an untested one that has a 33 percent chance of saving all 600 and a 67 percent chance of saving none (Vaccine B). Which do you choose? Now suppose instead that you have two therapeutic options for the disease: a known treatment that definitely will kill 67 percent of the villagers (Treatment C), and an untested one that has a 33 percent chance of killing none and a 67 percent chance of killing them all (Treatment D). Again, which do you choose? Most people choose the vaccine that will save 200 people for sure (Vaccine A) and the therapeutic intervention that has a chance of killing no one (Treatment D). Note, however, that the two decision situations are identical, with Vaccine A equivalent to Treatment C, and Vaccine B equivalent to Treatment D; the only difference is that one is framed in terms of saving and the other in terms of killing. (B) Range effects. When people are faced with a trade-off between money and time, people are much more likely to pay a cost in time (e.g., driving across town) to save money (e.g., $5) when the stakes are small (the first question shown here) than when the stakes are large, even though the cost-benefit ratio is the same in both cases.

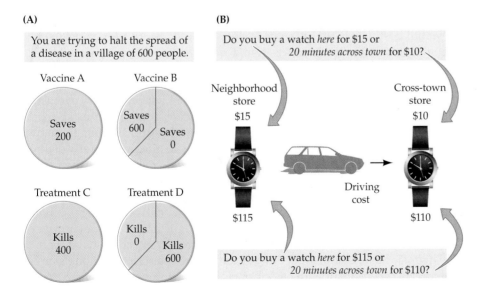

(A)

You are trying to halt the spread of a disease in a village of 600 people.

Vaccine A — Saves 200

Vaccine B — Saves 600 / Saves 0

Treatment C — Kills 400

Treatment D — Kills 0 / Kills 600

(B)

Do you buy a watch *here* for $15 or *20 minutes across town* for $10?

Neighborhood store $15

Cross-town store $10

Driving cost

$115

$110

Do you buy a watch *here* for $115 or *20 minutes across town* for $110?

■ BOX 24A Addiction to Gambling

The 2003 World Series of Poker was the scene of an unusual, even historic, championship match. One of the two finalists was Sam Farha, a professional poker player and veteran of hundreds of such tournaments. Sitting across the table was the improbably named Chris Moneymaker, an unknown who had never played in a face-to-face poker tournament before the series but was one of a "new breed" of online poker enthusiasts. Moneymaker bested more than 800 World Series entrants to reach the finals and, despite his inexperience at live tournament play, went on to defeat Farha and win a then-record $2.5 million. His victory signaled a turning point for the gambling industry. Within 2 years, there were more than 2 million online poker players (the majority from the United States), and today more than 100,000 players are logged on and playing at any given time. Whereas high-stakes poker was once a game played by professionals in smoky back rooms, now anyone with a computer and some skill can win

(or, far more likely, lose) a lot of money online.

This explosion of interest in online poker is simply the most visible example of a broader social problem. Taking into account all forms of gambling, estimates are that 3 to 4 percent of the U.S. population meet the criteria for problem gambling. A recent functional neuroimaging study found that, in pathological gamblers (a more serious diagnosis than problem gambling), activation of the ventromedial prefrontal cortex and the ventral striatum is reduced in response to winning and losing gambles. As discussed later in the chapter, these regions are critical for the evaluation of rewards, suggesting that gambling addicts may have reduced responsiveness to rewarding stimuli.

Adolescents, males especially, are particularly likely to suffer from problem gambling. The rate of problem gambling in males between 14 and 22 is approximately three times higher than in the population at large, and online gambling—with its ease of ac-

cess and cloak of privacy—represents a major source of abuse. Why adolescents are so susceptible to problem gambling is not clear. One possibility is the immaturity of executive control processes. Compared to other brain regions, the prefrontal cortex matures relatively late in development, with structural changes still observed in the late teens. Consistent with this delayed development, fMRI studies have frequently found differences between adolescents and adults in prefrontal cortex activation evoked by a variety of executive control paradigms, although whether more or less activation is observed in children differs across studies and tasks. Impairments in executive control processes may limit adolescents' abilities to inhibit the attractive effects of rewards and to evaluate the future consequences of behavior.

Ironically, a second demographic group that is disproportionately afflicted with problem gambling is the elderly. For many older adults, gambling provides a much desired social

---

Prospect theory is an example of a **descriptive theory** in that it attempts to predict what people *will* do, not what they *should* do.

Prospect theory differs from expected-utility theory in two important ways. First, it assumes that people make decisions in terms of the *anticipated gains and losses from their current state*, not in terms of the resulting absolute wealth. Increments in gains and losses are assumed to have diminishing value, as Bernoulli postulated, but the slope is steeper for losses than for gains. In general, people want to avoid losses more than they want to seek gains. Second, prospect theory proposes that probabilities themselves are subjective. That is, people tend to overestimate the chances of low-probability events (e.g., winning the lottery) and underestimate the chances of high-probability events.

A probability weighting function that incorporates these biases can be combined with the value function to determine subjective utility. When these two rules are combined, prospect theory predicts a distinctive pattern of risk-averse and risk-seeking behavior. People should be risk-averse when faced with high-probability gains (e.g., preferring safe to risky investments), risk-seeking for low-probability gains (e.g., buying lottery tickets), risk-averse for low-probability losses (e.g., buying insurance), and risk-seeking for high-probability losses (e.g., keeping losing stocks in the hope that they recover). All of these diverse predictions are now supported by experimental data.

The major tenets of prospect theory and related descriptive models are in several ways consonant with basic principles of cognitive neuroscience, espe-

Pathological Gambling in Patients with Parkinson's Disease

Before Treatment	On Dopamine Agonist	Off Dopamine Agonist
Patient A (age 54) gambled every few years	Gambled almost daily; lost about $2,500	Within a month, reported no interest in gambling
Patient B (age 63) gambled every 3 months or so, without problems	Reported "incredible compulsion" to gamble; gambled several times a week	After a month, frequency of gambling was back to every few months
Patient C (age 41) reported never having gambled	Became "consumed" with gambling; lost $5,000 within a few months; exhibited compulsions for shopping and sex	Two days after stopping treatment, reported no urge to gamble, and no other compulsions
Patient D (age 50) had no history of gambling	Gambled compulsively; remained at casinos for days at a time; exhibited hypersexuality and excessive drinking	Within a month, reported no interest in gambling

After Dodd et al. 2005.

opportunity, and retirees are frequent targets of casino marketing campaigns. As is the case for adolescents, multiple factors presumably contribute to the prevalence of gambling problems in the elderly. For example, older individuals are more likely than young adults to be impaired in decision-making tasks that rely on ventromedial prefrontal cortex. Gambling problems may also be associated with particular medications. Patients with Parkinson's disease who received therapy that included high doses of dopamine agonists had a higher incidence of pathological gambling than did control subjects (see the table for examples). As reviewed later in the chapter, the neurotransmitter dopamine is important for reward-based learning; its loss by the destruction of key dopaminergic systems in Parkinson's, and the sudden reintroduction of dopamine by means of medication, may result in hypersensitivity to gambling rewards.

References

Dodd, M. L., K. J. Klos, J. H. Bower, Y. E. Geda, K. A. Josephs and J. E. Ahlskog (2005) Pathological gambling caused by drugs used to treat Parkinson disease. *Arch. Neurol.* 62: 1377–1381.

Driver-Dunckley, E., J. Samanta and M. Stacy (2003) Pathological gambling associated with dopamine agonist therapy in Parkinson's disease. *Neurology* 61: 422–423.

Paus, T. (2005) Mapping brain maturation and cognitive development during adolescence. *Trends Cogn. Sci.* 9: 60–68.

cially as compared to expected utility theory. Estimating gains and losses according to the associated change in value rather than the final state of wealth accords with the general principle that the context rather than the absolute physical characteristics of a stimulus determines what people perceive (see Unit II). Overestimating the likelihood of extremely improbable events is also consistent with familiarity effects in studies of memory, suggesting that perceived frequency depends on how readily we can bring something to mind (see Unit IV). Although its details have been questioned by many economists and some psychologists, prospect theory describes many aspects of how people actually behave when making decisions.

Heuristics in decision making

Another reason for doubting the idea that people are essentially rational decision makers is that many decisions are made by the simple following of unstated rules referred to as **heuristics**. That heuristics play an important role in decision making was first popularized by the economist and psychologist Herbert Simon in the 1950s. Simon recognized that organisms have finite computational resources and must often make decisions under time constraints, rendering rational consideration impractical or even impossible. A simple example is the way we shop for things. Typically the shopper does not consider all the options but identifies a few important features, broadly considers price, identifies a few candidates for purchase, and buys an item that is acceptable. Such decisions involve determination not of the optimal choice, but of a choice that is simply "good enough." Simon called this heuristic *satisficing*, and proposed the idea of **bounded rationality** to emphasize that decisions that are formally irrational may nonetheless be adaptive. When humans and other animals use a satisficing heuristic, they still may be choosing the option with maximal expected utility, given their situational and computational limits.

Given the many heuristics that have been identified by psychologists and economists, it is clear that the rules that people exhibit when making decisions are not necessarily logical. For example, when using what has been called the **representativeness** heuristic (**Figure 24.3A**), people also make biased decisions based on matches with an expectation. Consider the following description of a student: "Amy has very strong mathematical skills, likes solving problems, and has always enjoyed building devices." Is it more likely that Amy's major is mechanical engineering or political science? The answer to this question comes easily, given that the description is more representative of engineering than of the social sciences. However, consider another description: "John is introverted and shy. He is very organized and meticulous, and he enjoys books." Which is more likely to be John's major: library science or psychology? When faced with choices like this, people usually select the option that most closely matches the description (i.e., that John is a library science major). But in many cases, this one included, the decision options have very different *prior probabilities*. The set of all students contains relatively few

Figure 24.3 Some problems with using heuristics in decision making. (A) Representativeness. If you could choose only one of these four tickets for tomorrow's $10 million lottery, which would you pick? All have equal probabilities of winning, yet when faced with such choices, most people select 4-13-17-24-37 because it appears more random than the others. The American psychologist Wendell Garner argued that this sort of bias occurs when a sequence seems representative of a random process. (B) Anchoring. Consider an advertisement that describes the features of a new car and states the manufacturer's suggested retail price (MSRP). If the suggested price is high, people's estimates of the value of the car will be high. But if the suggested price is low, then people's estimates of the value for the same car will be low.

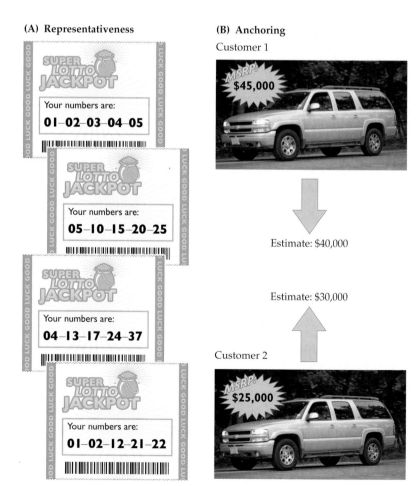

library science majors, and thus even a shy book lover is much more likely to be a psychology major. This example shows how following a heuristic can lead to a wrong decision, as well as to decisions that are simply irrational, such as the instance of representativeness in Figure 24.3A.

When using what has been called the **availability** heuristic, people make decisions on the basis of implicit assessments of how easily decision options can be brought to mind. A classic example of availability occurs in judgments of letter frequency. For example, which category of English words is more numerous—those that begin with *k* or those that have *k* as a third letter? Because it is much easier to generate words that begin with any given letter, people usually choose the former option, even though the latter is in fact more common. Advertisers take advantage of the availability heuristic by presenting their products repeatedly, so that they are available (both physically and mnemonically) when consumers are shopping. Availability biases are also often reported in memory tasks (see Unit V).

The **anchoring** heuristic refers to the tendency to bias the valuation of an option near an initial starting point (**Figure 24.3B**). When given a starting point, even a random one, people determine values by using that point as an anchor, as auctioneers know well.

We and many other animals make decisions in many real-world situations using heuristics rather than making more reflective, calculated choices. The reason is that following rules facilitates the sorts of constrained everyday decisions that we make on a regular basis. Such rules usually work to our advantage because they are statistically valid across a wide range of situations; but for the same reason, they often lead to wrong choices, as several of the examples here make clear.

Game theory

Most of the decisions discussed so far involve the judgments and preferences of individuals acting more or less alone. Many decisions, however, depend on other people. Consider, for example, a poker player who is dealt a good hand. Betting too much might scare potential opponents out of the game, and betting too little would minimize the potential winnings. To make good decisions, therefore, a player must evaluate not only his or her hand but the effects of potential actions on the decisions of others. Decision making can quickly become very complex when multiple individuals are involved, each with limited information and different preferences. The branch of decision science that studies how decisions are made in such circumstances is known as **game theory**, in part because many of its concepts can be easily expressed as simple interpersonal games.

Most games can be formalized in terms of a **payoff matrix** that plots the possible choices of each player along its axes and the outcomes for each player in its cells (**Figure 24.4A**). Games can be either cooperative or competitive. *Cooperative games* can also be called *coordination games* because subjects' interests are aligned and they must coordinate their decisions to receive the maximal reward. *Competitive games*, as the name implies, pit individuals with different goals against one another. Games can also be played in single-trial or repeated forms. A game that is simple when played only once may become very complex when played repeatedly, because a decision might be good in the short-term (i.e., results in a reward now) but bad in the long term (i.e., provides too much information to an opponent).

Probably the most famous scenario in game theory is the venerable **prisoner's dilemma** (see Figure 24.4A). The name comes from a criminally inspired backstory. The police have circumstantial evidence linking two thieves to a crime. If each confesses, either individual will do better regardless of what the accomplice says; but if both confess, they will do much worse than if both

Figure 24.4 Some commonly studied games. (A) The prisoner's dilemma. The terms *cooperate* and *defect*, typically used in descriptions of this game situation, refer, respectively, to cooperating with the partner by remaining quiet or defecting to the police by confessing. The numbers below each person indicate the personal utility of that outcome, from 4 ("going free") to 0 ("longest sentence"). (B) The ultimatum game. One player (the proposer) is given a sum of money (e.g., $10) that he may divide between himself and another player (the responder). The responder then decides to accept the division or reject it. If the division is rejected, neither player receives anything at all. (C) The trust game. Both players start the game with equivalent sums of money. The investor can keep the money or give any fraction of it to the trustee, whereupon the money is multiplied by some factor (e.g., tripling in value). The trustee then decides how much of the total amount to return to the investor.

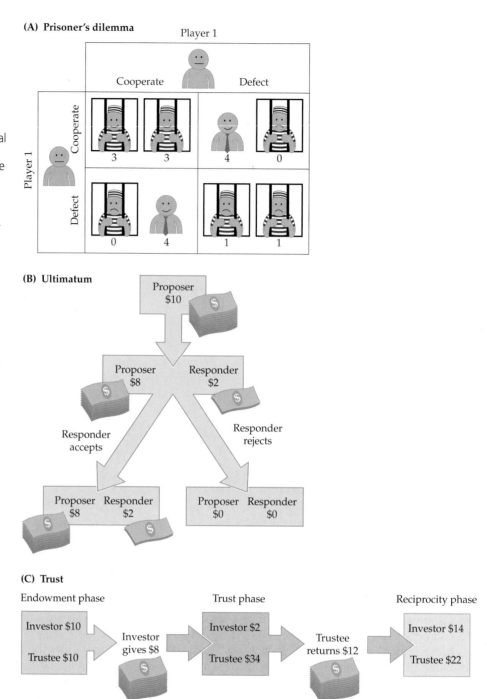

remain quiet. The paradox of the prisoner's dilemma is that a pair of truly rational decision makers would both choose to confess (or "defect" to the police, in the typical language of the game), resulting in the worst possible outcome for the pair. This "defect-defect" outcome is the **Nash equilibrium** solution for the game, meaning that if the players reached that solution, neither player would change his or her decision (i.e., from defect to cooperate) unilaterally. The Nash equilibria for a game reflect the strategies that should be adopted by rational decision makers. More complex scenarios and many sorts of games can have multiple Nash equilibria, including equilibria in which one or both players might mix their choices randomly among some of the strategies.

In another class of games that has been particularly well studied, resources are allocated by one decision maker and accepted by another. In the **ultimatum game** (**Figure 24.4B**), a purely rational responder would accept any offer, no matter how small, because rejecting it results in the worst monetary outcome. Yet many studies have shown that responders tend to reject offers that they deem unfair, even when relatively large stakes are involved (e.g., being offered $20 out of a total of $100). Perhaps expecting such rejections, proposers usually offer fair divisions. In a typical version of the related **trust game** (or *investment game*), depending on how confident the investor is in the trustee's reciprocity, more or less money might be invested (**Figure 24.4C**).

Studies using the ultimatum and trust games (and related games) have provided clear evidence for deviations from normative, rational behavior, notably by showing that decisions are predicated on more than just obtained rewards. As discussed in the following sections, both rewards and their emotional and cognitive consequences play important roles in making decisions.

Underlying Neural Mechanisms and Reward Systems

Understanding the neural basis of decision making requires first considering how the brain processes rewards that motivate choices. Rewards that have direct benefits for fitness, such as food, water, and sex, are called **primary** (or *unconditioned*) **reinforcers**. When decision-making experiments are conducted in non-human animals, the rewards are typically primary reinforcers, such as food or water, that are valued even in the absence of training. Many real-world decisions, at least for humans, do not involve primary reinforcers. Money, for example, has no value itself but can be used to obtain other rewards; thus it is described as a **secondary reinforcer**. Aversive outcomes are called **punishments**. For any animal to make good decisions, it must be able to predict the choices that lead to particular outcomes, and to evaluate the reinforcement value of those outcomes.

Midbrain

Studies of the neural mechanisms underlying reward and its evaluation have generally implicated the neurotransmitter **dopamine**. Two important structures in the midbrain contain dopaminergic neurons: the **substantia nigra** and the **ventral tegmental area** (**VTA**) (**Figure 24.5**). Axons from a subdivision of the substantia nigra called the **pars compacta** project to the basal ganglia, which are critical for the initiation and control of movement (see Chapter 8). Especially important for decision making are the VTA and its two major projections, the mesolimbic and mesocortical pathways. The **mesolimbic pathway** projects from the VTA to brain systems important for emotional and affective processing, such as the **nucleus accumbens** at the head of the caudate nucleus (sometimes referred to as the *ventral striatum*), the amygdala, and the hippocampus (see Chapter 17). The **mesocortical pathway** projects from the VTA to the cortex, especially the medial portions of the frontal lobe. The activity of dopaminergic neurons is affected by numerous drugs, most notably cocaine and amphetamine. This sort of pharmacological observation has further implicated dopamine as a central player in the neural evaluation of reward, as well as in the phenomenon of addiction.

The activity of dopamine neurons in the VTA reflects information about the reward value of stimuli. In a series of experiments, Wolfram Schultz and his colleagues at Cambridge University investigated how VTA neurons change their firing rate in response to rewarding stimuli. Monkeys with electrodes implanted in the VTA learned to press a lever when they saw a light, whereupon they would receive a squirt of juice (**Figure 24.6A**). At the beginning of

Figure 24.5 Dopaminergic pathways. The activity of neurons in the substantia nigra and ventral tegmental area of the midbrain is modulated by the neurotransmitter dopamine. These neurons project broadly throughout the brain, notably to the nucleus accumbens, the basal ganglia, and the ventral and medial parts of the prefrontal cortex.

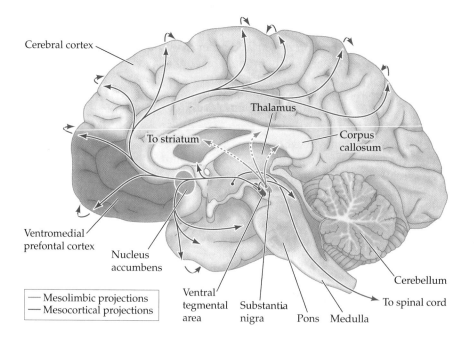

training, when the monkey was naive about the experimental task, the delivery of the juice reward evoked a significant increase in VTA activity. As the monkey learned the task, however, the VTA neurons fired less and less to the juice reward and began firing more and more to the light. With learning, therefore, the response of these particular dopamine neurons transfers from an unconditioned reinforcer to a conditioned stimulus that predicts that reinforcer. Moreover, if an expected reward was absent, then the activity of the neurons decreased below baseline firing rates. Subsequent studies by the same group suggested that the activation of VTA neurons is proportional both to the probability of reinforcement—with lower-probability rewards evoking greater activity—and to the magnitude of reinforcement.

Together these studies indicate that dopamine neuron activity provides an index of **reward prediction error**, defined as the difference between the expected reward and what was actually obtained. Subsequent functional neuroimaging studies have demonstrated that activation in the nucleus accumbens increases in response to unpredictable rewards compared to predictable rewards, consistent with the electrophysiological data in non-human primates. The dopamine error signal may generalize beyond simple reinforcers to other forms of novel or salient stimuli, but activity changes are not typically observed for aversive stimuli.

Given that activity in dopaminergic neurons is elicited for both drugs of abuse and conditioned reinforcers, one might infer that dopamine is associated with the pleasurable aspects of reward. This idea has been tested by intracranial self-stimulation of dopamine neurons. Rats were placed in a box with a lever, which, when pressed, delivered a train of electrical pulses to neurons in the VTA and substantia nigra. The animals repeatedly pressed the lever to receive the stimulation, indicating that it had considerable hedonic value. Although a natural interpretation is that the electrical stimulation was pleasurable, dopamine release was not observed. In another condition, stimulation was randomly and unexpectedly delivered by the experimenters, and dopamine release was observed. In short, dopamine neuron activity is associated with information about the motivational properties of rewards (wanting), but not the pleasurable aspects of the rewards per se (liking).

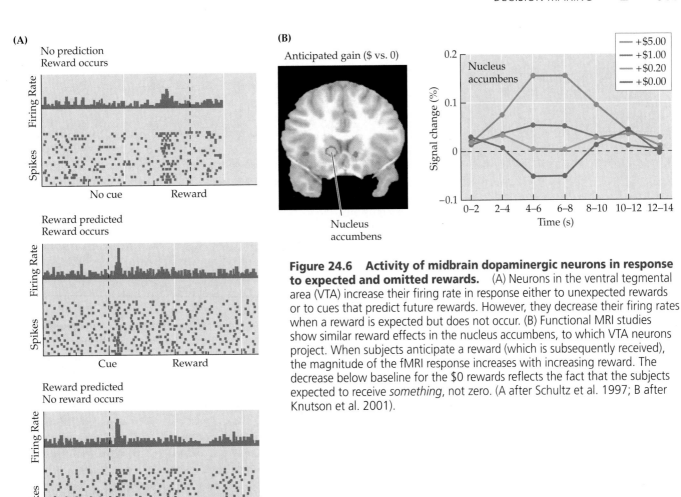

Figure 24.6 Activity of midbrain dopaminergic neurons in response to expected and omitted rewards. (A) Neurons in the ventral tegmental area (VTA) increase their firing rate in response either to unexpected rewards or to cues that predict future rewards. However, they decrease their firing rates when a reward is expected but does not occur. (B) Functional MRI studies show similar reward effects in the nucleus accumbens, to which VTA neurons project. When subjects anticipate a reward (which is subsequently received), the magnitude of the fMRI response increases with increasing reward. The decrease below baseline for the $0 rewards reflects the fact that the subjects expected to receive *something*, not zero. (A after Schultz et al. 1997; B after Knutson et al. 2001).

Basal ganglia and ventromedial prefrontal cortex

As described already, midbrain dopamine neurons project to many regions, most notably the basal ganglia and the ventromedial prefrontal cortex. These neurons, in conjunction with their projection targets in the basal ganglia, may be important for **temporal difference learning**. The key idea in temporal difference learning is that successive states of the world (and, in turn, predictions about those states) are correlated over time. Thus, it is computationally efficient to modify behavior according to changes in predictions (i.e., as cues and rewards occur unexpectedly) rather than keeping track of all cues and rewards over a long period of time.

Dopaminergic neurons in the ventral basal ganglia and the VTA exhibit increased activity both to cues that predict future rewards and to the delivery of rewards themselves. When cues or rewards occur unexpectedly, the ventral basal ganglia update ongoing predictions about how much reward can be expected in the future. In models of reinforcement learning, this evaluative role is sometimes referred to as the *critic*. Ventral striatal neurons exhibit more sensitivity to context than do VTA neurons. If a stimulus (e.g., a squirt of juice) is perceived by an experimental animal as relatively good in one context (e.g., when compared to a squirt of water) but bad in another (e.g., when compared to a dab of peanut butter), activity is greater in the context where the stimulus is more valued. Functional neuroimaging data in humans have indicated that the nucleus accumbens shows a transient increase in activity when a reward is expected, and the magnitude of that increase tracks the magnitude of expected reward (**Figure 24.6B**). If an expected reward fails to occur, activity in the nucleus accumbens decreases, as it does in VTA neurons.

A question of ongoing interest is whether activation of the ventral basal ganglia is specific to reward information or generalizes to other forms of salient stimuli. For example, unexpected and distracting events evoke activation in the basal ganglia, especially in ventral regions like the nucleus accumbens; and the magnitude of that activation increases as the events become more salient or interesting. It is not clear, however, how to reconcile saliency effects with reward-specific activity, since highly salient absences of expected reward result in decreases, not increases, in activity. Nor is it known whether and how salience influences other parts of the brain's reward circuitry. Recent fMRI studies suggest that novelty, but perhaps not other forms of salience, modulates activation of the substantia nigra and VTA in the midbrain, but more research will be needed to establish the relationship between salience and reward effects.

Although some neurons in the ventral striatum appear to evaluate rewards (thus playing the role of critic), the dorsal basal ganglia are important for the creation and modification of plans for action (see Chapter 9). This role is often labeled the *actor* in **actor-critic learning models**. Functional MRI studies support the functional distinction between these regions. Activation of the ventral basal ganglia follows rewards in both classical conditioning (passive) and instrumental conditioning (active) tasks, whereas activation of the dorsal basal ganglia is observed only in instrumental conditioning. Thus, the dorsal basal ganglia may be active only when reward information has implications for subsequent behavior. These observations are consistent with the perspective advanced in Chapter 23—namely, that the basal ganglia support the establishment of relatively direct links between specific stimuli and the required behavior.

Although the activity of striatal neurons is modulated by both informative cues and triggers for operant responses, activity of the ventromedial prefrontal cortex is typically associated with reward outcomes, but not with reward anticipation. As both neuroimaging and electrophysiological studies show, stimuli that are more valued by the subject tend to evoke increased activity in ventromedial prefrontal cortex. Conversely, lesion studies have shown that damage to this region reduces an individual's sensitivity to the negative consequences of actions. Evidence for this conclusion comes from the **Iowa Gambling Task**, which was developed by Antoine Bechara, Antonio Damasio, and their colleagues, then at the University of Iowa. Participants in this task are presented with four decks of cards, all face down. Decks A and B have large hypothetical rewards (e.g., $100) on every card, but also infrequent very large losses (e.g., about 10 percent of the cards in Deck B also have a loss of $1,250). Decks C and D are associated with small rewards (e.g., $50) on every card but only small losses on some of the cards. The decks are controlled so that A and B have negative expected values of –$25 per card, while C and D have positive expected values of +$25 per card. Subjects choose one card from one deck at a time to accumulate as much money as possible.

Patients with ventromedial prefrontal damage persist in choosing Decks A and B, even though those decks have a negative expected value. In addition, when selecting the bad decks, unlike normal individuals these patients exhibit no anticipatory skin conductance response (see the discussion of the somatic marker hypothesis in Chapter 18). The standard interpretation of these results is that damage to the ventromedial prefrontal cortex makes patients insensitive to signals of the risk or safety of upcoming choices; thus, their behavior is driven by the frequent large gains, whereas neurologically normal individuals learn from the infrequent losses.

Neuroeconomics

The integration of concepts from economics and neuroscience, as outlined in the previous two sections, has led to the emergence of a new field called **neuroeconomics**. The rapidly growing interest in neuroeconomics is a result of three converging trends in understanding the brain mechanisms underlying behavior. First, the increasing accessibility of functional neuroimaging has greatly facilitated studies of how people make decisions and evaluate rewards. Second, electrophysiological studies in non-human primates have demonstrated that neurons at multiple levels of perceptual and decision pathways encode motivationally relevant information (as we will see shortly). And third, the rise of behavioral economics has sparked renewed interest in the mechanisms of decision making.

A related factor is the evidence described earlier in the chapter that decisions are often irrational. They are primed by emotion, driven by fear of regret, shaped by social pressures, and grounded on a foundation of incomplete information. Once psychological variables became incorporated into standard models of decision making, studying the brain processes underlying those variables followed naturally, as described in the next few sections. As a result of these various influences, economic terms like *utility* and *subjective preference* are now part of the neuroscientific lexicon.

Basic value judgments

The simplest decisions in neuroeconomic research are **value judgments** (or *preference weightings*), which involve selecting one course of action from a set of possible courses on the basis of associated values and anticipated rewards. We make such judgments every day when we decide to eat a sandwich instead of a salad or to go canoeing rather than seeing a movie on a beautiful summer afternoon. Judgments of value, at first blush, may seem ephemeral. How could one study something as inherently personal as the relative values assigned to such options? Different people clearly have different tastes and will thus have different preferences about how to spend summer afternoons; moreover, circumstances can change a person's preferences, as anyone who has had to eat a favorite dish several days in a row can attest. Thus, there is often no objectively optimal choice in such decisions. Nevertheless, understanding how the brain incorporates value into decision making has become a vigorous area of research.

The first electrophysiological study of the effects of value on decision making was conducted by the neurophysiologists Michael Platt and Paul Glimcher, then at New York University (see Chapter 9 for a more extensive discussion of this experiment). They chose to record in a region of the parietal lobes called the **lateral intraparietal area** (*area LIP*) because that region had been theorized to represent a nexus between low-level attentional signals and high-level motor outputs. Expected value had a marked effect on neurons in this region. The firing rate increased to stimuli associated with larger or more probable rewards, especially early in the trials, before the monkey could execute a particular motor plan. Subsequent work from these and other investigators has now elucidated some of the functions of this region. When monkeys are placed in a simulated foraging task, in which the value of different responses changes dynamically, the activation of LIP neurons also changes dynamically as a function of the relative value of the possible actions.

Although this evidence shows that area LIP is important in at least some aspects of value-based decision making, its specific contributions are not yet clear. Given the sensitivity of this region to visuospatial input and to eye movements, one possibility is that LIP activation is specific to the modality of response (i.e., oculomotor control). Some evidence for this idea is provided by the observation that the probability of reward influences the activity of neurons within the superior colliculus, a structure directly concerned with the control of eye movements. More generally, LIP activity might reflect the transformation of value to action, consistent with demonstrations that LIP neurons track short-term fluctuations in the value of different response options. This latter perspective is consistent with neuroimaging studies showing that the parietal cortex supports the generation and modification of behavioral rules (see Chapter 23).

Mechanisms of interactive decision making

As is apparent from the earlier discussion in this chapter, a particular interest in neuroeconomics is decision making during economic games. So far, studies on this topic have investigated primarily the neural correlates of cooperative behavior and trust, for which the prisoner's dilemma (see Figure 24.4A) provides a natural framework. When this game is repeated over many trials, repeated cooperation by the two players yields the best mutual outcome. Although defection makes more money for a player on any given trial, it often causes the opponent to defect as well, lowering the total amount earned. Functional neuroimaging studies of the prisoner's dilemma game played over time have suggested that cooperation itself evokes activation in brain regions associated with rewards. When people choose to reciprocate following a cooperative action by their partner, activation increases in the ventral striatum (including the nucleus accumbens), the anterior caudate, and the anterior cingulate cortex. These regions have been associated with the evaluation of reward information; thus, one interpretation of the results is that subjects in these games find cooperation rewarding. Another interpretation is that cooperation generally predicts increased reward on subsequent trials, reflecting a ventral striatum response that reflects changes in future reward levels.

The neural basis of cooperation has also been studied through the use of variants of the trust game described earlier (see Figure 24.4C). A methodological development that promises to enhance future studies of interactive decision making is the *simultaneous* recording of fMRI data from individuals in two scanners who are playing a game against each other. This approach, which has been called **hyperscanning** by Read Montague and his group at Baylor College of Medicine, allows behavioral and brain changes in one individual to be predicted from the behavioral and brain changes in another. Data from a multiple-round trust game show that activation in the caudate (dorsal striatum) seems to signal an intention to subsequently trust one's opponent (**Figure 24.7**). In early rounds of the game, activation of the trustee's caudate increases in response to the actions of the investor. Once trust has been established in later rounds, however, the caudate is activated earlier in the trial.

This change from reactive to anticipatory activity in the caudate has been interpreted as the building of a model about the opponent, which then can be used to decide whether or not to trust that person. A hyperscanning approach has been used subsequently to demonstrate that the pattern of activation within the cingulate gyrus, which is linked to evaluations of the need for cognitive control (see Chapter 23), differs between evaluation of one's own decisions and presentation of the opponent's decisions. These and related results demonstrate the complex integration of information that is required in decision making.

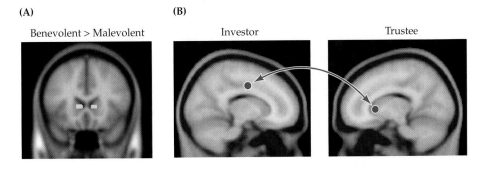

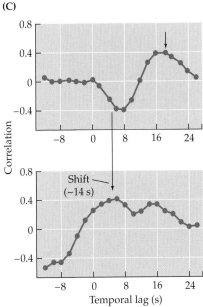

Figure 24.7 The neural correlates of trust in decision making.
(A) A variety of socially rewarding actions activate the basal ganglia, specifically in the head of the caudate nucleus. Shown here are voxels that exhibited greater fMRI activation to benevolent, cooperative actions than to malevolent, selfish actions in an investment game. (B) The researchers recorded fMRI data from the investor and the trustee simultaneously, examining the relations between fMRI activation in the cingulate cortex of the investor and in the caudate of the trustee. (C) On early trials, activation in the trustee lagged activation in the investor by about 16 seconds, which corresponds to the delay between the investor's decision and the trustee's decision. But after the two people had played the game six times, the trustee's brain was activated much earlier (arrows indicate the time lag with maximal correlation). The authors interpreted this change as reflecting the developing intention to trust, based on an expectation of fair behavior by the opponent. (After King-Casas et al. 2005.)

Activation in the dorsal striatum has also been associated with the intent to punish opponents who violate trust. In a game allowing people to punish noncooperators altruistically—by spending their own money to take away money of another person, whom they have not met and will not meet in the future—the caudate is activated when subjects can effectively punish their opponents, and that activation increases in subjects who are willing to spend more money to exert greater punishment. Taken together, these studies suggest that the dorsal striatum plays an important role in reward-directed decision making, at least in interactive settings.

Cooperation may result in large part from recognition that unfair behavior is likely to elicit *retaliation*. One form of retaliatory behavior is active punishment, which, as noted, evokes activation in the dorsal striatum. Another form is refusal to accept unfair offers; in the ultimatum game, for example, people reject a division of money if it seems unfair, even if it costs them money to do so (see Figure 24.4B). To understand why, researchers have studied how brain activation differs when people are given a fair or unfair offer in this game. The brain regions of most interest in these experiments are those associated with emotional processing, especially the anterior cingulate cortex and the insular cortex.

The **insular cortex** (the "island" of cortex created by the infolding of the ventral frontal lobe; see Chapter 1) contains neurons that support the sensations of taste and pain, amid other bodily information. Yet the insula also plays a role in decision making. Unfair offers activate the insular cortex, and the activation is greater for offers that are more unfair. Moreover, when insular activation is greater, unfair offers are more likely to be rejected. One interpretation of these results is that the insular activation provides an emotional signal that can override more rational evaluation of the outcomes. That interpretation is consistent with other studies showing that insular activation increases for risky decisions compared to safe decisions. One explanation for the seemingly disparate functions of the insula is that the brain has co-opted systems for aversive sensations (e.g., gustatory cortex within the insula), applying the same processing to emotionally aversive or risky behaviors (compare the somatic marker hypothesis introduced in Chapter 18).

Finally, decision-making processes depend on assessments of an opponent's goals and desires. In several neuroimaging studies, subjects have played the same game against human and computer opponents. When subjects play the games against computer opponents—and know that their opponents are computers—they are much less likely to evaluate the reasoning behind an opponent's actions or to retaliate against unfair behavior. Consistent with these behavioral effects, decision making in games against computers is often associated with reduced neural activation in the relevant areas. Depending on the study, the prefrontal cortex may be less activated, perhaps reflecting the absence of higher-level integrative or strategic reflection (see Box 25B) in the basal ganglia, because rewarding social signals are absent; and in regions that support emotional processes, because unfair offers made by computers elicit minimal affective reactions. Thus, decision making does not depend simply on the available choices and potential outcomes, but on how one interprets others' actions and uses that information to guide one's own decisions.

Decision preferences

An advantage of combining neuroimaging and economic studies of decision making is the opportunity to extend basic neuroscience approaches into real-world settings. For instance, when making decisions about what to buy, most people express a wide range of preferences—some that are relatively stable, and others that are easily influenced by context. The allocation of millions of advertising dollars rests on the empirical evidence that people's decisions can be altered by a change in how a given product is perceived, whether Volkswagens are associated with quirky individualism or McDonald's restaurants are associated with happy children.

Neuroeconomics research is unlikely to be of much value in specific advertising or marketing campaigns, given the amount of variability in how people perceive different products under different circumstances. It could provide insight, however, into the brain mechanisms underlying decision preferences, and how different types of information influence those mechanisms. For example, fMRI was used in one pertinent study to scan subjects while they awaited the delivery of squirts of either Coke or Pepsi. Activation in the ventromedial prefrontal cortex was correlated with subjects' behavioral preferences. Subjects who were more likely to choose Coke in a taste test showed greater activation when Coke was presented, and the reverse was observed for those who were more likely to choose Pepsi (**Figure 24.8**). This observation suggests that activity within a brain region known to be important for the evaluation of reward outcomes can be modulated by behavioral preferences. Furthermore, when subjects who preferred Coke were cued with an image of a Coke can before the squirt, activation in the hippocampus and in the dorsolateral prefrontal cortex increased, whereas no such change was observed for Pepsi cues. One interpretation of this result is that mnemonic associations, learned over years of exposure to advertising, are activated by hippocampal and prefrontal systems, thus modulating subjective preferences.

How strongly a person wants something often depends on how long it takes to obtain it. In general, people prefer immediate to delayed rewards and must overcome this **temporal discounting** tendency when saving for the future or avoiding impulse purchases. A paradox raised by temporal discounting is the development of time-inconsistent preferences. Most people prefer smaller immediate rewards to slightly larger delayed rewards—for example, $100 received now (A) versus $110 to be received a week from now (B). On the other hand, given the option of receiving $100 in 52 weeks (C) or $110 in 53 weeks (D), most people choose option D. The inconsistency in preferring A over B and D over C becomes apparent when one considers what would happen in 52 weeks. At that point in time, the person would still have

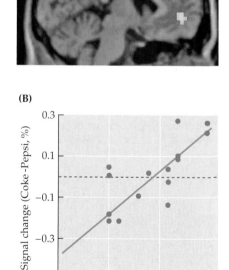

(A)

(B)

Figure 24.8 Activation in the ventromedial prefrontal cortex tracks subjective preferences. Functional MRI activation in the ventromedial prefrontal cortex (A) was different in subjects anticipating a squirt of Coke™ or Pepsi™ (B, y-axis), depending on whether the subject tended to prefer Coke™ or Pepsi™ in a prior taste test (B, x-axis). (After McClure et al. 2004.)

to wait another week to get $110 (now analogous to B), even after specifying a preference of getting an immediate $100 (now analogous to A).

Although temporal discounting is a challenging phenomenon to assess in the laboratory, recent studies suggest a possible resolution of this paradox. When subjects make choices between two monetary rewards that could be received at different times, choices that involve a reward that would be obtained today activate the ventral striatum and the medial and ventral prefrontal cortex. The magnitude of activation within the ventral striatum, in particular, tracks how much an individual subject values a particular delayed reward (i.e., there is less activation for future rewards in people whose behavioral data indicated that they are very averse to waiting). As discussed earlier, these regions receive significant input from dopaminergic neurons and are involved with representing reward information. In contrast, lateral prefrontal cortex is similarly active regardless of the time until reward. These results suggest that preferences for short- or long-term rewards, respectively, depend on the interaction between these brain regions. When faced with choices between immediate and delayed rewards, increased striatal and medial prefrontal activation results in a preference for the immediate reward. When faced with two delayed rewards, however, decision-making systems in the lateral prefrontal cortex may support the evaluation of reward magnitude rather than temporal proximity.

Information integration in decision making

Electrophysiological studies have suggested that multiple areas within both prefrontal and parietal cortices contribute to sensory integration in advance of a decision (for an example, see Figure 6.18). Information integration is harder to study with functional neuroimaging because of the spatial coarseness of its data. However, researchers have had some success using perceptual categories that elicit significantly different regional activations, such as in the different object category regions within the ventral temporal lobe (see Chapters 5 and 21). Photographs of faces and houses provide a natural pair of categories; and if sufficient noise is introduced, they can be made difficult to discriminate. When subjects make decisions about whether a given stimulus is a face or house, activation in the ventral temporal lobe increases in the stimulus-appropriate regions proportional to the clarity of the stimulus. However, concurrent activation is observed along the superior frontal sulcus in the dorsolateral prefrontal cortex that is independent of stimulus category, and greatest for simple discriminations (**Figure 24.9**). In contrast, regions supporting

Figure 24.9 Evidence that the prefrontal cortex integrates information in decisions about blurry stimuli. When subjects make decisions about whether a given stimulus is a face or house, activation increases in the stimulus-appropriate regions. (A) Activation of a region of the left dorsolateral prefrontal cortex (DLPFC) was correlated with activation of a face-selective region in the fusiform gyrus and a place-selective region in the parahippocampal gyrus. (B) When activity increased in the relevant region of the DLPFC, subjects tended to be correct in their decisions. When activity was reduced, subjects were often incorrect. These results suggest that this region is important for integrating perceptual information to reach a useful decision. (After Heekeren et al. 2004.)

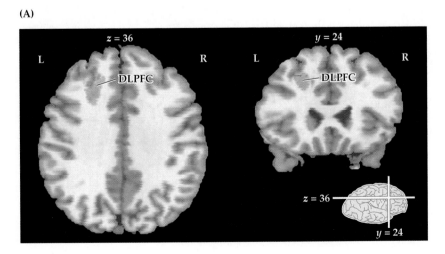

(A)

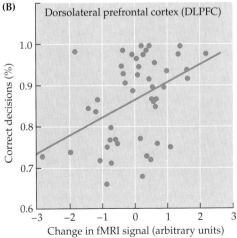

(B)

■ BOX 24B Uses and Abuses of Work in Neuroeconomics

To understand how neural processing contributes to economic behavior will require the synthesis of concepts from economics, psychology, and neuroscience. Popular accounts, however, often gloss over the limitations and difficulties involved, proffering breathless headlines such as "Researchers Discover Why Some People Seek Out Risks," or "Scientists Find the Part of the Brain That Makes People Cooperate." These sorts of reports are at best a mixed blessing; they promote new and exciting research but fail to alert readers to the ethical and practical issues that such research entails.

One pernicious issue in the popularization of neuroeconomics research—as well as of cognitive neuroscience studies generally—is the tendency to regard the brain activity elicited in a given paradigm as indicating a definitive answer about the basis of a particular cognitive function or question (see the figure for examples of simplistic interpretations of complex phenomena). This fallacy has sometimes been called *neurorealism*. The methods presently used in cognitive neuroscience are hardly definitive, and all have severe limitations (see Chapter 3). To the public, the identification of a specific brain area associated with a particular cognitive phenomenon can make research claims seem far more concrete and far-reaching than justifiable, much as in the pre-mature inferences drawn from discoveries about the genetic basis for Alzheimer's disease, major depression, or pathological aggression.

There has been an unfortunate and perhaps related groundswell of interest in *neuromarketing*, a term applied to the possible use of neuroscience data to help determine how best to brand and advertise commercial products. To many ethicists, the prospect of neuromarketing reflects a dangerous direction that abuses science, but some entrepreneurs see such information as just another source of marketing data. Of course, marketers do not need to measure brain activity to determine whether a particular advertisement causes more people to buy their product; they can simply measure purchasing behavior, as has been done for decades. Economists are thus understandably skeptical about whether neuroeconomics will have any practical consequences for commercial ventures.

Even so, in some arenas neuroscience does promise an impact on economic theory and social policy. For instance, cognitive neuroscience provides specific, biologically based constraints for economic models.

Some constraints are general, as in studies of executive function, or of the interactions between reasoning and emotion. Other constraints are specific to particular models. For instance, economists are increasingly interested in populations whose decision making is systematically maladaptive, such as addicts, habitual criminals, sociopaths, and others with behavioral pathologies. Because different neural deficits are found in each group, a policy of intervention that might be appropriate for one group would not necessarily be appropriate for others. Collaborations of economists, neuroscientists, and clinicians are beginning to tackle these difficult problems.

References

GLIMCHER, P. W. AND A. RUSTICHINI (2004) Neuroeconomics: The consilience of brain and decision. *Science* 306: 447–452.

RACINE, E., O. BAR-ILAN AND J. ILLES (2005) fMRI in the public eye. *Nature Rev. Neurosci.* 6: 159–164.

Studies of cognitive functions picked up by the popular media often lead to sensationalism. Because the intended audience knows neither the anatomy nor the jargon used to describe it, sweeping simplifications are commonplace (e.g., treating the frontal lobe as a unitary structure). Moreover, complex concepts like personality, intelligence, or emotion are falsely linked to specific areas, and erroneous inferences are drawn about behavior—for example, how one can become a better parent or investor in the stock market. (All headlines are taken from actual news reports from CNN or ABC.)

Can Personality be Traced to the Brain? Researchers Look for Signs

Science Journal

Do men really listen with just half a brain? Research sheds some light

Doctors: Front of brain controls fear

Prefrontal cortex *memory of safety*

Amygdala *memory of fear*

Fear

A measure of intelligence: Scientists say brain scans show locus for basic intelligence... ...Test preparation courses may be a waste of money after all.

processes related to attentional or cognitive control are more active for difficult discriminations. This result suggests that the dorsolateral prefrontal cortex may serve as a sensory integrator during at least some forms of decision-making tasks.

Despite these advances, questions remain about the correspondence between electrophysiological data in non-human primates (which suggest that a broad set of regions perform integrative functions) and human neuroimaging data (which support a more focal mechanism). One possible explanation of this discrepancy is methodological; fMRI could be insensitive to activity in particular regions, providing an incomplete picture of a distributed process. Alternatively, decision-making systems could have some fundamental differences in monkeys and humans, perhaps because of an increased capacity for abstraction in humans.

Resolving uncertainty

Neuroeconomic research on decision making has also been concerned with how people deal with *uncertainty*. This term means different things in different settings, but it can be thought of as the psychological state of having limited information, as often occurs in making real-world decisions. Functional MRI experiments have shown that when people make decisions fraught with uncertainty, activation increases in the posterior part of the medial frontal lobe. The area most reliably activated by uncertainty across experiments lies within Brodmann area 8, anterior to the premotor cortex—a region referred to as **frontomedian cortex**. Only some types of uncertain decision making activate this region, however. When uncertainty reflects limited information about what decisions should be made in response to a stimulus, then the magnitude of frontomedian cortex activation depends on the degree of uncertainty about the decision. But when the uncertainty of an outcome cannot be simplified further (e.g., when rolling dice), then frontomedian cortex activation does not increase with uncertainty. Instead, the lateral prefrontal and parietal regions become more active.

The approaches used in cognitive neuroscience can also inform economic theory and constrain economic modeling, although sometimes the implications of neuroscience are overstated (**Box 24B**). Consider, for instance two forms of uncertainty: risk and ambiguity. A decision involves *risk* if it has several potential outcomes with known probabilities. Betting on red or black in roulette is an example of a risky decision. In contrast, a decision involves *ambiguity* if the probabilities of its outcomes cannot be known. Many economic theorists have considered risk and ambiguity to be equivalent, assuming that all decisions involve subjective assessments of probability; others have argued for a distinction between these categories. If clear differences were to emerge between the patterns of brain activation evoked by risk and by ambiguity—especially within regions critical for decision making—then one could assume that the process of decision making differs for these conditions. Recent research suggests that this is indeed the case; ambiguity and risk have different effects on both ventral brain systems that support reward evaluation and lateral prefrontal and parietal regions associated with the resolution of uncertainty (**Figure 24.10**).

Such studies can also provide links between economic theory and real-world decisions. Perhaps the most pernicious form of maladaptive decision making is drug addiction. Addicts make repeated poor decisions that contribute to addiction, placing themselves in situations that offer the potential for relapse and engaging in self-destructive behavior despite experience with its long-term consequences. Economists have shown substantial enthusiasm for encapsulating these decision processes within models that can predict the

(A) Lateral orbitofrontal cortex   **(B)** Lateral prefrontal cortex

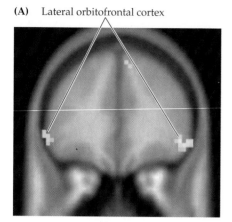
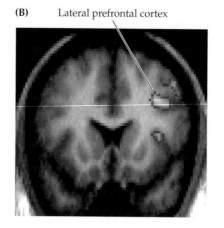
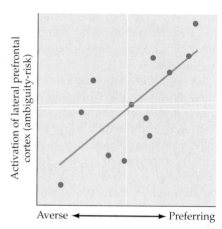

Averse ← → Preferring

Figure 24.10   Decision making in the face of economic ambiguity.   Many people are averse to ambiguity, which is defined by economists as a situation in which one must make a decision without knowing the probabilities of the possible outcomes. (A) Ambiguity in decision making evokes increased activation in the orbitofrontal cortex compared to risky decision making, perhaps because of its aversiveness. (B) Ambiguity also evokes increased activation in lateral prefrontal cortex, which may reflect the need to think about the possible probabilities and to construct a decision rule. Supporting this latter interpretation, the magnitude of activation in the lateral prefrontal cortex during decision making under ambiguous circumstances depends on whether the subject prefers or is averse to ambiguity. (A from Hsu et al. 2005; B from Huettel et al. 2006.)

course and consequences of addiction. Indeed, addictive decisions will be understood only when they are considered in the context of addiction's effects on brain systems for reward evaluation and decision making.

Summary

1. In decision making, one option is selected from a set based on prior knowledge, expectations about outcomes, and preferences about potential rewards.

2. Early research in economics combined ideas about expected value and probability weighting to create expected-utility models of rational decision makers. More recent economic research incorporates ideas from psychology about heuristics and biases, relaxing some of the assumptions of rationality in favor of the more realistic recognition that very little real-world decision making is rational.

3. Single-unit recording studies in non-human primates show that neurons can carry information about the expected values of stimuli, and that their activity can be used to predict an animal's decision preferences.

4. In parallel with this work, interest in reward systems in the brain, particularly the mesolimbic dopaminergic pathways, has exploded. Both electrophysiological and neuroimaging studies indicate that information about rewards is processed by a set of largely ventral brain regions that include the nucleus accumbens in the basal ganglia and the ventromedial prefrontal cortex.

5. Such methods have also been used to explore the neural correlates of phenomena like trust, altruism, unfairness, and subjective preferences.

6. Concepts derived from cognitive neuroscience and behavioral economics influence each other in the emerging discipline of neuroeconomics. Key areas of research within neuroeconomics include how the striatum facilitates learning and preference construction, how insular and orbitofrontal cortices shape risky decision making, how prefrontal and parietal cortices contribute to the resolution of uncertainty, and whether descriptive economic theories should be revised to reflect new data in neuroscience.

Additional Reading

Reviews

PLATT, M. L. (2002) Neural correlates of decisions. *Curr. Opin. Neurobiol.* 12: 141–148.

SCHULTZ, W., P. DAYAN AND P. R. MONTAGUE (1997) A neural substrate of prediction and reward. *Science* 275: 1593–1599.

TVERSKY, A. AND D. KAHNEMAN (1974) Judgment under uncertainty: Heuristics and biases. *Science* 185: 1124–1131.

Important Original Papers

BECHARA, A., H. DAMASIO, D. TRANEL AND A. R. DAMASIO (1997) Deciding advantageously before knowing the advantageous strategy. *Science* 275: 1293–1295.

DE QUERVAIN, D. J. AND 6 OTHERS (2004) The neural basis of altruistic punishment. *Science* 305: 1254–1258.

DE QUERVAIN, D. J. AND 6 OTHERS (2004) The neural basis of altruistic punishment. *Science* 305: 1254–1258.

GLIMCHER, P. A., J. KABLE, AND K. LOUIE (2007) Neuroeconomic studies of impulsivity: Now or just as soon as possible? *Amer. Econ. Rev.* 97: 142–147.

HSU, M., M. BHATT, R. ADOLPHS, D. TRANEL AND C. F. CAMERER (2005) Neural systems responding to degrees of uncertainty in human decision-making. *Science* 310: 1680–1683.

HUETTEL, S. A., C. J. STOWE, E. M. GORDON, B. T. WARNER AND M. L. PLATT (2006) Neural signatures of economic preferences for risk and ambiguity. *Neuron* 49: 765–775.

KAHNEMAN, D. AND A. TVERSKY (1979) Prospect theory: An analysis of decision under risk. *Econometrica* 47: 263–291.

KING-CASAS, B., D. TOMLIN, C. ANEN, C. F. CAMERER, S. R. QUARTZ AND P. R. MONTAGUE (2005) Getting to know you: Reputation and trust in a two-person economic exchange. *Science* 308: 78–83.

KNUTSON, B., G. W. FONG, C. M. ADAMS, J. L. VARNER AND D. HOMMER (2001) Dissociation of reward anticipation and outcome with event-related fMRI. *Neuroreport* 12: 3683–3687.

MCCLURE, S. M., D. I. LAIBSON, G. LOEWENSTEIN AND J. D. COHEN (2004) Separate neural systems value immediate and delayed monetary rewards. *Science* 306: 503–507.

MCCLURE, S. M., J. LI, D. TOMLIN, K. S. CYPERT, L. M. MONTAGUE AND P. R. MONTAGUE (2004) Neural correlates of behavioral preference for culturally familiar drinks. *Neuron* 44: 379–387.

O'DOHERTY, J. P., P. DAYAN, J. SCHULTZ, R. DEICHMANN, K. FRISTON AND R. J. DOLAN (2004) Dissociable roles of ventral and dorsal striatum in instrumental conditioning. *Science* 304: 452–454.

PLATT, M. L. AND P. W. GLIMCHER (1999) Neural correlates of decision variables in parietal cortex. *Nature* 400: 233–238.

RILLING, J., D. GUTMAN, T. ZEH, G. PAGNONI, G. BERNS AND C. KILTS (2002) A neural basis for social cooperation. *Neuron* 35: 395–405.

SANFEY, A. G., J. K. RILLING, J. A. ARONSON, L. E. NYSTROM AND J. D. COHEN (2003) The neural basis of economic decision-making in the Ultimatum Game. *Science* 300: 1755–1758.

SUGRUE, L. P., G. S. CORRADO AND W. T. NEWSOME (2004) Matching behavior and the representation of value in parietal cortex. *Science* 304: 1782–1787.

VOLZ, K. G., R. I. SCHUBOTZ AND D. Y. VON CRAMON (2003) Predicting events of varying probability: Uncertainty investigated by fMRI. *Neuroimage* 19: 271–280.

ZINK, C. F., G. PAGNONI, M. E. MARTIN-SKURSKI, J. C. CHAPPELOW AND G. S. BERNS (2004) Human striatal responses to monetary reward depend on saliency. *Neuron* 42: 509–517.

Books

CAMERER, C. (2003) *Behavioral Game Theory: Experiments in Strategic Interaction.* Princeton, NJ: Princeton University Press.

GIGERENZER, G., P. M. TODD AND THE ABC RESEARCH GROUP (1999) *Simple Heuristics That Make Us Smart.* New York: Oxford University Press.

GLIMCHER, P. W. (2003) *Decisions, Uncertainty, and the Brain: The Science of Neuroeconomics.* Cambridge, MA: MIT Press.

HASTIE, R. AND R. M. DAWES (2001) *Rational Choice in an Uncertain World: The Psychology of Judgment and Decision Making.* Thousand Oaks, CA: Sage.

MEYER, J. S. AND L. F. QUENZER (2005) *Psychopharmacology: Drugs, the Brain, and Behavior.* Sunderland, MA: Sinauer.

25

Reasoning and Problem Solving

Introduction

More than any other abilities, reasoning and problem solving embody what are commonly called *thinking* and *intelligence*. Indeed, the capacity to reason is often considered the essence of humanity, a point made most famously by René Descartes' dictum "I think, therefore I am." That reasoning and problem-solving skills are central to the cognition of *Homo sapiens* is clear, although similar abilities—albeit not so well developed—are apparent in non-human primates and in some other mammals and birds. Reasoning and problem solving share many similarities; they involve the planning and sequencing of actions, they often require foresight and logic, and they are expressly goal oriented. However, they can be roughly distinguished in terms of the processes, both cognitive and neural, that they require. Reasoning scenarios usually involve logical inferences based on well-defined rules. Consider, for example, Aristotle's syllogism "All men are mortal. Socrates is a man. Therefore, Socrates is mortal." Applying the rules of logic confirms that the syllogism's conclusion is true; Socrates is indeed mortal. Problem-solving scenarios, in contrast, present a starting point and a desired outcome, but do not specify the intervening steps. The problem solver often tries different approaches to see what works and what does not, abandoning strategies that seem initially successful. The very rules of the problem are frequently unspecified. Suppose you want to hang a light from a high ceiling, but you do not have a ladder. How could you fashion a tool that would help you solve this problem? Many problems, including this one, have a large number of potential solutions, making the problem solver's challenge not one of logical reasoning but one of creative and associative thinking. Understanding the mechanisms that underlie reasoning and problem solving remains an extraordinary challenge for cognitive neuroscience.

Deductive Reasoning

The simplest example of reasoning involves argument from premises to conclusions. This is known as **deductive reasoning** because the truth of a given conclusion must be deduced solely from a set of premises that are already in hand. A good example of deductive reasoning is the **syllogism**, which consists of two axiomatic premises and a single conclusion. Whether a syllogism is true or false depends only on the logical relations between its premises and the conclusion, and not on the truth or falsity of the premises. If the Aristotelian syllogism in the introduction to this chapter were reframed as "All men have blue hair. Socrates is a man. Therefore, Socrates has blue hair," it would remain equally valid. Premises in deductive arguments are expressed in relational terms (e.g., *is, greater than, below*), propositional terms (e.g., *if, and, or*), and quantifiable terms (e.g., *some, all, none*). These different terms can be expressed symbolically, and logicians have developed a system of notation that is used to express and evaluate many forms of deductive arguments.

The simple form of most syllogisms belies the difficulty of their solution. Consider this seemingly straightforward argument about a university campus: "If there is a final examination tomorrow, the library is full of students. There is no final examination tomorrow. Therefore, the library is not full of students." Does this conclusion logically follow from the premises? If not, why? When thinking about deductive arguments, it is often helpful to put them in abstract form so that prior knowledge about the truth of the premises does not contaminate the reasoning. (As discussed in the following sections, researchers have demonstrated that different brain systems support deductive reasoning in the presence and absence of content.) A common method of simplification is to replace all content terms with letters, so that the syllogism becomes: "If P, then Q. Not P. Therefore, not Q." For comparison, the Aristotelian syllogisms introduced here could be stated as follows: "If P, then Q. P. Therefore, Q."

Reducing these syllogisms to their basic logical structure allows us to quickly identify correct and incorrect forms of reasoning (**Figure 25.1**). The Aristotelian syllogism is clearly true and corresponds to a logical structure known as ***modus ponens***, or "the mode of argument that affirms." But what about the final exam syllogism? Note that the first premise states nothing about what happens if P is not true; that is, no information is given about the library's attendance on other days. The library could well be always full of students, even when no final is to be given. An error in logic of this form is known as **denying the antecedent** because the second premise denies the truth of the

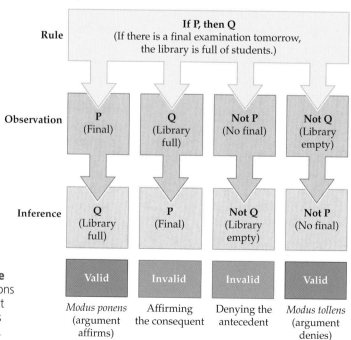

Figure 25.1 **Examples of correct and incorrect deductive reasoning.** A basic rule is shown, and four possible observations are indicated. Given the rule, some of the inferences made about the observations are valid and others are not. The logical process underlying each inference is given at the bottom of the diagram.

first term (antecedent) in the first premise. Another common error is to reverse the direction of inference: "If P, then Q. Q. Therefore, P." This error is known as **affirming the consequent** because the second premise affirms the truth of the second term (consequent) in the first premise. The final, and most frequently overlooked, form of deductive reasoning is known as *modus tollens*, "the mode that denies." A *modus tollens* argument takes the form "If P, then Q. Not Q. Therefore, not P." Note that if the premise Q is false (e.g., "The library is not full of students."), then the consequent of the first statement has not been met, which would have happened only if P were true. As discussed in **Box 25A**, people often have difficulty evaluating and using *modus tollens* arguments, especially when those arguments are framed in abstract form.

Theories of deductive reasoning

Although the basic principles of deductive reasoning have been recognized for millennia, the underlying neural processes remain the object of considerable debate. One interpretation of how humans can reason in this way is that people possess a faculty for rough **mental logic** that contains rules corresponding to basic forms of inference. When faced with a challenge that requires reasoning, they abstract the problem and then employ rules one after another until a solution is reached.

This perspective can explain much human reasoning but also has significant limitations. In fact, people do not seem to reason abstractly, but instead use prior knowledge to reach a solution. For example, performance suffers greatly when people are asked to evaluate the truth of syllogisms that have false premises, such as "No cigarettes are harmful." Indeed, even seemingly elementary logical statements can contain subtle assumptions that can be confounding. Imagine touring an art gallery and entering a room with four paintings by Italian masters. The Filippo Lippi painting is to the left of the Fra Angelico, the Veneziano is to the left of the Filippo Lippi, and the Gozzoli is to the left of the Veneziano. Therefore, the Gozzoli must be to the left of the Fra Angelico, right? Although such a conclusion is logically correct under the assumption that the four paintings are arranged on a single wall, it is incorrect in this example, because the four paintings are actually on separate walls of a square room in the National Gallery of Art in Washington DC. Simply applying the sorts of rules illustrated in Figure 25.1 would not be an efficient way to generate behavior in most ordinary circumstances, where experience rather than logic is a better guide to success.

These and similar objections make a strong mental-logic view of reasoning untenable. A contrasting **mental model** perspective has been proposed by the psychologist Philip Johnson-Laird, who suggested that real-world reasoning does not involve formal rules of logic (**Figure 25.2**). Instead, he speculated that people construct one or more models that assume the truth of the premises and then evaluate whether the conclusion would be true or false in each. If they cannot construct a model in which the conclusion is false, then its truth is assumed to follow from the premises.

The mental model theory predicts that some forms of reasoning errors are more likely than others. In particular, people should be relatively good at using information about what is true (i.e., hypothesis-confirming), but relatively poor at using information about what is false (hypothesis-falsifying). In the art

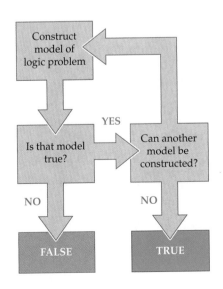

Figure 25.2 The mental model approach to deductive reasoning. A central concept in this approach is the idea that people are good at evaluating the truth of hypotheses (e.g., at falsifying possible models) but fail to create all possible models. This concept predicts the tendency to accept errors in logic.

■ BOX 25A Context Effects on Reasoning

Most conceptions of reasoning consider it to be abstract, logical, and domain-general. If this view were correct, the rules of logic should apply equally to any form of reasoning. Another possibility, however, is that the ways we reason differ according to what we are reasoning about. An important context for examining this issue is social reasoning, with which, compared to syllogisms and other abstract presentations, all humans have a great deal of experience. Social reasoning problems have sparked substantial interest—first among evolutionary biologists and now among neuroscientists. For example, it is important to identify people who violate mutually beneficial conventions for behavior, whether they are formal laws or informal social norms. A number of social scientists, notably Leda Cosmides and John Tooby at UC Santa Barbara, have argued that the importance of detecting such violators might be based on a specialized region or system within the brain.

To investigate whether reasoning processes differ in social and nonsocial situations, Cosmides, Tooby, and their colleagues used the Wason Card Sorting Task, which involves simple propositional reasoning (see Figures A–C). In this task, subjects are shown a set of four cards and must test the truth of a proposition, such as "Cards that have vowels on one side have even numbers on the other side." Since only one side of each card is visible, some of the cards must be turned over to learn what is on the other side and thus evaluate the merit of the proposition. The subjects must indicate which cards are necessary and sufficient for making this evaluation. Under standard forms of the task (Figure A), almost everyone selects cards that are consistent with the first clause (e.g., having vowels). But many people also make both commission and omission errors; they select cards consistent with the second clause (e.g., having even numbers), even though this is an affirming-the-consequent error, and they miss cards inconsistent with the second clause (e.g., having odd numbers). However, when the same task is reframed in a social context (specifically as a search for violations of a permission rule—i.e., cheating), subjects' performance improves dramatically. The example presented in Figure C is particularly salient, intuitive, and easily evaluated by young adults. Even unfamiliar social contexts lead to improved performance; when the permission rule involves the rituals of a fictional tribe of island people, performance is similarly good.

Although there has been considerable effort to exclude alternative explanations for these results, disagreements remain about what aspect of the social-framing manipulation contributes to improved performance and about whether social effects on reasoning extend to other tasks. Recent fMRI experiments have compared social and nonsocial versions of the Wason task. The results showed that both versions evoke activation in the left prefrontal cortex, as expected from prior research reviewed in this chapter. When subjects were reasoning about social rules, however, additional activation was observed in right prefrontal and parietal cortices, suggesting that additional brain regions were recruited. As is considered further in the discussion of inductive reasoning, experience can often trump logic in reaching decisions, particularly decisions about biologically important events and outcomes. To what extent such decisions fit a standard definition of reasoning is an open and interesting question.

---

gallery example, the natural model of the premises (all paintings on the same wall) implies a possibly true, but in this case incorrect, conclusion; only if another less obvious model is considered will the premature conclusion be rejected.

In summary, the basic building blocks of deductive reasoning seem to be extrapolations from inferences about the world that we commonly experience, much like the basis for inductive reasoning discussed later in the chapter. This conclusion implies that the way in which we reason, at its root, does not involve the abstractions and manipulations of formal logic. As will be considered in the following sections, converging evidence for this perspective comes from neuroimaging studies that demonstrate many similarities between the neural systems that support deductive and inductive reasoning.

Neural systems that support deductive reasoning

Some understanding of the brain systems that contribute to deductive reasoning has come from deficits in patients with cortical lesions, as well as from patterns of activation in neuroimaging studies. Nonetheless, the complexity of the reasoning process tempers the conclusions that can be drawn from these techniques.

In each example below, which cards should be turned to test the truth of the proposition?

(A) If a *vowel* is on one side, then an *even number* is on the other side.

2	7	A	K

(B) If working in *Washington DC*, then must be a *politician*.

Politician			Not a Politician

(C) If drinking *beer*, then must be *21+* years old.

Over 21   Under 21

Examples of the Wason Card Sorting Task. In these three versions of the task the rule is presented in an abstract context (A), a familiar context (B), and a social context (C). In all three cases, people tend to select the card consistent with the premise (e.g., a vowel in A), but only in the social context do they consistently select the card that is inconsistent with the conclusion (e.g., "under 21" in C).

References

BARKOW, J. H., L. COSMIDES AND J. TOOBY, EDS. (1992) *The Adapted Mind: Evolutionary Psychology and the Generation of Culture.* New York: Oxford University Press.

CANESSA, N. AND 6 OTHERS (2005) The effect of social content on deductive reasoning: An fMRI study. *Hum. Brain Mapp.* 26: 30–43.

WASON, P. AND P. JOHNSON-LAIRD (1966) *Psychology of Reasoning, Structure, and Content.* London: Batsford.

Like other executive processes, deductive reasoning requires functionally intact frontal lobes, and the lateral prefrontal cortex appears to be the most critical brain region. As discussed in **Box 25B**, however, damage to the most anterior parts of the frontal lobe impairs abstractive and reflective, not deductive, abilities. Most studies suggest that the left frontal lobe supports explicit language-based reasoning, consistent with the known contributions of this area to linguistic and syntactic processes (see Chapter 21).

Research by Vinod Goel and his colleagues at York University in Toronto indicates that deduction, in particular, involves inferior parts of the left frontal lobe, including Broca's area. Similarly, studies of split-brain patients by Michael Gazzaniga and colleagues at Dartmouth have led to the idea of a **left-brain interpreter** that can form inferences and associations among multiple concepts (**Figure 25.3**). Interestingly, patients with damage to the left frontal lobe perform similarly to control subjects in some reasoning tasks, but unlike controls, their performance does not improve when social information is present (compare the Wason Card Sorting Task introduced in Box 25A). Although the bulk of the evidence indicates that deductive reasoning is a primarily left-hemisphere ability, some neuroimaging data suggest that deduction may also involve right-hemisphere regions that are anatomically homologous to Broca's area. The conditions under which right-hemisphere activation is observed are not yet well established and may depend on the type of deduction being performed.

This evidence notwithstanding, it would be a mistake to conclude that deductive reasoning is based solely on processing in the left frontal lobes. The temporal lobe appears to be necessary when reasoning is based on semantic categories that are well known to subjects and for which there are existing beliefs (e.g., the characteristics of people or objects). Moreover, the parietal cortex appears to support reasoning about arbitrary categories, and the hippocampus contributes to spatial reasoning. Again, these contributing regions tend to be functionally lateralized; damage to the left temporal lobe causes broad impairments in syllogistic reasoning, and damage to the right temporal lobe impairs reasoning in which content manipulation is required. More broadly, damage to the right frontal lobe impairs the abilities to change the forms of a conclusion to match the premises ("X is larger than Y. Which is smaller?"), to perform multiple relations ("X is larger than Y. Y is larger than Z. Which is smallest?"), and to reach true conclusions from false premises.

Inductive Reasoning

Deductive reasoning has been of particular interest to philosophers and scientists because of its abstract, mathematical quality. Beginning from a simple set of axioms, one can determine truths from falsehoods. However, few chal-

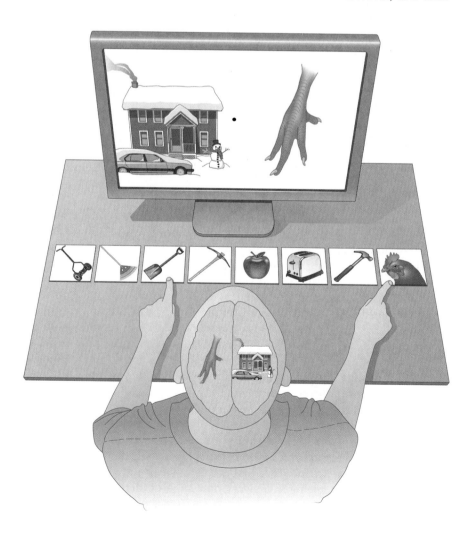

Figure 25.3 Evidence for the left-brain interpreter. Patient P.S. previously had most of the corpus callosum severed, so visual information could not travel between the two hemispheres. Compound images such as the one shown were flashed briefly while he looked at the center of the screen (black dot). Thus, each half of the image was processed within the contralateral hemisphere. When asked to explain why his left hand pointed to a picture that seemed unrelated to his verbal report, the patient's left hemisphere created a plausible, albeit inaccurate, story about shoveling the chicken coop. (After Gazzaniga and LeDoux 1978.)

■ BOX 25B The Role of Frontopolar Cortex

The most anterior part of the frontal lobes, the *frontopolar cortex*, is perhaps the least understood part of the cerebral cortex. Because it develops late, in both ontogenetic and phylogenetic senses, the frontopolar cortex has been associated historically with higher cognitive processes, such as reasoning and mental simulation. A classic test for deficits in frontal lobe function is the Raven's Progressive Matrices test, in which subjects view a matrix of shapes that "progress" along one or more dimensions (e.g., a three-by-three matrix with one dot in each cell of the left column, two dots in the cells of the middle column, and three dots in the cells of the right column). The subject's task is to identify what shape belongs in a blank cell of the matrix (i.e., what best completes the pattern). Depending on the complexity of the matrix, the task may require only simple logic (as in this example) or complex relational and integrative processes. Damage to the frontal lobes, particular to frontopolar cortex, impairs performance on this and similar tasks. Converging data comes from fMRI studies demonstrating that frontopolar activation is observed when abstract information from different sources must be integrated. Yet frontopolar cortex seems to be associated with much more than just integrating abstract information. Anterior frontal regions are activated in some forms of memory retrieval, in problem-solving tasks, even when people are simply daydreaming or letting their minds wander.

What, then, differentiates the functions supported by frontopolar cortex from those associated with other regions of the frontal lobe? One perspective is that the frontal lobe can be characterized along a posterior-to-anterior axis of function: from externally directed actions to internally directed thoughts (see Figures A–C). The frontopolar cortex, in this conceptualization, is necessary for operating on self-generated information, whereas more posterior regions respond to new external stimuli (e.g., lateral prefrontal cortex responds to unexpected, task-relevant events). Consistent with this interpretation, frontopolar activation is not generally observed when people make judgments about external stimuli, but it is observed when people must evaluate the relations between two or more judgments or concepts, as is necessary for inductive reasoning.

A novel perspective on frontopolar function comes from an fMRI comparison of information-seeking and reward-seeking behaviors, which are often characterized as *exploratory* and *exploitative*, respectively. Humans and other animals are often faced with trade-offs between taking a sure reward (which they want to exploit) and learning more about an unknown option (which they want to explore). When people engage in exploratory behavior to gain new information, activation of the frontopolar cortex and the intraparietal sulcus increases; when people choose to receive a sure reward, activation of the striatum and ventro-

medial prefrontal cortex (see Chapter 24) increases. Taken together with prior studies, this finding indicates that frontopolar cortex contributes to broad behavioral strategies, unlike other, more posterior parts of the frontal lobe that support more immediate behavioral control.

References

CHRISTOFF, K., J. M. REAM, L. P. GEDDES AND J. D. GABRIELI (2003) Evaluating self-generated information: Anterior prefrontal contributions to human cognition. *Behav. Neurosci.* 117: 1161–1168.

CHRISTOFF, K. AND 6 OTHERS (2001) Rostro-lateral prefrontal cortex involvement in relational integration during reasoning. *Neuroimage* 14: 1136–1149.

DAW, N. D., J. P. O'DOHERTY, P. DAYAN, B. SEYMOUR AND R. J. DOLAN (2006) Cortical substrates for exploratory decisions in humans. *Nature* 441: 876–879.

DOBBINS, I. G. AND A. D. WAGNER (2005) Domain-general and domain-sensitive prefrontal mechanisms for recollecting events and detecting novelty. *Cereb. Cortex* 15: 1768–1778.

Possible contributions of frontopolar cortex to executive function. (A) One theoretical perspective suggests that the frontal lobes are organized along a posterior-to-anterior axis, with the most anterior regions dealing with abstract, higher-order, and internally generated information. (B) Functional MRI studies have found activation in the frontopolar cortex when subjects compare two internally computed relations. (C) Activation is absent when the same comparisons are made while all stimuli are visible. (Adapted from Christoff et al. 2003.)

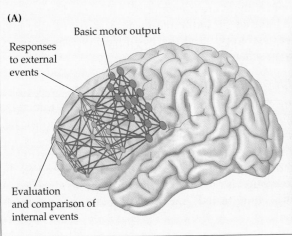

(A)

Basic motor output

Responses to external events

Evaluation and comparison of internal events

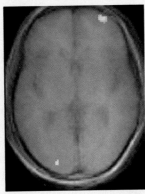

(B) Frontopolar cortex

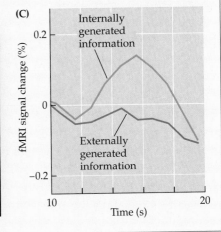

(C)

Internally generated information

Externally generated information

fMRI signal change (%)

Time (s)

lenges of daily life require deduction (the best examples are following laws and taboos). Much more common is **inductive reasoning**, in which one determines the likely truth of a conclusion from a set of probabilistic, often imperfect premises. Consider the following argument: "House cats purr when they are happy. Lions are related to house cats. Therefore, lions purr when they are happy." Is this conclusion true?

This example differs from deductive syllogisms in that its premises cannot be logically mapped onto each other. That lions are related to house cats does not mean that lions are a type of house cat, nor that the two share every attribute. Therefore, unlike deductive arguments, inductive arguments must be evaluated on the basis of prior knowledge and experience. In light of the preceding argument, knowledge that purring is an activity done by felines (of which the house cat is a prototypical member) might suggest that all felines, including lions, purr. Alternatively, knowledge that house cats are much smaller than lions could suggest that purring is a property of small felines with a particular vocal-tract structure, and knowledge that lions roar could suggest that they have a differently structured vocal system. For this and many other sorts of questions, truth cannot be derived from the premises alone. Only by considering additional empirical information can we draw accurate conclusions.

Perhaps the most common form of inductive argument is *argument from analogy*, of which the cat-lion syllogism is an example. Another is based on the prior probability of the conclusion for a specific exemplar, given information about a category. Here is an example: "Most birds can fly. A magpie is a bird. Therefore, a magpie can fly." Still other cases involve generalization from examples to classes, as in "Mary is a CIA employee. Mary has high-security clearance. Therefore, all CIA employees have high-security clearance."

Generalization in logical arguments may share cognitive processes with **sampling**, the determination of the likelihood of events from a set of presented examples. Regardless of the form of the argument, inductive reasoning involves making judgments about rules on the basis of examples, relations, and prior knowledge. The particular rules invoked may depend on many factors. For example, children often use highly salient object attributes in reasoning tasks: a wood chip floats because it is "light"; a battleship floats because it is "strong." Similarly, adult judgments about the likelihood or frequency of events are subject to the sorts of heuristic biases introduced in Chapter 24.

Although people are generally better at reasoning inductively than deductively, behavioral studies have demonstrated that inductive reasoning is less successful when events are separated in time, when an event has multiple causes, when causes or relations are abstract, when category shifts are required, or when conclusions contradict prior beliefs. Because of the complexity of inductive reasoning, there are no commonly accepted theories of induction, although some theories of deductive reasoning (e.g., the mental model theory described earlier) imply that the two forms of reasoning are based on the same processing schemes.

Neural systems that support inductive reasoning

Research on the neural mechanisms underlying induction has used techniques and reached conclusions that are generally similar to those in studies of deduction. Thus, damage to the prefrontal cortex, especially to the left hemisphere, has been found to impair the performance of a wide range of reasoning tasks, including inductive reasoning. If damage is restricted to the right hemisphere (or if information is provided to only the left hemisphere, as when a split-brain patient is being tested), inductive reasoning is relatively spared. Conversely, when someone engages in inductive reasoning, the left prefrontal cortex is activated, as measured by PET and fMRI. Taken broadly, the neural similarity between deduction and induction makes good sense in that the left prefrontal cortex is critical for both linguistic processing and executive functions, each of which would be necessary for all types of reasoning.

Damage to the prefrontal cortex evidently impairs all the various forms of inductive reasoning. Although a hallmark of damage to dorsolateral prefrontal cortex is the continued use of rules that are no longer applicable (the perseveration discussed in Chapter 23), such damage also causes difficulty in learning rules from examples and feedback. Thus, performance on the Tower of Hanoi task also becomes worse, reflecting problems with components of reasoning such as learning rules, planning ahead, and backtracking to reach a goal.

The left lateral prefrontal cortex is particularly important for the generation of new hypotheses, which is critical for inductive reasoning (but not needed for deductive reasoning). Neuroimaging studies show that deduction and induction both activate the left prefrontal cortex, although the specific foci of activation differ. In particular, when directly compared in an experiment undertaken by Vinod Goel and Raymond Dolan at University College London, induction activated dorsolateral prefrontal cortex, and deduction activated ventrolateral prefrontal cortex (**Figure 25.4**). This difference may reflect greater demands for generating and testing hypotheses during induction, but greater syntactic and linguistic demands during deduction.

Consistent with this distinction between the contributions of different regions of the frontal lobes is the report of a patient with damage to the inferior frontal lobe and the temporal lobe. The lesion rendered the patient severely agrammatical; although he could match words to pictures more or less nor-

(A) Deductive reasoning

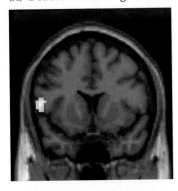
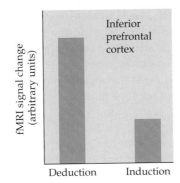

(B) Inductive reasoning

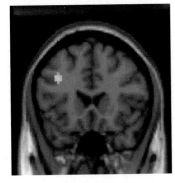
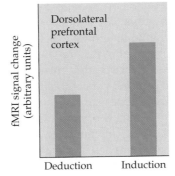

Figure 25.4 Prefrontal activation during deduction and induction tasks. Although both inductive and deductive reasoning involve the left prefrontal cortex, deduction evokes greater activation in an inferior region (A), and induction evokes greater activation in a superior region (B). (After Goel and Dolan 2004.)

mally, he could not speak in complete sentences, assess whether a sentence was structured correctly, or match sentences to pictures on the basis of their structure. Functions served by dorsolateral prefrontal cortex were intact, as evidenced by good performance on the Wisconsin Card Sorting Test. The patient's grammatical problems—presumably the result of damage to Broca's area—prevented him from completing standard written tests of reasoning. When inductive reasoning problems were presented aurally or pictorially, however, he was able to reach the correct conclusions. For example, he was given a book with a hidden compartment containing a necklace and then asked, "What does [a person seeing the book on a shelf] think is inside?" In answer to this question, the patient wrote, "Book!" Then, when asked, "What is really inside?" he drew a picture of a necklace, indicating that he could reason normally about true and false beliefs. His performance was similarly good on tests of reasoning that were presented as pictures. This case study provides an example of how inductive reasoning abilities can be expressed without intact functioning of brain areas that are important for language, syntax, and grammar.

Thus, inductive reasoning, like deduction, cannot be equated to prefrontal cortex function. The basal ganglia appear to be involved as well. Although damage to the basal ganglia is most commonly associated with deficits in motor control (see Chapter 9), patients with Parkinson's disease often have difficulty forming associations in inductive reasoning tasks. Some aspects of these reasoning deficits may be associated with accompanying frontal damage or damage to frontostriatal pathways. Yet there is also increasing evidence that the basal ganglia themselves—the caudate nucleus in particular—play a role in some forms of inductive reasoning.

Recent neuroimaging studies suggest that the contributions of the caudate to motor behavior and motor learning may extend to other forms of learning from examples—a function critical for inductive reasoning. Different parts of the caudate contribute to different components of learning: activation in the body and tail of the caudate (along with the putamen) increases as categories are learned, and activation in the head of the caudate is greatest when feedback is most informative. The basal ganglia may be most important for inductive reasoning related to specific motor responses (consistent with the contributions of these regions to motor behavior), and frontal regions may be more involved when verbal, logical reasoning is engaged.

Problem Solving

A celebrated example of problem solving occurred in the Greek city-state of Syracuse more than 2000 years ago. The king had commissioned the construction of a golden crown and provided a goldsmith with a quantity of gold sufficient for its creation. Although the completed crown was magnificent—and weighed as much as the original gold—rumors arose that the goldsmith had tricked the king by replacing some of the precious gold with silver. This allegation troubled the king, and he was left with a problem: how to determine the purity of the material in the crown without damaging or altering it in any way. He allegedly posed this problem to the young mathematician Archimedes, who puzzled over its solution for some time.

One day, as Archimedes sank into his bath, he noticed that the more his body sank into the water, the more water ran out over the tub. He is said to have jumped out of the tub shouting "Eureka, eureka!" ("I have found it! I have found it!"). Archimedes' insight was that the amount of water that an object displaces is determined by its density. Thus, if the crown displaced the same amount of water as a lump of pure gold of equivalent weight, then the crown must be constructed entirely of gold. Conversely, if the crown displaced more water, it must contain at least some amount of the less dense silver.

Several key components of problem solving are evident in this legend. Problems are generally framed in terms of a specific goal (e.g., to determine the composition of the crown), but the means for reaching that goal are not specified. The set of possible ways in which a problem can be represented is known as the **problem space**. For Archimedes, the problem space was large but constrained; he could do anything to the crown, as long as he did not damage it. In some scenarios, such as the best move at an early point in a chess match, the problem space is, for practical purposes, infinite (there are approximately 10^{120} ways that a chess game can unfold). Other scenarios have knowable problem spaces, such as in the chess endgame when only a few pieces remain, making the challenge properly one of reasoning rather than problem solving. When a problem space is very large, as in the early stages of a chess match, brute-force approaches are rarely successful (unlike when solving a logical or mathematical problem). Instead, subjects either must use heuristics to simplify the problem or must reorganize the problem space into a different form.

Heuristics in problem solving

When faced with complex problem spaces, people often use simple rules called *heuristics* (see Chapter 24 for examples in decision making). Though rarely optimal, heuristics are plausible strategies that tend to work well in a wide range of ecologically meaningful problems. The simplest sort of heuristic in problem solving, known as a *hill-climbing* or *best-available-option* approach, involves taking the step that minimizes the perceived difference between the current state of the problem and the eventual goal. Hill-climbing heuristics are often useful, especially for reducing a complex problem to a more tractable form. But many problems cannot be solved using hill climbing alone, because they involve **backtracking**. In chess, for instance, a player often has to sacrifice a piece (seemingly moving away from the goal) in order to gain a positional advantage over the opponent.

Another heuristic is the repeated application of a previously valid rule. Consider the classic water jar problems. To obtain a desired quantity of water, the person solving the problem must determine the sequence in which to fill and pour out water from a set of jars. For example, to obtain 4 units of water, given two jars of with capacities of 10 and 3 units, respectively (**Figure 25.5A**), one could fill the larger jar and then pour out enough water to fill the smaller one twice, leaving 4 units of water in the larger jar. (Note that the verbal description of such problems masks a simple algebraic form: find a set of coefficients a, b, c, … such that $ax + by + cz + \ldots = n$). **Figure 25.5B** gives some examples of water jar problems—for example, to obtain 100 units, given jars of 21, 127, and 3 units. After a bit of thinking, most people hit upon a solution for this example: fill the 127-unit jar, and then pour out 21 units once and 3 units twice.

When the psychologist Abraham Luchins gave subjects more problems that could be solved in this manner, they became increasingly quick at solving them. Then Luchins gave them another problem: obtain 20 units, given jars of 23, 49, and 3 units. More than 80 percent of his subjects continued to solve the problem in the same way (49 − 23 − 3 − 3 = 20), even though a much simpler solution existed (23 − 3 = 20).

The tendency to continue to use a working heuristic, even in situations in which it becomes suboptimal, has been given many names. The most evocative is **functional fixedness**, which conveys the idea that people tend to fixate on one conception of a problem (i.e., simplifying the problem space) at a cost of

Figure 25.5 Water jar problems. (A) The goal is to obtain a stated quantity of water; for this example, the quantity is 4 units. The problem solver can fill either jar at any time, can pour either jar into the other, or can empty either jar entirely, but has no other measuring tools that will allow accurate partial filling or pouring. (B) The table lists other, analogous water jar problems for the reader to complete.

(A)

(B)

Goal (units)	Water jars
100	21, 127, 3
99	14, 163, 25
5	18, 43, 10
21	9, 42, 6
31	22, 61, 4
20	23, 49, 3
18	15, 39, 3

missing other, potentially more efficient representations. The power of functional fixedness can be quite remarkable. To some of his subjects, Luchins presented a final problem: obtain 3 units of water, given jars of 3, 64, and 29 units. The majority persisted in the same rule as before: 64 – 3 – 29 – 29 = 3, while fewer than one-half of the subjects indicated that they would just fill the 3-unit jar! Functional fixedness can also be seen in other sorts of problems. To experience it, first rearrange the following arrangements of five letters into common English words: nedoz, nelin, and sdlen. Once you've solved those, try these: klsta, nolem, and dlsco. Now consider, by looking closely at the last anagrams, whether you experienced functional fixedness—at least unconsciously.

■ BOX 25C Problem Solving by Non-Human Animals

Whereas people often experience problem solving within artificial contexts like games or puzzles, animals face many problems in their daily lives, such as when extracting food while foraging. Imagine that a piece of fruit hangs in a nearby tree, on a branch too high to reach and too unsteady to climb. How can the fruit be obtained? Problems like this are difficult to solve by pure trial and error because the problem space is very large (see text). Instead, an animal must create a plan that uses objects in its environment in a coordinated manner. In the early twentieth century, the German psychologist Wolfgang Kohler studied how chimpanzees behave when faced with such challenges. He released his chimpanzees in an enclosure that had a piece of fruit out of reach, either because it was behind an impassable obstacle (e.g., a fence) or because it was hanging from a rope. Scattered around were numerous other objects, such as boxes and sticks. Although the chimpanzees were initially stymied, they eventually adopted

seemingly purposeful (and various) strategies for reaching the fruit. They stacked boxes to make a stable platform, they used sticks to extend their reach, and they used long sticks as effective, if precarious, climbing poles. One star chimpanzee even learned to create a long rake by inserting the end of one piece of bamboo into the hollow end of another.

Primatologists have subsequently observed numerous examples of chimpanzee problem solving in the wild. Many chimpanzees shape sticks to create simple tools for insect foraging (e.g., to reach deep into termite

mounds). Chimps have also been found to carry stones to common food-processing areas, so that the stones could be used to bash open nuts. Interestingly, the specific form and use of these tools seems to differ systematically across groups, perhaps reflecting cultural transmission. A recent experimental study supports this possibility (Figure A). Two high-ranking females from two different groups of chimpanzees were trained to use tools to open a food box, each in a different way. When the knowledgeable chimpanzees were reintroduced into their groups, the other chimps soon

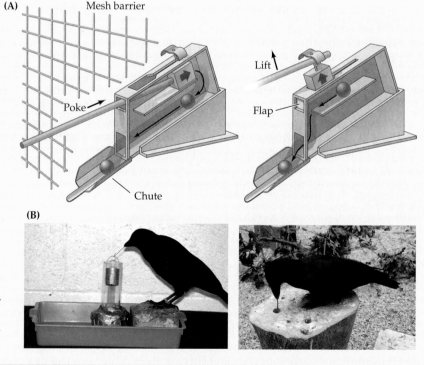

(A) Food extraction by chimpanzees. Dominant females were taught to obtain food from a complex apparatus either by poking a stick through a hole (left) or lifting a hook (right) to dislodge a barrier and get a food pellet. When the females were returned to their groups, the other chimpanzees observed the female using the stick and successfully mimicked her method for obtaining the food. (B) New Caledonian crows spontaneously shape natural materials (or wires, in the laboratory) into hooks that can be used to extract food. (B © The Behavioural Ecology Research Group, University of Oxford.)

learned how to extract the food as well, each group using the technique observed from its high-ranking female. A control group never used either technique.

That chimpanzees can discover and adopt complex strategies for solving problems is not especially surprising, since the prefrontal cortices of chimpanzees and the other great apes are well developed and in this sense are similar to the brains of humans (see Box 23A). More unexpected is the tool use that has been observed in animals whose brains differ considerably from ours. Good examples are found in the family Corvidae, which comprises species like crows, magpies, and

ravens. Crows from the islands of New Caledonia have been observed using multiple different types of tools while foraging, both in natural and laboratory settings (Figure B). To solve some problems, the crows use simple sticks chosen to match the distance to the food or the size of an opening. Other problems require more complex tools that the crows bend into complex shapes, sometimes using external objects for assistance. The good match between tool and problem suggests elements of planning and foresight. Why problem solving is manifest in such seemingly different animals as chimpanzees and crows and not in many other animals remains a mystery.

However, these observations suggest that problem solving is a widespread skill that is likely to depend on the interplay between a variety of brain systems in different species.

References

KENWARD, B., A. A. WEIR, C. RUTZ AND A. KACELNIK (2005) Behavioural ecology: Tool manufacture by naive juvenile crows. *Nature* 433: 121.

WEIR, A. A., J. CHAPPELL AND A. KACELNIK (2002) Shaping of hooks in New Caledonian crows. *Science* 297: 981.

WHITEN, A., V. HORNER AND F. B. DE WAAL (2005) Conformity to cultural norms of tool use in chimpanzees. *Nature* 437: 737–740.

Insight in problem solving

Although insight is rarely as dramatic as that experienced by Archimedes, everyone is familiar with the phenomenon of **insight** when solving a problem (**Figure 25.6**). In most cases, people experience insight only after attempting to solve a problem using other means—whether trial and error, or other heuristics—and reaching an impasse. At this point, they may experience functional fixedness. Then, without warning, the solution (or a clear path to the solution) leaps to mind, accompanied by a flash of excitement.

It is not known what sorts of information processing are necessary or sufficient for insightful problem solving. The idea most often advanced is *reorganization*. With reorganization, an insight occurs when one way of viewing the problem is replaced by another, more promising approach. Along these lines,

Figure 25.6 Classic insight problems. (A) On a table in front of you are a candle, a matchbook, and a box of tacks. How can you mount a lit candle on the wall, using only these objects? (B) Suppose you are placed in a room that has two ropes attached to the ceiling. The ropes are too far apart for you to reach both at the same time. How can you tie the ropes together without removing them from the ceiling, using only the tools provided?

(A)

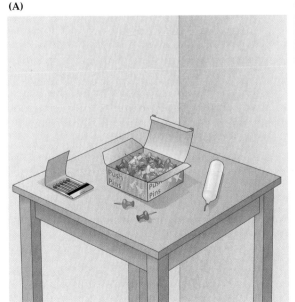

(B)

Wolfgang Kohler (whose work with apes is described in **Box 25C**) characterized the essence of problem solving as recognizing impasses and then taking detours (or backtracking) to get around them. He pointed out that when no detour or reorganization is necessary, the problem can be solved by a straightforward hill-climbing approach. An alternative view is that insight does not require reorganization, but instead occurs when the path to the solution is recognized. Also possible is the idea that insight occurs in both situations.

When people are struggling with a problem, they often rate their warmth, or closeness, to its solution as being very low, even in the moments immediately preceding an insight experience (thus the "eureka" quality of insight). This observation indicates that problem solvers have no explicit knowledge of the likely solution prior to the insight. However, when tested using implicit measures—such as by looking for whether words related to the solution exhibit semantic priming (see Chapter 15)—effects can be observed before the subjective experience of insight. Thus, although the conscious insight experience seems an all-or-none phenomenon, the unconscious progress to a solution may well have been gradual.

Because insight seems to come suddenly, self-help books have suggested many ways of approaching problems that require insight. Usually these suggestions take the form of vague blandishments to "think outside the box." More helpful are specific guidelines that take into account the limitations of normal problem-solving approaches. For example, one should first consider the perceived constraints of the problem and then think about which of those constraints could be relaxed. To do so, it is often helpful to think, "How else could this be used?" or "What other tools do I have?" In the famous Duncker candle problem illustrated in Figure 25.6A, the box containing the tacks could be used to hold other objects, such as the candle. Once that constraint is relaxed, the solution springs to mind quickly. Similarly, in the rope problem in Figure 25.6B, the seemingly useless flashlight could also serve as a pendulum weight, allowing one rope to swing back and forth to the outstretched arm of someone holding the other rope.

Neural systems that support problem solving

Problem solving can be a relatively slow process. When faced with the problem of weighing the king's crown, for example, Archimedes was said to have cogitated for days before inspiration struck. If not previously seen, the problems in Figure 25.6 may require many minutes to solve. Working on such a problem involves many types of cognitive processing. Some of these fall under the rubric of executive processing, pertinent to all problem solving, such as planning, simulating, choosing, and evaluating. Others are specific to the particular problem structure, perhaps involving perception, memory, and attention to different components in varying degrees and times. Because of the variety of processes required to complete a problem that has even a modicum of complexity, the neural underpinnings of problem solving (and of intelligence itself, as described in **Box 25D**) are difficult to address.

One approach has been to use highly structured scenarios (e.g., the Tower of Hanoi problem) that allow the steps to a solution to be quantified. These sorts of problems require a combination of planning and reasoning abilities, and thus the frontal lobes are critical for their solution. Another approach is to focus on a single aspect of problem solving, such as the insight experience that may reflect reorganization. Because the moment of insight can be reported by subjects, researchers can look for coincident neural changes. In general, insight has been associated with activation of the right hemisphere, perhaps because the right hemisphere plays a greater role in implicit association or emotional processing (see Chapters 17 and 18). Consistent with such findings,

■ BOX 25D The Neurobiology of Intelligence

The questions of how to measure and explain differences in intelligence have a long and controversial history. Some conceptions suggest that intelligence reflects the ability to reason and solve problems. The great thinkers of the ages, such as Leonardo da Vinci and Benjamin Franklin, are thus considered to have possessed very great intelligence. Other perspectives extend intelligence to include cognitive abilities (like vocabulary, mathematical skills, and memory), artistic talent, emotional and empathic traits, or even athletic excellence. Under these broader perspectives, a talented pianist or a world-famous painter or even a champion basketball player might be considered intelligent. In all of these domains, from art to sports, outstanding individuals are described by terms, such as *brilliant* or *gifted*, that are often synonyms for *intelligent*.

Given the breadth of ways in which behavioral and intellectual competence can be expressed, it seems an impossible task to characterize intelligence using a single measure. Even so, intelligence testing has a long history, whose best-known example is the IQ test developed by the French psychologist Alfred Binet in the early twentieth century. This test and its descendants ask a broad set of questions that tap reasoning, logic, math, vocabulary and general knowledge, resulting in an **intelligence quotient**, or **IQ**. The specific interpretation of an IQ score depends on the test that is used; in a typical scaling system, a mean score would be 100 with a standard deviation of 15 points.

Even though IQ scores seem authoritative, a person with an IQ of 130 may not necessarily be better at any particular task requiring intelligence than is someone else with an IQ of 120. One contemporary of Binet, the English psychologist Charles Spearman, recognized that there were still individual differences in specific contributors to intelligence. Some people may have very strong verbal aptitude but poor math skills; others may have exceptional spatial skills but a poor memory. Nevertheless, Spearman believed strongly in the existence of a central intelligence factor (which he labeled "g," for general ability). Although considerable disagreement about the specific constituent factors remains, there is now broad recognition (if not complete consensus) that intelligence comprises at least several separate components (e.g., verbal abilities, mathematical abilities) that are correlated in individuals.

(Continued on next page)

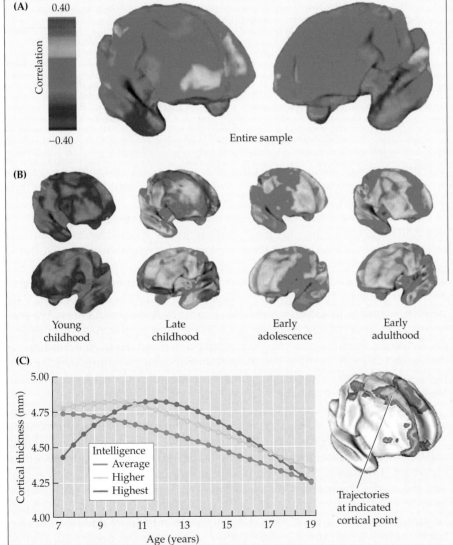

(A)

Correlation 0.40 to −0.40

Entire sample

(B)

Young childhood   Late childhood   Early adolescence   Early adulthood

(C)

Trajectories at indicated cortical point

Brain changes associated with the development of intelligence. (A) The color map indicates brain regions where the thickness of the cortex was correlated with the intelligence of children and adolescents. Note that few regions exhibited significant correlations across the age range. (B) More revealing were the correlations at specific age points, with young children of the highest intelligence having thinner cortices overall, and the adolescents of the highest intelligence having relatively thick prefrontal cortices. (C) The individuals of the highest intelligence exhibited a relatively late thickening and subsequent thinning of prefrontal cortex. (After Shaw et al. 2006.)

■ BOX 25D *(continued)*

The features of the human brain that correspond to intelligence have been equally contentious. Humans and other primates have large brains, modern adult humans have larger brains than our evolutionary ancestors had, and genes that control brain size are still evolving rapidly. Yet brain size does not predict intelligence among individuals; for example, males have larger brains than females, even though the average intelligence of males and females is essentially identical. Nor does brain size predict intelligence across species (see Chapter 27), as demonstrated by the intelligent behavior of tiny-brained crows. As might be expected, differences in the parts of the brain that organize complex behaviors may be the best predictors of intelligence. Unlike other mammals, humans and great apes have large frontal lobes (see Box 23A); the executive and other functions of these brain regions fit nicely with the idea that the frontal lobes are especially (although certainly not

uniquely) important in mediating intelligence. Converging evidence comes from fMRI studies that have found links between general intelligence (i.e., Spearman's "g") and differences in activation of the frontal and parietal cortices during reasoning tasks.

Differences in how the brain matures may also predict differences in intelligence across individuals. A recent developmental study scanned a large sample of children, adolescents, and young adults to assess whether IQ scores could be predicted from the thickness of the cerebral cortex in particular brain regions. Taking the entire age range as a whole, intelligence was only weakly related to the thickness of any particular brain region (Figure A). In specific age ranges, however, strong patterns were evident (Figure B). For example, children who eventually became most intelligent tended to show a rapid increase in cortical thickness until early adolescence (11–12 years of age), particularly in the prefrontal cor-

tex, followed by a rapid thinning thereafter (Figure C). This result suggests that adult intelligence is not simply a function of the size of the frontal lobes, but of their development as well, perhaps reflecting how synaptic connectivity is modulated by experience.

References

EVANS, P. D. AND 8 OTHERS (2005) Microcephalin, a gene regulating brain size, continues to evolve adaptively in humans. *Science* 309: 1717–1720.

GRAY, J. R., C. F. CHABRIS AND T. S. BRAVER (2003) Neural mechanisms of general fluid intelligence. *Nat. Neurosci.* 6: 316–322.

LEE, K. H. AND 6 OTHERS (2006) Neural correlates of superior intelligence: Stronger recruitment of posterior parietal cortex. *Neuroimage* 29: 578–586.

SHAW, P. AND 8 OTHERS (2006) Intellectual ability and cortical development in children and adolescents. *Nature* 440: 676–679.

THOMPSON, P. M. AND 12 OTHERS (2001) Genetic influences on brain structure. *Nat. Neurosci.* 4: 1253–1258.

priming effects in advance of explicit recognition of the solution are greater when cues are presented to the left visual field (i.e., right hemisphere) than when presented to the right visual field.

Several brain regions have been implicated in the experience of insight. In one fMRI study, subjects were given three words (e.g., *wedding, brass, aid*) and asked to think of a single word that could go with each of these in a two-word phrase. When subjects solved these problems and experienced insight, the anterior temporal cortex was activated more than when no insight was experienced (**Figure 25.7**). The anterior temporal cortex has been associated with building semantic associations, as when people must extract themes from passages, determine the gist of a story, or select a word appropriate to a particular sentence context. Converging evidence comes from the finding of increased EEG activity (in the gamma frequency range) within anterior temporal cortex, beginning about a third of a second before the report of an insight solution.

Although semantic association may reasonably be necessary for this task, association processes may be less relevant for other types of insight problems. When people solve riddles (e.g., "What can move heavy logs but not a small nail?"), insight is associated with increased activation in a broad set of regions, including cingulate cortex, lateral prefrontal cortex, posterior parietal cortex, and the medial temporal lobe. Note that—with the exception of the last—these regions are all critical for executive functions. Reorganization may also be supported by the anterior cingulate cortex. An intriguing finding from electrophysiological studies of riddle processing is that the presentation of an insight solution (e.g., showing the answer: *band* for the *wedding/brass/aid* prob-

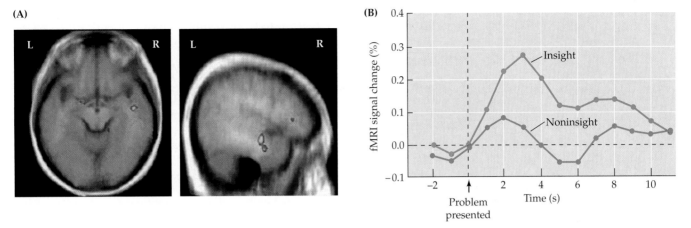

Figure 25.7 Neural correlates of insight. (A) When subjects solved a verbal problem and reported a feeling of insight, activation in the right anterior temporal lobe increased. (B) Comparing the fMRI signal for insight and non-insight solutions reveals a systematic increase in amplitude when insight was present. (After Jung-Beeman et al. 2004.)

lem, "a river" for the riddle) evokes a negative event-related potential at midline frontal sites with maximal amplitude of about 400 milliseconds.

As described in Chapter 23, the lateral prefrontal cortex supports the establishment of links between stimuli and the set of possible responses; for problem solving, establishing such links may involve determining what actions are afforded by the problem space. Many insight problems, however, are characterized by a misrepresentation of the problem space, as in the Duncker candle problem, in which people view the box as a container, not an option for support. Thus, the functioning of lateral prefrontal cortex might be beneficial or detrimental under different circumstances: beneficial if it pares the problem space effectively by eliminating unnecessary responses, detrimental if it eliminates the correct response and makes eventual reorganization necessary. This perspective was validated by a study showing that patients with lateral prefrontal damage performed worse than control subjects on most types of matchstick problems (**Figure 25.8**), but *better* than controls on problems that required breaking normal algebraic conventions. In essence, these patients did

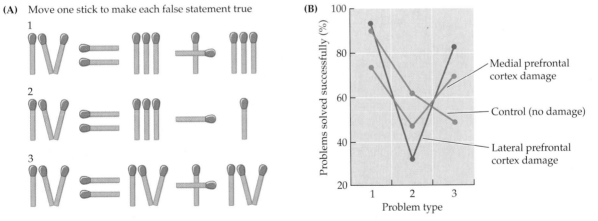

Figure 25.8 A counterintuitive example of improved problem solving. (A) Neurologically normal individuals and patients with damage to the prefrontal cortex of the brain were given matchstick problems like these. In each case, the matchsticks form a false arithmetic statement. The subject's task is to move one matchstick to make the statement true. (B) Patients with prefrontal damage did worse than neurologically normal subjects on problems that required changing a number (i.e., Type 1: where "IV" becomes "VI"). However, they did significantly better than normal individuals on the problems that required the logical but atypical step of creating a double equal sign (i.e., Type 3: which leads to "IV = IV = IV"). (After Reverberi et al. 2005.)

not need to think outside the box, because without an intact lateral prefrontal cortex, no constraining box existed.

Summary

1. Reasoning and problem solving are central to many aspects of cognition. Both involve processes like selection, inhibition, abstraction, and planning. Thus, like decision making, they can be considered aspects of the executive control of behavior.

2. Reasoning and problem solving differ from decision making in that they are not typically based on preferences for different outcomes. Two types of reasoning, deductive and inductive, are commonly studied.

3. Deductive reasoning entails determining which conclusions follow logically from a set of premises. Regions of the left hemisphere—especially the inferior frontal cortex—are especially (although not exclusively) important for the symbolic and syntactic manipulation necessary for deduction.

4. Induction is more commonplace than deduction in the "real world" of human reasoning. Inductive reasoning involves extrapolating rules from examples. The left frontal lobe is also important for inductive reasoning, but the specific regions activated differ from those that support deduction. In particular, dorsolateral and frontopolar regions of prefrontal cortex are more critical for induction than for deduction.

5. When solving a problem, people often first use heuristics or trial and error, reach an impasse, and finally recognize the solution in a flash of insight. The experience of insight is often associated with a reorganization of the problem into a solvable form, for which temporal and prefrontal brain regions are especially important.

Additional Reading

Reviews

BOWDEN, E. M., M. JUNG-BEEMAN, J. FLECK AND J. KOUNIOS (2005) New approaches to demystifying insight. *Trends Cogn. Sci.* 9: 322–328.

CHRISTOFF, K. AND J. D. E. GABRIELI (2000) The frontopolar cortex and human cognition: Evidence for a rostrocaudal hierarchical organization within the human prefrontal cortex. *Psychobiology* 28: 168–186.

GAZZANIGA, M. S. (2000) Cerebral specialization and interhemispheric communication: Does the corpus callosum enable the human condition? *Brain* 123: 1293–1325.

Important Original Papers

ANDERSON, J. R., M. V. ALBERT AND J. M. FINCHAM (2005) Tracing problem solving in real time: fMRI analysis of the subject-paced Tower of Hanoi. *J. Cogn. Neurosci.* 17: 1261–1274.

BUNGE, S. A., C. WENDELKEN, D. BADRE AND A. D. WAGNER (2004) Analogical reasoning and prefrontal cortex: Evidence for separable retrieval and integration mechanisms. *Cereb. Cortex* 15: 239–249.

CANESSA, N. AND 6 OTHERS (2005) The effect of social content on deductive reasoning: An fMRI study. *Hum. Brain Mapp.* 26: 30–43.

CHRISTOFF, K., J. M. REAM, L. P. GEDDES AND J. D. GABRIELI (2003) Evaluating self-generated information: Anterior prefrontal contributions to human cognition. *Behav. Neurosci.* 117: 1161–1168.

GOEL, V. AND R. J. DOLAN (2004) Differential involvement of left prefrontal cortex in inductive and deductive reasoning. *Cognition* 93: B109–121.

JOHNSON-LAIRD, P. N., P. LEGRENZI, V. GIROTTO AND M. S. LEGRENZI (2000) Illusions in reasoning about consistency. *Science* 288: 531–532.

JUNG-BEEMAN, M. AND 7 OTHERS (2004) Neural activity when people solve verbal problems with insight. *PLoS Biol.* 2: E97.

REVERBERI, C., A. TORALDO, S. D'AGOSTINI AND M. SKRAP (2005) Better without (lateral) frontal cortex? Insight problems solved by frontal patients. *Brain* 128: 2882–2890.

VARLEY, R. AND M. SIEGAL (2000) Evidence for cognition without grammar from causal reasoning and 'theory of mind' in an agrammatic aphasic patient. *Curr. Biol.* 10: 723–725.

Books

DUNCKER, K. (1945) On problem solving. (Translated by L. S. Lees from the 1935 original.) *Psych. Monogr.* 58: 270.

GAZZANIGA, M. S. AND J. E. LEDOUX (1978) *The Integrated Mind.* New York: Plenum.

GIGERENZER, G., P. M. TODD AND THE ABC RESEARCH GROUP (1999) *Simple Heuristics That Make Us Smart.* New York: Oxford University Press.

KOHLER, W. (1925) *The Mentality of Apes.* (Translated by E. Winter from the second revised edition.) New York: Harcourt, Brace & Company.

NEWELL, A. AND H. A. SIMON (1972) *Human Problem Solving.* Englewood Cliffs, NJ: Prentice-Hall.

UNIT IX

Evolution and Development of Cognitive Functions, Including Consciousness

A final consideration in this introduction to the principles of cognitive neuroscience is how and why cognitive abilities are present in many (although certainly not all) animals, and in particular how and why the cognitive abilities of humans have evolved and developed to such a significant degree in comparison to those of other species. As implied by their phrasing, these questions can be considered from two perspectives: the evolution of cognitive abilities over the eons (a process called phylogeny); and the development of cognitive abilities during the maturation of an individual member of a species (called ontogeny). These subjects are covered in Chapters 26 and 27, respectively.

Like all the biological features of an organism, an individual's cognitive abilities are determined in part by intrinsic developmental programs whose rules are inherited and are often referred to as the contribution of "nature". In addition, the experience of each maturing human or other animal shapes the development and maintenance of the neural circuitry underpinning cognitive abilities, and are often referred to as the contribution of "nurture."

Another broad, if anthropocentric, question underlying evolutionary and developmental considerations is the extent to which the cognitive abilities of humans set us apart from other species, if indeed they do. A closely related issue is whether other species are conscious. This controversial question, which has concerned philosophers and naturalists for millennia, is the subject of Chapter 28. Sorting out reasonable if still imperfect answers to these questions is the most straightforward way to understand what it means to be human, which is arguably the ultimate goal of cognitive neuroscience. ■

26

Evolution of Brain and Cognition

Introduction

The aim of cognitive neuroscience is to understand the neural circuits and computational processes underlying complex, flexible, goal-directed behavior. Any description of the present status of this effort would be incomplete without addressing the influence of evolutionary processes on the organization of cognitive functions and the neural circuits that mediate them; indeed the pressures of natural selection have presumably been the driving force for the emergence of all cognitive processes and their neural underpinnings. Just as the evolution of other morphological structures has enabled organisms to adapt to particular environmental challenges, brain evolution has shaped the ability of animals to respond successfully to specific information-processing challenges confronted in nature. The evolution of any new functional capacity builds on preexisting traits, and similar solutions to similar problems are often achieved in unrelated species. Understanding the organization of cognitive systems in the human brain thus profits from comparative studies of the brains and behaviors of other animals, as well as from examination of the fossil and archaeological record. Based on such observations, the increasing size and complexity of the neocortex appears to have been a key factor in the emergence of the increasingly sophisticated cognitive abilities in primates. The dual demands of foraging for hard-to-find foods and navigating complex social environments have been major selective forces in the evolution of complex cognitive abilities and their neural substrates. It is not surprising, then, that human culture has emerged in parallel with a gradual progression in brain size and behavioral complexity. The evidence reviewed in this chapter indicates that human cognition comprises a mosaic of abilities that are shared with many other animals, as well as highly specialized features that have arisen in humans, presumably as a result the special social and environmental challenges confronted by our primate and early human ancestors.

A Brief History of Ideas about the Evolution of Human Cognition

When Charles Darwin's *On the Origin of Species* was published in 1859, this monumental work recognized and carefully documented the now generally accepted idea that each organism's morphological features represent an amalgam of traits broadly shared with other animals (due to the descent of different species from a common ancestor), together with more specialized traits that adapt a given species to survival and reproduction in a particular ecological niche. Thus morphological evolution can be viewed, in Darwin's words, as "descent with modification," with increasing fitness of the characteristics of any plant or animal to its local environment. While subsequent empirical and theoretical work in biology and genetics has modified this scheme by recognizing the importance of genetic drift, developmental constraints, and other factors, the process of **adaptation** to specific features of the local environment remains the dominant theme in understanding the forces that have shaped any biological feature, including the human brain. *On the Origin of Species* remains one of the most influential and far-reaching works of scholarship ever published, and its legacy has importance for cognitive neuroscience.

While Darwin generally avoided discussing the evolution of behavior in his initial treatise, he was nonetheless convinced that these ideas about the body should apply equally to mental traits and abilities. In his "Notebook M," Darwin wrote: "Evolution of man now proved. Metaphysics must flourish. He who understands baboon would do more toward metaphysics than Locke." In his subsequent book, *The Expression of the Emotions in Man and Animals* published in 1872, Darwin endeavored to show that basic behavioral reactions to emotions such as anger, joy, and disgust are conserved across a variety of animals, including humans (**Figure 26.1**).

Although his ideas concerning the evolution of human cognitive traits were radical at the time, Darwin provided a biological framework for thinking about the relationship between brain and behavior that informs cognitive neuroscience today (**Box 26A**). Based on this framework, the task of documenting

(A)   **(B)**

Figure 26.1 Conserved behavioral reactions. In *The Expression of Emotions in Man and Animals*, Darwin endeavored to show that behavioral reactions to many basic emotions are similar (conserved) across different species. These drawings from the book compare (A) the aggressive and (B) submissive poses of a dog and a cat. (From Darwin 1871.)

■ BOX 26A Darwin and the Brain

The impact of Darwin's work on biology was revolutionary, and his prescient and wide-ranging scientific viewpoint is as applicable to the organization of the brain as to the body.

Before Darwin published his great trilogy (*On the Origin of Species*, *The Descent of Man and Selection in Relation to Sex*, and *The Expression of the Emotions in Man and Animals*), most anatomical studies of the brain were undertaken to support a special role for Man in God's Scheme of Creation, an enterprise called *natural theology*. The anatomist Richard Owen, for example, concluded that humans are not primates but are a taxonomically unique group of mammals based on the greater development of the cerebral cortex in comparison to apes and other animals. Similarly, Sir Charles Bell, a physician and theologian now remembered chiefly for his contributions to understanding the facial paralysis known as Bell's palsy, argued that humans possessed muscles of facial expression without counterpart in the animal kingdom. Bell declared that the corrugator supercillius muscle, which knits the brow in concern or sadness, was designed by the Creator precisely to convey the presence of a mind.

One of Darwin's main goals was to combat this naïve thinking by demonstrating continuity in morphology and behavior among humans and other animals. Thus, *The Expression of Emotions in Man and Animals* reads as a detailed catalog of similar facial expressions in humans and other animals, implying similar underlying emotional states and brain processes. Darwin's writings on brain and cognition, however, studiously avoided explanations for such things in terms of adaptation,

which was otherwise a central part of Darwin's evolutionary theory. As the modern psychologist Paul Ekman notes, this omission probably reflected Darwin's need to emphasize continuity over adaptive diversity in debates with creationists—a debate often played out then as now under intense public scrutiny.

Another reason for Darwin's reluctance to apply the principle of adaptation to the study of the brain was the difficulty of explaining how gradual changes in form could improve function enough to enhance reproductive fitness. Indeed, Darwin acknowledged this problem head-on in his explanation for the evolution of the vertebrate eye on page 190 of *On the Origin of Species*:

> To suppose that the eye, with all its inimitable contrivances for adjusting the focus to different distances, for admitting different amounts of light, and for the correction of spherical and chromatic aberration, could have been formed by natural selection, seems, I freely confess, absurd in the highest possible degree. Yet reason tells me, that if numerous gradations from a perfect and complex eye to one very imperfect and simple, each grade being useful to its possessor, can be shown to exist; and if further, the eye does vary ever so slightly; and if

any of the variations be inherited; and if any of the variations be ever useful to an animal under changing conditions of life, then the difficulty of believing that a perfect and complex eye could be formed by natural selection, though insuperable by our imagination, can hardly be considered real.

No doubt Darwin felt similarly about the brain, emotions, and other cognitive processes. Of course, Darwin and his contemporaries had no knowledge of the existence of genes per se—although Darwin's grasp of the nature of the hereditary mechanism was both presciently accurate and fundamental to the ideas he put forth. However, he could not have foreseen the discovery of *homeotic genes* and their wide-ranging role in creating evolutionary novelty, any more than he could have foreseen the technologies of functional neuroimaging.

References

BELL, C. (1824) *Essays on the Anatomy and Philosophy of Expression*. London: J. Murray.

DARWIN, C. (1872) *The Expression of Emotions in Man and Animals*. London: J. Murray.

OWEN, R. (1866) *On the Anatomy of Vertebrates*. London: Longmans, Green, and Co.

The debate over evolution, particularly as applied to human emotions and cognition, evoked strong reactions. Darwin was often depicted as part monkey to lampoon his argument that humans and non-human primates shared a common ancestor.

brain evolution was pursued with gusto by the great comparative neuroanatomists of the nineteenth and early twentieth centuries, including Darwin's defender and popularizer Thomas Henry Huxley, the neuroanatomist Korbinian Brodmann, and many others. Despite this initial enthusiasm, the study of behavior and cognition remained largely apart from the development of evolutionary theory for another 50 years. Not until the first half of the twentieth century did European scientists such as Karl von Frisch, Konrad Lorenz, and Niko Tinbergen elevate studies of animal behavior to the level of a serious scientific endeavor that took advantage of Darwin's prescient ideas about behavior. These and other biologists created a field of biologically and evolutionarily oriented ways to study behavior that is now known as **ethology**.

The fundamental tenet of ethology is that behavior, like morphology, reflects inheritance and is driven by the need to adapt to particular environmental and social challenges. This view was further elaborated late in the twentieth century by William D. Hamilton at Oxford, Edward O. Wilson at Harvard, Robert Trivers at the University of California at Santa Cruz, and other biologists, who developed quantitative models of behavioral evolution based on the same principles that govern genetic and morphological evolution. Today the evolutionary perspective on behavior has been extended to cognitive mechanisms as neurobiological studies have begun to reveal important similarities and differences in the neural circuits underlying species-specific behaviors. Together these intellectual developments have fostered an adaptive evolutionary approach to cognitive neuroscience that now informs the field.

The adaptive evolutionary approach to cognitive studies draws inspiration directly from Darwin's ideas by ascribing specific brain features and cognitive abilities to the joint influences of descent from a common ancestor and adaptation to local information processing challenges. The rest of this chapter focuses specifically on the question of how the human brain and its cognitive operations evolved from simpler forms through evolutionary adaptation, emphasizing both common descent and adaptive specialization.

Evolution of Brain Size

The first challenge in evolutionary studies of brain and cognition is to understand how these two biological features are related. Perhaps the most obvious aspect of brain morphology that could relate to cognitive abilities is absolute brain size. Since most studies of cognitive evolution focus on complex, flexible, goal-directed behavior, a global metric such as brain size is a reasonable starting point.

Among vertebrates, mammals and birds generally have larger brains (and certainly larger volumes of cerebral cortex; see below) than fish, amphibians, or reptiles, and no one would dispute the fact that these differences in brain volume are somehow related to differences in the cognitive abilities of these various taxonomic groups. Among the mammals, moreover, rats have smaller brains than cats or monkeys, which in turn have smaller brains than dolphins and humans, confirming the general tendency of cognitive abilities and brain size to track together (see Box 23A). Together these observations suggest that brain size is indeed an important determinant of behavioral complexity and flexibility. This conclusion makes good sense: as the number of neurons in the brain increases, the complexity of computations that the brain can perform must likewise increase, at least in principle.

A closer look at the relationship between absolute brain size and cognition, however, raises the troubling observation that some seemingly smart animals have smaller brains than other animals not known for their cognitive prowess (**Figure 26.2**). This observation implies that the notion about cognitive abilities

(A) Macaque

(B) Cow

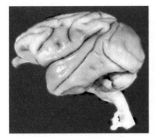
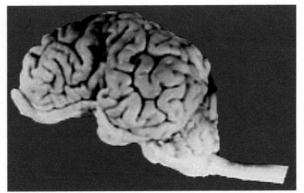

Figure 26.2 Brain size does not correlate absolutely with cognitive ability. Lateral views of the brains of a macaque monkey (A) and a cow (B), shown to scale. Even though its cognitive abilities are superior to those of the cow, the macaque brain is significantly smaller, as well as less folded. (Courtesy UW and MSU Comparative Mammalian Brains Collection.)

tracking absolute brain size is flawed, or that the relationship between absolute brain size and cognition is not simple. This issue has been further complicated by recent archaeological findings. For example, anthropologists have found skeletal remains of an anatomically modern but diminutive human on the Indonesian island of Flores that had brains only about one-third the size of their contemporaries on the mainland and were only about the size of a chimpanzee's brain (**Figure 26.3**). Despite this difference in absolute brain size, these microcephalic humans apparently made sophisticated stone tools, including long blades and possibly spear points, that were equal in complexity to those made by larger-brained humans of the same time period. Experts disagree as to whether these small-brained humans represent a case of island dwarfism—a common adaptation to the limited resources found on islands—or instead reflect some sort of skeletal pathology. Regardless of the outcome of the debate,

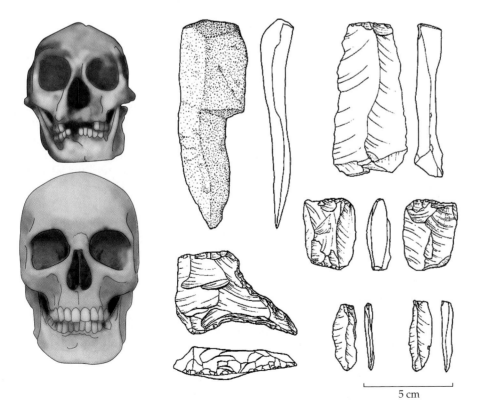

5 cm

Figure 26.3 A puzzling case of small-brained humans. The small human skull (compared here with the skull of a modern human) was found on the island of Flores in Indonesia and dates to about 18,000 years ago. Despite their smaller craniums, stone tools found in association with the microcephalic human remains on Flores include long blades and spear points similar in sophistication to those of mainland *Homo sapiens*. (After Brown et al. 2004.)

the Flores discovery highlights the related observation of large variation in the size of normal human brains today, which range in weight from about 1100 to about 1800 grams. Together, these observations reinforce the conclusion that, although absolute brain size is clearly important in determining cognitive capacity, other factors are important as well.

Allometry and relative brain size

The resolution of at least some of these puzzles is the relation of brain size and body size: it makes little sense to consider the size of an animal's brain without adjusting this metric for the size of the animal's body, since—cognitive abilities aside—the brain must be larger simply to organize the behavior of larger bodies. A detailed documentation of this relationship has been provided by Harry Jerison, a comparative neuroanatomist at UCLA who described a lawful relationship between absolute brain size and body size across a wide range of vertebrates. Differential measurements of individual body parts in relation to the whole to are known as **allometry** (the prefix *allo* means "other" in Greek), and the general proportionality of brain and body size reflects the fact that as the body grows larger, more brain neurons are needed to process sensory inputs, motor outputs, and their central interactions. Jerison noted that the allometric relationship of brain and body size is highly variable among species. Thus the regression line that fits to the scatter of brain size plotted against body size in **Figure 26.4A** makes obvious that some animals have brains that are larger than expected based on body size alone, whereas others do not. For instance, humans, porpoises, and crows have larger brains than expected for their average body size, whereas opossums, ostriches, and some other animals have smaller brains than we might expect. Moreover, birds and mammals have larger brains for their body size than do reptiles and fish. These deviations from allometrically predicted brain size, often referred to as *residual brain size*, correspond closely to relative cognitive ability. Within any particular group of vertebrates, relative brain size is also correlated, at least roughly, with apparent cognitive capacity (**Figure 26.4B**).

Relative brain size and cerebral complexity

Although the ratio of brain size to body size predicts cognitive abilities fairly well across a diversity of animals, this observation does not explain why or how the ratio of brain size to body size influences cognitive capacity. One reasonable argument is that the scaling relationship between brain size and body size in Figure 26.4 reflects the average amount of neural processing "machinery" necessary for maintaining a body of a particular size. According to this view, positive deviations in brain size from expectations based on body size would afford the animal extra neural processing capacity for additional abilities that transcended the usual housekeeping functions. The extra capacity could then be devoted to cognitive functions that are particularly advantageous for behavioral success in some ecological niches.

A second, not mutually exclusive, possibility is that changes in the relationship of brain and body size are associated with concomitant changes in the *structure* of the brain as well as its size. For example, the six-layered neocortex (see Chapter 1) is the most recently evolved part of the forebrain, is found only in mammals, and is widely agreed to be the seat of many advanced cognitive functions. Allometric analyses indicate that the size of the neocortex scales positively with the size of the rest of the brain: as the brain gets larger, the neocortex gets larger. This proportionality, however, varies among the different animal groups. That is, the allometric relationship relating neocortex size to brain size has the same slope, but different intercepts in different species. For example, simian primates (monkeys and apes) have proportion-

(A)

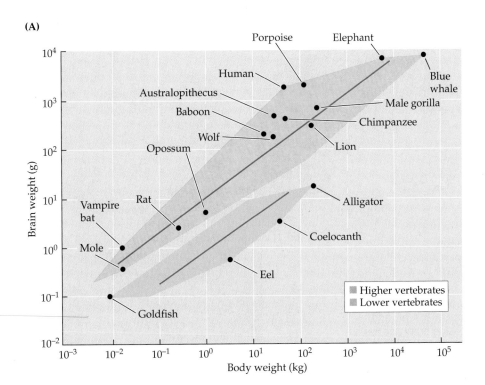

(B)

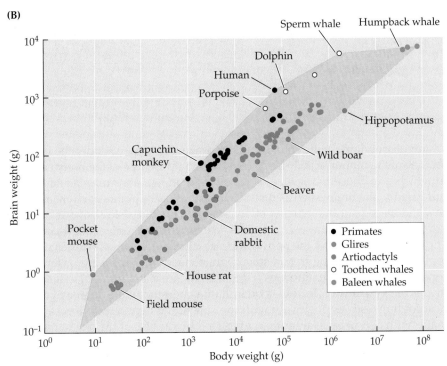

Figure 26.4 Importance of brain size relative to body size. Note that the scales are logarithmic in all cases. (A) Brain weight as a function of body weight. Heavy lines indicate the allometric scaling relationship between brain size and body size, determined by linear regression. The blue and green areas indicate minimal polygons enclosing the data points for mammals (blue) and for fishes and a reptile (green). (B) Allometric relationship of brain size and body size for placental (modern) mammals. Note that primates (black dots) have much larger brains given their body sizes than do rodents and rabbits (red dots) or artiodactyls (deer, antelope, etc.; blue dots), animals not known for their cognitive skills. (A after Jerison 1977; B after Striedter 2005.)

ately larger neocortices given the size of the rest of their brains than do prosimian primates (lemurs and lorises), which in turn have proportionately larger neocortices than expected compared to insectivores (**Figure 26.5**). Thus, as the size of the brain relative to body size increases, the relative size of the neocortex also increases. In at least this respect, the differential scaling of brain structures is important in the evolution of cognitive capacities.

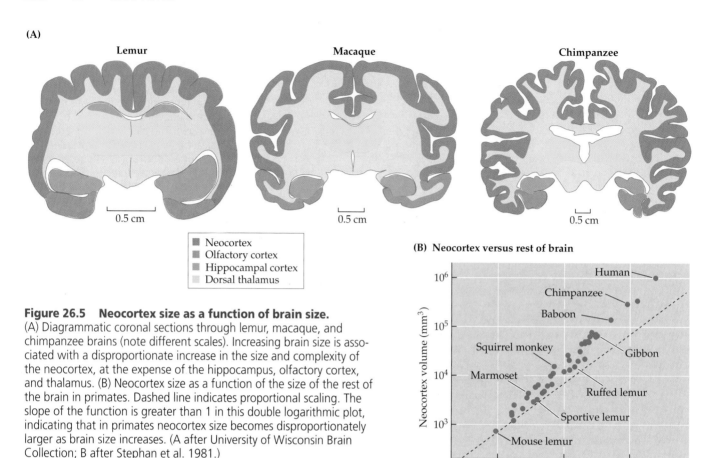

Figure 26.5 Neocortex size as a function of brain size.
(A) Diagrammatic coronal sections through lemur, macaque, and chimpanzee brains (note different scales). Increasing brain size is associated with a disproportionate increase in the size and complexity of the neocortex, at the expense of the hippocampus, olfactory cortex, and thalamus. (B) Neocortex size as a function of the size of the rest of the brain in primates. Dashed line indicates proportional scaling. The slope of the function is greater than 1 in this double logarithmic plot, indicating that in primates neocortex size becomes disproportionately larger as brain size increases. (A after University of Wisconsin Brain Collection; B after Stephan et al. 1981.)

Any discussion of the evolution of brain size must also consider the fact that the size of the mammalian brain is constrained by the size of the bony cranium in which it is housed. The size of the skull is limited by a number of factors unrelated to the brain, such as the size and attachment points of chewing muscles and the size of the female pelvic canal, which limits skull size at birth. In order to deal with these constraints, as the size of the neocortical sheet approaches the limits of the bony braincase in mammals, the cortex folds in on itself, thus creating the gyri and sulci characteristic of complex brains and more sophisticated cognitive functions (**Figure 26.6A**; see also Chapter 1). Across primates, the **gyrification index**—a quantitative measure of the degree of neocortical folding—scales positively with the size of the neocortex. Moreover, primates with neocortices larger than predicted by the size of the rest of the brain show even greater degrees of neocortical infolding (**Figure 26.6B**).

In addition to changes in the size of the brain itself and the relative size and complexity of structures like the neocortex, there is also evidence that the complexity of *neuronal circuitry* has increased during evolution. A family tree (properly called a *cladogram*) plotting the number of distinct neuronal cell types found in several vertebrate taxonomic group indicates that, as brain-to-body-weight ratios increased over evolutionary time, so did forebrain complexity (**Figure 26.7**). If the number of neuronal cell types found within a brain underlies the number and complexity of the computations it can perform, then the impact of brain size on cognitive capacity may also be due to increases the complexity of neuronal circuitry.

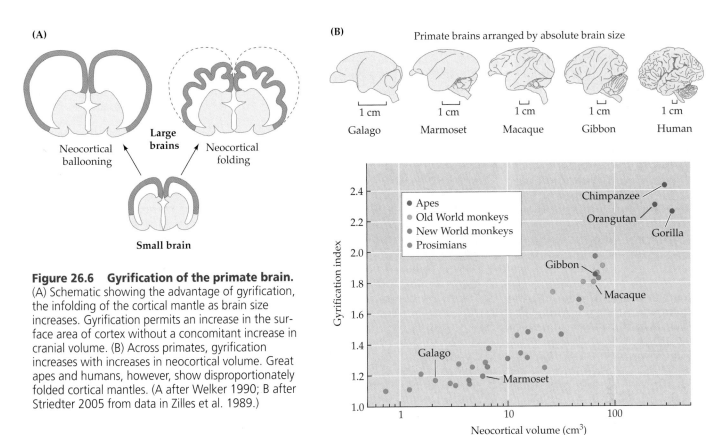

(A)

Neocortical ballooning

Large brains

Neocortical folding

Small brain

Figure 26.6 Gyrification of the primate brain.
(A) Schematic showing the advantage of gyrification, the infolding of the cortical mantle as brain size increases. Gyrification permits an increase in the surface area of cortex without a concomitant increase in cranial volume. (B) Across primates, gyrification increases with increases in neocortical volume. Great apes and humans, however, show disproportionately folded cortical mantles. (A after Welker 1990; B after Striedter 2005 from data in Zilles et al. 1989.)

(B) Primate brains arranged by absolute brain size

1 cm — Galago
1 cm — Marmoset
1 cm — Macaque
1 cm — Gibbon
1 cm — Human

- Apes
- Old World monkeys
- New World monkeys
- Prosimians

Chimpanzee, Orangutan, Gorilla, Gibbon, Macaque, Galago, Marmoset

Gyrification index (y-axis, 1.0 to 2.4), Neocortical volume (cm³) (x-axis, 1 to 100)

All told, these observations indicate that brain size scaling entails coordinated changes in the size and structural complexity of individual brain components. This is particularly true for neocortex, the most recently evolved component of the brain. Evolutionary changes in cognitive ability appear to be strongly related to the way brain size scales with body size across species,

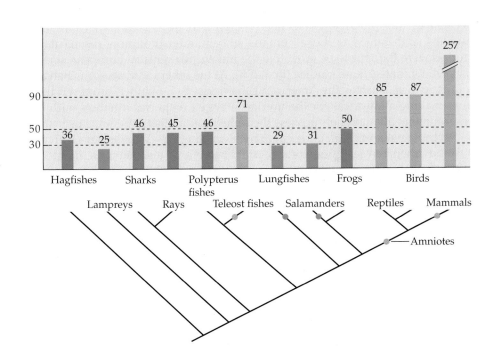

Hagfishes 36, Lampreys 25, Sharks 46, Rays 45, Polypterus fishes 46, Teleost fishes 71, Lungfishes 29, Salamanders 31, Frogs 50, Reptiles, Birds 85, 87, Mammals 257, Amniotes

Figure 26.7 Forebrain complexity.
In this cladogram, each bar indicates the number of different cell groups found in representative species of each major vertebrate group. Colors indicate when forebrain complexity is likely to have increased (orange) or decreased (green). (After Striedter 2005.)

(A)

(B)

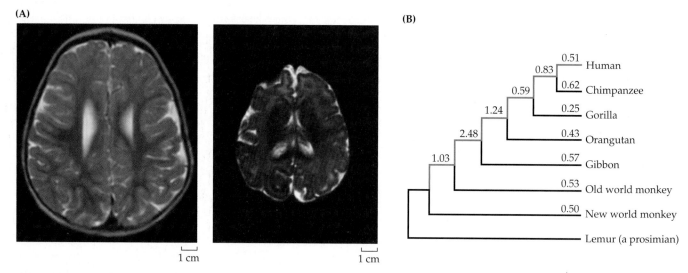

Figure 26.8 Genes may underlie evolutionary changes in brain size. (A) Brains of a normal 8-month-old child (left) and an 8-month-old child with microcephaly (right). (B) Cladogram based on the nucleotide substitution rate for the *microcephalin-1* (*MCPH1*) gene in primates. Higher ratios indicate more nonsynonymous mutations (i.e., mutations specifying a different amino acid than was originally present). The lineage leading to humans (red) shows the fastest substitution rate, suggesting accelerated adaptive evolution. (From Gilbert et al. 2005.)

suggesting that relatively small changes in the genetic programs controlling brain size could result in profound changes in cognition. This argument is endorsed by the recent finding that genes involved in determining brain size in humans have undergone extremely rapid evolution within the primate lineages leading to humans (**Figure 26.8**). Genes such as *microcephalin-1* (*MCPH1*) appear to underlie the growth and differentiation of neurons. Mutations in the microcephalin gene family lead to severe reductions in head and brain size, resulting in adults with brains about the size of chimpanzee brains who suffer from mental retardation. Relatively small changes in such genes could provide a mechanism for scaling brain size across primates.

Relative brain size and cognition

An important issue raised by the data on comparative brain size and complexity is whether the apparent differences in cognitive ability they predict are in fact measurable. Beginning with the battles fought by Darwin, this question has been the subject of ongoing debate. In part, controversy has persisted because greater intelligence has been ascribed to animals that are more like humans, and indeed to those humans who in older (and now discredited) studies were thought to be most like the nineteenth-century European scientists who initiated these studies (**Box 26B**). At the other extreme, some behavioral scientists, such as the American behaviorist B. F. Skinner, proposed that after making allowances for the myriad ways each species interacts with its environment, all mammals possess the same basic abilities.

Psychologist and primatologist Duane Rumbaugh at Georgia State University and others have suggested that certain behavioral tests, such as the speed with which an animal can learn to reverse its behavioral responses to a particular stimulus, do in fact reveal differences between species that reflect abstract cognitive ability. The problem with any single cognitive test, however, is that an animal might fail as a result of specific ways the test was administered rather than any limitations in its cognitive abilities.

A better way to assess cognitive differences would be to examine performance across a wide variety of problems. Robert Deaner, Carl van Schaik, and their colleagues at Duke University recently undertook an analysis of dozens of individual studies of behavioral task performance across an array of primate species (**Figure 26.9**). They found striking differences in general cognitive capacity that paralleled differences in relative brain size, as well as the

■ BOX 26B Brain Differences in Modern Humans: Implications for Cognition

A wealth of neuroanatomical, physiological, and behavioral data support the hypothesis that brain size and complexity predict cognitive abilities across a wide diversity of species. However, whether or not differences in brain size *within* a species are associated with differences in cognition remains a subject of debate. This is particularly true when considering differences in brain size and cognitive behavior in humans. Historically, scientists have often tried to link overall brain size to differences in performance on various global measures of cognitive performance such as intelligence (IQ) tests.

Several prominent nineteenth-century scientists—including the statistician Francis Galton (who, incidentally, was Darwin's cousin), the American physician Samuel Morton, and the French neuroanatomist Paul Broca (who determined that the left frontal lobe is responsible for articulate speech; see Chapter 21)—argued that individual differences in brain size, (often estimated by a method no more scientific than simply measuring the head) accurately predicted a person's intelligence. Unfortunately, this approach was used to support, either implicitly or explicitly, notions of racial and gender superiority that buttressed Western conventional wisdom of the time, according to which white European males were believed to have larger brains—and consequently greater intelligence—than everyone else in the world.

Careful reanalysis revealed much of this original research to be badly flawed. For example, Stephen Jay Gould demonstrated that Morton's measurements of cranial capacity (an index of brain size based on measuring the interior volume of the skull) in specimens of different races were inaccurate and highly biased towards finding larger brain sizes for European males. Moreover, it is now clear that it is difficult to measure general intelligence in individuals with different cultural, educational, and socioeconomic backgrounds. Despite recognition of these methodological problems, the legacy of this nineteenth-century mindset has continued to bedevil psychology, neuroscience, and society right into the twenty-first century.

Individual human beings clearly vary in cognitive ability as well as brain size. But such differences among human groups are small and often difficult to interpret, not least because the brain is a mosaic of interrelated modules and systems serving distinct behavioral functions. It thus makes more sense to consider more specifically whether variation in the size, physiology, cell structure, and molecular biology of such components corresponds to the efficiency or complexity of the behavioral functions they enable.

For example, the size of each of the various components of the visual system, including the optic tracts, lateral geniculate nucleus, and primary visual cortex, is intimately related within an individual; across subjects, however, these elements vary substantially in size. As described in Chapter 5, visual acuity corresponds closely to the cortical space allocated to each part of the visual field, suggesting (along with much other evidence) that the quality of cortical processing is a function of amount of cortical space given over to that function. Structural differences of this sort may also underlie gender differences in cognitive abilities such as language and spatial navigation. It has long been known, for example, that women are much less likely than men to suffer a debilitating loss of language (aphasia) following strokes involving cortical language areas in the left hemisphere. This gender difference suggests that women process language more bilaterally than men, a hypothesis supported by recent neuroimaging studies demonstrating stronger lateralization in language processing in males than females.

Stronger lateralization in males also extends to visuospatial information processing, as revealed by both lesion and functional neuroimaging studies.

These observed sex differences in brain organization could be related to differences in cognitive performance, specifically to the superior verbal abilities of females, on average, and the superior visuospatial navigation abilities in males revealed by standardized tests. Note, however, that such tests are subject to the same criticisms as the IQ tests described earlier.

As further discussed in Chapter 27, these and other differences in brain structure and cognitive performance in men and women seem likely to derive from the interplay of sex hormones and experience during development. Gender differences in the spatial navigation ability of experimental animals, for example, have been linked to differences in the size of the hippocampus in male and female voles and rats, which are known to be determined by the action of sex hormones during development.

These observations notwithstanding, the links between gender, hormones, experience, brain structure, and cognition in humans remain hotly debated. Given the enormous cultural, political, and educational implications of these kinds of findings, much more work will be required to understand the biological mechanisms that contribute to the wide range of differences in cognitive performance seen across groups and across individuals within groups.

References

ANDREWS, T. J., S. D. HALPERN AND D. PURVES (1997) Correlated size variations in human visual cortex, lateral geniculate nucleus, and optic tract. *J. Neurosci.* 17: 2859–2868.

BOYNTON, G. M. AND R. O. DUNCAN (2002) Visual acuity correlates with cortical magnification factors in human V1 [Abstract]. *J. Vision*, 2(10), 11a.

GOULD, S. J. (1981) *The Mismeasure of Man.* New York: W. W. Norton.

KIMURA, D. (1996) Sex, sexual orientation, and sex hormones influence human cognitive function. *Curr. Opin. Neurobiol.* 6: 259–263.

Figure 26.9 Cognitive ability across primate species. This meta-analysis of cognitive ability in primates was derived from performances by individuals from a large array of different taxa on a battery of different tasks. The work bears out that cognitive flexibility increases from prosimians to New World monkeys to Old World monkeys to the apes. (After Deaner et al. 2006.)

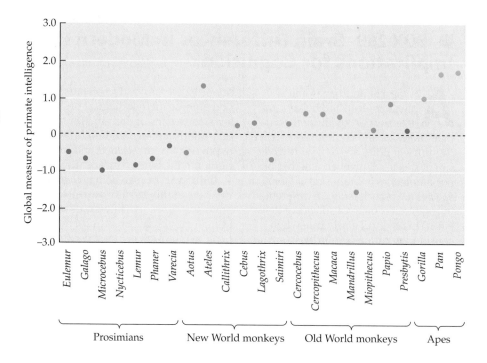

relative size of the neocortex. These data support the idea mentioned earlier that cognitive abilities scale with the amount of extra cortical space available to devote to cognitive functions.

Adaptive Specializations of Brain and Behavior

The discussion so far has focused on the evolution of overall cognitive capacities inferred from behavioral flexibility versus changes in total brain size and the size of some component structures. Just as important, however, are the specialized cognitive and behavioral mechanisms that have evolved to solve specific information-processing problems encountered in the natural environment. Adaptive specializations for particular types of behavior and cognitive functions have, until recently, received less attention than questions concerning the evolution of more general characteristics of the brain shared by many different species.

In the 1960s, one of the first indications that animals might preferentially process certain types of information at the expense of others was the observation made by John Garcia at UCLA that rats readily associate the taste of lithium chloride with the nausea induced by its ingestion, but have much greater trouble learning that bright lights predict nausea. In contrast, rats learn to associate bright lights with electric shock far more quickly than they learn to associate a specific taste with a shock. These findings challenged the then-dominant behaviorist notion that all behavior can be explained through simple associative learning, and suggested that, at the very least, animals are predisposed to learn particular types of stimulus-response relationships.

Later studies in birds further supported the idea that the adaptation of behavior to specific environmental and social contexts is a driving force behind brain evolution. For example, male songbirds produce a repertoire of species-specific songs during development, and adult males sing these songs to attract mates and to defend territory (see Chapter 20). Different songbird species show striking differences in the number of songs they can learn to produce. Even within a single species of songbirds, some individuals learn many more songs than others, and the number of songs a male produces affects his eventual reproductive success.

Such behavioral differences among species or individuals could be realized through changes in brain size, as described above, or through highly specific adaptations of the neural circuits involved in producing the behavior. The latter possibility is succinctly expressed in Jerison's **principle of proper mass**, which states that the mass of neural tissue controlling a particular function will be proportional and appropriate to the amount of information processing involved in performing the function in question. An example of Jerison's principle is the relative size of the superior and inferior colliculi, structures on the dorsal surface of the midbrain that are involved in visual and auditory processing, respectively (**Figure 26.10**). Tarsiers, which hunt insects using vision, have relatively large superior colliculi and small inferior colliculi; conversely, bats and dolphins use echolocation to capture their prey and have relatively large inferior colliculi and smalled superior colliculi. The superior and inferior colliculi of humans are roughly equal in size, consistent with our own reliance on both visual and auditory sensations to guide behavior.

Such specializations are sometimes referred to as *functional neural modules*, and the differential elaboration of modular regions is termed **mosaic brain evolution**. Functional and neuroanatomical studies indicate that neural modules can become exquisitely specialized for processing information vital to the ways a particular species interacts with its environment. For example, rats and mice navigate their environments at night by touch, and autoradiographic, histological, and electrophysiological studies of the primary somatosensory cortex show that mice and rats overrepresent tactile sensibility in the corresponding sensory cortex (see Chapter 7). These rodents possess an array of facial whiskers that is highly specialized to convey information about the size, shape, texture, and motion of objects around the head and face. Each whisker is represented by a corresponding module of cortex called a *whisker barrel*, and their overall representation is disproportionately large relative to the rest of

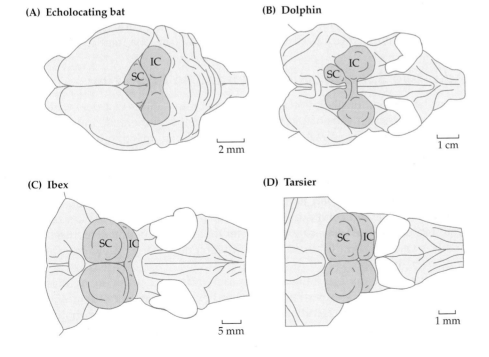

(A) Echolocating bat

(B) Dolphin

2 mm

1 cm

(C) Ibex

(D) Tarsier

5 mm

1 mm

Figure 26.10 The principle of proper mass. The relative size of the superior colliculus (SC, blue) and inferior colliculus (IC, green) varies according to the degree to which animals use visual and auditory information, respectively. Tarsiers, which hunt visually at night, and ibex, which use vision to detect predators, have larger SCs. On the other hand, bats and dolphins, which navigate using sonar, have larger ICs. (After Striedter 2005, adapted from A Baron et al. 1996; B Langworthy 1976; C Schober and Brauer 1974; D Tilney 1926.)

Figure 26.11 Overrepresentation of critical body parts in sensory and motor maps. (A) Barrels in mouse somatosensory cortex contain a precise, but disproportionately large, representation of the whiskers, the source of much sensory information in these animals. (B) Distorted topographic maps of the body surface in human somatosensory (left) and motor (right) cortex. (A from Woolsey et al. 1975; B after Penfield and Boldrey 1937.)

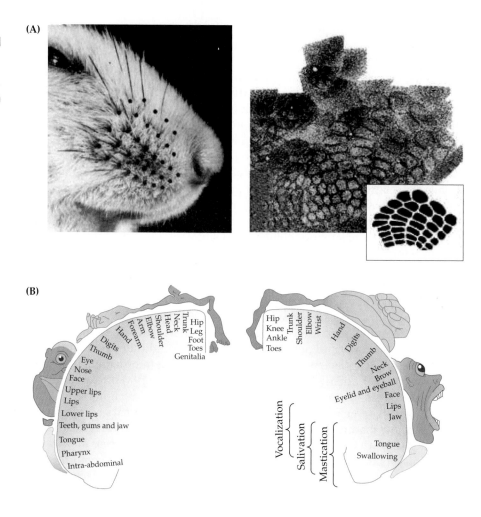

the body surface (**Figure 26.11A**). A similarly precise overrepresentation of the fingers and lips is apparent in the human somatosensory cortex, and underlies the fine sensory discrimination abilities of these structures (**Figure 26.11B**). Similarly their over-representation in the primary motor cortex contributes to the ability to move the fingers with high precision (see Chapter 8).

Adaptive Specializations Related to Cognition

As we have seen, the evolution of specialized brain regions that deal with the special processing needs of a given species is well documented, and many of these structural specializations are clearly related to cognitive abilities. Among warblers, for instance, the number of songs within a typical male's repertoire is directly proportional to the size of the *hyperstriatum ventrale pars caudale*, or *HVC*—the principal brain nucleus organizing song learning and production, and the avian homologue of the mammalian premotor cortex (**Figure 26.12**). The observation of a direct relationship between HVC size and song repertoire size in warblers suggests that specific neural structures are highly specialized for the particular information processing problems encountered by a given species.

The same general argument applies to neural structures contributing to memory formation, another key component of cognition. Several families of birds known for their overall cognitive flexibility also show morphological and behavioral specializations for storing and retrieving food. For instance,

(A) Relative volume correlation

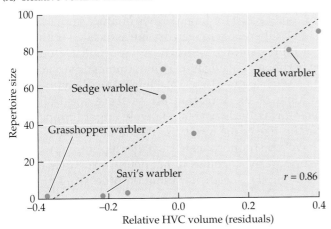

(B)

Figure 26.12 Brain nuclei control songbird behavior. Songbirds such as warblers display adaptive variation in motor brain structures related to vocalization and song repertoire size. (A) The size of the song control nucleus (HVC) in warblers is predicted by the number of songs each species sings. (B) The reed warbler, a bird known for its melodious song. (A after Szekely et al. 1996.)

members of the corvid (crow) family vary in the degree of their reliance on stored food, as well as on structural specializations of the mouth and throat for carrying food during storing. One such corvid, Clark's nutcracker, can carry dozens of seeds at a time and relies on stored seeds for up to 90 percent of its winter diet; in contrast, other corvids such as the scrub jay rely very little on stored food and show no morphological specializations for carrying food (**Figure 26.13A**).

Similar variation is seen within the parid bird family, which includes chickadees and other titmice, some species of which store food while others do not.

(A)

Clark's nutcracker

Scrub jay

(B) Absolute hippocampus size

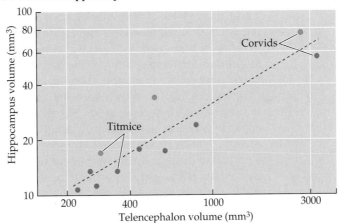

Figure 26.13 The size of some brain structures correlates with behavior. The hippocampus is specialized for remembering the location of stored food in birds, and its size varies accordingly. (A) Two members of the crow (corvid) family. Clark's nutcracker (top) displays highly specialized behavior for storing and retrieving food. In contrast, the Western scrub jay (bottom), a feeding generalist, is relatively unspecialized for food caching. (B) Hippocampal volume plotted against forebrain volume for two families of birds, corvids and parids (titmice). Food-storing species (red) tend to have larger hippocampal formations than expected based on the size of the forebrain as a whole. (After Krebs et al. 1989.)

Within both families, those species that rely on stored food and are morphologically specialized for food caching show greater capacity to remember the location and contents of food caches for long periods of time. And, central to the present argument, these differences in memory are associated with differences in the size of the hippocampus, a structure important for encoding information in memory pertinent to navigation in many animals (and declarative memory in humans; see Chapters 13 and 14). Hippocampal volume scales positively with the volume of the forebrain across these species (**Figure 26.13B**); moreover, food-storing birds have a relatively larger hippocampus than expected based on the size of the forebrain. By the same token, species that do not store food have a disproportionately smaller hippocampus. These observations strongly support the conclusion that neural structures become highly specialized for solving the specific information-processing problems faced by a species.

Engineering a Larger, More Complex Brain

It should by now be clear that the overall size, regional complexity, histological diversity, and modular specificity of the brain reflect both the prior adaptations of ancestral species and contemporary responses to adaptive pressures favoring the evolution of particular behavioral capacities. An important question raised by these observations is how these changes in brain size and structure are generated. This question becomes particularly interesting when one considers the relatively small number of coding sequences available in animal genomes for specifying the size and structure of the brain (keep in mind that there are fewer than 30,000 genes in the entire human genome).

Recent genetic discoveries have revealed a family of genes that appear to play some role in controlling brain size. Just how such a small number of genes might actually generate the diversity of brain size and complexity in different animals is not known. One model developed by Barbara Findlay and her collaborators at Cornell University suggests that changes in the timing of neurogenesis during brain development can account for regional diversity. To understand the merits of this model, it is useful to compare rats and macaque monkeys as to the developmental time at which neurons cease to be generated in different brain regions (**Figure 26.14A**). The sequence of neurogenesis in various brain structures follows the same pattern in both species, with locus coeruleus neurons born first, then septal neurons, and finally neocortical cells. In macaques, however, the neocortex develops at a later time relative to the rat than does the locus coeruleus. This differential timing might explain the large expansion of the neocortex in macaques and other primates compared with rodents (**Figure 26.14B**). Merely by stretching out the period of development of a particular brain area, the number of neurons generated—and thus the size of a given brain area—can effectively be increased.

Evolution of advanced cognition in primates

Abundant evidence supports the conclusion that primates are cognitively more advanced than most other animals. Moreover, the relative size of the brain, the disproportionate enhancement of neocortex, and the presence of several unique features of brain anatomy and neuronal cell types distinguish primates from other mammals. Several hypotheses have been offered to explain the elaboration of these brain features and the associated cognitive abilities in primates, including a propensity to use tools, the influence of a long neonatal period, and the relatively long life spans of most primate species. The more specific information-processing problems that have driven the evolution of high levels of cognitive function, however, are not clear.

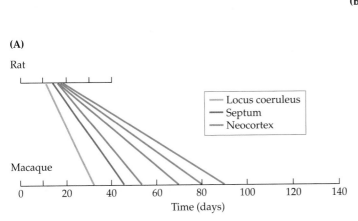

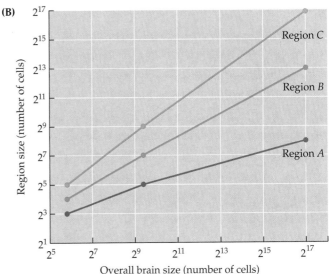

Figure 26.14 Developmental timing may explain differences in brain structure size.   (A) Comparison of the timing of the end of neuronal generation in different brain structures in rats and macaques. While the locus coeruleus develops at about the same time in both species, the neocortex takes much longer to mature in macaques. (B) Findlay and Darlington's "late equals large" model of timing effects on brain region size. Three different brain regions contain cells generated at different times (*A* first, *C* last) in three species with small, medium, and large brains. Region *C* is disproportionately large in the largest species as a result of having had more time for neuronal proliferation and maturation. (A after Clancy et al. 2001; B after Finlay and Darlington 1995.)

One hypothesis is that the demands of foraging for widely dispersed and ephemeral food sources favored the evolution of enhanced cognition and its neural correlates in primates. The **foraging hypothesis** was first suggested by the work of Timothy Clutton-Brock and Paul Harvey at Oxford, who showed that the allometric relationship between brain and body size differs in primates that forage for different types of foods.

Primates whose diet is high in ripe fruit tend to have larger brains for their body size than primates that eat mostly leaves or insects (**Figure 26.15A**). Enhanced brain size in fruit-eating primates compared with leaf- or insect-eating primates could represent an adaptation to the complex spatial and temporal information-processing problems posed by feeding on ripe fruits. In the tropics, fruit tends to ripen in a piecemeal fashion, and on trees dispersed over long distances throughout the forest. A diet rich in ripe fruit thus requires the ability to learn and remember both the temporal and spatial distribution of resources across a wide area. Leaf-eaters, on the other hand, typically possess specialized digestive mechanisms that permit them to extract energy from the abundant leaf matter located more or less anywhere in the forest. Insect-eaters tend to forage opportunistically, but are typically small enough in body size to satisfy their nutritional needs within a relatively small area.

This framework predicts that fruit-eating primates should possess better spatial learning and memory abilities than otherwise similar primates that forage on leaves, insects, or even tree sap. Michael Platt and his colleagues, then at the University of Nebraska, tested this model experimentally and found that fruit-eating tamarin monkeys can remember the location of food sources for much longer periods than sap-eating marmosets, despite the fact that the two species have a similar body size and possess the same cooperative social system. The foraging model is further supported by the observation that bats that eat fruit, flowers, or blood—all of which are difficult to obtain—have larger brains for their body size than insect-eating bats (**Figure 26.15B**).

Another important hypothesis posits that the demands of navigating a complex social group favored the evolution of cerebral and cognitive enhancement in primates. Most primates live in relatively large social groups structured around kinship, dominance hierarchies, and cooperative alliances. Managing these social relationships relies on individual recognition, status assessment, and long-term memory for prior interactions. Furthermore, it would be adaptive for primates to be able to infer the intentions of other individuals from their expressions and state of attention, as well as to be able to

Figure 26.15 The foraging hypothesis.
This concept posits that the demands of "specialized" feeding on widely dispersed and/or ephemeral food sources favor the evolution of enhanced cognition. (A) The brains of a howler monkey (a leaf-eating generalist feeder; left) and a spider monkey (a fruit-feeding specialist) are drawn to the same scale. Note the appreciably larger and more gyrified brain of the spider monkey. (B) Allometric plot of brain size against body size for bats. Bat species feeding on fruit, flowers or blood are plotted in red; insectivorous bats are plotted in black. The more generalist insectivorous bats have smaller brains for their body size than bats specialized for feeding on fruit, flowers, or blood. (B from Stephen et al. 1981.)

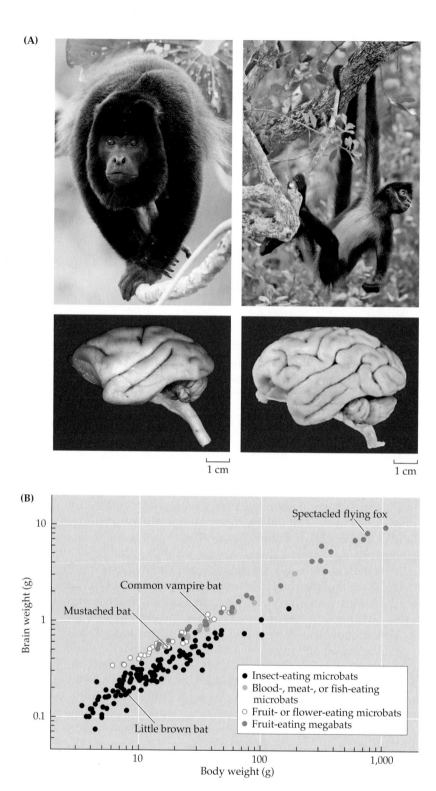

deceive others. Such socially sophisticated behavior implies an ability to infer the internal mental state of other individuals (see Chapter 19). This hypothesis of socially driven brain evolution is often referred to as the *Machiavellian intelligence hypothesis*, after the political theorist of the Italian Renaissance.

The suggestion that the more highly evolved cognitive abilities of primates have been socially driven is supported by several observations. First, primate

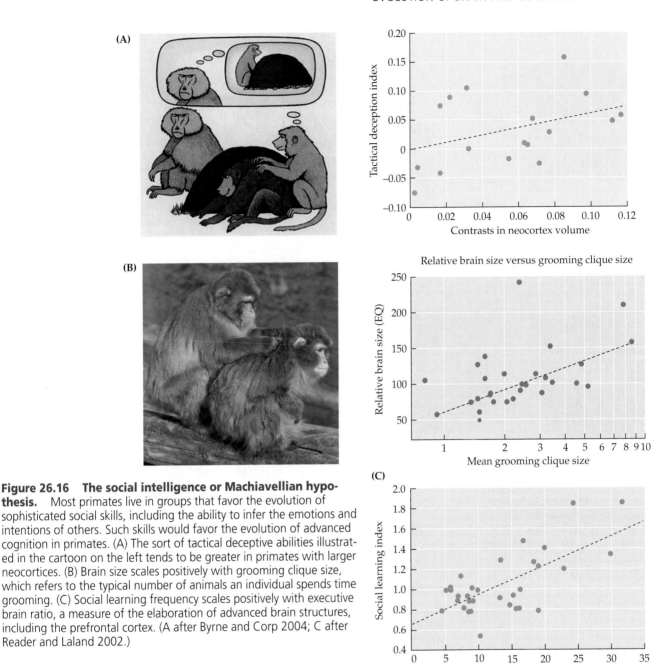

Figure 26.16 The social intelligence or Machiavellian hypothesis. Most primates live in groups that favor the evolution of sophisticated social skills, including the ability to infer the emotions and intentions of others. Such skills would favor the evolution of advanced cognition in primates. (A) The sort of tactical deceptive abilities illustrated in the cartoon on the left tends to be greater in primates with larger neocortices. (B) Brain size scales positively with grooming clique size, which refers to the typical number of animals an individual spends time grooming. (C) Social learning frequency scales positively with executive brain ratio, a measure of the elaboration of advanced brain structures, including the prefrontal cortex. (A after Byrne and Corp 2004; C after Reader and Laland 2002.)

societies are arguably among the most complex in the animal kingdom, and primates as a group possess relatively large forebrains. Moreover, other animals that live in complex social groups, such as dolphins and killer whales, also have relatively large brains. Second, various measures of advanced brain development among primates correlate with measures of social complexity such as deception rate, number of grooming partners, and frequency of social learning and innovation (**Figure 26.16**). And third, the primate brain also shows specializations for processing social information. Both human and nonhuman primates, for example, possess neurons selective for the identity and direction of gaze in a viewed face (**Figure 26.17A**). This last feature, however, is not unique to primates; sheep have similar face-selective neurons in their temporal cortices and, despite their simple social system, are adept at recognizing and remembering social identities (**Figure 26.17B**).

(A)

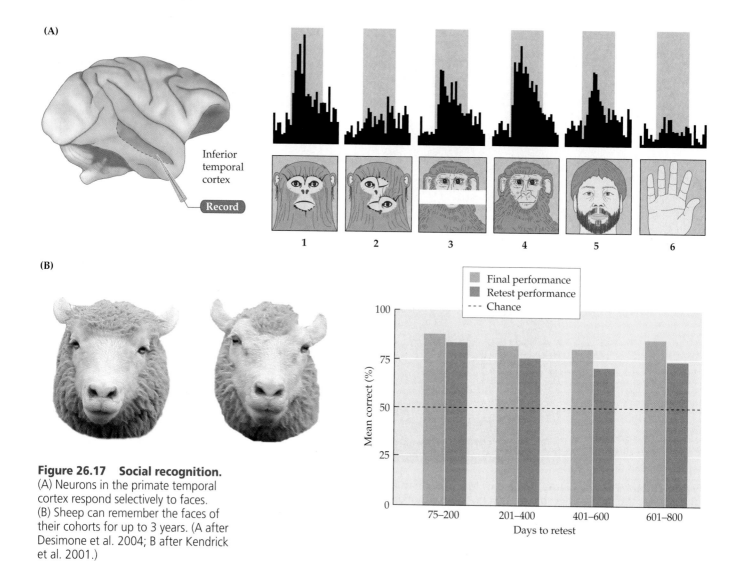

(B)

Figure 26.17 Social recognition. (A) Neurons in the primate temporal cortex respond selectively to faces. (B) Sheep can remember the faces of their cohorts for up to 3 years. (A after Desimone et al. 2004; B after Kendrick et al. 2001.)

Evolution of culture and cognition in the hominid lineage

It is clear that primates stand out among mammals for both their behavioral flexibility and the size and complexity of their brains. In many respects, human neural and cognitive evolution has simply elaborated on trends that are well established in non-human primates; in other respects, however, human brain evolution has been marked by distinctive deviations from other primates. For example, like other primates, the human brain represents a larger fraction of body size than among other mammals. Nonetheless, the trajectory of brain evolution relative to body size has been steeper within the lineage leading to modern humans (**Figure 26.18**).

The fossil (i.e., skeletal and other organismal remains) and archeological (i.e., stone tools and other artifacts of human activity) records provide clues about the coevolution of brain structure and cognition in humans. The primate lineage leading to humans first diverged from the great apes between 5 and 8 million years ago. Somewhat surprisingly, this divergence was not characterized by major neurological changes. The first adaptive change distinguishing ancestral humans, or **hominids**, from apes was not neurological but entailed upright bipedal walking. The first human ancestors, known as **Australopithecines** and found in eastern and southern African fossil beds dated to 3–4 million years ago, had brains about the same size as modern-day chim-

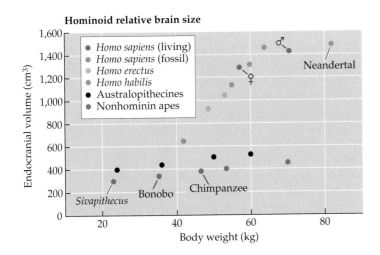

Hominoid relative brain size

- Homo sapiens (living)
- Homo sapiens (fossil)
- Homo erectus
- Homo habilis
- Australopithecines
- Nonhominin apes

Neandertal

Sivapithecus Bonobo Chimpanzee

Endocranial volume (cm³) vs *Body weight (kg)*

Figure 26.18 Trajectory of primate brain evolution relative to body size. Brain size is disproportionately large in relation to body size in humans and their immediate ancestors (hominids) compared to apes. (After Hofman, 1983.)

panzees (**Figure 26.19A**). However, the human evolutionary career thereafter is characterized by both gradual, progressive changes and relatively rapid advancements in brain size and cognition. The first member of the genus *Homo*, the group to which modern humans belong, diverged from an Australopithecine ancestor around 2.5 million years ago. This species, dubbed **Homo habilis** ("handy man") had a brain that was about 50 percent larger than its ancestors, and was the first human ancestor to produce crude stone tools (**Figure 26.19B**). About 800,000 years later, **Homo erectus** ("erect man") diverged from an earlier *Homo* species. Again, this evolutionary event was characterized by major advancements in brain size and cognition. Early *Homo erectus* fossils reveal brains that were about a third larger than the brains of early *Homo habilis*. Moreover, *Homo erectus* made stone tools of greater com-

(A)

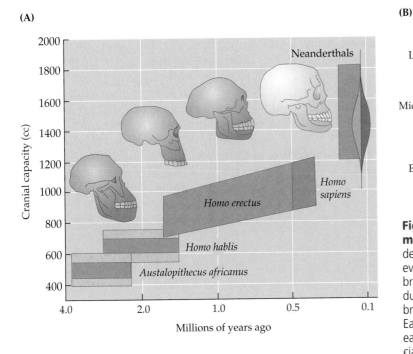

Neanderthals

Homo sapiens

Homo erectus

Homo hablis

Austalopithecus africanus

Cranial capacity (cc) vs *Millions of years ago*

(B)

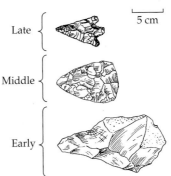

5 cm

Late

Middle

Early

Figure 26.19 Evolution of the human brain and material culture. (A) Brain size has increased in sudden jumps as well as gradual changes during hominid evolution. Shaded regions indicate range of variation in brain size. (B) The sophistication of the stone tools produced by hominids increased in parallel with increasing brain size over the course of evolutionary time. Bottom: Early Paleolithic tools associated with *Homo habilis* and early *Homo erectus*. Middle: Middle Paleolithic tools associated with late *Homo erectus* and early *Homo sapiens*. Top: Upper Paleolithic tools found with the skeletal remains of anatomically modern humans. (After Tattersall et al. 1988.)

plexity and symmetry than those made by earlier humans (see Figure 26.19B), and also began to use fire.

Homo erectus was an extremely successful species, persisting for about 2 million years and colonizing what is now Africa, Europe, and Asia. During that time, hominid brain size increased gradually and the stone tools produced by *Homo erectus* progressed in sophistication. These advances in brain and cognitive ability apparently permitted *Homo erectus* to survive in a wide variety of climates, utilize a variety of resources, and even navigate open oceans to reach Australia. Throughout the Old World, *Homo erectus* continued to evolve and adapt to local conditions until the late Pleistocene era, from 200,000 to about 50,000 years ago. In what is today Western Europe and the Middle East, *Homo erectus* evolved into **Neanderthals**, who, rather surprisingly, had brains that were even larger than those of modern humans (although it should be noted that their bodies were slightly heavier as well); in this instance, brain size does not align very well with the relatively primitive material culture of Neanderthals.

Modern humans, **Homo sapiens** ("wise man") evidently arose on the African continent about 200,000 years ago and rapidly spread throughout the world, eventually driving other hominid populations, including Neanderthals, to extinction. The competitive superiority of anatomically modern humans was almost certainly due, at least in part, to their superior cognitive abilities. Early *Homo sapiens* possessed an extremely sophisticated arsenal of stone tools, including long blades and hafted spear points (i.e., points with handles, which make much more effective weapons than a simple pointed implement with no handle). These were the first humans to produce symbolic representations and art (**Figure 26.20**). They buried their dead with jewelry and other items, indicating that they apparently had some type of religious beliefs.

Specialized neural systems supporting human culture

The explosion of creativity and technical sophistication displayed by hominids in general, and the first modern humans in particular, has important implications for understanding the organization of the human brain. In addition to the significant increases in brain size corresponding to advances in cognitive behavior in fossil humans, specific neural systems engaged by activities such as tool making and the visual arts must have also undergone dramatic evolutionary changes. Despite the fact that some non-human primates use and can even produce tools, no other animal produces artifacts nearly as sophisticated as those produced by even the earliest anatomically modern humans.

Another example of an evolutionary change with cultural implications is the development of fine motor control of the fingers needed for the production of improved stone tools and art (see Figures 26.19 and 26.20). As the size of the neocortex increases across taxa, so do the projections of the neocortex to the

(A)

(B)

(C)

Figure 26.20 Visual symbolism and art. Anatomically modern humans in Ice Age Europe began to produce symbolic art indicative of greatly enhanced cognitive abilities. (A) Carved woman's head from Brassempouy, in southern France, about 23,000 years old. (B) Lunar phases incised on a piece of bone, 30,000–40,000 years old. (C) Cave painting of a horse from Lascaux, France, approximately 15,000 years old.

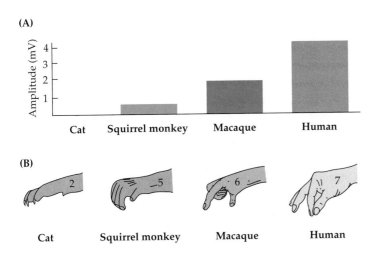

Figure 26.21 Motor system changes associated with enhanced manual coordination. (A) Amplitude of potentials recorded from populations of muscle fibers activated by spinal motor neurons following microstimulation in the primary motor cortex in cats, squirrel monkeys, macaques, and humans. These observations indicate that the efficacy of corticospinal synaptic connections increases in the human evolutionary lineage. (B) Hand morphology and dexterity in the same animals. Numbers indicate dexterity index, measured by the precision of grip. (After Nakajima et al. 2000.)

spinal cord. Moreover, these projections increasingly penetrate lower levels of the spinal cord and extend deeper into the lamina of spinal cord gray matter (see Chapters 8 and 9). This enhancement in corticospinal projections associated with increased neocortical volume results in larger-amplitude action potentials recorded extracellularly from populations of muscle fibers activated by spinal motor neurons in response to stimulation of the motor cortex—a phenomenon that correlates with greater manual dexterity (**Figure 26.21**).

Another feature of the primate brain that could arguably support advanced social cognition in both apes and humans is the presence of certain specialized neurons within the anterior cingulate cortex and insula. Known as **spindle cells** (or *von Economo neurons*, after the neuroanatomist who discovered them), these neurons are present only in great apes, humans, and some cetaceans. The density of these neurons is particularly high in the anterior cingulate cortex of humans and our closest living relative, the pygmy chimpanzee (**Figure 26.22**). Spindle cells have unique morphological characteristics and possess receptors for dopamine, serotonin, and vasopressin. As described in Chapter

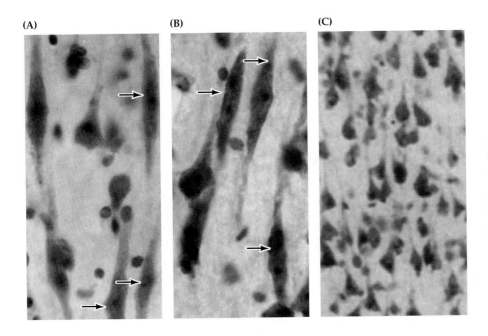

Figure 26.22 Spindle neurons may be a factor in enhanced cognitive abilities. Morphology of neurons in layer 5 of the anterior cingulate cortex is shown for (A) a human, (B) a pygmy chimpanzee, and (C) a gibbon. Clusters of spindle neurons (arrows) are clearly visible in the human and pygmy chimpanzee. The anterior cingulate cortex is believed to play an active role in attention, executive control processes, and decision making. (From Nimchinsky et al. 1999.)

24, dopamine and serotonin contribute to the processing of rewards and punishments, and vasopressin has been implicated in social bonding. Finally, neuroimaging studies have implicated the anterior cingulate cortex in attention, executive control processes, and decision making (see Unit VIII). Together, these observations endorse the possibility articulated by John Allman and his colleagues at Cal Tech that the anterior cingulate cortex has become specialized in hominoids, humans in particular, for processing the complex social information needed to guide the cognitive processes related to making appropriate social decisions.

Finally, no treatment of human brain evolution would be complete without mentioning the development of language. Humans obviously possess both the vocal and neurological apparatus to produce articulate speech. As discussed in Chapter 21, two brain regions in the left hemisphere appear to be major substrates for language processing in humans. Broca's area in the frontal cortex plays a critical role in language production, and lesions in this area produce an aphasia characterized by halting, inarticulate speech. Wernicke's area in the temporal lobe, on the other hand, contributes to language comprehension, and lesions to this area result in deficits in producing meaningful utterances.

Although it was initially thought that these two brain regions were unique to humans, it now appears that they represent elaborations of brain areas present in non-human primates (**Figure 26.23**). Field playback experiments of species-specific vocalizations in macaques have shown a right-ear response advantage (and thus a left-hemisphere processing bias) similar to the left-hemisphere lateralization of language in humans. Furthermore, the left temporoparietal area in macaques (roughly corresponding to Wernicke's area in humans) is larger in the left than right hemisphere. Similarly, the ventrolateral

(A) Macaque

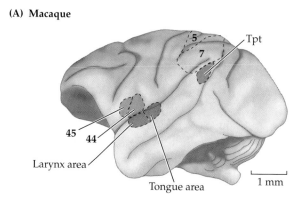

(B) Human

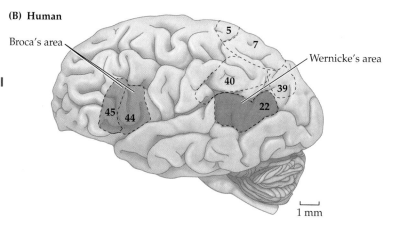

Figure 26.23 Vocal communication-related cortical areas in macaque and human.   Brodmann areas 44 and 45 in the macaque (A) correspond to Broca's area in humans (B), whereas the temporal parietal junction (Tpt) in macaques has apparently been elaborated as Wernicke's area in humans. Areas 39 and 40 in the human parietal lobe have no homologue in macaques, although some investigators contend that lateral area 7 in the macaque is homologous with these areas. (A after Preuss and Goldman-Rakic 1991; B after Petrides et al. 2005.)

frontal cortex of the macaque (roughly corresponding to Broca's area in humans) is specialized for fine control of the orofacial musculature and has a cellular structure generally similar to that found in Broca's area in humans. Recent PET studies have also revealed the homologue of Wernicke's area in rhesus monkeys to be activated when they hear species-specific vocalizations (see Figure 21.9). Together, these observations support the idea that specialized features of human speech are built on adaptations for social and perhaps vocal communication already present in non-human primates.

Despite these shared brain areas associated with vocal communication, it is quite clear that human language is both qualitatively and quantitatively distinct from animal communication. The linguistic complexity and cultural capacity of humans remains even more enigmatic when considered in light of the fact that most of the brain structures contributing to language and other cognitive abilities in humans are shared with other primates. These observations suggest that the neurobiological source of human language and culture might lie in unique patterns of neuronal connectivity, new cell types (such as spindle cells), or even morphological features outside the brain (such as the vocal tract), as well as novel features that have yet to be discovered.

Summary

1. Evolutionary theory states that biological structures, including the brain, are the product of inheritance from a common ancestor, the evolved phenotype having been shaped by reproductive success accruing from specialized adaptation to the challenges of an animal's ecological niche. The evidence discussed in this chapter about the evolution of the cognitive abilities of mammalian brains is consistent with the way natural selection is known to determine morphological form and function.

2. Comparative studies of brains and their cognitive abilities in a range of animals support the idea that increases in overall brain size—in particular the size and complexity of the neocortex relative to expectations based on body size—are fundamental for the emergence of enhanced cognition over evolutionary time.

3. The twin demands of foraging and navigating complex social environments appear to have been especially important selective forces in the evolution of complex cognitive abilities and their neural implementation in primates.

4. The emergence of human culture has been characterized by gradual increases in the complexity of behavior and parallel increases in the complexity of the relevant brain structures. In addition, human evolution has been marked by the relatively rapid development of new behavioral capabilities such as tool making, art, and language.

5. The degree to which these capacities tap ancestral systems or are mediated by completely novel neural structures is open to debate, but much evidence suggests that at least some of these abilities are built on homologues in the brains of non-human primates; the human cognitive brain thus represents a mosaic of primitive features shared with other animals, and highly specialized regions adapted to the social and environmental challenges confronting our primate and early human ancestors.

Additional Reading

Reviews

CHASE, P. G. AND H. L. DIBBLE (1987) Middle Palaeolithic symbolism: A review of current evidence and interpretations. *J. Anthropol. Archaeol.* 6: 263–296.

CLAYTON, N. S. AND J. R. KREBS (1995) Memory in food-storing birds: From behaviour to brain. *Curr. Opin. Neurobiol.* 5: 149–154.

GILBERT, S. L., W. B. DOBYNS AND B. T. LAHN (2005) Genetic links between brain development and brain evolution. *Nat. Rev. Genetics* 6: 581.

WYNN, T. (2002) Archaeology and cognitive evolution. *Behav. Brain Sci.* 25: 389–438.

Important Original Papers

CLUTTON-BROCK, T. H. AND P. H. HARVEY (1980) Primates, brains, and ecology. *J. Zool. Soc. London* 190: 309–323.

DUNBAR, R. I. M. (1993) Coevolution of neocortical size, group size and language in humans (with commentary). *Behav. Brain Sci.* 16: 681–735.

FINLAY, B. L. AND R. B. DARLINGTON (1995) Linked regularities in the development and evolution of mammalian brains. *Science* 268: 1578–1584.

JOLLY, A. (1966) Lemur social behavior and primate intelligence. *Science* 153: 501–506.

PLATT, M. L., E. M. BRANNON, T. BRIESE AND J. A. FRENCH (1996) Differences in feeding ecology predict differences in memory between lion tamarins (*Leontopithecus rosalia*) and marmosets (*Callithrix kuhli*). *Anim. Learn. Behav.* 24: 384–393.

SAWAGUCHI, T. (1989) Relationships between cerebral indices for "extra" cortical parts and ecological categories in anthropoids. *Brain Behav. Evol.* 43: 281–293.

Books

ALLMAN, J. (2000) *Evolving Brains*. New York: W. H. Freeman.

BYRNE, R. AND A. WHITEN, EDS. (1988) *Machiavellian Intelligence: Social Expertise and the Evolution of Intellect in Monkeys, Apes, and Humans*. Oxford: Oxford University Press.

JERISON, H. (1973) *Evolution of the Brain and Intelligence*. New York: Academic Press.

PURVES, D. (1988) *Body and Brain*. Cambridge, MA: Harvard University Press

STRIEDTER, G. F. (2005) *Principles of Brain Evolution*. Sunderland, MA: Sinauer.

Development of the Brain and Its Cognitive Functions

Introduction

To understand adult cognitive functions and the neural processes that underlie them, one must know how the organization of the adult brain emerges over the period of an individual's embryonic and childhood development (that is, over ontogenetic as distinct from evolutionary, or phylogenetic, time). A great deal is known about how the brain develops from an undifferentiated embryo into a highly specialized and complex information processing system. Much is also known about children's thought processes and how they develop (and in some instances deteriorate) over the human life span. The emerging field of developmental cognitive neuroscience is aimed at linking studies of physical changes in the developing brain to studies of cognitive development. It is thus important to characterize how brain maturation leads to cognitive change, and how in turn the relative strength and importance of various cognitive functions at different stages drives development. For example, aspects of neural development such as the myelination of nerve cell axons proceed at different rates in different cortical areas in a sequence consistent with developmental changes in cognitive abilities, and understanding this relationship is clearly of interest. Postnatal experience in the world also influences brain development and cognition in humans and other animals, and understanding this relationship presents another challenge for cognitive neuroscience. The relationship between neural development and cognitive development is thus both complex and bidirectional.

Development of the Nervous System

To appreciate the complexity of developmental processes that lead eventually to the adult brain and its cognitive abilities, it is useful to briefly review the major features of neural development in humans. This process begins as, over the first week or so of development, cell division transforms a single fertilized egg into a multicellular **blastocyst**. Over the following two weeks, the blastocyst differentiates into three distinct *germ layers* as its surface invaginates to form the three layers of the next embryonic stage, called the **gastrula** (**Figure 27.1**). The germ layers are called the endoderm, mesoderm, and ectoderm; the brain and the rest of the nervous system derive from the outer, or ectodermal component.

Figure 27.1 Early development in humans. Soon after the egg is fertilized by a sperm, the resulting zygote begins to divide. By the end of the first week, the dividing cells have formed a blastocyst with an inner cell mass of totipotent stem cells that will differentiate to form the embryo. Over the course of gastrulation, the inner cell mass forms three germ layers. The nervous system is generated by the cells of the ectoderm, or "outer" germ layer. (The color designations are those traditionally used for the germ layers.) (After Gilbert et al. 2005.)

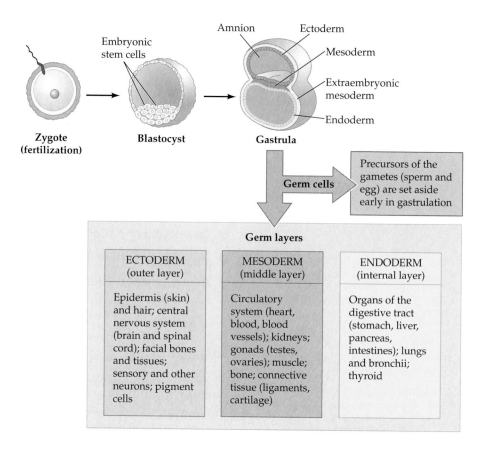

Somewhere around the twentieth day of embryogenesis, the nervous system begins to emerge. This stage is defined by a process called **neurulation,** in which the midline of the ectoderm develops into the **neural plate** (**Figure 27.2**). Under the influence of an underlying structure called the *notochord*, the neural plate folds inward on itself, and by 3 to 4 weeks postgestation has formed the **neural tube**; this is a landmark event, as the neural tube will eventually become the brain and spinal cord.

The cells of the neural tube are undifferentiated stem cells known as **neural precursor cells**; as stem cells, they are capable of producing any of the different neuronal or glial cells of the nervous system. These precursor cells divide to produce more precursor cells and somewhat more specialized **neuroblasts** that go on to further differentiate into their final cell type (see below). In humans, on the order of 100 billion neurons and several times that many glial cells are generated from these neural precursor cells, most between the sixth and eighth weeks of gestation. Remarkably, virtually all the neurons in the neocortex on which cognition will ultimately depend are present in the late-stage human embryo. With a few exceptions, no new neurons are generated after birth—a fact that must be taken into account in theories of cognitive development.

The rostral end of the neural tube begins to develop the components that can be recognized as those of the adult brain by generating three distinct vesicles that will eventually give rise to the forebrain, midbrain, and hindbrain (**Figure 27.3**). These vesicles emerge through disproportionately rapid cell proliferation at the rostral end of the neural tube. The locus of cell division is at the inner surface of the neural tube, a region called the *ventricular zone*. The neuronal precursor cells migrate outward (toward the surface of the neural tube) where they eventually differentiate into neurons. Those neurons in the

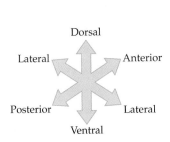

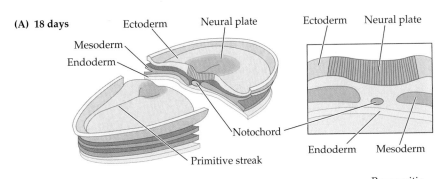

(A) 18 days

Ectoderm
Neural plate
Mesoderm
Endoderm
Notochord
Primitive streak

Ectoderm
Neural plate
Endoderm
Mesoderm

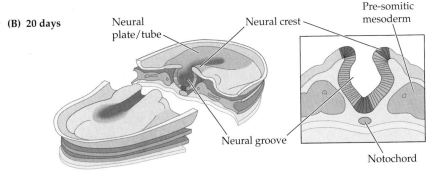

(B) 20 days

Neural plate/tube
Neural crest
Pre-somitic mesoderm
Neural groove
Notochord

Figure 27.2 Neurulation in the human embryo. (A) During late gastrulation and early neurulation, the notochord forms by invagination of the mesoderm. The ectoderm overlying the notochord becomes the neural plate (green). (B) The neural plate begins to fold at the midline, forming the neural groove and ultimately the neural tube. (C) Once the edges of the neural plate meet in the midline, the neural tube is complete. The mesoderm adjacent to the tube thickens and subdivides into structures called somites—the precursors of musculature and skeletal structures. (D) As development continues, the neural tube adjacent to the somites becomes the rudimentary spinal cord, and the neural crest gives rise to sensory and autonomic ganglia (the major elements of the peripheral nervous system). Finally, the anterior ends of the neural plate (the anterior neural folds) grow together at the midline and continue to expand, eventually giving rise to the brain.

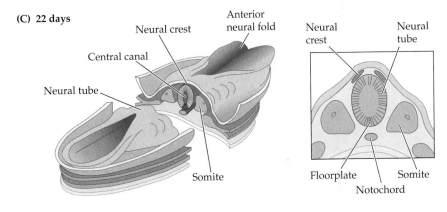

(C) 22 days

Anterior neural fold
Neural crest
Central canal
Neural tube
Somite

Neural crest
Neural tube
Floorplate
Somite
Notochord

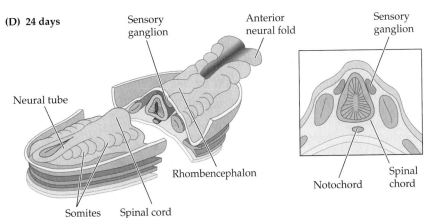

(D) 24 days

Sensory ganglion
Anterior neural fold
Sensory ganglion
Neural tube
Rhombencephalon
Notochord
Spinal chord
Somites
Spinal cord

emerging brain and spinal cord that are the last to be generated migrate to the most superficial layers of the gray matter (see Chapter 1), whereas neurons generated earlier in development remain in the deepest layers of the brain. In general, the development of the nervous system occurs in a rostrocaudal

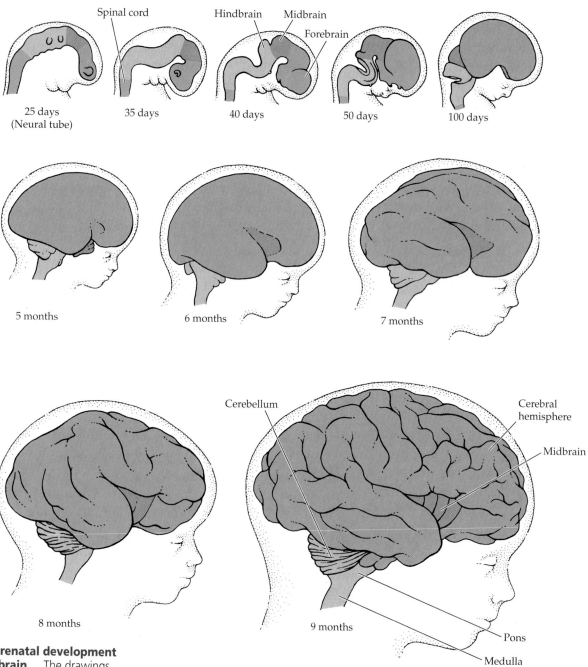

Figure 27.3 Prenatal development of the human brain. The drawings depict the development of the brain from the neural tube over the course of human gestation. Note the exceptional growth of the forebrain, which gives rise to the cerebral hemispheres. (After Cowan 1978.)

("head-to-tail") progression, as is apparent in Figure 27.3. A final point important in understanding the organization of the adult nervous system is that the central space of the neural tube remains as the adult ventricular system of the brain (see Chapter 1) and the central canal of the spinal cord.

Neuronal differentiation and the formation of neural connections

After reaching their destination in a given region of the brain or spinal cord, neuroblasts undergo **differentiation** whereby cell type is determined. Differentiation involves turning off some genes and turning on others by the action of transcription factors, a modulatory process determined by both the lineage of the neuron and local signals arising from its position in the developing brain. The result is the remarkable regional diversity of cell types that populate the adult brain. Most of these neural types are already present at birth. The key features that distinguish neuronal types are the signaling properties of the action potentials they generate, the transmitter agents that they employ, the receptor molecules they incorporate at postsynaptic sites, and the morphology of their axons and dendrites, which influence their ultimate connectivity.

In parallel with neuronal differentiation, glial cells differentiate and begin to perform their myriad functions. Particularly important is the differentiation of the glial class called oligodendrocytes, which elaborate the myelin that ensheaths many varieties of neuronal axons in the central nervous system. **Myelination** increases the speed of action potential conduction and thus improves the efficiency of neuronal signaling and processing generally. On the basis of this fact and correlative evidence, it is widely assumed that myelination is important in the emergence of cognitive functions in both evolution and individual development, as will be detailed later in the chapter.

Myelination begins relatively late in human gestation (at about 29 weeks), and many major tracts are not fully myelinated until adolescence (see Figure 27.5C). Indeed, some white matter tracts, such as the arcuate fascicularis that links Broca's and Wernicke's areas continue to myelinate into the third decade of life. As shown in **Figure 27.4A**, myelination more or less parallels the emergence of complex cognitive functions in different brain regions.

Once precursor cells have migrated to their destinations and differentiated into neurons, they send out axons to contact other cells and dendrites to receive the information that determines their ultimate function. The emerging axons reach their targets guided by molecular cues in the local environment. Having reached the target cells (which can be other neurons, muscle cells, or gland cells) the axon endings form *synapses* (see Chapter 1 and the Appendix). A great deal of cellular and molecular work has shown that synapse formation is primarily determined by surface and secreted molecules that are specific to each target.

The process of *synaptogenesis* begins early in gestation and peaks at different times in different brain regions. In assessing the development of synapses in the brain, two quite different issues are involved: the rate of synaptogenesis in a given brain region; and the maximum number of synapses per unit volume in a given region at different times over the human life span. The latter value is presumably a measure of the complexity of neural processing in the region of interest. The rate of synaptogenesis is straightforward in principle, but the number of synapses counted at any point in life in a given brain is subject to many factors, of which the rate of synapse formation is only one. Another obvious factor is synapse loss, which is evident throughout development and the rest of the human life span as synaptic contacts turn over and change under the influence of experience. As a result, the relationship between synaptogenesis and overall synaptic numbers in relation to cognitive functions is controversial. Extraordinarily careful microscopical studies of developing rhesus monkey brains carried out by the neuroanatomist Pasko Rakic and his colleagues at Yale University indicate that in primates the overall number of synapses increases progressively until adolescence and falls thereafter (**Figure 27.4B**).

The processes of synaptic production and change vary from region to region. Synaptogenesis tends to end earlier in brain regions whose functions are important early in life compared to regions whose functions are more dependent on postnatal experience, which develop more slowly and remain plastic longer (see below). Synaptogenesis is always paralleled by synapse loss and rearrangement, a process that presumably reflects the adjustment of

(A) Time course of myelination

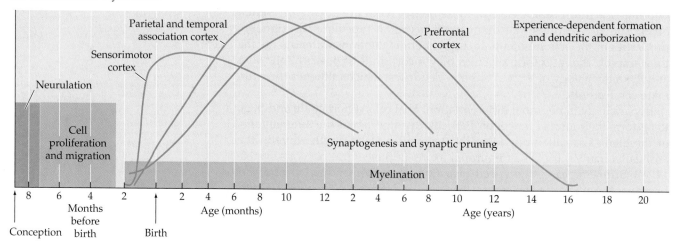

Figure 27.4 Time course of two key developmental processes. (A) Myelination in the human brain. (B) Density of synaptic contacts as a function of time, pooled across all cortical layers in a rhesus monkey. (A after Casey et al. 2005; B after Bourgeois and Rakic 1993.)

(B) Synaptic prevalence in rhesus development

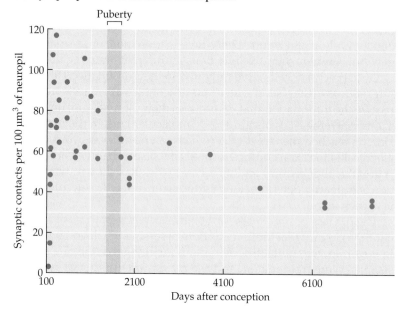

the numbers of synapses to the needs of the target cells. For similar reasons, some neuronal populations are overproduced and die in early development, although this phenomenon seems largely limited to the death of neurons in the spinal cord and plays relatively little part in the developing brain. Taken all in all, these variations are likely to influence cognitive development.

Another general aspect of cortical development is the importance of connectivity as a determinant of function. Since the organization of neocortex is broadly the same across all regions of the brain (see Chapter 1), the question arises whether neurons in one region might work just as well if they were transplanted to another region. In fact there is considerable evidence that this is indeed the case. For example, in experimental animals auditory cortex has been observed to process visual information after surgical rewiring of thalamic inputs. Similarly, as neurobiologist Dennis O'Leary and his colleagues at Washington University showed using experimental animals, when a region of embryonic visual cortex is transplanted into the somatosensory cortex, the visual cortex organization becomes similar to that of the somatosensory region.

Although cortical neurons are certainly not all the same, evidence of this sort implies that all neural processing across the neocortex must have much in common, and that what particular neurons end up doing is greatly dependant on their inputs, and the areas that they in turn innervate. More generally, the plasticity of neuronal function is greatest early in cortical development, and many transplantation experiments indicate that the ability of cortical progenitor cells to produce neurons of different phenotypes declines over time. Whereas early progenitors are multipotent, later progenitors become progressively restricted in their potential to assume different fates.

Later changes in the developing brain

By 2 years of age, a child's brain has reached about 80 percent of its adult weight, and by 5 years it is, on average, about 90 percent of adult size. However, longitudinal MRI studies show that some remodeling of gray and white matter in the cortex continues throughout life; indeed, average brain weight changes continually, peaking in the late teenage years and declining thereafter (**Figure 27.5A**). Psychiatrist Jay Giedd and his colleagues at the National Institutes for Mental Health have conducted a large-scale MRI project in which children's brains were visualized anatomically every two years in order to study changes in gray and white matter volume through adolescence. The researchers were specifically interested in how these changes were linked to cognitive abilities. Their results showed that total cerebral volume reaches a peak at approximately 11.5 years in females and 14.5 years in males, and that the rate of brain growth differs for different brain regions (**Figure 27.5B**).

Whereas white matter volume increases steadily and throughout the brain during childhood, adolescence and on into adulthood, gray matter volume follows an inverted U-shaped trajectory that peaks at somewhat different times in adolescence for different regions. The loss of gray matter in some brain regions in late adolescence and early adult life probably reflects the elimination of some neuronal connections, in keeping with Rakic's evidence in monkeys that the overall number of synapses in the neocortex increases through adolescence and then begins to slowly decline. This eventual decline also accords with average brain weight over the human life span, which as seen in Figure 27.5A decreases steadily during the adult years.

Anatomical changes seen in the MRI studies of children generally accord with the cognitive changes observed during development. For example, as shown in **Figure 27.5C**, regions that control primary functions such as motor and sensory systems develop first, followed by the temporal and parietal cortices associated with language and spatial attention. The last brain regions to mature are the prefrontal and lateral temporal cortices involved in the integration of sensorimotor processes, the modulation of attention and language, and critical aspects of decision making. These latter cognitive functions are also the latest to develop in behavioral studies.

Brain plasticity

An aspect of development especially pertinent to cognitive functions is the way the brain can be modified by developmental experience. Brain plasticity, as discussed in several earlier chapters, refers to the ability of the developing brain to respond to and be modified by experience. At the most general level, many studies have shown that enriched early environments influence brain development, memory, and the ability to learn. This phenomenon was first noted in the 1950s by neuroscientist Donald Hebb when he observed that when he took rats

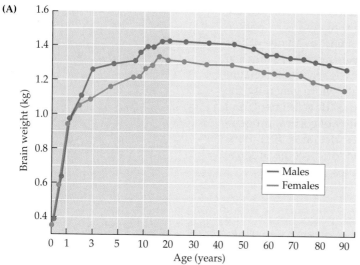

(A)

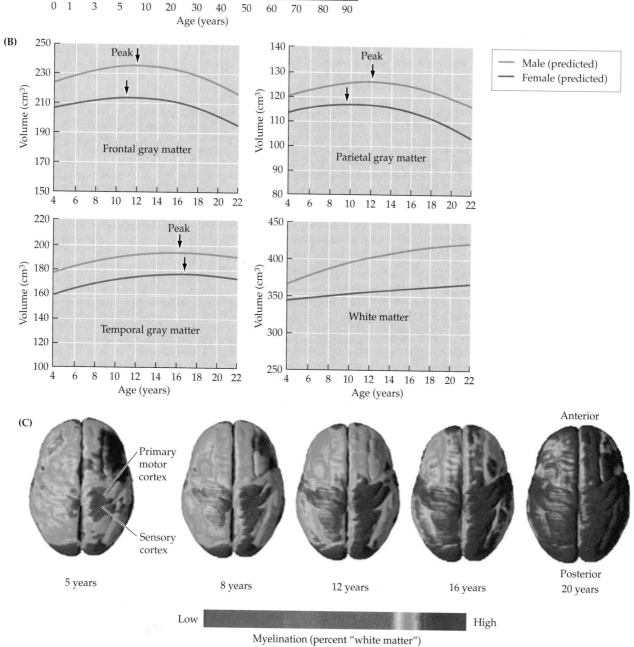

Figure 27.5 Anatomical measures of human brain development. (A) The average weight of the human brain over the life span. The brain continues to grow in mass for about two decades, then brain weight gradually declines, presumably representing a loss of neural circuitry in the aging brain. (B) Change in volume of frontal, parietal, and temporal gray matter, and white matter volume from ages 2 to 22 years. The data reflect 243 scans from 145 subjects scanned at 2-year intervals. (C) Dorsal view of the dynamic changes as gray matter matures over the cortical surface. The color changes in the figure are an amalgam and represent units of gray matter volume for 13 different subjects, each scanned 4 times at approximately 2-year intervals. (A after Dekaban and Sadowsky 1978; B,C after Lenroot and Giedd 2006, image C courtesy of N. Gogtay.)

from his laboratory home as pets, the animals showed superior performance to littermates raised in standard laboratory conditions. Since then more formal experiments, in particular the behavioral and anatomical work carried out by William Greenough and his colleagues at the University of Illinois, have examined how systematic manipulation of environmental complexity and physical activity in rats and other animals affects the developing brain.

For example, experiments have shown that environmental enrichment that enhances the prevalence of social interactions, nonsocial stimulation, and exercise in rats increases the survival of newborn neurons in the dentate gyrus of hippocampus (**Figure 27.6**). Such enrichment also results in improved per-

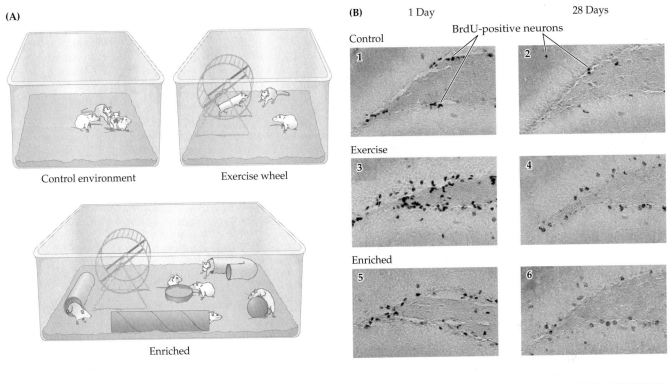

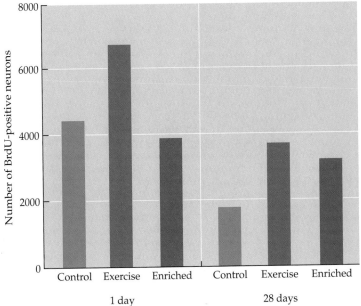

Figure 27.6 Environmental enrichment during development. (A) Rats were exposed for 12 days to one of three environments: a standard control environment, an environment that allowed voluntary exercise, or an environment enriched with both exercise equipment and varied objects. (B) Effects of enrichment on cell proliferation and neurogenesis in the dentate gyrus. Rats in all three conditions were given injections of bromo-deoxyuridine (BrdU), a chemical that labels dividing neurons (dark dots in micrographs). Animals were sacrificed and their brains sectioned for histological examination at two intervals. In both the short term (1 day) and the long term (28 days), control animals (1,2) showed fewer newly generated neurons compared to rats in the exercise wheel (3,4) and enriched (5,6) environments. Enrichment beyond the exercise wheel, however, appears to have had no effect on neurogenesis. (After van Praag et al. 2000.)

■ BOX 27A Sensory Deprivation Demonstrates Critical Periods in Cortical Development

An important principle of development is that environmental influences can have particularly strong effects on brain and behavior at particular times during development; these developmental time windows are called sensitive or critical periods. A classic example of a sensitive period is the phenomenon of *imprinting* in some waterfowl. A duckling or gosling will follow the first moving object they see after hatching, but forming these attachments occurs only during the first few days of posthatching life.

In mammals, the most carefully studied example of a critical period examined the development of neuronal connections in the primary visual cortex. Axons from the thalamus convey visual information from the left or right eye to cortical layer 4. Visual experience in the first few weeks in cats and the first few months after birth in monkeys is critical for normal formation of these connections. Landmark experiments performed on cats by David Hubel and Torstem Wiesel showed that if a kitten is deprived of normal visual experience by experimentally closing one eye during the first weeks of life, the arrangement of cortical connections in the adult cat is permanently altered; the inputs to layer 4 of the adult cat's primary visual cortex come to reflect connections predominantly from the eye that remained open. When single-cell recordings were made from neurons in the primary cortex of an adult cat who had suffered early monocular deprivation, the cells responded almost exclusively to input from the eye that had remained open. Thus, if visual input is interrupted during the critical period, the typical pattern of connectivity cannot be recovered even if normal input is later restored. By the same token, the effect of visual deprivation initiated in adulthood has little or no effect. Hubel and Wiesel described similar results in monkeys, which allowed them to demonstrate these effects anatomically by examining the left and right ocular dominance columns evident in many primates (see Chapter 5).

Effect of monocular deprivation on the number of cortical neurons driven by each eye. (A) Normal distribution of the influence of the two eyes on the number of neurons activated (i.e., firing) in the striate cortex of the adult cat. (B) Distribution of the influence of the two eyes on neuronal firing in the striate cortex of the adult cat when the animal had had one eye sutured shut as a kitten (during the period from 1 week to 2.5 months of age). No cells were driven by the previously sutured eye, and some cells could not be driven by either eye (NR, nonresponsive). (C) Distribution of the influence of the two eyes on neuronal activation after a lengthy monocular suture on an adult. Although the length of visual deprivation to the adult was much longer (from 12 to 38 months) than that to the kitten, there was little effect on the distribution of neuronal firing. Overall cortical activity, however, was somewhat diminished. (A, B, C after Hubel and Wiesel 1962, 1963, 1970, respectively.)

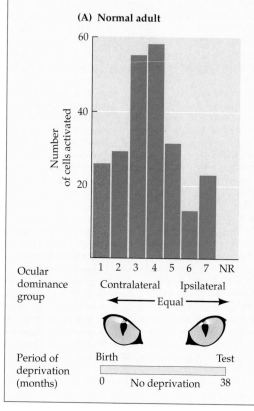

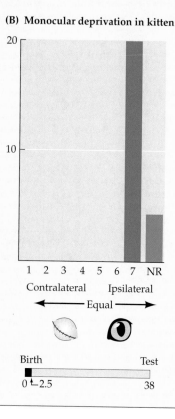

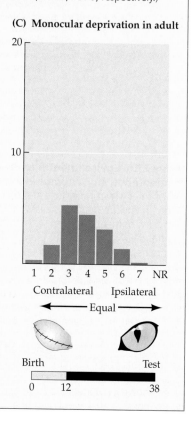

The importance of these observations for cognitive neuroscience is a clear demonstration that depriving the developing brain of experience during particular epochs in early life can have permanent effects on the connectivity of the neocortex, and deprivation of experience early on cannot easily be remedied later in life. The implications of this conclusion for child-rearing, education, and public policy should be self-evident.

References

HUBEL, D. H. AND T. N. WIESEL (1962) Receptive fields, binocular interaction and functional architecture in the cat's visual cortex. *J. Physiol. (Lond.)* 160: 106–154.

HUBEL, D. H. AND T. N. WIESEL (1970) The period of susceptibility to the physiological effects of unilateral eye closure in kittens. *J Physiol (Lond)* 206: 419–436.

HUBEL, D. H. AND T. N. WIESEL (1977) Ferrier Lecture: Functional architecture of macaque monkey visual cortex. *Proc. R. Soc. Lond. B* 198: 1–59.

JOHNSON, J. S. AND E. L. NEWPORT (1989) Critical period effects in second language learning: The influence of maturational state on the acquisition of English as a second language. *Cogn. Psychol.* 21: 60–99.

WIESEL, T. N. AND D. H. HUBEL (1963) Effects of visual deprivation of morphology and physiology of cells in the cat's lateral geniculate body. *J. Neurophysiol.* 26: 978–993.

formance on a variety of memory tasks such as the "Morris water maze" used to test spatial memory, in which a rat is placed in a small pool of murky water that contains a submerged escape platform (see Box 14A). Using electron microscopy, Greenough and colleagues further showed that the rats' improved behavior was correlated with a higher density of synapses and increased dendritic complexity in the hippocampus and other brain regions.

A further important point is that many effects of experience during development are most influential within a particular time window. These windows are referred to as **sensitive periods** or **critical periods**. For example, when infants fail to experience normal visual stimulation of one retina because of a lens defect (e.g., a cataract) or a misalignment of the eyes (*strabismus*) that causes the visual system to suppress input from one eye, the primary visual cortex develops abnormally, leading to a form of functional blindness called **amblyopia** (Greek for "dim sight"). The seminal work of David Hubel and Torsten Wiesel at Harvard Medical School showed that the underlying problem was a failure of the cortical neurons related to the deprived or suppressed eye to compete normally in establishing connections with their thalamic and other inputs. If the eyes are aligned early in development (or if the cataract is removed) the developmental failure and resulting deficit can be prevented.

Hubel and Wiesel's experiments with kittens and infant monkeys demonstrated that amblyopia is caused by altered wiring of the inputs from the two eyes to the primary visual cortex (**Box 27A**). Based on this basic and clinical evidence, ophthalmologists now commonly intervene early in development to prevent this effect by altering the eye muscles to achieve sufficient alignment to prevent suppression and resultant amblyopia. It is apparent from both clinical observations in humans and similar deprivation paradigms in experimental animals that prevention of a permanent deficiency requires intervention during a particular period of development that varies according to the developmental timetable of the species (see Box 27A).

Another observation that indicates the variability of neural plasticity over developmental time concerns the recovery of neurological function after brain injury. In general, recovery is better the earlier in development the injury has taken place. This generalization is known as the **Kennard principle** after Margaret Kennard, whose research on monkeys in the 1930s and 1940s showed that insults to motor cortex in infancy result in less severe deficits than the same insults in adulthood. More recent evidence has shown that, to some degree, changes in cortical organization can occur after injury, with intact regions taking over some of the functions of the injured areas. Again, such reorganization is dependent on the developmental stage at which the injury occurred. For example, in very young children with extensive left hemisphere damage, language functions can be instantiated in the right hemisphere, but this sort of reorganization is not seen in adults (see Chapter 21).

Perhaps the most commonly asked question about the determination of brain organization during development is the relative influence of learning and experience versus the role of an individual's genotype. In general terms, this issue is referred to as the **nature-nurture** debate. Earlier views in this long-standing controversy have ranged from the philosopher Jean-Jacques Rousseau's conclusion that humans come into the world as a *tabula rasa* (i.e., that the infant brain is "blank slate"), to the "preformationist" view that a completely formed being already exists within the germ cells (eggs and sperm), and that maturation is nothing more than growth. These historical debates about nature versus nurture have evolved in modern times into a more sophisticated investigation of the interaction between genes and environment. Although both psychologists and neurobiologists have long since agreed that both inheritance and the environment play important roles, differences of opinion about the degree to which each of these factor contributes to the development of cognitive abilities are still rife. The contribution of genes to complex human behaviors is still widely misunderstood and often exaggerated in popular accounts (see Chapter 21 for an account of the "language gene" controversy). In any event, it is abundantly clear that nature and nurture are joint contributors to all cognitive phenotypes.

Development of Cognitive Abilities Based on Behavior

As with other aspects of cognitive neuroscience, many classical studies have emerged from cognitive psychology in which relatively little attention was paid to brain development as such, simply because little information was available at the time. The Swiss developmental psychologist Jean Piaget, working in the 1940s and 1950s, is generally considered to be the most important figure in establishing the field of cognitive development. Even though prior to Piaget there were many published "baby diaries" in which parents and keen observers like Charles Darwin provided detailed accounts of their infants' behavioral development, the scientific study of infant cognition began with Piaget's efforts.

Piaget believed that children actively construct an understanding of the world as they adapt to their environment through processes he called **assimilation** and **accommodation**. In some circumstances, children assimilate new people, events, and objects into their preexisting schemes of thought. For example, a young child seeing an old man with a white beard and a pot belly might mistakenly call him Santa; this would be an example of *assimilating* a new person into a schema for Santa that the child already possessed. In other situations, a child might react to a new person, event, or object by changing or modifying their scheme of thought through *accommodation*. After learning that the man was just an ordinary person who happened to be overweight and have a white beard, the child would accommodate the concept of Santa to a more specific sort of individual.

Piaget's characterization of development involved four broad stages that in his view consisted of qualitatively different modes of thought.

1. In the **sensorimotor stage** (birth to 2 years), Piaget described infants as being dominated by reflex responses, with learning and intelligence being guided and constrained largely by the infant's sensory and motor abilities. Infants were postulated to learn about the consequences of their actions primarily through trial and error and in this way to begin to gain increasing voluntary control over their behavior.

2. In the **preoperational stage** (2 to 7 years), Piaget argued that children develop representational or symbolic abilities. The child begins to use both conventional and self-generated symbols in their play behavior (e.g., using a stick as a gun or rocking a doll in lieu of a baby). Piaget also described many limitations in the cognition of children during this stage. For example, he described preoperational children as egocentric in that they see the world only from their own perspective, and have difficulty appreciating differences in the knowledge base or values of other people. (Such egocentrism is illustrated by a child who holds a picture in such a way that only she can see it and says "Daddy, look at this!") Another well documented limitation of preoperational children is that they fail to show *conservation*—that is, they fail to appreciate transformations that neither add nor take away substance and thus have no effect on overall quantity **(Figure 27.7)**.

3. By the **concrete operations stage** (7 to 12 years), Piaget supposed that children begin to reason about the world, and can explain why rearranging objects has no effect on the number of objects in a line (i.e., the child now understands conservation and other simple principles of physics). However children of this age are still limited in their capacity for truly abstract thinking.

4. In the **formal operations stage** (12 and beyond) children become adept at reasoning hypothetically and thinking abstractly.

(A)

(B)

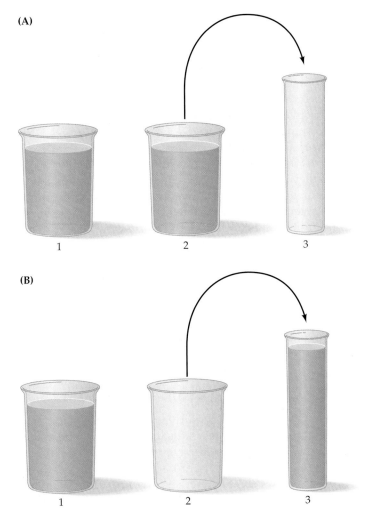

Figure 27.7 The concept of conservation. (A) Children are shown two beakers of the same shape and size that contain exactly the same amount of liquid. (B) Children watch as the liquid from beaker 2 is poured into a taller, thinner beaker. Children in the preoperational period believe that beaker 3 contains more liquid than beaker 1, reliably choosing the taller beaker as the amount they would prefer to receive.

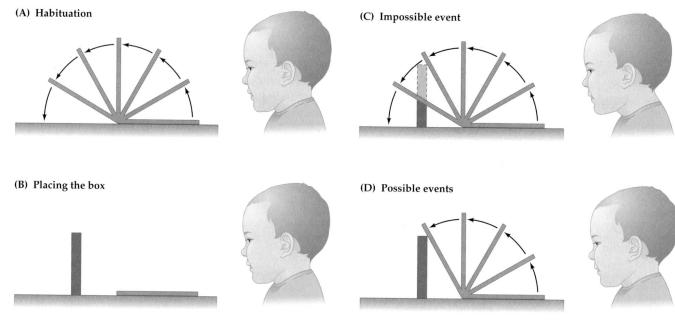

(A) Habituation

(B) Placing the box

(C) Impossible event

(D) Possible events

Figure 27.8 Screen-and-box study of object permanence.   (A) A young infant is habituated to a screen rotating back and forth on a table, making a 180° arc. (B) A box is placed in the path of the screen. (C) The infant gazes at the screen longer when it proceeds to rotate the full 180 degrees (i.e., as if it went right through the box) compared to the situation shown in (D), in which the screen stops where the box should have been. This finding suggests that infants expect the block to obstruct the screen, and that they visually represent the block despite the fact they can no longer see it.

Modern approaches using behavioral observation

Not surprisingly, not all psychologists have accepted Piaget's ideas. While the phenomena Piaget described have been replicated many times and are widely agreed on, his explanations are more controversial. One of the main challenges to Piagetian theory has come from studies showing that, during their first year, infants have a far richer mental life than Piaget attributed to his sensorimotor period. Much of this research makes use of methods such as *looking behavior* that rely on measuring behaviors in an infants' natural repertoire, thus bypassing infants' relatively undeveloped motor skills. Rochel Gelman of Rutgers University, for example, has emphasized the distinction between *performance* and *competence* (see also Chapter 2). The basic objection in this case is that infants may fail to perform a task that is not suited to their motor or linguistic skills, even when they possess the underlying conceptual competence.

An example of how looking behavior can reveal a competence that motor response tasks fail to uncover concerns what Piaget described as the concept of **object permanence**. Adult understanding of the world entails knowledge that objects do not cease to exist when they move out of view. However, babies less than 8 months of age, who are fascinated by a toy held in front of them, do not try to retrieve the toy when it is subsequently hidden from view. This observation was initially interpreted as evidence that, for a baby, when something is out of sight it is also out of mind. However, developmental psychologist Renee Baillargeon at the University of Illinois demonstrated that looking behavior by 3-month-old infants suggests that out-of-sight objects in fact *do* remain in mind (**Figure 27.8**).

Relating Cognitive Changes to Brain Maturation

One of the central aims in developmental cognitive neuroscience is to relate changes in cognition to maturational changes in the brain. One way to do this is to correlate the structural changes in the development of gray and white matter described earlier (see Figures 27.4 and 27.5) with behavioral measures. For example, short-term memory, rule learning, and cognitive control are all known to involve prefrontal cortex, and, as illustrated in Figure 27.5B, these and other cognitive abilities show age-related improvements that roughly parallel maturation of the prefrontal cortex. A recent study by Giedd and colleagues of a large population of normal adolescents indicated patterns of change in cortical thickness to be correlated with IQ. Specifically, children in the "superior IQ performance" part of their sample distribution initially showed thinner cortex in the superior prefrontal gyri, but showed a rapid increase in cortical thickness relative to the rest of the sample. Although such results are difficult to interpret, an important implication is that dynamic properties of cortical maturation need to be considered: it was not cortical thickness at any given time that was correlated with IQ, but rather the *changes* in cortical thickness.

Research with animals has also been helpful in understanding links between brain changes during development as they relate to cognition. Devising analogous tasks in animals and humans and determining the homologous brain regions in animal models is challenging but possible. A good example comes from studies of spatial memory in relation to the development of the hippocampus (recall from Chapters 13 and 14 that the hippocampus in rodents mediates this form of declarative memory). Before 19 days of age, rat pups are unable to solve the hidden platform version of the Morris water maze task, in which a rat is placed in opaque water and must find a submerged platform (rats of this age readily find the platform when the water is clear and the platform visible). By 21 days of age, however, rats can typically solve the Morris water maze. Correlated with these changes in cognitive ability, the number of granule cells in the dentate region of the rat hippocampus increases dramatically between about 19 and 25 days. These data imply that maturation of the hippocampus during this epoch is critical for the relational learning in this form of declarative memory.

A similar developmental sequence is apparent in children, although over a more protracted time course. When tested in a modified version of the Morris water maze task that involves a treasure hunt, all children tested between the ages of 3 and 9 years solved the platform problem when the goal was visible; in contrast, only children 7 years of age or older were proficient at finding a treasure when the platform equivalent in this paradigm was hidden. Consistent with these results, postmortem analysis of human brains shows that some aspects of hippocampal development do not reach completion until about 5 years of age. Thus the relatively late development of connectivity between the hippocampus and other regions may also be necessary for human relational learning and declarative memory. Clearly, however, these studies in humans are less decisive than those in rodents, and are complicated by the many other functions that the human hippocampus and the parahippocampal regions support.

Electroencephalography is another tool used by cognitive neuroscientists to link changes in brain and behavior in human development. This method is widely employed with infants because it is noninvasive, relatively easy, and inexpensive (**Figure 27.9A**). The amplitude of the EEG signal is high early in development and decreases with age, as a result of both increases in skull thickness and of white and gray matter maturation. There is also more power at low frequencies early in human development. Increases in higher-frequency bandwidths begin to show up during the first year and continue through adolescence. These relative changes in high and low frequencies in the EEG happen at different times in different cortical regions, providing a marker of normative cortical development. Children with learning and attention disorders tend to have relatively more spectral power at low frequencies and show a deficit in power at high-frequency bandwidths. Children who have been institutionalized in conditions of significant social deprivation (e.g., a Romanian orphanage) showed increased low-frequency power in posterior scalp regions and decreased high-frequency power, particularly at frontal and temporal electrode sites, relative to age-matched controls (**Figure 27.9B**). These observations suggest that abnormally low EEG frequencies may reflect delays in brain maturation, the relative lack of high frequencies reflecting failure to fully activate cortical processing circuits. Whatever the correct interpretation, these results accord with the evidence described earlier that impoverished environments early in life impede normal brain maturation.

Event-related potentials (i.e., time-locked EEG responses to a particular stimulus; see Chapter 3) have also been used to assess neural correlates of cognition during development. Of the positive and negative ERP components that have been found in infants and children, only some have clear counterparts in adults, making comparisons somewhat complicated. An example of a component found early in development that is also seen in adults is the mismatch negativity elicited by presenting a deviant stimulus in a train of similar stimuli (see Chapter 11). This response has been observed in newborn infants and is fully adultlike by about 5 to 7 years of age. However, in response to novel stimuli, infants also exhibit a consistent negative component (Nc) not seen in adults. The Nc peaks about 400–800 milliseconds poststimulus (see Figure 27.12) and probably reflects exogenous attention. Somewhere between the ages of 4 and 8 years, ERPs begin to resemble adultlike pattern, although changes in the form of ERPs continues until adulthood. The significance of this difference is not known.

(A)

Figure 27.9 EEG recording in infants.   (A) Child wearing an electrocap used to record EEG and ERP signals. (B) False-color topographic maps indicating the distribution of relative power across the scalp for children institutionalized in a Romanian orphanage, and for an age-matched Romanian control group. Color coding refers to the proportion of low-frequency bandwidths. (B from Marshall and Fox 2004.)

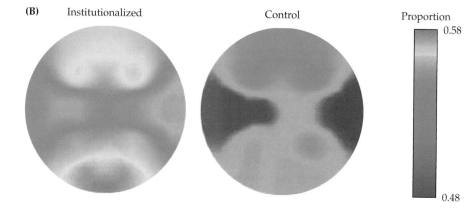

(B)   Institutionalized   Control   Proportion

Despite a number of special problems using the approach in children, functional MRI is being increasingly used to study the development of brain activity correlated with task performance. Most research to date has focused on children 7 years of age or older, since children of this age follow instructions more easily. A major challenge is adapting children to the loud and somewhat frightening atmosphere of the scanner; a mock scanner is often employed to get children used to lying still in a loud environment. Another challenge in fMRI research with young children is the need to warp each brain image to a standard template to allow comparisons between individuals. The fact that the template is usually an adult and that children younger than 6 show greater variability in activations elicited in different brain regions makes group averaging more problematic for data from children. A third issue is that the BOLD signal is influenced by the relative proportion of gray matter to white matter in the brain. As a result, changes in the proportion of gray to white matter during development increases variability in the BOLD signal as a function of age.

Despite these challenges, some important insights have emerged from fMRI studies. One general trend is that brain activity becomes more focal and less diffuse over development. For example, when children engage in tasks that require filtering out irrelevant information, a broader region of prefrontal cortex is recruited compared to the recruitment seen in adults. Another developmental trend is a decreasing reliance on subcortical systems. For example, adolescents show greater amygdala activation in a task that requires ignoring emotional information, whereas adults show greater prefrontal activation in the task.

Developmental Changes in Particular Cognitive Functions

These and other approaches have documented a number of specific changes over development in the major cognitive domains considered in previous chapters. The following sections review each of these areas in turn.

Perception

William James famously characterized the human baby as experiencing the sensory world as a "big, blooming, buzzing confusion." Since James's era, however, a great deal of research on perceptual abilities in children has shown that the newborn's experience of the world is actually quite organized. Although visual acuity is poor in a newborn infant, advances in behavioral techniques have determined that visual acuity develops rapidly so that by 8 months, vision is very nearly adultlike. The ways that acuity is assessed are quite ingenious. For instance, infants prefer to look at patterned compare to homogenous textures, so by varying the spatial frequency of a striped square one can determine the size of the stripe needed for an infant to show a bias toward a patterned as opposed to a homogenous square, thus demonstrating visual acuity (see also Box 27B). And although newborns have limited color vision, color vision is also almost adultlike by the time the child is 4 or 5 months old.

To navigate in the world, it is essential to perceive depth and distance accurately. One depth cue that is easy to test in infants is the *looming response* (i.e., the response to objects whose size increases rapidly, as if they were approaching the viewer). Infants as young as 1 month blink in response to an object that appears to be approaching. By about 4 months of age, infants are also able to use binocular disparity (i.e., the difference in retinal images on the two eyes; see Chapter 5) to determine the distance of nearby objects. And by 6 or 7 months of age, additional monocular cues to depth, such as occlusion and relative size, are used.

Another essential goal of the visual system is to integrate separate stimuli so that coherent objects are experienced and can be responded to. Any parent is intuitively aware that infants respond to objects, as indicated by behaviors such as smiling in response to a familiar face, grasping a desired object, and so on. Formal tests confirm that even infants early in the first year of life show this ability. For example, infants as young as 4 months can perceive a partially occluded object that moves independently behind its screen as a single intact object rather than as two separate parts. Bennett Bertenthal and colleagues at Indiana University have also shown that by 5 months babies look longer at points of light moving in darkness when these displays suggest human movement compared to when they do not, demonstrating that the infants are integrating the separate points of light into a coherent whole. By 7 months of age infants detect subjective contours such as the Kanizsa figures shown in **Figure 27.10**. By 8 months infants show 40-Hz oscillations when observing a Kanizsa figure, but not when they see the same elements in a control stimulus (**Figure 27.11**). Recall from Chapter 5 that such oscillations are associated with feature "binding," although the interpretation of this phenomenon remains controversial. Infants are also able to segregate objects from an early age; by 4 months of age infants routinely use object shape to segregate ambiguous displays of adjacent objects.

The infant auditory system is quite well developed at birth, indicating that the early maturation of perception is probably quite general. Newborns show evidence of an ability to localize sounds by turning their heads toward sound stimuli. Even before birth, fetuses hear extrauterine sounds, as indicated by changes in fetal heart rate; studies of this measurement show that infants habituate to a repeated sound and respond when a new sound occurs. Long-term memory for sounds heard in utero has also been demonstrated. In one study, expectant mothers read a Dr. Seuss story out loud daily during the last 6 weeks of their pregnancy. After birth their newborns were tested for their memory of this experience using a variant of the high-amplitude sucking procedure described in **Box 27B**. Lengthening the intervals between sucks relative to a baseline rate of sucking produced the familiar Dr. Seuss story whereas shortening the intervals between sucks produced a novel Dr. Seuss story (or vice versa). Both stories were read by the infants' mother and recorded on a tape. Thus regardless of whether infants were required to lengthen or shorten the intervals between sucks, they were found to change their sucking patterns relative to baseline to preferentially produce the familiar as opposed to the novel story.

(A) Kanizsa square   **(B) Control stimulus**

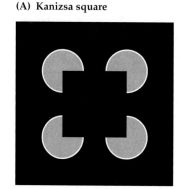

Figure 27.10 Integration of visual information to generate perceptions of form. (A) Stimuli known as "Kanizsa figures" composed of elements that imply a geometrical form elicit illusory form perception in adults (in this case filling in the lines that form a square). (B) The same elements placed in different orientations fail to elicit this percept. Infants as young as 7 months show evidence that they perceive a form when viewing a Kanizsa figure.

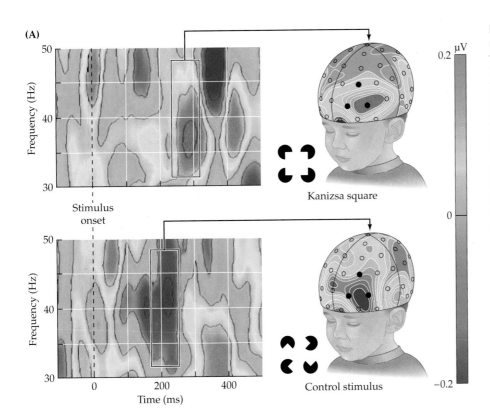

Figure 27.11 ERP responses in 8-month-old infants viewing Kanizsa figures. Time-frequency plots showing the brain activity in infants viewing the stimuli illustrated in Figure 27.10. (A) The different colors indicate changes in frequency compared to the prestimulus baseline period, with red representing maximum frequency enhancement. The amplitude of 40-Hz activity was significantly more when viewing the Kanizsa square compared to the control stimulus. (B) Overall amplitude changes at the three left frontal electrodes at 40 Hz. (From Csibra et al. 2000.)

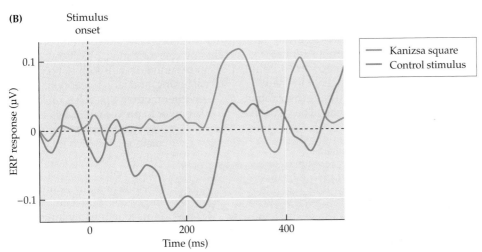

Although it has been more difficult to study, there is some evidence that fetuses also have significant chemosensory abilities (see Chapter 7). Thus newborns show an innate preference for sweet tastes, indicating some memory for tastes that they experienced in utero (i.e, sweet amniotic fluid). Indeed, newborns turn preferentially toward a cloth that smells like their mother's amniotic fluid as opposed to amniotic fluid from another woman.

Attention

The importance of the frontal and parietal cortices in governing attention was described in Unit IV. Studies of the development of attentional abilities suggest that posterior parietal and subcortical underpinnings of attention are already operative in the first year of life, and that these regions tend to support the orienting and/or investigative aspects of attention. Later during the

■ BOX 27B Methods Used to Study Infant Cognitive Behavior

Since Piaget's observations in the 1950s, a number of behavioral techniques have been developed to study preverbal cognition and perception in infancy in more quantitative and objective ways. Most of these methods rely on infant's looking behavior. In the *preferential looking technique*, infants are shown two visual displays on side-by-side computer screens. If the two screens display the same image, infants show no preference. Visual acuity in the infant (which may be clinically important) can be determined by varying the spatial frequency of alternating stripes and contrasting them with plain gray squares. In a variant of this procedure known as the *crossmodal preference paradigm*, infants are shown two different visual displays, one of which matches information presented in a second sensory modality. Infants preferentially look to the matching visual stimulus. For example, infants look preferentially at a pacifier with a texture that matches the pacifier they are sucking on.

In the *visual habituation* paradigms, infants are shown a stimulus (or exemplars from a category of stimuli) repeatedly until their looking time substantially decreases (Figure A). A new stimulus is then presented in alternation with the old stimulus (or new exemplars of the old category of stimuli). Infants who look longer at the new stimulus are taken to have discriminated the old from the new. The visual ha-

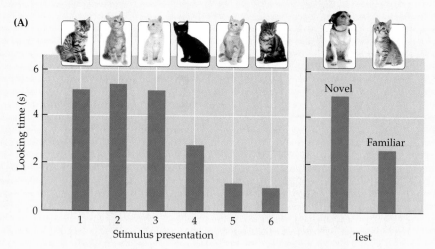

(A) Examples of habituation and test stimuli and idealized data for a visual habituation paradigm. Infants habituated to multiple cat pictures and then tested with new cats and new dogs. After showing a reduction in looking time over successive habituation stimuli infants then show a recovery of looking time to the novel exemplar of the new category but not the novel exemplar of the familiar category.

bituation method has been used to test many aspects of infant cognition including categorization, object concepts, memory, numerical discrimination, interval timing, and face perception.

Another method that relies on looking behavior in preverbal infants is the *violation of expectancy* method, in which infants witness an event that results in either a physically possible or a physically impossible outcome. If infants look reliably longer at the physically impossible outcome this is considered evidence that the event violated their expectations about the how the world works. (Figure B; also see Figure 27.8). At 3 months of age an infant has a simple all-or-none concept of support, and is surprised when an object

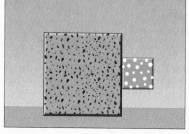

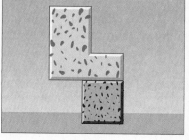

(B) Stimuli used to study infant understanding of support relationships. (After Needham and Baillargeon 1993.)

(C)

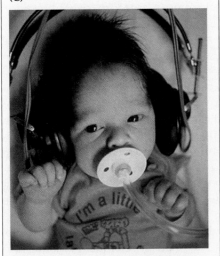

(C) Infant fitted with head phones and pacifier in the high-amplitude sucking procedure. (From Eimas et al. 1971.)

seems to float in midair without contacting another object. However, these infants are not perturbed if the object has any contact at all with another object, and do not take into account the physical improbability of support by the amount of contact and imbalance arising from gravity. By 12.5 months, infants consider the relative proportions and sizes of objects when judging whether or not one object is sufficient to support another.

High-amplitude sucking and *head turning* are widely used measures used in studies of infant speech and sound discrimination. In high-amplitude sucking (Figure C), the infant is fitted with a pacifier that can measure the strength and rate of sucking. Initially, a stimulus (such as a sound) is presented whenever the infant produces a high-amplitude suck. Typically infants increase their rate of sucking compared to a baseline period during which no sound was presented. Infants soon habituate to a given sound or category of sounds and their sucking rate decreases. Infants are then presented with either a new sound or the same sound they have already habituated to and the rate of sucking in the two conditions is compared.

In the head-turn procedure, infants learn that a change in sound indicates

(D)

(D) The head-turn procedure used to test phoneme discrimination in infants. (From Werker 1989.)

that an exciting event will occur. Figure D shows an experimenter manipulating a doll as an infant hears a constant stream of phonemes (e.g., Ba, Ba, Ba). When the phoneme changes (e.g., Pa) the rabbit in the glass case dances! Infants rapidly learn to anticipate the rabbit's dance when they hear a change in phonemes. In this way it is possible to examine whether infants hear particular phonemes as the same or different. (Chaper 21 describes some of the issues examined using this method.)

(E)

(E) The "conjugate mobile paradigm" used to test infant memory.

The *conjugate mobile paradigm* developed by Carolyn Rovee-Collier at Rutgers University also depends on learning a contingency between behavior and events in the world. A string is attached to an infant's leg and connected to a mobile suspended above the infant in its crib (Figure E). When the infant kicks, the mobile moves—a result infants like. After a delay, the same mobile or a new mobile is presented. Rate of kicking provides an index of memory and is heavily influenced by the similarity of the test mobile to the original. The more similar the mobiles and the shorter the delay from training to testing, the more infants kick.

These methods are only a small sample of the ingenious ways to assess the cognitive abilities of preverbal infants.

References

EIMAS, P. D., E. R. SIQUELAND, P. JUSCZYK AND J. VIGORITO (1971) Speech perception in infants. *Science* 171: 303–306.

FANTZ, R. L. (1961) The origin of form perception. *Scientific American*, 204(5): 66–72.

NEEDHAM, A. AND R. BAILLARGEON (1993) Intuitions about support in 4.5 month-old infants. *Cognition* 47: 121–148.

ROVEE-COLLIER, C. (1999) The development of infant memory. *Curr. Dir. Psychol. Sci.* 8(3): 80–85.

WERKER, J. (1989) Becoming a native listener. *Amer. Sci.* 77: 54–69.

first year and extending into the preschool years, the development of the frontal regions allow higher-level control systems for attention to emerge.

Much of the evidence for these conclusions is based on visual behavior. Although visual acuity develops rapidly in infants (see above), vision in newborns is relatively poor compared to adult vision, and infants spend the majority of each day asleep. Despite these facts, even newborns show nonrandom looking behavior. They prefer to look at patterned, high-contrast stimuli compared to solid patches, and have difficulty disengaging eye contact from an alluring stimulus. Newborns follow a moving stimulus with saccadic or steplike eye movements rather than the smooth pursuit seen in adults. In addition, their eye movements lag behind a moving target and are not anticipatory as those of older infants and adults are. One-month-old infants also have great difficulty disengaging from a stimulus that has caught their attention. It is not uncommon to observe a newborn staring at an object for as long as 2 or 3 minutes, beginning to cry while they seemingly are unable to move their gaze away from the object.

Mark Johnson and his colleagues at Birkbeck College suggested that this form of "obligatory attention" might be due to the development of tonic inhibition of the colliculus via the substantia nigra. An important shift in infant looking behavior takes place at about 2 months of age, which is when infants become able to track objects with smooth-pursuit eye movements presumably mediated by the middle temporal (MT) motion areas of the extrastriate cortex. By 3 to 4 months of age infants become able to make anticipatory eye movements and are able to learn sequences of looking patterns. In addition, 4-month-old infants are able to inhibit looking at a stimulus if they have learned that a more attractive stimulus will soon appear in a different location. These developments are thought to reflect maturation of the frontal eye fields and dendritic growth and myelination of the upper layers of primary visual cortex.

Thus the orienting and investigative behaviors and supporting neural pathways that emerge early in the first year of life allow infants to explore the world around them with increasing sophistication. This progressively more targeted ability to attend selectively appears to depend on the maturation of the posterior parietal cortex, the frontal eye fields, and the pathways that connect subcortical regions with posterior cortex, all of which are largely in place by about 6 months of age.

Memory

A paradox of early memory is that while infants clearly learn and store an enormous amount of information over the first few years of life (acquisition of language and motor skills, increasingly acceptable social behavior, and so on), adults have very little explicit memory of this period. Thus, even though a tremendous amount of learning takes place during infancy and early childhood, as adults we have almost no explicit memory of these experiences. Psychologists Daniel Schacter at Harvard University and Morris Moscovitch at the University of Toronto have suggested that this **infantile amnesia** indicates that declarative memory is late to develop, even though infants clearly have an enormous ability to acquire nondeclarative memories.

An alternative idea is that young children can in fact produce and store explicit memories that they retain for relatively long periods, even though these memories are not recalled later in life. A demonstration of explicit memory in infancy comes from the *elicited imitation paradigm* devised by Patricia Bauer and her colleagues at Emory University. In this paradigm, infants observe as an experimenter enacts an event using props. For example, an infant might observe an experimenter use a rod to roll a car down a ramp, causing a light to turn on. After a variable delay the child is given the opportunity to interact with the props and his or her behavior is compared to a baseline period in which the same child had the opportunity to interact with the props before witnessing the experimenter produce the action sequence, Memory is inferred if the number of reconstructed acts (i.e., using the rod to roll the car down the ramp) is higher in the experimental condition compared to the baseline comparisons or to a control group that did not witness the interaction.

Bauer and colleagues found significant changes in infants' ability to recall ordered sequences of events over the first year of life. Although infants as young as 9 months show reliable ordered recall of action sequences, the robustness of long-term recall was found to increase with age. Further research from this group indicated that infants as young as 13 months of age could remember 2- and 3-step sequences for as long as 8 months under the appropriate conditions. Importantly, the same factors that influence adult memory—such as the number of experiences with an event, the nature of the event, and the availability of cues that support event retrieval—were also found to influence children's ability to recall events. Thus even though adults do not remember experiences from early childhood, infants are forming robust memories that last for months and are influenced by the same factors that affect adult memories.

Charles Nelson and his colleagues at Harvard proposed a model of memory development in which implicit memory systems become available early in the first year of life, followed by a "pre-explicit" memory system, and finally the explicit memory system familiar in adult studies. In this scenario, pre-explicit memory in the form of novelty responses is thought to emerge early in the first few months of life, supported by the hippocampus. Toward the end of the first year of life, further development of the inferior temporal cortex is believed to allow for more sophisticated forms of explicit memory. Later on in the preschool years and early childhood, there is increasing development of the prefrontal cortex, and children begin to use more sophisticated mnemonic strategies (such as rehearsal) and show dramatic increases in retrieval and source memory (i.e., identifying the source from which information was learned).

At the end of the first year of life, changes in long-term memory (such as being able to successfully emulate a two-step action sequence) coincide with major changes in the development of the dentate gyrus of the hippocampus. As discussed in Unit V, the dentate gyrus is thought to be important for the temporal order of information stored as declarative memories, which may in turn support the emergence of episodic memory as it is understood in adults. Consistent with this idea, brain activity measured by ERPs predicts long-term memory for ordered sequences in infants. In this study, a group of 9-month-old infants was exposed to a live enactment of an ordered sequence of events; the infants were then immediately shown static images of either the same events or novel events while ERPs were measured. For all infants tested, the Nc component of the visual ERP showed greater negativity in response to static pictures from new action sequences compared with pictures from old sequences. However, when infants were shown the same static images a week later, there was more variability in this ERP component to novel versus familiar images, and this variability predicted infants' performance in the retrieval of action sequences as much as a month later (**Figure 27.12**). Specifically, infants who would later recall the two-step sequences showed more salient Nc divergences in the ERP waveforms to novel and familiar slides compared to infants who would later fail to recall the sequences they had observed. Since the variation in the Nc component was not present immediately but was visible only 1 week after encoding, these observations suggest that individual

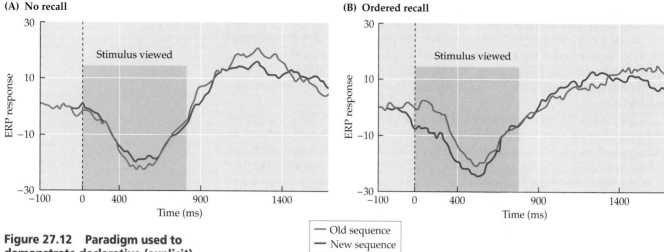

(A) No recall

(B) Ordered recall

Stimulus viewed

Stimulus viewed

— Old sequence
— New sequence

Figure 27.12 Paradigm used to demonstrate declarative (explicit) memory in infants. ERP waveforms recorded as infants viewed static images of an experimenter performing a two-step sequence with props. These data were collected a week after the infants had viewed a live demonstration of the experimenter acting out the two-step sequence. (A) The data reflect the subset of infants who later showed no recall for the two-step sequence. (B) Data from the subset of infants who later showed evidence of ordered recall. (After Bauer et al. 2003.)

differences in long-term memory for ordered sequences in 9-month-olds is a consequence of consolidation and storage failures rather than differences in encoding. This is a nice illustration of how brain indices may be used to predict behavioral indices in development.

Emotion and social cognition

At least since the 1872 publication of Darwin's book *The Expression of the Emotions in Man and Animals*, there has been discussion about which emotions are universal and present at birth, and which are culturally specific and learned. Newborn infants display many different facial expressions; adults can readily distinguish, for example, the face of an infant who has just seen her mother from the face of an infant who just received an injection. There is debate, however, about whether infants in the first year of life experience more complex emotions such as jealousy or guilt. A related question is whether infants can recognize and distinguish other people's emotions.

Using the visual habituation procedure described in Box 27B, researchers have shown that by 3 months of age infants can distinguish between frowning and smiling expressions in adults, and that by 4 to 7 months babies can differentiate surprise from happiness. Of course these demonstrations do not indicate whether infants actually understand the meaning of these perceptually distinct facial expressions. However, studies of crawling behavior in what has come to be called the *visual cliff paradigm* show that infants in the first year of life use their mothers' emotional expressions to make decisions about potentially perilous actions.

Eleanor Gibson at Smith College and later at Cornell developed the visual cliff apparatus, in which infants are allowed to crawl around on a glass tabletop. One end of the table has a checkered pattern surface placed on top of the glass (the "shallow" side), whereas the other end has the patterned surface underneath the glass, at floor level (the "deep" side). Infants around 12 months old show an aversion to crawling out over the "deep" side spontaneously, indicating that they have some awareness of vertical depth and its perils. When a 12-month-old infant's mother stands at the deep end of the table and coaxes her infant to crawl over the "danger," the probability that the baby will do so depends on whether the mother initially displays a fearful or a happy expression. Infants thus engage in social referencing whereby they assess their caregiver's emotions before deciding whether it is safe to crawl.

Research on infants and children has also contributed to the debate about whether faces are a special class of stimuli that recruit domain-specific neural processes (see Chapters 5 and 19). A logical suggestion is that exposure to faces during early development causes infants to become increasingly adept at face processing. If so, the routine exposure to faces should improve discrimination of upright compared to inverted faces (the *face inversion effect*), faces of one's own race compared to faces of another (the *own-race effect*), and discrimination of faces from one's own species compared to faces of another species (the *own-species effect*). Both behavioral and ERP data support this supposition, showing a gradual emergence of adultlike behavioral and ERP patterns of face processing. For example, infants do not show a behavioral inversion effect for faces until about 4 months of age. And although infants 3 months of age show an adultlike right-hemisphere bias for face processing and the usual ERP correlate of face processing (the N170 component; see Chapter 19), infants do not differentiate upright from inverted faces until sometime between 6 and 12 months of age.

The own-species effect also emerges gradually over development. Thus 6-month-old infants show about equal recognition memory for monkey faces and human faces, whereas by 9 months infants, like adults, are better able to recognize the human faces (**Figure 27.13**). This pattern of increasing specialization for own-species faces mirrors the phenomenon of perceptual narrowing seen in speech perception, in which infants initially perceive phonemes of all languages but gradually lose the ability to perceive phonemes not present in the language they are exposed to (see Chapter 20). Nevertheless, newborns visually track schematic drawings of faces significantly more than scrambled faces, showing that face stimuli already have a special status at birth.

Beyond face perception, a plethora of behavioral studies have examined children's emerging understanding of other minds. As Piaget described, young children often behave as if they do not reliably differentiate between their own experience and knowledge base and that of others. More recently, this deficiency and the resulting egocentric behavior of children has been described as a deficiency in a representational theory of mind (see Chapter 19). To examine this issue, Austrian psychologists Heinz Wimmer and Joseph Perner developed a **false belief task**, in which children between 3 and 7 years

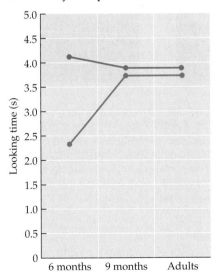

(A) Monkey faces presented

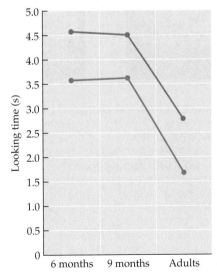

(B) Human faces presented

— Novel face
— Familiar face

Figure 27.13 The "own-species" effect. Six-month-old infants show longer looking times when presented with both novel monkey (A) and novel human (B) faces. In contrast, 9-month-old infants and adults only differentiate novel from familiar in human faces. (After Pascalis et al. 2002.)

old were presented with a story about a boy named Maxi and a bar of chocolate. Children are shown a picture of Maxi placing his chocolate bar in a kitchen cabinet and then leaving the room. Maxi's mother then enters and moves the chocolate bar to the refrigerator. The child being studied is asked where Maxi will look for the chocolate bar when he returns to the room. Wimmer and Perner found a large shift in the answers given by 3-year-olds versus 5-year-olds. Three-year-old children typically indicate that Maxi will look in the refrigerator, whereas 5-year-olds understand that Maxi does not know that his mother moved the candy, and therefore answer that Maxi will look in the kitchen cabinet.

Despite this shift in performance, it does not necessarily follow that 3-year-olds lack theory of mind. In fact, 3-year-olds are as adept as 5-year-olds at inferring desires from the behavior of others, and they use mental language to predict other people's actions. For example, a 3-year-old child will readily indicate Maxi will look in the refrigerator because he *wants* chocolate. The difficulty for a 3-year-old seems to be in distinguishing between reality and someone else's incorrect thoughts about reality.

The idea that attributing internal states such as wants and desires is dissociable from the ability to attribute thoughts and beliefs to others is supported by work by Rebecca Saxe at MIT. Saxe had subjects in an fMRI study read vignettes that described other people's thoughts, vignettes about other bodily sensations such as hunger, or descriptions of socially relevant information about personal appearance (**Figure 27.14A**). Saxe found that when adults read the vignettes that focused on other people's thoughts and intentions, the right

(A) Thoughts

Nicky knew that his sister's flight from San Francisco was delayed 10 hours. Only one flight was delayed that much that night, so when he got to the airport he knew that flight was hers.

Bodily sensation

Sheila skipped breakfast because she was late for the train to her mother's. By the time she got off the train, she was starving. Her stomach was rumbling, and she could smell food everywhere.

Appearance

Jose was a heavy-set man, with a gut that fell over his belt. He was balding and combed his blond hair over the top of his head. His face was pleasant, with large brown eyes.

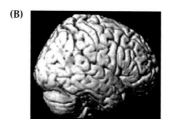 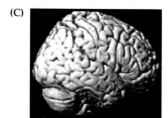 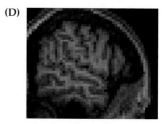

(B) **(C)** **(D)**

Figure 27.14 Appreciation of other minds. Adult subjects were scanned while presented with vignettes designed to test which brain regions are selectively recruited when a person thinks about other people's mental states. (A) Subjects read vignettes that described other people's thoughts, bodily sensations (such as hunger), or information about their personal appearance. (B) Red voxels indicate higher response when reading thought stories than either bodily-sensations or appearance stories. (C) Blue voxels indicate higher response when reading bodily-sensations stories than during appearance stories. (D) A single slice contrasts the right temporoparietal junction activation for thoughts stories (red) and right supramarginal gyrus activation for bodily-sensations stories (blue). Data suggest that the right temporoparietal junction is selectively recruited when adults read vignettes that require reasoning about other people's mental states. (From Saxe and Powell 2006.)

and left temporoparietal junction and the posterior cingulate were selectively recruited (**Figure 27.14B,D**). In contrast, these three brain regions were not especially active when subjects read vignettes about other subjective internal states or information about a person's looks (**Figure 27.14C,D**); in these circumstances the medial prefrontal cortex was recruited. Thus the early- and late-developing aspects of a theory of mind may rely on separate neural mechanisms that remain separate into adulthood. An alternative view suggested by Jason Mitchell at Harvard is that the right and left temporoparietal junction is actually used more broadly for nonsocial tasks that require redirecting attention to task-relevant stimuli. These questions are not yet resolved.

Another approach to understanding the neural bases of social cognition is to study developmental disorders that affect social cognition. An important developmental disorder in this context is autism. **Autism** is a disorder that affects about 3–6 in every 1000 children and, as described in Unit VI, involves many social deficits. Individuals with autism tend to avoid both physical and eye contact. They show heightened interest in the inanimate world, often fixating on particular objects. In addition, children with autism fail theory-of-mind tasks well beyond the age of 4 and fail to recognize biological motion from point-light displays. In contrast to typically developing children and adults, people with autism spend significantly less time examining people's eyes and instead focus on the mouth or body when shown images of people.

Cognitive neuroscientists have identified brain regions involved in social cognition for typically developing individuals that include the amygdala, the superior temporal sulcus, and the fusiform gyrus. Recent studies are beginning to suggest that autistic individuals may show dysfunctions in these brain regions. For example, when given a task that required judging mental or emotional states from photographs in which only the eyes of a person were visible, the left amygdala, superior temporal gyri, and insula of normal participants were activated; in contrast, high-functioning subjects with autism showed much less frontal and amygdala activation. In an fMRI study that compared autistic children with typically developing children, the autistic children showed less activity in the fusiform gyrus and higher precuneus activity when they were asked to match photos with the same facial expression. Of course, it is not clear whether the brain differences observed between autistic individuals and the general population are causally related to the autistic disorder, or if these differences are the result of differential exposure to social stimuli due to a lack of normal response to social stimuli over the autistic person's lifetime.

Another important disorder in this regard is **Williams' syndrome,** a genetic disorder characterized by distinctive facial features, mild retardation, an unusually cheerful demeanor, and a talkative personality. Children with this syndrome exhibit relatively normal social cognition, orienting to faces and successfully passing theory-of-mind tests. The contrast between children with Williams' syndrome, who are typically social and talkative, and children with autism, who are typically antisocial and reticent, has been interpreted by some as evidence that social cognition entails a distinct brain system that can be developmentally disturbed or spared. However, research by Annette Karmiloff-Smith and her colleagues at University College London suggests some caution in the interpretation of this contrast. For example, children with Down syndrome show impaired face processing but nonetheless pass of theory-of-mind tests. Karmiloff-Smith argues that segregation of social cognition may occur postnatally, through experience with normal social and speech input. In any event, developmental disorders of this sort are clearly complicated and are more likely to depend on a cascade of developmental events that has gone awry than on the loss of a specific regional function.

Language

It should be clear from that discussion and the discussion of brain evolution in Chapter 26 that human language has precedents, however rudimentary, in other animals, and that the cognitive foundations for language are present in infants at birth. The basis for this latter observation is of special interest from a developmental perspective.

As described in Chapter 21, the left hemisphere is the primary locus for language comprehension and production in the vast majority of adults. Both behavioral and neurobiological studies show that the left hemisphere is already the locus of speech processing in young infants. For example, behavioral studies have shown that infants show better speech discrimination when sounds are presented to their right ear (and thus preferentially processed by the left hemisphere). Functional imaging studies have confirmed that the left hemisphere is indeed predominant in speech processing in early infancy. Using infrared optical imaging (**Box 27C**), Jacques Mehler and his colleagues

---

■ BOX 27C Using Infrared Spectroscopy in Infants

A new addition to the suite of tools used by developmental neuroscientists is **near infra-red spectroscopy** (**NIRS**), in which optical signals related to brain activity are obtained through skull with laser *diodes* taped to the subject's head (Figure A). The method is based on the fact that light at certain wavelengths can measure the relative saturation of hemoglobin (this is the basis for both fMRI and conventional optical imaging of the exposed cortex). Differences in light absorption of oxyhemoglobin and deoxyhemoglobin are detected and reported by photodiodes sensitive to the relevant wavelengths. A computer algorithm then converts changes in optical density into changes in oxygenated and deoxygenated hemoglobin that in turn reflect the relative metabolic activity of the underlying cortex.

Infants are especially good subjects for NIRS because their skulls and scalp tissues are relatively thin and thus produce less light scattering than adult heads. Compared to other imaging methods, NIRS is much more practical in infants. The method is portable, far less expensive than fMRI, safer than

PET, and free from the motion artifacts that in other techniques are impossible to avoid because infants cannot be instructed to lie still.

A recent study using NIRS found that the right temporoparietal region in 3-month-old infants differentiates between "flattened" and normal

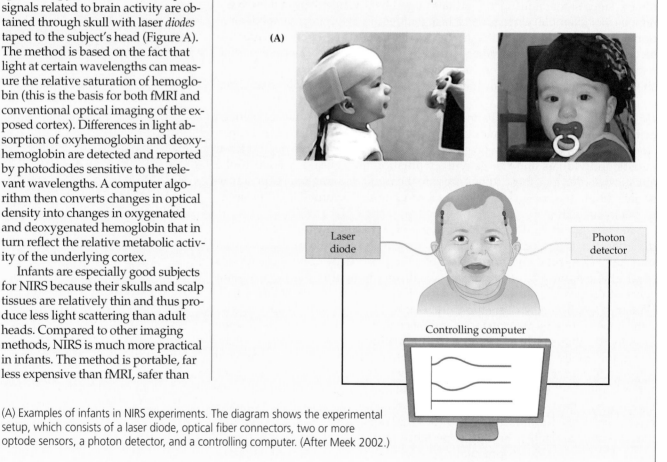

(A)

Laser diode

Photon detector

Controlling computer

(A) Examples of infants in NIRS experiments. The diagram shows the experimental setup, which consists of a laser diode, optical fiber connectors, two or more optode sensors, a photon detector, and a controlling computer. (After Meek 2002.)

found greater left-hemisphere activation in newborns for normal speech compared to speech played backwards. Similarly, fMRI shows that 3-month-old infants already exhibit left-biased brain activation when presented with forward speech. Although the complete network of brain regions needed for adult language processing described in Chapter 21 is not fully apparent in the infant brain, a subset of these regions are clearly active early in development. This evidence, together with the fact that newborns are responsive to speech and capable of learning the full range of phonemes in the world's languages (see Chapter 20), argues strongly for language circuitry arising from developmental programs that precede experience.

Despite this evidence, it is obvious that the relevant brain regions are influenced by language experience; after all, we learn a native or other languages during the early years of life and beyond, and do so more effectively before the end of a critical period that ends late in childhood (see also the review of language deprivation studies in children in Chapter 20). ERP studies in chil-

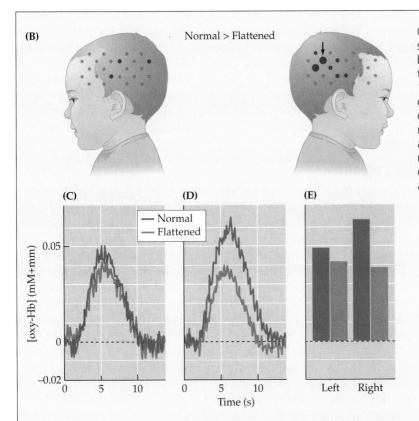

Comparing an infant brain's response to prosodic speech and speech without prosody. (B) Red- and blue-filled circles indicate optode channels with statistically significant activity. The arrow indicates channel 16 in the right hemisphere. (C) The average time course of optical signal changes over time recorded in channel 16 in the left hemisphere in response to normal and "flattened" (aprosodic) speech (D) The averaged time course of changes of channel 16 in the right hemisphere over time. (E) The mean changes in channel 16 in the two hemispheres. (After Homae et al. 2006.)

References

Baird, A. A., J. Kagan, T. Gaudette, K. Walz, N. Hershlag and D. Boas (2002) Frontal lobe activation during object permanence: Data from near-infrared spectroscopy. *Neuroimage* 16: 1120–1126.

Homae, F., H. Watanabe, T. Nakano, K. Asakawa and G. Taga (2006) The right hemisphere of sleeping infant perceives sentential prosody. *Neurosci. Res.* 54: 276–280.

Meek, J. (2002) Basic principles of optical imaging and application to the study of infant development. *Devel. Sci.* 5: 371–380.

Peña, M. and 6 others (2003) Sounds and silence: An optical topography study of language recognition at birth. *Proc. Natl. Acad. Sci. USA* 100: 11702–11705.

Taga, G., K. Asakawa, A. Maki, Y. Konishi and H. Koizumi (2003) Brain imaging in awake infants by near-infrared optical topography. *Proc. Natl. Acad. Sci. USA* 100: 10722–10727.

speech. Flattened speech is created by removing changes in the pitch contours of recorded speech; the purpose is to present stimulation that is speechlike but lacking the variations in pitch—the *prosody*—that convey emotional meaning (see Chapters 20 and 21). While both hemispheres showed activation in response to both flattened and normal speech, only the right hemisphere appeared to differentiate between speech with and without prosody (Figures B–E) . Thus, even by 3 months of age, the infant brain can analyze these acoustic properties of speech, suggesting that the processing of prosody information occurs early in language learning.

dren and adults further support this conclusion. Studies of language processing in adults show that posterior temporoparietal ERPs generated by the left hemisphere differentiate "open class" words (nouns and verbs) from "closed class" words that convey grammatical relationships (prepositions, determiners, and conjunctions).

Helen Neville and her colleagues at the University of Oregon carried out similar studies in children from 20 months to 3 years of age to investigate how this functional specialization develops. At 20 months, infants understand the meaning of open- and closed-class words but do not exhibit distinct ERP responses to the two classes. By 28 to 30 months, however—the point at which most children are beginning to speak in short sentences—ERPs differentiate open- and closed-class words. By 3 years of age, children are speaking in complete sentences and employing closed-class words correctly, and ERPs show the mature pattern of left-hemisphere asymmetry to closed-class words. These results suggest that brain systems for aspects of language become more specialized over development as the child masters increasingly complex linguistic challenges.

Another approach to these issues has been to study language development in patients with brain injuries (left- versus right-brain injuries in particular). Surprisingly, these studies reveal that language development is not much different for children with left- compared to right-hemisphere trauma when damage occurs very early in life. Thus, although behavioral and neuroimaging data demonstrate that laterality for speech processing emerges early in infancy and continues to develop with linguistic experience, other brain regions can take on language functions when the brain is injured early in development.

Numerical cognition

The cognitive neuroscience of timing and number processing in adults and non-human animals was described in Chapter 22. The further question considered here is how these capacities develop, and when during development the neural bases of adult number representation emerge.

Early studies addressed this question using the *visual habituation paradigm* (see Box 27B). Infants were shown repeated examples of one numerosity until the time they spent looking at each exemplar decreased, indicating that they had become habituated to that number of objects. Infants were then tested with alternating exemplars of the familiar and a new numerosity. If the infants look longer at the exemplars of the novel numerosity, they can be presumed to have discriminated between the two numerosities. Such tests showed that infants who had habituated to sets of three items looked longer at sets of two items, and vice versa. Babies only a few days old seem to discriminate arrays of dots or other objects based on number.

Although initial studies using this paradigm were later criticized because they did not rule out possible non-numerical cues in the stimuli, more recent work has carefully controlled for surface area, density, and perimeter—all variables that typically covary with number. These studies confirmed that infants can indeed discriminate both visual and auditory stimuli based solely on number. Thus Fei Xu at the University of British Columbia and Elizabeth Spelke at Harvard have shown that infants habituated to images that contain 8 dots look longer at new pictures with 16 dots than at new pictures with 8 dots when surface area, perimeter, and density are taken into account (**Figure 27.15**). Similarly, Spelke and colleagues have shown that infants preferentially orient toward a loudspeaker that plays a novel number of tones when duration, rate, and sound intensity are controlled for. While 6-month-old infants require a 1:2 ratio change in number (8 versus 16, 16 versus 32), by 9 months

Figure 27.15 Infant discrimination of numerosity. Stimuli like the examples illustrated here are shown to babies on a computer screen to test their numerical discrimination (i.e., their ability to discern the number of objects present) in a visual habituation paradigm. (After Xu and Spelke 2000.)

Habituation

Test

of age infants successfully discriminate visual and auditory arrays that have a 2:3 ratio, demonstrating that the precision with which infants discriminate number improves over the first year of life.

In addition to representing number, human infants can also manipulate numerical representations in rudimentary calculations. Karen Wynn at Yale has shown that babies look longer at the outcome of an event when the result is mathematically impossible and violates expectations. In this paradigm, infants watch a stage as dolls are sequentially placed behind a screen; the screen is then raised, and the expected number of dolls or an anomalous number is revealed. When infants see a 1 + 1 operation, they look longer at the unexpected outcome of 1 or 3 than at the expected outcome of 2. In contrast, when infants are shown a 2 – 1 operation (two dolls are hidden behind a screen and the infant then observes one being removed), they look longer at the outcome of 2 than at the expected outcome of 1. Using computer-animated displays that controlled for surface area, Wynn and colleagues further showed that when infants are shown a 5 + 5 operation they looked longer at the unexpected outcome of 5 than at the expected outcome of 10, but looked longer at 10 than 5 when they observed a 10 – 5 operation. In related studies infants do not show an increase in looking time when "Elmo" dolls are surreptitiously replaced with "Ernie" dolls, implying that babies do not represent the features of the dolls in this context, but are using numbers as such.

Only a few studies have investigated the neural bases of numerical cognition over developmental time. ERP differences were apparent when infants watched events that were arithmetically impossible versus events that were arithmetically possible (**Figure 27.16**). Other studies have found that children as young as 5 years show adultlike ERPs as a function of numerical distance when they make such judgments, and that both adults and children as young as 4 years recruit overlapping regions of the intraparietal sulcus when passively viewing numerosity arrays (**Figure 27.17**).

Executive processing and decision making

As described in Chapter 23, executive functions include planning for the future, deciding among alternative courses of action, inhibiting irrelevant information, and reasoning about complex problems. All of these cognitive abilities develop gradually and are not fully mature even in adolescence, as evidenced by the all too familiar prevalence of risk-taking behaviors in teenagers.

One essential component of executive function is the ability to delay gratification, and the development of this cognitive ability is of special interest. Walter Mischel of Columbia University demonstrated that young children have a great deal of difficulty delaying gratification. In the paradigm he used, a child is left in a room alone with a desirable item such as a cookie and told that if he or she is able to avoid eating or touching the cookie, two cookies will be given

Figure 27.16 Evidence that infants can add. (A) Stimuli used to test whether incorrect addition outcomes violate infants' expectations. (B) Infants wearing ERP recording caps while responding to the stimuli shown in the insets. (C) Average ERPs from 15 infants who looked longer at the unexpected outcome. ERPs showed a significant negativity between 330 and 530 ms in the incorrect condition, consistent with adult studies which typically show error-related negativity over anterior cingulate and other frontal areas at comparable post-stimulus times. (After Berger, Tzur and Posner, 2006.)

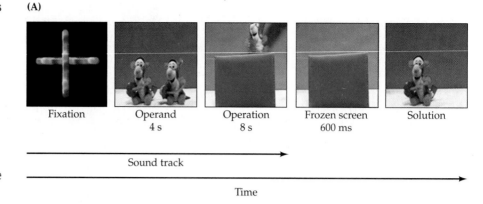

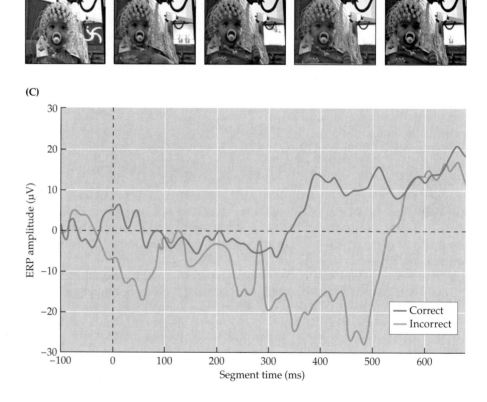

to the child when the experimenter returns. Although there is tremendous variation, younger children do not wait very long before they are unable to resist the inferior reward. However, by 6 years of age children will often wait as long as 25 minutes for the larger reward. Interestingly, the amount of time a child is able to resist such temptation is correlated with, among other things, academic achievement later in life (longer delays being associated with higher achievement).

Decision making typically involves estimating the risk associated with different potential outcomes, processing feedback, and assessing different strategies in working memory. As might be expected, the ability to carry out all of these functions also changes over development, with adolescents and children typically making less advantageous decisions and taking more risks than adults. Young children also are more likely to persist in making non-optimal

(A)

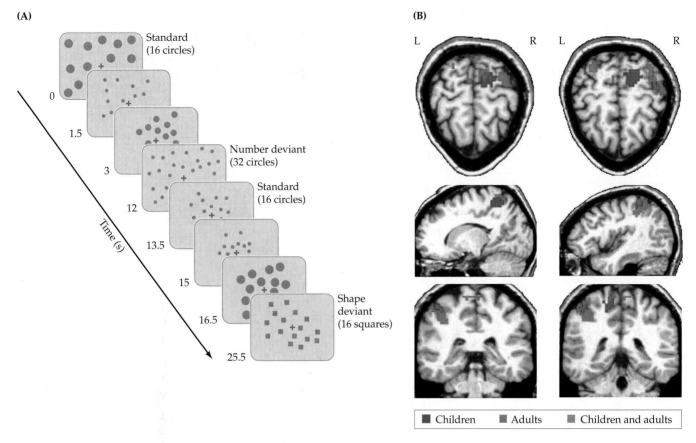

(B)

■ Children   ■ Adults   ■ Children and adults

Figure 27.17 Brain regions recruited when passively viewing numerical and shape changes. (A) Stimuli used in an fMRI study to test for brain regions that show number-specific activity. (B) Brain regions that responded more to numerical change than to a shape change. The intraparietal sulcus showed number selective activity in both children and adults. (From Cantlon et al. 2006.)

choices suggesting since they have less (or are unable to make use of) feedback from higher cortical processing areas. Using a child-friendly gambling task, Sylvia Bunge and her colleagues at Berkeley investigated the neural correlates of decision making in 9- to 12-year-old children and in adults. Participants in both age groups showed greater activation in orbitofrontal cortex, dorsolateral prefrontal cortex, and anterior cingulate cortex when making high-risk as compared to low-risk decisions. Participants also showed increased activation bilaterally in the ventrolateral prefrontal cortex when receiving negative as opposed to positive feedback. However, compared to adults, children showed greater engagement of anterior cingulate cortex during risk engagement and greater engagement of orbitofrontal cortex when processing negative feedback. These results are consistent with the idea that the circuitry relying on dorsolateral prefrontal cortex and orbitofrontal cortex and its connections with anterior cingulate cortex may not be fully developed by the age of 12, and that this situation may affect children's decision-making abilities.

The ability to use explicit rules also shows important developmental changes over childhood. Behavioral studies indicate that children's ability to use explicit rules follows a predictable pattern whereby they are first able to learn a single rule, then to learn bivalent rules that require flexibly switching between two compatible rules, and are finally able to learn higher order rules that require switching between two incompatible rules (**Figure 27.18**). For example, at age 2 children are able to sort objects according to one rule (e.g., color) but have difficulty sorting objects according to two rules (e.g., color and shape). By age 3, however, this type of sorting is relatively easy. Nonetheless, at age 3 children still have difficulty using two incompatible rules, such as required by the experimenter-determined rule changes in the Wisconsin Card Sorting Task discussed in Chapter 23 (e.g., first sort by color, then change the

Figure 27.18 Executive functions in children. Lateral view of the human brain; the lateral prefrontal cortex is highlighted. The orbitofrontal cortex, which represents rules that provide information about the value of the stimulus, is shown in red. Conditions that require learning a single rule (univalent rules) are represented by ventrolateral prefrontal cortex (Brodmann areas 44, 45, and 47). Conditions that require flexibly switching between two rules (C_1 and C_2) are represented by the dorsolateral prefrontal cortex (areas 9 and 46); higher-order conditions that require switching between two mutually incompatible rules (C_3 and C_4) are represented by the rostrolateral prefrontal cortex (area 10). (B after Bunge and Zelazo 2006.)

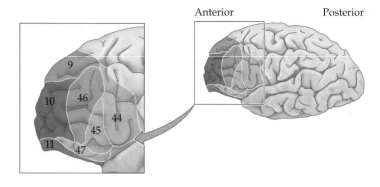

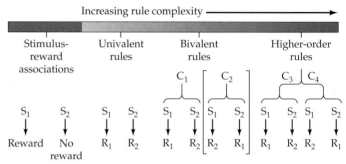

rule and sort by shape), and tend to keep persevering using whichever rule they were first asked to use. By age 5, however, children are able to switch flexibly between two incompatible rules. The longitudinal MRI studies of developing brains described earlier in the chapter indicate that within the prefrontal cortex, gray matter reaches adult levels first in orbitofrontal cortex, followed by ventrolateral PFC, and finally dorsolateral PFC. Sylvia Bunge and Philip Zelazo of the University of Toronto have argued that behavioral changes in the ability to use explicit rules track the maturation of these prefrontal regions.

In conclusion, then, although many issues remain to be clarified, a wealth of studies indicate that brain and behavior change together as individuals mature. This change is brought about through the interplay of genes and environmental influences. Much as in the development of the rest of the nervous system, each person's postnatal experience modulates the development of brain circuitry that is already prepared to carry out cognitive tasks. Although relative influence of nature and nurture is a source of continuing controversy, what each of us eventually becomes is clearly a product of both.

Summary

1. Understanding how changes in brain structure and function lead to changing cognitive abilities that are apparent during the course of infancy, childhood and adolescence remains an important goal. It is now clear that a great deal of brain development takes place prenatally, driven by intrinsic genetic and epigenetic programs that lay the foundation for adult cognitive skills.

2. The brain continues to develop and organize its connectivity postnatally, a process that continues through adolescence and to a diminished degree throughout adult life.

3. Different brain regions mature at different rates, and this variation appears to explain many of the changes evident in cognitive behavior during development. The tools of cognitive neuroscience applied in developmental contexts are rapidly enriching knowledge of these changes in the brain structure and function that underlie cognition.

4. Although many issues remain to be clarified, a wealth of studies indicates that brain and behavior change together through the interplay of genes and environmental influences as humans mature.

Additional Readings

Reviews

BUNGE, S. A. AND P. D. ZELAZO (2006) A brain-based account of the development of rule use in childhood. *Curr. Dir. Psychol. Sci.* 15: 118–121.

CASEY, B. J., N. TOTTENHAM, C. LISTON AND S. DURSTON (2005) Imaging the developing brain: What have we learned about cognitive development? *Trends Cogn. Sci.* 9: 104–110.

JOHNSON, M. H. (2001) Functional and brain development in humans. *Nat. Rev. Neurosci.* 2: 475–483.

LENROOT, R. K. AND J. N. GIEDD (2006) Brain development in children and adolescents: Insights from anatomical brain magnetic resonance imaging. *Neurosci. Behav. Rev.* 30: 718–729.

NELSON, C. (2001) The development and neural bases of face recognition. *Infant Child Devel.* 10: 3–18.

NEVILLE, H. J. AND D. BAVELIER (2002) Specificity and plasticity in neurocognitive development in humans. In *Brain Development and Cognition: A Reader*, 2nd ed. M. H. Johnson, Y. Munakata and R. O. Gilmore (eds.). Malden, MA: Blackwell Publishing, pp. 251–271.

PELPHREY, K. A. AND E. J. CARTER (2007) Brain mechanisms underlying social perception deficits in autism. In *Human Behavior and the Developing Brain*, 2nd Ed., D. Coch, G. Dawson and K. Fischer (eds.). New York: Guilford Press.

VAN PRAAG, H., G. KEMPERMANN AND F. H. GAGE (2000) Neural consequences of environmental enrichment. *Nat. Neurosci.* 1: 191–198.

Important Original Papers

BAILLARGEON, R. (1987) Object permanence in 3.5- to 4.5-month-old infants, *Devel. Psychol.* 23: 665–664.

BOURGEOIS, J. AND P. RAKIC (1993) Changes of synaptic density in the primary visual cortex of the macaque monkey from fetal to adult stage. *J. Neurosci.* 13: 2801–2820.

DEHAENE-LAMBERTZ, G., S. DEHAENE AND K. HERTZ-PANNIER (2002) Functional neuroimaging of speech perception in infants. *Science* 298: 2013–2015.

MILLS, D. L., C. PRAT, R. ZANGL, C. L. STAGER, H. J. NEVILLE AND J. F. WERKER (2004) Language experience and the organization of brain activity to phonetically similar words: ERP evidence from 14- and 20-month-olds. *J. Cogn. Neurosci.* 16: 1452–1464.

MISCHEL, W. (1981) Metacognition and the rules of delay. In *Social Cognitive Development*, J. H. Flavell and L. Ross (eds.). Cambridge: Cambridge University Press, pp. 240–271.

RAKIC, P. (1974) Neurons in rhesus monkey visual cortex: Systematic relation between time of origin and eventual disposition. *Science* 183: 425–427.

WIMMER, H. AND J. PERNER (1983) Beliefs about beliefs: Representation and constraining function of wrong beliefs in young children's understanding of deception. *Cognition* 13: 41–68.

WYNN, K. (1992). Addition and subtraction by human infants. *Nature* 358: 749–750.

Books

DE HAAN, M. AND M. H. JOHNSON (2003) *The Cognitive Neuroscience of Development*. London: Psychology Press.

JOHNSON, M. H. (2005) *Developmental Cognitive Neuroscience*. Malden, MA: Blackwell Publishing.

NELSON, C. A. AND M. LUCIANA (2001) *Handbook of Developmental Cognitive Neuroscience*. Cambridge, MA: MIT Press.

RUFF, H. A. AND M. K. ROTHBART (1996) *Attention in Early Development*. Oxford: Oxford University Press.

28

Consciousness

Introduction

Of all the cognitive abilities of the human brain, the one that has most deeply interested (and perplexed) thinkers over the centuries is the phenomenon of consciousness. Most people—whether neuroscientists, philosophers, or simply inquisitive individuals—will have asked questions such as "How and why are we conscious?" or "Are other animals conscious?" or "Can a machine be conscious?"; although none of these questions admits a definitive answer, there is nonetheless much to be said about them. Investigators in a variety of disciplines (neurobiology, psychology, ethology, anthropology, computer science, philosophy, and ethics) have in general moved from speculation to an increasingly solid foundation for exploring these and other questions about consciousness. In recent decades, a number of investigators have used modern techniques to explicitly search for the neural substrate(s) of consciousness. The purpose of this chapter is to review the different approaches to the question of consciousness, to consider the evidence that has been uncovered, and to indicate the general direction of present-day thinking about this highly charged issue. It is also fitting to end our account of the principles of cognitive neuroscience with a consideration of whether consciousness distinguishes the operation of the human brain from the cognitive abilities of other animals, or indeed from the non-biological information processing systems that are advancing at an extraordinary rate.

What Does It Mean To Be Conscious?

The first requirement for any sensible discussion of consciousness is to establish clear definitions of the terms involved. This is not an easy task, because the relevant words and phrases have meant different things in different fields that have significantly distinct intellectual traditions. Nevertheless, most definitions of **consciousness** refer to three different aspects of this phenomenon: being awake, being aware of the world, and being aware of oneself as an actor in the world. Each of these aspects of the concept of consciousness is pertinent to cognitive neuroscience:

1. A physiological meaning that describes consciousness in terms of the brain state we think of as **wakefulness**; this definition entails understanding the nature of brain activity that distinguishes wakefulness from sleep or other unconscious states.

2. A more abstract meaning that refers to a subjective **awareness** of the world, a brain state that must have a more subtle signature than wakefulness, since one can be awake and yet be unaware of some or most aspects of the external and internal environment.

3. A meaning that refers to **self-awareness,** a phrase that defines consciousness in the sense of being aware of oneself as distinct from other selves in the world.

Each of these meanings and its neural correlates (in so far as the neural correlates are known) is considered separately in the following sections, not least because each entails a different set of issues, different research agendas, and often different methodologies.

Consciousness as a Physiological State

Wakefulness and sleeping

Human beings spend each 24-hour solar cycle that defines a day on our planet in a variety of brain states, not all of which are conscious in any sense of this term. About a third of our lives are spent in the several stages of sleep, a state that (apart from periods of dreaming) is clearly unconscious. Even when we are fully awake, our awareness of the world around us and of our internal state in terms of thoughts, feelings, hopes, and desires varies greatly. These different brain states range from fully vigilant attention, through inattentiveness (e.g., boredom), drowsiness, and ultimately sleep; each of these states reflects different levels of consciousness in the sense of wakefulness (definition 1 above), which is in turn a prerequisite to consciousness in its other meanings (definitions 2 and 3). It is thus useful to review how the brain regulates changes from alert wakefulness to deep sleep, and to discuss what bearing, if any, this physiological regulation has on consciousness in its meanings of awareness of the world and of the self in the world.

As briefly described in Chapter 10, sleep is not simply the result of diminished brain activity or a "shutting off" of sensory input, but is a series of precisely controlled brain states. Humans descend into sleep in *stages* (as defined by electroencephalographic criteria) that succeed each other over the first hour or so after retiring (**Figure 28.1**).The control of these different states of consciousness is now fairly well understood as a result of many years of electrophysiological, anatomical, and pharmacological work. Observations dating from the 1940s show that electrically stimulating a group of cholinergic neurons that lies near the junction of the pons and midbrain causes wakefulness

(A)

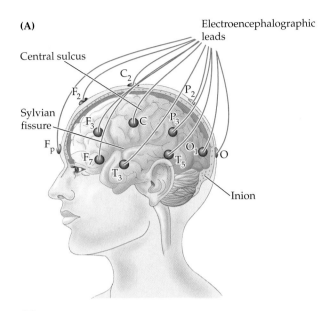

Electroencephalographic leads

Central sulcus

C_2

F_2

P_2

Sylvian fissure

F_3 C P_3

F_P

F_7 T_5 O_1 O

T_3

Inion

Figure 28.1 The stages of sleep. (A) Levels of wakefulness and sleep are usually monitored by electroencephalographic (EEG) activity. (B) The changes from alert wakefulness through boredom to drowsiness are indicated by shifts toward lower frequencies and higher amplitudes of the recorded signal. This pattern of lower frequency and higher amplitude waves continues throughout the progressive loss of consciousness that falling asleep entails. The entire sleep sequence from drowsiness to deep (stage IV) sleep usually takes about an hour. The descending stages into deep sleep are called non-rapid eye movement (non-REM) sleep. These stages contrast with periods of rapid eye movement (REM) sleep, a time when the brain again becomes active and most dreaming occurs.

(B)

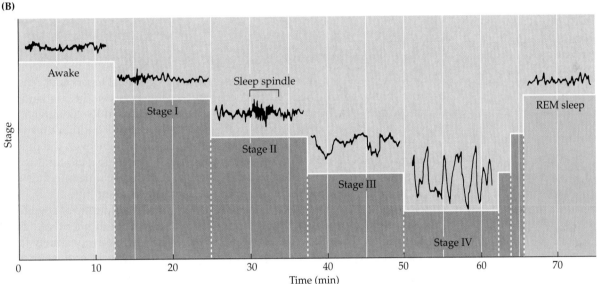

and arousal. These early observations revealed that wakefulness (or consciousness in this sense) is based on dedicated, active neural mechanisms.

Investigators now agree that the sequence of human brain states illustrated in Figure 28.1 is generated by a collection of nuclei in the central region of brainstem involved in arousal and motivation, a region called the **reticular activating system**. The most important of these controlling elements are the cells in the cholinergic nuclei of the **pons-midbrain junction**, the noradrenergic cells of the **locus coeruleus**, and the serotonergic neurons in the **raphe nuclei** (**Table 28.1**). Thus the activity of these brainstem nuclei modulates the degree of consciousness over the day on a continuum from alert wakefulness to deep sleep (**Figure 28.2**). These nuclei are in turn controlled by circadian clocks in the suprachiasmatic nucleus and the hypothalamus; these internal clocks are entrained to the light–dark cycles that define day and night (see Chapter 22).

Although being awake is clearly a prerequisite to being conscious in the sense of being aware of the world and the self, as explained in later sections these functions are not equivalent.

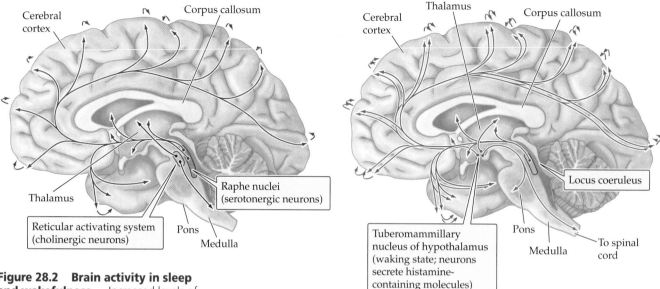

Figure 28.2 Brain activity in sleep and wakefulness. Increased levels of activity of cholinergic neurons in the reticular activating system are the primary cause of wakefulness, and their relative inactivity is the cause of physiological unconsciousness. Other brainstem nuclei involved in this complex regulatory scheme are noradrenergic neurons of the locus coeruleus and serotonergic neurons of the raphe nuclei. Both monoaminergic and cholinergic systems are active during the waking state (see Table 28.1). The neurons of the tuberomammillary nucleus produce the histamine-containing molecule orexin and are active during the awake state (which explains why antihistamines make people drowsy).

Consciousness as the neurophysiological present

Another aspect of consciousness defined in physiological terms concerns its temporal character. Consciousness occupies the time between the past and the future, and thus defines our sense of the *present*. We generally consider what happened some seconds ago to be in the *past*, and what will happen a few seconds hence to lie in the *future*. Looked at more critically, however, the precise temporal character of the present is problematic. Since there is no limit to the brevity of a moment in time, a puzzling issue is the specific time intervals that define the obvious and useful categories of past, present, and future.

A sensible position is that, while the present defined in terms of physics is indeed infinitely brief, our conscious sense of the present moment, or "right now," is defined by neural processing, which operates relatively slowly (milliseconds to seconds). Fuzzy though it may be, the subjective present does have a finite duration because of this limitation. The duration of the conscious moment that corresponds to our subjective sense of the present is of course impossible to measure with any precision, but based on knowledge about the various forms of neural processing described in earlier chapters, several hundred milliseconds to perhaps a second or so is a reasonable range.

This estimate of the conscious present is pertinent to the way in which we attend to objects and conditions in the world. Subjectively at least, it seems that we can consciously attend to only one thing at a time (or to a grouped collection of things), although the brain is unconsciously processing a very long list of items in parallel at any given moment. In a rough sense, then, the object of conscious attention is another way of defining the present moment. Of course, the "moments" that comprise the ongoing stream of the conscious present don't follow each other randomly, but are typically concatenated in purposeful sequences, as is apparent in working memory and thought processes generally (see Chapter 16 and Unit VIII).

This line of inquiry raises the question of how consciousness in the sense of a continually changing present moment is any different from the ever-changing focus of attention (see Unit IV). The simplest answer is that the conscious moment and the focus of attention are merely ways of examining the same general issue from somewhat different perspectives (see below). In any event,

■ TABLE 28.1 Brainstem Nuclei that Regulate Sleep and Wakefulness

Brainstem nuclei responsible	Neurotransmitter involved	Activity state of the relevant brainstem neurons
Wakefulness		
Cholinergic nuclei of pons-midbrain junction	Acetylcholine	Active
Locus coeruleus	Norepinephrine	Active
Raphe nuclei	Serotonin	Active
Tuberomammillary nuclei	Orexin (histamine)	Active
Non-REM sleep		
Cholinergic nuclei of pons-midbrain junction	Acetylcholine	Decreased
Locus coeruleus	Norepinephrine	Decreased
Raphe nuclei	Serotonin	Decreased
REM sleep on		
Cholinergic nuclei of pons-midbrain junction	Acetylcholine	Active
Raphe nuclei	Serotonin	Inactive
REM sleep off		
Locus coeruleus	Norepinephrine	Active

being physiologically awake and potentially responsive to information in the neurally defined present are necessary conditions for consciousness in its other senses: being aware of the world and of the self in it.

Consciousness as Awareness of the World and Self

These two other meanings of consciousness refer not to the neuroanatomical and physiological bases of wakefulness or a sense of the present, but to the deeply puzzling ability we all have to be subjectively aware of the world and of ourselves as actors in it. Whereas consciousness as wakefulness and its physiological basis fits easily in the conventional framework of neurobiological studies, consciousness as awareness or self-awareness raises difficult and contentious philosophical issues, and thus has been far more difficult to pursue with the techniques of cognitive neuroscience.

Attacking consciousness from this perspective is further complicated by the fact that being *aware* is not the same as being *self-aware*: one can imagine an animal that is aware of sense data without having the integrated sense of a separate self that humans possess. Indeed, as described in Chapter 27, this sense takes some time to emerge in developing humans. Whereas animals such as rats and pigeons seem clearly aware of the world, whether they are self-aware is debatable. On the other hand, based on the evidence described in Chapter 26, some non-human primates are both aware of the world and (at least to some degree) aware of themselves as participants in it, along with other selves (see discussion later in the chapter). Going further down the scale of brain (or nervous system) complexity, very simple animals presumably lack awareness altogether, at least in any conventional sense. In descending the continuum of nervous system complexity, the most neurally simple animals appear to operate as automatons, although it is not clear at what taxonomic level this occurs. And, lest a point made in earlier chapters be forgotten, recall that even in the human nervous system the great majority of neural processing is largely automatic, lying below the threshold of awareness. Indeed, an enormous amount of the cellular machinery in the human brain is devoted to neural processes that lie beyond the reach of cognition altogether.

Even within the domain of neural processing we are or can be aware of, it is obvious that the content of consciousness is limited to the bits and pieces that briefly enter awareness from the much greater reservoir of unconscious information that is only potentially accessible (for example, all the information stored as memories; see Chapter 13). The term *mind* rather vaguely but usefully refers to the sum of all the sense data, feelings, thoughts, and declarative memories that we *can* be aware of, as distinct from the much larger body of present and stored neural information that never penetrates awareness—and indeed was never intended to (think again of all the homeostatic mechanisms that insure your well-being in a thousand ways even while you ponder the significance of the sentence you have just read here).

Neural Correlates of Consciousness

These daunting issues notwithstanding, a number of cognitive neuroscientists have sought to address the basis of awareness by ferreting out some signature of the neural processing that occurs when we are aware of something (e.g., a visual stimulus) compared to when we are not (i.e., presentation of the same stimulus under circumstances in which it does not elicit any reportable percept).

Studies of normal subjects and patients with various pathological conditions have shed some light on this challenge (see also Unit IV). Most such work has, for practical reasons, been done in the context of visual perception, but the results may be assumed to apply to other sense modalities. Whether they can be further extrapolated to the awareness of feelings, thoughts, and desires that are not perceived by any sensory modalities has not yet been examined.

Neural correlates of awareness examined in normal subjects

In normal subjects, the approach most commonly taken to address this issue has been to assess the nature and location of neural activity when a particular sensory percept moves in and out of awareness. By asking the subject (or experimental animal) to report these perceptual transitions (typically by pressing a button or the equivalent when they perceive a visual stimulus), the investigator can compare neural events during awareness to the state of the brain when the subject is unaware of the stimulus in question.

The most widely used paradigms for this sort of study, all of which have been described in other chapters, include binocular rivalry, stimulus "crowding," inattentional blindness, attentional blinks, perceptual aftereffects, motion-induced blindness, and visual masking (see Chapters 5, 10, and 11). In many such paradigms, the physical stimulus remains unchanged and thus serves as its own control. A good example is viewing **bi-stable figures** such as the well known face/vase stimulus (**Figure 28.3A**). Transitions from one percept (face) to the other (vase) are universally seen, are stable for some seconds, and are easy for subjects to report. (Such figures also make the point that we can be aware of only one visual scene at a time.)

Another widely used paradigm is **binocular rivalry** (**Figure 28.3B**). As described in Chapter 5, binocular rivalry refers to the fact that when a particular stimulus pattern (e.g., vertical stripes) is presented to one eye while a discordant pattern (e.g., horizontal stripes) is presented to the other, the same

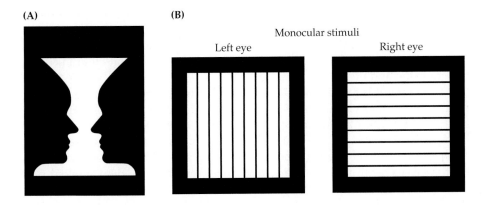

(A)

(B)

Monocular stimuli

Left eye   Right eye

Figure 28.3   Bi-stable and rivalrous visual stimuli.   Examples of the type of test stimuli used in assessing the neural correlates of awareness. (A) This classic example of a bi-stable image is alternately perceived as a face or a vase, but cannot be perceived as both at the same time. (B) These two linear stimuli elicit binocular rivalry when separately presented to the right and left eyes.

region of visual space is perceived to be alternately occupied by vertical or horizontal stripes, but not by both. Using human subjects or monkeys trained to report what they are seeing at any given moment, electrophysiological methods or fMRI can be used to assess what if any change in brain activity occurs when there is a switch of conscious content.

Recordings made from single neurons in at least some regions of the visual cortex tend to show increased activity when the animal is perceiving the view of one eye but not the other (see Figure 4.14). In accord with this observation, fMRI activity increases in the fusiform face area of the temporal lobe when a face is seen (see below), although stimuli such as those shown in Figure 28.3A have shown relatively little change in the activity of single neurons as awareness shifts from one percept to the other.

A different fMRI paradigm with the same aim of probing activity changes in the visual cortex during perception or its absence takes advantage of visual aftereffects (see Chapter 5). For example, orientation aftereffects can be induced by acutely exposing subjects to a series of lines (referred to as *gratings*) in a particular orientation (say, 45°) for a minute or two; following this exposure, "neutral" line stimuli (vertical lines) are perceived for a brief period as being slightly tilted in the direction opposite the angle of the inducing exposure. The same inducing stimulus can be presented without awareness by masking or stimulus-crowding during the presentation. One can then ask whether lack of awareness of the inducing stimulus abolishes the aftereffect. It does not, implying that visual cortical neurons sensitive to orientation are just as active when subjects are aware of the inducing stimulus as when they are not.

This lack of effect has been further confirmed in non-human primates by examining the activity of depth sensitive (disparity-tuned) neurons in V1 that are active in response to stereoscopic stimuli. Again, little or no difference in activity is apparent when the monkeys indicate behaviorally that they experienced a perception of depth compared to when they do not. In short, studies of activity in at least the early stages of visual cortical processing have not led to any clear hallmark of visual awareness (see also Chapters 10 and 11).

It may help in rationalizing these somewhat confusing results to distinguish lower-order visual processing from higher-order visual processing in the visual association cortices. Recall from Chapter 5 that the higher-order visual areas are divisible into a ventral stream running to the temporal lobe that is broadly concerned with the recognition of visual stimuli (the "what" pathway), and a dorsal stream that is more concerned with stimulus location (the "where" pathway). Nikos Logothetis and his colleagues at the Max Planck Institute in Tübingen have argued that correlations of neural activity with stimulus awareness in monkeys tend to increase as recording sites move away from V1 along the ventral pathway, toward the temporal lobe. This interpretation accords with the majority of the studies mentioned above, and with further human fMRI studies testing this idea carried out by Frank Tong at Princeton and others.

A final point is that the activity of some further cortical regions not generally thought of as visual are also correlated with visual awareness. Thus neuroimaging studies in humans carried out by Geraint Rees, Semir Zeki, and their collaborators at University College London showed that perceptual changes in both the face/vase and binocular rivalry paradigms are associated with activity in frontal and parietal cortical regions (i.e., they showed that altered activity in these cortical regions is time-locked to the subjects' reports of the perceptual changes). As described in Unit IV, these regions have been implicated in changes in attentional control. Consistent with this evidence, other perceptual effects such as "pop-out" of a visual stimulus (see Chapter 18), or the awareness of a previously missed stimulus feature, are also correlated activity changes in frontal and parietal areas. Transient functional disruption of processing in these areas by TMS also disturbs perception in normal subjects. Disturbances in perception following damage to these additional brain regions further confirm that they are somehow involved in awareness, although how and why remains unclear.

Taken together, this evidence is consistent with the generally accepted idea that any percept is based on altered activity of populations of cortical neurons in the regions of the association cortices that process the relevant stimulus and integrate it with information arising from other modalities and contextual influences. With respect to vision, the observed correlations described here suggest that activity in the visual association cortices is probably *necessary* for visual awareness. However, extrastriate activity is evidently not a *sufficient* cause of stimulus awareness, and no specific signature of awareness has yet been discerned.

Neural correlates of awareness examined in pathological conditions

Clinical pathological evidence, much of it discussed in other contexts in previous chapters, is also germane to understanding the neural basis of awareness. Some key examples are briefly reconsidered here insofar as they have informed the search for a neural signature of conscious awareness.

A pathological phenomenon that has been of particular interest in this regard is **blindsight,** most thoroughly described and studied over the last 40 years by psychologist Larry Weiskrantz and his colleagues at Oxford University. As described in Unit II, patients with damage to the primary visual cortex are blind in the affected area of the contralateral visual field (recall that as a result of the visual system anatomy, V1 in the right occipital lobe processes information arising from the left visual field, and V1 in left occipital lobe processes input from the right visual field). The area of blindness in the visual field affected is called a *scotoma*, and objects presented within this region are simply not seen as far as the patient is concerned. Nevertheless, when blindsight patients are forced by the experimenter to make a response to simple stimuli presented within their scotoma, the responses are often significantly above chance performance. For instance, if the patient is asked to guess whether a stimulus line presented within their scotoma is vertical or horizontal, they will answer correctly much of the time even though they claim to have seen nothing. Although this sort of paradigm does not apply for stimuli presented to the physiological blindspot* (since in that case no information is sent to any level of the visual system), Tony Ro and his collaborators at Rice University have shown that blindsight can be simulated in normal individuals by transient inactivation of V1. TMS applied over the occipital lobes creates a temporary scotoma, and the features of simple stimuli presented in the unseen region of the visual field are also guessed correctly at levels well above chance.

Functional neuroimaging studies of patients with blindsight show that the unseen stimuli elicit some activity in extrastriate regions, implying that these cortical areas are needed for successful behavior in the absence of awareness. This evidence underscores the conclusion of the previous section that extrastriate activity may be necessary for awareness, but is not a sufficient cause. The probable explanation of blindsight is that subcortical visual processing of the information in the stimulus (perhaps abetted by subliminal processing in extrastriate cortex) influences the patient's guesses. This interpretation accords with much other evidence that subliminal (unconscious) information processing influences behavior of all sorts.

Another example of neural pathology pertinent to understanding awareness is the experience of *split-brain patients* that was described in the context of language (see Chapter 21). When the corpus callosum is cut as a treatment for otherwise intractable epileptic seizures, direct communication between the right and left hemispheres is no longer possible. The perceptual consequences of this surgery were first studied by Roger Sperry and his student Michael Gazzaniga working at Cal Tech in the 1960s. Observations made on split-brain patients over subsequent decades have amply confirmed that the divided hemispheres function relatively independently, and that awareness generated by neural processing in one hemisphere is largely unavailable to the other. When simple written instructions such as "laugh" or "walk" are presented visually to left visual field—and thus to the right brain—of a split-brain patient, many subjects have enough rudimentary verbal understanding in the right hemisphere to execute the commanded action. However, when asked to report *why* they laughed or walked, they typically confabulate a response using the superior language skills in the left hemisphere, saying, for instance, that something the experimenter said struck them as funny, or that they were tired of sitting and needed to walk a bit. Thus the same individual can, under these circumstances, harbor two relatively independent domains of awareness. This evidence raises the provocative question of whether awareness is really the unified function we generally take it to be.

Whereas blindsight and hemispheric division lead to circumstances in which patients are unaware of stimulus processing that nonetheless influences their behavior, it is also possible to be fully aware of something that doesn't actually exist. Perhaps the most striking illustration of this sort of phenomenon is the *phantom limb* experiences of amputees described in Chapter 7. Recall that a common experience following amputation is the patient's subjective awareness of the missing arm or leg, despite the fact that the physical limb and its peripheral sensory input are absent. Although the interpretation of this bizarre condition is debated, the awareness of the missing limb and sensations arising from it (pain is especially problematic for some amputees) are quite real, emphasizing that processing of peripheral information is an active process in which the cortex constructs the percepts we experience. Hallucinations and visual illusions make the same point. In keeping with the evidence discussed in Unit II, awareness of the world does not simply arise by virtue of central representations that are generated by peripheral sense

---

*The *physiological blindspot* is a normal feature of vision arising from the absence of photoreceptors in the region of the retina from which the optic nerve emerges (see Figure 4.5). The physiological blindspot allows all of us to experience a scotoma and the invisibility of objects within it.

organs. Recognition of this fact adds a further challenge to the problem of understanding the bases of awareness.

Another clinical condition pertinent to consciousness is *coma*. **Coma** (Greek for "deep sleep") is the term applied to the brain state of individuals who have suffered brain injury that leaves them in a deeply unconscious state defined by apparent unresponsiveness to sensory stimuli. The condition typically involves compromised function of the brainstem and other deep brain structures, such that the normal interaction of these structures with the cerebral cortex is interrupted.

Coma can arise from varying degrees of brain damage, and the prognosis is often uncertain. Most comatose individuals recover consciousness within a few days or weeks as the compromised neurons and the circuits they contribute to gradually regain their functions. Coma can persist for much longer, however, if neural damage is more profound. Some patients recover consciousness after months, although typically with residual effects, and extremely rare cases have been reported in which consciousness was regained after some years. This variability has led to social, religious, and political controversy over the point at which a comatose patient should be considered to be in a *permanent vegetative state*, a diagnosis that argues for removing or withholding life-support measures. This sensitive issue means there has been, and will continue to be, great interest in techniques that could contribute to a better understanding of coma and a given patient's prognosis.

Electroencephalography has long been fundamental to diagnosing *irreversible brain death*, which occurs when brain trauma is so severe that no EEG activity can be recorded. More recently, functional neuroimaging has also been used to evaluate coma, sometimes with surprising results. For example, Adrian Owen and his colleagues Cambridge University imaged the brain of a 23-year-old woman who had been comatose for 5 months following a traffic accident. Despite her condition, fMRI imaging showed that she was to some degree able to understand verbal commands and to respond to them by generating appropriate brain activity in language areas.

All told, these studies of clinical conditions pertinent to awareness have in some instances been extraordinarily interesting and informative (split-brain studies) or clinically important (studies of coma), but they have not led to any consensus about the nature of consciousness. To judge from studies of normal subjects, awareness of sensory stimuli entails a modest modulation of activity in the sensory cortices (especially the higher-order association cortices) as well as in frontal and parietal cortices that support attention and many other cognitive functions. However, the efforts to identify a neural basis for awareness as such have not yet provided the sort of fundamental answer sought by many of the investigators in this field.

Is Consciousness Based on a Novel Neural Mechanism?

Given the relative inconclusiveness of studies seeking some signature of the neural basis of consciousness, some scientists have been attracted to the more radical idea that human consciousness might entail a mechanism that lies outside the realm of conventional thinking. This possibility has a long history in philosophy, where the **mind-body problem** has been a staple of discourse and debate for millenia.

In the seventeenth century, the central concern of natural philosophers was how an immaterial "soul" or "mind" could interact causally with a material body. This issue, evident even earlier in the philosophy of Aristotle (who in *De Motu Animalum* opined that the mind was located in the heart) was treated most famously in the writings of René Descartes. Descartes concluded that mind and body were fundamentally different, the body being subject to the laws of physics but the mind not. He thus championed what has ever since been referred to as Cartesian **dualism**. Beginning with the British empiricists of the eighteenth century (the major figures in this philosophical school were George Berkeley, John Locke, and David Hume), philosophers have increasingly taken the view that what one conceives to be "the mind" is an emergent property of the activity and operation of the brain. Modern mind-brain philosophers overlap greatly in their interests and knowledge base with cognitive neuroscientists, and the two fields have become increasingly allied.

Ironically, it has been practitioners of the hard sciences who have promulgated some of the most extreme ideas about mechanisms of consciousness. The highly accomplished mathematical physicist Roger Penrose, for example, has written extensively on the idea that quantum processes might lie at the heart of consciousness, and specifically suggested that quantum effects on the structure of axonal microtubules might be the basis for awareness. Some accomplished biologists have also been attracted to the idea that a special mechanism is likely to lie at the heart of consciousness. Like Penrose, John Eccles, who carried out pioneering work on the electrophysiology of synaptic transmission in the 1950s, suggested that quantum level events (quantum indeterminacy in particular) might provide a basis for the human sense of free will.

Other scientists have been less sanguine about the possible role of quantum physics, but nonetheless enthusiastic about the idea of consciousness requiring some special mechanism. Following his enormous contributions to molecular genetics, Francis Crick spent the last 25 years of his life working and writing on the basis of consciousness with the idea that something fundamentally new remained to be discovered. Crick's enormous prestige in science greatly encouraged the idea described earlier in this chapter that a neural correlate of awareness should be discernable in comparisons of brain activity when subjects are aware of a stimulus and when they are not. Gerald Edelman, another Nobel laureate distinguished for his work on the immune system and cell adhesion molecules, also devoted the later decades of his career to this problem, emphasizing computational models based on recurrent neural circuitry.

While quantum theories of consciousness are widely regarded as implausible (primarily because subatomic processes are so far removed from the well-understood mechanisms of neural signaling), the possibility of a novel mechanism or framework for understanding consciousness must certainly be entertained. The mechanism that has been most widely discussed as a novel framework for understanding consciousness is *high-frequency brain oscillations*. As described in Chapter 3, brain oscillations were discovered by the German neurologist and psychologist Hans Berger in 1924 when he first made the EEG recordings that, among other things, have provided so much useful insight into the physiology of the sleep-wake cycle (see above). Although the proximal basis of brain oscillations is well understood, the reason for their variety and behavior in different circumstances is not. As a result, a number of investigators have pursued the idea that particular components of oscillatory brain activity, which represents the coherent activity of large populations of widely distributed neurons, might be the key to understanding consciousness in terms of a new principle. In general, interest has focused on higher frequency oscillations, in the range of 40 Hz or higher.

Several lines of evidence suggest that synchronized neural activity might indeed have something to do with the perception of sensory stimuli. For example, as described in Chapter 11, attention to stimuli tends to synchronize neural activity in the sensory cortices, and perceptual transitions when viewing bi-stable stimuli are marked by some degree of long-distance synchronization among the relevant brain areas. As discussed in Chapter 4, the underlying idea is that neural synchrony may be important in generating cohesion among the object qualities (often called "binding"; see Box 4B), thus enabling a unified awareness of objects as such. Whether these observations are simply what one would expect as populations of cells process sensory information and extend their influence to related cell populations, or are the signature of a novel mechanism underlying awareness, is not clear. Many neuroscientists remain skeptical about the relevance of cortical oscillations to binding, let alone awareness.

In sum, there is as yet no compelling evidence that awareness entails any novel mechanisms, whether at the level of quantum physics or simply mainstream neurophysiology.

Are Other Animals Aware of World and Self?

The issue of whether non-human animals are aware was raised earlier, with the suggestion that at some taxonomic level of nervous system simplicity animals are automatons, responding in the same manner as a thermostat or similar device that reacts to an input without awareness or even behavioral flexibility. But even though we humans are inclined to place our cognitive functions on a plane well above the rest of the animal kingdom, it would be unreasonable to assume that we alone possess the biologically useful ability to be aware of the world. Awareness of present circumstances, and the consequent ability to react flexibly in light of specific goals, desires, and plans is an enormous advantage that the evolution of nervous systems would certainly have generated within the limits of constraints such brain size and the other demands on neural circuitry for a given species (see Chapter 26). Whereas mammals with small, simple brains presumably have rudimentary awareness, animals with brains of substantial size with extensive neocortices organized much like ours (**Figure 28.4**) would be expected to have a roughly similar degree of awareness of the world.

From a strictly a logical vantage point, of course, it is impossible to know whether *any* being other than one's own self is subjectively aware. This impasse is called "the problem of other minds." As philosophers like Alfred J. Ayer and computer scientists like Alan Turing have emphasized, we must inevitably take the consciousness of others on faith, or at least on the basis of empirical observations (thus the famous "Turing test" for distinguishing human from artificial intelligence; see the next section). By the same token, it is possible to take the philosophical position that even the most sophisticated human behavior could in principle occur without subjective awareness (after all, many or even most, complex human behaviors occur unconsciously), and that consciousness is an epiphenomenon without causal significance (see the discussion of free will below).

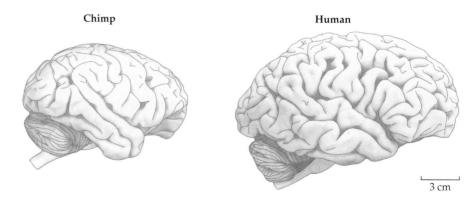

Figure 28.4 Awareness and brain size. Awareness of the world seems highly likely in animals such as chimpanzees, whose brains are organized very much like ours. In animals with smaller, less complex brains (e.g., rodents), awareness of the world is presumably limited, and absent altogether in species with a small number of neurons and no brains at all (e.g., invertebrates such as earthworms, whose nervous systems are simply chains of ganglia).

Chimp

Human

3 cm

A related question concerns not just whether some other species are aware of the world in roughly the same way we are, but whether they are aware of being a *self* in the world—an aspect of awareness that comes naturally to humans. As described in discussing theory of mind in Chapter 19, the significance of self-awareness is the ability to react to the motives of others based on an awareness of the motives and goals of oneself. Older evidence for self-awareness in other species was based largely on a **mirror test** devised in 1970 by psychologist Gordon Gallup, now at the University of Albany. In this paradigm, chimpanzees were allowed to see themselves in a full-length mirror. At first the chimps seemed to regard their mirror images as other chimps, as indicated by their performance of characteristic social displays (dogs and cats are said to show the same sort of reaction). After some days, however, Gallup reported that the chimps' behavior changed: the social displays stopped and they tended to groom themselves on the body parts apparent in the image. In a further step, Gallup placed a dye mark on the chimps' foreheads, where it could be seen only in the mirror. Whereas the animals rarely touched that spot on themselves otherwise, when they saw the mark in the mirror they touched it repeatedly. More recent work by Marc Hauser and colleagues, however, showed that some primates reported as having failed the mirror test in fact passed it, and questions have been raised about the validity of this general approach to evaluating self-awareness. Other investigators have argued that the level of frustration shown by rhesus monkeys in memory tests suggests an awareness of whether or not they know something. This phenomenon, called **metacognition**, has also been taken as an indication of of self-awareness in at least some non-human primates.

Although the challenge of demonstrating self-awareness is substantial and the evidence for this cognitive property in other primates is thus weak, it seems likely that consciousness in the sense of awareness of self is indeed present in non-human animals whose brains are organized much like ours, and whose social behavior would benefit from an awareness of being a self among other selves.

Can Machines Be Conscious?

A question that has long intrigued modern thinkers is whether awareness and self-awareness are inherently biological properties, or whether non-biological machines might someday incorporate these functions. Although a *machine* can be defined as any purposefully designed structure, for present purposes a machine means a computer or other information-processing device. The issue is thus whether such machines could, at some future time, be considered to have the property we call consciousness.

In principle at least, the answer to this question is yes. If one agrees, as virtually all contemporary neuroscientists do, that biological nervous systems and their elements operate according to the laws of chemistry and physics, then the human brain clearly falls into the category of a machine, albeit one made out of rather special parts (see Chapter 1 and the Appendix). If one rejects dualism—the Cartesian proposition that consciousness is not based on physical phenomena and is therefore beyond the ken of the rules that govern the behavior of matter—it follows that a structure could eventually be built that either mimicked our own awareness by being functionally isomorphic with the human brain, or that used physically different elements (e.g., the elements of digital computers) in sufficiently similar ways to allow awareness of the world and self (whatever the latter word might mean in this scenario). Thus the question really boils down to the issue of whether computers and computer scientists will ever be up to the task of such functional replication.

Despite the inexorable advance of computer science, this perspective tends to transform the question of machine awareness into a philosophical debate, and a number philosophers have joined it with gusto. Examples of philosophers whose ideas on this subject have been influential are Patricia and Paul Churchland at the University of California at San Diego, Daniel Dennett at Tufts University, and John Searle at Berkeley. An extreme position in this debate was famously proclaimed by the computer scientist John McCarthy, who argued that because the operations of computers as we know them today in some ways resemble mental processes, they can already be considered to have the rudiments of awareness. An equally famous argument that could be used to argue the other side of this issue is Searle's "Chinese Room" analogy, which emphasizes that the output of a machine does not necessarily indicate its internal workings or properties (e.g., its possible awareness). Searle describes a cubicle in which an English-speaking worker is given disordered Chinese symbols, which he then deals with according to a book of instructions in English. The person working in the room has no knowledge of Chinese; he simply manipulates symbols according to a set of rules (**Figure 28.5**). Although the output of the room is sensible statements in Chinese that duly impress external observers, the worker is oblivious to the meaning of the information he is dealing with and to the room's larger purpose. Although it should be noted that this analogy was initially devised to deal with other philosophical concerns, it makes clear that meaningful output does not provide unimpeachable evidence of consciousness or any other cognitive function.

What, then, would be needed to make a computer aware and/or self-aware? Or, to put the question another way, what are the essential features of animal brains underpinning these cognitive properties that computers today lack? One feature is the extraordinary interconnectedness of the components of the human brain, which supports recurrent activity as different regions of the brain communicate back and forth (recall from earlier chapters that the brain is in a state of continual activity, and that the overall activity level changes only modestly and in specific regions when we respond to a stimulus or carry out a specific task). Such ongoing back-and-forth signaling in brain circuits is referred to as **recursive processing** (*reentrant* or *reciprocal processing* are closely related terms). Recursive processing encompasses the sort of iterat-

Figure 28.5 Searle's Chinese room analogy. An English-speaking worker in a closed room manipulates symbols according to rules laid down in a manual, thus producing a narrative in Chinese that is intelligible (even highly impressive) to an external observer. The worker has no idea of the meaning of the symbols and is ignorant of the room's purpose, but the observer makes an incorrect inference and assumes cognizance of meaning and purpose on the part of the worker.

ed interactions that would presumably allow a brain or other information processing system to assess and reflect on its content.

Human brains differ from computers in their current form with respect to these characteristics: thus without input a computer's circuits are quiescent, and processing in one program does not typically affect another. For example, the word-processing program on your laptop does not interact with the graphics software, and vice versa. It seems reasonable to suppose that it is the ongoing activity and interconnectedness of the circuit loops in the human brain that allow us to consider circumstances, contexts, and contingencies, whether in terms of the present (perception), past (memory), or future (planning and decision making). The evolution of such circuitry and the recurrent activity it supports is arguably essential to awareness. Relatively simple animals (and computers in most current applications) have little or no need for the reflective abilities that such recursion allows. However, as animal nervous systems and the behavior they support become more complex, the ability to reflect more globally on the past, present, and future yields increasing benefits. At some point in their evolution, particularly as they interface with robotic devices, it seems likely that computers will also benefit from such reflection, and for the same general reasons. When they do, machines will be a step closer to doing what brains do and, in principle at least, nothing seems to stand in the way of this direction of development.

If computers eventually incorporate circuitry that allows them reflect on present and past experience and to extrapolate about the future, how will we (or could we) know that the machine has become aware? This question brings up the dilemma already mentioned: there is no way to be certain that another human other than ourselves is conscious, let alone a machine. More than 50 years ago, the computer scientist Alan Turing described what has come to be called the **Turing test**, an approach to this problem based on detailed interrogation. Turing asserted that if human judges could not discern by answers to their most challenging questions whether they were interacting with another human being or with a computer, then there would be no reason to withhold the attribution of consciousness to the machine answering the questions. Some programs already in operation allow computers to do fairly well by this criterion. But, as in the case of humans judging other humans, only the machine itself could know with certainty that it was conscious. At some time in the future the sophistication of computational devices may well force us to assume that a non-biological machine is truly aware, just as we now make that assumption when we interact with other people, and for much the same pragmatic reasons.

How Might Consciousness Have Evolved?

If awareness and self-awareness depend on brains (or machines) whose high degree of interconnectedness supports ongoing recurrent activity, how might these properties have evolved? In addition to the issues discussed in Chapter 26, the question of how such recursive circuitry might have evolved is informed by a long-standing debate in computer science. Modern computation began with, and is still largely based on, sequential operations that are formally specified in programming code. This approach was first implemented in nineteenth-century mechanical devices such as Charles Babbage's remarkable "analytical engine" (**Figure 28.6**), and ultimately in the hardware and software that enable today's computers to solve increasingly complex rule-based problems. In most applications, computer programs instruct the machine's hardware to carry out a sequence of logically defined steps to answer problems that have already been solved in principle by the program-

Figure 28.6 Charles Babbage's analytical engine. Babbage first designed this machine in 1837 and continued to improve it until his death in 1871. He is generally credited with pioneering the implementation of computational devices. This mechanical predecessor of electronic computers, which was designed to run on a version of what today would be called an assembler programming language, is instructive in that its visible parts convey the sequential and inflexible nature of traditional computation.

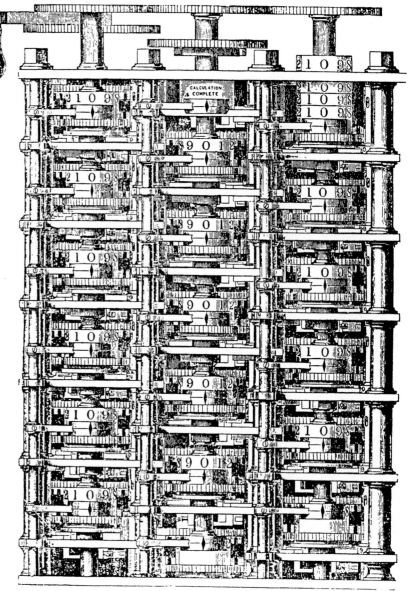

B. H. Babbage, del.

mer. As a result, the route to the solution of the vast majority of the challenges that computers deal with, from word processing to graphics to accounting, can be (indeed, are) laid out a priori. The enormous success of this general approach hardly needs to be emphasized, although all users of computers are well aware of the frustrating literalism of this style of operation.

Whatever the merits of analogies between information processing in the brains and digital computers, it is obvious that the operations of biological brains are not engineered in the rigid, rule-based style of Babbage's device or most modern computers and the programs they run. There is, however, another way that computers can solve complex problems that may be important in eventually understanding the sort of recursive activity and connectivity needed for awareness, and perhaps how and why these characteristics evolved in animal brains. Psychologist Warren McCulloch and logician Walter Pitts, two highly creative thinkers working at MIT in the early 1940s, were the

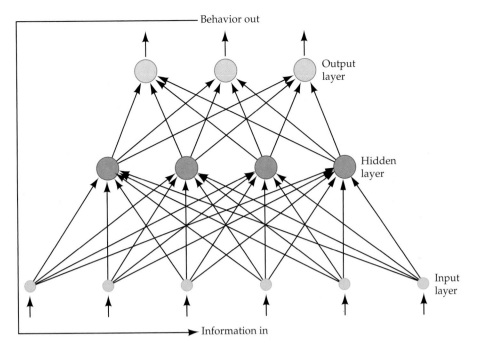

Behavior out

Output layer

Hidden layer

Input layer

Information in

Figure 28.7 A simple neural network. A typical artificial neural network comprises an input layer, an output layer, and a "hidden" layer. The common denominator of this and other far more complex artificial neural network architectures is a richly interconnected system of nodes or "neurons"; the system is programmed such that the strengths of the connections between the nodes are progressively changed according to the results of the trial and error responses of the output. The result is that the initially random connectivity of the system is gradually changed by feedback as the network deals more and more successfully with the task it has been given. The connectivity of the network that emerges is not readily predictable, nor is the way the network has solved a problem easily dissected. The network's operation may reduce to a logical algorithm if the problem is a simple one. But if the problem is very complex, the causal steps involved in solving it may be undecipherable, and would be uninformative in any practical sense even if they could be deciphered.

first to point out this alternative approach to computation. Rather than depending on a series of predetermined steps that dictate each operation, McCulloch and Pitts suggested that problems might also be solved by computing devices made up of units ("neurons" in their biologically inspired terminology) whose interconnections in a network could progressively change according to feedback about the success (or failure) of the network in dealing with the problem at hand (**Figure 28.7**).

The key attribute of such systems (which came to be called **artificial neural networks**, or just **neural nets**) is their ability to solve a problem without a priori knowledge of the answer, the steps needed to reach it, or even a clear conception on the part of the programmer about how the problem *might* be solved in some rational way. In effect, neural nets generate solutions by trial and error, gradually generating more and more useful responses according to operational success. As a result, the architecture of the trained network (arguably analogous to an evolved or trained neural circuit) is effectively a result of the network's history—i.e., its experience.

Understanding the relevant processing by analyzing the connectivity of the machine after training in logical terms is difficult in practice, making neural networks unappealing to many computer scientists. Because the operation of such systems is not easily reduced to a series of logical steps that make sense in human terms, and because the training is empirical, it is sometimes said that using a neural network to deal with any given problem is always the "second-best solution." For some types of problems, however, an empirical solution may be the only viable avenue (consider, for instance, the quandary posed by inverse problem in vision, which appears to have led to the empirical perceptual strategies described in Unit II).

A further extension of this empirical approach to computation has been to "evolve" neural networks in virtual environments. This approach employs **genetic algorithms** that mimic the biology of gene replication, mutation, and recombination (**Figure 28.8**). In this scheme, a population of artificial neural networks representing virtual organisms gradually changes by the selection and reproduction of those networks that perform better by criteria of behavioral success in a computer-simulated environment. Random changes in the structure and function of connectivity of "ancestral forms" persists or not in

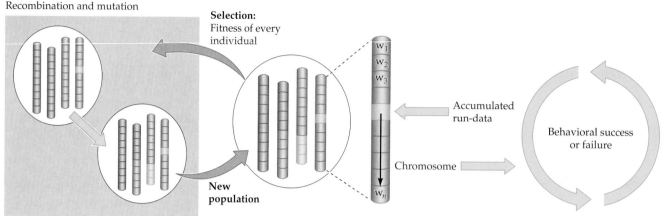

Reproduction
Recombination and mutation

Selection:
Fitness of every individual

w_1
w_2
w_3

Accumulated run-data

Chromosome

Behavioral success or failure

New population

w_n

Figure 28.8   Using genetic algorithms to evolve neural networks. The weights of the connections in a neural network (see Figure 28.7) can be modeled as genes that mutate. These random changes lead to corresponding changes in the behavior of the network, which can then be selected for according to behavioral success in a virtual environment.

the descendants, according to their operational success. This scheme continually updates the network circuitry according to the empirical success or failure of the behavior it produces. As a result, configurations of neural circuitry that better exemplify behavioral success wax in the evolving networks, whereas circuit configurations that are less useful wane.

This approach is particularly pertinent to the evolution of neuronal networks that could reflect on their content through the evolution of recursive operations. Natural selection is the major force that has instantiated the recursive brain wiring that presumably supports human awareness. If the ability of an organism to reflect on the content of the information it is processing is indeed the advantage it seems to be in the natural world, then this property might be expected to gradually emerge when sufficiently complex artificial neural networks were allowed to "evolve" in environments realistic enough to make awareness a valuable asset.

Despite the highly speculative nature of these considerations, it is at least possible to imagine ways that awareness could have evolved; and articulating the way human consciousness presumably evolved could be useful in creating similar properties in non-biological information processing systems.

Some General Issues Raised by Studies of Consciousness

As cognitive neuroscientists have become increasingly thoughtful about the neural basis of awareness, some long held perspectives about human cognitive functions have begun to change. One arena of change concerns the idea that cognitive functions operate on the basis of a processing hierarchy. As discussed in Unit II, a traditional perspective has been that environmental stimuli generate "sense data" at the level of sensory receptors (the "bottom" of the bottom-up conception of sensory processing), and that this information then ascends (the "up" in bottom-up) through stages of further processing to higher-order regions of the cerebral cortex (the "top" in the top-down notion of cortical influences). In this view, percepts, together with whatever further cortical activity they elicit (e.g., memories, emotions, desires, etc.), then influence lower stations in the nervous system (the "down" in top-down). This traditional conceptualization of neural processing is attractive because the relevant signaling events obviously begin in the periphery, travel centrally, are to some degree sequential, and have widespread influences in the brain. However, this scheme can also be misleading. As noted here and in earlier accounts of perception and attention (see Chapters 4, 5, and 10), there is no evidence that awareness is the province of any particular cortical locus or mechanism, or that any given station in a sensory pathway is less important in the generation of awareness than any other. Awareness of the world and the self evidently depends on the integrated operation of multiple elements in neural networks, sensory and otherwise, and should not be thought of as representing the apex of a processing hierarchy.

A second concern is that most studies of awareness depend on evidence derived from sensory perception, typically visual perception. Would the same arguments hold for awareness generated by neural systems that process information related to thoughts, feelings, memories, and desires? Although even the most abstract thought is arguably based on sensory input at some level, the links may be so remote as to render the influence of sensory stimuli difficult or impossible to discern. Since we are clearly aware of these other categories of non-sensory mental content, the question of whether they can be assumed to have the same basis as our awareness of sensory percepts cannot be avoided. It seems likely that awareness of these further categories of mental content ("mind") will lead to the same conclusions derived from paradigms based on awareness of sensory stimuli, but this remains to be shown. The neural correlates of the awareness of mental content that is not primarily sensory has been little studied. Remedying this gap in knowledge is likely to have an increasing influence on the direction of research on the neural basis of awareness.

A third concern is sorting out the differences, if any, between awareness and attention. In Unit IV, attention was considered as a separate cognitive function governed by controlling networks defined primarily on the basis of sensory paradigms. But how does *attending* to a sensory stimulus differ from being *aware* of it? One answer might be couched in terms of an active versus a passive process: we think of awareness as a sort of default condition of wakefulness, whereas attention is often thought of as requiring an active focus or "searchlight." Recall, however, that outside the laboratory attention is more often driven by ongoing events than any voluntary process in response to an explicit instruction, whether external or internal (see Chapter 10). It could be argued that attention is simply another word for awareness, or at least the two are heavily intertwined. If this is so, then conceptualizations of attention will have to address the concerns about awareness and its neural correlates discussed in this chapter.

Finally, the apparent absence of loci or neural processes specific to awareness raises the question of how the things we can be aware of (sensory percepts, feelings, abstract thoughts, memories etc.) are actually *represented* in the brain. Although this question has come up in the more restricted contexts of previous chapters, it is worth considering in general terms here. It has long been accepted that the activity of some subset of neural circuitry is the basis of any mental content. Thus all neural representations are definable in terms of the relative activity of populations of nerve cells. Historically, the inclination of neuroscientists has been to imagine that representation in the brain rests on the activity of small neuronal populations. Indeed, even within the last few decades the concept of a "grandmother cell"—the notion that the representation of a specific object such as a person's grandmother might reside in one or a few highly specialized cortical neurons—has been seriously considered.

Although the grandmother cell concept is now dismissed as both naïve and inconsistent with present evidence, the concept that percepts, feelings, thoughts, and memories are represented by the activity of relatively small, specialized nerve cell populations remains the conventional wisdom for many neuroscientists. From the evidence discussed here and in other chapters, however, it seems more likely that the representation of specific objects or any other mental content we are aware of at a given moment entails neural activity in multiple brain regions, and that this activity is influenced—directly or indirectly—by the activity at the same moment of much of the rest of the nervous system. This conclusion derives from the extensive range of different qualities that we attribute to or associate with even the simplest object or thought, and the enormous interconnectedness of any brain region. Objects or other mental content are thus inevitably represented by varying degrees of activity in large populations of neurons distributed throughout the brain. A corollary is that, far from being grandmother cells, each of the cortical and subcortical neurons involved in cognitive functions contributes to a great many different representations of the sorts of things we can be aware of.

What Does it Mean to Be Human?

In light of all the topics discussed in this unit, a final question is, "What does it mean to be human?" In the not-too-distant past, the answer would have been predicated on the notion that many of the cognitive properties seen in humans are lacking in other animals. These missing attributes, depending on the discipline and/or biases of the scholar making such a pronouncement, might have included consciousness in the sense of awareness; a sense of self-awareness; and a variety of more specific functions such as language, the ability to reason, and a sense of right and wrong (i.e., morality). As neuroscience (and biology generally) has become more sophisticated, these and other cognitive abilities taken to be uniquely human have become fewer and fewer. Thus, antecedents of language and the rudiments of culture are well established in some other species (see Unit VII), higher apes and some other animals are capable of limited reasoning and problem solving (see Unit VIII), and there is evidence for awareness and self-awareness in a variety of species. Indeed, there is no compelling reason for concluding that other animals with brains much like ours lack any of the attributes believed in centuries or even decades past to distinguish *Homo sapiens* from all other species. The differences between ourselves and our fellow animals seem more and more to be a matter of degree (admittedly quite large in some instances) than of kind.

One cognitive property that many would still argue is uniquely human, however, is the sense that our conscious decisions and subsequent actions are self-determined, signifying *free will*. Since legal codes and penal systems are based on the idea that a mentally healthy person's actions are freely made, this issue is of fundamental importance in human societies and social contracts. Could free will, then, be the touchstone of humanity?

Although a subjective sense of freedom might well be unique to our species, Harvard psychologist Daniel Wegner and others have argued that free will is simply a chimera. The problem with the conviction that we freely make decisions is the implication that at least some aspects of brain function are governed by an entity (sometimes derisively referred to as a *homunculus*, or "little man") that is independent of the causal chains of events that determine any other physical behavior. Skeptics like Wegner rightly ask what is really meant when we postulate a "self" that makes decisions, and how choices thought to be "freely made" could be any different from the "choices" being made by the nervous system all the time about homeostatic or other unconscious neural functions that we accept as arising from more primitive "reflexive" neural processing. When the nervous system responds to sensory input and "decides" to adjust blood pressure or heart rate to some new level based on highly complex circumstances, we don't think of the resulting physiological behavior as the consequence of a decision in the usual sense, let alone one that involves free will; it is simply the result of a complex causal chain involving sensory receptors that provide information that the cardiovascular system needs to adapt to altered conditions. It is difficult to escape the conclusion that if we accept the concept of free will, we must do so on the basis of belief, or a pragmatic sense of its utility in social contracts, rather than evidence for it in any aspect of brain function.

A closely related issue is how to define the difference between *voluntary* and *involuntary* behavior. As a context for thinking about this question, consider the neural basis of a voluntary (willed) action that we have in some sense "decided" to carry out that can also occur as an involuntary reflex— for example, voluntary extension of the leg compared to the involuntary "knee-jerk reaction" described in Chapter 1. The input to the spinal motor neurons that causes the extension in the knee-jerk reflex is relatively well understood although, as pointed out in Unit III, a great deal of complex higher-order control of motor circuitry is involved in this or any sort of motor response. The input to the relevant spinal motor neurons in voluntary extension of the leg is also a product of a causal linkage from stimulus to response, although the stimulus in this case is less immediate and may be difficult to discern. For instance, the stimulus arising from seeing a ball might trigger neural activity that represented the awareness of the reward (pleasure) that would be derived from kicking it, and this activity might in turn trigger a decision to extend the leg to reap the reward by actually kicking the ball. Further obscuring the causal chain underlying such voluntary actions is that part or all of the process is often unconscious: a person might kick the ball but be unaware of the underlying motivation because they were thinking of something else.

Although long, complex, and often unconscious causal chains between stimulus and response can lead to voluntary leg extension or some other act, there is no getting around the fact that a causal chain of neural linkages always underlies a voluntary behavior. From this perspective, actions we think of as voluntary are as determined as the knee jerk elicited by the physician's reflex hammer. The difference seems again to be a matter of degree rather than kind, degree in this case referring to the immediacy and obviousness of the relevant causal chain. Perhaps our deeply rooted sense of a higher-order self that freely determines our most important actions has arisen from the undeniable evolutionary advantages that accrue to a species like ours whose individual members have a strong sense of personal responsibility.

To sum up the difficult and contentious issues considered in this chapter, it may be that the question "What is consciousness?" will fade from the preeminence it has had for so long, much in the way the question "What is life?"—a question natural scientists considered paramount until quite recently—is no longer asked by biologists. As knowledge about the cellular and molecular bases of living organisms increased exponentially over the course of the twentieth century, biologists came to recognize that "What is life?" is an ill-posed question and admits no definitive answer. As the present century progresses and cognitive neuroscientists learn more and more about the detailed ways in which the human brain works, the question "What is consciousness?" may well meet the same fate. In any event, recognition that the human brain and its cognitive properties are no more and no less amenable to explanation than any other aspect of biology should eventually lead us to a clearer and healthier understanding of our place in the universe, as well as to a better understanding of cognitive neuroscience.

Summary

1. This chapter has considered a series of controversial issues whose common denominator is consciousness, and what this phenomenon tells us about the nature of the human brain.

2. Although these issues will be debated for many years to come, the thrust of present evidence is that consciousness, both as awareness of the world and awareness of the self as an actor in the world, is not a special feature of *Homo sapiens*, or even a property that will always be limited to brains as we know them in biology.

3. The evidence so far has not succeeded in identifying any specific signature or locus of awareness, nor has it suggested any new principle or neural mechanism for consciousness.

4. The output of an information processing system that is capable of reflecting on its content in the way that we reflect on the past, present, and future would be difficult or impossible to distinguish from the behavioral output of another human being.

5. Since, as a logical proposition, we can only be certain that we ourselves are conscious, there would be no reason in principle to withhold the assumption of awareness from a non-biological information processing system that eventually operated like the human brain.

Additional Reading

Reviews

CHURCHLAND, P. M. AND P. S. CHURCHLAND (1990) Could a machine think? *Sci. Am.* 262(Jan.): 32–37.

CRICK, F. AND C. KOCH (1998) Consciousness and neuroscience. *Cerebral Cortex* 8: 97–107.

HAMPTON, R. R. AND B. M. HEMPSTEAD (2006) Spontaneous behavior of a rhesus monkey (*Macaca mulatta*) during memory tests suggests memory awareness. *Behav. Proc.* 72: 184–189.

HANNULA, D. E., D. J. SIMONS AND N.J. COHEN (2005) Imaging implicit perception: Promise and pitfalls. *Nat. Rev. Neurosci.* 6: 247–255.

KIM, C. H. AND R. BLAKE (2005) Psychophysical magic: Rendering the visible "invisible." *Trends Cogn. Sci.* 9: 381–388.

LLINÁS, R., U. RIBARY, D. CONTRERAS AND C. PEDROARENA (1998) The neuronal basis for consciousness. *Philos. Trans. R. Soc. Lond. B* 353: 1841–1849.

MCCARLEY, R. W. (1995) Sleep, dreams and states of consciousness. In *Neuroscience in Medicine*, P. M. Conn (ed.). Philadelphia: J. B. Lippincott, pp. 535–554.

REES, G., G. KREIMAN AND C. KOCH (2002) Neural correlates of consciousness in humans. *Nat. Rev. Neurosci.* 3: 261–270.

SAPER, C. B. AND F. PLUM (1985) Disorders of consciousness. In *Handbook of Clinical Neurology*, Volume 1(45): *Clinical Neuropsychology*, J. A. M. Frederiks (ed.).

Amsterdam: Elsevier Science, pp. 107–128.

SEARLE, J. R. (2000) Consciousness. *Annu. Rev. Neurosci.* 23: 557–578.

SMITH, J. D. AND D. A. WASHBURN (2005) Uncertainty monitoring and metacognition by animals. *Curr. Dir. Psycholog. Sci.* 14: 19–24.

STERIADE, M. (1992) Basic mechanisms of sleep generation. *Neurology* 42: 9–18.

STOERIG, P. AND A. COWEY (1997) Blindsight in man and monkey. *Brain* 120: 535–559.

TONG, F. (2004) Primary visual cortex and visual awareness. *Nat. Rev. Neurosci.* 4: 219–228.

TONONI, G. AND G. EDELMAN (1998) Consciousness and complexity. *Science* 282: 1846–1851.

Important Original Papers

ASCHOFF, J. (1965) Circadian rhythms in man. *Science* 148: 1427–1432.

ASERINSKY, E. AND N. KLEITMAN (1953) Regularly occurring periods of eye motility, and concomitant phenomena during sleep. *Science* 118: 273–274.

BOYER, J. L., S. HARRISON AND T. RO (2005) Unconscious processing of orientation and color without primary visual cortex. *Proc. Natl. Acad. Sci. USA* 102: 16875–16879.

GALLUP, G. G. (1970) Chimpanzees: Self–recognition. *Science* 167: 86–87.

HAUSER, M. D. (1995) Self-recognition in primates: Phylogeny and the salience of species-typical features. *Proc. Natl. Acad. Sci. USA* 92: 10811–10814.

HAUSER, M. D. AND J. KRALIK (1997) Life beyond the mirror: A reply to Anderson and Gallup. *Anim. Behav.* 54: 1568–1571.

LEE, S.-H., R. BLAKE AND D. J. HEEGER (2005) Traveling waves of activity in early visual cortex during binocular rivalry. *Nat. Neurosci.* 8: 22–23.

MCCULLOCH, W. S. AND W. PITTS (1943) A logical calculus of the ideas immanent in nervous activity. *Bull. Math. Biophys.* 5: 115–133.

MORUZZI, G. AND H. W. MAGOUN (1949) Brain stem reticular formation and activation of the EEG. *Electroenceph. Clin. Neurophysiol.* 1: 455–473.

OWEN, A. M., M. R. COLEMAN, M. BOLY, M. H. DAVIS, S. LAUREYS AND J. D. PICKARD (2006) Detecting awareness in the vegetative state. *Science* 313: 1402.

TURING, A. (1950) Computing machinery and intelligence. *Mind* 59: 433–460.

WEIR, A. A. S., B. KENWOOD, B. CHAPPELL AND A. KACELNIK (2002) Shaping of hooks in New Caledonian crows. *Science* 297: 981.

Books

CRICK, F. (1995) *The Astonishing Hypothesis: The Scientific Search for the Soul.* New York: Touchstone.

DENNETT, D. C. (1991) *Consciousness Explained.* Boston: Little, Brown & Co.

PENROSE, R. (1996) *Shadows of the Mind: A Search for the Missing Science of Consciousness.* Oxford: Oxford University Press.

SEARLE, J. R. (1992) *The Rediscovery of the Mind*. Cambridge, MA: MIT Press.

SCHRÖDINGER, E. (1967) *What Is Life?* and *Mind and Matter*. Cambridge: Cambridge University Press.

WEGNER, D. M. (2002) *The Illusion of Conscious Will*. Cambridge, MA: MIT Press.

WEISKRANTZ, L. (1986) *Blindsight: A Case Study and Its Implications*. Oxford: Oxford University Press.

WEISKRANTZ, L. (1997) *Consciousness Lost and Found: A Neuropsychological Explanation*. Oxford: Oxford University Press.

Appendix | *Neural Signaling*

Overview

Nerve cells generate electrical signals that transmit information. Although they are not intrinsically good conductors of electricity, elaborate mechanisms for generating these signals have evolved in neurons based on the flow of ions across their plasma membranes. Ordinarily, neurons generate a negative potential called the resting membrane potential that can be measured by recording the voltage between the inside and outside of nerve cells. The action potential is the fundamental signal that carries information from one place to another in the nervous system; action potentials transiently abolish the negative resting potential, briefly rendering the transmembrane potential positive. For most nerve cells, this occurs by means of a rapid rise in sodium ion (Na^+) permeability, followed by a slower but more prolonged rise in potassium ion (K^+) permeability. Both permeabilities are voltage-dependent, increasing as the membrane potential depolarizes; however, the Na^+ permeability increase is rapidly inactivated and thus short-lived. These same ionic mechanisms permit action potentials to be propagated along the length of neuronal axons, explaining how electrical signals are conveyed along the nerves of the body and within the brain and spinal cord.

The generation of electrical signals requires that neuronal plasma membranes establish concentration gradients for specific ions and that these membranes undergo rapid and selective changes in the membrane permeability to these ions. The membrane proteins that generate ion gradients are called active transporters, whereas other proteins called ion channels give rise to selective ion permeability changes. Thus, transporters create the concentration gradients that help drive ion fluxes through open ion channels, generating the electrical signals of nerve cells.

Appendix by Leonard E. White and George Augustine
Adapted from the Fourth Edition of *Neuroscience* (Purves et al. 2008)

Communication among nerve cells or between nerve cells and effector tissues is facilitated by synapses, which are the functional contacts between excitable cells. Two categories of synapses—electrical and chemical—can be distinguished on the basis of their mechanism of transmission. At electrical synapses, current flows through gap junctions, which are specialized membrane channels that connect two cells. In contrast, chemical synapses enable cell-to-cell communication via the secretion of neurotransmitters; these chemical agents released by the presynaptic neurons produce secondary current flow in postsynaptic neurons by activating specific receptor molecules. There are two major classes of receptors: those in which the receptor is part of an ion channel, and those in which the receptor and the ion channel are separate molecules. In addition to very rapid effects that alter postsynaptic excitability, neural signaling may also stimulate slower cascades of intracellular reactions involving GTP-binding proteins, second messenger molecules, protein kinases, ion channels, and many other effector proteins. The modulation of these signaling cascades temporarily changes the physiological state of the postsynaptic cell and the strength of its synaptic connections. These same intracellular signal transduction pathways can also cause longer-lasting changes by altering the transcription of genes, thus affecting the protein composition of target cells on a more permanent basis.

Electrical Potentials across Nerve Cell Membranes

Neurons employ several different types of electrical signal to encode and transfer information. When a microelectrode is inserted through the membrane of the neuron at rest, the microelectrode reports a negative potential, indicating that neurons have a means of generating a constant voltage across their membranes (see Box 1A). This voltage, called the **resting membrane potential**, depends on the type of neuron being examined, but it is always a fraction of a volt (typically in the –40 to –90 mV range). The electrical signals produced by neurons are caused by responses to stimuli, which then change the resting membrane potential.

For primary sensory neurons, **receptor potentials** are due to the activation of sensory neurons by external stimuli, including light, sound, heat, and self-generated stimuli such as the movements of our bodies (see Chapters 4–9). For example, touching the fingertip to a hard surface generates a brief receptor potential in underlying Pacinian corpuscles, which are the receptor terminals of one class of neurons that sense mechanical disturbances of the skin (**Figure A1A**).

Another type of electrical signal is associated with intercellular communication at **synapses**, which are specialized junctions between two individual neurons and between neurons and effector (e.g., muscle) tissues. Activation of synapses (discussed in detail below) generates **synaptic potentials**, which allow transmission of information from one neuron to another (**Figure A1B**). Synaptic potentials are the means of exchanging information in complex neural circuits in both the central and peripheral nervous systems. In addition, use-dependent modulation of synapses is thought to provide a cellular basis for learning and memory, as described in Chapter 13.

Both receptor potentials and synaptic potentials can trigger **action potentials**, the fundamental electrical signals by which information is passed from one location to another along the axons of nerve cells (**Figure A1C**). Thus, action potentials are the principal means by which electrical signals generated near the cell bodies of neurons are able to influence the synaptic contacts at the ends of axons, which, for many neurons, may be located a considerable distance away (nearly a meter for some spinal motor neurons). An action

(A) Receptor potential

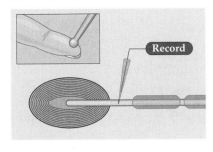

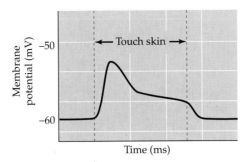

(B) Synaptic potential

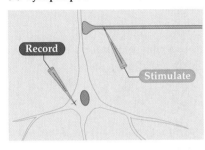

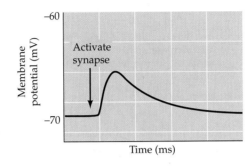

(C) Action potential

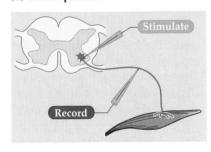

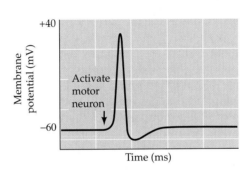

Figure A1 Types of electrical signals in neurons. In all cases, microelectrodes are used to measure changes in the resting membrane potential during the indicated signals. (A) A brief touch causes a receptor potential in a Pacinian corpuscle in the skin. (B) Activation of a synaptic contact onto a hippocampal pyramidal neuron elicits a synaptic potential. (C) Stimulation of a spinal motor neuron produces an action potential in the neuron's axon.

potential is the product of specialized proteins embedded in nerve cell membranes. The actions of these proteins result in the movement of electrically charged ions across the membranes, thus overcoming the relatively poor conductive properties of axons (as compared to, say, a copper wire). Thus, action potentials are critical for the production of observable behavior—requiring the activation of muscle by motor neurons—as well as the generation of thought, emotion, memory, and all the types of cognitive activity that become possible when networks of neurons in disparate brain structures interact with great speed and efficiency. Remarkably, all the electrical signals described above are produced by similar mechanisms that rely on the movement of ions across the neuronal membrane.

How Ion Movements Produce Electrical Signals

Electrical potentials are generated across the membranes of neurons—and, indeed, all cells—because (1) there are *differences in the concentrations* of specific ions across nerve cell membranes, and (2) the membranes are *selectively permeable* to some of these ions. These two facts depend in turn on two different kinds of proteins in the cell membrane (**Figure A2**).

Figure A2 Ion transporters and ion channels. (A) Transporter proteins embedded in the nerve cell membrane create ion concentration differences by actively transporting ions from one side of the membrane to the other against their concentration gradients. (B) Channel proteins take advantage of the concentration gradients established by active ion transport to allow selected ions to move across the membrane via passive diffusion (i.e., from the side of higher to the side of lower concentration). Together these two types of membrane proteins are responsible for the transmembrane traffic in ions that generates electrical impulses and results in neural signaling.

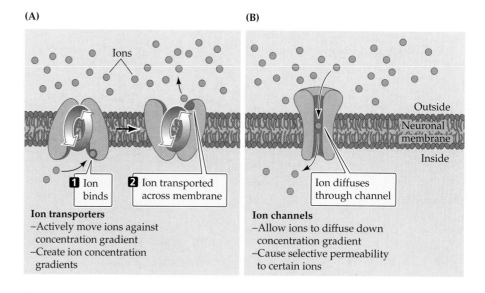

Differences in ion concentrations, or *concentration gradients*, are established by proteins known as **active transporters** that are embedded in the cell's membrane. As their name suggests, these proteins actively move ions into or out of cells against their concentration gradients. This "uphill" transport of ions requires the consumption of energy, and active transporters fall into two classes based on their energy sources. Some acquire energy directly from the hydrolysis of ATP and are called **ATPase pumps**, the most prominent example being the sodium/potassium pump, more accurately designated as the **Na⁺/K⁺ ATPase pump**, which is responsible for maintaining transmembrane concentration gradients for both Na^+ and K^+. The second class of active transporter does not use ATP directly, but depends instead on the electrochemical gradients of other ions as an energy source. This type of transporter carries one or more ions *up* its electrochemical gradient while simultaneously taking another ion (most often Na^+) *down* its gradient. Because at least two species of ions are involved in such transactions, these transporters are usually called **ion exchangers**.

The selective permeability of membranes is due largely to **ion channels**, a different class of membrane protein that allows only certain kinds of ions to cross the membrane in the direction of their concentration gradients (i.e., to flow from a region of higher concentration to a region of lower concentration). Thus active transporters gradually store energy in the form of ion concentration gradients, while the opening of ion channels uses and rapidly dissipates this stored energy. Relatively brief electrical signaling events are the net result. Thus, channels and transporters work against each other, and in so doing they generate the resting membrane potential, action potentials, and the synaptic potentials and receptor potentials that trigger action potentials.

Before considering the structure and function of membrane channels and pumps, consider a simple system in which an artificial membrane separates two compartments containing solutions of ions. In such a system, it is possible to determine the composition of the two solutions, and thereby control the ion gradients across the membrane. For example, take the case of a membrane that is permeable only to potassium ions (K^+). If the concentration of K^+ on each side of this membrane is equal, then no electrical potential is measurable across it (**Figure A3A**). However, if the concentration of K^+ on one side of the membrane (compartment 1) is 10 times higher than the K^+ concentration in

(A)

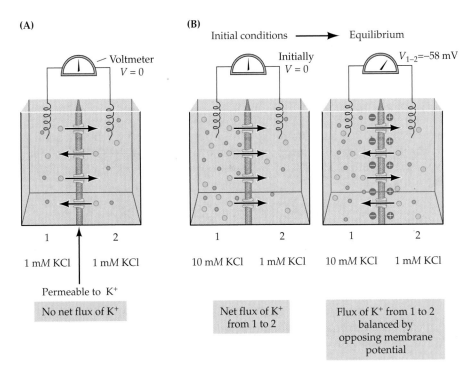

(B)

Initial conditions $\longrightarrow$ Equilibrium

Figure A3   Electrochemical equilibrium. (A) A membrane permeable only to K^+ (yellow spheres) separates compartments 1 and 2, shown here at an equilibrium concentration of potassium chloride (KCl; green spheres represent Cl^-). (B) Increasing the KCl concentration in compartment 1 to 10 mM initially causes a small movement of K^+ into compartment 2 until the electromotive force acting on K^+ balances the concentration gradient, and the net movement of K^+ becomes zero (i.e., reaches equilibrium).

compartment 2, K^+ ions will flow down their concentration gradient and take their electrical charge (one positive charge per ion) with them as they go, and the electrical potential of compartment 1 will become negative relative to compartment 2 (**Figure A3B**). Because neuronal membranes contain active transporters that accumulate K^+ in the cell cytoplasm, and because K^+-permeable channels in the plasma membrane allow a transmembrane flow of K^+, an analogous situation exists in living nerve cells. A continual efflux of K^+ is therefore responsible for the resting membrane potential.

In the hypothetical case just described, equilibrium is reached quickly. As K^+ moves from compartment 1 to compartment 2 (the left panel in Figure A3B), a potential is generated that tends to impede further flow of K^+. This impediment results from the fact that the potential gradient across the membrane tends to repel the positive K^+ that would otherwise move across the membrane. Thus, as compartment 2 becomes positive relative to compartment 1, the increasing positivity makes compartment 2 less attractive to the positively charged K^+. The net movement (or *flux*) of K^+ will stop at the point (equilibrium; right panel in Figure A3B) where the change in potential across the membrane (the relative positivity of compartment 2) exactly offsets the concentration gradient (the tenfold excess of K^+ in compartment 1). At this point, called **electrochemical equilibrium**, there is an exact balance between two opposing forces: (1) the concentration gradient that causes K^+ to move from compartment 1 to compartment 2; and (2) an opposing electrical gradient that increasingly tends to stop K^+ from moving across the membrane.

The number of ions that needs to flow to generate this electrical potential is very small, a fact that is significant in two ways. First, it means that the overall concentrations of permeant ions in the solutions on each side of the membrane remain essentially constant, even after the flow of ions has generated the resting potential. Second, the tiny fluxes of ions required to establish the membrane potential do not disrupt chemical electroneutrality because each ion has an oppositely charged counter-ion (chloride ions, Cl^-) to maintain the neutrality of the solutions on each side of the membrane (which is important for maintaining the integrity of the membrane and the functions of its associated proteins). The concentration of K⁺ remains equal to the concentration of chloride ions in the solutions in compartments 1 and 2 and the separation of charge that creates the potential difference is restricted to the immediate vicinity of the membrane.

The forces that create membrane potentials

The electrical potential generated across the membrane at electrochemical equilibrium, the **equilibrium potential**, can be predicted by a formula called the **Nernst equation**. With simplifying assumptions, this relationship may be expressed:

$$E_X = \frac{58}{z} \log \frac{[X]_2}{[X]_1}$$

where E_X is the equilibrium potential (in millivolts, mV) for any ion X, the value 58 is a constant derived from physical considerations that govern the behavior of molecules near room temperature, z is the valence (electrical charge) of the permeant ion (+1 in the case of K⁺), and the bracketed terms indicate the concentrations of ion X on each side of the membrane. Thus, for K⁺, the potential across the membrane at electrochemical equilibrium is –58 mV (i.e., $58 \times \log 1/10$). For such a simple hypothetical system with only one type of permeant ion, the Nernst equation allows the electrical potential across the membrane at equilibrium to be predicted exactly.

Now consider a somewhat more complex situation in which sodium and potassium ions, Na⁺ and K⁺, are unequally distributed across the membrane (**Figure A4A**). In this case the membrane potential would depend on the *relative permeability* of the membrane to both K⁺ and Na⁺. In Figure A4A, we see that solutions of 10 mM K⁺ and 1 mM Na⁺ are present in compartment 1, while compartment 2 holds 1 mM K⁺ and 10 mM Na⁺. If the membrane were permeable only to K⁺, the membrane potential would be –58 mV; if the membrane were permeable only to Na⁺, the potential predicted by the Nernst equation would be +58 mV. But what would the potential be if the membrane were permeable to *both* K⁺ and Na⁺? In this case, the potential would depend on the *relative permeability* of the membrane to K⁺ and Na⁺. If it were more permeable to K⁺, the potential would approach –58 mV, and if it were more permeable to Na⁺, the potential would be closer to +58 mV.

Because there is no permeability term in the Nernst equation, a more elaborate equation is needed that takes into account both the concentration gradients of the permeant ions and the relative permeability of the membrane to each permeant species. The **Goldman equation** accounts for the case most relevant to neurons, in which K⁺, Na⁺, and Cl⁻ are the primary permeant ions:

$$V = 58 \log \frac{P_K[K]_2 + P_{Na}[Na]_2 + P_{Cl}[Cl]_1}{P_K[K]_1 + P_{Na}[Na]_1 + P_{Cl}[Cl]_2}$$

In the Goldman equation, V is the voltage across the membrane and P indicates the permeability of the membrane to each ion of interest. The Goldman equation is thus an extended version of the Nernst equation that takes into account the relative permeabilities of each of the ions involved. It is important to note that the valence factor (z) has been eliminated; this is why the concentrations of negatively charged Cl⁻ have been inverted relative to the concentrations of the positively charged ions [remember that $-\log (A/B) = \log (B/A)$]. If the membrane in Figure A4A is permeable to K⁺ and Na⁺ only, the terms involving Cl⁻ drop out because P_{Cl} is 0. In this case, solution of the Goldman equation yields a potential of –58 mV when only K⁺ is permeant,

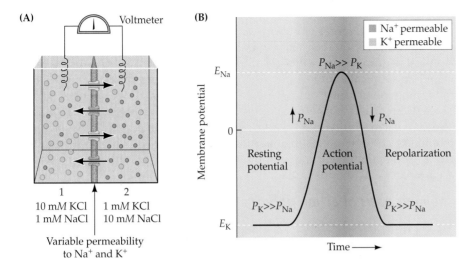

Figure A4 Resting and action potentials entail permeabilities to different ions. (A) Hypothetical situation in which a membrane variably permeable to Na⁺ (red) and K⁺ (yellow) separates two compartments that contain both ions. (For simplicity, Cl⁻ ions are not shown.) (B) At rest, neuronal membranes are more permeable to K⁺ (yellow) than to Na⁺ (red); accordingly, the resting membrane potential is negative and approaches the equilibrium potential for K⁺, E_K. During an action potential, the membrane briefly becomes very permeable to Na⁺ (red) and the membrane potential becomes positive, approaching the equilibrium potential for Na⁺, E_{Na}. The rise in Na⁺ permeability is transient, however, so that the membrane again becomes permeable primarily to K⁺ and the potential returns to its resting (negative) value.

+58 mV when only Na⁺ is permeant, and some intermediate value if both ions are permeant.

With respect to neural signaling, it is particularly pertinent to ask what would happen if the membrane started out being permeable to K⁺, and then temporarily switched to become most permeable to Na⁺. In this circumstance, the membrane potential would start out at a negative level, become positive while the Na⁺ permeability remained high, and then fall back to a negative level as the Na⁺ permeability decreased again. In fact, this scenario essentially describes what goes on in a neuron during the generation of an action potential.

In the resting state, P_K of the neuronal plasma membrane is much higher than P_{Na} and, as a result of the action of ion transporters, there is always more K⁺ inside the cell than outside. Taken together, these two facts account for the negative resting membrane potential (**Figure A4B**). As the membrane potential becomes more positive than the resting potential—an effect called **depolarization**—P_{Na} increases. The transient increase in Na⁺ permeability causes the membrane potential to become even more positive (the red region in Figure A4B), due to the inrushing Na⁺ (there is typically much more Na⁺ outside a neuron than inside, again as a result of ion pumps). Because of this positive feedback loop, an action potential occurs. The rise in Na⁺ permeability during the action potential is transient, however; as the membrane once again becomes more permeable to K⁺ than Na⁺, the membrane potential quickly returns to its resting level.

Armed with an appreciation of these simple electrochemical principles, it will be much easier to understand the following more detailed account of how neurons generate both resting potentials and action potentials.

The ionic basis of the resting membrane potential

The action of ion transporters creates substantial transmembrane gradients for most ions. **Table A1** summarizes the ion concentrations found in typical mammalian neurons. Such ion concentration data provide the basis for stating that there is much more K⁺ inside the neuron than out, and much more Na⁺ outside than in. These transporter-dependent concentration gradients of permeant ions are, indirectly, the source of the resting neuronal membrane potential and the action potential.

■ TABLE A1 Ion Concentrations in a Typical Mammalian Neuron

Ion	Concentration (m*M*)	
	Inside cell	Outside cell
Potassium (K⁺)	140	5
Sodium (Na⁺)	5–15	145
Chloride (Cl⁻)	4–30	110
Calcium (Ca²⁺)	0.0001	1–2

Once the ion concentration gradients across various neuronal membranes are known, the Nernst equation can be used to calculate the equilibrium potential for K^+ and other major ions. Since the resting membrane potential of a typical neuron is approximately –65 mV, K^+ is the ion that is closest to being in electrochemical equilibrium when the cell is at rest. This fact implies that the resting membrane is more permeable to K^+ than to the other ions listed in Table A1, and that this permeability is the source of the resting potential. The selective permeability to K^+ is caused by K^+-permeable membrane channels that tend to be open in resting neurons, and the large K^+ concentration gradient is, as noted above, produced by membrane transporters that selectively accumulate K^+ within neurons.

The ionic basis of action potentials

What causes the membrane potential of a neuron to depolarize during an action potential? Although a general answer to this question has been given (i.e., increased permeability to Na^+), it is well worth examining this change in membrane permeability to Na^+ in more detail.

Given the data presented in Table A1, one can use the Nernst equation to calculate the equilibrium potential for Na^+ (E_{Na}). If the membrane were to become highly permeable to Na^+, the membrane potential would approach a positive value. Based on this consideration (and a series of seminal experimental findings), we know that the action potential arises because the neuronal membrane becomes temporarily permeable to Na^+. Thus, the resting neuronal membrane is only slightly permeable to Na^+, but it becomes extraordinarily permeable to Na^+ during the **rising phase** and the **overshoot phase** of the action potential (when the membrane potential "overshoots" 0 mV and becomes positive). This temporary increase in Na^+ permeability results from the *voltage-dependent activation* (opening) of Na^+-selective channels that are essentially closed in the resting state (**Figure A5**). When the Na^+ channels activate, Na^+ flows into the neuron—down its concentration gradient—causing the membrane potential to depolarize and approach E_{Na}.

The time that the membrane potential lingers near E_{Na} (about +58 mV) during the overshoot phase of an action potential is extremely brief because the increased membrane permeability to Na^+ is short-lived. This is because the Na^+-selective channels quickly *inactivate*, thereby limiting the duration of Na^+ influx to a fraction of a millisecond. Na^+ channel inactivation is explained by the closure of a molecular *inactivation gate* on the cytoplasmic side of the channel. As the neuron depolarizes during the rising phase, the accumulation of positive charge along the inner surface of the neuronal plasma membrane repels the normal positive charge on this molecular structure (which is an extension of the Na^+-selective channel itself). This electrorepulsive force pushes the inactivation gate into the pore of the channel, effectively plugging the channel and preventing further flux of Na^+ (see Figure A5).

During the rising phase of the action potential, depolarization also causes the voltage-dependent activation of K^+-selective channels; however, the activation of K^+ channels proceeds much more slowly than the activation of Na^+ channels. This relatively delayed activation of K^+ channels allows K^+ to leave the cell, but the outgoing current does not achieve its maximum until after the peak of the action potential. Unlike Na^+-selective channels, K^+ channels (at least the type of K^+ channel under consideration here) lack an inactivation gate. Therefore, K^+ is free to diffuse down its concentration gradient as long as depolarizing conditions persist and K^+ channels remain open (see Figure A5). K^+ channel activation—together with the inactivation of Na^+ channels—accounts for the **falling phase** of the action potential as the membrane potential repolarizes toward E_K. Because E_K is slightly below the resting membrane

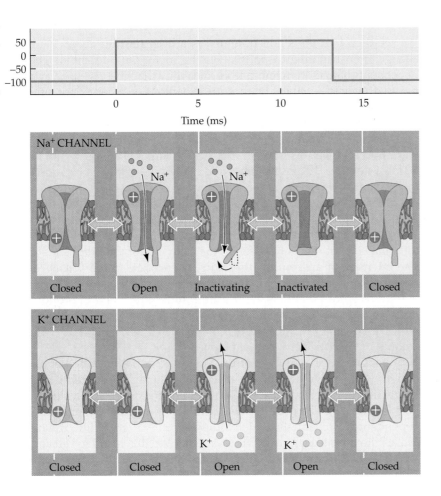

Figure A5 Functional states of voltage-gated Na+ and K+ channels. The gates of both channels are closed when the membrane potential is hyperpolarized (i.e., at rest). When the potential is depolarized (top trace), voltage sensors (indicated by + in the drawings) allow the channel gates to open; the Na+ channels open first, followed by the K+ channels. Na+ channels inactivate during prolonged depolarization, whereas many types of K+ channels do not.

potential and more K+-selective channels are open during the falling phase than in the resting condition, the membrane potential becomes **hyperpolarized**—that is, it briefly becomes more negative than the normal resting potential. This phase, occurring near the end of the action potential, is called **undershoot**. Hyperpolarization causes K+-selective channels to close, allowing the membrane potential to return to its resting level. Hyperpolarization also allows the inactivation gates of Na+-selective channels to return to their resting ("open gate") configuration, which prepares these channels for another cycle of activation.

Figure A6 depicts the temporal relations between the changes in membrane permeability that underlie the action potential (expressed in terms of *conductance*, which as used here is essentially synonymous with permeability) and the membrane potential itself.

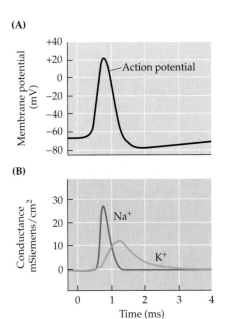

Figure A6 Changes in membrane permeability underlie the action potential. (A) Mathematical reconstruction of an action potential. (B) The underlying changes in Na+ (red curve) and K+ (yellow curve) conductance (conductance in this case is synonymous with permeability). Note the correspondence in time between the sharp increase in Na+ conductance and the rising phase of the action potential, and the correspondence between the falling phase of the action potential and the steep decline (inactivation) of the Na+ conductance and slow increase in K+ conductance. Near the end of the action potential, K+ conductance is elevated and Na+ conductance is zero, and the membrane potential "undershoots" the resting potential.

Action potentials are both self-perpetuating and self-limiting

We see then that an action potential is a brief (lasting about 1 millisecond) change from negative to positive in the membrane potential. The voltage-dependent changes in membrane permeability that give rise to an action potential are triggered—usually by receptor potentials or synaptic potentials—when the neuronal membrane is depolarized beyond a certain **threshold potential**.

For purposes of study, depolarization can be achieved—and action potentials elicited—by an injection of electrical current in experimental preparations (**Figure A7**). When this done, it is clear that larger currents do not elicit larger action potentials. Thus, the amplitude of the action potential is independent of the magnitude of the current used to evoke it. The action potentials of a given neuron are therefore said to be **all-or-none**, because they occur fully or not at all. If the amplitude or duration of the stimulus current is increased sufficiently, multiple action potentials occur, as can be seen in the responses to the three different current intensities seen at the right end of the graphs in Figure A7B. The intensity of a stimulus, therefore, is encoded in the *frequency* of action potentials rather than in their amplitude. This arrangement differs dramatically from receptor potentials, whose amplitudes are *graded* in proportion to the magnitude of the sensory stimulus, and synaptic potentials, whose amplitude varies according to the number of synapses activated and the previous amount of synaptic activity (see below).

The all-or-none character of the action potential and the behavior of the underlying voltage-dependent mechanisms may be conceptualized as the interaction of two feedback loops: a fast positive loop, and a slower negative loop (**Figure A8**). The positive feedback loop is initiated by activating voltage-dependent Na⁺ channels, which allows rapid Na⁺ entry into the neuron and causes the membrane potential to depolarize; this leads to the activation of still more Na⁺ channels, more Na⁺ entry, and still further depolarization (top loop in Figure A8). Because this positive loop, once initiated, is sustained by

Figure A7 Recording passive and active electrical signals in a nerve cell. (A) Two microelectrodes are inserted into a neuron; one measures membrane potential while the other injects current into the neuron. (B) Inserting the voltage-measuring microelectrode into the neuron reveals a negative potential (the resting membrane potential); injecting current through the microelectrode (top trace) alters the transmembrane potential (bottom trace). Hyperpolarizing current pulses produce only passive changes in the membrane potential. While small depolarizing currents also elicit only passive responses, depolarizations that cause the membrane potential to meet or exceed threshold evoke action potentials.

(A)

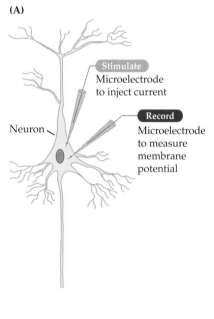

(B)

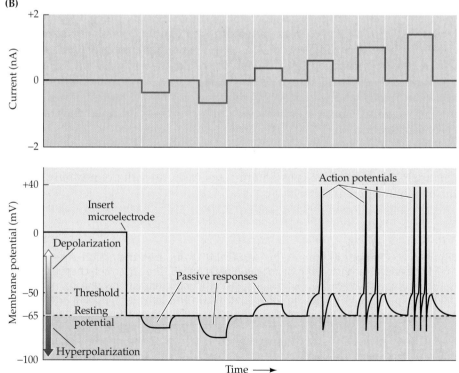

Figure A8 Positive and negative feedback loops during an action potential. Membrane depolarization rapidly activates a positive feedback loop fueled by the voltage-dependent activation of Na⁺ conductance. This phenomenon is followed by the slower activation of a negative loop as depolarization activates a K⁺ conductance, which helps to repolarize the membrane potential and terminate the action potential.

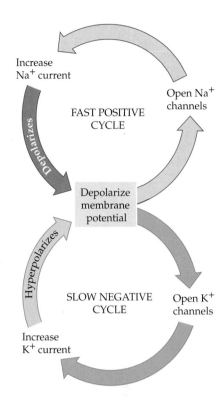

the intrinsic properties of the neuron—namely, the voltage dependence of the ion channels—the action potential is self-supporting, or **regenerative**. The fast positive feedback loop continues unabated until Na⁺ channel inactivation and the delayed activation of K⁺ channels begin to restore the membrane potential to the resting level. These later events account for a slower negative feedback loop (bottom loop in Figure A8) that ensures the self-limiting nature of the action potential.

Long-Distance Signaling by Means of Action Potentials

Passive current flow and action potential generation

The voltage-dependent mechanisms of action potential generation also explain the long-distance transmission of these electrical signals. Recall that neurons are relatively poor conductors of electricity, at least compared to a copper wire. Current conduction by wires, and by neurons in the absence of action potentials, is called **passive current flow**. The passive electrical properties of a nerve cell axon can be determined by measuring the voltage change resulting from a pulse of electrical current passed across the axonal membrane (**Figure A9A**). If this current pulse is not large enough to generate an action potential, the magnitude of the resulting potential change decays exponentially with increasing distance from the site of current injection (**Figure A9B**). Typically, the potential falls to a small fraction of its initial value at a distance of no more than a couple of millimeters away from the site of injection (**Figure A9C**). The progressive decrease in the amplitude of the induced potential change occurs because the injected current leaks out across the axonal membrane. The leakiness of the axonal membrane prevents effective passive transmission of electrical signals in all but the shortest axons. Likewise, the leakiness of the membrane slows the time course of the responses measured at increasing distances from the site where current was injected.

If the experiment shown in Figure A9 is repeated with a depolarizing current pulse large enough to produce an action potential, the result is dramatically different (**Figure A10A,B**). In this case, an action potential occurs without decrement along the entire length of the axon—even along the axons of peripheral nerves, some of which are almost a meter in length. Thus, action potentials must somehow circumvent the inherent leakiness of neurons.

How, then, do action potentials traverse great distances along such a poor passive conductor? The answer is provided in part by all-or-none behavior described in the previous section: that is, the amplitude of the action potentials recorded at different distances is constant (**Figure A10C**). This all-or-none behavior indicates that there must be more than simple passive flow of current involved in action potential propagation. A second clue comes from examination of the time of occurrence of the action potentials recorded at different distances from the site of stimulation: action potentials occur later and later at greater distances along the axon (see Figure A10B). Thus, the action potential has a measurable rate of transmission, called the **conduction velocity**.

The mechanism of action potential propagation is easy to grasp once one understands how action potentials are generated and how current flows pas-

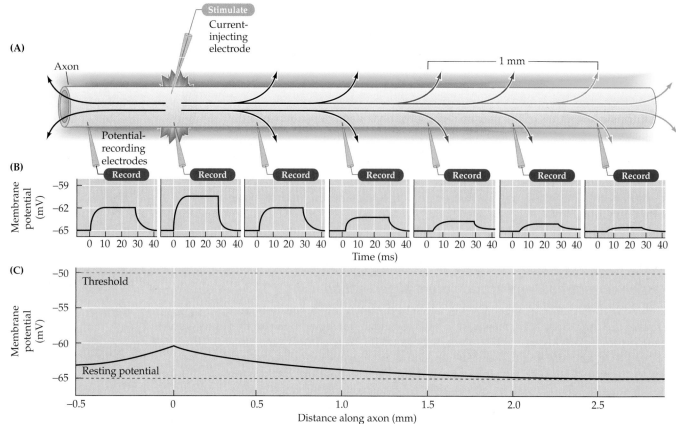

(A)

Axon

Stimulate
Current-injecting electrode

1 mm

Potential-recording electrodes

(B)

Record | Record | Record | Record | Record | Record | Record

Membrane potential (mV)

−59
−62
−65

0 10 20 30 40

Time (ms)

(C)

Membrane potential (mV)

−50 Threshold
−55
−60
−65 Resting potential

−0.5   0   0.5   1.0   1.5   2.0   2.5

Distance along axon (mm)

Figure A9 Passive current flow in an axon. (A) Experimental arrangement for examining the local flow of electrical current in an axon. A current-injecting electrode produces a subthreshold change in membrane potential, which spreads passively along the axon. (B) Potential responses recorded at the positions indicated by microelectrodes. With increasing distance from the site of current injection, the amplitude of the potential change is attenuated. (C) Relationship between the amplitude of potential responses and distance. (After Hodgkin and Rushton 1938.)

sively along an axon (**Figure A11**). A depolarizing stimulus (e.g., a receptor or synaptic potential, or an experimenter's electrode) locally depolarizes the axon, opening the voltage-sensitive Na⁺ channels in that region. The opening of the channels causes inward movement of Na⁺, and the resulting depolarization of the membrane potential generates an action potential at that site. Some of the local current generated by the action potential will then flow passively down the axon, in the same way that subthreshold currents spread along the axon (see Figure A9). This passive current flow does not require the movement of Na⁺ along the axon, but instead occurs by a shuttling of charge, somewhat similar to what happens when wires passively conduct electricity. This passive current flow depolarizes the membrane potential in the adjacent region of the axon, thus opening the Na⁺ channels in the neighboring membrane and triggering an action potential in this region, which then spreads again and again in a continuing cycle until the end of the axon is reached. The regenerative properties of Na⁺ channel opening allow action potentials to continue to propagate by acting as a booster at each point along the axon, thus ensuring the long-distance transmission of electrical signals.

In the wake of this traveling wave of depolarization, the action potential briefly leaves Na⁺ channels inactivated and K⁺ channels activated. These transitory changes make it hard for the axon to produce subsequent action potentials during this interval, which is called the **refractory period**. The refractoriness of the membrane explains why action potentials do not normally propagate backward, toward the point of initiation, but always travel forward along an axon. The refractory period also limits the number of action potentials that a given nerve cell can produce per unit time.

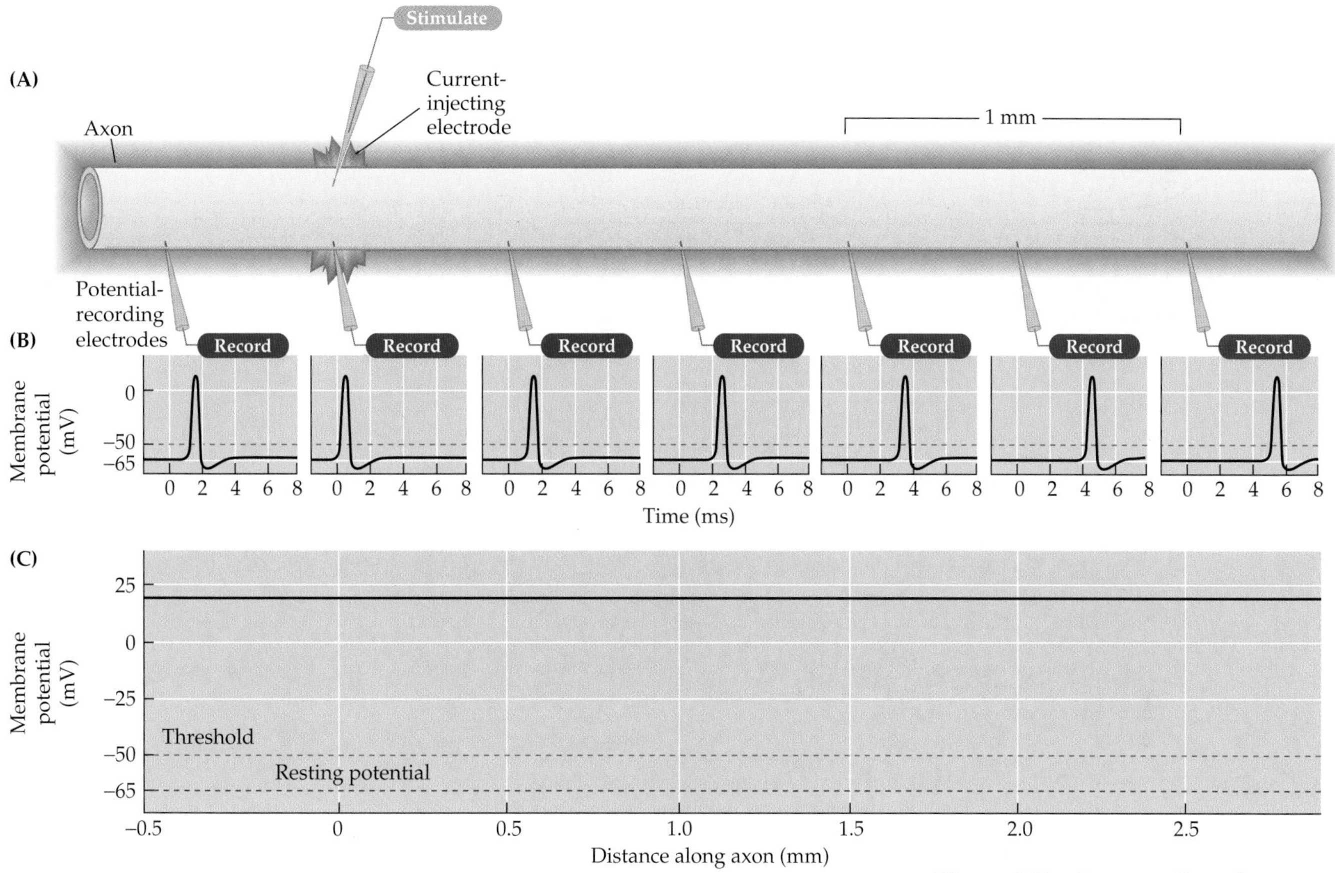

(A)

(B)

(C)

Figure A10 Propagation of an action potential. (A) In this experimental arrangement, an electrode evokes an action potential by injecting a suprathreshold current. (B) Potential responses recorded at the positions indicated by microelectrodes. The amplitude of the action potential is constant along the length of the axon, although the time of appearance of the action potential is delayed with increasing distance. (C) The constant amplitude of an action potential (solid black line) measured at different distances.

Myelination and saltatory conduction

Action potential propagation requires the coordinated action of two forms of current flow: the passive flow of current, and active currents flowing through voltage-dependent ion channels. The rate of action potential propagation is influenced by both of these phenomena, and it should not come as a surprise that a number of different mechanisms have evolved that optimize action-potential propagation of action potentials along axons. One very straightforward way of improving passive current flow is simply to increase the diameter of an axon, which effectively decreases the internal resistance to passive current flow. Another strategy to improve the passive flow of electrical current is to insulate the axonal membrane against current leakage. Reducing the ability of current to leak out of the axon increases the distance along the axon that a local current can flow passively. This strategy is evident in the **myelination** of axons, a process by which oligodendrocytes in the central nervous system and Schwann cells in the peripheral nervous system wrap the axon in **myelin**, which consists of multiple layers of closely opposed glial membranes (**Figure A12A**; see also Chapter 1). By acting as an electrical insulator, myelin greatly speeds up action potential conduction.

The major reason underlying this marked increase in speed is that the time-consuming process of action potential generation occurs only at specific points along the axon, called **nodes of Ranvier**, where there is a gap in the myelin wrapping (**Figure A12B**). If the entire surface of an axon were insulated, there would be no place for current to flow out of the axon and action potentials could not be generated. As it happens, an action potential generated at one node of Ranvier elicits current that flows passively within the myeli-

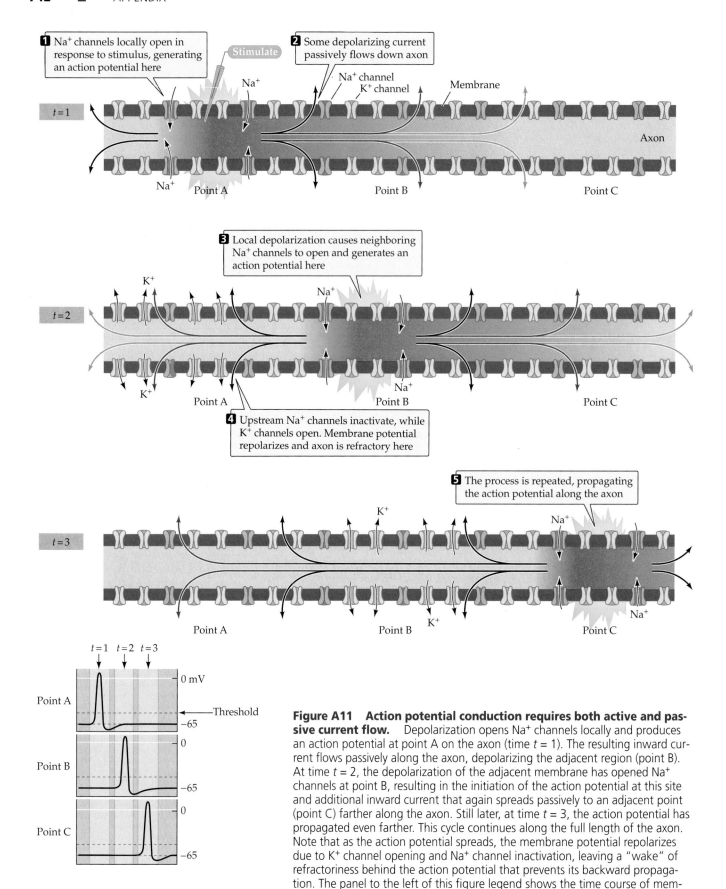

1 Na⁺ channels locally open in response to stimulus, generating an action potential here

Stimulate

2 Some depolarizing current passively flows down axon

Na⁺ channel
K⁺ channel
Membrane

Na⁺

$t = 1$

Axon

Na⁺   Point A   Point B   Point C

3 Local depolarization causes neighboring Na⁺ channels to open and generates an action potential here

K⁺

Na⁺

$t = 2$

K⁺   Point A   Na⁺   Point B   Point C

4 Upstream Na⁺ channels inactivate, while K⁺ channels open. Membrane potential repolarizes and axon is refractory here

5 The process is repeated, propagating the action potential along the axon

K⁺

Na⁺

$t = 3$

Point A   Point B   K⁺   Point C   Na⁺

$t = 1$ $t = 2$ $t = 3$

Point A

0 mV
Threshold
−65

Point B

0
−65

Point C

0
−65

Figure A11 Action potential conduction requires both active and passive current flow.   Depolarization opens Na⁺ channels locally and produces an action potential at point A on the axon (time $t = 1$). The resulting inward current flows passively along the axon, depolarizing the adjacent region (point B). At time $t = 2$, the depolarization of the adjacent membrane has opened Na⁺ channels at point B, resulting in the initiation of the action potential at this site and additional inward current that again spreads passively to an adjacent point (point C) farther along the axon. Still later, at time $t = 3$, the action potential has propagated even farther. This cycle continues along the full length of the axon. Note that as the action potential spreads, the membrane potential repolarizes due to K⁺ channel opening and Na⁺ channel inactivation, leaving a "wake" of refractoriness behind the action potential that prevents its backward propagation. The panel to the left of this figure legend shows the time course of membrane potential changes at the points indicated.

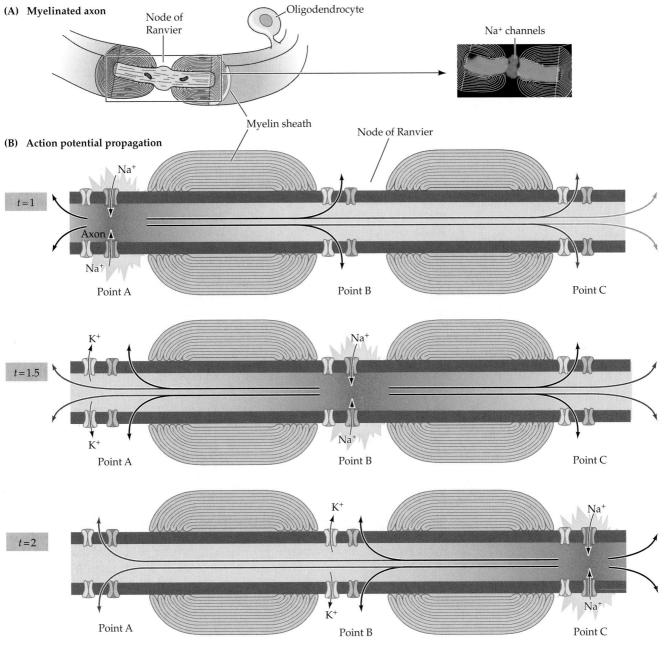

(A) Myelinated axon

Node of Ranvier

Oligodendrocyte

Na+ channels

Myelin sheath

Node of Ranvier

(B) Action potential propagation

$t = 1$

Na+

Axon

Na+

Point A

Point B

Point C

$t = 1.5$

K+

Na+

K+

Na+

Point A

Point B

Point C

$t = 2$

K+

Na+

K+

Na+

Point A

Point B

Point C

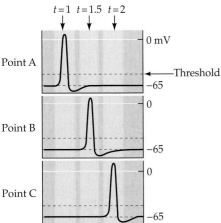

$t=1$ $t=1.5$ $t=2$

Point A

0 mV

Threshold

−65

Point B

0

−65

Point C

0

−65

Figure A12 Saltatory action potential conduction along a myelinated axon. (A) Diagram and micrograph of a myelinated axon. The micrograph shows the voltage-gated Na+ channels (red) at a node of Ranvier in a myelinated axon of the optic nerve. Green indicates a protein called Caspr, which is found adjacent to the node of Ranvier. (B) Local current in response to action potential initiation at a particular site flows locally, as described in Figure A11. Myelin, however, prevents the local current from leaking across the internodal membrane, so the current travels farther along the axon than it would in the absence of myelin. Voltage-gated Na+ and K+ channels are present only at nodes of Ranvier, so the generation of active, voltage-gated Na+ currents need occur only at these unmyelinated regions. The result is a greatly enhanced velocity of action potential conduction. (Micrograph from Chen et al. 2004.)

nated segment until the next node is reached. This local current flow then generates an action potential in the neighboring segment, and the cycle is repeated along the length of the axon in a process known as **saltatory conduction**, meaning that the action potential jumps from node to node. Not surprisingly, loss of myelin, as occurs in demyelinating diseases such as multiple sclerosis, causes a variety of serious neurological problems.

Synaptic Transmission

The preceding account explains how neural signals generated near the cell body of one neuron may propagate—by means of action potential regeneration—to a distant target cell. The function of neural circuits and the ability of the central nervous system to control effector tissues (such as skeletal or smooth muscle) depends on the ability of nerve cells to communicate with one another and, for motor neurons, to motivate the contractions of muscle fibers.

So what happens when the action potential reaches the "end of the line," or *axon terminal*? Here the neural signal has reached a **synapse**, a specialized junction between a neuron and a target cell. The neuron conveying the neural signal contributes the **presynaptic element**, which is usually a specialized region of the axon terminal, and the target cell provides the **postsynaptic element,** which is one of many such sites along the length of the target cell's dendrites or its cell body.

The many different kinds of synapses within the human brain can be divided into two general classes, electrical and chemical. While the structure and function of electrical synapses are relatively simple, the subcellular structures and molecular mechanisms that govern neural signaling at the far more common chemical synapses are profoundly complex; this complexity is instrumental in facilitating the development of neural circuits in early life and the neural functions that underlie learning and memory throughout an individual's life span.

Electrical synapses

Electrical synapses are prominent in developing nervous systems and in certain populations of neurons and glia in the mature nervous system. At an electrical synapse, the presynaptic neuron is the source of current that flows into the postsynaptic neuron. The membranes of the two communicating neurons come extremely close at the synapse and are actually linked together by an intercellular specialization called a **gap junction** (**Figure A13A**). Gap junctions contain precisely aligned, paired channels in the membrane of the pre- and postsynaptic neurons, such that each channel pair forms a pore. Electrical synapses thus work by allowing ionic current to flow passively through the gap junction pores from one neuron to another. The usual source of this current is the potential difference generated locally by an action potential in the presynaptic neuron.

The pore of a gap junction channel is much larger than the pores of the voltage-gated ion channels described above. As a result, a variety of substances in addition to ions can simply diffuse between the cytoplasm of the pre- and postsynaptic neurons, including some fairly large molecules such as the energy source ATP and other important intracellular molecules.

Communication via gap junctions has a number of interesting consequences. One is that transmission can go in either direction; another is that transmission is extraordinarily fast because passive current flow across the gap junction is virtually instantaneous. Consequently, electrical synapses play an important role in synchronizing electrical activity among small populations of neurons. For example, the brainstem neurons that generate rhythmic electrical

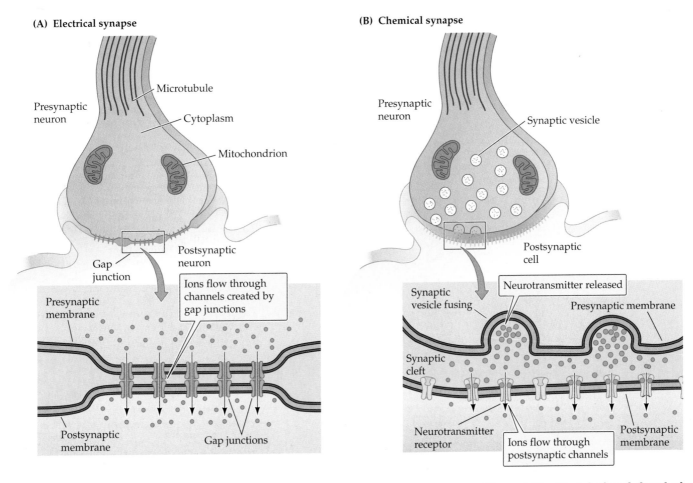

(A) Electrical synapse

Presynaptic neuron

Microtubule

Cytoplasm

Mitochondrion

Gap junction

Postsynaptic neuron

Ions flow through channels created by gap junctions

Presynaptic membrane

Postsynaptic membrane

Gap junctions

(B) Chemical synapse

Presynaptic neuron

Synaptic vesicle

Postsynaptic cell

Synaptic vesicle fusing

Neurotransmitter released

Presynaptic membrane

Synaptic cleft

Neurotransmitter receptor

Ions flow through postsynaptic channels

Postsynaptic membrane

Figure A13   Electrical and chemical synapses.   (A) At electrical synapses, gap junctions between pre- and postsynaptic membranes permit ions (red circles) to flow passively through intercellular channels. The flow changes the postsynaptic membrane potential, initiating (or in rare instances inhibiting) the generation of action potentials in the postsynaptic cell. (B) At chemical synapses, there is no intercellular continuity, and thus no direct flow of current from pre- to postsynaptic cell. Synaptic current flows across the postsynaptic membrane only in response to the secretion of neurotransmitters (green circles), which open or close postsynaptic ion channels after binding to receptor molecules.

activity underlying breathing are synchronized by electrical synapses, and electrical transmission between certain hormone-secreting neurons within the hypothalamus ensures that all cells fire action potentials at about the same time, thus facilitating a burst of hormone secretion into the circulation.

Chemical synapses

Chemical synapses are the primary means of intercellular signaling among neurons, and between neurons and effector tissues. The general structure of a chemical synapse is shown schematically in **Figure A13B**. The space between the pre- and postsynaptic neurons is substantially greater at chemical synapses than at electrical synapses and is called the **synaptic cleft**. The key feature of all chemical synapses is the presence of small, membrane-bounded organelles called **synaptic vesicles** within the presynaptic terminal. These tiny spheres are filled with one or more **neurotransmitters**—biochemical signal molecules that will be secreted from the presynaptic neuron.

Transmission at chemical synapses is based on an elaborate sequence of events (**Figure A14**). The process is initiated when an action potential reaches the presynaptic axon terminal. The change in membrane potential caused by the arrival of the action potential leads to the opening of **voltage-gated calcium channels** in the presynaptic membrane. Because of the steep concentration gradient of calcium ions (Ca^{2+}) across the presynaptic membrane, the opening of these channels causes a rapid influx of Ca^{2+} into the presynaptic terminal, with the result that the Ca^{2+} concentration of the cytoplasm in the terminal rises steeply, albeit transiently. This elevation of presynaptic Ca^{2+}

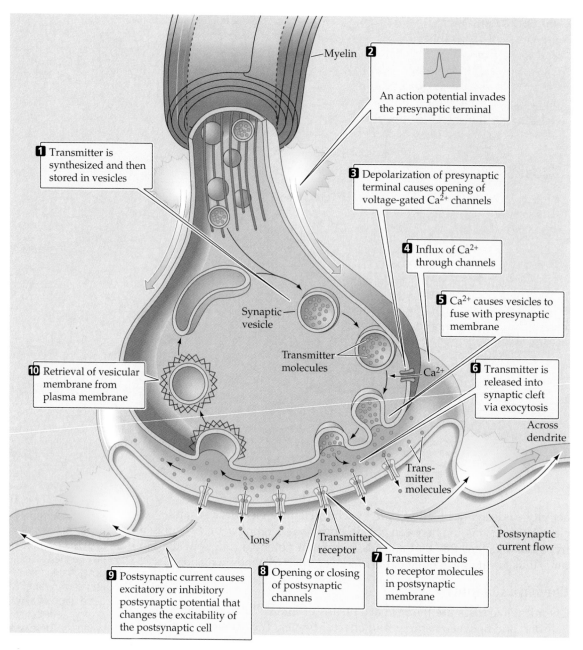

Myelin

2 An action potential invades the presynaptic terminal

1 Transmitter is synthesized and then stored in vesicles

3 Depolarization of presynaptic terminal causes opening of voltage-gated Ca^{2+} channels

4 Influx of Ca^{2+} through channels

5 Ca^{2+} causes vesicles to fuse with presynaptic membrane

Synaptic vesicle

Transmitter molecules

Ca^{2+}

10 Retrieval of vesicular membrane from plasma membrane

6 Transmitter is released into synaptic cleft via exocytosis

Across dendrite

Transmitter molecules

Postsynaptic current flow

Ions

Transmitter receptor

9 Postsynaptic current causes excitatory or inhibitory postsynaptic potential that changes the excitability of the postsynaptic cell

8 Opening or closing of postsynaptic channels

7 Transmitter binds to receptor molecules in postsynaptic membrane

Figure A14 Sequence of events at a typical chemical synapse. The arrival of an action potential at a presynaptic axon terminal sets off a cascade that results in the release of neurotransmitter molecules to the synaptic cleft. Membrane proteins in the postsynaptic cell then bind the neurotransmitter, resulting in the opening or closing of ion channels and changes in the electrical potential of the postsynaptic cell.

concentration triggers a complex set of molecular events that allows synaptic vesicles to fuse with the membrane of the presynaptic neuron and then to release their neurotransmitters into the synaptic cleft.

Following this exocytosis, transmitters diffuse across the synaptic cleft and bind to specific receptors on the membrane of the postsynaptic neuron. The binding of neurotransmitter to the receptors causes channels in the postsynaptic membrane to open or close (among other possible effects; see below), thus changing the ability of ions to flow across the postsynaptic membrane. The resulting neurotransmitter-induced current flow usually alters the membrane potential of the postsynaptic neuron, thereby inducing a synaptic potential that will either increase or decrease the probability that the postsynaptic neuron will fire an action potential. In this way, information is transmitted from one neuron to another.

After a neurotransmitter has been secreted into the synaptic cleft, it must be removed quickly so that the postsynaptic cell can engage in another cycle of synaptic transmission. The removal of a neurotransmitter involves diffusion away from the postsynaptic receptors, as well as reuptake into presynaptic terminals or surrounding glial cells, degradation by specific enzymes, or a combination of these mechanisms. Specific transporter proteins remove most neurotransmitters (or their metabolic by-products) from the synaptic cleft, ultimately delivering them back to the presynaptic terminal for reuse.

Neurotransmitters and Their Receptors

Studies of chemical synapses have led to the identification of more than 100 different neurotransmitter molecules, which can be classified into two broad categories based on size: small-molecule neurotransmitters and the much larger neuropeptides (**Figure A15**). **Small-molecule neurotransmitters** are often individual amino acids, such as glutamate and gamma-aminobutyric acid (GABA), the brain's major excitatory and inhibitory neurotransmitters, respectively. Some neurotransmitters in this group are small organic molecules such as acetylcholine or adenosine triphosphate (ATP); this category also includes the biogenic amines dopamine, epinephrine, serotonin, and histamine (to name a few). **Neuropeptides** are relatively large protein molecules made up of anywhere from 3 to 36 amino acids.

■ TABLE A2 Features of the Major Neurotransmitters

Neurotransmitter	Postsynaptic effect[a]	Precursor(s)	Rate-limiting step in synthesis	Removal mechanism
Acetylcholine (ACh)	Excitatory	Choline + acetyl CoA	Choline acetyltransferase (CAT)	Acetylcholinesterase (AChE)
Glutamate	Excitatory	Glutamine	Glutaminase	Transporters
Gamma-aminobutyric acid (GABA)	Inhibitory	Glutamate	Glutamic acid decarboxylase (GAD)	Transporters
Glycine	Inhibitory	Serine	Phosphoserine	Transporters
Catecholamines (epinephrine, norepinephrine, dopamine)	Excitatory	Tyrosine	Tyrosine hydroxylase	Transporters, monoamine oxidase (MAO), catechol O-methyltransferase (COMT)
Serotonin (5-HT)	Excitatory	Tryptophan	Tryptophan hydroxylase	Transporters, monoamine oxidase (MAO)
Histamine	Excitatory	Histidine	Histidine decarboxylase	Transporters
Adenosine triphosphate (ATP)	Excitatory	ADP	Mitochondrial oxidative phosphorylation; glycolysis	Hydrolysis to AMP and adenosine
Neuropeptides	Excitatory and inhibitory	Amino acids (protein synthesis)	Synthesis and transport	Proteases
Endocannabinoids	Inhibits inhibition	Membrane lipids	Enzymatic modification of lipids	Hydrolysis
Nitric oxide	Excitatory and inhibitory	Arginine	Nitric oxide synthase	Spontaneous oxidation

[a]The most common postsynaptic effect is indicated; the same transmitter can elicit postsynaptic excitation or inhibition depending on the nature of the ion channels affected by transmitter binding.

SMALL-MOLECULE NEUROTRANSMITTERS

Acetylcholine $(CH_3)_3\overset{+}{N}-CH_2-CH_2-O-\overset{O}{\overset{\|}{C}}-CH_3$

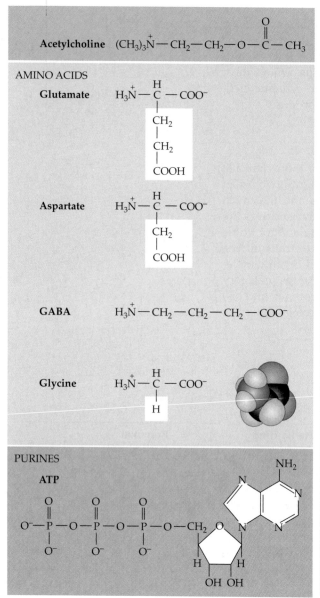

AMINO ACIDS

Glutamate

$$H_3\overset{+}{N}-\underset{\underset{\underset{\underset{COOH}{|}}{CH_2}}{\underset{|}{CH_2}}}{\overset{\overset{H}{|}}{C}}-COO^-$$

Aspartate

$$H_3\overset{+}{N}-\underset{\underset{COOH}{\underset{|}{CH_2}}}{\overset{\overset{H}{|}}{C}}-COO^-$$

GABA $\quad H_3\overset{+}{N}-CH_2-CH_2-CH_2-COO^-$

Glycine

$$H_3\overset{+}{N}-\underset{\underset{H}{|}}{\overset{\overset{H}{|}}{C}}-COO^-$$

PURINES

ATP

BIOGENIC AMINES

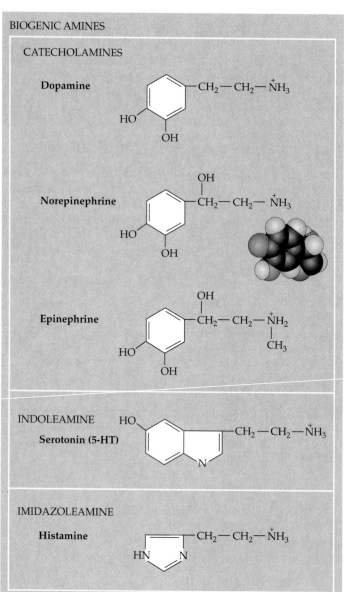

CATECHOLAMINES

Dopamine

Norepinephrine

Epinephrine

INDOLEAMINE
Serotonin (5-HT)

IMIDAZOLEAMINE

Histamine

PEPTIDE NEUROTRANSMITTERS (more than 100 peptides, usually 3–30 amino acids long)

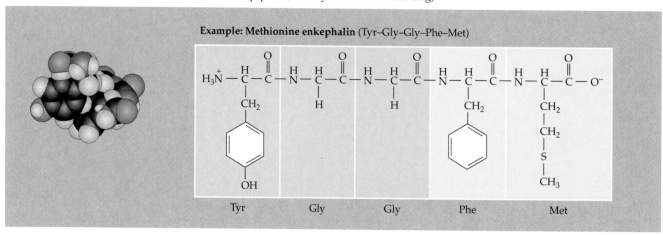

Example: Methionine enkephalin (Tyr–Gly–Gly–Phe–Met)

Tyr   Gly   Gly   Phe   Met

◀ **Figure A15 Examples of small-molecule and peptide neurotransmitters.**
Small-molecule transmitters can be subdivided into acetylcholine, the amino acids, purines, and biogenic amines. The catecholamines, so named because they all share the catechol moiety (the hydroxylated benzene ring), are a distinctive subgroup within the biogenic amines. Serotonin and histamine contain an indole and an imidazole ring, respectively. Size differences between the small-molecule neurotransmitters and the peptide neurotransmitters are indicated by the space-filling models for glycine, norepinephrine, and methionine enkephalin. (In these molecular diagrams, carbon atoms are shown in black, nitrogen atoms in blue, and oxygen atoms in red.)

This wide array of neurotransmitters gives synapses a diverse physiological repertoire: different neurotransmitters and combinations of multiple neurotransmitters can produce different types of responses on individual postsynaptic cells. For example, a neuron can be excited by one type of neurotransmitter and inhibited by another type. The speed of postsynaptic responses produced by different transmitters varies, allowing control of electrical signaling over different time scales. In general, small-molecule neurotransmitters mediate rapid synaptic actions, whereas neuropeptides tend to modulate slower, ongoing synaptic functions. Many types of neurons are known to synthesize and release two or more different neurotransmitters, most often a small-molecule neurotransmitter and one or more neuropeptides. **Table A2** catalogues the functional properties of some of the most important and best understood neurotransmitters.

Neurotransmitter receptors

Neurotransmitter receptors are proteins embedded in the plasma membrane of postsynaptic cells. Domains of receptor molecules that extend into the synaptic cleft bind neurotransmitters that are released by the presynaptic neuron. The binding of neurotransmitters, either directly or indirectly, causes ion channels in the postsynaptic membrane to open or close. The opening or closing of postsynaptic ion channels is accomplished in different ways by two broad families of neurotransmitter receptor proteins, **ionotropic receptors** and **metabotropic receptors**.

Ionotropic receptors are linked directly to ion channels (the Greek word *tropos* means "to turn" and signifies movement in response to a stimulus). These receptors contain two functional domains: an extracellular site that binds neurotransmitters, and a membrane-spanning domain that forms an ion channel. Thus, ionotropic receptors combine transmitter binding (ligand) and channel functions into a single molecular entity; reflecting this, they are also known as *ligand-gated ion channels*. Ionotropic receptors are made up of at least four or five individual protein subunits, each of which contributes to the pore of the ion channel (**Figure A16A**).

The second family of neurotransmitter receptors comprises the **metabotropic receptors**, so called because the eventual movement of ions through a channel depends on one or more metabolic steps. These receptors do not have ion channels as part of their structure; instead, they affect channels by the activation of intermediate effector molecules called **G-proteins** (**Figure A16B**). For this reason, metabotropic receptors are also called *G-protein-coupled receptors*. Metabotropic receptors are monomeric (i.e., single, as opposed to made up of subunits) proteins with an extracellular domain that contains a neurotransmitter binding site and an intracellular domain that binds to G-proteins. When a neurotransmitter binds to a metabotropic receptor, G-proteins are activated and then dissociate from the receptor. The G-proteins can then interact directly with ion channels, or else bind to other effector proteins, such as enzymes,

(A) Ionotropic receptors

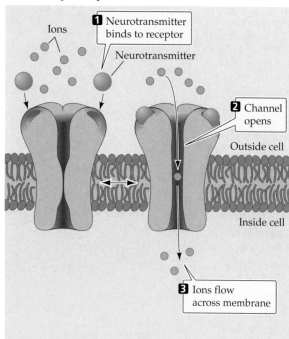

(B) Metabotropic receptors

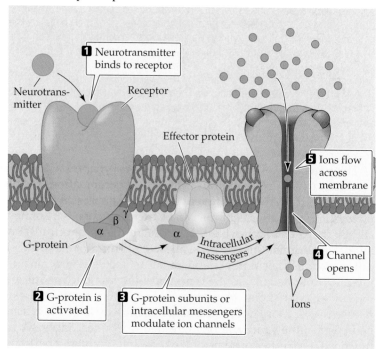

Figure A16 Neurotransmitter receptors in the postsynaptic cell.
A neurotransmitter can affect the activity of a postsynaptic cell via two different types of receptor proteins. (A) Ionotropic receptors (also called ligand-gated ion channels) combine receptor and channel functions in a single protein complex. (B) Metabotropic receptors usually activate G-proteins, which modulate ion channels directly or indirectly through intracellular effector enzymes and second messengers.

that make intracellular messengers that open or close ion channels. Thus, G-proteins can be thought of as transducers that couple neurotransmitter binding to the regulation of postsynaptic ion channels.

These two families of postsynaptic receptors give rise to synaptic potentials—also called **postsynaptic potentials**, or **PSPs**, to emphasize their genesis in the postsynaptic element—with very different time courses. The actions resulting from PSPs range from less than a millisecond to minutes, hours, or even days. Ionotropic receptors generally mediate rapid postsynaptic effects: PSPs arise within a millisecond or two of an action potential invading the presynaptic terminal and last for a few tens of milliseconds or less. In contrast, the activation of metabotropic receptors typically produces much slower responses, ranging from hundreds of milliseconds to minutes or even longer. The comparative slowness of metabotropic receptor actions reflects the fact that multiple proteins need to bind to each other sequentially in order to produce the final physiological response. A given transmitter may activate both ionotropic and metabotropic receptors to produce both fast and slow PSPs at the same synapse, as is illustrated below for the neurotransmitter glutamate.

Perhaps the most important principle to keep in mind is that the response elicited at a given synapse depends on the neurotransmitter released and the postsynaptic complement of receptors, associated channels and the second messenger systems that transduce the activity of neurotransmitters into signals that affect postsynaptic structure and function.

Glutamate: The major excitatory neurotransmitter of the central nervous system

The amino acid glutamate is the most important neurotransmitter in normal brain function. Nearly all excitatory neurons in the central nervous system are glutamatergic (i.e., use glutamate as a neurotransmitter), and it is estimated that over half of all brain synapses release this agent. Glutamate plays an especially important role in clinical neurology because elevated concentrations of extracellular glutamate, released as a result of excessive excitation and/or neural injury, are toxic to neurons. A detailed consideration of this chemical messenger illustrates general principles that govern the life cycles and functions of other small-molecule neurotransmitters.

Glutamate cannot cross the blood-brain barrier and therefore must be synthesized within neurons from local precursor molecules that are already present in the cell. The most prevalent precursor for glutamate synthesis is glutamine, which is released by glial cells. Once released, glutamine is taken up into presynaptic terminals and metabolized to glutamate by the mitochondrial enzyme glutaminase (**Figure A17**). Some of the glucose metabolized by neurons can also be used for glutamate synthesis.

The glutamate synthesized in the presynaptic cytoplasm is packaged into synaptic vesicles by *vesicular glutamate transporters*, or VGLUT. Once released, glutamate is removed from the synaptic cleft by the *excitatory amino acid transporters* (EAATs) in surrounding glial processes and presynaptic terminals (see Figure A17). Glutamate taken up by glia is converted into glutamine by the enzyme glutamine synthetase; glutamine is then transported out of the glial cells and into nerve terminals. In this way, synaptic terminals cooperate with glial cells to maintain an adequate supply of the neurotransmitter.

Several types of glutamate receptors have been identified, including three types of ionotropic receptors called, respectively, **NMDA receptors**, **AMPA receptors**, and **kainate receptors** (named after the agonists that activate them). All of the ionotropic glutamate receptors are nonselective cation channels that allow the passage of Na^+ and K^+, and in some cases small amounts of Ca^{2+}. Like most ionotropic receptors, AMPA, kainate, and NMDA receptors are formed from the association of several protein subunits that can combine in many ways to produce a large number of receptor isoforms with varying neurophysiological properties. Activation of any of these three receptor types always produces excitatory postsynaptic responses, for reasons that are discussed below.

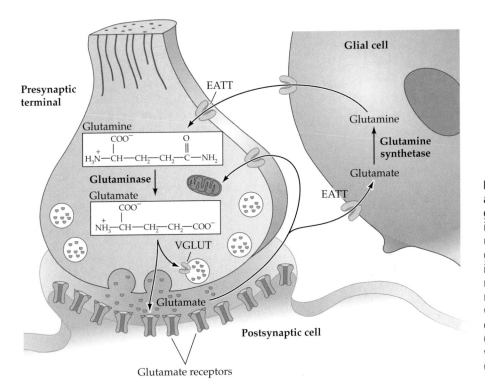

Figure A17 Glutamate synthesis and cycling between neurons and glia. The action of glutamate released into the synaptic cleft is terminated by uptake into neurons and surrounding glial cells via specific transporters. Within the nerve terminal, the glutamine released by glial cells and taken up by neurons is converted back to glutamate. Glutamate is transported into cells via excitatory amino acid transporters (EATTs) and loaded into synaptic vesicles via vesicular glutamate transporters (VGLUT).

The functional properties of NMDA receptors are especially interesting. Perhaps most significant is the fact that NMDA receptor ion channels allow the entry of Ca^{2+} in addition to monovalent cations such as Na^+ and K^+ (**Figure A18A**). As a result, excitatory postsynaptic potentials produced by NMDA receptors can increase the concentration of Ca^{2+} within the postsynaptic neuron; the Ca^{2+} concentration change can then act as a second messenger to activate diverse intracellular signaling cascades.

Another key property of NMDA receptors is that they bind extracellular magnesium, Mg^{2+}. At membrane potentials near resting levels, Mg^{2+} blocks the pore of the NMDA receptor channel (**Figure A18B**). Depolarization, however, pushes Mg^{2+} out of the pore, allowing other cations to flow through. This property provides the basis for a voltage-dependence to current flow through the receptor (dashed line in Figure A18B) and means that NMDA

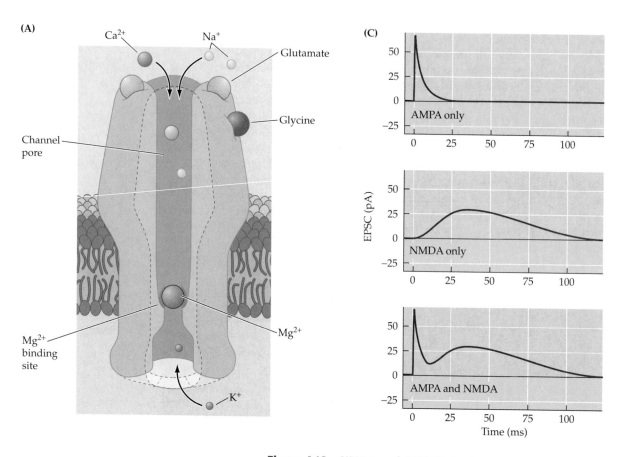

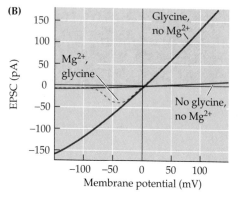

Figure A18   NMDA and AMPA/kainate receptors.
(A) NMDA receptors contain binding sites for glutamate and the co-activator glycine, as well as an Mg^{2+}-binding site in the pore of the channel. At hyperpolarized potentials, the electrical driving force on Mg^{2+} drives this ion into the pore of the receptor and blocks it. (B) Current flow across NMDA receptors at a range of postsynaptic voltages, showing the requirement for glycine, and Mg^{2+} block at hyperpolarized potentials (dotted line). (C) The differential effects of glutamate receptor antagonists indicate that activation of AMPA or kainate receptors produces very fast excitatory postsynaptic currents (EPSCs; top panel) and activation of NMDA receptors causes slower EPSCs (middle panel), so that EPSCs recorded in the absence of antagonists have two kinetic components due to the contribution of both types of response (bottom panel).

receptors pass cations (most notably Ca^{2+}) only during depolarization of the postsynaptic cell. Depolarization may result from either activation of a large number of excitatory inputs and/or repetitive firing of action potentials in the presynaptic cell. These properties are widely thought to be the basis for some forms of synaptic plasticity (see Chapter 13).

Whereas some glutamatergic synapses have only AMPA or NMDA receptors, most possess both. Antagonists of NMDA receptors have been used to reveal differences between the electrical signals produced by the two receptor types, such as the fact that the synaptic currents produced by NMDA receptors are slower and longer lasting than those produced by AMPA receptors (**Figure A18C**). The physiological roles of kainate receptors are less well defined; in some cases, these receptors are found on presynaptic terminals and serve as a feedback mechanism to regulate glutamate release.

In addition to these ionotropic glutamate receptors, there are three types of metabotropic glutamate receptor (mGluRs). These receptors differ in their coupling to intracellular signal transduction pathways and in their sensitivity to pharmacological agents. Unlike the excitatory ionotropic glutamate receptors, mGluRs cause slower postsynaptic responses that can either increase or decrease the excitability of postsynaptic cells. As a result the physiological roles of mGluRs are particularly varied.

Excitatory and Inhibitory Postsynaptic Potentials

Postsynaptic potentials (such as those that arise following interactions between glutamate and its ionotropic receptors) ultimately alter the probability that an action potential will be produced in the postsynaptic cell. Postsynaptic potentials are called **excitatory** (**EPSPs**) if they increase the likelihood of an action potential occurring in the postsynaptic cell, and **inhibitory** (**IPSPs**) if they decrease this likelihood. In both cases, neurotransmitters binding to receptors open or close ion channels in the postsynaptic cell (see Figure A14). Whether an EPSP or an IPSP results depends on the type of channel that is coupled to the receptor and the concentration of permeant ions inside and outside the postsynaptic cell.

In fact, the only distinction between postsynaptic excitation and inhibition is the **reversal potential** of the current that underlies the PSP in relation to the threshold voltage for generating action potentials in the postsynaptic cell. The reversal potential for a postsynaptic current flowing through a ligand-gated ion channel is analogous to a Nernst equilibrium potential for a current flowing through a voltage-gated ion channel: it is the membrane potential where no net current flows through open channels. This is because the membrane potential counterbalances the net movement of charge carried by the diffusing ions, even when more than one ionic species is permeant (as is the case for most ligand-gated ion channels).

Consider again a synapse that uses glutamate as a transmitter. When, for example, AMPA receptors are activated, both Na^+ and K^+ flow across the postsynaptic membrane, yielding an E_{rev} of approximately 0 mV for the resulting postsynaptic current (when the channel is open, Na^+ flows in, K^+ flows out and the reversal potential is somewhere between E_{Na} and E_K). If the resting potential of the postsynaptic neuron is –60 mV, the resulting EPSP will depolarize by bringing the postsynaptic membrane potential toward 0 mV. For the hypothetical neuron shown in **Figure A19A**, the action potential threshold voltage is –40 mV. Thus, a glutamate-induced EPSP will increase the probability that this neuron produces an action potential, defining the synapse as excitatory.

As an example of inhibitory postsynaptic action, consider a neuronal synapse that uses GABA as its transmitter. At such synapses, the GABA recep-

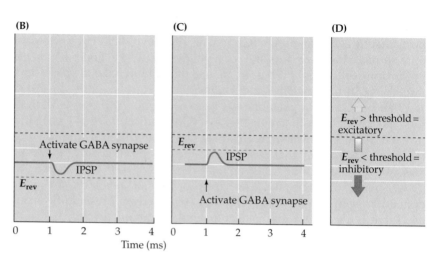

Figure A19 Reversal and threshold potentials determine postsynaptic excitation and inhibition. (A) If the reversal potential for a postsynaptic potential (PSP) is more positive (0 mV) than the action potential threshold (−40 mV), the effect of a transmitter is excitatory, and it generates excitatory PSPs (EPSPs). (B) If the reversal potential for a PSP is more negative than the action potential threshold, the transmitter is inhibitory and generates inhibitory PSPs (IPSPs). (C) IPSPs can nonetheless depolarize the postsynaptic cell if their reversal potential is between the resting potential and the action potential threshold. (D) The general rule of postsynaptic action is: If the reversal potential is more positive than threshold, excitation results; inhibition occurs if the reversal potential is more negative than threshold.

tors typically open ionotropic channels that are selectively permeable to chloride ions, Cl^-, and the action of GABA causes Cl^- to flow across the postsynaptic membrane. Consider a case where E_{Cl} is −70 mV, as is typical for many neurons, so that the postsynaptic resting potential of −60 mV is less negative than E_{Cl}. When such GABA receptor-channels are open, the positive electrochemical driving force will cause negatively charged Cl^- to flow into the cell and produce a hyperpolarizing IPSP (**Figure A19B**). This hyperpolarizing IPSP will take the postsynaptic membrane away from the action potential threshold of −40 mV, clearly inhibiting the postsynaptic cell. Surprisingly, inhibitory synapses need not produce hyperpolarizing IPSPs. If E_{Cl} were −50 mV instead of −70 mV, then the negative electrochemical driving force would cause Cl^- to flow out of the cell and produce a depolarizing IPSP (**Figure A19C**). However, the synapse would still be inhibitory: given that the reversal potential of the IPSP still is more negative than the action potential threshold (−40 mV), the depolarizing IPSP would inhibit because the postsynaptic membrane potential would be kept more negative than the threshold for action potential initiation.

Although the particulars of postsynaptic action can be complex, a simple rule distinguishes postsynaptic excitation from inhibition: an EPSP has a reversal potential more positive than the action potential threshold, whereas an IPSP has a reversal potential more negative than threshold (**Figure A19D**). Intuitively, this rule can be understood by realizing that an EPSP will tend to depolarize the membrane potential so that it exceeds threshold, whereas an IPSP will always act to keep the membrane potential more negative than the threshold potential.

Surprisingly, PSPs produced at most synapses in the brain are well below the threshold for generating postsynaptic action potentials; how, then, can neurons use PSPs to transmit information? The answer is that neurons in the central nervous system are typically innervated by thousands of synapses, and the PSPs produced by each active synapse can *sum together* in space and in time to determine the behavior of the postsynaptic neuron.

Consider the highly simplified case of a neuron that is innervated by two excitatory synapses, each generating a subthreshold EPSP, and by an inhibitory synapse that produces an IPSP (**Figure A20A**). While activation of either one of the excitatory synapses alone produces a subthreshold EPSP, activation of *both* excitatory synapses at about the same time causes the two EPSPs to sum together (E1 + E2). If E1 + E2 is sufficient to depolarize the postsynaptic neuron to threshold, a postsynaptic action potential results. **Summation** thus allows subthreshold EPSPs to influence action potential production. Likewise,

(A)

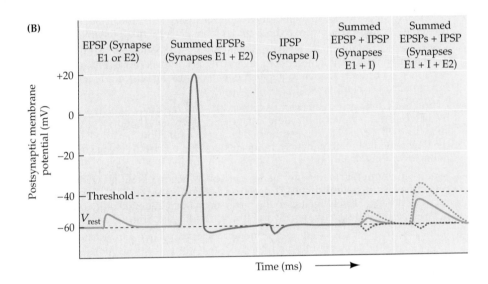

Figure A20 Summation of postsynaptic potentials.
(A) A microelectrode records the postsynaptic potentials produced by the activity of two excitatory synapses (E1 and E2) and an inhibitory synapse (I). (B) Electrical responses to synaptic activation. Stimulating either excitatory synapse (E1 or E2) produces a subthreshold EPSP, whereas stimulating both synapses at the same time (E1 + E2) produces a suprathreshold EPSP that evokes a postsynaptic action potential (blue line). Activation of the inhibitory synapse alone (I) results in a hyperpolarizing IPSP. Summing this IPSP (dashed red line) with the EPSP (dashed green line) produced by one excitatory synapse (E1 + I) reduces the amplitude of the EPSP (orange line). Summing the IPSP with the suprathreshold EPSP produced by activating synapses E1 and E2 keeps the postsynaptic neuron below threshold so that no action potential is evoked.

an IPSP generated by an inhibitory synapse (I) can sum with a subthreshold EPSP to reduce its amplitude (E1 + I), or it can sum with suprathreshold EPSPs to prevent the postsynaptic neuron from reaching threshold (E1 + I + E2). In short, the summation of EPSPs and IPSPs by a postsynaptic neuron permits a neuron to integrate the electrical information provided by all the inhibitory and excitatory synapses acting on it at any moment (**Figure A20B**). Whether the sum of active synaptic inputs results in the production of an action potential depends on the balance between excitation and inhibition.

Synaptic connectivity between neurons is a dynamic entity that is constantly changing in response to ongoing patterns of neural activity that are modulated by the accrual of life experience. Such changes in synaptic transmission arise from a number of forms of plasticity that vary in time scale from milliseconds to years. For students of cognitive neuroscience, it is especially pertinent to appreciate the means by which neuronal connections can be strengthened or weakened over time scales of 30 minutes or longer. This category of synaptic plasticity is germane to understanding the basis of learning, memory and the persistent influence of experience on brain function. See Chapter 13 for a detailed consideration of these and other phenomena related to use-dependent alterations in synaptic strength.

Summary

1. Nerve cells generate electrical signals that convey information over substantial distances and are transmitted to other cells by means of synaptic connections. These signals ultimately depend on changes in electrical potential across the neuronal membrane.

2. Neural signaling is facilitated by the complementary functions of ion transporters and channels, which maintain a resting membrane potential and account for the transient changes in transmembrane potential that generate and propagate neural signals. The primary purpose of transporters is to generate transmembrane concentration gradients, which are then exploited by ion channels to generate electrical signals.

3. The resting potential occurs because nerve cell membranes are permeable to one or more ion species subject to an electrochemical gradient. More specifically, a negative membrane potential at rest results from a net efflux of K^+ across neuronal membranes that are predominantly permeable to K^+.

4. An action potential is a sudden shift from the negative resting potential to a positive polarity. Action potentials are triggered when a transient rise in Na^+ permeability allows a net influx of Na^+ across the membrane that is now predominantly permeable to Na^+. The brief rise in membrane Na^+ permeability is followed by a secondary, transient rise in membrane K^+ permeability that repolarizes the neuronal membrane and produces a brief undershoot of the action potential.

5. During an action potential, the neuronal membrane is depolarized in an all-or-none fashion. Thus, the action potential and all its complex properties can be explained by time- and voltage-dependent changes in the Na^+ and K^+ permeabilities of neuronal membranes.

6. Action potentials propagate along axons by the passive flow of current as well as by active currents flowing through voltage-dependent ion channels, with the speed and efficiency of propagation being largely a function of axon diameter and the degree of axonal myelination. In this way, action potentials enable neural signaling over long distances.

7. Synapses communicate the information carried by action potentials from one neuron to the next in neural circuits. The cellular mechanisms that underlie synaptic transmission are closely related to the mechanisms that generate other types of neuronal electrical signals, namely ion flow through membrane channels.

8. In the case of electrical synapses, the membrane channels are gap junctions; direct but passive flow of current through the gap junctions is the basis for this type of synaptic transmission.

9. In the case of chemical synapses, membrane channels with smaller and more selective pores than gap junctions are activated by the binding of neurotransmitters (released from the presynaptic axon terminal) to postsynaptic receptors. The large number of neurotransmitters extant in the human nervous system can be divided into two broad classes: small-molecule neurotransmitters and neuropeptides.

10. Vesicles containing neurotransmitters discharge their contents into the synaptic cleft when depolarization generated by an action potential opens voltage-gated calcium channels, allowing Ca^{2+} to enter the presynaptic terminal.

11. Postsynaptic neurotransmitter receptors are a diverse group of proteins that bind neurotransmitters secreted into the synaptic cleft from the presynaptic terminal. Postsynaptic receptors then transduce the bound neurotransmitter into electrical signals by opening or closing ion channels, thus increasing or decreasing postsynaptic excitability.

12. Because postsynaptic neurons are usually innervated by many different inputs, the integrated effect of the conductance changes underlying all the excitatory and inhibitory potentials (EPSPs and IPSPs) produced in a postsynaptic cell at any moment determines whether or not the cell fires an action potential.

13. The strength of synaptic connections may be modified over time, and these modifications are the basis of memory and other use-dependent changes in brain function.

Additional Reading

Reviews

ARMSTRONG, C. M. AND B. HILLE (1998) Voltage-gated ion channels and electrical excitability. *Neuron* 20: 371–80.

AUGUSTINE, G. J. AND H. KASAI (2007) Bernard Katz, quantal transmitter release, and the foundations of presynaptic physiology. *J. Physiol. (Lond.)* 578: 623–625.

BAILEY, C. H., E. R. KANDEL AND K. SI (2004) The persistence of long-term memory: A molecular approach to self-sustaining changes in learning-induced synaptic growth. *Neuron* 44: 49–57.

BLISS, T. V. P. AND G. L. COLLINGRIDGE (1993) A synaptic model of memory: Long-term potentiation in the hippocampus. *Nature* 361: 31–39.

BREDT, D. S. AND R. A. NICOLL (2003) AMPA receptor trafficking at excitatory synapses. *Neuron* 40: 361–379.

CATTERALL, W. A. (1988) Structure and function of voltage-sensitive ion channels. *Science* 242: 50–61.

CONNORS, B. W. AND M. A. LONG (2004) Electrical synapses in the mammalian brain. *Annu. Rev. Neurosci.* 27: 393-418.

DAN, Y. AND M. M. POO (2006) Spike timing-dependent plasticity: from synapse to perception. *Physiol. Rev.* 86: 1033–1048.

EMSON, P. C. (1979) Peptides as neurotransmitter candidates in the CNS. *Prog. Neurobiol.* 13: 61–116.

HÖKFELT, T. D. AND 10 OTHERS (1987) Coexistence of peptides with classical neurotransmitters. *Experientia* Suppl. 56: 154–179.

HODGKIN, A. L. (1951) The ionic basis of electrical activity in nerve and muscle. *Biol. Rev.* 26: 339–409.

HODGKIN, A. L. (1958) The Croonian Lecture: Ionic movements and electrical activity in giant nerve fibres. *Proc. R. Soc. Lond. B* 148: 1–37.

HYLAND, K. (1999) Neurochemistry and defects of biogenic amine neurotransmitter metabolism. *J. Inher. Metab. Dis.* 22: 353–363.

KAPLAN, J. H. (2002) Biochemistry of Na,K-ATPase. *Annu. Rev. Biochem.* 71: 511–535.

MALENKA, R. C. AND S. A. SIEGELBAUM (2001) Synaptic plasticity: Diverse targets and mechanisms for regulating synaptic efficacy. In *Synapses*, W. M. Cowan, T. C. Sudhof and C. F. Stevens (eds.). Baltimore: Johns Hopkins University Press, pp. 393–413.

NAKANISHI, S. (1992) Molecular diversity of glutamate receptors and implication for brain function. *Science* 258: 597–603.

NEHER, E. (1992) Nobel lecture: Ion channels for communication between and within cells. *Neuron* 8: 605–612.

NICOLL, R. A. (2003) Expression mechanisms underlying long-term potentiation: A postsynaptic view. *Philos. Trans. Roy. Soc. Lond. B* 358: 721–726.

PIERCE, K. L., R. T. PREMONT AND R. J. LEFKOWITZ (2002) Seven-transmembrane receptors. *Nat. Rev. Mol. Cell Biol.* 3: 639–650.

SÜDHOF, T. (2004) The synaptic vesicle cycle. *Annu. Rev. Neurosci.* 27: 509–547.

ZUCKER, R. S. AND W. G. REGEHR (2002) Short-term synaptic plasticity. *Annu. Rev. Physiol.* 64: 355–405.

Books

BAUDRY, M. AND J. D. DAVIS (1991) *Long-Term Potentiation: A Debate of Current Issues.* Cambridge, MA: MIT Press.

COOPER, J. R., F. E. BLOOM AND R. H. ROTH (2003) *The Biochemical Basis of Neuropharmacology.* New York: Oxford University Press.

HILLE, B. (2002) *Ion Channels of Excitable Membranes*, 3rd Ed. Sunderland, MA: Sinauer.

KATZ, B. (1966) *Nerve, Muscle, and Synapse.* New York: McGraw-Hill.

KATZ, B. (1969) *The Release of Neural Transmitter Substances.* Liverpool: Liverpool University Press.

LANDFIELD, P. W. AND S. A. DEADWYLER (EDS.) (1988) *Long-Term Potentiation: From Biophysics to Behavior.* New York: A. R. Liss.

NICHOLLS, D. G. (1994) *Proteins, Transmitters, and Synapses.* Boston: Blackwell Scientific.

PETERS, A., S. L. PALAY AND H. DEF. WEBSTER (1991) *The Fine Structure of the Nervous System: Neurons and their Supporting Cells*, 3rd Ed. Oxford: Oxford University Press.

SIEGEL, G. J., B. W. AGRANOFF, R. W. ALBERS, S. K. FISHER AND M. D. UHLER (1999) *Basic Neurochemistry.* Philadelphia: Lippincott-Raven.

SQUIRE, L. R. AND E. R. KANDEL (1999) *Memory: From Mind to Molecules.* New York: Scientific American Library.

Glossary

A1 See *primary auditory cortex*.

A2 See *secondary auditory cortex*.

abulia A symptom of brain damage, often to the frontal lobes, that manifests as flat affect, limited willpower, and reduced motivation. [23]

accommodation A stage of child development in which the child learns to react to novel entities by modifying their scheme of thought. Compare *assimilation*. [27]

acquired sociopathy A personality change, often following focal damage to the frontal lobes, in which a person's behavior becomes sociopathic. [23]

action potential The electrical signal conducted along neuronal axons by which information is conveyed from one place to another in the nervous system. [1, Appendix]

acuity The ability of a sensory system to accurately discriminate spatial detail; usually tested by the ability to spatially discriminate two points, as in the Snellen eye chart exam for vision. Applies to all the sensory systems, but most obviously to vision and somatic sensation. [4]

adaptation The adjustment of sensory receptors or other elements in a sensory system to different levels of stimulus intensity; allows sensory systems to operate over a wide range of stimulus intensities. [4,26]

ADHD See *attention deficit hyperactivity disorder*.

aerial perspective The diminution of contrast (i.e., the increasing haziness of contour boundaries) as a function of distance from the observer; occurs as a result of the imperfect transmittance of the atmosphere, and is a monocular cue to depth. [5]

affect The outward display of emotion, which typically reflects a subjective feeling (often used synonymously with *emotion*). Compare *temperament*. [17]

affect intensity See *arousal* (definition 2).

affective neuroscience The study of the neurobiological basis of emotions. [17,18]

afferent neuron An axon that conducts action potentials from the periphery to more central parts of the nervous system. Compare *efferent neuron*. [1]

affirming the consequent An error in deductive logic caused by reversing the direction of inference (e.g., "If P, then Q. Q is true. Therefore, P.") Compare *denying the antecedent*. [25]

aftereffect The influence on visual perception that arises from looking at any sort of repetitive stimulus, such as a continuous motion stimulus. The classic example is the waterfall effect: the apparent upward movement seen after staring at falling water. [5]

afterimage The altered image that follows the presentation and removal of a visual stimulus—for example, the residual image after a flash, or after looking for many seconds at a chromatic stimulus (in which case a complementary-color afterimage is seen). [4,5]

agonist A neuropharmacological agent that mimics the action of a neurotransmitter. Compare *antagonist*. [3]

AI See *artificial intelligence*.

alexithymia A clinical condition marked by a lack of words to describe one's own emotions.

algorithm A set of rules or procedures set down in logical notation, and typically (but not necessarily) carried out by a computer.

allometry The study of differential growth rates. [26]

alpha motor neurons Spinal cord neurons that innervate skeletal muscle fibers. Compare *gamma motor neurons*. [8]

amblyopia Diminished visual acuity arising from a failure to establish appropriate visual cortical connections in early life as a result of visual deprivation. [27]

amnesia The pathological inability to remember or to establish memories. See also *anterograde amnesia* and *retrograde amnesia*. [13]

amygdala A nuclear complex in the temporal lobe that forms part of the limbic system; its major functions concern autonomic, emotional, and sexual behavior. [1,17,18]

analog magnitude system A cognitive system that represents the number of elements in a set in a continuous or analog fashion as opposed to a digital or discrete fashion. [22]

analytical Derived according to a set of principles, such as the features of an image. Compare *empirical*.

antagonist A neuropharmacological agent that opposes or interferes with the action of a neurotransmitter. Compare *agonist*. [3]

anterior In front of. [1]

anterior cingulate cortex A cortical structure in the midline frontal lobe, usually considered to be part of the limbic cortex; its dorsal regions are associated with the detection of conflicting information or stimuli and with the attentional control invoked to resolve such conflict. [23]

anterior commissure A small midline fiber tract that lies at the anterior end of the corpus callosum; like the callosum, it connects the two hemispheres. [1]

anterior horn See *ventral horn*.

anterograde amnesia The inability to lay down new memories. Compare *retrograde amnesia*. [13]

anthropoid primates Non-human primates that have characteristics especially similar to those of humans; generally refers to monkeys and great apes. [26]

aperture problem The challenge of determining the speed and direction of a moving line when its ends are obscured by an opening such as a circular hole or a vertical rectangle. [5]

aphasias Language deficits that arise from damage to one of the cortical language areas, typically in the left hemisphere. [21]

apparent motion The sensation of motion elicited by presentation of a stimulus in two positions over a brief interval. [5]

appendicular ataxia Uncoordinated, jerky movements of the limbs, typically associated with damage to the cerebellum. [9]

aprosodia The inability to inflect speech with the usual emotional color that typically arises from the contribution of the right hemisphere to language. Results in a monotonic or "robotic" speech pattern. [21]

area LIP See *lateral intraparietal area.*

arousal 1. A global state of the brain (or the body) reflecting an overall level of responsiveness. Compare *attention.* [2,10] 2. Also known as *affect intensity.* The degree of intensity of an emotion. [17]

artificial intelligence (AI) A computational approach to mimicking brain function that generally depends on the analytical solving of problems. [2, 28]

artificial neural network A computer architecture for solving problems by feedback from trial and error, rather than by a predetermined algorithmic solution. [28]

ascending pathway A pathway that extends from a more peripheral processing station to a higher one, typically in a sensory system. Compare *descending pathway.*

assimilation A developmental stage in which young children deal with novel entities by encompassing them into their preexisting thought schemes (for example, assuming any woman who seems to be the child's mother's age is also a mother). Compare *accommodation.* [27]

association An approach employed in cognitive neuroscience in which experimental evidence is used to show that a particular cognitive function is associated with a specific brain area or brain activity. Compare *dissociation.* [3]

association cortices See *cortical association areas.*

associativity In the hippocampus, the enhancement of a weakly activated group of synapses when a nearby group is strongly activated. [13]

attention The marshalling of cognitive processing resources on a particular aspect of the external or internal environment, or on internal processes such as thoughts or memories. Compare *arousal* (definition 1). [10]

attention deficit hyperactivity disorder (ADHD) A childhood disorder of unknown cause characterized by impulsiveness, short attention span, and continual activity. [23]

attentional blink A cognitive phenomenon, typically observed in a rapidly presented stream of stimuli, in which the ability to successfully report a second target stimulus occurring within 100 to 300 milliseconds of a successfully reported first target in the stream is decreased. [10]

attentional orienting The process by which attentional resources are directed toward specific aspects of the environment. [11,12]

attentional stream paradigm A paradigm used in attention research in which two or more segregated series of stimuli are presented and subjects selectively attend to one of the series to perform a task. [11]

auditory N1 Also called *N100 wave.* The first major negative ERP wave elicited by an auditory stimulus, arising from secondary auditory cortex and peaking at about 100 mil-

liseconds after the stimulus; can be strongly modulated by auditory spatial attention. [11]

auditory nerve The eighth cranial nerve, which carries information from the inner ear and vestibular system centrally to the cochlear nuclei and other processing stations in the brainstem. [6]

auditory system The peripheral and central neural apparatus for hearing. [6]

autism A childhood disorder of unknown cause, characterized by social disengagement that varies greatly in severity. [27]

autobiographical memory Memory of one's personal experience. [14]

autonomic ganglia Collections of autonomic motor neurons outside the central nervous system that innervate visceral smooth muscles, cardiac muscle, and glands. [1]

autonomic motor system Also called *visceral motor system.* The very large component of the nervous system that is dedicated to proper functioning of the viscera (all the organs that maintain the well-being of the body and brain). [1,8]

autonomic nervous system Also called the *visceral nervous system.* All of the neural apparatus that controls visceral behavior; includes the sympathetic, parasympathetic, and enteric systems. [1,8,17]

availability heuristic A simplified rule for gauging the frequency or importance of an event by the ease with which it can be accessed in memory. [24]

awareness The subjective aspects of consciousness. [28]

axial section See *horizontal section.*

axon The extension of a neuron that carries the action potential from the nerve cell body to a target. Compare *dendrite.* [1, Appendix]

axon hillock The initial portion of an axon, closest to the cell body; the point where action potentials are typically initiated. [1]

axon terminal The presynaptic ending of an axon; the point at which an action potential affects the postsynaptic target cell. [Appendix]

background In visual perception, pertaining to the part or parts of a scene that are farther away from an observer and/or less salient. [5]

backtracking In problem solving, moving temporarily farther from the end goal in order to set up a path to the solution. [2,25]

Baddeley model A model, proposed by Alan Baddeley, positing that working memory consists of three memory buffers that briefly maintain information (the phonological loop, the visuospatial sketchpad, and the episodic buffer) and a central executive that allocates attentional resources to the buffers. [16]

Balint's syndrome A neurological syndrome, caused by bilateral damage to the posterior parietal and lateral occipital cortex, that has three hallmark symptoms: simultanagnosia, optic ataxia, and oculomotor apraxia. Simultanagnosia is the sign most closely associated with the syndrome, and the one most studied from a cognitive neuroscience standpoint. [12]

bandwidth A frequency range within a spectrum; a measure of stimulus duration. [3,6]

basal forebrain nuclei Also called *septal forebrain nuclei.* A complex of primarily cholinergic nuclei that lies between the hypothalamus in the diencephalon and the orbital cortex of the frontal lobes; concerned with alertness and memory, among other functions. [1]

basal ganglia A group of nuclei lying deep in the subcortical white matter of the frontal lobes that organize motor behavior. The caudate, putamen, and globus pallidus are major components of the basal ganglia; the subthalamic nucleus and substantia nigra are often included. [1,9,23]

basic emotions Emotions that are innate, pan-cultural, evolutionarily old, shared with other species, and expressed by particular physiological patterns and facial configurations. Compare *complex emotions*. [17, 26]

basilar membrane The membranous sheet in the cochlea of the inner ear that contains the receptor cells (hair cells) that initiate audition. [6]

behavioral LTP A change in synaptic efficacy similar to LTP that follows an actual learning experience. [13]

behavioral facilitation The phenomenon in an exogenously cued spatial attention paradigm of faster behavioral response to a target stimulus presented at the (validly) cued location earlier than 300 milliseconds after the cue. Compare *inhibition of return*. [10]

behaviorism A perspective in cognitive psychology that holds that only directly observable behavior, and not internal mental states, can be studied scientifically. [2]

belt area See *secondary auditory cortex*.

BER See *brainstem-evoked response*.

beta A measure of a processing system's response bias in the performance of a discrimination or detection (i.e., being more or less likely to press the response button even when very unsure versus only when very sure). Compare *d-prime*. [10]

bi-stable figures Visual stimuli that elicit perceptual changes that fluctuate back and forth between the perception one of two different objects (e.g., between seeing a face and a vase in Figure 28.3A). [28]

binding 1. The postulated mechanisms by which the various features and qualities of an object are bound together to bring about a holistic perception of the object. [4,10] 2. The attachment of a biochemical molecule such as an odorant, tastant, or neurotransmitter to a protein in the cell membrane. [7, Appendix]

binocular Pertaining to both eyes. Compare *monocular*. [5]

binocular disparity The geometric difference between the view of the left and right eyes in animals with frontal eyes and stereoscopic depth perception. [5, 27]

binocular rivalry The bi-stable visual experience that occurs when the right and left eye are presented with incompatible or conflicting images. [5,28]

bipolar cells Cells in the vertebrate retina that receive input from the photoreceptors and communicate that input directly or indirectly to retinal ganglion cells. [4]

blastocyst A stage of embryonic development intermediate between the zygote (fertilized egg) and the embryo; differentiates into the three layers that make up the gastrula. [27]

blind spot The region of visual space that falls on the optic disk in the view generated by each eye; because photoreceptors are lacking in this part of the retina, objects that lie completely within the blind spot are not perceived in monocular view. [4,28]

blindsight The ability of people who are blind, usually because of damage to their cortex, to identify the properties of simple visual stimuli when forced to guess. [18,28]

block design An experimental design in which the integrated brain activity over an extended period in one experi-

mental condition (a block) is measured; the experimental block can then be compared to the integrated brain activity recorded during a block with a different experimental or a control condition. [3]

blood oxygenation level-dependent (BOLD) Pertaining to the signal typically measured with fMRI to measure brain activity; based on the local variations of the blood concentration of deoxygenated hemoglobin that result from the changes in blood flow induced by neural activity. [3]

bottom-up processing Peripheral sensory processing; or, more generally, processing that occurs in the lower stations of a sensory system. Compare *top-down processing*.

bounded rationality The idea that biological limitations on cognitive processing prevent people from making decisions or reasoning in a fully rational manner. [24]

brain The cerebral hemispheres and brainstem. [1]

brain activity The physiological processes that occur in the brain. Recent technologies that allow us to noninvasively measure brain activity in humans has revolutionized studies of how such activity may underlie cognitive functions (and behavior in general). [3]

brain lesion A localized region of brain damage.

brainstem The portion of the brain that lies between the diencephalon and the spinal cord; comprises the midbrain, pons, and medulla. [1,8]

brainstem-evoked response (BER) A small electrical brain wave elicited during the first 10 milliseconds after onset of a brief auditory stimulus that can be detected at the scalp; BERs reflect activity in the auditory brainstem nuclei as the sound stimulus information reaches them in sequence via the auditory afferent pathway. [11]

brainstem nucleus A collection of anatomically identifiable neurons in the brainstem that carries out specific functions.

brightness Technically, the apparent intensity of a source of light; more generally, a sense of the effective overall intensity of a light stimulus. Compare *lightness*, *hue*, and *saturation*. [5]

Broca's aphasia Also called *expressive aphasia*, *motor aphasia*, or *production aphasia*. A language deficit arising from damage to Broca's area in the frontal lobe and characterized by difficulty in the production of speech. Compare *Wernicke's aphasia*. [21]

Broca's area Cytoarchitectonic areas 44 and 45 in the ventral posterior region of the frontal lobe in the left hemisphere; named after the nineteenth-century anatomist and neurologist Paul Broca. Compare *Wernicke's area*. [1,21,26]

Brodmann areas Approximately 50 anatomically distinct subdivisions of the cerebral cortex identified in the early twentieth century by Korbinian Brodmann. [1]

Brodmann area 17 See *primary visual cortex*.

CA Abbreviation for *cornus Ammon* ("horn of Ammon"), an area of the hippocampus. Subregions CA1, CA2, and CA3 are important in memory processing. [13]

calcarine sulcus The major sulcus on the medial aspect of the human occipital lobe; the primary visual cortex lies largely within this sulcus. [1]

Cannon-Bard theory A theory of emotion, developed by Walter Cannon and Philip Bard, that emphasized the role of the hypothalamus and related parallel processing routes for emotional expression and emotional experience. [17]

categorical theories Theories of emotion positing that emotions are organized into discrete categories. Compare *dimensional theories*. [17]

caudal Posterior, or "tailward" (toward the back of the head when speaking of the brain). Compare *rostral*. [1]

caudate A nucleus that, together with the putamen, serves as the input structure for the globus pallidus. Damage to the caudate nucleus leads to hyperkinetic movement disorders such as Huntington's disease. [1]

cell The basic biological unit of life, defined by a membrane or wall that encloses cytoplasm and, in eukaryote organisms (including all plants and animals), a nucleus.

cell body Also called *soma*. The portion of a neuron that houses the cell's nucleus; axons and dendrites typically extend from the neuronal cell body. [1]

central nervous system The brain and spinal cord of vertebrates (by analogy, the central nerve cord and ganglia of invertebrates). Compare *peripheral nervous system*. [1]

central pattern generator The oscillatory activity found in the spinal cord of vertebrates (or the central nerve cord of invertebrates) that generates specific patterns of motor activity. [8]

central sulcus A major sulcus on the lateral aspect of the hemispheres that forms the boundary between the frontal and parietal lobes. Its anterior bank contains the primary motor cortex; the posterior bank contains the primary sensory cortex. [1]

cerebellar cortex The superficial gray matter of the cerebellum. [1]

cerebellum The prominent hindbrain structure that is concerned with motor coordination, posture, balance, and some cognitive processes; composed of a three-layered cortex and deep nuclei, and attached to the brainstem by the cerebellar peduncles. [1,9]

cerebral achromatopsia Loss of color vision as a result of damage to the visual cortex. [5]

cerebral aqueduct The portion of the ventricular system that connects the third and fourth ventricles. [1]

cerebral cortex The superficial gray matter of the cerebral hemispheres. [1]

cerebral hemispheres The two halves of the forebrain. [1]

cerebral peduncles The major fiber bundles that connect the brainstem to the cerebral hemispheres. [1]

cerebrocerebellum The part of the cerebellar cortex that receives input from the cerebral cortex via axons from the pontine relay nuclei. [9]

cerebrospinal fluid A normally clear and cell-free fluid that fills the ventricular system of the central nervous system; produced by the choroid plexus in the lateral ventricles. [1]

cerebrum The largest and most rostral part of the brain in humans and other mammals, consisting of the two cerebral hemispheres. [1]

change blindness Also called *inattentional blindness*. The normal inability to see a particular alteration in a changing scene because the change is not noticed. [28]

channel A protein in a cell membrane that creates a pore through which ions can pass [Appendix]

channel capacity In information theory, the maximum number of bits that a communication channel can carry. [2]

chiasm See *optic chiasm*.

cholinergic nuclei of the pons-midbrain junction Nuclei that play a central role in the regulation of sleep and wakefulness. [28]

chord In audition, a combination of two or more consonant tones sounded simultaneously (typically three simultaneously sounded notes, called a *triad*). [6]

choreiform movement Uncontrollable, dancelike ("choreiform") writhing or twisting movements associated with damage to the basal ganglia as occurs in disorders such as Huntington's disease. [9]

choroid plexus Specialized epithelium in the ventricular system that produces cerebrospinal fluid. [1]

chromatic scale A 12-tone musical scale that divides octaves into 12 approximately equal parts . [6]

chunking A method of increasing working memory capacity by packing more information into each remembered item. [2,16]

cingulate gyrus The gyrus that surrounds the corpus callosum. [1,17]

cingulate sulcus A sulcus on the medial aspect of the cerebral hemispheres defined by the cingulate gyrus. [1]

circadian rhythm Periodic variations over the 24-hour cycle of light and darkness (i.e., a day). [22]

circle of Willis A ring of arteries at the base of the midbrain; connects the posterior and anterior cerebral circulation. [1]

circuitry The connections between neurons; usually used in reference to a particular neural function (as in *visual circuitry*; see Chapters 4 and 5; or a *spinal reflex circuit*; see Chapter 1).

circumplex model A way to graphically represent the relationships among emotions by ordering them along the circumference of a circle formed by intersecting two orthogonal axes of valence and arousal at the circle's center. Compare *vector model*. [17]

classical conditioning Also called *conditioned reflex*. The modification of an innate reflex by associating its normal triggering stimulus with an unrelated stimulus. The unrelated stimulus comes to trigger the original response by virtue of this repeated association. [15]

clinical-pathological correlation A method in which damage to the brain is correlated with behavioral signs and symptoms to draw conclusions about the nature of a patient's problems and the function of the relevant brain area. [3]

cochlea The portion of the inner ear specialized for transducing sound energy into neural signals. [6]

cochlear nucleus The initial processing station in the brainstem for auditory nerve signals. [6]

cocktail party effect An attentional phenomenon in which an individual can selectively focus attention on one particular speaker and tune out other simultaneously occurring conversations. [2,10]

cognition "Higher-order" mental processes.

cognitive map theory A theory positing that the hippocampus mediates memory for spatial relations among objects in the environment. [14]

cognitive skill learning Gradual improvement in the performance of cognitive operations through practice. Compare *perceptual skill learning*. [15]

coincidence detectors Neurons that detect simultaneous events, as in sound localization. [6]

color The subjective sensations elicited in humans (and presumably many other animals) by different spectral distributions of light. [5]

color-blind See *color-deficient*.

color constancy The similar appearance of surfaces despite different spectral return from them; usually applied to the approximate maintenance of object appearances in different illuminants. Compare *lightness constancy*. [5]

color contrast The different color appearance of surfaces despite similar spectral returns from them. [5]

color-deficient Describing an individual who has abnormal color vision as a result of the absence of (or abnormalities in) one or more of the three types of human cone cells. [5]

color space The depiction of a human color experience in diagrammatic form by a space with three axes representing the perceptual attributes of hue, saturation, and brightness. [5]

coma A pathological state of profound and persistent unconsciousness. [28]

competence The knowledge or cognitive capacity that an organism possesses. Compare *performance*. [2]

complex emotions Emotions that are learned, socially and culturally shaped, evolutionarily new, and typically expressed by combinations of the response patterns that characterize basic emotions. Compare *basic emotions*. [17]

component process theories of emotion Theories that attempt to classify emotions according to the extent to which they recruit similar cognitive appraisals of emotion-eliciting situations. [17]

comprehension aphasia See *Wernicke's aphasia*.

computerized tomography (CT) An imaging method in which X-rays acquired at multiple angles are used to build a three-dimensional image of biological tissue. [3]

conceptual priming A form of direct priming in which the test cue and the target are semantically related. Compare *perceptual priming*. [15]

concrete operations stage In Jean Piaget's theory of cognitive development, the stage from ages 7 to 12 years in which a child begins to reason about the world; precedes the *formal operations stage*. [27]

conditioned reflex See *classical conditioning*.

conditioned response (CR) In classical conditioning, the reflex (normally innate in response to a particular unconditioned stimulus) that is triggered by a novel stimulus by virtue of repeated association. Compare *unconditioned response*. [15]

conditioned stimulus (CS) In classical conditioning, the novel stimulus that eventually comes to trigger the innate reflex by virtue of repeated association. Compare *unconditioned stimulus*. [15]

conditioning The generation of a novel response that is gradually elicited by repeated pairing of a novel stimulus (the conditioned stimulus) with a stimulus that normally elicits the response being studied (the unconditioned stimulus). [13,15]

cone opsins The three distinct photopigment proteins found in cones; the basis for color vision. [5]

cones Photoreceptor cells (i.e., cells that respond to light energy signals) that are specialized for high visual acuity and the perception of color. Compare *rods*. [4,5]

connectionist Pertaining to the connectivity of neural networks whose connection weights vary according to experience. [20]

connectionist models Information-processing models based on neural networks, in which problems are solved by changing the "weights" of the network connections. [2]

consciousness A contentious concept that includes the ideas of wakefulness, awareness of the world, and awareness of the self as an actor in the world. [28]

conservation The understanding that some physical transformations preserve quantity despite changes in apparent size or shape. [27]

consolidation The strengthening of memory traces following encoding. [2,13]

consonance The pleasing quality of two notes sounded together. [6]

content-based model of prefrontal organization A model of prefrontal cortex organization proposing that ventrolateral regions are involved primarily in object working memory, whereas dorsolateral regions are involved more in spatial working memory. Compare *process-based model*. [16]

context The information provided by the surroundings of a "target." The division of a scene into target and surround is useful, but arbitrary, since any part of a scene provides contextual information for any other part. [4,5]

contextual fear conditioning A form of emotional learning in which fear responses are acquired in response to environments that predict the presence of an aversive stimulus. [18]

continuity effect Also called *filling in*. The perceptual attribution of a property or properties to a region of visual space when the information from that space is either absent or physically different from what is actually seen. [2,20]

continuous mental magnitudes A mental representation that is continuous in format, as opposed to discrete. [22]

contralateral On the opposite side. Compare *ipsilateral*.

contrast The difference, usually expressed as a percentage, between the luminance (or spectral distribution, in the case of color) of two surfaces.

coronal section Also called *frontal section*. A brain section in the plane of the face; the term comes not from the concept of a crown but from a halo, which is classically depicted in that plane. Compare *horizontal section*, *sagittal section*. [1]

cornus Ammon See *CA*.

corpus callosum The large midline fiber bundle that connects the cortices of the two cerebral hemispheres. [1]

correspondence problem The problem presented in a random dot stereogram (or any image for that matter) of matching a dot in the retinal image in one eye to the corresponding dot in the retinal image of the other eye.

cortex The gray matter of the cerebral hemispheres and cerebellum, where most of the neurons in the brain are located.

cortical association areas Also called *association cortices*. The regions of cerebral neocortex that are not involved in primary sensory or motor processing. [4]

cortical columns See *cortical modules*.

cortical magnification Also called *magnification factor*. The disproportionate representation of cortical space according to peripheral receptor density (such as occurs for the central representation of the fovea of the human eye). [4]

cortical modules Also called *cortical columns*. Vertically organized groups of cortical neurons that process the same or similar information; examples are ocular dominance columns and orientation columns in the primary visual cortex. [4]

cortisol A steroid hormone released by the adrenal gland that is involved in the stress response. Called *corticosterone* in rodents. [18]

counting A serial enumeration process that results in a cardinal representation of the number of objects in a set. [22]

covert attention The directing of visual attention without shifting the direction of gaze to the attended region. Can apply to other sensory modalities or to attentional paradigms. Compare *overt attention*. [10]

Cowan model A model positing that working memory is organized in two embedded levels: (1) long-term memory representations in an activated state, and (2) activated representations that fall within the focus of attention. [16]

CR See *conditioned response.*

cranial motor nerves Nerves projecting from the cranial motor nuclei to muscles of the face, head, eyes, or neck. [1]

cranial nerve ganglia The sensory or motor ganglia associated with the 12 cranial nerves. Compare *dorsal root ganglia.* [1]

cranial nerves The 12 pairs of nerves arising from the brainstem that carry sensory information toward and motor information away from the central nervous system. [1]

critical period Also called *sensitive period.* A restricted developmental period during which the nervous systems of humans and other mammals are particularly sensitive to the effects of experience. [20,27]

crossed extension reflex A complex reflex arc that flexes a limb on one side of the body while simultaneously extending the limb on the opposite side of the body, thereby maintaining postural stability. Compare *flexion reflex.* [8]

CS See *conditioned stimulus.*

CT See *computerized tomography.*

cue See *retrieval cue.*

cutaneous withdrawal reflex A reflex initiated by a noxious stimulus that moves the affected body part away from the stimulus.

cyclopean fusion The normal sense when looking at the world with both eyes that we see it as if with a single eye. [5]

d-prime (d′) A measure of a processing system's ability to discriminate or detect; developed from information theory, it is based on the numbers of correctly detected/discriminated targets (hits), missed targets (misses), and nontargets that were incorrectly identified as targets (false alarms). Compare *beta.* [10]

dark adaptation Adjustment of the sensitivity of the visual system to scotopic conditions; based on the reactivation of bleached rhodopsin. Compare *light adaptation.* [4]

dB See *decibel.*

deactivations Regional decreases in brain activity measured in response to a cognitive task or event.

decibel (dB) A logarithmic unit of sound stimulus intensity based on the threshold of human hearing. [6]

declarative memory Also called *explicit memory.* Memory available to consciousness that can be expressed by language. Compare *nondeclarative memory.* [2,13]

declarative memory theory A theory positing that the hippocampus mediates all declarative memories, regardless of whether they are spatial, nonspatial, relational, nonrelational, episodic or semantic. [14]

deductive reasoning Deriving a logical inference by considering only a set of premises. Compare *inductive reasoning.* [2,25]

deep tendon reflex See *stretch reflex.*

default mode Brain processes that occur in the absence of active executive control; a pattern of brain activation that reflects a set of cognitive processes that are typically more engaged during passive experience. [19]

default-mode network A network of the brain that includes the posterior cingulate cortex, the ventral anterior cingulate cortex, and the medial inferior prefrontal cortex and that has been proposed to be engaged when the brain is either "idling" or not engaged in any specific cognitive task. [12]

degree A unit in terms of which visual space is measured; 1 degree is approximately the width of the thumbnail held at arm's length and covers about 0.2 mm on the retina.

delay conditioning A form of classical conditioning in which the conditioned stimulus is still ongoing when the unconditioned stimulus starts, and they both terminate at the same time. [15]

delay lines The time delay generated by axons of different lengths—a mechanism important in coincidence detection. [6]

delay phase The second of three phases of working memory, in which the information is maintained for several seconds. Compare *encoding phase* and *response phase.* [16]

delayed match-to-sample task Also called *delayed recognition task.* A memory test, often used with monkeys, in which the subject must maintain memory for a single object over a delay and then, when given the option between that object and a new one, must select the new object. [16]

delayed recognition task See *delayed match-to-sample task.*

delayed response task A task in which the appropriate response is known during the delay phase. [16]

dendrite The extension of a neuron that receives synaptic input; usually branches near the cell body. Compare *axon.* [1]

dendritic field potential An electrical potential induced in the dendritic tree of a neuron by input from the axons of other neurons. Called *local field potential (LFP)* when recorded locally, this electrical activity can often also be detected at the scalp as an EEG or ERP. [3]

dendritic spines Small extensions from the surfaces of dendrites that receive synapses. [13]

denying the antecedent An error in deductive logic caused by reasoning from a false premise (e.g., "If P, then Q. P is false. Therefore, Q is false."). Compare *affirming the consequent.* [25]

deoxyglucose technique A method for marking neurons according to their level of activity by incorporating a radioactively tagged, nonmetabolized sugar.

depolarization Changing the membrane potential of a neuron in the positive direction, which initiates an action potential if threshold is reached. Compare *hyperpolarization.* [1]

depth perception The perception of distance from the observer (either monocular or stereoscopic).

descending pathway A pathway that extends from the cerebral cortex to subcortical structures. Compare *ascending pathway.* [4]

descriptive model A model that attempts to describe how things are, as opposed to how they should be. Compare *normative model.* [2]

development See *ontogeny.*

developmental amnesia Amnesia that is due to brain damage occurring early during childhood development and is characterized by a deficit in episodic memory but relatively normal semantic memory. [14]

developmental dissociations Different rates of change during childhood and adult aging. [15]

developmental dyscalculia A learning disability in children that is characterized by the inability to learn simple arithmetic. [22]

dichotic listening A paradigm used in auditory attention research in which two different streams of auditory input are presented, one to each ear, and the subject is instructed to attend selectively to one of them. [18]

dichromat A color-deficient human (or the majority of mammals) whose color vision depends on only two cone types. Compare *monochromat* and *trichromat*. [5]

diencephalon The portion of the brain that lies just rostral to the brainstem; comprises the thalamus and hypothalamus. [1]

difference-in-memory (Dm) effects Greater study-phase activity for items that are remembered than for items that are forgotten in a subsequent memory test. Regions showing Dm effects are assumed to mediate successful encoding operations. [14]

differentiation The progressive specialization of developing cells. [27]

digit-span task A working memory test in which the subject is asked to immediately recall a random string of numbers, which is gradually increased until recall fails. [13]

dimensional theories Theories of emotion positing that emotions are organized according to two fundamental orthogonal axes of arousal and valence. Compare *categorical theories*. [17]

direct pathway A neural circuit in the basal ganglia that releases movement from inhibition when activated. Compare *indirect pathway*. [9]

direct priming The facilitation of recall in which the prime and the target are identical or have the same name. Compare *indirect priming*. [15]

direction The trajectory taken by something (e.g., a point moving within a frame of reference); together with speed, defines velocity. [23]

disinhibition The arranging of inhibitory and excitatory cells in a circuit that generates excitation by transiently inhibiting tonically active inhibitory neuron. [23]

dissociation An method in which experimental evidence is used to show that a particular cognitive function is *not* associated with a specific brain area or brain activity. See also *double dissociation*. Compare *association*. [3]

dissonance A combination of simultaneous sounds or notes heard by most people as suggesting tension or lack of resolution.

distal Farther away from a point of reference. In anatomy, often refers to a position toward the extremities as opposed to the trunk of the body. Compare *proximal*.

Dm effects See *difference-in-memory effects*.

dopamine A catecholamine neurotransmitter involved in learning and reward evaluation, among other roles in the nervous system of humans and other animals. [24]

dorsal When pertaining to the long body axis, refers to the back (as in *dorsal columns*). When pertaining to the brain, refers to the top (e.g., a "dorsal view" would be from the top of the head looking down). Compare *ventral*. [1]

dorsal columns Major ascending tracts in the spinal cord that carry mechanosensory information from the spinal cord to the thalamus; comprise the cuneate and gracile nuclei. [1,8]

dorsal horn The dorsal portion of the spinal cord gray matter, which contains neurons that process sensory information. Compare *lateral horn* and *ventral horn*. [1]

dorsal lateral geniculate nucleus Usually called the *lateral geniculate*. The thalamic nucleus that relays information from the retina to the cerebral cortex. [5]

dorsal root ganglia The segmental sensory ganglia of the spinal cord that contain the first-order sensory neurons whose axons project centrally via the dorsal

column/medial lemniscus and spinothalamic pathways. Compare *cranial nerve ganglia*. [1]

dorsal spinal roots The bundle of axons that runs from the dorsal root ganglia to the dorsal horn of the spinal cord, carrying sensory information from the periphery. Compare *ventral spinal roots*. [1,8]

dorsal stream A partially segregated visual processing pathway passing from primary visual cortex through extrastriate areas to the higher-order association cortices of the parietal cortex; thought to be concerned primarily with spatial aspects of visual processing. Compare *ventral stream*. [4]

dorsolateral prefrontal cortex Typically, the part of the lateral surface of frontal lobes that is anterior to motor cortex and the frontal eye fields. [23]

dorsolateral prefrontal syndrome See *frontal dysexecutive syndrome*.

double dissociation An approach in which one area of the brain is experimentally shown to be associated with a particular task or cognitive function, whereas another area is shown not to be involved in the same task or function. This demonstration thus distinguishes the cognitive roles of different regions in a more rigorous way than does simply showing that the two regions in question respond differently. [3]

dyslexia A common disorder characterized by difficulty reading. [21]

early selection A model of attention postulating that attentional mechanisms can selectively filter out or attenuate irrelevant sensory input at an early processing stage, before the completion of sensory and perceptual analysis. Compare *late selection*. [10]

eccentricity The distance from the center; in vision, typically refers to the distance in degrees away from the line of sight. [5]

EEG See *electroencephalographic recording*.

efferent neuron An axon that conducts information away from the central nervous system. Compare *afferent neuron*. [1]

electroencephalographic (EEG) recording A method of recording electrical brain activity, typically noninvasively from the scalp. EEG activity is thought to reflect mainly the currents produced in the dendritic trees of the large pyramidal cells in underlying cortex. [3]

electromagnetic radiation The full spectrum of radiated energy found in the universe; includes light, X-rays, gamma rays, and so on.

electrophysiological recording Referring to various methods of recording electrical activity in the nervous system. [1,3]

embodiment A sense of physical location of the self within one's own body. [19]

emotion A set of physiological responses, action tendencies, and subjective feelings that adaptively engage humans and other animals to react to events of biological and/or individual significance. Compare *affect* and *mood*. [17]

emotion family A group of emotions that share similar properties. [17]

emotion regulation The voluntary or involuntary deployment of resources to gain control over emotional responses. [18]

emotional perseveration The continuation of an emotional response to a stimulus after the emotional significance of the stimulus has changed and the response is no longer appropriate. [18]

empathy The ability to share the same feelings expressed by another individual. Compare *sympathy*. [19]

empirical Derived on the basis of past experience, effectively by trial and error. Compare *analytical*.

encoding The incorporation of new information into a memory store, which requires the modification or creation of memory traces. Compare *retrieval*. [2,13]

encoding phase The first of three phases of working memory, in which information is incorporated into memory. Compare *delay phase* and *response phase*. [16]

endogenous attention A form of attention in which processing resources are directed voluntarily to specific aspects of the environment, typically based on experimental instructions or more normally on an individual's goals, expectations, and/or knowledge. Compare *exogenous attention*. [2,10]

engram Also called *memory trace*. The physical basis of a stored memory. [13]

enteric division The division of the autonomic nervous system that is specifically concerned with regulating the behavior of the gut. [1]

epiphenomenon An effect taken to be an incidental consequence of a more basic property or principle.

episodic memory A component of declarative memory that refers to memory for personally experienced past events. Compare *semantic memory*. [2,13,14]

episodic memory theory A theory positing that the hippocampus is critical for episodic memory but not for semantic memory. [14]

episodic retrieval mode Also called simply *retrieval mode*. The mental state of episodic retrieval (the retrieval of episodic memories), which is assumed to be qualitatively different than the mental states of other cognitive abilities. [14]

EPSP See *excitatory postsynaptic potential*.

ERF See *event-related magnetic-field response*.

EROS See *event-related optical signals*.

ERP See *event-related potential*.

error-related negativity (ERN) An electrophysiological marker that occurs when participants make errors in cognitive tasks. [19,23]

ethology An approach to understanding behavior by determining its evolutionary origins, current function, developmental trajectory, and underlying physiological mechanisms. [26]

event-related magnetic-field response (ERF) Magnetic-field fluctuations in an ongoing brain MEG recording that are triggered by sensory and cognitive events, reflecting the summed activity of neuronal populations specifically responding to those events. [3]

event-related optical signals (EROS) A noninvasive optical imaging approach based on the fact that when brain tissue is illuminated, even through the skull, the amount of transmitted versus scattered light varies as a function of whether the neuronal tissue is electrically active. [3]

event-related potential (ERP) Voltage fluctuations in an ongoing brain EEG that are triggered by sensory and/or cognitive events; the changes reflect the summed electrical activity of neuronal populations specifically responding to those events and are extracted from the ongoing EEG by time-locked averaging. [3]

excitatory Pertaining to a synaptic effect that brings the membrane of the postsynaptic cell closer to threshold, thereby making firing of the postsynaptic cell more likely. Compare *inhibitory*. [1]

excitatory postsynaptic potential Usually abbreviated EPSP. A synaptic potential that increases the likelihood of an action potential occurring in the postsynaptic (target) cell. Compare *inhibitory postsynaptic potential, synaptic potential*. [Appendix]

executive control The cognitive function associated with altering thought and behavior in a goal-directed, context-dependent, and flexible manner. [23]

executive processes The cognitive functions that allow flexible and goal-directed control. The major executive processes are initiation, inhibition, task switching, and monitoring. [2,23]

exogenous attention Also called *reflexive attention*. A form of attention in which processing resources are directed to specific aspects of the environment as the result of a sudden stimulus change, such as a loud noise or sudden movement, that attracts attention automatically. Compare *endogenous attention*. [2,10]

expected utility The personal value (i.e., utility) placed on the potential outcome of a decision. Compare *expected value*. [2,24]

expected-utility theory A normative model for decision making in which individuals select the option that provides the greatest expected utility, regardless of other factors. Compare *expected-value theory* and *prospect theory*. [24]

expected value The absolute value in a particular currency (e.g., dollars) of the potential outcome of a decision. Compare *expected utility*. [2,24]

expected-value theory A normative model for decision making in which individuals select the option that provides the greatest expected value, regardless of other factors. Compare *expected-utility theory*. [24]

explicit memory See *declarative memory*. [13]

explicit memory test A memory test in which subjects are instructed to intentionally remember information from a particular past event. Compare *implicit memory test*. [2]

expressive aphasia See *Broca's aphasia*.

external ear The cartilaginous elements of the visible ear (the pinna and concha). [6]

extinction 1. The gradual disappearance of a conditioned response that is no longer being rewarded. [15] 2. A phenomenon, found in patients with hemispatial neglect, in which a stimulus on the right side of the body or right visual field (processed by the intact left hemisphere) dominates perception, "extinguishing" the ability to perceive the simultaneous stimulus on the left. [12]

extrastriate visual cortical areas Regions of the visual cortex that lie outside the primary (striate) visual cortex; includes higher-order visual processing areas such as V4, MT, and MST. [4,5]

eyeblink conditioning A paradigm in which a puff of air is repeatedly paired with a tone until the tone by itself elicits blinking. [15]

face-in-a-crowd effect The phenomenon in visual search behavior in which it is easier to identify an angry face dispersed among many happy ones compared to a happy face dispersed among many angry ones. Compare *snake-in-the-grass effect*. [18]

facial expressions of emotion Facial movements that express emotions including surprise, fear, disgust, anger, happiness, and sadness. [2]

facilitation model of repetition suppression A model positing that suppression reflects faster processing of stimuli because of shorter latencies and/or shower duration of neural firing. Compare *fatigue model* and *sharpening model*. [15]

false-belief task A task used to test whether a child comprehends that another person can hold a false belief. [27]

familiarity The feeling that one has experienced an event at some point in the past, even though no specific associations or contextual detail come to mind. Compare *recollection*. [14]

fatigue model of repetition suppression A model positing that when a stimulus is repeated, all initially responsive neurons show a proportionally equivalent reduction in their response. Compare *facilitation model* and *sharpening model*. [15]

fear conditioning A form of emotional learning in which fear responses are acquired to cues that predict the occurrence of an aversive stimulus. See also *contextual fear conditioning*. Compare *fear extinction*. [18]

fear extinction A form of emotional learning in which fear responses are reduced by repeated presentation of a feared stimulus without any unpleasant consequences. Compare *fear conditioning*. [18]

feature detection The concept that sensory percepts entail the processing of physical features of the stimuli arising from objects in the world. [2]

feature integration theory An attention model postulating that the visual perceptual system is organized as a set of feature maps, each providing information about the location(s) in the visual field of a particular feature. [10]

feature similarity gain model A model in which the attentional modulation of the amplitude (gain) of a sensory neuron's response depends on the similarity of the features of the currently relevant target and the feature preferences of that neuron. [11]

feedback Information that is projected backward from a higher-order station to a lower one in a neural processing system. Compare *feedforward*. [4]

feedforward Information that is projected forward from a lower-order station to a higher one in a neural processing system. Compare *feedback*. [4]

FFA See *fusiform face area*.

fight-or-flight response A rapid reaction to a threatening stimulus that causes engagement of the sympathetic branch of the autonomic nervous system in preparation for action. [18]

filling in See *continuity effect*.

fissure A deep cleft in the surface of the brain; can be between two lobes (e.g., the lateral fissure between the frontal and temporal lobes), or an especially deep sulcus (e.g., the calcarine fissure in the occipital lobe). [1]

flanker task An attentional paradigm used to study stimulus-processing interference that arises when irrelevant flanking stimuli conflict on a particular dimension with the features of a task-relevant visual stimulus. [10]

flashbulb memory The concept that traumatic memories are vividly and accurately represented in the brain as though the event were recorded through the flash of a camera. [18]

flexion reflex A polysynaptic reflex mediating withdrawal from a painful stimulus. Compare *crossed extension reflex*. [8]

fMRI See *functional magnetic resonance imaging*.

FN400 effect In ERP studies of recognition memory, the greater negativity that is elicited by new items than by old items over midfrontal regions about 300 to 500 milliseconds after the stimulus. [14]

folia The ridges and valleys that are apparent in the cerebellar cortex. [1]

foraging hypothesis The proposal that the information-processing demands of finding scarce foods such as ripe fruit stimulated the evolution of enhanced cognition in some species of primates relative to others that feed on more evenly distributed foods, such as leaves or grass. [26]

forebrain The anterior portion of the brain that includes the cerebral hemispheres (the telencephalon and diencephalon). [1]

form The perception of object geometry or shape; one of the major visual perceptual qualities. [5]

formal operations stage In Jean Piaget's theory of cognitive development, the stage from 12 years old and beyond in which reasoning children become able to engage in abstract problem solving; follows the *concrete operations stage*. [27]

formant One of several frequencies that represent the natural resonances of different components of the vocal tract. [20]

fornix (pl. fornices) An axon tract, best seen from the medial surface of the divided brain, that interconnects the hypothalamus and hippocampus. [1]

Fourier analysis A mathematical procedure for representing a function as the sum of a series of sinusoids. Based on *Fourier's theorem*, the idea established by Jean-Baptiste-Joseph Fourier in the late eighteenth century, that any periodic function can be decomposed into a series of sine or cosine waves that are harmonically related (and thus that any spectrum can be represented as the sum of a series of appropriate sine waves). [6]

fourth ventricle The ventricular space that lies between the pons and the cerebellum. [1]

fovea The area of the human retina specialized for high acuity; contains a high density of cones and few rods. Most mammals do not have a well-defined fovea, although many have an area of central vision (called the *area centralis*) in which acuity is higher than in more eccentric retinal regions. [4]

framing effect A mode of representing a decision-making scenario that changes the decisions that people make, even though the basic structure of the problem is left unchanged. [2,24]

frequency How often something occurs in a unit of time and/or space.

frequency band See *bandwidth*.

frequency distribution A histogram or other graphical representation showing the relative frequency of occurrence of an event.

frontal disinhibition syndrome A collection of behavioral signs and symptoms, typically caused by damage to the ventral prefrontal cortex; manifested by a loss of control, inappropriate outbursts, and a lack of inhibition in social settings. [23]

frontal dysexecutive syndrome Also called *dorsolateral prefrontal syndrome*. A collection of behavioral signs and symptoms, typically caused by damage to the dorsolateral prefrontal cortex; manifested by an inability to change behavior willfully and flexibly according to context. [23]

frontal eye fields A region of the prefrontal cortex in human and nonhuman primates, often associated with Brodmann area 8a, that plays a key role in voluntary visual orienting movements. [8]

frontal lobe The lobe of the brain that includes all the cortex lying anterior to the central sulcus and superior to the lateral fissure. [1]

frontal section See *coronal section*.

frontomedian cortex The region of the superior and medial frontal lobe that is immediately anterior to supplementary motor cortex. [24]

frontopolar cortex The most anterior part of the prefrontal cortex. [23]

functional brain imaging A technique for imaging brain activity that depends on the metabolic activity of the relevant brain tissue to reveal the location of neural functions; major types include positron emission tomography (PET) and functional magnetic resonance imaging (fMRI). [3]

functional dissociation Differential effects of experimental factors manipulated in the laboratory. For example, a functional dissociation between episodic memory and perceptual priming is that semantic processing during encoding enhances the former but not the latter. [15]

functional fixedness Focusing on one reasonable, but incorrect, solution to a problem. [25]

functional magnetic resonance imaging (fMRI) A noninvasive method for imaging brain activity that uses imaging pulse sequences generated by an MRI scanner; the signal measured is caused by hemoglobin-based changes in blood oxygenation and blood flow that are induced by local neural activity. [3]

fundamental frequency (f_0) The first harmonic in the harmonic series evident in the sound spectra generated by a vibrating string or column of air. Compare *harmonic*. [6,20]

fusiform face area (FFA) A region of the fusiform gyrus that shows enhanced responses to faces relative to other objects. [19]

game theory A subfield of behavioral economics that investigates how people make decisions in simple, well-controlled games. [2,24]

gamma motor neurons Spinal motor neurons that are specifically concerned with the regulation of muscle spindle length; they innervate the intrafusal muscle fibers of the spindle. Compare *alpha motor neurons*. [8]

ganglion (pl. ganglia) A structurally and functionally discrete collection of neurons (individually referred to as *ganglion cells*) in the periphery (i.e., outside the central nervous system). Not to be confused with the *basal ganglia*, a group of structures that lie within the brain (see Chapter 1). Compare *nucleus*. [1,8]

gastrula A phase of embryonic development that follows the blastocyst phase and is characterized by three layers (endoderm, mesoderm, and ectoderm). [27]

gating Allowing or permitting. The basal ganglia, for example, gate movement initiation. Channels through the neuronal membrane are often gated, allowing the access of certain ions under certain conditions. [9, Appendix]

gaze-triggered shift of attention A shift of visual attention that is induced by viewing another individual's gaze being directed to a location in space. [10]

gene A hereditary unit located on a chromosome and defined in the simplest case by encoding the information for a particular protein; the genetic information is carried by linear sequences of nucleotides in DNA that code for corresponding sequences of amino acids.

generator potential See *receptor potential*.

genetic algorithms A computer-based scheme for simulating evolution using artificial neural networks. [28]

genome The complete set of an animal's genes.

genotype The genetic makeup of an individual. Compare *phenotype*.

geometric illusion A discrepancy between a visual stimulus and the resulting percept based on geometric measurements (measurements of length, angle, etc.). [5]

geon An abbreviation for "geometric icon." A hypothetical feature detector that is sensitive to simple three-dimensional shapes such as cylinders or cubes. [2]

Gestalt laws Generalizations about the rules of perception as applied to stimulus categories; not widely accepted today but of historical interest. [2]

Gestalt school An early-twentieth-century school of psychology promulgating the theory that the overall set of features of a scene determine its perception according to simple rules. (The German *Gestalt* means "an integrated perceptual whole.") [2]

glia See *neuroglial cells*.

globus pallidus One of the three major nuclei that make up the basal ganglia in the cerebral hemispheres; relays information from the caudate and putamen to the thalamus. [1]

glomeruli Characteristic collections of neurons in the olfactory bulb; formed by dendrites of mitral cells and terminals of olfactory receptor cells, as well as processes from local interneurons. [7]

glottis The space or opening between the vocal cords. [20]

goal state The solution to a problem. [24]

G-protein-coupled receptors See *metabotropic receptors*.

grammar The system of rules implicit in a language. [2,20]

grandmother cell A hypothetical neuron whose activity would indicate the presence of a specific object in the environment (e.g., one's grandmother). [28]

grapheme A symbol used in the written representation of speech. The symbol may represent a whole word, a syllable, or a speech sound, as in the letters of an alphabet. [20]

gray matter Regions of the central nervous system that are rich in neuronal cell bodies; includes the cerebral and cerebellar cortices, the nuclei of the brain, and the central portion of the spinal cord. Compare *white matter*. [1, 27]

guided search An attention theory positing that top-down mechanisms based on behavioral goals can be used to set priorities and facilitate processing during visual search. [10]

gustatory system Also called *taste system*. The peripheral and central components of the nervous system dedicated to processing and perceiving taste stimuli. [7]

gyrification index A quantitative measure of the degree of neocortical folding. [26]

gyrus A ridge in the folded cerebral cortex. Compare *sulcus*. [1]

habituation The process by which a behavioral response to the same stimulus decreases in intensity, frequency, or duration when a stimulus is repeated over and over. Compare *sensitization* (definition 1). [13]

hair cell The receptor cell in the inner ear for transducing sound stimuli (or other mechanical stimuli in the case of vestibular hair cells) into neural signals. [6]

hardware The mechanical components (machinery) of a computer. Compare *software*. [28]

harmonic Also called *overtone*. A natural frequency of resonant vibration in a harmonic series; always an integer multiple of the fundamental frequency of the vibrating object. Compare *fundamental frequency*. [20]

harmonic series The series of vibratory modes evident in the spectra produced by resonating objects. [6]

harmony The perceptual responses to presenting simultaneous tones that comprise consonant musical intervals. See *chord*. [6]

Hebbian learning The idea, proposed by Donald Hebb in the late 1940s, that when presynaptic and postsynaptic neurons fire action potentials together, the strength of the synaptic connections between them is enhanced. *Hebb's rule* is often state as "Cells that fire together wire together." [2,13]

hemiballismus A neurological disorder resulting from unilateral damage to the basal ganglia; manifested by flinging movements of the limbs contralateral to the lesion. [9]

hertz (Hz) A measure of frequency; 1 hertz equals 1 cycle per second.

heuristic A rule of procedure derived from past experience that can be used to solve a problem; in vision, heuristics are sometimes taken to determine perception. [2,24]

heuristic process A process used for simple tasks or decisions that is based on a set of rules and a decision criterion. Compare *systematic process*. [14]

hidden unit In connectionist models, the elements in the layer or layers of an artificial neural network between the input and the output. [2]

hierarchy A system of interconnected higher and lower ranks. In vision, the idea that neurons in initial stations of the visual system determine the properties of higher-order neurons. [4]

higher-order Pertaining to processes and/or areas taken to be further removed from the input stages of a system; in neuroscience, sometimes used as a synonym for *cognitive*.

higher-order neurons Neurons that are relatively remote from peripheral sensory receptors or motor effectors; often refers to neurons in the cerebral cortex.

hill climbing A strategy for solving a problem that entails choosing the action that brings one closest to the goal state, without backtracking. [2]

hippocampal-perirhinal theory The idea that the hippocampus processes information relatively slowly and is associational and spatial, whereas the perirhinal cortex processes information more rapidly and is automatic and item-based. [14]

hippocampus (pl. hippocampi) A specialized cortical structure located in the medial portion of the temporal lobe; in humans, concerned with short-term declarative memory, among many other functions. [1,17]

homeostasis Pertaining to the steady maintenance at optimal levels of essential physiological processes such as heart rate, blood pressure, and breathing rate. Myriad feedback and feedforward loops in the nervous system serve to maintain homeostasis. [8]

hominids The family of primates that includes humans and their bipedal ancestors but not great apes (although some taxonomists include all African apes, humans, and human ancestors within the hominid family). [26]

Homo The genus of humans and their ancestors characterized by upright walking, a relatively large brain, certain advanced dental features, and toolmaking. [26]

homologue A biological feature or trait shared by two organisms because it was inherited from a common ancestor. Homologous traits may differ in their function, but they derive from the same genetic and developmental programs. [26]

homonyms Words that sound the same and have the same spelling but different meanings (e.g., *bank*). [20]

homophones Words that sound the same but are spelled differently (e.g., *kernel* and *colonel*). [20]

homunculus (pl. homunculi) Literally "little man" (Greek), often used in referring to the shape of a primary sensory or motor cortical map; also used to refer (often derisively) to the dualist notion of an "I" that stands above neural processing. [7,28]

horizontal section Also called an *axial section*. Brain sections taken parallel to the rostral-caudal (i.e, nose to back of head) axis. Compare *coronal section*, *sagittal section*. [1]

HPA axis See *hypothalamic-pituitary-adrenal axis.*

hue The aspect of color sensation that pertains specifically to judgments about a color with respect to its redness, greenness, blueness, or yellowness. Compare *brightness* and *saturation*. [5]

Huntington's disease An autosomal dominant genetic disorder in which a single gene mutation results in damage to the basal ganglia that causes personality changes, progressive loss of the control of voluntary movement, and eventually death. [9]

hyperpolarization Changing the membrane potential of a neuron in the negative direction, driving it away from threshold and making it less likely to initiate an action potential. Compare *depolarization*. [1]

hyperscanning An fMRI technique that involves the simultaneous collection of data across more than one MRI scanner, often while individuals are playing a multiplayer game. [24]

hypothalamic-pituitary-adrenal (HPA) axis The primary information-processing pathway for stress responses; connects the hypothalamus, pituitary gland, and adrenal gland. [18]

hypothalamus A collection of small but critical nuclei in the diencephalon that lies just inferior to the thalamus; governs reproductive, homeostatic, and circadian functions. [1,17]

Hz See *hertz.*

illumination The light that falls on a scene or surface. [5]

illusion A discrepancy between the physically measured properties of a stimulus and what is actually perceived.

illusory conjunction A perceptual process in which sensory features from different objects in a scene are falsely perceived as being part of the same object. [10]

image The representation in art, on the retina, or in perception, of an external form.

imagery The mental representation of an image without the physical presence of sensory stimuli. [16]

implicit memory See *nondeclarative memory.*

implicit memory test A memory test in which subjects are asked to perform a task that is seemingly unrelated to the encoding event but nonetheless reveals memory for it. Compare *explicit memory test*. [2]

in vitro Literally "in glass" (Latin). Pertaining to any biological process studied outside of the organism. Compare *in vivo*.

in vivo Literally "in life" (Latin). Pertaining to any biological process studied in an intact living organism. Compare *in vitro*.

inattentional blindness See *change blindness*.

incidental learning Learning that occurs when participants do not know that they are encoding information. Compare *intentional learning*. [2]

indirect pathway A neural circuit in the basal ganglia that inhibits movement when activated. Compare *direct pathway*. [9]

indirect priming The facilitation of recall by an item (the prime) that is not directly related to the item. For example, the word *winter* may indirectly prime both *summer* and *snow*. Compare *direct priming*. [9]

inductive reasoning Deriving an inference about a larger category by considering examples from within that category. Compare *deductive reasoning*. [2,25]

infantile amnesia In adults, the inability to remember the early years of childhood. [27]

inferior Below. [1]

inferior colliculi Paired hillocks on the dorsal surface of the midbrain; concerned with auditory processing. Compare *superior colliculi*. [1,6]

information The systematic arrangement of a parameter such that an observer (or a receiver) can, in principle, extract a signal from the background noise.

information theory A theory of communication channel efficiency first elaborated by Claude Shannon in the late 1940s. [2]

inhibition Also called *inhibitory response*. Any effect that leads to a decrease in neuronal signaling. [2,23]

inhibition of return (IOR) A phenomenon in an exogenously cued spatial attention paradigm that is apparent as a slower behavioral response to a target stimulus presented at the (validly) cued location later than 300 milliseconds after the cue. Compare *behavioral facilitation*. [10]

inhibitory postsynaptic potential Abbreviated *IPSP*. A synaptic potential that increases the likelihood of an action potential occurring in the postsynaptic (target) cell. Compare *excitatory postsynaptic potential, synaptic potential*. [Appendix]

initiation The executive control process associated with starting a behavior. [2,23]

inner ear The cochlea and semicircular canals. [6]

innervate To establish synaptic contact with another neuron or target cell.

innervation All the synaptic contacts made on a particular target.

input The information supplied to a neural processing or other information-processing system.

insight The experience felt when one suddenly perceives the solution of a problem. [2,25]

insula Literally "island" (Latin). The portion of the cerebral cortex that is buried within the depths of the lateral fissure. [1,4,19]

insular cortex The hidden portion of the cerebrum formed by the conjunction of the frontal and temporal lobes. [24]

intelligence quotient (IQ) A standardized but controversial measure of intelligence. [25]

intention tremor A tremor that occurs during performance of a voluntary motor act. Characteristic of cerebellar pathology. [9]

intentional learning Learning that occurs when participants know that their memory will be tested and hence try to encode the information efficiently. Compare *incidental learning*. [2]

interaural intensity difference The difference in the intensity of a sound stimulus at the two ears, which contributes to sound localization. Compare *interaural time difference*. [6]

interaural time difference The difference in the time of arrival of a sound stimulus at the two ears, which contributes to the ability to localize sounds. Compare *interaural intensity difference*. [6]

intercellular communication Signaling interactions between cells; in neurons, typically by means of synaptic transmission. [1, Appendix]

interleaved learning Learning in which a particular item is learned not all at once but through a series of presentations intermixed with exposure to other examples of the same general domain. [13]

intermodal attention The ability to focus attention on the stimulus information in one modality and relatively tune out the stimulus information in the sensory input in another modality. Compare *supramodal attention*. [11]

internal capsule A large white matter tract that lies between the diencephalon and the basal ganglia; contains, among others, sensory axons that run from the thalamus to the cortex and motor axons that run from the cortex to the brainstem and spinal cord. [1]

interneuron Literally, a neuron in a circuit that lies between primary sensory and primary effecter neurons; more generally, a neuron that branches locally to innervate other neurons. [1]

interval timing The postulated mechanisms that allow us and other animals to track durations over the range of seconds to minutes. [2]

intracellular recording Recording the potential between the inside and outside of a neuron with a microelectrode. [1]

invalidly cued Pertaining an attentional cuing paradigm in which the target following a cue occurs in a location different from the one in which it was cued. Compare *validly cued*. [10]

inverse optics problem The impossibility of knowing the world directly by means of light stimuli; the problem arises because of the ambiguity of light patterns projected onto the retina. [5]

investment game See *trust game*.

ion An atom or group of atoms in which the number of electrons is either greater or less than the number of protons, resulting in an electrical charge on the atom. The primary ions of the nervous system are potassium (K^+), sodium (Na^+), calcium (Ca^{2+}), and chloride (Cl^-). Movement of ions across neuronal membranes in response to stimuli creates the electrical signals that result in action potentials and synaptic transmission. [Appendix]

ion channel A membrane protein that uses the passive energy of concentration gradients (created by ion exchangers) to allow the passage of ions across the cell membrane. Compare *ion exchanger*. [1, Appendix]

ion exchanger Also called *ion pumps*. A membrane protein that uses metabolic energy to create ion concentration gradients across neuronal membranes. Compare *ion channel* [1, Appendix]

ionotropic receptors Also called *ligand-gated ion channels*. Class of postsynaptic neurotransmitter receptors that link binding of neurotransmitter with the action of ion channels. Compare *metabotropic receptors*. [Appendix]

IOR See *inhibition of return*.

Iowa Gambling Task An experimental paradigm, developed by Antonio Damasio and colleagues at the University of Iowa, that tests subjects' sensitivity to risk and reward; the test reveals that patients with damage to the inferior prefrontal cortex tend to make risk-seeking choices. [24]

ipsilateral On the same side. Compare *contralateral*.

IPSP See *inhibitory postsynaptic potential*.

IQ See *intelligence quotient*.

ischemia A paucity or complete lack of blood supply. A common cause of stroke. [1]

isoluminance Also called *equiluminance*. The condition in which two surfaces have the same luminance. [5]

item-in-context theory A theory positing that the perirhinal cortex and the associated lateral entorhinal cortex are concerned with *memory for items*, that the parahippocampal cortex and associated medial entorhinal cortex are involved in *memory for context*, and that the hippocampus interacts with both regions and is involved in *memory for items in context*. [14]

item memory test An explicit memory test that asks participants to remember *what* happened during a particular event. Compare *source memory test*. [2]

James-Lange theory A theory, developed by William James and Carl Lange, positing that emotions are determined by the pattern of feedback from the body periphery to the cerebral cortex. [17]

Kennard principle The principle that cortical injuries in infancy are often less deleterious compared to the same injury in adulthood; named after Margaret Kennard. [27]

Klüver-Bucy syndrome A rare behavioral syndrome following anterior temporal lobe damage that includes the lack of appreciation for the motivational significance of objects in the environment, hyperorality, and altered sexual behavior; named after Heinrich Klüver and Paul Bucy. [17]

labyrinth The bony portion of the inner ear that contains the vestibular apparatus. [7]

lamina A layer, typically one of the cell layers that characterize the neocortex, hippocampus, cerebellar cortex, spinal cord, or retina. [1,5]

laminated Layered.

language The system of communication used in the speech of any group of people. [2]

larynx The upper part of the respiratory tract that lies between the trachea and the pharynx. [20]

late selection A theory of attention postulating that all stimuli are processed through the completion of sensory and perceptual analysis before any selection or influence of attention occurs. Compare *early selection*. [10]

lateral Located away from the midline. Compare *medial*. [1]

lateral column The lateral regions of spinal cord white matter that convey motor information from the brain to the spinal cord. [1]

lateral fissure Also called *Sylvian fissure*. The cleft on the lateral surface of the human brain that separates the temporal and frontal lobes. [1]

lateral geniculate See *dorsal lateral geniculate nucleus*.

lateral horn The lateral portion of the spinal cord gray matter, which mediates sympathetic motor responses. Compare *dorsal horn* and *ventral horn*. [1]

lateral inhibition Inhibitory effects extending laterally in the plane of any neural tissue (e.g., the retina or the visual cortex).

lateral intraparietal area Also called *area LIP*. Part of the inferior parietal lobule, typically associated with Brodmann area 7 in primates, which plays a key role in orienting attention and the eyes to a location in space. [23,24]

lateral olfactory tract The projection from the olfactory bulbs to higher olfactory centers. [7]

lateral ventricles The major ventricles in each cerebral hemisphere. [1]

learning The acquisition of novel information and behavior through experience.

left-brain interpreter A hypothesis postulating that the prefrontal cortex in the left hemisphere supports the construction of coherent mental narratives. [25]

left-parietal effect In ERP studies of recognition memory, the phenomenon whereby old items elicit a greater positivity over parietal electrodes than do new items at about 400 to 800 milliseconds after the stimulus. Compare *right-frontal effect*. [14]

levels of processing framework The idea that semantic processing leads to better retention than does nonsemantic (e.g., perceptual) processing. [2]

lexeme The key word in a group of words that have the same basic meaning. For example, *being*, *been*, *am*, and *is* refer to the lexeme *be*. [2]

ligand-gated ion channels See *ionotropic receptors*.

light The wavelength range in the electromagnetic spectrum that elicits visual sensations in humans (photons having a wavelength of about 400 to 700 nanometers). [4,5]

light adaptation Adjustment of the sensitivity of the visual system according to ambient light conditions. Compare *dark adaptation*. [4]

lightness In vision, the apparent reflectance of a surface. Compare *brightness*. [5]

lightness constancy The similar grayscale appearance of two surfaces, despite differences in their spectral return. Compare *color constancy*. [5]

limbic system The cortical and subcortical structures concerned with the emotions that lie along the medial wall of the forebrain. [17]

limbic system theory The theory that structures of the limbic forebrain constitute a system that generates emotions. [17]

LIP See *lateral intraparietal area*.

lobes The four major regions of the cerebral cortex: the frontal, parietal, occipital, and temporal lobes. [1]

local circuit neuron A neuron whose local connections contribute to processing circuitry. [8]

locus coeruleus A small adrenergic nucleus in the rostral brainstem that projects widely in the brain; it plays a role in the sleep-waking cycle, mediating alertness and perhaps attention. [28]

long-term depression (LTD) A particular kind of diminishment of synaptic strength as a result of repetitive activity. Compare *long-term potentiation*. [13]

long-term memory Memory that last days, weeks, months, years, or a lifetime. Compare *short-term memory*. [2,13]

long-term potentiation (LTP) A particular kind of enhancement of synaptic strength as a result of repetitive activity. Compare *long-term depression*. [13]

loudness The sensory quality elicited by the intensity of sound stimuli. [6]

lower motor neuron so called *primary motor neuron* or *spinal motor neuron*. motor neuron that directly innervates muscle. Compare *upper motor neuron*. [8]

lower motor neuron syndrome A clinical condition characterized by signs and symptoms arising from direct damage to motor neurons; includes paralysis or paresis, muscle atrophy, areflexia, and fibrillations. Compare *upper motor neuron syndrome*. [8]

LTD See *long-term depression*.

LTP See *long-term potentiation*.

luminance The physical measure of light intensity. [5]

Machiavellian intelligence hypothesis The proposal that the information-processing demands of navigating large, complex social groups are responsible for the evolution of enhanced cognition in primates relative to other mammals. [26]

machine Any man-made device, or more broadly, any apparatus that accomplishes a purpose by the operation of a series of causally connected parts. In cognitive neuroscience, often refers to a digital computer. [28]

macula Also called *macula lutea*. The central region of the retina that includes the fovea; distinguished by is pale appearance when the retina is viewed through an ophthalmoscope. [4]

magnetic resonance imaging (MRI) A noninvasive imaging method based on the behavior of atomic nuclei (particularly hydrogen) within a strong magnetic field; provides excellent soft tissue contrast of brain anatomy, and can also be used to measure functional brain activity noninvasively. See also *functional magnetic resonance imaging*. [3]

magnetoencephalographic (MEG) recording A method of recording electrical brain activity from the scalp based on the detection of magnetic fields. Like EEG, MEG activity is thought to reflect mainly the electrical currents produced in the dendritic trees of the large pyramidal cells in cortex, which in turn produce the magnetic effects. [3]

magnification factor See *cortical magnification*.

magnocellular system The component of the primary visual processing pathway that is specialized in part for the perception of motion and other aspects of stimulus change; so named because of the relatively large neurons involved. Compare *parvocellular system*. [5]

mammal An animal whose embryos develop in a uterus, and whose young suckle at birth; technically, a member of the class Mammalia.

mammillary bodies Small prominences on the ventral surface of the diencephalon; functionally, part of the caudal hypothalamus. [1]

map A systematic arrangement of information in space. In neurobiology, the ordered projection of axons from one region of the nervous system to another, by which the organization of a relatively peripheral part of the body (e.g., the retina) is reflected in the organization of the nervous system (e.g., the primary visual cortex). [4]

mapping The corresponding arrangement of the peripheral and central components of a sensory or motor system. [4]

mask An interfering stimulus that follows shortly after a prime. [15]

masked priming A technique in which conscious awareness of a prime is prevented by an interfering mask that follows shortly after the prime. [15]

mass action principle A principle stating that when the brain is damaged, the ensuing reduction in learning ability is proportional to the amount of tissue destroyed. [13]

McGurk effect The misperception of speech sounds due to conflicting visual stimuli. [20]

medial Located nearer to the midline of an animal. Compare *lateral*. [1]

medial geniculate nucleus The thalamic nucleus in the primary auditory pathway. [1,6]

median section See *sagittal section*.

medulla The caudal portion of the mammalian brainstem, extending from the pons to the spinal cord. [1]

medullary pyramids Longitudinal bulges on the ventral aspect of the medulla that signify the corticospinal tracts at this level of the neuraxis. [8]

MEG See *magnetoencephalographic recording*.

melody A sequence of tones in a musical composition; typically structured in the diatonic scale for a given key. [6]

memory load See *working memory load*.

memory modulation hypothesis A hypothesis positing that the basolateral amygdala is important for modulating memory processing in other brain regions to enhance the retention of emotional events. [18]

memory trace See *engram*.

mental number line A spatially organized representation of numbers. [22]

mentalizing See *theory of mind*.

mesopic Pertaining to light levels at which both the rod and cone systems are active. [4]

metabotropic receptors Also called *G-protein-coupled receptors*. Class of postsynaptic neurotransmitter receptors in which neurotransmitter binding activates G-proteins, triggering metabolic molecular cascades whose actions regulate the opening and closing of ion channels. Compare *ionotropic receptors*. [Appendix]

metacognition Knowing that one knows something. [28]

microelectrode A recording device (typically made of wire, or of a glass tube pulled to a point and filled with an electrolyte) used to monitor electrical potentials from individual or small groups of nerve cells. [1]

midbrain The most rostral portion of the brainstem; identified by the superior and inferior colliculi on its dorsal surface, and the cerebral peduncles on its ventral aspect. [1,23]

middle ear The portion of the ear between the eardrum and the oval window; contains the three small bones that amplify sound stimuli mechanically. [6]

midlatency response The second major phase of the auditory ERP, 10 to 50 milliseconds following an auditory stimulus; it reflects early evoked activity in auditory cortex. [11]

midsagittal The midline; that plane that divides a structure into mirror-image halves. Compare *sagittal section*.

mind The full spectrum of a person's awareness (one aspect of consciousness) at any point in time, reflecting sensory percepts, as well as thoughts, feelings, goals, desires, and so on. [28]

mind-body problem The age-old problem of understanding how the body (i.e., the brain) is related to the contents of consciousness (mind). [28]

mirror neurons Neurons in the frontal and parietal cortices that show similar electrophysiological responses to actions executed oneself or to observation of the same actions being executed by another. [19]

mirror test A test that supposedly determines whether a non-human animal sees its reflection in a mirror as an image of itself; taken as a measure of self-awareness. [28]

mismatch negativity (MMN) A negative ERP wave peaking at about 150 to 200 milliseconds following a deviant stimulus in a stream of otherwise identical stimuli (usually sound stimuli). [11]

missing fundamental Hearing the pitch of the fundamental frequency of a harmonic series when the energy of the fundamental has been removed. [6]

MMN See *mismatch negativity*.

modality A category of function; for example, vision, hearing, and touch are different sensory modalities.

modality-specific Pertaining to a specific sensory modality; opposite of *supramodal*. [11]

mode control model A model of nonverbal enumeration that results in an analog magnitude representation of number. Compare *object file model*. [22]

modification theory of priming The theory proposing that priming reflects an alteration in preexisting memory representations. [15]

modularity The principle of iterated (repeating) units. The anatomical organization of sensory cortices into iterated groups of neurons (modules, columns, or "blobs") with similar functional properties. [4]

modus ponens A form of valid logical reasoning in which the antecedent of a conditional relation is true (i.e., "If P, then Q. P is true. Therefore, Q.") Compare *modus tollens*. [25]

modus tollens A form of valid logical reasoning in which the consequent of a conditional relation is false (i.e., "If P, then Q. Q is false. Therefore, P is false.") Compare *modus ponens*. [25]

monitoring process A process during memory retrieval that evaluates the appropriateness and accuracy of answers generated by search during a memory test. [14]

monochromat A color-deficient individual who has only one or no cone opsins, and therefore has no color vision. Compare *dichromat* and *trichromat*.

monochromatic Referring to light comprising a single wavelength; in practice, often a narrow band of wavelengths generated by an interference filter [5]

monocular Pertaining to one eye. Compare *binocular*. [5]

mood A prolonged feeling state. Compare *emotion*. [17]

mood regulation The long-term balance between emotional and attentional processing of emotions. When these processes become skewed, mood disorders such as depression can occur. [18]

morpheme A linguistic unit that cannot be divided into smaller meaningful parts (e.g., *dog*). [2]

Morris water maze A task used to test spatial memory, developed by Richard Morris, in which an animal is placed in water and required to swim to a hidden platform. [14]

mosaic brain evolution The proposal that different functional parts of the brain, or modules, evolve at different rates in response to different selective pressures in the environment. [26]

motion The changing position of an object defined by speed and direction within a frame of reference. [5]

motion aftereffects The persistence of perceived motion in the opposite direction when a motion stimulus has ceased. [5]

motion parallax The different degree of movement of near and far objects as a function of moving the head or body while observing a scene. [5]

motivation The desire to attain a particular goal. [17]

motives Basic needs or drives that influence goal-directed behavior.

motor Pertaining to movement.

motor aphasia See *Broca's aphasia*.

motor cortex In humans and other mammals, the region of the cerebral cortex anterior to the central sulcus that is concerned with motor behavior; includes the primary motor cortex in the precentral gyrus, and associated premotor cortical areas in the frontal lobe. [1,8]

motor neuron A nerve cell that innervates skeletal or smooth muscle. [1,8]

motor neuron pool The collection of motor neurons that innervates a single muscle. [8]

motor program The plan to produce a particular motor action, such as writing one's name, that occurs independently of the effectors used to carry out the movement. [8]

motor system All the central and peripheral structures that support motor behavior. [1]

motor unit A motor neuron and the skeletal muscle fibers that it innervates; more loosely, the collection of skeletal muscle fibers innervated by a single motor neuron. [8]

MRI See *magnetic resonance imaging*.

MST An extrastriate cortical region in primates that is in part specialized for motion processing. [4,5]

MT In primates, an extrastriate cortical region related to the MST that is also in part specialized for motion processing. [4,5]

MT+ Also called *V5*. The more inclusive name given the MT area in humans because of its poor definition. [5]

Müller-Lyer illusion A geometric effect, first described by the nineteenth-century German philosopher and sociologist F. D. Müller-Lyer, in which the length of a line terminated by arrowheads appears shorter than the same line terminated by arrow tails.

multiple-trace theory A theory positing that episodic memories, consolidated or otherwise, always depend on the hippocampus. [13]

multisensory integration The combining of sensory information from different sensory modalities. [4,11]

muscle fibers The striated, smooth, or cardiac muscle cells that generate biological movements. [8]

muscle spindles Specialized sensory organs found in most skeletal muscles that provide the central nervous system with information about muscle strength. [7,8]

music Sounds produced by a wide variety of physical objects that are appreciated as pleasing to humans and that are implemented formally in the chromatic scale. [6]

myelin The membranous wrapping of axons by certain classes of glial cells that makes brain regions with axonal pathways look whitish. See *white matter*. [1,27, Appendix]

myelination The process by which glial cells wrap axons to form multiple layers of glial cell membrane that electrically insulate the axon, thereby speeding up the conduction of action potentials. [1,27, Appendix]

myotatic reflex See *stretch reflex*.

N-back tasks Tasks in which subjects must indicate whether each item in a continuous stream matches an item presented one, two, or more items "back" in the series. [16]

N100 wave See *auditory N1* and *visual N1*.

N2pc wave An ERP component elicited by the detection of a feature pop-out target in a visual search array, thought to reflect either the shift of attention to the location of the pop-out or the filtering of the nearby distracter items. [12]

Nash equilibrium In an interactive game, a set of decisions by the players of that game from which no player would deviate unilaterally (thus the game is at an equilibrium). [24]

natural resonance frequency The fundamental frequency at which strings, air columns, or other objects tend to vibrate when mechanically perturbed. [6]

Neanderthals A subspecies of *Homo sapiens* that lived between 200,000 and 30,000 years ago in the Middle East and Europe. [26]

neglect syndrome A neurological syndrome due to damage to the right inferior parietal lobe that causes deficits in spatial attention to the left side of personal and extrapersonal space. [12]

neocortex The six-layered cortex that covers the bulk of the cerebral hemispheres. [1,26]

nerve A collection of peripheral axons that are bundled together and travel a common route. [1]

nerve cell Also called *neuron*. A cell specialized for the conduction and transmission of electrical signals in the nervous system. [1]

neural circuit A collection of interconnected neurons mediating a specific function. [1]

neural network An artificial network of interconnected nodes whose connections change in strength as a means of solving problems. [20]

neural plasticity The ability of the nervous system to change as a function of experience; typically applied to changes in the fully formed adult nervous system. [13]

neural plate The thickened region of the dorsal ectoderm of a neurula that gives rise to the neural tube. [27]

neural precursor cells Undifferentiated stem cells in the neural tube that will divide to produce more precursor cells and neuroblasts that develop into neurons. [27]

neural processing All the operations carried out by neural circuitry.

neural system A collection of peripheral and central neural circuits dedicated to a particular function (e.g., the visual system, the auditory system). [1]

neural tube The primordium of the brain and spinal cord; derived from the neural ectoderm. [27]

neuroblast A dividing cell, the progeny of which develop into neurons. [27]

neuroeconomics An emerging discipline that combines theoretical perspectives from neuroscience and economics, as well as other of the social sciences, in the creation of mechanistic models for behavior. [24]

neuroglial cells Also called *neuroglia* or *glia*. Any of several types of non-neural cells found in the peripheral and central nervous system that carry out a variety of functions that do not directly entail signaling. [1]

neuromuscular junction The synapse made by a motor axon on a skeletal muscle fiber. [8, Appendix]

neuron See *nerve cell*.

neuronal receptive field See *receptive field*.

neuroscience The study of the structure and function of the nervous system.

neurotransmitter A chemical agent released at synapses that mediates signaling between nerve cells. [1, Appendix]

neurotransmitter receptor A molecule embedded in the membrane of a postsynaptic cells that binds a neurotransmitter. Compare *ionotropic receptors, metabotropic receptors*. [1, Appendix]

neurulation The process by which the neural plate folds to form the neural tube. [27]

nociceptive system See *pain system*.

nociceptor A cell that specifically responds to potentially harmful stimuli. [7]

noise A signal that does not carry information. [6]

nondeclarative memory Also called *implicit memory*. Memory expressed through performance; assumed to operate unconsciously. Compare *declarative memory*. [2,13]

noradrenaline See *norepinephrine*.

norepinephrine Also called *noradrenaline*. A catecholaminergic neurotransmitter released across synapses in postganglionic neurons of the sympathetic nervous system, in the adrenal medulla, and in some parts of the central nervous system. [18]

normative model A model for a particular phenomenon that attempts to describe how things should be, as opposed to how they are. Compare *descriptive model*. [2,24]

nucleus An anatomically discrete collection of neurons within the brain; typically serves a particular function. [1]

nucleus accumbens A subdivision of the ventral striatum that contains neurons sensitive to the neurotransmitter dopamine and that contributes to learning and reward evaluation. [24]

nucleus of the lateral lemniscus A brainstem nucleus in the primary auditory pathway. [6]

nucleus of the solitary tract A brainstem nucleus that integrates gustatory and other information relevant to the autonomic control of the gut and other autonomic target organs. [7]

numerical distance effect The greater ease of discriminating two numbers that differ significantly in magnitude compared to two numbers close in magnitude. Compare *numerical size effect*. [22]

numerical size effect The greater ease of discriminating smaller values compared to larger values if numerical distance is held constant. Compare *numerical distance effect*. [22]

numerons Nonverbal representations of number that are arbitrarily related to the value they represent, but are applied according to the counting principles offered by psychologists Rochel Gelman and Charles Gallistel. [22,27]

object A physical entity that gives rise to a visual stimulus by reflecting illumination (or by emitting light if, as more rarely happens, it is itself a generator of light). [5]

object file model A model of nonverbal enumeration that allows the representation of small sets of objects by the opening of an "object file" for each event or item; numerical equivalence is established through a process of one-to-one correspondence. Compare *mode control model*. [22]

object permanence The awareness that objects continue to exist even when they are out of sight. [27]

occipital cortex Part of the brain nearest the back of the head, containing mainly visual processing areas. [3,5]

occipital lobe The most posterior lobe of the brain; devoted primarily to vision. [1,5]

octave The frequency or pitch interval between any starting (or fundamental) frequency and its multiplication by two. [6]

ocular dominance columns The segregated termination patterns of thalamic inputs representing the two eyes in the primary visual cortex of some species of primates and carnivores. [5]

oculomotor apraxia Impairment of voluntarily directing gaze toward objects in the visual field by means of a saccade; seen in Balint's patients, who have suffered bilateral damage in lateral parieto-occipital cortex. [12]

odorant An airborne molecule in the environment that when bound to a receptor neuron in the olfactory epithelium elicits the sensation of a specific odor, or smell. [7]

olfactory bulb The olfactory relay station that receives axons from the olfactory cranial nerve and transmits this information via the olfactory tract to higher centers. [1,7]

olfactory epithelium Pseudostratified epithelium that contains olfactory receptor cells, supporting cells, and mucus-secreting glands in the nasal cavity. [7]

olfactory nerve The first cranial nerve; runs from the olfactory mucosa to the olfactory bulb. [1]

olfactory receptor neurons Bipolar neurons in olfactory epithelium that contain receptors for odorants. [7]

olfactory system The sensory system that includes the olfactory epithelium of the nasal cavity, the olfactory tract and olfactory bulbs; mediates the perception of odors. [7]

olfactory tract See *lateral olfactory tract*. [1]

one-to-one correspondence principle A counting principle indicating that only one label must be applied to each item that is to be counted. [22]

ontogeny Also called *development*. The developmental history of an individual animal. [26,27]

operant conditioning The altered probability of a behavioral response engendered by associating responses with rewards (or punishments). [15]

opponent colors Colors that appear to be perceptual opposites, (e.g., red and green, or blue and yellow), with no way to reach one from the other by gradual steps. [5]

opsins Proteins (pigments) in photoreceptors that absorb light (in humans, rhodopsin and the three specialized cone opsins). [5]

optic ataxia A neurological condition associated with damage to the dorsal parietal cortex and characterized by deficits in visually guided reaching. [9,12]

optic chiasm The crossing of optic nerve axons from the nasal portions of the retinas in humans and other mammals such that the temporal visual fields are represented in the contralateral cerebral hemispheres. [1,4,5]

optic nerve Cranial nerve II, containing the axons of retinal ganglion cells; extends from the eye to the optic chiasm. [4,5]

optic radiation The portion of the internal capsule containing the axons from lateral geniculate neurons that carry visual information to the striate cortex. [4,5]

optic tract The axons of retinal ganglion cells after they have passed through the region of the optic chiasm en route to the lateral geniculate nucleus of the thalamus. [4,5]

optical axis See *line of sight*.

optical brain imaging A set of methods based on the fact that active and inactive brain tissues absorb and transmit light differently, and that these differences can be picked up and imaged by optical recording devices. Optical brain imaging signals can derive from hemodynamic changes, voltage changes, or membrane-swelling changes induced by neural activity. [3]

orbitofrontal cortex The division of the prefrontal cortex that lies above the orbits in the most rostral and ventral extension of the sagittal fissure; important in emotional processing and rational decision making. [17,23]

organelle A subcellular component visible in a light or electron microscope (e.g., nucleus, ribosome, endoplasmic reticulum).

orientation selectivity The propensity of certain neurons to respond selectively to edges presented over a relatively narrow range of stimulus orientations. [5]

orientation tuning curve See *tuning curve*.

oval window Site where the middle-ear bones transfer vibrational energy to the cochlea. [6]

overt attention The directing of attention (typically visual) by voluntarily shifting gaze. Compare *covert attention*. [10]

overtone See *harmonic*.

P100 wave See *visual P1*.

P20–50 attention effect An enhanced positive ERP wave 20 to 50 milliseconds after the stimulus elicited by attended relative to unattended auditory stimuli from. [11]

P300 A positive ERP wave peaking at about 300 to 500 milliseconds, elicited by stimuli that are infrequent or surprising, typically occurring within a stream of other sensory events. [19]

pain The highly unpleasant percepts generated by stimuli that are potentially damaging. [7]

pain system Also called *nociceptive system*. The mechanosensory system that mediates the perception of pain. [7]

parahippocampal gyrus Cortical gyrus in the medial temporal lobe adjacent to the hippocampus; plays a role in declarative memory, emotion, and responses to olfactory stimuli. [1]

parallel processing Also called *parallel distributed processing*. Simultaneous information processing by different components of a neural or artificial system. [2]

paramedian pontine reticular formation (PPRF) A loose aggregation of neurons in the pons that organizes the activation of oculomotor neurons to produce coherent movements of both eyes. [8]

paramedian section See *sagittal section*.

parasympathetic division The component of the autonomic nervous system that mediates restorative metabolic functions. Compare *sympathetic division*. [1,8]

parietal lobe The lobe of the brain that lies between the frontal lobe anteriorly and the occipital lobe posteriorly. [1]

Parkinson's disease A neurodegenerative process affecting the substantia nigra that results in a characteristic tremor at rest and a general paucity of movement. [9,23]

pars compacta See *substantia nigra pars compacta*.

pars reticulata See *substantia nigra pars reticulata*.

parvocellular system The component of the primary visual processing pathway that is specialized in part for the detection of detail and color; so named because of the relatively small size of the neurons involved. Compare *magnocellular system*. [5]

pathological dissociations Abnormal dissociational effects observed in patients with brain lesions or other perturbations of brain function. [15]

patient H.M. A well-studied patient whose severe memory deficits (i.e., amnesia) following the removal of his temporal lobes highlighted the critical role of these regions for declarative memory. [13]

payoff matrix In an interactive game, the set of rewards that can be obtained depending on the choices of the experimental subjects. [24]

percept The subjective, conscious experience initiated by activation of the receptors of a sensory system. See also *sensation*. [4]

perception The subjective awareness (taken to be conscious) of any aspect of the external or internal environment. [2,4]

perceptual load The level of processing difficulty or complexity of a task being performed by an individual; usually measured by the time it takes for perceptual analyses of the stimuli. [10]

perceptual priming A form of direct priming in which the test cue and the target are perceptually related. Compare *conceptual priming*. [2,15]

perceptual skill learning Improvements in processing perceptual stimuli, whether familiar, transformed, or entirely novel. Compare *cognitive skill learning*. [15]

performance Measurable indices of skill in performing a task. Compare *competence*.

peripheral nervous system All the nerves and neurons that lie outside the brain and spinal cord. Compare *central nervous system*. [6]

peristimulus histogram A graph that plots neuronal activity, typically firing rate or number of spikes, as a function of the time of stimulus presentation. [3]

perseveration The repetition of a response despite changing stimuli or rules that make a different response more appropriate. [23]

perspective The effects of representing three-dimensional objects and depth relationships on a two-dimensional surface. [5]

perspective taking The ability to adopt the viewpoint of another individual. [19]

PET See *positron emission tomography*.

PFC See *prefrontal cortex*.

phantom limb phenomenon The sensation that a limb or other missing part is present even though it is not (e.g., because of amputation). [7]

pharmacological manipulation An experimental method in which drugs are used to examine the function of neurochemical systems and interactions in the brain. [3]

phase Temporal characteristics of a repeating wave, especially important when two waves interact and either cancel or sum according to their relative phases. [3, 6]

phenotype The visible (or otherwise discernible) characteristics of an animal that arise during development. Compare *genotype*.

pheromone A chemical signal produced by an animal such as a rodent, typically from glands, that mediates aspects of social communication. [7]

phoneme One of the set of basic perceptual units that distinguish one utterance from another in a given language. [20]

phonetic Representing sounds with symbols. [20]

phonological similarity effect The fact that working memory for letters is worse when the letters sound similar to each other than when they sound different. [16]

photopic Pertaining to daylight levels of light, in which the predominant information is provided by cones. Compare *scotopic*. [4]

photopic system The components of the visual system activated at relatively high light levels. Compare *scotopic system*. [4]

photoreceptors Cells in the retina of the eye that are specialized to absorb photons, and thus to generate neural signals in response to light stimuli. See *cones*, *rods* [4,5]

phrenology Originating in the early nineteenth century, the attempt to create maps of brain function based on the pattern of bumps and valleys on the surface of the skull. [23]

phylogeny The evolutionary history of a species or other taxonomic category. [26]

pitch The perception of a periodic sound as being higher or lower on an ordinal scale; roughly, but only roughly, corresponds to sound frequency. [6]

pituitary gland An endocrine structure comprising an anterior lobe made up of many different types of hormone-secreting cells, and a posterior lobe that secretes neuropeptides produced by neurons in the hypothalamus. [1]

pixel Any one of the array of discrete elements that make up a two-dimensional digital image. [5]

place cells Neurons found in the hippocampus that fire depending on the specific location of the animal. [14]

place coding The idea that the meaning of a sensory stimulus derives from the locus that it activates on a sensory receptor sheet such as the retina or basilar membrane. [4]

plasticity See *neural plasticity*.

point of subjective equality In a bisection task, the stimulus value that subjects are equally likely to classify as an exemplar of either of the two anchor values. [22]

polymodal Pertaining to more than one sensory modality.

pons One of the three components of the brainstem, lying between the midbrain rostrally and the medulla caudally. [1]

population vector A computational variable representing the weighted average response of a group or population of neurons. [8]

positron emission tomography (PET) A method of noninvasive, hemodynamically based brain imaging that uses radioactively labeled molecules injected into the bloodstream that are taken up to a greater degree by active neurons . [3]

postcentral gyrus The gyrus that lies just posterior to the central sulcus; contains the primary somatosensory cortex. [1]

posterior In back of. [1]

posterior parietal cortex The region of the parietal cortex surrounding the intraparietal sulcus. [23]

postsynaptic Referring to the cell receiving the signal generated by the axon terminal of the presynaptic cell. Compare *presynaptic*. [1, Appendix]

postsynaptic potential Abbreviated *PSP*. A synaptic potential originating in the postsynaptic cell. See also *excitatory postsynaptic potential, inhibitory postsynaptic potential*. [Appendix]

power The rate of energy generation.

PPRF See *paramedian pontine reticular formation*.

pre-neural apparatus The components of a peripheral sensory system that amplify and filter stimuli before they reach the stage of neural transduction. [4]

precentral gyrus The gyrus that lies just anterior to the central sulcus; contains the primary motor cortex. [1]

prefrontal cortex Abbreviated *PFC*. Cortical regions in the frontal lobe that are anterior to the primary motor and premotor cortices; thought to be involved in planning complex cognitive behaviors and in the expression of personality and appropriate social behavior. [1]

premotor cortex Part of the prefrontal cortex lying just anterior to the primary motor cortex; involved in planning movement. [8]

premotor cortical areas Cortical areas, including the premotor cortex, supplementary motor cortex, and parts of the parietal cortex, that provide motor programming signals to the primary motor cortex. [8]

premotor theory of attention A cognitive theory proposing that shifts of attention and preparation of goal-directed action are closely linked because they are controlled by shared sensorimotor mechanisms. [12]

preoperational stage In Jean Piaget's theory of cognitive development, the stage from ages 2 through 7 years in which children develop representational or symbolic abilities; follows the *sensorimotor stage* and precedes the *concrete operations stage*. [27]

presynaptic Referring to the axonal ending that contacts (transmits a signal to) a target (postsynaptic) cell. [1, Appendix]

primary auditory cortex (A1) The cortical target of the neurons in the medial geniculate nucleus; the terminus of the primary auditory pathway. [4,6]

primary auditory pathway The pathway from the inner ear to the primary auditory cortex in the temporal lobe. [6]

primary colors The four perceptual qualities or categories of human color vision (red, green, blue, and yellow) that are defined by a unique color sensation. [5]

primary motor cortex A major source of descending projections to motor neurons in the spinal cord and cranial nerve nuclei; located in the precentral gyrus (Brodmann area 4) and essential for the voluntary control of movement. [8]

primary motor neuron See *lower motor neuron*.

primary reinforcer Also called *unconditioned reinforcer*. A stimulus whose rewarding properties come from its salutary effects on homeostatic processes; food, water, warmth, and sex are examples. Compare *secondary reinforcer*. [24]

primary sensory cortex Any one of several cortical areas that directly receives the thalamic input for a particular sensory modality. [4]

primary somatosensory cortex (S1) The cortex of the postcentral gyrus of the parietal lobe that receives mechanosensory input from the thalamus. Compare *secondary somatosensory cortex*. [4,7]

primary visual cortex (V1) Also called *Brodmann area 17* or *striate cortex*. The cortex in the calcarine fissure of the parietal lobe that receives visual input from the thalamus. [4]

primary visual pathway The pathway from the retina via the lateral geniculate nucleus of the thalamus to the primary visual cortex; carries the information that allows conscious visual perception. [5]

primate Any member of the order of mammals that includes lemurs, tarsiers, marmosets, monkeys, apes, and humans.

priming Facilitated processing of a particular stimulus based on previous encounters with the same or a related stimulus. Compare *skill learning*. [2,13,15]

principle of proper mass Principle stating that the mass of neural tissue controlling a particular function will be proportional and appropriate to the amount of information processing involved in performing the function in question. [26]

prisoner's dilemma An interactive game in which two players must decide whether to cooperate or to defect and take advantage of the other; the dilemma arises because its equilibrium solution—both players defecting—results in the worst overall outcome. [24]

probabilistic classification learning An example of cognitive skill learning in which participants learn to classify stimuli on the basis of statistical information. [15]

probability The likelihood of an event, usually expressed as a value from 0 (will never occur) to 1 (will always occur).

probability distribution The probability of a variable having a particular value, expressed as a function of all the possible values of that variable.

problem space The set of possible states of a problem; can be vast in complex games like chess. [25]

procedural memory Unconscious memories such as motor skills and associations. [2]

process-based model of prefrontal organization A model of prefrontal cortex organization proposing that ventrolateral regions are involved primarily in simple maintenance operations, whereas dorsolateral regions are involved in more complex processes involving monitoring and manipulating information within working memory. Compare *content-based model*. [16]

processing All of the neural activity mediating a particular function.

processing negativity A slow, long-lasting negative-wave activity that is elicited during auditory selective attention, the amplitude of which may reflect how much each stimulus matches an attentional "template." [11]

production aphasia See *Broca's aphasia*.

propranolol An antagonist of the β-adrenergic system. [18]

proprioceptive system The mechanosensory subsystem that processes information arising from mechanical forces acting on muscles, tendons, and joints. [7]

proprioceptors Sensory receptors (usually limited to mechanosensory receptors) that sense the internal forces acting on the body; muscle spindles and Golgi tendon organs are the preeminent examples. [7]

prosodic Pertaining to the inflection in speech, often associated with emotion. [21]

prosody The fluctuating pitch of speech. Gives emotional and other information to speech. [17]

prosopagnosia The inability to recognize faces; usually associated with lesions of the right inferior temporal cortex. [19]

prospect theory A quantitative decision-making model proposing that people make decisions in terms of the anticipated gains and losses from their current state, and that probabilities are subjective. Compare *expected-utility theory*. [24]

proximal Closer to a point of reference In anatomy, often refers to a position close to the trunk of the body as opposed to at the extremities of the limbs. Compare *distal*.

PSP See *postsynaptic potential*.

psychoactive drug A chemical substance that acts primarily on the central nervous system, where it alters brain function, resulting in changes in perception, mood, consciousness, and/or behavior. [3]

psychological refractory period The time interval proposed to reflect an attention-related processing bottleneck at the response selection stage, during which the selection of one response precludes the selection of another. [10]

psychology The study of mental processes in humans and other animals.

psychophysics The study of mental processes by quantitative methods, typically involving reports by human subjects of the percepts elicited by carefully measured stimuli.

psychosomatic Pertaining to medical problems arising from the influence of the nervous system on bodily functions. This term is now out of fashion.

pulvinar A nucleus of the thalamus that mediates interactions among several sensory association areas of the cortex. [1]

punishment The delivery of an aversive stimulus. [24]

pupillary light reflex The decrease in the diameter of the pupil that follows stimulation of the retina by light.

putamen One of the three major nuclei that make up the basal ganglia. [1]

pyriform cortex A component of the cerebral cortex in the temporal lobe pertinent to olfaction; so named because of its pearlike shape. [1,7]

radial arm maze A device used to test spatial memory in animals.

radial glial cells Glial cells that contact both the luminal and pial surfaces of the neural tube, providing a substrate for neuronal migration.

raphe nuclei Brainstem nuclei involved in the control of the sleep-waking cycle, among other functions. [28]

rapid serial visual presentation (RSVP) A method of presenting stimuli in quick succession (about 5 to 15 per second) that is used in studies of visual processing and attention. [10]

rate coding A computational principle in which information is encoded by the firing rate of neurons or other elements. [4]

rationality Consistency in decision making that is based on a conscious evaluation of the circumstances. [24]

reaction time The time it takes to initiate behavior in response to a stimulus.

readiness potential An electrical potential recorded from the motor and premotor cortices with EEG electrodes that signals the intention to initiate a voluntary movement well in advance of the actual production of the movement. [9]

real-world Pertaining to an external world that determines what we perceive, even though it is not directly knowable.

recency effect The better immediate recall that is displayed for the last few items in a list compared to the items in the middle of the list. [13]

receptive aphasia See *Wernicke's aphasia*.

receptive field The region of the receptor surface of a sensory neuron that, when stimulated, elicits a response in the neuron being examined. [4]

receptive-field properties The defining characteristics of a neuron's responses to stimuli within its receptive field. [4]

receptor cells The cells in a sensory system that transduce environmental energy into neural signals (e.g., photoreceptors in the retina, hair cells in the inner ear). [4,6]

receptor potential Also called *generator potential*. A membrane potential (hyperpolarizing or depolarizing) elicited by the interaction of energy with a sensory receptor cell. [1]

receptor proteins The proteins in receptor cells that capture the energy in the process of sensory transduction (e.g., the opsins on photoreceptors). [7]

reciprocal innervation A motor control process in which contraction of a particular muscle (e.g., the biceps) is coupled with simultaneous relaxation of its opposing muscle (e.g., the triceps). [8]

recollection Remembering a past event, as well as specific associations and contextual details. Compare *familiarity*. [14]

recursive processing Neural processing that enables reflection on other neural processes, arguably allowing humans or other animals to be aware of themselves and their mental content. [28]

reentrant process Following a stimulus or event, a process in which neural activity is fed back to the same brain region activated earlier in the processing sequence. [11]

reflectance The percentage of incident light reflected from a surface (often expressed as the *reflectance efficiency function*, in which the reflectance of a surface is measured at different wavelengths). [5]

reflex A stereotyped response elicited by a defined stimulus. Usually taken to be restricted to "involuntary" actions (an assumption that is not necessarily appropriate).

reflex arc The circuitry that connects a sensory input to a motor output. [1]

reflexive attention See *exogenous attention*.

refreshing Maintaining a piece of information active within working memory by briefly thinking about it. Compare *rehearsal*. [16]

rehearsal Maintaining a piece of information active within working memory by thinking about it over and over. Compare *refreshing*. [2,16]

relational memory theory The theory that the hippocampus is involved primarily in encoding and retrieving associations between items, including spatial associations but also other types of associations. [14]

repetition enhancement The creation of new representations and the increase in activity that result from the repetition of stimuli during priming; associated with priming for novel stimuli. [15]

repetition suppression A phenomenon observed in functional neuroimaging studies in which previously encountered stimuli evoke smaller hemodynamic responses than do novel stimuli. [15]

representation 1. The way in which the brain encodes and processes symbolic information. Compare *symbolic representation*. [2] 2. The neural activity taken to underlie perception at the level of the association cortices.

representativeness A heuristic for decision making and reasoning that evaluates the likelihood of an event according to how well it matches a particular category. [24]

resolution The ability to distinguish two points in space. See also *acuity*. [5]

resonance The tendency of any physical object to vibrate maximally at a certain frequency. [6,20]

response conflict A state in which two or more possible responses are potentiated. [23]

response phase The last of three phases of working memory, in which an action is executed on the basis of information that has been incorporated and maintained. Compare *encoding phase* and *delay phase*. [16]

response selection A putative later stage of information processing in which an appropriate behavioral response to an event is selected. [10]

reticular activating system A large region in the brainstem core whose many nuclei mediate overall arousal and level of awareness. [28]

reticular formation A network of neurons and axons that occupies the core of the brainstem, giving it a reticulated appearance in myelin-stained material; major functions include control of respiration and heart rate, posture, and state of consciousness. [1,8]

reticulospinal tract A pathway from the reticular formation in the brainstem to the spinal cord that plays an important role in anticipatory postural adjustments preceding voluntary movement. [8]

retina The laminated neural component of the eye that contains the photoreceptors (rods and cones) and the initial processing circuitry for vision. [4,5]

retinal disparity The geometric difference between the same points in the images projected on the two retinas, measured in degrees with respect to the fovea. [5]

retinal ganglion cells The output neurons of the retina, whose axons form the optic nerve. [5]

retinal image The image focused on the retina by the cornea and lens of the eye. [5]

retrieval The recovery or accessing of stored memory traces. Compare *encoding*. [2,13]

retrieval cue Any information that leads to the retrieval of memories, such as the hits provided by memory tests. [2,14]

retrieval effort In functional neuroimaging studies, brain activity that is greater when recovery is low; possibly related to demanding search or monitoring processes. [14]

retrieval mode See *episodic retrieval mode*.

retrograde amnesia The inability to recall memories for events that happened before the lesion or brain disorder that caused the memory loss. Compare *anterograde amnesia*. [13]

reward prediction error A quantity given by the difference between the reward that was expected and what actually occurs; the activity of some dopaminergic neurons seems to convey this quantity. [24]

reward processing The cognitive processing that goes into determining goals and optimal outcomes and the behaviors most appropriate to achieving them, and evaluating the feedback when desired goals and outcomes have been achieved. [2,24]

reward value The likelihood that a particular movement will yield a reward, multiplied by the amount of reward expected. [9]

rhinencephalon Called *visceral brain* by James Papez. A historical term for the limbic system that emphasized its olfactory functions. [17]

rhodopsin The photopigment found in vertebrate rods. Compare *cone opsins*. [5]

right-frontal effect In ERP studies of recognition memory, the phenomenon whereby old items elicit greater positivity over right frontal regions 600 to 1200 milliseconds after the stimulus than do new items. Compare *left-parietal effect*. [14]

right-hemisphere hypothesis A hypothesis that the right hemisphere is specialized for emotional functions. [17]

risk Known probabilistic variation in the distribution of reward outcomes. [24]

rods Photoreceptors that are specialized to operate at low light levels. Compare *cones*. [5]

rostral Toward the nose, or anterior, when pertaining to the brain. Compare *caudal*. [1]

RSVP See *rapid serial visual presentation*.

S1 See *primary somatosensory cortex*.

S2 See *secondary somatosensory cortex*.

saccades Ballistic eye movements that change the point of binocular visual fixation; normally occur at a rate of about three to four per second. [4,8]

sagittal section Brain section taken in the plane that divides the two hemispheres; can be *midsagittal* (at the midline), *median* (near the midline), or *paramedian* (at some distance from the midline). Compare *coronal section, horizontal section, midsagittal*. [1]

saliency maps A theoretical construct of visual attention in which the importance of different stimuli in the visual field is set by a combination of top-down processes based on behavioral goals and bottom-up processes resulting from how distinctive the different elements of a stimulus are compared to the background. [10]

sampling The regular recording of the state of a system. [25]

saturation The aspect of color sensation pertaining to the subjective sense of the perceptual distance of the color from neutrality (an unsaturated color is one that approaches a neutral gray). Compare *brightness* and *hue*. [5]

scalar timing theory An information-processing model of interval timing comprising clock, memory, and decision stages. [22]

scalar variability Variability (as measured by the standard deviation) that increases proportionally with the mean value. [22]

schizophrenia A heterogeneous psychiatric condition characterized by disordered thought, withdrawal symptoms, and inaccurate beliefs about reality. [23]

SCN See *suprachiasmatic nucleus*.

scotoma A defect in the visual field resulting from injury or disease to a component of the primary visual pathway. [4,28]

scotopic Pertaining to vision in dim light, where only the rods are operative. Compare *photopic*. [4]

scotopic system The components of the visual system operating at relatively low levels of light. Compare *photopic system*. [4]

SCR See *skin conductance response*.

secondary auditory cortex (A2) Also called *belt area*. The cortical region surrounding the primary auditory cortex. [6]

secondary reinforcer A stimulus that has no direct effects on homeostatic processes but is nevertheless rewarding; money is a paradigmatic example. Compare *primary reinforcer*. [24]

secondary somatosensory cortex (S2) A higher-order somatosensory map in the parietal lobe adjacent to S1. Compare *primary somatosensory cortex*. [7]

selection negativity A slow, later negative ERP wave elicited over visual sensory cortices that may reflect attention to a nonspatial visual feature. [11]

selective attention The selective focusing of processing resources on a particular location or aspect of the external or internal environment. [10]

self The subjective sense of existing as an individual. [19]

self-awareness An awareness of oneself as a separate actor in the world. [28]

semantic dementia A memory deficit that impairs semantic memory rather than episodic memory and is associated with left-lateralized atrophy of the anterior temporal cortex. [14]

semantic memory A component of declarative memory that refers to general knowledge about the world, including knowledge of language, facts, and the properties of objects. Compare *episodic memory*. [2,13,14]

semantic priming A form of indirect priming in which the prime and the target are semantically related. [15]

semicircular canals The three elements of the vestibular component of the inner ear that provide a sense of acceleration and the position of the head in space. [7]

sensation A confusing word that is often used to refer to the sense data that initiates sensory processing. In ordinary speech, however, it is used as a synonym for *percept*. [4]

sensitive period See *critical period*.

sensitivity The ability of a sensory system to respond to the energy in a stimulus. [6]

sensitization The process by which a behavioral response to an otherwise benign stimulus increases in intensity, frequency, or duration when that stimulus is paired with an aversive stimulus. Compare *habituation*. [13]

sensorimotor stage In Jean Piaget's theory of cognitive development, the stage from birth to 2 years old that is dominated by reflex responses, with learning and intelligence guided and constrained largely by the infant's sensory and motor abilities; precedes the *preoperational stage*. [27]

sensory Pertaining to mechanisms or processes related to neural processing in sensory systems.

sensory aphasia See *Wernicke's aphasia*.

sensory coding The manner in which information is generated in sensory systems. [4]

sensory ganglia (sing. ganglion) Collections of neurons in the peripheral nervous system that comprise the cell bodies of afferent sensory neurons. [1]

sensory memory Memory that receives information from sensory systems and holds a large amount of precategorical (i.e., not yet interpreted) information for a very brief interval, presumably in different stores for the different sensory modalities. [2]

sensory neuron Any neuron involved in sensory processing. [1]

sensory plasticity The ability of a sensory system to change as a result of experience or injury.[7]

sensory stimulus Any pattern of energy impinging on a sensory receptor sheet such as the retina, skin, or basilar membrane. [4]

sensory system All the components of the central and peripheral nervous system concerned with processing information arising from a particular stimulus category (e.g., light, sound stimuli). [1]

sensory transduction The process by which energy in the environment is converted into electrical signals by sensory receptors. [4]

sentence A sequence of words that expresses a complete and meaningful thought;. [20]

septal forebrain nuclei See *basal forebrain nuclei*.

septum pellucidum A sheet of tissue in the midline of the brain's ventricular system (within the third ventricle). [1]

sequential processing model A model in which a particular cognitive task is assumed to involve a series of sequential and independent processing stages. [2]

sham rage An emotional reaction elicited in cats by electrical stimulation of the hypothalamus. [17]

shared attention The allocation of processing resources toward an object or region of space cued by another individual. [19]

sharpening model of repetition suppression A model positing that when a stimulus is repeated, neurons that carry critical information about the stimulus continue to fire vigorously, whereas neurons that are not essential for processing the stimulus respond less and less. Compare *facilitation model* and *fatigue model*. [15]

short-term memory Memory that lasts seconds to minutes. Compare *long-term memory*. [2]

sign language A means of communication by specific hand gestures. [21]

signal detection theory A theoretical approach to extracting signal from noise using mathematical and statistical tools. [2]

simulation The cognitive process involved in generating a potential future state, given knowledge of the current state of a system; critical for planning and reasoning. [23]

simultanagnosia The inability to attend to, and/or perceive, more than one visual object at a time; a primary deficit seen in patients with Balint's syndrome as a result of bilateral damage to lateral occipitoparietal cortex. [12]

simultaneous contrast The ability of contextual information to alter the perception of a visual target, especially in regard to its luminance (i.e., lightness or brightness; *simultaneous brightness contrast*) or its color (*simultaneous color contrast*). [5]

single-unit recording Also called simply *unit recording*. A method of studying the activity of single neurons using a microelectrode. [3,4]

sinusoid The pattern defined by a sine (or cosine) function. [3,6]

size constancy The sense that familiar objects maintain their size despite being seen at different distances from an observer. [5]

size-distance relationship The diminished size of a retinal projection as a function of distance from the observer. [5]

size principle The orderly recruitment of motor neurons by size to generate increasing amounts of muscle tension. [8]

skeletal muscle Also called *striated muscle*. Muscle typically connected to bones of the skeleton that causes movement by applying force across joints. One notable exception is the extraocular muscles, which attach to the eyeball and move it within the eye socket. Compare *smooth muscle*. [8]

skill learning Gradual improvement in the performance of a motor or cognitive task as a result of extensive experience and repeated practice. Compare *priming*. [13,15]

skin conductance response (SCR) A stimulus-induced increase in the electrical conductance of the skin due to increased hydration. [17,18]

Skinner box A device used in operant conditioning, in which animals such as pigeons or rats learn to press a lever to receive a food pellet. [15]

smooth muscle Muscle within the internal viscera that is controlled by the autonomic nervous system. Compare *skeletal muscle*. [8]

snake-in-the-grass effect The phenomenon in visual search behavior in which it is easier to identify an emotional target object dispersed among many neutral ones compared to a neutral object dispersed among many emotional ones. Compare *face-in-a-crowd effect*. [18]

SNARC (spatial-numerical association of response codes) A behavioral effect whereby subjects are faster to make an oddity judgment when responding with the left hand compared to the right hand with small numerical values and conversely faster with the right hand with large numerical values. [22]

SNc See *substantia nigra pars compacta*.

SNr See *substantia nigra pars reticulata*.

social cognition Information processing that contributes to behavior in interpersonal settings. [2]

social referencing The use of emotions expressed by another individual to guide behavior. [19]

software The programs that run computers. Compare *hardware*. [28]

soma See *cell body*.

somatic marker hypothesis 1. A theory, first advocated by Antonio Damasio and his colleagues, that motivated behavior is influenced by neural representations of body states (i.e., the "somatic markers"), whose reexperiencing can shape behavior positively or negatively; the hypothesis that evaluation of one's own bodily states makes important contributions to decision making. [18,23]

somatic motor system The components of the motor system that support skeletal movements mediated by the contraction of skeletal muscles. [1,8]

somatosensory cortex That region of the mammalian neocortex that is concerned with processing sensory information from the body surface, subcutaneous tissues, muscles, and joints; in humans, located primarily in the posterior bank of the central sulcus and on the postcentral gyrus. [1,7]

somatosensory system The parts of the nervous system that are involved in processing sensory information about the mechanical forces that act on both the body surface and on deeper structures, such as muscles and joints. [7]

somatotopic map The corresponding anatomical arrangement of the sensory periphery and its central representation. [7]

sound In common usage, both the physical characteristics of a sound stimulus and the perception that it generates. [6]

sound spectrum The analysis of a sound stimulus showing the distribution of power as a function of frequency. [6]

sound stimuli See *sound*. [6]

sound wave The periodic compression and rarefaction of air molecules underlying a sound stimulus. [6]

source-filter model A generally accepted model for the production of speech sound stimuli that entails the vocal-fold vibrations as a source and the rest of the vocal tract as a dynamic filter. [20]

source memory test An explicit memory test that asks participants to remember not merely what events happened in the past but *where*, *when*, or *how* they happened. Compare *item memory test*. [2]

spasticity A motor system disorder in which muscles are continuously contracted because of the loss of descending inhibitory inputs from upper motor neurons in the cortex and brainstem. [8]

spatial-numerical association of response codes See *SNARC*.

species A taxonomic category subordinate to genus; members of a species are defined by extensive similarities and the ability to interbreed.

spectral differences Differences in the distribution of spectral power in a visual stimulus that give rise to perceptions of color. [4,5]

spectrophotometer A device for measuring the spectral power distribution in light—that is, electromagnetic radiation with wavelengths between about 400 and 700 nanometers. [5]

spectrum (pl. spectra) A plot of the amplitude of a stimulus such as light or sound as a function of frequency over a particular period of sampling time. [4,5,6]

spinal column See *vertebral column*.

spinal cord The portion of the central nervous system that extends from the lower end of the brainstem (the medulla) to the cauda equina. It sits within a protective tube, or, column created by the vertebrae of the spine. See *vertebral column*. [1,8]

spinal motor neuron See *lower motor neuron*.

spindle cells Unusual elongated bipolar neurons found in the anterior cingulate cortex and insula of humans and African apes, characterized by a single dendrite at one end and a single dendrite at the other. Because of their phylogenetic distribution and anatomical location, hypothesized to play an important role in higher cognitive function. Also called *von Economo neurons*, after the Romanian-Austrian neurologist Constantin von Economo. [26]

spinocerebellum The region of the cerebellar cortex that receives input from the spinal cord. [9]

spiral ganglion A ganglion associated with the auditory component of cranial nerve VIII. [6]

split-brain patient An individual whose corpus callosum has been surgically interrupted as a treatment for epilepsy, functionally separating the left and right hemispheres. See also *patient H.M.* [13,21]

stable order principle One of the five counting principles offered by psychologists Rochel Gelman and Charles Gallistel, stating that arbitrary symbols for number such as the count words *one*, *two*, and *three* must be used in the counting process. [22]

standard consolidation theory A theory postulating that the hippocampus rapidly encodes an integrated representation of an event or concept, which is then slowly transferred to the cortex and eventually becomes independent of the hippocampus. [13]

startle response A behavioral reaction to a sudden, intense auditory or visual stimulus that is mediated by a subcortical reflex circuit. [17]

stereogram A pair of pictures of the same scene taken from slightly different angles that, when fused, create a sensation of stereoscopic depth. [5]

stereopsis The special sensation of depth that results from fusion of the two eyes' views of relatively nearby objects. [5]

storage The retention of information over time. [2,13]

strabismus Misalignment of the two eyes (often congenital); compromises normal binocular vision unless corrected at an early age. [27]

stress An emotional reaction to a stimulus that causes intense physical or mental tension. [18]

stress hormone See *cortisol*.

stretch reflex Also called *deep tendon reflex* or *myotatic reflex*. A spinal reflex comprising the motor response to afferent sensory information arising from muscle spindles. [8]

striate cortex See *primary visual cortex*.

striated muscle See *skeletal muscle*.

striatum The input nuclei of the basal ganglia, consisting of the caudate and putamen. So called because of the striped appearance of these structures in brain sections. [1,9]

stroke The clinical and neuropathological results of interruption of the blood supply to one or another region of the brain. [1]

Stroop task A paradigm used to study the effects of stimulus conflict and attention, in which the experimenter presents a series of color words whose font color either matches or does not match the word meaning; subjects are faster to identify the font color when the word meaning is congruent, and slower when it is incongruent. [4,10,19,23]

subcortical Pertaining to brain structures other than the cerebral cortex. [1]

subitizing A cognitive operation distinct from counting that allows the fast and accurate perception of the numerosity of small sets of events or objects. [22]

subliminal Pertaining to a stimulus that is below the threshold for detection.

subsequent memory paradigm A method to determine the neural processes that predict whether an item will be remembered or forgotten on a subsequent memory test. [14]

substantia nigra A nucleus at the base of the midbrain that receives input form a number of cortical and subcortical structures. The dopaminergic cells of the substantia nigra send their output to the caudate or putamen, and the GABA-ergic cells send their output to the thalamus. [1,24]

substantia nigra pars compacta (SNc) A component of the midbrain substantia nigra nucleus that is important for dopamine production. [24]

substantia nigra pars reticulata (SNr) A component of the midbrain substantia nigra nucleus that plays a key role in the suppression and initiation of saccadic eye movements. [9]

sulcus Any of the valleys that arise from the enfolding of the cerebral hemisphere between the gyral ridges. See also *fissure*. Compare *gyrus*. [1]

summation The additive effects of postsynaptic potentials (EPSPs and IPSPs) that are sequential in space and/or time. [Appendix]

superior Above. [1]

superior colliculi Paired structures that form part of the roof of the midbrain; important in orienting movements of the head and eyes. Compare *inferior colliculi*. [1,8]

superior olivary complex A complex of brainstem nuclei in the primary auditory pathway. [6]

supplementary motor cortex Also called *supplementary motor area*. A premotor area, lying anterior to the primary motor cortex on the medial surface of the cerebral hemisphere, that plays an important role in movement planning. [8,9]

suprachiasmatic nucleus (SCN) A region of the brain, located in the hypothalamus, that is critical for regulating circadian rhythms. [22]

supramodal attention The ability to focus attention on the stimulus information from multiple modalities at the same time. Compare *intermodal attention*. [11]

syllable An elemental component of word. [20]

syllogism A simple logical argument typically consisting of two premises and a conclusion. [25]

Sylvian fissure See *lateral fissure*.

symbolic representation A broad set of cognitive skills by which ideas are communicated using agreed-on stimuli (symbols) that stand for distinctive objects, conditions, or concepts. Compare *representation* (definition 1). [2]

sympathetic division Part of the autonomic motor system that contributes to the mobilization of energy to prepare the body for action. Compare *parasympathetic division*. [1,8]

sympathy Feelings of pity or concern for another individual's plight. Compare *empathy*. [19]

synapse A specialized point of contact between the axon of a neuron (the presynaptic cell) and a target (postsynaptic) cell. Information is transferred between the presynaptic and postsynaptic cells by the release and receipt of biochemical neurotransmitters. [1, Appendix]

synaptic consolidation Consolidation involving changes in synapses that presumably allow the persistence of some forms of memory traces at the cellular level. Compare *system consolidation*. [13]

synaptic potential A membrane potential generated by the action of a chemical transmitter agent. Synaptic potentials allow the transmission of information from one neuron to another. [1, Appendix]

synaptic vesicles The organelles at synaptic endings that contain neurotransmitter agents. [1, Appendix]

synaptogenesis The elaboration of synapses during neural development. [27]

synesthesia A condition in which two sensory modalities interact abnormally such that, for example, numbers or musical notes elicit perceptions of color. [4]

syntax The way in which words are combined to form sentences or phrases. [2,20]

system consolidation Consolidation involving a reorganization of the brain regions that support the memory in question. In the case of declarative memory, refers to a decrease in the role of the hippocampus and an increase in the role of the cortex over time. Compare *synaptic consolidation*. [13]

systematic process A process used for tasks or decisions that involves detailed, deliberate analyses of activated information during episodic memory retrieval. Compare *heuristic process*. [14]

task switching The executive control process that is required when changing behavior rapidly and repeatedly between two different forms. [23]

tastant An environmental molecule that, when bound to a receptor in the taste cells, elicits a taste percept. [7]

taste The sensory modality comprising the perception of substances placed in the mouth. [7]

taste buds Onion-shaped structures in the mouth and pharynx that contain taste cells. [7]

taste cells The chemoreceptor cells in taste buds. [7]

taste system See *gustatory system*.

tectum Literally "roof" (Latin). The dorsal region of the brainstem. [1]

tegmentum The central gray matter of the brainstem. [1]

temperament A disposition to react to emotional situations either positively or negatively. Compare *affect*. [17]

template matching The strategy that explains sensory perception through the recognition of patterns of sensory stimulation that correlate with stored information about objects and conditions experienced in the past. [2]

temporal coding A computational principle in which information is encoded by the precise timing of neuronal activity. [4]

temporal difference learning A form of learning that modulates behavior according to the difference between an obtained reward and an estimate, compiled over the recent past, of an expected reward. [24]

temporal discounting The reduction in how strongly a person wants something over time. [24]

temporal lobe The lobe of the brain that lies inferior to the lateral fissure. [1]

temporoparietal junction A region of the neocortex that includes the posterior portion of the superior temporal gyrus and the angular gyrus of the parietal lobe. [19]

thalamus A collection of nuclei that forms the major component of the diencephalon. Although its functions are many, a primary role of the thalamus is to relay sensory information from the periphery to the cerebral cortex. [1]

theory of mind Also called *mentalizing*. The ability to represent the internal mental states of other individuals. [2,19]

threshold 1. The lowest energy level of a stimulus that causes a perceptual response. [4] 2. The level of membrane potential at which an action potential is generated. [Appendix]

timbre The quality of sound by which stimuli that elicit the same pitch and loudness are distinguished; often taken to arise from the distribution of power in the waveform, as opposed to its periodicity. [6]

TMS See *transcranial magnetic stimulation.*

tonal Pertaining to a sound stimulus that, by virtue of its periodic repetition, produces the perception of a tone. [20]

tone The sound heard in response to a particular frequency of vibration or combination of vibrations. [6]

tonic Pertaining to sustained activity in response to an ongoing stimulus. Compare *phasic.*

tonotopic organization The central arrangement of tone analysis in the auditory system that roughly corresponds to the peripheral responsiveness of the basilar membrane. [6]

top-down processing The idea that cognitive influences arising from higher-order cortical regions influence lower-order cortical or subcortical processing. Compare *bottom-up processing.*

topographic representation A mapping that reflects the organization of the sensory periphery. [4]

trace conditioning A form of classical conditioning in which there is a brief time interval between the end of the conditioned stimulus and the start of the unconditioned stimulus. [15]

tract A major white matter (axonal) pathway in the brain. [1]

transcranial magnetic stimulation (TMS) A method in which a rapidly changing, strong magnetic field is generated next to the skull, thereby delivering transient electrical stimulation to the underlying cortex; the electrical stimulation typically disrupts the local cortical activity, thereby facilitating inferences concerning the cognitive function(s) in which that brain area is involved. [3]

transduction The cellular and molecular process by which energy is converted into neural signals.

transfer-appropriate processing The hypothesis that memory performance depends on a match between the conditions surrounding the encoding and retrieval of a stimulus. [2]

trial A single occurrence of an event in an experiment. [3]

trichromat A person or other animal whose color vision depends on three retinal cone types that absorb long, medium, and short wavelengths of light, respectively. Compare *dichromat* and *monochromat.* [5]

trigeminal chemosensory system The chemosensory system that responds to irritating chemicals that enter the nose or mouth. [7]

triune brain The theory that the brain evolved in three stages, from reptiles (subcortical) to older mammals (three-layered cortex) to newer mammals (six-layered cortex). [17]

trophic Pertaining to the ability of one tissue or cell to support the growth and/or function of another.

tropic Pertaining to the influence of one tissue or cell on the direction of movement (or outgrowth) of another.

truncal ataxia A neurological disorder characterized by poorly coordinated locomotion and associated with damage to the medial portions of the cerebellum. [9]

trust game Also called *investment game.* An experimental paradigm in behavioral economics in which one player (an investor) offers money to another (a trustee), in hopes of reciprocation. [24]

tuning curve The function obtained when a neuron's receptive field is tested with stimuli at different orientations; the peak of the tuning curve defines the maximum sensitivity of the neuron in question. [3,4]

Turing test A hypothetical test in which, through detailed interrogation, subjects judge whether they interacting with a human or a computer. [28]

tympanic membrane The eardrum. [6]

ultimatum game An experimental paradigm in behavioral economics in which one player proposes a fixed transaction, which the other player may either accept or reject; if the transaction is rejected, then neither player receives anything. [24]

uncertainty The psychological state of having limited information when making a decision. [24]

unconditioned reinforcer See *primary reinforcer.*

unconditioned response (UR) In classical conditioning, the innate reflex that is naturally triggered by a particular stimulus. Compare *conditioned response.* [15]

unconditioned stimulus (US) In classical conditioning, the stimulus that naturally triggers the innate reflex. Compare *conditioned stimulus.* [15]

unit recording See *single-unit recording.*

universal grammar The hypothesis that all human languages share fundamental rules. [2,20]

upper motor neuron A neuron that gives rise to a descending projection that controls the activity of *lower motor neurons* in the brainstem and spinal cord. [8]

upper motor neuron syndrome A clinical condition characterized by signs and symptoms that result from damage to descending motor systems, including paralysis, spasticity, and a positive Babinski sign. Compare *lower motor neuron syndrome.* [8]

UR See *unconditioned response.*

US See *unconditioned stimulus.*

utility The personal worth associated with a good; may deviate from the stated value of that good depending on an individual's preferences, biases, or current state. [24]

utilization behavior A cognitive dysfunction, typically associated with frontal lobe damage, in which an individual reflexively uses objects presented to them (e.g., spontaneously pounding a hammer).

V1 See *primary visual cortex.*

V2 See *secondary visual cortex.*

V4 An area of extrastriate visual cortex that is probably important in color vision, although it processes other information as well. [4,5]

V5 See *MT+.*

valence The degree of pleasantness or unpleasantness of a stimulus. [2,17]

valence hypothesis A hypothesis about the hemispheric organization of emotions in the cerebral cortex postulating that positive emotions are preferentially processed in the left hemisphere and negative emotions are preferentially processed in the right hemisphere. [17]

validly cued Pertaining to an attentional cuing paradigm in which the target following a cue occurs in the location indicated by the cue. Compare *invalidly cued*. [10]

variable A measurement that can, in principle, assume any value within an appropriate range.

vector model A way to graphically represent the relationships among emotions by ordering them along two orthogonal axes of positive and negative valence. Compare *circumplex model*. [17]

ventral For the long body axis, stipulates the direction toward the belly (as in *ventral horn*). When speaking of the brain, pertains to the bottom (e.g, a view of the brain from the bottom looking up). Compare *dorsal*. [1]

ventral horn Also called *anterior horn*. The ventral portion of the spinal cord gray matter, which contains the primary motor neurons. Compare *dorsal horn* and *lateral horn*. [1,8]

ventral posterior nuclear complex (VPN) A group of thalamic nuclei that receives the somatosensory projections from the dorsal column nuclei and the trigeminal nuclear complex. [7]

ventral roots See *ventral spinal roots*.

ventral spinal roots The collection of nerve fibers containing motor axons that exit ventrally from the spinal cord and contribute the motor component of each segmental spinal nerve. Compare *dorsal spinal roots*. [1,8]

ventral stream The stream of visual information directed from the primary visual cortex toward the temporal lobe that is especially pertinent to object recognition. Compare *dorsal stream*. [4]

ventral tegmental area (VTA) A part of the midbrain that contains many dopaminergic neurons and that is important for reward and learning. [1,24]

ventricles The spaces in the vertebrate brain that represent the lumen of the embryonic neural tube. [1]

ventricular system The system of fluid spaces in the brain that contain cerebrospinal fluid arising from the central space in the embryonic brain rudiment. [1]

ventromedial prefrontal cortex The ventral portion of the prefrontal cortex surrounding the hemispheric midline; plays a key role in the control of emotions and social behavior. [23]

vermis Medial portion of the cerebrocerebellum that plays a key role in the unconscious correction of movement errors based on inputs from muscle proprioceptors and vestibular inputs. [9]

vertebral column Also called the *spinal column*. The skeletal structure that encloses the spinal cord. It is divided into five regions: cervical (neck; 8 vertebrae), thoracic (chest; 12 vertebrae), lumbar (abdominal region; 5 vertebrae), sacrum (pelvis; 5 vertebrae), and coccyx (the tailbone). [1]

vertebrate An animal with a vertebral column, or "backbone" (technically, a member of the subphylum Vertebrata).

vestibular nuclei Brainstem nuclei that process information about the position of the head and about body acceleration. [7]

vestibular system The sensory system dedicated to generating information about the position of the head in space and the acceleration of the body. [7,8]

vestibulo-ocular reflex (VOR) An involuntary movement of the eyes in response to displacement of the head; allows retinal images to remain stable while the head is moved. [9]

vestibulocerebellum The part of the cerebellar cortex that receives direct input from the vestibular nuclei or vestibular nerve. [9]

vestibulospinal pathways Medial and lateral projections from the vestibular nuclei in the brainstem to the spinal cord that play a key role in postural and locomotor control. [8]

visceral nervous system See *autonomic nervous system*.

vision The process by which the visual system (eye and brain) uses information conveyed by light to generate appropriate percepts and visually guided responses. [4,5]

visual acuity See *acuity*.

visual association cortices The neocortex in occipital lobe, and in the adjacent regions of the parietal and temporal lobes, devoted to higher-order visual processing. [5]

visual cliff paradigm An experimental paradigm that is used to study depth perception in infants. [27]

visual field The area of visual space normally seen by one or both eyes (referred to, respectively, as the monocular and binocular fields). [5]

visual habituation paradigm A paradigm used to test infant perception and cognition. Infants are habituated to a single stimulus or multiple exemplars from a category; they are then shown new exemplars of the familiar category or a novel category and longer looking at the exemplars from the novel category is taken as evidence that the infant can discriminate the two categories. [27]

visual N1 Also called *N100 wave*. The first major negative ERP wave elicited by a visual stimulus, peaking at about 180 milliseconds after a stimulus over the parietal-occipital scalp; thought to derive from visual cortical regions in parietal and occipital cortex. Compare *visual P1*. [11]

visual P1 Also called *P100 wave*. The first major positive ERP wave elicited by a visual stimulus, peaking at about 100 milliseconds after a stimulus over the occipital scalp contralateral to the side of the visual stimulus; thought to derive mainly from the low-level extrastriate visual areas V2, V3, and V4, it is the earliest-latency ERP component affected by attention. Compare *visual N1*. [11]

visual perception The manifestation in consciousness of the empirical significance of visual stimuli (and not, therefore, a necessary accompaniment of visually guided behavior, which often occurs without any particular awareness of what is being seen). [5]

visual percepts Mental constructs that represent the empirical significance of light stimuli. [5]

visual pigment Also called *opsins*. A pigment—in humans, rhodopsin or one of the three cone opsins—that absorbs light and initiates the process of vision. [4,5]

visual processing Transformations carried out by the visual system on information in the retinal stimulus. [4,5]

visual qualities The descriptors of visual percepts (e.g., brightness, color, depth, form, and motion). [5]

visual search The searching in a visual scene with multiple stimulus items for a particular type of item possessing one or more specific feature attributes. [10]

visual spatial attention Attention directed to a location in visual space. The observer's actions undertaken to deal with the object or objects in the scene giving rise to the visual stimuli. [10]

vocal cords Also called *vocal folds*. The bands or folds in the larynx that oscillate as air passes through the glottis, thus producing a vibration that is subsequently shaped by the rest of the vocal tract. [20]

vocal folds See *vocal cords*.

vocal tract The vocal pathway that shapes speech sounds; comprises the larynx, pharynx, and buccal cavity. [20]

vocalization Any sound produced by the vocal tract, which may or may not qualify as speech. [20]

voiced Pertaining to a speech sound stimulus characterized by laryngeal harmonics; typically a vowel sound. [20]

von Economo neurons See *spindle cells*.

VOR See *vestibulo-ocular reflex*.

voxel An imaging volume unit; its exact size parameters vary with the technology used. (In fMRI, a voxel often represents a volume of about 27 mm^3.) [3]

VPN See *ventral posterior nuclear complex*.

VTA See *ventral tegmental area*.

wakefulness The state in which one is not asleep. [28]

wavelength The interval between two wave crests or troughs in any periodic function; for light, the standard measure of the energy of different photons. [4,5,6]

Weber's law The principle that the just noticeable difference in a stimulus increment is a constant fraction (the *Weber fraction*) of the stimulus; named after the nineteenth-century German physiologist and anatomist Ernst Weber. [22]

Wernicke's aphasia Also called *comprehension aphasia*, *receptive aphasia*, or *sensory aphasia*. A language deficit arising from damage to Wernicke's area in the posterior temporal lobe and characterized by an inability to link objects or ideas and the words that signify them and to subjectively comprehend this relationship. Compare *Broca's aphasia*. [21]

Wernicke's area A region of cortex in the superior and posterior region of the left temporal lobe that helps mediate language comprehension; named after the nineteenth-century neurologist Carl Wernicke. Compare *Broca's area*. [6,21]

white light Broadband light that is perceived as lacking color (i.e., as neutral). [5]

white matter The large axon tracts in the brain and spinal cord; these tracts have a whitish cast when viewed in freshly cut material. Compare *gray matter*. [1,27]

Williams' syndrome A rare genetic disorder that is characterized by distinctive facial features and a cheerful personality. [27]

Wisconsin Card Sorting Test A cognitive test that involves classifying a set of cards, each showing one or more simple shapes, into categories based on rules that periodically change throughout the session. [23]

word A speech sound or combination of sounds that communicates a meaning; an elemental component of a sentence. [20]

word length effect The fact that people can hold more words in working memory when the words are short than when they are long. [16]

working memory Memory held briefly in the mind that enables a particular task to be accomplished (e.g., efficiently searching a room for a lost object). [13]

working memory load Also called simply *memory load*. The number of items being held in working memory. [16]

working memory maintenance Retaining information in an active state for a relatively brief time, in order to achieve specific goals. This central function of working memory corresponds to the traditional concept of *short-term memory*. [16]

Illustration Credits

Credits for Unit-Opening Images

Unit I © AJPhoto/Photo Researchers, Inc.
Unit II © Elena Elisseeva/istockphoto.com
Unit III © imagebroker/Alamy
Unit IV © Skip O'Donnell/istockphoto.com
Unit V © Susan Stewart/istockphoto.com
Unit VI © Rainer Raffalski/Alamy
Unit VII © Alexey Buhantsov/
istockphoto.com
Unit VIII © David McIntyre
Unit IX © Ben Conlan/istockphoto.com

Chapter 1: The Human Nervous System

The art in Chapter 1, along with much of the anatomical art in the rest of the book, is adapted from the Fourth Edition of Neuroscience (2008) by D. Purves, G. J. Augustine, D. Fitzpatrick, W. C. Hall, A.-S. LaMantia, J. O. McNamara, and L. E. White. Sunderland, MA: Sinauer Associates, Inc., Publishers.

Chapter 2: Relevant Principles of Cognitive Psychology

Figure 2.4 STERNBERG, S. (1966) High-speed memory scanning in human memory. *Science* 153: 652–654. **Figure 2.5A** GREGORY, R. (1970) *The Intelligent Eye.* New York: McGraw-Hill. **Figure 2.6** JOHNSTON, W. A. and S. P. HEINZ (1978). Flexibility and capacity demands of attention, *J. Exp. Psychol.* 107: 420–435. **Figure 2.8** KISSIN, B. (1986) Conscious and unconscious programs in the brain. *Psychology of Human Behavior.* New York: Plenum. **Figure 2.9** LIBERMAN, A. M., K. S. HARRIS, H. HOFFMAN AND B. GRIFFITH (1957) The discrimination of speech sounds within and across phoneme boundaries. *J. Exp. Psychol.* 54: 358–368.

Chapter 3: Exploring Cognitive Processes in Neural Terms

Figure 3.2 GEORGE, M. S., S. H. LISANBY AND H. A. SACKEIM (1999) Transcranial magnetic stimulation: Applications in neuropsychiatry. *Arch. Gen. Psychiatry* 56: 300–311. **Figure 3.3B** COLBY, C. L., J. R. DUHAMEL AND M. E. GOLDBERG (1996) Visual, presaccadic, and cognitive activation of single neurons in monkey lateral intraparietal area. *J. Neurophysiol.* 76: 2841–2852. **Figure 3.8D** WOLDORFF, M. G., M. MATZKE, F. ZAMARRIPA AND P. T. FOX (1999) Procedure to extract a weekly pattern of performance of human reaction time. *Human Brain Mapping* 8: 121–127. **Figure 3.10B** HUETTEL, S. A., A. W. SONG AND G. MCCARTHY (2004) *Functional Magnetic Resonance Imaging.* Sunderland, MA: Sinauer. **Figure 3.12** BUROCK, M. A., R. L. BUCKNER, M. G. WOLDORFF, B. R. ROSEN AND A. M. DALE (1998) Randomized event-related experimental designs allow for extremely rapid presentation rates using functional MRI. *NeuroReport* 9: 3735–3739. **Figure 3.14** CHURCHLAND, P. S. AND T. J. SEJNOWSKI (1988) Perspectives on cognitive neuroscience. *Science* 242: 741–745.

Chapter 4: Overview of Sensory Processing

Figure 4.1C JOHANSSON, R. S. AND A. B. VALLBO (1983) Tactile sensory coding in the glabrous skin of the human. *Trends Neurosci.* 6: 27–32. **Figure 4.3** SAKMANN, B. AND O. D. CREUTZFELDT (1969) Scotopic and mesopic light adaptation in the cat's retina. *Pflügers Arch.* 313: 168–185. **Figure 4.5C** WEINSTEIN, S. (1968) Neuropsychological studies of the phantom. In *Contributions to Clinical Neuropsychology*, A. L. Benton (ed.). Chicago: Aldine Publishing Company, pp. 73–106. **Figure 4.7** BLUMENFELD, H. (2002) *Neuroanatomy through Clinical Cases.* Sunderland: Sinauer. **Figure 4.13A–D** Purves, D., D. Riddle and A.-S. LaMantia (1992) Iterated patterns of brain circuitry (or how the cortex got its spots). *Trends Neurosci.* 15: 362–369.

Chapter 5: The Perception of Visual Stimuli

Figure 5.2A ANDREWS, T. J., S. D. HALPERN AND D. PURVES (1997) Correlated size variations in human visual cortex, lateral geniculate nucleus, and optic tract. *J. Neurosci.* 17: 2859–2868. **Figure 5.2B** WATANABE, M. AND R. W. RODIECK (1989) Parasol and midget ganglion cells of the primate retina. *J. Comp. Neurol.* 289: 434–454. **Figure 5.3** SERENO, M. I. AND 7 OTHERS (1995) Borders of multiple visual areas in humans revealed by functional magnetic resonance imaging. *Science* 268: 889–893. **Figure 5.4B, 5.10 and 5.12** PURVES, D. AND R. B. LOTTO (2003) *Why We See What We Do.* Sunderland, MA: Sinauer. **Figure 5.6** WHITE, M. (1979) A new effect of pattern on perceived lightness. *Perception* 8: 413–416. **Figure 5.9** BOUVIER, S. E. AND S. A. ENGEL (2006) Behavioral deficits and cortical damage in cerebral achromatopsia. *Cereb. Cortex* 16: 183–191. **Figure 5.11** HOWE, C. Q. AND D. PURVES (2005) *Perceiving Geometry: Geometrical Illusions Explained by Natural Scene Statistics.* New York: Springer Verlag. **Figure 5.13** MURRAY, S. O., H. BOYACI AND D. KERSTEN (2006) The representation of perceived angular size in primary visual cortex. *Nat. Neurosci.* 9: 429–434. **Figure 5.17** BLAKE, R. AND N. K. LOGOTHETIS (2002) Visual competition. *Nat. Rev. Neurosci.* 3: 1–11. **Figure 5.18** SUGRUE, L. P., G. S. CORRADO AND W. T. NEWSOME (2005) Choosing the greater of two goods: Neural currencies for valuation and decision making. *Nat. Rev. Neurosci.* 6: 363–375. **Figure 5.21** TOOTELL, R. B. AND 6 OTHERS (1995) Visual motion aftereffect in human cortical area MT revealed by functional magnetic resonance imaging. *Nature* 375: 139–141. **Figure 5. 23** ISHAI, A., L. G. UNGERLEIDER AND J. V. HAXBY (2000) Distributed neural systems for the generation of visual images. *Neuron* 28: 979–990.

Chapter 6: The Perception of Auditory Stimuli

Figure 6.1, micrograph KESSEL, R. G. AND R. H. KARDON (1979) *Tissue and Organs: A Text-Atlas of Scanning Electron Microscopy.* San Francisco: W. H. Freeman. **Figure 6.7** BENDOR, D. AND X. WANG (2006) Cortical representations of pitch in monkeys and humans. *Curr. Opin. Neurobiol.* 16: 391–399. **Figure 6.14** TRAMO, M. J. (2001) Biology and music: Music of the hemispheres. *Science* 291: 54–56. **Figure 6.15** ALAIN, C., S. R. ARNOTT AND T. W. PICTON (2001) Bottom-up and top-down influences on auditory scene analysis: Evidence from event-related brain potentials. *J. Exp. Psych.: Human Perception and Performance* 27: 1072–1089.

Chapter 7: Mechanosensory and Chemosensory Perception

Figure 7.8 ROSS, M. H., L. J. ROMMELL AND G. I. KAYE (1995) *Histology, A Text and Atlas.* Baltimore: Williams and Wilkins. **Figure 7.11**

JENKINS, W. M., M. M. MERZENICH, M. T. OCHS, T. ALLARD AND E. GUIC-ROBLES (1990) Functional reorganization of primary somatosensory cortex in adult owl monkeys after behaviorally controlled tactile stimulation. *J. Neurophysiol.* 63: 82–104.

Chapter 8: Motor Systems and Motor Control

Figures 8.1 BERNSTEIN, N. A. (1947). *On the Formation of Movement.* English translation of Russian original. Hillsdale, NJ: Lawrence Erlbaum, p. 83. **Figure 8.3** FUCHS, A. F. (1967) Saccadic and smooth pursuit movements in the monkey. *J. Physiol.* (Lond.) 191: 609–630. **Figure 8.4** BURKE, R. E., P. L. STRICK, K. KANDA, C. C. KIM AND B. WALMSLEY (1977) Anatomy of medial gastrocnemius and soleus motor nuclei in cat spinal cord. *J. Neurophysiol.* 40: 667–680. **Figure 8.7A** WALMSLEY, B., J. A. HODGSON AND R. E. BURKE (1978) Forces produced by medial gastrocnemius and soleus muscles during locomotion in freely moving cats. *J. Neurophysiol.* 41: 1203–1215. **Figure 8.7B** MONSTER, A. W. AND H. CHAN (1977) Isometric force production by motor units of extensor digitorum communis muscle in man. *J. Neurophysiol.* 40: 1432–1443. **Figure 8.10** PEARSON, K. (1976) The control of walking. *Sci. Am.* 235: 72–86. **Figure 8.11** BLUMENFELD, H. (2002) *Neuroanatomy through Clinical Cases.* Sunderland, MA: Sinauer. **Figure 8.14** BREEDLOVE, S. M., M. R. ROSENZWEIG AND N. V. WATSON (2007) *Biological Psychology: An Introduction to Behavioral, Cognitive, and Clinical Neuroscience,* 5th Ed. Sunderland, MA: Sinauer. **Figure 8.15** GRAZIANO, M. S. A. (2006) The organization of behavioral repertoire in motor cortex. *Ann. Rev. Neurosci.* 29: 105–134. **Figure 8.16A** EVARTS, E. V. (1981) Functional studies of the motor cortex. In *The Organization of the Cerebral Cortex,* F. O. Schmitt, F. G. Worden, G. Adelman and S. G. Dennis (eds.). Cambridge, MA: MIT Press, pp. 199–236. **Figure 8.16B** PORTER, R. AND R. LEMON (1993) *Corticospinal Function and Voluntary Movement.* Oxford: Oxford University Press. **Figure 8.17** LEE, D. L., W. H. ROHRER AND D. L. SPARKS (1988) Population coding of saccadic eye movements by neurons in the superior colliculus. *Nature* 332: 357–360. **Figure 8.18** GEORGOPOLOUS, A. P., A. B. SCHWARTZ AND R. E. KETTNER (1986) Neuronal population coding of movement direction. *Science* 233: 1416–1418.

Chapter 9: Computation and Cognition in the Motor System

Figure 9.2 EAGLEMAN, D. M. (2004) The where and when of intention. *Science* 303: 1144–1146. **Figure 9.3** SHADLEN, M. N. AND W. T. NEWSOME (1996) Motion perception: Seeing and deciding. *Proc. Natl. Acad. Sci. USA* 93: 628–633. **Figure 9.4** GOLD, J. AND M. SHADLEN (2002) Banburismus and the brain: Decoding the relationship between sensory stimuli, decisions, and reward. *Neuron* 36: 299–308. **Figure 9.5A,B** PLATT, M. L. AND P. W. GLIMCHER (1999) Neural correlates of decision variables in parietal cortex. *Nature* 400: 233–238. **Figure 9.6** TANJI, J. AND K. SHIMA (1994) Role for supplementary motor area cells in planning several movements ahead. *Nature* 371: 413–416. **Figure 9.7** FUJII, N. AND A. M. GRAYBIEL (2003) Representation of action sequence boundaries by macaque prefrontal cortical neurons. *Science* 301: 1246–1249. **Figure 9.8** DEIBER, M. P., M. HONDA, V. IBAÑEZ, N. SADATO AND M. HALLETT (1999) Mesial motor areas in self-initiated versus externally triggered movements examined with fMRI: Effect of movement type and rate. *J. Neurophysiol.* 81: 3065–3077. **Figure 9.9A** http://psychology.uwo.ca/faculty/goodale/research. **Figure 9.9B** MILNER, A. D. AND M. A. GOODALE (1995) *The Visual Brain in Action.* Oxford: Oxford University Press. **Figure 9.11** HIKOSAKA, O. AND R. H. WURTZ (1989) The basal ganglia. In *The Neurobiology of Saccadic Eye Movements,* R. H. Wurtz and M. E. Goldberg (eds.). New York: Elsevier, pp. 257–281. **Figure 9.12** GRAYDON, F. X., K. J. FRISTON, C. G. THOMAS, V. B. BROOKS AND R. S. MENON (2005) Learning-related fMRI activation associated with a rotational visuo-motor transformation. *Brain Res. Cogn. Brain Res.* 22: 373–383. **Figure 9.15** BLUMENFELD, H. (2002) *Neuroanatomy through Clinical Cases.* Sunderland, MA: Sinauer. **Figure 9.16** PURVES, D. AND 6 OTHERS (2008) *Neuroscience,* 4th Ed. Sunderland, MA: Sinauer. **Figure 9.17** IMAMIZU, H. AND 7 OTHERS (2000) Human cerebellar activity reflecting an acquired internal model of a novel tool. *Nature* 403: 192–195.

Chapter 10: Overview of Attention

Figure 10.3 CHERRY, E. C. (1953) Some experiments on the recognition of speech, with one and with two ears. *J. Acoust. Soc. Amer.* 25: 975–979. **Figure 10.4A** BROADBENT, D. E. (1958) *Perception and Communication.* London: Pergamon. **Figure 10.4B** TREISMAN, A. (1960) Contextual cues in selective listening. *Q. J. Exp. Psychol.* 12: 242–248. **Figure 10.5** PASHLER, H. (1994) Overlapping mental operations in serial performance with preview. *Q. J. Exp. Psychol.* 47: 161–191. **Figure 10.6** RAYMOND, J. E., K. L. SHAPIRO AND K. M. ARNELL (1992) Temporary suppression of visual processing in an RSVP task: An attentional blink? *J. Exp. Psychol. Hum. Percept. Perform.* 18: 849–860. **Figure 10.7** POSNER, M. I., C. R. R. SNYDER AND B. J. DAVIDSON (1980) Attention and the detection of signals. *J. Exp. Psychol. Gen.* 109: 160–174. **Figure 10.8** KLEIN, R. M. (2000) Inhibition of return. *Trends Cogn. Sci.* 4: 138–147; POSNER, M. I. AND Y. COHEN (1984) Components of visual orienting. In *Attention and Performance,* Vol. 10: *Control of Language Processes,* H. Bouma and D. Bouwhuis (eds.). London: Erlbaum, pp. 531–556. **Figure 10.9** TREISMAN, A. AND G. GELADE (1980) A feature integration theory of attention. *Cognit. Psychol.* 12: 97–136.

Chapter 11: Effects of Attention on Stimulus Processing

Figure 11.1 PICTON, T. P., S. A. HILLYARD, H. I. KRANSZ AND R. GALAMBOS (1974) Human auditory-evoked potentials. I. Evaluation of components. *Electroenceph. Clin. Neurophysiol.* 36: 179–190. **Figure 11.2** HILLYARD, S. A., R. F. HINK, V. L. SCHWENT AND T. W. PICTON (1973) Electrical signs of selective attention in the human brain. *Science* 182: 177–180. **Figure 11.3A,B** WOLDORFF, M., J. C. HANSEN AND S. A. HILLYARD (1987) Evidence for effects of selective attention in the mid-latency range of the human auditory event-related potential. In *Current Trends in Event-Related Potential Research,* R. Johnson Jr., R. Parasuraman, and J. W. Rohrbaugh (eds.). Amsterdam: Elsevier, pp. 146–154. **Figure 11.3C** WOLDORFF, M. G. AND 6 OTHERS (1993) Modulation of early sensory processing in human auditory cortex during auditory selective attention. *Proc. Natl. Acad. Sci. USA* 90: 8722–8726. **Figure 11.4** PETKOV, C. I., X. KANG, K. ALHO, O. BERTRAND, E. W. YUND AND D. L. WOODS (2004) Attentional modulation of human auditory cortex. *Nat. Neurosci.* 7: 658–663. **Figure 11.5** WOLDORFF, M. G., S. A. HACKLEY AND S. A. HILLYARD (1991) The effects of channel-selective attention on the mismatch negativity wave elicited by deviant tones. *Psychophysiology* 28: 30–42. **Figure 11.8** HEINZE, H. J. AND 11 OTHERS (1994) Combined spatial and temporal imaging of brain activity during visual selective attention in humans. *Nature* 372: 543–546. **Figure 11.9** NOESSELT, T. AND 8 OTHERS (2002) Delayed striate cortical activation during spatial attention. *Neuron* 35: 575–587. **Figure 11.10** MORAN, J. AND R. DESIMONE (1985) Selective attention gates visual processing in the extrastriate cortex. *Science* 229: 782–784. **Figure 11.11** McADAMS, C. J. AND J. H. R. MAUNSELL (1999) Effects of attention on reliability of individual neurons in monkey visual cortex. *Neuron* 23: 765–773. **Figure 11.12** REYNOLDS, J. H., T. PASTERNAK AND R. DESIMONE (2000) Attention increases sensitivity of V4 neurons. *Neuron* 26: 703–714. **Figure 11.13** REES, G., C. D. FRITH AND N. LAVIE (1997) Modulating irrelevant motion perception by varying attentional load in an unrelated task. *Science* 278: 1616–1618. **Figure 11.14** ZATORRE, R. J., A. C. EVANS, E. MEYER AND A. GJEDDE (1992) Lateralization of phonetic and pitch discrimination in speech processing. *Science* 256: 846–849. **Figure 11.15** O'CRAVEN, K. M., B. R. ROSEN, K. K. KWONG, A. TREISMAN AND R. L. SAVOY (1997) Voluntary attention modulates fMRI activity in human MT-MST. *Neuron* 18: 591–598. **Figure 11.16** TREUE, S. AND

J. C. Martinez Trujillo (1999) Feature-based attention influences motion processing gain in macaque visual cortex. *Nature* 399: 575–579.

Chapter 12: Attentional Control and Attentional Systems

Figure 12.1 Heilman, H. and E. Valenstein (1985) *Clinical Neuropsychology*, 2nd Ed. New York: Oxford University Press. **Figure 12.2A,C** Posner, M. I. and M. E. Raichle (1994) *Images of Mind.* New York: Scientific American Library. **Figure 12.2B** Blumenfeld, H. (2002) *Neuroanatomy through Clinical Cases.* Sunderland: Sinauer. **Figure 12.2D** Grabowecky, M., L. C. Robertson and A. Treisman (1993) Preattentive processes guide visual search: evidence from patients with unilateral visual neglect. *J. Cogn. Neuerosci.* 5: 288–302. **Figure 12.3** Friedman-Hill, S. R., L. C. Robertson and A. Treisman (1995) Parietal contributions to visual feature binding: Evidence from a patient with bilateral lesions. *Science* 269: 853–855. **Figure 12.4A** Humphreys, G. W. and M. J. Riddoch (1993) Interactions between object and space systems revealed through neuropsychology. In *Attention and Performance*, Vol. 14: *Synergies in Experimental Psychology, Artificial Intelligence, and Cognitive Neuroscience*, D. E. Meyer and S. Kornblum (eds.). Cambridge, MA: MIT Press, pp. 183–218. **Figure 12.4B** Cooper, A. A. and G. W. Humphreys (2000) Coding space within but not between objects: Evidence from Balint's syndrome. *Neuropsychologia* 38: 723–733. **Figure 12.5** Hopfinger, J. B., M. H. Buonocore and G. R. Mangun (2000) The neural mechanisms of top-down attentional control. *Nat. Neurosci.* 3: 284–291. **Figure 12.6A** Liu, T., S. D. Slotnick, J. T. Serences and S. Yantis (2003) Cortical mechanisms of feature-based attentional control. *Cereb. Cortex* 13: 1334–1343. **Figure 12.6B** Serences, J. T., J. Schwartbach, S. M. Courtney, X. Colay and S. Yantis (2004) Control of object-based attention in human cortex. *Cereb. Cortex* 14: 1346–1357. **Figure 12.7** Woldorff, M. G., C. J. Hazlett, H. M. Fichtenholtz, D. H. Weissman, A. M. Dale and A. W. Song (2004) Functional parcellation of attentional control regions of the brain. *J. Cogn. Neurosci.* 16: 149–165. Grent-'t-Jong, T. and M. G. Woldorff (2007) Timing and sequence of brain activity in top-down control of visual-spatial attention. *PLoS Biol.* 5: 114–126. **Figure 12.8** Colby, C. L., J. R. Duhamel and M. E. Goldberg (1996) Visual, presaccadic, and cognitive activation of single neurons in monkey lateral intraparietal area. *J. Neurophysiol.* 76: 2841–2852. **Figure 12.9** Thompson, K. G., K. L. Biscoe and T. R. Sato (2005) Neuronal basis of covert spatial attention in the frontal eye field. *J. Neurosci.* 25: 9479–9487. **Figure 12.10A** Hopfinger, J. B., M. H. Buonocore and G. R. Mangun (2000) The neural mechanisms of top-down

attentional control. *Nat. Neurosci.* 3: 284–291. **Figure 12.10B** Luck, S. J., L. Chelazzi, S. A. Hillyard and R. Desimone (1997) Neural mechanisms of spatial selective attention in areas V1, V2, and V4 of macaque visual cortex. *J. Neurophysiol.* 77: 24–42. **Figure 12.10C** Grent-'t-Jong, T. and M. G. Woldorff (2007) Timing and sequence of brain activity in top-down control of visual-spatial attention. *PLoS Biol.* 5: 114–126. **Figure 12.11** Corbetta, M., J. M. Kincade, J. M. Ollinger, M. P. McAvoy and G. L. Shulman (2000) Voluntary orienting is dissociated from target detection in human posterior parietal cortex. *Nat. Neurosci.* 3: 292–297. **Figure 12.12** Corbetta, M. and G. L. Shulman (2002) Control of goal-directed and stimulus-driven attention in the brain. *Nat. Rev. Neurosci.* 3: 201–215. **Figure 12.13** Moore, T., K. M. Armstrong and M. Fallah (2003) Visuomotor origins of covert spatial attention. *Neuron* 40: 671–683. **Figure 12.14** Corbetta, M., and 10 others (1998) A common network of functional areas for attention and eye movements. *Neuron* 21: 761–773.

Chapter 13: Memory and the Brain: From Cells to Systems

Figure 13.1 University of Rome Psychobiology Lab Web Site: http://darwin41.bio.uniroma1.it/~Psychobiology/Psicobiologia/didattica/materiale/psicobio/introduz/introduz.htm **Figure 13.2** Squire, L. R. and E. R. Kandel (1999) *Memory: From Mind to Molecules.* New York: Scientific American Library. **Figure 13.3** Malinow, R., H. Schulman and R. W. Tsien (1989) Inhibition of postsynaptic PKC or CaMKII blocks induction but not expression of LTP. *Science* 245: 862–866. **Figure 13.5** Tsien, J. Z., P. T. Huerta and S. Tonegawa (1996) The essential role of hippocampal CA1 NMDA receptor-dependent synaptic plasticity in spatial memory. *Cell* 87: 1327–1338. **Figure 13.6A–C** Lamprecht, R. and J. LeDoux (2004) Structural plasticity and memory. *Nat. Rev. Neurosci.* 5: 45–54. **Figure 13.6D** Engert, F. and T. Bonhoeffer (1999) Dendritic spine changes associated with hippocampal long-term synaptic plasticity. *Nature* 399: 66–70. **Figure 13.7** Corkin, S., D. G. Amaral, R. G. González, K. A. Johnson and B. T. Hyman (1997) H.M.'s medial temporal lobe lesion: Findings from MRI. *J. Neurosci.* 17: 3964–3979. **Figure 13.9** Milner, B., S. Corkin and H.-L. Teuber (1968) Further analysis of the hippocampal amnesic syndrome: A 14-year follow-up study of H.M. *Neuropsychologia* 6: 215–234. **Figure 13.12A** Warrington, E. K. and T. Shallice (1969) The selective impairment of auditory-verbal short-term memory. *Brain* 92: 885–896. **Figure 13.12B** Drachman, D. A. and J. Arbit (1966). Memory and the hippocampal complex. II. Is memory a multiple process? *Arch. Neurol.* 15: 52–61. **Figure 13.13** Graf, P., L.

R. Squire and R. Mandler (1984). The information that amnesic patients do not forget. *J. Exp. Psychol.: Learning, Memory and Cognition* 10: 164–178. **Figure 13.14** Gabrieli, J. D. E., D. A. Fleishman, M. M. Keane, S. L. Reminger and F. Morrell (1995) Double dissociation between memory systems underlying explicit and implicit memory in the human brain. *Psychol. Sci.* 6: 76-82. **Figure 13.16** Dudai, Y. (2004). The neurobiology of consolidations, or, how stable is the engram? *Annu. Rev. Psychol.* 55: 51–86; Agranoff, B., R. Davis and J. Brink (1966) Chemical studies on memory formation in goldfish. *Brain Res.* 1: 303–309; Kim, J. J. and M. S. Fanselow (1992) Modality-specific retrograde amnesia of fear following hippocampal lesions. *Science* 256: 675–677. **Figure 13.17** Frankland, P. W. and B. Bontempi (2005) The organization of recent and remote memories. *Nat. Rev. Neurosci.* 6: 119–130.

Chapter 14: Declarative Memory

Figure 14.1B Ekstrom, A. and 6 others (2003) Cellular networks underlying human spatial navigation. *Nature* 425: 184–187. **Figure 14.1C** Maguire, E. A. and 6 others (2000) Navigation-related structural change in the hippocampi of taxi drivers. *Proc. Natl. Acad. Sci. USA* 97: 4398–4403. **Figure 14.3** Eichenbaum, H., P. Dudchenko, E. Wood, M. Shapiro and H. Tanila (1999) The hippocampus, memory, and place cells: Is it spatial memory or a memory space? *Neuron* 23: 209–226. **Figure 14.4** Dusek, J. and H. Eichenbaum (1997) The hippocampus and memory for orderly stimulus relations. *Proc. Natl. Acad. Sci. USA* 94: 7109–7114. **Figure 14.5A** Tulving, E. (2002) Episodic memory: From mind to brain. *Annu. Rev. Psychol.* 53: 1–25. **Figure 14.5B** Rosenbaum, R. S. and 6 others (2000) Remote spatial memory in amnesic person with extensive bilateral hippocampal lesions. *Nat. Neurosci.* 3: 1044–1048. **Figure 14.6** Vargha-Khadem, F., D. G. Gadian, K. E. Watkins, A. Connelly, W. Van Paesschen and M. Mishkin (1997) Differential effects of early hippocampal pathology on episodic and semantic memory. *Science* 277: 376–380. **Figure 14.8A** Eldridge, L. L., B. J. Knowlton, C. S. Furmanski, S. Y. Bookheimer and S. A. Engle (2000) Remembering episodes: A selective role for the hippocampus during retrieval. *Nat. Neurosci.* 3: 1149–1152. **Figure 14.8B** Prince, S. E., S. M. Daselaar and R. Cabeza (2005) Neural correlates of relational memory: Successful encoding and retrieval of semantic and perceptual associations. *J. Neurosci.* 25: 1203–1210. **Figure 14.8C** Yonelinas, A. P. and 6 others (2002) Effects of extensive temporal lobe damage or mild hypoxia on recollection and familiarity. *Nat. Neurosci.* 5: 1236–1241. **Figure 14.9A** Xiang, J.-Z. and M. W. Brown (1998) Differential neuronal encoding of novelty, familiarity, and recency in regions of the anterior temporal lobe.

Neuropharmacology 37: 657–676. **Figure 14.9B** DASELAAR, S. M., M. S. FLECK AND R. CABEZA (2006) Triple dissociation within the medial temporal lobes: Recollection, familiarity, and novelty. *J. Neurophysiol.* 96: 1902–1911. **Figure 14.10** EICHENBAUM, H., A. R. YONELINAS AND C. RANGANATH (2007). The medial temporal lobe and recognition memory. *Annu. Rev. Neurosci.* 30: 123–152. **Figure 14.11** JANOWSKY, J. S., A. P. SHIMAMURA, M. KRITCHEVSKY AND L. R. SQUIRE (1989) Cognitive impairment following frontal lobe damage and its relevance to human amnesia. *Behav. Neurosci.* 103: 548–560. **Figure 14.12A** KAPUR, S., F. I. CRAIK, E. TULVING, A. A. WILSON, S. HOULE AND G. M. BROWN (1994) Neuroanatomical correlates of encoding in episodic memory: Levels of processing effect. *Proc. Natl. Acad. Sci. USA* 91: 2008–2011. **Figure 14.12B** PALLER, K. A. AND 7 OTHERS (2002) Neural correlates of person recognition. *Learn. Mem.* 10: 253–260. **Figure 14.13** MCDERMOTT, K. B., S. E. PETERSEN, J. M. WATSON AND J. G. OJEMANN (2003) A procedure for identifying regions preferentially activated by attention to semantic and phonological relations using fMRI. *Neuropsychologia* 41: 293–304. **Figure 14.14** BLUMENFELD, R. S. AND C. RANGANATH (2006) Dorsolateral prefrontal cortex promotes long-term memory formation through its role in working memory organization. *J. Neurosci.* 26: 916–925. **Figure 14.15A** DÜZEL, E. AND 6 OTHERS (1999) Task-related and item-related brain processes of memory retrieval. *Proc. Natl. Acad. Sci. USA* 96: 1794–1799. **Figure 14.15B** VELANOVA, K., L. L. JACOBY, M. E. WHEELER, M. P. MCAVOY, S. E. PETERSEN AND R. L. BUCKNER (2003) Functional-anatomic correlates of sustained and transient processing components engaged during controlled retrieval. *J. Neurosci.* 23: 8460–8470. **Figure 14.16A** HENSON, R. N. A., T. SHALLICE AND R. J. DOLAN (1999) Right prefrontal cortex and episodic memory retrieval: A functional MRI test of the monitoring hypothesis. *Brain* 122: 1367–1381. **Figure 14.16B** DOBBINS, I. G., H. J. RICE, A. D. WAGNER AND D. L. SCHACTER (2003) Memory orientation and success: Separable neurocognitive components underlying episodic recognition. *Neuropsychologia* 41: 318–333. **Figure 14.17A** FLECK, M. S., S. M. DASELAAR, I. G. DOBBINS AND R. CABEZA (2006) Role of prefrontal and anterior cingulate regions in decision-making processes shared by memory and nonmemory tasks. *Cerebral Cortex* 16: 1623–1630. **Figure 14.17B** SCHACTER, D. L., N. M. ALPERT, C. R. SAVAGE, S. L. RAUCH AND M. S. ALBERT (1996) Conscious recollection and the human hippocampal formation: Evidence from positron emission tomography. *Proc. Natl. Acad. Sci. USA* 93: 321–325. **Figure 14.18A** WAGNER, A. D., B. J. SHANNON, I. KAHN AND R. L. BUCKNER (2005) Parietal lobe contributions to episodic memory retrieval. *Trends*

Cogn. Sci. 9: 445–453. **Figure 14.18B** DASELAAR, S. M., S. E. PRINCE AND R. CABEZA (2004) When less means more: deactivations during encoding that predict subsequent memory. *NeuroImage* 23: 921–927. **Figure 14.18C** GUSNARD, D. A. AND M. E. RAICHLE (2001) Searching for a baseline: Functional imaging and the resting human brain. *Nat. Rev. Neurosci.* 2: 685–694. **Figure 14.19** KAHN, I., L. DAVACHI AND A. D. WAGNER (2004). Functional-neuroanatomic correlates of recollection: Implications for models of recognition memory. *J. Neurosci.* 24: 4172–4180.

Chapter 15: Nondeclarative Memory

Figure 15.3A GRAF, P. AND G. MANDLER (1984) Activation makes words more accessible, but not necessarily more retrievable. *J. Verb. Learn. Verb. Behav.* 23: 553–568. **Figure 15.3B** WELDON, M. S. AND H. L. ROEDIGER (1987) Altering retrieval demands reverses the picture superiority effect. *Mem. Cogn.* 15: 269–280. **Figure 15.4A** PARKIN, A. J., AND S. STREETE (1988) Implicit memory in young children and adults. *Brit. J. Psychol.* 79: 361–369. **Figure 15.4B** LIGHT, L. L. AND A. SINGH (1987) Implicit and explicit memory in young and older adults. *J. Exp. Psychol. Learn. Mem. Cogn.* 4: 531–541. **Figure 15.5** BUCKNER, R. L., W. KOUTSTAAL,, D. L. SCHACTER AND B. R. ROSEN (2000) fMRI evidence for a role of frontal and inferior temporal cortex in amodal components of priming. *Brain* 123: 620–640. **Figure 15.6A,B** KOUTSTAAL, W., A. D. WAGNER, M. ROTTE, A. MARIL, R. L. BUCKNER AND D. L. SCHACTER (2001) Perceptual specificity in visual object priming: Functional magnetic resonance imaging evidence for a laterality difference in fusiform cortex. *Neuropsychologia* 39: 184–199. **Figure 15.6C,D** DEHAENE, S., L. AND 6 OTHERS. (2001) Cerebral mechanisms of word masking and unconscious repetition priming. *Nat. Neurosci.* 4: 752–758. **Figure 15.7** WAGNER, A. D., W. KOUTSTAAL, A. MARIL, D. L. SCHACTER AND R. L. BUCKNER (2000) Task-specific repetition priming in left inferior prefrontal cortex. *Cereb. Cortex* 10: 1176–1184. **Figure 15.9** ROSSELL, S. L., C. J. PRICE AND A. C. NOBRE (2003) The anatomy and time course of semantic priming investigated by fMRI and ERPs. *Neuropsychologia* 41: 550–564. **Figure 15.10** HENSON, R., T. SHALLICE AND R. DOLAN (2000) Neuroimaging evidence for dissociable forms of repetition priming. *Science* 287: 1269–1272. **Figure 15.11** GRILL-SPECTOR, K., R. HENSON AND A. MARTIN (2006) Repetition and the brain: Neural models of stimulus-specific effects. *Trends Cogn. Sci.* 10: 14–23. **Figure 15.13** DELLA-MAGGIORE, V., N. MALFAIT, D. J. OSTRY AND T. PAUS (2004) Stimulation of the posterior parietal cortex interferes with arm trajectory adjustments during the learning of new dynamics. *J. Neurosci.* 24: 9971–9976. **Figure 15.14A,B** GAUTHIER, I., M. J. TARR, A.

W. ANDERSON, P. SKUDLARSKI AND J. C. GORE (1999) Activation of the middle fusiform "face area" increases with expertise in recognizing novel objects. *Nat. Neurosci.* 2: 568–573. **Figure 15.14C** GAUTHIER, I., P. SKUDLARSKI, J. C. GORE AND A. W. ANDERSON (2000) Expertise for cars and birds recruits brain areas involved in face recognition. *Nat. Neurosci.* 3: 191–197. **Figure 15.15** POLLMANN, S. AND M. MAERTENS (2005) Shift of activity from attention to motor-related brain areas during visual learning. *Nat. Neurosci.* 8: 1494–1496. **Figure 15.16** KNOWLTON, B. J., J. A. MANGELS AND L. R. SQUIRE (1996) A neostriatal habit learning system in humans. *Science* 262: 1747–1749. **Figure 15.17** POLDRACK, R. A. AND 7 OTHERS (2001) Interactive memory systems in the human brain. *Nature* 414: 546–550.**Box 15B** KOURTZI, Z. AND K. GRILL-SPECTOR (2005) fMRI adaptation: A tool for studying visual representations in the primate brain. In *Fitting the Mind into the World: Adaptation and After-Effects in High-Level Vision*, G. Rhodes and C. Clifford (eds.) New York: Oxford University Press. PHOTOS © Elnur/Fotolia.com (teacup) and © Eric Isselée/Fotolia.com (dog).

Chapter 16: Working Memory

Figure 16.1 Photo © Paul Piebinga/istock-photo.com **Figure 16.2** BADDELEY, A. (2003) Working memory: Looking back and looking forward. *Nat. Rev. Neurosci.* 4: 829–839. **Figure 16.3** COWAN, N. (1998) Visual and auditory working memory capacity. *Trends Cogn. Sci.* 2: 77–78. **Figure 16.5A** LEUNG, H. C., J. C. GORE AND P. S. GOLDMAN-RAKIC (2002) Sustained mnemonic response in the human middle frontal gyrus during on-line storage of spatial memoranda. *J. Cogn. Neurosci.* 14: 659–671. **Figure 16.5B** PESSOA, L., E. GUTIERREZ, P. A. BANDETTINI AND L. G. UNGERLEIDER (2002) Neural correlates of visual working memory: fMRI amplitude predicts task performance. *Neuron* 35: 975–987. **Figure 16.6** CHEIN, J. M. AND J. A. FIEZ (2001) Dissociation of verbal working memory system components using a delayed serial recall task. *Cereb. Cortex* 11:1003–1014. **Figure 16.7** FIEBACH, C. J., J. RISSMAN AND M. D'ESPOSITO (2006) Modulation of inferotemporal cortex activation during verbal working memory maintenance. *Neuron.* 51 :251–261. **Figure 16.8** SHIVDE, G. S. AND S. L. THOMPSON-SCHILL (2004) Dissociating semantic and phonological maintenance using fMRI. *Cogn. Affect. Behav. Neurosci.* 4: 10–19. **Figure 16.9** FUNAHASHI, S., C. J. BRUCE AND P. S. GOLDMAN-RAKIC (1989) Mnemonic coding of visual space in the monkey's dorsolateral prefrontal cortex. *J. Neurophysiol.* 61: 331. **Figure 16.10C** CURTIS, C. E., V. Y. RAO AND M. D'ESPOSITO (2004) Maintenance of spatial and motor codes during oculomotor delayed response tasks. *J. Neurosci.* 24: 3944–3952. **Figure 16.11A,B** FUSTER, J. M. AND J. P. JERVEY (1982) Neuronal firing in the inferotemporal cortex of the monkey in a visual memory task. *J. Neurosci.* 2: 361–375. **Figure 16.11C** MIYASHITA, Y. AND H.-S. CHANG (1988) Neuronal correlate of pictorial short-term memory in the primate temporal cortex. *Nature.* 331: 68–70. **Figure 16.12A** SALA, J. B., P. RÄMÄ AND S. M. COURTNEY (2003) Functional topography of a distributed neural system for spatial and nonspatial information maintenance in working memory. *Neuropsychologia* 41: 341–356. **Figure 16.12B** ISHAI, A., L. G. UNGERLEIDER AND J. V. HAXBY (2000) Distributed neural systems for the generation of visual images. *Neuron* 28: 379–390. **Figure 16.13** KOSSLYN, S. M. AND 8 OTHERS (1999) The role of area 17 in visual imagery: Convergent evidence from PET and rTMS. *Science* 284: 167–170. **Figure 16.14** BADDELEY, A. (2003) Working memory: Looking back and looking forward. *Nat. Rev. Neurosci.* 4: 829–839. **Figure 16.15A** COURTNEY, S. M., L. G. UNGERLEIDER, K. KEIL AND J. V. HAXBY (1997) Transient and sustained activity in a distributed neural system for human working memory. *Nature* 386: 608–611. **Figures 16.15B and 16.17** HARRIS, J. A., C. MINIUSSI, I. M. HARRIS AND M. E. DIAMOND (2002) Transient storage of a tactile memory trace in primary somatosensory cortex. *J. Neurosci.* 22: 8720–8725. **Figure 16.16** KRAEMER, D. J., C. N. MACRAE, A. E. GREEN AND W. M. KELLEY (2005) Musical imagery: Sound of silence activates auditory cortex. *Nature* 434: 158. **Figure 16.19** D'ESPOSITO M., B. R. POSTLE AND B. RYPMA (2000) Prefrontal cortical contributions to working memory: evidence from event–related fMRI studies. *Exp. Brain Res.* 133: 3–11. **Figure 16.20** SAKAI, K., J. B. ROWE AND R. E. PASSINGHAM (2002) Active maintenance in prefrontal area 46 creates distractor-resistant memory. *Nat. Neurosci.* 5: 479–484. **Figure 16.21** ROWE, J. B., I. TONI, O. JOSEPHS, R. S. FRACKOWIAK AND R. E. PASSINGHAM 2000. The prefrontal cortex: Response selection or maintenance within working memory? *Science* 288: 1656–1660.

Chapter 17: Overview of Emotions

Figure 17.3A LANG, P. J., M. K. GREENWALD, M. M. BRADLEY AND A. O. HAMM (1993) Looking at pictures: Affective, facial, visceral, and behavioral reactions. *Psychophysiology* 30: 261–273. **Figure 17.3B** RUSSELL, J. A. (1980) A circumplex model of affect. *J. Pers. Soc. Psychol.* 39: 1161–1178. **Figure 17.8** MacLEAN, P. D. (1949) Psychosomatic disease and the "visceral brain": Recent developments bearing on the Papez theory of emotion. *Psychosom. Med.* 11: 338–353. **Figure 17.9** MacLEAN, P. D. (1970) The triune brain, emotion and scientific bias. In *The Neurosciences: Second Study Program*, F. O. Schmitt (ed.). New York: Rockefeller University Press, pp. 336–349. **Figure 17.11** ROSS, E. D. (1997) The aprosodias. In *Behavioral Neurology and Neuropsychology*, T. E. Feinberg

and M. J. Farah (eds.). New York: McGraw-Hill, pp. 699–710. **Figure 17.12A** DAVIDSON, R. J. (1995) Cerebral asymmetry, emotion, and affective style. In *Brain Asymmetry*, R. J. Davidson and K. Hugdahl (eds.). Cambridge, MA: MIT Press, pp. 361–387. **Figure 17.12B** KALIN, N. H., C. LARSON, S. E. SHELTON AND R. J. DAVIDSON (1998) Asymmetric frontal brain activity, cortisol, and behavior associated with fearful temperament in rhesus monkeys. *Behav. Neurosci.* 112: 286–292.

Chapter 18: Emotional Influences on Cognitive Functions

Figure 18.1 BUCK, R. (1984) *The Communication of Emotion.* New York: Guilford. **Figure 18.3A** WHALEN, P. J. AND 10 OTHERS (2004) Human amygdala responsivity to masked fearful eye whites. *Science* 306: 2061. **Figure 18.3B** WILLIAMS, M. A., A. P. MORRIS, F. McGLONE, D. F. ABBOTT AND J. B. MATTINGLEY (2004) Amygdala responses to fearful and happy facial expressions under conditions of binocular suppression. *J. Neurosci.* 24: 2898–2904. **Figure 18.4** ANDERSON, A. K. AND E. A. PHELPS (2001) Lesions of the human amygdala impair enhanced perception of emotionally salient events. *Nature* 411: 305–309. **Figure 18.5** LaBAR, K. S., M. M. MESULAM, D. R. GITELMAN AND S. WEINTRAUB (2000) Emotional curiosity: Arousal modulation of visuospatial attention is preserved in aging and early-stage Alzheimer's disease. *Neuropsychologia* 38: 1734–1740. **Figure 18.7** YAMASAKI, H., K. S. LaBAR AND G. McCARTHY (2002) Dissociable prefrontal brain systems for attention and emotion. *Proc. Natl. Acad. Sci. USA* 99: 11447–11451; FICHTENHOLTZ, H. M., H. L. DEAN, D. G. DILLON, H. YAMASAKI, G. McCARTHY AND K. S. LaBAR (2004) Emotion-attention network interactions during a visual oddball task. *Brain Res. Cogn. Brain Res.* 20: 67–80. PHOTOS © Marcin Balcerzak/istockphoto.com and rarpia/istockphoto.com **Figure 18.9** LaBAR, K. S. AND R. CABEZA (2006) Cognitive neuroscience of emotional memory. *Nat. Rev Neurosci.* 7: 54–64. **Figure 18.10** DOLCOS, F., K. S. LaBAR AND R. CABEZA (2004) Interaction between the amygdala and the medial temporal lobe memory system predicts better memory for emotional events. *Neuron* 42: 855–863. **Figure 18.12** BECHARA, A., D. TRANEL, H. DAMASIO, R. ADOLPHS, C. ROCKLAND AND A. R. DAMASIO (1995) Double dissociation of conditioning and declarative knowledge relative to the amygdala and hippocampus in humans. *Science* 269: 1115–1118.

Chapter 19: Social Cognition

Figure 19.1A HEATHERTON, T. F., C. L. WYLAND, C. N. MACRAE, K. E. DEMOS, B. T. DENNY AND W. M. KELLEY (2006) Medial prefrontal activity differentiates self from close

others. *Soc. Cogn. Affect. Neurosci.* 1: 18–24. **Figure 19.1B** CABEZA, R. AND 7 OTHERS (2004) Brain activity during episodic retrieval of autobiographical and laboratory events: An fMRI study using a novel photo paradigm. *J. Cogn. Neurosci.* 16: 1583–1594. **Figure 19.2A** ARZY, S., G. THUT, C. MOHR, C. M. MICHEL AND O. BLANKE (2006) Neural basis of embodiment: Distinct contributions of temporoparietal junction and extrastriate body area. *J. Neurosci.* 26: 8074–8081. **Figure 19.2B** BLANKE, O. AND 7 OTHERS (2005) Linking out-of-body experience and self processing to mental own-body imagery at the temporoparietal junction. *J. Neurosci.* 25: 550–557. **Figure 19.3A** HAXBY, J. V., E. A. HOFFMAN AND I. GOBBINI (2000) The distributed human neural system for face perception. *Trends Cogn. Sci.* 4: 223–233. **Figure 19.3B** HASSELMO, M. E., E. T. ROLLS AND G. C. BAYLIS (1989) The role of expression and identity in the face-selective responses of neurons in the temporal visual cortex of the monkey. *Behav. Brain Res.* 32: 203–218. **Figure 19.3C** LaBAR, K. S., M. J. CRUPAIN, J. B. VOYVODIC AND G. McCARTHY (2003) Dynamic perception of facial affect and identity in the human brain. *Cereb. Cortex* 13: 1023–1033. **Figure 19.4** ADAMS, R. B., JR., H. L. GORDON, A. A. BAIRD, N. AMBADY AND R. E. KLECK (2003) Effects of gaze on amygdala sensitivity to anger and fear faces. *Science* 300: 1536. **Figure 19.5** ALLISON, T., A. PUCE AND G. McCARTHY (2000) Social perception from visual cues: Role of the superior temporal sulcus region. *Trends Cogn. Sci.* 4: 267–278. **Figure 19.6** SCHULLER, A. M. AND B. ROSSION (2001) Spatial attention triggered by eye gaze increases and speeds up early visual activity. *Neuroreport* 12: 2381–2386. **Figure 19.7** PHELPS, E. A. AND 6 OTHERS (2000) Performance on indirect measures of race evaluation predicts amygdala activation. *J. Cogn. Neurosci.* 12: 729–738. **Figure 19.8** RICHESON, J. A. AND 6 OTHERS (2003) An fMRI investigation of the impact of interracial contact on executive function. *Nat. Neurosci.* 6: 1323–1328. **Figure 19.9** RIZZOLATTI, G., L. FADIGA, V. GALLESE AND L. FOGASSI (1996) Premotor cortex and the recognition of motor actions. *Cogn. Brain Res.* 3: 131–141. **Figure 19.10** FRITH, U. AND C. D. FRITH (2003) Development and neurophysiology of mentalizing. *Philos. Trans. R. Soc. Lond. B* 358: 459–473. **Figure 19.11** HARE, B., J. CALL AND M. TOMASELLO (2001) Do chimpanzees know what conspecifics know? *Anim. Behav.* 61: 139–151.

Chapter 20: Speech and Language

Figure 20.3 MILLER, G. A. (1991) *The Science of Words.* New York: Scientific American Library. **Figure 20.4** SCHWARTZ, D. A., C. Q. HOWE AND D. PURVES (2003) The statistical structure of human speech sounds predicts musical universals. *J. Neurosci.* 23: 7160–7168. **Figure 20.7A** JOHNSON, J. S.

AND E. L. NEWPORT (1989) Critical period effects in second language learning: The influence of maturational state on the acquisition of English as a second language. *Cogn. Psychol.* 21: 60–99. **Figure 20.7B** BROWN, T. T., H. M. LUGAR, R. S. COALSON, F. M. MIEZIN, S. E. PETERESEN AND B. L. SCHLAGGER (2005) Developmental changes in human cerebral functional organization for word generation. *Cereb. Cortex* 15: 275–290. **Figure 20.8** KUHL, P. K., K. A. WILLIAMS, F. LACERDA, K. N. STEVENS AND B. LINDBLOM (1992) Linguistic experience alters phonetic perception in infants 6 months of age. *Science* 255: 606–608. **Figure 20.10** GENTNER, T. Q., K. M. FENN, D. MARGOLIASH AND H. C. NUSBAUM (2006) Recursive syntactic pattern learning by songbirds. *Nature* 440: 1204–1207. **Figure 20.11** GHAZANFAR, A. A. AND N. LOGOTHETIS (2003) Facial expressions linked to monkey calls. *Nature* 423: 937. **Figure 20.12** SAVAGE-RUMBAUGH, S., S. G. SHANKER AND T. J. TAYLOR (1998) *Apes, Language, and the Human Mind.* New York: Oxford University Press. **Box 20C** Photograph by David McIntyre.

Chapter 21: The Neural Bases of Language

Figure 21.4A PENFIELD, W. AND L. ROBERTS (1959) *Speech and Brain Mechanisms.* Princeton, NJ: Princeton University Press, 1959. **Figure 21.4B** OJEMANN, G. A., I. FRIED AND E. LETTICH (1989) Electrocorticographic (EcoG) correlates of language. *Electroencephalogr. Clin. Neurophysiol.* 73: 453–463. **Figure 21.5** KUTAS, M. AND S. A. HILLYARD (1980) Reading senseless sentences: Brain potentials reflect semantic incongruity. *Science* 207: 203–205. **Figure 21.6** POSNER, M. I. AND M. E. RAICHLE (1994) *Images of Mind.* New York: Scientific American Library. **Figure 21.7** CHAO, L. L., J. V. HAXBY AND A. MARTIN (1999) Attribute-based neural substrates in temporal cortex for perceiving and knowing about objects. *Nature Neurosci.* 2: 913–919. **Figure 21.8** BELLUGI, U., H. POIZNER AND E. S. KLIMA (1989) Language, modality, and the brain. *Trends Neurosci.* 12: 380–388. **Figure 21.9** GIL-DA-COSTA, R., A. MARTIN, M. A. LOPES, M. MUNOZ, J. FRITZ AND A. R. BRAUN (2006) Species-specific calls activate homologs of Broca's and Wernicke's areas in the macaque. *Nat. Neurosci.* 9: 1064–1070.

Chapter 22: Representation of Time and Number

Figure 22.2 HENDERSON, J., T. A. HURLY, M. BATESON AND S. D. HEALY (2006) Timing in free-living rufous hummingbirds, *Selasphorus rufus. Curr. Biol.* 16: 512–515. **Figure 22.3** RAKITIN, B. C., J. GIBBON, T. B. PENNEY, C. MALAPANI, S. C. HINTON AND W. H. MECK (1998) Scalar expectancy theory and peak-interval timing in humans. *J. Exp. Psychol. Anim. Behav. Process.* 24: 15–33. **Figure 22.4** GIBBON, J., R. M. CHURCH AND W. H. MECK

(1984) Scalar timing in memory. *Ann. N. Y. Acad. Sci.* 423: 52–77. **Figure 22.5** COULL, J. T., F. VIDAL, B. NAZARIAN AND F. MACAR (2004) Functional anatomy of the attentional modulation of time estimation. *Science* 5: 1506–1508. **Figure 22.6B** MOYER, R. S. AND T. K. LANDAUER (1967) Time required for judgements of numerical inequality. *Nature* 215: 1519–1520. **Figure 22.6C** MOYER, R. S. AND S. T. DUMAIS (1978) Mental comparisons. In *The Psychology of Learning and Motivation*, Vol. 12, G. H. Bower (ed.). New York: Academic Press, pp. 117–155. **Figure 22.7** PICA, P., C. LEMER, W. IZARD AND S. DEHAENE (2004) Exact and approximate arithmetic in an Amazonian indigene group. *Science* 306: 499–503. **Figure 22.8** CANTLON, J. AND E. M. BRANNON (2006) Shared system for ordering small and large numbers in monkeys and humans. *Psychol. Sci.* 17: 401–406. **Figure 22.9A** PLATT, J. R. AND D. M. JOHNSON (1971) Localization of position within a homogeneous behavior chain: Effects of error contingencies. *Learn. Motiv.* 2: 386–414. **Figure 22.9B** WHALEN, J., R. GELMAN AND C. R. GALLISTEL (1999) Non-verbal counting in humans: The psychophysics of number representation. *Psychol. Sci.* 10: 130–137. **Figure 22.10** DEHAENE, S. AND J. CHANGEUX (1993) Development of elementary numerical abilities: A neuronal model. *J. Cogn. Neurosci.* 5: 390–407. **Figure 22.12** MOLKO, N. AND 7 OTHERS (2003) Functional and structural alterations of the intraparietal sulcus in a developmental dyscalculia of genetic origin. *Neuron* 40: 847–858. **Figure 22.13** PIAZZA, M., V. IZARD, P. PINEL, D. LE BIHAN AND S. DEHAENE (2004) Tuning curves for approximate numerosity in the human intraparietal sulcus. *Neuron* 44: 547–555. **Figure 22.14** NIEDER, A. AND E. K. MILLER (2004) A parieto-frontal network for visual numerical information in the monkey. *Proc. Natl. Acad. Sci. USA* 101: 7457–7462.

Chapter 23: Executive Control Systems

Figure 23.1 MILLER, E. K. AND J. D. COHEN (2001) An integrative theory of prefrontal cortex function. *Annu. Rev. Neurosci.* 24: 167–202. **Figure 23.6** HUETTEL, S. A., P. B. MACK AND G. MCCARTHY (2002) Perceiving patterns in random series: Dynamic processing of sequence in prefrontal cortex. *Nat. Neurosci.* 5: 485–490. **Figure 23.7** SHALLICE, T. (1982) Specific impairments of planning. *Philos. Trans. R. Soc. Lond. B Biol. Sci.* 298: 199–209. **Figure 23.8** WALLIS, J. D., K. C. ANDERSON AND E. K. MILLER (2001) Single neurons in prefrontal cortex encode abstract rules. *Nature* 411: 953–956. **Figure 23.9B** BUSH, G., P. J. WHALEN, B. R. ROSEN, M. A. JENIKE, S. C. MCINERNEY AND S. L. RAUCH (1998) The counting Stroop: An interference task specialized for functional neuroimaging—Validation study with functional MRI. *Hum. Brain Mapp.* 6: 270–282. **Figure 23.9C** BUSH, G., P. LUU AND M. I. POSNER (2000)

Cognitive and emotional influences in anterior cingulate cortex. *Trends Cogn. Sci.* 4: 215–222. **Figure 23.10** KERNS, J. G., J. D. COHEN, A. W. MACDONALD III, R. Y. CHO, V. A. STENGER AND C. S. CARTER (2004) Anterior cingulate conflict monitoring and adjustments in control. *Science* 303: 1023–1026. **Figure 23.11** FELLOWS, L. K. AND M. J. FARAH (2005) Is anterior cingulate cortex necessary for cognitive control? *Brain* 128: 788–796.

Chapter 24: Decision Making

Figure 24.6A SCHULTZ, W., P. DAYAN AND P. R. MONTAGUE (1997) A neural substrate of prediction and reward. *Science* 275: 1593–1599. **Figure 24.6B** KNUTSON, B., G. W. FONG, C. M. ADAMS, J. L. VARNER AND D. HOMMER (2001) Dissociation of reward anticipation and outcome with event-related fMRI. *Neuroreport* 12: 3683–3687. **Figure 24.7** KING-CASAS, B., D. TOMLIN, C. ANEN, C. F. CAMERER, S. R. QUARTZ AND P. R. MONTAGUE (2005) Getting to know you: Reputation and trust in a two-person economic exchange. *Science* 308: 78–83. **Figure 24.8** MCCLURE, S. M., J. LI, D. TOMLIN, K. S. CYPERT, L. M. MONTAGUE AND P. R. MONTAGUE (2004) Neural correlates of behavioral preference for culturally familiar drinks. *Neuron* 44: 379–387. **Figure 24.9** HEEKEREN, H. R., S. MARRETT, P. A. BANDETTINI AND L. G. UNGERLEIDER (2004) A general mechanism for perceptual decision-making in the human brain. *Nature* 431: 859–862. **Figure 24.10A** HSU, M., M. BHATT, R. ADOLPHS, D. TRANEL AND C. F. CAMERER (2005) Neural systems responding to degrees of uncertainty in human decision-making. *Science* 310: 1680–1683. **Figure 24.10B,C** HUETTEL, S. A., C. J. STOWE, E. M. GORDON, B. T. WARNER AND M. L. PLATT (2006) Neural signatures of economic preferences for risk and ambiguity. *Neuron* 49: 765–775.

Chapter 25: Reasoning and Problem Solving

Figure 25.3 GAZZANIGA, M. S. AND J. E. LEDOUX (1978) *The Integrated Mind.* New York: Plenum. **Figure 25.4** GOEL, V. AND R. J. DOLAN (2004) Differential involvement of left prefrontal cortex in inductive and deductive reasoning. *Cognition* 93: B109–121. **Figure 25.7** JUNG-BEEMAN, M. AND 7 OTHERS (2004) Neural activity when people solve verbal problems with insight. *PLoS Biol* 2: E97. **Figure 25.8** REVERBERI, C., A. TORALDO, S. D'AGOSTINI AND M. SKRAP (2005) Better without (lateral) frontal cortex? Insight problems solved by frontal patients. *Brain* 128: 2882–2890. **Box 25A** Photo of Washington DC © Jonathan Larsen/istockphoto.com; photo of New York City © Franky Sze/istockphoto.com **Box 25C** Photographs courtesy of The Behavioural Ecology Research Group, University of Oxford.

Chapter 26: Evolution of Brain and Cognition

Figure 26.2 Courtesy of the University of Wisconsin and Michigan State Comparative Mammalian Brain Collections. **Figure 26.3** BROWN, P. AND 6 OTHERS (2004) A new small-bodied hominin from the Late Pleistocene of Flores, Indonesia. *Nature* 431: 1055–1061. **Figure 26.4A** JERISON, H. J. (1977) The theory of encephalization. *Ann. N.Y. Acad. Sci.* 299: 146–160. **Figure 26.4B** STREIDTER, G. F. (2005) *Principles of Brain Evolution.* Sunderland, MA: Sinauer. **Figure 26.5A** Courtesy of the University of Wisconsin and Michigan State Comparative Mammalian Brain Collections. **Figure 26.5B** STEPHAN, H., H. FRAHM AND G. BARON. 1981. New and revised data on volumes of brain structures in insectivores and primates. *Folia Primatol.* 35: 1-29. **Figure 26.6A** WELKER, W. (1990) Why does cerebral cortex fissure and fold? In *Cerebral Cortex*, Vol 8B, E. G. Jones and A. Peters (eds.). New York: Plenum, pp. 3-136. **Figure 26.6B** STREIDTER, G. F. (2005) *Principles of Brain Evolution.* Sunderland, MA: Sinauer; ZILLES, K., E. ARMSTRONG, K. H. MOSER, A. SCHLEICHER AND H. STEPHAN (1989) Gyrification in the cerebral cortex of primates. *Brain Behav. Evol.* 34: 143–150. **Figure 26.7** STREIDTER, G. F. (2005) *Principles of Brain Evolution.* Sunderland, MA: Sinauer. **Figure 26.8** GILBERT, S. L., W. B. DOBYNS AND B. T. LAHN (2005) Genetic links between brain development and brain evolution. *Nat. Rev. Genetics* 6: 581. **Figure 26.9** DEANER, R. O., K. ISLER, J. BURKART AND C. VAN SCHAIK (2007) Overall brain size, and not encephalization quotient, best predicts cognitive ability across non-human primates. *Brain, Behav. Evol.* 70: 115–124. **Figure 26.10** STREIDTER, G. F. (2005) *Principles of Brain Evolution.* Sunderland, MA: Sinauer. **Figure 26.11B** PENFIELD, W., AND E. BOULDREY (1937) Somatic motor and sensory representation in the cerebral cortex of man as studied by electrical stimulation. *Brain* 60: 389-443. **Figure 26.12A** SZEKELY, T. A., A. CATCHPOLE, A. DEVOOGD, Z. MARCHL, AND T. J. DEVOOGD (1996) Evolutionary changes in a song control area of the brain (HVC) are associated with evolutionary changes in song repertoire among European warblers (Sylviidae). *Proc. R. Soc. (London) B:* 263: 607–610; photo © Iurii Konoval/istockphoto.com. **Figure 26.13** KREBS, J. R., D. F. SHERRY, S. D. HEALY, V. H. PERRY AND A. L. VACCARINO (1989) Hippocampal specialization of food-storing birds. *Proc. Natl. Acad. Sci. USA* 86: 1388–1392; photos courtesy of John and Karen Hollingsworth (Clark's nutcracker) and Lee Carney (scrub jay), U.S. Fish and Wildlife Service. **Figure 26.14A** Clancy, B., R. B. Darlington and B. L. Finlay. (2000) The course of human events: predicting the timing of primate neural development. *Dev. Sci.* 3: 57–66. **Figure 26.14B** FINLAY, B. AND R. DARLINGTON (1995) Linked regularities in the development and evolution of mammalian brains. *Science* 268: 1578–1584. **Figure 26.15** ALLMAN, J. M. *Evolving Brains.* New York: Scientific American Library. 2000; photos © David Tipling (howler monkey) and Mike Lane (spider monkey) Alamy Photo; brain images Courtesy of the University of Wisconsin and Michigan State Comparative Mammalian Brain Collections. **Figure 26.16A** BYRNE, R. W. AND N. CORP (2004) Neocortex size predicts deception rate in primates. *Proc. R. Biol. Soc.* 271: 1693–1699. **Figure 26.16B** KUDO, H. AND R. I. M. DUNBAR (2001). Neocortex size and social network size in primates. *Anim. Behav.* 62: 711–722; photo © Andrey Novikov/istockphoto.com **Figure 26.16C** READER, S. M. AND K. N. LELAND (2002) Social intelligence, innovation, and enhanced brain size in primates. *Proc. Natl. Acad. Sci. USA* 99: 4436–4441. **Figure 26.18** HOFMAN, M. A. (1983) Evolution of brain size in neonatal and adult placental mammals: A theoretical approach. *J. Theor. Biol.* 105: 317–332. **Figure 26.19** TATTERSALL, I., E. DELSON AND J. VAN COUVERING, EDS. (1988) *Encyclopedia of Human Evolution and Prehistory.* New York: Garland. **Figure 26.20C** Photo © Robert Harding Picture Library Ltd/Alamy. **Figure 26.22** NIMCHINSKY, E. A., E. GILISSEN, J. M. ALLMAN, D. P. PERL, J. M. ERWIN AND P. R. HOFF (1999) A neuronal morphologic type unique to humans and great apes. *Proc. Natl. Acad. Sci. USA* 96: 5268-5273. **Figure 26.23A** PREUSS, T. M., AND P. S. GOLDMAN-RAKIC (1991) Myelo- and cytoarchitecture of the granular frontal cortex and surrounding regions in the strepsirhine primate *Galago* and the anthropoid primate *Macaca. J. Comp. Neurol.* 310: 429–474. **Figure 26.23B** PETRIDES, M., G. CADORET AND S. MACKEY (2005) Orofacial somatomotor responses in the macaque monkey homologue of Broca's area. *Nature* 435: 1235–1238.

Chapter 27: Development of the Brain and Its Cognitive Functions

Figure 27.1 GILBERT, S. G., A. L. TYLER AND E. J. ZACKIN (2005) *Bioethics and the New Embryology.* Sunderland: Sinauer. **Figure 27.3** COWAN, W. M. (1979) The development of the brain. *Sci. Am.* 241(3): 106–117. **Figure 27.4A** CASEY, B. J., N. TOTTENHAM, C. LISTON AND S. DURSTON (2005) Imaging the developing brain: What have we learned about cognitive development? *Trends Cogn. Sci.* 9: 104–110. **Figure 27.4B** BOURGEOIS, J. AND P. RAKIC (1993) Changes of synaptic density in the primary visual cortex of the macaque monkey from fetal to adult stage. *J. Neurosci.* 13: 2801–2820. **Figure 27.5A** DEKABAN, A. S. AND D. SADOWSKY (1978) Changes in brain weights during the span of human life: relation of brain weights to body heights and body weights. *Ann. Neurol.* 4: 345–356. **Figure 27.5B** LENROOT, R. K. AND J. N. GIEDD (2006) Brain development in children and adolescents: Insights from anatomical brain magnetic resonance imaging. *Neurosci. Behav. Rev.* 30: 718–729. **Figure 27.6** VAN PRAAG, H., G. KEMPERMANN AND F. H. GAGE (2000) Neural consequences of environmental enrichment. *Nat. Neurosci.* 1: 191–198. **Figure 27.9** MARSHALL, P. J., N. A. FOX AND THE BEIP CORE GROUP (2004) A comparison of the electroencephalogram between institutionalized and community children in Romania. *J. Cogn. Neurosci.* 16: 1327–1338. **Figure 27.11** CSIBRA, G., G. DAVIS AND M. W. JOHNSON (2000) Gamma oscillations and object processing in the infant brain. *Science* 290: 1582–1585. **Figure 27.12** BAUER, P. J., S. A. WIEBE, L. J. CARVER, J. M. WATERS AND C. A. NELSON (2003) Developments in long-term explicit memory late in the first year of life: Behavioral and electrophysiological indices. *Psychol. Sci.* 14: 629–635. **Figure 27.13** PASCALIS, O., M. DE HAAN AND C. A. NELSON (2002) Is face processing species-specific during the first year of life? *Science* 296: 1321–1323. **Figure 27.14** SAXE, R. AND I. J. POWELL (2006) It's the thought that counts: Brain regions for one component of theory of mind. *Psychol. Sci.* 17: 692–699. **Figure 27.15** XU, F. AND E. S. SPELKE (2000) Large number discrimination in 6-month-old infants. *Cognition* 74: B1–B11. **Figure 27.16** BERGER, A., G. TZUR AND M. I. POSNER (2006) Infant babies detect arithmetic error. *Proc. Natl. Acad. Sci. USA* 103: 12649–12553. **Figure 27.17** CANTLON, J., E. M. BRANNON, E. J. CARTER AND K. PELPHREY (2006) Notation-independent number processing in the intraparietal sulcus in adults and young children. PLoS Biology 4: e125, 1–11. **Figure 27.18** BUNGE, S. A. AND P. D. ZELAZO (2006) A brain-based account of the development of rule use in childhood. *Curr. Dir. Psychol. Sci.* 15: 118–121. **Box 27B, Figure A** Cat photos © Larysa Dodz, Jose Manuel Gelpi Diaz, and Tony Campbell/istockphoto.com; dog photo © Eric Isselée - Fotolia.com **Box 27B, Figure E** © Michael Newman/PhotoEdit.

APPENDIX

Figure A9 HODGKIN, A. L. AND W. A. RUSHTON (1938) The electrical constants of a crustacean nerve fibre. *Proc. R. Soc. Lond. B* 133: 444–478. **Figure A12 micrograph** CHEN, C. AND 17 OTHERS (2004) Mice lacking sodium channel β1 subunits display defects in neuronal excitability, sodium channel expression, and nodal architecture. *J. Neurosci.* 24: 4030–4042.

Name Index

Subject Index

About the Book

Editor: Graig Donini

Project Editor: Kathaleen Emerson

Copy Editors: Carol Wigg and Stephanie Hiebert

Production Manager: Christopher Small

Photo Researcher: David McIntyre

Book Design and Layout: Jefferson Johnson

Illustration Program: Dragonfly Media Group

Indexer: Grant Hackett

Cover and Book Manufacturer: Courier Companies, Inc.